PSYCHOLOGY
CONCEPTS AND APPLICATIONS
MORRIS MAISTO DUNN

Charles G. Morris

University of Michigan

Albert A. Maisto

University of North Carolina at Charlotte

Wendy L. Dunn

Coe College

PEARSON

Prentice
Hall

Upper Saddle River, NJ 07458

Library of Congress Cataloging-in-Publication Data
Morris, Charles G.
    Psychology: concepts and applications / Charles G. Morris, Albert A. Maisto, Wendy Dunn. —1st ed.
    p.   cm.
    ISBN 0-13-240324-2
    Includes bibliographical references and indexes.
    1.   Psychology—Textbooks.   I. Maisto, Albert A. (Albert Anthony)   II. Dunn, Wendy.   III.   Title.
    BF121.M5983 2007
    150 —dc22   2006030317

Editorial Director: Leah Jewell
Executive Editor: Jessica Mosher
Editorial Assistant: Jessica Kupetz
Senior Media Editor: Brian Hyland
Supplements Editor: Richard Virginia
Assessment Editor: Keri Scott
Director of Marketing: Brandy Dawson
Senior Marketing Manager: Jeanette Moyer
Assistant Marketing Manager: Billy Grieco
Marketing Assistant: Laura Kennedy
Editor in Chief, Development: Rochelle Diogenes
Senior Development Editor: Jeannine Ciliotta
Managing Editor (Production): Maureen Richardson

Production Liaison: Randy Pettit
Prepress and Manufacturing Manager: Nick Sklitsis
Prepress and Manufacturing Buyer: Sherry Lewis
Creative Design Director: Leslie Osher
Interior Cover Design: Ilze Lemesis
Cover Illustration/Photo: Getty Images
Image Rights and Permissions Manager: Zina Arabia
Image Researcher: Rachel Lucas
Image Permission Coordinator: Annette Linder
Text Permission Specialist: The Permissions Group
Composition/Full-Service Project Management: Preparé
Printer/Binder: The Courier Companies
Cover Printer: Phoenix Color Corp.

Credits and acknowledgments borrowed from other sources and reproduced, with permission, in this textbook appear on appropriate page within text (or on page C-1–C-2).

Pearson Education, Ltd.
Pearson Education Australia PTY, Limited
Pearson Education Singapore, Pte., Ltd.
Pearson Education North Asia Ltd.
Pearson Education, Canada, Ltd.

Pearson Educación de Mexico, S.A. de C.V.
Pearson Education–Japan
Pearson Education Malaysia, Pte., Ltd.
Pearson Education, Upper Saddle River, New Jersey.

10   9   8
ISBN 978-0-13-240324-5
ISBN 0-13-240324-2

>BRIEF CONTENTS<

>CONTENTS<

6 Motivation and Emotion   200

7 Human Development Across the Lifespan   232

8 Personality, Stress, and Health   276

>PREFACE<

Focus on Understanding and Applying Basic Concepts

The idea to publish Morris/Maisto/Dunn *Psychology: Concepts and Applications* came about as we read reviews for the latest edition of Morris/Maisto's *Understanding Psychology*, a best-selling introductory psychology text in its seventh edition. Response from our readers indicated that *Understanding Psychology* is valued for "getting it right" and paring down the voluminous psychological literature to present the most important research and topics. What we noted when analyzing these reviews was a growing demand from our readers for more material to better illustrate the link between psychological concepts and everyday life examples. Introductory psychology is a challenging course for many students. It is important that students understand the important and fascinating link between what they are reading and how it will apply to their own lives. The result is a "new" book that truly retains the best of *Understanding Psychology 7/e* while offering a new eleven-chapter format including a full chapter on "Psychology Applied to Work".

Our purposes in writing this book are several. Our central goal has been to prepare a book that presents a scientific, accurate, and concise overview of the essential concepts within the field of psychology in a style and format that is easy for students to comprehend and learn from. We have tried to write clearly about psychology and its fascinating applications without being trendy, while being sensitive to the concerns and challenges faced by students in what is likely to be their first psychology course. We have emphasized the promise of psychology as a means to explain everyday human behavior and thinking, especially in the context of the important aspects of our lives pertaining to our work and our family interactions.

Pedagogy that Makes Material More Accessible

The book includes a number of features designed to help students understand the material and how it applies to them, especially in the parts of their lives that are dedicated to jobs and careers. The result is that students don't just process lists of unrelated, empty facts and definitions. Rather, our focus has been on explaining the content we present, and setting it in the context of the everyday concerns and questions that psychological research has attempted to address. We have created several pedagogical features and embedded these in the text to help students develop a thorough and deep understanding of and appreciation for the field of psychology. These features include:

- **Opening case studies** start each chapter with a real-life example demonstrating the most important ideas in the chapter. These case studies link the study of psychology with important aspects of corporate policies and provide examples of practical applications of psychological principles and research findings. Exam-

ples of these chapter opening case studies include a discussion of the sleep-enhancing drug Ambien, an exploration of how video games are being used to train U. S. soldiers for combat, and an analysis of how Trader Joe's, the popular grocery store chain, is using psychological principles to create an organization oriented toward a very different view of how businesses should run.

- **"Understanding Ourselves"** boxes are included in each chapter to highlight the most recent research and the specific applications of core ideas to areas that are likely to be of especially high, and perhaps even personal, interest to students. See the Chapter-by-Chapter Highlights section on pp. xi-xiii for examples of these boxes.
- **Learning objectives** accompany each major section of the chapters to give students an idea about how to focus their attention and study.
- **Questions** are used to orient students' attention within the various sections of chapters, and these same questions are answered in the Chapter Review that appears at the end of each chapter.
- **Figures, Tables, and Summary Tables** are presented along with the content of the text to help students visualize and summarize important points to be learned.
- **"Check Your Understanding"** boxes are presented at the end of each major section within chapters. These boxes contain questions testing the students' mastery of facts and definitions and also their ability to apply their knowledge to novel situations and examples.
- **"Talking graphics"** clarify complex processes with step-by step explanations, particularly in the areas of neuroscience in Chapter 2: The Biological Basis Behavior.
- **Key terms** are printed in boldface and defined in the margin of the page where they first appear – a technique that helps students master the basic vocabulary of the field.
- **Chapter Reviews,** organized around the questions that are embedded in the text, are presented at the conclusion of each chapter, along with a list of vocabulary terms that the chapter have been presented in the chapter.
- **Concept Maps** conclude each chapter a visually organized overview of the main ideas and facts presented in the chapter, arranged in a clear, engaging, and integrated format. Concept Maps assist students in forming a more sophisticated and clearer understanding of and appreciation for the material presented in the text.

Chapter-by-Chapter Highlights

CHAPTER 1: THE SCIENCE OF PSYCHOLOGY

- Chapter-opening case study: Toyota
- "Understanding Ourselves: The Benefits of Studying Psychology" feature box shows students how the science of psychology applies to questions they have likely asked themselves
- High interest discussions on the role of women in psychology and sections on human diversity—gender, race and ethnicity, and culture

CHAPTER 2: THE BIOLOGICAL BASIS OF BEHAVIOR

- Chapter-opening case study: The Pepsi Challenge
- "Understanding Ourselves: Drugs and Behavior" box on how some psychoactive drugs and poisons work by affecting neurotransmitters
- High-interest discussions of stem cell research, neuroscience, tools for studying the brain, the endocrine system, and the human genome

CHAPTER 3: SENSATION, PERCEPTION AND CONSCIOUS EXPERIENCE

- Chapter-opening case study: Ambien
- "Understanding Ourselves: Massage: Benefits of Massage"
- Chapter covers sensation, perception, and conscious experience, sleep, drug-altered consciousness, and meditation and hypnosis in a brief, streamlined, but complete discussion
- Includes a decibel scale for common sounds
- Up to date discussion of adequate sleep, sleep deprivation, and sleep disorders
- Up to date discussion of substance abuse and dependence, addiction

CHAPTER 4: LEARNING AND MEMORY

- Chapter-opening case study: Every Soldier a Sensor
- "Understanding Ourselves: Improving Your Memory"
- Chapter covers both learning and memory topics in a streamlined but complete discussion
- Includes practical tips for modifying your own behavior
- Includes such topics as the role of money as a reinforcer, the drawbacks of punishment, examples of reinforcement in everyday life

CHAPTER 5: COGNITION AND MENTAL ABILITIES

- Chapter-opening case study: The Rainbow Project
- "Understanding Ourselves: Becoming A More Skillful Problem Solver"
- Section on problem solving with many practical problem-solving techniques
- Discussion of decision making includes many practical techniques
- Discussion of the relationship between IQ and success
- Discussion of the interaction of heredity and environment

CHAPTER 6: MOTIVATION AND EMOTION

- Chapter-opening case study: Work-Life Balance
- "Understanding Ourselves: The Slow but Lasting Fix for Weight Gain"
- Coverage of the issue of work-life balance
- How intrinsic and extrinsic motivation affect job success
- Section on Motivating Employees
- Section on eating disorders and obesity
- Voice quality, facial expression, body language, personal space, and gestures
- Culture and emotion

CHAPTER 7: HUMAN DEVELOPMENT ACROSS THE LIFESPAN

- Chapter-opening case study: The Boomerang Generation
- "Understanding Ourselves: Resolving Conflicts in Intimate Relationships"
- Discussion of children in dual-career families, TV and children
- Managing intimate adult relationships
- Women in the work force
- Section on the demographics of aging

CHAPTER 8: PERSONALITY, STRESS, AND HEALTH

- Chapter-opening case study: Workplace Wellness
- "Understanding Ourselves: Evaluating Your Personality"
- Chapter combines discussion of theories of personality and assessment with up-to-date coverage of stress: sources, coping techniques, and the relationship between stress and health
- Critical discussion of Freud's work
- Personality traits and job performance
- Sources of stress: change, everyday hassles, self-imposed stress
- Extreme stress, including posttraumatic stress disorder
- Strategies for coping with stress and for staying healthy

CHAPTER 9: PSYCHOLOGICAL DISORDERS AND THEIR TREATMENT

- Chapter-opening Case Study: Lincoln's "Melancholy"
- "Understanding Ourselves: Recognizing Depression"
- Defining abnormality, models of abnormality
- Chapter provides comprehensive discussion of current psychotherapies and biological therapies, including current drug therapies and issues such as deinstitutionalization

CHAPTER 10: SOCIAL PSYCHOLOGY

- Chapter-opening Case Study: Hidden Biases
- "Understanding Ourselves: Beliefs and Binge Drinking"
- Prejudice and discrimination in work situations
- Strategies for reducing prejudice and discrimination in real situations
- Conformity and culture
- Section on social forces in organizations that focuses on decision making, leadership, productivity, and communication in work based organizations.
- Using psychology to increase worker output and satisfaction.

CHAPTER 11: PSYCHOLOGY APPLIED TO WORK

- Chapter-opening case study: Trader Joe's
- "Understanding Ourselves: How do We Determine What Is Fair?"
- Techniques for predicting job performance, including tests
- Strategies and techniques for evaluating performance
- Training employees: on the job, simulation training, management development
- Types of work teams
- Job satisfaction and organizational justice
- Creating a healthy work environment
- Managing job-related stress

Enhanced Supplements Package

It is increasingly true today that, as valuable as a good textbook is, it is still only one element of a comprehensive learning package. We have made every effort to provide high-quality instructor and student supplements that will save you preparation time and will enhance the classroom experience

FOR ACCESS TO ALL INSTRUCTOR SUPPLEMENTS FOR MORRIS/MAISTO/DUNN PSYCHOLOGY: CONCEPTS AND APPLICATIONS AND ANY OTHER PEARSON TEXT SIMPLY GO TO *http://prenhall.com/irc* and follow the directions to register (or log in if you already have a user name and password). Once you have registered and your status as an instructor is verified, you will be e-mailed a login name and password. Use your login name and password to access the catalogue. Click on the "online catalogue" link, click on "psychology" followed by "introductory psychology" and then the Morris/Maisto/Dunn *Psychology: Concepts and Applications* text. Under the description of each supplement is a link that allows you to download and save the supplement to your desktop.

Hard copies of the supplements can be requested through your Pearson sales representative. If you do not know your sales representative, go to *http://prenhall.com/replocator/* and follow the directions to locate your sales representative.

For technical support for any of your Pearson products, you and your students can contact *http://247.prenhall.com/* or call customer technical support at 1-800-677-6337.

SUPPLEMENTS FOR INSTRUCTORS

TEST ITEM FILE (978-0-13-232594-3): Created from one of the most respected test banks on the market today by Gary Piggrem of DeVry University, this test file contains over 2,500 multiple-choice, true/false, and essay questions. To facilitate your selection of items, each question is page referenced to the textbook. A two-page Total Assessment Guide chapter overview makes creating tests easier by listing all of the test items in an easy-to-reference grid. The Total Assessment Guide organizes all test items by text section and question type/level of difficulty. All multiple-choice questions are categorized as either factual, conceptual, or applied. Many of the items also include statistics indicating how many students answered that question correctly in class-testing at both 2-year and 4-year schools. In addition, the text author, Charles Morris, has carefully reviewed the test file and has indicated a number of "Author's Choice" questions because of their challenging nature or interesting focus.

PRENTICE HALL'S TESTGEN (978-0-13-232623-0): Available on one dual-platform CD-ROM, this computerized test generator program provides instructors "best in class" features in an easy-to-use program. Create tests using the TestGen Wizard and easily select questions with drag-and-drop or point-and-click functionality. Add or modify test questions using the built-in Question Editor. TestGen also offers algorithmic functionality, which allows for the creation of unlimited versions of a single test. The Quiz Master feature allows for online test delivery. Complete with an instructor gradebook and full technical support. Available online through the Instructor's Resources Center or on the Instructor's Resource CD-ROM.

ALSO AVAILABLE, PEARSON'S NEW TESTING PLATFORM *MyTest* is an alternative program to Test Gen. A powerful assessment generation program that helps instructors easily create and print quizzes, tests, exams, as well as homework or practice handouts. Questions, assessments, or assignments can all be authored online, allowing instructors ultimate flexibility and the ability to efficiently manage assessments at anytime, from anywhere. Contact your local Pearson representative for more information.

POWERPOINT PRESENTATION AND CLASSROOM RESPONSE QUESTIONS (on Instructor's CD-ROM or on-line at *http://prenhall.com*): A completely redesigned PowerPoint presentation by Katie Scott (Miami-Jacobs Career College) created especially for the Eighth Edition incorporating the text art and outlining the key points for each text chapter. Also available,

CLASSROOM RESPONSE SYSTEMS Pearson Education is pleased to offer the benefits of our partnership with Training Masters an award-winning team dedicated to helping schools, businesses, and organizations reach their full growth potential. The Training Masters team consists of experts in leadership, career school management, instructor training, professional development, communications and technology (*http://www.trainingmasters.com*). The Klickerz Remote Response System developed by Training Masters allows you to quiz students, take attendance and ask questions to gauge student understanding and promote interaction in the classroom. Classroom Response questions ("clicker" questions) created by Theresa Tuttle (ECPI College of Technology) for *Psychology: Concepts and Applications* help promote interaction and student engagement in the classroom. Ask your local Pearson sales representative for more information.

INSTRUCTOR'S RESOURCE MANUAL (978-0-13-232593-6): An abundant collection of resources prepared by Joy Easton (DeVry University) For each chapter, you'll find activities, exercises, assignments, handouts, and demos for in-class use, as well as guidelines on integrating the many Morris media resources into your classroom and syllabus. The material for each chapter is organized in an easy-to-use Chapter Lecture Outline. This resource saves prep work and helps you make the maximum use of your classroom time.

PH COLOR TRANSPARENCIES (978-0-13-192699-8): A set of full-color transparencies is designed to be used in large lecture settings. Available on the Instructor's Resource Center online at *http://prenhall.com/irc* or on CD-ROM, as well as in acetate format. Lecture notes to accompany the transparencies created by Theresa Tuttle (ECPI College of Technology) for easy use in the classroom also available on-line.

INSTRUCTOR'S CD-ROM (978-0-13-232622-3): Bringing all of the instructor resources together in one place, the Instructor's Resource CD-ROM offers the PowerPoint presentations, the electronic files for the Instructor's Resource Manual materials and the Test Item File to help you customize your lecture notes. (Note that all of these resources can be downloaded from the Instructor's Resource center online by following the directions at *http://prenhall.com/irc.*

COLLEGE TEACHING TIPS (978-0-13-614317-8) This guide by Fred W. Whitford helps new instructors or graduate teaching assistants to manage the myriad complex tasks required to teach an introductory course effectively. The author has used his own teaching experiences over the last 25 years to help illustrate some of the types of problems that a new instructor can expect to face. The guide has been completely revised and updated from the former *Teaching Psychology: A Guide for the New Instructor, Fourth Edition* to include content applicable to a number of disciplines with introductory courses.

MOVIES AS ILLUSTRATIONS FOR INTRODUCTORY PSYCHOLOGY (978-0-13-145510-8) This teaching guide suggests 45 different movie scenes, several for each chapter of a typical introductory psychology textbook that can be used to spark discussion and clarify concepts covered in class. Includes Scene Notes, which summarize the scenes and provide context; Topic Notes, which tie in the movie scenes to topics likely covered in introductory psychology classes, and Discussion Questions, which suggest ways of engaging the class in conversation about the scene.

MEDIA AND ONLINE RESOURCES FOR INSTRUCTORS AND STUDENTS

 SELF-ASSESSMENT LIBRARY CD-ROM (978-0-13-221793-4) ISBN FOR BOOK AND CD-ROM (978-0-13-233354-2):

The Self-Assessment Library by best-selling organizational behavior and management author Stephen P. Robbins and Timothy A. Judge (University of Florida, Warrington College of Business) is a unique learning tool that helps students to create a personal skills portfolio. It is an interactive library of 51 behavioral questionnaires that helps students discover things about themselves, their attitudes, and their personal strengths and weaknesses. Learning about themselves gives students interesting insights into how they behave in real world situations and motivates them to learn more about psychological theories and practices that can help them better understand what it takes to be successful in everyday life. Results from student responses are automatically graded; self-scoring exercises generate immediate, individual analysis and feedback. Topics include *What's My Basic Personality? How Satisfied Am I with My Job? What is My Decision-Making Style? What's My Leadership Style? How Well Do I Manage Impressions? What's the Right Organizational Culture for Me? How Stressful is My Life?*.

 **VANGONOTES (www.VangoNotes.com):**

With VangoNotes students can study "in between" all the other things they need to get done. Students download chapter reviews from their text and listen to them on any mp3 player. VangoNotes gives students the confidence needed to succeed in the classroom. They're flexible; just download and go. And, they're efficient. Use them in the car, at the gym, walking to class, wherever; for more information or to download go to *www.VangoNotes.com*.

 **NEW *MyPsychLab* FOR *Psychology: Concepts* AND *Applications* (www.mypsychlab.com)**

Continual feedback is an important component to successful student progress. New to this edition is Pearson's *MyPsychLab*, an easy-to-use online resource that allows instructors to assess student progress and adapt course material to meet the specific needs of the class. *MyPsychLab* enables students to assess their progress by completing online self-assessment tests. The tests have a large base of questions, distinct from the test bank and other supplementary materials. A variety of question types are used for the pre- and post-tests, including multiple choice, text match, ranking, fill in the blank, and drag and drop.

Based on the results of the pre-test, students are provided with a customized study plan that includes a variety of tools to help them fully master the material such as e-book exercises, simulations and activities. Students can use the activities to study key content areas and they can also continue to quiz themselves by taking the post-test as many times as they want. Pre- and post-tests are randomized so if students opt to take the post-test again, they have exposure to more questions for the same content area.

MyPsychLab records the pre-test, study plan and post-test results for the instructor, as individual student grades as well as an aggregate report of class progress. Based on these reports, the instructor can adapt course material to suit the needs of individual students or the class as a whole. Having instructor course materials such as extra lecture notes, PPT slides, and activities available in *MyPsychLab* saves instructors time since they can choose to use only those resources, based on the results of the pre-test, that reflect the areas their students are having difficulty with.

MyPsychLab provides a more compelling classroom experience by allowing students to better assess their own progress and by providing instructors materials specific to the needs of their class. *MyPsychLab* saves instructors time by cataloguing student progress and providing tools to help students achieve success in their introductory psychology class. Students access *MyPsychLab* through an access code packaged with their text, or purchased online at *www.mypsychlab.com*. Contact your local Pearson representative for an instructor's code and for more information.

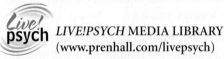 **LIVE!PSYCH MEDIA LIBRARY (www.prenhall.com/livepsych)**

The *Live!Psych* media library is a series of experiments, simulations and activities developed to offer students an interactive way to master the major concepts presented in introductory psychology and to reinforce the scientific nature of the discipline. Designed to get students to interact with the material and to appeal to different learning styles, these media activities were created in consultation with psychology instructors and carefully reviewed by a board of experts to ensure accuracy and pedagogical effectiveness. For the development of the *Live!Psych* Experiments, a special thank you goes to Linda Lockwood, Metro State College, the content author, and to the members of our *Live!Psych* review board. The *Live!Psych* media library is available through *MyPsychLab* or on a CD-ROM (0131947745). Contact your local Pearson sales representative for more information.

 **RESEARCH NAVIGATOR™ (*WWW. RESEARCHNAVIGATOR.COM*)** Research Navigator helps students find, cite, and conduct research with three exclusive databases: EBSCO's ContentSelect Academic Journal Database; *The New York Times* Search by Subject Archive; and Best of the Web Link Library. Available through *MyPsychLab* or packaged with the text, ask your Pearson sales representative for ordering information.

VIDEO CLASSICS IN PSYCHOLOGY CD-ROM (978-0-13-189154-8): Using the power of video to clarify key concepts in the text, this CD-ROM offers original footage of some of the best-known classic experiments in psychology, including Milgram's obedience study, Watson's Little Albert, Bandura's BoBo doll, Pavlov's dog, Harlow's monkey, and others. In addition, students can see interviews with renowned contributors to the field like B. F. Skinner, Carl Rogers, Erik Erickson, Carl Jung, and others. Each video is preceded by background information on the importance of the experiment or researcher to the field and is followed by questions that connect the video to concepts presented in the text. Contact your local sales representative for the package ISBN of the text and CD ROM.

SAFARIX WEBBOOK (*WWW.SAFARIX.COM*): Students can buy an online subscription to *Psychology: Concepts and Applications* at a 50 percent savings. With the SafariX WebBook, students can search the text, make notes online, print out reading assignments that incorporate lecture notes, and bookmark important passages. Ask your local Pearson representative for details of visit *www.safarix.com*.

COMPANION WEBSITE (*WWW.PRENHALL.COM/ MORRIS*): Visit the Prentice Hall Introductory Psychology website, your guide to exploring the fascinating and diverse world of psychology. On this site you can find information on what psychology is about and help in gaining an understanding of the history of psychology; examples of the types of research done in the major fields of psychology; links to useful sites in the major areas of psychology; news links to current real-world issues in psychology; and online quizzes providing immediate scoring and feedback. The Prentice Hall Introductory Psychology web site for the Morris/Maisto/Dunn text is an open access site available to all.

VIDEO RESOURCES FOR INSTRUCTORS

Prentice Hall is proud to present you with the following video packages, available exclusively to qualified adopters of the Morris/ Maisto text.

INTRODUCTORY PSYCHOLOGY TEACHING FILMS BOXED SET (978-0-13-192687-5) Offering you an easy-to-use multi-DVD set of videos, organized by chapter topics, to incorporate into your Introductory Psychology course, this resource offers approximately 100 short video clips of 5–15 minutes in length from many of the most popular video sources for Psychology content, such as ABC News; the *Films for the Humanities* series; *PBS*, and more. Available to qualified adopters, contact your local Prentice Hall representative for more information.

PRENTICE HALL LECTURE LAUNCHER VIDEO FOR INTRODUCTORY PSYCHOLOGY (978-0-13-048640-0) Adopters can receive this video ideal for launching lecture topics. The video includes short clips covering all major topics in Introductory Psychology. The clips have been carefully selected from the *Films for Humanities and Sciences* library and edited to provide brief and compelling video content for enhancing your lectures. Contact your local representative for a full list of video clips on this tape.

Other video series are available; ask your Pearson sales representative for more details.

SUPPLEMENTARY TEXTS

Contact your Prentice Hall representative to package any of these supplementary texts with *Psychology: Concepts and Applications* (note a package ISBN is required for your bookstore order):

Current Directions in Introductory Psychology: Readings from the American Psychological Society (978-0-13-152367-8) This exciting reader includes over 20 articles carefully selected for the undergraduate audience, and taken from the very accessible *Current Directions in Psychological Science* journal. These timely, cutting-edge articles allow instructors to bring their students real-world perspective about today's most current and pressing issues in psychology.

TIME **Special Edition: Psychology (978-0-13-109024-8)** Prentice Hall and *TIME* magazine are pleased to offer you and your students a chance to examine today's most current and compelling issues in an exciting and new way. *TIME* Special Edition: Psychology offers a selection of 15 *TIME* articles on today's most current issues and debates in the field of psychology, perfect for discussion groups, in-class debates, or research assignments.

Forty Studies That Changed Psychology, Fifth Edition **(978-0-13-114729-4)** by Roger Hock (Mendocino College). Presenting the seminal research studies that have shaped modern psychological study, this brief supplement provides an overview of the environment that gave rise to each study, its experimental design, its findings, and its impact on current thinking in the discipline.

How to Think Like a Psychologist: Critical Thinking in Psychology, Second Edition(978-0-13-015046-2) by Donald McBurney (University of Pittsburgh). This unique supplementary text uses a question and answer format to explore some of the most common questions students ask about psychology.

Acknowledgements

Many people have contributed to the production of *Psychology: Concepts and Applications*. First, we would like to acknowledge the efforts of those who have added to the success of the various editions of *Understanding Psychology*, since many of these contributions have been incorporated into this text as well. We are grateful for the assistance we received from those who reviewed the text and supplements of *Understanding Psychology 7/e* and suggested improvements for the new text. Their thoughtful comments helped greatly to identify areas in need of special attention.

Cheryl Bluestone, Queensborough Community College
Dixon A. Bramblett, Lindenwood University
Thomas Bruce, F.M.U
Linda Bruff, Strayer University
Christina Bumgardner, MSB College
Kelly Charlton, University of North Carolina, Pembroke
Stephen M. Colarelli, Central Michigan University
Stacy Crawford, AIB College of Business
Jim Dalton, Sanford-Brown College
Daniel Dickman, Ivy Tech Community College
Michael Durnam, Montana State University - Bozeman
Joy Easton, De Vry University
Jane El-Jacoubi, Strayer University (Manassas Campus)
Christian Fossa-Anderson, De Vry University South Florida
Tom Frangicetto, Northampton Community College
John Gambon, Ozarks Technical Community College
Jennifer Georgen, Missouri College
Andrea Goldstein, Keiser College
Joe Grisham, Indian River Community College
Jack Harnett, Virginia Commonwealth University
Amy Hickman, Collins College
Aleyenne Johnson-Jonas, The Art Institute of California- SD
Jason Kaufman, Ph.D, Inver Hills Community College
Joseph Lao, Borough of Manhattan Community College
Gregory Manley, University of Texas San Antonio
Leslie Oja, Argosy University- Seattle
Barbara B. Oswald, University of South Carolina
Jennifer Peluso, Mercer University
Terry Pettijohn, Ohio State University
Kate Sawyer, Lincoln Educational Services
Karen Tinsley, Guilford College
Thomas Todd, Adler School of Professional Psychology
Theresa Tuttle, ECPI College of Technology
Carolyn Tremblay, Orlando Culinary Academy
Fred Whitford, Montana State University

Special thanks goes to several excellent full manuscript reviewers. Joy Easton (DeVry University) and Theresa Tuttle (ECPI College of Technology) provided comprehensive reviews of all the content included in the book, as well as suggestions for improvements and for the topics illustrated in the opening case statements. Their excellent judgment about which content was especially critical guided the creation of this text from establishing the table of contents on forward through every phase of creation. Sara Farrell (Coe College) provided exceptionally thoughtful and well-grounded advice about the content for Chapter 11: Psychology Applied to Work. Her critiques of various versions of this chapter and her suggestions about content coverage helped to shape this chapter in terms of topics as well as contemporary perspectives in the field. David Hayes and Daniel Lehn (both at Coe College) also read this work carefully and added to its precision and coverage.

Special thanks must go to two talented writers who contributed, in somewhat different ways, to the material included. John Gambon (Ozarks Technical Community College) prepared an early draft of Chapter 11 that was valuable in shaping the content ultimately presented in this chapter. Many of John's ideas have been retained in this chapter, and his synthesis of the broad topics in the field of I/O psychology was especially useful. Nancy Brandwein provided the research and text for all of the chapter opener Case Studies. Nancy's work provided a creative, focused, and applied perspective that contributes very importantly to the text's overarching themes. Her ability to generate topical ideas that successfully illustrate the link between basic psychological principles and the applications they generate in the world of work today represents a truly impressive creative and thoughtful approach for this book.

At Prentice Hall, a rather large team of professional editors and project directors deserves recognition for excellent work. First, Jessica Mosher, Executive Editor, merits our special thanks and appreciation for identifying the need for this book and for conceptualizing the overall approach we have taken. Her thoughtful, forward-thinking, creative work has oriented the project throughout its development. In particular, the integrated set of Web-based support materials that have been created to support students and instructors who use this text is the most exciting in the industry today, and Jessica deserves special recognition for her role in creating and implementing this system. Jeannine Ciliotta is an exceptionally talented and responsible developmental editor, and she, too, deserves special recognition for her insight, her knowledge base, her persistence, and her dedication to high standards and tough deadlines, not to mention her kind, steady, and optimistic support of others involved in the project. Rochelle Diogenes, Editor in Chief of Development, has provided especially valued support and advice concerning the overall project and its associated market, context, and production. She is a consummate professional and a voice of wisdom, experience, encouragement, and good sense.

Thanks as well to Billy Grieco and Jessica Kupetz for their editorial assistance during this development of the text. Kerri Scott, Assessment Editor, and Brian Hyland, Media Editor, oversaw the development of all of the print and media supplements for the text. The production was handled by Maureen Richardson, Assistant Managing Editor; Randy Pettit, Production Liaison; and Stefania Magaldi, Production Editor, Preparè. Thanks also to Ilze Lemesis, Interior and Cover Design, and Leslie Osher, Creative Design Director. Finally, our sincere thanks to the Pearson sales staff for their enthusiastic support of our text and for the excellent service they provide to our adopters.

Others who deserve our thanks include Beth Valenta and Kim Pierson at Coe College, who provided excellent, prompt, and accurate technical support in the production of the manuscript, and Shari Saari, who handled the shipping arrangements for various iterations of chapters and materials, a job not nearly so simple as it might at first seem. The authors are grateful for the support of many other people at Coe College, including, but not limited to, Mike Baker, Tom Moye, Nükhet Yarbrough, Marc Roy, and Jim Phifer. Finally, Wendy Dunn would like to note that, if the book were to be dedicated, it would undoubtedly be, as always, to Greg.

Charles G. Morris
Albert A. Maisto
Wendy L. Dunn

Welcome to Psychology!

How does the brain command a finger to move? Do our dreams mean anything? What do genes have to do with intelligence? How do babies learn to talk? What is love? In this book, you will learn about the full range of human behavior, how psychologists go about trying to answer the preceding questions, and so much more. You will also learn about learning itself. Do you know how *you* learn? How many times have you sat down to read your textbook and found your mind just wandering off? You know that your eyes have picked up every word on the page, but by the end of the page, you have no memory of reading anything! Remember this saying by Thomas Alva Edison: "I have not failed. I've just found 10,000 ways that won't work." You are about to learn some ways of studying that *do* work, techniques that are based on what psychologists know about learning and memory.

Knowing how you learn—your personal "learning style"—is the first step. Your learning style has nothing to do with how intelligent you are. There is no "good" or "bad" learning style—there are simply different ways of learning. For example, some people are best at remembering information they hear. Other people are better at remembering information that they see. Your preferred learning style is simply the way you learn best. Once you know your preferred learning style, you can use that knowledge to your advantage to make your studying more efficient and effective. You will remember more information in a shorter amount of time, thus paving the way for you to do better in all of your classes.

Analyze Your Learning Style

Psychologists have identified a number of learning styles (Suskie, 2003). We will mention just four of them here. To understand these styles, think about how you usually carry out a new task—say, putting together a piece of furniture with the dreaded "some assembly required." The furniture comes with a printed set of directions with words and pictures. Do you read the directions word for word and go through the steps in an orderly way? If so, you are probably a *visual/verbal learner*. Or are you the type of learner who just looks at the pictures and doesn't need the written instructions? If so, you are most likely a *visual/nonverbal learner*. How about those of you who prefer to read the instructions out loud or have a friend read them to you while you work on the piece of furniture? You are most likely an *auditory learner* who learns best when you hear something. Finally, how about those of you who don't need directions at all—you study the pieces and then just start putting the furniture together? Chances are that you are a *tactile/kinesthetic learner* who learns best by "doing" a hands-on task.

Now think about some of the classes you have had in the past. You may have had some classes in which the material made perfect sense and was easy to remember. In those classes, it is likely that the teaching style and your learning style were well matched. Then there may have been other classes in which you tried and tried to remember the material, but nothing seemed to work—you probably had difficulty staying interested and perhaps had difficulty even staying awake! In those instances, in all likelihood your learning style and the teaching style did not match. The sooner you can figure out your own "best" learning style, the easier your studying and learning will become because you will be able to adapt any information you are given to your optimal learning style.

One of the simplest ways to assess your preferred learning style is online (and it's free!). Simply point your web browser to *http://www.metamath.com/lsweb/dvclearn.htm*. You will find much more information about these four learning styles. At the bottom of the page you can click on "Learning Styles Survey" to assess your preferred style and learn about study techniques that are particularly appropriate for that style. If you click on "Four Learning Styles" you can learn much more about the four learning styles and their respective learning strategies.

Arousal and Optimal Learning

Do you ever get drowsy just as you start to study, during class or during an exam? It may have something to do with your sleep habits. But it may also be that you are not getting the stimulation you need to concentrate. The traditional study method is to sit in a quiet place and just read. This works well for some people but not others. You may find that you need some "noise" in the background to study and remember effectively. This could be noise from a television program in the background, the chatter in a local coffeehouse, or music that you are listening to. If you need more noise than quiet to help you concentrate then use it! While you are studying, listen to your CD player with headphones. Or turn on the television or the radio. Experiment a little to find your optimum level of stimulation for learning.

Reading the Text and Actually Remembering It!

One tried-and-true method psychologists have found that helps students to remember concepts from printed material is called the SQ3R Method: *Survey, Question, Read, Recite,* and *Review.* The text has been prepared with a number of tools that will help you use this effective method of studying printed material. You can use the knowledge of your preferred learning style to make the SQ3R method more effective for you.

SURVEY: Surveying, or previewing, prepares your brain to receive information in an organized way. Properly done, it will help you read faster and comprehend better. Before you begin a chapter, survey the topics it covers by reading the **Overview** on the chapter title page. If you are a visual/verbal learner (the most traditional learning style), reading the overview while thinking about what the topics mean should work just fine. However, if you are primarily an auditory learner, you may want to read the overview out loud and ask yourself questions about what each section of the chapter might be about. Visual/nonverbal learners should read the overview, perhaps highlight the key concepts or write questions in the margin in bright colors, and look over the illustrations in the chapter as they survey the material. The tactile/kinesthetic learner might walk around with the textbook and read it, maybe even reading out loud while walking. If possible, write out questions about the chapter topics in your text or on a separate piece of paper while you read. Yes, you really need to get used to writing in your textbooks! Those nice wide margins are there for a reason: notes, stars, marks, doodles . . . just about anything can be written there that will help you to remember the material.

QUESTION: Be sure to read the **Questions** that appear in color at the beginning of each major section in the chapter. These opening questions indicate what key ideas you should be looking for as you read that section. Again, the same learning-style techniques used in surveying will help here. Compare those opening questions to the questions you thought up when you were surveying the chapter. If you think that writing information down or typing it out helps you to remember, then write down or type out these questions as well. They help you to identify what is especially important in each chapter.

READ: As you read each section, keep the opening question in mind and actively look for answers to it. The key terms in the margins provide clear definitions of the most important terms in the text, so study them, too, as you go along, rather than waiting until you have finished reading the chapter. Now you know that "to study" means "to use the techniques for your primary learning style" . . . don't just sit there passively and let your eyes touch the words while nothing goes into your brain! Figures and photos will help you visualize concepts that are described in the text, and summary tables will aid in organizing the information for you.

RECITE: After each main section, be sure to take the **Check Your Understanding** and **Apply Your Understanding** quizzes. These brief quizzes will help you process the material you just read, making it more likely that you will understand it fully and remember it later. The quiz questions are typical of the questions that are likely to appear on multiple-choice and fill-in-the-blank exams. Think of them as mini pretests.

REVIEW: At the end of each chapter is a list of **Key Terms** with page references. Review each term carefully and refer back to the appropriate page if there are any such terms you can't recall. Use your preferred learning method to help ensure that you remember the meaning of these terms. Next, read through the detailed **Chapter Review**, which summarizes the key concepts in the chapter. Again, reviewing and reading passively while sitting in a quiet room works for some students but not all. During your review, you need to use the methods that work for your learning style. If you know you study well with another person, then these key terms and the chapter review are perfect for reviewing with your "study buddy."

Improving Your Memory and Recall (also Known as "Getting to the Exam with Your Memory Intact!")

Are there ways you can actually improve your memory and recall for material in class and in the text? Absolutely! Knowing your learning style, being aware of how much "noise" you need for optimal stimulation, and using the SQ3R method will all help to improve your memory for course material. However, there are other steps you can take as well.

Perhaps you have noticed that you remember the material discussed in class more easily than the material in the text. If so, it is probably because you build multiple retrieval cues for the class material. Here is how it works: You hear the material, you may also see it (if the instructor writes on the board or puts it into an electronic presentation), you think about it and decide it is important, you write it down when you take notes, and you probably are given examples of the concept or asked to come up with some examples in class. All of those actions provide you with cues for retrieving the material later when you need it. In contrast, if you passively read the text, assuming the information ever gets into long–term memory, you have few if any cues for retrieving it later. The mystery has been solved: You need to build *multiple* retrieval cues for material you want to remember. This can be done in a number of ways, some of which we have already mentioned. Here is a new one: Have you ever tried reading the textbook out loud into a mirror? Actors often use this technique to learn their lines. It may work for you, too. You will see the information when you read it, you will hear it when you speak it, and you will probably also have a mental picture of yourself reading while looking in the mirror. You will be amazed how well this simple technique works to provide those retrieval cues!

The most important step you can take to improve your memory is to make connections between new material and other information already stored in your long-term memory. Using examples, discussing things you want to remember, and applying the material to real-life events help to form bonds between new and old information in long-term memory. Special memory techniques called *mnemonics* (pronounced ni-MON-iks) work in the same way. Some of the simplest mnemonic techniques are rhymes and jingles that we use for remembering dates. For example," Thirty days hath September, . . . April, June, and November . . . " helps us to recall how many days are in a month. Also, forming mental images or making up a story using the material to be remembered really can help. Similarly, making up a story (rather than writing out a list) that uses the items you need to remember at the market can help your memory by providing retrieval cues as you are shopping.

Insider Tips on Note Taking during Class and on Test Taking

You will be able to take notes more efficiently if you have an idea of what will be going on in class on a particular day. Always check the date of the class for the topic and chapter(s) to be covered. Then read at least the chapter objectives and summary for the day's lesson if you don't have time to read the full chapter. Be sure to bring all of your favorite note-taking tools to class, such as different-color pens, highlighter markers, and note cards. Try to get to class early. Relax a little and get yourself ready to learn. To get in the mood for learning, it may help to review your notes from the previous class. Other tips that will help with note taking and remembering the material include sitting close to the front of the class where there will be fewer distractions. Also, try to be active in class. Take part in demonstrations, join the class discussions, and ask questions. Try to relate the topic being discussed to an interest of yours or to an event that happened to you or a friend. Be on the lookout for clues to what is important (for example, the instructor repeats something several times or says "The important point is . . ."). Other clues to particularly important information are summary statements, information written on the board, and handouts. If you miss a few key words while taking lecture notes, just leave a blank space and ask the instructor or teaching assistant after class to help you fill in the missing material.

Well before your first exam, ask about testing procedures if you are not clear about them. Is it possible to ask questions during the exam? Are any notes allowed? Is the test timed? When you first receive the quiz or exam, read the directions carefully. Then reread them! When actually starting the test, you may not want to complete the questions in the order they are presented in the exam. You may want to read through all the questions once and then skip around and answer first the easiest, shortest questions and the ones that you know for sure. Then move on to the questions you are a little less sure of. By using this technique, you won't get stuck in one area of the exam if you don't remember that particular material. Use your memory techniques when you're stuck and don't dwell on any one question too long. Be sure to watch your time if the quiz or exam must be completed in a specified period. Budget your time on the basis of how many points each question or section is worth. Here are a few more words to the wise: If you are having trouble with a particular question, look for helpful clues in other test questions. A term, name, date, or other fact that you can't seem to remember might appear in the test itself. Or something in another question might serve as a retrieval cue and trigger your memory for the missing information. Also think back to the quizzes in the textbook and on the Web site—it's possible that they contained a similar question (that is another reason to use those resources). More **Tips on Test Taking** can be found in the preface of the student study guide that accompanies this text.

MORE INSIDER INFORMATION: GENERAL STUDY TECHNIQUES FOR ANY COLLEGE CLASS

You should plan at least two hours of study time for every hour you spend in class. Using the knowledge and techniques associated with your primary learning style will make this time more effective for you. Study the subjects that you find boring or difficult first. Take short breaks as you study; long study sessions can make you overly tired, and your attention will go downhill fast. Be aware of your best time of the day or night for studying. Cramming right before an exam is not a good study method. You do need some sleep after you study and before you take an exam. Sleeping and dreaming help to solidify new memories. If you find that studying with other people helps you, then, by all means, start a study group. Look for other dedicated students who share your academic goals as well as your time schedule. You might ask your instructor for help in forming these groups, or just write a note on the board before class saying that you want to start a study group. Limit the group to about five or six people. People of similar learning styles seem to work best to-

gether, so you may want to ask about the other students' learning styles. Initially, plan a one-time-only study session. If that works out, then plan additional sessions.

How to Have an "A" College Student Attitude

Optimism helps! Approach your studying with an optimistic, positive, "can do" attitude. If you get a low grade on an exam, put it behind you and set about doing better next time. A famous cartoon figure, Ziggy, says, "You can complain because roses have thorns, or you can rejoice because thorns have roses." Optimists do the latter. An optimistic attitude helps you to meet challenges head-on and conquer just about any task!

In the world of academia, you are playing the part of the student. Are you playing the part of an "A" student or a failing student? Here are some tips on playing the part of an "A" student both inside and outside of the classroom: While in class, make eye contact with the instructor often. Don't be afraid to ask questions in class (if that is permitted) or during office hours. Take notes and nod your head in approval when the instructor says something interesting or helpful. Don't engage in distracting side conversations with other students.

Outside of the classroom, be well-organized. Get a calendar that you can write in and carry with you. You need to have a clear idea of due dates and exam dates. Your handouts and notes should be organized by class and date. Get a three-ring binder for a class notebook that has pockets for handouts; if it doesn't, use a three-hole punch to put handouts where they belong. Always bring the handouts from the previous class with you unless otherwise instructed. Early in the term, go through the course syllabus carefully. Highlight sections that give you specific instructions about assignments such as term papers, quizzes, and exams. Also, make a note indicating how to get in touch with your instructor if you have questions outside of class. The instructor's e-mail address or phone number is usually on the syllabus. If your class has an accompanying Web site, use it! If you don't have Internet access at home, use your college's or local library's computer facility. And whatever you do, make one or more backup copies of any work you do on the computer. There seems to be an unwritten law that if a computer is going to crash, or a disk is going to become unreadable, it will happen the night before something important is due!

Getting to know your professor or teaching assistant is also important, and they also should get to know you and understand that you are an interested and highly motivated student. Letting them get to know you can be quite challenging if you are in a large class. So introduce yourself during posted office hours and let this important person know that you are eager to do well in the class. If he or she doesn't have office hours, then send an email or introduce yourself after class.

Most students do not think they need tutoring until after they do poorly on an exam or paper. The "A" students know how to get tutoring *before* they do poorly! Tutoring serves multiple goals. First, it will give you insight into what is important in the course and perhaps what is important for an exam, paper, or other assignment.

Second, it will make the subject matter more real and personal, and we already know that this alone will help your recall. Last, but not least, when you show up for tutoring, you are reinforcing the message that you are motivated to do well.

Closing the Deal: Learning What You Need to Know and Getting an "A"

After reading this introductory section you may be feeling more overwhelmed with information than helped! There is so much more to being a good learner and knowledgeable person than meets the eye. Sitting passively listening to a lecture and regurgitating information back onto a test is just not enough anymore, if it ever was. You should now feel very well equipped with new techniques and tools to reach your goals in school as well as in life. Just knowing your preferred style of learning and using even a few of the techniques presented here will work wonders for you. Now that you have the tools and techniques, match them with your optimistic attitude and you will greatly increase your chances of being successful. Once again, **Welcome to psychology!**

More Study Tools Available for You

Check out the following study tools online at *www.myPearsonstore.com*

 **SELF-ASSESSMENT LIBRARY CD-ROM (978-0-13-221793-4):** The Self-Assessment Library is a unique learning tool that allows you to assess your knowledge, beliefs, feelings, and actions with regard to a wide range of personal skills, abilities, and interests. Automatically grades, self-scoring exercises generate immediate, individual analysis and feedback. Topics include *What's My Basic Personality? How Satisfied Am I with My Job? What is My Decision-Making Style? What's My Leadership Style? How Well Do I Manage Impressions? What's the Right Organizational Culture for Me? How Stressful is My Life?.*

VANGONOTES Study on the go with VangoNotes. Just download chapter reviews from your text and listen to them on any mp3 player. Now wherever you are—whatever you're doing—you can study by listening to the following for each chapter of your textbook:

- **Big Ideas:** Your "need to know" for each chapter
- **Practice Test:** A gut check for the Big Ideas – tells you if you need to keep studying
- **Key Terms:** Audio "flashcards" to help you review key concepts and terms
- **Rapid Review:** A quick drill session – use it right before your test

VangoNotes are flexible; download all the material directly to your player, or only the chapters you need. And they're efficient. Use them in your car, at the gym, walking to class, wherever. So get yours today. And get studying. Check it out at *http://www.VangoNotes.com.*

 NEW *MYPSYCHLAB* FOR *PSYCHOLOGY: CONCEPTS AND APPLICATIONS* Pearson's *MyPsychLab* is an easy-to-use online resource that helps you understand how you are doing in your class. The program contains multiple quizzes tied to your textbook. Based on the results of a content pre-test, you are provided with your own customized study plan. The study plan contains a variety of activities such as e-book exercises, simulations and activities that help you master key content. You can continue to quiz yourself by taking the post-test as many times as you want. Pre- and post-tests are randomized so if you opt to take the post-test again, you have access to more questions for the same content area. Find out more at *http://www.mypsychlab.com.*

 COMPANION WEBSITE (www.prenhall.com/morris): Visit the Prentice Hall Introductory Psychology website, your guide to exploring the fascinating and diverse world of psychology. On this site you can find information on what psychology is about and help in gaining an understanding of the history of psychology; examples of the types of research done in the major fields of psychology; links to useful sites in the major areas of psychology; news links to current real-world issues in psychology; and online quizzes providing immediate scoring and feedback. The Prentice Hall Introductory Psychology web site for Morris is an open access site available to all.

PSYCHOLOGY
CONCEPTS AND APPLICATIONS

The Science of Psychology

Overview

TOYOTA

There's a problem on the Toyota assembly line: A Toyota employee with a small build is having a hard time lifting up parts to bolt them onto the chassis. She talks with her supervisor and the two of them quickly come up with a simple setup that allows her to do her work without straining her muscles—a solution that improves safety, quality, and ergonomics.

This seemingly unremarkable interaction is part of the **scientific method** that has catapulted Toyota from a tiny Japanese carmaker in the 1940s—its production was a fraction of Ford's—to become the world's largest car company, in volume. Its earnings are $11.4 billion today—more than all other major automakers combined. From the beginning, Toyota didn't have the money to invest in the expensive presses and other machinery American automakers had. This forced it to focus more on process and in particular, to focus more on how to get employees to solve problems on the assembly room floor.

Years ago, two Harvard professors followed some managers around the factory to see what makes Toyota run so well. They promptly coined the term "Community of Scientists" for Toyota's workers because, like the woman with the aching back, each employee—from the line worker to the design engineer—uses the scientific method to solve daily problems. This method entails first defining specifications—making a plan—and then establishing hypotheses, or predictions, about what will happen if the plan is put in place. Then the employees—or, rather, team members—must continually test the plan and measure the outcomes. In Toyota terminology, it's called "A3 Thinking" and has four simple steps: "Plan-do-check-adjust."

Here's how A3 thinking works in practice: Say employees in the fabrication shop have a problem with the changeover time of a certain press. It should take only 20 minutes, but it actually takes 60—40 minutes of lost production time. A team of Toyota employees develops a hypothesis that goes something like this: "If we alter our changeover process in "X" way, and if it includes these steps, these elements, these times, and this walk pattern, we believe we will reduce changeover time by 40 minutes." Next, they test the hypothesis, and in the "check"

phase they study what actually happens. If changeover time is reduced by only 37 minutes, they adjust the process until they meet their target.

"Plan-do-check-adjust" seems simple, and that's why so many companies think they can copy Toyota's techniques and enjoy the same success. But former Toyota president Fujio Cho is quick to point out that those who try often fail. No mere process can turn a poor performer into a star. "Rather, you have to address employees' fundamental way of thinking." At the heart of the Toyota way is an investment in people. The company hires as few people as possible and expects to keep an employee for 30 years or more. "To involve people, to get them to solve problems, you have to have the [right] atmosphere," says Pascal Dennis, a former Toyota employee who now teaches Toyota's techniques. Treating people well is part of what makes the atmosphere so special. "It's a different relationship between [management and labor] that's based on mutual trust," says Dennis. The Toyota system presumes that people will be team players and put the group's needs in front of their own.[1]

What Is Psychology?

1.1 Define psychology and describe the most important issues and topics that present-day psychologists study.

So what does *psychology*, the subject of this textbook, have to do with how a group of employees work to build an even better version of the Toyota Prius, the company's popular hybrid car? Like Toyota employees, like white-coated scientists in a biotech lab, or even like a group of fourth graders working on a science fair project, psychologists rely on the scientific method to answer questions. **Psychology** is, after all, the scientific study of all kinds of behavior and mental processes. As such, viewed from a wealth of different perspectives, it encompasses every aspect of human thoughts, feelings, and actions. It is not confined to investigating abnormal behavior, as many people mistakenly assume. In fact, with new research technologies, new areas of inquiry to explore, and more collaboration with other sciences, psychology is continually redefining itself more broadly (Evans, 1999).

THE FIELDS OF PSYCHOLOGY

How is psychology defined and what topics do psychologists study?

Psychology is not so much a single, unified field of study as it is an umbrella concept for a loose amalgamation of different subfields (Evans, 1999). The American Psychological Association has over 50 divisions, each representing a specialized area of research and interest. These are identified in **Table 1-1**. Several of these subfields may be familiar to you, including perhaps seven of the largest, which we describe here.

psychology The scientific study of behavior and mental processes.

3

>TABLE 1-1   AMERICAN PSYCHOLOGICAL ASSOCIATION DIVISIONS (2004)

The two major organizations of psychologists in the United States are the American Psychological Association (APA), founded over 100 years ago, and the American Psychological Society (APS), founded in 1988. Members of both groups work in a wide variety of areas. The following list of divisions of the APA reflects the enormous diversity of the field of psychology:

Division*

1. Society for General Psychology	30. Society of Psychological Hypnosis
2. Society for the Teaching of Psychology	31. State, Provincial, and Territorial Psychological Association Affairs
3. Experimental Psychology	32. Humanistic Psychology
5. Evaluation, Measurement, and Statistics	33. Mental Retardation and Developmental Disabilities
6. Behavioral Neuroscience and Comparative Psychology	34. Population and Environmental Psychology
7. Developmental Psychology	35. Society for the Psychology of Women
8. Society for Personality and Social Psychology	36. Psychology of Religion
9. Society for the Psychological Study of Social Issues (SPSSI)	37. Child, Youth, and Family Services
10. Society for the Psychology of Aesthetics, Creativity and the Arts	38. Health Psychology
12. Society of Clinical Psychology	39. Psychoanalysis
13. Society of Consulting Psychology	40. Clinical Neuropsychology
14. Society for Industrial and Organizational Psychology	41. American Psychology—Law Society
15. Educational Psychology	42. Psychologists in Independent Practice
16. School Psychology	43. Family Psychology
17. Society of Counseling Psychology	44. Society for the Psychological Study of Lesbian, Gay, and Bisexual Issues
18. Psychologists in Public Service	45. Society for the Psychological Study of Ethnic Minority Issues
19. Society of Military Psychology	46. Media Psychology
20. Adult Development and Aging	47. Exercise and Sport Psychology
21. Applied Experimental and Engineering Psychology	48. Society for the Study of Peace, Conflict, and Violence: Peace Psychology Division
22. Rehabilitation Psychology	49. Group Psychology and Group Psychotherapy
23. Society for Consumer Psychology	50. Addictions
24. Society for Theoretical and Philosophical Psychology	51. Society for the Psychological Study of Men and Masculinity
25. Behavior Analysis	52. International Psychology
26. Society for the History of Psychology	53. Society of Clinical Child and Adolescent Psychology
27. Society for Community Research and Action: Division of Community Psychology	54. Society of Pediatric Psychology
28. Psychopharmacology and Substance Abuse	55. American Society for the Advancement of Pharmacotherapy
29. Psychotherapy	56. Trauma Psychology

*There are no divisions 4 or 11.

For information on a division, e-mail the APA at division@apa.org, or locate them on the Internet at http://www.apa.org/about/division.html.

Source: American Psychological Association (2004). Divisions of the American Psychological Association. Retrieved March 9, 2004, from the Internet at http://www.apa.org/about/division.html.

DEVELOPMENTAL PSYCHOLOGY *Developmental psychologists* study all aspects of human growth and change—physical, mental, social, and emotional—from the prenatal period through old age. Most specialize in a particular stage of human development. *Child psychologists* focus on infants and children, concerning themselves with issues such as whether babies are born with distinct temperaments, how infants become attached to their caregivers, at what age sex differences in behavior emerge, and what changes occur in the meaning and importance of friendship during childhood. *Adolescent psychologists*, who study changes that occur during the teenage years, primarily look at how puberty affects a whole range of developmental topics, from relationships with peers and parents to the search for a personal identity. Finally, *life-span psychologists* focus on the challenges and changes of adulthood, from marrying and having children, to meeting demands at work, to facing the transitions related to aging and eventual death.

PHYSIOLOGICAL PSYCHOLOGY *Physiological psychologists* investigate the biological basis of human behavior, thoughts, and emotions. Those who are known as *neuropsychologists* are interested in the workings of the brain and nervous system. How does the brain enable us to perceive the world through our senses? How does it allow us to think, speak, sleep, move our bodies, and feel emotions such as anger, sadness, and joy? Neuropsychologists help to answer these and many other fundamental questions about how thoughts, feelings, and behaviors are controlled. Their colleagues known as *psychobiologists* study the body's biochemistry and the ways that hormones, psychoactive medications, and "social drugs" affect us. They investigate topics such as how the hormones of puberty are related to mood swings and how alcohol consumption by a pregnant woman impairs the development of her unborn child. *Behavioral geneticists* add yet another dimension: They explore the impact of heredity on both normal and abnormal behavior. To what degree is individual intelligence hereditary? Do illnesses such as alcoholism and depression have a genetic component? What about differences in the ways that men and women think, act, and feel?

EXPERIMENTAL PSYCHOLOGY *Experimental psychologists* conduct research on basic psychological processes, including learning, memory, sensation, perception, thinking, motivation, and emotion. They are interested in answering questions such as: How do people remember information and what makes them forget? How do they go about making decisions and solving various kinds of problems? Do men and women solve complex problems in different ways? Why are some people much more motivated than others? Work in the field of experimental psychology often serves as the basis for developing applications of psychological principles, such as those used by Toyota to create its unique organizational culture.

PERSONALITY PSYCHOLOGY *Personality psychologists* study the differences among individuals in such traits as sociability, conscientiousness, emotional stability, self-esteem, agreeableness, aggressive inclinations, and openness to new experiences. Psychologists in this field attempt to determine what causes some people to be optimists and others to be pessimists, why some people are outgoing and friendly, whereas others are shy and reserved, as well as whether there are consistent differences in the personality characteristics of males and females. As is the case in experimental psychology, research in personality psychology often is applied to solving real-world problems. At Toyota, for example, job applicants who are flexible, creative, and work well with others are more likely to be hired.

CLINICAL AND COUNSELING PSYCHOLOGY When asked to describe a "psychologist," most people think of a therapist who sees troubled patients in an office, clinic, or hospital. This popular view is half correct. About 50 percent of psychologists specialize in clinical or counseling psychology, both of which seek to help people deal more successfully with their lives. The two areas also differ, however. *Clinical psychologists* are interested primarily in the diagnosis, causes, and treatment of psychological disorders, such as depression or acute anxiety. *Counseling psychologists*, in contrast, are concerned mainly with the "normal" everyday problems of adjustment that most of us face at some point in life, such as making a difficult career choice or coping with a troubled marriage. Clinical and counseling psychologists often divide their time between treating patients and conducting research on the causes of psychological disorders and on the effectiveness of different types of therapy.

SOCIAL PSYCHOLOGY Social psychologists start with the assumption that a person's personality characteristics are insufficient to predict that person's thoughts, feelings, and behaviors. This is because, like it or not, we are all greatly influenced by other people. Social psychology is the scientific study of just how these social influences are exerted and the effects they have. Social psychologists investigate issues such as interpersonal attraction, persuasive communications and attitude formation, obedience to authority, conformity to group norms, and how people often behave differently in crowds. At Toyota, social psychologists are especially interested in studying the interactions of work team members.

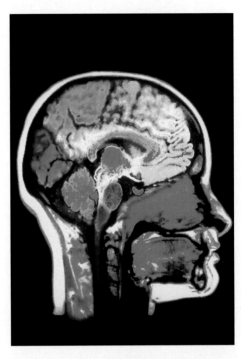

Recent advances in neuroimaging techniques enable physiological psychologists to investigate how specific regions of the brain are involved in complex behaviors and mental processes.

INDUSTRIAL AND ORGANIZATIONAL (I/O) PSYCHOLOGY *Industrial and organizational (I/O) psychologists* apply the principles of psychology to the work place. They are concerned with practical issues such as selecting and training personnel, improving productivity and working conditions, and managing the impact of computerization and automation on workers. I/O psychologists seek to determine in advance who will be effective as a salesperson, as an airline pilot, or in any other career. They ask whether organizations tend to operate differently under highly structured versus participative leadership and, if so, what the drawbacks or benefits of each might be. And because research shows that high morale fosters more productive workers, I/O psychologists also search for specific strategies that managers can use to improve group morale. In the case of Toyota, they are interested in how a new and different type of organizational culture affects productivity and many other work place behaviors. I/O psychology plays an important role in the modern world of work. Wherever you might eventually find a job, that work place will probably have been shaped to some extent by the efforts of I/O psychologists.

ENDURING ISSUES

Given this broad range of careers and interests, what holds psychology together?

What do psychologists who study organizations, psychological disorders, memory and cognition, behavioral genetics, or attachment in infants have in common? All psychologists share a common interest in five enduring issues that override their areas of specialization and that cut to the core of what it means to be human.

PERSON–SITUATION To what extent is behavior caused by processes that occur inside the person (such as thoughts, emotions, motives, attitudes, values, personality, and genes)? In contrast, to what extent is behavior caused or triggered by factors outside the person (such as incentives, cues in the environment, and the presence of other people)? Put another way, are we masters of our fate, or victims of circumstances? We will encounter these questions most directly in our consideration of behavior genetics, learning, emotion and motivation, personality, social, and industrial/organizational psychology.

NATURE–NURTURE Is the person we become a product of innate, inborn tendencies, or a reflection of experiences and upbringing? This is the famous "nature versus nurture" debate. For decades, psychologists argued about the degree of influence that heredity, or genes, versus environment, or experience, has on thought and behavior. This issue appears in our discussions of behavior genetics, intelligence, development, personality, and abnormal psychology, and it will arise elsewhere as well.

STABILITY–CHANGE Are the characteristics we develop in childhood more or less permanent and fixed, or do we change in predictable (and unpredictable) ways over the course of our lives? Do the same traits that guide our choices as adolescents continue to influence our selection of mates, careers, and hobbies throughout adulthood, or do our personalities change as we move through the life span? Developmental psychologists are especially interested in these questions (as are psychologists who specialize in personality, adjustment, abnormal psychology and therapy, and industrial/organizational psychology), as well as other areas.

DIVERSITY–UNIVERSALITY To what extent is every person in certain respects similar to all other people, similar to some other people, or similar to no other person? (Adapted from Kluckhohn, Murray, & Schneider, 1961, p. 53.) Human diversity is a central concern for psychologists. Throughout the book, we will encounter these questions: Does our understanding apply equally well to every human being? Does it apply only to men or just to women, or only to particular racial or ethnic groups or particular societies (especially our own)? Do we need to hire different types of workers to do different types of jobs? Do we perhaps need "different psychologies" to account for the wide diversity of human behaviors?

MIND–BODY Finally, how are mind and body connected? Many psychologists are fascinated by the relationship between what we experience (such as thoughts and feelings) and

"I told my parents that if grades were so important they should have paid for a smarter egg donor."

what our biological processes are (such as activity in the nervous system). This mind-body issue will arise most clearly in our discussions of the biological basis of behavior, sensation and perception, altered states of consciousness, emotion and motivation, health psychology, and psychological disorders and therapy.

Philosophers have pondered the significance of these five issues for centuries, and they also have been a running theme throughout the history of psychology. Depending on what subject they are studying, psychologists in one subfield or one school of thought may emphasize the person or the situation, heredity or environment, stability or change, diversity or universality, or subjective experience or biological processes. These same questions of emphasis are seen throughout the historical development of psychology as a scientific field of inquiry. Viewpoints about what the proper scope and subject matter of psychology should be oftentimes crystallized around these central, enduring issues.

To understand human behavior, we must appreciate the rich diversity of culture throughout the world.

▶ CHECK YOUR UNDERSTANDING

1. Indicate whether each of the following statements is true (T) or false (F):
   a. _____ The study of how others influence an individual's actions would fall most clearly within the subfield of social psychology.
   b. _____ Developmental psychologists most often study how organizations, such as schools and companies, grow and change.
   c. _____ Behaviorial geneticists do not typically employ the methods of science in their work.
   d. _____ If Damon wanted to call in an expert to figure out how to hire more successful salespeople for his company,

   he would most likely hire an industrial/organizational psychologist.
   e. _____ The mind-body issue pertains to the question, "Are all of our thoughts and feelings the result of only the action of the neurons in our brain?"

2. If Julia believes that workers' ability to handle stress is controlled by the genes they inherit, her viewpoint emphasizes which enduring issue?
   a. Nature–nuture
   b. Stability–change
   c. Person–situation
   d. Diversity–universality

Answers: 1. a. (T), b. (F), c. (F), d. (T), e. (T)., 2. a.

▶ APPLY YOUR UNDERSTANDING

1. Caroline is interested in the question of whether our personality characteristics are determined for life by genetics or can be changed as a result of the experiences of our lives. Which of the enduring issues discussed in this chapter best describes Caroline's interests?
   a. Mind–body
   b. Diversity–universality
   c. Nature–nurture
   d. Person–situation

2. Dakota spends most of his work time in his office developing training programs to teach workers how to better perform their jobs. Dakota is most likely a(n) _____ psychologist.
   a. industrial/organizational
   b. developmental
   c. clinical
   d. experimental

Answers: 1. c., 2. a.

The Growth of Psychology

1.2 Describe the origins of psychology and identify the major historical views that have guided its development as a discipline up to the present time.

In the West, since the time of Plato and Aristotle, people have wondered and written about human behavior and mental processes. But not until the late 1800s did they begin to apply the scientific method to questions that had puzzled philosophers for centuries. Only then did psychology come into being as a formal, scientific discipline separate from philosophy. The history of psychology can be divided into three main stages: the emergence of a science of the mind, the behaviorist decades, and the "cognitive revolution."

THE "NEW PSYCHOLOGY": A SCIENCE OF THE MIND

How did the work of Wundt and Titchener, of James, and of Freud contribute to the early development of psychology as a field of study?

At the beginning of the twentieth century, most university psychology programs were located in philosophy departments. But the foundations of the "new psychology"—the science of psychology—had been laid.

WILHELM WUNDT AND EDWARD BRADFORD TITCHENER: VOLUNTARISM AND STRUCTURALISM Most psychologists agree that psychology was born in 1879, the year that Wilhelm Wundt founded the first psychological laboratory at the University of Leipzig in Germany. In the public eye, a laboratory identified a field of inquiry as "science" (Benjamin, 2000). At the outset, Wundt did not attract much attention; only four students attended his first lecture. By the mid-1890s, however, his classes were filled to capacity.

Wundt set about trying to explain the conscious experience we often refer to as "thought" and to develop ways to study it scientifically. By establishing a laboratory and insisting on measurement and experimentation, Wundt moved psychology out of the realm of philosophy and into the world of science (Benjamin, 2000).

One important product of the Leipzig lab was its students who carried the new science of psychology to universities in other countries, including the United States: G. Stanley Hall (who established the first American psychology laboratory at Johns Hopkins University in 1883), J. M. Cattell (a professor at the University of Pennsylvania in 1888, who was the first American to be called a "professor of psychology"), and British-born Edward Bradford Titchener, who went to Cornell University. Titchener's ideas differed sharply in many respects from those of his mentor (Zehr, 2001). Titchener was impressed by recent advances in chemistry and physics, achieved by analyzing complex compounds (molecules) in terms of their basic elements (atoms). Similarly, Titchener reasoned, psychologists should analyze complex conscious experiences in terms of their simplest components. For example, when people look at a banana they immediately think, "Here is a fruit, something to peel and eat." But this perception is based on associations with past experience. Titchener asked, "What are the most fundamental elements, or "atoms," of thought?"

Titchener broke down consciousness into three basic elements: physical sensations (what we see), feelings (such as liking or disliking bananas), and images (memories of other bananas). Even the most complex thoughts and feelings, he argued, can be reduced to these simple elements. Titchener saw psychology's role as identifying these elements and showing how they can be combined and integrated—an approach known as **structuralism**. Although the structuralist school of psychology was relatively short-lived and has had little long-term effect, the study of perception and sensation continues to be very much a part of contemporary psychology, as you will see in Chapter 3: "Sensation, Perception, and Conscious Experience".

WILLIAM JAMES: FUNCTIONALISM One of the first academics to challenge structuralism was an American, William James (son of the transcendentalist philosopher Henry James, Sr., and brother of novelist Henry James). As a young man, James earned a degree in

Wilhelm Wundt

structuralism School of psychology that stresses the basic units of experience and the combinations in which they occur.

physiology and also studied philosophy on his own, unable to decide which interested him more. In psychology, he found the link between the two. In 1875, James offered a class in psychology at Harvard. He later commented that the first lecture he ever heard on the subject was his own.

James argued that Titchener's "atoms of experience"—pure sensations without associations—simply do not exist in real-life experience. Our minds are constantly weaving associations, revising experience, starting, stopping, and jumping back and forth in time. Perceptions, emotions, and images cannot be separated, James argued; consciousness flows in a continuous stream. Furthermore, mental associations allow us to benefit from previous experience. If we could not recognize a banana, we would have to figure out what it was each time we saw one. When we get up in the morning, get dressed, open the door, and walk down the street, we don't have to think about what we are doing: We act out of habit. James suggested that when we repeat something, our nervous systems are changed so that each repetition is easier than the last.

James developed a **functionalist theory** of mental processes and behavior that raised questions about learning, the complexities of mental life, the impact of experience on the brain, and humankind's place in the natural world that still seem current today. Although impatient with experiments, James shared Wundt and Titchener's belief that the goal of psychology was to analyze experience. Wundt was not impressed. After reading James's *The Principles of Psychology* (1890), he commented, "It is literature, it is beautiful, but it is not psychology" (M. Hunt, 1994, p. 139).

SIGMUND FREUD: PSYCHODYNAMIC PSYCHOLOGY Of all psychology's pioneers, Sigmund Freud is by far the best known—and the most controversial. A medical doctor, unlike the other figures we have introduced, Freud was fascinated by the central nervous system. He spent many years conducting research in the physiology laboratory of the University of Vienna and only reluctantly became a practicing physician. After a trip to Paris, where he studied with a neurologist who was using hypnosis to treat nervous disorders, Freud established a private practice in Vienna. His work with patients convinced him that many nervous ailments are psychological, rather than physiological in origin. Freud's clinical observations led him to develop a comprehensive theory of mental life that differed radically from the views of his predecessors.

Freud held that human beings are not as rational as they imagine, and that "free will," which was so important to Wundt, is largely an illusion. Rather, we are motivated by unconscious instincts and urges that are not available to the rational, conscious part of our mind. Other psychologists had referred to the unconscious in passing, as a dusty warehouse of old experiences and information we could retrieve as needed. In contrast, Freud saw the unconscious as a dynamic cauldron of primitive sexual and aggressive drives, forbidden desires, nameless fears and wishes, and traumatic childhood memories. Although *repressed* (or hidden from awareness), unconscious impulses press on the conscious mind and find expression in disguised or altered form, including dreams, mannerisms, slips of the tongue, and symptoms of mental illness, as well as in socially acceptable pursuits such as art and literature. To uncover the unconscious, Freud developed the technique of *free association*, in which the patient lies on a couch, recounts dreams, and says whatever comes to mind.

Freud's psychodynamic theory was as controversial at the turn of the century as Darwin's theory of evolution had been twenty-five years earlier. Many of Freud's Victorian contemporaries were shocked, not only by his emphasis on sexuality, but also by his suggestion that we are often unaware of our true motives and thus are not entirely in control of our thoughts and behavior. Conversely, members of the medical community in Vienna at that time generally held Freud's new theory in high regard, nominating him for the position of *Professor Extraordinarious* at the University of Vienna (Esterson, 2002). Freud's lectures and writings attracted considerable attention in the United States as well as in Europe; he had a profound impact on the arts and philosophy, as well as on psychology. Freud's theories and methods, however, continue to inspire heated debate.

Psychodynamic theory, as expanded and revised by Freud's colleagues and successors, laid the foundation for the study of personality and psychological disorders, and

William James

Sigmund Freud

functionalist theory Theory of mental life and behavior that is concerned with how an organism uses its perceptual abilities to function in its environment.

psychodynamic theories Personality theories contending that behavior results from psychological factors that interact within the individual, often outside conscious awareness.

we will discuss them in Chapters 8: "Personality, Stress, and Health" and 9: "Psychological Disorders and Their Treatments." His revolutionary notion of the unconscious and his portrayal of human beings as constantly at war with themselves are taken for granted today, at least in literary and artistic circles. Freud's theories were never totally accepted by mainstream psychology, however, and in recent decades his influence on clinical psychology and psychotherapy has declined (Robins, Gosling, & Craik, 1999; see also Westen, 1998).

REDEFINING PSYCHOLOGY: THE STUDY OF BEHAVIOR

How was the approach to human behavior taken by Watson and Skinner different from Freud's?

Until the beginning of the twentieth century, psychology saw itself as the study of mental processes. The primary method of collecting data was introspection or self-observation, in a laboratory, or on an analyst's couch. At the beginning of the twentieth century, however, a new generation of psychologists rebelled against this "soft" approach. The leader of the challenge was the American psychologist John B. Watson.

JOHN B. WATSON: BEHAVIORISM John B. Watson argued that the whole idea of mental life was superstition, a relic left over from the Middle Ages. In *Psychology as a Behaviorist Views It* (1913), Watson contended that you cannot see or even define consciousness any more than you can observe a soul. And if you cannot locate or measure something, it cannot be the object of scientific study. For Watson, psychology was the study of observable, measurable behavior—and nothing more.

Watson's view of psychology, known as **behaviorism**, was based on the work of the Russian physiologist Ivan Pavlov, who had won a Nobel Prize for his research on digestion. In the course of his experiments, Pavlov noticed that the dogs in his laboratory began to salivate as soon as they heard their feeder coming, even before they could see their dinner. Pavlov decided to find out whether salivation, an automatic reflex, could be shaped by learning. He began by repeatedly pairing the sound of a buzzer with the presence of food. The next step was to observe what happened when the buzzer was sounded without introducing food. This experiment clearly demonstrated what Pavlov had noticed incidentally: After repeated pairings, the dogs salivated in response to the buzzer alone. Pavlov called this simple form of training *conditioning*. Thus a new school of psychology was inspired by a casual observation—followed by rigorous experiments. In this respect, Pavlov's approach is similar to that used at Toyota: Observe what works, develop a system based on that observation, and test the system using scientific experimentation. We will learn more about the principles of conditioning in Chapter 4: "Learning and Memory."

Watson came to believe that all mental experiences—thinking, feeling, awareness of self—are nothing more than physiological changes that occur in response to accumulated experiences. An infant, he argued, is a *tabula rasa* (Latin for "blank slate") on which experience may write virtually anything:

> Give me a dozen healthy infants, well-formed, and my own specialized world to bring them up in, and I'll guarantee to take any one at random and train him to become any type of specialist I might select—doctor, lawyer, artist, merchant chief and, yes, even beggar man, and thief, regardless of his talents, penchants, tendencies, abilities, vocations, and race. (Watson, 1924, p. 104)

Watson attempted to demonstrate that all psychological phenomena—even Freud's unconscious motivations—are the result of conditioning (Rilling, 2000). In one of the most infamous experiments in psychology's history, Watson attempted to create a conditioned fear response in an 11-month-old boy. "Little Albert" was a secure, happy baby who enjoyed new places and experiences. On his first visit to Watson's laboratory, Albert was delighted by a tame, furry white rat, but he became visibly frightened when Watson banged a steel bar with a hammer just behind the infant's head. On his second visit, Watson placed the rat near Albert, and the moment the baby reached out and touched the rat, Watson

John B. Watson

behaviorism School of psychology that studies only observable and measurable behavior.

banged the hammer. After half a dozen pairings, little Albert began crying the instant the rat was introduced, without any banging. Further experiments found that Albert as frightened by anything white and furry—a rabbit, a dog, a sealskin coat, cotton wool, and Watson wearing a Santa Claus mask (Watson & Rayner, 1920). Freud had labeled the transfer of emotions from one person or object to another "displacement," a neurotic response that he traced to the unconscious. Drawing on Pavlov, Watson called the same phenomenon "generalization," a simple matter of conditioning (Rilling, 2000). As far as Watson was concerned, psychodynamic theory and psychoanalysis were "voodooism."

Watson was also interested in showing that fears could be eliminated by conditioning. Mary Cover Jones (Jones, 1924), one of his graduate students, successfully reconditioned a boy who showed a fear of rabbits (not caused by laboratory conditioning) to overcome this fear. Her technique, which involved presenting the rabbit at a great distance and then gradually bringing it closer while the child was eating, is similar to conditioning techniques used by psychologists today which are described in Chapter 4: "Learning and Memory."

B. F. SKINNER: BEHAVIORISM REVISITED B. F. Skinner became one of the leaders of the behaviorist school of psychology. Similar to Watson, Skinner fervently believed that psychologists should study only observable and measurable behavior (Skinner, 1938, 1987, 1989, 1990). He, too, was primarily interested in changing behavior through conditioning—and in discovering natural laws of behavior in the process. But Skinner added a new element to the behaviorist repertoire: reinforcement. He rewarded his subjects for behaving the way he wanted them to behave. For example, an animal (rats and pigeons were Skinner's favorite subjects) was put into a special cage and allowed to explore it. Eventually, the animal reached up and pressed a lever or pecked at a disk on the wall, whereupon a food pellet dropped into the box. Gradually, the animal learned that pressing the bar or pecking at the disk always brought food. Why did the animal learn this? Because it was *reinforced*, or rewarded, for doing so. Skinner thus made the animal an active agent in its own conditioning.

Behaviorism dominated academic psychology in the United States well into the 1960s. One unintended and, at the time, largely unnoticed consequence was that psychology developed an *environmental bias*: Virtually every aspect of human behavior was attributed to learning and experience. Investigating evolutionary influences on behavior or studying hereditary, genetic influences on individual and group differences was considered taboo (Evans, 1999).

THE COGNITIVE REVOLUTION

How have Gestalt psychologists, humanistic psychologists, and cognitive psychologists extended the definition of psychology?

In the 1960s, behaviorism's grip on the field of psychology began to loosen. On the one hand, research on perception, personality, child development, interpersonal relations, and other topics that behaviorists had ignored raised questions they couldn't readily explain. On the other hand, research in other fields (especially anthropology, linguistics, neurobiology, and computer science) was beginning to shed new light on the workings of the mind. Psychologists came to view behaviorism not as an all-encompassing theory or paradigm, but as only one piece of the explanation of human behavior and mental processes (Robins et al., 1999). They began to look into the "black box" of the human mind, and put more emphasis on humans (and other animals) as sentient—conscious, perceptive, and alert—beings; that is, as active learners, not passive recipients of life's lessons.

THE PRECURSORS: GESTALT AND HUMANISTIC PSYCHOLOGY Even during the period that behaviorism dominated American psychology, not all psychologists had accepted behaviorist doctrines. Two schools that paved the way for the cognitive revolution were Gestalt psychology and humanistic psychology.

In Germany, Max Wertheimer, Wolfgang Köhler, and Kurt Koffka were all interested in perception, but particularly in certain tricks that the mind plays on itself. For example,

Mary Cover Jones

B. F. Skinner

Gestalt psychologists argued that perception involves more than a simple summation of sensory elements. We see this picture not as merely a set of black and white dots, but rather as a Dalmatian dog, separated perceptually from its background.

Gestalt psychology School of psychology that studies how people perceive and experience objects as whole patterns.

humanistic psychology School of psychology that emphasizes mental health and well-being, self-understanding, and realizing one's full human potential.

cognitive psychology School of psychology devoted to the study of mental processes in the broadest sense.

when we see a series of still pictures flashed at a constant rate (for example, movies or "moving" neon signs), why do the pictures seem to move?

Phenomena like these launched a new school of thought, **Gestalt psychology**. Roughly translated from German, *Gestalt* means "whole" or "form." When applied to perception, it refers to our tendency to see patterns, to distinguish an object from its background, to complete a picture from a few cues. Similar to William James, the Gestalt psychologists rejected the structuralists' attempt to break down perception and thought into their elements. When we look at a tree, we see just that, a tree, not a series of isolated leaves and branches.

During the same period, the American psychologist Abraham Maslow, who studied under Gestalt psychologist Max Wertheimer and anthropologist Ruth Benedict, developed a more holistic approach to psychology in which feelings and yearnings play a key role. Maslow referred to **humanistic psychology** as the "third force"—beyond Freudian theory and behaviorism. Humanistic psychologists emphasize human potential and the importance of love, belonging, self-esteem and self-expression, peak experiences (when one becomes so involved in an activity that self-consciousness fades), and self-actualization (the spontaneity and creativity that result from focusing on problems outside oneself and looking beyond the boundaries of social conventions). They focus on mental health and well-being, and on self-understanding and self-improvement, rather than on mental illness.

Humanistic psychology has made important contributions to the study of motivation and emotions (see Chapter 6: "Motivation and Emotion," as well as to the subfields of personality and psychotherapy (See Chapters 8: "Personality, Stress, and Health" and 9: "Psychological Disorders and Their Treatment"). But it has never been totally accepted by mainstream psychology. Because humanistic psychology is interested in questions of meaning, values, and ethics, many people—including its own members—see this school of psychology more as a cultural and spiritual movement than as a branch of science. In recent years, however, *positive psychologists* (whom we discuss later in this chapter) have begun to reinvestigate some of the questions that humanistic psychologists raised a half century ago (Bohart & Greening, 2001) but within the context and using the method of a scientific approach.

THE RISE OF COGNITIVE PSYCHOLOGY In the 1960s, psychology began to come full circle. The phrase "cognitive revolution" refers to a general shift away from a limited focus on behavior toward a broad interest in mental processes such as thought, attention, and problem-solving. The field returned from a period in which consciousness was considered to be inaccessible to scientific inquiry and began to investigate and theorize about the mind—but now with new research methods and behaviorism's commitment to objective, empirical research. Even the definition of psychology changed. Psychology is still the study of human "behavior," but psychologists' definition of "behavior" has been expanded to include thoughts, feelings, and states of consciousness.

This new focus holds for both existing and new subfields of psychology. In developmental psychology, for example, the idea that a child is a blank slate, whose development is shaped entirely by his or her environment, was replaced by a new view of babies and children as aware, competent, social beings. According to this new cognitive view, children actively seek to learn about and make sense of their world. Moreover, all healthy children are "equipped" with such distinctively human characteristics as the ability to acquire language, without formal education, through exposure. Developmental psychology is only one subfield that both contributed to and benefited from the emergence of cognitive psychology.

Cognitive psychology is the study of our mental processes in the broadest sense: thinking, feeling, learning, remembering, making decisions and judgments, and so on. If the behaviorist model of learning resembled an old-fashioned telephone switchboard (a call or a stimulus comes in, is relayed along various circuits in the brain, and an answer or a response goes out), the cognitive model resembles a high-powered, modern computer. Cognitive psychologists are interested in the ways in which people "process information"—that is, how we acquire information, process or transform bits of information into programs, and use those programs to solve problems.

In contrast to behaviorists, cognitive psychologists believe that mental processes can and should be studied scientifically. Although we cannot observe memories or thoughts directly, we can observe behavior and make inferences about the kinds of cognitive processes that underlie that behavior. For example, we can read a lengthy story to people and then observe the kinds of things that they remember from that story, the ways in which their recollections change over time, and the sorts of errors in recall that they are prone to make. On the basis of systematic research of this kind, we can gain insight into the cognitive processes underlying human memory (which we discuss in Chapter 4: "Learning and Memory"). Moreover, with the advent of new brain-imaging techniques (described in Chapter 2: "The Biological Basis of Behaviors"), cognitive psychologists have begun to address questions about the neurological mechanisms that underlie such cognitive processes as learning, memory, intelligence, and emotion, giving rise to the rapidly expanding field of *cognitive neuroscience* (D'Esposito, Zarahn, & Aguirre, 1999; Schacter, 1999).

In just a short time, cognitive psychology has had an enormous impact on almost every area of psychology (Sperry, 1988, 1995) and has become the most prominent school in contemporary scientific psychology (Johnson & Erneling, 1997; Robins et al., 1999).

NEW DIRECTIONS

How is the field of psychology being defined today?

During much of the twentieth century, psychology was divided into competing theoretical schools: structuralism, functionalism, psychodynamic perspectives, and so forth. Crossing theoretical lines was considered intellectual heresy. Today, however, psychologists are more flexible in considering the merits of new approaches, combining elements of different perspectives as their interests or research findings dictate. As a result, new theories and initiatives are emerging.

EVOLUTIONARY PSYCHOLOGY As the name indicates, **evolutionary psychology** focuses on the evolutionary origins of behavior patterns and mental processes, the adaptive value they have or had, and the functions they serve or served in our emergence as a distinct species (DeKay & Buss, 1992; Wright, 1994). All of the theoretical views we have discussed so far seek to explain humans as we exist today. In contrast, evolutionary psychologists ask, how did human beings get to be the way we are? They study such diverse topics as perception, language, helping others (altruism), parenting, happiness, sexual attraction and mate selection, jealousy, and violence (Bernhard & Penton-Voak, 2002; Buss, 2000a, 2000b; Caporael, 2001; Miller, 2000). By studying such phenomena in different species, different habitats, different cultures, and in males and females, evolutionary psychologists seek to understand the basic biological programs that guide thinking and behavior (Archer, 1996; Buss & Malamuth, 1996; Byrne, 2002; Cartwright, 2000).

A common view among evolutionary psychologists is that the mind is "hardwired," meaning that human beings are biologically predisposed to think and act in certain ways (Cosmides, Tooby, & Barkow, 1992; Goode, 2000b; Siegert & Ward, 2002). Further, they contend that these fixed programs evolved hundreds of thousands of years ago when our ancestors lived as hunter-gatherers, although the problem-solving strategies that benefited early humans may or may not be adaptive in the modern era. Whether evolutionary psychology finds a place among the major fields of psychology or stays on the sidelines remains to be seen (see Bjorklund, 2003; Buss & Reeve, 2003; Crawford, 2003; Krebs, 2003; Lickliter & Honeycutt, 2003a, 2003b; Tooby, Cosmides, & Barrett, 2003).

Cognitive psychologists emphasize the complex interplay of mental processes, such as those involved in "multi-tasking"—performing many different tasks, all at the same time.

evolutionary psychology An approach to, and subfield of, psychology that is concerned with the evolutionary origins of behaviors and mental processes, their adaptive value, and the purposes they continue to serve.

Positive psychologists believe we should learn more about "the good life," including happiness and the development of such traits as wisdom.

POSITIVE PSYCHOLOGY Another emerging perspective is **positive psychology**, the view that psychology should devote more attention to "the good life," that being the study of subjective feelings of happiness and well-being; the development of such individual traits as intimacy, integrity, leadership, altruism, and wisdom; and the kinds of families, work settings, and communities that encourage individuals to flourish (Schmuck & Sheldon, 2001; Seligman & Csikszentmihalyi, 2000).

Positive psychologists argue that psychologists have learned a great deal about the origins, diagnosis, and treatment of mental illness but relatively little about the origins and nurturance of mental wellness. In recent decades, for example, psychologists have made great strides in understanding the neurology of depression, schizophrenia, and other disorders. We have come to understand a lot about how individuals survive and endure under conditions of extreme adversity, but far less about ordinary human strengths and virtues (Sheldon & King, 2001). We know more about intelligence than about wisdom; more about conformity than originality; and more about stress than about tranquility. There have been many studies of prejudice and intergroup hostility, for example, but very few about tolerance and intergroup harmony.

Today's positivists do not argue that psychologists should abandon their role in the science of healing. To the contrary, they support efforts to promote better, more widespread use of what psychologists have learned. But they argue that psychology has reached a point where building positive qualities should receive as much emphasis as repairing damage. Positive psychology approaches are discussed in more detail in Chapter 10: "Personality, Stress, and Health."

MULTIPLE PERSPECTIVES OF PSYCHOLOGY TODAY As we've seen, contemporary psychologists tend to see different perspectives as complementary, with each perspective contributing to our understanding of human behavior (Friman, Allen, Kerwin, & Larzelere, 1993). When they study aggression, for example, psychologists no longer limit their explanations to the behavioral view (aggressive behavior is learned as a consequence of reward and punishment) or the Freudian perspective (aggression is an expression of unconscious hostility toward a parent). Instead, most contemporary psychologists trace aggression to a number of factors, including long-standing adaptations to the environment (evolutionary psychology) and the influences of culture, gender, and socioeconomic status on how people perceive and interpret events—"That guy is making fun of me" or "She's asking for it"—(cognitive and social psychology). Likewise, physiological psychologists no longer limit themselves to identifying the genetic and biochemical roots of aggression. Instead, they study how heredity and the environment interact.

Sometimes these theoretical perspectives mesh beautifully, with each one enhancing the others; at other times, adherents of one approach challenge their peers, arguing for one viewpoint over all the others. But all psychologists agree that the field advances only with the addition of new evidence to support or challenge existing theories and, hence, they embrace the scientific foundation of the field.

WHERE ARE THE WOMEN?

In psychology's early years, why were relatively few women prominent in the field?

As you read the brief history of modern psychology, you may have concluded that the founders of the new discipline were all men. But did psychology really have only fathers and no mothers? If there were women pioneers, why are their names and accomplishments missing from historical accounts?

In fact, women have contributed to psychology from its beginnings. In the United States, women presented papers and joined the national professional association as soon as it was formed in 1892. Often, however, they faced discrimination. Some colleges and universities did not grant degrees to women, professional journals were reluctant to publish their work, and teaching positions were often closed to them (Kite et al., 2001; Minton,

positive psychology An emerging field of psychology that focuses on positive experiences, including subjective well-being, self-determination, the relationship between positive emotions and physical health, and the factors that allow individuals, communities, and societies to flourish.

2002). Despite these barriers, a number of early women psychologists made important contributions and were acknowledged by at least some of the men in the growing discipline of psychology.

In 1906, James McKeen Cattell published *American Men of Science*, which, despite its title, included a number of women, among them 22 female psychologists. Cattell rated three of these women as among the 1,000 most distinguished scientists in the country: Mary Whiton Calkins (1863–1930), for her analysis of how we learn verbal material and her contributions to self-psychology; Christine Ladd-Franklin (1847–1930), for her work in color vision; and Margaret Floy Washburn (1871–1939), for her pioneering research examining the role of imagery in thought processes. In addition, Mary Whiton Calkins was elected and served as the first female president of APA in 1905, a position also held by Margaret Floy Washburn in 1921. Because the doors to an academic career remained mostly closed, however, other early female psychologists found positions in therapeutic and other nonacademic settings; pursued careers in allied professions, such as child development and education, which were considered acceptable fields for women; or gained recognition by collaborating on research projects and books with their spouses (Evans, 1999).

In recent decades, the situation has changed dramatically. The number of women who receive Ph.D.s in psychology has grown by leaps and bounds. (See Figure 1-1.) Indeed, women have begun to outnumber men in psychology. According to a recent APA survey, women receive three-fourths of the baccalaureate degrees awarded in psychology; represent just under three-fourths of psychology graduate students; and earned two out of three doctorate degrees in psychology awarded in 1997 (APA, 2000). Because female psychologists perform key research in all of the psychology subfields, you will find their work referred to throughout this text. For example, Terry Amabile has studied creativity, in particular the positive effects that exposure to creative role models can have on people. Elizabeth Loftus's research on memory has uncovered how unreliable eyewitness accounts of a crime can be. Carol Nagy Jaklin has studied the role that parents' expectations can play in girls' (and boys') perceptions of the value of mathematics. Judith Rodin's research examines eating behavior, in particular bulimia and obesity. Eleanor Maccoby, Alice Eagly, and Jacqueline Eccles are prominent among the growing number of women and men who are studying sex differences in a variety of areas, such as emotionality, math and verbal ability, and helping behavior. Clearly, today both women and men are making important contributions to the field of psychology.

Margaret Floy Washburn

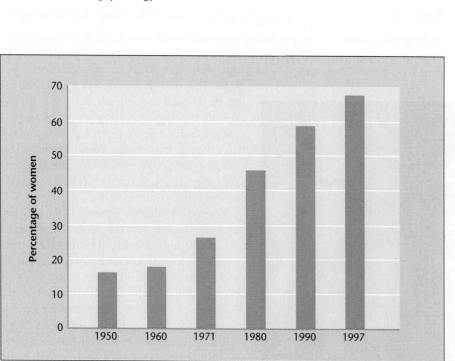

Figure 1-1

Percentage of women recipients of Ph.D.s in psychology, 1950–1997.

Source: Summary Report: Doctorate Recipients from United States Universities (Selected Years). National Research Council. Figure compiled by the APA Research Office. Copyright © 2000.

Human Diversity

1.3   Suggest why the study of human diversity is essential to the field of psychology.

The absence of women from much of the early history of psychology is only one aspect of a much bigger and more troubling concern: The relative inattention to human diversity that characterized psychology through most of the twentieth century. Only recently have psychologists looked closely at the ways in which culture, gender, race, and ethnicity can affect virtually all aspects of human behavior.

THE VALUE OF STUDYING DIVERSITY

Why is the study of human diversity important in the field of psychology?

In the early twentieth century, psychology was a white male profession with a distinctly American accent (Strickland, 2000). The great majority of research studies were conducted by white male professors at American universities, using white male American college students as participants. This arrangement was not a conscious or deliberate decision to study just one particular group. Like other sciences and prestigious professions in Europe and North America, psychology took for granted that what was true of white Western males would be true for other people as well. One critical history of psychology during this period was entitled *Even the Rat Was White!* (Guthrie, 1976).

For today's students however—who will be tomorrow's citizens of the world—understanding human diversity is essential. The reason for that urgency is all around you. Our major cities are home to people from diverse backgrounds, with diverse values and goals, living side by side. But proximity does not always produce harmony; sometimes it leads to aggression, prejudice, and conflict. Understanding cultural, racial, ethnic, and gender differences in thinking and behavior gives us the tools to reduce some of these interpersonal tensions. Looking at human diver-

Today's work force includes men and women who represent many different groups. An understanding of human diversity helps us appreciate the values and needs of others and become more effective in our own work.

[UNDERSTANDING OURSELVES]

THE BENEFITS OF STUDYING PSYCHOLOGY

We know that many students, rather than out of a strong initial interest in the subject, take psychology classes to fulfill a requirement for their degree. Those students, and even some who are keenly interested in psychology, may wonder, "What am I going to gain from taking this course?" There are several benefits that you can gain from studying psychology:

- *Self-understanding.* Almost all of us want to understand ourselves and others better. In our daily lives, we often look for answers by relying on our own experience, knowledge, and assumptions. But as you will see, that barely scratches the surface. As a psychology student, you will be challenged to go beyond the superficial in your life and to confront what really lies behind your most basic actions. You will learn to look deeply into human behavior and to ask complex and precise questions. In the process, you will not only achieve a better understanding of yourself and your fellow human beings, but also come to realize that much of what we consider "just plain common sense about people" doesn't hold up under close scrutiny.

- *Critical thinking skills.* In addition to greater understanding of yourself and others, by studying psychology, you will also

have an opportunity to acquire some specific skills. One of those skills is the ability to think critically about psychological issues: To clearly define issues, to examine the evidence bearing on them, to become more aware of hidden assumptions, to resist the temptation to oversimplify, to draw conclusions carefully, and above all to realize the relevance of empirical research to understanding psychological issues. As a result of practicing critical thinking, you will become a more sophisticated consumer of the information that is available to you in the mass media. We hope that you will also become more cautious about too quickly accepting what looks like "common sense."

- *Study skills.* You will also have the opportunity to acquire better study skills that will serve you well in all your courses. You will find an entire chapter on learning and memory (Chapter 4) that contains excellent information about making the most of your study time. But you will also find information about the relationship between sleep and learning and the effects of drugs on memory (Chapter 3), about the nature of intelligence and its relation to success in school and in later life (Chapter 5), about the effects of motivation and arousal on the ability to learn and

to perform (Chapter 6), and about age differences in the ability to learn and remember (Chapter 7).

- *Job skills.* Finally, you may acquire some skills that will help you find a job. This chapter lists many career possibilities for students who earn degrees in psychology. In addition, many careers outside psychology draw on a person's knowledge of psychology. For example, personnel administrators deal with employee relations; vocational rehabilitation counselors help people with disabilities to find employment; directors of volunteer services recruit and train volunteers; probation officers work with parolees; and supervisors of day-care centers oversee the care of preschool children of working parents. Indeed, employers in many areas of business seek out psychology majors because of their knowledge of the principles of human behavior and their skills in experimental design and data collection and analysis.

Of course, all of these benefits are much more likely to accrue to students who regularly attend class, study, and try to apply what they learn to their own lives. As with many other opportunities, the benefits you receive are, in large part, up to you.

sity from a scientific perspective will allow you to separate fact from fiction in your daily interactions with people. Moreover, after you understand how and why groups differ in their values, behaviors, approaches to the world, thought processes, and responses to situations, you will be better able to savor the diversity around you. Finally, the better your awareness is of human diversity, the more you will appreciate the many universal features of humanity (See the box, Understanding Ourselves, for other benefits of studying psychology.)

Examining and overcoming past assumptions and biases has been a slow and uneven process, but a new appreciation of human diversity is taking shape (Ocampo et al., 2003; Phinney, 1996; also see Tucker & Herman, 2002). Psychologists have begun to question assumptions that are explicitly based on gender, race, and culture. As you saw in the opening description of Toyota's corporate strategy, all workers—and all people—can make important contributions.

GENDER

How are psychologists helping us to understand the differences between men and women?

Gender has many layers. The words *male* and *female* refer to one's biological makeup, the physical and genetic facts of being one sex or the other. Scientists often use the term *sex* to

Today, women occupy important positions in industry, government, and world politics. Here, Meg Whitman, President and CEO of eBay, addresses a group.

refer exclusively to biological differences in anatomy, genetics, or physical functioning, and **gender** to refer to the psychological and social meanings attached to being biologically male or female. Because distinguishing what is biologically produced from what is socially influenced is almost impossible, in our discussion of these issues, we will use the terms *sex* and *gender* interchangeably.

In the past, men and women typically led very different lives. Today, women in many societies are as likely as men to obtain higher education; to work full-time, pursue careers, and start businesses; and to be active in politics. And men are more likely to be more active parents and homemakers than their fathers were. Yet, stereotypes about how the "typical male" looks and acts or the "accepted social roles" for females still lead to confusion and misunderstandings between the sexes. Beyond our stereotypes about what males and females "typically" are like, we also have general beliefs about *gender roles*—that is, cultural expectations regarding acceptable behavior and activities for males and females, respectively.

The study of gender similarities and differences and of the influence of gender stereotypes and gender roles has become part of mainstream psychology. Psychologists in virtually every subfield conduct research to determine whether their findings apply equally to males and females, and if not, why not. Furthermore, the field of **feminist theory** explores how general views on the social roles of women and men can influence the treatment of all people, and women in particular.

RACE AND ETHNICITY

Why are psychologists interested in racial and ethnic differences?

One of the first things we notice about someone (along with sex) is that person's race or ethnicity (Omi & Winant, 1994). **Race** is a biological term used to refer to a subpopulation whose members have reproduced exclusively among themselves and therefore are genetically similar to each other but distinct from other members of the same species (Betancourt & López, 1993; Diamond, 1994; Macionis, 1993). Most people simply take for granted the idea that the human species can be divided into a number of distinct races (Asians, Africans, Caucasians, Native Americans, and so on). However, human beings have migrated, intermarried, and commingled so frequently over time that it is impossible to identify biologically separate races. To a greater or lesser degree, all humans are "racial hybrids." Moreover, the criteria people use to differentiate among different races are arbitrary. In the United States, we assign people to different races primarily on the basis of skin color and facial features. In central Africa, members of the Tutsi and Hutu tribes see themselves as different races, although they are similar in skin color and facial features. In spite of these different definitions, most people continue to believe that racial categories are meaningful, and as a result, race shapes people's social identities, their sense of self, their experiences in their own and other societies, and their interactions with others.

Whereas racial categories are based on physical differences, **ethnicity** is based on cultural characteristics. An ethnic group is a category of people who have migrated to another country, but still see themselves—and are perceived by others—as distinctive because of a common homeland and history, language, religion, or traditional cultural beliefs and social practices. For example, Latino Americans may be black, white, or any shade in between. What unites them is their language and culture. By the mid-1980s, there was sufficient interest among psychologists in ethnicity that APA created a new division devoted to the psychological study of ethnic minority issues (Division 45). Increasing numbers of psychologists are now studying why ethnicity is so important both in our country and in others, and how individuals select or create an ethnic identity and respond to ethnic stereotypes.

RACIAL AND ETHNIC MINORITIES IN PSYCHOLOGY Most ethnic minorities are still underrepresented among the ranks of American psychologists. According to the APA, ethnic-minority students account for almost 25 percent of college entrants, but

---

gender The psychological and social meanings attached to being biologically male or female.

feminist theory Feminist theories offer a wide variety of views on the social roles of women and men, the problems and rewards of those roles, and prescriptions for changing those roles.

race A subpopulation of a species, defined according to an identifiable characteristic (that is, geographic location, skin color, hair texture, genes, facial features, and so forth).

ethnicity A common cultural heritage—including religion, language, or ancestry—that is shared by a group of individuals.

only 16 percent of graduates who majored in psychology, 14 percent of those who enroll in graduate school in psychology, 12 percent of those who receive master's degrees in psychology, and 9 percent of those who earn doctorates (Sleek, 1999). Why? One possibility is that when black, Hispanic American, Native American, and other students look at the history of psychology or at the psychology faculties of today's universities, they find few role models; likewise, when they look at psychological research, they find little about themselves and their realities (Strickland, 2000). As recently as the 1990s, a survey of psychology journals found that less than 2 percent of the articles focused on U.S. racial and ethnic minorities (Iwamasa & Smith, 1996). Nonetheless, their small numbers have not prevented them from achieving prominence and making significant contributions to the field (see Pickren, 2004). For example, Kenneth Clark, a former president of the American Psychological Association, received national recognition for the important work he and his wife, Mamie Clark, did on the effects of segregation on black children (Lal, 2002). This research was cited by the Supreme Court in the *Brown v. Board of Education* decision of 1954 that outlawed segregated schools in the United States (Keppel, 2002).

In an effort to remedy the underrepresentation of ethnic minorities, the APA's Office of Ethnic Minority Affairs is sponsoring programs to attract ethnic-minority students to psychology (Rabasca, 2000a). This initiative includes summer programs for high school students, recruitment at the high school and college levels, mentor and other guidance programs, and a clearinghouse for college students who meet the requirements for graduate programs.

Psychologists are also working to uncover and overcome biases in psychological research that are related to gender, race, and ethnicity. The field of psychology is broadening its scope to probe the full range and richness of human diversity, and this text mirrors that expansive and inclusive approach. We consider the problem of bias in psychological research later in the chapter and deal with this topic again in Chapter 11: "Psychology Applied to Work."

Kenneth Clark's research on the effects of segregation influenced the Supreme Court to outlaw segregated schools in Brown v. Board of Education.

CULTURE

How does culture contribute to human diversity?

A classic definition of culture is a people's "design for living" (Kluckhohn, 1949). A **culture** provides modes of thinking, acting, and communicating; ideas about how the world works and why people behave as they do; beliefs and ideals that shape our individual dreams and desires; information about how to use and improve technology; and perhaps most important, criteria for evaluating what natural events, human actions, and life itself mean. All large, complex modern societies also include subcultures—groups whose values, attitudes, behavior, and vocabulary or accent distinguish them from the cultural mainstream. Most Americans participate in a number of subcultures as well as in mainstream culture.

Culture is often defined according to a person's gender and ethnicity; however, subcultures can sometimes be quite specific. For example, the "corporate culture" of a particular work environment may be formal or casual; supervision can be hierarchical or distributed more evenly to members of work teams. Consider how the corporate culture of the Toyota organization described at the beginning of this chapter differs from that of more traditional manufacturing organizations with which you may be familiar. Psychologists are interested in studying all aspects of culture, both broadly and narrowly defined. Throughout this book, we discuss the impact of culture on human behavior and thought.

Corporate cultures may be strict and formal, or may be more casual and informal, as represented by this worker's office.

culture The tangible goods and the values, attitudes, behaviors, and beliefs that are passed from one generation to another.

Psychology as a Science

1.4   Describe the basic premises on which a scientific field is based and suggest how the scientific method accomplishes the purposes of science.

Earlier in this chapter, psychology was defined as the science of behavior and mental processes. The key word in this definition is science. What does it mean to define a field as a *science*?

SCIENCE AND THE SCIENTIFIC METHOD

What features distinguish a scientific field from a field not based in science?

First, all scientific fields, including chemistry, biology, and psychology, are based on *empirical observation*. By empirical, we mean that the phenomena that are of interest can be observed and measured. For example, when an industrial psychologist is studying how various types of keyboard designs affect how quickly typists can enter data, the behavior of interest is observable and measurable: The number of keystrokes per minute is directly quantifiable. If an ergonomically improved keyboard allows typists to enter 10 percent more keystrokes per minute, those results can be used to make decisions about keyboard design. Sometimes the topics of interest to psychologists are not so directly observable. Consider how the mental process of creativity might be observed or measured. Although creative thought cannot be "seen" or measured directly, psychologists nonetheless consider it to be an empirical construct since the results of creative thought processes can be observed. One way that creativity can be measured would be by asking people to solve a problem that requires creative thought. When asked, for example, "How many uses can you think of for a piece of bubble gum?" creative people can generate many more possible ideas. This task, thus, can be used to measure a person's creativity.

A second characteristic of scientific disciplines is that they rely on the **scientific method** as the basis of study. Science progresses when observations are carefully collected, the data they yield are appropriately analyzed, and conclusions are made that stem directly from that data. The scientific method defines all fields of science including psychology.

Oftentimes the scientific method implies an order to the way in which scientists approach the problems they wish to study. Usually a first step is to conceptualize the problem in the form of a **hypothesis**, or educated guess as to what the scientist thinks the predicted results will be. For example, in the case of the keyboard study mentioned earlier, the psychologist might reason that people have more mobility in their first finger than in their

scientific method An approach to knowledge that relies on collecting data, generating a theory to explain the data, producing testable hypotheses based on the theory, and testing those hypotheses empirically.

hypothesis A specific, testable prediction derived from a theory.

third finger. This might lead to the hypothesis that if a keyboard is constructed such that letters that are typed more frequently (like "a" and "s") are positioned on the keyboard so that the first finger strikes those keys, and letters that are typed infrequently (like "q" or "z") are positioned for the third finger, typing speed will be increased.

The next step in the scientific method involves designing an approach to testing the hypothesis under study. Psychologists employ several different methods in their work, and these are more fully described in the next section of the text. In the keyboard example, the psychologist might design two different keyboards, one in which commonly-occurring letters are struck by the first finger and another in which they are placed where the third finger will strike them. Then the hypothesis is *tested*; that is, results are collected which will allow the scientist to determine whether or not the original hypothesis is supported or disconfirmed. The testability of scientific investigations is a critically important aspect of science and is, in part, what distinguishes a scientific approach from other non-scientific methods of inquiry. These results are then analyzed, oftentimes by using statistical techniques, some of which are further discussed in Appendix A of this text.

A key feature of the scientific method is that the results of tested hypotheses are eventually organized into more general explanations, called **theories**. Theories not only summarize the results of several streams of experimentation; they also allow scientists to formulate new hypotheses that can be tested in order to expand the scope of theory. For example, if results demonstrate that humans can respond more quickly to some types of tasks than others, a general theory of information processing within the brain might result. This theory might then lead to additional hypotheses about how humans might respond, think, and act in a wider variety of situations, not just at the computer keyboard. Like hypotheses, theories are always testable, and they are conceptualized in such a way that they can be proven wrong, a feature of science referred to as its *falsifiability requirement*. Theories are never considered to be "finished;" rather they are treated as the best explanations at the time, given the limited amount of information that is available. Many famous examples of erroneous theories come to mind, for example the theories that the Earth was the center of the solar system and that all matter was composed of four basic elements (earth, air, fire, and water). Both theories guided scientific thought for centuries, yet today we have discarded them because they cannot explain the additional data scientists have collected more recently. Overall, the goals of science are these: to describe, to predict, to explain, and to understand. Theories help psychologists meet these goals as they study behavior and mental processes using the methods of science.

theory General, systematic explanation of a phenomenon that organizes known facts and allows us to predict relationships.

► CHECK YOUR UNDERSTANDING

1. Scientific disciplines are considered to be "empirical." This means that the phenomena that are studied are:
   a. reliable
   b. valid
   c. correlated with each other
   d. observable

2. In science, a general explanation is called a(n) _____.

Answers: 1. d, 2. theory.

► APPLY YOUR UNDERSTANDING

1. If Dr. Ames states that no evidence can be obtained that will ever render her theory incorrect, we know that she is not engaged in a scientific study because her statement violates:
   a. the falsibility requirement
   b. the requirement that data be based on empirical observation
   c. scientific logic
   d. ethical principles of science

2. Mr. Julestrom develops a training method he believes will improve the error rate in operating a complex machine. His prediction about how this training program will work would, in the language of science, be called a(n):
   a. theory
   b. hypothesis
   c. correlation
   d. scientific method

Answers: 1. a, 2. b

Research Methods in Psychology

1.5 Identify the strengths and limitations of each of the major scientific methods of research employed by psychologists: naturalistic observation, case studies, surveys, correlational research, experimental research, and multimethod research.

All sciences—including psychology, sociology, economics, political science, biology, and physics—require evidence based on careful observation and experimentation. To collect data systematically and objectively, psychologists use a variety of research methods, including naturalistic observation, case studies, surveys, correlational research, and experimental research.

NATURALISTIC OBSERVATION

Why is a natural setting sometimes better than a laboratory for observing behavior?

Psychologists use **naturalistic observation** to study human or animal behavior in its natural context. One psychologist with this real-life orientation might observe behavior in a school or a factory; another might actually join a family to study the behavior of its members; still another might observe monkeys in the wild rather than in cages. The primary advantage of naturalistic observation is that the behavior observed in everyday life is likely to be more natural, spontaneous, and varied than that observed in a laboratory.

For example, naturalistic observation was used in a recent study (Hammen, Gitlin, & Altshuler, 2000) designed to understand why some patients with bipolar disorder (a mental disorder discussed more fully in Chapter 9, "Psychological Disorders and Their Treatments") are more likely to adjust successfully to the work place than others. By carefully studying 52 people over a two-year period in their natural settings, these authors found that the people who displayed the most successful work adjustment were those who also had strong supportive personal relationships with other people. Surprisingly, stressful life events did not seem to play an important role in how well these people adjusted to work. Because simulating a genuine workplace environment in a laboratory would have been extremely difficult (especially over an extended period of time), naturalistic observation provided a practical alternative for exploring this issue.

Naturalistic observation is not without its drawbacks. Psychologists using naturalistic observation have to take behavior as it comes. They cannot suddenly yell, "Freeze!" when they want to study in more detail what is going on. Nor can psychologists tell people to stop what they are doing because it is not what the psychologists are interested in researching. Moreover, simply describing one's impressions of "a day in the life" of a particular group or the way that different people behave in the same setting is not science. Observers must measure behavior in a systematic way, for example, by devising a form that enables them to check at timed intervals what people are doing.

The main drawback in naturalistic observation is **observer bias**. As we will see in Chapter 4: "Learning and Memory," eyewitnesses to a crime are often very unreliable sources of information. Even psychologists who are trained observers may subtly distort what they see to make it conform to what they were hoping to see. For this reason, contemporary researchers often use videotapes that can be analyzed and scored by other researchers who do not know what the study is designed to find out. Another potential problem is that psychologists may not be able to observe or record all important behavior; therefore, many observational studies employ a team of trained observers who pool their notes. This strategy often generates a more complete picture than one observer could draw alone.

Naturalistic observation is a valuable tool. After all, real-life behavior is what psychology is all about. Naturalistic observation often provides new ideas and suggests new theories, which can then be studied more systematically and in more detail in the laboratory. This method also helps researchers maintain their perspective by reminding them of the larger world outside the lab.

naturalistic observation Research method involving the systematic study of animal or human behavior in natural settings rather than in the laboratory.

observer bias Expectations or biases of the observer that might distort or influence his or her interpretation of what was actually observed.

CASE STUDIES

When can a case study be most useful?

A second research method is the **case study**: a detailed description of one person or a few individuals. Although in some ways this method is similar to naturalistic observation, the researcher here uses a variety of methods to collect information that yields a detailed, in-depth portrait of the individual. A case study usually includes real-life observation, interviews, scores on various psychological tests, and whatever other measures the researcher considers revealing. For example, the Swiss psychologist Jean Piaget developed a comprehensive theory of cognitive development by carefully studying each of his three children as they grew and changed during childhood. Case studies can also be applied to the study of work groups or even entire organizations. Business schools often ask students to read case studies based on successful organizations to help them learn important principles related to organizational effectiveness and success.

Like naturalistic observation, case studies can provide valuable insights, but also have significant drawbacks. Observer bias is as much a problem here as it is with naturalistic observation. Moreover, because each person, or each group, is unique, we cannot confidently draw general conclusions from a single case. Nevertheless, case studies figure prominently in psychological research. For example, the famous case of Phineas Gage, who suffered severe and unusual brain damage, led researchers to identify the front portion of the brain as important for the control of emotions and the ability to plan and carry out complex tasks (see Chapter 3: "The Biological Basis of Behavior.") The case study of another brain-damaged patient (Milner, 1959), called "H. M.," who could remember events that preceded his injury, but nothing that happened after it, prompted psychologists to suggest that we have several distinct kinds of memory. (see Chapter 4: "Learning and Memory").

SURVEYS

What are some of the benefits of survey research?

In some respects, surveys address the shortcomings of naturalistic observation and case studies. In **survey research**, a carefully selected group of people is asked a set of predetermined questions in face-to-face interviews or in questionnaires. Surveys, even those with a low-response rate, can generate a great deal of interesting and useful information at relatively low cost, but for results to be accurate, researchers must pay close attention to the survey questions (Tourangeau, Rips, & Rasinski, 2000). In addition, the people surveyed must be selected with great care, and the people must be motivated to respond to the survey thoughtfully and truthfully (Krosnick, 1999). For example, asking workers, "Do you ever engage in sabatoge against your company?" may elicit the socially correct answer, "No." Asking "Have you ever called in sick when you were not ill?" is more likely to elicit an honest response, because the question is specific and implies that most workers do occasionally violate company sick leave policies; the researcher is merely asking when and why. At the same time, survey researchers must be careful not to ask leading questions, such as "Most Americans abuse their sick leave priveleges; do you?" Guaranteeing anonymity to participants in a survey can also be important.

Naturalistic observations, case studies, and surveys can provide a rich set of raw data that describes behaviors, beliefs, opinions, and attitudes. But these research methods are not ideal for making predictions, or for explaining or determining the causes of behavior. For these purposes, psychologists use more powerful research methods, as we will see in the next two sections.

CORRELATIONAL RESEARCH

What is the difference between correlation and cause and effect?

A psychologist, under contract to the U.S. Air Force, is asked to predict which applicants for a pilot-training program will make good pilots. An excellent approach to this

Surveys can generate a great deal of useful data, but only if the questions are clear and the people surveyed are carefully selected and answer the questions honestly.

case study Intensive description and analysis of a single individual or just a few individuals.

survey research Research technique in which questionnaires or interviews are administered to a selected group of people.

Industrial psychologists study the correlations between scores on tests that measure important psychological traits and abilities and workers' subsequent performance on the job.

problem would be **correlational research**. The psychologist might select several hundred trainees, give them a variety of aptitude and personality tests, and compare their test results with their performance in training school. This approach would tell the psychologist whether some characteristic or set of characteristics is closely related to, or correlated with, eventual success as a pilot.

Suppose that the psychologist finds that the most successful trainees score higher than the unsuccessful trainees on mechanical aptitude tests and that they are also cautious people who do not like to take unnecessary risks. The psychologist has discovered that there is a *correlation*, or relationship, between these traits and success as a pilot trainee: High scores on tests of mechanical aptitude and caution predict success as a pilot trainee. If these correlations are confirmed in new groups of trainees, the psychologist could recommend with some confidence that the Air Force consider using these tests to select future trainees.

Correlational data are useful for many purposes, but they do not permit the researcher to explain cause and effect. This important distinction is often overlooked. Correlation means that two phenomena are related: When one goes up, the other goes up (or down). For example, young people with high IQ scores usually earn higher grades in school than do students with average or below-average scores. The presence of such a correlation allows researchers to predict that children with high IQ scores will do well on tests and other classwork. But correlation does not identify what causes a relationship to exist. For example, a high IQ might cause or enable a child to be a good student. But the reverse might also be true: Working hard in school might cause children to score higher on IQ tests. Or a third, unidentified factor might intervene: Growing up in a middle-class family that places a high value on education might cause both higher IQ scores and higher school grades. (See Appendix A for more discussion about correlation.)

So it is with our example. This psychologist has *described* a relationship between skill as a pilot and two other characteristics, and as a result he is able to use those relationships to predict with some accuracy which trainees will and will not become skilled pilots. But he has no basis for drawing conclusions about cause and effect. Does the tendency to shy away from taking risks make a trainee a good pilot? Or is it the other way around: Learning to be a skillful pilot makes people cautious? Or is there some unknown factor that causes people to be both cautious and capable of acquiring the different skills needed in the cockpit?

Despite limitations, correlational research often sheds light on important psychological phenomena. In this book, you will come across many examples of correlational research: People who are experiencing severe stress are more prone to develop physical illnesses than people who are not; children whose parent(s) have schizophrenia are more likely to develop this disorder than are other children; and when someone needs help, the more bystanders there are, the less likely it is that any one of them will come forward to offer help. These interesting findings allow us to make some predictions, but psychologists want to move beyond simply making predictions. To explain the causes of psychological phenomena, psychologists most often use experimental research.

EXPERIMENTAL RESEARCH

What kinds of research questions are best studied using experimental research?

A corporate trainer notices that on Monday mornings, most students in her class do not remember materials as well as they do later in the week. She has discovered a correlation between the day of the week and memory for course-related material. On the basis of this correlation, she could predict that next Monday and every Monday thereafter, the students in her class will not absorb material as well as on other days. But she wants to go beyond simply predicting her students' behavior, she wants to understand and explain why their memories are poorer on Mondays than on other days of the week.

correlational research Research technique based on the naturally occurring relationship between two or more variables.

As a result of her own experiences and some informal interviews with students, she suspects that students stay up late on weekends and that their difficulty remembering facts and ideas presented on Mondays is due to lack of sleep. This hypothesis appears to make sense, but the trainer wants to prove that it is correct. To gather evidence that lack of sleep actually causes memory deficits, she turns to the **experimental method**.

Her first step is to select **participants**, people whom she can observe to find out whether or not her hypothesis is correct. She decides to use training program volunteers. To keep her results from being influenced by sex differences or intelligence levels, she chooses a group made up of equal numbers of men and women, all of whom scored between the 75th and the 80th percentile ranks on their entrance exam for the training program.

The trainer then needs to know which participants are sleep deprived. Simply asking people whether they have slept well is not ideal: Some may say "no" so that they will have an excuse for doing poorly on the test, and others may say "yes" because they do not want her to think they are so anxious that they cannot sleep. And two people who both say they "slept well" may not mean the same thing by that phrase. So the trainer decides to intervene—that is, to *control* the situation more closely. Everyone in the experiment, she decides, will spend the night in the same hotel. They will be kept awake until 4:00 A.M. and then awakened at 7:00 A.M. sharp. She and some colleagues will patrol the halls to make sure that no one falls asleep ahead of schedule. By manipulating the amount of time the participants sleep, the trainer is introducing and controlling an essential element of the experimental method: an independent variable.

Next, the trainer needs to know how well the students remember new information after they are deprived of sleep. For this, she designs a memory task. She needs something that none of her participants will know in advance. If she chooses questions from a mechanical aptitude test, for example, she runs the risk that some of her participants will be gifted in these skills. Given the various possibilities, the psychologist decides to print a page of geometric shapes, each labeled with a nonsense word. Circles are "glucks," triangles are "rogs," and so on. She gives students half an hour to learn the names from this page, then takes it away and asks them to assign those same labels to geometric shapes on a new page. The trainer believes that the students' ability to learn and remember labels for geometric shapes will depend on their having had a good night's sleep. Performance on the memory task (the number of correct answers) thus becomes the dependent variable. According to the hypothesis, changing the **independent variable** (the amount of sleep) should also change the **dependent variable** (performance on the memory task). Her prediction is that this group of participants, who get no more than three hours of sleep, should do quite poorly on the memory test.

At this point, the trainer begins looking for loopholes in her experimental design. How can she be sure that poor test results mean that the participants did less well than they would have done if they had more sleep? For example, their poor performance could simply be the result of knowing that they were being closely observed. To be sure that her experiment measures only the effects of inadequate sleep, the trainer creates two groups, containing equal numbers of males and females of the same ages and with the same entrance exam scores. One of the groups, the **experimental group**, will be kept awake, as described, until 4:00 A.M. That is, they will be subjected to the trainer's manipulation of the independent variable—amount of sleep. Members of the other group, the **control group**, will be allowed to go to sleep whenever they please. If the only consistent difference between the two groups is the amount of sleep they get, the trainer can be much more confident that if the groups differ in their test performance, the difference is due to the length of time they slept the night before.

Finally, the trainer questions her own objectivity. Because she believes that lack of sleep inhibits students' learning and memory, she does not want to prejudice the results of her experiment; that is, she wants to avoid **experimenter bias**. So she decides to ask a neutral person, someone who does not know which participants did or did not sleep all night, to score the tests. Experimenter bias can sometimes be quite subtle, and may reflect cultural stereotypes. For example, male and female experimenters can sometimes unintentionally

experimental method Research technique in which an investigator deliberately manipulates selected events or circumstances and then measures the effects of those manipulations on subsequent behavior.

participants Individuals whose reactions or responses are observed in an experiment.

independent variable In an experiment, the variable that is manipulated to test its effects on the other, dependent variable.

dependent variable In an experiment, the variable that is measured to see how it is changed by manipulations in the independent variable.

experimental group In a controlled experiment, the group subjected to a change in the independent variable.

control group In a controlled experiment, the group not subjected to a change in the independent variable; used for comparison with the experimental group.

experimenter bias Expectations by the experimenter that might influence the results of an experiment or its interpretation.

produce different outcomes among their participants (Crutchfield, 1955; Eagly & Carli, 1981). Similarly, research with African-American participants may be significantly affected by the race of the experimenter (Graham, 1992). Thus, researchers must be sensitive to the impact even their presence can have on how experimental participants behave.

The experimental method is a powerful tool, but it, too, has limitations. Many intriguing psychological variables, such as love, hatred, or grief, do not readily lend themselves to experimental manipulation. And even if it were possible to induce such strong emotions as part of a psychological experiment, this treatment would raise serious ethical questions. In some cases, psychologists may use animals rather than humans for experiments. But some topics, such as the emergence of language in children or the expression of emotions, cannot be studied with other species. Also, because experiments are conducted in an artificial setting, participants—whether human or nonhuman animals—may behave differently than they would in real life.

The accompanying Summary Table groups the main advantages and disadvantages of each of the research methods we have discussed. Because each method has drawbacks, psychologists often use more than one method to study a single problem.

SUMMARY TABLE

BASIC METHODS OF RESEARCH

RESEARCH METHOD	ADVANTAGES	LIMITATIONS
Naturalistic Observation Behavior is observed in the environment in which it occurs naturally.	Provides a great deal of firsthand behavioral information that is more likely to be accurate than reports after the fact. The participant's behavior is more natural, spontaneous, and varied than behaviors taking place in the laboratory. A rich source of hypotheses as well.	The presence of an observer may alter the participants' behavior; the observer's recording of the behavior may reflect a preexisting bias; and it is often unclear whether the observations can be generalized to other settings and other people.
Case Studies Behavior of one person or a few people is studied in depth, often using multiple methods.	Yields a great deal of detailed descriptive information. Useful for forming hypotheses.	The case(s) studied may not be a representative sample. This method can be time consuming and expensive. Observer bias is a potential problem.
Surveys A large number of participants are asked a standard set of questions.	Enables an immense amount of data to be gathered quickly and inexpensively.	Sampling biases can skew results. Poorly constructed questions can result in answers that are ambiguous, so data are not clear. Accuracy depends on ability and willingness of participants to answer questions honestly.
Correlational Research This approach employs statistical methods to examine the relationship between two or more variables.	May clarify relationships between variables that cannot be examined by other research methods. Allows prediction of behavior.	This method does not permit researchers to draw conclusions regarding cause-and-effect relationships.
Experimental Research One or more variables are systematically manipulated, and the effect of that manipulation on other variables is studied.	Because of strict control of variables, offers researchers the opportunity to draw conclusions about cause-and-effect relationships.	The artificiality of the lab setting may influence subjects' behavior; unexpected and uncontrolled variables may confound results; many variables cannot be controlled and manipulated.

MULTIMETHOD RESEARCH

What does multimethod research allow psychologists to do?

Suppose that a psychologist was interested in studying creativity. She would probably combine several of the methods we have described. She might begin her research by giving a group of college students a creativity test that she had created to measure their capacity to discover or produce something new, and look for *correlations* among the students' scores on her test, their grades, and their scores on commonly used intelligence tests. She might then spend several weeks *observing* a college class and *interviewing* teachers, students, and parents to correlate classroom behavior and her interview data with the students' scores on the creativity test. She could go on to test some of her ideas with an *experiment* by using a group of students as participants. Her findings at any point in this research program might prompt her to revise her creativity test or her hypotheses. Eventually, her research might be able to give the general public new insights into creativity.

THE IMPORTANCE OF SAMPLING

How can sampling affect the results of a research study?

One obvious drawback to every form of research is that it is usually impossible, or at least impractical, to measure every single occurrence of the variables under study. No one could expect to measure the memory of every human being, to study the responses of all individuals who suffer from the irrational fears known as phobias, or to record the maternal behavior of all female monkeys. No matter what research method is used, whenever researchers conduct a study, they examine only a relatively small number of people or animals in the population they seek to understand. In other words, researchers almost always study a small *sample* and then use the results of that limited study to generalize about larger *populations*. For example, the corporate trainer who studied the effect of lack of sleep on memory assumed that her results would apply to other students in her training classes (past and future), as well as to students in other programs at other companies.

How realistic are these assumptions? How confident can researchers be that the results of research conducted on a relatively small sample of people apply to the much larger population from which the sample was drawn? Social scientists have developed several techniques to reduce sampling errors and improve the generalizability of their results. One is to select participants at random from the larger population. For example, the researcher studying pilot trainees might begin with an alphabetical list of all trainees and then select every third name or every fifth name on the list to be in his study. These participants would constitute a **random sample** from the larger group of trainees because every trainee had an equal chance of being chosen for the study.

Another way to make sure that conclusions apply to the larger population is to pick a **representative sample** of the population being studied. For example, researchers looking for a representative cross section of Americans would want to ensure that the proportion of males and females in the study matched the national proportion, that the number of participants from each state matched the national population distribution, and so on. Even with these precautions, however, unintended bias may influence psychological research.

random sample Sample in which each potential participant has an equal chance of being selected.

representative sample Sample carefully chosen so that the characteristics of the participants correspond closely to the characteristics of the larger population.

▶ CHECK YOUR UNDERSTANDING

1. A method of research known as _____ allows psychologists to study behavior as it occurs in real-life settings.

2. Psychologists use _____ research to examine relationships between two or more variables without manipulating any variable.

3. The method of research best suited to explaining behavior is _____ research.

4. The _____ variable in an experiment is manipulated to see how it affects a second variable; the _____ variable is the one observed for any possible effects.

5. To ensure that the results of a particular study apply to a larger population, researchers use _____ or _____ samples.

Answers: 1. naturalistic observation, 2. correlational, 3. experimental, 4. independent, dependent, 5. random; representative.

Ethics and Psychology

1.6   Summarize the major principles that govern the ethical standards adopted by psychologists and describe their importance in guiding research in the field.

Ethical issues—those that cause us to consider the difference between right and wrong—surround us in everyday life. On the job, for example, workers are called on frequently to make decisions that raise questions of ethics. Should a manager be told that a co-worker is abusing sick leave or using illegal drugs? Psychologists, too, must struggle with ethical issues, and oftentimes these are raised by the type of research that psychologists conduct.

RESEARCH ON HUMANS: THE MILGRAM EXPERIMENTS

Why did Milgram's experiments on obedience raise ethical questions about his research?

Consider the ethical debate that flared up in 1963 when psychologist Stanley Milgram published the results of several experiments he had conducted. Milgram paid people to participate in what he said was a learning experiment. In a typical session, a young man would arrive at the laboratory to participate. He was met by a stern-faced researcher in a lab coat; another man in street clothes was sitting in the waiting room. The researcher explained that he was studying the effects of punishment on learning and that the men would be assigned the roles of teacher and learner. When the two men drew slips out of a hat, the participant's slip always said "teacher." The teacher watched as the "learner" was strapped into a chair and an electrode attached to his wrist. The teacher was then taken into an adjacent room and seated at an impressive-looking "shock generator" with switches from 15 to 450 volts, labeled "Slight Shock," "Very Strong Shock," up to "Danger: Severe Shock," and, finally, "XXX." The teacher's job was to read a list of paired words that the learner would attempt to memorize and repeat. The teacher was instructed to deliver a shock whenever the learner gave a wrong answer and to increase the intensity of the shock each time the learner made a mistake. At 90 volts, the learner began to grunt; at 120 volts, he shouted, "Hey, this really hurts!" At 150 volts, he demanded to be released, and at 270 volts, his protests became screams of agony. Beyond 330 volts, the learner appeared to pass out. If the teacher became concerned and asked whether he could stop, the experimenter politely but firmly replied that he was expected to continue, that this experiment was being conducted in the interests of science.

In reality, Milgram was studying obedience, not learning. He wanted to find out whether ordinary people would obey orders to cause another person pain. As part of his research, Milgram (1974) described the experiment to 110 psychiatrists, college students, and middle-class adults, and he asked them at what point they thought participants would stop. Members of all three groups guessed that most people would refuse to continue beyond 130 volts and that no one would go beyond 300 volts. The psychiatrists estimated that only one in a thousand people would continue to the XXX shock level. Astonishingly, 65 percent of Milgram's participants administered the highest level of

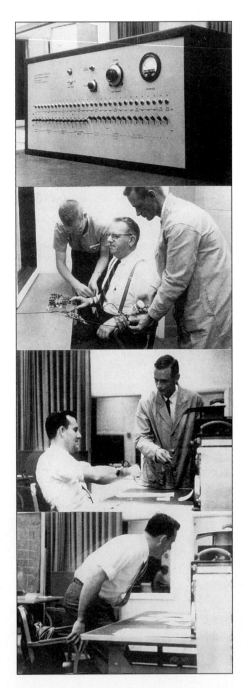

Stanley Milgram's Obedience Experiment. (A) The shock generator used in the experiment. (B) With electrodes attached to his wrists, the learner provides answers by pressing switches that light up on an answer box. (C) The subject administers a shock to the learner. (D) The subject breaks off the experiment. Milgram's study yielded interesting results, but it also raised serious questions about the ethics of such experimentation.

shock, even though many worried aloud that the shocks might be causing serious damage to the learners.

To find out what he wanted to know, Milgram had to deceive his participants. The stated purpose of the experiment—to test learning—was a lie. The "learners" were Milgram's accomplices, who had been trained to act as though they were being hurt; the machines were fake; and the learners received no shocks at all (Milgram, 1963). But, critics argued, the "teachers"—the real subjects of the study—were hurt. Not only did most voice concern, but they also showed clear signs of stress: They sweated, bit their lips, trembled, stuttered, or in a few cases, broke into uncontrollable nervous laughter. Critics also worried about the effect of the experiment on the participants' self-esteem. How would you like to be compared with the people who ran the death camps in Nazi Germany?

THE APA CODE OF ETHICS

Are there ethical guidelines for conducting psychological research?

Although the design of Milgram's experiment was not typical of the vast majority of psychological experiments, it sparked such a public uproar that the American Psychological Association (APA) re-evaluated its ethical guidelines, first published in 1953. A new code of ethics on psychological experimentation was approved. This code is assessed each year and periodically revised to ensure that it adequately protects participants in research studies. In addition to outlining the ethical principles guiding research and teaching, the code spells out a set of **ethical standards** for psychologists who offer therapy and other professional services, such as psychological testing.

The APA code of ethics requires that researchers obtain informed consent from participants and stipulates the following:

- Participants must be informed of the nature of research in clearly understandable language.

- Informed consent must be documented.

- Risks, possible adverse effects, and limitations on confidentiality must be spelled out in advance.

- If participation is a condition of course credit, equitable alternative activities must be offered.

- Participants cannot be deceived about aspects of the research that would affect their willingness to participate, such as risks or unpleasant emotional experiences.

- Deception about the goals of the research can be used only when absolutely necessary to the integrity of the research.

In addition, psychological researchers are required to follow the U.S. government's Code of Federal Regulations, which includes an extensive set of requirements concerning the protection of human participants in all kinds of research. Failure to abide by these federal regulations may result in the termination of federal funding for the researcher and penalties for the research institution.

RESEARCH ON ANIMALS

What objections have been raised regarding research on animal subjects?

In recent years, questions have also been raised about the ethics of using animals in psychological research (Herzog, 1995; Plous, 1996; Rowan & Shapiro, 1996; Shapiro, 1991). Psychologists study animal behavior in order to shed light on human behavior. Crowding mice into small cages, for example, has yielded valuable insights into the effects of overcrowding on humans. Animals are used in experiments in which it would be clearly

ethical standards Ethical requirements that psychologists who offer therapy or other professional services must adhere to.

unethical to use human participants—for instance, studies involving brain lesions (requiring cutting into the brain) or electric stimulation of parts of the brain. In fact, much of what we know about sensation, perception, drugs, emotional attachment, and the neural basis of behavior is derived from animal research (Domjan & Purdy, 1995). Yet, animal protectionists and others question whether it is ethical to use nonhuman animals, which cannot give their consent to serve as subjects, in psychological research.

Their opponents contend that the goals of scientific research—in essence, to reduce or eliminate human suffering—justify the means, even though they agree that animals should be made to suffer as little as possible (Gallistel, 1981; Novak, 1991). They argue that procedures now in place, including the use of anesthesia in many experiments, already minimize animal suffering. The APA has addressed this issue in its ethical guidelines, noting that psychologists using animals in research must ensure "appropriate consideration of [the animal's] comfort, health, and humane treatment" (APA, 1992).

Throughout this text you will be learning about research studies conducted on a wide array of topics. It is useful to keep in mind that these investigations are part of the scientific enterprise which guides the field of psychology—the scientific study of behavior and mental processes.

▶ CHECK YOUR UNDERSTANDING

Are the following statements true (T) or false (F)?

1. Controversy over ethical standards in psychology has almost disappeared.
2. The APA code of ethics used today is unchanged since 1953.
3. Researchers who fail to follow the federal code of regulations are subject to penalties.

Answers: 1. (F), 2. (F), 3. (T).

▶ APPLY YOUR UNDERSTANDING

1. Your classmate Jared says he does not need to be concerned about ethical standards because he is using a naturalistic observation method, not an experiment. On the basis of what you have learned from this chapter, your reply should be
   a. "You're right, but only if the subjects of the study are animals."
   b. "You're right. Only laboratory experiments must conform to ethics standards."
   c. "That's incorrect. All psychological research is subject to ethical guidelines."
   d. "That's incorrect. Actually, naturalistic observation is the only kind of research subject to ethics rules."

2. Before she asks co-workers to volunteer for an unpleasant work assignment, LaNae makes sure that they all understand exactly what the work entails, how long the assignment will last, and how much extra pay volunteers will receive. The key ethical protection LaNae is providing is most similar to which of the following ethical guidelines that psychologists embrace?
   a. informed consent
   b. deception
   c. limiting risk
   d. limiting experimental bias

Answers: 1. c, 2. a.

>KEY TERMS<

What is psychology?

psychology, *p. 3*

The growth of psychology

structuralism, *p. 8*
functionalist theory, *p. 9*
psychodynamic theories, *p. 9*
behaviorism, *p. 10*
Gestalt psychology, *p. 12*
humanistic psychology, *p. 12*
cognitive psychology, *p. 12*

evolutionary psychology, *p. 13*
positive psychology, *p. 14*

Human diversity

gender, *p. 18*
feminist theory, *p. 18*
race, *p. 18*
ethnicity, *p. 18*
culture, *p. 19*

Psychology as a science

scientific method, *p. 20*

hypothesis, *p. 20*
theory, *p. 21*

Research methods in psychology

naturalistic observation, *p. 22*
observer bias, *p. 22*
case study, *p. 23*
survey research, *p. 23*
correlational research, *p. 24*
experimental method, *p. 25*
participants, *p. 25*

independent variable, *p. 25*
dependent variable, *p. 25*
experimental group, *p. 25*
control group, *p. 25*
experimenter bias, *p. 25*
random sample, *p. 27*
representative sample, *p. 27*

Ethics and psychology

ethical standards, *p. 29*

>CHAPTER REVIEW<

What Is Psychology?

How is psychology defined and what topics do psychologists study? **Psychology** is the scientific study of behavior and mental processes. It seeks to both describe and explain every aspect of human thought, feelings, perceptions, and actions, and is not confined to investigating only abnormal behavior.

Psychology has many major subdivisions. Developmental psychology is concerned with processes of growth and change over the life course, from the prenatal period through old age and death. Neuroscience and physiological psychology focus on the body's neural and chemical systems, studying how these affect thought and behavior. Experimental psychology investigates basic psychological processes, such as learning, memory, sensation, perception, cognition, motivation, and emotion. Personality psychology looks at differences among people in traits such as anxiety, aggressiveness, and self-esteem. Clinical and counseling psychology specializes in diagnosing and treating psychological disorders; social psychology focuses on how people influence one another's thoughts and actions. Finally, industrial and organizational psychology studies problems in the work place and other kinds of organizations.

Given this broad range of careers and interests, what holds psychology together? A number of fundamental questions cut across the various subfields of psychology, unifying them with similar themes. Five fundamental questions are:

1. Person–Situation—Is behavior caused more by inner traits or by external situations?

2. Nature–Nurture—How do genes and experiences interact to influence people?

3. Stability–Change—How much do we stay the same as we develop and how much do we change?

4. Diversity–Universality—In what ways do people differ in how they think and act?

5. Mind–Body—What is the relationship between our internal experiences and our biological processes?

The Growth of Psychology

As a subject of interest to people, psychology has a long past because humans have wondered about behavior and mental processes since ancient times. As a scientific discipline, however, psychology has a short history, dating back only to the late-nineteenth century.

How did the work of Wundt and Titchener, of James, and of Freud contribute to the early development of psychology as a field of study? Two of the earliest leading psychological researchers were Wilhelm Wundt and Edward Titchener. Wundt established the first psychology laboratory in 1879 at the University of Leipzig in Germany. His use of experiment and measurement marked the beginnings of psychology as a science. One of Wundt's students, Edward Titchener, established a perspective called **structuralism**, which was based on the belief that psychology's role was to identify the basic elements of experience and how they combine.

The American psychologist William James criticized structuralism, arguing that sensations cannot be separated from the mental associations that allow us to benefit from past experiences. Our rich storehouse of ideas and memories is what enables us to function in our environment, James believed. His perspective became known as **functionalism**.

The theories of Sigmund Freud added another new dimension to psychology: The idea that much of our behavior is governed by unconscious conflicts, motives, and desires. Freud's work gave rise to **psychodynamic theories**.

How was the approach to human behavior taken by Watson and Skinner different from Freud's? John B. Watson, a spokesman for the school of thought called **behaviorism**, argued that psychology should concern itself only with observable, measurable behavior. Watson based much of his work on the conditioning experiments of Ivan Pavlov.

B. F. Skinner's beliefs were similar to Watson's, but he added the concept of reinforcement, or reward. Skinner's views dominated American psychology into the 1960s.

How have Gestalt psychologists, humanistic psychologists, and cognitive psychologists extended the definition of psychology? According to **Gestalt psychology**, perception depends on the human tendency to see patterns, to distinguish objects from their backgrounds, and to complete pictures from a few clues. In this emphasis on wholeness, the Gestalt school radically differed from structuralism.

Humanistic psychology is another perspective, one that emphasizes the goal of reaching one's fullest potential. **Cognitive psychology** is the study of mental processes in the broadest sense, focusing on how people perceive, interpret, store, and retrieve information. Unlike behaviorists, cognitive psychologists believe that mental processes can and should be studied scientifically. This view has dramatically changed American psychology from its previous behaviorist focus by expanding the scope of the subject matter of psychology.

How is the field of psychology being defined today? **Evolutionary psychology** focuses on the functions and adaptive value of various human behaviors, emphasizing how those behaviors may have evolved. **Positive psychology** studies subjective feelings of happiness and well-being; the development of individual traits such as integrity and leadership; and the settings that encourage individuals to flourish. In this way, it seeks to add a new dimension to psychological research. Most contemporary psychologists do not adhere to just one school of thought. They believe that different theories can often complement one another and together enrich our understanding of human behavior.

In psychology's early years, why were relatively few women prominent in the field? Although psychology has profited from the contributions of women from its beginnings, women often faced discrimination: Some colleges and universities did not grant degrees to women, professional journals were often reluctant to publish their work, and teaching positions were often closed to them. More recently, many women have entered the field and are making important contributions.

Human Diversity

Why is the study of human diversity important in the field of psychology? A rich diversity of behavior and thought exists in the human species, among individuals and groups. A knowledge of this diversity can help reduce the tensions that arise when people misunderstand one another. It can also help us to define what humans have in common.

How are psychologists helping us to understand the differences between men and women? Psychologists sometimes find it useful to distinguish between biological sex and the more encompassing term *gender*. Today, social roles ascribed to men versus women are more blurred than in the past, but differences in our expectations of men and women—called *gender stereotypes*—continue to exist. Psychologists are trying to determine the causes of gender differences by considering the contributions of both heredity and culturally learned gender roles. The field of **feminist theory** explores how views of women can influence the treatment of all people.

Why are psychologists interested in racial and ethnic differences? **Race** and **ethnicity** are two traditional dimensions of diversity in humans. Because it is so difficult to define race, most psychologists have abandoned the term as a scientific concept. Ethnicity and ethnic identity, however, remain meaningful. They involve a shared cultural heritage based on common ancestry, can affect norms of behavior.

How does culture contribute to human diversity? The various aspects of **culture**—the beliefs, values, traditions, and norms of behavior that a particular people share—make an important contribution to human diversity. In a society as large and diversified as ours, there are many subcultural groups with their own identities.

Psychology as a Science

What features distinguish a scientific field from a field not based in science? All fields of science are based on empirical observation and rely on the **scientific method**, which involves formulating **hypotheses**, collecting data, and constructing **theories** to explain results. A key feature of scientific theories is that they are falsifiable, meaning that new evidence can disconfirm them.

Research Methods in Psychology

Psychologists use a variety of methods to study behavior and mental processes. These include naturalistic observation, case studies, surveys, correlational research, and experiments. Each method has its own advantages and limitations.

Why is a natural setting sometimes better than a laboratory for observing behavior? Psychologists use **naturalistic observation** to study behavior in natural settings. Because there is minimal interference from the researcher, the behavior observed is likely to be more accurate, spontaneous, and varied than behavior studied in a laboratory. Researchers using this method must be careful to avoid **observer bias**.

When can a case study be most useful? Researchers conduct a **case study** to investigate the behavior of one person or a few persons in depth. This method can yield a great deal of detailed, descriptive information that is useful for forming hypotheses.

What are some of the benefits of survey research? **Survey research** generates a large amount of data quickly and inexpensively by asking a standard set of questions of a large number of people. Great care must be taken, however, in how the questions are worded and in obtaining an unbiased sample of participants.

What is the difference between correlation and cause and effect? **Correlational research** investigates the relationship, or correlation, between two or more variables. Although two variables may be *related* to each other, that does not imply that one *causes* the other.

What kinds of research questions are best studied using experimental research? An **experiment** is called for when a researcher wants to draw conclusions about cause and effect. In an experiment, the impact of one factor can be studied, while all other factors are held constant. The factor whose effects are being studied is called the **independent variable**, since the researcher is free to manipulate it at will. The factor on which there is apt to be an impact is called the **dependent variable**. Usually an experiment includes both an **experimental group** of subjects or **participants** and a **control group** for comparison purposes. Often a neutral person records data and scores results, so **experimenter bias** doesn't creep in.

What does multimethod research allow psychologists to do? Many psychologists overcome the limitations of using a single research method by using multiple methods to study a single problem.

How can sampling affect the results of a research study? Regardless of the particular research method used, psychologists almost always study a small sample of participants and then generalize their results to larger populations. Proper sampling is critical to ensure that results have broader application. **Random samples**, in which subjects are chosen randomly, and **representative samples**, in which subjects are chosen to reflect the general characteristics of the population as a whole, are two ways of doing this.

Ethics and Psychology

Why did Milgram's experiments on obedience raise ethical questions about his research? Milgram's obedience studies involved asking human volunteers to press buttons that they believed would deliver increasingly painful and harmful electrical shocks to other volunteers. Even though no shocks were actually delivered, the ethics of deceiving people so that they believed they might be seriously injuring others is questionable.

Are there ethical guidelines for conducting psychological research? The American Psychological Association (APA) has a code of ethics for conducting research involving human participants. Researchers must obtain informed consent from participants in their studies. Participants must be told in advance about the nature of the research and the possible risks involved. People should not feel pressured to participate if they do not want to. Psychologists who offer therapy or other psychological services must adhere to **ethical standards** that serve as guidelines for the ethical treatment of clients.

What objections have been raised regarding research on animal subjects? Although much of what we know about certain areas of psychology has come from animal research, the practice of experimenting on animals has strong opponents because of the pain and suffering that are sometimes involved. Both APA and the federal government have issued guidelines for the humane treatment of laboratory animals that protect their comfort and health.

>CHAPTER 1< The Science of Psychology

1.1 WHAT IS PSYCHOLOGY?

PSYCHOLOGY is the scientific study of behavior and mental processes.

FIELDS OF SPECIALIZATION:

Developmental — How humans grow and change

Physiological — The biological bases of behavior, thought, and emotion

Experimental — Basic explanations for human behavior and mental processes

Personality — How individuals differ in basic traits

Clinical and Counseling — How mental illnesses and adjustment problems are diagnosed and treated

Social — How others influence our own behavior and thinking

Industrial and Organizational — How the principles of psychology can be applied in the workplace

ENDURING ISSUES IN PSYCHOLOGY:

Person-Situation — How important are internal thoughts and feelings versus external events?

Nature-Nurture — Is behavior the result of hereditary or environmental forces?

Stability-Change — Is the behavior of an individual stable throughout the lifespan or does it change in response to life events?

Diversity-Universality — To what extent are all people alike?

Mind-Body — To what extent is our sense of personal awareness a consequence of biological processes occurring in the nervous system?

1.2 THE GROWTH OF PSYCHOLOGY

EARLY VIEWS OF PSYCHOLOGY AND PSYCHOLOGICAL PROCESSES:

- In Germany, in 1879, **Wundt** sets up a laboratory to study mental processes scientifically: establishes the **Structuralist view**

- In the United States, **William James** argues that conscious experience is ever-changing: establishes the **Functionalist view**

- **Sigmund Freud** emphasizes the role of unconcious processes: establishes the **Psychodynamic view**

- **John B. Watson** redefines psychology as the science limited to the study of observable behavior: Establishes **Behaviorism**, a view later popularized by **B. F. Skinner**

THE COGNITIVE REVOLUTION AND NEW DIRECTIONS

- **Gestalt** and **Humanistic** psychologists expand the scope of psychology to include the study of perception and human emotions, respectively

- **Cognitive psychologists** use scientific methods to study mental processes such as thinking and feeling

- **Evolutionary psychologists** examine how human behavior has evolved and focus on how behavior helps us adapt to our surroundings

- **Positive psychologists** study mental wellness and successful adjustment patterns

1.3 HUMAN DIVERSITY

DIVERSITY IN THE FIELD:

- Psychologists encourage women and members of racial and ethnic minority groups to enter the field

ISSUES:

- Psychologists study gender, race, ethnicity, and culture as they affect behavior

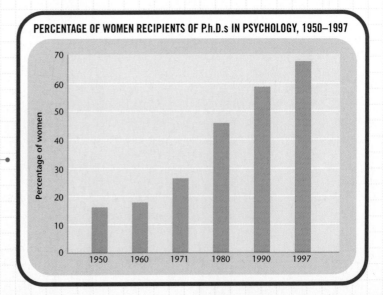

PERCENTAGE OF WOMEN RECIPIENTS OF P.h.D.s IN PSYCHOLOGY, 1950–1997

1.4 PSYCHOLOGY AS A SCIENCE

HOW PSYCHOLOGISTS USE THE SCIENTIFIC METHOD:
Psychologists rely on the scientific method to describe, understand, predict, and explain behavior and mental processes.

HOW THE SCIENTIFIC METHOD WORKS:
As data are collected, patterns of results are explained with **theories**, which in turn generate additional testable **hypotheses**.

1.5 RESEARCH METHODS IN PSYCHOLOGY

DESCRIPTIVE METHODS:
- **Naturalistic Observation:** Systematic study of behavior in natural rather than laboratory settings, but with limited control
- **Case Study:** Detailed description of an individual, but open to potential observer bias
- **Survey:** Use of interviews or questionnaires to collect information about a group of people, but open to sampling bias

CORRELATIONAL RESEARCH:
- **Correlation:** Numerical expression of the degree to which two variables are related to each other
- Correlation can be used to describe a relationship, but not to establish cause-and-effect

EXPERIMENTAL RESEARCH:
- Can be used to study cause-and-effect relationships
- Often involves the manipulation of an **Independent Variable** by the experimenter to see if it affects the **Dependent Variable** of interest
- Results obtained on participants in the **Experimental Group** are compared to those obtained on participants in a **Control Group**
- **Experimenter bias** must be limited through careful planning and control of the experiment
- Results in all methods depend on who is included in the sample of participants studied.
  Random sample: All potential participants have an equal chance of being selected.
  Representative sample: Sample chosen so that the characteristics of its participants match those in the larger population
- Care must be taken in generalizing from results obtained for one group of people to other groups

1.6 ETHICS AND PSYCHOLOGY

ETHICAL PRINCIPLES THAT GUIDE RESEARCH IN PSYCHOLOGY
- Informed consent must be given by participants
- Confidentiality must be maintained
- Participants have the right to not participate or discontinue participation
- Deception can be employed only in carefully limited ways

Concept Map

The Biological Basis of Behavior

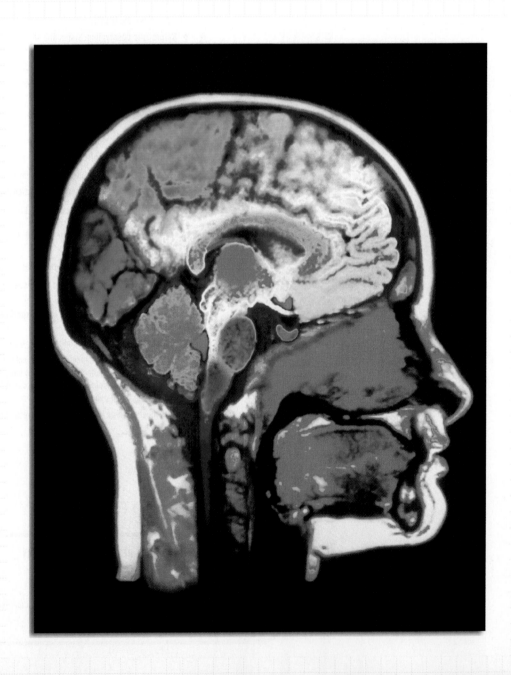

THE PEPSI CHALLENGE

What makes people choose one soft drink over another? And how do we find the mechanism? In the summer of 2003, neuroscientist Read Montague's 17-year-old daughter was interning at his Human Neuroimaging Lab at Baylor College of Medicine in Houston, where the focus is on the brain and the nervous system. To make her experience more interesting and more practical, he came up with a study he named the Pepsi Challenge.

Using a brain-scanning tool called *Functional Magnetic Resonance Imaging* (fMRI) to monitor activity in the brain, Montague gave 67 people a blind taste test using Coca-Cola and Pepsi. When volunteers relied on taste alone to choose a drink, the brain's reward circuits lit up, and they were evenly split as to which drink they preferred. When the same participants were shown images of soda cans as they sipped, they overwhelmingly preferred Coke—no matter which soda they were sipping. When Montague and his team analyzed the fMRIs, they saw that the Coke label seemed to activate different regions of the brain than the blind taste test had. A memory region called the hippocampus and another part of the brain, the prefrontal cortex, lit up. Their conclusion: Marketing, not taste, made the difference. For this group, Coca-Cola was more effective than Pepsi in embedding its brand image deep into consumers' brains. More important, the study showed that consumers'

conscious and subconscious can conflict when they interact with a brand.

Montague's Pepsi Challenge helped launch the field known as neuromarketing. Organizations—ranging from The Metropolitan Museum of Art to Daimler-Chrysler and Home Depot—now pay neuroscientists to search for the "buy button" in consumers' brains. Advertisers have a huge incentive to do so: In our media-saturated culture, the average American consumer is bombarded with 3,000 advertising messages a day, on which advertisers spend $117 billion a year. In all likelihood you don't even remember which product is featured in the tiny percentage of ads you *do* recall. So advertisers need to come up with a more reliable means of figuring out what works—and what doesn't.

Still, consumer and civil liberties groups question the morality of what they see as the ultimate invasion of privacy. They are concerned about the idea of political groups or corporations figuring out how to change brain activity to serve their own ends. The fear is not unfounded. As researchers have begun to map the brain, they have realized that it is more malleable than anyone had guessed. Studies such as the Pepsi Challenge show that not only do marketing messages change minds, but they do so by altering the brain's circuits.

All the organs of our body—not only the brain—depend on intricate feedback-and-control

patterns between external events and internal controls. Our biological systems are geared to make adjustments that keep us in tune with our surroundings—whether that means drinking Coke instead of Pepsi or considering certain celebrities "cool" and others "uncool." If practicing a musical instrument can physically alter areas of the cerebral cortex, intense, repetitive marketing messages might shape the brain circuits involved in decision-making.

This chapter introduces **psychobiology**, the branch of psychology that deals with the biological bases of behavior and mental processes. Psychobiology overlaps with a much larger interdisciplinary field of study called **neuroscience**, which specifically focuses on the study of the brain and the nervous system. Many psychobiologists who study the brain's influence on behavior call themselves **neuropsychologists**.

We begin our journey by looking at the basic building blocks of the brain and nervous system: nerve cells, called *neurons*. Then we will explore the two major systems that integrate and coordinate our behavior, keeping us in constant touch with what is going on "out there." One is the *nervous system*, of which the brain is part. The other is the *endocrine system*, made up of glands that secrete chemical messages, called *hormones*, into the blood. Last, we examine the influence on behavior of the genetic instructions we inherit. ◼

Neurons: The Messengers

2.1 Identify the main structural features of neurons, explain how they function, and describe how they respond to environmental enrichment and to injury.

The brain of an average human being contains as many as 100 billion nerve cells, or **neurons**. Billions more neurons are found in other parts of the nervous system. Neurons vary widely in size and shape, but they are all specialized to receive and transmit information.

THE STRUCTURE OF NEURONS

What types of cells are found in the nervous system?

A typical neuron is shown in **Figure 2–1**. Like other cells, the neuron's cell body is made up of a nucleus, which contains a complete set of chromosomes and genes; cytoplasm, which keeps the cell alive; and a cell membrane, which encloses the whole cell. What makes a neuron different from other cells is the tiny fibers that extend out from the cell body, enabling

neuropsychologists Psychobiologists who study the brain's influence on behavior.

neuroscience The study of the brain and the nervous system.

psychobiology The area of psychology that focuses on the biological foundations of behavior and mental processes.

neurons Individual cells that are the smallest unit of the nervous system.

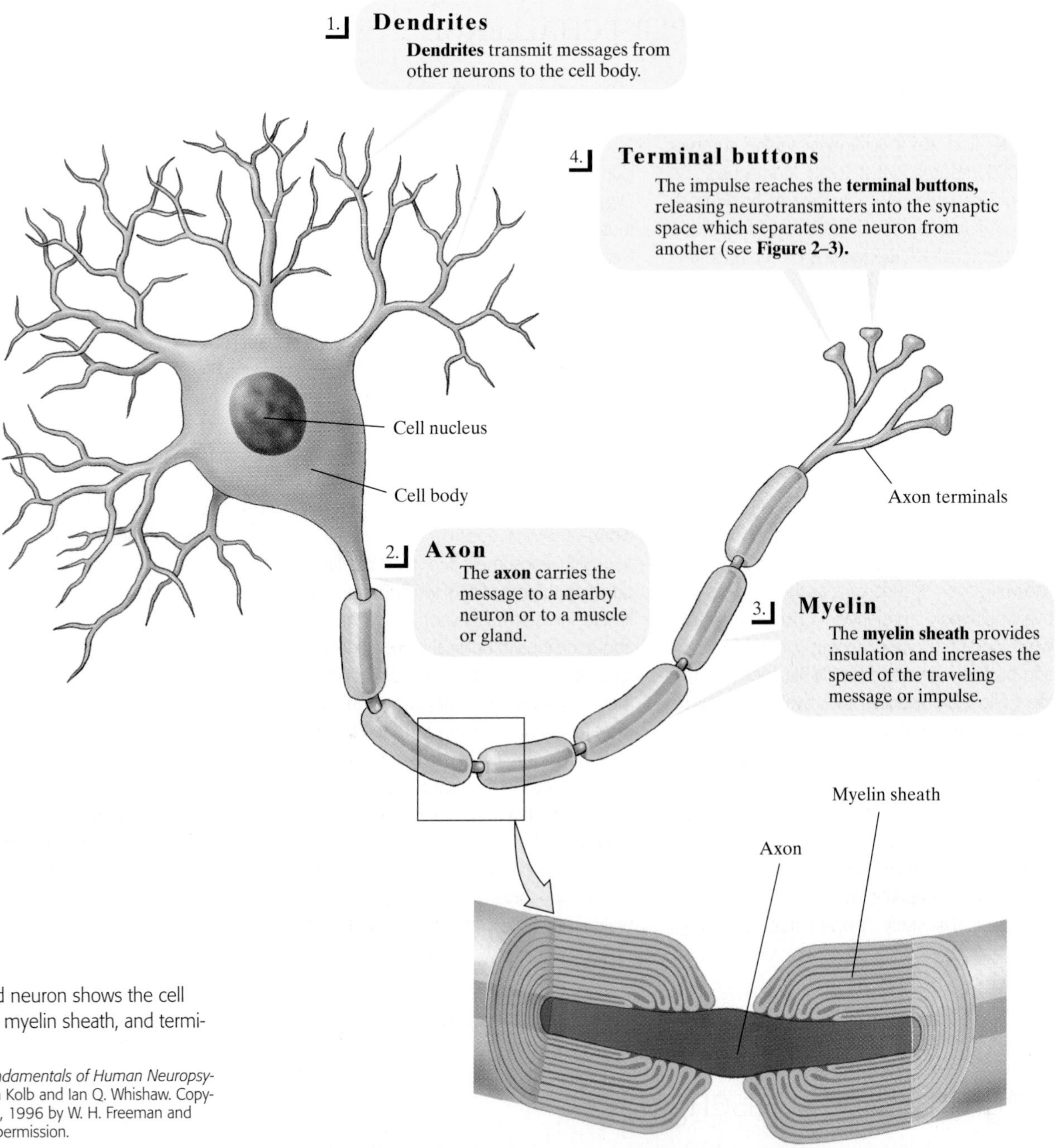

1.| Dendrites

Dendrites transmit messages from other neurons to the cell body.

4.| Terminal buttons

The impulse reaches the **terminal buttons**, releasing neurotransmitters into the synaptic space which separates one neuron from another (see **Figure 2–3**).

Cell nucleus

Cell body

Axon terminals

2.| Axon

The **axon** carries the message to a nearby neuron or to a muscle or gland.

3.| Myelin

The **myelin sheath** provides insulation and increases the speed of the traveling message or impulse.

Myelin sheath

Axon

Figure 2–1

This typical myelinated neuron shows the cell body, dendrites, axon, myelin sheath, and terminal buttons.

Source: Adapted from *Fundamentals of Human Neuropsychology* (4th ed.), by Brian Kolb and Ian Q. Whishaw. Copyright © 1980, 1985, 1990, 1996 by W. H. Freeman and Company. Reprinted with permission.

dendrites Short fibers that branch out from the cell body and pick up incoming messages.

axon Single long fiber extending from the cell body; it carries outgoing messages.

nerve (or tract) Group of axons bundled together.

myelin sheath White fatty covering found on some axons.

a neuron to perform its special job: receiving and transmitting messages. The short fibers branching out around the cell body are **dendrites**. Their role is to pick up incoming messages from other neurons and transmit them to the cell body. The single long fiber extending from the cell body is an **axon**. The axon's job is to carry outgoing messages to neighboring neurons or to a muscle or gland. Axons vary in length from 1 or 2 millimeters (about the length of the word "or" in this sentence) to 3 feet. (In adults, a single axon may run from the brain to the base of the spinal cord or from the spinal cord to the tip of the thumb.) Although a neuron typically has only one axon, near its end the axon splits into many terminal branches. When we talk about a **nerve** (or **tract**), we are referring to a group of axons bundled together like wires in an electrical cable.

The axon in **Figure 2–1** is surrounded by a white, fatty covering called a **myelin sheath**. The myelin sheath is "pinched" at intervals, making the axon resemble a string of microscopic sausages. Not all axons have this covering, but myelinated axons are found in all parts of the body. (Because of this white covering, tissues made up primarily of myelinated axons are known as "white matter," whereas tissues made up primarily of unmyelinated axons are called "gray matter.") The myelin sheath has two functions: It provides insulation so that signals from adjacent neurons do not interfere with each other, and it increases the speed at which signals are transmitted.

Neurons that collect messages from sense organs and carry those messages to the spinal cord or the brain are called **sensory** (or **afferent**) **neurons**. Neurons that carry messages from the spinal cord or the brain to the muscles and glands are called **motor** (or **efferent**) **neurons**. And neurons that carry messages from one neuron to another are called **interneurons** (or **association neurons**).

The nervous system also contains a vast number of **glial cells**, or **glia** (the word *glia* means "glue"). Glial cells hold the neurons in place, provide nourishment and remove waste products, prevent harmful substances from passing from the bloodstream into the brain, and form the myelin sheath that insulates and protects neurons. Recent evidence suggests that glial cells may play an important role in learning and memory, and thereby may affect the brain's response to new experiences (Featherstone, Fleming, & Ivy, 2000; Roitbak, 1993).

THE NEURAL IMPULSE

What "language" do neurons speak?

How do neurons "talk" to one another? What form do their messages take? Neurons speak in a language that all cells in the body understand: simple "yes–no," "on–off" electrochemical impulses.

When a neuron is at rest, the membrane surrounding the cell forms a partial barrier between the fluids that are inside and outside the neuron. Both solutions contain electrically charged particles, or **ions**. (See **Figure 2–2A**.) Because there are more negative ions inside the neuron than outside, there is a small electrical charge (called the **resting potential**) across the cell membrane. Thus, the resting neuron is said to be in a state of **polarization**. A resting, or polarized, neuron is like a spring that has been compressed or a guitar string that has been pulled, but not released. All that is needed to generate a neuron's signal is the release of this tension.

When a small area on the cell membrane is adequately stimulated by an incoming message, pores (or channels) in the membrane at the stimulated area open, allowing a sudden inflow of positively charged sodium ions. (See **Figure 2–2B**.) This process is called *depolarization*; now the inside of the neuron is positively charged relative to the outside. Depolarization sets off a chain reaction. When the membrane allows sodium to enter the neuron at one point, the next point on the membrane opens. More sodium ions flow into the neuron at the second spot and depolarize this part of the neuron, and so on, along the entire length of the neuron. As a result, an electrical charge, called a **neural impulse** or **action potential**, travels down the axon, much like a fuse burning from one end to the other. (See **Figure 2–2C**.) When this happens, we say that the neuron has "fired." The speed at which neurons carry impulses varies widely, from as fast as nearly 400 feet per second on largely myelinated axons to as slow as about 3 feet per second on those with no myelin.

A single neuron may have many hundreds of dendrites and its axon may branch out in numerous directions, so that it is in touch with hundreds or thousands of other cells at both its input end (dendrites) and its output end (axon). At any given moment, a neuron may be receiving messages from other neurons, some of which are primarily *excitatory* (telling it to "fire"), and from others, primarily *inhibitory* (telling it to "rest"). The constant interplay of excitation and inhibition determines whether the neuron is likely to fire or not.

As a rule, single impulses received from neighboring neurons do not make a neuron fire. The incoming message causes a small, temporary shift in the electrical charge, called a **graded potential**, which is transmitted along the cell membrane and may simply fade away, leaving the neuron in its normal polarized state. For a neuron to fire, graded potentials caused by impulses from many neighboring neurons—or from one neuron firing repeatedly—must exceed a certain minimum **threshold of excitation**. Just as a light switch requires a minimum amount of pressure to be turned on, an incoming message must be above the minimum threshold to make a neuron fire.

sensory (or afferent) neurons Neurons that carry messages from sense organs to the spinal cord or brain.

motor (or efferent) neurons Neurons that carry messages from the spinal cord or brain to the muscles and glands.

interneurons (or association neurons) Neurons that carry messages from one neuron to another.

glial cells (or glia) Cells that insulate and support neurons by holding them together, provide nourishment and remove waste products, prevent harmful substances from passing into the brain, and form the myelin sheath.

ions Electrically charged particles found both inside and outside the neuron.

resting potential Electrical charge across a neuron membrane resulting from more positive ions concentrated on the outside and more negative ions on the inside.

polarization The condition of a neuron when the inside is negatively charged relative to the outside; for example, when the neuron is at rest.

neural impulse (or action potential) The firing of a nerve cell.

graded potential A shift in the electrical charge in a tiny area of a neuron.

threshold of excitation The level an impulse must exceed to cause a neuron to fire.

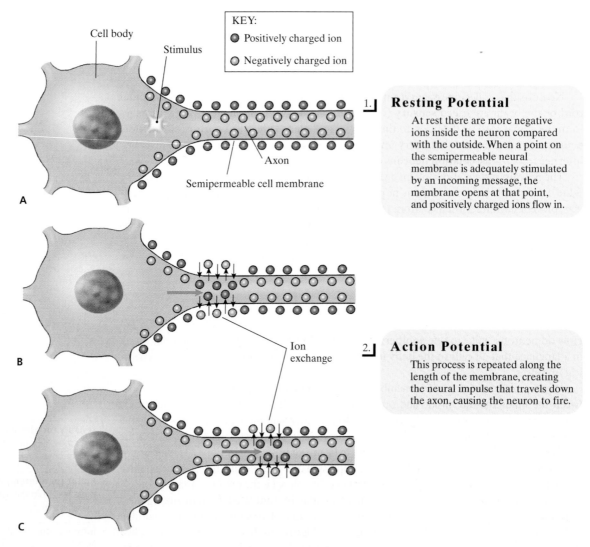

KEY:
- ● Positively charged ion
- ○ Negatively charged ion

Cell body

Stimulus

Axon

Semipermeable cell membrane

A

1. **Resting Potential**

At rest there are more negative ions inside the neuron compared with the outside. When a point on the semipermeable neural membrane is adequately stimulated by an incoming message, the membrane opens at that point, and positively charged ions flow in.

B

Ion exchange

2. **Action Potential**

This process is repeated along the length of the membrane, creating the neural impulse that travels down the axon, causing the neuron to fire.

C

Figure 2–2
The neural impulse—communication within the neuron.

Either neurons fire, or they do not; and every firing of a particular neuron produces an impulse of the same strength. This is called the **all-or-none law**. However, the neuron is likely to fire *more often* when stimulated by a strong signal. The result is rapid neural firing that communicates the message "There's a very strong stimulus out here!" Immediately after firing, the neuron goes through an *absolute refractory period:* For about a thousandth of a second, the neuron will not fire again, no matter how strong the incoming messages may be. Following that is a *relative refractory period,* when the cell is returning to the resting state. During this period, the neuron will fire, but only if the incoming message is considerably stronger than is normally necessary to make it fire. Finally, the neuron returns to its resting state, ready to fire again.

NEUROTRANSMITTERS AND THE SYNAPSE

What happens as information moves from one neuron to the next?

Neurons are not directly connected like links in a chain. Rather, they are separated from each other by a tiny gap, called a **synaptic space** or **synaptic cleft**, where the axon terminals of one neuron *almost* touch the dendrites or cell body of other neurons. The entire area composed of the axon terminals of one neuron, the synaptic space, and the dendrites and cell body of the next neuron is called the **synapse**. (See **Figure 2-3**.)

all-or-none law Principle that the action potential in a neuron does not vary in strength; either the neuron fires at full strength, or it does not fire at all.

synaptic space (or synaptic cleft) Tiny gap between the axon terminal of one neuron and the dendrites or cell body of the next neuron.

synapse Area composed of the axon terminal of one neuron, the synaptic space, and the dendrite or cell body of the next neuron.

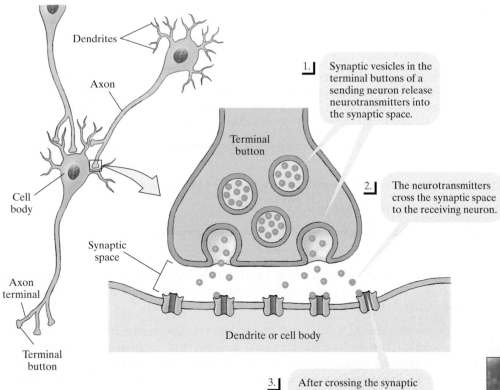

1. Synaptic vesicles in the terminal buttons of a sending neuron release neurotransmitters into the synaptic space.

2. The neurotransmitters cross the synaptic space to the receiving neuron.

3. After crossing the synaptic space the neurotransmitters fit into receptor sites located on the dendrites or cell body of the receiving neuron.

Figure 2–3
Synaptic transmission—communication between neurons. When a neural impulse reaches the end of an axon, tiny oval sacs, called synaptic vesicles, at the end of most axons release varying amounts of chemical substances called neurotransmitters. These substances travel across the synaptic space and affect the next neuron.

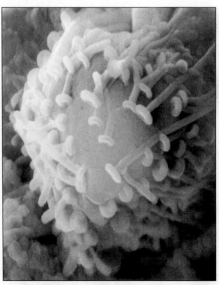

A photograph taken with a scanning electron microscope, showing the synaptic knobs at the ends of axons. Inside the knobs are the vesicles that contain neurotransmitters.

NEUROTRANSMITTERS For the neural impulse to move on to the next neuron, it must somehow cross the synaptic space. It is tempting to imagine that the neural impulse simply leaps across the gap like an electrical spark, but in reality the transfer is made by chemicals. What actually happens is this: When a neuron fires, an impulse travels down the axon, out through the axon terminals, into a tiny swelling called a **terminal button**, or **synaptic knob**. Most terminal buttons contain a number of tiny oval sacs called **synaptic vesicles**. (See **Figure 2–3**.) When the neural impulse reaches the end of the terminals, it causes these vesicles to release varying amounts of chemicals called **neurotransmitters** into the synaptic space. Each neurotransmitter has specific matching **receptor sites** on the other side of the synaptic space. Neurotransmitters fit into their corresponding receptor sites just as a key fits into a lock. This lock-and-key system ensures that neurotransmitters do not randomly stimulate other neurons, but follow orderly pathways.

After their job is complete, neurotransmitters detach from the receptor site. In most cases, they are either reabsorbed into the axon terminals to be used again, broken down and recycled to make new neurotransmitters, or disposed of by the body as waste. The synapse is cleared and returned to its normal state.

terminal button (or synaptic knob) Structure at the end of an axon terminal branch.

synaptic vesicles Tiny sacs in a terminal button that release chemicals into the synapse.

neurotransmitters Chemicals released by the synaptic vesicles that travel across the synaptic space and affect adjacent neurons.

receptor sites Locations on a receptor neuron into which a specific neurotransmitter fits like a key into a lock.

SUMMARY TABLE

MAJOR NEUROTRANSMITTERS AND THEIR EFFECTS

Acetylcholine (ACh)	Distributed widely throughout the central nervous system, where it is involved in arousal, attention, memory, motivation, and movement. Involved in muscle action through presence at neuromuscular junctions (specialized type of synapse where neurons connect to muscle cells). Degeneration of neurons that produce ACh has been linked to Alzheimer's disease. Too much ACh can lead to spasms and tremors; too little, to paralysis or torpor.
Dopamine	Involved in a wide variety of behaviors and emotions, including pleasure. Implicated in schizophrenia and Parkinson's disease.
Serotonin	Involved in the regulation of sleep, dreaming, mood, eating, pain, and aggressive behavior. Implicated in depression.
Norepinephrine	Affects arousal, wakefulness, learning, memory, and mood.
Endorphins	Involved in the inhibition of pain. Released during strenuous exercise. May be responsible for "runner's high."

In recent decades, neuroscientists have identified hundreds of neurotransmitters; their exact functions are still being studied. (See "**Summary Table**: Major Neurotransmitters and Their Effects.") However, a few brain chemicals are well known.

- *Acetylcholine* (ACh) acts where neurons meet skeletal muscles. It also appears to play a critical role in arousal, attention, memory, and motivation (Panksepp, 1986). Alzheimer's disease, which involves loss of memory and severe language problems, has been linked to degeneration of the brain cells that produce and respond to ACh (Froelich & Hoyer, 2002).
- *Dopamine* generally affects neurons associated with voluntary movement, learning, memory, and emotions. The symptoms of Parkinson's disease—tremors, muscle spasms, and increasing muscular rigidity—have been traced to loss of the brain cells that produce dopamine (Costa et al., 2003).
- *Serotonin* is popularly known as "the mood molecule" because it is often involved in emotional experiences. Serotonin is an example of a neurotransmitter that has widespread effects. Serotonin is like a master key that opens many locks—that is, it attaches to as many as a dozen receptor sites (Mintun et al., 2004; Thierry et al., 2004).
- *Endorphins* appear to reduce pain by inhibiting, or "turning down," the neurons that transmit pain messages in the brain. One endorphin was found to be 48 times more potent than morphine when injected into the brain and three times more potent when injected into the bloodstream (S. H. Snyder, 1977).

Endorphins and other brain chemicals regulate the sensitivity of large numbers of synapses, in effect "turning up" or "turning down" the activity level of whole portions of the nervous system. Endorphins were discovered in the early 1970s. Researchers Candace Pert and Solomon Snyder (1973) were attempting to explain the effects of *opiates*—painkilling drugs such as morphine and heroin that are derived from the poppy plant—when they discovered that the central nervous system contained receptor sites for these substances. They reasoned that these receptor sites would not exist unless the body produced its own natural painkillers. Not long after, researchers discovered the endorphins. Morphine and other narcotics lock into the receptors for endorphins and have the same painkilling effects. Research on endorphins has provided clues to why people become addicted to morphine, heroin, and other opiates. When a person takes one of these drugs repeatedly, the body's production of *natural* painkillers slows down. As a result, an addict needs more of the artificial drug to feel "normal."

Imbalances in neurotransmitters appear to contribute to many types of mental illness. Schizophrenia, for example, has been associated with an overabundance of, or hypersensitivity to, dopamine. An undersupply of serotonin and norepinephrine has been linked to depression and other disorders. As in the case of endorphins, the design and testing of drugs has helped neuroscientists to identify the functions of neurotransmitters. (For more on the relationship between drugs and behavior, see "**Understanding Ourselves**.")

Endorphins, which are released into the brain and body during strenuous exercise, are neurotransmitters that act as natural painkillers.

[UNDERSTANDING OURSELVES]

DRUGS AND BEHAVIOR

Understanding how neurotransmitters work can also help you understand how chemical substances, including some common ones that you may use, affect your brain. You have already seen in this chapter how opiates such as morphine and heroin work because they fit into the same receptors as naturally occurring endorphins. Other psychoactive drugs as well as many toxins (or poisons) also work by either blocking or enhancing the transmission of chemicals across synapses. Consider the following examples:

- *Botulism* (produced by the bacteria in improperly canned or frozen food) prevents the release of Acetylcholine (Ach), which carries signals to the muscles. The result is paralysis and, sometimes, rapid death.

- *Curare*, a poison that some native people of South America traditionally used to tip their arrows, instantly stuns and sometimes kills their prey or enemies. Curare blocks the ACh *receptors*—that is, it has the same effect as botulism, but acts at the other side of the synapse.

- The poison of the *black widow spider* produces the opposite effect. It causes ACh to spew into the synapses of the nervous system. As a result, neurons fire repeatedly, causing spasms and tremors.

- Antipsychotic medications *chlorpromazine* (trade name Thorazine) and *clozapine* prevent dopamine from binding to receptor sites; this reduction in stimulation apparently reduces schizophrenic hallucinations.

- *Caffeine* works in a slightly more complex way. It blocks the action of adenosine, a transmitter that inhibits the release of other neurotransmitters such as epinephrine (Nehlig, Daval, & Debry, 1992). Without the restraining effects of adenosine, more of these other excitatory, arousing neurotransmitters are released. Two or three cups of coffee contain enough caffeine to block half the adenosine receptors for several hours, producing a high state of arousal and, in some cases, anxiety and insomnia.

- *Cocaine* works in yet another way. It prevents dopamine from being reabsorbed from the synapse after it has done its job of stimulating the next neuron. As a result, excess amounts of dopamine accumulate in the synapses, producing heightened arousal of the entire nervous system (Freeman et al., 2002).

- Some *antidepressant medications* also work by preventing or slowing the removal of neurotransmitters from the synapse. We will say more about these "miracle drugs" that help reduce the hopelessness of severe depression in Chapter 9: "Psychological Disorders and Their Treatments."

We will have much more to say about drugs and their effects in Chapter 3: "Sensation, Perception, and Conscious Experience" and in Appendix B: "Drugs."

NEURAL PLASTICITY AND NEUROGENESIS

How can experience and the development of new neurons change the brain?

In a classic series of experiments, M. R. Rosenzweig (1984) demonstrated the importance of experience to neural development in the laboratory. Rosenzweig assigned baby rats into two groups. Members of one group were raised in an impoverished environment, isolated in barren cages. Members of the second group were raised in an enriched environment; they lived in cages with other rats and a variety of toys that offered opportunities for exploration, manipulation, and social interaction. Rosenzweig found that the rats raised in enriched environments had larger neurons with more synaptic connections than those raised in impoverished environments. (See **Figure 2-4.**) In more recent experiments, Rosenzweig (1996) showed that similar changes occur in rats of any age. Other researchers have found that rats raised in stimulating environments perform better on a variety of problem-solving tests and develop more synapses when required to perform complex tasks (Kleim, Vig, Ballard, & Greenough, 1997). These combined results suggest that the brain changes in response to the experiences that the organism has, a principle called **neural plasticity**. Furthermore, they demonstrate that neural plasticity is a feedback loop: Experience leads to changes in the brain, which, in turn, facilitate new learning, which leads to further neural change, and so on (Nelson, 1999).

Reorganization of the brain as a result of experience is not limited to rats (Kolb, Gibb, & Robinson, 2003). For example, violinists, cellists, and other string musicians spend years developing precise left-hand sensitivity and dexterity. Researchers have found that the area of these musicians' brains associated with left-hand sensation is larger than the area that represents the right hand (which string musicians use for bowing), and larger than the

neural plasticity The ability of the brain to change in response to experience.

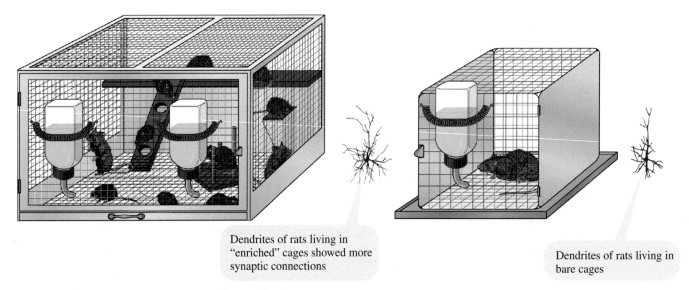

Dendrites of rats living in "enriched" cages showed more synaptic connections

Dendrites of rats living in bare cages

Figure 2–4

Brain growth and experience. In Rosenzweig's experiment, young rats lived in two kinds of cages: "impoverished," with nothing to manipulate or explore, or "enriched," with a variety of objects. When Rosenzweig examined the rats' brains, he found that the enriched group had larger neurons with more synaptic connections (shown as dendrites in the drawing) than the rats that lived in the bare cages. Experience, then, can actually affect the structure of the brain.

Source: From "Brain changes in response to experience" by M. R. Rosenzweig, E. L. Bennett, and M. C. Diamond. Copyright © 1972, Scientific American, Inc. All rights reserved. Adapted with permission of the estate of Bunji Tagawa.

left-hand area in nonmusicians (Elbert, Pantev, Wienbruch, Rockstroh, & Taub, 1995). In deaf people, an area of the brain usually responsible for hearing rewires itself to read lips and sign language (Bosworth & Dobkins, 1999). Brain reorganization is most likely the fundamental mechanism described in the Pepsi Challenge research outlined at the beginning of this chapter.

We have seen that experience can lead to dramatic changes in the number and complexity of synaptic connections in the brain—that is, in the connections between neurons. Might experience also produce new neurons? For many years, psychologists believed that organisms are born with all the brain cells they will ever have. New research appears to overturn this traditional view. A number of studies conducted in the 1990s showed that adult brains are capable of **neurogenesis**, the production of new brain cells (Gage, 2003; Prickaerts, Koopmans, Blokland, & Scheepens, 2004).

The discovery of lifelong neurogenesis has widespread implications for treating neurological disorders. Traditionally, injuries to the brain and spinal cord have been considered permanent; treatment was limited to stabilizing the patient to prevent further damage, treating related infections, and using rehabilitation to maximize remaining capabilities (McDonald, 1999). Some individuals with brain damage recovered over time, but they were the exception. The discovery of adult neurogenesis, however, raises new possibilities.

One of these possibilities, the use of fetal stem cells, has been the focus of recent debate in Congress and the media. Scientists have long known that embryos contain large numbers of stem cells: Undifferentiated, precursor cells or "precells" that, under the right conditions, can give rise to any specialized cell in the body—liver, kidney, blood, heart, or neurons (Bjornson, Rietze, Reynolds, Magli, & Vescovi, 1999). Remarkably, in tests with animals, stem cells transplanted into a brain or spinal cord spontaneously migrated to damaged areas and began to generate specialized neurons for replacement (McKay, 1997). It was as if stem cells moved through the brain, going from one neuron to the next looking for

neurogenesis The growth of new neurons.

damage. If damage was found, the stem cells began to divide and produce specialized neurons appropriate for that area of the brain.

In clinical trials with human patients suffering from Parkinson's disease, fetal nerve cell transplants have improved motor control for periods of five to ten years (Barinaga, 2000a). But the supply of fetal tissue is limited, and its harvest and use raise ethical questions (Patenaude, Guttmacher, & Collins, 2002).

Another potential use of new research findings is to stimulate the brain's own stem cells to provide "self-repair." After the chemicals that regulate neurogenesis are more fully understood, it may be possible to increase the amounts of these substances in areas of the central nervous system where neural growth needs to occur (Gage, 2000). Some researchers have already begun to identify substances and environmental conditions that show promise of stimulating neural regrowth (Auvergne et al., 2002; Rasika, Alvarez-Buylla, & Nottebohm, 1999). One substance in particular, inosine, has been shown in rats to stimulate undamaged nerve fibers to grow new connections and restore motor functioning following strokes (Chen, Goldberg, Kolb, Lanser, & Benowitz, 2002). Specific treatments for humans may take years to develop, but people suffering from neurological disorders such as Parkinson's and Alzheimer's diseases, as well as victims of spinal cord injuries and stroke, now have hope (Barinaga, 2000a; Gage, 2000; McMillan, Robertson, & Wilson, 1999; Van Praag & Gage, 2002).

Severing the spinal cord at the neck typically causes paralysis of everything below the head because nerves connecting to the body's muscles no longer have a cable to the brain. The late actor Christopher Reeve suffered from paralysis of everything below the head when his spinal cord was severed after he was thrown from a horse, and the nerves connected to his body's muscles no longer had a cable to the brain. Others with similar injuries may someday benefit from research on neurogenesis.

▶ CHECK YOUR UNDERSTANDING

Match each term with the appropriate definition.

1. _____ neuron
2. _____ neural plasticity
3. _____ dendrites
4. _____ axons
5. _____ neural impulse
6. _____ resting potential
7. _____ absolute refractory period
8. _____ neurogenesis
9. _____ synapse
10. _____ neurotransmitters
11. _____ dopamine
12. _____ serotonin
13. _____ all-or-none law

a. growth of new neurons
b. long cellular fibers carrying outgoing messages
c. when a nerve cell cannot fire again
d. affects emotions, arousal, and sleep
e. cell that transmits information
f. experience changes the brain
g. chemicals that carry messages across synapses
h. short cellular fibers that pick up incoming messages
i. neurotransmitter with a role in schizophrenia and Parkinson's disease
j. action potential
k. a neuron either fires at full strength or not at all
l. terminal button, synaptic space, and dendrite of neighboring neuron
m. electrical imbalance across a neural membrane at rest

Answers: 1. e. 2. f. 3. h. 4. b. 5. j. 6. m. 7. c. 8. a. 9. l. 10. g. 11. i. 12. d. 13. k.

▶ APPLY YOUR UNDERSTANDING

1. You return from a day at the beach to find you have developed a severe sunburn. Which neurons are sending messages from your burned skin to your brain informing you of the pain from the burn?
   a. Afferent neurons
   b. Efferent neurons
   c. Interaction neurons
   d. Motor neurons

2. John is a 75-year-old male who is in the early stages of Alzheimer's disease. The cause of his disorder is most likely a deficiency of
   a. acetylcholine
   b. dopamine
   c. serotonin
   d. norepinephrine

Answers: 1. a. 2. a.

central nervous system (CNS) Division of the nervous system that consists of the brain and spinal cord.

peripheral nervous system (PNS) Division of the nervous system that connects the central nervous system to the rest of the body.

The Central Nervous System

2.2 Explain how the central nervous system is organized and describe how it is studied.

The nervous system is an elegantly interconnected network of neurons comprised of billions of cells. To better understand how the nervous system works, it is useful to label its different parts according to their location and their primary function. **Figure 2–5** displays the major structural and functional divisions of the human nervous system.

THE ORGANIZATION OF THE NERVOUS SYSTEM

How is the nervous system organized?

One of the most useful approaches to understanding how the nervous system functions is to conceptualize it as being composed of two major divisions: the central nervous system and the peripheral nervous system. The **central nervous system** includes the brain and spinal cord, which together contain more than 90 percent of the body's neurons. The **peripheral nervous system** consists of nerves that connect the brain and spinal cord to every other part of the body, carrying messages back and forth between the central nervous system and the sense organs, muscles, and glands. The peripheral nervous system is subdivided into the *somatic nervous system*, which transmits information about body movements and the external environment, and the *autonomic nervous system*, which transmits information to and from the internal organs and glands. (We will discuss the endocrine system, which works hand in hand with the nervous system, later in the chapter.)

THE BRAIN

What are the major structures and areas of the brain, and what functions do they serve?

The brain is the seat of awareness and reason, the place where learning, memory, and emotions are centered. It is the part of us that decides what to do and whether that decision was right or wrong, and it imagines how things might have turned out if we had acted differently.

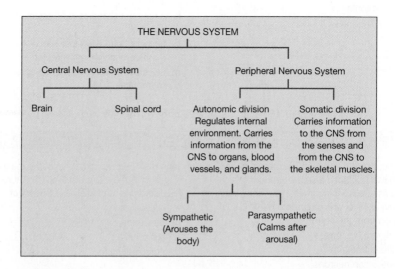

Figure 2–5

A schematic diagram of the divisions of the nervous system and their various subparts.

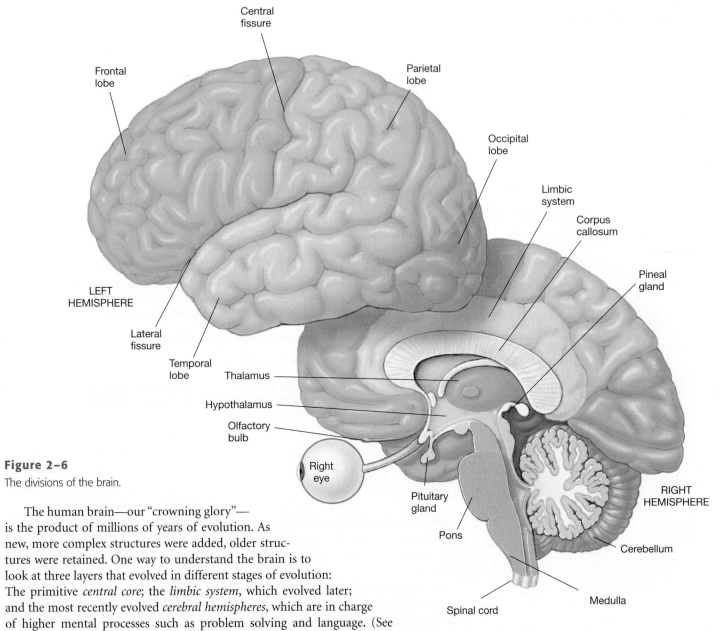

Figure 2–6
The divisions of the brain.

The human brain—our "crowning glory"—is the product of millions of years of evolution. As new, more complex structures were added, older structures were retained. One way to understand the brain is to look at three layers that evolved in different stages of evolution: The primitive *central core*; the *limbic system*, which evolved later; and the most recently evolved *cerebral hemispheres*, which are in charge of higher mental processes such as problem solving and language. (See **Figure 2–6**.) We will use these three basic divisions to describe the parts of the brain, what they do, and how they interact to influence our behavior. (See "**Summary Table**: Parts of the Brain and Their Functions.")

THE CENTRAL CORE At the point where the spinal cord enters the skull, it becomes the hindbrain. Because the **hindbrain** is found in even the most primitive vertebrates, it is believed to have been the earliest part of the brain to evolve. The part of the hindbrain nearest to the spinal cord is the *medulla*, a narrow structure about 1.5 inches long. The medulla controls such bodily functions as breathing, heart rate, and blood pressure. The medulla is also the point at which many of the nerves from the body cross over on their way to and from the higher brain centers; nerves from the left part of the body cross to the right side of the brain and vice versa

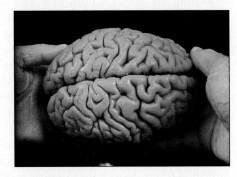

The human brain, viewed from the top. Its relatively small size belies its enormous complexity.

hindbrain Area containing the medulla, pons, and cerebellum.

SUMMARY TABLE

PARTS OF THE BRAIN AND THEIR FUNCTIONS

Central Core	Medulla	Regulates respiration, heart rate, blood pressure.
Hind-brain	Pons	Regulates sleep–wake cycles.
	Cerebellum	Regulates reflexes and balance; coordinates movement.
Mid-brain	Thalamus	Major sensory relay center; regulates higher brain centers and peripheral nervous system.
	Hypothalamus	Influences emotion and motivation; governs stress reactions.
	Reticular formation	Regulates attention and alertness.
Limbic System	Hippocampus	Regulates formation of new memories.
	Amygdala	Governs emotions related to self-preservation.
Cerebral Cortex	Frontal lobe	Goal-directed behavior; concentration; emotional control and temperament; voluntary movements; coordinates messages from other lobes; complex problem solving; involved in many aspects of personality.
	Parietal lobe	Receives sensory information; visual/spatial abilities.
	Occipital lobe	Receives and processes visual information.
	Temporal lobe	Smell and hearing; balance and equilibrium; emotion and motivation; some language comprehension; complex visual processing and face recognition.

cerebellum Structure in the hindbrain that controls certain reflexes and coordinates the body's movements.

midbrain Region between the hindbrain and the forebrain; it is important for hearing and sight, and it is one of several places in the brain where pain is registered.

(a topic to which we will return). Near the medulla lies the *pons*, which produces chemicals that help maintain our sleep–wake cycle. (See Chapter 3: "Sensation, Perception, and Conscious Experience.") Both the medulla and the pons transmit messages to the upper areas of the brain.

The part of the hindbrain at the top and back of the brain stem is the **cerebellum**. The cerebellum is sometimes called the "little brain," but in this case, appearances are deceiving. Although the cerebellum takes up only a small space, its surface area is almost two-thirds that of the much larger cerebral cortex. Traditionally, it has been thought that the cerebellum is simply responsible for our sense of balance and for coordinating the body's actions to ensure that movements go together in efficient sequences. Damage to the cerebellum in adults does indeed cause severe problems in movement, such as jerky motions and stumbling. Recent research suggests, however, that the cerebellum is also involved in many more psychological processes, including emotional control, attention, memory, and coordinating sensory information (Bower & Parsons, 2003; Highstein & Thatch, 2002).

Above the cerebellum, the brain stem widens to form the **midbrain**. The midbrain is especially important for hearing and sight. It is also one of several places in the brain where pain is registered.

More or less directly over the brain stem are the two egg-shaped structures that make up the *thalamus*. The thalamus is often described as a relay station: Almost all sensory information passes through the thalamus on the way to higher levels of the brain, where it is translated and routed to the appropriate brain location. Directly below the thalamus is the smaller *hypothalamus*, which exerts an enormous influence on many kinds of motivation. Portions of the hypothalamus govern hunger, thirst, sexual drive, and body temperature

(Sewards & Sewards, 2003; Winn, 1995) and are directly involved in emotional behavior such as experiencing rage, terror, or pleasure.

The *reticular formation (RF)* is a netlike system of neurons that weaves through all of these structures. Its main job seems to be to send "Alert!" signals to the higher parts of the brain in response to incoming messages. The RF can be subdued, however; during sleep, the RF is turned down. Anesthetics work largely by temporarily shutting this system off, and permanent damage to the RF can even induce a coma.

THE LIMBIC SYSTEM The **limbic system** is a ring of loosely connected structures located between the central core and the cerebral hemispheres. (See **Figure 2–7.**) In evolutionary terms, the limbic system is more recent than the central core and is fully developed only in mammals.

The limbic system appears to play a central role in times of stress, co-ordinating and integrating the activity of the nervous system. One part of the limbic system, the *hippocampus,* plays an essential role in the forma-tion of new memories. People with severe damage to this area can still re-member names, faces, and events that they recorded in memory before they were injured, but they cannot remember anything new. Another structure, the *amygdala* (working together with the hippocampus) is in-volved in governing and regulating emotions (Davidson, Jackson, & Kalin, 2002; Hamann, Ely, Hoffman, & Kilts, 2002), particularly those re-lated to self-preservation (MacLean, 1970). When portions of these struc-tures are damaged or removed, aggressive animals become tame and docile. In contrast, stimulation of some portions of these structures causes animals to exhibit signs of fear and panic, whereas stimulation of other por-tions triggers unprovoked attacks.

Other limbic structures heighten the experience of pleasure. Given the op-portunity to press a bar that electrically stimulates one such region, animals do so endlessly, ignoring food and water. Humans also experience pleasure when some areas of the limbic system are electrically stimulated, though apparently not as intensely (Kupfermann, 1991; Olds & Forbes, 1981). Even our ability to read the facial ex-pressions of emotion in other people (such as smiling or frowning) is registered in the lim-bic system (Lange et al., 2003). (We will return to the limbic system in Chapter 6: "Motivation and Emotion.")

THE CEREBRAL CORTEX Ballooning out over and around the central core and limbic system, virtually hiding them, is the *cerebrum.* The cerebrum is divided into two hemi-spheres and covered by a thin layer of gray matter (unmyelinated cells) called the **cerebral cortex**. This is what most people think of first when they talk about "the brain"; it is the part of the brain that processes thought, vision, language, memory, and emotions. The cerebral cortex takes up most of the room inside the skull, accounting for about 80 percent of the weight of the human brain and containing about 70 percent of the neurons in the central nervous system.

The cerebral cortex, which is the most recently evolved part of the nervous system, is more highly developed in humans than in any other animal. Spread out, the human cortex would cover two to three square feet and be about as thick as the letter "T." To fit inside the skull, in humans the cerebral cortex has developed intricate folds—hills and valleys called *convolutions.* In each person, these convolutions form a pattern that is as unique as a fingerprint.

A number of landmarks on the cortex allow us to identify distinct areas each with dif-ferent functions. The first is a deep cleft, running from front to back, that divides the brain into *right* and *left* hemispheres. As seen in **Figure 2–6**, each of these hemispheres can be di-vided into four *lobes* (described later), which are separated from one another by crevices, or fissures, such as the *central fissure.* In addition, there are large areas on the cortex of all four lobes called **association areas** that integrate information from diverse parts of the cortex and are involved in mental processes such as learning, thinking, and remembering.

The different lobes of the cerebral hemispheres are specialized for different functions. (See **Figure 2–8**). The **frontal lobe**, located just behind the forehead, accounts for about half the

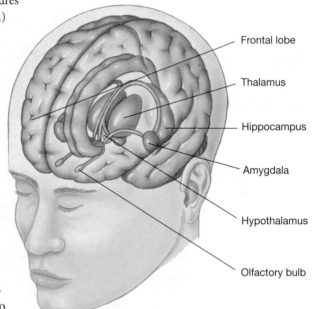

Figure 2–7
The limbic system. A system of brain structures, including the thalamus, hippocampus, amygdala, hypothalamus, and olfactory bulb. This system is primarily involved in regulating behaviors having to do with motivation and emotion.

limbic system Ring of structures that play a role in learning and emotional behavior.

cerebral cortex The outer surface of the two cerebral hemispheres that regulates most complex behavior.

association areas Areas of the cerebral cortex where incoming messages from the separate senses are combined into meaningful impressions and outgoing messages from the motor areas are integrated.

frontal lobe Part of the cerebral cortex that is responsible for voluntary movement; it is also important for attention, goal-directed behavior, and appropriate emotional experiences.

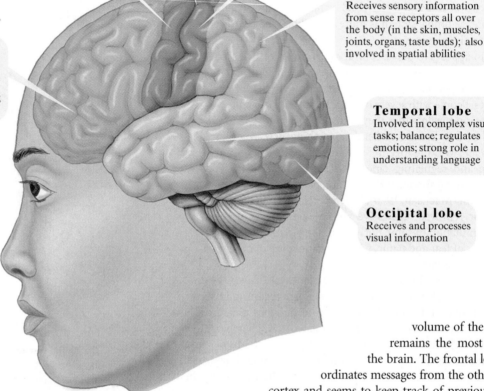

Central fissure
Separates the primary somatosensory cortex from the primary motor cortex

Primary somatosensory cortex
Registers sensory messages from the entire body

Primary motor cortex
Part of the frontal lobe; sends messages to muscles and glands; key role in voluntary movement

Parietal lobe
Receives sensory information from sense receptors all over the body (in the skin, muscles, joints, organs, taste buds); also involved in spatial abilities

Frontal lobe
Coordinates messages from the other cerebral lobes; involved in complex problem-solving tasks

Temporal lobe
Involved in complex visual tasks; balance; regulates emotions; strong role in understanding language

Occipital lobe
Receives and processes visual information

Figure 2–8
The four lobes of the cerebral cortex. Deep fissures in the cortex separate these areas or lobes. Also shown are the primary somatosensory and motor areas.

volume of the human brain, yet it remains the most mysterious part of the brain. The frontal lobe receives and coordinates messages from the other three lobes of the cortex and seems to keep track of previous and future movements of the body. This ability to monitor and integrate the complex tasks that are going on in the rest of the brain has led some investigators to hypothesize that the frontal lobe serves as an "executive control center" for the brain (Kimberg, D'Esposito, & Farah, 1997; Waltz et al., 1999) and is involved in a wide range of problem-solving tasks, including answering both verbal and spatial IQ-test questions (Duncan et al., 2000). The section of the frontal lobe known as the **primary motor cortex** plays a key role in voluntary action. The frontal lobe also seems to play an important role in the behaviors we associate with personality, including motivation, persistence, affect (emotional responses), character, and even moral decision making (Greene & Haidt, 2002; Jackson et al., 2003).

Until recently, our knowledge of the frontal lobes was based on research with nonhuman animals, whose frontal lobes are relatively undeveloped, and on studies of rare cases of people with frontal lobe damage. One famous case, involving a bizarre accident, was reported in 1848. Phineas Gage, the foreman of a railroad construction gang, made a mistake while using some blasting powder. The explosion blew a nearly four-foot-long tamping iron more than an inch thick into his cheek and all the way through the top of his head, severely damaging his frontal lobes. To the amazement of those who witnessed the accident, Gage remained conscious, walked part of the way to a doctor, and suffered few physical aftereffects. He did, however, suffer lasting psychological changes, including difficulty reasoning and making decisions, as well as difficulty controlling his emotions. These changes were so radical that, in the view of his friends, he was no longer the same man. (See Macmillan, 2000; Wagar & Thagard, 2004.)

A century later, most neuroscientists agree that personality change—especially loss of motivation and ability to concentrate—is the major outcome of frontal lobe damage. The frontal lobes are involved in goal-directed behavior and the ability to lead a mature emotional life (Rule,

primary motor cortex The section of each frontal lobe responsible for voluntary movement.

Figure 2–9

The two cerebral hemispheres. Each hemisphere specializes in processing specific types of information, as shown on the diagram.

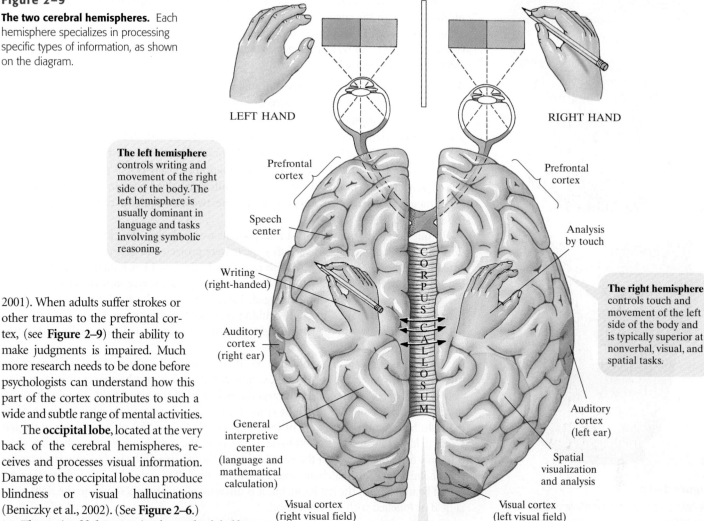

The left hemisphere controls writing and movement of the right side of the body. The left hemisphere is usually dominant in language and tasks involving symbolic reasoning.

LEFT HAND

RIGHT HAND

Prefrontal cortex

Speech center

Writing (right-handed)

Auditory cortex (right ear)

General interpretive center (language and mathematical calculation)

Visual cortex (right visual field)

CORPUS CALLOSUM

Prefrontal cortex

Analysis by touch

The right hemisphere controls touch and movement of the left side of the body and is typically superior at nonverbal, visual, and spatial tasks.

Auditory cortex (left ear)

Spatial visualization and analysis

Visual cortex (left visual field)

The corpus callosum permits the exchange of information between the two hemispheres.

2001). When adults suffer strokes or other traumas to the prefrontal cortex, (see **Figure 2–9**) their ability to make judgments is impaired. Much more research needs to be done before psychologists can understand how this part of the cortex contributes to such a wide and subtle range of mental activities.

The **occipital lobe**, located at the very back of the cerebral hemispheres, receives and processes visual information. Damage to the occipital lobe can produce blindness or visual hallucinations (Beniczky et al., 2002). (See **Figure 2–6**.)

The **parietal lobe** occupies the top back half of each hemisphere. This lobe receives sensory information from all over the body—from sense receptors in the skin, muscles, joints, internal organs, and taste buds. Messages from these sense receptors are registered in the **primary somatosensory cortex**. The parietal lobe also seems to oversee spatial abilities, such as the ability to follow a map or to tell someone how to get from one place to another (A. Cohen & Raffal, 1991).

The **temporal lobe**, located in front of the occipital lobe, roughly behind the temples, plays an important role in complex visual tasks such as recognizing faces. The temporal lobe also receives and processes information from the ears, contributes to balance and equilibrium, and regulates emotions and motivations such as anxiety, pleasure, and anger. In addition, the ability to understand and comprehend language is thought to be concentrated primarily in the rear portion of the temporal lobes, though some language comprehension may also occur in the parietal and frontal lobes (Ojemann, Ojemann, Lettich, & Berger, 1989).

HEMISPHERIC SPECIALIZATION

How are the left and right hemispheres specialized for different functions?

The cerebrum, as noted earlier, consists of two separate cerebral hemispheres. Quite literally, humans have a "right half-brain" and a "left half-brain." The primary connection between the left and the right hemispheres is a thick, ribbonlike band of nerve fibers under the cortex called the **corpus callosum**. (See **Figure 2–9**.)

occipital lobe Part of the cerebral hemisphere that receives and interprets visual information.

parietal lobe Part of the cerebral cortex that receives sensory information from throughout the body.

primary somatosensory cortex Area of the parietal lobe where messages from the sense receptors are registered.

temporal lobe Part of the cerebral hemisphere that helps regulate hearing, balance and equilibrium, and certain emotions and motivations.

corpus callosum A thick band of nerve fibers connecting the left and right cerebral cortex.

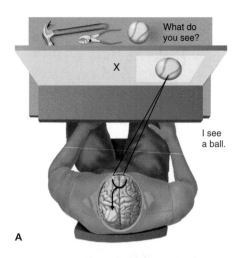

A

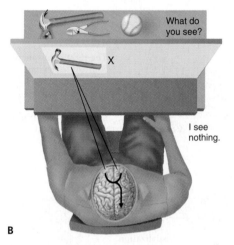

B

Figure 2–10

(A) When split-brain patients stare at the "X" in the center of the screen, visual information projected on the right side of the screen goes to the patient's left hemisphere, which controls language. When asked what they see, patients can reply correctly. (B) When split-brain patients stare at the "X" in the center of the screen, visual information projected on the left side of the screen goes to the patient's right hemisphere, which does not control language. When asked what they see, patients cannot name the object, but can pick it out by touch with the left hand.

Source: Adapted from Carol Ward, © 1987, Discover Publications.

Under normal conditions, the left and right cerebral hemispheres are in close communication through the corpus callosum and work together as a coordinated unit (Banich, 1998; Hellige, 1993; Hoptman & Davidson, 1994; Saint-Amour, Lepore, Lassonde, & Guillemot, 2004). But research suggests that the cerebral hemispheres are not really equivalent. (See again **Figure 2–9**.)

SPLIT-BRAIN PATIENTS The most dramatic evidence comes from "split-brain" patients. In some cases of severe epilepsy, surgeons cut the corpus callosum to stop the spread of epileptic seizures from one hemisphere to the other. In general, this procedure is successful: The patients' seizures are reduced and sometimes eliminated. But their two hemispheres are functionally isolated; in effect, their right brain doesn't know what their left brain is doing (and vice versa). Because sensory information typically is sent to both hemispheres, in everyday life, split-brain patients function quite normally; however, a series of ingenious experiments revealed what happens when the two hemispheres cannot communicate (Sperry, 1964, 1968, 1970).

In one such experiment, split-brain patients were asked to stare at a spot on a projection screen. When pictures of various objects were projected to the *right* of that spot, they could name the objects. And, with their right hands, they could pick them out of a group of hidden objects. (See **Figure 2–10A**.) When pictures of objects were shown on the *left* side of the screen, however, something changed. Patients could pick out the objects by feeling them with their left hands, but they couldn't say what the objects were! In fact, when asked what objects they saw on the left side of the screen, split-brain patients usually said "nothing." (See **Figure 2–10B**.)

The explanation for these unusual results is found in the way each hemisphere of the brain operates. When the corpus callosum is cut, the *left hemisphere* receives information only from the right side of the body and the right half of the visual field. As a result, it can match an object shown in the right visual field with information received by touch from the right hand, but it is unaware of (and thus unable to identify) objects shown in the left visual field or touched by the left hand. Conversely, the *right hemisphere* receives information only from the left side of the visual field and the left side of the body. Consequently, the right hemisphere can match an object shown in the left visual field with information received by touch from the left hand, but it is unaware of any objects shown in the right visual field or touched with the right hand.

But why can't the right hemisphere verbally identify an object that is shown in the left visual field? The answer is that for the great majority of people (even for most left-handers), in the process of learning to read, language ability becomes concentrated primarily in the *left* hemisphere (Hellige, 1990, 1993; Turkeltaub, Gareau, Flowers, Zeffiro, & Eden, 2003). As a result, when an object is in the left visual field, the nonverbal right hemisphere can see the object, but can't name it. The verbal left hemisphere, in contrast, can't see an object in this location, so when asked what it sees, it answers that nothing is on the screen.

OTHER DIFFERENCES BETWEEN HEMISPHERES Does the left hemisphere specialize in any other tasks besides language? Some researchers think that it may also operate more analytically, logically, rationally, and sequentially than the right hemisphere does (Kingstone, Enns, Mangun, & Gazzaniga, 1995). In contrast, the right hemisphere excels at visual and spatial tasks—nonverbal imagery, including music, face recognition, and the perception of emotions (Hellige, 1990, 1993; Metcalfe, Funnell, & Gazzaniga, 1995; Semrud-Clikeman & Hynd, 1990). Put another way, the left hemisphere specializes in analyzing sequences and details, whereas the right hemisphere specializes in holistic processing (Reuter-Lorenz & Miller, 1998) and in solving problems that require *insight* or creative solutions (Bowden & Jung-Beeman, 2003; Bowden & Beeman, 1998). The right hemisphere is also more likely than the left hemisphere to respond emotionally to spoken words, interpreting whether a message conveys happiness, sadness or anger (Vingerhoets, Berckmoes, & Stroobant, 2003).

The frontal lobes of the two hemispheres may also influence temperament in distinctive ways. People whose left frontal lobe is more active than the right tend to be more cheerful, sociable, ebullient, and self-confident, whereas people with more right frontal lobe activity are more easily stressed, frightened, and upset by unpleasant things. They also tend to be more suspicious and depressed than people with predominantly left frontal lobe activity (Henriques & Davidson, 1990; Rotenberg, 2004).

Although such research is fascinating and fun to speculate about, it is necessary to be cautious in interpreting it. Not everyone shows the same pattern of differences between the left and right hemispheres. In particular, the differences between the hemispheres may be greater in men than in women (Hellige, 1993; Seamon & Kenrick, 1992; Semrud-Clikeman & Hynd, 1990). Also it is easy to oversimplify and exaggerate differences between the two sides of the brain. Split-brain research has given rise to several popular but misguided books that classify people as "right-brain" or "left-brain" thinkers. It is important to remember that under normal conditions, the right and left hemispheres are in close communication through the corpus callosum and so work together in a coordinated, integrated way (Hoptman & Davidson, 1994). Furthermore, the plasticity of the brain means that both hemispheres have the potential to perform a range of tasks.

LANGUAGE The notion that human language is controlled primarily by the left cerebral hemisphere was first set forth in the 1860s by a French physician named Paul Broca. Broca's ideas were modified a decade later by the scientist Karl Wernicke. Thus, it should come as no surprise that the two major language areas in the brain have traditionally been called Broca's area and Wernicke's area. (See **Figure 2–11.**)

Wernicke's area lies toward the back of the temporal lobe. This area is crucial in processing and understanding what others are saying. By contrast, Broca's area, found in the frontal lobe, is considered to be essential to our ability to talk. To oversimplify a bit, Wernicke's area seems to be important for listening, and Broca's area seems to be important for talking. Support for these distinctions comes from patients who have suffered left-hemisphere strokes and resulting brain damage. Such strokes often produce predictable language problems, called *aphasias*. If the brain damage primarily affects Broca's area, the aphasia tends to be "expressive." That is, the patients' language difficulties lie predominantly in sequencing and producing language (talking). If the damage primarily affects Wernicke's area, the aphasia tends to be "receptive," and patients generally have profound difficulties understanding language (listening). Neuroimaging studies of people without brain damage confirm the role of Broca's and Wernicke's areas in language production and reception (Gernsbacher & Kaschak, 2003), as well as in the auditory hallucinations that torment people suffering from schizophrenia (Hoffman et al., 2003).

TOOLS FOR STUDYING THE BRAIN

What methods have been developed to study the brain?

For centuries, our understanding of the human brain depended mostly on observing patients who had suffered brain injury or from examining the brains of cadavers. Another approach (and one that is still in use) was to remove or damage the brains of nonhuman animals and study the effects. But the human cerebral cortex is far more complicated than that of any other animal. How can scientists study the living, fully functioning human brain? Contemporary neuroscientists have four basic techniques—microelectrodes, macroelectrodes, structural imaging, and functional imaging. New, more accurate techniques have appeared almost every year and are used for both diagnosis and research. (The "**Summary Table**: Tools for Studying the Nervous System" reviews these techniques and their uses.)

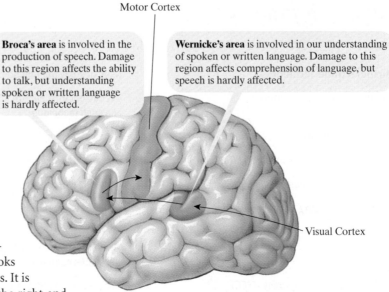

Motor Cortex

Broca's area is involved in the production of speech. Damage to this region affects the ability to talk, but understanding spoken or written language is hardly affected.

Wernicke's area is involved in our understanding of spoken or written language. Damage to this region affects comprehension of language, but speech is hardly affected.

Visual Cortex

Figure 2–11

Processing of speech and language. Broca's and Wernicke's areas, generally found only on the left side of the brain, work together, enabling us to produce and understand speech and language.

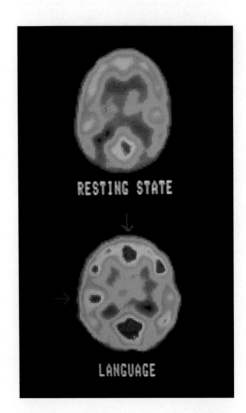

RESTING STATE

LANGUAGE

PET scans of a person at rest (top) and using language (bottom). The "hot" colors (red and yellow) indicate greater brain activity. These scans show that language activity is located primarily, but not exclusively, in the brain's left hemisphere.

SUMMARY TABLE

TOOLS FOR STUDYING THE NERVOUS SYSTEM

Microelectrode Techniques	Used to study the functions of individual neurons.
Macroelectrode Techniques	Used to obtain a picture of the activity in a particular region of the brain. The EEG is one such technique.
Structural Imaging	Family of techniques used to map structures in a living brain.
Computerized axial tomography (CAT or CT)	Permits three-dimensional imaging of a living human brain.
Magnetic resonance imaging (MRI)	Produces pictures of inner brain structures.
Functional Imaging Techniques	Family of techniques that can image activity in the brain as it responds to various stimuli.
EEG imaging	Measures general brain activity on a millisecond-by-millisecond basis through electrodes pasted to the scalp.
Magnetoencephalography (MEG) *Magnetic source imaging (MSI)*	Two procedures that are similar to EEG imaging but have greater accuracy.
Positron emission tomography (PET) scanning *Single photon emission computed tomography (SPECT)*	Two techniques that use radioactive energy to map exact regions of brain activity.
Functional magnetic resonance imaging (fMRI)	Measures the movement of blood molecules in the brain, pinpointing specific sites and details of neuronal activity.

MICROELECTRODE TECHNIQUES *Microelectrode* recording techniques are used to study the functions of single neurons. A microelectrode is a tiny glass or quartz pipette or tube (smaller in diameter than a human hair) that is filled with a conducting liquid. When technicians place the tip of this electrode near a neuron, they can study changes in the electrical conditions of that neuron. Microelectrode techniques have been used to understand action potentials, the effects of drugs or toxins on neurons, and even processes that occur in the neural membrane.

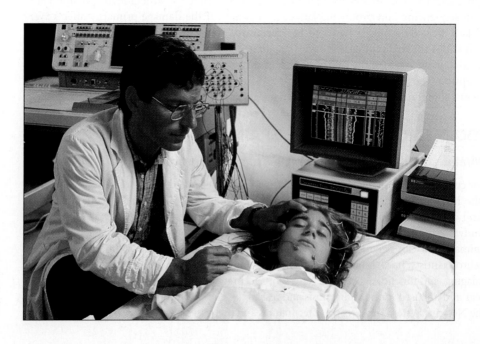

In an EEG, electrodes attached to the scalp are used to create a picture of neural activity in the brain.

MACROELECTRODE TECHNIQUES *Macroelectrode* recording techniques are used to obtain an overall picture of the activity in particular regions of the brain, which may contain millions of neurons. The first such device—the *electroencephalograph* (EEG)—is still in use today. Flat electrodes, taped to the scalp, are linked by wires to a device that translates electrical activity into lines on a moving roll of paper (or, more recently, images on a computer screen). This graph of so-called brain waves provides an index of both the strength and the rhythm of neural activity. As we will see in Chapter 3: "Sensation, Perception, and Conscious Experience," this technique has given researchers valuable insights into changes in brain waves during sleep and dreaming.

The macroelectrode technique enables researchers to "listen" to what is going on in the brain, but it does not allow them to *look* through the skull and see what is happening. Some newer techniques, however, do just that.

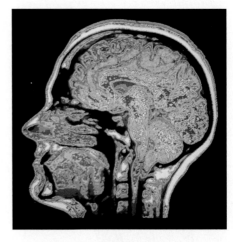

MRI image of the human head.

STRUCTURAL IMAGING When researchers want to map the structures in a living human brain, they turn to two newer techniques. *Computerized axial tomography* (CAT or CT) *scanning* allows scientists to create three-dimensional images of a human brain without performing surgery. To produce a CAT scan, an X-ray photography unit rotates around the person, moving from the top of the head to the bottom; a computer then combines the resulting images. *Magnetic resonance imaging* (MRI) is even more successful at producing pictures of the inner regions of the brain, with its ridges, folds, and fissures. Here the person's head is surrounded by a magnetic field, and the brain is exposed to radio waves, which causes hydrogen atoms in the brain to release energy. The energy released by different structures in the brain generates an image that appears on a computer screen.

FUNCTIONAL IMAGING In many cases, researchers are interested in more than structure; they want to look at the brain's *activity* as it actually reacts to sensory stimuli such as pain, tones, and words. Such is the goal of several *functional imaging* methods. Functional EEG imaging measures brain activity "on a millisecond-by-millisecond basis" (Fischman, 1985, p. 18). In this technique, more than two dozen electrodes are placed at important locations on the scalp. These electrodes record brain activities, which are then converted by a computer into colored images on a television screen. The technique has been extremely useful in detecting abnormal cortical activity such as that observed during epileptic seizures.

Two related techniques, called *magnetoencephalography* (MEG) and *magnetic source imaging* (MSI), take the procedure a step further. In standard EEG, electrical signals are distorted as they pass through the skull, and their exact source is difficult to determine; however, those same electrical signals create magnetic fields that are unaffected by bone. Both MEG and MSI measure the strength of the magnetic field and identify its source with considerable accuracy. By using these procedures, neuroscientists have begun to determine exactly which parts of the brain do most of the work in such psychological processes as memory (Gabrieli et al., 1996), language processing (Tulving et al., 1994), and reading.

Another family of functional imaging techniques—including *positron emission tomography* (PET) *scanning*—uses radioactive energy to map brain activity. In these techniques, a person first receives an injection of a radioactive substance. Brain structures that are especially active absorb most of the substance, which releases subatomic particles. By studying where most of the particles come from, researchers can determine exactly which portions of the brain are most active. Some of the findings produced by these techniques have been surprising. For example, one study found that, in general, the brains of people with higher IQ scores are *less* active than those of people with lower IQ scores, perhaps because they process information more efficiently (Haier, 1993). Progress has also been made in locating the damaged brain region in Parkinson's disease. Other researchers have used these techniques to investigate how our memory for words and images is stored in the brain (Cabeza & Nyberg, 2000; Craik et al., 1999). These techniques also are used to study the effects of psychoactive drugs, such as antidepressants.

One of the newest and most powerful techniques for recording activity in the brain is called *functional magnetic resonance imaging* (fMRI). This is the imaging technique that was used to study brain activity in the Pepsi Challenge experiment described at the

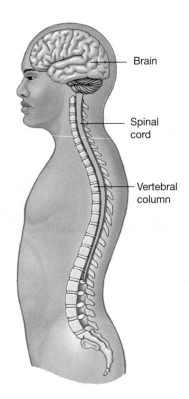

Figure 2–12

Brain and spinal cord.

Source: Human Physiology, An Integrated Approach by A. C. Silverthorn, © 1989. Reprinted by permission of Pearson Education, Inc., Upper Saddle River, NJ.

spinal cord Complex cable of neurons that runs down the spine, connecting the brain to most of the rest of the body.

beginning of this chapter. Functional MRI measures the movement of blood molecules (which is related to neuron activity) in the brain, permitting neuroscientists to pinpoint specific sites and details of neuronal activity. By comparing brain activity in normal learners with brain activity in children with learning problems, researchers have begun to identify the biological origins of attention-deficit hyperactivity disorder (ADHD) (Sowell et al., 2003); dyslexia (Ackerman, 2004; Shaywitz et al., 1998); and difficulties with math (Dehaene, Spelke, Stanescu, Pinel, & Tsivkin, 1999). It is even possible to determine with some accuracy what a person is thinking about and whether he or she is lying (Ross, 2003). Because fMRI enables us to collect extremely precise images rapidly and does not require the injection of radioactive chemicals (making it less invasive), it is especially promising as a new research tool (Esposito, Zarahn, & Aguirre, 1999; Nelson et al., 2000).

By combining these various techniques, neuroscientists can simultaneously observe anatomical structures (from CAT and MRI), sites of energy use (PET and MEG), blood and water movement (fMRI), and areas of electrical activity in the brain (EEG). These techniques are helping researchers better understand a wide variety of diseases and disorders, as well as how the brains of healthy, normal humans work. Table 2-1 provides a brief summary of the causes of and symptoms associated with some of the most common nervous system diseases and disorders, along with a brief outline of new approaches being developed for their treatment.

THE SPINAL CORD

How does the spinal cord work with the brain to sense events and act on them?

We talk of the brain and the spinal cord as two distinct structures, but in fact, there is no clear boundary between them; at its upper end, the spinal cord enlarges into the brain stem. (See **Figure 2–12**.)

The **spinal cord** is our communications superhighway, connecting the brain to most of the rest of the body. Without it, we would be literally helpless. More than 400,000 Americans are partially or fully paralyzed—about half as a result of sudden traumas to the spinal cord (most often due to car crashes, gunshot wounds, falls, or sports injuries); and half as a result of tumors, infections, and such disorders as multiple sclerosis (McDonald, 1999). When the spinal cord is severed, parts of the body are literally disconnected from the brain. These victims lose all sensations from the parts of the body that can no longer send information to higher brain areas, and they can no longer control the movements of those body parts.

The spinal cord is made up of soft, jellylike bundles of long axons, wrapped in insulating myelin (white matter), and is surrounded and protected by the bones in the spine. There are two major neural pathways in the spinal cord. One consists of motor neurons, descending from the brain, that control internal organs and muscles and help to regulate the autonomic nervous system (described later). The other consists of ascending, sensory

>TABLE 2-1 CAUSES AND TREATMENTS OF COMMONLY OCCURRING NEUROLOGICAL DISEASES AND DISORDERS			
Disorder/Disease	**Cause**	**Symptoms**	**New Directions in Treatments and Research**
Stroke	A severe interruption of blood flow to the brain that kills cells. *Ischemic strokes* are caused by a blocked blood vessel; *Hemorrhagic strokes* result from a burst blood vessel.	Most stoke victims have some residual motor, sensory, or cognitive deficit, according to the region of the brain damaged. The actor Kirk Douglas has suffered from serious strokes.	If treated within 3 hours, ischemic strokes can now be treated with a drug (tissue plasminogen activator) that breaks up clots and allows normal blood flow to return, limiting damage. Better drugs with longer windows of treatment are being developed as are treatments that will allow the brain to initiate its own repair. At present there are no effective treatments for hemorrhagic strokes.

Disorder/Disease	Cause	Symptoms	New Directions in Treatments and Research
Parkinson's Disease	Disease caused by degeneration of neurons in a region of the midbrain (called the substantia nigra) that are active in neural pathways that involve the neurotransmitter dopamine.	Symptoms usually begin with uncontrollable shaking of the hands, which later on extends into the entire body, and is accompanied by difficulty with eating, swallowing, balance, and other muscular control. Symptoms include tremor, rigidity, loss of spontaneous movement, and disturbances of posture. The actor Michael J. Fox is a national spokesperson for research on Parkinson's Disease, which he has.	Treatment with drugs that increase dopamine levels, such as L-dopa, can improve symptoms, but also have long-term side effects. In some cases "lesioning (surgical destruction of specific brain tissue) can lessen the severity of symptoms. Also, some patients respond well to the surgical insertion of electrodes into the brain that can be used to stimulate neural activity. New therapies involving transplanting stem cells into the brain show promise, but are a tpresent highly experimental.
Alzheimer's Disease	Degenerative disease of unknown cause in which neuritic plaques (scars) form, mostly in the cerebral cortex, and neurons degenerate. Also, neurofibrillary tangles are found in the cortex and hippocampus and the size of the brain shrinks, losing as much as one-third of its volume.	First symptoms usually include progressively greater memory loss. President Ronald Reagan suffered from Alzheimer's Disease in his later years.	Since the neural pathways primarily affected involve the neurotransmitter acetylcholine, one current stream of research is aimed at developing drugs, such as Cognex, that enhance activity in these pathways. Currently, such drugs appear to provide temporary relief in the progression of symptoms, but other drugs are being developed that may be more effective. Neuron degeneration and the development of tangles may be the result of loss of acetylcholine sources, so Alzheimer's Disease may also respond positively to drugs that counteract this neurotransmitter deficiency.
Multiple sclerosis (MS)	Disorder caused by the progressive degeneration of the myelin surrounding axons, largely in motor and sensory tracts. This deterioration allows plaques (scars) to form, impeding neural conduction in affected pathways.	Disorder is often characterized by periods of active disease, followed by remissions, with relapses. Although symptoms vary widely among affected individuals, most involve motor and sensory abilities, often leading to paralysis. Actress Annette Funicello, one of the original "Mouseketeers," has multiple sclerosis.	MS may be caused by the body's misguided immune response, which begins to attack myelin. One stream of research is to build up the body's tolerance to its own immunological attacks by injecting myelin antigens. Other drug therapies using biotechnological agents (usually interferon drugs) aimed at slowing disease progression and limiting the severity of attacks. Temporary relief of symptoms can sometimes be accomplished with steroid therapy to reduce brain inflammation, such as treatment with Prednisone.
Spinal cord injury	Trauma to the spinal cord, sometimes involving complete severing of the cord, which prevents peripheral nervous system impulses below the site of damage from reaching the brain.	Loss of function for body functions controlled below the site of damage is often complete, and usually involves paralysis and loss of sensation. Actor Christopher Reeve recently died from the secondary effects resulting from a serious spinal cord injury	Nerve fibers are prevented from growing across the cut in the spinal cord by formation of scar tissue, a lack of blood supply, and the absence of chemicalsthat encourage neuronal regrowth. Stem cell research provides considerable hope for overcoming these obstacles and there is considerable optimism for treatments in the not-distant future.

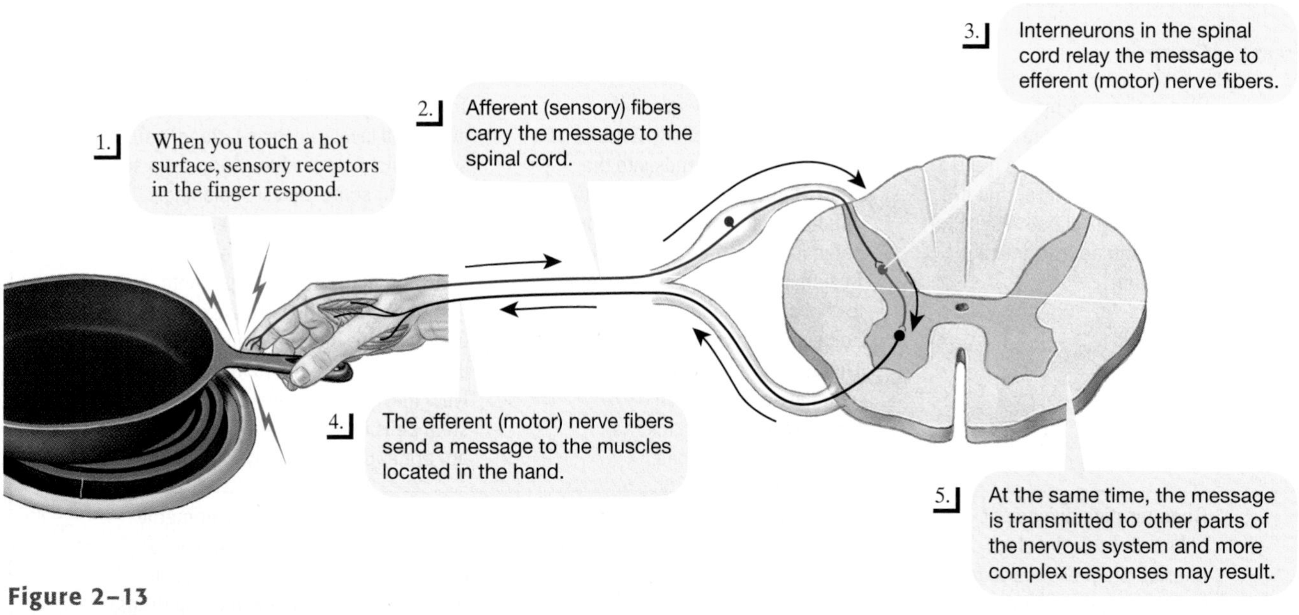

1. When you touch a hot surface, sensory receptors in the finger respond.

2. Afferent (sensory) fibers carry the message to the spinal cord.

3. Interneurons in the spinal cord relay the message to efferent (motor) nerve fibers.

4. The efferent (motor) nerve fibers send a message to the muscles located in the hand.

5. At the same time, the message is transmitted to other parts of the nervous system and more complex responses may result.

Figure 2–13
The spinal cord and reflex action.

neurons that carry information from the extremities and internal organs to the brain. In addition, the spinal cord contains neural circuits that produce reflex movements (and control some aspects of walking). These circuits do not require input from the brain.

To understand how the spinal cord works, consider the simple act of burning your finger on a hot pan. (See **Figure 2–13**.) You pull your hand away without thinking, but that quick response was the last event in a series of reactions in your nervous system. Special sensory cells pick up the message that your finger is burned. They pass this information along to *interneurons* located in the spinal cord. The interneurons, in turn, connect to motor neurons, triggering a quick withdrawal of your hand. (A similar reaction occurs when the doctor taps your knee with a rubber mallet.) At the same time, the message is being sent to other parts of your nervous system. Your body goes on "emergency alert": You breathe faster, your heart pounds, your entire body (including the endocrine system) mobilizes itself against the wound. Meanwhile, your brain is interpreting the messages it receives: You feel pain, you look at the burn, and you run cold water over your hand. A simple, small burn, then, triggers a complex, coordinated sequence of activities.

► CHECK YOUR UNDERSTANDING

Match the lobes of the cerebral cortex with their functions.

1. _____ frontal lobes
2. _____ occipital lobes
3. _____ temporal lobes
4. _____ parietal lobes

   a. process language and information from the ears
   b. process body sensations and spatial information
   c. plan goal-directed behavior
   d. process visual information

5. Which of the following brain structures is most recent, in an evolutionary sense?

   a. pons
   b. reticular formation
   c. frontal lobe of the cerebral cortex
   d. cerebellum

6. Which of the following is a task most closely associated with activity in the left cerebral hemisphere?

   a. language functions
   b. control of the left side of the body
   c. sensory experiences from the left side of the body
   d. vision

Answers: 1. c, 2. d, 3. a, 4. b, 5. c, 6. a.

▶ APPLY YOUR UNDERSTANDING

1. Susan has a degenerative disease that causes her to lose her balance easily and to move in a jerky and uncoordinated way. She cannot drink from a glass without spilling or touch her toes without falling over. This disease is probably affecting her
   a. hypothalamus
   b. midbrain
   c. cerebellum
   d. reticular formation

2. After a head injury a woman reports that she is unable to see, although her eyes are uninjured. A doctor would suspect an injury in the _____ lobe.
   a. frontal
   b. occipital
   c. parietal
   d. temporal

3. Suppose you interview a neuroscientist who is studying how the brains of children of various ages react when they see violent versus nonviolent images on TV. The scanning device most likely used in this research is:
   a. a CAT scanner
   b. functional magnetic resonance imaging
   c. an MRI
   d. an EEG

4. If you compared a spinal cord reflex to the way a computer processes information, which part of the reflex would correspond to the entry of data from the keyboard?
   a. the interneuron connections
   b. the efferent pathway
   c. the afferent pathway
   d. the cortical activation

Answers: 1. c., 2. b., 3. b., 4. c.

The Peripheral Nervous System

2.3 Describe the function of the peripheral nervous system and explain how it operates.

The origins of the quick response your body makes to touching a hot pan are in your peripheral nervous system. The peripheral nervous system (PNS) links the brain and spinal cord to the rest of the body, including the sensory receptors, glands, internal organs, and skeletal muscles.

THE STRUCTURE AND FUNCTION OF THE PNS

How does the brain communicate with the rest of the body?

The peripheral nervous system consists of both **afferent neurons**, which carry messages *to* the central nervous system (CNS), and **efferent neurons**, which carry messages *from* the CNS. The afferent neurons carry sensory information. All the things that register through your senses—sights, sounds, smells, temperature, pressure, and so on—travel to your brain via afferent neurons. The efferent neurons carry signals from the brain to the body's muscles and glands.

Some neurons belong to a part of the PNS called the **somatic nervous system**. Neurons in this system are involved in making voluntary movements of the skeletal muscles. Every deliberate action you make, from pedaling a bike to scratching a toe, involves neurons in the somatic nervous system. Other neurons belong to a part of the PNS called the autonomic nervous system. Neurons in the **autonomic nervous system** govern involuntary activities of your internal organs, from the beating of your heart to the hormone secretions of your glands.

The autonomic nervous system is of special interest to psychologists because it is involved not only in vital body functions, such as breathing and blood flow, but also in important emotions as well. To understand the workings of the autonomic nervous system, you must know about the system's two parts: the *sympathetic* and the *parasympathetic* divisions. (See **Figure 2–14**.)

The nerve fibers of the **sympathetic division** are busiest when you are intensely aroused, such as being enraged or very frightened. For example, if you were hiking through a forest and suddenly encountered a large, growling bear, your sympathetic division would be instantaneously triggered. In response to messages from it, your heart would begin to

afferent neurons Neurons that carry messages from sense organs to the spinal cord or brain.

efferent neurons Neurons that carry messages from the spinal cord or brain to the muscles and glands.

somatic nervous system The part of the peripheral nervous system that carries messages from the senses to the central nervous system and between the central nervous system and the skeletal muscles.

autonomic nervous system The part of the peripheral nervous system that carries messages between the central nervous system and the internal organs.

sympathetic division Branch of the autonomic nervous system; it prepares the body for quick action in an emergency.

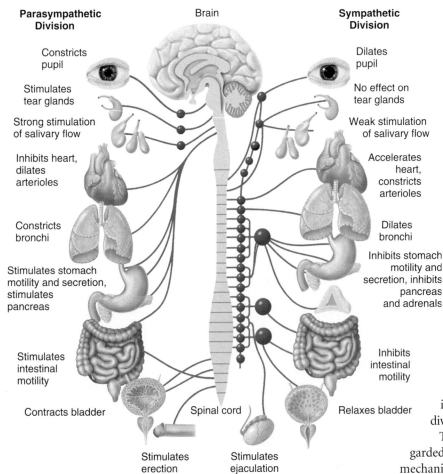

Parasympathetic Division

Constricts pupil

Stimulates tear glands

Strong stimulation of salivary flow

Inhibits heart, dilates arterioles

Constricts bronchi

Stimulates stomach motility and secretion, stimulates pancreas

Stimulates intestinal motility

Contracts bladder

Stimulates erection

Brain

Spinal cord

Sympathetic Division

Dilates pupil

No effect on tear glands

Weak stimulation of salivary flow

Accelerates heart, constricts arterioles

Dilates bronchi

Inhibits stomach motility and secretion, inhibits pancreas and adrenals

Inhibits intestinal motility

Relaxes bladder

Stimulates ejaculation

Figure 2–14

The sympathetic and parasympathetic divisions of the autonomic nervous system.

The sympathetic division generally acts to arouse the body, preparing it for "fight or flight." The parasympathetic follows with messages to relax.

Source: Adapted from *General Biology*, revised edition, 1st edition by Willis Johnson, Richard A. Laubengayer, and Louis E. Delanney, Copyright © 1961. Reprinted with permission of Brooks/Cole, an imprint of the Wadsworth Group, a division of Thomson Learning.

pound, your breathing would quicken, your pupils would enlarge, and your digestion would stop. All these changes would help direct your energy and attention to the emergency you faced, giving you the keen senses, stamina, and strength needed to flee from the danger or to stand and fight it. Your sympathetic division would also tell your glands to start pumping hormones into your blood to further strengthen your body's reactions. Sympathetic nerve fibers connect to every internal organ—a fact that explains why the body's response to sudden danger is so widespread.

Although sympathetic reactions are often sustained even after danger is passed, eventually even the most intense sympathetic division reaction fades, and the body calms down, returning to normal. The heart then goes back to beating at its regular rate, the stomach muscles relax, digestion resumes, breathing slows down, and the pupils contract. This calming effect is promoted by the **parasympathetic division** of the autonomic nervous system. Parasympathetic nerve fibers connect to the same organs as sympathetic nerve fibers do, but they cause the opposite reaction. So, whereas the sympathetic division arouses the body's organs in response to danger and stress, the parasympathetic division calms them once the threat has passed.

Traditionally, the autonomic nervous system was regarded as the "automatic" part of the body's response mechanism (hence its name). You could not, it was believed, tell your own autonomic nervous system when to speed up or slow down your heartbeat or when to stop or start your digestive processes. Studies in the 1960s and 1970s, however, showed that humans (and animals) have some control over the autonomic nervous system. For example, people can learn to moderate the severity of high blood pressure (Buist, 2002) or migraine headaches (Hermann & Blanchard,

parasympathetic division Branch of the autonomic nervous system; it calms and relaxes the body.

During times of stress, the sympathetic branch of the autonomic nervous system is especially active.

2002), and even to regulate their own heart rate and brain waves (Monastra, Monastra, & George, 2002) through *biofeedback*, a subject we will look at more closely in Chapter 4: "Learning and Memory."

▶ CHECK YOUR UNDERSTANDING

Indicate whether each function is associated with the sympathetic (S) or the parasympathetic (P) division of the autonomic nervous system.

1. _____heartbeat increases
2. _____stomach starts digesting food
3. _____breathing speeds up
4. _____body recovers from an emergency situation

Answers: 1. (S)., 2. (P)., 3. (S)., 4. (P).

▶ APPLY YOUR UNDERSTANDING

1. The heavy footsteps on the stairs get closer and closer. Slowly, the door to the bedroom creaks open. As a stranger lunges in, you let out an ear-piercing scream. Which of the following most accurately describes your nervous system at this point?
   a. Your sympathetic nervous system is more active than your parasympathetic nervous system.
   b. Your parasympathetic nervous system is more active than your sympathetic nervous system.
   c. Both your sympathetic and your parasympathetic nervous systems are extremely active.
   d. Neither your sympathetic nor your parasympathetic nervous systems are unusually active.

2. John started jogging to lose weight. The first day he ran two miles. The next morning, as he lay in bed relaxing and trying to recover, the nerves of his _____ nervous system made him painfully aware that he had overexercised.
   a. parasympathetic
   b. somatic
   c. autonomic
   d. sympathetic

Answers: 1. a., 2. b.

The Endocrine System

2.4   Compare the operation of the endocrine system to that of the nervous system.

The nervous system is not the only mechanism that regulates the functioning of our bodies. The endocrine system plays a key role in helping to coordinate and integrate complex psychological reactions. In fact, as we've noted throughout this chapter, the nervous system and the endocrine system work together in a constant chemical conversation.

FUNCTIONING OF THE ENDOCRINE SYSTEM

Why are psychologists interested in hormones?

The **endocrine glands** release chemical substances called **hormones** that are carried throughout your body by the bloodstream. Hormones serve a similar function to neurotransmitters: They carry messages. Indeed, the same substance—for example, norepinephrine—may serve both as a neurotransmitter and as a hormone. A main difference between the nervous and the endocrine systems is speed. A nerve impulse may travel through the body in a few hundredths of a second. Traveling through the bloodstream is a slower process: Hormones may take seconds, even minutes, to reach their target.

Hormones interest psychologists for two reasons. At certain stages of development, hormones *organize* the nervous system and body tissues. At puberty, for example, hormone surges trigger the development of secondary sex characteristics, including breasts in females, a deeper voice in males, and pubic and underarm hair in both sexes. Also hormones *activate* behaviors. They affect such things as alertness or sleepiness, excitability, sexual

endocrine glands Glands of the endocrine system that release hormones into the bloodstream.

hormones Chemical substances released by the endocrine glands; they help regulate bodily activities.

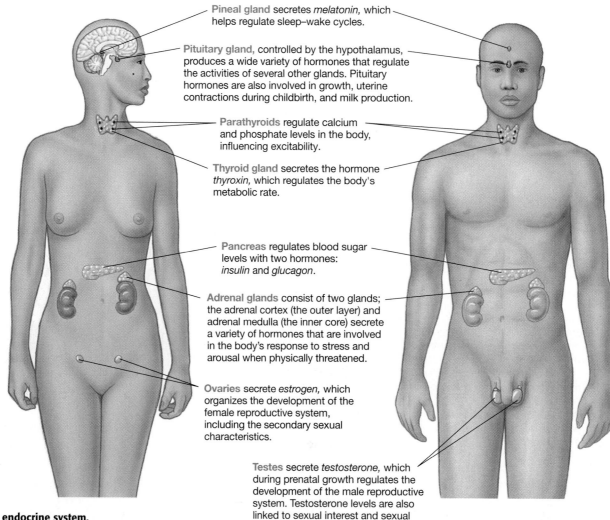

Pineal gland secretes *melatonin,* which helps regulate sleep–wake cycles.

Pituitary gland, controlled by the hypothalamus, produces a wide variety of hormones that regulate the activities of several other glands. Pituitary hormones are also involved in growth, uterine contractions during childbirth, and milk production.

Parathyroids regulate calcium and phosphate levels in the body, influencing excitability.

Thyroid gland secretes the hormone *thyroxin,* which regulates the body's metabolic rate.

Pancreas regulates blood sugar levels with two hormones: *insulin* and *glucagon.*

Adrenal glands consist of two glands; the adrenal cortex (the outer layer) and adrenal medulla (the inner core) secrete a variety of hormones that are involved in the body's response to stress and arousal when physically threatened.

Ovaries secrete *estrogen,* which organizes the development of the female reproductive system, including the secondary sexual characteristics.

Testes secrete *testosterone,* which during prenatal growth regulates the development of the male reproductive system. Testosterone levels are also linked to sexual interest and sexual behavior in adults.

Figure 2–15

The glands of the endocrine system.
Endocrine glands secrete hormones that produce widespread effects on the body.

behavior, ability to concentrate, aggressiveness, reactions to stress, even desire for companionship. Hormones can also have dramatic effects on mood, emotional reactivity, ability to learn, and ability to resist disease. Radical changes in some hormones may also contribute to serious psychological disorders, such as depression. The locations and primary functions of the endocrine glands are shown in **Figure 2–15**. Because specific hormones can have important consequences for many of the phenomena that psychologists study, these will be discussed in more detail in several chapters of this book.

▶ CHECK YOUR UNDERSTANDING

1. Communication in the endocrine system depends on _____, which are chemicals secreted directly into the bloodstream.

2. Match each gland with its major function.

 _____ thyroid gland
 _____ parathyroid glands
 _____ pineal gland
 _____ pancreas
 _____ pituitary gland
 _____ ovaries and testes
 _____ adrenal glands

a. balance calcium and phosphate in the body
b. controls sugar level in the blood
c. involved in stress response
d. produce estrogen and testosterone
e. regulates rate of metabolism
f. controls other endocrine glands
g. controls daily cycle of activity levels

Answers: 1. hormones, **2.** thyroid gland (e); parathyroid glands (a); pineal gland (g); pancreas (b); pituitary gland (f); ovaries and testes (d); adrenal glands (c).

1. On a biology test, Samantha is asked whether norepinephrine is a neurotransmitter or a hormone. Her answer should be, "It is _____."
   a. a neurotransmitter
   b. a hormone
   c. both a neurotransmitter and a hormone
   d. neither a neurotransmitter nor a hormone

2. Mary has been under a great deal of stress lately. Her blood pressure has increased, she has lost her appetite, and her heart is beating faster than usual. These changes are most likely the result of
   a. increased activity in the pineal gland
   b. reduced activity in the pancreas
   c. increased activity in the adrenal glands
   d. reduced activity in the thyroid gland

Answers: 1. c, 2. c.

Genes and Behavior

2.5 **Describe the basic mechanism of heredity and explain how psychologists study the relative influence of heredity and environment in shaping behavior.**

Our brain, nervous system, and endocrine system keep us aware of what is happening outside (and inside) our bodies; enable us to use language, think, and solve problems; affect our emotions; and thus guide our behavior. To understand why they function as they do, we need to look at our genetic heritage, as individuals and as members of the human species. Discussions about the role heredity plays in shaping behavior and mental processes form the basis of the field of **behavior genetics**, the final topic we explore in this chapter.

GENETICS

How are traits passed from one generation to the next?

Genetics is the study of how living things pass on traits from one generation to the next. Offspring are not carbon copies or "clones" of their parents, yet some traits reappear from generation to generation in predictable patterns. Around the beginning of the twentieth century, scientists named the basic units of inheritance **genes**. But they did not know what genes were or how they were transmitted.

Today we know much more about genes and the way they work. Genes are carried by **chromosomes**, tiny threadlike bodies found in the nucleus of all cells. Chromosomes vary in size and shape, and usually come in pairs. Each species has a constant number: Mice have 20 pairs, monkeys have 27, and peas have 7. Human beings have 23 pairs of chromosomes in every normal cell, except the sex cells (eggs and sperm), which have only half a set of chromosomes. At fertilization, the chromosomes from the father's sperm link to the chromosomes from the mother's egg, creating a new cell called a *zygote*. That single cell and all of the billions of body cells that develop from it (except sperm and eggs) contain 46 chromosomes, arranged as 23 pairs.

The main ingredient of chromosomes is **deoxyribonucleic acid (DNA)**, a complex organic molecule that looks like two chains twisted around each other in a double-helix pattern. Amazingly, a six-foot strand of DNA is crammed into the nucleus of every cell of your body (Travis, 2004). DNA is also the only known molecule that can replicate or reproduce itself, and this happens each time a cell divides.

A gene is a small segment of DNA that carries directions for a particular trait or group of traits. Each human chromosome contains thousands of genes in fixed locations. The **human genome**, the sum total of all the genes necessary to build a human being, is approximately 30,000 genes. The goal of the Human Genome Project, launched in 1990, is to map all 23 pairs of human chromosomes and to determine which genes influence which characteristics (Johnson, 1990; Plomin & Rende, 1991). In June 2000—ahead of schedule—researchers announced the first rough map of the entire genome. Already, researchers have identified genes on specific chromosomes that are associated with Alzheimer's disease (Corder et al., 1993; Papassotiropoulos et al., 2002), alcoholism (Uhl, Blum, Nobel, &

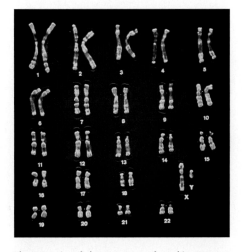

The 23 pairs of chromosomes found in every normal human cell. The two members of 22 of these pairs look exactly alike. The two members of the 23rd pair, the sex chromosomes, may or may not look alike. Females have equivalent X chromosomes, while males have one X and one Y chromosome, which look very different.

behavior genetics Study of the relationship between heredity and behavior.

genetics Study of how traits are transmitted from one generation to the next.

genes Segments of DNA that control the transmission of traits; they are found on the chromosomes.

chromosomes Pairs of threadlike bodies within the cell nucleus that contain the genes.

deoxyribonucleic acid (DNA) Complex molecule in a double-helix configuration that is the main ingredient of chromosomes and genes and that forms the code for all genetic information.

human genome The full complement of genes within a human cell.

Smith, 1993), schizophrenia, (Blouin et al., 1998; Kendler et al., 2000), suicide (Abbar, et al., 2001; Du et al., 1999), cognitive functioning (Gécz & Mulley, 2000), intelligence (Plomin et al., 1994), and even aging (Migliaccio et al., 1999). By using these genetic markers, researchers expect not only to prevent or reverse some genetic diseases, but also to understand better the role of heredity in even the most complex behaviors (Plomin & Crabbe, 2000; Plomin, DeFries, Craig, & McGuffin, 2003; Plomin, DeFries, & McClearn, 1990; Wahlsten, 1999).

It appears that there are only a handful of traits that are dictated by a single gene. Most of the characteristics we inherit are **polygenic**, meaning that they are determined through the combined action of several genes. Weight, height, skin pigmentation, and countless other characteristics are polygenic. Just as each of the instruments in a symphony orchestra contributes separate notes to the sound that reaches the audience, each of the genes in a polygenic system contributes separately to the total effect (McClearn et al., 1991).

Heredity need not be immediately or fully apparent. In some cases, expression of a trait is delayed until later in life. For example, many men inherit "male-pattern baldness" that does not show up until middle age. Moreover, quite often genes may predispose a person to developing a particular trait, but full expression of the characteristic depends on environmental factors. For example, people with an inherited tendency to gain weight may or may not become obese, depending on their diet, exercise program, and overall health. Put another way, genes establish a range of potential outcomes. For many traits, the actual outcome you end up with depends on the interactions of many genes with the environment. Given the same environment, for example, a person who inherits "tall" genes will be tall, and a person who inherits "short" genes, short. But if the first person is malnourished in childhood and the second person well nourished as a child, they may be the same height as adults. On average, Americans today are taller than their grandparents and great-grandparents, whose genes they share. The reason is that they enjoyed better food as children and were less likely to contract growth-stunting childhood diseases.

So far, we have used physical characteristics as examples. Behavior geneticists apply the same principles to *psychological* characteristics.

People clearly do inherit physical traits from their parents. Whether—and to what extent—they also inherit behavioral traits remains uncertain.

polygenic inheritance Process that occurs when traits are determined through the combined action of several genes.

BEHAVIOR GENETICS

What methods do psychologists use to study the effects of genes on behavior?

Behavior geneticists study the topics that interest all psychologists—perception, learning and memory, motivation and emotions, personality, and psychological disorders—but from a genetic perspective. Their goal is to identify what genes contribute to intelligence, temperament, talents, and other characteristics, as well as genetic predispositions to psychological and neurological disorders (Brunner, Nelen, Breakefield, Ropers, & Van Oost, 1993; Cunningham, 2003; Plomin, 1999; Plomin, DeFries, & McClearn, 1990; Plomin & Rende, 1991; Spinath, Harlaar, Ronald, & Plomin, 2004). Of course, genes do not directly cause behavior; rather, they affect the development and operation of the nervous system and the endocrine system, which, in turn, influence the likelihood that a certain behavior will occur under certain circumstances (Wahlsten, 1999).

In the remainder of this chapter, we will look at some of the methods used by behavior geneticists as well as some of their more interesting discoveries. We will start with methods appropriate for animal studies and then examine the techniques used to study behavior genetics in humans.

ANIMAL BEHAVIOR GENETICS Much of what we know about behavior genetics comes from studies of nonhuman animals. Mice are favorite subjects because they breed quickly and have relatively complex behavior patterns. In *strain studies,* close relatives, such as siblings, are intensively inbred over many generations to create strains of animals that are genetically similar to one another, but different from other strains. When animals from different strains are raised together in the same environment, differences between them largely reflect genetic differences in the strains. This method has shown that performance on learning tasks, as well as sense of smell and susceptibility to seizures, are affected by heredity.

Selection studies are another way to assess **heritability**, the degree to which a trait is inherited. If a trait is closely regulated by genes, when animals with the trait are interbred, more of their offspring should have the trait than one would find in the general population. Humans have practiced selective breeding for thousands of years to create breeds of dogs and other domesticated animals that have desirable traits—both physical and psychological. Today, with more than 400 breeds, dogs are more variable in size and shape than any other species.

HUMAN BEHAVIOR GENETICS For obvious reasons, scientists cannot conduct strain or selection studies with human beings. But there are a number of ways to study behavioral techniques indirectly (Dick & Rose, 2002; Hutchison, Stallings, McGeary, & Bryan, 2004).

Family studies are based on the assumption that if genes influence a trait, close relatives should share that trait more often than distant relatives because close relatives have more genes in common. For example, overall, schizophrenia occurs in only 1 to 2 percent of the general population (Robins & Regier, 1991). Siblings of people with schizophrenia, however, are about eight times more likely (and children of schizophrenic parents about 10 times more likely) to develop the disorder than someone chosen randomly from the general population. Unfortunately, because family members share not only some genes but also similar environments, family studies alone cannot clearly distinguish the effects of heredity and environment (Plomin, DeFries, & McClearn, 1990).

To obtain a clearer picture of the influences of heredity and environment, psychologists often use **twin studies. Identical twins** develop from a single fertilized ovum and are therefore identical in genetic makeup. Any differences between them must be due to environmental influences. **Fraternal twins**, however, develop from two separate fertilized egg cells and are no more similar genetically than are other brothers and sisters. If twin pairs grow up in similar environments and if identical twins are no more alike in a particular characteristic than fraternal twins, heredity cannot be very important for that trait.

Twin studies suggest that heredity plays a crucial role in schizophrenia. When one identical twin develops schizophrenia, the chances that the other twin will develop the disorder are about 50 percent. For fraternal twins, the chances are about 15 percent (Gottesman, 1991). Such studies have also provided evidence for the heritability of a wide variety of other behaviors, including verbal skills (Eley, Bishop, et al., 1999; Viding et al., 2004), mild intellectual impairment (Spinath, Harlaar, Ronald, & Plomin, 2004), aggressiveness (Eley, Lichenstein, & Stevenson, 1999), depression and anxiety (Eley & Stevenson, 1999; O'Connor, McGuire, Reiss, Hetherington, & Plomin, 1998), and even mannerisms such as the strength of a handshake (Farber, 1981).

Similarities between twins, even identical twins, cannot automatically be attributed to genes, however; twins nearly always grow up together. Parents and others may treat them alike—or try to emphasize their differences, so that they grow up as separate individuals. In either case, the data for heritability may be biased. To avoid this problem, researchers attempt to locate identical twins who were separated at birth or in very early childhood and then raised in different homes. A University of Minnesota team led by Thomas Bouchard followed separated twins for more than 10 years (Bouchard, 1984, 1996; Bouchard et al., 1990). They confirmed that genetics plays a major role in mental retardation, schizophrenia, depression, and intelligence. Bouchard and his colleagues have also found that complex personality traits, interests, and talents, and even the structure of brain waves, are guided by genetics.

Studies of twins separated shortly after birth have also drawn criticism. For example, the environment in the uterus may be more traumatic for one twin than the other (Phelps, Davis, & Schartz, 1997). Also, because adoption agencies usually try to place twins in similar families, their environments may not be much different (Ford, 1993;

Identical twins develop from a single ovum and consequently start out with the same genetic material.

heritability Degree to which a given trait results from hereditary, genetic instructions.

family studies Studies of heritability in humans based on the assumption that if genes influence a certain trait, close relatives should be more similar on that trait than distant relatives.

twin studies Studies of identical and fraternal twins to determine the relative influence of heredity and environment on human behavior.

identical twins Twins developed from a single fertilized ovum and therefore identical in genetic makeup at the time of conception.

fraternal twins Twins developed from two separate fertilized ova and therefore different in genetic makeup.

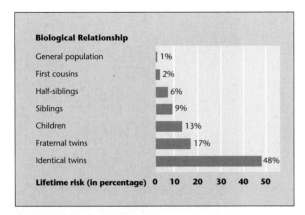

Figure 2–16

Average risk of schizophrenia among biological relatives of people with schizophrenia.

Source: The Origins of Madness by Irving I. Gottesman, 1991, p.96. Henry Holt and Company, LLC.

adoption studies Research carried out on children, adopted at birth by parents not genetically related to them, to determine the relative influence of heredity and environment on human behavior.

Wyatt, 1993). Finally, the number of twin pairs separated at birth is fairly small. For these reasons, scientists sometimes rely on other types of studies to investigate the influence of heredity.

Adoption studies focus on children who were adopted at birth and brought up by parents not genetically related to them. Adoption studies provide additional evidence for the heritability of intelligence and some forms of mental illness (Horn, 1983; Scarr & Weinberg, 1983) as well as for the role of genetics in behavior previously thought to be solely determined by environmental influences, even smoking (Boomsma, Koopman, Van Doornen, & Orlebeke, 1994; Heath & Martin, 1993; Lerman et al., 1999).

By combining the results of *twin, adoption,* and *family* studies, psychologists have obtained a clearer picture of the role of heredity in many human characteristics, including schizophrenia. As shown in **Figure 2–16**, the average risk of schizophrenia steadily increases in direct relation to the closeness of one's biological relationship to an individual with the disorder.

So far, we have been talking about the environment as if it were something *out there*, something that happens *to* people, over which they have little control. But individuals also shape their environments. The genes and predispositions individuals inherit alter the environment in several ways (Plomin, DeFries, Craig, & McGuffin, 2003). For example, people tend to seek out environments in which they feel comfortable. A shy person might prefer an occupation with less social interaction and more opportunity for individual work activities, whereas a more outgoing person might be happier in a job that emphasizes teamwork and interpersonal communication. In addition, our own behavior causes others to respond in particular ways. A manager's approach to correcting the behavior of a sensitive coworker might be quite different from how a more extraverted and socially confident employee would be treated. Because genes and environments interact in so many intricate ways, trying to separate and isolate the effects of heredity and environment—nature and nurture—is artificial (Collins, Maccoby, Steinberg, Hetherington & Bornstein, 2000, 2001; McGuire, 2001; Plomin, 1997). The interaction of heredity and environment, however, is fundamental in shaping human behavior and thought, and it will be further explored in many chapters throughout this text.

>KEY TERMS<

neuropsychologists, *p. 37*
psychobiology, *p. 37*
neuroscience, *p. 37*

Neurons: the messengers

neurons, *p. 37*
dendrites, *p. 38*
axon, *p. 38*
nerve (or tract), *p. 38*
myelin sheath, *p. 38*
sensory (or afferent) neurons, *p. 39*
motor (or efferent) neurons, *p. 39*
interneurons (or association neurons), *p. 39*
glial cells (or glia), *p. 39*
ions, *p. 39*
resting potential, *p. 39*
polarization, *p. 39*
neural impulse (or action potential), *p. 39*

graded potential, *p. 39*
threshold of excitation, *p. 39*
all-or-none law, *p. 40*
synaptic space (or synaptic cleft), *p. 40*
synapse, *p. 40*
terminal button (or synaptic knob), *p. 41*
synaptic vesicles, *p. 41*
neurotransmitters, *p. 41*
receptor sites, *p. 41*
neural plasticity, *p. 43*
neurogenesis, *p. 44*

The central nervous system

central nervous system (CNS), *p. 46*
peripheral nervous system (PNS), *p. 46*
hindbrain, *p. 47*
cerebellum, *p. 48*
midbrain, *p. 48*

limbic system, *p. 49*
cerebral cortex, *p. 49*
association areas, *p. 49*
frontal lobes, *p. 49*
primary motor cortex, *p. 50*
occipital lobe, *p. 51*
parietal lobe, *p. 51*
primary somatosensory cortex, *p. 51*
temporal lobes, *p. 51*
corpus callosum, *p. 51*
spinal cord, *p. 56*

The peripheral nervous system

afferent neurons, *p. 59*
efferent neurons, *p. 59*
somatic nervous system, *p. 59*
autonomic nervous system, *p. 59*
sympathetic division, *p. 59*
parasympathetic division, *p. 60*

The endocrine system

endocrine glands, *p. 61*
hormones, *p. 61*

Genes, evolution, and behavior

behavior genetics, *p. 63*
genetics, *p. 63*
genes, *p. 63*
chromosomes, *p. 63*
deoxyribonucleic acid (DNA), *p. 63*
human genome, *p. 63*
polygenic inheritance, *p. 64*
heritability, *p. 65*
family studies, *p. 65*
twin studies, *p. 65*
identical twins, *p. 65*
fraternal twins, *p. 65*
adoption studies, *p. 66*

>CHAPTER REVIEW<

Biological processes are the basis of our thoughts, feelings, and actions. All of our behaviors are kept in tune with our surroundings and coordinated with one another through the work of two interacting systems: the nervous system and the endocrine system. **Neuropsychologists** study how the brain influences behavior.

Neurons: The Messengers

What types of cells are found in the nervous system? The basic building block of the nervous system is the **neuron**, or nerve cell. Neurons have several characteristics that distinguish them from other cells. Neurons receive messages from other neurons through short fibers called **dendrites**. A longer fiber, called an **axon**, carries outgoing messages from the cell. A group of axons bundled together forms a **nerve** or **tract**. Some axons are covered with a myelin sheath made up of **glial cells**; this increases neuron efficiency and provides insulation.

What "language" do neurons speak? When a neuron is at rest (a state called the **resting potential**), there is a slightly higher concentration of negatively charged **ions** inside its membrane than there is outside. The membrane is said to be **polarized**—that is, the electrical charge inside it is negative relative to its outside. When an incoming message is strong enough, this electrical imbalance abruptly changes (the membrane is depolarized), and an **action potential** (**neural impulse**) is generated. Incoming messages cause **graded potentials**, which, when combined, may exceed the minimum **threshold of excitation** and make the neuron "fire." After firing, the neuron briefly goes through the **absolute refractory period**, when it will not fire again, and then through the **relative refractory period**, when firing will occur only if the incoming message is much stronger than usual. According to the **all-or-none law**, every firing of a particular neuron produces an impulse of equal strength. More rapid firing of neurons is what communicates the strength of a message.

What happens as information moves from one neuron to the next? **Neurotransmitter** molecules, released by **synaptic vesicles**, cross the tiny **synaptic space** (or **cleft**) between an **axon terminal** (or **terminal button**) of a sending neuron and a dendrite of a receiving neuron. Here they latch on to **receptor sites**, much as keys fit into locks, and pass on their excitatory or inhibitory messages. Psychologists need to understand how **synapses** function because neurotransmitters affect an enormous range of physical and emotional responses.

How can experience and the development of new neurons change the brain? Research demonstrates that experiences in our environments can produce changes in the brain, a principle called **neural plasticity**. Human brains also are capable of **neurogenesis**—

the production of new brain cells. The study of neurogenesis may help treat neurological disorders, but also raises ethical questions.

The Central Nervous System

How is the nervous system organized? The nervous system is organized into two parts: The **central nervous system (CNS)**, which consists of the brain and spinal cord, and the **peripheral nervous system (PNS)**, made up of nerves that radiate throughout the body, linking all of the body's parts to the CNS.

What are the major structures and areas of the brain, and what functions do they serve? Physically, the brain has three more-or-less distinct areas: the central core, the limbic system, and the cerebrum.

The central core consists of the hindbrain, cerebellum, midbrain, thalamus and hypothalamus, and reticular formation. The **hindbrain** is made up of the medulla, a narrow structure nearest the spinal cord that controls breathing, heart rate, and blood pressure, and the pons, which produces chemicals that maintain our sleep–wake cycle. The medulla is the point at which many of the nerves from the left part of the body cross to the right side of the brain and vice versa. The **cerebellum** controls the sense of balance and coordinates the body's actions. The **midbrain**, which is above the cerebellum, is important for hearing and sight and is one of the places in which pain is registered. Within the midbrain, the structures of the *thalamus* serve as relay station that integrates and shapes incoming sensory signals before transmitting them to the higher levels of the brain. The *hypothalamus* is important to motivation and emotional behavior. The *reticular formation*, which is woven through all of these structures, alerts the higher parts of the brain to incoming messages.

The **limbic system**, a ring of structures located between the central core and the cerebral hemispheres, is a more recent evolutionary development than the central core. It includes the hippocampus, which is essential to the formation of new memories, and the amygdala, which, together with the hippocampus, governs emotions related to self-preservation. Other portions of the limbic system heighten the experience of pleasure. In times of stress, the limbic system coordinates and integrates the nervous system's response.

The cerebrum takes up most of the room inside the skull. The outer covering of the cerebral hemispheres is known as the **cerebral cortex**. They are the most recently evolved portion of the brain, and they regulate the most complex behavior. Each cerebral hemisphere is divided into four lobes, delineated by deep fissures on the surface of the brain. The **occipital lobe** of the cortex, located at the back of the head, receives and processes visual information. The **temporal lobe**, located roughly behind the temples, helps us perform complex visual tasks, such as recognizing faces. The **parietal lobe**, which sits on top of the temporal and occipital lobes, receives sensory information from all over the body and oversees spatial abilities. Messages from sensory receptors are registered in the **primary somatosensory cortex**. The **frontal lobe** receives and coordinates messages from the other lobes and keeps track of past and future body movement. It is primarily responsible for goal-directed behavior and is key to the ability to lead a mature emotional life. The **primary motor cortex** is responsible for voluntary movement. The

association areas—areas that are free to process all kinds of information—make up most of the cerebral cortex and enable the brain to produce behaviors requiring the coordination of many brain areas.

How are the left and right hemispheres specialized for different functions? The two cerebral hemispheres are linked by the **corpus callosum**, through which they communicate and coordinate their activities. Nevertheless, each hemisphere appears to specialize in certain tasks (although they also have overlapping functions). The right hemisphere excels at visual and spatial tasks, nonverbal imagery, and the perception of emotion, whereas the left hemisphere excels at language and perhaps analytical thinking, too. The right hemisphere controls the left side of the body, and the left hemisphere controls the right side.

What methods have been developed to study the brain? An increasingly sophisticated technology exists for investigating the brain. Among the most important tools are microelectrode techniques, macroelectrode techniques (EEG), structural imaging (CT scanning and MRI), and functional imaging (EEG imaging, MEG, and MSI). Two new functional imaging techniques, PET scanning and fMRI, allow us to observe not only the structure, but also the functioning of parts of the brain. Scientists often combine these techniques to study brain activity in unprecedented detail—information that can help in the treatment of medical and psychological disorders.

How does the spinal cord work with the brain to sense events and act on them? The **spinal cord** is a complex cable of nerves that extends from the brain and connects it to most of the rest of the body. It is made up of bundles of long nerve fibers and has two basic functions: to permit some reflex movements and to carry messages to and from the brain. A break in the cord disrupts the flow of impulses from the brain below that point, causing paralysis and lack of sensation.

The Peripheral Nervous System

How does the brain communicate with the rest of the body? The peripheral nervous system (PNS) contains two types of neurons: **afferent neurons**, which carry sensory messages *to* the central nervous system, and **efferent neurons**, which carry messages *from* the CNS. Neurons involved in making voluntary movements of the skeletal muscles belong to a part of the PNS called the **somatic nervous system**, whereas neurons involved in governing the actions of internal organs belong to a part of the PNS called the autonomic nervous system. The **autonomic nervous system** is itself divided into two parts: the **sympathetic division**, which acts primarily to arouse the body when it is faced with threat, and the **parasympathetic division**, which acts to calm the body down, restoring it to normal levels of arousal.

The Endocrine System

Why are psychologists interested in hormones? The endocrine system is the other communication system in the body. It is made up of **endocrine glands** that produce **hormones**, chemical substances released into the bloodstream to either trigger developmental changes in the body or to activate certain behavioral responses. Endocrine glands are located in various parts of the body, and each secretes specific hormones that regulate behavior and direct developmental process.

Genes and Behavior

How are traits passed from one generation to the next? The field of **behavior genetics** explores the influences of heredity on human behavior and addresses questions pertaining to the nature-versus-nurture debate over the relative contributions of genes and the environment to human similarities and differences. **Genetics** is the study of how traits are passed on from one generation to the next via genes. This process is called heredity. Each **gene** is lined up on tiny threadlike bodies called **chromosomes**, which in turn are made up predominantly of **deoxyribonucleic acid (DNA)**. The **Human Genome** Project has produced a rough map of the genes on the 23 pairs of human chromosomes. Most inherited characteristics are polygenic; in **polygenic inheritance** a number of genes interact to produce a trait.

What methods do psychologists use to study the effects of genes on behavior? Psychologists use a variety of methods to study **heritability**—that is, the contribution of genes in determining variations in certain traits. *Strain studies* approach the problem by observing strains of highly inbred, genetically similar animals, whereas *selection studies* try to determine the extent to which an animal's traits can be passed on from one generation to another. In the study of humans, **family studies** tackle heritability by looking for similarities in traits as a function of biological relatedness. Also useful in studying human heritability are **twin studies** and **adoption studies**. Understanding the interaction of heredity and environmental forces is critically important throughout the study of psychology.

2.1 NEURONS: THE MESSENGERS

Concept Map

TYPES OF CELLS

- **Sensory (afferent) neurons:** Messages from sense organs to brain and spinal cord
- **Motor (efferent) neurons:** Messages from brain and spinal cord to muscles and glands
- **Interneurons (association neurons):** Messages from one neuron to another
- **Glial cells (glia):** Support and nourish neurons

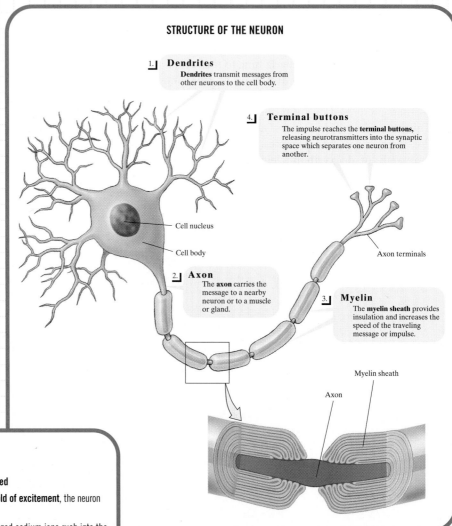

STRUCTURE OF THE NEURON

1. **Dendrites**
   Dendrites transmit messages from other neurons to the cell body.

4. **Terminal buttons**
   The impulse reaches the **terminal buttons,** releasing neurotransmitters into the synaptic space which separates one neuron from another.

Cell nucleus

Cell body

Axon terminals

2. **Axon**
   The **axon** carries the message to a nearby neuron or to a muscle or gland.

3. **Myelin**
   The **myelin sheath** provides insulation and increases the speed of the traveling message or impulse.

Myelin sheath

Axon

FUNCTIONS OF THE NEURON

Action Potential

- When at rest, the neuron is **polarized**
- When stimulation exceeds a **threshold of excitement**, the neuron depolarizes (fires)
- With depolarization, positively charged sodium ions rush into the neuron, creating an **action potential**
- The action potential travels the length of the axon and causes **neurotransmitters** to be released from **synaptic vesicles** into the synaptic cleft

Synaptic Transmission

- Neurons are separated by a **synaptic space** (synaptic cleft)
- Neurotransmitter molecules convey messages across the synaptic space by locking onto **receptor sites** on the receiving neuron, creating a **graded potential** that may be sufficient to depolarize the receiving neuron

NEUROPLASTICITY AND NEUROGENESIS

- Neurons can develop in response to environmental stimulation or deprivation, a feature called **neural plasticity**. Even adult brains can produce new neurons, a process called **neurogenesis**.

2.2 THE CENTRAL NERVOUS SYSTEM

THE BRAIN

The Central Core

- **Hindbrain:** Medulla, Pons, Cerebellum
- **Midbrain:** Thalamus, Hypothalamus, Reticular Formation

The Limbic System

- Plays a central role in times of stress
- Integrates the activity of the nervous system through the hippocampus and amygdala

THE CEREBRAL CORTEX

Brain: Cerebral Cortex

- Two **hemispheres** (left and right)
- Four **lobes** (frontal, parietal, temporal, occipital)

STUDYING THE BRAIN

- Microelectrode techniques used to study individual neurons.
- Macroelectrode techniques: EEG
- Structural Imaging techniques: CAT (CT) Scan, MRI Scan
- Functional Imaging techniques: PET scans, fMRI scans

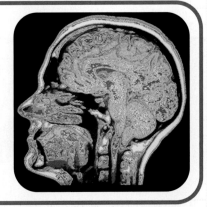

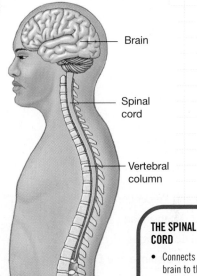

Brain

Spinal cord

Vertebral column

THE SPINAL CORD

- Connects brain to the rest of the nervous system
- Coordinates reflexes

Concept Map

2.3 THE PERIPHERAL NERVOUS SYSTEM

SOMATIC NERVOUS SYSTEM

- Afferent (sensory) neurons bring sensory messages to the brain and spinal cord; efferent (motor) neurons bring motor messages from the brain and spinal cord to muscles and glands

AUTONOMIC NERVOUS SYSTEM

- Sympathetic and parasympathetic divisions govern involuntary activities of organs

2.4 THE ENDOCRINE SYSTEM

- Communicates messages that regulate body functions
- Chemical messengers called **hormones** are produced by a wide variety of **endocrine glands**
- Action of the endocrine system is slower, but longer lasting, than the nervous system

2.5 GENES AND BEHAVIOR

THE GENETIC CODE

- Humans have 23 pairs of **chromosomes**, which each consist of a molecule of **DNA (deoxyribonucleic acid)**
- The 46 chromosomes contain about 30,000 **genes**, small segments of DNA that carry instructions; these comprise the **human genome**
- Many genetic traits are **polygenic**, regulated by multiple genes

BEHAVIORAL GENETICS

- Researchers study genetically-related individuals to estimate the importance of heredity in producing a given trait
- Studies of **identical** and **fraternal** twins, and of adopted children, help researchers understand the relative impact of heredity and environment

Sensation, Perception, and Conscious Experience

Christina Brothers, a financial analyst who was prescribed a sleeping pill for insomnia in May 2005, had a rude awakening on the concrete floor of a jail cell, after only three days of taking the prescribed dose. Brothers learned from a police report that she got out of bed around 6:00 a.m., left her house, drove her mother's car into a parked vehicle, left the scene, and ran into another vehicle. Brothers left that scene, too, returned home, had a chat with her mother as if nothing had happened, and was arrested in her bedroom later that morning, which she didn't remember either.

Sleep driving is a bizarre, if rare, side effect of Ambien, the nation's best-selling prescription sleeping pill. Yet, however alarming this incident is, it is but a tiny detail in a larger, more disturbing picture. Americans' use of prescription sleeping pills has shot up steeply in recent years. In 2005, 42 million sleeping pill prescriptions were filled (with Ambien making up 31 million), up by nearly 60 percent since 2000. The rise can be attributed, in part, to the enormous amount of TV and print ads for Ambien and competing drugs like Sonata and Lunesta.

But we respond to the ads from a deep and very real need. According to a major new government study, there is an epidemic of sleeplessness in the country, with 50 to 70 million Americans experiencing chronic sleep disorders, while millions more are sleep deprived. Why are we sleepless? Experts surmise that our "modern lifestyle" is to blame, what one sleep scientist calls "a 24-hour-a-day-seven-days-a-week society." Sleep schedules are shifted ever later to accommodate later work schedules, and a good night's rest loses out to everything from finishing household chores to Internet surfing, e-mail, late night cable, and other distractions.

The irony is that the more hours we work, the less productive we are because more sleep—the recommended seven to nine hours per night—has been shown to make the mind function better. Sleep helps consolidate memory, improve judgment, promote learning and concentration, boost mood, speed reaction time, and sharpen problem solving and accuracy. Sleep's benefits to the body can also be seen when you read studies of what happens when the body *does not* get its recommended slumber. Recent physiological studies suggest that a sleep deficit may put the body into a state of high alert, increasing the production of stress hormones, driving up blood pressure, and even causing a heightened state of inflammation—all major risk factors for heart attacks, heart disease, strokes, cancer, and diabetes.

In short, those who sleep less don't end up saving a lot of time because they are more likely to die sooner than those who sleep more. Popping a little five-milligram pill at night may seem like an easy solution, yet the danger lies in not exploring the underlying causes of *insomnia*, the inability to fall or remain asleep.

In this chapter we introduce the varieties of human sensation, perception, and consciousness. *Sensations*, which include smells, sights, sounds, tastes, balance, touch, and pain, are the raw data of experience. Our various sense organs are continuously bombarded by bits of information, all competing for attention and, by themselves, as meaningless as pieces of a giant jigsaw puzzle. *Perception* is the mental process of sorting, identifying, and arranging these bits into meaningful patterns. Sensation and perception are the foundation of *consciousness*; our awareness of how we think, feel, and perceive the world. Sleep and wakefulness are both states of consciousness.

We begin this chapter by looking at the basic principles involved in sensation. We will examine the body's different sense organs to see how each converts physical energy—light or sound waves, for example—into nerve impulses. We then explore how our brain organizes this sensory information so that it has meaning for us—a process called *perception*. Finally, we will discuss consciousness, in its several forms: waking, sleeping, and the altered states that are associated with the use of psychoactive drugs or the techniques of meditation and hypnosis. Each of these three phenomena—sensation, perception, and consciousness—is intimately tied to how we experience the world, and each serves as a useful reference in understanding behavior and mental processes. ◼

The Nature of Sensation

3.1   Identify the ways in which the human sensory system is limited and suggest the impact these limits have on how humans experience the world.

Sensation is the process of receiving sensory data from the environment and translating it to the brain. Sensory processes begin when energy, either from an external source or from inside the body, stimulates a receptor cell in one of the sense organs, such as the eye or the ear. Each **receptor cell** responds to one particular form of energy—for example, light waves (in the case of vision) or vibration of air molecules (in the case of hearing). When there is sufficient energy, the receptor cell "fires" and sends to the brain, via a sensory nerve pathway to which it is connected, a coded signal that varies according to the characteristics of the stimulus. The specific sensation produced depends on *how many* neurons fire, *which* neurons fire, and *how rapidly* these neurons fire.

sensation The process of receiving sensory data from the environment and translating it to the brain.

receptor cell A specialized cell that responds to a particular type of energy.

SENSORY THRESHOLDS

How is physical energy from the environment converted into a message carried to the brain and what limitations are there on this process, called sensation?

To produce any sensation at all, the physical energy reaching a receptor cell must achieve a minimum intensity, or **absolute threshold**. Any stimulation below the absolute threshold will not be experienced. But how much sensory stimulation is enough? How loud must a sound be, for example, for a person to hear it? How bright does a blip on a radar screen have to be for the operator to see it?

To answer such questions, psychologists present a stimulus at different intensities and ask people whether they sense anything. You might expect that there would come a point at which people would suddenly say, "Now I see the flash" or "Now I hear a sound." But actually there is a range of intensities over which a person sometimes—but not always—can sense a stimulus. The absolute threshold is defined as the point at which a person can detect the stimulus 50 percent of the time that it is presented. Although there are differences among people—and even from moment to moment for the same person—the absolute threshold for each of our senses is remarkably low. The approximate absolute thresholds under ideal circumstances are as follows (McBurney & Collings, 1984):

* Hearing: The tick of a watch from 6 meters (20 feet) in very quiet conditions
* Vision: A candle flame seen from 50 kilometers (30 miles) on a clear, dark night
* Taste: 1 gram (0.0356 ounce) of table salt in 500 liters (529 quarts) of water
* Smell: One drop of perfume diffused throughout a three-room apartment
* Touch: The wing of a bee falling on the cheek from a height of 1 centimeter (0.39 inch)

Under normal conditions, absolute thresholds vary according to the level and nature of ongoing sensory stimulation. For example, your threshold for the taste of salt would be considerably higher after you eat salted peanuts, and your vision threshold would be much higher in the middle of a sunny day than at midnight on a moonless night. In both cases, the absolute threshold would rise because of sensory **adaptation**, in which our senses automatically adjust to the overall average level of stimulation in a particular setting. When confronted by a great deal of stimulation, they become much less sensitive than when the overall level of stimulation is low. Similarly, when the level of stimulation drops, our sensory apparatus becomes much more sensitive than under conditions of high stimulation.

This process of adaptation allows all of our senses to be keenly attuned to a multitude of environmental cues without getting overloaded. We can hear the breathing of a sleeping baby when we enter a quiet room, but if we are on a city street during rush hour, the traffic noise would be deafening if our ears did not become less sensitive to stimulation. Similarly, adaptation lets us go from a dark room into bright sunshine without experiencing great pain. (Later in this chapter, we look more closely at adaptation.)

Imagine now that you can hear a particular sound. How much stronger must the sound become before you notice that it has grown louder? The smallest change in stimulation that you can detect 50 percent of the time is called the **difference threshold**, or the **just-noticeable difference (jnd)**. Like the absolute threshold, the difference threshold varies from person to person and from moment to moment for the same person. And, like absolute thresholds, difference thresholds tell us something about the flexibility of sensory systems. For example, adding 1 pound to a 5-pound load will certainly be noticed, so we might assume that the difference threshold must be considerably less than 1 pound. Yet adding 1 pound to a 100-pound load probably would not make much of a difference, so we might conclude that the difference threshold must be considerably more than 1 pound. But how can the difference threshold (jnd) be both less than and greater than 1 pound? It turns out that the difference threshold varies according to the strength or intensity of the original stimulus. The greater the stimulus, the greater the change necessary to produce a jnd.

In the 1830s, Ernst Weber concluded that the difference threshold is a constant *fraction* or *proportion* of the original stimulus, a theory known as **Weber's law**. The values of these fractions vary significantly for the different senses. Hearing, for example, is very sensitive:

During a hearing test, this woman's absolute threshold and difference threshold would be measured by asking her whether or not she could hear sounds of varying intensities and frequencies.

absolute threshold The least amount of energy that can be detected as a stimulation 50 percent of the time.

adaptation An adjustment of the senses to the level of stimulation they are receiving.

difference threshold or just-noticeable difference (jnd) The smallest change in stimulation that can be detected 50 percent of the time.

Weber's law The principle that the jnd for any given sense is a constant fraction or proportion of the stimulation being judged.

We can detect a change in sound of 0.3 percent (of 1 percent). By contrast, producing a jnd in taste requires a 20 percent change. To return to our earlier example of weight, a change in weight of 2 percent is necessary to produce a jnd. So adding 1 pound to a 50-pound load would produce a noticeable difference half of the time; adding 1 pound to a 100-pound load would not.

SUBLIMINAL AND EXTRASENSORY PERCEPTION

Under what circumstances might messages outside our awareness affect our behavior?

The idea of an absolute threshold implies that some events occur *subliminally*—below our level of awareness. Can subliminal messages used in advertisements and self-help tapes, for example, change people's behavior? We should think critically about these questions. For decades, the story has circulated that refreshment sales increased dramatically when a movie theater in New Jersey flashed subliminal messages to "Drink Coca-Cola" and "Eat Popcorn." In fact, sales of Coke and popcorn did not change.

Similarly, audiotapes with subliminal self-help messages (which make up between one-quarter and one-third of all spoken-word audiocassette sales) often promise more than they deliver. In one series of studies, volunteers used such tapes for several weeks. About half said they had improved as a result of listening to the tapes, but objective tests detected no measurable change. Moreover, the perceived improvement had more to do with the label on the tape than its subliminal content: About half the people who received a tape labeled "Improve Memory" said that their memory had improved even though many of them had actually received a tape intended to boost self-esteem. About one-third of the people who listened to tapes labeled "Increase Self-Esteem" said that their self-esteem had gone up, though many of them had actually been listening to tapes designed to improve memory (Greenwald et al., 1991).

Although some studies (Arndt, Greenberg, Pyszczynski, & Solomon, 1997; Bar & Biederman, 1998; Kunst-Wilson & Zajonc, 1980; Monahan, Murphy, & Zajonc, 2000; Rensink, 2004) have indicated that, *in a controlled laboratory setting*, people can process and respond to information outside of awareness, this does *not* mean that people automatically or mindlessly obey subliminal messages in advertisements, rock music, self-help tapes, or any other form. To the contrary, independent scientific studies show that hidden messages *outside* the laboratory have no significant effect on behavior (Beatty & Hawkins, 1989; Greenwald et al., 1991; T. G. Russell, Rowe, & Smouse, 1991; Smith & Rogers, 1994; Underwood, 1994).

Similarly, claims for *extrasensory perception*, or *ESP*, have also generally not been confirmed by scientific research. Much of the research into ESP has been criticized for poor experimental design, failure to control for dishonesty, or selective reporting of results. Even carefully designed experiments have failed to produce consistent results (Milton & Wiseman, 1999; Storm & Ertel, 2001). Thus, despite decades of research, experimentation has not provided clear scientific support for the existence of ESP.

So far, we have been talking about the general characteristics of sensation, but each of the body's sensory systems works a little differently. Individual sensory systems contain receptor cells that specialize in converting a particular kind of energy into neural signals. The threshold at which this conversion occurs varies from system to system. So do the mechanisms by which sensory data are sent to the brain for additional processing. In some cases, such as in hearing, sensory processes are mechanical; in others, such as in vision, they involve chemical reactions. We now turn to the unique features of each of the major sensory systems.

According to Weber's law, adding an additional weight to a heavy load is much less noticeable than adding the same weight to a light load.

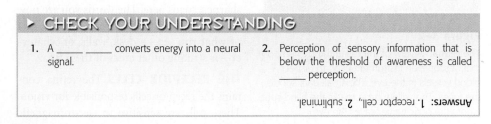

▶ CHECK YOUR UNDERSTANDING

1. A _____ _____ converts energy into a neural signal.

2. Perception of sensory information that is below the threshold of awareness is called _____ perception.

Answers: 1. receptor cell, 2. subliminal.

The Senses

3.2   Describe the basic mechanisms involved in vision, hearing, and the other major senses and explain the theories that describe how these sensory processes work.

Different animal species depend more on some senses than on others. Dogs rely heavily on the sense of smell, bats on hearing, and some fish on taste. But for humans, vision is the most important sense. To understand vision, we need to look first at the parts of the visual system, beginning with the structure of the eye.

VISION

How is light energy converted to sensory information in the process of vision?

The structure of the human eye is shown in **Figure 3–1**. Light enters the eye through the **cornea**, the transparent protective coating over the front part of the eye. It then passes through the **pupil**, the opening in the center of the **iris**, the colored part of the eye. In very bright light, the muscles in the iris contract to make the pupil smaller and thus protect the eye from damage. This contraction also helps us to see better in bright light. In dim light, the muscles relax to open the pupil wider and let in as much light as possible.

Inside the pupil, light moves through the **lens**, which focuses it onto the **retina**, the light-sensitive inner lining of the back of the eyeball. Normally, the lens is focused on a middle distance, and it changes shape to focus on objects that are closer or farther away. To focus on a very close object, tiny muscles contract and make the lens rounder. To focus on something far away, the muscles flatten the lens. Directly behind the lens is a depressed spot in the retina called the **fovea**. (See **Figure 3–2**.) The fovea occupies the center of the visual field, and images that pass through the lens are in sharpest focus here. The words you are now reading are hitting the fovea, while the rest of what you see—a desk, walls, or whatever—is striking other areas of the retina.

THE RECEPTOR CELLS The retina contains the receptor cells responsible for vision. These cells are sensitive to electromagnetic

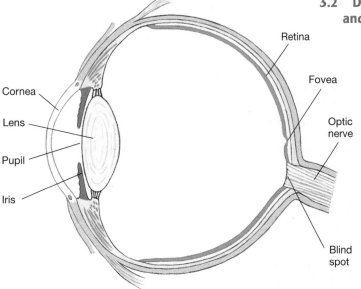

Figure 3–1

A cross section of the human eye. Light enters the eye through the cornea, passes through the pupil, and is focused by the lens onto the retina.

Source: Adapted from Hubel, 1963.

---

cornea The transparent protective coating over the front part of the eye.

---

pupil A small opening in the iris through which light enters the eye.

---

iris The colored part of the eye that regulates the size of the pupil.

---

lens The transparent part of the eye behind the pupil that focuses light onto the retina.

---

retina The lining of the eye containing receptor cells that are sensitive to light.

---

fovea The area of the retina that is the center of the visual field.

Figure 3–2

The retina. A view of the retina through an oph-thalmoscope, an instrument used to inspect blood vessels in the eye. The small dark spot is the fovea. The yellow circle marks the blind spot, where the optic nerve leaves the eye.

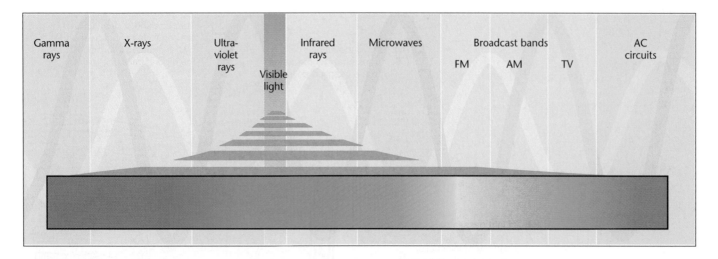

Figure 3–3

The electromagnetic spectrum. The eye is sensitive to only a very small segment of the spectrum, known as visible light.

energy, commonly referred to as light. Although we receive light waves across the full spectrum of wavelengths (See **Figure 3–3**), only a portion of it is *visible light* to us; the rest is other energies. The shortest wavelengths that humans can see are experienced as violet–blue colors; the longest appear as reds.

There are two kinds of receptor cells in the retina—**rods** and **cones**—named for their characteristic shapes. (See **Figure 3–4**.) About 120 million rods and 8 million cones are present in the retina of each eye. Rods and cones differ from each other in a number of ways (see "Summary Table: Rods and Cones"). Rods, chiefly responsible for *night vision*, respond only to varying degrees or intensities of light and dark. Cones, in contrast, allow us to see colors. Operating chiefly in daylight, cones are also less sensitive to light than rods are (MacLeod, 1978). Cones, like color film, work best in relatively bright light. The more sensitive rods, like black-and-white film, respond to much lower levels of illumination.

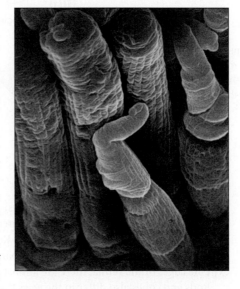

Figure 3–4

Rods and cones. As you can see from this photomicrograph, the rods and cones are named for their shape.

Source: E. R. Lewis, Y. Y. Zeevi, F. S. Werblin. *Brain Research 15* (1969): 559–562. Scanning electron microscopy of vertebrate receptors.

rods Receptor cells in the retina responsible for night vision and perception of brightness.

cones Receptor cells in the retina responsible for color vision.

SUMMARY TABLE

RODS AND CONES

TYPE OF RECEPTOR CELL	FEATURES AND FUNCTIONS	LOCATION	CONNECTIONS
Rods	• Highly sensitive to light • Responsible for night vision • Responsible for perception of brightness	• Missing from the fovea • Concentrated just outside the fovea	Typically, many rods connect to a single bipolar cell.
Cones	• Moderately sensitive to light • Most useful in daylight • Responsible for color vision	• Located mainly in the fovea • Concentrated in the center of the fovea	In the fovea, a single cone typically connects to a single bipolar cell.

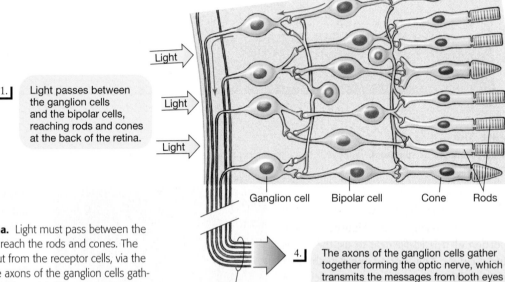

3. Now, the bipolar cells transmit this information to the ganglion cells.

2. The rods and cones, which are sensitive to light, respond by transmitting information to the bipolar cells.

1. Light passes between the ganglion cells and the bipolar cells, reaching rods and cones at the back of the retina.

Light

Light

Light

Ganglion cell   Bipolar cell   Cone   Rods

4. The axons of the ganglion cells gather together forming the optic nerve, which transmits the messages from both eyes to the brain, where they are interpreted as sight.

Optic nerve

Figure 3–5

A close-up of the layers of the retina. Light must pass between the ganglion cells and the bipolar cells to reach the rods and cones. The sensory messages then travel back out from the receptor cells, via the bipolar cells, to the ganglion cells. The axons of the ganglion cells gather together to form the optic nerve, which carries the messages from both eyes to the brain. (See **Figure 3–2**.)

Cones are found mainly, but not exclusively, in the fovea, which contains no rods. The greatest density of cones is in the very center of the fovea, which is where images are projected onto the retina in sharpest focus. Rods predominate just outside the fovea. The greater the distance from the fovea, the sparser both rods and cones become, until, at the extreme edges of the retina, there are almost no cones and only a few rods.

Rods and cones also differ in the ways that they connect to the nerve cells leading to the brain. Both rods and cones connect to specialized neurons called **bipolar cells**, which have only one axon and one dendrite. (See **Figure 3–5**.) In the fovea, cones generally connect with only one bipolar cell—a sort of "private line" arrangement. In contrast, it is normal for several rods to share a single bipolar cell.

The one-to-one connection between cones and bipolar cells in the fovea allows for maximum **visual acuity**—the ability to distinguish fine visual details. To see this for yourself, hold this book about 18 inches from your eyes and look at the "X" in the center of the following line:

This is a test to show how visual X acuity varies across the retina.

Your fovea picks up the "X" and about four letters to each side. This is the area of greatest visual acuity. Notice how your vision drops off for words and letters toward the left or right end of the line. Outside the fovea, visual acuity drops by as much as 50 percent.

When we want to examine something closely, we move it into the sunlight or under a lamp. For activities such as reading, sewing, and writing, the more light, the better: Stronger light stimulates more cones, increasing the likelihood that bipolar cells will start a message to the brain. Several eye diseases and disorders involve difficulties associated with focusing light on the fovea or with degeneration of cells there. Some of these are identified in **Table 3-1**.

bipolar cells Neurons that have only one axon and one dendrite; in the eye, these neurons connect the receptors on the retina to the ganglion cells.

visual acuity The ability to distinguish fine details visually.

> TABLE 3-1 COMMON PROBLEMS OF VISION

Condition	Description	Treatment
Myopia (near-sightedness)	difficulty seeing objects at a distance	corrective lenses or corrective surgery (Lasix)
Presbyopia (far-sightedness)	difficulty seeing close or highly detailed objects	corrective lenses or corrective surgery (Lasix)
Astigmatism	blurred vision due to irregularities in the shape of the lens or retina	corrective lenses or corrective surgery (Lasix)
Cataract	a thin cloudy covering develops on the surface of the eye	surgery to remove the cataract
Glaucoma	build up of pressure within the eye that can lead to blindness	diet and/or medication
Macular degeneration	degeneration of retinal cells, usually in and around the fovea; eventually causes blindness	no treatment at present
Retinitis pigmentosa	hereditary disorder that involves deterioration of cells in the retina; eventually causes blindness	no treatment at present

ADAPTATION Earlier in the chapter, we introduced the term *adaptation*, the process by which our senses adjust to different levels of stimulation. In the case of vision, adaptation occurs as the sensitivity of rods and cones changes according to how much light is available. When you go from bright sunlight into a dimly lit theater, your cones are initially fairly insensitive to light, and you can see little as you look for a seat. During the first 10 minutes in the dark, the cones become increasingly sensitive to the dim light, and your vision improves. After about 10 minutes, the cones do not become any more sensitive. But the rods continue adapting until they reach their maximum sensitivity, about 30 minutes after you enter a darkened room; your best vision will be after the rods have adapted. There is usually not enough energy in very dim light, however, to stimulate many cones, so you see the world in only black, white, and gray. The process by which rods and cones become more sensitive to light in response to lowered levels of illumination is called **dark adaptation**.

Problems with dark adaptation account in part for the much greater incidence of highway accidents at night (Leibowitz & Owens, 1977). When people drive at night, their eyes shift from the darkened interior of the car, to the road area illuminated by headlights, to the darker areas at the side of the road. Unlike the situation in a darkened movie theater, these changing night-driving conditions do not permit complete adaptation of either rods or cones, so neither system is operating at maximum efficiency. Because most drivers are generally unaware of the deterioration of their vision at night, they may overestimate their ability to stop in time to avoid an accident.

In the reverse process, **light adaptation**, the rods and cones become less sensitive to light. By the time you leave a movie theater, your rods and cones have grown very sensitive, and all the neurons fire at once when you go into bright outdoor light. You squint and shield your eyes, and your irises contract—all of which reduces the amount of light entering your pupils and striking your retinas. As light adaptation proceeds, the rods and cones become less sensitive to stimulation by light. Within about a minute, both rods and cones are fully adapted to the light, and you no longer need to shield your eyes.

You can observe the effects of dark and light adaptation by staring continuously at the dot in the center of the upper square in **Figure 3–6** for about 20 seconds and then shifting your gaze to the dot in the lower square. A gray-and-white pattern should appear in the lower square. (When looking at the lower square, if you blink your eyes or shade the book from bright light, the illusion will be even stronger.) When you look at the lower square, the striped areas that were black in the upper square will now seem to be white, and the areas that were white in the upper square will now appear gray. This **afterimage** appears because the part of the retina that was exposed to the dark stripes of the upper square becomes

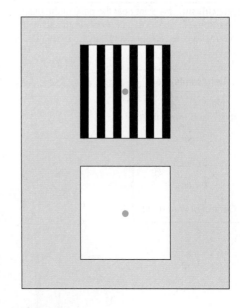

Figure 3–6

An afterimage. First stare continuously at the center of the upper square for about 20 seconds, then look at the dot in the lower square. Within a moment, a gray-and-white afterimage should appear inside the lower square.

dark adaptation Increased sensitivity of rods and cones in darkness.

light adaptation Decreased sensitivity of rods and cones in bright light.

afterimage Sensory experience that occurs after a visual stimulus has been removed.

Figure 3–7

Finding your blind spot. To locate your blind spot, hold the book about a foot away from your eyes. Then close your right eye, stare at the "X," and slowly move the book toward you and away from you until the red dot disappears.

ganglion cells Neurons that connect the bipolar cells in the eyes to the brain.

optic nerve The bundle of axons of ganglion cells that carries neural messages from each eye to the brain.

blind spot The place on the retina where the axons of all the ganglion cells leave the eye and where there are no receptors.

optic chiasm The point near the base of the brain where some fibers in the optic nerve from each eye cross to the other side of the brain.

Left visual field   Right visual field

| **Left Hemisphere** |
| Right side of body touch and movement |
| Language |
| Speech |
| Writing |
| Control of right hand |

| **Right Hemisphere** |
| Left side of body touch and movement |
| Spatial abilities |
| Control of left hand |

Eye

Optic nerve

Optic chiasm

Neural pathways

Left occipital lobe   Right occipital lobe

Figure 3–8

The neural connections of the visual system. Messages about the red-colored area in the left visual field of each eye travel to the right occipital lobe; information about the blue area in the right visual field of each eye goes to the left occipital lobe. The crossover point is the optic chiasm.

Source: Adapted from "The Split Brain of Man," by Michael S. Gazzaniga. Copyright © 1967. Adapted with permission.

more sensitive. (It becomes adapted to the dark.) The area exposed to the white part of the upper square becomes less sensitive. (It becomes adapted to the light.) When you shift your eyes to the lower square, the less sensitive parts of the retina produces the sensation of gray rather than white. This afterimage fades within a minute as the retina adapts again, this time to the solid white square.

In the real world, our eyes seldom adapt completely, because light stimulation is rarely focused on the same receptor cells long enough for them to become totally insensitive. Rather, small involuntary eye movements keep the image moving slightly on the retina, so the receptor cells never have time to adapt completely.

FROM EYE TO BRAIN We have so far directed our attention to the eye, but messages from the eye must travel to the brain in order for a visual experience to occur. To begin with, rods and cones are connected to bipolar cells in many different numbers and combinations. (See again **Figure 3–5**). Eventually, these bipolar cells hook up with the **ganglion cells** leading out of the eye. The axons of the ganglion cells join to form the **optic nerve**, which carries messages from each eye to the brain. The place on the retina where the axons of all the ganglion cells join to form the optic nerve is called the **blind spot**. This area contains no receptor cells. Hence, even when light from a small object is focused directly on the blind spot, the object will not be seen. (See **Figure 3–7**).

Although there are more than 125 million rods and cones in each retina, there are only about 1 million ganglion cells in the optic nerve. The information collected by the 125 million receptor cells must be combined and reduced to fit the mere 1 million "wires" that lead from each eye to the brain. Research indicates that most of this consolidation takes place in the interconnection between receptors and ganglion cells (Hubel & Livingstone, 1990; Kolb, 2003).

After the nerve fibers that make up the optic nerves leave the eyes, they separate, and some of them cross to the other side of the head at the **optic chiasm**. (See **Figure 3–8**.) The nerve fibers from the right side of each eye travel to the right hemisphere of the brain; those from the left side of each eye travel to the left hemisphere. Thus, visual information about any object in the left visual field, the area to the left of the viewer, will go to the right hemisphere (the pathway traced by the red line in Figure 3–8). Similarly, information about any object in the right visual field, the area to the right of the viewer, will go to the left hemisphere (the pathway traced by the blue line). (You can refer back to Figures 2–9 and 2–10 in Chapter 2, "The Biological Basis of Behavior," to recall how researchers took advantage of the split processing of the two visual fields to study split-brain patients.)

The optic nerves carry their messages to various parts of the brain. Some messages reach the area of the brain that controls the reflex movements that adjust the size of the pupil. Others go to the region that directs the eye muscles to change the shape of the lens. But the main destinations for messages from the retina are the visual projection areas of the occipital lobe of the cerebral cortex, where the complex coded messages from the retina are registered and interpreted in the process called visual perception.

How does the brain register and interpret these signals, "translating" light into visual images? In research for which they received a Nobel Prize, David H. Hubel and Torsten N. Wiesel (1959, 1979) found that certain brain cells—called **feature detectors**—are highly specialized to detect particular elements of the visual field, such as horizontal or vertical lines. Other feature-detector cells register more complex information, with some being sensitive to movement, others to depth, and still others to color. These different types of feature detectors send messages to specific, but nearby, regions of the cortex. Visual experience, then, depends on the brain's ability to combine these pieces of information into a meaningful image.

COLOR VISION Humans, like many other animals, see in color, at least during the day. Color vision is highly adaptive for an animal that needs to know when fruit is ripe or how to avoid poisonous plants and berries (which tend to be brightly hued), as our ancestors did. There are different ideas, however, about how it is that we are able to see colors.

If you look closely at a color television screen, you will see that the picture is actually made up of tiny red, green, and blue dots that blend together to give all possible hues. The same principle is at work in our own ability to see thousands of colors. For centuries, scientists have known that they could produce all of the basic hues humans can see by mixing together only a few lights of different colors. (See **Figure 3–9**.) Red, green, and blue lights—the primary colors for light mixtures—can be combined to create any hue. For example, red and green lights combine to give yellow; red and blue lights combine to make magenta. Combining red, green, and blue lights in equal intensities produces white. The process of mixing lights of different wavelengths is called **additive color mixing**, because each light adds additional wavelengths to the overall mix.

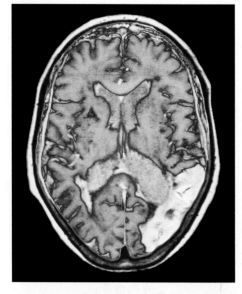

This scan shows extensive damage to the right occipital cortex of the brain. Such damage probably would result in impaired vision for objects in the right visual field.

feature detectors Specialized brain cells that only respond to particular elements in the visual field such as movement or lines of specific orientation.

additive color mixing The process of mixing lights of different wavelengths to create new hues.

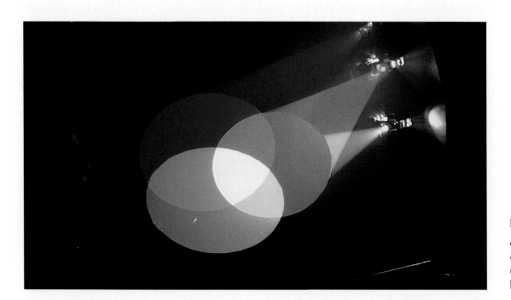

Figure 3–9

Additive color mixing. Mixing light waves is an additive process. When red and green lights are combined, the resulting hue is yellow. Adding blue light to the other two yields white light.

trichromatic theory The theory of color vision that holds that all color perception derives from three different color receptors in the retina (usually red, green, and blue receptors).

color blindness Partial or total inability to perceive hues.

opponent-process theory Theory of color vision that holds that three sets of color receptors (yellow–blue, red–green, black–white) respond to determine the color you experience.

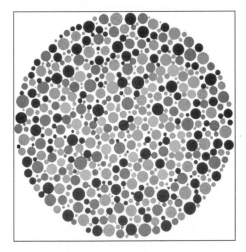

Figure 3–10

Experiencing color blindness. Perceiving the number 96 embedded in the mass of green circles is easy, except for people who have red–green color blindness.

Source: Ishihara, *Test for Color Deficiency.* Courtesy of the Isshinkai Foundation founded by Prof. Ishihara, Tokyo, Japan.

Color mixing with paint follows different rules than color mixing with light. With light, different wavelengths add together, but the color of paint depends not on which wavelengths are *present*, but rather on which are *absorbed* and which are *reflected*. For example, red paint absorbs light from the blue end of the spectrum and reflects light from the red end. Since paint mixing depends on what colors are absorbed, or subtracted, and which are reflected, the process is called subtractive color mixing.

In the early 1800s, the German physiologist Hermann von Helmholtz proposed a theory of color vision based on additive color mixing. Helmholtz reasoned that, since there are three primary colors of light, the eye must contain three types of cones: some that are sensitive to red light, others that pick up green, and still others that respond most strongly to blue–violet. According to this view, color experiences come from the combination of signals from these three receptors. Helmholtz's explanation of color vision is known as **trichromatic** (or **three-color**) **theory**.

Trichromatic theory explains how three primary colors can be combined to produce any other hue. In fact, people with normal color vision are called *trichromats* because they sense all three primary colors of light. However, approximately 10 percent of men and 1 percent of women display some form of **color blindness**, which is not well explained by trichromatic theory. People with the two most common forms of color blindness are called *dichromats* because they see the world in terms of only reds and greens (the red–green dichromats) or of blues and yellows (the blue–yellow dichromats). (See **Figure 3–10**.) Among humans, *monochromats*, who see no color at all, but respond only to shades of light and dark, are extremely rare.

Trichromatic theory also does not explain some aspects of normal color vision. Why, for example, don't people with normal color vision ever see a light or a pigment that can be described as "reddish green" or "yellowish blue"? And what accounts for *color afterimages*? (See **Figure 3–11**.) In the later nineteenth century, another German scientist, Edward Hering, proposed an alternative theory of color vision that can explain these phenomena. Hering proposed the existence of three *pairs* of color receptors: a yellow–blue pair and a red–green pair that determine the color you see; and a black–white pair that determine the brightness of the colors you see. The yellow–blue pair can relay messages about yellow *or* blue, but not messages about yellow *and* blue light at the same time; the same is true for red–green receptors. Thus, the members of each pair work in opposition to each other, which explains why we never see yellowish blue or reddish green. Hering's theory is now known as the **opponent-process theory**.

Opponent-process theory also explains color afterimages. While you were looking at the green stripes in Figure 3–11, the red–green receptors were sending "green" messages to your brain, but they were also adapting to the stimulation by becoming less sensitive to green light. When you later looked at the white page (made up of light from all parts of the spectrum), the red–green receptors responded vigorously to wavelengths in the

Figure 3–11

Afterimage. Stare at the white spot in the center of the flag for about 30 seconds. Then look at a blank piece of white paper, and you will see an afterimage in complementary colors. Although the flag is printed in green, yellow, and black, its afterimage will appear in red, blue, and white.

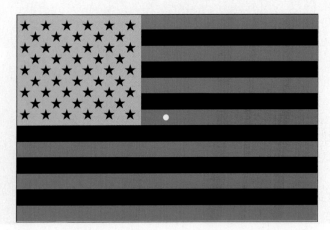

red portion of the spectrum, so you saw red stripes instead of green. Hering's opponent-process theory also explains the color experiences of dichromats. If the red–green system fails, then all that is left is the yellow–blue system, and vice versa.

Today, psychologists believe that both the trichromatic and opponent-process theories are valid, but at different stages of the visual process. As trichromatic theory asserts, there are three kinds of cones for color. (Some are most sensitive to violet–blue light, others are most responsive to green light, and still others are most sensitive to yellow light—not red light, as Helmholtz contended.) Thus, trichromatic theory corresponds fairly closely to the types of color receptors that actually exist in the retina. The opponent-process theory, however, closely reflects what happens along the neural pathways that connect the eye and the brain. Together, trichromatic theory and opponent-process theory can account for most color phenomena.

HEARING

How is sound energy converted to sensory information in the process of hearing (audition)?

If a tree falls in the forest and no one is there, does the tree make a sound? A psychologist would answer the philosopher's question about the tree falling in the forest this way: "There are sound waves, but there is no sound or noise." Sounds and noise are psychological experiences created by the brain.

SOUND The sensation we call **sound** is our brain's interpretation of the ebb and flow of air molecules pounding on our eardrums. When something in the environment moves, pressure is caused as molecules of air or fluid collide with one another and then move apart again. This pressure transmits energy at every collision, creating **sound waves**. The simplest sound wave—what we hear as a pure tone—can be pictured as the wave shown in **Figure 3–12**. The tuning fork vibrates, causing the molecules of air first to contract and then to expand. The **frequency** of the waves is measured in cycles per second, expressed in a unit called hertz (Hz). Frequency primarily determines the **pitch** of the sound—how high or how low it is. The human ear responds to frequencies from approximately 20 Hz to 20,000 Hz. A double bass can reach down to about 50 Hz; a piano can reach as high as 5,000 Hz.

The height of the sound wave represents its **amplitude**, which, together with frequency, determines the perceived loudness of a sound. Sound intensity is measured in *decibels*. (See **Figure 3–13**.) As we grow older, we typically lose some of our ability to hear soft sounds, but we can hear loud sounds as well as ever.

Like our other senses, hearing undergoes adaptation and can function optimally under a wide variety of conditions. City residents enjoying a weekend in the country, for example, may be struck at first by how quiet everything seems. But after a while they may find that the country starts to sound very noisy because they have adapted to the quieter environment.

sound A psychological experience created by the brain in response to changes in air pressure that are received by the auditory system.

sound waves Changes in pressure caused when molecules of air or fluid collide with one another and then move apart again.

frequency The number of cycles per second in a wave; in sound, the primary determinant of pitch.

pitch Auditory experience corresponding primarily to frequency of sound vibrations, resulting in a higher or lower tone.

amplitude The magnitude of a wave; in sound, the primary determinant of loudness.

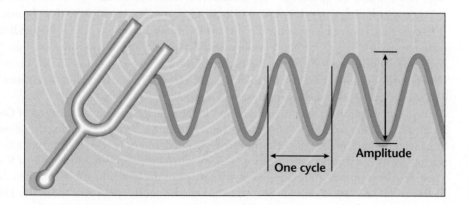

Figure 3–12

Sound waves. As the tuning fork vibrates, it alternately compresses and expands the molecules of air, creating a sound wave.

Figure 3–13

A decibel scale for several common sounds.
Prolonged exposure to sounds above 85 decibels can cause permanent damage to the ears, as can even brief exposure to sounds near the pain threshold.

Source: Adapted from Dunkle, 1982.

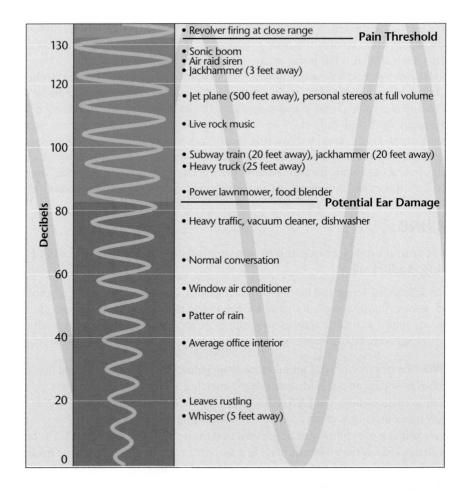

Decibels	
130	• Revolver firing at close range — **Pain Threshold**
	• Sonic boom
	• Air raid siren
120	• Jackhammer (3 feet away)
	• Jet plane (500 feet away), personal stereos at full volume
100	• Live rock music
	• Subway train (20 feet away), jackhammer (20 feet away)
	• Heavy truck (25 feet away)
	• Power lawnmower, food blender — **Potential Ear Damage**
80	• Heavy traffic, vacuum cleaner, dishwasher
	• Normal conversation
60	• Window air conditioner
	• Patter of rain
40	• Average office interior
20	• Leaves rustling
	• Whisper (5 feet away)
0	

timbre The quality or texture of sound; caused by overtones.

oval window Membrane across the opening between the middle ear and inner ear that conducts vibrations to the cochlea.

cochlea Part of the inner ear containing fluid that can vibrate, which in turn causes the basilar membrane to vibrate.

basilar membrane Membrane in the cochlea of the inner ear that responds to vibrations; it contains sense receptors for sound.

organ of Corti Structure on the surface of the basilar membrane that contains the receptor cells for hearing.

auditory nerve The bundle of axons that carries signals from each ear to the brain.

The sounds that we hear seldom result from pure tones. Unlike a tuning fork, which can produce a tone that is almost pure, musical instruments produce *overtones*—accompanying sound waves that are different multiples of the frequency of the basic tone. This complex pattern of overtones determines the **timbre**, or texture, of the sound. When playing the same note, a piano sounds different from a violin because of differences in the overtones of the two instruments. Music synthesizers can mimic different instruments electronically because they produce not only pure tones, but also the overtones that correspond to the timbre of different musical instruments.

THE EAR Hearing begins when sound waves are gathered by the *outer* ear and passed along to the eardrum (see **Figure 3–14**) causing it to vibrate. The quivering of the eardrum prompts three tiny bones in the *middle* ear—the *hammer*, the *anvil*, and the *stirrup*—to hit each other in sequence and thus carry the vibrations to the *inner* ear. The last of these three bones, the stirrup, is attached to a membrane called the **oval window**. Vibrations of the oval window, in turn, are transmitted to the fluid inside a snail-shaped structure called the **cochlea**. The cochlea is divided lengthwise by the **basilar membrane**, which is stiff near the oval window but gradually becomes more flexible toward its other end. When the fluid in the cochlea begins to move, the basilar membrane ripples in response.

Lying on top of the basilar membrane and moving in sync with it is the **organ of Corti**. Here the messages from the sound waves finally reach the receptor cells for the sense of hearing: thousands of tiny hair cells that are embedded in the organ of Corti (Spoendlin & Schrott, 1989). As you can see in **Figure 3–15**, each hair cell is topped by a bundle of fibers. These fibers are pushed and pulled by the vibrations of the basilar membrane. When these fibers move, the receptor cells send a signal through the **auditory nerve** to the brain. There, auditory messages are routed to several locations. Some go to the brain centers that coordinate the movements of the eyes, head, and ears. Others travel through the reticular

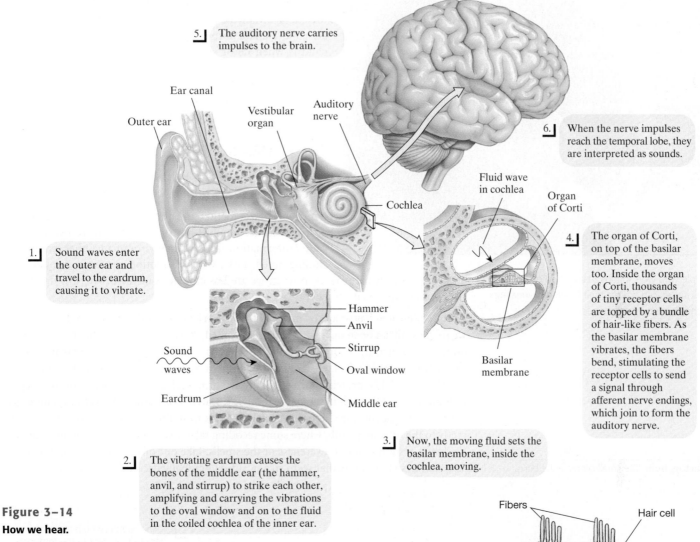

5. The auditory nerve carries impulses to the brain.

6. When the nerve impulses reach the temporal lobe, they are interpreted as sounds.

Ear canal

Outer ear

Vestibular organ

Auditory nerve

Cochlea

Fluid wave in cochlea

Organ of Corti

Basilar membrane

1. Sound waves enter the outer ear and travel to the eardrum, causing it to vibrate.

4. The organ of Corti, on top of the basilar membrane, moves too. Inside the organ of Corti, thousands of tiny receptor cells are topped by a bundle of hair-like fibers. As the basilar membrane vibrates, the fibers bend, stimulating the receptor cells to send a signal through afferent nerve endings, which join to form the auditory nerve.

Hammer
Anvil
Stirrup
Oval window
Middle ear

Sound waves

Eardrum

3. Now, the moving fluid sets the basilar membrane, inside the cochlea, moving.

2. The vibrating eardrum causes the bones of the middle ear (the hammer, anvil, and stirrup) to strike each other, amplifying and carrying the vibrations to the oval window and on to the fluid in the coiled cochlea of the inner ear.

Figure 3–14
How we hear.

formation (which we examined in Chapter 2: "The Biological Basis of Behavior"). But the primary destinations for these auditory messages are the auditory areas in the temporal lobes of the two cerebral hemispheres. (See **Figure 2–8**.) Our sensory experience of hearing is processed for the most part in these brain regions.

HEARING DISORDERS Because the mechanisms that allow us to hear are so complicated, a large number of problems can interfere with hearing. Deafness, one of the most common concerns, may result from defects in the middle ear—for example, the eardrum may be damaged, or the small bones of the middle ear may not work properly. Deafness may also occur because of damage to the basilar membrane, the hair cells, or the auditory nerve, caused by disease, infections, and even long-term overexposure to loud noise. Of the 28 million Americans with hearing loss, about 10 million are victims of overexposure to noise. The chief culprits are leaf blowers, chain saws, snowmobiles, jet planes, and personal stereo systems including iPods. (Refer back to **Figure 3–13**; Goldstein, 1999; Leary, 1990.)

A number of remedies are available for irreversible hearing loss. New digital technology has made hearing aids, which simply amplify sound, more precise by enhancing only those frequencies the person does not hear. Surgery can help people with conductive hearing loss due to a stiffening of the connections between the bones (hammer, anvil, and stirrup) of the middle ear. Cochlear implants offer hope to people who suffer from deafness due to hair cell damage within the cochlea (Clark, 1998; Fischetti, 2003). Platinum electrodes are inserted into the cochlea to bypass the damaged hair cells and convey electrical

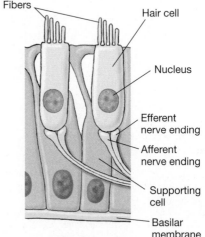

Fibers

Hair cell

Nucleus

Efferent nerve ending

Afferent nerve ending

Supporting cell

Basilar membrane

Figure 3–15

A detailed drawing of a hair cell. At the top of each hair cell is a bundle of fibers. If the fibers bend as much as 100 trillionths of a meter, the receptor cells transmit a sensory message to the brain.

Source: Adapted from "The Hair Cells of the Inner Ear," by A. J. Hudspeth, © 1983. Illustrated by Bunji Tagawa for *Scientific American*. Adapted with permission from the Estate of Bunji Tagawa.

People who work in jobs that involve exposure to loud noises can protect their hearing by wearing sound-deadening earphones.

olfactory bulb The smell center in the brain.

signals from a miniature sound synthesizer directly to the auditory nerve. Many of the people who receive cochlear implants are children. Not surprisingly, the younger a hearing-impaired child is when he or she receives cochlear implants, the more speech recognition and language development are improved (Kileny, Zwolan, & Ashbaugh, 2001). Cochlear implants can also be used to treat severe causes of tinnitus, a high-pitched ringing in the ears. (Johansson & Arlinger, 2003.)

THE OTHER SENSES

What mechanisms are involved in the chemical, the kinesthetic and vestibular, and the skin senses?

Researchers have focused most of their attention on vision and hearing because humans rely primarily on these two senses to gather information about their environment. Other senses—including smell, taste, balance, motion, pressure, temperature, and pain—are also at play, even when we are less conscious of them. We turn first to the chemical senses: smell and taste.

SMELL Research has unlocked many of the mysteries of our other senses, but exactly how we smell is still an open question (Keller & Vosshall, 2004). Our sense of smell for common odors is activated by a complex protein produced in a nasal gland. As we breathe, a fine mist of this protein, called odorant binding protein (OBP), is sprayed through a duct in the tip of the nose. The protein binds with tiny airborne molecules that then activate receptor cells located high in each nasal cavity, though researchers are still at a loss to explain exactly how that happens. (See **Figure 3–16**.) The axons from these millions of receptors go directly to the **olfactory bulb**, where some recoding takes place. Then messages are routed to the brain, resulting in our awareness of the smells. Like our other senses, smell undergoes adaptation, so that odors that seem strong at first gradually become less noticeable.

Figure 3–16

The human olfactory system. The sense of smell is triggered when odor molecules in the air reach the olfactory receptors located inside the top of the nose. Inhaling and exhaling odor molecules from food does much to give food its flavorful "taste."

Source: Human Anatomy and Physiology by Anthony J. Gaudin and Kenneth C. Jones. Copyright © 1989. Reprinted by permission.

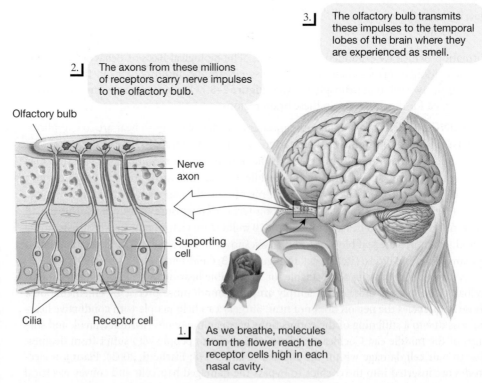

3. The olfactory bulb transmits these impulses to the temporal lobes of the brain where they are experienced as smell.

2. The axons from these millions of receptors carry nerve impulses to the olfactory bulb.

Olfactory bulb

Nerve axon

Supporting cell

Cilia

Receptor cell

1. As we breathe, molecules from the flower reach the receptor cells high in each nasal cavity.

Humans rely less on their sense of smell than do many animals, especially mammals. Hamsters and ground squirrels, for example, can recognize members of their families by their smell, even if they have been separated from them at birth (Mateo & Johnston, 2000). Odors that are produced to communicate with others are called **pheromones**.

Humans, like other mammals, have receptors for pheromones (Mateo, 2002). Although we are seldom aware of these smells, they can have an effect on our behavior. For example, pheromones can affect the menstrual cycles of women (McClintock, 1999; Stern & McClintock, 1998). Also, both men and women provide higher ratings of sexual attractiveness of members of the opposite sex when they are exposed to their pheromones (Scholey, Bosworth, & Dimitraki, 1999; Thorne, Neave, Scholey, Moss, & Fink, 2002). Yet, pheromones do not appear to instigate sexual behavior in humans in as direct a way as they operate in other mammals, indicating that the sense of smell in humans is often secondary to vision and hearing.

TASTE To understand taste, we must distinguish it from flavor—a complex interaction of taste and smell. Try holding your nose when you eat. You will notice that most of the food's flavor will disappear, and you will experience only the basic taste qualities: *sweet, sour, salty,* and *bitter*.

The receptor cells for the sense of taste are housed in the **taste buds**, most of which are found on the tip, sides, and back of the tongue. The tip of the tongue is most sensitive to sweetness and saltiness; the back, to bitterness; and the sides, to sourness (see **Figure 3–17**), although each area can distinguish all taste qualities to some degree (Bartoshuk & Beauchamp, 1994). Because the number of taste buds decreases with age, older people often lose interest in food—they simply cannot taste it as well as they used to.

The taste buds are embedded in the tongue's papillae, bumps that you can see if you look at your tongue in the mirror. When we eat something, the chemical substances in the food dissolve in saliva and go into the crevices between the papillae, where they come into contact with the taste receptors. The chemical interaction between food substances and the taste cells causes adjacent neurons to fire, sending a nerve impulse to the parietal lobe of the brain and to the limbic system.

Taste, like the other senses, undergoes adaptation. For example, when you first start eating salted peanuts or potato chips, the saltiness is quite strong, but after a while it becomes less noticeable. Furthermore, exposure to one quality of taste can modify other taste sensations—after brushing your teeth in the morning, for instance, you may notice that your orange juice has lost its sweetness.

KINESTHETIC AND VESTIBULAR SENSES

The **kinesthetic senses** provide information about the speed and direction of our movement in space (Carello & Turvey, 2003). More specifically, they relay information about muscle movement, changes in posture, and strain on muscles and joints. Specialized nerve endings called **stretch receptors** are attached to muscle fibers, and different nerve endings called **Golgi tendon organs** are attached to the tendons, which connect muscles to bones. Together these two types of receptors provide constant feedback from the stretching and contraction of individual muscles. The information from these receptors travels via the spinal cord to the cortex of the parietal lobes, the same brain area that perceives the sense of touch.

Certain animal species rely more on their sense of smell than humans do. This dog has been trained to use its keen sense of smell to help security forces at the airport.

pheromones Chemicals that communicate information to other organisms through smell.

taste buds Structures on the tongue that contain the receptor cells for taste.

kinesthetic senses Senses of muscle movement, posture, and strain on muscles and joints.

stretch receptors Receptors that sense muscle stretch and contraction.

Golgi tendon organs Receptors that sense movement of the tendons, which connect muscle to bone.

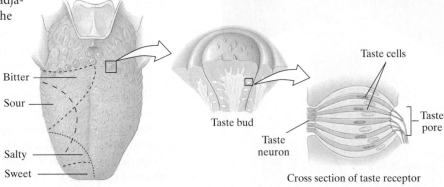

Bitter
Sour
Salty
Sweet

Taste cells
Taste bud
Taste neuron
Taste pore
Cross section of taste receptor

1. Different areas on the tongue are slightly more sensitive to different tastes.

2. When we eat, chemicals in the food dissolve in saliva and come into contact with the taste cells (receptors) within the taste buds.

3. Now, adjacent neurons fire, sending nerve impulses to the brain's parietal lobe, where the messages are perceived as taste.

Figure 3–17

The structure of a taste bud. The sensory receptors for taste are found primarily on the tongue. Taste cells can detect only sweet, sour, salty, and bitter qualities. All other tastes result from different combinations of these taste sensations.

This dancer is utilizing information provided by both her kinesthetic and her vestibular senses. Her kinesthetic senses are relaying messages pertaining to muscle strain and movements; her vestibular senses are supplying feedback about her body position in space.

vestibular senses The senses of equilibrium and body position in space.

People who have impairments in one sensory system must rely on their other senses. This blind man is using a Braille device, which uses raised patterns of dots to represent letters of the alphabet, to read.

The **vestibular senses** provide information about our orientation or position in space (Leigh, 1994). We use this information to determine which way is up and which way is down. Birds and fish also rely on these senses to determine in which direction they are heading when they cannot see well. Like hearing, the vestibular senses originate in the inner ear, where hair cells serve as the sense organs. There are actually two kinds of vestibular sensation. The first one, which relays messages about the speed and direction of body rotation, arises in the three *semicircular canals* of the inner ear. As in the cochlea, each canal is filled with fluid that shifts hair bundles, which in turn stimulate hair cells, sending a message to the brain about the speed and direction of body rotation.

The second vestibular sense gives us information about gravitation and movement forward and backward, up and down. This sense arises from the two *vestibular sacs* that lie between the semicircular canals and the cochlea. Both sacs are filled with a jellylike fluid that contains millions of tiny crystals. When the body moves horizontally or vertically, the crystals bend hair bundles, prompting a sensory message.

The nerve impulses from both vestibular organs travel to the brain along the auditory nerve, but their ultimate destinations in the brain are still something of a mystery. Certain messages from the vestibular system go to the cerebellum, which controls many of the reflexes involved in coordinated movement. Others reach the areas that regulate the internal body organs, and some find their way to the parietal lobe of the cerebral cortex for analysis and response.

Perhaps we are most acutely aware of our vestibular senses when we experience *motion sickness*. Certain kinds of motion, such as riding in ships, cars, airplanes, even on camels and elephants, trigger strong reactions in some people. According to one theory, motion sickness stems from discrepancies between visual information and vestibular sensations (Stern & Koch, 1996). In other words, our eyes and our body are sending our brain contradictory information. The same thing occurs when we watch an automobile chase scene that was filmed from inside a moving car: Our eyes tell our brain that we are moving, but the organs in our inner ear insist that we are sitting still. Susceptibility to motion sickness appears to be related to both race and genetics: People of Asian ancestry are particularly susceptible to motion sickness, which also seems to be inherited (Muth et al., 1994).

THE SKIN SENSES Our skin is our largest sense organ—a person 6 feet tall has about 21 square feet of skin. Our skin protects us from the environment, holds in body fluids, regulates our internal temperature, and contains receptors for our sense of touch, which plays an important role in human interaction and emotion.

Skin receptors give rise to sensations of pressure, temperature, and pain, but the relationship between the receptors and our sensory experiences is a subtle one. Researchers believe that our brains draw on complex information about the patterns of activity received from many different receptors to detect and discriminate among skin sensations. For example, our skin has "cold fibers" that increase their firing rate as the skin cools down and that slow their firing when the skin heats up. Conversely, we have "warm fibers" that accelerate their firing rate when the skin gets warm and

[UNDERSTANDING OURSELVES]

MASSAGE: RUBBING PEOPLE THE WRONG WAY?

Therapeutic massage is one of the most ancient practices related to medicine. The first book on the subject was written in China approximately 3000 B.C. For some time, however, the reputation of massage suffered, and it came to be regarded as something of an unproven, "alternative" practice. Recently, however, medical and psychological researchers have started taking another look at some of the benefits of a "hands-on" approach. Recent research indicates that massage therapy can

- *Help babies grow.* In a now-famous study, researchers compared premature infants who were massaged three times a day for 15 minutes at a time with a control group that was left untouched in their incubators. (Field, 1986). Their results have had significant effects on the way parents and hospital staff care for premature infants (Dieter, Field, Hernandez, Emory, & Redzepi, 2003). The researchers found that:
  - Babies who were massaged gained weight much more quickly than those who were not. Significantly, the mas-

saged infants did not eat more than the others: Their accelerated weight gain appeared to be due solely to the effect of physical touch on their metabolism.

- The massaged babies were subsequently more responsive to faces and rattles and were generally more active than other babies.
- Because of their comparatively rapid growth, the massaged infants were discharged from the hospital an average of six days earlier than the nonmassaged infants were.
- Eight months later, the massaged infants maintained their weight advantage while performing better on tests of motor ability.
- *Reduce pain.* Adults also benefit from touching (Field, 2001). A study of 129 patients suffering from long-term musculoskeletal pain also found that massage therapy was effective in reducing pain. A three-month follow-up of these patients revealed, however, that their symptoms

reappeared after the therapy had been discontinued (Hasson, Arnetz, Jelveus, & Edelstam, 2004). Thus, the long-term benefits of massage therapy are still open to question.

- *Alleviate anxiety and depression.* One review of 37 studies evaluating massage therapy for adults with anxiety and depression (Moyer, Rounds, & Hannum, 2004) found that a single massage therapy session could effectively reduce immediate feelings of anxiety. Multiple sessions were effective at reducing long-term anxiety and depression, as well as alleviating pain. The authors of this study concluded that multiple applications of massage therapy produced benefits similar to those of psychotherapy when used to treat anxiety and depression. Although additional research is needed before the benefits of massage therapy are fully understood and begin to gain widespread acceptance among therapists, results like these show promise.

---

that slow down when the skin cools. The brain may use the combined information from these two sets of fibers as the basis for determining skin temperature. If both sets are activated at once, the brain may read their combined pattern of firings as "hot" (Craig & Bushnell, 1994). Thus, you might sometimes think that you are touching something hot when you are really touching something warm and something cool at the same time, a phenomenon known as *paradoxical heat.* (See **Figure 3–18**.)

The skin senses are remarkably sensitive. For example, skin displacement of as little as 0.00004 of an inch can result in a sensation of pressure. Moreover, various parts of the body differ greatly in their sensitivity to pressure: Your face and fingertips are extremely sensitive, whereas your legs, feet, and back are much less so (Weinstein, 1968). It is this remarkable sensitivity in our fingertips that makes possible Braille touch reading, which requires identifying patterns of tiny raised dots distributed over a very small area. Therapeutic massage also depends for success on the skin senses (See **Box**, Understanding Ourselves).

Like other senses, the skin senses undergo various kinds of sensory adaptation. When we first get into a bath, it may be uncomfortably hot, but in a few minutes, we adapt to the heat, just as our eyes adapt to darkness. Skin senses are also influenced by our expectations. When someone

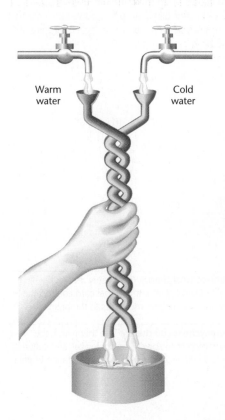

Figure 3–18

Paradoxical heat. Touching a warm pipe and a cold pipe at the same time causes two sets of skin receptors to signal at once to the brain. The brain reads their combined pattern of firings as "hot," a phenomenon known as paradoxical heat.

tickles us, our skin senses respond with excitement, but tickling ourselves produces no effect. Clearly, the brain draws on many sources of information in interpreting the sense of touch.

PAIN Individuals vary widely in both their *pain threshold* (the amount of stimulation required to feel pain) and their *pain tolerance* (the amount of pain with which they can cope). Culture and belief systems also play an important role in how pain is experienced. How do psychologists explain why the experience of pain differs among individuals?

One commonly accepted view is the **gate-control theory** of pain (Melzack, 1980; Wall & Melzack, 1989). According to this theory, a "neurological gate" in the spinal cord controls the transmission of pain impulses to the brain. If the gate is open, we experience more pain than we do if it is closed. Whether the gate is closed or open depends on a complex competition between two different types of sensory nerve fibers—large fibers that tend to "close the gate" and small fibers that "open the gate" when they are stimulated, letting the pain messages get through to the brain. Moreover, certain areas of the brain stem can also close the gate from above by sending down signals to fibers in the spinal cord to close the gate. Differences in how individuals experience pain may be due to the number of small and large fibers a person has. Also, some people may have faulty neurological gates, thereby experiencing more or less pain than others do.

Some psychologists believe that the gate-control theory oversimplifies the complex experience we call pain. **Biopsychosocial theory** holds that pain sensations involve three interrelated mechanisms. *Biological mechanisms* involve the degree to which tissue is injured and the way that our pain pathways have adapted. Genetics also appears to account for some of the individual differences in the perception of pain. Scientists have recently identified a small variation in a specific gene which seems to account for at least some of the reason why different people experience different amounts of pain. Not surprisingly, this gene produces an enzyme involved in the production of endorphins in the brain, which, as we saw in Chapter 2, are implicated in regulating pain and mood (Zubieta et al., 2003).

Psychological mechanisms involve our thoughts, beliefs, and emotions concerning pain. For example, when hospital patients were led to believe that a medical procedure was not painful, they actually reported experiencing less pain than people who had not been given this information (DiMatteo & Friedman, 1982).

Social mechanisms, such as the degree of family support or cultural expectations, can influence our experience of pain. For example, when people believe that their pain is manageable and that they can cope, they often experience less pain, perhaps because these positive beliefs cause higher brain centers to reduce or block pain signals (Wall & Melzack, 1996).

An example of how the biopsychosocial theory can provide a useful explanation involves the phenomenon of *phantom limb pain*: When people undergo amputation of an arm or a leg, they usually continue to feel that the limb is still there, and often they experience itching, burning, and pain in the missing limb (Sherman, 1996). Fortunately, phantom limb pain usually subsides with time, as the brain slowly reorganizes the neurons associated with the amputated limb (Flov, Elbert, Knecht, Weinbruch, & Panter, 1995), and as psychological and social mechanisms also adjust habits and expectations.

Because the experience of pain is at best unpleasant and at worst debilitating, many approaches are used to relieve it. Some, like medications and acupuncture, appear to affect the biological processes involved. Other techniques based on psychological and social mechanisms can also be effective. These will be discussed more fully in Chapter 4: "Learning and Memory", and Chapter 9: "Psychological Disorders and Their Treatments."

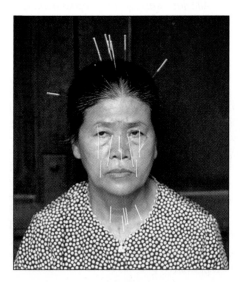

Traditional Asian medicine has used acupuncture to reduce or eliminate pain. Studies indicate that acupuncture works by releasing endorphins into the body.

gate-control theory The theory that a "neurological gate" in the spinal cord controls the transmission of pain messages to the brain.

biopsychosocial theory The theory that the interaction of biological, psychological, and cultural factors influences the intensity and duration of pain.

▶ CHECK YOUR UNDERSTANDING

Match the terms with the appropriate definitions.

1. _____ cornea
2. _____ pupil
3. _____ iris
4. _____ lens
5. _____ fovea
6. _____ retina

a. colored part of the eye
b. center of the visual field
c. opening in the iris through which light enters
d. protective layer over front part of the eye
e. part that contains the rods and cones that respond to light
f. part that focuses light onto the retina

7. Arrange the following terms in the order in which a sound wave would reach them when traveling from the outer ear to the inner ear: oval window, anvil, cochlea, auditory nerve, eardrum.

8. The basic tastes are _____, _____, _____, and _____.

9. Skin senses include sensations of _____, _____, and _____.

10. Our _____ sense provides awareness of our body's position.

Answers: 1. d, **2.** c, **3.** a, **4.** f, **5.** b, **6.** e, **7.** eardrum, anvil, oval window, cochlea, auditory nerve, **8.** sweet, sour, salty, and bitter, **9.** pressure, temperature, and pain, **10.** kinesthetic.

▶ APPLY YOUR UNDERSTANDING

1. Imagine that you are wearing a multicolored shirt when you go out for a short walk on a dark night. During the walk you look down and notice that the colors all look like patches of gray. The reason that you no longer see the colors as different hues is that
   a. you are seeing primarily with the cones
   b. you are seeing primarily with the rods
   c. the image of your shirt is falling on your blind spot
   d. you have converted from being a trichromat to a dichromat

2. As you sit in front of a sound generator, the frequency of the sound is gradually increased. You are most likely to notice an increase in
   a. pitch
   b. loudness
   c. saturation
   d. overtones

3. A friend says, "I hear this loud ringing in my ears. Sometimes it's so loud I have trouble sleeping. It's driving me crazy!" Your friend is most likely describing
   a. cochlear degeneration
   b. timbre
   c. rippling of the basilar membrane
   d. tinnitus

4. George suffers from chronic back pain. His doctor suggests that he try a form of therapy in which electrical stimulation is applied to his back. You recognize that this therapy is based on the idea that stimulating large sensory nerves in the spinal cord can prevent the sensation of pain, and that it is an application of the _____ theory of pain.
   a. gate-control
   b. contra-stimulation
   c. free nerve ending
   d. patterned-firing

Answers: 1. b, **2.** a, **3.** d, **4.** a.

Perception

3.3 Distinguish between sensation and perception and describe the general principles that organize human perceptual processes.

Our senses provide us with raw data about the external world. But unless we interpret this raw information, it is nothing more than what William James (1890) called a "booming, buzzing confusion." The eye records patterns of lightness and darkness, but it does not "see" a bird flittering from branch to branch. The eardrum vibrates in a particular fashion, but it does not "hear" a symphony. Deciphering *meaningful* patterns in the jumble of sensory information is what we mean by **perception**. But how does perception differ from sensation?

perception The brain's interpretation of sensory information so as to give it meaning.

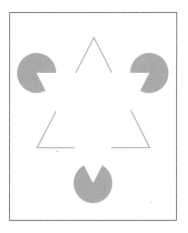

Figure 3–19

An illusory triangle. When sensory information is incomplete, we tend to create a complete perception by supplying the missing details. In this figure we fill in the lines that let us perceive a white triangle in the center of the pattern.

Figure 3–20

Perceiving a pattern. Knowing beforehand that the black blotches in this figure represent a person riding a horse changes our perception of it.

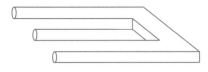

Figure 3–21

An optical illusion. In the case of the trident, we go beyond what is sensed (blue lines on flat white paper) to perceive a three-dimensional object that isn't really there.

Figure 3–22

Figure–ground relationship ... How do you perceive this figure? Do you see a vase or the silhouettes of a man and a woman? Both interpretations are possible, but not at the same time. Reversible figures like this work because it is unclear which part of the stimulus is the figure and which is the neutral ground against which the figure is perceived.

SENSATION AND PERCEPTION

How is perception different from sensation?

Perception takes place in the brain. Using sensory information as raw material, the brain creates perceptual experiences that go beyond what is sensed directly. For example, looking at **Figure 3–19**, we tend to perceive a white triangle in the center of the pattern, although the sensory input consists only of three circles from which "pie slices" have been cut and three 60-degree angles. Or take **Figure 3–20**. At first glance most people see only an assortment of black blotches. If you are told that the blotches represent a person riding a horse, suddenly your perceptual experience changes. What was meaningless sensory information now takes shape as a horse and rider.

Sometimes, as in certain optical illusions, you perceive things that could not possibly exist. The trident shown in **Figure 3–21** exemplifies such an "impossible" figure. On closer inspection, you discover that the object that you "recognized" is not really there. In all these cases, the brain actively creates and organizes perceptual experiences out of raw sensory data—sometimes even from data we are not aware of receiving. We now explore how perceptual processes organize sensory experience.

PERCEPTUAL ORGANIZATION

How do we organize our perceptual experiences?

Early in this century, a group of German psychologists calling themselves *Gestalt psychologists* set out to discover the principles through which we interpret sensory information. The German word *Gestalt* has no exact English equivalent, but essentially it means "whole," "form," or "pattern." The Gestalt psychologists believed that the brain creates a coherent perceptual experience that is more than simply the sum of the available sensory information and that it does so in predictable ways.

In one important facet of the perceptual process, we distinguish *figures* from the *ground* against which they appear. A colorfully upholstered chair stands out from the bare walls of a room. A marble statue is perceived as a whole figure separate from the red brick wall behind it. The figure–ground distinction pertains to all of our senses, not just vision. We can distinguish a violin solo against the ground of a symphony orchestra, a single voice amid cocktail-party chatter, and the smell of roses in a florist's shop. In all these instances, we perceive some objects as "figures" and other sensory information as "background."

Sometimes, however, there are not enough cues in a pattern to permit us easily to distinguish a figure from its ground. The horse and rider in **Figure 3–20** illustrate this problem. This is the principle behind camouflage: to make a figure blend into its background.

Sometimes a figure with clear contours can be perceived in two very different ways because it is unclear which part of the stimulus is the figure and which is the ground. (See **Figure 3–22**.) At first glance, you perceive figures against a specific background, but as you stare at the illustration, you will discover that the figures and the ground reverse, making for two very different perceptions of the same illustration. The stimulus hasn't changed, but your perception has (Adelson, 2002; Vecera, Vogel, & Woodman, 2002).

Figure 3–23 demonstrates some other important principles of perceptual organization. As these illustrations demonstrate, we use sensory information to create a percep-

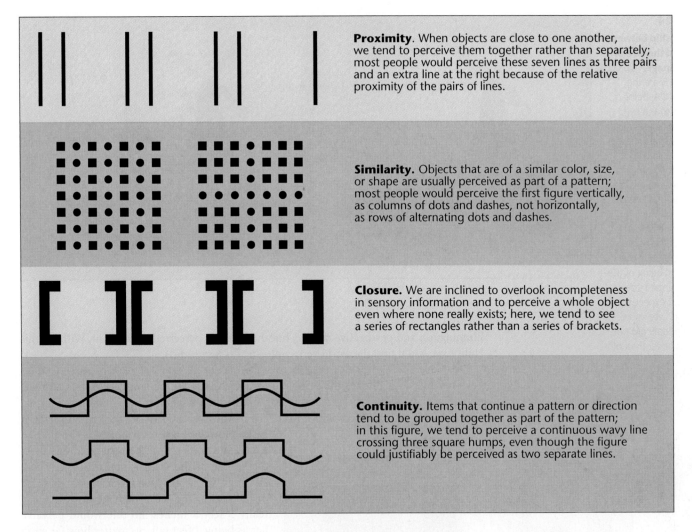

Proximity. When objects are close to one another, we tend to perceive them together rather than separately; most people would perceive these seven lines as three pairs and an extra line at the right because of the relative proximity of the pairs of lines.

Similarity. Objects that are of a similar color, size, or shape are usually perceived as part of a pattern; most people would perceive the first figure vertically, as columns of dots and dashes, not horizontally, as rows of alternating dots and dashes.

Closure. We are inclined to overlook incompleteness in sensory information and to perceive a whole object even where none really exists; here, we tend to see a series of rectangles rather than a series of brackets.

Continuity. Items that continue a pattern or direction tend to be grouped together as part of the pattern; in this figure, we tend to perceive a continuous wavy line crossing three square humps, even though the figure could justifiably be perceived as two separate lines.

Figure 3–23
Gestalt principles of perceptual organization.

tion that is more than just the sum of the parts. Although sometimes perceptual processes can cause problems, the tendency to "fill in the blanks" usually broadens our understanding of the world. As we search for meaning, our brain tries to fill in missing information, to group various objects together, to see whole objects, and to hear meaningful sounds, rather than just random bits and pieces of raw sensory data.

PERCEPTUAL CONSTANCIES

How do we perceive things as unchanging despite changing sensory information?

When anthropologist Colin Turnbull (1961) studied the Mbuti pygmies of Zaire, most of them had never left the dense Ituri rain forest and had rarely encountered objects that were more than a few feet away. On one occasion, Turnbull took a pygmy guide named Kenge on a trip onto the African plains. When Kenge looked across the plain and saw a distant herd of buffalo, he asked what kind of insects they were. He refused to believe that the tiny black spots he saw were buffalo. As he and Turnbull drove toward the herd, Kenge believed that magic was making the animals grow larger. Because he had no experience of distant objects, he could not perceive the buffalo as having constant size.

Perceptual constancy refers to the tendency to perceive objects as relatively stable and unchanging despite changing sensory information. After we have formed a stable perception of an object, we can recognize it from almost any position, at almost any distance, under almost any illumination. A white house looks like a white house by day or by night and from any angle. We see it as the same house. The sensory information may change as

perceptual constancy A tendency to perceive objects as stable and unchanging despite changes in sensory stimulation.

Figure 3–24

The relationship between distance and the size of the retinal image. Object A and object B are the same size, but A, being much closer to the eye, casts a much larger image on the retina. Even though the size of the image projected onto the retina of the two people in this photograph is quite different (the person on the left takes up a much greater proportion of the photo's space), we perceive the two people of being of the same approximate size. Based on our experience with "people," we know that some people are not many times larger than others. The principle of size constancy describes this perceptual process..

illumination and perspective change, but the object is perceived as constant. Without this ability, we would find the world very confusing (as Kenge did).

Memory and experience play important roles in all types of perceptual constancy. For example, according to the principle of **size constancy**, we tend to perceive familiar objects at their true size regardless of the size of the image that they cast on the retina. The farther away an object is from the lens of the eye, the smaller the retinal image it casts. However, when an object is familiar to us, we judge its size to be constant, regardless of the size of the retinal image it casts. Thus, although we might guess that a woman some distance away is 5 feet 4 inches tall when she is really 5 feet 8 inches, no one would perceive her as being 2 feet tall, no matter how far away she is. We know from experience that adults are seldom that short. (See **Figure 3–24**). Size constancy depends partly on experience—information about the relative sizes of objects stored in memory—and partly on distance cues.

Figure 3–25

Examples of shape constancy. Even though the image of the door on the retina changes greatly as the door opens, we still perceive the door as being rectangular.

Source: Boring, E.G., Langfeld, H.S., & Weld, H.P., 1976.

---

size constancy The perception of an object as the same size regardless of the distance from which it is viewed.

---

shape constancy A tendency to see an object as the same shape no matter what angle it is viewed from.

Familiar objects also tend to be seen as having a constant shape, even though the retinal images they cast change as they are viewed from different angles. This is called **shape constancy**. A dinner plate is perceived as a circle even when it is tilted and the retinal image is oval. A rectangular door will project a rectangular image on the retina only when it is viewed directly from the front. From any other angle, it casts a trapezoidal image on the retina, but it is not perceived as having suddenly become a trapezoidal door. (See **Figure 3–25**.) Perceptual constancies also apply to other dimensions of perception, such as color and brightness. The study of perceptual constancies makes clear the point that perceptions are constructions imposed by our brain on sensory information. Perceptions are heavily dependent on our experiences, as was clearly demonstrated by Kenge's perception of buffalo as insects. Our perceptions are also heavily influenced by not only our experiences, but by our motivations, our expectations, our cognitive style of thinking, our personality, and by many aspects of the culture in which we live. We will discuss the influence these factors have on our perceptions and our other cognitive processes more fully in Chapter 5: "Cognition and Mental Abilities."

PERCEPTION OF DISTANCE AND DEPTH

How do we know how far away something is?

We are constantly judging the distance between ourselves and other objects. When we walk through a classroom, our perception of distance helps us to avoid bumping into desks or tripping over the wastebasket. If we reach out to pick up a pencil, we automatically judge how far to extend our hand. We also assess the depth of objects—how much total space they occupy. We use many cues to determine the distance and the depth of objects. Some of these cues depend on visual messages that one eye alone can transmit; these are called **monocular cues**. Others, known as **binocular cues**, require the use of both eyes. Having two eyes allows us to make more accurate judgments about distance and depth, particularly when objects are relatively close. But monocular cues alone are often enough to allow us to judge distance and depth quite accurately, as we see in the next section.

MONOCULAR CUES One important monocular distance cue that provides us with information about relative position is called **interposition**. Interposition occurs when one object partly blocks a second object. The first object is perceived as being closer, the second as more distant. (See **Figure 3–26**.)

As art students learn, there are several ways in which **perspective** can help in estimating distance and depth. In *linear perspective*, two parallel lines that extend into the distance seem to come together at some point on the horizon. In *aerial perspective*, distant objects have a hazy appearance and a somewhat blurred outline. On a clear day, mountains often seem to be much closer than on a hazy day, when their outlines become blurred. The *elevation* of an object also serves as a perspective cue to depth: An object that is on a higher horizontal plane seems to be farther away than one on a lower plane. (See **Figure 3–27**.)

Another useful monocular cue to distance and depth is **texture gradient**. An object that is close seems to have a rough or detailed texture. As distance increases, the texture becomes finer, until finally the original texture cannot be distinguished clearly, if at all. For example, when standing on a pebbly beach, you can distinguish among the gray stones and the gravel in front of your feet. As you look down the beach, however, the stones appear to become smaller and finer until eventually you cannot make out individual stones at all. **Shadowing**, another important cue to the distance, depth, and solidity of an object, is illustrated in **Figure 3–28**.

People traveling on buses or trains often notice that nearby trees or telephone poles seem to flash past the windows, whereas buildings and other objects farther away seem to move slowly. These differences in the speeds of movement of images across the retina as you move give an important cue to distance and depth. You can observe the same effect if you stand still and move your head from side to side as you focus your gaze on something in the middle distance: Objects close to you seem to move in the direction opposite to the

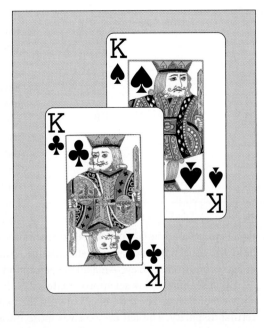

Figure 3–26

Interposition. Because the king of clubs appears to have been interposed on the king of spades, we perceive it to be closer to us.

monocular cues Visual cues requiring the use of one eye.

binocular cues Visual cues requiring the use of both eyes.

interposition Monocular distance cue in which one object, by partly blocking a second object, is perceived as being closer.

perspective Monocular distance and depth cues that involve the convergence of lines, the haziness of images, and the relative elevation of objects.

texture gradient Monocular cue to distance and depth based on the fact that objects seen at greater distances appear to be smoother and less textured.

shadowing Monocular cue to distance and depth based on the fact that shadows often appear on the parts of objects that are more distant.

Figure 3–27

Perspective Cues. Because of the higher elevation and the suggestion of depth provided by the road, the tree on the right is perceived as being more distant and about the same size as the tree at lower left. Actually, it is appreciably smaller, as you can see if you measure the heights of the two drawings.

Figure 3-28

Shadowing. Shadowing on the outer edges of a spherical object, such as a ball or globe, gives it a three-dimensional quality (A). Without shadowing (B), it might be perceived as a flat disk. Shadowing can also affect our perception of the direction of depth. In the absence of other cues, we tend to assume overhead lighting, so image C appears to be a bump because its top edge is lit, whereas image D appears to be a dent. If you turn the book upside down, the direction of depth is reversed.

---

motion parallax Monocular distance cue in which objects closer than the point of visual focus seem to move in the direction opposite to the viewer's moving head, and objects beyond the focus point appear to move in the same direction as the viewer's head.

---

stereoscopic vision Combination of two retinal images to give a three-dimensional perceptual experience.

---

retinal disparity Binocular distance cue based on the difference between the images cast on the two retinas when both eyes are focused on the same object.

---

convergence A visual depth cue that comes from muscles controlling eye movement as the eyes turn inward to view a nearby stimulus.

---

monaural cue Cue to sound location that requires just one ear.

---

binaural cue Cue to sound location that involves both ears working together.

Figure 3-29

Cues used in sound localization. Sound waves coming from source B will reach both ears simultaneously. A sound wave from source A reaches the left ear first, where it is also louder. The head casts a "shadow" over the other ear, thus reducing the intensity of the delayed sound in that ear.

Source: Boring, E.G., Langfeld, H.S., & Weld, H.P., 1976 *Foundations of Psychology.* New York: Wiley, 1948.

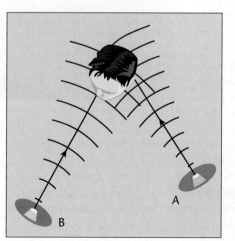

direction in which your head is moving, whereas objects far away seem to move in the same direction as your head. This distance cue is known as **motion parallax**.

BINOCULAR CUES All the visual cues examined so far depend on the action of only one eye. Many animals—such as horses, deer, and fish—rely entirely on monocular cues. Although they have two eyes, the two visual fields do not overlap, because their eyes are located on the sides of the head rather than in front. Humans, apes, and many predatory animals—such as lions, tigers, and wolves—have a distinct perceptual advantage over these other animals. Because both eyes are set in the front of the head, the visual fields overlap. The **stereoscopic vision** derived from combining the two retinal images—one from each eye—makes the perception of depth and distance more accurate.

Because our eyes are set approximately 2 ½ inches apart, each one has a slightly different view of things. The difference between the two images that the eyes receive is known as **retinal disparity**. The left eye receives more information about the left side of an object, and the right eye receives more information about the right side. You can easily prove that each of your eyes receives a different image. Close one eye and line up a finger with some vertical line, like the edge of a door. Then open that eye and close the other one. Your finger will appear to have moved a great distance. When you look at the finger with both eyes, however, the two different images become one.

A second important binocular cue to distance, especially when objects are close to us, comes from the muscles that control the **convergence** of the eyes. When we look at objects that are fairly close to us, our eyes tend to *converge*—to turn slightly inward toward each other. The sensations from the muscles that control the movement of the eyes thus provide the brain with a cue for distance.

LOCATION OF SOUNDS Most of us rely so heavily on visual cues that we seldom pay much attention to the rich array of auditory information available around us. However, just as we use monocular and binocular cues to establish visual depth and distance, we draw on **monaural** (single-ear) and **binaural** (two-ear) **cues** to locate the source of sounds. (See **Figure 3–29**.) In one monaural cue, loud sounds are perceived as closer than faint sounds, with changes in loudness translating into changes in distance. Binaural cues work on the principle that because sounds off to one side of the head reach one ear slightly ahead of the other (in the range of 1/1,000th of a second), the time difference between sound waves reaching the two ears registers in the brain and helps us to make accurate judgments of location.

In a second binaural cue, sound signals arriving from a source off to one side of you are slightly louder in the nearer ear than in the ear farther from the source. The slight difference occurs because your head, in effect, blocks the sound, reducing the intensity of sound in the opposite ear. This relative loudness difference between signals heard separately by the two ears is enough for the brain to locate the sound source and to judge its distance. When sound engineers record a musical group, they may place microphones at many different locations. On playback, the speakers project sounds from voices or instruments at slightly different instants to mimic the sound patterns you would hear if you were actually listening to the group perform right in front of you.

VISUAL ILLUSIONS

What causes visual illusions?

Visual illusions graphically demonstrate the ways in which we use a variety of sensory cues to create perceptual experiences that may (or may not) correspond to what is out there in the real world. By understanding how we are fooled into "seeing" something that isn't there, psychologists can figure out how perceptual processes work in the everyday world and under normal circumstances.

Psychologists generally distinguish between physical and perceptual illusions. One example of a *physical illusion* is the bent appearance of a stick when it is placed in water—an illusion easily understood because the water acts like a prism, bending the light waves before they reach our eyes. *Perceptual illusions* occur because the stimulus contains misleading cues that give rise to inaccurate or impossible perceptions.

The illusions in **Figure 3–30** result from false and misleading depth cues (Spehar & Gillam, 2002). For example, in **Figure 3–30F** both monsters cast the same size image on the

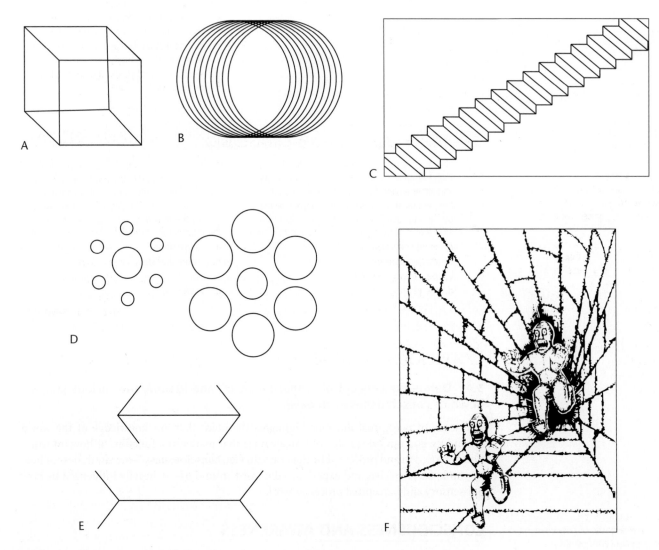

Figure 3–30

Reversible figures and misleading depth cues. Images A, B, and C are examples of reversible figures—drawings that we can perceive two different ways, but not at the same time. Images D, E, and F show how, through the use of misleading depth cues, we misjudge the size of objects. The middle circles in image D are exactly the same size, as are the lines in image E and the monsters in image F.

retina in our eyes. But the depth cues in the tunnel suggest that we are looking at a three-dimensional scene and that therefore the top monster is much farther away. In the real world, this perception would mean that the top monster is actually much larger than the bottom monster. Therefore we "correct" for the distance and actually perceive the top monster as larger, despite other cues to the contrary. We know that the image is actually two dimensional, but we still respond to it as if it were three dimensional.

There are also "real-world" illusions that illustrate how perceptual processes work, such as the illusion of *induced movement*. When you are sitting in a stationary train and the train next to you begins to move forward, you seem to be moving backward. Because you have no reference point by which to tell whether you are standing still, you are confused as to which train is actually moving. However, if you look down at the ground, you can establish an unambiguous frame of reference and make the situation clear to yourself.

► CHECK YOUR UNDERSTANDING

Match the following principles of perception with the appropriate definitions.

1. _____ similarity
2. _____ continuity
3. _____ proximity
4. _____ closure

a. tendency to perceive a whole object even where none exists
b. elements that continue a pattern are likely to be seen as part of the pattern
c. objects that are like one another tend to be grouped together
d. elements found close together tend to be perceived as a unit

Answers: 1. c, 2. b, 3. d, 4. a.

► APPLY YOUR UNDERSTANDING

1. You are seated at a small table talking to a friend opposite you who is drinking coffee. As she lifts the cup off the saucer and raises it to her mouth, the image made on your retina by the cup actually changes shape, but you still "see" it as being a cup. This is due to
   a. good continuation
   b. motion parallax
   c. perceptual constancy
   d. the phi phenomenon

2. As you study a painting, you notice that a pathway in the painting is made up of stones that become smaller and smaller as you look "down the lane." The artist has used which one of the following distance cues to create the impression of depth?
   a. interposition
   b. texture gradient
   c. elevation
   d. shadowing

Answers: 1. c, 2. b.

Conscious Experience

3.4 Define the concept of "consciousness" and identify the various states in which consciousness can exist.

The study of perceptual illusions highlights the point that our knowledge of the world around us, and our knowledge of ourselves for that matter, is a function of how information is carried to and processed by the brain. In fact, **consciousness**—our awareness of how we think, feel, perceive, and experience the word around us—is heavily influenced by how our sensory and perceptual processes work.

CONSCIOUSNESS AND AWARENESS

How does our awareness of the environment contribute to the various states of consciousness we experience?

Psychologists who study consciousness are interested in a wide array of cognitive activities, including those mentioned above, which are often referred to as our **waking consciousness**,

---

consciousness Our awareness of how we think, feel, perceive, and experience the world.

waking consciousness Mental state that encompasses the thoughts, feelings, and perceptions that occur when we are awake and reasonably alert.

to distinguish that these are modes of mental activities that occur while we are awake and fully aware of our surroundings. Waking consciousness is usually action- or plan-oriented and tuned in to the external environment, hence the link between consciousness and sensation and perception. However, sometimes our conscious experience differs from that of normal waking consciousness, as when we are detached, in varying degrees, from the external environment. Such **altered states of consciousness**, including sleep, daydreaming, dreaming, and other mind-altered states that may result from the use of psychoactive drugs or hypnosis, also comprise our conscious experience, broadly defined.

One of the most important characteristics of consciousness is that it is *limited*. Even when we are fully awake and alert, we are usually conscious of only a small portion of what is going on around us. At any given moment, we are exposed to a great variety of sounds, sights, and smells from the outside world. At the same time, we experience all sorts of internal sensations, such as heat and cold, touch, pressure, pain, and equilibrium, as well as an array of thoughts, memories, emotions, and needs. Normally, however, we are not aware of all these competing stimuli. To make sense of our environment, we must select only the most important information to attend to and then filter out everything else. At times we pay such close attention to what we are doing that we are oblivious to what is going on around us. How the process of attention works is examined at some length in Chapter 4, "Learning and Memory." Here it is enough to note that the hallmark of normal waking consciousness is the highly selective nature of attention.

The selective nature of attention can be seen in the number of processes that go on without drawing our conscious attention. We are rarely attuned to such vital bodily processes as blood pressure and respiration, for example, and we can walk down the street or ride a bicycle without consciously thinking about every movement. In fact, we carry out certain tasks, such as signing our name, better when we are *not* consciously aware of performing each movement. Similarly, when we drive or walk along a familiar route that we always take to work or school, the process may be so automatic that we remain largely unaware of our surroundings.

Many psychologists believe that certain key mental processes, such as recognizing a word or a friend's face, also go on outside of normal waking consciousness. As we saw in the first chapter, Sigmund Freud thought that many of the most important influences on our behavior—such as erotic feelings for our parents—are screened from our consciousness and may be accessible only through altered states such as dreaming. We explore the notion of nonconscious mental processes as we consider various altered states of consciousness, beginning with natural ones such as daydreaming.

DAYDREAMING AND FANTASY

Do daydreams serve any useful function?

In James Thurber's classic short story *The Secret Life of Walter Mitty* (1942), the meek, painfully shy central character spends much of his time weaving elaborate fantasies in which he stars as a bold, dashing adventurer. Daydreams are his reality—and his waking-conscious experience something of a nightmare. Few people live in their imaginations to the extent that Walter Mitty does. Thurber deliberately used exaggeration to explore the secret life that all of us share, but that few of us discuss: our fantasies. Everyone has **daydreams**—apparently effortless, spontaneous shifts in attention away from the here and now into a private world of make-believe.

The urge to daydream seems to come in waves, surging about every 90 minutes and peaking between noon and 2 P.M. (Ford-Mitchell, 1997). According to some estimates, the average person spends almost half of his or her waking hours fantasizing, though this proportion varies from person to person and situation to situation. Are daydreams random paths that your mind travels? Not at

altered states of consciousness Mental states that differ noticeably from normal waking consciousness.

daydreams Apparently effortless shifts in attention away from the here and now into a private world of make-believe.

Daydreaming, which all people do, can provide a refreshing break in a stressful day and an opportunity to solve problems and attend to personal concerns.

all. Studies show that most daydreams are variations on a central theme—thoughts and images of unfulfilled goals and wishes, accompanied by emotions arising from an appraisal of where we are now compared with where we want to be (Baars & McGovern, 1994).

Does daydreaming serve any useful function? Some psychologists view daydreaming as nothing more than a retreat from the real world, especially when that world is not meeting our needs. As such, daydreaming can interfere with productive activities and make those problems worse. Although most daydreaming is quite normal, it is considered maladaptive when it involves extensive fantasizing, replacing human interaction and interfering with vocational or academic success (Somer, 2002). Clearly, people who have difficulty distinguishing between fantasy and reality and who begin replacing real-life relationships with imaginary family and friends may need professional help.

Other psychologists stress the positive value of daydreaming and fantasy (Klinger, 1990). Daydreams may provide a refreshing break from a stressful day and serve to remind us of neglected personal needs. Freudian theorists tend to view daydreams as a harmless way of working through hostile feelings or satisfying guilty desires. Cognitive psychologists emphasize that daydreaming can build problem-solving and interpersonal skills, as well as encourage creativity. Moreover, daydreaming helps people endure difficult situations: Prisoners of war have used fantasies to survive torture and deprivation. Daydreaming and fantasy, then, may provide welcome relief from unpleasant reality and reduce internal tension and external aggression.

➤ CHECK YOUR UNDERSTANDING

1. Our awareness of the mental processes of our everyday life is called _____.
2. Consciousness is often divided into _____ consciousness, which represents our awareness of the world around us, and _____ _____ of consciousness, which includes states such as sleep, daydreaming, dreaming, and drug-altered experiences.

Answers: 1. consciousness; 2. waking; altered states.

➤ APPLY YOUR UNDERSTANDING

1. Waking consciousness is limited by which of the following processes?
   a. circadian ryhthms
   b. attention
   c. REM patterns
   d. apnea

2. Jason argues that he daydreams about as much as the typical person. He explains that he experiences daydreams about every:
   a. 10–15 minutes
   b. 90 minutes or so
   c. 3–4 hours
   d. morning and evening, averaging 2 daydreams per day

Answers: 1. b., 2. b.

Sleep

3.5 Describe the phenomena we call sleep and dreaming and identify the various functions these altered states of consciousness might serve.

Human beings spend about one-third of their lives in the altered state of consciousness known as sleep: a natural state of rest characterized by a reduction in voluntary body movement and decreased awareness of the surroundings. No one who has tried to stay awake longer than 20 hours at a time could doubt the necessity of sleep. Some people claim they never sleep, but when observed under laboratory conditions, they actually sleep soundly without being aware of it. When people are deprived of sleep, they crave sleep just as strongly as they would food or water after a period of deprivation.

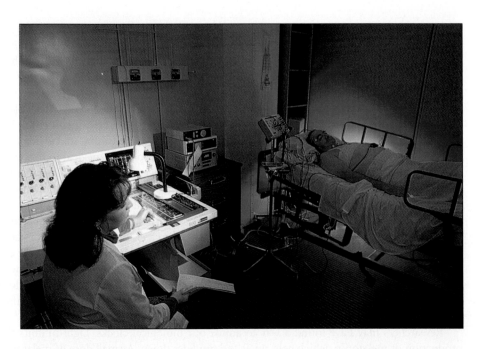

Sleep researchers monitor volunteers' brain waves, muscle tension, and other physiological changes during sleep.

Our need for sleep is sometimes frustrated when we have trouble falling asleep or staying asleep. As the opening paragraphs of this chapter make clear, Americans' inability to sleep well is a widespread and serious problem. Merely resting doesn't satisfy us.

All birds and mammals sleep, although scientists are not sure about other species. However, reptiles, frogs, fish, and even insects go into "rest states" similar to sleep. How long organisms sleep, where, in what positions, and other details about sleep states vary from species to species. In general, large animals sleep less than small animals, perhaps because eating enough to support their size requires more time awake. Evolutionary psychologists see sleep as an adaptive mechanism that evolved to allow organisms to conserve and restore energy (Tobler, 1997). In support of this theory, researchers have shown that people use less energy when they are asleep than when they are awake (Madsen, 1993).

Nobody knows exactly why we need to sleep, although evidence has begun to accumulate that sleep may play an important restorative function, both physically and mentally. For instance, one study has shown that getting adequate sleep boosts our immune response, making us less susceptible to disease (Lange, Perras, Fehm, & Born, 2003). In addition, recent research has revealed that when people are presented with complex problems and are permitted to sleep prior to solving them, they are more likely to generate insightful solutions than if they are kept from sleeping (Wagner, Gais, Haider, Verleger, & Born, 2004). This latter finding supports the idea that creativity and problem-solving skills may be enhanced by getting adequate sleep.

CIRCADIAN CYCLES: THE BIOLOGICAL CLOCK

What is the biological clock and what does it have to do with jet lag?

Like many other biological functions, sleep and waking follow a daily, or *circadian*, cycle (from the Latin expression *circa diem*, meaning "about a day") (Moore-Ede, Czeisler, & Richardson, 1983). **Circadian rhythms** are an ancient and fundamental adaptation to the 24-hour solar cycle of light and dark, found not only in humans and other animals, but also in plants and even one-celled organisms (Moore, 1999; Refinetti, 2000). The human *biological clock* is largely governed by a tiny cluster of neurons in our brain. In response to light and dark cycles detected by the eye, this region of the brain triggers the release of specific neurotransmitters that control body temperature, metabolism, blood pressure, hormone levels, and hunger, which vary predictably through the course of the day. For example, the level of the hormone epinephrine (which causes the body to go on alert) reaches a peak in the late morning hours and then steadily declines until around midnight,

circadian rhythm A regular biological rhythm with a period of approximately 24 hours.

when it suddenly drops to a very low level and remains there until morning. By contrast, levels of melatonin (which promotes sleep) surge at night and drop off during the day. Animal studies have shown that the brain even responds to seasonal variations in the length of the day, regulating the production of various hormones and behaviors, like mating, that are linked to seasonal changes in many species (Sumova, Sladek, Jac, & Illnerova, 2002).

However, day length is not the only determinant of circadian rhythms, because the biological clock can continue to function even in the absence of external cues (Refinetti, 2000). For example, Czeisler, Duffy, and Shanahan (1999) studied 24 people who volunteered to live in an artificial environment for three weeks. The only time cues that participants had were a weak cycle of light and dark set at 28 hours and a bedtime signal. Even in this misleading environment, their body temperatures, hormone levels, and other biological processes showed that their bodies continued to function according to their own internal 24-hour cycle.

We rarely notice circadian rhythms until they are disturbed. Jet lag is a familiar example. Travelers who cross several time zones in one day often feel "out of it" for several days. The reason for jet lag is not so much lack of sleep as *desynchronization*. Sleep-and-wake cycles adapt quickly, but hormones, body temperature, and digestive cycles change more slowly. As a result, bodily functions are out of synch. Likewise, shift workers often lose weight and suffer from irritability, insomnia, and extreme drowsiness for some time after changing to a new shift (Richardson, Miner, & Czeisler, 1989–1990).

Researchers may have found a way to adjust our biological clocks. Light inhibits the production of melatonin, which goes up as the sun goes down. A small dose of melatonin taken in the morning (the time when the hormone is usually tapering off) sets back or slows down the biological clock (Liu et al., 1997). Taken in the evening, melatonin speeds up the biological clock, making the person fall asleep earlier than usual (Lewy, Ahmed, Latham, & Sack, 1992). Applying this knowledge, melatonin has been successfully used as an aid to persons with blindness, who sometimes are unable to sense dark–light cycles, causing insomnia or daytime sleepiness. Carefully timed doses of melatonin seem to "reset" the biological clocks of such people, enabling them to sleep better at night and remain alert during the day (Sack, Brandes, Kendall, & Lewy, 2001).

RHYTHMS OF SLEEP

What physical changes mark the rhythms of sleep?

Over the years, researchers have accumulated a large body of observations about what happens in our bodies and brains during sleep. In a typical study, researchers recruit volunteers who spend one or more nights in a "sleep lab." With electrodes painlessly attached to their skulls, the volunteers sleep comfortably as their brain waves, eye movements, muscle tension, and other physiological functions are monitored. Data from such studies show that although there are significant individual differences in sleep behavior, almost everyone goes through the same stages of sleep (Anch et al., 1988). Each stage is marked by characteristic patterns of brain waves, muscular activity, blood pressure, and body temperature (Carlson, 2000). **Figure 3–31** illustrates the electrical activity related to the brain, heart, and facial muscles at each stage.

"Going to sleep" means losing awareness and failing to respond to a stimulus that would produce a response in the waking state. As measured by an EEG, brain waves during this "twilight" state are characterized by irregular, low-voltage alpha waves. This brain-wave pattern mirrors the sense of relaxed wakefulness that we experience while lying on a beach or in a hammock or when resting after a big meal. In this twilight state with the eyes closed, people often report seeing flashing lights and colors, geometric patterns, and visions of landscapes. Sometimes they also experience a floating or falling sensation, followed by a quick jolt back to consciousness.

After this initial twilight phase, the sleeper enters *Stage 1* of sleep. Stage-1 brain waves are tight and of very low amplitude (height), resembling those recorded when a person is alert or excited. But, in contrast to normal waking consciousness, Stage 1 of the sleep cycle is marked by a slowing of the pulse, muscle relaxation, and side-to-side rolling movements of the eyes—the last being the most reliable indication of this first stage of sleep (Dement,

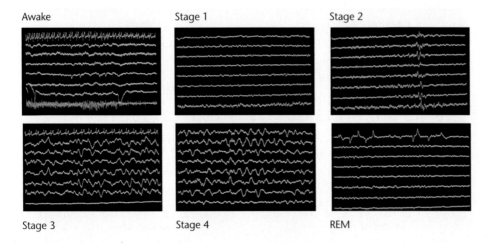

Awake   Stage 1   Stage 2

Stage 3   Stage 4   REM

Figure 3–31

Waves of sleep. This series of printouts illustrates electrical activity in the brain, heart, and facial muscles during the various stages of sleep. Note the characteristic delta waves that begin to appear during Stage 3 and become more pronounced during Stage 4.

1974). Stage 1 usually lasts only a few moments. The sleeper is easily aroused at this stage and, once awake, may be unaware of having slept at all.

Stages 2 and *3* are characterized by progressively deeper sleep. During Stage 2, short rhythmic bursts of brain-wave activity called *sleep spindles* periodically appear. In Stage 3, *delta waves*—slow waves with very high peaks—begin to emerge. During these stages, the sleeper is hard to awaken and does not respond to stimuli such as noises or lights. Heart rate, blood pressure, and temperature continue to drop.

In *Stage 4* sleep, the brain emits very slow delta waves. Heart rate, breathing rate, blood pressure, and body temperature are as low as they will get during the night. In young adults, delta sleep occurs in 15- to 20-minute segments—interspersed with lighter sleep—mostly during the first half of the night. Delta sleep time lessens with age, but continues to be the first sleep to be made up after sleep has been lost.

About an hour after falling asleep, the sleeper begins to ascend from Stage 4 sleep to Stage 3, Stage 2, and back to Stage 1—a process that takes about 40 minutes. The brain waves return to the low-amplitude, saw-toothed shape characteristic of Stage 1 sleep and waking alertness. Heart rate and blood pressure also increase, yet the muscles are more relaxed than at any other point in the sleep cycle, and the person is very difficult to awaken. The eyes move rapidly under closed eyelids. This **rapid-eye movement (REM)** sleep stage is distinguished from all other stages of sleep (called **non-REM** or **NREM**) that precede and follow it.

REM sleep is also called *paradoxical sleep* because although measures of brain activity, heart rate, blood pressure, and other physiological functions closely resemble those recorded during waking consciousness, the person in this stage appears to be deeply asleep and is incapable of moving; the body's voluntary muscles are essentially paralyzed. Some research suggests that REM sleep is also the stage when most dreaming occurs, though dreams take place during NREM sleep as well (Stickgold, Rittenhouse, & Hobson, 1994). The first Stage 1–REM period lasts about 10 minutes and is followed by Stages 2, 3, and 4 of NREM sleep. This sequence of sleep stages repeats itself all night, averaging 90 minutes from Stage 1–REM to Stage 4 and back again. Normally, a night's sleep consists of four to five sleep cycles of this sort. But the pattern of sleep changes as the night progresses. At first, Stages 3 and 4 dominate; but as time passes, the Stage 1–REM periods gradually become longer, and Stages 3 and 4 become shorter, eventually disappearing altogether. Over the course of a night, then, about 45 to 50 percent of the sleeper's time is spent in Stage 2, whereas REM sleep takes up another 20 to 25 percent of the total.

Sleep requirements and patterns vary considerably from person to person. Some adults need hardly any sleep. Researchers have documented the case of a Stanford University professor who slept for only three to four hours a night over the course of 50 years and that of a woman who lived a healthy life on only one hour of sleep per night (Rosenzweig & Leiman, 1982). Sleep patterns also change with age. (See **Figure 3–32**; Sadeh, Raviv, & Gruber, 2000.) Infants sleep much longer than adults—13 to 16 hours during the first year—and much more of their sleep is REM sleep.

REM (paradoxical) sleep Sleep stage characterized by rapid-eye movements and increased dreaming.

non-REM (NREM) sleep Non-rapid-eye-movement stages of sleep that alternate with REM stages during the sleep cycle.

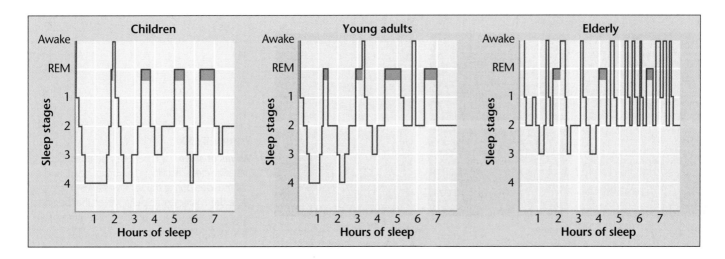

Figure 3–32

A night's sleep across the life span. Sleep patterns change from childhood to young adulthood to old age. The red areas represent REM sleep, the stage of sleep that varies most dramatically across age groups. Note how many times older adults awaken during their hours of sleep.

Source: Adapted by permission of *The New England Journal of Medicine, 290*, p. 487, 1974. Copyright © 1974 Massachusetts Medical Society. All rights reserved.

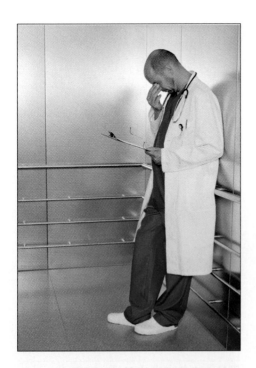

When people are deprived of sleep, they often are less able to solve complex problems and more likely to make errors. Many states are imposing restrictions on how many consecutive hours employees can work, especially in high risk occupations.

ADEQUATE SLEEP

What are the consequences of sleep deprivation?

As the opening paragraphs of this chapter make clear, inadequate sleep has become a "national epidemic" in the United States. Between one-third and one-half of all adults regularly fail to get enough sleep. High school students report that they fall asleep in class about once a week (Acebo & Carskadon, 2002; Maas, 1998).

Despite common beliefs, people do not adapt to chronic sleep loss (Hébert, 2003; Van Dongen, Maislin, Mullington, & Dinges, 2003). Extensive research shows that losing an hour or two of sleep every night, week after week, month after month, makes it more difficult for people to pay attention (especially to monotonous tasks) and to remember things (Johnsen, Laberg, Eid, & Hugdahl, 2002). Reaction time slows down, behavior becomes unpredictable, logical reasoning is impaired, and accidents and errors in judgment increase, while productivity and the ability to make decisions decline (Babkoff et al., 1991; Blagrove & Akehurst, 2000, 2001; Webb & Levy, 1984). These findings have important implications. For example, experts estimate that sleep loss is a contributing factor in between 200,000 and 400,000 automobile accidents each year, resulting in approximately 1,500 deaths (Carskadon, 2002). Research suggests that driving while sleepy is just as dangerous as driving while drunk (Powell et al., 2001). Combining sleep deprivation with drinking, even moderate drinking, is especially dangerous (Horne, Reyner, & Barrett, 2003).

Sleep deprivation may also routinely affect the performance of people in high-risk positions, such as pilots, truck drivers, emergency medical technicians, firefighters, and hospital workers. Awareness of the relationship between sleep deprivation and accidents has led to changes in the working patterns of people whose jobs can have life-and-death consequences. Several states have shortened the shifts of hospital residents to prevent errors caused by sleep deprivation. Similarly, the number of hours a pilot can fly or a truck driver can drive without having time off to sleep has come under federal regulation. Sleep deprivation is also clearly related to depression in high school and college students. According to Mary Alice Carskadon, a leading researcher in the area of sleep among college students, "Every study we have ever done over the past decade on high school and college students shows the less sleep they get the more depressed mood they report" (Markel, 2003, p. D6).

Unfortunately, people do not always know when they are not getting enough sleep. Most truck drivers involved in accidents that resulted from their falling asleep at the wheel claimed that they felt rested at the time (Wald, 1995). In a laboratory study, one group of healthy college students who were getting seven to eight hours of sleep a night showed no apparent signs of sleep deprivation. Yet 20 percent of them fell asleep immediately when they were put into a dark room, a symptom of chronic sleep loss. Another group for a period of time went to bed 60 to 90 minutes earlier than their normal bedtime. These students reported that they felt much more vigorous and alert—indeed, they performed significantly better on tests of psychological and mental acuity (Carskadon & Dement, 1982).

According to a well-known sleep researcher, Dr. William Dement, one way to reduce your sleep debt is to take short naps. Even a 20-minute nap can increase alertness, reduce irritability, and improve efficiency, while one-hour naps lead to more marked increases in performance (Mednick et al., 2002). Unfortunately, while in many cultures midafternoon is seen as siesta time, in America we often reach for a cup of coffee to keep us going.

SLEEP DISORDERS

What types of sleep disorders do people experience?

At any given time, at least 40 million Americans suffer from chronic, long-term sleep disorders, and 20 million other Americans experience occasional sleep problems. Also, there is a link between sleep and a large number of diseases, including asthma, stroke, and heart disease (National Institute of Neurological Disorders and Stroke, 2003; Ayas et al., 2003). The scientific study of typical sleep patterns has yielded further insights into several sleep disorders, including the ones we discuss in this chapter: insomnia, sleeptalking, sleepwalking, night terrors, apnea, and narcolepsy.

INSOMNIA **Insomnia**, the inability to fall or remain asleep, afflicts as many as 50 million Americans. Most episodes of insomnia grow out of stressful events and are temporary and many cases of insomnia yield to drug therapy or behavioral therapy (M. T. Smith et al., 2002). However, treatments can create problems for some susceptible individuals. Some prescription medications for insomnia can cause anxiety, memory loss, hallucinations, and violent behavior (Gathchel & Oordt, 2003; Morin, Bastien, Brink, & Brown, 2003). In a few rare cases, sleep-inducing medicines, such as Ambien, can cause serious problems for users, as the opening paragraphs of this chapter make clear.

The causes of insomnia vary for different individuals (Lichstein, Wilson, & Johnson, 2000). For some people, insomnia is part of a larger psychological problem, such as depression, so its cure requires treating the underlying disorder. Research indicates that interpersonal difficulties, such as loneliness, also can contribute to difficulty sleeping (Cacioppo et al., 2002). For others, insomnia results from an over-aroused biological system. A physical predisposition to insomnia may combine with distress over chronic sleeplessness to create a cycle in which biological and emotional factors reinforce one another. People may worry so much about not sleeping that their bedtime rituals, such as brushing teeth and getting dressed for bed, "become harbingers of frustration, rather than stimuli for relaxation" (Hauri, 1982). Furthermore, bad sleep habits—such as varying bedtimes and awakening times—and distracting sleep settings may aggravate or even cause insomnia. For a list of suggestions that can help address occasional bouts of insomnia, see **Table 3–2**.

insomnia Sleep disorder characterized by difficulty in falling asleep or remaining asleep throughout the night.

>TABLE 3–2 TIPS FOR TREATING INSOMNIA

What can people who have trouble sleeping do to ease their insomnia? Here are some suggestions:

- Maintain regular bedtime hours.
- Establish a regular routine of activities performed just before going to bed.
- Abstain from drugs, including those with alcohol or caffeine.
- Adjust the room temperature to a comfortable level.
- Avoid foods, such as chocolate, that contain caffeine.
- Engage in regular daytime exercise, but avoid exercising just before bedtime.
- Learn to relax and avoid anxiety-provoking thoughts at bedtime.
- Don't fight insomnia: If you can't sleep, get up, work or read for an hour or so, and then try to sleep again.

SLEEPTALKING, SLEEPWALKING, AND NIGHT TERRORS *Sleeptalking* and *sleepwalking* usually occur during Stage 4. Both are more common among children than adults: About 20 percent of children have at least one episode of either sleepwalking or sleeptalking. Boys are more likely to walk in their sleep than girls. Contrary to popular belief, waking a sleepwalker is not dangerous, but because sleepwalking commonly takes place during a very deep stage of sleep, waking a sleepwalker is not easy (Hobson, 1994).

Sometimes sleep can be frightening, when people experience **nightmares** or *sleep terrors*, which are also known as **night terrors**. Although both these phenomena are bad dreams, they are very different (Zadra & Donderi, 2000). Nightmares occur during REM sleep, and we can remember them in the morning. These frightening dreams are also very common; virtually everyone has them occasionally. Night terrors, a form of nocturnal fright that makes the dreamer suddenly sit up in bed, often screaming out in fear, occur during NREM sleep. People generally cannot be awakened from night terrors and will push away anyone trying to comfort them. Unlike nightmares, night terrors cannot be recalled the next morning. Night terrors are fairly rare, occurring in fewer than 10 percent of children, although they occur more often if the person is very tired. Although nightmares and night terrors are more common in children, adults can have them during times of stress (Muris, Merckelbach, Gadet, & Moulaert, 2000).

APNEA AND NARCOLEPSY The sleep disorder called **apnea** affects 10 to 12 million Americans, many of whom have inherited the condition (Kadotani et al., 2001). Apnea is associated with breathing difficulties at night: In severe cases, the victim actually stops breathing after falling asleep (Vgontzas & Kales, 1999). When the level of carbon dioxide in the blood rises to a certain point, apnea sufferers are spurred to a state of arousal just short of waking consciousness. Because this process may happen hundreds of times a night, apnea patients typically feel exhausted and fall asleep repeatedly the next day. They may also complain of depression, sexual dysfunction, difficulty concentrating, and headaches. Moreover, sleep-related breathing disorders have been shown to be related to hyperactivity, conduct disorders, and aggressiveness among children and adolescents (Chervin, Killion, Archbold, & Ruzicka, 2003).

People suffering from insomnia and apnea may envy those who have no trouble sleeping. But too much sleep has serious repercussions as well. **Narcolepsy** is a hereditary disorder whose victims nod off without warning in the middle of a conversation or other alert activity. People with narcolepsy often experience a sudden loss of muscle tone upon expression of any sort of emotion. A joke, anger, sexual stimulation—all bring on the muscle paralysis associated with deep sleep. Suddenly, without warning, they collapse. Another symptom of the disorder is immediate entry into REM sleep, which produces frightening hallucinations that are, in fact, dreams that the person is experiencing while still partly awake. Narcolepsy is believed to arise from a defect in the central nervous system (Bassetti & Aldrich, 1996).

DREAMS

What are dreams?

Every person dreams, and every culture, including our own, attributes meaning to dreams. Some people believe that dreams contain messages from their gods; some that dreams predict the future. Psychologists define **dreams** as visual and auditory experiences that our minds create during sleep. The average person has four or five dreams a night, accounting for about one to two hours of the total time spent sleeping. People awakened during REM sleep report graphic dreams about 80 to 85 percent of the time (Berger, 1969). Less striking dreamlike experiences that resemble normal wakeful consciousness are reported about 50 percent of the time during NREM sleep.

Most dreams last about as long as the events would in real life; they do not flash on your mental screen just before waking, as was once believed. Generally, dreams consist of a sequential story or a series of stories. Stimuli, both external (such as a train whistle or a low-

---

nightmares Frightening dreams that occur during REM sleep and are remembered.

night terrors Frightening, often terrifying dreams that occur during NREM sleep from which a person is difficult to awaken and doesn't remember the content.

apnea Sleep disorder characterized by breathing difficulty during the night and feelings of exhaustion during the day.

narcolepsy Hereditary sleep disorder characterized by sudden nodding off during the day and sudden loss of muscle tone, often following moments of emotional excitement.

dreams Vivid visual and auditory experiences that occur primarily during REM periods of sleep.

flying airplane) and internal (say, hunger pangs), may modify an ongoing dream, but they do not initiate dreams. Often, dreams are so vivid that it is difficult to distinguish them from reality.

WHY DO WE DREAM? Psychologists have long been fascinated by dream activity and the contents of dreams, and a number of explanations have been proposed.

- **Dreams as Unconscious Wishes** Sigmund Freud (1900), the first modern theorist to investigate this topic, called dreams the "royal road to the unconscious." Believing that dreams represent wishes that have not been fulfilled in reality, he asserted that people's dreams reflect the motives guiding their behavior—motives of which they may not be consciously aware. Freud distinguished between the *manifest*, or surface, *content* of dreams and their *latent content*—the hidden, unconscious thoughts or desires that he believed were expressed indirectly through dreams. In dreams, according to Freud, people permit themselves to express primitive desires that are relatively free of moral controls. For example, someone who is not consciously aware of hostile feelings toward a sister may dream about murdering her. However, even in a dream, such hostile feelings may be censored and transformed into a symbolic form. For example, the desire to do away with one's sister (the dream's latent content) may be recast into the dream image of seeing her off at a train "terminal" (the dream's manifest content). According to Freud, this process of censorship and symbolic transformation accounts for the highly illogical nature of many dreams. Deciphering the disguised meanings of dreams is one of the principal tasks of psychoanalysts (Hill et al., 2000; Mazzoni, Lombardo, Malvagia, & Loftus, 1999).

- **Dreams and Information Processing** Another explanation for dreaming holds that, in our dreams, we reprocess information gathered during the day as a way of strengthening the memory of information crucial to survival (Carpenter, 2001; Winson, 1990). During our waking hours, our brains are bombarded with sensory data. We need a "time out" to decide what information is valuable, whether it should be filed in long-term memory, where it should be filed (with which older memories, ideas, desires, and anxieties), and what information should be erased so that it doesn't clutter neural pathways (Crick & Mitchison, 1995). According to this view, dreams seem illogical because the brain is rapidly scanning old files and comparing them with new, unsorted "clippings."

    In support of this view, research has demonstrated that both humans and nonhumans spend more time in REM sleep after learning difficult material; furthermore, interfering with REM sleep immediately after learning severely disrupts the memory for the newly learned material (Smith, 1985; Smith & Kelly, 1988; Smith & Lapp, 1986). Brain-imaging studies have also found that the specific area of the brain most active while learning new material is also active during subsequent REM sleep (Maquet et al., 2000).

    Other psychologists think dreams may involve emotional processing. Some (Cartwright, 1996) have suggested that we work through problems in our dreams—indeed, that dreams are part of the healing process after a divorce, the death of a loved one, or other emotional crises. But critics argue that these breakthroughs may be more the result of foresight or hindsight than of dreams themselves (Domhoff, 1996).

The fanciful images of Marc Chagall's paintings capture the quality of many of our dreams. Is a dream of an entwined man and woman floating high above a city symbolic of some subconscious sexual desire, as Freud would have suggested? Or is it just an illogical image caused by random brain cell activity during sleep? As yet, psychologists have no conclusive answer. Perhaps both views have merit.

Source: Marc Chagall (Russian, 1887–1985), "Above the City." Tretyakov Gallery, Moscow, Russia. SuperStock, Inc. / © Artists Rights Society (ARS), New York.

- **Dreams and Waking Life** Still another theory maintains that dreams are an extension of the conscious concerns of daily life in altered (but not disguised) form (Domhoff, 1996). Most often, dream content reflects an individual's unique conceptions, interests, and concerns. For example, a parent who is having problems with a child may dream about childhood confrontations with his or her own parents. Dream content is also related to where you are in your sleep cycle, what you've been doing before you sleep, your gender, your age, and even your socioeconomic status. For example, men more often dream about weapons, unfamiliar characters, male characters, aggressive interactions, and failure outcomes, whereas women are more likely to dream about being the victims of aggression (Bursik, 1998; Domhoff, 1996; Kolchakian & Hill, 2002). Dream content also appears to be relatively "consistent" for most individuals, displaying similar themes across years and even decades (Domhoff, 1996).
- **Dreams and Neural Activity** New research, using advanced brain-imaging techniques, has indicated that the limbic system, which is involved with emotions, motivations, and memories, is "wildly" active during dreams; so, to a lesser extent, are the visual and auditory areas of the forebrain that process sensory information. However, areas of the forebrain involved in working memory, attention, logic, and self-monitoring are relatively inactive (Braun et al., 1998). This fact would explain the highly emotional texture of dreams, as well as bizarre imagery, and the loss of critical insight, logic, and self-reflection. This uncensored mixture of desires, fears, and memories comes very close to the psychoanalytic concept of unconscious wishes, suggesting that Freud may have come closer to the meaning of dreams than many contemporary psychologists have acknowledged.

> ► CHECK YOUR UNDERSTANDING

1. In humans, sleeping and waking follow a _____ cycle.
2. Most vivid dreaming takes place during the _____ stage of sleep.
3. We normally spend about _____ hours each night dreaming.
4. Freud distinguished between the _____ and _____ content of dreams.

Answers: 1. circadian, 2. REM, 3. two, 4. manifest, latent.

> ► APPLY YOUR UNDERSTANDING

1. Suppose you are a nurse studying an elderly person's sleep cycle. Compared with a younger person, you would expect to find that this older person spends _____ time in Stage 3 and Stage 4 sleep.
   a. less
   b. more
   c. about the same
   d. zero

2. Recently, your office coworker has found it difficult to stay awake during the day. In the middle of a conversation, she will suddenly nod off. At night when she goes to bed, she often describes frightening hallucinations. Your coworker is probably suffering from
   a. sleep apnea
   b. REM deprivation
   c. narcolepsy
   d. insomnia

Answers: 1. a, 2. c.

Drug-Altered Consciousness

3.6   Provide a historical perspective on the use of psychoactive drugs and explain how and why people sometimes become addicted to them

The use of **psychoactive drugs**—substances that change people's moods, perceptions, mental functioning, or behavior—is almost universal. In nearly every known culture throughout history, people have sought ways to alter waking consciousness.

DRUG USE IN HISTORICAL PERSPECTIVE

How is today's drug problem different from the drug use in other societies and times?

Many of the drugs available today, legally or illegally, have been used for thousands of years. For example, marijuana is mentioned in the herbal recipe book of a Chinese emperor, dat-

---

psychoactive drugs Chemical substances that change moods and perceptions.

ing from 2737 B.C. Natives of the Andes Mountains in South America chew leaves of the coca plant (which contain cocaine) as a stimulant—a custom dating back at least to the Inca Empire of the fifteenth century.

Is today's drug problem different from the drug use in other societies and times? In many ways, the answer is yes. First, motives for using psychoactive drugs have changed. Historically in most cultures, psychoactive substances have been used as part of religious rituals, as medicines and tonics, as nutrient beverages, or as culturally approved stimulants (much as we drink coffee). In contrast, the use of alcohol and other drugs in our society today is primarily recreational. For the most part, people do not raise their glasses in praise of God or inhale hallucinogens to get in touch with the spirit world, but to relax, have fun with friends (and strangers), and get high. Moreover, Americans most often use drugs in settings specifically designed for recreation and inebriation: bars, clubs, beer parties, cocktail parties, "raves" (large, all-night dance parties), and so-called crack houses. In addition, people use and abuse drugs privately and secretly in their homes, sometimes without the knowledge of family and friends—possibly leading to hidden addiction. Whether social or solitary, the use of psychoactive substances today is largely divorced from religious and family traditions.

Second, the drugs themselves have changed. Today's psychoactive substances often are stronger than those used in other cultures and times. For most of Western history, wine (12 percent alcohol) was often diluted with water. Hard liquor (40 to 75 percent alcohol) appeared only in the tenth century A.D. And the heroin available on the streets today is stronger and more addictive than that available in the 1930s and 1940s.

In addition, new, synthetic drugs appear regularly, with unpredictable consequences. In the 1990s, the National Institute for Drug Abuse created a new category, "Club Drugs," for increasingly popular psychoactive substances manufactured in small laboratories or even home kitchens (from recipes available on the Internet). Because the source, the psychoactive ingredients, and any possible contaminants are unknown, the symptoms, toxicity, and short- or long-term consequences are also unknown—making these drugs especially dangerous. The fact that they are often consumed with alcohol multiplies the risks. Examples include "Ecstasy" (methylenedioxymethamphetamine [MDMA]), a combination of the stimulant amphetamine and a hallucinogen; "Grievous Bodily Harm" (gammahydroxybutyrate [GHB]), a combination of sedatives and growth hormone stimulant; "Special K" (ketamine), an anesthetic approved for veterinary use that induces dreamlike states and hallucinations in humans; and "Roofies" (flunitrazepam), a tasteless, odorless sedative/anesthesia that can cause temporary amnesia, which is why it is also known as the "Forget-Me Pill" and is associated with sexual assault.

Finally, scientists and the public know more about the effects of psychoactive drugs than in the past. Cigarettes are an obvious example. The Surgeon General's Report issued in 1964 confirmed a direct link between smoking and heart disease, as well as lung cancer. Subsequent research, establishing that cigarettes are harmful not only to smokers, but also to people around them (secondhand smoke) and to their unborn babies (Ness et al., 1999), transformed a personal health decision into a moral issue. Nonetheless, tens of millions of Americans still smoke, and millions of others use drugs they know to be harmful.

In the U.S. today, psychoactive drugs are usually used recreationally, rather than as part of a religious or cultural tradition.

SUBSTANCE USE, ABUSE, AND DEPENDENCE

How can we tell whether someone is dependent on a psychoactive substance?

If we define drugs broadly, as we did earlier, to include caffeine, tobacco, and alcohol, then most people throughout the world use some type of drug on an occasional or a regular basis. The majority of these people use such drugs in moderation and do not suffer ill effects. But for many, substance use escalates into **substance abuse**—a pattern of drug use that diminishes a person's ability to fulfill responsibilities, that results in repeated use of the drug in dangerous situations, or that leads to legal difficulties related to drug use. For example, people whose drinking causes ill health and problems within their families or on their jobs are abusing alcohol (D. Smith, 2001). Substance abuse is America's leading health problem (Martin, 2001).

substance abuse A pattern of drug use that diminishes the ability to fulfill responsibilities at home, work, or school; that results in repeated use of a drug in dangerous situations; or that leads to legal difficulties related to drug use.

> **TABLE** 3-3 SIGNS OF SUBSTANCE DEPENDENCE

The most recent clinical definition of dependence (American Psychiatric Association, 1994; Anthony & Helzer, 2002) describes a broad pattern of drug-related behaviors characterized by at least three of the following seven symptoms over a 12-month period:

1. Developing tolerance, that is, needing increasing amounts of the substance to gain the desired effect or experiencing a diminished effect when using the same amount of the substance. For example, the person might have to drink an entire six-pack to get the same effect formerly experienced after drinking just one or two beers.

2. Experiencing withdrawal symptoms, which are physical and psychological problems that occur if the person tries to stop using the substance. Withdrawal symptoms range from anxiety and nausea to convulsions and hallucinations.

3. Using the substance for a longer period or in greater quantities than intended.

4. Having a persistent desire or making repeated efforts to cut back on the use of the substance.

5. Devoting a great deal of time to obtaining or using the substance.

6. Giving up or reducing social, occupational, or recreational activities as a result of drug use.

7. Continuing to use the substance even in the face of ongoing or recurring physical or psychological problems likely to be caused or made worse by the use of the substance.

The ongoing abuse of drugs, including alcohol, may lead to compulsive use of the substance, or **substance dependence**, which is also known as addiction. (See **Table 3–3**.) Although not everyone who abuses a substance develops dependence, dependence usually follows a period of abuse. Dependence often includes *tolerance*, the phenomenon whereby higher doses of the drug are required to produce its original effects or to prevent *withdrawal symptoms*, the unpleasant physical or psychological effects following discontinuance of the substance. Many organizations publicize self-tests based on these and other elements in the definition of substance abuse. For example, a self-test from the National Council on Alcoholism includes the questions, "Can you handle more alcohol now than when you first started to drink?" and "When drinking with other people, do you try to have a few extra drinks the others won't know about?" (The Web site that accompanies this book includes a link to this entire self-test, as well as information on where to get help if you are concerned about problems with alcohol or other substances.)

The causes of substance abuse and dependence are a complex combination of biological, psychological, and social factors that varies for each individual and for each substance (Finn, Sharkansky, Brandt, & Turcotte, 2000; Zucker & Gomberg, 1990). Generally, psychoactive drugs are categorized according to the major effects they have on the nervous system. For example, alcohol, tranquilizers, and opiate-derivative drugs (such as heroin) depress, or slow down, the conduction of neural impulses, and therefore are categorized as **depressants** (see **Summary Table: "Drugs: Characteristics and Effects"**). Drugs such as amphetamines, cocaine, nicotine, and caffeine stimulate, or increase, neural conduction, especially in the sympathetic pathways in the brain. These drugs are usually categorized as **stimulants**. When drugs produce a significant disruption of normal waking consciousness, they usually are included in the group called **hallucinogens**. Examples of drugs in this group include LSD (lysergic acid diethylamide) and marijuana. (For a more detailed discussion of the specific action of the more commonly used drugs in each of these categories, please see Appendix B.) Each type of drug, and each specific drug within each category, has somewhat unique addictive properties which affect individuals in varying ways and to varying degrees.

Also, the development of substance dependence does not follow an established timetable. One person might drink socially for years before abusing alcohol, whereas someone else might become addicted to cocaine in a matter of days. But psychologists have identified a number of factors that, especially in combination, make it more likely that a person will abuse drugs.

substance dependence A pattern of compulsive drug-taking that results in tolerance, withdrawal symptoms, or other specific symptoms for at least a year.

depressants Chemicals that slow down the action of the nervous system and its associated behaviors and cognitive processes.

stimulants Chemicals that speed up the action of the nervous system and its associated behaviors and cognitive processes.

hallucinogens Chemicals that produce a significant disruption in waking consciousness.

SUMMARY TABLE

DRUGS: CHARACTERISTICS AND EFFECTS

	TYPICAL EFFECTS	EFFECTS OF OVERDOSE	TOLERANCE/DEPENDENCE
Depressants			
Alcohol	Two phases: tension-reduction "high," followed by depressed physical and psychological functioning.	Disorientation, loss of consciousness, death at extremely high blood-alcohol levels.	Tolerance; physical and psychological dependence; withdrawal symptoms.
Barbiturates Tranquilizers	Depressed reflexes and impaired motor functioning, tension reduction.	Shallow respiration, clammy skin, dilated pupils, weak and rapid pulse, coma, possible death.	Tolerance; high psychological and physical dependence on barbiturates, low to moderate physical dependence on such tranquilizers as Valium, although high psychological dependence; withdrawal symptoms.
Opiates	Euphoria, drowsiness, "rush" of pleasure, little impairment of psychological functions.	Slow shallow breathing, clammy skin, nausea, vomiting, pinpoint pupils, convulsions, coma, possible death.	High tolerance; physical and psychological dependence; severe withdrawal symptoms.
Stimulants			
Amphetamines Cocaine Caffeine Nicotine	Increased alertness, excitation, euphoria, increased pulse rate and blood pressure, sleeplessness.	For amphetamines and cocaine: agitation and, with chronic high doses, hallucinations (e.g., "cocaine bugs"), paranoid delusions, convulsions, death. For caffeine and nicotine: physical and psychological dependence; withdrawal symptoms.	For amphetamines, cocaine and nicotine: tolerance, psychological and physical dependence. For caffeine and nicotine: restlessness, insomnia, rambling thoughts, heart arrhythmia, possible circulatory failure. For nicotine: increased blood pressure.
Hallucinogens			
LSD	Illusions, hallucinations, distortions in time perception, loss of contact with reality.	Psychotic reactions.	No physical dependence; degree of psychological dependence unknown.
Marijuana	Euphoria, relaxed inhibitions, increased appetite, possible disorientation.	Fatigue, disoriented behavior, possible psychosis.	Psychological dependence.

EXPLAINING ABUSE AND ADDICTION

What combination of factors makes it more likely that someone will abuse drugs?

Many factors contribute to drug abuse and addiction. Among these are biological predispositions and psychological, social, and cultural forces.

BIOLOGICAL FACTORS Are some individuals biologically vulnerable to drug abuse because of hereditary factors? There is evidence of a genetic basis for alcohol abuse. People whose biological parents have alcohol-abuse problems are more likely to abuse alcohol—even if they are adopted and are raised by people who do not abuse alcohol. Identical twins are far more likely to have similar patterns relating to alcohol, tobacco, and marijuana use than are fraternal twins (Gordis, 1996; Lerman, et al., 1999; McGue, 1993; National Institute on Drug Abuse, 2000a), further strengthening biological explanation for drug and alcohol abuse.

Is addiction a disease, like diabetes or high blood pressure? Alcoholics Anonymous (AA), the oldest and probably the most successful self-help organization in this country, has long endorsed this view. According to the disease model, alcoholism is not a moral issue, but a medical one, and alcohol abuse is not a sign of character flaws, but is a symptom of a physiological condition. The disease model has been applied to many addictions. For example, a new organization called *Nicotine Anonymous*, dedicated to helping smokers quit, now operates over 450 active groups nationwide (Lichtenstein, 1999). To some degree, the disease model has become part of conventional wisdom: Many Americans view substance abuse as a biological problem, often the result of "bad" genes that requires medical treatment. Many health professionals share this viewpoint. Miller and Brown (1997) point out that clinical psychologists tend to view substance abuse as a medical problem, beyond their area of expertise, and either refer clients to substance abuse programs or focus on the consequences of substance abuse, rather than on the abuse itself. Regardless of the initial source of the addiction, drug use dramatically changes the brain. To reverse these changes can take months or years and, during that time, cravings to use the drug can be intense (Nestler & Malenka, 2004; Vastag, 2003).

Counseling can be an important component of treatment for drug or alcohol abuse.

PSYCHOLOGICAL, SOCIAL, AND CULTURAL FACTORS Whether a person uses a psychoactive drug and what effects that drug has also depend on the person's expectations, the social setting, and cultural beliefs and values.

A number of studies have shown that people use or abuse alcohol because they expect that drinking will help them to feel better (Cooper, Frone, Russell, & Mudar, 1995). During the 1960s and 1970s, members of the counterculture held similar expectations for marijuana, as do a significant number of young people today.

The setting in which drugs are taken is another important determinant of their effects. Every year thousands of hospital patients are given opiate-based painkillers before and after surgery. They may have experiences that a heroin or cocaine user would label as a "high," but they are more likely to consider them confusing than pleasant. In this setting, psychoactive substances are defined as medicine, dosage is supervised by physicians, and patients take these drugs to get well, not to get high. In contrast, at teenage raves, college beer parties, and all-night clubs, people drink specifically to get drunk and take other drugs to get high. But even in these settings, some individuals participate without using or abusing drugs. Motives for using drugs also vary. People who drink or smoke marijuana because they think that they need a drug also to overcome social inhibitions and be accepted are more likely to slip into abuse than people who use the same substances in the same amounts because they want to have more fun.

The family in which a child grows up also shapes attitudes and beliefs about drugs. For example, children whose parents do not use alcohol tend to abstain or to drink only moderately; children whose parents abuse alcohol tend to drink heavily (Chassin, Pitts, Delucia, & Todd, 1999; Gordis, 1996; Harburg, Gleiberman, DiFranceisco, Schork, & Weissfeld, 1990). Such children are most likely to abuse alcohol if their family tolerates deviance in general or encourages excitement and pleasure seeking (Finn et al., 2000). Moreover, adolescents who have been physically assaulted or sexually abused in their homes are at increased risk for drug abuse (Kilpatrick et al., 2000). Parents are not the only influence: Research indicates that siblings' and peers' attitudes and behavior also can have a major impact on young people's use of drugs (Ary, Duncan, Duncan, & Hops, 1999; also see Harris, 1998).

Culture, too, may steer people toward or away from alcoholism. Alcohol is also more acceptable in some ethnic cultures than in others—for example, Orthodox Jews frown on the use of alcohol, and Muslims prohibit it. Culture also exerts an influence on how many people view other psychologically-induced methods of altering waking conscious experience. Two such methods that have received considerable attention, both from psychologists and the public, are meditation and hypnosis.

Meditation and Hypnosis

3.7 Describe meditation and hypnosis and suggest how these states of consciousness are achieved and how they differ from normal waking consciousness

At one time, Western scientists viewed meditation and hypnosis with great skepticism. However, research has shown that both techniques can produce alterations in consciousness that can be measured through such sophisticated methods as brain imaging.

MEDITATION

What are the effects of meditation?

For centuries, people have used various forms of **meditation** to experience an alteration in consciousness (Benson, 1975). Each form of meditation focuses the meditator's attention in a slightly different way. *Zen meditation* concentrates on respiration, for example, whereas *Sufism* relies on frenzied dancing and prayer (Schwartz, 1974). In *transcendental meditation* (TM), practitioners intone a mantra, which is a sound specially selected for each person, to keep all other images and problems at bay and to allow the meditator to relax more deeply (Deikman, 1973; Schwartz, 1974). The increasingly popular practice of *yoga* involves stretching and bending exercises, and may also encourage practitioners to engage in meditative mental relaxation.

In all its forms, meditation suppresses the activity of the sympathetic nervous system, the part of the nervous system that prepares the body for strenuous activity during an emergency. (See Chapter 2; Davidson et al., 2003.) Meditation also lowers the rate of metabolism, reduces heart and respiratory rates, and decreases blood lactate, a chemical

Many forms of meditation combine physical exercises with mental relaxation techniques to produce a state of calm and peacefulness.

linked to stress. Alpha brain waves (which accompany relaxed wakefulness) increase noticeably during meditation.

Meditation has been used to treat certain medical problems, especially so-called functional complaints (those for which no physical cause can be found). For example, stress often leads to muscle tension and, sometimes, to pressure on nerves—and pain. In other cases, pain leads to muscle tension, which makes the pain worse. Relaxation techniques such as meditation may bring relief (Blanchard et al., 1990). Several studies have found that people stopped using drugs after taking up meditation (Alexander, Robinson, & Rainforth, 1994). Finally, some recent evidence indicates that meditation may increase the effectiveness of the immune system (Davidson et al., 2003).

Besides physiological benefits, people who regularly practice some form of meditation report emotional and even spiritual gains, including increased sensory awareness and a sense of timelessness, well-being, and being at peace with oneself and the universe (Hameroff, Kaszniak, & Scott, 1996; Lantz, Buchalter, & McBee, 1997).

HYPNOSIS

What clinical uses have been found for hypnosis?

In mid-eighteenth-century Europe, Anton Mesmer, a Viennese physician, fascinated audiences by putting patients into trances in order to cure their illnesses. Mesmerism—now known as **hypnosis**—was initially discredited by a French commission chaired by Benjamin Franklin. But some respectable nineteenth-century physicians revived interest in hypnosis when they discovered that it could be used to treat certain forms of mental illness. Nevertheless, even today considerable disagreement persists about how to define hypnosis and even about whether it is a valid altered state of consciousness.

One reason for the controversy is that from a behavioral standpoint, there is no simple definition of what it means to be hypnotized. (See Kihlström, 1998; Kirsch & Lynn, 1998; Kirsch & Braffman, 2001.) Different people who are believed to have undergone hypnosis describe their experiences in very different ways (Farthing, 1992, p. 349):

"Hypnosis is just one thing going on, like a thread . . . focusing on a single thread of one's existence. . . ."

"I felt as if I were 'inside' myself; none of my body was touching anything. . . ."

"I was very much aware of the split in my consciousness. One part of me was analytic and listening to you (the hypnotist). The other part was feeling the things that the analytic part decided I should have."

HYPNOTIC SUGGESTIONS Individuals also vary in their susceptibility to hypnosis. Several studies have shown that, while susceptibility to hypnosis is not related to personal characteristics such as trust, gullibility, submissiveness, and social compliance, it is related to the ability of an individual to become absorbed in reading, music, and daydreaming. (See Nash, 2001.)

One measure of susceptibility is whether people respond to hypnotic suggestion. Some people who are told that they cannot move their arms or that their pain has vanished do, in fact, experience paralysis or anesthesia; if told that they are hearing a certain piece of music or are unable to hear anything, they may hallucinate or become deaf temporarily (Montgomery, DuHamel, & Redd, 2000). When hypnotized subjects are told, "You will remember nothing that happened under hypnosis until I tell you," some people do experience amnesia. But, contrary to rumors, hypnotic suggestion cannot force people to do something foolish and embarrassing—or dangerous—against their will.

Another measure of the success of hypnosis is whether people respond to *posthypnotic commands*. For example, under hypnosis, a person suffering from back pain may be instructed that when he feels a twinge, he will imagine that he is floating on a cloud, his body

meditation Any of the various methods of concentration, reflection, or focusing of thoughts undertaken to suppress the activity of the sympathetic nervous system.

hypnosis Trancelike state in which a person responds readily to suggestions.

is weightless, and the pain will stop—a technique also called "imaging." A runner may be told that when she pulls on her ear, she will block out the noise of the crowd and the runners on either side of her to heighten her concentration—a form of *self-hypnosis*. As the last example suggests, hypnosis has become increasingly popular among professional athletes and their weekend counterparts (Liggett, 2000).

CLINICAL APPLICATIONS OF HYPNOSIS Because hypnotic susceptibility varies significantly from one person to another, its value in clinical and therapeutic settings is difficult to assess. Nevertheless, hypnosis is used in a variety of medical and counseling situations. (See Rhue, Lynn, & Kirsch, 1993; also see Nash, 2004.) Some research indicates that it can enhance the effectiveness of traditional forms of psychotherapy (Kirsch, Montgomery, & Sapirstein, 1995), but psychologists do not all agree on this issue. Hypnosis has been shown to be effective in controlling various types of physical pain (Patterson & Jensen, 2003; Patterson & Ptacek, 1997). Dentists have used it as an anesthetic for years. Hypnosis has also been used to alleviate pain in children with leukemia who have to undergo repeated bone-marrow biopsies (Hilgard, Hilgard, & Kaufmann, 1983). Moreover, it also has a role in treating some medical conditions, such as irritable bowel syndrome (Gonsalkorale, Miller, Afzal, & Whorwell, 2003).

Susceptibility to hypnosis varies from person to person, but many people have found it useful in a variety of medical and counseling situations.

Can hypnosis make someone change or eliminate bad habits? In some cases, posthypnotic commands temporarily diminish a person's desire to smoke or overeat (Elkins & Rajab, 2004; Green & Lynn, 2000; Griffiths & Channon-Little, 1995). But even certified hypnotists agree that this treatment is effective only if people are motivated to change their behavior. Hypnosis may shore up their will, but so might joining a support group, such as Nicotine Anonymous or Weight Watchers.

▸ CHECK YOUR UNDERSTANDING

Match the following terms with the appropriate description:

1. meditation
2. hypnosis
3. hypnotic susceptibility

a. varies tremendously over time
b. is a controversial altered state of consciousness
c. suppresses sympathetic nervous system

Answers: 1. c, 2. b, 3. a.

▸ APPLY YOUR UNDERSTANDING

1. Marie works in a high-pressure, competitive job. She regularly practices transcendental meditation. The most likely reason she finds this practice beneficial is that meditation
   a. increases the rate of metabolism
   b. increases the activity of the sympathetic nervous system
   c. produces deep relaxation
   d. allows her to sleep fewer hours and still feel refreshed

2. You overhear some people discussing the effects of hypnosis. On the basis of what you have learned in this chapter, you agree with everything they say EXCEPT
   a. "Some people can easily be hypnotized and some people can't."
   b. "If you tell someone under hypnosis to forget everything that happens, some people will actually do that."
   c. "Under hypnosis, people can be forced to do foolish or embarrassing things against their will."
   d. "Hypnosis can actually be used to control some kinds of pain."

Answers: 1. c, 2. c.

>KEY TERMS<

The nature of sensation

sensation, *p. 73*
receptor cell, *p. 73*
absolute threshold, *p. 74*
adaptation, *p. 74*
difference threshold or just-noticeable difference (jnd), *p. 74*
Weber's law, *p. 74*

The senses

cornea, *p. 76*
pupil, *p. 76*
iris, *p. 76*
lens, *p. 76*
retina, *p. 76*
fovea, *p. 76*
rods, *p. 77*
cones, *p. 77*
bipolar cells, *p. 78*
visual acuity, *p. 78*
dark adaptation, *p. 79*
light adaptation, *p. 79*
afterimage, *p. 79*
ganglion cells, *p. 80*

optic nerve, *p. 80*
blind spot, *p. 80*
optic chiasm, *p. 80*
feature detectors, *p. 81*
additive color mixing, *p. 81*
trichromatic theory, *p. 82*
color blindness, *p. 82*
opponent-process theory, *p. 82*
sound, *p. 83*
sound waves, *p. 83*
frequency, *p. 83*
pitch, *p. 83*
amplitude, *p. 83*
timbre, *p. 84*
oval window, *p. 84*
cochlea, *p. 84*
basilar membrane, *p. 84*
organ of Corti, *p. 84*
auditory nerve, *p. 84*
olfactory bulb, *p. 86*
pheromones, *p. 87*
taste buds, *p. 87*
kinesthetic senses, *p. 87*
stretch receptors, *p. 87*
Golgi tendon organs, *p. 87*

vestibular senses, *p. 88*
gate-control theory, *p. 90*
biopsychosocial theory, *p. 90*

Perception

perception, *p. 91*
perceptual constancy, *p. 93*
size constancy, *p. 94*
shape constancy, *p. 94*
monocular cues, *p. 95*
binocular cues, *p. 95*
interposition, *p. 95*
perspective, *p. 95*
texture gradient, *p. 95*
shadowing, *p. 95*
motion parallax, *p. 96*
stereoscopic vision, *p. 96*
retinal disparity, *p. 96*
convergence, *p. 96*
monaural cue, *p. 96*
binaural cue, *p. 96*

Consciousness experience

consciousness, *p. 98*
waking consciouness, *p. 98*

altered states of consciousness, *p. 99*
daydreams, *p. 99*

Sleep

circadian rhythms, *p. 101*
REM (paradoxical) sleep, *p. 103*
non-REM (NREM) sleep, *p. 103*
insomnia, *p. 105*
nightmares, *p. 106*
night terrors, *p. 106*
apnea, *p. 106*
narcolepsy, *p. 106*
dreams, *p. 106*

Drug-altered consciousness

psychoactive drugs, *p. 108*
substance abuse, *p. 109*
substance dependence, *p. 110*
depressants, *p. 110*
stimulants, *p. 110*
hallucinogens, *p. 110*

Meditation and hypnosis

meditation, *p. 113*
hypnosis, *p. 114*

>CHAPTER REVIEW<

The Nature of Sensation

How is physical energy from the environment converted into a message carried to the brain and what limitations are there on this process, called sensation? Humans have sensory experiences of sight, hearing, smell, taste, touch, pain, and balance, which are known as **sensations**. These experiences begin when the body's sensory receptors are stimulated. In each case, some form of physical energy is converted into neural impulses that are carried to the brain. The process of sending a sensory message to the brain begins when energy stimulates **receptor cells** in one of the sense organs. The receptor cells then send the brain a coded neural signal that varies according to the characteristics of the stimulus. Further coding occurs as the signal passes along sensory nerve fibers, so that the message finally reaching the brain is very detailed and precise.

The amount of physical energy that reaches sensory receptors must be of a minimal intensity to produce a detectable sensation.

The least amount of energy needed to produce a sensation 50 percent of the time is called the **absolute threshold**. For hearing, the absolute threshold is roughly the tick of a watch from 6 meters (20 feet) away in a very quiet room, and for vision, it is a candle flame seen from 50 kilometers (30 miles) on a clear, dark night. Absolute thresholds vary according to the intensity of the stimulus present at any given time—a process called **adaptation**. Also, we are very sensitive to *changes* in the stimulus intensity. The **difference threshold**, also called the **just-noticeable difference (jnd)**, is the smallest change in stimulation that can be detected 50 percent of the time.

Under what circumstances might messages outside our awareness affect our behavior? When people respond to sensory messages that are below their threshold level of awareness, they are said to be responding subliminally. Such subliminal processing can occur in controlled laboratory settings, but there is no scientific evidence that subliminal messages have any effect in everyday life.

The Senses: Vision

How is light energy converted to sensory information in process of vision? In humans, vision is probably the most important sense, which is why it has received the most research attention. Visual processing begins when light enters an eye through the **cornea** (a transparent protective coating) and passes through the **pupil** (the opening in the **iris**) and then the **lens**, which focuses it onto the eye's light-sensitive inner lining called the **retina**. Neural impulses are generated in the retina by receptor cells known as **rods** and **cones**. The rods and cones connect to nerve cells called **bipolar cells**, which in turn connect to **ganglion cells**. The axons of ganglion cells converge to form the **optic nerve**, which carries to the brain the neural impulses triggered in the retina.

Two theories have been proposed to explain color vision. One theory, the **trichromatic theory**, is based on the principles of **additive color mixing**. It holds that the eyes contain three different kinds of color receptors, one of which is most responsive to red, another to green, and another to blue–violet. By combining signals from these three types of receptors, the brain can detect a wide range of colors. In contrast, the **opponent-process theory** of color vision maintains that receptors in the eyes are specialized to respond to one half of three basic color pairs: red–green, yellow–blue, and black–white (or light–dark). Research gives some support for both these theories; there are indeed three kinds of color receptors in the retinas, but the messages they initiate are coded by other neurons into opponent-process form.

The Senses: Hearing

How is sound energy converted to sensory information in the process of hearing (audition)? The physical stimuli for the sense of hearing are **sound waves**, which produce vibration in the eardrums. **Frequency**, the number of cycles per second in a sound wave, is the primary determinant of **pitch** (how high or low the tones seems to be). **Amplitude**, the magnitude of a wave, largely determines the loudness of a sound. When complex overtones of sound waves are generated along with a pure tone, we perceive the combination as **timbre**. Timbre explains why two musical instruments playing tha same note do not sound identical.

When sound waves strike an eardrum and cause it to vibrate, three bones in the middle ear—the hammer, the anvil, and the stirrup—are stimulated to vibrate in sequence. These vibrations are magnified in their passage through the middle ear and into the inner ear beyond it. In the inner ear, movement of the **basilar membrane** stimulates sensory receptors in the **organ of Corti**. This stimulation of the hair cells produces auditory signals that travel to the temporal lobes of the brain via the **auditory nerve**.

Deafness may result from several causes and can be treated with hearing aids that amplify sound, or by surgically implanted electrodes in the cochlea. Cochlear implants can sometimes be used to treat tinnitus, a high-pitched ringing in the ears.

The Other Senses

What mechanisms are involved in the chemical, kinesthetic and vestibular, and skin senses? The senses of smell and taste involve the detection of various chemical substances in the air and in foods that we eat. Substances carried by airborne molecules into the nasal cavities activate highly specialized receptors for smell. From here, messages are carried directly to the **olfactory bulb** in the brain, where they are sent to the brain's temporal lobe, resulting in our awareness of smell. The receptors for taste are housed in the **taste buds** on the tongue. When these receptors are activated by the chemical substances in food, their adjacent neurons fire, sending nerve impulses to the brain. There are four basic tastes that we sense—sweet, sour, salty, and bitter—and other tastes derive from combinations of these. The overall flavor of something is a complex blend of taste and smell.

The **vestibular senses** provide information about our orientation or position in space, such as whether we are rightside up or upside down. The receptors for these senses are in two vestibular organs in the inner ear—the semicircular canals and the vestibular sacs. The kinesthetic senses provide information about the speed and direction of our movements. They rely on feedback from two sets of specialized nerve endings—**stretch receptors**, which are attached to muscle fibers, and **Golgi tendon organs**, which are attached to the tendons that connect muscle to bone. The vestibular organs are responsible for motion sickness. This queasy feeling may be triggered by discrepancies between visual information and vestibular sensations.

The skin is the largest sense organ, and sensations that arise from the receptors embedded in it produce our sensation of touch, which includes pressure, temperature, and pain. Research has not yet established a simple, direct connection between these three sensations and the various types of skin receptors whose nerve fibers lead to the brain. People have varying degrees of sensitivity to pain based partly on their physiological makeup, but also on their current mental and emotional state, their expectations about what they will experience, and their cultural beliefs and values. One commonly accepted explanation of pain is the **gate-control theory**, which holds that a "neurological gate" in the spinal cord controls the transmission of pain messages to the brain. **Biopsychosocial theory** proposes that pain results from a complex interaction of biological, psychological, and social mechanisms.

Perception

How is perception different from sensation? Sensation refers to the raw sensory data that the brain receives from the senses of sight, hearing, smell, taste, balance, touch, and pain. **Perception**, which takes place in the brain, is the process of organizing, interpreting, and giving meaning to that raw data in order to understand what is going on around us.

How do we organize our perceptual experiences? Early in the twentieth century, a group of Gestalt psychologists in Germany set out to discover the principles through which we interpret sensory information. They believed that the brain creates a coherent perceptual experience that is more than simply the sum of the available sensory data. The brain imposes order on the data it receives partly by distinguishing patterns such as figure and ground, proximity, similarity, closure, and continuity.

How do we perceive things as unchanging despite changing sensory information? **Perceptual constancy** is our tendency to perceive objects as unchanging even given many changes in sensory stimulation. After we have formed a stable perception of something, we see it as essentially the same regardless of differences in viewing angle, distance, lighting, and so forth.

How do we know how far away something is? We perceive distance and depth through both **monocular cues** (which can be received even by one eye alone) and **binocular cues** (which depend on the interaction of both eyes). Examples of monocular cues are **interposition** (in which one object partly covers another), **linear perspective**, **elevation** (or closeness of something to the horizon), **texture gradient** (from coarser to finer depending on distance), **shadowing**, and **motion parallax** (differences in the relative movement of close and distant objects as we change position). Two binocular cues are **retinal disparity** (the fact that each eye receives a slightly different view from the other) and **convergence** of the eyes as viewing distance decreases. **Stereoscopic vision**, which is derived from combining our two retinal images, produces a three-dimensional perception of two-dimensional images. Just as we use monocular and binocular cues to sense depth and distance, we use **monaural** (one-ear) and **binaural** (two-ear) cues to locate sound.

What causes visual illusions? Visual illusions occur when we use a variety of sensory cues to create perceptual experiences that do not actually exist. Some are *physical illusions*, such as the bent appearance of a stick in water. Others are *perceptual illusions*, which occur because a stimulus contains misleading cues that lead to inaccurate perceptions.

Conscious Experience

How does our awareness of the environment contribute to the various states of consciousness we experience? To make sense of our complex environment, we choose what to attend to from the myriad happenings around us and filter out the rest. This process applies to both external stimuli such as sounds, sights, and smells, and internal sensations such as heat, cold, pressure, and pain. Even our thoughts, memories, emotions, and needs are subjected to this selective process. We also perform familiar tasks, such as signing our names, without deliberate attention. Many psychologists believe that important mental processes go on outside normal **waking consciousness.**

Do daydreams serve any useful function? **Daydreaming** occurs without effort, often when we seek briefly to escape the demands of the real world. Some psychologists see no positive or practical value in daydreaming. Others contend that daydreams and fantasies allow us to express and deal with hidden desires without guilt or anxiety. Still others believe that daydreams build cognitive and creative skills that help us survive difficult situations, and that they can serve as a beneficial way of relieving tension.

Sleep

What is the biological clock and what does it have to do with jet lag? Like many other biological functions, sleep and waking follow a daily, biological cycle known as a **circadian rhythm**. The human *biological clock* is governed by a tiny cluster of neurons in the brain. Normally, the rhythms and chemistry of the body's cycles interact smoothly, but when we cross several time zones in one day, hormonal, temperature, and digestive cycles become desynchronized.

What physical changes mark the rhythms of sleep? Normal sleep consists of several stages. During *Stage 1*, the pulse slows, muscles relax, and the eyes move from side to side. The sleeper is easily awakened from Stage 1 sleep. In *Stages 2 and 3*, the sleeper is hard to awaken and does not respond to noise or light. Heart rate, blood pressure, and temperature continue to drop. During *Stage 4* sleep, heart and breathing rates, blood pressure, and body temperature are at their lowest points of the night. About an hour after first falling asleep, the sleeper begins to ascend through the stages back to Stage 1—a process that takes about 40 minutes. At this stage in the sleep cycle, heart rate and blood pressure increase, the muscles become more relaxed than at any other time in the cycle, and the eyes move rapidly under closed eyelids. It is during this **rapid-eye movement (REM)** stage, also called paradoxical sleep, that much of our dreaming occurs.

What are the consequences of sleep deprivation? When people are deprived of sleep, they have more difficulty paying attention, their reaction times slow, their memory suffers, and their judgements become impaired. People do not adapt to chronic sleep loss, which can be especially problematic for those in high-risk occupations.

What types of sleep disorders to people experience? Sleep disorders include **insomnia**, sleeptalking, sleepwalking, **night terrors, apnea,** and **narcolepsy**. Insomnia is characterized by difficulty in falling asleep or remaining asleep throughout the night. Insomnia can be treated with prescription medicines but these sometimes have negative side effects. Most episodes of sleeptalking and sleepwalking occur during a deep stage of sleep. Unlike **nightmares**, night terrors, which are more common among children than adults, prove difficult to be awakened from and are rarely remembered the next morning.

What are dreams? **Dreams** are visual or auditory experiences that occur primarily during REM periods of sleep. Less vivid experiences that resemble conscious thinking tend to occur during NREM sleep. Several theories have been developed to explain the nature and content of dreams. According to Freud, dreams have two kinds of contents: *manifest* (the surface content of the dream itself) and *latent* (the disguised, unconscious meaning of the dream). One recent hypothesis suggests that dreams arise out of the mind's reprocessing of information absorbed during the day.

Drug-altered Consciousness

How is today's drug problem different from drug use in other societies and times? Although many of the **psychoactive drugs** available today have been used for thousands of years, the motivation for using drugs is different today. Traditionally, these drugs were used in religious rituals, as nutrient beverages, or as culturally approved stimulants. Today, most psychoactive drug use is recreational, divorced from religious or family traditions. Drugs today are also stronger.

How can we tell whether someone is dependent on a psychoactive substance? **Substance abuse** is a pattern of drug use that diminishes the person's ability to fulfill responsibilities at home, work, or school and that results in repeated use of a drug in dangerous situations or that leads to legal difficulties related to drug use. Continued abuse over time can lead to **substance dependence**, a pattern of compulsive drug taking that is much more serious than substance abuse. It is often marked by tolerance, the need to take higher doses of a drug to produce its original effects or to prevent withdrawal symptoms. Withdrawal symptoms are the unpleasant physical or psychological effects that follow discontinuance of the psychoactive substance.

Drugs are usually categorized according to the major effect they have on the nervous system. **Depressants**, like alcohol, barbiturates, and opium-derivatives, slow down central nervous system functioning. **Stimulants**, like amphetamines, cocaine, nicotine, and caffeine, speed up neural activity, especially in the sympathetic branch. **Hallucinogens**, like LSD and marijuana, usually produce significant alterations in normal waking consciousness.

What combination of factors makes it more likely that someone will abuse drugs? Different drugs are associated with various patterns of abuse and dependence. Several general factors also make it more likely that a person will abuse drugs. They include a possible genetic predisposition, the person's expectations, the social setting, and cultural beliefs and values.

Meditation and Hypnosis

What are the effects of meditation? **Meditation** refers to any of several methods of concentration, reflection, or focusing of thoughts intended to suppress the activity of the sympathetic nervous system. Meditation not only lowers the rate of metabolism, but also reduces heart and respiratory rates. Brain activity during meditation resembles that experienced during relaxed wakefulness, and the accompanying decrease in blood lactate reduces stress.

What clinical uses have been found for hypnosis? Hypnosis is a trancelike state in which the person responds readily to suggestions. People's susceptibility to hypnosis depends on how easily they can become absorbed in concentration. Hypnosis has several practical applications; for instance, it eases the pain of certain medical conditions and can help people stop smoking and break other habits.

>CHAPTER 3<

Sensation, Perception, and Conscious Experience

3.1 THE NATURE OF SENSATION

HOW SENSATION HAPPENS

- **Receptor cells** in sense organs code stimuli into neural impulses that travel to the brain and are interpreted as **sensations**
- Sensory **thresholds** limit what humans can sense
- **Absolute threshold**: Least amount of energy that can be detected 50% of the time
- **Difference threshold**: Smallest change in energy that can be detected 50% of the time

3.2 THE SENSES

HOW VISION OCCURS

- **Light** enters through the **cornea** and **pupil** and is focused by the **lens** on the **retina**, where it activates **rod** and **cone receptor cells**.
- **Rods**: Work in low light; code for black-and-white vision
- **Cones**: Work in bright light; code for color vision
- Impulses are conveyed via the **bipolar cells, ganglion cells**, and neurons in the **optic nerve**, are rerouted at the **optic chiasm**, and end up at the **occipital cortex** of the brain

THEORIES OF COLOR VISION

- **Trichromatic theory:** Three types of cones (red, blue, green) sense different wavelengths of light, and their combined impulses are interpreted as color.
- **Opponent process theory:** Three pairs of color receptors in neural pathways (red-green, blue-yellow, black-white) create the sensation of color.

COLOR BLINDNESS

People who cannot see the number 96 here have red-green color blindness

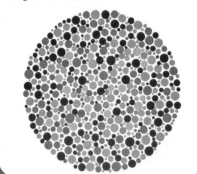

HOW HEARING OCCURS

- Vibrations of air molecules produce **sound waves**, which travel into the ear
- They vibrate the **eardrum**, three tiny connected bones (the hammer, anvil, and stirrup), and the **oval window**
- This sets up vibrations of fluid in the **cochlea**, which triggers the firing of **hair cells** embedded in the **organ of Corti** that lies along the basilar membrane
- The **auditory nerve** carries impulses to the brain
- Frequency theory better explains lower-frequency sounds and Place theory better explains higher-frequency (above 4,000 Hz) sounds

3.3 PERCEPTION

GESTALT PRINCIPLES OF PERCEPTION

- Figure-Ground
- Proximity
- Similarity
- Closure
- Continuity

PERCEPTUAL CONSTANCIES

- **Size constancy:** Objects appear to be the same size, regardless of their distance from us
- **Shape constancy:** Objects appear to be the same shape, regardless of the angle from which we view them

OTHER SENSES

- **Smell:** Airborne molecules bind with a protein in the nose, where messages are relayed to the **olfactory bulb**, and then to the brain
- **Taste:** Receptors in the **taste buds** on the tongue code messages for four basic taste qualities: sweet, sour, salty, and bitter
- **Kinesthetic senses:** The body's movements in space are recorded by stretch receptors embedded in muscles and **Golgi tendon organs** attached to tendons
- **Vestibular senses:** The body's position in space is sensed by hair cells in the **semicircular canals** and **vestibular sacs** in the inner ear and travel to the brain
- **Skin senses:** Receptors in the skin give rise to sensations of pressure, temperature, and pain.
  - **Gate-control theory of pain:** Pain signals can be blocked with neurological signals
  - **Biopsychosocial theory:** Pain is a multi-faceted and complex phenomenon

PERCEPTION OF DISTANCE AND DEPTH

Our eyes help us locate objects in space.

Monocular (1-eye) Cues	Binocular (2-eye) Cues
Interposition	Stereoscopic vision
Perspective	Retinal disparity
Texture gradient	
Shadowing	
Motion parallax	

VISUAL ILLUSIONS

- **Physical illusions:** Caused by distortions of stimuli
- **Perceptual illusions:** Caused by misleading or confusing stimulus cues

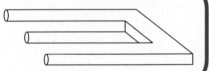

3.4 CONSCIOUS EXPERIENCE

STATES OF CONSCIOUSNESS

- **Waking consciousness:** Mental state that encompasses thoughts, feelings, and perceptions when we are awake and alert
- **Altered states of consciousness:** Mental states that differ noticeably from normal waking consciousness

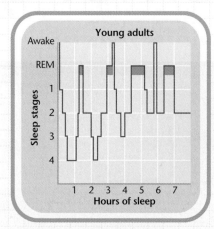

3.5 SLEEP

THE BIOLOGICAL CLOCK

- Sleep and waking occur in a **circadian rhythm**, or biological clock, about every 24 hours
- Governed by neurotransmitters affecting body temperature, metabolism, blood pressure, hormone levels, and hunger

RHYTHMS OF SLEEP

- **Stage 1:** Light sleep, with increasing relaxation and brain waves that are tight and low amplitude
- **Stage 2:** Deeper sleep than Stage 1, with short bursts of brain wave activity (sleep spindles)
- **Stage 3:** Delta waves in EEG; very relaxed and hard to awaken
- **Stage 4:** Deepest sleep, slowest body functions, delta waves common
- **REM (Rapid Eye Movement) Sleep paradoxical sleep:** Physical responses (blood pressure, heart rate) similar to waking state, but muscles relaxed; eyes move under eyelids, person difficult to awaken. Most dreaming occurs in REM sleep.

SLEEP DISORDERS

- Sleep talking and sleepwalking: Stage 4
- Nightmares: REM sleep, dreamer remembers
- Night Terrors: Non-REM sleep, dreamer doesn't remember
- Insomnia: Inability to fall asleep or stay asleep; treated with counseling or medicines
- Apnea: Breathing irregularities that disrupt sleep
- Narcolepsy: Hereditary disorder involving abrupt periods of sleep during waking activities

3.6 DRUG-ALTERED CONCIOUSNESS

SUBSTANCE USE AND DEPENDENCE

- Today's drugs are usually used for recreation, are more powerful, and their better understood than before
- **Signs of substance dependence:** tolerance, withdrawal symptoms, greater use than intended, persistently trying to stop, compulsion to use

TYPES OF PSYCHOACTIVE DRUGS

- **Depressants** (alcohol, barbiturates, opium derivatives): Slow down nervous system functioning
- **Stimulants** (amphetamines, cocaine, nicotine, caffeine): Speed up nervous system functioning
- **Hallucinogens** (LSD, marijuana): Distort aspects of waking consciousness

3.7 MEDITATION AND HYPNOSIS

- **Meditation:** Any of the various methods of concentration, reflection, or focusing of thoughts to suppress activity of the sympathetic nervous system
- **Hypnosis:** Trancelike state in which the person responds readily to suggestions

Concept Map

Learning and Memory

Overview

EVERY SOLDIER A SENSOR

Private Jones is gathering intelligence in the Iraqi city of Mosul. Mopeds whiz by, car horns honk, there are small knots of men on street corners, groups of black-clad women carrying parcels, children on a dusty field playing a soccer game, and graffiti emblazoned on nearby walls. The soldier moves toward a group of old men who tell him that the neighborhood needs to be "cleared up." Private Jones has a decision to make. Should he listen to them, detain them, or ignore them? If they have news of a hidden explosive device, the consequences of ignoring them could be life-threatening—that is, if Private Jones were really in Mosul and not sitting in front of his laptop in Fort Jackson, South Carolina.

Pvt. Jones is playing *Every Soldier a Sensor*, a video game developed to teach soldiers an untraditional but absolutely critical combat skill, using observations and judgments to bring the right details back to base. Like the popular *Civilization* or *The Sims*, in which players design civilizations and cities, *Every Soldier a Sensor* is an *epistemic* game, a game that immerses players in virtual worlds. Although familiar to the average 21-year-old "digital native" who has played 10,000 hours of video games in his lifetime, these games are finally being used as learning tools—not just in the U.S. military, but in business management training seminars and elementary school classrooms. Game developers estimate that at least 10 percent of classrooms in the nation's 2,500 major school districts use mainstream video game titles for learning.

It makes sense. Students are more willing to learn and practice a skill when they are having fun and interacting with the content. If you were Pvt. Jones, what would you rather do—sit in a dark lecture hall watching a PowerPoint presentation on military intelligence or rove through the virtual streets of Iraq trying to uncover hidden explosives? And after a player interacts within a game, he or she is lured to learn and practice skills by the promise of rewards. Pop culture defender and writer Steven Johnson, author of *Everything Bad is Good for You*, says, "In the game world reward is everywhere. The universe is literally teeming with rewards." In *The Sims*, for example, Johnson says, ". . . the game has a subtle reward architecture" in which "the software withholds a trove of objects and activities until you've reached certain predefined levels, either of population, money, or popularity."

Video games stimulate a basic form of learning, operant conditioning, in which behaviors are produced to earn rewards or avoid punishments. In *Every Soldier a Sensor*, for example, players gain points by collecting information and spotting improvised explosive devices. Putting the soldier in a real-life sweat, the game clock ticks down second-by-second, challenging the player to do the right thing quickly. Because each action a player takes consumes additional time, players learn that if they check out everyone and everything, time will run out. As they accrue points, a big human brain symbol glows more brightly on the computer screen, reflecting their increasing ability to gather intelligence quickly and effectively.

Dr. Henry Jenkins, principal investigator of Microsoft's Games-to-Teach Project has identified several ways that games promote learning: They can create a social context among players, accommodate a variety of learning styles, keep students engaged through immersion, and provide a jumping-off point for additional research and learning. Video games, thus, provide ample opportunities for gamers to perfect their learning strategies and refine their memory for key information.[1]

In this chapter, we begin our exploration of learning and memory by examining several approaches to **learning**. One basic way in which we learn involves forming associations between events. Both *operant conditioning* and *classical conditioning* involve learning associations, or contingencies, among events. But forming associations is not all there is to human learning. Our learning also involves the construction of concepts, theories, ideas, and other mental abstractions—the type of thinking referred to as *cognitive learning*. And all forms of learning, of course, rely on our ability to remember. We therefore conclude the chapter with an exploration of human **memory**, including a discussion of not only how we remember but also why we sometimes forget. ◼

Classical Conditioning

4.1 Describe the way in which classically conditioned responses become established and suggest what kinds of responses are most easily conditioned in humans.

The Russian physiologist Ivan Pavlov (1849–1936) discovered **classical conditioning** almost by accident. Working in his laboratory at the turn of the twentieth century, Pavlov was studying digestion, which begins when saliva mixes with food in the mouth. While measuring how much saliva dogs produce when given food, he noticed that they began to salivate even before they tasted the food. The mere sight of food made them drool. In fact, they even drooled at the sound of the experimenter's footsteps. This aroused Pavlov's curiosity. What was causing these responses? How had the dogs learned to salivate to sights and sounds?

learning The process by which experience or practice results in a relatively permanent change in behavior or potential behavior.

memory The ability to remember the things that we have experienced, imagined, and learned

classical (or Pavlovian) conditioning The type of learning in which a response naturally elicited by one stimulus comes to be elicited by a different, formerly neutral stimulus.

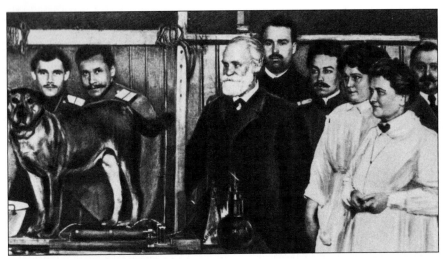

Ivan Pavlov (center) identified the basic mechanisms involved in classical conditioning while investigating digestive processes in dogs.

unconditioned stimulus (US) A stimulus that invariably causes an organism to respond in a specific way.

unconditioned response (UR) A response that takes place in an organism whenever an unconditioned stimulus occurs.

conditioned stimulus (CS) An originally neutral stimulus that is paired with an unconditioned stimulus and eventually produces the desired response in an organism when presented alone.

conditioned response (CR) After conditioning, the response an organism produces when a conditioned stimulus is presented.

To answer this question, Pavlov sounded a bell just before presenting his dogs with food. A ringing bell does not usually make a dog's mouth water, but after hearing the bell many times right before getting fed, Pavlov's dogs began to salivate as soon as the bell rang. It was as if they had learned that the bell signaled the appearance of food, and their mouths watered on cue even if no food followed. The dogs had been conditioned to salivate in response to a new stimulus: the bell, which normally would not prompt salivation (Pavlov, 1927).

ELEMENTS OF CLASSICAL CONDITIONING

How does classical conditioning occur?

Figure 4–1 diagrams the four basic elements in classical conditioning: (1) the unconditioned stimulus, (2) the unconditioned response, (3) the conditioned stimulus, and (4) the conditioned response. The **unconditioned stimulus (US)** is an event that automatically elicits a certain reflex reaction, which is the **unconditioned response (UR)**. In Pavlov's studies, food in the mouth was the unconditioned stimulus, and salivation to it was the unconditioned response. The third element in classical conditioning, the **conditioned stimulus (CS)**, is an event that is repeatedly paired with the unconditioned stimulus. For a conditioned stimulus, Pavlov often used a bell. At first, the conditioned stimulus does not elicit the desired response. But eventually, after repeatedly being paired with the unconditioned stimulus, the conditioned stimulus alone comes to trigger a reaction similar to the unconditioned response. This learned reaction is the **conditioned response (CR)**.

Classical conditioning has been demonstrated in virtually every animal species, even squid and spiders (Krasne & Glanzman, 1995). It is one of the basic learning processes for humans as well: Consider how your mouth begins to water when you smell your favorite food cooking on the stove, or how you get "butterflies" in your stomach before you give a presentation or performance.

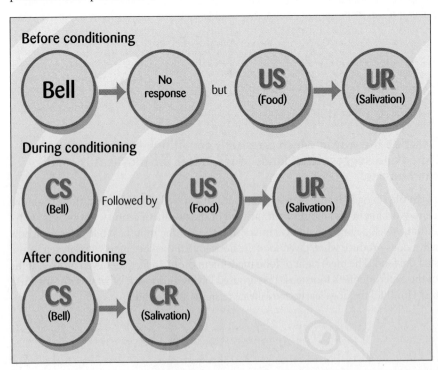

Figure 4–1
A model of the classical conditioning process.

CLASSICAL CONDITIONING AND FEAR RESPONSES

How is classical conditioning involved in learning and unlearning emotional responses such as fear?

In some cases, *phobias*—which are intense, irrational fears of particular things or situations, such as spiders, snakes, flying, or being in enclosed places—can be learned through classical conditioning. In Chapter 1, we discussed the study in which John Watson and his assistant Rosalie Rayner used classical conditioning to instill a phobia of white rats in a one-year-old baby named Albert (Watson & Rayner, 1920). They started by showing Albert a white rat, which he happily tried to play with. But every time he approached the rat, the experimenters made a loud frightening noise by striking a steel bar behind the baby's head. After a few pairings of the rat and the frightening noise, Albert began to cry in fear at the sight of the rat alone. By being paired with the unconditioned stimulus of the loud noise, the rat had become a conditioned stimulus for a conditioned fear response.

Several years later, psychologist Mary Cover Jones demonstrated a way that fears can be unlearned by means of classical conditioning (Jones, 1924). Her subject was a three-year-old boy named Peter who, like Albert, had a fear of white rats. Jones paired the sight of a rat with an intrinsically pleasant experience—eating candy. While Peter sat alone in a room, a caged white rat was brought in and placed far enough away so that the boy would not be frightened. At this point, Peter was given plenty of candy to eat. On each successive day, the cage was moved closer to Peter, after which, he was given candy. Eventually, he showed no fear of the rat, even without any candy. By being repeatedly paired with a stimulus that evoked a pleasant emotional response, the rat had become a conditioned stimulus for pleasure.

In more recent times, psychiatrist Joseph Wolpe (1915–1997) adapted Jones's method to the treatment of certain kinds of anxiety (Wolpe, 1973, 1982). Wolpe reasoned that because irrational fears are learned or conditioned, they also could be unlearned through conditioning. He noted that it is not possible to be both fearful and relaxed at the same time. Therefore, if people could be taught to relax in fearful or anxious situations, their anxiety should disappear. Wolpe's **desensitization therapy** begins by teaching a system of deep-muscle relaxation. Then the person constructs a list of situations that prompt various degrees of fear or anxiety, from intensely frightening to only mildly so. A person with a fear of heights, for example, might construct a list that begins with standing on the edge of the Grand Canyon and ends with climbing two rungs on a ladder. While deeply relaxed, the person imagines the least distressing situation on the list first. If he or she succeeds in remaining relaxed, the person proceeds to the next item on the list, and so on until no anxiety is felt, even when imagining the most frightening situation. In this way, classical conditioning is used to change an undesired reaction: A fear-arousing thought is repeatedly paired with a muscular state that produces calmness until eventually the formerly fearful thought no longer triggers anxiety. Desensitization therapy has been used successfully to treat a variety of disorders such as phobias and posttraumatic stress disorder (Everly & Lating, 2004; Travis, 2004), topics we will turn our attention to again in Chapter 9: "Psychological Disorders and Their Treatments."

CLASSICAL CONDITIONING IS SELECTIVE

Why are people more likely to develop a phobia of snakes than of flowers?

If people can develop phobias through classical conditioning, as Little Albert did, why don't we acquire phobias of virtually everything that is paired with harm? For example, many people get shocks from electric sockets, but almost no one develops a socket phobia. Why should this be the case? Why shouldn't most carpenters have phobias of hammers due to accidentally pounding their fingers with them?

One reason is that classically conditioned responses usually require many pairings of the CS and the UCS to become learned. Psychologist Martin Seligman has offered a second answer: The key, he says, lies in the concept of **preparedness**. Some things readily become conditioned stimuli for fear responses because we are biologically prepared to learn those associations.

Desensitization therapy is based on the belief that we can overcome fears by learning to remain calm in the face of increasingly fear-arousing situations. Here people being desensitized for a fear of heights are able to swing high above the ground without panicking.

desensitization therapy A conditioning technique designed to gradually reduce anxiety about a particular object or situation.

preparedness A biological readiness to learn certain associations because of their survival advantages.

Seligman's theory of preparedness argues that we are biologically prepared to associate certain stimuli, such as heights, the dark, and snakes, with fear responses. In our evolutionary past, fear of these potential dangers probably offered a survival advantage

Among the common objects of phobias are heights, snakes, and the dark. In our evolutionary past, fear of these potential dangers probably offered a survival advantage, and so a readiness to form such fears may have become "wired into" our species (Mineka & Oehman, 2002).

Preparedness, for example, underlies **conditioned taste aversion**, a learned association between the taste of a certain food and a feeling of nausea and revulsion. Perhaps you know someone who has developed a very strong aversion to a particular food after becoming ill a few hours after consuming it. Conditioned taste aversions are acquired very quickly. They differ from most classically conditioned responses in that it usually takes only one pairing of a distinctive flavor and subsequent illness to develop a learned aversion to the taste of that food. Learning connections between distinctive flavors and illness has clear benefits. If we can quickly learn which foods are poisonous and avoid those foods in the future, we greatly increase our chances of survival. Other animals with a well-developed sense of taste, such as rats and mice, also readily develop conditioned taste aversions, just as humans do (Brooks, Bowker, Anderson, & Palmatier, 2003; Chester, Lumeng, Li, & Grahame, 2003; Cross-Mellor, Kavaliers, & Ossenkopp, 2004).

Even knowing that a certain food paired with nausea wasn't the cause of the illness doesn't spare us from developing a conditioned taste aversion. For example, cancer patients often develop strong taste aversions to foods eaten right before nausea-inducing chemotherapy, even though they know that it is the drug that triggered their nauseous reaction. These patients can't prevent themselves from automatically learning a connection that they are biologically prepared to learn (Jacobsen et al., 1994).

► CHECK YOUR UNDERSTANDING

Match the following in Pavlov's experiment with dogs:

1. _____ unconditioned stimulus
2. _____ unconditioned response
3. _____ conditioned stimulus
4. _____ conditioned response
   a. bell
   b. food
   c. salivating to bell
   d. salivating to food

5. A learned association between the taste of a certain food and a feeling of nausea is called _____ _____ _____.

6. Teaching someone to relax even when he or she encounters a distressing situation is called _____ therapy.

7. In the classic experiment in which Little Albert learned to fear a harmless white rat, the unconditioned stimulus was a _____ _____.

Answers: 1. b, 2. d, 3. a, 4. c, 5. conditioned taste aversion, 6. desensitization, 7. loud noise

► APPLY YOUR UNDERSTANDING

1. You feel nervous when your overly critical boss walks into the lunchroom, even though your recent performance has been excellent. For you in this situation, your boss's presence is the
   a. US
   b. CS
   c. CR
   d. UCR

2. Which of the following are examples of classical conditioning?
   a. Eating when not hungry just because we know it is lunchtime
   b. A specific smell triggering a bad memory
   c. A cat running into the kitchen to the sound of a can opener
   d. All of the above are examples of classical conditioning

Answers: 1. b., 2. d.

Operant Conditioning

4.2 Describe the basic mechanism of operant conditioning and distinguish between reinforcers and punishers.

Around the turn of the century, while Pavlov was busy with his dogs, the American psychologist Edward Lee Thorndike (1874–1949) was using a "puzzle box," or simple wooden cage, to study how cats learn (Thorndike, 1898). As illustrated in **Figure 4–2**, Thorndike confined a hungry cat in the puzzle box, with food just outside where the cat could see and

conditioned taste aversion Learned revulsion of certain foods because they have been associated with subsequent nausea; based on classical conditioning, conditioned teste aversions are acquired very quickly, sometimes in only one trial.

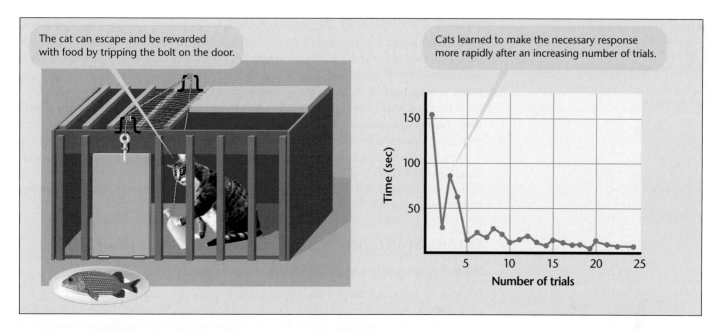

The cat can escape and be rewarded with food by tripping the bolt on the door.

Cats learned to make the necessary response more rapidly after an increasing number of trials.

Figure 4–2

A cat in a Thorndike "puzzle box." The cat can escape and be rewarded with food by tripping the bolt on the door. As the graph shows, Thorndike's cats learned to make the necessary response more rapidly after an increasing number of trials.

smell it. To get to the food, the cat had to figure out how to open the latch on the box door, a process that Thorndike timed. In the beginning, it took the cat quite a while to discover how to open the door. But on each trial, it took the cat less time, until eventually, it could escape from the box in almost no time at all. Thorndike was a pioneer in studying the kind of learning that involves making a certain response due to the consequences it brings. This form of learning has come to be called **operant** or **instrumental conditioning**.

ELEMENTS OF OPERANT CONDITIONING

What two essential elements are involved in operant conditioning?

One essential element in operant conditioning is *emitted behavior*. This is one way in which operant conditioning is different from classical conditioning. In classical conditioning, a response is automatically triggered by some stimulus. Food in the mouth automatically triggers salivation; a loud noise automatically triggers fear. In this sense, classical conditioning is passive: The behaviors are elicited by stimuli. In operant conditioning, behaviors are not triggered by stimuli; rather, they are *freely emitted* to obtain some desired outcome. Thus they are called **operant behaviors** because they involve "operating" on the environment. In the *Every Soldier a Sensor* game described at the beginning of this chapter, the game-playing behaviors are all emitted—they are not triggered through a reflex action, but rather are carefully considered to produce a particular outcome.

CONSEQUENCES: REINFORCERS AND PUNISHERS A second essential element in operant conditioning is a *consequence* following a behavior. Thorndike's cats gained freedom and a piece of fish for escaping from the puzzle boxes; your dog may receive a food treat for sitting on command; a child may receive praise or a chance to watch television for helping to clear the table. Consequences like these that increase the likelihood that a behavior will be repeated are called **reinforcers**.

In contrast, consequences that *decrease* the chances that a behavior will be repeated are called **punishers**. Imagine how Thorndike's cats might have acted had they been greeted by a large, snarling dog when they escaped from the puzzle boxes. Or consider what might happen if a dog that sits on command is scolded for doing so, or if a child who has helped to clear the table is sent to sit in a "time-out" corner. Thorndike summarized the influence of consequences in his **law of effect**: Behavior that brings about a satisfying effect (reinforcement) is likely to be performed again, whereas behavior that brings about a negative effect (punishment) is likely to be suppressed. Contemporary psychologists often refer to the **principle of reinforcement**, rather than the law of effect, but the two terms mean the same thing.

operant (or instrumental) conditioning The type of learning in which behaviors are emitted (in the presence of specific stimuli) to earn rewards or avoid punishments.

operant behavior Behavior designed to operate on the environment in a way that will gain something desired or avoid something unpleasant.

reinforcer A stimulus that follows a behavior and increases the likelihood that the behavior will be repeated.

punisher A stimulus that follows a behavior and decreases the likelihood that the behavior will be repeated.

law of effect Thorndike's theory that behavior consistently rewarded will be "stamped in" as learned behavior, and behavior that brings about discomfort will be "stamped out."

principle of reinforcement Same as law of effect

Skinner box A box often used in operant conditioning of animals; it limits the available responses and thus increases the likelihood that the desired response will occur.

WHAT IS PUNISHMENT? We do not know whether something is reinforcing or punishing until we see whether it increases or decreases the occurrence of a response with which it is paired. We might assume that candy, for example, is a reinforcer for children, but some children don't like candy. We might also assume that having to work alone, rather than in a group of peers, would be punishing, but some employees prefer to work alone. Managers must understand the employees in their units as individuals before they decide how to reward or punish them. For example, what is reinforcing for men may not be reinforcing for women, and what is reinforcing for people in one culture might not have the same effect for people in other cultures.

In addition, an event or object might not be consistently rewarding or punishing over time. So even if candy is initially reinforcing for some children, if they eat large amounts of it, it can become neutral or even punishing. We must therefore be very careful in labeling items or events as reinforcers or punishers.

ESTABLISHING AN OPERANTLY CONDITIONED RESPONSE

How are operantly conditioned responses acquired?

Because the behaviors involved in operant conditioning are voluntary behaviors, it is not always easy to establish an operantly conditioned response. The desired behavior must first be performed spontaneously in order for it to be rewarded and strengthened. Sometimes you can simply wait for this action to happen. Thorndike, for example, waited for his cats to trip the latch that opened the door to his puzzle boxes; then he rewarded them with fish.

But when there are many opportunities for making irrelevant responses, waiting can be slow and tedious. If you were an animal trainer for a circus, imagine how long you would have to wait for a tiger to decide to jump through a flaming hoop so you could reward it. One way to speed up the process of operant learning is to increase motivation, as Thorndike did by allowing his cats to become hungry and by placing a piece of fish outside the box. Even without food in sight, a hungry animal is more active than a well-fed one and so it is more likely, just by chance, to make the response you're looking for. Another strategy is to reduce opportunities for irrelevant responses, as Thorndike did by making his puzzle boxes small and bare.

Many researchers use Skinner boxes to train small animals. A **Skinner box**, named after B. F. Skinner, another pioneer in the study of operant conditioning, is a small cage with solid walls that is relatively empty, except for a food cup and an activating device, such as a bar or a button. (See **Figure 4–3.**) In this simple environment, it doesn't take long for an active, hungry rat or a pigeon to press the bar or peck the button that releases food into the cup, thereby reinforcing the desired behavior.

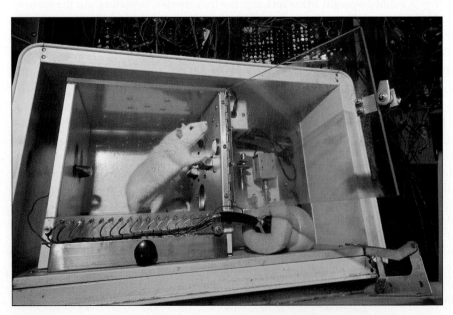

Figure 4–3

A rat in a Skinner box. By pressing the bar, the rat releases food pellets into the box; this procedure reinforces the rat's bar-pressing behavior.

> TABLE 4-1 MODIFY YOUR OWN BEHAVIOR

If you wish to change your own habits, you may find it useful to apply the principles of operant conditioning, as outlined below.

1. Identify the behavior you wish to acquire or eliminate.	"I want to study more."
2. Define the target behavior precisely.	"I want to study at least two hours every weekday."
3. Monitor your present behavior.	"I currently study, on average, 40 minutes each weekday."
4. Provide yourself with a positive reinforcement that is contingent on performing the target behavior (or a punishment that is contingent, if the target behavior is to be eliminated.)	"For every day I study two hours or more, I will reward myself with an hour of relaxation (like watching TV)."

Usually, however, the environment cannot be controlled so easily; hence a different approach is called for. Another way to speed up operant conditioning is to reinforce successive approximations of the desired behavior. This approach is called **shaping**. The circus is a wonderful place to see the results of shaping. To teach a tiger to jump through a flaming hoop, the trainer might first reinforce the animal for jumping up on a pedestal. After that behavior has been learned, the tiger might be required to leap from that pedestal to another before reinforcement is given. Next, the tiger might be required to jump through a hoop between the pedestals to gain a reward. And finally, the hoop is set on fire, and the tiger must leap through it to be rewarded. In much the same way, a speech therapist might reward a child with a lisp for closer and closer approximations of the correct sound of "s."

As in classical conditioning, the learning of an operantly conditioned response eventually reaches a point of diminishing returns. If you look back at **Figure 4–2**, you'll see that the first few reinforcements produced quite large improvements in performance, as indicated by the rapid drop in time required to escape from the puzzle box. But each successive reinforcement produced less of an effect until, eventually, continued reinforcement brought no evidence of further learning. After 25 trials, for example, Thorndike's cats were escaping from the box no more quickly than they had been after 15 trials. The operantly conditioned response has now been fully established. The principle of operant conditioning can be used to successfully modify a wide range of human behavior. See **Table 4-1** to learn about how you can use operant conditioning to modify your own behavior.

A CLOSER LOOK AT REINFORCEMENT

How do various types of reinforcement work?

We have been talking about reinforcement as if all reinforcers are alike, but in fact this is not the case. Think about the many kinds of consequences that would encourage you to perform some behavior. Certainly these include some positive outcomes, like praise, recognition, or money. But the removal of a negative stimulus is also a good reinforcer of behavior. When new parents discover that rocking a baby will stop the infant's persistent crying, they sit down and rock the baby deep into the night; the removal of the infant's crying is a powerful reinforcer for their "rocking" behavior.

POSITIVE AND NEGATIVE REINFORCERS These examples show that there are two kinds of reinforcers. **Positive reinforcers**, such as food, praise, or money, add something rewarding to a situation, whereas **negative reinforcers**, such as stopping an aversive noise, subtract something unpleasant. You might find it helpful to use a plus sign (+) to refer to a positive reinforcer that *adds* something rewarding and a minus sign (−) to refer to a negative reinforcer that *subtracts* something noxious. Animals will learn to press bars and open doors not only to obtain food and water (positive reinforcement), but also to turn off a loud buzzer or to avoid an electric shock (negative reinforcement).

shaping Reinforcing successive approximations to a desired behavior.

positive reinforcer Any event whose presence increases the likelihood that ongoing behavior will recur.

negative reinforcer Any event whose reduction or termination increases the likelihood that ongoing behavior will recur.

Motion picture film consists of a series of still-frame photos, taken a fraction of a second apart. When these still-frame images are projected, one after another, on a screen at the same speed at which they were taken, we perceive continuous motion. This is because the image from one frame is still present in the visual sensory register while the next image is projected, and the images blur together in our visual memory, thereby creating the illusion of motion.

Both positive and negative reinforcement result in the learning of new behaviors or the strengthening of existing ones. In operant conditioning, reinforcement—whether positive or negative—always strengthens or encourages a behavior. An employee might work hard because she receives praise for good work (positive reinforcement) or because it gives her a break from the boss's criticism (negative reinforcement), but in either case the end result is a higher level of performance.

But what if a particular behavior is just *accidentally* reinforced because it happens by chance to be followed by some rewarding incident? Will the behavior still be more likely to occur again? B. F. Skinner (1948) showed that the answer is yes. He put a pigeon in a Skinner box and at random intervals dropped a few grains of food into the food cup. The pigeon began repeating whatever it had been doing just before the food was given: standing on one foot, hopping around, or strutting with its neck stretched out. None of these actions had anything to do with getting the food, of course. But still the bird repeated them over and over again. Skinner called the bird's behavior superstitious because it was learned in a way that is similar to how some human superstitions are learned (Aeschleman, Rosen, & Williams, 2003). If you happen to be wearing an Albert Einstein T-shirt when you get your first A on an exam, you may come to believe that wearing this shirt was a factor. Even though the connection was pure coincidence, you may keep on wearing your "lucky" shirt to every test thereafter.

In the case of superstitious behaviors, the effect of unintended reinforcement is generally harmless. However, some psychologists believe that reinforcement can also lead inadvertently to negative results. They believe that offering certain kinds of reinforcers (candy, money, play time) for a task that could be intrinsically rewarding (that is, reinforcing in and of itself) can undermine the intrinsic motivation to perform it. People may begin to think that they are working only for the reward and lose enthusiasm for what they are doing. They may no longer see their work as an intrinsically interesting challenge in which to invest creative effort and strive for excellence. Instead, they may see work as a chore that must be done to earn some tangible payoff. This warning can be applied to many situations, such as offering large rewards to students for their work in the classroom, or giving employees a large "pay for performance" incentive to meet company goals (Kohn, 1993; Tagano, Moran, & Sawyers, 1991). Other psychologists, however, suggest that this concern that tangible reinforcers may diminish creativity and motivation is exaggerated. In fact, one extensive review of more than 100 studies showed that when used appropriately, rewards do not compromise intrinsic motivation, and under some circumstances, they may even help to encourage creativity (Eisenberger & Cameron, 1996). For example, research has shown that rewarding highly creative behavior on one task often enhances subsequent creativity on other tasks (Eisenberger & Rhoades, 2001).

PRIMARY AND SECONDARY REINFORCERS Some reinforcers, such as food, water, and sex, are intrinsically rewarding in and of themselves. These are called **primary reinforcers**. No prior learning is required to make them reinforcing. Other reinforcers have no intrinsic value. They have acquired value only through association with primary reinforcers. These are the **secondary reinforcers** we mentioned earlier. They are called secondary not because they are less important, but because prior learning is needed before they will function as reinforcers. Suppose a rat learns to get food by pressing a bar; then a buzzer is sounded every time food drops into the dish. Even if the rat stops getting the food, it will continue to press the bar for a while just to hear the buzzer. Although the buzzer by itself has no intrinsic value to the rat, it has become a secondary reinforcer through association with food, a primary reinforcer. In the *Every Soldier a Sensor* video training game described in the opening paragraphs of this chapter, the rewards are all secondary reinforcers, and highly motivating ones at that!

Note how, in creating a secondary reinforcer, classical conditioning is involved. Because it has been paired with an intrinsically pleasurable stimulus, a formerly neutral stimulus comes to elicit pleasure, too. This stimulus can then serve as a reinforcer to establish an operantly conditioned response.

primary reinforcer A reinforcer that is rewarding in itself, such as food, water, and sex.

secondary reinforcer A reinforcer whose value is acquired through association with other primary or secondary reinforcers.

For humans, money is one of the best examples of a secondary reinforcer. Although money is just paper or metal, through its exchange value for food, clothing, and other primary reinforcers, it becomes a powerful reinforcer. Children come to value money only after they learn that it will buy such things as candy (a primary reinforcer); then the money becomes a secondary reinforcer. Stimuli paired with secondary reinforcers can likewise acquire reinforcing properties through a process called *higher-order conditioning*. Checks and credit cards, for example, are one step removed from money, but they can also be highly reinforcing.

A CLOSER LOOK AT PUNISHMENT

What problems can punishment create?

Although we all hate to be subjected to it, **punishment** is a powerful controller of behavior. After receiving a heavy fine for failing to report extra income to the IRS, we are less likely to make that mistake again. After being rudely turned down when we ask someone for a favor, we are less likely to ask that person for another favor. In both cases, an unpleasant consequence reduces the likelihood that we will repeat a behavior. This is the definition of punishment.

Punishment is different from negative reinforcement. Reinforcement of whatever kind *strengthens* (reinforces) behavior. Negative reinforcement strengthens behavior by removing something unpleasant from the environment. In contrast, punishment adds something unpleasant to the environment, and as a result, it tends to *weaken* the behavior that caused it.

Is punishment effective? Does it always work? We can all think of instances when it doesn't seem to. Children often continue to misbehave even after they have been punished repeatedly for that particular misbehavior. Some drivers persist in driving recklessly despite repeated fines. The family dog may sleep on the couch at night despite being punished for being on the couch every morning. Why are there these seeming exceptions to the law of effect? Why, in these cases, isn't punishment having the result it is supposed to?

For punishment to be effective, it must be imposed properly (Gershoff, 2002). First, punishment should be *swift*. If it is delayed, it doesn't work as well. Correcting an employee's inappropriate behavior immediately after it takes place (even when it is not convenient to do so) is much more effective than waiting for a "better" time to punish. Punishment should also be *sufficient* without being cruel. If a head nurse gently criticizes the technique of a subordinate, the criticism must be sufficient to change the way the technique is performed. At the same time, punishment should be *consistent*. It should be imposed for all infractions of a rule, not just for some. If supervisors allow some acts of aggression to go unpunished, additional aggressive acts are likely to follow.

Punishment is particularly useful in situations in which a behavior is dangerous and must be changed quickly. A child who likes to poke things into electric outlets must be stopped immediately, so punishment may be the best course of action. Similarly, punishment may be called for to stop severely disturbed children from repeatedly banging their heads against walls or hitting themselves in the face with their fists. Once this self-destructive behavior is under control, other forms of therapy can be more effective.

But even in situations like these, punishment has drawbacks (Gershoff, 2002; Skinner, 1953). First, it only *suppresses* the undesired behavior; it doesn't prompt someone to "unlearn" the behavior, and it doesn't teach a more desirable one. If the threat of punishment is removed, the negative behavior is likely to recur. This result is apparent on the highway. Speeders slow down when they see a police car (the threat of punishment), but speed up again as soon as the threat is passed. Punishment, then, rarely works when long-term changes in behavior are wanted (Pogarsky & Piquero, 2003).

Second, punishment often stirs up negative feelings (frustration, resentment, self-doubt), which can impede the learning of new, more desirable behaviors. For example, when a worker who is learning a new task is criticized for every mistake, he may become very frustrated and hesitant. This frustration and doubt about ability can prompt more errors, which lead to more corrections. In time, the negative feelings that punishment has caused can become so unpleasant that the worker may develop a negative attitude toward the entire work setting, and may be unable to learn the new task.

The use of punishment has potential drawbacks. It cannot "unteach" unwanted behavior, only suppress it. Punishment may also stir up negative feelings in the person who is punished or inadvertently provide a model of aggressive behavior.

punishment Any event whose presence decreases the likelihood that ongoing behavior will recur.

learned helplessness Failure to take steps to avoid or escape from an unpleasant or aversive stimulus that occurs as a result of previous exposure to unavoidable painful stimuli.

A third drawback of punishment, when it is harsh, is the unintended lesson that it teaches: Harsh punishment may encourage the learner to copy that same harsh and aggressive behavior toward other people (Gershoff, 2002). In laboratory studies, monkeys that are harshly punished tend to attack other monkeys, pigeons other pigeons, and so on (B. Schwartz, 1989). In addition, punishment often makes people angry, and angry people frequently become more aggressive and hostile.

Because of these drawbacks, punishment should be used carefully and always together with reinforcement of desirable behavior. After a more desirable response is established, punishment should be removed to reinforce negatively that new behavior. Positive reinforcement (praise, rewards) should also be used to strengthen the desired behavior. This approach is more productive than punishment alone because it teaches an alternative behavior to replace the punished one. Positive reinforcement also makes the learning environment less threatening.

LEARNED HELPLESSNESS

What happens when punishment cannot be avoided?

By changing their behavior, people learn to prevent themselves from being punished, but what happens when the avoidance of punishment for some reason isn't possible? The answer is often a "giving up" response that can generalize to other situations. This response is known as **learned helplessness**.

Martin Seligman and his colleagues first studied learned helplessness in experiments with dogs (Seligman & Maier, 1967). They placed two groups of dogs in chambers that delivered a series of electric shocks to the dogs' feet at random intervals. The dogs in the control group could turn off (escape) the shock by pushing a panel with their nose. The dogs in the experimental group could not turn off the shock—they were, in effect, helpless. Next, both the experimental and the control animals were placed in a different situation, one in which they could escape shock by jumping over a hurdle. A warning light always came on 10 seconds before each 50-second shock was given. The dogs in the control group quickly learned to jump the hurdle as soon as the warning light flashed, but the dogs in the experimental group didn't. These dogs, which had previously experienced unavoidable shocks, didn't even jump the hurdle *after* the shock started. They just lay there and accepted the pain. Also, many of these dogs were generally listless, suffered loss of appetite, and displayed other symptoms associated with depression.

Many subsequent studies have shown that learned helplessness can occur both in animals and in humans (Maier & Seligman, 1976; Peterson, Maier, & Seligman, 1993b; Overmier, 2002). When established, the condition generalizes to new situations and can be very persistent, even when the animal or person is given evidence that an unpleasant circumstance can now be avoided (Peterson, Maier, & Seligman, 1993). For example, after being faced with a series of unsolvable problems, a college student may give up trying and make only halfhearted efforts to solve new problems, even when the new problems are solvable.

▶ CHECK YOUR UNDERSTANDING

1. An event whose reduction or termination increases the likelihood that ongoing behavior will recur is called _____ reinforcement, whereas any event whose presence increases the likelihood that ongoing behavior will recur is called _____ reinforcement.

2. When a person has learned that exposure to an adverse event is unavoidable and no longer makes any effort to escape it, this is called _____ _____.

3. A reinforcer that acquires its value because it is associated with other reinforcers is called a _____ reinforcer.

4. Any stimulus that follows a behavior and decreases the likelihood that the behavior will be repeated is called a _____.

Answers: 1. negative; positive, 2. learned helplessness, 3. secondary, 4. punishment.

Common Features of Classical and Operant Conditioning

4.3   Compare and contrast classical with operant conditioning, commenting on the significance of contingencies, and on the conditions that lead to extinction, spontaneous recovery, generalization, and discrimination.

Because classical and operant conditioning are both forms of associative learning, they both involve perceived contingencies. A **contingency** is a relationship in which one event *depends* on another. Graduating from college is *contingent* on passing a certain number of courses. Earning a paycheck is *contingent* on working at a job. In both classical and operant conditioning, perceived contingencies are very important.

THE IMPORTANCE OF CONTINGENCIES

What contingencies are particularly important in classical and operant conditioning?

CONTINGENCIES IN CLASSICAL CONDITIONING   In classical conditioning, a contingency is perceived between the CS and the US. The CS comes to be viewed as a signal that the US is about to happen. This is why, in classical conditioning, the CS not only must occur in close proximity to the US, but also should precede the US and provide predictive information about it (Rescorla, 1966, 1967, 1988).

Imagine an experiment in which animals are exposed to a tone (the CS) and a mild electric shock (the US). One group always hears the tone a fraction of a second before it is shocked. Another group sometimes hears the tone first, but other times the tone sounds a fraction of a second *after* the shock, and still other times the tone and shock occur together. Soon the first group will show a fear response upon hearing the tone alone, but the second group will not. This is because the first group has learned a contingency between the tone and the shock: The tone has always preceded the shock, so it has come to mean that the shock is about to be given. For the second group, in contrast, the tone has signaled little or nothing about the shock. Sometimes the tone has meant that a shock is coming, sometimes it has meant that the shock is here, and sometimes it has meant that the shock is over and "the coast is clear." Because the meaning of the tone has been ambiguous for the members of this group, they have not developed a conditioned fear response to it. Classical conditioning occurs when a stimulus tells the learner something about the likelihood that a US will occur.

CONTINGENCIES IN OPERANT CONDITIONING   Contingencies also figure prominently in operant conditioning. The learner must come to perceive a connection between performing a certain voluntary action and receiving a certain reward or punishment. If no contingency is perceived, there is no reason to increase or decrease the behavior.

contingency A reliable "if–then" relationship between two events, such as a CS and a US.

>TABLE 4-2 EXAMPLES OF REINFORCEMENT IN EVERYDAY LIFE

Continuous reinforcement (reinforcement every time the response is made)	Getting additional pay for every hour of overtime work. Putting coins in a vending machine to get candy or soda.
Fixed-ratio schedule (reinforcement after a fixed number of responses)	Being paid on a piecework basis. In the garment industry, for example, workers may be paid a fee per 100 dresses sewn.
Variable-ratio schedule (reinforcement after a varying number of responses)	Playing a slot machine. The machine is programmed to pay off after a certain number of responses have been made, but that number keeps changing. This type of schedule creates a steady rate of responding, because players know that if they play long enough, they will win. Sales commissions. You have to talk to many customers before you make a sale, and you never know whether the next one will buy. The number of sales calls you make, not how much time passes, will determine when you are reinforced by a sale, and the number of sales calls will vary.
Fixed-interval schedule (reinforcement of first response after a fixed amount of time has passed)	You have an exam coming up, and as time goes by and you haven't studied, you have to make up for it all by a certain time, and that means cramming. Picking up a salary check, which occurs every week or every two weeks.
Variable-interval schedule (reinforcement of first response after varying amounts of time)	Surprise quizzes in a course cause a steady rate of studying because you never know when they'll occur; you have to be prepared all the time. Watching a football game, waiting for a touchdown. It could happen anytime. If you leave the room, you may miss it, so you have to keep watching continuously.

Source: From Landy, 1987, p. 212. Adapted by permission.

---

schedule of reinforcement In operant conditioning, the rule for determining when and how often reinforcers will be delivered.

fixed-interval schedule A reinforcement schedule in which the correct response is reinforced after a fixed length of time since the last reinforcement.

variable-interval schedule A reinforcement schedule in which the correct response is reinforced after varying lengths of time following the last reinforcement.

fixed-ratio schedule A reinforcement schedule in which the correct response is reinforced after a fixed number of correct responses.

But after a contingency is perceived, does it matter how often a consequence is actually delivered? When it comes to rewards, the answer is yes and, interestingly enough, fewer rewards are often better than more. In the language of operant conditioning, *partial* or *intermittent reinforcement* results in behavior that will persist longer than behavior learned by *continuous reinforcement*. Why would this be the case? The answer has to do with expectations. When people receive only occasional reinforcement, they learn not to expect reinforcement with every response, so they continue responding in the hopes that eventually they will gain the desired reward.

Psychologists refer to a pattern of reward payoffs as a **schedule of reinforcement**. Partial or intermittent reinforcement schedules are either fixed or variable, and they may be based on either the number of correct responses or the time elapsed between correct responses. **Table 4-2** gives some everyday examples of different reinforcement schedules.

On a **fixed-interval schedule**, learners are reinforced for the first response after a certain amount of time has passed since that response was previously rewarded. That is, they have to wait for a set period before they will be reinforced again. With a fixed-interval schedule, performance tends to fall off immediately after each reinforcement and then tends to pick up again as the time for the next reinforcement draws near. For example, when exams are given at fixed intervals—like midterms and finals—students tend to decrease their studying right after one test is over and then increase studying as the next test approaches.

A **variable-interval schedule** reinforces correct responses after varying lengths of time following the last reinforcement. One reinforcement might be given after six minutes, the next after four minutes, the next after five minutes, and the next after three minutes. The learner typically gives a slow, steady pattern of responses, being careful not to be so slow as to miss all the rewards. For example, if exams are given during a semester at unpredictable intervals, students have to keep studying at a steady rate because on any given day there might be a test.

On a **fixed-ratio schedule**, a certain number of correct responses must occur before reinforcement is provided, resulting in a high response rate because making many responses in a short time yields more rewards. Being paid on a piecework basis is an example of a fixed-ratio schedule. Farmworkers might get $3 for every 10 baskets of cherries they pick. The more they pick the more money they make. Under a fixed-ratio schedule, a brief pause after reinforcement is followed by a rapid and steady response rate until the next reinforcement.

On a **variable-ratio schedule**, the number of correct responses needed to gain reinforcement is not constant. The casino slot machine is a good example of a variable-ratio schedule. It will eventually pay off, but you have no idea when. Because there is always a chance of hitting the jackpot, the temptation to keep playing is great. Learners on a variable-ratio schedule tend not to pause after reinforcement and have a high rate of response over a long period of time. Because they never know when reinforcement may come, they keep on working in anticipation of a reward.

EXTINCTION AND SPONTANEOUS RECOVERY

Under what circumstances might old learned associations suddenly reappear?

Another factor shared by classical and operant conditioning is that learned responses sometimes weaken and may even disappear. If a CS and a US are never paired again or if a consequence that followed a certain behavior is discontinued, the learned association will begin to fade until eventually the effects of prior learning are no longer seen. This outcome is called **extinction** of a response.

EXTINCTION AND SPONTANEOUS RECOVERY IN CLASSICAL CONDITIONING As an example of extinction in classical conditioning, let's go back to Pavlov's dogs, which had learned to salivate upon hearing a bell. What would you predict happened over time when the dogs heard the bell (the CS), but food (the US) was no longer given? The conditioned response to the bell—salivation—gradually decreased until eventually it stopped altogether. The dogs no longer salivated when they heard the bell. Extinction had taken place. Extinction of classically conditioned responses also occurs in your own life. If speaking in public (a CS) is no longer paired with feeling humiliated (a US), you will eventually stop becoming tense and anxious (a CR) when you are called on to make a presentation. Your classically conditioned response to public speaking has undergone extinction.

After such a response has been extinguished, is the learning gone forever? Pavlov trained his dogs to salivate when they heard a bell and then extinguished this conditioned response. A few days later, the dogs were exposed to the bell again in the laboratory setting. As soon as they heard it, their mouths began to water. The response that had been learned and then extinguished reappeared on its own with no retraining. This phenomenon is known as **spontaneous recovery**. The dogs' response was now only about half as strong as it had been before extinction, and it was very easy to extinguish a second time. Nevertheless, the fact that the response occurred at all indicated that the original learning was not completely forgotten. Similarly, if you stop making public presentations for a while, you may find that the next time you do, standing up to speak once again makes you tense and anxious. A response that was extinguished has returned spontaneously after the passage of time.

EXTINCTION AND SPONTANEOUS RECOVERY IN OPERANT CONDITIONING Extinction and spontaneous recovery also occur in operant conditioning. In operant conditioning, extinction happens as a result of withholding reinforcement. The effect usually isn't immediate. In fact, when reinforcement is first discontinued, there is often a brief *increase* in the strength or frequency of responding before a decline sets in. For example, if you put coins in a vending machine and it fails to deliver the goods, you may pull the lever more forcefully and in rapid succession before you finally give up.

Just as in classical conditioning, extinction in operant conditioning doesn't completely erase what has been learned. Even though much time has passed since a behavior was last

The slot machine is a classic example of a variable-ratio schedule of reinforcement. The machine eventually pays off, but always after a variable number of plays. Because people keep hoping that the next play will be rewarded, they maintain a high rate of response over a long period of time.

variable-ratio schedule A reinforcement schedule in which a varying number of correct responses must occur before reinforcement is presented.

extinction A decrease in the strength or frequency, or stopping, of a learned response because of failure to continue pairing the US and CS (classical conditioning) or withholding of reinforcement (operant conditioning).

spontaneous recovery The reappearance of an extinguished response after the passage of time, without training.

rewarded and the behavior seems extinguished, it may suddenly reappear. This spontaneous recovery may be somewhat dependent on interference from new behaviors. If a rat is no longer reinforced for pressing a lever, it will start to engage in other behaviors—turning away from the lever, biting at the corners of the Skinner box, attempting to escape, and so on. These new behaviors will interfere with the operant response of lever pressing, causing it to extinguish. Spontaneous recovery is a brief victory of the original learning over interfering responses. The rat decides to give the previous "reward" lever one more try, as if testing again for a reward.

The difficulty of extinguishing an operantly conditioned response depends on a number of factors:

- **Strength of the original learning.** The stronger the original learning, the longer it takes the response to extinguish. If you spend many hours training a puppy to sit on command, you will not need to reinforce this behavior very often once the dog grows up.
- **Pattern of reinforcement.** As you learned earlier, responses that were reinforced only occasionally when acquired are usually more resistant to extinction than responses that were reinforced every time they occurred.
- **Variety of settings in which the original learning took place.** The greater the variety of settings, the harder it is to extinguish the response. Rats trained to run several different types of alleys to reach a food reward will keep running longer after food is withdrawn than will rats trained in a single alley.
- **Complexity of the behavior.** Complex behavior is much more difficult to extinguish than simple behavior is. Complex behavior consists of many actions put together, and each of those actions must be extinguished for the whole to be extinguished.
- **Learning through punishment versus reinforcement.** Behaviors learned through punishment rather than reinforcement are especially hard to extinguish. If you avoid jogging down a particular street because a vicious dog there attacked you, you may never venture down that street again, so your avoidance of the street may never extinguish.

One way to speed up the extinction of an operantly conditioned response is to put the learner in a situation that is different from the one in which the response was originally learned. The response is likely to be weaker in the new situation, and therefore it will extinguish more quickly. Of course, when the learner is returned to the original learning setting after extinction has occurred elsewhere, the response may undergo spontaneous recovery, just as in classical conditioning. But now the response is likely to be weaker than it was initially, and it should be relatively easy to extinguish once and for all. You may have experienced this phenomenon yourself when you began working at a new job. A habit that you thought you had overcome—perhaps biting your fingernails—may have suddenly reappeared. The new work setting serves as a "reminder" stimulus, encouraging the response, just as we mentioned when discussing classical conditioning. Because you have already extinguished the habit in another setting, however, extinguishing it here shouldn't be difficult.

STIMULUS CONTROL, GENERALIZATION, AND DISCRIMINATION

How do the processes of discrimination and generalization work?

The previous examples demonstrate how cues in the environment can influence conditioned responses. This phenomenon is called **stimulus control**, and it occurs in both classical and operant conditioning. In classical conditioning, the conditioned response (CR) is under the control of the conditioned stimulus (CS) that triggers it. Salivation, for example, might be controlled by the sound of a bell. In operant conditioning, the learned response is under the control of whatever stimuli come to be associated with delivery of reward or punishment. A leap to avoid electric shock might come under the control of a flashing light, for example. In both classical and operant conditioning, moreover, the learner may respond to cues that are merely similar (but not identical) to the ones that prevailed during the original learning. This tendency to respond to similar cues is known as **stimulus generalization**.

stimulus control Control of conditioned responses by cues or stimuli in the environment.

stimulus generalization The transfer of a learned response to different but similar stimuli.

GENERALIZATION AND DISCRIMINATION IN CLASSICAL CONDITIONING There are many examples of stimulus generalization in classical conditioning. One example is the case of Little Albert, who was conditioned to fear white rats. When the experimenters later showed him a white rabbit, he cried and tried to crawl away, even though he had not been taught to fear rabbits. He also showed fear of other white, furry objects—cotton balls, a fur coat, even a bearded Santa Claus mask. Similarly, Pavlov noticed that after his dogs had been conditioned to salivate when they heard a bell, their mouths would often water when they heard a buzzer or the ticking of a metronome. Both Pavlov's dogs and Albert had generalized their learned reactions from rats and bells to similar stimuli. In much the same way, a person who learned to feel anxious over math tests in grade school might come to feel anxious about any task involving numbers, even balancing a checkbook.

Stimulus generalization is not inevitable, however. Through a process called **stimulus discrimination**, learners can be trained not to generalize, but rather to make a conditioned response only to a single specific stimulus. This process involves presenting several similar stimuli, only one of which is followed by the unconditioned stimulus. For instance, Albert might have been shown a rat, a rabbit, cotton balls, and other white, furry objects, but only the rat would be followed by a loud noise (the US). Given this procedure, Albert would have learned to discriminate the white rat from the other objects, and the fear response would not have generalized as it did.

Learning to discriminate is essential in everyday life. We prefer for children to learn not to fear *every* loud noise, *every* insect, *every* dog, and so forth, but only those that are potentially harmful. Through stimulus discrimination, behavior becomes more finely tuned to the demands of our environment.

GENERALIZATION AND DISCRIMINATION IN OPERANT CONDITIONING Stimulus generalization also occurs in operant conditioning. For example, you may apply the study behaviors that are effective in one class to other similar learning situations.

In operant conditioning, responses, too, can be generalized, not just stimuli. For example, a person who learns to operate a complex piece of equipment may be able to generalize, or adapt, these skills to other similar machines. This is called **response generalization**. You may recall that response generalization doesn't occur in classical conditioning. If a dog is taught to salivate when it hears a high-pitched tone, it will salivate less when it hears a low-pitched tone, but the response is still salivation.

Just as discrimination is useful in classical conditioning, it is also useful in operant conditioning. Learning *what* to do has little value if you do not know *when* to do it. Discrimination training in operant conditioning consists of reinforcing *only* a specific, desired response and *only* in the presence of a specific stimulus. For example, a manager may need to discriminate between situations in which criticism is helpful and those in which it diminishes productivity. Using stimulus discrimination procedures, pigeons have been trained to peck at a red disk, but not at a green one. First they are taught to peck at a disk. Then they are presented with two disks, one red and one green. They get food when they peck at the red one, but not when they peck at the green. Eventually they learn to discriminate between the two colors, pecking only at the red. In much the same way, equipment operators learn to vary their responses depending on the specific machine they are operating.

The skills a person learns in playing tennis may generalize to similar sports, such as Ping-Pong, squash, and badminton.

stimulus discrimination Learning to respond to only one stimulus and to inhibit the response to all other stimuli.

response generalization Giving a response that is somewhat different from the response originally learned to that stimulus.

► CHECK YOUR UNDERSTANDING

1. After extinction and a period of rest, a conditioned response may suddenly reappear. This phenomenon is called _____ _____.

2. If reward occurs after every response, this schedule of reinforcement is called _____.

3. If the contingency between response and reinforcement no longer exists, the process of _____ has occurred.

4. The process by which a learned response to a specific stimulus comes to be associated with different, but similar stimuli is known as _____ _____.

5. Being able to tell the difference between two similar stimuli is called stimulus _____.

Answers: 1. spontaneous recovery, **2.** continuous, **3.** extinction, **4.** stimulus generalization, **5.** discrimination.

Cognitive Learning

cognitive learning Learning that depends on mental processes that are not directly observable.

latent learning Learning that is not immediately reflected in a behavior change.

4.4 Define cognitive learning and suggest how it differs from classical and operant conditioning.

Although many important aspects of human behavior can be explained by the principles of classical and operant conditioning, others depend on an understanding of how people think and solve problems. The principles of **cognitive learning** help us understand how mental processes are involved in learning.

LATENT LEARNING AND COGNITIVE MAPS

Did you learn your way around campus solely through operant conditioning (rewards for correct turns, punishments for wrong ones), or was something more involved?

Interest in cognitive learning began shortly after the earliest work in classical and operant conditioning (Eichenbaum & Cohen, 2001). In the 1930s, Edward Chace Tolman, one of the pioneers in the study of cognitive learning, argued that learning can occur, even if it is not directly reflected in observable responses. Tolman called learning that isn't apparent because it is not yet demonstrated **latent learning**.

Tolman studied latent learning in a famous experiment (Tolman & Honzik, 1930). Two groups of hungry rats were placed in a maze and allowed to find their way from a start box to an end box. The first group found food pellets (a reward) in the end box; the second group found nothing there. According to the principles of operant conditioning, the first group would learn the maze better than the second group—which is, indeed, what happened. But when Tolman took some of the rats from the second, unreinforced group and started to give them food at the goal box, almost immediately they ran the maze as well as the rats in the first group. (See **Figure 4–4**.) Tolman argued that the unrewarded rats had actually learned a great deal about the maze as they wandered around inside it. In fact, they may have even learned *more* about it than the rats that had been trained with food rewards, but their learning was *latent*—stored internally, but not yet reflected in their behavior. It was not until they were given a motivation to run the maze that they put their latent learning to use.

Since Tolman's time, much work has been done on the nature of latent learning regarding spatial layouts and relationships. From studies of how animals or humans find their way around a maze, a building, or a neighborhood with many available routes, psychologists have proposed that this kind of learning is stored in the form of a mental image, or **cognitive map**. When the proper time comes, the learner can call up the stored image and put it to use.

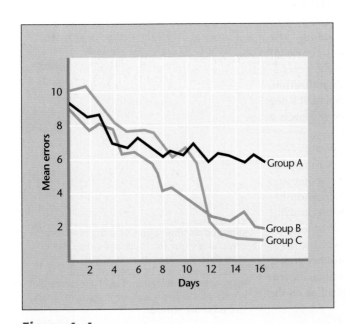

Figure 4–4

Maze used to study latent learning in rats.
The results of the classic Tolman-Honzik study are revealed in the graph. Group A never received a food reward. Group B was rewarded each day. Group C was not rewarded until the eleventh day, but note the significant change in the rats' behavior on Day 12. The results suggest that Group C had been learning all along, although this learning was not reflected in their performance until they were rewarded with food for demonstrating the desired behaviors.

Source: Tolman & Honzik, 1930.

Consider the *Every Soldier a Sensor* training game described in the opening paragraphs of this chapter. Participants must construct elaborate cognitive maps to remember where enemies are hiding, where weapons are located, and where to go to escape from danger. Humans have considerable ability to remember places and locations. We frequently rely on our cognitive maps in everyday life.

INSIGHT AND LEARNING SETS

How does establishing a learning set prepare the way in problem solving that involves insight?

During World War I, the German Gestalt psychologist Wolfgang Köhler conducted a classic series of studies into another aspect of cognitive learning: sudden **insight** into a problem's solution. Outside a chimpanzee's cage, Köhler placed a banana on the ground, not quite within the animal's reach. When the chimp realized that it couldn't reach the banana, it reacted with frustration. But then it started looking at what was in the cage, including a stick left there by Köhler. Sometimes quite suddenly the chimp would grab the stick, poke it through the bars of the cage, and drag the banana within reach. The same kind of sudden insight occurred when the banana was hung from the roof of the cage, too high for the chimp to grasp. This time the cage contained some boxes, which the chimp quickly learned to stack up under the banana so that it could climb up to pull the fruit down. Subsequent studies have shown that even pigeons can solve the box-and-banana problem through insight if they are properly motivated, given the right tools, and taught how to use them (R. Epstein et al., 1984).

Apparently, Köhler's chimps had also "learned how to learn," that is, they had established a **learning set** regarding this problem. When they were presented with the second version of the "banana" problem, they simply called upon past learning in the first situation (reaching a banana on the ground versus reaching one hanging from the ceiling), and used it in a new, insightful way.

Insightful learning is particularly important in humans, who must learn not only where to obtain food and how to escape from predators, but also such complex ethical and cultural ideas as the value of working hard, helping others, overcoming addictions, or dealing with a life crisis. In Chapter 5, "Cognition and Individual Differences," we will explore the role of insight in creative problem solving. As we will see, there are times when formal problem-solving techniques fail to produce a solution; in such cases, it is not unusual for the solution suddenly to "pop up" in a moment of insight (Novick & Sherman, 2003). Moreover, once people gain insight into their own behavior, they should be capable of changing significantly over the course of their lives (Bornstein & Masling, 1998). Indeed, as we will see in Chapter 9: "Psychological Disorders and Their Treatments," the common goal of the various *insight therapies*, such as psychoanalysis, is to give people a better awareness and understanding of their feelings, motivations, and actions in the hope that this will lead to better adjustment (Pine, 1998).

LEARNING BY OBSERVING

Why would it be harder to learn to drive a car if you had never been in one before?

The first time you drove a car, you probably successfully turned the key in the ignition, put the car in gear, and pressed the gas pedal without having ever done any of those things before. How were you able to do that without step-by-step shaping of the correct behaviors? The answer is that you had often watched other people driving, and had learned by observing their actions. There are countless things we learn by watching other people and listening to what they say. This process is called **observational** or **vicarious learning** because, although we are learning, we don't have to do the learned behaviors firsthand; we merely look or listen. Observational learning is a form of "social learning," as it involves interaction with other people. Psychologists who study it are known as **social learning theorists**.

Köhler's experiments with chimpanzees illustrate learning through insight. In this photo, one of the chimps has arranged a stack of boxes to reach bananas hanging from the ceiling. Insights gained in this problem-solving experience may transfer to similar situations.

cognitive map A learned mental image of a spatial environment that may be called on to solve problems when stimuli in the environment change.

insight Learning that occurs rapidly as a result of understanding all the elements of a problem.

learning set The ability to become increasingly more effective in solving problems as more problems are solved.

observational (or vicarious) learning Learning by observing other people's behavior.

social learning theorists Psychologists whose view of learning emphasizes the ability to learn by observing a model or receiving instructions, without firsthand experience by the learner.

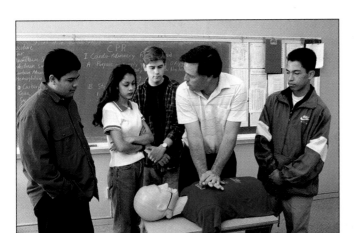

In observational or vicarious learning, we learn by watching a model perform a particular action and then trying to imitate that action correctly. Some actions would be very difficult to master without observational learning.

Observational learning is very common. By watching other people who model, or demonstrate, new behaviors, we can learn such things as how to start a lawn mower and how to saw wood. We also learn how to show love, respect, or concern, as well as how to show hostility and aggression (Blackmore, 1999). We can even learn bad habits, such as smoking. When the Federal Communications Commission (FCC) banned cigarette commercials on television, it was acting on the belief that providing models of smokers would prompt people to imitate smoking. The FCC removed the models to discourage the behavior.

Of course, we do not imitate *everything* that other people do. Why are we selective in our imitation? There are several reasons (Bandura, 1977, 1986). First, we can't pay attention to everything going on around us. The behaviors we are most likely to imitate are those that are modeled by someone who commands our attention (as does a famous or attractive person, or an expert). In a famous series of studies, Albert Bandura (1965; 1973; 1977; 1986) showed that young children can learn aggressive actions by watching adults perform them. Research such as this raises serious concerns about the effects that media violence may have, especially on young viewers. Second, we must make an effort to convert what we see into action. If we have no motivation to perform an observed behavior, we probably won't show what we've learned. This is a distinction between *learning* and *performance*, which is crucial to social learning theorists: We can learn without any change in overt behavior that demonstrates our learning. Whether or not we act depends on our motivation. Finally, we must remember what a model does to imitate it. If a behavior isn't memorable, it won't be learned.

▶ CHECK YOUR UNDERSTANDING

Match the following terms with the appropriate definition.

1. ___ latent learning
2. ___ insight
3. ___ observational learning

a. new, suddenly occurring idea to solve a problem
b. learning by watching a model
c. learning that has not yet been demonstrated in behavior

Answers: 1. c, 2. a, 3. b.

▶ APPLY YOUR UNDERSTANDING

1. An ape examines a problem and the tools available for solving it. Suddenly the animal leaps up and quickly executes a successful solution. This is best considered to be an example of
   a. insight
   b. operant conditioning
   c. latent learning
   d. secondary reinforcement

2. On his job interview, Connor noticed that all men in the office wore jackets and neckties. He decides to wear a jacket and tie to work his first day on the job, which demonstrates the principle of
   a. insight
   b. vicarious learning
   c. latent learning
   d. stimulus discrimination

Answers: 1. a, 2. b.

Forming Memories

4.5 Describe how the sensory registers and short-term memory (STM) work and state how attention is involved in selecting information from the sensory registers for further memory processing.

Just how does our memory work? How is it that we remember the things we have experienced, imagined, and learned? And why is it that some things are remembered so easily and effortlessly, whereas other things require concerted effort to store in memory?

Today, many psychologists find it useful to think about memory as a series of steps in which we process information, much as a computer stores and retrieves data (Massaro & Cowan, 1993). Together, these steps are known as the **information-processing model** of

information-processing model A computerlike model used to describe the way humans encode, store, and retrieve information.

Motion picture film consists of a series of still-frame photos, taken a fraction of a second apart. When these still-frame images are projected, one after another, onto a screen at the same speed at which they were taken, we perceive continuous motion. This is because the image from one frame is still present in the visual sensory register while the next image is projected, and the images blur together in our visual memory, thereby creating the illusion of motion.

memory. Psychologists use terms like *encoding*, *storage*, and *retrieval* to describe the various processes involved in memory.

According to the information-processing model, memories are formed by first selecting important information from the massive amount of stimuli that constantly bombards our senses. After we have directed our attention to what is important—a process that takes place in our sensory registers—that information receives further processing in the next stage of memory, called short-term memory.

THE SENSORY REGISTERS

What is the role of sensory registers?

Look slowly around the room. Each glance takes in an enormous amount of visual information, including colors, shapes, textures, relative brightness, and shadows. At the same time, you pick up sounds, smells, and other kinds of sensory data. All of this raw information flows from your senses into what are known as the **sensory registers**. These registers are like waiting rooms in which information enters and stays for only a short time. Although there are registers for each of our senses, the visual and auditory registers have been studied most extensively.

Although the sensory registers have virtually unlimited capacity (Cowan, 1988), information disappears from them quite rapidly, especially from the sensory register that is associated with vision. (Rainer & Miller, 2002) A simple experiment can demonstrate how much visual information we take in—and how quickly it is lost. Bring a digital camera into an unfamiliar darkened room, and then take a photograph with a flash. During the split second that the room is lit up by the flash, your visual register will absorb a surprising amount of information about the room and its contents. Try to hold on to that visual image, or *icon*, as long as you can. You will find that in a few seconds, it is gone. Then compare your remembered image of the room with what you actually saw, as captured in the photograph. You will discover that your visual register took in far more information than you were able to retain for even a few seconds.

Experiments by George Sperling (1960) clearly demonstrate how quickly information disappears from the visual register. Sperling flashed groups of letters, organized into three rows, on a screen for just a fraction of a second. When the letters were gone, he sounded a tone to tell his participants which row of letters to recall: A high-pitched tone indicated that they should try to remember the top row of letters, a low-pitched tone meant that they should recall the bottom row, and a medium-pitched tone signaled them to recall the middle row. Using this *partial-report technique*, Sperling found that if he sounded the tone immediately after the letters were flashed, people could usually recall three or four of the letters in *any* of the three rows; that is, they seemed to have at least nine of the original 12 letters in their visual registers. But if he waited for even one second before sounding the tone, his participants were able to recall only one or two letters from any single row—in just one second, then, all but four or five of the original set of 12 letters had vanished from their visual registers.

Visual information may disappear from the visual register even more rapidly than Sperling thought (Cowan, 1988). In everyday life, new visual information keeps coming into the register, and the new information replaces the old information almost immediately, a process often called *masking*. This is just as well, because otherwise the visual information would simply pile up in the sensory register and get hopelessly scrambled. Under normal viewing conditions, visual information is erased from the sensory register in about a quarter of a second as it is replaced by new information.

Auditory information fades more slowly than visual information. The auditory equivalent of the icon, the *echo*, tends to last for several seconds, which, given the nature of speech,

sensory registers Entry points in memory for raw information from the senses.

attention The selection of some incoming information for further processing in memory.

is certainly lucky for us. Otherwise, "*You* did it!" would be indistinguishable from "You *did* it!" because we would be unable to remember the emphasis on the first words by the time the last words were registered.

ATTENTION

Why does some information capture our attention, whereas other information goes unnoticed?

If information disappears from the sensory registers so rapidly, how do we remember anything for more than a second or two? One way is that we select some of the incoming information for further processing by means of **attention**. (See **Figure 4–5**.) Attention is the process of selectively looking, listening, smelling, tasting, and feeling (Egeth & Lamy, 2003). At the same time, we give meaning to the information that is coming in. Look at the page in front of you. You will see a series of black lines on a white page. If you did not know how to read English, they would be just meaningless marks. For you to make sense of this jumble of data, you process the information in the sensory registers for meaning.

How do we select what we are going to pay attention to at any given moment, and how do we give that information meaning? Donald Broadbent (1958) suggested that a filtering process at the entrance to the nervous system allows only those stimuli that meet certain requirements to pass through. For example, if you and a friend are sitting in a busy restaurant talking, you would hear several conversations that people seated around you are having. Yet, although you might be able to describe certain characteristics of those other conversations, such as whether the people speaking were men or women and whether the words were spoken loudly or softly, you normally cannot recall what was being discussed, even at neighboring tables. Since you filtered out those other conversations, the processing of that information did not proceed far enough for you to understand what you heard.

Broadbent's filtering theory helps explain some aspects of attention, but sometimes unattended stimuli do capture our attention. To return to the restaurant example, if someone nearby were to mention your name, your attention probably would shift to that conversation, at least briefly. This is known as the *cocktail-party phenomenon* (Cherry, 1966; Conway, Cowan, & Bunting, 2001; Wood & Cowan, 1995).

This student is working attentively in spite of other activity in the classroom. If the teacher calls her name, though, the student's attention will be quickly diverted to attend to the teacher's voice.

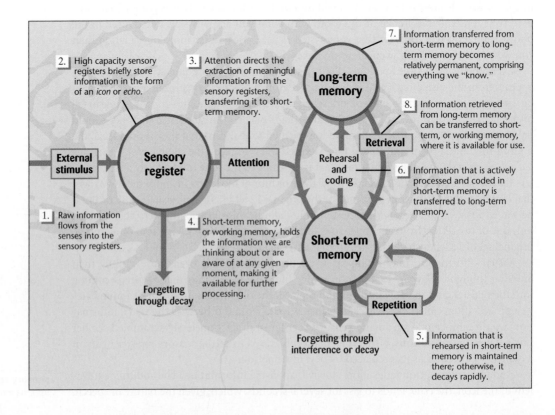

Figure 4–5

The sequence of information processing.

2. High capacity sensory registers briefly store information in the form of an *icon* or *echo*.

3. Attention directs the extraction of meaningful information from the sensory registers, transferring it to short-term memory.

7. Information transferred from short-term memory to long-term memory becomes relatively permanent, comprising everything we "know."

8. Information retrieved from long-term memory can be transferred to short-term, or working memory, where it is available for use.

6. Information that is actively processed and coded in short-term memory is transferred to long-term memory.

1. Raw information flows from the senses into the sensory registers.

4. Short-term memory, or working memory, holds the information we are thinking about or are aware of at any given moment, making it available for further processing.

5. Information that is rehearsed in short-term memory is maintained there; otherwise, it decays rapidly.

External stimulus

Sensory register

Attention

Long-term memory

Retrieval

Rehearsal and coding

Short-term memory

Repetition

Forgetting through decay

Forgetting through interference or decay

Thus, the filter is not a simple on and off switch, but rather a variable control, like the volume control on a radio, which can "turn down" unwanted signals without rejecting them entirely (Treisman 1960, 1964). According to this view, although we may be paying attention to only some incoming information, we monitor the other signals at a low volume and we can shift our attention if we pick up something particularly meaningful. This automatic processing can work even when we are asleep: Parents often wake up immediately when they hear their baby crying, but sleep through other, louder noises. At times, however, our automatic processing monitor fails, and we can overlook even meaningful information. In research studies, for example, some experienced pilots landing an aircraft in a simulator failed to see another aircraft in plain view that was blocking the runway; and some people watching a video of a ball-passing game failed to notice a person dressed as a gorilla who was plainly visible for nearly 10 seconds (Mark, 2003). This is not quite as strange as it seems: For example, most of us, when concentrating on driving in heavy traffic or a severe storm, have failed to hear something important that a passenger said or that was on the radio. As another example, it's certainly not unheard of for sports fans, engrossed in watching a particularly intense game, to fail to hear things that are said to them (Engle, 2002).

To summarize, we consciously attend to very little of the information in our sensory registers; instead, we select some information and process those signals further as we work to recognize and understand them. Unattended information receives at least some initial processing, however, so that normally we can shift our attention to any element of our surroundings that strikes us as potentially meaningful. The information that we do attend to enters our short-term memory.

SHORT-TERM MEMORY

What are the most important tasks performed by short-term memory?

Short-term memory (STM) holds the information that we are thinking about or are aware of at any given moment (Stern, 1985). When you listen to a conversation or a song on the radio, when you watch a television show or a football game, when you become aware of a leg cramp or a headache—in all these cases, you are using STM both to hold onto and to think about new information coming in from the sensory registers. STM has two primary tasks: to store new information briefly and to work on that (and other) information. STM is sometimes called *working memory*, to emphasize the active or working component of this memory system (Baddeley & Hitch, 1994; Nairne, 2003).

CAPACITY OF STM The video-game fanatic is oblivious to the outside world. Chess masters at tournaments demand complete silence while they ponder their next move. You shut yourself in a quiet room to study for final exams. As these examples illustrate, STM can handle only so much information at any given moment. Research suggests that STM can hold about as much information as can be repeated or rehearsed in 1.5 to 2 seconds (Baddeley, 1986, 2002).

To get a better idea of the limits of STM, read the first row of letters in the list that follows just once. Then close your eyes, and try to remember the letters in the correct sequence. Repeat the procedure for each subsequent row.

1. C X W
2. M N K T Y
3. R P J H B Z S
4. G B M P V Q F J D
5. E G Q W J P B R H K A

Like most other people, you probably found rows 1 and 2 fairly easy, row 3 a bit harder, row 4 extremely difficult, and row 5 impossible to remember after just one reading. You have just experienced the relatively limited capacity of STM.

Now try reading through the following set of 12 letters just once, and see whether you can repeat them:
TJYFAVMCFKIB

short-term memory (STM) Working memory; briefly stores and processes selected information from the sensory registers.

Chess players often demand complete silence as they consider their next move. This is because there is a definite limit to the amount of information STM can handle at any given moment.

chunking The grouping of information into meaningful units for easier handling by short-term memory.

rote rehearsal Retaining information in memory simply by repeating it over and over.

How many letters were you able to recall? In all likelihood, not all 12. But what if you had been asked to remember the following 12 letters instead?

TV   FBI   JFK   YMCA

Could you remember them? Almost certainly the answer is yes. These are the same 12 letters as before, but here they are grouped into four separate "words." This way of grouping and organizing information so that it fits into meaningful units is called **chunking** (Gobet et al., 2001). The 12 letters have been chunked into four meaningful elements that can readily be handled by STM—they can be repeated in less than two seconds. Now try to remember this list of numbers:

106619451812

Remembering 12 separate digits is usually very difficult, but try chunking the list into three groups of four:

1066   1945   1812

For those who take an interest in military history, these three chunks (which are dates of important battles) will be much easier to remember than 12 unrelated digits.

By chunking words into sentences or sentence fragments, we can process an even greater amount of information in STM (Baddeley, 1994; Carter, Hardy, & Hardy, 2001). For example, suppose that you want to remember the following list of words: *tree, song, hat, sparrow, box, lilac, cat*. One strategy would be to cluster as many of them as possible into phrases or sentences: "The sparrow in the tree sings a song"; "a lilac hat in the box"; "the cat in the hat." But isn't there a limit to this strategy? Would five sentences be as easy to remember for a short time as five single words? No. As the size of any individual chunk increases, the number of chunks that can be held in STM declines (Simon, 1974). STM can easily handle five unrelated letters or words at once, but five unrelated sentences are much harder to remember.

Another way we can hold information in STM for longer periods is through **rote rehearsal**, also called *maintenance rehearsal* (Greene, 1987). Rote rehearsal consists of repeating information over and over, silently or out loud. Although it may not be the most efficient way to remember something permanently, it can be quite effective for a short time.

Keep in mind that STM usually has to perform more than one task at a time (Baddeley & Hitch, 1994). During the brief moments you spent memorizing the preceding rows of letters in the previous task, you probably gave them your full attention. But normally you have to attend to new incoming information while you work on whatever is already present in short-term memory. Competition between these two tasks for the limited work space in STM means that neither task will be done as well as it could be. Try counting backward from 100 while trying to learn the rows of letters in our earlier example. What happens?

Now turn on some music and try to learn the rows of letters. You'll find that the music doesn't interfere much, if at all, with learning the letters. Interestingly, when two memory tasks are presented in different sensory modalities (for instance, visual and auditory), they are less likely to interfere with each other than if they are in the same modality (Cocchini, Logie, Sala, MacPherson, & Baddeley, 2002). This suggests the existence of *domain-specific* working memory systems that can operate at the same time with very little interference.

ENCODING IN STM We generally encode verbal information for storage in STM *phonologically*—that is, according to how it sounds. This is the case even if we see the word, letter, or number on a page, rather than hear it spoken (Baddeley, 1986; Pollatasěk, Rayner, & Lee, 2000). We know this because numerous experiments have shown that when people try to retrieve material from STM, they generally mix up items

"Hold on a second, Bob. I'm putting you on a stickie."

that sound alike (Sperling, 1960). A list of words such as mad, man, mat, map is harder for most people to recall accurately than is a list such as pit, day, cow, bar (Baddeley, 1986).

But not all material in short-term memory is stored phonologically. At least some material is stored in visual form, and other information is retained on the basis of its meaning (Cowan, 1988; Matlin, 1989). For example, we don't have to convert visual data such as maps, diagrams, and paintings into sound before we can code them into STM and think about them. Moreover, research has shown that memory for images is generally better than memory for words because we often store images both phonologically and as images, while words are usually stored only phonologically (Paivio, 1986). The *dual coding* of images accounts for the reason it is sometimes helpful to form a mental picture of something you are trying to learn (Sadoski & Paivio, 2001).

▶ CHECK YOUR UNDERSTANDING

1. Indicate whether the following statements are true (T) or false (F):
   a. ___ The sensory registers have virtually unlimited capacity.
   b. ___ Some kinds of information are stored permanently in the sensory registers.
   c. ___ Auditory information fades from the sensory registers more quickly than visual information does.

2. ___ memory is what we are thinking about at any given moment. Its function is briefly to store new information and to work on that and other information.

3. ___ enables us to group items held in short-term memory into compact meaningful units.

Answers: 1. a. (T), b. (F), c. (F), 2. short-term, or working, 3. chunking

▶ APPLY YOUR UNDERSTANDING

1. You are in a large, noisy group in which everyone seems to be talking at once. In order to concentrate on the conversation you are having with one of the people, you "tune out" all the other conversations that are going on around you. A few minutes later, while talking to someone else, you suddenly hear someone nearby mention your name. This time your attention is immediately drawn to that other conversation. This is an example of
   a. the auditory sensory register
   b. the partial-report technique
   c. the cocktail-party phenomenon
   d. masking

2. Your sister looks up a phone number in the phone book, but then can't find the phone. By the time she finds the phone, she has forgotten the number. While she was looking for the phone, she apparently failed to engage in
   a. rote rehearsal
   b. parallel processing
   c. phonological coding
   d. categorizing

Answers: 1. c, 2. a.

Long-Term Memory

4.6   Suggest how long-term memories are stored and distinguish between explicit and implicit memories by providing two examples of each of these types of memory.

Everything that we learn is stored in **long-term memory** (**LTM**): The words to a popular song; the results of the last election; the meaning of *justice*; how to roller skate or draw a face; your enjoyment of opera or your disgust at the sight of raw oysters; and what you are supposed to be doing tomorrow at 4:00 P.M. Long-term memory can store a vast amount of information for many years. In one study, for example, adults who had graduated from high school more than 40 years earlier were still able to recognize the names of 75 percent of their classmates (Bahrick, Bahrick, & Wittlinger, 1974). And some people are able to remember their high school Spanish after 50 years, even if they have had little opportunity to practice it (Bahrick, 1984).

long-term memory (LTM) The portion of memory that is more or less permanent, corresponding to everything we "know."

serial position effect The finding that, when asked to recall a list of unrelated items, performance is better for the items at the beginning and end of the list than for items in the middle.

ENCODING IN LTM

How are most memories encoded in LTM?

Can you picture the shape of Florida? Do you know what a trumpet sounds like? Can you imagine the smell of a rose or the taste of coffee? When you answer the telephone, can you sometimes identify the caller immediately, just from the sound of the voice? Your ability to do most of these things means that at least some long-term memories are coded in terms of nonverbal images: shapes, sounds, smells, tastes, and so on (Cowan, 1988).

Yet, most of the information in LTM seems to be encoded in terms of *meaning*. If material is especially familiar (the words of the national anthem, say, or the opening of the Gettysburg Address), you may have stored it verbatim in LTM, and you can often retrieve it word for word when you need it. Generally speaking, however, we do not use verbatim storage in LTM. If someone tells you a long, rambling story, you may listen to every word, but you certainly will not try to remember the story verbatim. Instead, you will extract the main points of the story and try to remember those. Even simple sentences are usually encoded in terms of their meaning. Thus, when people are asked to remember that "Tom called John," they often find it impossible to remember later whether they were told "Tom called John" or "John was called by Tom." They usually remember the meaning of the message, but not the exact words (Bourne, Dominowski, Loftus, & Healy, 1986).

MAINTAINING LTM

What three ways are used to hold information in LTM?

ROTE REHEARSAL Rote rehearsal, the principal tool for holding information in STM, is also useful for transferring information from STM to LTM. The old saying that practice makes perfect has some merit. Millions of students have learned the alphabet and multiplication tables by doggedly repeating letters and numbers. Rote rehearsal is probably the standard method of storing away largely meaningless material, such as phone numbers, Social Security numbers, security codes, computer passwords, birth dates, and people's names. The impact of rote rehearsal on memory is demonstrated in studies that involve the **serial position effect**. When given a list of items to remember (such as a list of grocery items), people tend to do better at recalling the first items (*primacy effect*) and the last items (*recency effect*) in the list. They also tend to do poorest of all on the items in the middle of the list. (See **Figure 4–6**.)

The explanation for this serial position effect resides in understanding how short- and long-term memory work together. The *recency effect* occurs because the last items that were presented are still contained in STM and thus are available for recall. The *primacy effect*, on the other hand, reflects the opportunity to rehearse the first few items in the list—increasing their likelihood of being transferred to LTM.

Poor performance on the items in the middle of the list occurs because they were presented too long ago to still be in STM, and because so many items requiring attention were presented before and after them that there was little opportunity for rehearsal.

Although everyone hates rote drill, there seems to be no escaping its use in mastering a wide variety of skills, from memorizing the alphabet to playing a work of Mozart on the piano or doing a back flip on the balance beam. Mastering a skill means achieving *automaticity*, the word that researchers use to describe fluid, immediate performance. Expert typing, for example, means being able to hit the right keys accurately without having to think about it. And automaticity is achieved only through long, hard practice.

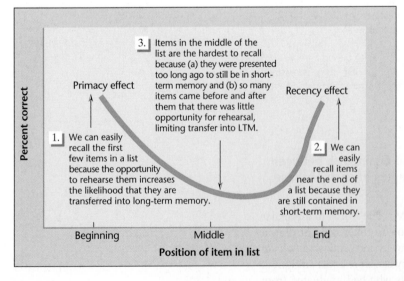

Figure 4–6

The serial position effect. The serial position effect demonstrates how short- and long-term memory work together.

Figure 4–7

A penny for your thoughts. Which of these accurately illustrates a real U.S. penny? The answer is on page 148.

ELABORATIVE REHEARSAL As we have seen, rote rehearsal with the intent to learn is sometimes useful in storing information in LTM. But often, an even more effective procedure is **elaborative rehearsal** (Craik & Lockhart, 1972; Craik, 2002; Postman, 1975), the act of relating new information to something that we already know. Through elaborative rehearsal, you extract the meaning of the new information and then link it to as much of the material already in LTM as possible. We tend to remember meaningful material better than arbitrary facts, and the more links or associations of meaning you can make, the more likely you are to remember the new information later. To demonstrate this point, stop for a moment and try to imagine from memory the front side of a U.S. penny. Now look at **Figure 4–7**, and pick the illustration that matches your memory. For most people, this task is surprisingly difficult: Despite the repetition of seeing thousands of pennies, most people cannot accurately draw one, or even pick one out from among other, similar objects (Nickerson & Adams, 1979). For most people, the specific details on a penny are not meaningful, so even with thousands of chances to remember them, we do not.

Clearly, elaborative rehearsal calls for a deeper and more meaningful processing of new data than does simple rote rehearsal (Craik & Lockhart, 1972). Unless we rehearse material elaboratively, we often soon forget it. Effective study strategies are generally based on interpreting new information in the context of what is already known—a form of elaborative rehearsal. (**See the Understanding Ourselves box, "Improving Your Memory"**)

In some situations, special techniques called **mnemonics** (pronounced ni-MON-iks) may help you to tie new material to information already in LTM. Some of the simplest mnemonic techniques are the rhymes and jingles that we often use to remember dates and other facts. "Thirty days hath September, April, June, and November . . ." enables us to recall how many days are in a month. We are also familiar with other simple mnemonic devices in which we make up words or sentences out of the material to be recalled. We can remember the colors of the visible spectrum—red, orange, yellow, green, blue, indigo, and violet—by using their first letters to form the name ROY G. BIV. In addition, several studies have shown that when you can relate a mnemonic to personal information, such as your hobbies or interests, you are even more likely to be able to recall it later (Symons & Johnson, 1997).

SCHEMATA A variation on the idea of elaborative rehearsal is the concept of **schema** (plural: **schemata**). A schema is like a script that past experience has begun writing for you, with details to be filled in by your present experience. It is a mental representation of an event, an object, a situation, a person, a process, or a relationship that is stored in memory and that leads you to expect your experience to be organized in certain ways. For example, you may have a schema for going to the mall, for eating in a restaurant, for driving a car, or for attending a class lecture. A class lecture schema might include sitting down in a large room with seats arranged in rows, opening your notebook, and expecting the professor or lecturer to come in and address the class from the front of the room. Schemata such as these provide a framework into which incoming information is fitted.

Information in LTM is highly organized and cross-referenced, like a cataloging system in a library. The more carefully we organize information, the more likely we will be to retrieve it later.

elaborative rehearsal The linking of new information in short-term memory to familiar material stored in long-term memory.

mnemonics Techniques that make material easier to remember.

schema (plural: schemata) A set of beliefs or expectations about something that is based on past experience.

[UNDERSTANDING OURSELVES]

IMPROVING YOUR MEMORY

What can you do to improve your memory? It's the active decision to get better and the number of hours that you push yourself to improve that makes the difference. Here are some tips that can help.

- **Develop motivation.** Without a strong desire to learn or remember something, you probably won't. But if you find a way to keep yourself alert and stimulated, you will have an easier time learning and remembering things.

- **Practice memory skills.** To stay sharp, memory skills, like all other skills, must be practiced and used. Memory experts recommend games such as crossword puzzles, Sudoku, anagrams, Scrabble, Monopoly, Trivial Pursuit, and bridge. You might learn a new language or make a point of discussing current events regularly with friends.

- **Be confident in your ability to remember.** If you're convinced that you won't remember something, you probably won't. Self-doubt often leads to anxiety, which, in turn, interferes with the ability to retrieve information from memory. Relaxation exercises, experts agree, may substantially boost your ability to retrieve information from memory.

- **Minimize distractions.** Although some people can study for an exam and listen to the radio simultaneously, most people find that outside distractions interfere with both learning and remembering.

- **Stay focused.** Paying close attention to details, and focusing on your surroundings, emotions, and other elements associated with an event, will help you remember it clearly.

- **Make connections between new material and other information already stored in your long-term memory.** The more links you forge between new information and old information already in LTM, the more likely you are to remember the new material. Discuss things that you want to remember with other people. Think about or write down ways in which the new information is related to things you already know.

- **Use mental imagery.** Imagery works wonders as an aid to recalling information from memory. Whenever possible, form mental pictures of the items, people, words, or activities you want to remember.

- **Use retrieval cues.** The more retrieval cues that you have, the more likely it is that you will remember something. One way to establish automatic retrieval cues is to create routines and structure. For example, when you come in the door, put your house and car keys in the same place every time. Then when you ask yourself, "Where did I put my keys?" the fact that you have a special place for the keys serves as a retrieval cue. Sometimes something that is clearly *not* routine or structured can serve as a retrieval cue. For example, if you want to remember to do something before you go to bed, leave an unusual item on your bed (perhaps a shoe or sock); when it's time to go to bed, you'll see the unusual object, and that sighting should help remind you of what you wanted to do.

- **Rely on more than memory alone.** Use other tools. Write down things you need to remember, and then post a list of things somewhere obvious, such as on your bulletin board or refrigerator door. Put all the dates you want to remember on a calendar in a conspicuous place.

- **Be aware that your own personal schemata may distort your recall event.** As we've seen, people sometimes unknowingly "rewrite" past events to fit their current image or their desired image of themselves and their past decisions (Lyubomirsky & Ross, 1999; Mather, Shafir, & Johnson, 2000). Being on guard against such distortions may help you avoid them.

To summarize, the three stages of memory we have described here—the sensory registers, STM, and LTM—comprise the information-processing view of memory, as reviewed in the **"Summary Table."** (The accurate illustration of a penny in **Figure 4–7** is the third from the left.)

TYPES OF LTM

How do different types of LTM differ?

Regardless of how memories have been encoded into LTM, the information stored there can take many forms. However, most long-term memories can be classified into one of several types: episodic, semantic, procedural, and emotional memories.

Episodic memories (Tulving, 1985) are memories for events experienced in a specific time and place. These are *personal* memories, not historical facts. If you can recall what you ate for dinner last night, what presents you got at your sixteenth birthday party, or how you learned to ride a bike when you were young, then you are calling up episodic memories. Episodic memories are like a diary or daily journal that lets you "go back in time" (Wheeler, Stuss, & Tulving, 1997).

One particular type of episodic memory is called a *flashbulb memory* because it involves the experience of remembering vividly a certain event and the incidents surround it, even after a

---

episodic memory The portion of long-term memory that stores personally experienced events.

SUMMARY TABLE

MEMORY AS AN INFORMATION-PROCESSING SYSTEM

SYSTEM	MEANS BY WHICH INFORMATION IS ENCODED	FORM IN WHICH INFORMATION IS STORED	STORAGE ORGANIZATION	STORAGE DURATION	MEANS BY WHICH INFORMATION IS RETRIEVED	FACTORS IN FORGETTING
Sensory Register	Visual and auditory registers	Raw sensory data	None	From less than 1 second to only a few seconds	Reconsideration of registered information	Decay or masking
Short-Term Memory	Rote or maintenance rehearsal	Visual and phonological representation	None	Usually 15 to 20 seconds	Rote or maintenance rehearsal	Interference or decay
Long-Term Memory	Rote rehearsal, elaborative rehearsal, schemata	Some nonverbal representations, mostly stored by meaning (semantics)	Logical frameworks, such as hierarchies or categories	Perhaps for an entire lifetime	Retrieval cues linked to organized information	Retrieval failure or interference

long time has passed (Davidson & Glisky, 2002). Many people reading this text will remember in detail the image of airliners flying into the World Trade Center in New York City on September 11, 2001—an example of a flashbulb memory (Edery & Nachson, 2004; Talarico & Rubin, 2003).

Semantic memories are facts and concepts not linked to a particular time. If episodic memory is like a daily journal, semantic memory is like a dictionary or an encyclopedia, filled with facts and concepts, such as the meaning of the word *semantic*, the name of the inventor of the light bulb, the location of the Empire State Building, the value of 2 times 7, and the identity of George Washington.

Procedural memories are motor skills and habits (Johnson, 2003). They are not memories *about* skills and habits; they *are* the skills and habits. Procedural memories have to do with knowing *how*: how to ride a bicycle, swim, play a violin, type a letter, make coffee, write your name, comb your hair, walk across a room, or slam on a car's brakes. The information involved usually consists of a precise sequence of coordinated movements that are often difficult to describe in words. Repetition and, in many cases, deliberate practice are often required to master skills and habits, but when learned, they are rarely completely lost. The saying "You never forget how to ride a bicycle" illustrates the durability of procedural memories.

Emotional memories are learned emotional responses to various stimuli: all of our loves and hates, our rational and irrational fears, our feelings of disgust and anxiety. If you are afraid of flying insects, become enraged at the sight of a Nazi flag, or are ashamed of something you did, you have emotional memories.

EXPLICIT AND IMPLICIT MEMORY Because of the differences among types of memories, psychologists distinguish between **explicit memory**, which includes episodic and semantic memories, and **implicit memory**, which includes procedural and emotional memories (Nelson, 1999). These terms reflect the fact that sometimes we are aware that we know something (explicit memory) and that sometimes we are not (implicit memory).

Serious interest in the distinction between explicit and implicit memory began as a result of experiments with amnesic patients. These patients had suffered brain damage that, it was thought, prevented them from forming new long-term memories. They could recall things learned prior to their injury, but not afterward.

For example, Brenda Milner (Milner, Corkin, & Teuber, 1968) studied the now famous case of patient H. M., a young man who had severe, uncontrollable epileptic seizures. The seizures became life threatening, so that as a last resort, surgeons removed most of the afflicted area of his brain. The surgery greatly reduced the frequency and severity of seizures, but it left behind a new problem: H. M. could no longer form new memories. He could meet someone again and again, and each time it was as if he were meeting the person for the first time. He could read the same magazine day after day and not recall ever having seen it before. Old memories were intact: He could remember things that he had learned long before the operation, but he could not learn anything new. Or so it seemed!

Experienced typists have well developed procedural memories for keyboard skills.

semantic memory The portion of long-term memory that stores general facts and information.

procedural memory The portion of long-term memory that stores information relating to skills, habits, and other perceptual-motor tasks.

emotional memory Learned emotional responses to various stimuli.

explicit memory Memory for information that we can readily express in words and are aware of having; these memories can be intentionally retrieved from memory.

implicit memory Memory for information that we cannot readily express in words and may not be aware of having; these memories cannot be intentionally retrieved from memory.

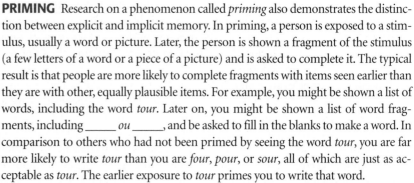

>TABLE 4-3 TYPES OF MEMORIES

Explicit		Implicit	
Semantic	**Episodic**	**Procedural**	**Emotional**
Memories of facts and concepts	Memories of personally experienced events	Motor skills and habits	Learned emotional reactions
Example: recalling that Albany is the capital of New York	*Example:* recalling a trip to Albany	*Example:* remembering how to ice skate	*Example:* feeling anxious at the sight of a rat

Then one day Milner asked H. M. to trace the outline of a star while looking in a mirror. This simple task is surprisingly difficult, but with practice most people show steady progress. Surprisingly, so did H. M. Each day he got better and better at tracing the star, just as a person with an undamaged brain would do—yet each day he had no recollection of ever having attempted the task. H. M.'s performance demonstrated not only that he could learn, but also that there are different kinds of memories. Some are explicit: We know things, and we know that we know them. And some are implicit: We know things, but that knowledge is unconscious. (See **Table 4-3** for a summary of the various types of long-term memory.)

Looking into a bakery window, perhaps smelling the aromas of the cakes inside, may prime the memory, triggering distinct memories associated with those sights and smells, formed many years ago.

PRIMING Research on a phenomenon called *priming* also demonstrates the distinction between explicit and implicit memory. In priming, a person is exposed to a stimulus, usually a word or picture. Later, the person is shown a fragment of the stimulus (a few letters of a word or a piece of a picture) and is asked to complete it. The typical result is that people are more likely to complete fragments with items seen earlier than they are with other, equally plausible items. For example, you might be shown a list of words, including the word *tour*. Later on, you might be shown a list of word fragments, including _____ *ou* _____, and be asked to fill in the blanks to make a word. In comparison to others who had not been primed by seeing the word *tour*, you are far more likely to write *tour* than you are *four*, *pour*, or *sour*, all of which are just as acceptable as *tour*. The earlier exposure to *tour* primes you to write that word.

The distinction between explicit and implicit memories means that some knowledge is literally unconscious. Moreover, explicit and implicit memories also seem to involve different neural structures and pathways. However, memories typically work together. When we remember going to a Chinese restaurant, we recall not only when and where we ate and whom we were with (episodic memory), but also the nature of the food we ate (semantic memory), the skills we learned such as eating with chopsticks (procedural memory), and the embarrassment we felt when we spilled the tea (emotional memory). When we recall events, we typically do not experience these kinds of memories as distinct and separate; rather, they are integrally connected, just as the original experiences were. Whether we will continue to remember the experiences accurately in the future depends to a large extent on what happens in our brain.

► CHECK YOUR UNDERSTANDING

1. The primacy effect accounts for why we remember items at the _____ of a list, while the recency effect accounts for why we remember items at the _____ of the list.

2. If information is learned through repetition, this process is _____ rehearsal; if it is learned by linking it to other memories, this process is _____ rehearsal.

3. A schema is a framework in memory into which new information is fit. Is this statement true (T) or false (F)?

4. Sometimes we retain memories that we are not aware we have. These are called ___ memories.

Answers: 1. beginning; end, 2. rote; elaborative, 3. T, 4. implicit.

1. You run into a business acquaintance who gives you his phone number and asks you to call. You want to be sure to remember the phone number, so you relate the number to things that you already know. "555" is the same as the combination to your bicycle lock. "12" is your brother's age. And "34" is the size of your belt. This technique for getting information into long-term memory is called

   a. rote rehearsal
   b. serial position rehearsal
   c. elaborative rehearsal
   d. episodic rehearsal

2. He: "We've been to this restaurant before."
   She: "I don't think so."

   He: "Didn't we eat here last summer with your brother?"

   She: "That was a different restaurant, and I think it was last fall, not last summer."

   This couple is trying to remember an event they shared and, obviously, their memories differ. The information they are seeking is most likely stored in

   a. procedural memory
   b. emotional memory
   c. semantic memory
   d. episodic memory

Answers: 1. c., 2. d.

The Biology of Memory

4.7   Identify the regions of the brain that appear to be involved in different types of memory.

Research on the biology of memory focuses mainly on the question, how and where are memories stored? Simple as the question is, it has proved enormously difficult to answer and our answers are still not entirely complete.

HOW ARE MEMORIES STORED?

What changes occur in the brain as memories are stored?

Current research indicates that memories consist of changes in the synaptic connections among neurons (Squire & Kandel, 1999). When we learn new things, new connections are formed in the brain; when we review or practice previously learned things, old connections are strengthened. These chemical and structural changes can continue over a period of months or years (Gold & Greenough, 2001; Squire, Slater & Chace, 1975), during which the number of connections among neurons increases as does the likelihood that cells will excite one another through electrical discharges, a process known as **long-term potentiation (LTP)**.

The fact that changes in the brain occur when memories are stored provides one explanation for **childhood amnesia**, or *infantile amnesia*, which refers to the finding that adults usually cannot remember experiences from their first two years of life. Exactly why people have difficulty remembering events from their first years of life is not well understood, although several explanations have been advanced (Wang, 2003). One hypothesis holds that childhood amnesia is a result of the child's brain not being fully developed at birth. An immature brain structure, such as the prefrontal cortex, may be incapable of efficiently processing and storing information in memory. In fact, the hippocampus, which is so important in the formation of episodic and semantic memories, is not fully formed until about age two (Jacobs & Nadel, 1998).

WHERE ARE MEMORIES STORED?

Are STM and LTM found in the same parts of the brain?

Not all memories are stored in one place (Brewer, Zhao, Desmond, Glover, & Gabriel, 1998); however, this characteristic does not mean that memories are randomly distributed

long-term potentiation (LTP) A long-lasting change in the structure or function of a synapse that increases the efficiency of neural transmission and is thought to be related to how information is stored by neurons.

childhood amnesia The difficulty adults have remembering experiences from their first two years of life.

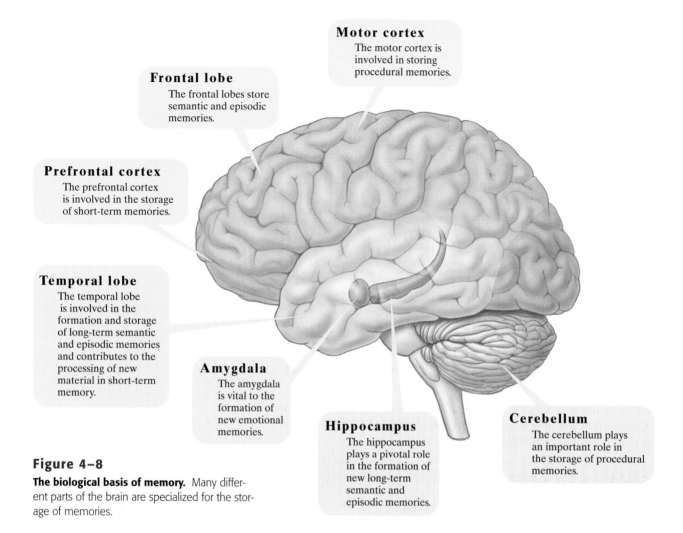

Motor cortex
The motor cortex is involved in storing procedural memories.

Frontal lobe
The frontal lobes store semantic and episodic memories.

Prefrontal cortex
The prefrontal cortex is involved in the storage of short-term memories.

Temporal lobe
The temporal lobe is involved in the formation and storage of long-term semantic and episodic memories and contributes to the processing of new material in short-term memory.

Amygdala
The amygdala is vital to the formation of new emotional memories.

Hippocampus
The hippocampus plays a pivotal role in the formation of new long-term semantic and episodic memories.

Cerebellum
The cerebellum plays an important role in the storage of procedural memories.

Figure 4–8
The biological basis of memory. Many different parts of the brain are specialized for the storage of memories.

throughout the brain. In fact, different parts of the brain are specialized for the storage of memories (See **Figure 4–8**; Rolls, 2000).

Short-term memories, for example, seem to be located primarily in the prefrontal cortex and temporal lobe. (See again **Figure 4–8**; Rainer & Miller, 2002; Scheibel & Levin, 2004; Rolls, Tovee, & Panzeri, 1999; Szatkowska, Grabowska, & Szymanska, 2001.) Long-term semantic memories seem to be located primarily in the frontal and temporal lobes of the cortex which, interestingly, also seem to play a prominent role in consciousness and awareness. (See again **Figure 4–8**.) Research shows increased activity in a particular area of the left temporal lobe—for example, when people are asked to recall the names of people. A nearby area shows increased activity when they are asked to recall the names of animals, and another neighboring area becomes active when they are asked to recall the names of tools (Damasio, Grabowski, Tranel, Hichawa, & Damasio, 1996). (See **Figure 4–9**.) Destruction of these areas of the cortex (through head injury, surgery, stroke, or disease) results in selective memory loss (e.g., Damasio et al., 1996).

Episodic memories also find their home in the frontal and temporal lobes (Nyberg et al., 2003; Wheeler, Stuss, & Tulving, 1997). But some evidence shows that episodic and semantic memories involve different portions of these brain structures. Wood and colleagues (1980) compared blood flow in the brain as people worked on two different kinds of tasks. (Blood flow to an area is associated with activity in that area.) Some people performed a task involving episodic memory; others performed a task involving semantic memory. The researchers found that the two kinds of tasks resulted in increased blood flow to somewhat different areas of the brain.

Procedural memories appear to be located primarily in the cerebellum (an area required for balance and motor coordination) and in the motor cortex (Gabrieli, 1998).

When people perform a task that requires them to follow a rotating object with a hand-held stylus, activity in their motor cortex increases (Grafton et al., 1992).

Subcortical structures also play a role in long-term memory. For example, the hippocampus has been implicated in the functioning of both semantic and episodic memory (Eichenbaum & Fortin, 2003; Manns, Hopkins, & Squire, 2003; Rolls, 2000), as well as being involved in the ability to remember spatial relationships (Astur, Taylor, Marnelak, Philpott, & Sutherland, 2002; Robertson, Rolls, & Georges-Francois, 1998). If the hippocampus is damaged, people can remember events that have just occurred (and are in STM), but their long-term recall of those same events is impaired. The amygdala, a structure that lies near the hippocampus, seems to play a role in emotional memory that is similar to the role the hippocampus plays in episodic, semantic, and procedural memory (Cahill & McGaugh, 1998; Pare, Collins, & Guillaume, 2002; Vermetten & Bremner, 2002). For example, damage to the amygdala reduces the ability to recall new emotional experiences, but it does not prevent the recall of emotional events that occurred prior to the damage, although they are often remembered as neutral facts, devoid of emotional content. This may explain why people with amygdala damage are sometimes unable to "read" facial expressions, even though they recognize the person's face (Young, Hellawell, Wan de Wal, & Johnson, 1996).

Clearly, psychologists have a long way to go before they will fully understand the biology of memory, but progress is being made in this fascinating area. As we will see in the next section, another problem that is beginning to succumb to scientific analysis is, why do we forget?

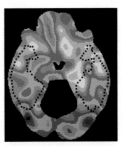

Persons

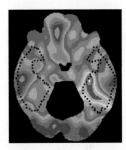

Animals

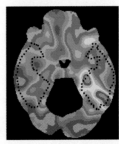

Tools

► CHECK YOUR UNDERSTANDING

Match the following types of memory to the location in the brain where they appear to be stored:

1. ___ short-term memories
2. ___ long-term semantic and episodic memories
3. ___ procedural memories
4. ___ emotional memories

a. frontal and temporal lobes
b. cerebellum and motor cortex
c. amygdala
d. prefrontal cortex and temporal lobe

Answers: 1. d, 2. a, 3. b, 4. c.

► APPLY YOUR UNDERSTANDING

1. Oliver Sacks, in his book *The Man Who Mistook His Wife for a Hat*, describes Jimmie G. who was an otherwise healthy 49-year-old man whose long-term memory stopped changing when he was 19. New information in his short-term memory simply never got stored in long-term memory. Which part of his brain was most likely not working correctly?

   a. the prefrontal cortex
   b. the hippocampus
   c. Broca's area
   d. the occipital lobe

2. Imagine now that you encounter someone like Jimmie G., but in this case, the person cannot form new emotional memories. He has emotional reactions to things he encountered early in his life, but he has no such reactions to things he encountered more recently—no new loves or hates, no new fears, no new sources of anger or happiness. Which part of his brain is most likely not working correctly?

   a. the amygdala
   b. the temporal lobe
   c. the prefrontal cortex
   d. the cerebellum

Answers: 1. b, 2. a.

Figure 4–9

PET scan of brain activity. PET scanning shows increased activity (as indicated by "warm" colors of red and yellow) in different areas of the brain when people are asked to recall the names of people, animals, and tools.

Source: Damaio, H., Grabowski, T. J., Tranel, D., Hichwa, R. D., & Damasio, A. R. "A neural basis for lexical retrieval." *Nature, 380,* 499–505, 1996. Department of Neurology and Image Analysis Facility. University of Iowa. Reprinted by permission of Nature. http://www.nature.com/.

Forgetting

4.8 Describe how memories might decay, how they can interfere with each other, and how our motivational state can cause us to experience memory problems or distortions.

Why do memories, once formed, not remain forever in the brain? Part of the answer has to do with the biology of memory, and another part has to do with the experiences that we have before and after learning.

THE BIOLOGY OF FORGETTING

How does the deterioration of the brain help to explain forgetting?

According to the **decay theory**, memories deteriorate because of the passage of time. Most of the evidence supporting decay theory comes from experiments known as *distractor studies*. For example, in one experiment, participants learned a sequence of letters, such as PSQ. Then they were given a three-digit number, such as 167, and asked to count backwards by threes: 167, 164, 161, and so on, for up to 18 seconds (Peterson & Peterson, 1959). At the end of that period, they were asked to recall the three letters. The results of this test astonished the experimenters. The participants showed a rapid decline in their ability to remember the letters. Because the researchers assumed that counting backwards would not *interfere* with remembering, they could only account for the forgotten letters by noting that they had simply faded from short-term memory in a matter of seconds. Decay, then, seems to be at least partly responsible for forgetting in short-term memory.

Information in LTM also can be lost if the storage process is disrupted. Head injuries often result in **retrograde amnesia**, a condition in which people cannot remember what happened to them shortly before their injury. In such cases, forgetting may occur because memories are not fully *consolidated*, or stored, in the brain. The problem is analogous to something that every computer user has experienced: A momentary power outage results in the loss of information that has not been saved to the hard drive. One moment the information is there before you, and readily accessed; in the next, it is gone.

Severe memory loss is invariably traced to brain damage caused by accidents, surgery, poor diet, or disease (Roncadin, Guger, Archibald, Barnes, & Dennis, 2004). For example, chronic alcoholism can lead to a form of amnesia called *Korsakoff's syndrome* caused by a vitamin deficiency in the poor diet typically eaten by people who abuse alcohol (Baddeley, 1987; Hildebrandt, Brokate, Eling, & Lanz, 2004). Other studies show the importance of the hippocampus to long-term memory formation. Studies of elderly people who are having trouble remembering new material, for example, show that the hippocampus is smaller than normal (Golomb et al., 1994). Brain scans also reveal a diminished hippocampus in people suffering from *Alzheimer's disease*, a neurological disorder that causes severe memory loss. (See Chapter 7, "Human Development Across the Lifespan," for more information about Alzheimer's disease; Bennett & Knopman, 1994).

Alzheimer's may also involve below-normal levels of the neurotransmitter acetylcholine in the brain. Indeed, some research suggests that drugs and surgical procedures that increase acetylcholine levels may serve as effective treatments for age-related memory problems (Hall, 2003; Li & Low, 1997; Parnetti, Senin, & Mecocci, 1997; D. E. Smith, Roberts, Gage, & Tuszynski, 1999; McIntyre, Marriott, & Gold, 2003).

EXPERIENCE AND FORGETTING

What environmental factors contribute to our inability to remember?

Although sometimes caused by biological factors, forgetting can also result from inadequate learning. A lack of attention to critical cues, for example, is a cause of the forgetting commonly referred to as absentmindedness (Schacter, 1999). For example, if you can't remember where you parked your car, most likely you can't remember because you didn't pay attention to where you parked it.

Forgetting also occurs because although we attended to the matter to be recalled, we did not rehearse the material enough. Merely "going through the motions" of rehearsal does little good. Prolonged, intense practice results in less forgetting than a few, halfhearted repetitions. Elaborative rehearsal can also help make new memories more durable. When you park your car in space G-47, you will be more likely to remember its location if you think, "G-47. My uncle *George* is about *47* years old." In short, we cannot expect to remember information for long if we have not learned it well in the first place.

INTERFERENCE Inadequate learning accounts for many memory failures, but learning itself can cause forgetting. This is the case because learning one thing can interfere with

---

decay theory A theory that argues that the passage of time causes forgetting.

retrograde amnesia The inability to recall events preceding an accident or injury, but without loss of earlier memory.

learning another. Information gets mixed up with, or pushed aside by, other information and thus becomes harder to remember. Such forgetting is said to be due to *interference*. There are two kinds of interference. In **retroactive interference**, new material interferes with information already in long-term memory. Retroactive interference occurs every day. For example, after you learn a new telephone number, you may find it difficult to recall your old number, even though you used that old number for years.

In the second kind of interference, old material interferes with new material being learned; this is called **proactive interference**. Like retroactive interference, proactive interference is an everyday phenomenon. Suppose you always park your car in the lot behind the building where you work, but one day all those spaces are full, so you have to park across the street. When you leave for the day, you are likely to head for the lot behind the building—and may even be surprised at first that your car is not there. Learning to look for your car behind the building has interfered with your memory that today you parked the car across the street.

The most important factor in determining the degree of interference is the similarity of the competing items. Learning to swing a golf club may interfere with your ability to hit a baseball, but probably won't affect your ability to make a free throw on the basketball courts. The more dissimilar something is from other things that you have already learned, the less likely it will be to mingle and interfere with other material in memory (Bower & Mann, 1992).

SITUATIONAL FACTORS Whenever we try to memorize something, we are also unintentionally picking up information about the context in which the learning is taking place. That information becomes useful when we later try to retrieve the corresponding information from LTM. If those environmental cues are absent when we try to recall what we learned, the effort to remember is often unsuccessful. Context-dependent memory effects tend to be small, so studying in the same classroom where you are scheduled to take an exam will probably not do too much to improve your grade. Nevertheless, contextual cues are occasionally used by police who sometimes take witnesses back to the scene of a crime in the hope that they will recall crucial details that can be used to solve the crime.

In addition to being influenced by environmental cues, our ability to accurately recall information is affected by internal cues. This phenomenon is known as **state-dependent memory**. State-dependent memory refers to the finding that people who learn material in a particular physiological state tend to recall that material better if they return to the same state they were in during learning (de-l'Etoile, 2002; Kelemen & Creeley, 2003; Riccio, Millin, & Gisquet-Verrier, 2003). For example, if people learn material while under the influence of caffeine, recall of the material is slightly improved when they are again under the influence of caffeine (Keleman & Creeley, 2003). Similarly, if you discovered the location of a particularly scrumptious bakery when you were really hungry, you may find it easier to remember the way there when you're hungry than when you are not.

THE RECONSTRUCTIVE PROCESS Forgetting also occurs because of what is called the "reconstructive" nature of remembering. Earlier, we talked about how schemata are used in storing information in long-term memory. Bartlett proposed that people also use schemata to "reconstruct" memories (Bartlett, 1932; Schacter, Norman, & Koutstaal, 1998). This reconstructive process can lead to huge errors. Indeed, we are sometimes more likely to recall events that never happened than events that actually took place (Brainerd & Reyna, 1998)! The original memory is not destroyed; instead, people are sometimes unable to tell the difference between what actually happened and what they merely heard about or imagined (Garry & Polaschek, 2000; Lindsay & Johnson, 1989; Reyna & Titcomb, 1997; Taylor, Pham, Rivkin, & Armor, 1998). In other words, sometimes people combine the elements of both real and imagined events (Henkel, Franklin, & Johnson, 2000). People also unknowingly "rewrite" past events to fit their current image or their desired image of themselves and their past decisions (Lyubomirsky & Ross, 1999; Mather, Shafir, & Johnson, 2000).

We may also reconstruct memories for social or personal self-defense. Each time you tell someone the story of an incident, you may unconsciously make subtle changes in the

People who work in the legal system must be careful to interview witnesses without leading them to reconstruct their memory about a crime.

retroactive interference The process by which new information interferes with information already in memory.

proactive interference The process by which information already in memory interferes with new information.

state-dependent memory The finding that people who learn material in a particular physiological state tend to recall that material better if they return to the same state they were in during learning.

Millions of people will forever have a vivid flash-bulb memory of planes flying into the twin towers of the World Trade Center in New York City on September 11, 2001.

details of the story, with the result that these changes then become part of your memory of the event. When an experience doesn't fit our view of the world or ourselves, we tend, unconsciously, to adjust it or to blot it out of memory altogether (Bremner & Marmar, 1998). Such distortions of memory become critically important in criminal trials, in which a person's guilt or innocence may depend on the testimony of an eyewitness.

RECOVERED MEMORIES Memory reconstruction processes may also be involved in the controversial phenomenon referred to as *recovered memory* (McNally, 2003a, 2003b). The idea is that people experience an event, then lose all memory of it, and then later recall it, often in the course of psychotherapy or under hypnosis. Frequently, the recovered memories concern physical or sexual abuse during childhood. The issue is important not only for theoretical reasons, but also because of the fact that people have been imprisoned for abuse solely on the basis of the recovered memories of their "victims." No one denies the reality of childhood abuse or the damage that such experiences cause. But are the recovered memories real? Did the remembered abuse really occur?

The answer is by no means obvious. There is ample evidence that people can be induced to "remember" events that never happened (Smith, Gleaves, Pierce, Williams, Gilliland, & Gerkens, 2003). For example, when Elizabeth Loftus and her colleagues told people that relatives had mentioned an event in their lives, a fourth of the participants "remembered" the events even though they had never actually happened Elizabeth (Loftus, Coan, & Pickrell, 1996; Loftus & Pickrell, 1995). And as we have seen, simply imagining that something happened can increase the likelihood that people will "remember" that the event actually happened (Garry & Polaschek, 2000; Mazzoni & Memon, 2003). Other research confirms that it is relatively easy to implant memories of an experience merely by asking about it. The more times that people are asked about the event, the more likely they are to "remember" it. Sometimes these memories become quite real to the participant. In one experiment, 25 percent of adults "remembered" fictitious events by the third time they were interviewed about them. One of the fictitious events involved knocking over a punch bowl onto the parents of the bride at a wedding reception. At the first interview, one participant said that she had no recollection whatsoever of the event; by the second interview, she "remembered" that the reception was outdoors and that she had knocked over the bowl while running around. Some people even "remembered" details about the event, such as what people looked like and what they wore. Yet, the researchers documented that these events never happened (Hyman, Husband, & Billings, 1995). Other research shows that people can even become convinced that they remember experiences from infancy that never happened (Spanos, 1996; Spanos, Burgess, Burgess, Samuels, & Blois, 1997).

The implication of this and similar research is that it is quite possible for people to "remember" abusive experiences that never happened. And some people who have "recovered" abuse memories have later realized that the events never occurred. Some of these people have brought suit against the therapists who, they came to believe, implanted the memories. In one case, a woman won such a suit and was awarded $850,000 (Imrie, 1999).

There is reason to believe; however, that not all recovered memories are merely the products of suggestion. There are numerous case studies of people who have lived through traumatic experiences, including natural disasters, accidents, combat, assault, and rape, who then apparently forgot these events for many years, but who later remembered them (Arrigo & Pezdek, 1997). For example, Wilbur J. Scott, a sociologist, claimed to remember nothing of his tour of duty in Vietnam during 1968–1969, but during a divorce in 1983, he discovered his medals and souvenirs from Vietnam, and the memories then came back to him (Arrigo & Pezdek, 1997).

What is needed is a reliable way of separating real memories from false ones, but so far no such test is available (Gleaves, Smith, Butler, & Spiegel, 2004). The sincerity and conviction of the person who "remembers" long-forgotten childhood abuse is no indication of the reality of that abuse. We are left with the conclusion that recovered memories are not, in themselves, sufficiently trustworthy to justify criminal convictions. There must also be corroborative evidence, since without corroboration, there is no way that even the most experienced examiner can separate real memories from false ones (Loftus, 1997).

► CHECK YOUR UNDERSTANDING

Match the following terms with their appropriate definitions:

1. ___ retrograde amnesia
2. ___ retroactive interference
3. ___ proactive interference
4. ___ recovered memory

   a. Forgetting because new information makes it harder to remember information already in memory

b. Forgetting because old information in memory makes it harder to learn new information
c. Linked to head injury or electroconvulsive therapy
d. Occurs when memory is forgotten, but later remembered

Answers: 1. c., 2. a., 3. b., 4. d.

► APPLY YOUR UNDERSTANDING

1. You are trying to explain to someone that "forgetting" sometimes occurs because of the reconstructive nature of long-term memory. Which of the following would be an example that you might use to support your position?

   a. People can distinguish between real and fictional accounts in stories.
   b. People who learn material in a particular setting tend to recall that material better if they return to that same setting.
   c. Rote rehearsal with no intention to remember has little effect on long-term memory.
   d. People often rewrite their memories of past events to fit their current view or desired view of themselves.

2. You are given a chance to earn $10 if you can correctly learn a list of 20 words. You have five minutes to learn the entire list. At the end of that time, you can recite the list perfectly. But before you are given a chance to show what you have learned, you are required to learn a second list of similar words. When it comes time to show how well you learned the first list, to your dismay, you discover that you have forgotten half the words that you once knew perfectly. What is the most likely cause of your forgetting the words on the first list?

   a. Negative transference
   b. Retroactive interference
   c. Retroactive facilitation
   d. Proactive interference

Answers: 1. d., 2. b.

>KEY TERMS<

learning, *p. 123*
memory, *p. 123*

Classical conditioning

classical (or Pavlovian) conditioning, *p. 123*
unconditioned stimulus (US), *p. 124*
unconditioned response (UR), *p. 124*
conditioned stimulus (CS), *p. 124*
conditioned response (CR), *p. 124*
desensitization therapy, *p. 125*
preparedness, *p. 125*
conditioned taste aversion, *p. 126*

Operant conditioning

operant (or instrumental) conditioning, *p. 127*
operant behavior, *p. 127*
reinforcer, *p. 127*
punisher, *p. 127*
law of effect, *p. 127*

principle of reinforcement, *p. 127*
Skinner box, *p. 128*
shaping, *p. 129*
positive reinforcer, *p. 129*
negative reinforcer, *p. 129*
primary reinforcer, *p. 130*
secondary reinforcer, *p. 130*
punishment, *p. 131*
learned helplessness, *p. 132*

Common Features of classical and operant conditioning

contingency, *p. 133*
schedule of reinforcement, *p. 134*
fixed-interval schedule, *p. 134*
variable-interval schedule, *p. 134*
fixed-ratio schedule, *p. 134*
variable-ratio schedule, *p. 135*
extinction, *p. 135*
spontaneous recovery, *p. 135*
stimulus control, *p. 136*
stimulus generalization, *p. 136*
stimulus discrimination, *p. 137*

response generalization, *p. 137*

Cognitive learning

cognitive learning, *p. 138*
latent learning, *p. 138*
cognitive map, *p. 139*
insight, *p. 139*
learning set, *p. 139*
observational (or vicarious) learning, *p. 139*
social learning theorists, *p. 140*

Forming Memories

information-processing model, *p. 140*
sensory registers, *p. 141*
attention, *p. 142*
short-term memory (STM), *p. 143*
chunking, *p. 144*
rote rehearsal, *p. 144*

Long-term memory

Long-term memory (LTM), *p. 145*
serial position effect, *p. 146*

elaborative rehearsal, *p. 147*
mnemonics, *p. 147*
schema, *p. 147*
episodic memory, *p. 148*
semantic memory, *p. 149*
procedural memory, *p. 149*
emotional memory, *p. 149*
explicit memory, *p. 149*
implicit memory, *p. 149*

The biology of memory

long-term potentiation (LTP), *p. 151*
childhood amnesia, *p. 151*

Forgetting

decay theory, *p. 154*
retrograde amnesia, *p. 154*
retroactive interference, *p. 155*
proactive interference, *p. 155*
state-dependent memory, *p. 155*

>CHAPTER REVIEW<

Classical Conditioning

How does classical conditioning occur? **Learning** is the process by which experience or practice produces a relatively permanent change in behavior or potential behavior. One basic form of learning involves learning to associate one event with another. **Classical conditioning** is a type of associative learning that Pavlov discovered while studying digestion. Pavlov trained a dog to salivate at the sound of a bell when he rang the bell just before food was given. The dog learned to associate the bell with food and began to salivate at the sound of the bell alone.

In Pavlov's studies food served as an **unconditioned stimulus (US)** that automatically evoked the **unconditioned response (UR)** of salivation. By repeatedly pairing food with a second, initially neutral stimulus (such as a bell) that doesn't at first cause salivation, the second stimulus eventually became a **conditioned stimulus (CS),** which became capable of eliciting the **conditioned response (CR)** of salivation.

How is classical conditioning involved in learning and unlearning emotional responses such as fear? John Watson conditioned a little boy, Albert, to fear white rats by making a loud, frightening noise every time the boy was shown a rat. In your own life, you may have acquired a classically conditioned fear or anxiety (to the sound of a dentist's drill, for instance) in much the same way. Perhaps you have also unlearned a conditioned fear by repeatedly pairing the feared object with something pleasant. Mary Cover Jones pioneered this procedure by pairing the sight of a feared rat (at gradually decreasing distances) with a child's pleasant experience of eating candy. This procedure evolved into **desensitization therapy.**

Why are people more likely to develop a phobia of snakes than of flowers? Martin Seligman has used the concept of **preparedness** to account for the fact that certain conditioned responses are acquired very easily. The ease with which we develop **conditioned taste aversions** illustrates preparedness. Because animals are biologically prepared to learn them, conditioned taste aversions can occur with only one pairing of the taste of a tainted food and later illness, and even when there is a lengthy interval between eating the food and becoming ill. A fear of snakes may also be something that humans are prepared to learn.

Operant Conditioning

What two essential elements are involved in operant conditioning? **Operant** or **instrumental conditioning** involves learning to make or withhold a certain response because of its consequences. One essential element in operant conditioning is an **operant behavior,** or a behavior performed by one's own volition while "operating" on the environment. The second essential element is a consequence associated with that operant behavior. When a consequence increases the likelihood of an operant behavior's being emitted, it is called a **reinforcer.** When a consequence decreases the likelihood of an operant behavior, it is called a **punisher.** These relationships are the basis of the **law of effect,** or **principle of reinforcement**: Consistently rewarded behaviors are likely to be repeated, whereas consistently punished behaviors are likely to be suppressed.

How are operantly conditioned responses acquired? To speed up establishing an operantly conditioned response in the laboratory, the number of potential responses may be reduced by restricting the environment, as in a **Skinner box.** For behaviors outside the laboratory, which cannot be controlled so conveniently, the process of **shaping** is often useful. In shaping, reinforcement is given for successive approximations to the desired response.

How do various types of reinforcement work? There are several kinds of reinforcers, all of which strengthen behavior. **Positive reinforcers** (like food) increase the likelihood of a behavior by adding something rewarding to a situation. **Negative reinforcers** (such as stopping an electric shock) increase the likelihood of a behavior by subtracting something unpleasant. When an action is followed closely by a reinforcer, we tend to repeat the action, even if it did not actually produce the reinforcement. Such behaviors are called superstitious.

In operant conditioning, initially neutral stimuli can **become reinforcers** by being associated with other reinforcers. A **primary reinforcer** is one that, like food and water, is rewarding in and of itself. A **secondary reinforcer** is one whose value is learned through its association with primary reinforcers or with other secondary reinforcers. Money is such a good secondary reinforcer because it can be exchanged for so many different primary and secondary rewards.

What problems can punishment create? **Punishment** is any event that decreases the likelihood that the behavior that precedes it will occur again. Whereas negative reinforcement strengthens behavior, punishment weakens it. Although punishment can be effective, it also has drawbacks, such as stirring up negative feelings and sometimes modeling aggressive behavior. Also, punishment doesn't teach a more desirable response; it only suppresses an undesirable one.

What is the result when punishment cannot be avoided? When people or other animals are unable to escape from a punishing situation, they may acquire a "giving up" response, called **learned helplessness.** Learned helplessness can generalize to new situations, causing resignation in the face of unpleasant outcomes, even when the outcomes can be avoided. A college student who gives up trying to do well in school after a few poor grades on tests is exhibiting learned helplessness.

Common Features of Classical and Operant Conditioning

What contingencies are particularly important in classical and operant conditioning? In both classical and operant conditioning, an "if–then" relationship, or **contingency**, exists either between two stimuli or between a stimulus and a response. In both these kinds of learning, perceived contingencies are very important.

In classical conditioning, the contingency is between the CS and the US. The CS comes to be viewed as a signal that the US is about to happen. For that reason, the CS must not only occur in close proximity to the US, but must also precede the US and provide predictive information about it. If the CS occurs *after* the US, it will come to serve as a signal that the US is over, not that the US is imminent.

In operant conditioning, contingencies exist between responses and consequences. Contingencies between responses and rewards are called **schedules of reinforcement**. *Partial reinforcement*, in which rewards are given for some correct responses, but not for every one, generates behavior that persists longer than behavior learned by continuous reinforcement. This is the case because partial reinforcement encourages learners to keep "testing" for a reward. The type of partial reinforcement schedule also matters. A **fixed-interval schedule**, by which reinforcement is given for the first correct response after a fixed time period, tends to result in a flurry of responding right before a reward is due. A **variable-interval schedule**, which reinforces the first correct response after an unpredictable period of time, tends to result in a slow, but steady pattern of responding as the learner keeps testing for the next payoff. In a **fixed-ratio schedule**, behavior is rewarded after a fixed number of correct responses, so the result is usually a high rate of responding, since faster responses yield quicker payoffs. Finally, a **variable-ratio schedule** provides reinforcement after a varying number of correct responses. It encourages a high rate of response that is especially persistent, as the person keeps harboring the hope that the next response will bring a reward.

Under what circumstances might old learned associations suddenly reappear? Another factor shared by classical and operant conditioning is that learned responses sometimes weaken and may even disappear, a phenomenon called **extinction**. The learning is not necessarily completely forgotten, however. Sometimes a **spontaneous recovery** occurs, in which the learned response suddenly reappears on its own, with no retraining.

Extinction is produced in classical conditioning by failure to continue pairing the CS and the US. The CS no longer serves as a signal that the US is about to happen, and so the conditioned response dies out. An important contributing factor is often new learned associations that interfere with the old one. In situations in which you are reminded of the old association, spontaneous recovery may occur.

Extinction occurs in operant conditioning when reinforcement is withheld until the learned response is no longer emitted. The ease with which an operantly conditioned behavior is extinguished varies according to several factors: the strength of the original learning, the variety of settings in which learning took place, and the schedule of reinforcement used during conditioning. Especially hard to extinguish is behavior learned through punishment.

How do the processes of discrimination and generalization work? When conditioned responses are influenced by surrounding cues in the environment, **stimulus control** occurs. The tendency to respond to cues that are similar, but not identical, to those that prevailed during the original learning is known as **stimulus generalization**. **Stimulus discrimination** enables learners to perceive differences among cues so as not to respond to all of them.

In classical conditioning, the conditioned response (CR) is under the control of the conditioned stimulus (CS) that triggers it. An example of stimulus generalization in classical conditioning is a student's feeling anxious about studying math in college because he or she had a bad experience learning math in grade school.

In operant conditioning, the learned response is under the control of whatever cues come to be associated with delivery of reward or punishment. Learners often generalize about these cues, responding to others that are broadly similar to the ones that prevailed during the original learning. An example is slapping any face card in a game of slapjack. Learners may also generalize their responses by performing behaviors that are similar to the ones that were originally reinforced. This result is called **response generalization**. Discrimination in operant conditioning is taught by reinforcing only a certain response and only in the presence of a certain stimulus.

Cognitive Learning

Did you learn your way around campus solely through operant conditioning (rewards for correct turns, punishments for wrong ones) or was something more involved? **Cognitive learning** refers to the mental processes that go on inside us when we learn. **Latent learning** is any knowledge we acquire that has not yet been demonstrated in behavior. Your knowledge of psychology is latent if you have not yet displayed it in what you say, write, and do. One kind of latent learning is knowledge of spatial layouts and relationships, which is usually stored in the form of a **cognitive map**. Rewards or punishments aren't essential for latent learning to take place. You did not need rewards and punishments to learn the layout of your campus, for example. You acquired this cognitive map simply by storing your visual perceptions.

How does establishing a learning set prepare the way for problem solving that involves insight? A **learning set** is a concept or procedure that provides a key to solving a problem even when its demands are slightly different from those of problems you have solved in the past. As a student, you probably have a learning set for writing a term paper that allows you successfully to develop papers on many different topics. A learning set can sometimes encourage **insight** or the sudden perception of a solution even to a problem that at first seems totally new. In this case, you are perceiving similarities between old and new problems that weren't initially apparent.

Why would it be harder to learn to drive a car if you had never been in one before? **Social learning theorists** argue that we learn much by observing other people who model a behavior or by simply hearing about something. This process is called **observational** (or **vicarious**) **learning**. It would be harder to learn to drive a car without ever having been in one because you would lack a model of "driving behavior". The extent to which we imitate behaviors learned through observation depends on our motivation to do so. One important motivation is any reward or punishment that we have seen the behavior bring.

Forming Memories

What is the role of sensory registers? Many psychologists view **memory** as a series of steps in which we encode, store, and retrieve information, much as a computer does. This is called the **information-processing** model of memory. The first step in the model is inputting data through our senses into temporary holding bins, called **sensory registers**. These registers give us a brief moment to decide whether something deserves our attention.

Information entering a sensory register disappears very quickly if it isn't processed further. Information in the visual register lasts for only about a quarter of a second before it is replaced by new information. If sounds faded from our auditory register as rapidly as this, spoken language would be more difficult to understand. Luckily, information in the auditory register can linger for several seconds.

Why does some information capture our attention, while other information goes unnoticed? The next step in the memory process is **attention**—selectively looking at, listening to, smelling, tasting, or feeling what we deem to be important. The nervous system seems to automatically filter out peripheral information, allowing us to zero in on what is essential at a particular time. Unattended information receives at least some processing, however, so that we can quickly shift attention to it if it suddenly strikes us as significant.

What are the most important tasks performed by short-term memory? **Short-term memory (STM)** holds whatever information we are actively attending to at any given time. Its two primary tasks are to store new information briefly and to "work" on information that we currently have in mind. This second function is why STM is also called *working memory*.

Research suggests that STM lasts about 1.5 to 2 seconds, and its capacity can be expanded by **chunking**, which involves fitting information into meaningful units. Short-term memories can be maintained through repetition, called **rote rehearsal.** Information can be stored in STM according to the way it sounds, the way it looks, or its meaning. Verbal information is encoded by sound, even if we see the words written rather than hear them spoken. It is interesting that the capacity for visual encoding in STM seems to be greater than for encoding by sound.

Long-Term Memory

How are most memories encoded in LTM? **Long-term memory (LTM)** is more or less permanent and stores everything we "know." Long-term memory can store a vast amount of information that can last for many years.

Most of the information in LTM seems to be encoded according to its meaning.

What three ways are used to hold information in LTM? The way in which we encode material for storage in LTM affects the ease with which we can retrieve it later on. **Rote rehearsal** is useful for holding information in LTM, particularly meaningless material such as phone numbers. Short- and long-term memory work together to explain the **serial position effect**, the fact that when given a list of items to remember, people tend to recall the first and last items in the list better than words in the middle. The *recency effect* explains that items at the end are still held in STM, whereas the *primacy effect* describes the extra LTM rehearsal given to items early in the list.

Through **elaborative rehearsal**, we extract the meaning of information and link it to as much material that is already in LTM as possible. Elaborative rehearsal processes new data in a deeper and more meaningful way than simple rote repetition. Memory techniques such as **mnemonics** rely on elaborative processing.

A **schema** is a mental representation of an object or event that is stored in memory. Schemata provide a framework into which incoming information is fitted. They may prompt the formation of stereotypes and the drawing of inferences.

How do different types of LTM differ? **Episodic memories** are memories for events experienced in a specific time and place. **Semantic memories** are facts and concepts not linked to a particular time. **Procedural memories** are motor skills and habits. **Emotional memories** are learned emotional responses to various stimuli.

Explicit memory refers to memories we are aware of, including episodic and semantic memories. A particularly vivid type of episodic memory is a *flashbulb memory*, which typically is associated with a dramatic or significant event. **Implicit memory** refers to memories for information that either was not intentionally committed to LTM or is retrieved unintentionally from LTM, including procedural and emotional memories. This distinction is illustrated by research on *priming*, which finds that people are more likely to complete fragments with items seen earlier than with other, equally plausible items.

The Biology of Memory

What changes occur in the brain as memories are stored? Memories consist of changes in the chemistry and structure of neurons. The process by which these changes occur is called **long-term potentiation (LTP)**. Adults usually cannot remember experiences from their first two years of life, a phenomenon called **childhood** (or infantile) **amnesia**. One explanation is that these early memories were not encoded in the developing brain.

Are STM and LTM found in the same parts of the brain? There is no one place where all memories are stored, but research has shown that different parts of the brain are specialized for the storage of memories. Short-term memories seem to be located primarily in the prefrontal cortex and temporal lobe. Long-term memories seem to involve both subcortical and cortical structures. Semantic and episodic memories seem to be located primarily in the frontal and temporal lobes of the cortex, and procedural memories appear to be located primarily in the cerebellum and motor cortex. A brain structure called the hippocampus seems especially important in the formation of semantic, episodic, and procedural memories. Emotional memories are dependent on the amygdala.

Forgetting

How does the deterioration of the brain help to explain forgetting? Both biological and environmental factors can contribute to our inability to recall information. According to the decay theory, memories deteriorate because of the passage of time. Severe memory loss can be traced to brain damage caused by accidents, surgery, poor diet, or disease. Head injuries can cause **retrograde amnesia**, the inability of people to remember what happened shortly before their accident. Some studies have focused on the role of the hippocampus in long-term memory formation. Other research has emphasized the role of neurotransmitters, especially acetylcholine, in the memory process.

What environmental factors contribute to our inability to remember? To the extent that information is apparently lost from LTM, researchers attribute the cause to inadequate learning or to interference from competing information. Interference may come from two directions: In **retroactive interference**, new information interferes with old information already in LTM; **proactive interference** refers to the process by which old information already in LTM interferes with new information.

When environmental cues that were present during learning are absent during recall, context-dependent forgetting may occur. The ability to recall information is also affected by one's physiological state when the material was learned; this process is known as **state-dependent memory**.

Sometimes we "reconstruct" memories for social or personal self-defense as demonstrated in research about eyewitness testimony. Sometimes, too, memory reconstruction can be involved with recovered memories, which are stored, then forgotten, and then recalled at a later time. Such recovered memories are highly controversial because research shows that people can be induced to "remember" events that never happened. So far there is no clear way to distinguish real recovered memories from false ones.

Concept Map

4.1 CLASSICAL CONDITIONING

HOW CLASSICAL CONDITIONING HAPPENS

- A stimulus occurs just before an **unconditioned stimulus (UCS)–unconditioned response (UCR)** reflex
- Through repeated pairings, an association forms between this stimulus, which is now called the **conditioned stimulus (CS)**, and the UCS-UCR reflex
- After learning, the CS elicits a **conditioned response (CR)**
- **Preparedness:** A biological readiness to learn certain associations for survival

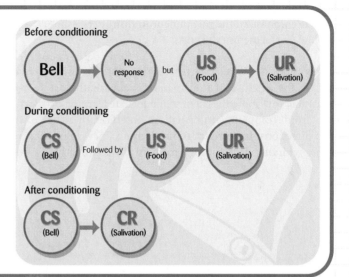

Before conditioning

Bell → No response but US (Food) → UR (Salivation)

During conditioning

CS (Bell) Followed by US (Food) → UR (Salivation)

After conditioning

CS (Bell) → CR (Salivation)

4.2 OPERANT CONDITIONING

HOW OPERANT CONDITIONING HAPPENS

Operant, or instrumental, **conditioning** occurs when an emitted response is followed by a consequence.

- **Positive reinforcement**: A pleasant consequence that increases the likelihood of the response it follows
- **Negative reinforcement**: Removal of an unpleasant consequence that increases the likelihood of the response it follows
- **Punishment**: An unpleasant consequence that decreases the likelihood of the response it follows
- **Shaping**: Reinforcing successive approximations to a desired behavior
- **Learned helplessness**: A failure to respond to escape or avoid unpleasant circumstances because earlier experience has taught that unpleasant consequences cannot be avoided

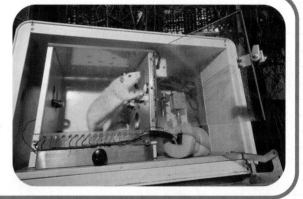

4.3 COMMON FEATURES OF CLASSICAL AND OPERANT CONDITIONING

	CLASSICAL CONDITIONING	OPERATIONAL CONDITIONING
Contingencies	The CS occurs just before the UCS-UCR reflex, thereby predicting the onset of the UCS	Consequences that follow a behavior can increase or decrease the likelihood that the behavior will be repeated
Extinction	When CS is presented but not followed by UCS-UCR, it eventually loses its power to elicit the CR	When the response is no longer followed by a reinforcement or punishment; occurs most quickly in continuous schedules of reinforcement

SCHEDULES OF REINFORCEMENT

- **Continuous**: Every response is followed by a reinforcement (or punishment)
- **Fixed ratio**: Reinforcement after a fixed number of responses
- **Variable ratio**: Reinforcement after a varying number of responses
- **Fixed interval**: Reinforcement of the first response after a fixed amount of time has passed
- **Variable interval**: Reinforcement after the first response after varying amounts of time

GENERALIZATION, DISCRIMINATION AND SPONTANEOUS RECOVERY

- **Generalization**: When similar stimuli elicit the same response, or when similar responses are produced by the same stimuli
- **Discrimination**: When stimuli are judged to be different, and therefore produce different responses
- **Spontaneous recovery**: The reappearance of an extinguished response after the passage of time, without training

4.4 COGNITIVE LEARNING

TYPES OF COGNITIVE LEARNING
- **Latent learning**: Learning that is not immediately reflected in behavior
- **Insight**: Learning that occurs rapidly as the result of understanding all elements of a problem
- **Observational (vicarious) learning**: Learning by observing other peoples' behavior

4.6 LONG-TERM MEMORY

Long-term memory (LTM) is our permanent store for information, much of which is encoded in terms of meaning

TYPES OF LTM
- **Explicit**: Memories of which we are aware
  - **Episodic**: Memories of personally experienced events, such as flash-bulb memories
- **Semantic**: General facts and information
- **Implicit**: Memories of which we are not generally aware
  - **Procedural**: Memories for how to do something
  - **Emotional**: Learned emotional responses

MAINTAINING LONG-TERM MEMORIES
- Rote rehearsal (repetition)
- Elaborative rehearsal, where new information is linked to familiar material in LTM
- Use of schemata (scripts based on past experience)

4.7 THE BIOLOGY OF MEMORY

REGIONS OF THE BRAIN AND PARTICULAR TYPES OF MEMORY
- **Short-term memory (STM)**: Prefrontal cortex and temporal lobes
- **Long-term memory (LTM)**: Frontal and temporal lobes and hippocampus
- **Episodic memory**: Frontal and temporal lobes and hippocampus
- **Semantic memory**: Frontal and temporal lobes and hippocampus
- **Procedural memory**: Cerebellum and motor cortex
- **Emotional memory**: Amygdala

4.5 FORMING MEMORIES

THE INFORMATION PROCESSING MODEL OF MEMORY

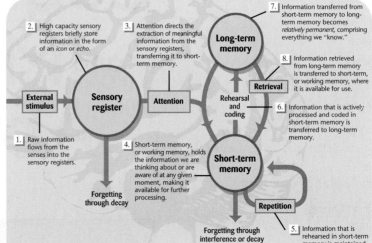

1. Raw information flows from the senses into the sensory registers.
2. High capacity sensory registers briefly store information in the form of an *icon* or *echo*.
3. Attention directs the extraction of meaningful information from the sensory registers, transferring it to short-term memory.
4. Short-term memory, or working memory, holds the information we are thinking about or are aware of at any given moment, making it available for further processing.
5. Information that is rehearsed in short-term memory is maintained there; otherwise, it decays rapidly.
6. Information that is actively processed and coded in short-term memory is transferred to long-term memory.
7. Information transferred from short-term memory to long-term memory becomes *relatively permanent*, comprising everything we "know."
8. Information retrieved from long-term memory is transferred to short-term, or working memory, where it is available for use.

SENSORY REGISTERS
- Correspond to each sense
- Brief (1.5–2 second) store of information
- Attention processes select most important information for futher processing in **STM**

SHORT-TERM MEMORY (WORKING MEMORY)
- Where we "work" with information; our "thinking" memory
- Capacity can be increased by "chunking" (giving meaning) to information
- Information can be maintained in STM by repetition, called **rote rehearsal**
- Encoding is primarily phonological (in terms of how words sound)

4.8 FORGETTING

THEORIES OF FORGETTING
- **Decay**: Memory traces fade away in STM, or their storage in the brain is disrupted, resulting in **retrograde amnesia**.
- **Interference**: Learning something new interferes with remembering something already stored (**retroactive interference**) or previous learning makes it difficult to learn new things (**proactive interference**).
- **State-dependent memory**: We remember things better if we are in the same motivational or emotional state as when they were learned.
- **Reconstructive memory**: Our memories change after they are stored so they become more consistent with other information or with what we wish would have happened.

Cognition and Mental Abilities

How would you persuade your friends to haul a bulky mattress up a flight of stairs? What would you do if you were assigned to a dorm triple, in which one bedroom is bigger than the other, and all three roommates wanted it? Confronted with a title like "The Octopus's Sneakers" what would you write?

Questions such as these are designed to measure the practical and creative knowledge that can be crucial to success in college and in life. Yet you won't see anything like them on even the newest version of the College Board's Scholastic Aptitude Test (SAT), which is designed to test analytical and reasoning skills. Starting in 2007, however, Tufts University in Boston, MA, will introduce questions like these into its admissions process, becoming the first college in the country to explicitly measure creative and practical skills.

The brainchild behind the new admissions process at Tufts is psychologist Robert Sternberg, who left Yale University to become Tufts' Dean of Arts and Sciences. While at Yale, Sternberg started the Rainbow Project that developed new assessment tools to supplement the usual admissions process, which puts enormous weight on applicants' SAT scores and high school grades. These assessment tools (funded by The College Board, the SAT's creator) were introduced at 1,000 colleges and the results, published in the journal *Intelligence*, were refreshing: The Rainbow Project assessment tools not only were a more accurate predictor of freshman performance than the SAT, but they also significantly narrowed the differences between white students and minorities.

The SAT was originally created in the 1940s to level the playing field between the Northeastern social elite who attended prestigious prep schools and those who didn't have connections or means. Although the SAT resulted in creating opportunities for students of more modest backgrounds, the test has not embraced new theories of intelligence that emphasize diverse human abilities. Sternberg's theory of *triarchic intelligence*, for example, says there are three kinds of human intelligence: analytical, creative, and practical.

Sternberg's own experience as a college student compelled him to study students' diverse learning styles and use that information to improve teaching methods. "I had planned to be a psychology major, but I bombed introductory psychology," says Sternberg. After being told to try math, Sternberg failed the midterm. He returned to psychology and ended up doing very well in higher-level courses. "I'm more of a cre-

ative learner," says Sternberg, "I do very well in projects, but I was not good at memorizing all of that material in the introductory classes."

No doubt if more universities make the Rainbow Project assessment tools part of their admissions process, it will be a boon and comfort to the much maligned middle—the C students who often go on to run corporations, colleges and even countries. "… my concern," says Robert Sternberg, "given the relatively low predictability of the standardized tests is that there may be people who have tremendous talents, creative and practical talents, who, because they don't do well on these tests, never get the chance to show what they really could do in important jobs." Now, at least at Tufts University, they will.[1]

Psychologists use the term **cognition** to refer to all the processes that we use to acquire and apply information. We have already considered the cognitive processes of perception, learning, and memory. In later chapters, we examine cognition's crucial relation to coping and adjustment, abnormal behavior, and interpersonal relations. In this chapter, we focus on three cognitive processes that we think of as characteristically human: thinking, problem solving, and decision making. We also discuss two mental abilities that psychologists have tried to measure: intelligence and creativity. ◼

Building Blocks of Thought

5.1 Describe how language, images, concepts, and culture each contribute to how we think.

When you think about a close friend, you may have in mind complex statements about her, such as "I'd like to talk to her soon" or "I wish I could be more like her." You may also have an image of her—probably her face, but perhaps the sound of her voice as well. Or you may think of your friend by using various concepts or categories such as *woman*, *kind*, *strong*, *dynamic*, and *gentle*. When we think, we make use of all these things—language, images, and concepts—often simultaneously. These are the three most important building blocks of thought.

---

cognition The processes whereby we acquire and use knowledge.

language A flexible system of communication that uses sounds, rules, gestures, or symbols to convey information.

phonemes The basic sounds that make up any language.

morphemes The smallest meaningful units of speech, such as simple words, prefixes, and suffixes.

grammar The language rules that determine how sounds and words can be combined and used to communicate meaning within a language.

LANGUAGE

What steps do we go through to turn a thought into a statement?

Human **language** is a flexible system of symbols that enables us to communicate our ideas, thoughts, and feelings. Language is a unique human ability that sets us apart from other animals (Savage-Rumbaugh & Brakke, 1996). Although all animals communicate with each other, human language is a far more complex system. Chimpanzees—our closest relatives in the animal kingdom—use some three dozen different vocalizations plus an array of gestures, postures, and facial expressions to communicate, a system far simpler than the speech of a normal three-year-old child.

One way to understand the uniquely human system of language is to consider its basic structure. Spoken language is based on units of sound called **phonemes**. The sounds of *t*, *th*, and *k*, for example, are all phonemes in English. There are about 45 phonemes in the English language and as many as 85 in some other languages (Bourne, Dominowski, Loftus, & Healy, 1986). By themselves, phonemes are meaningless and seldom play an important role in helping us to think. The sound *b*, for example, has no inherent meaning. But phonemes can be grouped together to form words, prefixes (such as *un-* and *pre-*), and suffixes (such as *-ed* and *-ing*). These meaningful combinations of phonemes are known as **morphemes**—the smallest meaningful units in a language. Morphemes play a key role in human thought. They can represent important ideas such as "red" or "calm" or "hot." The suffix *-ed* captures the idea of "in the past" (as in *visited* or *liked*). The prefix *pre-* conveys the idea of "before" or "prior to" (as in *preview* or *predetermined*).

We can combine morphemes to create words that represent quite complex ideas, such as *pre-exist-ing, un-excell-ed, psycho-logy*. In turn, words can be joined into even more complex thoughts. Just as there are rules for combining phonemes and morphemes, there are also rules for structuring sentences and their meaning. These rules are what linguists call **grammar**. The two major components of grammar are *syntax* and *semantics*. *Syntax* is the system of rules that governs how we combine words to form meaningful phrases and sentences. For example, in English and many other languages, the meaning of a sentence is often determined by word order. "Sally hit the car" means one thing; "The car hit Sally" means something quite different; and "Hit Sally car the" is meaningless.

Semantics describes how we assign meaning to morphemes, words, phrases, and sentences—in other words, the content of language. When we are thinking about something—say, the ocean—our ideas usually consist of phrases and sentences, such as "The ocean is unusually calm tonight." Sentences have both a *surface structure*—the particular words and phrases—and a *deep structure*—the underlying meaning. The same deep structure can be conveyed by different surface structures:

The ocean is unusually calm tonight.

Tonight the ocean is particularly calm.

Compared with most other nights, tonight the ocean is calm.

Syntax and semantics enable speakers and listeners to perform what linguist Noam Chomsky calls *transformations* between the surface and the deep structure. According to Chomsky (1957; Chomsky, Place, & Schoneberger, 2000), when you want to communicate an idea, you start with a thought, choose words and phrases that will express the idea, and finally produce the speech sounds that make up those words and phrases. Speaking requires *top-down processing*, and you can see from the left arrow in **Figure 5–1** that the movement is indeed from top to bottom. When you want to understand a sentence, your task is reversed. You must start with

Figure 5–1

The direction of movement in speech production and comprehension. Producing a sentence involves movement from thoughts and ideas to basic sounds; comprehending a sentence requires movement from basic sounds back to the underlying thoughts and ideas.

Meaning
(thought, idea)

Sentences
(phrases)

Morphemes
(words, prefixes, suffixes)

Phonemes
(basic sounds)

Producing speech

Comprehending speech

speech sounds and work your way up to the meaning of those sounds. This method is called *bottom-up processing*, as shown by the right arrow in **Figure 5–1**.

IMAGES

What role do images play in thinking?

Think for a moment about Abraham Lincoln. Then think about being outside in a summer thunderstorm. Your thoughts of Lincoln may have included such phrases as "wrote the Gettysburg Address," "president during the Civil War," and "assassinated by John Wilkes Booth." You probably also had some mental images about him: bearded face, lanky body, or log cabin. When you thought about the thunderstorm, you probably formed mental images of wind, rain, and lightning—perhaps even the smell of wet leaves and earth. An **image** is a mental representation of some sensory experience, and it can be used to think about things. We can visualize the Statue of Liberty; we can smell Thanksgiving dinner or the scent of a Christmas tree; we can hear Martin Luther King, Jr., saying, "I have a dream!" In short, we can think by using images.

Images allow us to think about things in nonverbal ways. Albert Einstein relied heavily on his powers of visualization to understand phenomena he would later describe by using complex mathematical formulas. Einstein believed that his extraordinary genius resulted in part from his skill in visualizing possibilities (Miller, 1992; Shepard, 1978). Although few of us can match Einstein's brilliance, we all use images to think about and solve problems. We have all seen a teacher clarify a difficult concept by drawing a quick, simple sketch on a blackboard. Many times, when words make a tangled knot of an issue, a graphic image drawn on paper straightens out the confusion. Images also allow us to use concrete forms to represent complex and abstract ideas, as when newspapers use pie charts and graphs to illustrate how people voted in an election (Yang, Chen, & Hong, 2003; Stylianou, 2002).

Experiments that use the brain-imaging techniques we learned about in Chapter 2 have shown that we often use the same brain centers for thinking about images as we do for visual perception (Kreiman, Koch, & Freid, 2000). This research supports the idea that we do not simply remember images; rather, we also think pictorially.

CONCEPTS

How do concepts help us to think more efficiently?

Concepts are mental categories for classifying specific people, things, or events (Komatsu, 1992). *Dogs*, *books*, and *mountains* are all concepts for classifying things, whereas *fast*, *beautiful*, and *interesting* can classify things, events, or people. When you think about a specific object—say, Mt. Everest—you usually think of the concepts that apply to it, such as *highest* and *dangerous to climb*. Concepts can also be used to create and organize hierarchies or groups of subordinate categories. For example, the general concept of *plants* can be broken down into the subordinate categories of *trees*, *bushes*, and *grasses*, just as the subordinate concept of *trees* can be further subdivided into *oaks*, *maples*, *pines*, and so forth (Reed, 1996). If we could not form concepts, we would need a different name for every object. Concepts help us to think efficiently about things and how they relate to one another.

Concepts also give meaning to new experiences. We do not stop and form a new concept for every new experience that we have. We draw on concepts we have already formed and place the new event into the appropriate categories. As we do so, we may modify some of our concepts to better match our experiences. Consider the concept of a job interview. You probably have some concept of this process even before your first interview, but your concept will probably change somewhat after you actually look for a job. After you have formed a concept of *job interview*, you will not have to respond to each interview as a totally new experience; you will know what to expect and how you are expected to behave. Conceptualizing *job interview* or anything else is a way of organizing experiences.

Although it is tempting to think of concepts as simple and clear-cut, most of the concepts that we use are rather "fuzzy": They overlap one another and are often poorly defined.

"Well, you don't look like an experimental psychologist to me."

"Well, you don't look like an experimental psychologist to me."

Source: © The New Yorker Collection, 1994. Sam Gross from www.cartoonbank.com. All Rights Reserved.

Pablo Picasso, the great 20th-century artist, developed a style of painting known as Cubism. In paintings such as *Nude with Bunch of Irises and Mirror*, 1934, shown here, he reformed objects into basic geometric shapes. We recognize the figure in this painting as a woman because its shapes represent the "concept" of a female.

Source: Picasso, Pablo (1881-1973). Nude with bunch of irises and mirror. 1934. 162 × 130 cm. © Copyright Succession Picasso/ARS, NY Photo: R.G. Ojeda. Musee Picasso, Paris, France.

image A mental representation of a sensory experience.

concept A mental category for classifying objects, people, or experiences.

For example, most people can tell a mouse from a rat, but listing the critical differences between the two would be difficult (Rosch, 1973, 2002).

If we cannot explain the difference between mouse and rat, how can we use these *fuzzy concepts* in our thinking? We may construct a model, or **prototype**, of a representative mouse and one of a representative rat, and then use those prototypes in our thinking (Rosch, 1978, 1998, 2002). Our concept of bird, for example, does not consist of a list of a bird's key attributes, like *feathered, winged, two-footed,* and *lives in trees*. Instead, most of us have a model bird, or prototype, in mind—such as a robin or a sparrow—that captures for us the essence of *bird*. When we encounter new objects, we compare them with this prototype to determine whether they are, in fact, birds. And when we think about birds, we usually think about our prototypical bird.

Concepts, then, such as words and images, help us to formulate thoughts. But human cognition involves more than just passively thinking about things. It also involves actively using words, images, and concepts to fashion an understanding of the world, to solve problems, and to make decisions. In the next three sections, we see how this is done.

LANGUAGE, THOUGHT, AND CULTURE

How do language, thought, and culture influence each other?

Concepts can correspond to ideas that we express verbally, and also to actions, such as the skill sets required to operate complex pieces of equipment, as this man is doing.

Language is closely tied to the expression and understanding of thoughts. Words—such as *friend, family, airplane,* and *love*—correspond to concepts, which are the building blocks of thought. By combining words into sentences, we can link concepts to other concepts and can express complex ideas.

Is it possible that language also influences how we think and what we can think about? Benjamin Whorf (1956) strongly believed that it does. According to Whorf's **linguistic relativity hypothesis**, the language that we speak determines the pattern of our thinking and our view of the world. For Whorf, if a language lacks a particular expression, the thought to which the expression corresponds will probably not occur to the people who speak that language. For example, the Hopi, a Native American people of the southwestern United States, have only two nouns for things that fly. One noun refers to birds; the other is used for everything else. A plane and a dragonfly, for example are both referred to with the same noun. According to Whorf, Hopi speakers would not see as great a difference between planes and dragonflies as we do because their language labels the two similarly.

The linguistic relativity hypothesis has intuitive appeal—it makes sense to think that limits of language will produce limits in thinking; however, researchers have found several flaws in Whorf's theory.

For example, the Dani people of New Guinea have only two words for colors—"dark" and "light"—yet they see and can easily learn to label other basic colors like red, yellow, and green. They also judge the similarity of colors much as English-speaking people do (E. R. Heider, 1972; E. R. Heider & Oliver, 1972; Rosch, 1973). Thus, the ability to think about colors is quite similar across cultures, even when these cultures have quite different color terms in their languages (Roberson, Davies, & Jules, 2000; Ross, 2004).

Other critics say that it is the need to think about things differently that changes a language, not that language changes the way we think (Berlin & Kay, 1969). For example, English-speaking skiers, realizing that different textures of snow can affect their downhill run, refer to snow as *powder, corn,* and *ice*. The growth of personal computers and the Internet has inspired a vocabulary of its own, such as *hard drive, RAM, gigabyte, software, online,* and *CD-ROM*. In short, people create new words when they need them—experience shapes language.

Psychologists have not dismissed the Whorf hypothesis altogether, but rather have softened it, recognizing that language, thought, and culture are intertwined (Giovanni, 2003;

prototype According to Rosch, a mental model containing the most typical features of a concept.

linguistic relativity hypothesis Whorf's idea that patterns of thinking are determined by the specific language one speaks.

Matsumoto, 1996). This realization has caused us to examine more carefully how we use our language. Traditionally, the English language has used masculine terms such as "man" and "he" to describe people of both genders—"all 'men' are created equal." Research has shown, however, that when people are asked to make judgments about a person, their opinions were influenced by whether the person was referred to as "he" or "she" (Greenwald & Banaji, 1995; Hyde, 1984a). Findings such as these have led many people (including textbook authors!) to refer to others in gender-neutral language (for example, "he or she").

▶ CHECK YOUR UNDERSTANDING

1. _____, _____, and _____ are the three most important building blocks of thought.

2. In language, units of sound, called _____, are combined to form the smallest units of meaning, called _____. These smallest meaningful units can then be combined to create words, which in turn can be used to build phrases and sentences.

3. Language rules that specify how sounds and words can be combined into meaningful sentences are called rules of _____.

4. According to Whorf's _____ _____ hypothesis, the language we speak shapes our thinking.

5. Indicate whether the following statements are true (T) or false (F).

   a. ___ Images help us to think about things because images use concrete forms to represent complex ideas.

   b. ___ People decide which objects belong to a concept by comparing the object's features to a model or prototype of the concept.

   c. ___ Concepts help us give meaning to new experiences.

   d. ___ Thoughts are limited to the words in the languages that a person speaks.

Answers: 1. language, images, concepts, 2. phonemes, morphemes, 3. grammar, 4. linguistic relativity, 5. a. (T); b. (T); c. (T); d. (F).

▶ APPLY YOUR UNDERSTANDING

1. "I will spend tonight working." "Tonight I will be working." These two sentences exhibit the same
   a. surface structure
   b. syntax
   c. phonology
   d. deep structure

2. Harry cannot list the essential differences between dogs and cats, but he has no trouble thinking about dogs and cats. This is most likely due to the fact that he
   a. has a prototype of a representative dog and another of a representative cat
   b. has developed a morpheme for a dog and another morpheme for a cat

   c. is able to use bottom-up processing
   d. is able to use the linguistic relativity hypothesis

3. Cross-cultural studies indicate that people from different cultures with very different languages nonetheless perceive and are able to think about such things as colors in very similar ways even if their language contains no words for these things. These data _____ Whorf's linguistic relativity theory.
   a. support
   b. contradict
   b. neither support nor contradict
   d. are unrelated to

Answers: 1. d, 2. a, 3. b.

Figure 5–2
Problem 1

Problem Solving

5.2   Describe why interpreting a problem correctly is important to its ultimate solution and identify factors that either encourage or limit our problem-solving abilities.

Solve the following problems:

Problem 1   You have three measuring spoons. (See **Figure 5–2**.) One is filled with eight teaspoons of salt; the other two are empty, but have a capacity of two teaspoons each. Divide the salt among the spoons so that only four teaspoons of salt remain in the largest spoon.

Problem 2   You have a five-minute hourglass and a nine-minute hourglass. (See **Figure 5–3**.) How can you use them to time a 14-minute barbecue? (Adapted from Sternberg, 1986.)

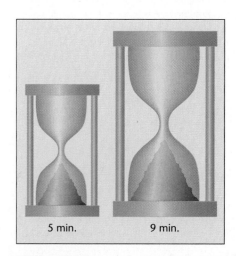

5 min.   9 min.

Figure 5–3
Problem 2 and Problem 4

Figure 5–4
Problem 3.

Most people find these problems very easy. Now try solving more elaborate versions of them (answers to all the problems are at the end of this chapter).

Problem 3 You have three measuring spoons. (See **Figure 5–4**.) One (spoon A) is filled with eight teaspoons of salt. The second and third spoons are both empty. The second spoon (spoon B) can hold five teaspoons, and the third (spoon C) can hold three teaspoons. Divide the salt among the spoons so that spoon A and spoon B each have exactly four teaspoons of salt and spoon C is empty.

Problem 4 You have a five-minute hourglass and a nine-minute hourglass. (See again **Figure 5–3**.) (Note: the answers to these and other problems are provided at the end of this chapter.)

Most people find these two problems much more difficult than the first two. Why? The answer lies in interpretation, strategy, and evaluation. Problems 1 and 2 are considered trivial because it is so easy to interpret what is needed, the strategies for solving them are simple, and you can effortlessly verify that each step you take moves you closer to a solution. Problems 3 and 4, in contrast, require some thought to interpret what is needed, the strategies for solving them are not immediately apparent, and it is harder to evaluate whether any given step has actually made progress toward your goal. These three aspects of problem solving—interpretation, strategy, and evaluation—provide a useful framework for investigating this topic.

THE INTERPRETATION OF PROBLEMS

Why is representing the problem so important to finding an effective solution?

The first step in solving a problem is called **problem representation**, which means interpreting or defining the problem. It is tempting to leap ahead and try to solve a problem just as it is presented, but this impulse often leads to poor solutions. For example, if your business is losing money, you might define the problem as deciphering how to cut costs. But by defining the problem so narrowly, you have ruled out other options. A better representation of this problem would be to figure out ways to boost profits—by cutting costs, by increasing income, or both. Problems that have no single correct solution and that require a flexible, inventive approach call for **divergent thinking**—or thinking that involves generating many different possible answers. In contrast, **convergent thinking** is thinking that narrows its focus in a particular direction, assuming that there is only one solution, or at most a limited number of correct solutions (Guilford, 1967). Many business and engineering schools stress divergent thinking skills to encourage more creative problem solving (Kaplan & Simon, 1990).

To see the importance of problem representation, consider these two problems:

Problem 5 You have four pieces of chain, each of which is made up of three links. (See **Figure 5–5**.) All links are closed at the beginning of the problem. It costs two cents to open

problem representation The first step in solving a problem; it involves interpreting or defining the problem.

divergent thinking Thinking that meets the criteria of originality, inventiveness, and flexibility and is directed at generating many possible solutions.

convergent thinking Thinking that is directed toward one correct solution to a problem.

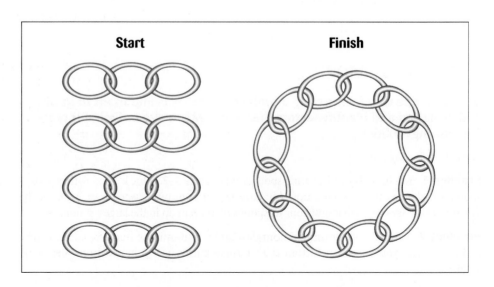

Figure 5–5
Problem 5.

a link and three cents to close a link. How can you join all 12 links together into a single, continuous circle without paying more than 15 cents?

Problem 6 You have six kitchen matches. (See **Figure 5–6**.) Arrange these matches into four equilateral triangles. Each side of every triangle must be only one match in length.

These two problems are difficult because people tend to represent them in ways that impede solutions. For example, in Problem 5, most people assume that the best way to proceed is to open and close the end links on the pieces of chain. As long as they persist with this "conceptual block," they will be unable to solve the problem. If the problem is represented differently, the solution is almost immediately obvious. Similarly, for the kitchen match problem, most people assume that they can work only in two dimensions—that is, that the triangles must lie flat on a surface—or that one match cannot serve as the side of two triangles. When the problem is represented differently, the solution becomes much easier. (The solutions to both problems appear at the end of this chapter.)

If you have successfully interpreted Problems 5 and 6, give number 7 a try:

Problem 7 A monk wishes to get to a retreat at the top of a mountain. He starts climbing the mountain at sunrise and arrives at the top at sunset of the same day. During the course of his ascent, he travels at various speeds and stops often to rest. He spends the night engaged in meditation. The next day, he starts his descent at sunrise, following the same narrow path that he used to climb the mountain. As before, he travels at various speeds and stops often to rest. Because he takes great care not to trip and fall on the way down, the descent takes as long as the ascent, and he does not arrive at the bottom until sunset. Prove that there is one place on the path that the monk passes at exactly the same time of day on the ascent and on the descent.

This problem is extremely difficult to solve if it is represented verbally or mathematically. It is considerably easier to solve if it is represented visually, as you can see from the explanation that appears at the end of this chapter.

Another aspect of successfully representing a problem is deciding to which category the problem belongs. Properly categorizing a problem can provide clues about how to solve it. In fact, after a problem has been properly categorized, its solution may be very easy. Quite often, people who seem to have a knack for solving problems are actually just very skilled at categorizing them in effective ways. Star chess players, for example, can readily categorize a game situation by comparing it with various standard situations stored in their long-term memories (Huffman, Matthews, & Gagne, 2001; also see Waters, Gobet, & Leyden, 2002). This strategy helps them interpret the current pattern of chess pieces with greater speed and precision than the novice chess player can. Similarly, a seasoned football coach may quickly call for a particular play because the coach has interpreted a situation on the field in terms of familiar categories. Gaining expertise in any field, from football to physics, consists primarily of increasing your ability to represent and categorize problems so that they can be solved quickly and effectively (Haberlandt, 1997).

PRODUCING STRATEGIES AND EVALUATING PROGRESS

Why is an algorithm often better for solving a problem than is the process of trial and error?

After you have properly interpreted a problem, the next steps needed are selecting a solution strategy and evaluating progress toward your goal. One of the simplest problem-solving approaches is to retrieve information from long-term memory about how such a problem was solved in the past. Information retrieval is an especially important option when a solution is needed quickly. For example, pilots simply memorize the slowest speed at which a particular airplane can fly before it stalls. Another relatively simple strategy for solving problems is trial and error. Trial and error is a strategy that works best when there are only limited choices. For example, if you have only three or four keys from which to choose, trial and error is the best way to find out which one unlocks your friend's garage door. In most cases, however, trial and error wastes time because there are so many different options to test.

Figure 5–6

Problem 6. Arrange the six matches so that they form four equilateral triangles. The solution is given in Figure 5–11.

An experienced football coach can analyze a situation on the field in terms of familiar categories. The coach can then call plays based on this knowledge. This is an example of how expertise can contribute to problem solving.

algorithm A step-by-step method of problem solving that guarantees a correct solution.

heuristics Rules of thumb that help in simplifying and solving problems, although they do not guarantee a correct solution.

ALGORITHMS AND HEURISTICS More complex problems require more complex strategies. An **algorithm** is a problem-solving method that guarantees a solution if it is appropriate for the problem and is properly carried out. For example, to calculate the product of 323 and 546, we multiply the numbers according to the rules of multiplication (the algorithm). If we do it accurately, we are guaranteed to get the right answer. Similarly, to convert temperatures from Fahrenheit to Celsius, we use the algorithm: C = 5/9 (F − 32).

Because we don't have algorithms for every kind of problem, we often turn to **heuristics**, or rules of thumb. Heuristics do not guarantee a solution, but they may bring it within reach. Several types of heuristics can be used to solve problems (see **Table 5–1**). Part of problem solving is to decide which heuristic is most appropriate for a given problem (Bourne et al., 1986).

For example, consider the problem of the Hobbits and the Orcs:

Problem 8 Three Hobbits and three Orcs are on the bank of a river. They all want to get to the other side, but their boat will carry only two creatures at a time. Moreover, if at any time the Orcs outnumber the Hobbits, the Orcs will attack the Hobbits. How can all the creatures get across the river without danger to the Hobbits?

The solution to this problem may be found by thinking of it in terms of a series of subgoals. What has to be done to get just one or two creatures across the river safely, temporarily leaving aside the main goal of getting everyone across? We could first send two of the Orcs across and have one of them return. That gets one Orc across the river. Now we can

>TABLE 5–1   COMMON HEURISTIC STRATEGIES

Heuristic Strategy	Definition	Example
Hill climbing	Moving closer and closer to the goal without going "backward".	On a multiple-choice test, eliminating the alternatives that are incorrect.
Creating subgoals	Breaking a complex problem into smaller, more manageable pieces, each of which is simpler to solve than the whole problem.	A large marketing proposal is broken down into smaller tasks: identifying competing products; hiring a consulting firm to conduct a market analysis; hiring an advertising agency to develop an ad campaign; developing a production line to manufacture the product, etc.
Means-end analysis	Combination of hill climbing and creating subgoals that includes both identifying the gap between the present status and the final goal and then developing steps that will eventually move toward the final goal, even if they temporarily lead away from it.	A pitcher in a baseball game may intentionally walk a home-run-hitter, even though this appears to work against the goal of preventing runners from getting on base.
Working backwards	Starting at the final goal and then working from there backwards to the present status.	In creating a monthly budget, a person, first subtracts all required monthly expenses (e.g., rent, utilities), then apportions what is left to various discretionary expenses (e.g., groceries, entertainment, charity contributions).

think about the next trip. It's clear that we can't then send a single Hobbit across with an Orc because the Hobbit would be outnumbered as soon as the boat landed. Therefore, we have to send either two Hobbits or two Orcs. By working on the problem in this fashion—concentrating on subgoals—we can eventually get everyone across. (One possible solution is presented at the end of this chapter.)

TROUBLESHOOTING Understanding how to conceptualize a problem is often the first step in *troubleshooting* a problem. Troubleshooting is a strategy that involves anticipating what problems may arise before they actually develop. For example, if you are concerned that your schedule will be so busy that you may not have time to prepare for an upcoming test, you might troubleshoot the situation and attempt to identify, before it is too late to respond, how you can rearrange some commitments to make time for reading and studying. By anticipating a problem before it actually happens, people also can prepare in advance to address it, should it occur.

Troubleshooting is a valuable skill, especially in work-related settings. Employees who can see what problems might arise, who can represent such problems accurately and then develop appropriate strategies for addressing them, are better able to keep small problems from becoming large ones. The heuristic strategies outlined in **Table 5–1** are especially useful in troubleshooting. Complex problems often are best addressed by breaking them down into component parts (*subgoal analysis*), by analyzing how the current situation differs from the desired end result, and by developing a strategy to move toward a successful solution to the problem by *hill-climbing*, *means-end analysis*, or *working backwards* (See again **Table 5–1**).

OBSTACLES TO SOLVING PROBLEMS

How can a "mental set" both help and hinder problem solving?

In everyday life, many factors can either help or hinder problem solving. One factor is a person's level of motivation, or emotional arousal. Generally, we must generate a certain surge of excitement to motivate ourselves to solve a problem, yet too much arousal can hamper our ability to find a solution. (See Chapter 6, "Motivation and Emotion.")

Another factor that can either help or hinder problem solving is **mental set**—our tendency to perceive and to approach problems in certain ways. Set determines which information we tend to retrieve from memory to help us find a solution. Set can be helpful if we have learned operations that we can apply to the present situation. Much of our formal education involves learning sets and ways to solve problems (that is, learning heuristics and algorithms). But sets can also create obstacles, especially when we need a new approach. The most successful problem solvers can choose from many different sets and can judge when to change sets or when to abandon them entirely. Great ideas and inventions come out of such flexibility.

One type of mental set that can seriously hinder problem solving is called **functional fixedness**. Consider this problem: You are placed in a room and are given a box of thumb tacks, two candles, and a box full of match books. Can you think of a way to mount a candle on the side wall of the room? If not, you are probably stymied by functional fixedness. (The solution to this problem appears in **Figure 5–14** at the end of the chapter.) The more you use an object in only one way, the harder it is to see new uses for it, because you have "assigned" the object to a fixed function. To some extent, part of the learning process is to assign correct functions to objects—this is how we form concepts. But we need to be open to seeing that an object can be used for an entirely different function.

Because creative problem solving requires thinking up original ideas, deliberate strategies don't always help. Solutions to many problems rely on insight, often a seemingly arbitrary flash "out of the blue." (See Chapter 4, "Learning and Memory.") Psychologists have only recently begun to investigate such spontaneous and unplanned problem-solving processes as insight and intuition (Bechara et al., 1997; Novick & Sherman, 2003; Underwood, 1996).

mental set The tendency to perceive and to approach problems in certain ways.

functional fixedness The tendency to perceive only a limited number of uses for an object, thus interfering with the process of problem solving.

[UNDERSTANDING OURSELVES]

BECOMING A MORE SKILLFUL PROBLEM SOLVER

Even the best problem solvers occasionally get stumped, but you can do some things that will help you find a solution. These tactics encourage you to discard unproductive approaches and find strategies that are more effective.

- *Eliminate poor choices.* When we are surer of what won't work than what will, the *tactic of elimination* can be very helpful. List all the possible solutions you can think of, and then discard all the solutions that seem to lead in the wrong direction. Now, examine the list more closely. Some solutions seem to be inef-

fective but may turn out to be good on closer examination.

- *Visualize a solution.* Sometimes people who are stumped by a problem can find a solution by using a basic building block of thought: Visual images. *Visualizing* often involves diagramming courses of action (J. L. Adams, 1980). For example, in the Hobbit and Orc problem, draw a picture of the river, and show the Hobbits and Orcs at each stage of the solution as they are ferried across. Drawing a diagram can help you grasp what a problem calls for. You also can visualize mentally.

- *Develop expertise.* People get stumped on problems because they lack the knowledge to find a quick solution. Experts not only know more about a particular subject but also organize their information in larger "chunks" that are extensively interconnected, much like a cross-referencing system in a library.

- *Think flexibly.* Striving to be more flexible and creative is an excellent tactic for becoming a better problem solver. Many problems require some original thinking. For example, how many unusual uses can you think of for a brick?

However, it is not always possible to wait for a flash of insight: Some problems need a faster solution and can't be solved through intuition. Several other problem-solving strategies can be useful in such circumstances. For example, sometimes we get so enmeshed in the details of a problem that we lose sight of the obvious. If we stop thinking about the problem for a while, we may return to it from a new angle (H. G. Murray & Denny, 1969). We may then be able to redefine the problem and circumvent an unproductive mind-set. For other strategies that sometime can be useful in solving problems, see "Understanding Ourselves."

The value of looking for new ways to represent a difficult problem cannot be overstressed. Ask yourself, "What is the real problem here? Can the problem be interpreted in other ways?" Also be open to potential solutions that at first seem unproductive. The solution may turn out to be more effective, or it may suggest related solutions that will work. This is the rationale behind the technique called **brainstorming**: When solving a problem, generate a lot of ideas before you review and evaluate them (McGlynn, McGurk, Effland, Johll, & Harding, 2004; Park-Gates, 2002).

brainstorming A problem-solving strategy in which an individual or a group produces numerous ideas and evaluates them only after all ideas have been collected.

Complex jobs often require flexible approaches to solving problems. Brainstorming with knowledgeable coworkers often can provide good alternatives to consider.

Finally, people often become more creative when exposed to creative peers and teachers (Amabile, 1983). Although some creative people work well alone, many others are stimulated by working in teams with other creative people.

> CHECK YOUR UNDERSTANDING

1. Match each form of thinking with its definition and the kind of problems to which it is suited.
   ___ divergent thinking
   ___ convergent thinking
   a. suited to problems for which there is one correct solution or a limited number of solutions
   b. thinking that involves generating many different ideas
   c. suited to problems that have no one right solution and require an inventive approach
   d. thinking that limits its focus to a particular direction

Match each problem-solving strategy with the appropriate definition.

2. ___ algorithm
3. ___ heuristic
4. ___ hill climbing

5. ___ means-end analysis
6. ___ working backward
7. ___ subgoal creation
   a. rule-of-thumb approach that helps in simplifying and solving problems, although it doesn't guarantee a correct solution
   b. strategy in which each step moves you closer to a solution
   c. step-by-step method that guarantees a solution
   d. strategy in which one moves from the goal to the starting point
   e. strategy that aims to reduce the discrepancy between the current situation and the desired goal at a number of intermediate points
   f. breaking down the solution to a larger problem into a set of smaller, more manageable steps

Answers: 1. divergent thinking-b and c; convergent thinking-a and d., 2. c., 3. a., 4. b., 5. e., 6. d., 7. f.

> APPLY YOUR UNDERSTANDING

1. Your car is not operating correctly. The mechanic opens the hood and says, "We've been seeing lots of cars recently with fouled plugs or dirty fuel filters. Let's start there and see if that's your problem, too." The mechanic is using a(n)
   a. heuristic
   b. algorithm
   c. compensatory decision model
   d. noncompensatory decision model

2. You are at a football game when it begins to rain heavily. As you get soaked, you see the person next to you pull a folded plastic garbage bag out of her pocket to use as a temporary "raincoat." Your failure to realize that the garbage bag might also be used as rain protection is an example of
   a. an algorithm
   b. a heuristic
   c. means-end analysis
   d. functional fixedness

Answers: 1. a., 2. d.

Decision Making

5.3 Compare and contrast the benefits and limitations of logical models of decision making with those based on some common heuristic approaches.

Decision making is a special kind of problem solving in which we already know all the possible solutions or choices. The task is not to come up with new solutions, but rather to identify the best available one based on whatever criteria we are using. This might sound like a fairly simple process, but sometimes we have to juggle a large and complex set of criteria as well as many possible options. For example, suppose that you are looking for an apartment and there are hundreds available. A reasonable rent is important to you, but so are good neighbors, a good location, a low noise level, and cleanliness. If you find a noisy apartment with undesirable neighbors but at a cheap rent, should you take it? Is it a better choice than an apartment in a better location with less noise but a higher rent? How can you weigh your various criteria and make the best choice?

compensatory model A rational decision-making model in which choices are systematically evaluated on various criteria.

representativeness A heuristic by which a new situation is judged on the basis of its resemblance to a stereotypical model.

availability A heuristic by which a judgment or decision is based on information that is most easily retrieved from memory.

LOGICAL DECISION MAKING

How would you go about making a truly logical decision?

The logical way to make a decision is to rate each of the available choices on all the criteria you are using, arriving at some overall measure of the extent to which each choice matches your criteria. For each choice, the attractive features can offset or compensate for the unattractive features. This approach to decision making is therefore called a **compensatory model**.

Table 5–2 illustrates one of the most useful compensatory models, applied to the decision of what kind of car to buy. The buyer has three criteria, which are weighted in terms of importance: price (not weighted heavily), gas mileage, and service record (both weighted more heavily). Each car is then rated from 1 (poor) to 5 (excellent) on each of the criteria. You can see that Car 1 has an excellent price (5) but relatively poor gas mileage (2) and service record (1); Car 2 has a less desirable price but fairly good mileage and service record. Each rating is then multiplied by the weight for that criterion (e.g., for Car 1, the price rating of 5 is multiplied by the weight of 4, and the result is put in parentheses next to the rating). Then, ratings are added to give a total for each car. Clearly, Car 2 is the better choice: It has a less desirable price, but that disadvantage is offset by the fact that its mileage and service record are better, and these two criteria are more important than price to this particular buyer.

The use of a table like this one allows individuals to evaluate a large number of choices on a large number of criteria. If the criteria are weighted properly and the choices rated correctly, the alternative with the highest total score is the most rational choice, given the information available. Does this outcome mean that most day-to-day decision making is rational? Not necessarily. Many, if not most, decisions—choosing a college, deciding whom to marry—involve a high degree of ambiguity (Mellers, Schwartz, & Cooke, 1998). Often we must rely on our intuition to make the right choice and take a heuristic rather than a purely logical approach.

DECISION-MAKING HEURISTICS

How can heuristic approaches lead us to make bad decisions?

Research has identified a number of common heuristics that people use to make decisions. We use these because, for the most part, they have worked in the past and because they simplify decision making, even though they may lead to less-than-optimal decisions (Dhami, 2003).

We use the **representativeness** heuristic whenever we make a decision on the basis of certain information that matches our model of the typical member of a category. For example, if every time you went shopping you bought the least expensive items, and if all of these items turned out to be poorly made, you might eventually decide not to buy anything that seems typical of the category "very cheap." Another common heuristic is **availability** (Schwarz & Vaughn, 2002). In the absence of full and accurate information, we often base decisions on whatever information is most readily available to memory, even though this information may not be accurate.

> **TABLE 5-2 COMPENSATORY DECISION TABLE FOR PURCHASE OF A NEW CAR**

	Price (weight = 4)	Gas mileage (weight = 8)	Service record (weight = 10)	Weighted Total
Car 1	5 (5 × 4 = 20)	2 (2 × 8 = 16)	1 (1 × 10 = 10)	(20 + 16 + 10 = 46)
Car 2	1 (1 × 4 = 4)	4 (4 × 8 = 32)	4 (4 × 10 = 40)	(4 + 32 + 40 = 76)

Ratings: 5 = excellent; 1 = poor

A familiar example of the availability heuristic is the so-called *subway effect* (Gilovich, 1991). It seems to be a law of nature that if you are waiting at a subway station, one train after another will come along headed in the opposite direction from the direction that you want to go. Similarly, if you need a taxi in a hurry, inevitably an unusually long string of occupied or off-duty taxis will pass by. The problem here is that once a subway train or a taxi does come along, we leave the scene, so we never get to see the opposite situation: Several subway trains going in our direction before one comes the other way, or a long string of empty taxis. As a result, we tend to assume that those situations seldom or never occur, and so we make our decisions accordingly.

Confirmation biases may hinder effective decision making. If you believe that everyone who owns a minivan is a bad driver, for example, you may avoid buying one, even though it might be the best vehicle for your needs.

Another heuristic, closely related to availability, is **confirmation bias**—the tendency to notice and remember evidence that supports our beliefs and to ignore evidence that contradicts them (Myers, 1996). For example, individuals who believe that AIDS is something that happens to "other people" (homosexual men and intravenous drug users, not middle-class heterosexuals) are more likely to remember articles about rates of HIV infection in these groups or in third-world countries than articles about AIDS cases among people like themselves (Fischhoff & Downs, 1997). Convinced that HIV is not something that they personally need to worry about, they ignore evidence to the contrary.

A related phenomenon is our tendency to see *connections* or *patterns of cause and effect* where none exist (Kahneman & Tversky, 1996; Rottenstreich & Tversky, 1997). For example, many people still believe that chocolate causes acne to flare up in susceptible teenagers, yet this myth was disproved almost half a century ago; acne is a bacterial infection, although the tendency to get acne has a strong genetic component (Kolata, 1996a). Many parents strongly believe that sugar may cause hyperactivity in children—despite research evidence to the contrary. The list of commonsense beliefs that persist in the face of contrary evidence is long.

EXPLAINING OUR DECISIONS

How do we explain to ourselves the decisions we make?

FRAMING For the most part, people are reasonably satisfied with the decisions they make in the real world (Kleinmuntz, 1991); however, these decisions can be intentionally or unintentiontially influenced by how the information provided to make the decision is presented, or *framed*. Psychologists use the term **framing** to refer to the perspective or phrasing of information that is used to make a decision. Numerous studies have shown that subtle changes in the way information is presented can dramatically affect the final decision (Jones, Sinclair, & Courneya, 2003; LeBoeuf & Shafir, 2003; Mann, Sherman, & Updegraff, 2004).

A classic study (McNeil, Pauker, Sox, & Tversky, 1982) illustrates how framing may influence a medical decision. In this study, experimental participants were asked to choose between surgery and radiation therapy to treat lung cancer; however, the framing of information provided to make this choice was manipulated. In the *survival frame*, the participants were given the statistical outcomes of both procedures in the form of survival statistics, thus emphasizing the number of people who would survive each procedure one year and five years after treatment. In the *mortality frame*, the participants were given the same information, although this time it was presented (or framed) according to the number of people who would *die* after one year and after five years. It is interesting that although the actual number of deaths and survivors associated with each procedure was identical in both the survival and mortality frames, the percentage of participants who chose one procedure over another varied dramatically depending on how the information was framed. Probably most surprising was that this framing effect was found even when 424 experienced physicians with a specialty in radiology served as the experimental participants!

confirmation bias The tendency to look for evidence in support of a belief and to ignore evidence that would disprove a belief.

framing The perspective from which we interpret information before making a decision.

hindsight bias The tendency to see outcomes as inevitable and predictable after we know the outcome.

counterfactual thinking Thinking about alternative realities and things that never happened.

HINDSIGHT Whether a choice is exceptionally good, extraordinarily foolish, or somewhere in between, most people think about their decisions after the fact. The term **hindsight bias** refers to the tendency to view outcomes as inevitable and predictable after we know the outcome, and to believe that we could have predicted what happened, or perhaps that we did (Azar, 1999b; Fischoff, 1975; Pohl, Schwarz, Sczesny, & Stahlberg, 2003). For example, physicians remember being more confident about their diagnoses when they learn that they were correct than they were at the time of the actual diagnoses.

Psychologists have long viewed the hindsight bias as a cognitive flaw—a way of explaining away bad decisions and maintaining our confidence (see Louie, Curren, & Harich, 2000). A team of researchers in Berlin, however, argues that the hindsight bias serves a useful function (Hoffrage, Hertwig, & Gigerenzer, 2000). "Correcting" memory is a quick and efficient way to replace misinformation or faulty assumptions, so that our future decisions and judgments will be closer to the mark. In a sense, hindsight functions like the "find and replace" function in a word processing program, eliminating extra, time-consuming keystrokes and mental effort.

"IF ONLY" At times, everyone imagines alternatives to reality and mentally plays out the consequences. Psychologists refer to such thoughts about things that never happened as **counterfactual thinking**—the thoughts are counter to the facts (Roese, 1997; Segura & McCloy, 2003; Walchle & Landman, 2003). Counterfactual thinking often takes the form of "If only" constructions, in which we mentally revise the events or actions that led to a particular outcome: "If only I had studied harder"; "If only I had said no"; "If only I had driven straight home." Research shows that counterfactual thinking usually centers around a small number of themes: reversing a course of events that led to a negative experience; explaining unusual events by assigning responsibility to someone or something; and regaining a sense of personal control (Roese, 1997).

▸ CHECK YOUR UNDERSTANDING

Match each decision-making heuristic with the appropriate definition.

1. ___ representativeness heuristic
2. ___ availability heuristic
3. ___ confirmation bias
   a. making judgments on the basis of whatever information can be most readily retrieved from memory
   b. attending to evidence that supports your existing beliefs and ignoring other evidence

   c. making decisions on the basis of information that matches your model of what is "typical" of a certain category
4. The way a question is framed usually will not affect its answer. Is this statement true (T) or false (F)?
5. Julio's girlfriend gets a speeding ticket, and he blames himself, saying, "If only I hadn't let her borrow my car." His thinking is an example of _____ _____.

Answers: 1. c, 2. a, 3. b, 4. F, 5. counterfactual thinking

▸ APPLY YOUR UNDERSTANDING

1. In deciding where to go on vacation, you decide you want a place where you can relax, a place that is warm, and a place that you can reach inexpensively. But you will not consider any place that is more than 1,000 miles away. What kind of decision-making model are you using?
   a. visualization
   b. brainstorming
   c. noncompensatory
   d. compensatory

2. When airplanes crash, media often display graphic, emotional stories. This may be one reason that many people believe flying is more dangerous than driving (although the reverse is actually true). Erroneous conclusions such as this one are most likely due to
   a. "if only" thinking
   b. hindsight bias
   c. mental set
   d. the availability heuristic

Answers: 1. c, 2. d.

Intelligence and Mental Abilities

5.4 Define what is meant by the term "intelligence" and describe how intelligence can be measured.

Consider the questions posed in **Table 5–3**. These questions were taken from various tests of **intelligence**, or general mental ability. (The answers appear at the end of the chapter.) Because intelligence is a fundamental human ability, it has long been the subject matter of psychology.

THEORIES OF INTELLIGENCE

What are some of the major theories of intelligence?

For more than a century, psychologists have argued about what constitutes general intelligence—or even if "general" intelligence actually exists. One of their basic questions is whether intelligence is a single, general mental ability or whether it is composed of many separate abilities (see Lubinski, 2000).

Charles Spearman, one of the first psychologists to study intelligence in the early 1900s, maintained that intelligence is quite general—a kind of well, or spring, of mental energy that flows through every action. Spearman believed that people who are bright in one area are often bright in other areas as well. The intelligent person understands things quickly, makes sound decisions, carries on interesting conversations, and tends to behave intelligently in a variety of situations.

THE TRIARCHIC THEORY Today, psychologists are more likely to emphasize the various kinds of mental abilities that comprise intelligence. Contemporary psychologists have considerably broadened the concept of intelligence and how it can best be measured (Benson, 2003). For example, Robert Sternberg (1986, 2003) has proposed a **triarchic theory of intelligence**, the basis for Rainbow Project described in the opening paragraphs of this chapter. Sternberg argues that human intelligence encompasses a broad variety of skills, among which are skills that influence our effectiveness in many areas of life. These, says Sternberg, are just as important as the more limited skills assessed by traditional intelligence tests. As the name implies, the theory suggests that there are three basic kinds of intelligence. *Analytical intelligence* refers to the mental processes emphasized by most theories of intelligence, such as the ability to learn how to do things, acquire new knowledge, solve problems, and carry out tasks effectively. According to Sternberg, this is the aspect of intelligence assessed by most intelligence tests. *Creative intelligence* is the ability to adjust to new tasks, use new concepts, respond effectively in new situations, gain insight, and adapt creatively. People who score high in *practical intelligence* are very good at finding solutions to practical and personal problems. They make the most of their talents by seeking out situations that match their skills, shaping those situations so they can make optimal use of their skills, and knowing when to change situations to better fit their talents. Sternberg points out that while practical intelligence is not taught in school, it is sometimes more important than analytical intelligence because it enables people to get along successfully in the world. The use of Stenberg's theory for making admissions decisions about students at Tufts is an exciting application of this contemporary perspective.

THE THEORY OF MULTIPLE INTELLIGENCES Another influential theory of intelligence is the **theory of multiple intelligences** advanced by Howard Gardner and his associates at Harvard (Gardner, 1983a, 1993, 1999). Gardner believes that intelligence is made up of several distinct abilities, each of which is relatively independent of the others. Precisely how many separate intelligences might exist is difficult to determine, but Gardner lists eight: *logical-mathematical, linguistic, spatial, musical, bodily-kinesthetic, interpersonal, intrapersonal,* and *naturalistic*. The first four are self-explanatory. Bodily-kinesthetic intelligence is the ability to manipulate one's body in space; a

intelligence A general term referring to the ability or abilities involved in learning and adaptive behavior.

triarchic theory of intelligence Sternberg's theory that intelligence involves mental skills (analytical intelligence), insight and creative adaptability (creative intelligence), and environmental responsiveness (practical intelligence).

theory of multiple intelligences Howard Gardner's theory that there is not one intelligence, but rather many intelligences, each of which is relatively independent of the others.

>TABLE 5-3 QUESTIONS FROM TESTS OF INTELLIGENCE

Answer the following questions:

1. Describe the difference between *laziness* and *idleness*.

2. Which direction would you have to face so that your right ear would be facing north

3. What does *obliterate* mean?

4. In what way are an hour and a week alike?

5. Choose the lettered block that best completes the pattern in the following figure.

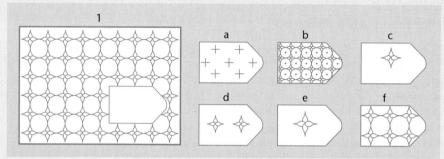

6. If three pencils cost 25 cents, how many pencils can you buy for 75 cents?

7. Select the lettered pair that best expresses a relationship similar to that expressed in the original pair:

   CRUTCH: LOCOMOTION:

   (a) paddle: canoe

   (b) hero: worship

   (c) horse: carriage

   (d) spectacles: vision

   (e) statement: contention

8. Decide how the first two items in the following figure are related to each other. Then find the one item at the right that goes with the third item in the same way that the second item goes with the first.

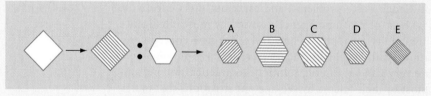

9. For each item in the following figure, decide whether it can be completely covered by using some or all of the given pieces without overlapping any.

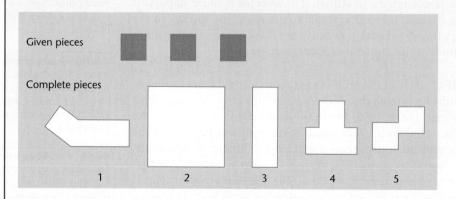

skilled athlete shows high levels of this kind of intelligence. People who are extraordinarily talented at understanding and communicating with others, such as exceptional teachers and parents, have strong interpersonal intelligence. Intrapersonal intelligence reflects the ancient adage, "Know thyself." People who understand themselves and who use this knowledge effectively to attain their goals rank high in intrapersonal intelligence. Finally, naturalistic intelligence reflects an individual's ability to understand, relate to, and interact with the world of nature.

Gardner's approach has become quite influential, largely because he emphasizes the unique abilities that each person possesses. Gardner also notes that the different forms of intelligence often have different values placed on them by different cultures. For example, many traditional Native American cultures placed a much higher value on naturalistic intelligence than does contemporary mainstream American culture. Because we have unique patterns of strengths and weaknesses in separate abilities, Gardner believes that education should be designed to suit the profile of abilities demonstrated by each child. Individuals might then wish to pursue jobs that emphasize the specific kinds of abilities in which they excel.

Mariel Zagunis, the first U.S. woman to ever win an Olympic gold medal for fencing, possesses an abundance of what Howard Garner calls bodily-kinesthetic intelligence.

EMOTIONAL INTELLIGENCE Daniel Goleman (1997) has proposed a theory of **emotional intelligence**, which refers to how effectively people perceive and understand their own emotions and the emotions of others and can manage their emotional behavior. Goleman was puzzled about the fact that people with high IQ scores sometimes fail in life, whereas those with more modest intellectual skills prosper. He contends that one of the reasons IQ tests sometimes fail to predict success accurately is that they do not take into account an individual's emotional competence.

Five traits are generally recognized as contributing to emotional intelligence (Goleman, 1997; Goleman, Boyatzis, & McKee, 2002):

1. **Knowing one's own emotions.** The ability to monitor and recognize our own feelings is of central importance to self-awareness and all other dimensions of emotional intelligence.

2. **Managing one's emotions.** The ability to control impulses; to cope effectively with sadness, depression, and minor setbacks, as well as to control how long emotions last.

3. **Using emotions to motivate oneself.** The capacity to harness emotions toward achieving personal goals.

4. **Recognizing the emotions of other people.** The ability to read subtle, nonverbal cues that reveal what other people really want and need.

5. **Managing relationships.** The ability to acknowledge and display one's own emotions accurately as well as be sensitive to the emotions of others.

The concept of emotional intelligence is relatively new, and researchers have only begun to evaluate its scientific merit (Bar-On & Parker, 2000; Matthews, Zeidner, & Roberts, 2002). Nevertheless, as you might expect, the ability to manage and regulate one's emotions in the workplace and in other relationships appears to be important (Cherniss & Goleman, 2001; Grandey, 2000).

Some investigators, however, remain skeptical about identifying emotional intelligence as a major component of overall ability, arguing that it is no different from traits that are already described by more traditional measures of intelligence and personality (Davies, Stankov, & Roberts, 1998). More research is needed before we can assess the scientific validity and usefulness of this intriguing and potentially important new theory of intelligence.

The "**Summary Table**" reviews the contemporary theories described here. Theories of intelligence such as these shape the content of intelligence tests and other measures of mental abilities which are used to help evaluate the abilities of millions of people.

emotional intelligence According to Goleman, a form of intelligence that refers to how effectively people perceive and understand their own emotions and the emotions of others, and how well they can regulate and manage their emotional behavior.

SUMMARY TABLE

COMPARING GARDNER'S, STERNBERG'S, AND GOLEMAN'S THEORIES OF INTELLIGENCE

Gardner's multiple intelligences	Sternberg's triarchic intelligences	Goleman's emotional intelligence
Logical-mathematical Linguistic	Analytical	
Spatial Musical Bodily-kinesthetic	Creative	
Interpersonal		Recognizing emotions in others and managing relationships
	Practical	
Intrapersonal		Knowing, managing, and motivating yourself with emotions
Naturalistic		

INTELLIGENCE TESTS

What kinds of intelligence tests are in use today?

THE STANFORD–BINET INTELLIGENCE SCALE The first test developed to measure intelligence was designed by two Frenchmen, Alfred Binet and Theodore Simon. The test, first used in Paris in 1905, was designed to identify children who might have difficulty in school.

The first *Binet–Simon Scale* consisted of 30 tests arranged in order of increasing difficulty. With each child, the examiner started with the easiest tests and worked down the list until the child could no longer answer questions. By 1908, enough children had been tested to predict how the average child would perform at each age level. From these scores, Binet developed the concept of *mental age*. A child who scores as well as an average 4-year-old has a mental age of 4; a child who scores as well as an average 12-year-old has a mental age of 12.

A well-known adaptation of the *Binet–Simon Scale*, the **Stanford–Binet Intelligence Scale**, was prepared at Stanford University by L. M. Terman and published in 1916. Terman introduced the now famous term **intelligence quotient (IQ)** to establish a numerical value of intelligence, setting the score of 100 for a person of average intelligence. **Figure 5–7** shows an approximate distribution of IQ scores in the population.

The current Stanford–Binet Intelligence Scale is designed to measure four kinds of mental abilities that are almost universally considered to be part of intelligence: *verbal reasoning, abstract/visual reasoning, quantitative reasoning,* and *short-term memory*. Test items vary with the subject's age. For example, a three-year-old might be asked to describe the purpose of a cup and to name objects such as a chair and a key. A six-year-old might be asked to define words such as *orange* and *envelope* and to complete a sentence such as "An inch is short; a mile is _____." A 12-year-old might be asked to define *skill* and *juggler* and to complete the sentence "The streams are dry _____ there has been little rain" (Cronbach, 1990).

The Stanford–Binet test is given individually by a trained examiner. It is best suited for children, adolescents, and very young adults.

THE WECHSLER INTELLIGENCE SCALES The most commonly used individual test of intelligence for adults is the **Wechsler Adult Intelligence Scale—Third Edition (WAIS-III)**, originally developed in the late 1930s by David Wechsler, a psychologist. The Stanford–Binet emphasizes verbal skills, but Wechsler felt that adult intelligence consists more of the ability to handle life situations than to solve verbal and abstract problems.

Stanford-Binet Intelligence Scale Test of intelligence, developed from Binet and Simon's original scale, which set the average intelligence quotient (IQ) at 100.

intelligence quotient (IQ) A numerical value given to intelligence that is determined from the scores on an intelligence test on the basis of a score of 100 for average intelligence.

Wechsler Adult Intelligence Scale—Third Edition (WAIS-III) An individual intelligence test developed especially for adults; measures both verbal and performance abilities.

The WAIS-III is divided into two parts, one stressing verbal skills, the other performance skills. The verbal scale includes tests of information ("Who wrote *Paradise Lost*?"); tests of simple arithmetic ("Sam had three pieces of candy, and Joe gave him four more. How many pieces of candy did Sam have then?"); and tests of comprehension ("What should you do if you see someone forget a book on a bus?"). The performance scale also measures routine tasks. People are asked to "find the missing part" (buttonholes in a coat, for example), to copy patterns, and to arrange three to five pictures so that they tell a story.

Although the content of the WAIS-III is somewhat more sophisticated than that of the Stanford–Binet, Wechsler's chief innovation was in scoring. His test gives separate verbal and performance scores as well as an overall IQ score. On some items, one or two extra points can be earned, depending on the complexity of the answer given. This unique scoring system gives credit for the reflective qualities that we expect to find in intelligent adults. On some questions, both speed and accuracy affect the score.

Wechsler also developed a similar intelligence test for use with school-age children. Like the WAIS-III, the 1991 version of the **Wechsler Intelligence Scale for Children–Third Edition (WISC-III)** yields separate verbal and performance scores as well as an overall IQ score.

GROUP TESTS The Stanford–Binet, the WAIS-III, and the WISC-III are individual tests. The examiner takes a person to an isolated room, spreads the materials on a table, and spends from 30 to 90 minutes administering the test. The examiner may then take another hour or so to score the test according to detailed instructions in the manual. This is a time-consuming, costly operation, and the examiner's behavior can under some circumstances influence the score. For these reasons, test makers have devised **group tests**. These are written tests that a single examiner can administer to a large group of people at the same time. Instead of sitting across the table from a person who asks you questions, you receive a test booklet that contains questions for you to answer within a certain amount of time.

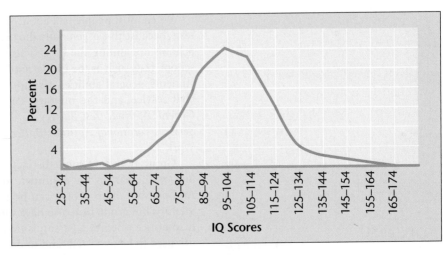

Figure 5–7

The approximate distribution of IQ scores in the population. Note that the greatest percentage of scores fall around 100. Very low percentages of people score at the two extremes of the curve.

Wechsler Intelligence Scale for Children–Third Edition (WISC-III) An individual intelligence test developed especially for school-aged children; measures verbal and performance abilities and also yields an overall IQ score.

group tests Written intelligence tests administered by one examiner to many people at one time.

The Wechsler Intelligence Scales, developed by David Wechsler, are individual intelligence tests administered to one person at a time. There are versions of the Wechsler Scales for both adults and children. Here, a child and an adult are being asked to copy a pattern using blocks.

When most people talk about "intelligence" tests, they are usually referring to group tests, because this is generally the means by which they were themselves tested in school. Schools are among the biggest users of group tests. From fourth grade through high school, tests such as the *California Test of Mental Maturity (CTMM)* are used to measure students' general abilities. Group tests are also widely used in different industries, the civil service, and the military. People who apply for government jobs are given the *General Aptitude Test Battery (GATB)*; those who enlist in the military take the *Armed Services Vocational Aptitude Battery (ASVAB)* (See Chapter 11: "Psychology Applied to Work").

Group tests have some distinct advantages over individualized tests. They eliminate bias on the part of the examiner. Answer sheets can be scored quickly and objectively. And because more people can be tested in this way, comparison groups are easier to identify. But group tests also have some distinct disadvantages. The examiner is less likely to notice whether a person is tired, ill, or confused by the directions. People who are not used to being tested tend to do less well on group tests than on individual tests. Finally, emotionally disturbed people and those with learning disabilities often do better on individual tests than on group tests (Anastasi & Urbina, 1997).

PERFORMANCE AND CULTURE-FAIR TESTS To perform well on the intelligence tests that we have discussed, people must be fluent in the language in which the test is given and be familiar with the culture to which test items may refer. Tests given today are constructed with care so that they do not yield test scores that are unfairly biased. For example, the latest version of the Stanford–Binet, released in 1986, replaced items that had been found to be biased against members of ethnic groups or against males or females with unbiased items. New items were added that permitted testers to better identify mentally retarded and intellectually gifted people, as well as people with specific learning disabilities (Sattler, 2002).

Another approach to addressing concerns about unfair bias in testing has led to the development of performance tests and culture-fair tests. **Performance tests** consist of problems that minimize or eliminate the use of words. One of the earliest performance tests, the *Seguin Form Board*, was devised in 1866 to test people with mental retardation. The form board is essentially a puzzle. The examiner removes specifically designed cutouts, stacks them in a predetermined order, and asks the person to replace them as quickly as possible. A more recent performance test, the *Porteus Maze*, consists of a series of increasingly difficult printed mazes. People trace their way through the maze without lifting the pencil from the paper. Such tests require the test taker to pay close attention to a task for an extended period and continuously plan ahead to make the correct choices.

Culture-fair tests are designed to measure the intelligence of people who are outside the culture in which the test was devised. Like performance tests, culture-fair tests minimize or eliminate the use of language. Culture-fair tests also try to downplay skills and values—such as the need for speed—that vary from culture to culture. In the *Goodenough–Harris Drawing Test*, people are asked to draw the best picture of a person that they can. Drawings are scored for proportions, correct and complete representation of the parts of the body, detail in clothing, and so on. An example of a culture-fair item from the *Progressive Matrices* is Question 5 in **Table 5–3**. This test consists of 60 designs, each with a missing part. The person is given six to eight possible choices to replace the part. The test involves various logical relationships, requires discrimination, and can be given to one person or to a group.

WHAT MAKES A GOOD TEST?

What are some important characteristics of a good test?

How can we tell whether intelligence tests will produce consistent results no matter when they are given? And how can we tell whether they really measure what they claim to measure?

---

performance tests Intelligence tests that minimize the use of language.

---

culture-fair tests Intelligence tests designed to eliminate cultural bias by minimizing skills and values that vary from one culture to another.

Psychologists address these questions by referring to a test's reliability and validity. Issues of reliability and validity apply equally to all psychological tests, not just to tests of mental abilities. In Chapter 8, for example, we reexamine these issues as they apply to personality assessment.

RELIABILITY By **reliability**, psychologists mean the dependability and consistency of the scores that a test yields. If your alarm clock is set for 8:15 A.M. and it goes off at that time every morning, it is reliable. But if it is set for 8:15 and rings at 8:00 one morning and 8:40 the next, you cannot depend on it; it is unreliable. Similarly, a test has reliability when it yields consistent results.

How do we know whether a test is reliable? The simplest way to find out is to give the test to a group and then, after a short time, to give the same people the same test again. If they score approximately the same each time, the test is reliable. There is a drawback, however. How do we know that people have not simply remembered the answers from the first testing and repeated them the second time around? To avoid this possibility, psychologists prefer to give two equivalent tests, both designed to measure the same thing. If people score the same on both forms, the tests are considered reliable. One way to create alternate forms is to split a single test into two parts—for example, to assign odd-numbered items to one part and even-numbered items to the other. If scores on the two halves agree, the test has **split-half reliability**. Most intelligence tests do, in fact, have alternate equivalent forms, just as college admission tests like the SAT and ACT have many versions.

How reliable are intelligence tests? In general, people's IQ scores on most intelligence tests are quite stable (Meyer et al., 2001). Performance and culture-fair tests are somewhat less reliable. Scores on even the best tests, however, vary somewhat from one day to another. Therefore, many testing services now report a person's score along with a range of scores that allows for some day-to-day variation. For example, a score of 110 might be reported with a range of 104–116. This implies that the person's true score is most likely within a few points of 110, but almost certainly does not fall lower than 104 or higher than 116.

VALIDITY Generally, intelligence tests are quite reliable, but do these tests really measure "intelligence"? When psychologists ask this question, they are concerned with test validity. **Validity** refers to a test's ability to measure what it has been designed to measure. How do we know whether a given test actually measures what it claims to measure?

One measure of validity is known as **content validity**—whether the test contains an adequate sample of the skills or knowledge that it is supposed to measure. Most widely used intelligence tests, such as those from which the questions at the beginning of this chapter were taken, seem to measure at least some of the mental abilities that we think of as part of intelligence. These include planning, memory, understanding, reasoning, concentration, and the use of language. Although they may not adequately sample all aspects of intelligence equally well, they at least seem to have some content validity.

Another way to measure a test's validity is to see whether a person's score on that test closely matches his or her score on another test designed to measure the same thing. The two different scores should be very similar if they are both measures of the same ability. Various intelligence tests seem to show this kind of validity as well. Despite differences in test content, people who score high on one test tend to score high on others.

Still, this outcome doesn't necessarily mean that the two tests measure intelligence. Conceivably, they could both be measuring the same thing, but that thing is not necessarily intelligence. To demonstrate that the tests are valid, we need an independent measure of intelligence against which to compare intelligence test scores. Determining test validity in this way is called **criterion-related validity**. Ever since Binet invented the intelligence test, the main criterion against which intelligence test scores have been compared has been school achievement. Even the strongest critics agree that IQ tests predict school achievement well (Aiken, 1988; Anastasi & Urbina, 1997).

CRITICISMS OF IQ TESTS What is it about IQ tests, then, that makes them controversial? One major criticism concerns the narrowness of their content. Many critics believe that intelligence tests assess only a very limited set of skills: passive verbal understanding, the

reliability Ability of a test to produce consistent and stable scores.

split-half reliability A method of determining test reliability by dividing the test into two parts and checking the agreement of scores on both parts.

validity Ability of a test to measure what it has been designed to measure.

content validity Refers to a test's having an adequate sample of questions measuring the skills or knowledge it is supposed to measure.

criterion-related validity Validity of a test as measured by a comparison of the test score and independent measures of what the test is designed to measure.

Many organizations require job applicants to complete tests of mental ability as part of the hiring process. Sometimes these tests are administered via a computer, as is the case in this photo.

ability to follow instructions, common sense, and, at best, scholastic aptitude (Ginsberg, 1972; Sattler, 1992). One critic observes, "Intelligence tests measure how quickly people can solve relatively unimportant problems making as few errors as possible, rather than measuring how people grapple with relatively important problems, making as many productive errors as necessary with no time factor" (Blum, 1979, p. 83). A test score is also a very simplistic way of summing up an extremely complex set of abilities. Maloney and Ward (1976) point out that we do not describe a person's personality with a two- or three-digit number. Why, then, they ask, should we try to sum up something as complex as intelligence by labeling someone "90" or "110"? Furthermore, it is important to remember that an IQ is not the same thing as intelligence. Tests measure our ability level at a certain point in time. Test scores do not tell us why someone performs poorly or well.

Another major criticism of IQ tests is that their content and administration do not sufficiently take into account cultural variations and, in fact, may discriminate against minorities. For example, certain questions may have very different meanings for children of different social classes. The WISC-III, for instance, asks, "What are you supposed to do if a child younger than you hits you?" The "correct" answer is "Walk away." But for a child who lives in an environment where survival depends on being tough, the "correct" answer might be "Hit him back." This answer, however, receives zero credit.

Even presumably culture-fair tests may accentuate the very cultural differences that they were designed to minimize, to the detriment of some test takers (Linn, 1982). For example, when given a picture of a head with the mouth missing, one group of Asian-American children responded by saying that the body was missing, thus receiving no credit. To them, the absence of a body under the head was more remarkable than the absence of the mouth (Ortar, 1963). Although some investigations argue that the most widely used and thoroughly studied tests are not unfairly biased against minorities (Damas, 2002; Herrnstein & Murray, 1994), others argue that a proper study of cultural bias in testing has yet to be made (Helms, 1992).

One response to concerns about unfair test bias is to treat test scores as only *one* source of information about a person. For example, it seems reasonable that abilities beyond those measured by intelligence tests contribute to success on the job and to success in school. Job performance may be better predicted by tests of actual job knowledge than by paper-and-pencil tests that measure general intelligence. In schools IQ scores should be used in conjunction with other kinds of information that help us to interpret what these scores mean. One such approach is the System of Multicultural Pluralistic Adjustment (SOMPA). SOMPA involves collecting a wide range of data on a child, such as overall health status and socioeconomic background. This information on the students' characteristics and their environment is used to provide a context within which intelligence test scores can be interpreted. Another approach, the Rainbow Project, was described at the beginning of this chapter.

IQ AND SUCCESS As we've seen, IQ scores predict success in school with some accuracy. In many ways, it isn't surprising that scores on these tests correlate well with academic achievement, since both involve some intellectual activity and both stress verbal ability. Moreover, both academic achievement and high IQ scores require similar kinds of motivation, attention, perseverance, and test-taking ability.

Attitudes and beliefs may also play a role. Alfred Binet developed the first IQ test to help the Paris public school system identify students who needed to be put in special classes. When IQ tests are used to put a person into a "track" or "slot" in school, however, students' performance may reflect the tracking more than it shows their ability. Students in special classes apart from "normal" students may come to doubt their abilities. Tracking may also have the opposite effect on high IQ scorers. In a self-fulfilling prophecy, such children may come to believe that they will be high achievers, and this expectation may figure prominently in their subsequent success (Dahlström, 1993). Teachers, too, may come to expect particular students to do well or poorly on the basis of IQ scores and so encourage or neglect those students. IQ scores, then, may not simply predict future achievement or failure; they may also contribute to it.

IQ tests also tend to predict success after people finish their schooling. People with high IQ scores tend to enter high-status occupations: Physicians and lawyers tend to have higher IQs than truck drivers and janitors. Critics point out, however, that this pattern can be explained in various ways. For one thing, because people with higher IQs tend to do better in school, they stay in school longer and earn advanced degrees, thereby opening the door to high-status jobs. Moreover, children from wealthy families generally grow up in environments that encourage academic success and reward good performance on tests (Blum, 1979; Ceci & Williams, 1997). In addition, they are more likely to have the money needed for graduate school and advanced occupational training, as well as helpful family connections that contribute to occupational success. Still, higher grades and intelligence test scores do predict occupational success and performance on the job (Barret & Depinet, 1991; Kuncel, Hezlett, & Ones, 2004; Ree & Earles, 1992), a topic we will address more fully in Chapter 11: "Psychology Applied to Work."

▶ CHECK YOUR UNDERSTANDING

1. Indicate whether the following statements are true (T) or false (F).
   a. ___Intelligence is synonymous with problem-solving ability.
   b. ___Intrapersonal intelligence reflects the adage, "Know thyself."
   c. ___Sternberg's and Gardner's theories of intelligence both emphasize practical abilities.
   d. ___The consistency with which a test measures is called validity.

2. In 1916, the Stanford psychologist L. M. Terman introduced the term _____ _____, abbreviated as _____, and set the score of _____ for a person of average intelligence.

3. _____ tests eliminate or minimize the use of words in assessing mental abilities. Like these tests, _____-_____ tests minimize the use of language, but they also include questions that minimize skills and values that vary across cultures.

Answers: 1. a. (F); b. (T); c. (T); d. (F). 2. intelligence quotient, I.Q., 100. 3. Performance, culture fair.

▶ APPLY YOUR UNDERSTANDING

1. A friend of yours says, "Everyone has different talents and abilities. Some people are really good at math but just kind of average at everything else. Other people are really good at music or athletics or dancing but can't add two numbers to save their lives. Because you have an ability in one area doesn't mean you're talented at other things." Your friend's view of abilities most closely matches which of the following theorists discussed in this section of the chapter?
   a. Spearman
   b. Gardner
   c. Goleman
   d. Sternberg

2. Dr. Atem is trying to create a 10-item intelligence test. She compares scores from her test to scores on the Stanford–Binet test in an attempt to determine her test's
   a. reliability
   b. validity
   c. practicality
   d. standard deviation

Answers: 1. b., 2. b.

Heredity, Environment, and Intelligence

5.5   Explain how hereditary and environmental forces interact to produce an individual's level of intelligence and describe the characteristics that are associated with mental retardation, giftedness, and creativity.

Is intelligence inherited, or is it the product of the environment? Sorting out the importance of each factor as it contributes to intelligence is a complex task.

HEREDITY

Why are twin studies useful in studying intelligence?

As we saw in Chapter 2, "The Biological Basis of Behavior," scientists can use studies of identical twins to measure the effects of heredity in humans. Twin studies of intelligence typically begin by comparing the IQ scores of identical twins who have been raised together. As **Figure 5–8** shows, the correlation between their IQ scores is very high. In addition to

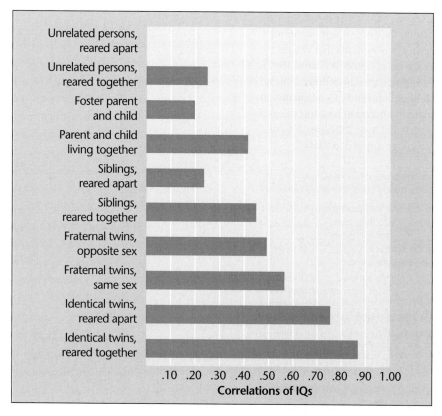

Figure 5–8

Correlations of IQ scores and family relationships. Identical twins who grow up in the same household have IQ scores that are almost identical to each other. Even when they are reared apart, their scores are highly correlated.

Source: Adapted from "Genetics and intelligence: A review," by Erienmeyer–Kimling and L. F. Jarvik 1963, *Science, 142,* pp. 1477–79. Copyright © 1963 by the American Association for the Advancement of Science. Reprinted with permission of the author.

Individual differences in intelligence can be partly explained by differences in environmental stimulation and encouragement. The specific forms of stimulation given vary from culture to culture. Because our culture assigns importance to developing academic skills, the stimulation of reading and exploring information in books can give children an edge over those who are not so encouraged.

identical genes, however, these twins grew up in very similar environments: They shared parents, home, teachers, vacations, and probably friends. These common experiences could explain their similar IQ scores. To check this possibility, researchers have tested identical twins who were separated early in life—generally before they were six months old—and raised in different families. As **Figure 5–8** shows, even when identical twins are raised in different families, they tend to have very similar test scores; in fact, the similarity is much greater than that between non-twin siblings who grow up in the *same* environment.

These findings make a strong case for the heritability of intelligence. Although, for reasons identified in Chapter 2, twin studies do not constitute "final proof," other evidence also demonstrates the role of heredity. For example, adopted children have been found to have IQ scores that are more similar to those of their *biological* mothers than to those of the mothers who are raising them (Loehlin, Horn, & Willerman, 1997). Researcher John Loehlin finds these results particularly interesting because "[they] reflect genetic resemblance in the absence of shared environment: These birth mothers had no contact with their children after the first few days of life" (Loehlin et al., 1997, p. 113). Do psychologists, then, conclude that intelligence is an inherited trait and that environment plays little, if any, role?

ENVIRONMENT

What have we learned from early intervention programs about the influence of the environment on intellectual development?

Although our genes provide a base or starting point, experience plays an important role in the development of intellect, as is also the case for many human characteristics (Garlick, 2003). For example, each of us inherits a certain body build from our parents, but our actual weight is greatly determined by what we eat and how much we exercise. Similarly, although we inherit certain mental capacities, the development of those inherited intellectual abilities depends on what we see around us as infants, how our parents respond to our first attempts to talk, what schools we attend, which books we read, which television programs we watch—even what we eat (Sternberg & Grigorenko, 2001).

Quite by chance, psychologist H. M. Skeels found evidence in the 1930s that IQ scores among children depend on environmental stimulation. While investigating orphanages for the state of Iowa, Skeels observed that the children lived in very overcrowded wards and that the few adults there had almost no time to play with the children, to talk to them, or to read them stories. Many of these children were classified as "subnormal" in intelligence. Skeels followed the cases of two girls who, after 18 months in an orphanage, were sent to a ward for women with severe retardation. Originally, the girls' IQs were in the range of retardation, but after a year on the adult ward, as if by magic, their IQs had risen to normal (Skeels, 1938). Skeels regarded this fact as quite remarkable—after all, the women with whom the girls had lived were themselves severely retarded. When he placed 13 other "slow" children as houseguests in such adult wards, within 18 months their mean IQ rose from 64 to 92 (within the normal range)—all because they had had someone (even someone of below-normal intelligence) to play with them, to read to them, to cheer them on when they took their first steps, and to encourage them to talk (Skeels, 1942). During the same period, the mean IQ of a group of children who had been left in orphanages dropped from 86 to 61. Thirty years later, Skeels found that all 13 of the children raised on adult wards were self-supporting, their occupations ranging from waiting on tables to real estate sales. Of the contrasting group, half were unemployed, four were still in institutions, and all of those who had jobs were dishwashers (Skeels, 1966).

Later studies have reinforced Skeels's findings on the importance of intellectually stimulating surroundings as well as the importance of good nutrition (Capron & Duyme, 1989). For example, researchers have found that the socioeconomic status (SES) of adoptive parents has an effect on their adopted children's IQs. Regardless of the socioeconomic status of the child's biological parents, those children adopted by high-SES parents had higher IQs than did those children adopted by low-SES parents, because high-SES families tend to provide children with better nutrition and heightened stimulation. Do such findings mean that intervention programs that enhance the environments of impoverished children can have a positive impact on their IQ?

INTERVENTION PROGRAMS: HOW MUCH CAN WE BOOST IQ? *Head Start*, the nation's largest intervention program, began in 1965. Today, it provides comprehensive child care services for 739,000 children, (Kassebaum, 1994; Ripple, Gilliam, Chanana, & Zigler, 1999). Head Start focuses on preschoolers between the ages of three and five from low-income families and has two key goals: To provide the children with some educational and social skills before they go to school, and to provide information about nutrition and health to both the children and their families. Head Start involves parents in all its aspects, from daily activities to administration of the program itself. This parental involvement has been crucial to Head Start's success (Cronan, Walen, & Cruz, 1994; Mendez & Martha, 2001).

Several studies evaluating the long-term effects of Head Start have found that it boosts cognitive abilities (Barnett, 1998; B. Brown & Grotberg, 1981; Zigler, 1998; Zigler & Styfco, 2001), but some experts are concerned that these improvements may be modest or short

Head Start, the nation's largest federally funded early intervention program, provides preschool education and support to at-risk children.

term. Nevertheless, children leaving Head Start are in a better position to profit from schooling than they would be otherwise (Zigler & Styfco, 1994). Studies following Head Start graduates until age 27 revealed several benefits, including higher academic achievement; the Head Start graduates also tended to stay in school longer, and were more likely to graduate from college. They also had a lower level of delinquency. Thus, even if the mental ability gains due to Head Start are not long lasting, the program still seems to provide long-term, practical benefits (Schweinhart, Barnes, & Weikart, 1993; Zigler & Styfco, 2001; Zigler, 2003).

Overall, the effectiveness of early intervention appears to depend on the quality of the particular program (Collins, 1993; Ramey, 1999; Zigler & Muenchow, 1992; Zigler & Styfco, 1993). Intervention programs that have clearly defined goals; that explicitly teach basic skills, such as counting, naming colors, and writing the alphabet; and that take into account the broad context of human development, including health care and other social services; achieve the biggest and most durable gains. Also, interventions that begin in the preschool years and include a high degree of parental involvement (to ensure continuity after the official program ends) are generally more successful (Zigler, Finn–Stevenson, & Hall, 2002).

UNDERSTANDING THE INTERACTION OF HEREDITY AND ENVIRONMENT Both heredity and environment have important effects on individual differences in intelligence, but is one of these factors more important than the other? The answer depends on the IQs that you are comparing. A useful analogy comes from studies of plants (Turkheimer, 1991).

Suppose that you grow one group of randomly assigned plants in enriched soil, and another group in poor soil. The enriched group will grow to be taller and stronger than the nonenriched group; the difference between the two groups in this case is due entirely to differences in their environment. *Within* each group of plants, however, differences among individual plants are likely to be primarily due to genetics, because all plants in the same group share essentially the same environment. Thus, the height and strength of any single plant reflects both heredity *and* environment.

Similarly, group differences in IQ scores might be due to environmental factors, but differences among people *within* groups could be due primarily to genetics. At the same time, the IQ scores of particular people would reflect the effects of both heredity *and* environment. Robert Plomin, an influential researcher in the field of human intelligence, concludes that "the world's literature suggests that about half of the total variance in IQ scores can be accounted for by genetic variance" (Plomin, 1997, p. 89). This finding means that environment accounts for the other half. Heredity and environment both contribute to human differences.

THE FLYNN EFFECT An interesting side note to this discussion is the fact that IQ scores have *gone up* in the population as a whole (Daley, Whaley, Sigman, Espinosa, & Neumann, 2003; Humphreys, 1992; Jensen, 1992; Neisser et al., 1996; Neisser, 1998; Resing & Nijland, 2002). Because James Flynn (Flynn, 1984, 1987) of the University of Otago in New Zealand was the first to report this finding, it is often called the *Flynn Effect*. In his original research, Professor Flynn gathered evidence showing that, between 1932 and 1978, intelligence test scores rose about three points per decade. More recently, by pulling together data from five nations (Britain, Netherlands, Israel, Norway, and Belgium), Flynn (1999) has shown that the average increase in IQ may be as high as six points per decade. Consistent with this result is a finding by Flieller (1999) that children today between the ages of 10 and 15 years old display significant cognitive advancement compared with children of the same age tested 20 and 30 years ago. And, as Neisser (1998) points out, accompanying this general increase in IQ scores is a decrease in the difference in intelligence scores between blacks and whites.

Although this finding has many possible explanations, none of them seem to account entirely for the magnitude of the effect (Flynn, 1999; Rowe & Rodgers, 2002). Rather than getting smarter, maybe people are simply getting better at taking tests. Environmental factors, such as improved nutrition and health care, may also contribute to this trend (Lynn, 1989). Some psychologists have suggested that the sheer complexity of the modern world is responsible (Schooler, 1998). For example, the proliferation of televisions, computers, and video games could be contributing to the rise in IQ scores (Greenfield, 1998; Neisser, 1998). Continued research on the Flynn Effect will undoubtedly shed more light on our understanding of the nature of intelligence and the factors that influence its development.

EXTREMES OF INTELLIGENCE

What do psychologists know about the two extremes of human intelligence: very high and very low?

The average IQ score on intelligence tests is 100. Nearly 70 percent of all people have IQs between 85 and 115, and all but 5 percent of the population have IQs between 70 and 130. In this section, we focus on people who score at the two extremes of intelligence—those with mental retardation and those who are intellectually gifted—as well as those who are highly creative.

MENTAL RETARDATION **Mental retardation** encompasses a vast array of mental deficits with a wide variety of causes, treatments, and outcomes. The American Psychiatric Association (1994) defines mental retardation as "significantly subaverage general intellectual functioning... that is accompanied by significant limitations in adaptive functioning" that appears before the age of 21 (p. 39). There are also various degrees of mental retardation. Mild retardation corresponds to Stanford–Binet IQ scores ranging from a high of about 70 to a low near 50. Moderate retardation corresponds to IQ scores from the low 50s to the middle 30s. People with IQ scores between the middle 30s and 20 are considered severely retarded, and the profoundly retarded are those whose scores are below 20. (See **Table 5–4**.)

The Flynn Effect, which notes that IQ scores are steadily rising in the population, may be the result of better nutrition and health care, as well as more time spent with technology and on problem solving tasks.

mental retardation Condition of significantly subaverage intelligence accompanied by deficiencies in adaptive behavior.

>TABLE 5-4 LEVELS OF MENTAL RETARDATION

Type of Retardation	IQ Range	Attainable Skill Level (Approximate)
Mild retardation	Low 50s to low 70s	People may be able to function adequately in society and learn skills comparable to a sixth-grader, but they need special help at times of unusual stress.
Moderate retardation	Mid-30s to low 50s	People profit from vocational training and may be able to travel alone. They can learn on a second-grade level and perform skilled work in a sheltered workshop under supervision.
Severe retardation	Low 20s to mid-30s	People do not learn to talk or to practice basic hygiene until after age 6. They cannot learn vocational skills but can perform simple tasks under supervision.
Profound retardation	Below 20 or 25	Constant care is needed. Usually, people in this group have a diagnosed neurological disorder.

Source: Based on APA, DSM-IV, 1994.

But a low IQ is not in itself sufficient for diagnosing mental retardation. The person must also be unable to perform the daily tasks needed to function independently (Wielkiewicz & Calvert, 1989). A person who is able to live independently, for example, is not considered to have mental retardation even if his or her IQ may be quite low. To fully assess individuals and to place them in appropriate treatment and educational programs, mental health professionals need information on physical health and on emotional and social adjustment.

What causes mental retardation? In most cases, the causes are unknown (Beirne–Smith, Patton, & Ittenbach, 1994)—especially in cases of mild retardation, which account for nearly 90 percent of all retardation. When causes can be identified, most often they stem from a wide variety of genetic, environmental, social, nutritional, and other risk factors (Baumeister & Baumeister, 2000).

About 25 percent of cases—especially the more severe forms of retardation—appear to involve genetic or biological disorders. Scientists have identified more than 100 forms of mental retardation caused by single defective genes (Plomin, 1997). One is the genetically based disease *phenylketonuria*, or *PKU*, which occurs in about one person out of 25,000 (Minton & Schneider, 1980). In people suffering from PKU, the liver fails to produce an enzyme necessary for early brain development. Fortunately, placing a PKU baby on a special diet can prevent mental retardation from developing. Another form of hereditary mental retardation is *fragile-X syndrome* (Hagerman & Hagerman, 2002), which affects about one in every 1,250 males and one in every 2,500 females (Plomin, 1997). A defect in the X chromosome, passed on between generations, seems to be caused by a specific gene (M. Hoffman, 1991). In the disorder known as *Down syndrome*, which affects one in 600 newborns, an extra 21st chromosome is the cause. Down syndrome, named for the physician who first described its symptoms, is typically marked by moderate to severe mental retardation.

Biologically caused mental retardation can be addressed through education and training (Ramey, Ramey, & Lanzi, 2001). The prognosis for those with no underlying physical causes is even better. People whose retardation is due to a history of social and educational deprivation may respond dramatically to appropriate interventions. Today, the majority of children with physical or mental disabilities are educated in local school systems (Lipsky & Gartner, 1996; Schroeder, Schroeder, & Landesman, 1987), in *inclusion* arrangements (Kavale, 2002) (previously known as *mainstreaming*), which help these students to socialize with their nondisabled peers. The principle of mainstreaming has also been applied to adults with mental retardation, by taking them out of large, impersonal institutions and placing them in smaller community homes that provide more normal life experiences (Conroy, 1996; Landesman & Butterfield, 1987; Maisto & Hughes, 1995; Stancliffe, 1997). Although the benefits of mainstreaming are debatable, most psychologists and educators support the effort (Zigler & Hodapp, 1991).

GIFTEDNESS At the other extreme of the intelligence scale are "the gifted"—those with exceptional mental abilities, as measured by very high scores on standard intelligence tests. As with mental retardation, the causes of **giftedness** are largely unknown.

The first and now-classic study of giftedness was begun by Lewis Terman and his colleagues in the early 1920s. They defined giftedness in terms of academic talent and measured it by an IQ score in the top 2 percentiles (1925). More recently, some experts have sought to broaden the definition of giftedness beyond that of simply high IQ (Coleman & Cross, 2001; Csikszentmihalyi, Rathunde, & Whalen, 1993; Subotnik & Arnold, 1994). One view is that giftedness is often an interaction of above-average general intelligence, exceptional creativity, and high levels of commitment (Renzulli, 1978). Congress has defined gifted children as those with demonstrated achievement or potential ability in any of the following areas, singly or in combination: (1) general intellectual ability, (2) specific academic aptitude, (3) creative or productive thinking, (4) leadership ability, and (5) fine arts.

People have used various criteria to identify gifted students, including scores on intelligence tests, teacher recommendations, and achievement test results. School systems generally use diagnostic testing, interviews, and evaluation of academic and creative work (Sattler, 1992). These selection methods can identify students with a broad range of talent, but they can miss students with specific abilities, such as a talent for mathematics or music. This is an important factor because research suggests that most gifted individuals display special abilities in only a few areas. "Globally" gifted people are rare (Achter, Lubinski, & Benbow, 1996; Lubinski & Benbow, 2000; Olzewski-Kubilius, 2003; Winner, 1998, 2000).

A common view of the gifted is that they have poor social skills and are emotionally maladjusted; however, research does not support this stereotype (Richards, Encel, & Shute, 2003; Robinson & Clinkenbeard, 1998). Indeed, one review (Janos & Robinson, 1985) concluded that "being intellectually gifted, at least at moderate levels of ability, is clearly an asset in terms of psychosocial adjustment in most situations" (p. 181). Nevertheless, children who are exceptionally gifted sometimes do experience difficulty "fitting in" with their peers.

CREATIVITY

What is creativity?

Definitions of both mental retardation and giftedness rely for the most part on assessments of an individual's intelligence. However, most researchers today would argue that intelligence is not a unitary, singular trait. Rather, it is composed of different types of abilities, including **creativity**, the ability to produce novel and socially valued ideas or objects ranging from philosophy to painting, from music to mousetraps (Mumford & Gustafson, 1988; Runco, 2004; Sternberg, 2001). Although some researchers, including Robert Sternberg, consider creativity and insight to be important elements in human intelligence, many researchers would argue that intelligence and creativity are not the same thing. One way of exploring the difference between these two constructs is to investigate how creativity is measured. Measuring creativity, however, poses special problems (Naglieri & Kaufman, 2001). Because creativity involves original responses to situations, questions that can be answered *true* or *false* or *a* or *b* are not good measures. Open-ended tests are better: Instead of asking for one predetermined answer to a problem, the examiner asks the test takers to let their imaginations run free. Scores are based on such factors as the originality of a person's answers and the number of total answers given.

In one such test, the *Torrance Test of Creative Thinking*, people must explain what is happening in a picture, how the scene came about, and what its consequences are likely to be. In the *Christensen–Guilford Test*, they are to list as many words containing a given letter as possible, to name things belonging to a certain category (such as liquids that will burn), and to write four-word sentences beginning with the letters RDLS—"Rainy days look sad, Red

Down syndrome is a common biological cause of mental retardation, affecting one in 600 newborns. The prognosis for Down syndrome children today is much better than it was in the past. With adequate support, many children with the disorder can participate in regular classrooms and other childhood activities.

giftedness Refers to superior IQ combined with demonstrated or potential ability in such areas as academic aptitude, creativity, and leadership.

creativity The ability to produce novel and socially valued ideas or objects.

dogs like soup, Renaissance dramas lack symmetry," and so on. One of the most widely used creativity tests, S. A. Mednick's (1962) *Remote Associates Test (RAT)*, asks people to relate three apparently unrelated words. For example, the three stimulus words might be *poke*, *go*, and *molasses*, and one response is to relate them through the word *slow*: "Slowpoke, go slow, slow as molasses." In the newer *Wallach and Kogan Creative Battery*, people form associative groupings. For example children are asked to "name all the round things you can think of" and to find similarities between objects, such as between a potato and a carrot.

The study of creativity demonstrates mental abilities are indeed complex and multi-faceted. It also suggests that they may be linked to personality dimensions and motivational levels. For example, creative people are *problem finders* as well as problem solvers (Getzels, 1975; Mackworth, 1965). The more creative people are, the more they like to work on problems that they have set for themselves. Creative scientists (such as Charles Darwin and Albert Einstein) often work for years on a problem that has sprung from their own curiosity (Gruber & Wallace, 2001). Creativity also involves cultural and social dimensions (Csikszentmihalyi, 1999). Finally, "greatness" rests not just on "talent" or "genius"; such people also have intense dedication, ambition, and perseverance. These are topics we address in upcoming chapters of this text.

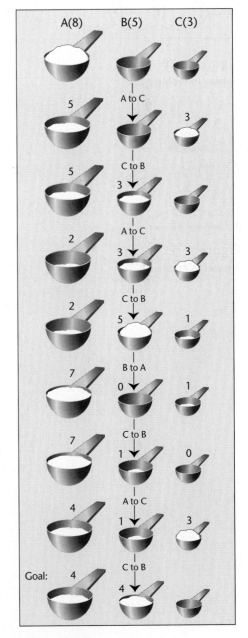

Figure 5–9

Answer to Problem 3.

▶ CHECK YOUR UNDERSTANDING

1. Indicate whether the following statements are true (T) or false (F):
   a. ___ When identical twins are raised apart, their IQ scores are not highly correlated.
   b. ___ Environmental stimulation has little, if any, effect on IQ.
   c. ___ Head Start graduates are more likely than their peers to graduate from college.

2. As psychologists have learned more about giftedness, the definition of this term has become (broader/narrower) _____.

3. The ability to produce novel and unique ideas or objects, ranging from philosophy to painting, from music to mousetraps, is termed _____.

4. _____-_____ tests are the best type for measuring creativity.

Answers: 1. a. (F); b. (F); c. (T), 2. broader, 3. creativity, 4. Open ended.

▶ APPLY YOUR UNDERSTANDING

1. Which of the following pairs of individuals would be expected to have IQs most similar to each other?
   a. Sara and Susan, who are identical twins.
   b. Janice and Jeannette, who are sisters.
   c. Bob and Tom, who have worked together at the same job for thirty years.
   d. Greg and his son Jason.

2. Ten-year-old John has an IQ score of 60 on the Wechsler Intelligence Scale for Children.

Which of the following would you need to know before you could determine whether John is mildly retarded?
   a. Whether his score on the Stanford–Binet Intelligence Scale is also below 70
   b. Whether he can perform the daily tasks needed to function independently
   c. Whether he has a genetic defect in the X chromosome
   d. Whether he suffered from malnutrition before birth

Answers: 1. a., 2. b.

Answers to Problems in the Chapter

Problem 1 Fill each of the smaller spoons with salt from the larger spoon. That step will require four teaspoons of salt, leaving exactly four teaspoons of salt in the larger spoon.

Problem 2 Turn the five-minute hourglass over; when it runs out, turn over the nine-minute hourglass. When it runs out, 14 minutes have passed.

Problem 3 As shown in **Figure 5–9**, fill spoon C with the salt from spoon A (now A has five teaspoons of salt and C has three). Pour the salt from spoon C into spoon B (now A has

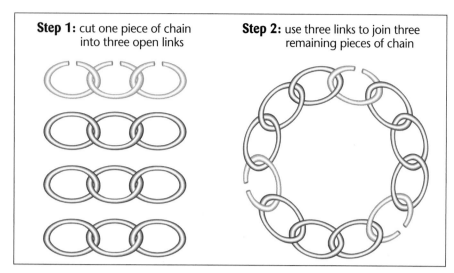

Step 1: cut one piece of chain into three open links

Step 2: use three links to join three remaining pieces of chain

Figure 5–10
Answer to Problem 5.

Figure 5–11
Answer to Problem 6.

five teaspoons of salt, and B has three). Again fill spoon C with the salt from spoon A. (This leaves A with only two teaspoons of salt, while B and C each have three.) Fill spoon B with the salt from spoon C. (This step leaves one teaspoon of salt in spoon C, while B has five teaspoons, and A has only two.) Pour all of the salt from spoon B into spoon A. (Now A has seven teaspoons of salt, and C has one.) Pour all of the salt from spoon C into spoon B, and then fill spoon C from spoon A. (This step leaves four teaspoons of salt in A, one teaspoon in B, and three teaspoons in C.) Finally, pour all of the salt from spoon C into spoon B. (This step leaves four teaspoons of salt in spoons A and B, which is the solution.)

Problem 4 Start both hourglasses. When the five-minute hourglass runs out, turn it over to start it again. When the nine-minute hourglass runs out, turn over the five-minute hourglass. Because there is one minute left in the five-minute hourglass when you turn it over, it will run for only four minutes. Those four minutes, together with the original nine minutes, add up to the required 13 minutes for the barbecue.

Problem 5 Take one of the short pieces of chain shown in **Figure 5–10**, and open all three links. (This step costs six cents.) Use those three links to connect the remaining three pieces of chain. (Hence, closing the three links costs nine cents.)

Problem 6 Join the matches to form a three-dimensional pyramid as seen in **Figure 5–11**.

Problem 7 One way to solve this problem is to draw a diagram of the ascent and the descent, as in **Figure 5–12**. From this drawing, you can see that indeed there is a point that the monk passes at exactly the same time on both days. Another way to approach this problem is to imagine that there are two monks on the mountain; one starts ascending at 7 A.M., while the other starts descending at 7 A.M. on the same day. Clearly, sometime during the day the monks must meet somewhere along the route.

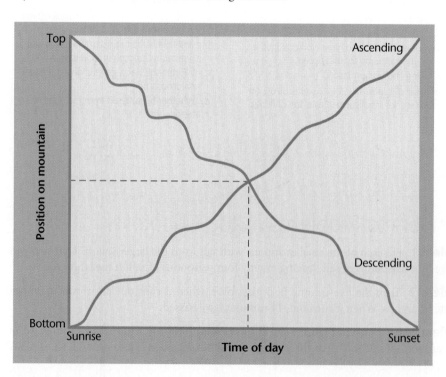

Figure 5–12
Answer to Problem 7.

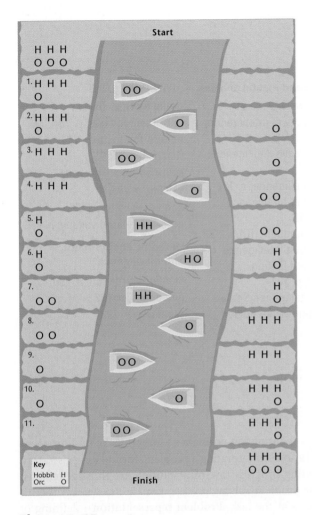

Figure 5–13
Answer to Problem 8: The Hobbits and the Orcs.

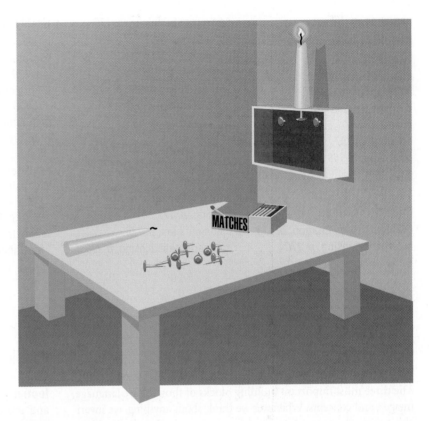

Figure 5–14
Solution to a Problem Limited by Functional Fixedness. In solving the "Candle and tacks" problem presented in the text, many people have trouble realizing that the box of tacks can also be used as a candleholder, as shown here.

Problem 8 This problem has four possible solutions, one of which is shown in **Figure 5–13**.

Answers to Intelligence Test Questions

1. *Idleness* refers to the state of being inactive, not busy, unoccupied; *laziness* means an unwillingness or a reluctance to work. Laziness is one possible cause of idleness, but not the only cause.

2. If you face west, your right ear will face north.

3. *Obliterate* means to erase or destroy something completely.

4. Both an hour and a week are measures of time.

5. Alternative (f) is the correct pattern.

6. 75 cents will buy nine pencils.

7. Alternative (d) is correct. A crutch is used to help someone who has difficulty with locomotion; spectacles are used to help someone who has difficulty with vision.

8. Alternative D is correct. The second figure is the same shape and size but with diagonal cross-hatching from upper left to lower right.

9. Figures 3, 4, and 5 can all be completely covered by using some or all of the given pieces.

>KEY TERMS<

>CHAPTER REVIEW<

Building Blocks of Thought

What steps do we go through to turn a thought into a statement? The three most important building blocks of thought are language, images, and concepts. Whenever we think about anything, we invariably use words, sensory "snapshots," and categories that classify things.

Language is a flexible system of symbols that allows us to communicate ideas to others. When we express thoughts as statements, we must conform to our language's rules. Every language has rules indicating which sounds (or **phonemes**) are part of that particular language, how those sounds can be combined into meaningful units (or **morphemes**), and how those meaningful units can be ordered into phrases and sentences (rules of **grammar**). When we wish to communicate an idea, we start with a thought, then choose sounds, words, and phrases that will express the idea in an understandable way. To understand the speech of others, the task is reversed.

What role do images play in thinking? **Images** are mental representations of sensory experiences. Visual images in particular can be powerful aids in thinking about the relationships between things. Picturing things in our mind's eye can sometimes help us solve problems.

How do concepts help us to think more efficiently? **Concepts** are categories for classifying objects, people, and experiences based on their common elements. Without the ability to form concepts, we would need a different name for every new thing we encounter. Concepts also help clarify new experiences, as we can draw on them to anticipate what new experiences will be like.

How do language, thought, and culture influence each other? According to Benjamin Whorf's **linguistic relativity hypothesis**, thought is greatly influenced by the language a person speaks. But critics contend that Whorf overstated his case. Thought, they say, can shape and change a language as much as a language can shape and change thought.

Problem Solving

Why is representing the problem so important to finding an effective solution? Interpreting a problem, formulating a strategy, and evaluating progress toward a solution are three general aspects of the problem-solving process. Each in its own way is critical to success at the task. **Problem representation**—defining or interpreting the problem—is the first step in problem solving. We must decide whether to view the problem verbally, mathematically, or visually, and we must decide to which category of problems it belongs in order to get clues about how to solve it. Some problems require **convergent thinking**, or searching for a single correct solution, while others call for **divergent thinking**, generating many possible solutions. Representing a problem in an unproductive way can block progress completely.

Why is an algorithm often better for solving a problem than is the process of trial and error? Selecting a solution strategy and evaluating progress toward the goal are also important steps in the problem-solving process. A solution strategy can be anything from simple trial and error, to information retrieval based on similar problems, to a set of step-by-step procedures guaranteed to work (called an **algorithm**), to rule-of-thumb approaches known as **heuristics**. An algorithm is often preferable over trial and error because it guarantees a solution and does not waste time. But because there are so many things for which we don't have algorithms, heuristics are vital to human problem solving. Some useful heuristics are *hill climbing*, creating *subgoals*, *means-end analysis*, and *working backward*.

How can a "mental set" both help and hinder problem solving? A **mental set** is a tendency to perceive and approach a problem in a certain way. Although sets can enable us to draw on past experience to help solve problems, a strong set can also prevent us from using creative new approaches. One set that can seriously hamper problem solving is **functional fixedness**—the tendency to perceive only traditional uses for an object.

Decision Making

How would you go about making a truly logical decision? Decision making is a special kind of problem solving in which we already know all the possible solutions or choices. The task is not to come up with new solutions, but rather to identify the best available one on the basis of whatever criteria we are using. The logical way to make a decision is to rate each of the available choices in terms of criteria you have weighted based on how important they are to you. Then total the ratings for each choice to arrive at a "best" option. Because heavily weighted attractive features can compensate for lightly weighted unattractive ones, this decision-making approach is called a **compensatory model**.

How can heuristic approaches lead us to make bad decisions? When people use heuristics or rule-of-thumb approaches to help them make decisions, they can save a great deal of time and effort, but they do not always make the best choices. One example is errors in judgment based on the **representativeness** heuristic, which involves making decisions based on information that matches our model of the "typical" member of a category. Other examples are overreliance on the **availability** heuristic (making choices based on whatever information we can most easily retrieve from memory, even though it may not be accurate) and the **confirmation bias** (the tendency to seek evidence in support of our existing beliefs and to ignore evidence that contradicts them).

How do we explain to ourselves the decisions we make? **Framing**, or setting the context in which a problem is presented, can also affect the outcome of a decision. And regardless of whether a decision proves to be good or bad, we often use **hindsight bias** to "correct" our memories so that the decision seems to be a good one. **Counterfactual thinking** involves revisiting our decisions by considering "what if" alternatives.

Intelligence and Mental Abilities

What are some of the major theories of intelligence? Psychologists who study **intelligence** ask what intelligence entails and how it can be measured. They also wonder about the relationship between intelligence and creativity. Intelligence theories fall into two categories: those that argue in favor of a "general intelligence," which affects all aspects of cognitive functioning, and those that say intelligence is composed of many separate abilities, with a person not necessarily scoring high in all of them. Spearman's theory of intelligence is an example of the first category. Sternberg's **triarchic theory of intelligence** and Gardner's **theory of multiple intelligences** both view intelligence as being comprised of multiple factors. Goleman's theory of **emotional intelligence** emphasizes skill in social relationships and awareness of others' and one's own emotions.

What kinds of intelligence tests are in use today? The *Binet–Simon Scale*, developed in France by Alfred Binet and Theodore Simon, was adapted by Stanford University's L. M. Terman to create a test that yields an **intelligence quotient (IQ)**, the **Stanford–Binet Intelligence Scale**. **The Wechsler Adult Intelligence Scale** was developed by David Wechsler especially for adults. He also created the **Wechsler Intelligence Scale for Children**. In contrast to these individual intelligence tests, there are also **group tests** of intelligence, which are administered by one examiner to many people at a time. In addition, some psychologists who criticize traditional IQ tests have developed alternatives to them. Some are **performance tests** of mental abilities, which don't involve the use of language, and others are **culture-fair tests** that reduce cultural bias in a variety of ways.

What are some important characteristics of a good test? **Reliability**, the ability of a test to produce consistent and stable scores, and **validity**, the ability of a test to measure what it has been designed to measure, are two important characteristics of a good test. Although the reliability of IQ tests is seldom questioned, their validity is questioned. Critics charge that these tests assess only a very limited set of mental skills—for example passive verbal understanding, the ability to follow instructions, and the ability to give correct answers in a limited time frame. They point out that some tests may be unfairly biased against members of some minority groups. Also, poor school performance may be *the result of*, rather than caused by, low test scores, an example of a self-fulfilling prophecy. New tests are being developed to address these concerns.

Heredity, Environment, and Intelligence

Why are twin studies useful in studying intelligence? Although there has been extended debate about the extent to which heredity and environment contribute to IQ, studies comparing the IQ scores of identical and fraternal twins raised in the same families and in different families indicate that approximately 50 percent of the differences in intelligence are due to genetics and the other half are due to differences in environment and education.

What have we learned from early intervention programs about the influence of the environment on intellectual development? With such a sizable percentage of the differences in IQ scores being attributable to the environment and education, many psychologists are strongly in favor of compensatory education programs for young children from disadvantaged homes. Head Start is one such program. Although they may not boost IQ scores greatly in the long run, intervention programs do seem to have significant educational benefits.

Both heredity and environment have important effects on the development of intelligence. Research indicates that IQ scores have gone up in the population as a whole—a finding referred to as the Flynn Effect.

What do psychologists know about the two extremes of human intelligence: very high and very low? The IQs of nearly 70 percent of the general population fall between 85 and 115, and all but 5 percent of the population have IQs between 70 and 130. **Mental retardation** and **giftedness** are the two extremes of intelligence. About a quarter of the cases of mental retardation can be traced to biological causes, including Down syndrome, but the causes of the other 75 percent of cases are not fully understood. Neither are the causes of giftedness. Gifted people do not necessarily excel in all mental abilities. Sometimes they are gifted in one area without being gifted in others.

What is creativity? **Creativity** is the ability to produce novel and socially valued ideas or objects.

A number of tests of creativity have been developed. These tests measure divergent thinking and are scored on such factors as the originality of answers and the number of responses given. Creativity is dependent on a host of factors including mental ability, personality, motivation, and culture.

Concept Map

5.1 BUILDING BLOCKS OF THOUGHT

LANGUAGE: A flexible system of symbols that allows us to communicate ideas.

- **Phonemes:** Basic sounds of language
- **Morphemes:** Meaningful units of language
- **Grammar:** Rules for combining morphemes
- Speaking requires top-down processing to convert ideas into words
- Understanding requires bottom-up processing to convert words into ideas

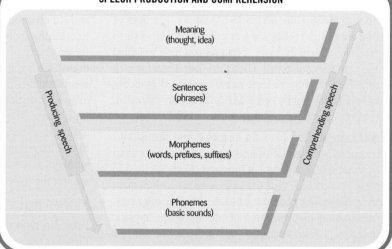

SPEECH PRODUCTION AND COMPREHENSION

Meaning (thought, idea)

Sentences (phrases)

Morphemes (words, prefixes, suffixes)

Phonemes (basic sounds)

Producing speech

Comprehending speech

IMAGES AND CONCEPTS

- **Image:** A mental representation of a sensory experience
- **Concept:** A mental category for classification
- **Prototype:** A representative example of a category

LANGUAGE AND THOUGHT

- Language may determine in part how we think about the world according to the **Linguistic Relativity Hypothesis**
- Other theorists say that how we think influences language

5.2 PROBLEM SOLVING

PROBLEM INTERPRETATION

- Problem representation: How the problem is interpreted or defined
- Divergent thinking: Generating many possible solutions
- Convergent thinking: Selecting a correct answer

PROBLEM STRATEGIES

- Information retrieval: Remembering how a problem was previously solved
- Trial and error: Using different solutions until a correct one is reached
- **Algorithms:** Step-by-step problem solving that guarantees a correct solution
- **Heuristics:** Rules of thumb that help in simplifying and solving problems
- **Troubleshooting:** Anticipating problems
- **Brainstorming:** Producing numerous possible solutions in a group and evaluating them only after all ideas have been collected

OBSTACLES TO SOLVING PROBLEMS

- Mental set: Tendency to perceive and approach problems a certain way
- Functional fixedness: Tendency to perceive only a limited number of uses for an object

5.3 DECISION MAKING

THE COMPENSATORY MODEL

- Identify all options
- Weigh each in terms of importance
- Add ratings and compare

HEURISTICS

- **Representativeness:** Decisions are based on what has worked before in similar situations
- **Availability:** Decisions are made based on what is most easily remembered
- **Confirmation bias:** Evidence that contradicts a decision tends to be ignored

DECISION BIASES

- **Framing:** Decisions depend on how the situation is perceived, or "framed"
- **Hindsight bias:** The tendency to see an outcome as inevitable and predictable
- **Counterfactual thinking:** "If only" thinking about outcomes

5.4 INTELLIGENCE AND MENTAL ABILITIES

THEORIES OF INTELLIGENCE

- **Spearman:** Intelligence is a general, global activity
- **Sternberg's Triarchic Theory:** Intelligence is comprised of analytical, creative, and practical intelligence
- **Gardner's Theory of Multiple Intelligences:** Intelligence is comprised of eight distinct abilities
- **Goleman's Emotional Intelligence:** How well people perceive and understand their own and other's emotions, how well they manage their emotional behavior

INTELLIGENCE TESTS

- Intelligence can be represented numerically with an IQ (Intelligence Quotient) score
- Average IQ is 100
- Cultural bias in IQ testing can be minimized by eliminating biased questions, by giving nonverbal **performance tests**, or by giving **culture-fair tests**

CHARACTERISTICS OF GOOD TESTS

- Reliability: Test yields consistent and stable scores
- Validity: Test measures what it is intended to

5.5 HEREDITY, ENVIRONMENT, AND INTELLIGENCE

INFLUENCES ON INTELLIGENCE

- Heredity plays an important role in establishing an individual's level of intelligence, as documented with twin studies
- Environmental factors

    Diet and learning opportunities are both important

    Early intervention programs can help improve academic outcomes

EXTREMES OF INTELLIGENCE

- Mental retardation: Mental deficits corresponding to low IQ and limited ability to function
- Giftedness: High IQ together with potential for high academic aptitude, creativity, and leadership

CREATIVITY: Mental ability to produce novel and socially valued ideas or objects

- Creativity tests require open-ended questions
- Creativity also has personality, motivational, and cultural dimensions

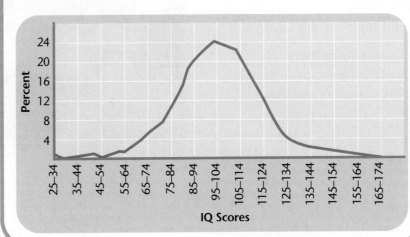

RANGE OF IQs

Most scores fall around 100

[CHAPTER 6]

Overview

Motivation and Emotion

Everyone who manages people—from CEOs to line managers at your local McDonalds—knows that motivated employees are more productive. Yet the million-dollar question is "how do you motivate today's employees?" In its world-wide survey, the consulting firm Towers-Perrin isolated these top five "global attraction drivers" that spur employee engagement in 16 countries:

1. Competitive base pay
2. Work-life balance
3. Challenging work
4. Career advancement opportunities
5. Salary increases linked to individual performance

Perhaps the most notable finding is the importance of work-life balance to today's workforce. Working hours are increasing everywhere in the world—with 57 percent of employees surveyed working more than 40 hours a week—and there is an increasing sense that perhaps our priorities need shifting. Penny Webb, a partner at business consulting firm Whitehead Mann, explains: "Ever since 9/11 people have reassessed their values and views on what is really important. For years, people talked about work-life balance taking precedence over pay; now it is really happening. The top executives are choosing healthcare benefits, extra holidays, sabbaticals, and commitment to extra education over financial incentives."

Having stretched themselves to the limit, baby boomer executives are just now crying out for a more balanced life. Yet, for college graduates, work-life balance may already trump pay as a motivator. Tony Giles, a campus recruiting coordinator for Target Corp. says, "They want to work hard, but they also want to be able to play hard. They are definitely looking for a work-life balance." Gordon Green, a human resource consultant, puts it this way: "The older generations 'worked to live.' Boomers 'live to work,'" but Green says that Gamers, young people raised on computer and video games, "expect harmonization in their life and work. They want a whole approach, not just balance. Work needs to fit into their life plans. They want to be engaged and treated as a whole person, not just used as an employee or worker for a task."

The need to be treated as a "whole person" and not just a cog in a well-functioning machine has spurred some companies to use a workforce practice known as "personalized motivation," or "how would you like to be managed?" profiling. After all, while one employee may be motivated by "work-life balance," another may be spurred to higher levels of achievement by "competitive pay," or "challenging work." Baptist Health Care of Florida is breaking new ground in this area by distributing a simple but effective survey to employees asking them how they would like to be rewarded and recognized.[1]

The study of motivation, whether spurred by a practical attempt to motivate workers in an organization like Baptist Health Care or studied in a psychologist's laboratory, is intimately tied to the study of emotion as well. A **motive** is a specific need or desire that arouses the organism and directs its behavior toward a goal. All motives are triggered by some kind of stimulus: a bodily condition, such as low levels of blood sugar or dehydration; a cue in the environment, such as a "Sale" sign; or a feeling, such as loneliness, guilt, or anger. When a stimulus induces goal-directed behavior, we say that it has motivated the person. **Emotion** refers to the experience of feelings such as fear, joy, surprise, and anger. Similar to motives, emotions also activate and affect behavior, but it is more difficult to predict the kind of behavior that a particular emotion will prompt. If a man is hungry, we can be reasonably sure that he will seek food. If, however, this same man experiences a feeling of joy or surprise, we cannot know with certainty how he will act.

The important thing to remember about both motives and emotions is that they push us to take some kind of action—from an act as drastic as murder to a habit as mundane as drumming our fingers on a table when we are nervous. Motivation occurs whether or not we are aware of it. We do not need to think about feeling hungry to make a beeline for the refrigerator or to focus on our need for achievement to study for an exam. Similarly, we do not have to recognize consciously that we are afraid to step back from a growling dog or to know that we are angry before raising our voice at someone. Moreover, the same motivation or emotion may produce different behaviors in different people. Ambition might motivate one person to go to law school and another to join a crime ring. Feeling sad might lead one person to cry alone and another to seek out a friend. On the other hand, the same behavior might arise from different motives or emotions: You may go to a movie because you are happy, bored, or lonely. In short, the workings of motives and emotions are very complex.

In this chapter, we will first look at some specific motives that play important roles in human behavior. Then we will turn our attention to emotions and the various ways they are expressed. We begin our discussion of motivation with a few general concepts. ◼

Perspectives on Motivation

6.1 Explain the different perspectives involved in instinctual, drive-reduction, and arousal theories of motivation and describe how a hierarchical view of motivation can accommodate both intrinsic and extrinsic motivational factors.

The study of human motivation addresses the fundamental question: Why do humans act the way they do? Many perspectives have contributed to our present understanding about

motive Specific need or desire, such as hunger, thirst, or achievement, that prompts goal-directed behavior.

emotion Feeling, such as fear, joy, or surprise, that underlies behavior.

motivation. Some focus on biological needs and drives; others emphasize external, environmental conditions as the sources that trigger motives to arise. Today, psychologists recognize the role that both nature and nurture play in human motivational processes.

INSTINCTS, DRIVE REDUCTION, AND AROUSAL

How well do theories based on the biological concepts of instinct, homeostasis, and arousal explain human motivation?

All living organisms have biological needs that must be satisfied in order to stay alive, such as the need for food, for water, for air, and so forth. Several theories of motivation emphasize the idea that biological forces—such as needs, drives, instincts, and arousal levels—influence our behavior to an important degree.

INSTINCT THEORY Early in the 20th century, psychologists often emphasized the role of biologically-based instincts in influencing human behavior. **Instincts** are specific, inborn behavior patterns that are characteristic of an entire species. Just as instincts motivate salmon to swim upstream to spawn and spiders to spin webs, instincts were thought to explain much of human behavior. In 1890, William James compiled a list of human instincts that included hunting, rivalry, fear, curiosity, shyness, love, shame, and resentment. But by the 1920s, instinct theory began to fall out of favor as an explanation of human behavior for three reasons: (1) most important human behavior is learned; (2) human behavior is rarely rigid, inflexible, unchanging, and found throughout the species, as is the case with instincts; and (3) ascribing every conceivable human behavior to a corresponding instinct explains nothing (calling a preference to be alone an "antisocial instinct," for example, merely names the behavior without pinpointing its origins). So, after World War I, psychologists started looking for more credible explanations of human behavior.

DRIVE-REDUCTION THEORY An alternative view of motivation holds that bodily needs (such as the need for food or the need for water) create a state of tension or arousal called a **drive** (such as hunger or thirst). According to **drive-reduction theory**, motivated behavior is an attempt to reduce this unpleasant state of tension in the body and to return the body to a state of **homeostasis**, or balance. When we are hungry, we look for food to reduce the hunger drive. When we are tired, we find a place to rest. When we are thirsty, we find something to drink. In each of these cases, behavior is directed toward reducing a state of bodily tension or arousal.

According to drive-reduction theory, drives can generally be divided into two categories. **Primary drives** are unlearned, are found in all animals (including humans), and motivate behavior that is vital to the survival of the individual or species. Primary drives include hunger, thirst, and sex. Not all motivation stems from the need to reduce or satisfy primary drives, however. Humans, in particular, are also motivated by **secondary drives**, drives that are acquired through learning. For example, no one is born with a drive to acquire great wealth, yet many people are motivated by money. Other secondary drives include getting good grades in school and career success.

AROUSAL THEORY Drive-reduction theory is appealing, but it cannot explain all kinds of behavior. It implies, for example, that, if able, people would spend as much time as possible at rest. They would seek food when hungry, water when thirsty, and so on, but after the active drives were satisfied, they would do little. They would literally have no motivation. Yet this is obviously not the case. People work, play, chat with one another, and do many things for which there is no known biological need that they are striving to satisfy.

Some psychologists suggest that motivation might have to do with arousal or state of alertness. The level of arousal at any given moment falls along a continuum from extreme alertness to sleep.

Arousal theory suggests that each of us has an optimum level of arousal that varies from one situation to another and over the course of the day. According to the theory, behavior is motivated by the desire to maintain the optimum level of arousal for a given moment. Sometimes behavior seems to be motivated by a desire to reduce the state of arousal. For example,

---

instinct Inborn, inflexible, goal-directed behavior that is characteristic of an entire species.

drive State of tension or arousal that motivates behavior.

drive-reduction theory States that motivated behavior is aimed at reducing a state of bodily tension or arousal and at returning the organism to homeostasis.

homeostasis State of balance and stability in which the organism functions effectively.

primary drive An unlearned drive, such as hunger, that is based on a physiological state.

secondary drive A learned drive, such as ambition, that is not based on a physiological state.

arousal theory Theory of motivation that proposes that organisms seek an optimal level of arousal.

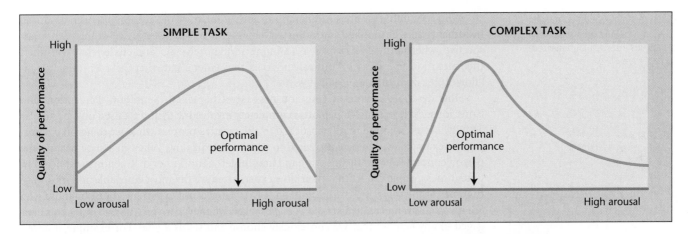

Oftentimes people volunteer to help others for the satisfaction and enjoyment they feel when providing assistance—an example of the power of intrinsic motivation.

when you are sleepy, you are likely to turn off the television and turn off the light. Other times, behavior appears to be motivated by a desire to increase the state of arousal. For example, when you are bored, you may turn on the television, take a walk, or call a friend.

It is not surprising that an individual's arousal level also affects how well he or she performs in different situations. Psychologists agree that there is no "best" level of arousal necessary to perform all tasks (Gray, Braver, & Raichle, 2002). Rather, it is largely a question of degree—of both the level of arousal and the complexity of the task. The **Yerkes–Dodson law** puts it this way: The more complex the task, the lower the level of arousal that can be tolerated without interfering with performance. Thus, higher levels of arousal are optimal when one is required to perform simple tasks, and relatively lower levels of arousal are best when performing complex tasks. (see **Figure 6–1.**)

INTRINSIC AND EXTRINSIC MOTIVATION

How can you use intrinsic and extrinsic motivation to help you succeed in your job?

Some psychologists further distinguish between extrinsic and intrinsic motivation. **Extrinsic motivation** refers to motivation that derives from the consequences of an activity. For example, a worker may perform well on the job not because he enjoys it, but because doing so results in a paycheck; and an adult who hates golf may play a round with a client because doing so may help close a sale. **Intrinsic motivation** refers to motivation provided by an activity itself. Play is a good example. People go bowling, play cards, and play video games for no other reason than the fun they get from the activity itself. In the same way, they solve crossword puzzles, learn to knit, or tinker in a workshop largely for the enjoyment they get from the activity. As the opening paragraphs of this chapter describe, knowing what factors—both extrinsic and intrinsic—are motivating to workers helps to shape organizational policies and expectations, a topic discussed more fully in Chapter 11, "Psychology Applied to Work."

Whether behavior is intrinsically or extrinsically motivated can have important consequences. For example, if parents offer a reward to their young daughter for writing to her grandparents, the likelihood of her writing to them when rewards are no longer available may actually decrease. One recent analysis of some 128 studies that examined the effect of extrinsic rewards on the behavior of children, adolescents, and adults found that when extrinsic rewards are offered for a behavior, intrinsic motivation and a sense of personal responsibility for that behavior are likely to decrease, at least for a short time (Deci, Koestner, & Ryan, 1999, 2001). This finding helps explain why workers who are well paid and in secure jobs sometimes feel unmotivated to do their best work.

Figure 6–1

The Yerkes–Dodson law. A certain amount of arousal is needed to perform most tasks, but a very high level of arousal interferes with the performance of complicated activities. That is, the level of arousal that can be tolerated is higher for a simple task than for a complex one.

Source: After Hebb, 1955.

Yerkes–Dodson law States that there is an optimal level of arousal for the best performance of any task; the more complex the task, the lower the level of arousal that can be tolerated before performance deteriorates.

extrinsic motivation A desire to perform a behavior to obtain an external reward or avoid punishment.

intrinsic motivation A desire to perform a behavior that stems from the enjoyment derived from the behavior itself.

flow According to Csikszentmihalyi, a state of mind characterized by complete and consuming focus on an activity that provides a sense of internalized motivation and happiness.

A viewpoint that emphasizes the importance of intrinsic motivation has been advanced by Mihaly Csikszentmihalyi (pronounced "chick-sent-me-high-ee"). According to this perspective, when individuals are able to immerse themselves in an activity that consumes their attention and focuses it on realistic goals, they enter a state that Csikszentmihalyi calls "flow" (Csikszentmihalyi, 1990; 1996).

Flow describes a state of consciousness (see Chapter 3: "Sensation, Perception, and Consciousness") in which a person is completely involved with and focused on a particular activity. Artists who are totally absorbed in the creative process while working on a painting, for example, would be considered to be in a state of flow. When in a state of flow, the person concentrates on the task at hand and forgets about other distractions and projects. Oftentimes, people report that their flow experiences are the most enjoyable and meaningful times of their lives (Csikszentmihalyi, 1990). Flow is not experienced just by those who are involved in the creative arts: It is experienced whenever we are fully absorbed and engaged in any activity that we consciously choose and set as a goal. For example, a bookkeeper who is completely focused on balancing a set of books or a student who is absorbed with writing a paper may also be experiencing the state of flow.

Flow involves several characteristics. When people are experiencing flow, they usually report being completely involved in and focused on a specific task—thus their level of intrinsic motivation is high. They also report experiencing a sense of ecstasy—being completely happy with their present state. Oftentimes, individuals describe their flow experiences as involving a sense of inner clarity and serenity, and they typically report the sense that time is irrelevant. For example, in a state of flow, hours may pass like minutes and the person may be surprised to learn that so much time has passed while working.

A HIERARCHY OF MOTIVES

How does Maslow's theory of motivation organize the various types of human motives?

The concept of flow bears certain similarities to *self-actualization*—the highest level of motivation in Abraham Maslow's (1954) hierarchy of needs theory. According to Maslow, motives can be arranged in a hierarchy, from lower to higher. The lower motives spring from bodily needs that must be satisfied. For example, *physiological needs* include such things as the need for food, water, air, and an environment that is not too hot or too cold. *Safety needs* involves securing an environment that is safe—from danger, from threat, and from the unknown. As we move higher in Maslow's hierarchy of needs (see **Figure 6–2**), the motives have more subtle origins: the desire to feel that we belong to a group, such as our family or our friends (*belongingness*), and the need to make the best possible impression on others and to feel that we are competent (*esteem*). According to Maslow's theory, higher motives emerge only after the more basic ones have been largely satisfied: A person who is starving doesn't care what people think of her table manners. As noted, the highest level of need in Maslow's theory is *self-actualization*—the drive to realize one's full potential.

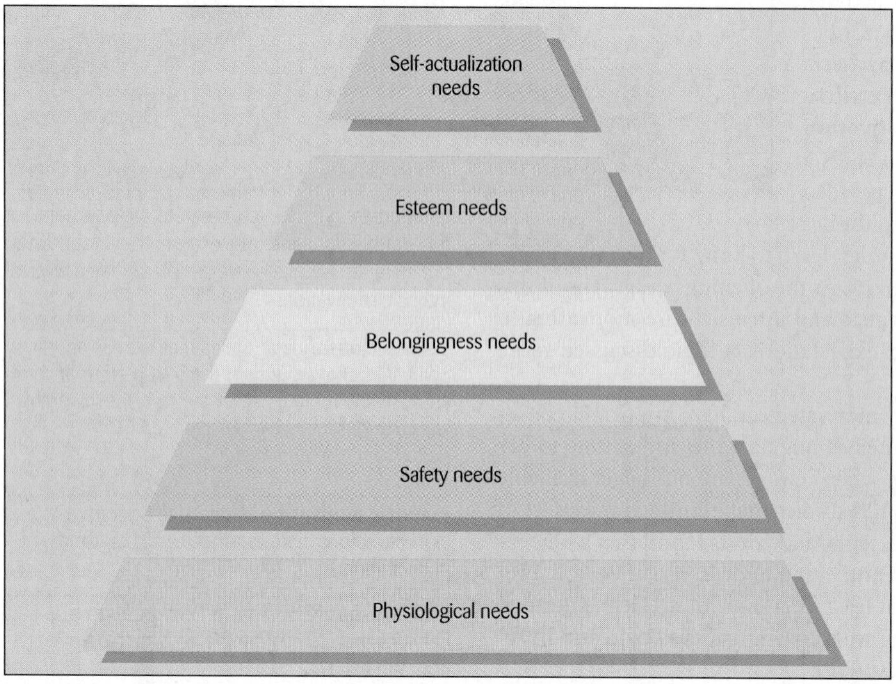

Maslow's model offers an appealing way to organize a wide range of motives into a coherent structure. But recent research challenges the universality of his views. Maslow based his hierarchical model on observations of historical figures, famous living individuals, and even friends whom he admired greatly; however, the majority of these people were white males living

Figure 6–2

A pyramid representing Maslow's hierarchy of needs. From bottom to top, the stages correspond to how fundamental the motive is for survival and how early it appears in both the evolution of the species and the development of the individual. According to Maslow, the more basic needs must largely be satisfied before higher motives can emerge.

Source: After Maslow, 1954.

in Western society. In many simpler societies, people often live on the very edge of survival, yet they form strong and meaningful social ties and possess a firm sense of self-esteem (Neher, 1991).

In fact, difficulty in meeting basic needs can actually foster the satisfaction of higher needs: A couple struggling financially to raise a family may grow closer as a result of the experience. Also, in some cases higher-order needs must be met before lower-order needs can be addressed: Sometimes, for example, we need to feel confident in ourselves (esteem) before we can forge successful relationships with others (belongingness). As a result of such research findings, many psychologists now view Maslow's model with a measure of skepticism, although it continues to be a convenient way to think of the wide range of human motives.

MOTIVATING EMPLOYEES

What theories have been proposed to explain motivation in the work place?

The topic of motivation concerns the question of why individuals behave the way they do. In an organizational context, motivation usually addresses issues related to effort: How can workers be encouraged to do their best work?

Over the years, a variety of theories have been proposed to explain why workers work, and what factors motivate them to give their best. One way of understanding how these theories approach the topic of motivation is to categorize them into groups (Donovan, 2001).

MOTIVATION AS A PERSONALITY TRAIT Several theories suggest that differences in the amount of effort workers expend in their jobs is linked in some way to characteristic patterns of behavior. According to this view, some people are "hard-chargers," "dedicated workers," or "highly competitive in the workplace." Of particular interest to psychologists studying motivation is the personality trait called *conscientiousness,* which has also been described as "the will to achieve" (Digman & Takemoto-Chock, 1981). (See Chapter 8: "Personality, Stress, and Health" for a further discussion of conscientiousness.) Workers with a high level of conscientiousness are not only more attentive to detail and aware of their progress in completing tasks assigned to them, they also are highly ambitious (Barrick & Mount, 1991): They are, in short, more highly motivated.

Theories that view motivation as being linked to one or more personality traits imply that motivational style is a relatively stable characteristic, perhaps of genetic origin. In fact, the fastest growing area of research in human motivation concerns the degree to which motivational differences among individuals stem from basic dispositions or stable personality traits (Mitchell & Daniels, 2003). This view, if correct, has important implications. For example, if motivation is a characteristic of the worker, it should be possible for an organization to hire workers who possess the personal qualities associated with highly motivated behavior (Kanfer & Ackerman, 2000).

REINFORCEMENT THEORY Some motivational theories focus more on the outcomes associated with an employee's work, rather than the personal traits that workers possess. **Reinforcement theory,** which is based on the principles of operant conditioning (see Chapter 4: "Learning and Memory"), has been used to explain how all workers—regardless of their personality traits—can be motivated toward high levels of performance (Komaki, 1986).

According to reinforcement theory, workers' behavior is controlled by outcomes involving reinforcement or punishment. Simply put, when work is followed by positive outcomes (reinforcements), the behaviors that led to these outcomes will be maintained and strengthened; when work is punished, the worker will change the behavior that is associated with punishment. Reinforcement theories suggest that the use of the term, "motivation," merely describes the reinforcement contingencies that control a worker's behavior.

An example of how reinforcement theory can be applied in a production setting is a *piece-rate system* of compensation. In a piece-rate system, workers are paid according to the number of "pieces" they assemble. Thus, a worker who can build 25 pieces in a day will be paid more than one who can build only 20 pieces. A sales commission system, where sales

reinforcement theory Theory based on the principles of operant conditioning which specifies that workers will modify their behavior based on the outcomes that are associated with it.

agents are paid a percentage of the price of the products they sell, is another type of compensation system based on reinforcement theory. According to reinforcement theory, rewards can be used to "motivate" productive behavior.

Can reinforcement theory be applied successfully to organizations? Most research suggests the answer is, "yes." Research that examined the effect of reinforcement-based performance systems over the span of 20 years showed a 17 percent improvement in productivity when reinforcements were used to motivate workers' behavior (Stajkovic & Luthans, 1997). In another study, when reinforcement theory was applied to work settings, more than 90 percent of organizations included in the study were found to experience sustainable improvements in productivity (Komaki, 2003). When workers are paid according to performance, their sense of autonomy and control over their work is enhanced (Eisenberger, Rhoades, & Cameron, 1999).

Although reinforcement theory clearly has advocates, it also poses some challenges (Yukl & Latham, 1975). For example, when workers are paid according to their own individual successes, they may be reluctant to participate in activities that require cooperation with others. Such "pay-for-performance" systems can encourage competitive behavior, which, at the extreme, may involve sabotage of co-workers' efforts and an overall decline in work place productivity. Also, some people question the ethics of systems that equate results to rewards without considering individual differences in abilities. In any situation, some individuals will not be able to produce as much work as others are capable of, and the self-concept of workers who are not able to produce at high levels may suffer in performance-based systems. The impact of placing workers in highly stressful, competitive work environments must be considered when evaluating the desirability of reinforcement-based motivational approaches (see Chapter 11: "Psychology Applied to Work"). Others criticize reinforcement theories as being too mechanistic, noting that humans do not simply respond like robots to rewards and punishments; they also think about their situations, often in complex ways.

COGNITIVE THEORIES OF MOTIVATION Cognitive-based theories of motivation emphasize how workers' beliefs about the work place influence their attitudes and behaviors. In cognitive theories of motivation, how workers think about their jobs is of central importance. Three cognitive views that have received considerable attention from psychologists are equity theory, expectancy theory, and goal setting theory.

Equity theory holds that individual workers monitor two key features of the work place: the amount of effort they and their co-workers expend on the job, and the rewards that they and their co-workers receive for this effort. In the simplest case, equity theory predicts that when workers believe they are expending equal amounts of effort, they should benefit from equal levels of reward. Motivation to work hard depends on the worker's sense of fairness, or *equity*. When workers are either over-rewarded or under-rewarded relative to their co-workers, their motivation suffers and they will decrease the quality or quantity of work they produce correspondingly.

Equity theory is appealing because it describes a motivational process that many people have experienced firsthand. Perhaps you have worked at a job in which you expended a large measure of effort, but were not appropriately rewarded for your hard work. Such a situation is particularly aggravating when co-workers do less, but receive greater rewards. These are inequitable situations, and equity theory predicts that under-rewarded workers will reduce their level of motivation in order to re-establish an equitable situation where low rewards are matched with low effort.

Expectancy theory also emphasizes the cognitive processes workers use in evaluating their level of effort and the rewards they receive. However, in expectancy theory, the comparison we make is not to how our own effort and rewards compare to those of others, but rather is centered on how we view the connection between our own behavior and the likelihood of attaining desired rewards. According to expectancy theory, individuals are aware of the value of work-related rewards, and they also are aware of how their behavior on the job is connected with attaining those rewards. Based on their assessment of the value of the rewards they seek and of the degree to which they expect they can attain those rewards by working harder, they will expend the corresponding amount of effort on the job (Vroom,

equity theory Theory of motivation that emphasizes the belief that effort expended should match rewards received for work.

expectancy theory Theory of motivation that emphasizes workers' awareness of the value of work-related rewards and of how their behaviors are linked to receiving those rewards.

SUMMARY TABLE

THEORIES OF WORK PLACE MOTIVATION

THEORY	SOURCE OF MOTIVATION
Personality Trait Theory	Individuals differ in the basic personality traits they possess, and some traits, such as conscientiousness, are directly related to work place motivation and effort.
Reinforcement Theory	Based on principles of operant conditioning; motivated behavior is maintained by making rewards contingent on work performance.
Equity Theory	Workers monitor the effort and rewards they and co-workers expend and receive and they will increase or decrease their effort in order to achieve fairness, or equity.
Expectancy Theory	Workers are aware of the rewards provided for work and of the link between their effort and the attainment of these rewards. When rewards are valued and effort is clearly linked to attaining them, motivation is high.
Goal Theory	Motivation is maximized when work goals are clearly stated and work place behavior is clearly linked to the attainment of goals; similar to expectancy theory but with an emphasis on explicitly stated work goals.

1964; Van Eerde & Thierry, 1996). For example, if workers attach high value to a promotion, and if they believe that through hard work they will be promoted, this *expectancy* will serve to motivate them to perform at a high level. Conversely, if the rewards offered on the job are not perceived by workers to be valuable (a worker does not want a promotion), or if workers do not believe that their efforts will result in the attainment of valued rewards (a worker believes that no amount of effort will result in a promotion), motivation will diminish and effort with not be expended.

Goal-setting theory emphasizes the role that clearly articulated, formally stated goals can have on motivation. When goals are clearly stated, and when workers believe that their efforts on the job will lead to the attainment of these goals, their behavior will be highly motivated toward meeting the goals (Locke & Latham, 2002). Many people apply goal setting theory in their own lives. For example, you may work extra hours at a second part-time job in order to reach the goal of buying a car or paying the rent on a new apartment. The keys in goal-setting theory are (1) to identify clearly stated, appropriate, attainable goals, and (2) to clearly communicate to workers what they need to do to reach those goals. A summary of these work-related theories of motivation is presented in "**Summary Table: Theories of Work Place Motivation.**"

► CHECK YOUR UNDERSTANDING

Match the following terms with the appropriate definition.

1. _____ drive
2. _____ drive reduction
3. _____ homeostasis
4. _____ instinct
5. _____ intrinsic motivation
6. _____ extrinsic motivation
7. _____ flow
8. The personality trait most closely linked to motivation is _____.
9. If real estate sales agents are paid a percentage of the selling price for the houses they sell, the theory of motivation being used to encourage their work is_____theory.

a. inborn, inflexible, goal directed behavior that characterizes all members of a species
b. state of balance in which the organism functions effectively
c. theory that motivated behavior is focused on reducing bodily tension
d. tending to perform behavior to receive some external reward or avoid punishment
e. state of tension brought on by biological needs
f. motivation arising from behavior itself
g. state of mind characterized by complete focus on an activity

Answers: 1. e, 2. c, 3. b, 4. a, 5. f, 6. d, 7. g, 8. conscientiousness, 9. reinforcement theory

goal-setting theory Theory of motivation that emphasizes that when goals are clearly stated, and when workers believe that their efforts on the job will lead to the attainment of these goals, their behavior will be highly motivated toward meeting the goals.

1. You are home alone and have nothing to do. You find yourself walking around. You look for something to read, but nothing seems quite right. Then you check to see if anything interesting is on TV, but again nothing seems worth watching. Finally, you decide to go jogging. This kind of motivated behavior that increases the state of arousal is most difficult to explain using
   a. the instinct theory of motivation
   b. the concept of intrinsic motivation
   c. the drive-reduction theory of motivation
   d. the Yerkes–Dodson law

2. While you are working on a complex task, your boss stops by your desk and says, "You've only got 10 more minutes to finish that up. It's really important that it be done right. I know you can do it and I'm depending on you." When you complain that he's mak-ing you nervous and your performance will suffer, he replies, "I'm just trying to motivate you." Which of the following does your boss apparently not understand?
   a. drive-reduction theory
   b. homeostasis
   c. extrinsic motivation
   d. the Yerkes–Dodson law

3. Renee tells her roommate that she is dissatisfied at work because she works harder than her co-workers but is paid at the same rate. The motivational theory that most directly addresses Renee's complaint is:
   a. drive-reduction theory
   b. goal-setting theory
   c. equity theory
   d. expectancy theory

Answers: 1. c, 2. d, 3. c.

Hunger and Thirst

6.2 Desribe how both internal biological factors and external social and cultural factors are involved in the regulation of thirst and hunger.

The motivational theories described in the preceding section emphasize several basic concepts that pertain to motivation as a general construct. However, psychologists also are concerned with specific motives that are important aspects of human behavior. Foremost among these are the specific motives of hunger and thirst.

Hunger is a psychological state that usually leads us to eat, thereby satisfying our biological need to consume the food necessary for survival. Hunger, however, is influenced by factors in addition to our biological needs. Sometimes we feel hungry when we smell a delicious food cooking, even when our stomachs are full. Sometimes, too, we need to eat, but feel no hunger—for example, if we are emotionally upset. Thus, hunger results from a combination of biological and psychological forces.

Similar to hunger, *thirst* is stimulated by both internal and external cues. Internally, thirst is controlled by two regulators that monitor the level of fluids inside and outside the cells. Both regulators stimulate thirst when fluid levels are too low. Just as we become hungry in response to external cues, the experience of thirst can also be affected by environmental factors (W. G. Hall, Arnold, & Myers, 2000; Rowland, 2002). We may get thirsty when we see a TV commercial featuring people savoring tall, cool drinks in a lush, tropical setting. Seasonal customs and weather conditions also affect our thirst-quenching habits: Ice-cold lemonade is a summer staple, whereas hot chocolate warms cold winter nights.

BIOLOGICAL FACTORS INVOLVED IN HUNGER

How is the brain involved in hunger?

Because hunger is a topic of considerable interest and concern to many people, we will focus our attention on this basic drive. Early research established the importance of the hypothalamus as the brain center involved in hunger and eating. Initially, researchers identified two regions in the hypothalamus as controlling our experience of hunger and satiety (*satiety* means being full to satisfaction). One of these centers appeared to act as the feeding center because when it was stimulated, animals began to eat. When it was destroyed, the animals stopped eating to the point of starvation. Another area of the hypothalamus was thought to be the satiety center: When it was stimulated, animals stopped eating; when it was destroyed, animals ate to the point of extreme obesity. The hypothalamus seemed to be a kind of "switch" that turned eating on or off, at least in rats.

More recent studies, however, have challenged this simple "on–off" explanation for the control of eating by showing that a number of other areas of the brain are also involved (Winn, 1995). A third center in the hypothalamus appears to influence the drive to eat specific foods. Studies have also shown that regions of the cortex and spinal cord play an important role in regulating food intake. Moreover, the connections among brain centers that control hunger are now known to be considerably more complex than were once thought—involving more than a dozen different neurotransmitters (Flier & Maratos-Flier, 1998; Woods, Seeley, Porte, & Schwartz, 1998). Some of these neurotransmitters act to increase the consumption of specific foods such as carbohydrates or fats, whereas others suppress the appetite for these foods (Blundell & Halford, 1998; Lin, Umahara, York, & Bray, 1998).

How do these various areas of the brain know when to stimulate hunger? It turns out that the brain monitors the blood levels of glucose (a simple sugar used by the body for energy), fats, carbohydrates, and insulin. Changes in the blood levels of these substances signal the need for food (Seeley & Schwartz, 1997). The presence of a particular hormone, leptin, also influences our desire to eat (Chua et al., 1996; Holtkamp et al., 2003; Leroy et al., 1996; Ravussin et al., 1997; Vaisse et al., 1996). Fat cells within our body produce leptin that travels in the bloodstream and is sensed by the hypothalamus. High levels of leptin signal the brain to reduce appetite, or to increase the rate at which fat is burned.

The brain also monitors the amount and kind of food that has been eaten. Receptors in the stomach sense not only how much food the stomach is holding, but also how many calories that food contains. Signals from these receptors travel to the brain. When food enters the small intestine, a hormone is released into the bloodstream and carried to the brain, where it serves as an additional source of information about the body's nutritional needs (Albus, 1989; Takaki, Nagai, Takaki, & Yanaihara, 1990).

How and when you satisfy hunger and thirst depends on social, psychological, environmental, and cultural influences as well as on physiological needs. For example, the Japanese tea ceremony is concerned more with restoring inner harmony than with satisfying thirst.

EXTERNAL HUNGER CUES

How can external cues influence our desire to eat?

As we noted earlier, a biological need for food is not always directly tied to hunger. One external factor that sometimes is involved is previous learning, especially classical conditioning (see Chapter 4: "Learning and Memory"). The smell of a cake baking in the oven, for example, may trigger the desire to eat whether the body needs fuel or not. Sometimes just looking at the clock and realizing that it is dinnertime can make us feel hungry. One intriguing line of research suggests that such external cues may set off internal biological processes that mimic those associated with the need for food. For example, the mere sight, smell, or thought of food causes an increase in insulin production, which, in turn, lowers glucose levels in the body's cells, mirroring the body's response to a physical need for food (Rodin, 1985). Thus, the aroma from a nearby restaurant may serve as more than an **incentive** to eat; it may actually trigger an apparent need for food.

How you respond when you are hungry will vary according to your experiences with food, which are mostly governed by learning and social conditioning. The majority of Americans eat three meals a day at regular intervals. A typical American family eats breakfast at 7 A.M., lunch around noon, and dinner about 6 P.M. But in Europe, people often have dinner much later in the evening. Italians, for example, rarely eat dinner before 9 P.M. Numerous studies with both humans and animals have shown that regularly eating at particular times during the day leads to the release at those times of the hormones and neurotransmitters that cause hunger (Woods, Schwartz, Baskin, & Seeley, 2000). In other words, we get hungry around noon partly because the body "learns" that if it's noon, it's time to eat.

Social situations also affect our motivation to eat. Say that you are at an important business lunch where you need to impress a prospective client. You may not feel very hungry, even though this lunch is taking place an hour past your usual lunchtime. Conversely, social

incentive External stimulus that prompts goal-directed behavior.

situations may prompt you to eat even when you are not hungry. Imagine that on a day when you have slept late and eaten a large breakfast, you visit friends. When you arrive, you discover that a wonderful meal is being served in a few minutes. Although you are not at all hungry, you may decide to eat merely out of courtesy. Recent research also shows that people tend to eat more when they are with other people, especially if those other people are eating a lot (Herman, Roth, & Polivy, 2003).

The hunger drive also is tied to emotions, often in complex ways. Some people head for the refrigerator whenever they are depressed, bored, anxious, or angry. Others lose all interest in food at these times and complain that they are "too upset to eat." One student studying for an important exam spends as much time eating as reading; another student studying for the same exam lives on coffee until the exam is over. Under emotionally arousing conditions, what one person craves may turn another person's stomach. Culture also influences what we choose to eat and how much. Although most Americans will not eat horsemeat, it is very popular in some European countries. Yet many Americans consume pork, which violates both Islamic and Jewish dietary laws (Scupin, 1995). So, although hunger is basically a biological drive, it is not merely an internal state that we satisfy when our body tells us to. Hunger is the product of the complex interaction of both environmental and biological forces.

EATING DISORDERS AND OBESITY

What factors define and are involved in the common eating disorders of anorexia, bulimia, and obesity?

The importance of non-biological factors is especially apparent when explaining various types of eating disorders. In cases of *anorexia nervosa* and *bulimia nervosa*, individuals become overly concerned about eating too much food, and they attempt to regulate the amount of food they consume, either by severely restricting the amount they eat or by excessive binge eating followed by purging. In cases involving obesity, individuals consume more food than their bodies can metabolize without excessive weight gain. Both eating disorders and obesity pose problems for many people living in the United States and in developing nations around the world.

ANOREXIA NERVOSA AND BULIMIA NERVOSA "When people told me I looked like someone from Auschwitz [the Nazi concentration camp], I thought that was the highest compliment anyone could give me." This confession comes from a young woman who as a teenager suffered from a serious eating disorder known as **anorexia nervosa**. She was 18 years old, 5 feet 3 inches tall, and weighed 68 pounds. This young woman was lucky. She managed to overcome the disorder and has since maintained normal body weight. Others are less fortunate. The world-class gymnast Christy Henrich succumbed to the disease, weighing just 61 pounds at her death (Pace, 1994).

People with anorexia nervosa perceive themselves as overweight and strive to lose weight, usually by severely limiting their intake of food. Even after they become very thin, they constantly worry about weight gain. The following four symptoms are used in the diagnosis of anorexia nervosa (APA, 1994):

1. Intense fear of becoming obese, which does not diminish as weight loss progresses.
2. Disturbance of body image (for example, claiming to "feel fat" even when emaciated).
3. Refusal to maintain body weight at or above a minimal normal weight for age and height.
4. In females, the absence of at least three consecutive menstrual cycles.

Approximately 1 percent of all adolescents suffer from anorexia nervosa; about 90 percent of these are white upper- or middle-class females (Rosenvinge, Borgen, & Boerresen, 1999). Generally, people suffering from anorexia enjoy an otherwise normal childhood and adolescence. They are usually successful students and cooperative, well-behaved children. They have an intense interest in food, but view eating with disgust. They also have a very distorted view of their own body (Grant, Kim, & Eckert, 2002), although this characteristic is less prevalent among African-American woman with this disorder (White, Kohlmaier, Varnado, & Williamson, 2003).

anorexia nervosa A serious eating disorder that is associated with an intense fear of weight gain and a distorted body image.

Anorexia is frequently compounded by another eating disorder known as **bulimia nervosa** (Fairburn & Wilson, 1993; O'Brien & Vincent, 2003). The following criteria are used for the diagnosis of bulimia nervosa (APA, 1994):

1. Recurrent episodes of binge eating (rapid consumption of a large amount of food, usually in less than two hours).

2. Recurrent inappropriate behaviors to try to prevent weight gain, such as self-induced vomiting or excessive use of laxatives.

3. The binge eating and compensatory behaviors must occur at least twice a week for three months.

4. Body shape and weight excessively influence the person's self-image.

5. These types of behavior occur at least sometimes in the absence of anorexia.

Approximately 1 to 2 percent of all adolescent females suffer from bulimia nervosa (Gotesdam & Agras, 1995). The binge-eating behavior usually begins at about age 18, when adolescents are facing the challenge of new life situations. Not surprisingly, residence on a college campus is associated with a higher incidence of bulimia (Squire, 1983). The socio-economic group at high risk for bulimia—again, primarily upper-middle- and upper-class women—is highly represented on college campuses.

Does the American obsession with super-slimness lead adolescents to become anorexic?

Although anorexia and bulimia are apparently much more prevalent among females than males (S. Turnbull, Ward, Treasure, Jick, & Derby, 1996), many more men are affected by these disorders than was once suspected (Al Dawi, 2002; Tanofsky, Wilfley, Spurrell, Welch, & Brownell, 1997). For example, in a 1992 survey of people who had graduated from Harvard University in 1982, reported cases of eating disorders had dropped by half for women over the decade, but had doubled for men (Seligman, Rogers, & Annin, 1994). Interestingly, a related phenomenon called *muscle dysmorphia* appears to be on the increase among young men (Pope, 2000). Muscle dysmorphia is an obsessive concern with one's muscle size. Men with muscle dysmorphia, many of whom are well-muscled, are distressed at their perceived puniness, and spend an inordinate amount of time fretting over their diet and exercising to increase their muscle mass (Leit, Gray, & Pope, 2002).

Because studies of eating disorders have focused almost entirely on females, we know very little about what might predispose an adolescent male to develop such a disorder. Among adolescent women, several factors appear likely (Brooks–Gunn, 1993; Bruch, 2001). The media promote the idea that a woman must be thin to be attractive (Crandall, 1994). How often have you seen a fashion magazine cover feature a well-proportioned woman of normal weight for her height? Perhaps because of this emphasis on thinness, American women are prone to overestimate their body size (Bruch, 1980; Fallon & Rozin, 1985). One study found that over 95 percent of the female participants believed they were about 25 percent larger than they actually were in the waist, thighs, and hips (Thompson & Thompson, 1986).

Psychological factors also contribute to the risk of eating disorders (Walters & Kendler, 1995; Zonnevylle–Bender, 2004). Women with bulimia commonly have low self-esteem, and they often are hypersensitive to social interactions (Steiger, Gauvin, Jabalpurwala, Seguin, & Stotland, 1999). Many have experienced some form of clinical depression or obsessive–compulsive disorder (see Chapter 9, "Psychological Disorders and Their Treatments") prior to the development of the eating disorder (Klingenspor, 1994; Phelps & Bajorek, 1991; Wade, Bulik, Neale, & Kendler, 2000). Feelings of vulnerability and helplessness apparently dispose many people to adopt inappropriate strategies for one area where they can exercise control—their own eating habits.

Finally, there is growing evidence that genetics plays a role in both anorexia nervosa and bulimia nervosa, although the two eating disorders may have a very different genetic basis (Jacobi, Hayward, de Zwaan, Kraemer, & Agras, 2004; Keel & Klump, 2003).

Anorexia and bulimia are notoriously hard to treat, and there is considerable disagreement on the most effective approach to therapy (BenTovim, 2003; Fairburn, Cooper, & Shafran, 2003; Russell, 2004). In fact, some psychologists doubt that we can ever eliminate eating disorders in a culture bombarded with the message that "thin is in." Regrettably, in many developing countries such as Taiwan, Singapore, and China, where dieting is becoming a fad, eating disorders, once little known, are now becoming a serious problem (Hsu, 1996; Lee, Chan, & Hsu, 2003).

bulimia nervosa An eating disorder characterized by binges of eating followed by self-induced vomiting or the excessive use of laxatives.

OBESITY According to the U.S. Surgeon General, obesity is the most pressing health problem in America today (Johnson, 2003). *Obesity* refers to an excess of body fat in relation to lean body mass, while *overweight* refers to weighing more than a desirable standard, whether from high amounts of fat or being very muscular. Obesity has increased by more than 50 percent during the last decade, with more than two-thirds of Americans being either overweight or obese. In contrast to anorexia nervosa and bulimia nervosa, obesity is more prevalent among poor black women than among white women with higher incomes (White, Kohlmaier, Varnado, & Williamson, 2003).

Even more disturbing, the rate of obesity among young people has more than tripled since 1980, with over 9 million overweight adolescents in America today. This problem is particularly serious because children and adolescents who are overweight are more likely to grow up to become overweight adults who are at an increased risk for serious diseases such as hypertension, cardiovascular disease, diabetes, and sleep apnea (Nishimura et al., 2003).

Many factors contribute to overeating and obesity (Fairburn & Brownell, 2002). Some people inherit a tendency to be overweight (Bulik, Sullivan, & Kendler, 2003; Yanovski & Yanovski, 2002). Children born to two obese parents are seven times more likely to become obese than children born to parents of normal weight. A sedentary life style contributes to the problem. U.S. children today are more likely to watch television and play video games than play tag or dodgeball, and many adults lack physical activity, too. Abundant opportunities and encouragement to overeat in American culture are also factors. Portion size has increased in recent years, as has the constant availability of food from vending machines and fast-food restaurants.

Adding to the medical difficulties that accompany obesity, overweight people often face ridicule and discrimination, resulting in significant economic, social, and educational loss (Waite, 1995). Despite federal laws prohibiting employment bias against people who are overweight, studies have shown they are nevertheless discriminated against in school and in the workplace. For example, in one study overweight women reported feelings of lowered self-confidence and being victimized in school and at work because of their weight (Rothblum, Brand, Miller, & Oetjen, 1990). In another study, obese male lawyers were found to earn less than male lawyers of normal weight (Saporta & Halpern, 2002). Thus, it is not surprising that men and women who are overweight are more likely to be plagued by feelings of lowered self-esteem and helplessness (Johnson, 2002). Even children who are overweight display increased rates of behavior problems, including aggression, lack of discipline, immaturity, anxiety, and depression, when compared with their normal-weight peers (Yang & Chen, 2001).

With all of the problems associated with being overweight, it is not surprising that so many people are constantly trying to lose weight. There are no quick fixes for weight loss, but the suggestions in "**Understanding Ourselves: The Slow but Lasting Fix for Weight Control**," can help people lose weight and keep it off.

▶ **CHECK YOUR UNDERSTANDING**

1. The levels of _____ and the hormone _____ in the blood signals hunger.
2. Hunger can be stimulated by both _____ and _____ cues.

Match the following terms with the appropriate definition.

3. _____ hypothalamus
4. _____ anorexia nervosa
5. _____ bulimia nervosa

a. recurrent episodes of binge eating, followed by vomiting, taking laxatives, or excessively exercising
b. contains both a hunger center and a satiety center
c. intense fear of obesity, disturbance of body image, and very little intake of food, with resulting weight well below normal minimums

Answers: 1. glucose, leptin, 2. internal, external, 3. b, 4. c, 5. a.

▶ APPLY YOUR UNDERSTANDING

1. You are on your way to an important business meeting, and you notice that you are hungry. While you are at the meeting, you no longer feel hungry. But when the meeting is over, you notice that you are hungry again. This demonstrates that
   a. the biological need for food causes hunger
   b. if you are distracted, primary drives but not secondary drives will decrease
   c. hunger does not necessarily correspond to a biological need for food
   d. primary drives are unlearned and are essential to survival of the individual or species

2. You've noticed that when you are hungry, eating a carrot doesn't satisfy you, but eating a chocolate bar does. This is probably because the chocolate bar, to a greater extent than the carrot,
   a. increases the amount of glucose in your bloodstream, which in turn reduces hunger
   b. reduces your biological need for food
   c. represents a higher level in Maslow's hierarchy of motives
   d. serves as an incentive

Answers: 1. c, 2. a.

[UNDERSTANDING OURSELVES]

THE SLOW (BUT LASTING) FIX FOR WEIGHT CONTROL

The study of hunger and eating has led to some interesting insights into the problem of weight control. It appears that our bodies are genetically "set" to maintain a certain weight (Bennett & Gurin, 1982). Thus, according to this *set point theory*, if you consume more calories than you need for that weight, your metabolic rate will go up, and you will feel an increase in energy that will prompt you to be more active, thereby burning more calories. If you eat fewer calories than you need for your weight, your metabolic rate will go down, and you will feel tired and become less active, thereby burning fewer calories. This mechanism was no doubt helpful during the thousands of years that our species lived literally hand to mouth, but it is less helpful where food is abundant, as in modern industrialized nations.

An implication of our current understanding of hunger and weight regulation is that a successful weight-control program must be long term and must work with, rather than against, the body's normal tendency to maintain weight. It should be undertaken only after consultation with a doctor. On the basis of studies of the hunger drive and the relationship between eating and body weight, here is our formula for weight control:

1. First, check with your doctor before you start. People want quick fixes, so they often go overboard on dieting or exercise, sometimes with disastrous consequences. Make sure your weight loss program will be safe.

2. Increase your body's metabolism through regular exercise. The most effective metabolism raiser is 20–30 minutes of moderate activity several times a week. Only about 200–300 calories are burned off during each exercise session (Craighead, 1990), but the exercise increases the resting metabolic rate. This means that you burn more calories when not exercising. Thus, exercise is an important part of a weight reduction program (Wadden et al., 1997).

3. Modify your diet. A moderate reduction in calories is beneficial. Also, reduce your consumption of fats (particularly saturated fats) and sugars. Sugars trigger an increase in the body's level of insulin, and high levels of fat and insulin in the blood stimulate hunger.

4. Reduce external cues that encourage you to eat undesirable foods. The mere sight or smell of food can increase the amount of insulin in the body, thus triggering hunger. Many people find that if they do their grocery shopping on a full stomach, it is easier to resist the temptation to buy junk foods.

5. Set realistic goals. Focus at least as much on preventing weight gain as on losing weight. If you must lose weight, try to shed just one pound a week for two or three months, then concentrate on maintaining that new, lower weight for several months before moving on to further weight loss.

6. Reward yourself—in ways unrelated to food—for small improvements. Use some of the behavior-modification techniques described in Chapter 5: Reward yourself not only for each pound of weight lost but also for each day or week that you maintain that weight loss. And remember, the only way you can keep the weight off is by continuing to adhere to a reasonable diet and exercise plan (Abdel, 2003; McGuire, Wing, Klem, Lang, & Hill, 1999).

To learn more about weight control visit our Web site at www.prenhall.com/morris.

Sex

6.3 Explain how biological forces and environmental factors are involved in sexual motivations, sexual behaviors, and homosexuality.

Sex is the primary drive that motivates reproductive behavior. Similar to the other primary drives, it can be turned on and off by biological conditions in the body and by environmental cues. The human sexual response is also affected by social experience, sexual experience, nutrition, emotions (particularly feelings about one's sex partner), and age. In fact, just thinking about or having fantasies about sex can lead to sexual arousal in humans (Laan, Everaerd, van Berlo, & Rijs, 1995; Leitenberg & Henning, 1995). Sex differs from other primary drives in one important way: Hunger and thirst are vital to the survival of the individual, but sex is vital only to the survival of the species. The sex drive, like hunger, is the result of both biological and environmental factors.

BIOLOGICAL, CULTURAL, AND ENVIRONMENTAL FACTORS

Is sexual behavior more the result of biological urges or of cultural and environmental factors?

Biology clearly plays a major role in sexual motivation. In fact, early in the twentieth century, the level of hormones such as *testosterone*—the male sex hormone—was believed to *determine* sex drive. Today, scientists recognize that hormonal influences on human sexual arousal are considerably more complex. Testosterone does play a role in early sexual development (such as the onset of puberty), in differentiating male and female sex organs during prenatal development and, to some extent, in establishing characteristic patterns of adult sexual behavior (Kalat, 1988). But moment-to-moment fluctuations in testosterone levels are not necessarily linked to sex drive. In fact, adult males who have been castrated (resulting in a significant decrease in testosterone levels) often report little decrease in sex drive (Persky, 1983). Unlike lower animals, whose sexual activity is largely controlled by hormones and is tied to the female's reproductive cycle, humans are capable of sexual arousal at any time.

Many animals secrete substances called *pheromones* that promote sexual readiness in potential partners. (See Chapter 3: "Sensation, Perception, and Conscious Experience.") Some indirect evidence suggests that humans, too, secrete pheromones in the sweat glands of the armpits and in the genitals and that these may influence human sexual attraction (Lundstrom, Goncalves, Esteyes, & Olsson, 2003; Thornhill & Gangestad, 1999; Wedeking, Seebeck, Bettens, & Paepke, 1995). The brain also exerts a powerful influence on the sex drive. In particular, the limbic system, located deep within the brain, is involved in sexual excitement. (See Chapter 2, "Biological Basis of Behavior"; Heath, 1972; Hyden, 1982.)

The biology of sexual behavior is better understood than the mechanism of the sex drive itself. Sex researchers William Masters and Virginia Johnson long ago identified a *sexual response cycle* that consists of four phases: *excitement, plateau, orgasm,* and *resolution* (Masters & Johnson, 1966). In the *excitement phase,* the genitals become engorged with blood. In the male, this causes erection of the penis; in the female, it causes erection of the clitoris and nipples. This engorgement of the sexual organs continues into the *plateau phase,* in which sexual tension levels off. During this phase, breathing becomes more rapid and genital secretions and muscle tension increase. During *orgasm,* the male ejaculates, and the woman's uterus contracts rhythmically, and both men and women experience some loss of muscle control. The *resolution phase* is one of relaxation in which muscle tension decreases and the engorged genitals return to normal. Heart rate, breathing, and blood pressure also return to normal. **Figure 6–3** displays the pattern of sexual responses for men and women.

Although hormones and the nervous system do figure in the sex drive, human sexual motivation, especially in the early stages of excitement and arousal, is much more dependent on experience and learning than on biology. What kind of stimuli activate the sex drive? It need not be anything as immediate as a sexual partner. The thought of one's lover, as well as the smell of perfume or after-shave lotion, can stimulate sexual excitement. People respond differently, however, to environmental cues. One person may be unmoved by

The stimuli that trigger sexual interest and arousal are often heavily dependent on culture. Do you find that body piercings and tattoos increase or decrease the sexual attractiveness of others?

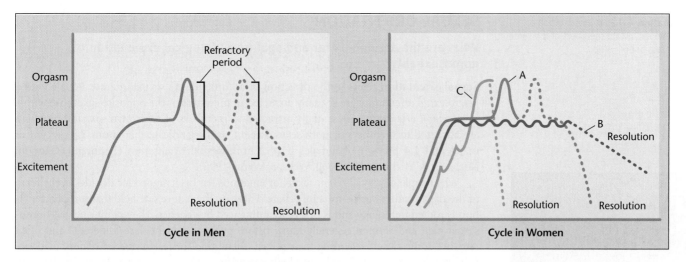

Cycle in Men

Cycle in Women

Figure 6–3

The sexual response cycle in males and females. As the illustration shows, males typically go through one complete response cycle and are then capable of becoming excited again after a refractory period. Females have three characteristic patterns: one similar to the male cycle, with the added possibility of multiple orgasms (A); one that includes a lengthy plateau phase with no orgasm (B); and a rapid cycle including several increases and decreases of excitement before reaching orgasm (C).

Source: Adapted from Masters & Johnson, *Human Sexual Response* 1966. Reprinted by permission of The Masters and Johnson Institute.

an explicit pornographic movie, but aroused by a romantic love story, whereas another may respond in just the opposite way. Ideas about what is moral, appropriate, and pleasurable also influence our sexual behavior.

Just as society dictates standards for sexual conduct, culture guides our views of sexual attractiveness. Culture and experience may influence the extent to which we find particular articles of clothing or body shapes sexually arousing (Furnham, McClelland, & Omar, 2003). In some cultures, most men prefer women with very large breasts, but in other cultures, small and delicate breasts are preferred. Among some African cultures, elongated earlobes are considered very attractive. In our own culture, what we find attractive often depends on the styles of the time.

PATTERNS OF SEXUAL BEHAVIOR AMONG AMERICANS

What constitutes a "typical" sexual response?

Contrary to media portrayals of sexual behavior in publications such as *Playboy* or TV shows like *Sex in the City*, which depict Americans as oversexed and unwilling to commit to long-term relationships, research indicates that most people are far more conservative in their sex lives. One carefully designed study (Michael, Gagnon, Laumann, & Kolata, 1994) of 3,480 randomly selected people between the ages of 18 and 59 revealed the following patterns in the sexual activity of American men and women:

- About one-third of those sampled had sex twice a week or more, one-third a few times a month, and the remaining third a few times a year or not at all.
- The overwhelming majority of respondents did not engage in "kinky" sex. Instead, vaginal intercourse was the preferred form of sex for over 90 percent of those sampled. Interestingly, watching their partner undress was ranked second, and oral sex third.
- Married couples reported having sex more often, and being more satisfied with their sex lives, than did unmarried persons.
- The average duration of sexual intercourse reported by most people was roughly 15 minutes.
- The median number of partners over the lifetime for males was six and for females two (17 percent of the men and 3 percent of the women reported having sex with over 20 partners).
- About 25 percent of the men and 15 percent of the women had committed adultery.

Extensive research has also documented at least four significant differences in sexuality between American men and women: Men are more interested in sex than are women; women are more likely than men to link sex to a close, committed relationship; aggression, power, dominance, and assertiveness are more closely linked to sex among men than among women; and women's sexuality is more malleable (more open to change over time and more closely associated with such things as level of education and religion) (Peplau, 2003).

sexual orientation Refers to the direction of one's sexual interest toward members of the same sex, the other sex, or both sexes.

Homosexual activity is common among animals. For example, male giraffes often engage in extreme necking, entwining, and rubbing, becoming sexually aroused as they do.

SEXUAL ORIENTATION

What are the arguments for and against a biological explanation of homosexuality?

Sexual orientation refers to the direction of an individual's sexual interest. People with a *heterosexual orientation* are sexually attracted to members of the opposite sex; those with a *homosexual orientation* are sexually attracted to members of their own sex; and *bisexuals* are attracted to members of both sexes. Recent studies indicate that about 2.8 percent of males and 1.4 percent of females have a homosexual orientation (Laumann, Gagnon, Michaels, & Michaels, 1994; Sell, Wells, & Wypij, 1995).

Why people display different sexual orientations has been argued for decades in the form of the classic nature-versus-nurture debate. Those on the nature side hold that sexual orientation is rooted in biology and is primarily influenced by genetics. They point out that homosexual men and women generally know before puberty that they are "different" and often remain "in the closet" regarding their sexual orientation for fear of recrimination. Evidence from family and twin studies shows a higher incidence of male homosexuality in families with other gay men, and a higher rate of homosexuality among men with a homosexual twin even when the twins were raised separately (LeVay & Hamer, 1994). Moreover, they contend if homosexuality were the result of early learning and socialization, children raised by gay or lesbian parents would be more likely to become homosexual. Research, however, has clearly demonstrated that this is not the case (Patterson, 2000). The nature position also derives some support from studies suggesting differences between the brains of homosexual and heterosexual men (Allen & Gorski, 1992; LeVay, 1991; Swaab & Hoffman, 1995).

It is interesting to note that among other animals, homosexual activity seems to occur with some degree of regularity. For example, among pygmy chimpanzees, about 50 percent of all observed sexual activity is between members of the same sex. Even male giraffes commonly entwine their necks until both become sexually stimulated. And among some birds, such as greylag geese, homosexual unions have been found to last up to 15 years (Bagemihl, 2000).

Those on the nurture side argue that sexual orientation is primarily a learned behavior, influenced by early experience and largely under voluntary control. They criticize research supporting the biological position as methodologically flawed—sometimes confusing what causes homosexuality with what results from homosexuality (Byne, 1994). Also, they contend that early socialization determines sexual orientation. Moreover, they find support for their position from cross-cultural studies that show sexual orientations occurring at different frequencies in various cultures.

To date, neither the biological nor the socialization theory has provided a completely satisfactory explanation for the origin of sexual orientation. As with most complex behaviors, a more likely explanation probably involves a combination of these two forces (Garnets, 2002; Kelley & Dawson, 1994).

▶ **CHECK YOUR UNDERSTANDING**

1. The sex drive is necessary for the survival of the (individual/species).
2. The four stages of the sexual response cycle are _____, _____, _____, and _____.

Match the following terms with the appropriate definitions.

3. _____ pheromones
4. _____ testosterone
5. _____ limbic system

a. brain center involved in sexual excitement
b. hormone that influences some aspects of sexual development
c. scents that may cause sexual attraction

Answers: 1. species, 2. excitement, plateau, orgasm, and resolution, 3. c, 4. b, 5. a.

1. Barbie has just "come out" to her friend Ken, telling him that she is a lesbian. She says she has known since she was a child that she was different from other girls because she was never attracted to boys, and she has concluded that this is just the way she is meant to be. Ken's reaction, however, is negative. He suggests that Barbie just isn't trying hard enough and that counseling could help her learn new patterns of attraction. Barbie is expressing the _____ view of homosexual orientation, while Ken's response demonstrates the _____ view.

   a. interventionist; interactionist
   b. interactionist; interventionist
   c. nurture; nature
   d. nature; nurture

2. You are reading an article in the newspaper when you come across the following statement: "The extent to which a male is interested in sex is determined by his level of the hormone testosterone at that moment." Which of the following would be an accurate response, based on what you have learned in this chapter?

   a. "That would be true only for adolescent and young adult males, not older adults."
   b. "Actually there is very little relationship between moment-to-moment levels of testosterone and sex drive in males."
   c. "That's true, but testosterone is a pheromone, not a hormone."
   d. "That's true, but only during the excitement phase of the sexual response cycle."

Answers: 1. d., 2. b.

Other Important Motives

6.4 Describe how both hereditary and environmental factors are involved in curiosity, contact, aggression, achievement, and affiliation motives.

So far, our discussion has moved from motives that depend on biological needs (hunger and thirst) to a motive that is far more sensitive to external cues—sex. Now, we consider motives that are even more responsive to environmental stimuli. These motives, called **stimulus motives**, include exploration, curiosity, manipulation, and contact. They push us to investigate and often to change our environment.

EXPLORATION AND CURIOSITY

What motives cause people to explore and change their environment?

Where does that road go? What is in that dark little shop? How does a television set work? Answering these questions has no obvious benefit: You do not expect the road to take you anywhere you need to go or the shop to contain anything you really want. Nor are you about to start a TV repair service. You just want to know. Exploration and curiosity are motives sparked by the new and unknown and are directed toward no more specific goal than "finding out." They are not unique to humans. The family dog will run around a new house, sniffing and checking things out before it settles down to eat its dinner. Even rats, when given a choice, will opt to explore an unknown maze rather than run through a familiar one. But although curiosity is not uniquely human, it is perhaps particularly characteristic of humans.

Psychologists disagree about the nature and causes of curiosity (Loewenstein, 1994). William James viewed it as an emotion; Freud considered it a socially acceptable expression of the sex drive. Others have seen it as a response to the unexpected and as evidence of a human need to find meaning in life. We might assume that curiosity is a key component of intelligence, but studies attempting to establish a positive correlation between the two have been inconclusive; however, curiosity has been linked to creativity (Kashdan & Fincham, 2002).

Curiosity can also vary according to our familiarity with events and circumstances. As we continually explore and learn from our environment, we raise our threshold for the new and complex, and in turn our explorations and our curiosity become much more

This toddler is exhibiting curiosity, a stimulus motive.

stimulus motive Unlearned motive, such as curiosity or contact, that prompts us to explore or change the world around us.

An infant monkey with Harlow's surrogate "mothers"—one made of bare wire, the other covered with soft terry cloth. The baby monkey clings to the terry-cloth mother, even though only the wire mother dispenses food. Apparently, there is contact comfort in the cuddly terry cloth that the bare wire mother can't provide.

ambitious. In this respect, curiosity is linked to cognition. A gap in our understanding may stimulate our curiosity. But as our curiosity is satisfied and the unfamiliar becomes familiar, we tend to become bored. This outcome, in turn, prompts us to explore our surroundings further (Loewenstein, 1994).

MANIPULATION AND CONTACT

Is the human need for contact universal?

Why do museums have "Do Not Touch" signs everywhere? It is because the staff knows from experience that the urge to touch is almost irresistible. Unlike curiosity and exploration, *manipulation* focuses on a specific object that must be touched, handled, played with, and felt before we are satisfied. Manipulation is a motive limited to primates, who have agile fingers and toes. In contrast, the need for *contact* is more universal than the need for manipulation. Furthermore, it is not limited to touching with the fingers—it may involve the whole body. Manipulation is an active process, but contact may be passive.

In a classic series of experiments, Harry Harlow demonstrated the importance of the need for contact (Harlow, 1958; Harlow & Zimmerman, 1959). Newborn baby monkeys were separated from their mothers and given two "surrogate mothers." Both surrogate mothers were the same shape, but one was made of wire mesh and had no soft surfaces. The other was cuddly—layered with foam rubber and covered with terry cloth. Both surrogate mothers were warmed by means of an electric light placed inside them, but only the wire-mesh mother was equipped with a nursing bottle. Thus, the wire-mesh mother fulfilled two physiological needs for the infant monkeys: the need for food and the need for warmth. But baby monkeys most often gravitated to the terry-cloth mother, which did not provide food. When they were frightened, they would run and cling to it as they would to a real mother. Because both surrogate mothers were warm, the researchers concluded that the need for closeness goes deeper than a need for mere warmth. The importance of contact has also been demonstrated with premature infants. Low-birth-weight babies who are held and massaged gain weight faster and are calmer than those who are seldom touched (Field, 1986).

AGGRESSION

Is aggression a biological or a learned response?

Where people are concerned, the term **aggression** encompasses all behavior that is intended to inflict physical or psychological harm on others. Intent is a key element of aggression (R. Beck, 1983). Accidentally hitting a pedestrian with your car is not an act of aggression, but deliberately running down a person is.

Judging from the statistics (which often reflect underreporting of certain types of crimes), aggression is disturbingly common in this country. According to the FBI's *Uniform Crime Reports*, there were nearly 1.4 million reported violent crimes in the United States in 2003. These crimes included more than 16,000 murders, over 93,000 forcible rapes, 412,000 robberies, and nearly 860,000 aggravated assaults (Federal Bureau of Investigation, 2004). Family life also has a violent underside: One-quarter of families experience some form of violence. Some 3 to 4 million women are battered by their partners each year; more than 25 percent of these battered women seek medical attention for their injuries. In addition, over 900,000 cases of child abuse were reported in 2001, with more than 1,300 children dying as a result of abuse. Children younger than 1 year accounted for 41 percent of the fatalities (National Clearing House on Child Abuse and Neglect, 2003).

Why are people aggressive? Freud considered aggression an innate drive, similar to hunger and thirst, that builds up until it is released. In his view, one important function of society is to channel the aggressive drive into constructive and socially acceptable avenues, such as sports, debating, and other forms of competition. If Freud's analysis is correct, expressing aggression should reduce the aggressive drive. Research shows, however, that under many circumstances, venting one's anger is more likely to increase than to reduce future aggression (Bushman, Baumeister, & Stack, 1999).

aggression Behavior intended to do harm to others; also, the motive to behave aggressively.

According to another view, aggression is a vestige of our evolutionary past (Buss & Shackelford, 1997) that is triggered by pain or frustration (Lorenz, 1968). Some evidence shows that pain can prompt aggressive behavior. In one experiment, for example, when a pair of rats received electric shocks through the grid floor of their cage, they immediately attacked each other. As the frequency and intensity of the shocks increased, so did the fighting (Ulrich & Azrin, 1962).

Frustration often plays a role in aggression. In one experiment, researchers told people that they could earn money by soliciting charitable donations over the telephone (Kulik & Brown, 1979). Some participants were told that previous callers had been quite successful in eliciting pledges; others were led to expect only scant success. Each group was given a list of prospective donors, all of whom were confederates of the experimenters and had instructions to refuse to pledge any money. The researchers assumed that people who expected to have an easy time would experience more frustration than those who anticipated difficulty. The results showed that the more frustrated group tended to argue with uncooperative respondents and even to slam down the phone. They expressed considerably more frustration than the other group.

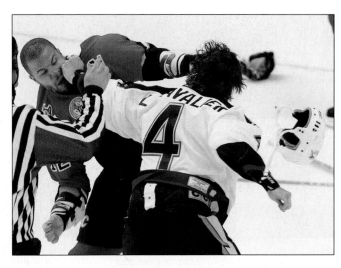

Some psychologists believe that aggression is largely a learned behavior. Professional athletes in contact sports often serve as models of aggressive behavior.

Although studies like this one reveal a link between frustration and aggression, frustration does not always produce aggression. In fact, individuals have very different responses to frustration: some seek help and support, others withdraw from the source of frustration, and some choose to escape into drugs or alcohol. Frustration seems to generate aggression only in people who have learned to be aggressive as a means of coping with unpleasant situations (Bandura, 1973).

One way we learn aggression is by observing aggressive models, especially those who get what they want (and avoid punishment) when they behave aggressively. For example, in contact sports, we often applaud acts of aggression (Bredemeier & Shields, 1985). In professional hockey, fistfights between players may elicit as much fan fervor as goal scoring.

But what if the aggressive model does not come out ahead or is even punished for aggressive actions? Past research has demonstrated that when children view aggressive behavior, they learn it regardless of whether the aggressive model was rewarded or punished. The same results were obtained in a study in which children were shown films of aggressive behavior. Those children who saw the aggressive model being punished were less aggressive than those who saw the aggressive model rewarded, but both groups of children were more aggressive than those who saw no aggressive model at all. These data are consistent with research showing that exposure to cinematic violence of any sort causes a small to moderate increase in aggressive behavior among children and adolescents (Wood, Wong, & Chachere, 1991). So, simply seeing an aggressive model seems to increase aggression among children, even if the model is punished; it also makes little difference whether the model is live or shown on film (C. A. Anderson, 1997). Children who grow up in homes where aggression and violence are prevalent are at particular risk (Feldman et al., 1995; Onyskiw, 2000).

ACHIEVEMENT

Is being highly competitive important to high achievement?

Climbing Mount Everest, sending rockets into space, making the dean's list, rising to the top of a giant corporation—all these actions may have mixed underlying motives. But in all of them there is a desire to excel, "to overcome obstacles, to exercise power, to strive to do something difficult as well and as quickly as possible" (Murray, 1938, pp. 80–81). It is this desire for achievement for its own sake that leads psychologists to suggest that there is a separate **achievement motive**.

Using a self-report questionnaire called the Work and Family Orientation scale (WOFO) to study achievement motivation, researchers discovered three separate but interrelated aspects of achievement-oriented behavior: *work orientation*, the desire to work hard and do a good job; *mastery*, the preference for difficult or challenging feats, with an emphasis on

achievement motive The need to excel, to overcome obstacles.

High achievement is partly a matter of great commitment and effort. Just as this student keeps working late into the night, so those who excel in any field are willing to work hard for success. The desire to excel not for tangible rewards but for the pleasure of being "one of the best" is called achievement motivation.

improving one's past performance; and *competitiveness*, the enjoyment of pitting one's skills against those of other people (Helmreich & Spence, 1978). How do individual differences in the three aspects of achievement motivation relate to people's attainment of goals? In one study, students' grade-point averages (GPAs) were compared with their WOFO scores. As you might expect, students who scored low in work, mastery, and competitiveness had lower GPAs. But students who scored high in all three areas did not have the highest GPAs. It turned out that the students with the highest grades were those who had high work and mastery scores, but low competitiveness scores. In this study, having a high degree of competitiveness actually interfered with achievement.

The counterproductive effect of competitiveness curbs achievement in other groups of people as well, including businesspeople, elementary-school students, and scientists. What accounts for this phenomenon? No one knows for sure, but some researchers speculate that highly competitive people alienate the very people who would otherwise help them achieve their goals; others suggest that preoccupation with winning distracts them from taking the actions necessary to attain their goals.

From psychological tests and personal histories, psychologists have developed a profile of people with a high level of achievement motivation. These people are fast learners. They relish the opportunity to develop new strategies for unique and challenging tasks, whereas people with a low need for achievement rarely deviate from methods that worked for them in the past. Driven less by the desire for fame or fortune than by the need to live up to a high, self-imposed standard of performance (Carr, Borkowski, & Maxwell, 1991), those motivated by high achievement are self-confident, willingly take on responsibility, and do not readily bow to outside social pressures. However, although they are energetic and allow few things to stand in the way of their goals, they are also apt to be tense and to suffer from stress-related ailments, such as headaches. They may also feel like impostors even—or especially—when they achieve their goals.

AFFILIATION

How do psychologists explain the human need to be with other people?

Generally, people have a need for *affiliation*—to be with other people. If they are isolated from social contact for a long time, they may become anxious. Why do human beings seek one another out?

For one thing, the **affiliation motive** is aroused when people feel threatened. Cues that signal danger, such as illness or catastrophe, appear to increase our desire to be with others (Rofe, 1984). Esprit de corps—the feeling of being part of a sympathetic group—is critical among troops going into a battle, just as a football coach's pregame pep talk fuels team spirit. Both are designed to make people feel they are working for a common cause or against a common foe.

Fear and anxiety may also be closely tied to the affiliation motive. When rats, monkeys, or humans are placed in anxiety-producing situations, the presence of a member of the same species who remains calm will reduce the fear of the anxious ones. Patients with critical illnesses tend to prefer being with healthy people, rather than with other seriously ill patients or by themselves (Rofe, Hoffman, & Lewin, 1985). In the same way, if you are nervous on a plane during a bumpy flight, you may strike up a conversation with the calm-looking woman sitting next to you.

On the basis of these facts, some theorists have argued that our need for affiliation has an evolutionary basis (see Ainsworth, 1989; Baumeister & Leary, 1995; Buss, 1990, 1991), although cultural and social factors are also undoubtedly involved. In this view, the formation and maintenance of social bonds provided our ancestors with both survival and reproductive benefits. Social groups can share resources such as food and shelter, provide opportunities for reproduction, and assist in the care of offspring. Children who chose to stay with adults were probably more likely to survive (and ultimately reproduce) than those who wandered away from their groups. Thus, it is understandable that people in general tend to seek out other people.

affiliation motive The need to be with others.

▶ CHECK YOUR UNDERSTANDING

1. Motives such as explanation, curiosity, manipulation, and contact are called _____ motives.

2. Harlow's research with newborn monkeys who were separated from their mothers and given the choice of a wire or a cloth surrogate mother demonstrated the importance of the need for _____.

Indicate whether the following statements are true (T) or false (F).

_____ a. Curiosity has been linked to creativity.

_____ b. Research shows that low-birth-weight babies gain weight faster with frequent physical contact.

_____ c. Aggression may be a learned response to numerous stimuli.

_____ d. Competitiveness leads to higher achievement.

_____ e. Need for affiliation may have an evolutionary basis.

Answers: 1. stimulus, 2. contact, 3. a. (T); b. (T); c. (T); d. (F); e. (T).

▶ APPLY YOUR UNDERSTANDING

1. You are watching a children's TV show in which the "bad guys" eventually are punished for their aggressive behavior. Your friend says, "It's a good thing the bad guys always lose. Otherwise, kids would learn to be aggressive from watching TV shows like this." You think about that for a minute and then, on the basis of what you have learned in this chapter, you reply,

   a. "Actually, seeing an aggressor punished for his or her actions leads to more aggression than seeing no aggression at all."

   b. "You're right. Seeing aggressors punished for their actions is a good way to reduce the amount of aggressiveness in children."

   c. "Aggression is an instinctual response to frustration, so it really doesn't matter what children see on TV. If they are frustrated, they will respond with aggression."

   d. "Viewing violence actually makes children less aggressive."

2. Susan scores high on tests of achievement motivation. Which of the following would you LEAST expect to be true of her?

   a. She is a person who willingly takes on extra responsibility.

   b. She seldom deviates from methods that have worked for her in the past.

   c. She has a strong desire to live up to high, self-imposed standards of excellence.

   d. She is self-confident and resists outside social pressures.

Answers: 1. a., 2. b.

Emotions

6.5 Compare and contrast primary and secondary emotions and cite research evidence supporting the existence of both.

Many motives are closely tied to *emotions*—the feelings we experience that underlie our behavior. For example, when we are motivated to behave aggressively, we *feel* aggressive—we may become angry, agitated, energized, and anxious; when our need for affiliation is activated, we may *feel* lonely, sad, and fearful. Psychologists have long studied human emotional responses, which are intimately tied to many topics within the field—for example, dealing with stress (see Chapter 8: "Personality, Stress, and Health") and treating mental disorders (see Chapter 9: "Psychological Disorders and Their Treatments"). One approach to the study of emotions is to distinguish among the various emotional states we experience, identifying which appear to be of fundamental importance in human behavior.

BASIC EMOTIONS

Are there basic emotions that all people experience regardless of their culture?

Many people have attempted to identify and describe the basic emotions experienced by humans (Cornelius, 1996; Plutchik, 1980). Some years ago, Robert Plutchik (1980), for example, proposed that there are eight basic emotions: *fear, surprise, sadness, disgust, anger, anticipation, joy,* and *acceptance.* Each of these emotions helps us adjust to the demands of our environment, although in different ways. Fear, for example, underlies flight, which helps protect animals from their enemies; anger propels animals to attack or destroy.

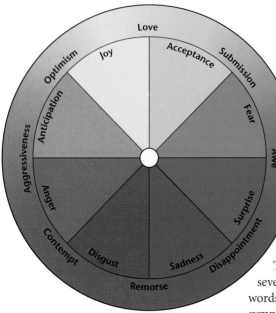

Figure 6–4

Plutchik's eight basic categories of emotion.

Source: Plutchik, 1980.

---

primary emotions Emotions, such as fear, anger, and pleasure, that are found in all cultures.

---

secondary emotions Emotions found in some but not all cultures.

Figure 6–5

Display of anger in animal and human.
Compare the facial expressions. The human face is that of a Kabuki player who is simulating anger. Note how the actor bares his teeth, copying the mandrill's display of emotion.

Emotions adjacent to each other on Plutchik's emotion "circle" (see **Figure 6–4**) are more alike than those situated opposite each other or that are farther away from each other. Surprise is more closely related to fear than to anger; joy and acceptance are more similar to each other than either is to disgust. Moreover, according to Plutchik's model, different emotions may combine to produce an even wider and richer spectrum of experience. Occurring together, anticipation and joy, for example, yield optimism; joy and acceptance fuse into love; and surprise and sadness make for disappointment. Within any of Plutchik's eight categories, emotions vary in intensity.

Some scientists challenge Plutchik's model, noting that it may apply only to the emotional experience of English-speaking people. Anthropologists report enormous differences in the ways that other cultures view and categorize emotions. Some languages, in fact, do not even have a word for "emotion" (Russell, 1991). Languages also differ in the number of words they have to name emotions. English includes over 2,000 words to describe emotional experiences, but Taiwanese Chinese has only 750 such descriptive words. One tribal language has only seven words that could be translated into categories of emotion. Some cultures lack words for "anxiety" or "depression" or "guilt." Samoans have one word encompassing love, sympathy, pity, and liking—all distinct emotions in our own culture (Russell, 1991).

Of interest is that words used to name or describe an emotion may influence how that emotion is experienced. For example, the Tahitian language has no direct translation for the concept of sadness. Instead, Tahitians experience sadness in terms of physical illness. The sadness we feel over the departure of a close friend would be experienced by a Tahitian as, say, exhaustion.

PRIMARY AND SECONDARY EMOTIONS

How are primary emotions different from secondary emotions?

Because of the differences in emotions from one culture to another, the tendency now is to distinguish between primary and secondary emotions. **Primary emotions** are those shared by people throughout the world, regardless of culture. Most researchers use four criteria to identify primary emotions (see Plutchick, 1994): The emotion must (1) be evident in all cultures, (2) contribute to survival, (3) be associated with a distinct facial expression, and (4) be evident in nonhuman primates (see **Figure 6–5**.) As yet no consensus exists about what emotions qualify as primary, but the number is small, very likely no more than a dozen. They include, at a minimum, fear, anger, and pleasure, but may also include sadness, disgust, surprise, and other emotions.

Secondary emotions are those that are found throughout one or more cultures, but not throughout all cultures. They may be thought of as subtle combinations of the primary emotions. There are many more secondary emotions than primary emotions, but there is, again, no consensus about which of those emotions are or how many they number.

Attempts to identify primary emotions have generally used cross-cultural studies (Ekman et al., 1987; Izard, 1994). For example, one group of researchers asked participants from 10 countries to interpret photographs depicting various facial expressions of emotions (Ekman et al., 1987). The percentage of participants from each country who correctly identified the emotions ranged from 60 to 98 percent. (See **Figure 6–6**.) The researchers used this and other evidence to argue for the existence of six primary emotions—*happiness*, *surprise*, *sadness*, *fear*, *disgust*, and *anger* (Cornelius, 1996). Notice that love is not included in this list. Although Ekman did not find a universally recognized facial expression for love, many psychologists nevertheless hold that love is a primary emotion (Hendrick & Hendrick, 2003). Its outward expression, however, may owe much to the stereotypes promoted by a culture's media (Fehr, 1994). In one study in which American college students were asked to display a facial expression for love, the participants mimicked the conventional "Hollywood" prototypes such as sighing deeply, gazing skyward, and holding their hand over their heart (Cornelius, 1996)

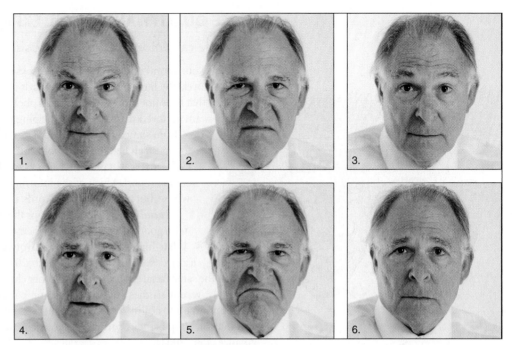

Figure 6–6

Name that face. Dr. Paul Ekman believes that facial expressions are distinct, predictable, and easy to read for someone who has studied them. His research involved breaking the expressions down into their specific muscular components and developing programs to help train people to become more accurate observers of the feelings that flit briefly across others' faces. Here, he demonstrates six emotional states. How many of them can you match to the pictures? The answers follow the figure.

   a. fear
   b. neutral (no emotion)
   c. sadness
   d. anger
   e. surprise
   f. disgust

Answers: 1. b. (neutral) 2. f. (disgust) 3. e. (surprise) 4. a. (fear) 5. d. (anger) 6. c. (sadness).

> ### CHECK YOUR UNDERSTANDING

1. In Plutchik's theory, if two emotions are next to each other on the emotional "circle", then they are *less alike* than those that are opposite each other. True or False?

2. _____ emotions are those experienced by members of every culture.

Answers: 1. F, 2. Primary

> ### APPLY YOUR UNDERSTANDING

1. Dr. Roth suggests that every culture experiences emotions in different and unique ways, thereby emphasizing the significance of _____ emotions.
  a. primary
  b. secondary
  c. core
  d. homeostatic

2. If a researcher found that every culture had an emotion that corresponded to fear, this evidence would support the existence of _____ emotions.
  a. primary
  b. secondary
  c. homeostatic
  d. developmental

Answers: 1. b, 2. a.

Communicating Emotion

6.6 Identify four different ways in which emotions can be communicated and analyze the role that heredity and environment play in how emotions are displayed.

Sometimes you are vaguely aware that a person makes you feel uncomfortable. When pressed to be more precise, you might say, "You never know what she is thinking." But you do not mean that you never know her opinion of a film or what she thought about the last election. It would probably be more accurate to say that you do not know what she is feeling. Almost all of us conceal our emotions to some extent, but usually people can tell what we are feeling. Although emotions can often be expressed in words, much of the time we communicate our feelings nonverbally. We do so through, among other things, voice quality, facial expression, body language, personal space, and explicit acts.

VOICE QUALITY AND FACIAL EXPRESSION

What role can voice and facial expression play in expressing emotion?

If your roommate is washing the dishes and says acidly, "I *hope* you're enjoying your novel," the literal meaning of his words is quite clear, but you probably know very well that he is not expressing a concern about your reading pleasure. He is really saying, "I am annoyed that you are not helping to clean up." Similarly, if you receive a phone call from someone who has had very good or very bad news, you will probably know how she feels before she has told you what happened. In the same way, we can literally hear fear in a person's voice, as we do when we listen to a nervous student give an oral report. Much of the information we convey is not contained in the words we use, but in the way those words are expressed (Gobl & Chasaide, 2003).

Facial expressions are perhaps the most obvious emotional indicators. We can tell a good deal about a person's emotional state by observing whether that person is laughing, crying, smiling, or frowning. Many facial expressions are innate, not learned (Ekman, 1994; Goldsmith, 2002). Children who are born deaf and blind use the same facial expressions as do other children to express the same emotions. Interestingly, recent studies suggest that some patients with severe depressive disorder may have an impaired ability to accurately judge another person's facial expression of emotion, and that this impairment contributes to their difficulty in interpersonal functioning (Surguladze et al., 2004).

Charles Darwin first advanced the idea that most animals share a common pattern of muscular facial movements. For example, dogs, tigers, and humans all bare their teeth in rage. Darwin also observed that expressive behaviors serve a basic biological as well as social function. Darwin's notion that emotions have an evolutionary history and can be traced across cultures as part of our biological heritage laid the groundwork for many modern investigations of emotional expression (see **Figure 6–7**; Izard, 1992, 1994).

Figure 6–7

Universal facial expressions. People throughout the world use the "brow-raise" greeting when a friend approaches.

BODY LANGUAGE, PERSONAL SPACE, AND GESTURES

How can posture and personal space communicate emotion?

Body language is another way that we communicate messages nonverbally. How we hold our back, for example, communicates a great deal. When we are relaxed, we tend to stretch back into a chair; when we are tense, we sit more stiffly with our feet together.

The distance we maintain between ourselves and others is called *personal space*. This distance varies depending on the nature of the activity and the emotions felt. If someone stands closer to you than is customary, that proximity may indicate either anger or affection; if farther away than usual, it may indicate fear or dislike. The normal conversing distance between people varies from culture to culture. Two Swedes conversing would ordinarily stand much farther apart than would two Arabs or Greeks.

Explicit acts, of course, can also serve as nonverbal clues to emotions. A slammed door may tell us that the person who just left the room is angry. If friends drop in for a visit and you invite them into your living room, you are probably less at ease with them than with friends who generally sit down with you at the kitchen table. Gestures, such as a slap on the back or an embrace, can also indicate feelings. Whether people shake your hand briefly or for a long time, firmly or limply, tells you something about how they feel about you.

You can see from this discussion that nonverbal communication of emotions is important; however, a word of caution is needed here. Although nonverbal behavior may offer a clue to a person's feelings, it is not an *infallible* clue. Laughing and crying can sound alike, yet crying may signal sorrow, joy, anger, or nostalgia—or that you are slicing an onion. Moreover, as with verbal reports, people sometimes "say" things nonverbally that they do not mean. We all have done things thoughtlessly—turned our backs, frowned when thinking about something else, or laughed at the wrong time—that have given offense because our actions were interpreted as an expression of an emotion that we were not, in fact, feeling.

Also, many of us overestimate our ability to interpret nonverbal cues. For example, in one study of several hundred "professional lie catchers," including members of the Secret Service,

When having a conversation, most Arabs stand closer to one another than most Americans do. In our society, two men would not usually stand as close together as these two Arabs unless they were very aggressively arguing with each other (a baseball player heatedly arguing with an umpire, for example).

government lie detector experts, judges, police officers, and psychiatrists, every group except for the psychiatrists rated themselves above average in their ability to tell whether another person was lying. Only the Secret Service agents managed to identify the liars at a better-than-chance rate (Ekman & O'Sullivan, 1991). Similar results have been obtained with other groups of people (DePaulo & Pfeifer, 1986). In part, the reason seems to be that many behaviors that might seem to be associated with lying (such as avoiding eye contact, rapid blinking, or shrugs) are not in fact associated with lying; and other behaviors that are associated with lying (such as tenseness and fidgeting) also occur frequently when people are not lying (DePaulo et al., 2003). Thus, even the best nonverbal cues only indicate that a person *may* be lying.

GENDER AND EMOTION

Are men less emotional than women?

Men are often said to be less emotional than women (DeAngelis, 2001). But do men feel less emotion, or are they simply less likely to express the emotions they feel? And are there some emotions that men are more likely than women to express?

Research sheds some light on these issues. In one study, when men and women saw depictions of people in distress, the men showed little emotion, but the women expressed feelings of concern for those in distress (Eisenberg & Lennon, 1983). Physiological measures of emotional arousal (such as heart rate and blood pressure), however, showed that the men in the study were actually just as affected as the women were. The men simply inhibited the expression of their emotions, whereas the women were more open about their feelings. Emotions such as sympathy, sadness, empathy, and distress are often considered "unmanly," and traditionally, in Western culture, boys are trained from an early age to suppress those emotions in public (O'Leary & Smith, 1988). The fact that men are less likely than women to seek help in dealing with emotional issues (Komiya, Good, & Sherrod, 2000) is probably a result of this early training. In addition, women tend to have stronger emotional reactions to self-generated thoughts and memories (see **Figure 6–8**; Carter, 1998.)

Men and women are also likely to react with very different emotions to the same situation. For example, being betrayed or criticized by another person would make males feel angry, whereas females are more likely to feel hurt, sad, or disappointed (Brody, 1985; Fischer, Rodriguez-Mosquera, van-Vianen, & Manstead, 2004). And, when men get angry, they generally turn their anger outward, against other people and against the situation in which they find themselves. Women are more likely to see themselves as the source of the problem and to turn their anger inward, against themselves. These gender-specific reactions are consistent with the fact that men are four times more likely than women to become violent in the face of life crises; women are much more likely to become depressed.

Men and women also differ in their ability to interpret nonverbal cues of emotion. Women are more skilled than men at decoding the facial expressions, body cues, and tones of voice of others (Hall, 1984). How can we explain these differences? One possibility is that because women tend to be the primary caregivers for preverbal infants, they need to become more attuned than men to the subtleties of emotional expressions. Some psychologists have even suggested that this skill may be genetically programmed into females. Consistent with this evolutionary perspective, research has shown that male and female infants do express and self-regulate emotions differently (McClure, 2000; Weinberg, Tronick, Cohn, & Olson, 1999).

Another explanation of gender differences in emotional sensitivity is based on the relative power of women and men. Because women historically have occupied less powerful positions, they may have felt the need to become acutely attuned to the emotional displays of others, particularly those in more powerful positions (namely, men). This idea is supported by evidence that, regardless of gender, followers are more sensitive to the emotions of leaders than vice versa (Snodgrass, 1992).

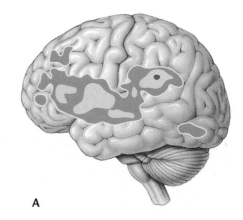

A

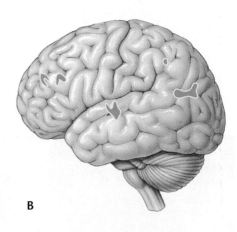

B

Figure 6–8

Emotion and brain activity in men and women. When asked to think of something sad, women (A) generate more activity in their brains than men (B).

Why do flight attendants always look happy? Because they must. Even while showing passengers how to use an oxygen mask, flight attendants are expected to trade genuine emotions—perhaps of fear or sadness—for an automatic, reassuring smile.

The fact that men are more likely than women to hold positions of power may affect emotional experience in other ways as well. In the types of jobs traditionally held by women, workers are often called on to regulate, manage, or otherwise alter their emotional expression. Sociologist Arlie Hochschild (1983) described this process as emotional labor. In a study of flight attendants, the majority of whom were women, Hochschild found clear guidelines regarding which emotions were to be displayed, to whom, by whom, and how often. Most of the flight attendants felt that they were being robbed of genuine emotional experiences on the job: "... [I]n the flight attendant's work, smiling is separated from its usual function, which is to express a personal feeling, and attached to another one—expressing a company feeling" (p. 127). Hochschild also noted that the people who hold jobs that are high in emotional labor—such as secretaries, registered nurses, cashiers, social workers, and bank tellers—tend to be women.

CULTURE AND EMOTION

How can culture influence the way we interpret and express emotion?

Studies that identify gender differences in emotionality raise the more general question about the role that culture plays in the interpretation and expression of emotion. Among nonverbal channels of communication, facial expressions seem to communicate the most specific information. Hand gestures or posture can communicate general emotional states (e.g., feeling bad), but the complexity of the muscles in the face allows facial expressions to communicate very specific feelings (e.g., feeling sad, angry, or fearful). Some researchers have argued that across cultures, peoples,

and societies, the face looks the same whenever certain emotions are expressed: This phenomenon is known as the *universalist* position. Charles Darwin subscribed to this view, arguing that as part of our common evolutionary heritage, people use the same expressions to convey the same emotions. In contrast, other researchers support the *culture-learning* position, which holds that members of a culture learn the appropriate facial expressions for emotions. These expressions, then, can differ greatly from one culture to the next. Which view is more accurate?

As we saw earlier, Ekman and his colleagues have concluded from cross-cultural studies that at least six emotions are accompanied by universal facial expressions: happiness, sadness, anger, surprise, fear, and disgust. Carroll Izard (1980) conducted similar studies in England, Germany, Switzerland, France, Sweden, Greece, and Japan with similar results. These studies seem to support the universalist position: Regardless of culture, people tended to agree on which emotions others were expressing facially; however, this research does not completely rule out the culture-learning view. Because the participants were all members of developed countries that likely had been exposed to one another through movies, magazines, and tourism, they might simply have become familiar with the facial expressions seen in other cultures. A stronger test was needed that reduced or eliminated this possibility.

Such a test was made possible by the discovery of several contemporary cultures that had been totally isolated from Western culture for most of their existence.

Can you identify the emotions being expressed by this man from New Guinea? The finding that U.S. college students could recognize the emotional expressions of people who had been largely isolated from Western cultures—and vice versa—lends support to the universalist position of facial expression.

Members of the Fore and the Dani cultures of New Guinea, for example, had their first contact with anthropologists only a few years before Ekman's research took place. They provided a nearly perfect opportunity to test the universalist/culture-learning debate. If members of these cultures gave the same interpretation of facial expressions and produced the same expressions on their own faces as people in Western cultures, there would be much stronger evidence for the universality of facial expressions of emotion. Ekman and his colleagues presented members of the Fore culture with three photographs of people from outside their culture and asked them to point to the picture that represented how they would feel in a certain situation. For example, if a participant was told "Your child has died, and you feel very sad," he or she would have the opportunity to choose which of the three pictures most closely corresponded to sadness. The results indicated very high rates of agreement on facial expressions of emotions (Ekman & Friesen, 1971; Ekman, Sorenson, & Friesen, 1969). Moreover, when photographs of the Fore and Dani posing the primary emotions were shown to college students in the United States, the same high agreement was found (Ekman & Friesen, 1975). This finding suggests that at least some emotional expressions are inborn.

If this is true, why are people so often confused about the emotions being expressed by people in other cultures? It turns out that the answer is not simple. Part of the explanation involves **display rules** (Ekman & Friesen, 1975). Display rules concern the circumstances under which it is appropriate for people to show emotion. Display rules differ substantially from culture to culture (Matsumoto & Kupperbusch, 2001). In a study of Japanese and American college students, the participants watched graphic films of surgical procedures, either by themselves or in the presence of an experimenter. The students' facial expressions were secretly videotaped as they viewed the films. The results showed that when the students were by themselves, both the Japanese and the Americans showed facial expressions of disgust, as expected. But when the participants watched the films in the presence of an experimenter, the two groups displayed different responses. American students continued to show disgust on their faces, but the Japanese students showed facial expressions that were more neutral, even somewhat pleasant (Ekman, Friesen, & Ellsworth, 1972). Why the sudden switch? The answer in this case appears to lie in the different display rules of the two cultures. The Japanese norm says, "Don't display strong negative emotion in the presence of a respected elder" (in this case, the experimenter). Americans typically don't honor this display rule; hence, they expressed their true emotions whether they were alone or with someone else.

However, display rules don't tell the whole story. In a comprehensive review of the literature, researchers demonstrated that differences in language, familiarity, majority or minority status within a culture, cultural learning, expressive style, and a number of other factors also may account for the fact that we understand emotions more accurately when they are expressed by members of our own cultural or subcultural group (Elfenbein & Ambady, 2002; 2003). Much more research is needed before we can fully understand this "in-group advantage" in emotion recognition.

display rules Culture-specific rules that govern how, when, and why expressions of emotion are appropriate.

▶ CHECK YOUR UNDERSTANDING

1. Cultural differences, particularly _____, influence how we experience emotion.

2. Two important nonverbal cues to emotions are _____ _____ and _____ _____.

3. Men tend to interpret the source of their anger to be in their _____.

4. Research shows that some _____ _____ are recognized universally.

5. _____ _____ are the cultural circumstances under which it is appropriate to show emotions on the face.

6. _____ Overt behavior is an infallible clue to emotions. Is this statement true (T) or false (F)?

Answers: 1. language, 2. facial expression, body language, 3. environment, 4. facial expressions, 5. Display rules, 6. (F).

▶ APPLY YOUR UNDERSTANDING

1. Which of the following people would probably be best at "reading" nonverbal emotional cues?
   a. a young man
   b. an older woman
   c. an older man
   d. they would all be equally accurate since gender and age are not related to the ability to understand nonverbal cues to emotion.

2. You are studying gender differences in emotion. You show men and women various films of people in distress. On the basis of what you have read in this chapter, you would predict that the men will show _____ amount of physiological arousal, and _____ emotional expression as the women.
   a. the same; the same
   b. the same; less
   c. a greater; less
   d. a smaller; less

Answers: 1. b., 2. b.

>KEY TERMS<

motive, *p. 201*
emotion, *p. 201*

Perspectives on motivation

instinct, *p. 202*
drive, *p. 202*
drive-reduction theory, *p. 202*
homeostasis, *p. 202*
primary drive, *p. 202*
secondary drive, *p. 202*

arousal theory, *p. 202*
Yerkes–Dodson law, *p. 203*
extrinsic motivation, *p. 203*
intrinsic motivation, *p. 203*
flow, *p. 204*
reinforcement theory, *p. 205*
equity theory, *p. 206*
expectaney theory, *p. 206*
goal-setting theory, *p. 207*

Hunger and thirst

incentive, *p. 209*
anorexia nervosa, *p. 210*
bulimia nervosa, *p. 211*

Sex

sexual orientation, *p. 216*

Other important motives

stimulus motive, *p. 217*

aggression, *p. 218*
achievement motive, *p. 219*
affiliation motive, *p. 220*

Emotions

Primary emotions, *p. 222*
Secondary emotions, *p. 222*

Communicating emotion

display rules, *p. 227*

>CHAPTER REVIEW<

Perspectives on Motivation

How well do theories based on the biological concepts of instinct, homeostasis, and arousal explain human motivation?
There are many ways of viewing human motivation. The idea that our motivations are largely based on **instincts** was popular in the early twentieth century but has since fallen out of favor. Human motivation has also been viewed as an effort toward **drive reduction** and **homeostasis**, or balance in the body, as well as an effort to maintain an optimum level of arousal. Drive–reduction theories often distinguish between **primary drives**, which are needed for survival, and **secondary drives**, which are acquired through learning. The **Yerkes–Dodson law** explains that the relationship between arousal level and performance depends on task complexity.

How can you use intrinsic and extrinsic motivation to help you succeed in your job? Another perspective is that of motivational inducements, or **incentives**. When inducements originate from within the person, they are called **intrinsic motivation**, and when they come from outside, they are called **extrinsic motivation**. Extrinsic motivation can certainly help you succeed in your job, as when your manager offers you a raise for good performance. Developing intrinsic motivation to succeed, however, will have a greater, more long-lasting effect. The concept of **flow**, a state of mind characterized by a complete and consuming focus on an activity, is a powerful example of instrinsic motivation.

How does Maslow's theory of motivation organize the various types of human motives? Abraham Maslow suggested that human motives can be arranged in a hierarchy, with basic motives based on physical needs positioned at the bottom, and higher motives such as self-esteem positioned toward the top. Maslow believed that the higher motives don't emerge until the more basic ones have been met, but recent research challenges his view. For example, difficulty in meeting basic needs can actually foster the satisfaction of higher motives.

What theories have been proposed to explain motivation in the work place? Theories that focus on individual differences in motivation often identify personality traits, such as conscientiousness, as being responsible for why some workers are more highly motivated than others. **Reinforcement theory,** based on the principles of operant conditioning, centers on the idea that when workers are rewarded for work, they will continue working hard. Other theories focus more on cognitive processes. For example, **equity theory** suggests that workers compare their own effort and rewards to those of others; inequitable situations lead to lack of motivation. **Expectancy theory** focuses on how workers perceive the link between their actions and rewards and how valuable the rewards associated with work are. When rewards are valued and work is believed to lead to rewards, motivation is high. **Goal-setting theory** emphasizes the motivating effect that setting clear and attainable goals can have for workers.

Hunger and Thirst

How is the brain involved in hunger? Hunger is regulated by several centers within the brain. These centers are stimulated by receptors that monitor stomach contents, as well as by receptors that monitor the contents of the blood, especially its levels of glucose, fats, and carbohydrates.

How can external cues influence our desire to eat? Hunger is also stimulated by factors outside the body, such as cooking aromas, and by emotional, cultural, and social factors.

What factors define and are involved in the common eating disorders of anorexia, bulimia, and obesity? The eating disorders, identified as **anorexia nervosa** and **bulimia nervosa** are more prevalent among females than among males. They are characterized by extreme preoccupation with body image and weight. Another food-related problem, obesity, is affecting millions of Americans. Obesity has complex causes and negative consequences, particularly for obese children, who are more likely to have health problems as adults.

Sex

Is sexual behavior more the result of biological urges or of cultural and environmental factors? Sex is a primary drive that gives rise to reproductive behavior essential for the survival of the species. Although hormones are involved in human sexual responses, they don't play as dominant a role as they do in some other species. In humans, the brain exerts a powerful influence on the sex drive as well.

Human sexual motivation, however, is highly dependent on experience and learning. Because people have different experiences, they also have different preferences for sexually arousing stimuli. What is sexually attractive is also influenced by culture.

What constitutes a "typical" sexual response? Research indicates that most Americans are far more conservative in their own sex lives than popular culture suggests. Men generally are more interested in sex than women, and are more likely to link it with power and dominance. Women have more flexible definitions of sex and usually associate it with a close, committed relationship.

What are the arguments for and against a biological explanation of homosexuality? People with a heterosexual orientation are sexually attracted to members of the opposite sex; those with a homosexual orientation are sexually attracted to members of their own sex. It is likely that both biological and environmental factors play a role in explaining sexual orientation.

Other Important Motives

What motives cause people to explore and change their environment? In contrast to primary drives, stimulus motives and social motives are less obviously associated with the survival of the organism or the species, even though they often help human beings adapt successfully to their environments. **Stimulus motives**, such as the urge to explore and manipulate things, are associated with obtaining information about the world. Social motives, such as the desire to affiliate with other people, center on human interactions with one another. Exploration and curiosity are two human motivations that encourage to explore our environment and often to change it.

Is the human need for contact universal? Another important stimulus motive in humans and other primates is to seek various forms of tactile stimulation. This contact motive can be seen in the child's urge to cling and cuddle.

Is aggression a biological or a learned response? Any behavior intended to inflict physical or psychological harm on others is an act of **aggression**. Some psychologists see aggression as an innate drive in humans that must be channeled to constructive ends, but others see it more as a learned response that is greatly influenced by modeling. The fact that levels of aggression differ markedly across cultures tends to support the view of human aggression as encouraged and shaped by learning.

Is being highly competitive important to high achievement? People who display a desire to excel, to overcome obstacles, and to accomplish difficult things score high in what psychologists call **achievement motive**. Although hard work and a strong desire to master challenges both contribute to achievement, competitiveness toward others often does not. In fact, competitiveness can actually interfere with achievement.

How do psychologists explain the human need to be with other people? The **affiliation motive**, or need to be with other people, is especially pronounced when we feel threatened or anxious. Affiliation with others in this situation can counteract fear and bolster spirits.

Emotions

Are there basic emotions that all people experience regardless of their culture? Robert Plutchik's classification system for **emotions** uses a circle to position eight basic emotional categories. But not all cultures categorize emotions the way that Plutchik does.

How are primary emotions different from secondary emotions? When emotions are found in all cultures, they are called **primary emotions**. Examples includes fear, anger, and pleasure. **Secondary emotions** are those that are found in some, but not all, cultures. A cross-cultural analysis of emotional expression has led Paul Ekman to argue for the universality of at least six primary emotions—happiness, surprise, sadness, fear, disgust, and anger. Many psychologists add love to this list.

Communicating Emotion

What role can voice and facial expression play in expressing emotion? People sometimes express their emotions verbally through their words, tone of voice, exclamations, and other sounds. Facial expressions are the most obvious nonverbal indicators of emotion.

How can posture and personal space communicate emotion? Other indicators involve body language—our posture, the way we move, our preferred personal distance from others when talking to them, our degree of eye contact. Explicit acts, such as slamming a door, express emotions, too. People vary in their skill at reading these nonverbal cues.

Are men less emotional than women? Research confirms some gender differences in expressing and perceiving emotions. For example, when confronted with a person in distress, women are more likely than men to express emotion, even though the levels of physiological arousal are the same for the two sexes. Also, in some stressful situations, such as being betrayed or criticized, men tend to report more anger, and women more disappointment and hurt. There is also some truth to the common stereotype that women are generally better than men at reading other people's emotions. This skill may be sharpened by their role as caretakers of infants and their traditional subordinate status to men.

How can culture influence the way we interpret and express emotion? The facial expressions associated with certain basic emotions appear to be universal: The expressions are the same regardless of a person's cultural background. This cross-cultural finding contradicts the culture-learning view, which suggests that facial expressions of emotion are learned within a particular culture. This is not to say that there are no cultural differences in emotional expression, however. Overlaying the universal expression of certain emotions are culturally varying **display rules** that govern when it is appropriate to show emotion—to whom, by whom, and under what circumstances. Other forms of nonverbal communication of emotion vary more from culture to culture than facial expressions do.

>CHAPTER 6< Motivation and Emotion

6.1 PERSPECTIVES ON MOTIVATION

THEORIES OF MOTIVATION

- **Instinct:** Motives are inborn and present in all members of a species
- **Drive-reduction theory:** Bodily needs produce states of tension called drives that motivate behavior so need state is reduced
- **Arousal theory:** View that organisms seek an optimal, usually intermediate, level of arousal

INTRINSIC AND EXTRINSIC MOTIVATION

- **Extrinsic motivation:** Motivation that derives from the consequences of an activity
- **INTRINSIC MOTIVATION:** Motivation provided by an activity itself, such as in a state of flow

MASLOW'S HIERARCHY OF MOTIVES

More basic, physiologically based needs must be satisfied before higher-level needs are satisfied.

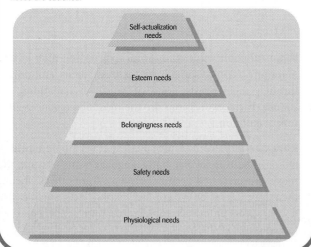

Self-actualization needs

Esteem needs

Belongingness needs

Safety needs

Physiological needs

MOTIVATION IN THE WORK PLACE

- Personality traits are linked to motivation in the work place
- **Reinforcement theory:** Work behaviors are strengthened with positive outcomes
- **Equity theory:** Motivation depends on how people evaluate their effort and rewards in comparison to those of others
- **Expectancy theory:** Motivation depends on how people value rewards and on how they understand the link between their own behavior and receiving those rewards
- **Goal-setting theory:** Clearly articulated valuable goals motivate goal-seeking behavior

6.3 SEX

BIOLOGICAL FACTORS RELATED TO SEX

- Testosterone plays a role in sexual development
- Scents called pheromones can trigger sexual excitation in animals
- Limbic system is involved in sexual excitement
- Biological sequence of arousal in both men and women: Excitement, plateau, orgasm, resolution

SEXUAL ORIENTATION

- Heterosexuals: Attracted to members of the opposite sex
- Homosexuals: Attracted to members of their own sex
- Sexual orientation is most likely explained by the interaction of biological and environmental factors

6.2 HUNGER AND THIRST

FACTORS RELATED TO HUNGER

Biological Hunger Cues	External
Hypothalamus	Learned associations
Regions in the cortex and spinal cord	Eating habits
Neurotransmitters	Social settings, emotional states
Brain, blood levels of nutrients and insulin	Cultural expectations
Hormone leptin	
Receptors in the stomach	

EATING DISORDERS AND OBESITY

- **Anorexia nervosa:** Serious eating disorder characterized by extreme thinness, intense fear of weight gain, and a distorted body image
- **Bulimia nervosa:** Eating disorder characterized by eating binges followed by purging
- **Obesity:** An excess of body fat

6.4 OTHER IMPORTANT MOTIVES

EXPLORATION AND CURIOSITY

- Not unique to humans
- Linked to creativity

MANIPULATION AND CONTACT

- Manipulation is limited to primates
- Contact is more universal
- Harlow's monkeys demonstrated the need for contact

AGGRESSION

- May serve an evolutionary purpose
- Can be triggered by frustration
- Can be learned by watching aggressive models

ACHIEVEMENT AND AFFILIATION

- **Achievement motive:** High work orientation, high mastery, and low competitiveness yield best performance
- **Affiliation motive:** Need to be around others, which is aroused when people feel threatened
- Like other motives, achievement and affiliation have both a biological and experiential basis

6.5 EMOTIONS

EMOTIONS

Feelings we experience that underlie our behavior

HOW MANY EMOTIONS?

- Plutchik proposes 8 basic emotions: fear, surprise, sadness, disgust, anger, anticipation, joy, acceptance
- Emotions help us adjust to the demands of our environment
- Cultures view and categorize emotions in vastly different ways
- Words used to name or describe an emotion may influence how that emotion is experienced

TYPES OF EMOTIONS

- **Primary:** Emotions found in all cultures
- **Secondary:** Emotions found in some, but not all, cultures

6.6 COMMUNICATING EMOTION

HOW EMOTIONS ARE COMMUNICATED

- Facial expressions: How the person looks
- Voice quality: How the person sounds
- Body language: How the person holds his or her body
- Personal space: The distance we maintain between ourselves and others
- Explicit acts: Nonverbal cues such as a slammed door, gestures

GENDER DIFFERENCES

- Men generally show less emotion
- Women are sometimes more skilled at decoding nonverbal communications
- Women may be more emotionally sensitive

CULTURAL DIFFERENCES

- **Universalist position:** Evolutionary forces have established some communication patterns that are common across cultures
- **Culture-learning position:** People learn appropriate emotional responses by observing others in their culture
- Cross-cultural differences in **display rules** arise from cultural rules about showing emotion

Concept Map

[CHAPTER 7]

Human Development Across the Lifespan

aitlin's room is small: It has only a twin bed piled high with stuffed penguins, and shelves lined with old swimming trophies—a bit out-of-step with her 23-year-old self. Yet, you can't beat the rent—a mere $400 a month and within easy reach of San Francisco, where one-bedroom apartments go for $1500 a month. Caitlin also gets home-cooked meals almost every night, and has someone to clean her room and wash her clothes. And she's managing to sock away another $400 a month in savings, an awesome amount compared to most of her peers, who are deep in credit card debt.

Caitlin is a rookie elementary school teacher who has moved back home with her parents after two years on her own—and she's in good company. Called alternately "Boomerang Kids," or "Generation Yo-Yo" for their habit of going back and forth between independence and their parents' nests, an increasing number of young adults in their 20s and even 30s are coming back home to roost. In 2004, for instance 57 percent of American men and 47 percent of women ages 18–24 were living at home.

The major forces driving young adults to seek refuge under their parents' roofs are economic. Housing prices are skyrocketing, with one-bedroom apartments and even studios in major cities from Los Angeles to Atlanta going for over $1,000 a month. College tuition likewise is rising—the typical college graduate accumulates $19,000 in college loan debt, double

that of a 1997 graduate—while the pay for entry-level or low wage jobs has not kept pace with inflation. As economic forces make it difficult for young adults to make it on their own, other factors have made coming home easier and less stigmatizing that it would have been in, say, the 1970s. Trend tracker Yankelovich Partners has found that parents and children today have different relationships than those in previous generations. Children regard parents as friends, and vice versa. Recent Williams college graduate Bobby Jackson says, "I love hanging out with my parents," and hang out he will, while looking for a PR job from the comfort of his parents' home.

That's not to say all is comfy-cozy after young people come home to roost in the empty nest. Parents often resent taking up their old roles—cooking, laundering, and picking up after their kids—at a time when they're ready for respite and renewal. Grown children chafe at the lack of independence—curfews or cell phone calls home—and the lack of autonomy. And there's a generational difference in how these Boomerangers are viewed. Young people and younger parents see coming home as a sound and strategic step toward getting a firm footing for one's career. Older people, especially those who left home after high school and never came back, ask questions like "You live where?! At your age?! What's wrong with you?!"[1]

The phenomenon of the Boomerang Generation is part of a larger trend in **develop-**

mental psychology, the broad field of study that investigates the changes that occur in people as they move through life. As you'll see in this chapter, *adolescence* and *adulthood* are two distinct stages of development. Yet, 20-somethings are delaying typical stages of adulthood by going to college longer and getting married and having children later in life. Demographers, people who study the changing characteristics of human population, have begun talking about a new life stage for people 18 to 25 who have moved beyond adolescence but are not quite mature enough to be adults. How do developmental psychologists study the patterns of life change that occur across the lifespan?

Because developmental changes take place across the entire lifespan, which for some individuals can be more than 100 years, developmental psychologists often use special methods to study behavior and mental processes. Sometimes they use a **cross-sectional approach**, which compares different age **cohorts**—groups of people all of the same ages. However, people of different ages often have quite different life experience: Consider how your life is being shaped by forces different from those your grandparents likely experienced. Consequently, developmental psychologists also use **longitudinal approaches**, in which the same group of individuals is studied at various points across time. Examples of both types of studies will be described in this chapter. ◻

Prenatal Development

7.1 Define the concept of "critical period" as it relates to the major developments that occur during the prenatal period.

Regardless of the specific methods they choose, developmental psychologists recognize that many forces—some hereditary and some environmental—shape each individual's life. Many of these forces are set in motion when conception occurs, and the period of *prenatal development* begins.

FROM EMBRYO TO FETUS

What major events take place during the fetal and embryonic stages of prenatal development?

During the earliest period of **prenatal development**—the stage of development from conception to birth—the fertilized egg divides, embarking on the process that will transform

developmental psychology The study of the changes that occur in people from conception to death.

cross-sectional approach A method of studying developmental changes by comparing people of different ages at about the same time.

cohort A group of people born during the same period in historical time.

longitudinal approach A method of studying developmental changes by evaluating the same people at different points in their lives.

prenatal development Development from conception to birth.

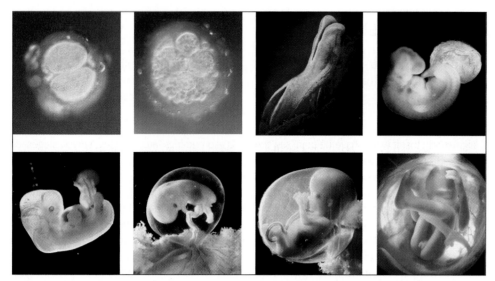

Figure 7–1
Stages in prenatal developmet.

embryo A developing human between 2 weeks and 3 months after conception.

fetus A developing human between 3 months after conception and birth.

critical period A time when certain internal and external influences have a major effect on development; at other periods, the same influences will have little or no effect.

fetal alcohol syndrome (FAS) A disorder that occurs in children of women who drink alcohol during pregnancy; this disorder is characterized by facial deformities, heart defects, stunted growth, and cognitive impairments.

it, in just nine months, from a one-celled organism into a complex human being (see **Figure 7–1**.) The dividing cells form a hollow ball, which implants itself in the wall of the uterus. Two weeks after conception, the cells begin to specialize: Some will form the baby's internal organs, others will form muscles and bones, and still others will form the skin and the nervous system. No longer an undifferentiated mass of cells, the developing organism is now called an **embryo**.

The embryo stage ends three months after conception, when the *fetal stage* begins. At this point, although it is only one inch long, the **fetus** roughly resembles a human being, with arms and legs, a large head, and a heart that has begun to beat. Although it can already move various parts of its body, another month is likely to pass before the mother feels those movements.

An organ called the *placenta* nourishes the embryo and the fetus. Within the placenta, the mother's blood vessels transmit nutritive substances to the embryo or fetus, and carry waste products away from it. Although the mother's blood never actually mingles with that of her unborn child, toxic agents that she eats, drinks, or inhales (known as *teratogens*) are capable of crossing the placenta and compromising the baby's development (Newland & Rasmussen, 2003; Roy, Seidler, & Slotkin, 2002; Wass, Simmons, Thomas, & Riley, 2002). Diseases can also cross the placenta and infect the fetus, often with disastrous results.

CRITICAL PERIODS IN DEVELOPMENT

Why can a toxic agent cause devastating effects at one point in prenatal development but not at others?

Many potentially harmful substances have a **critical period** when they are most likely to have a major effect on the fetus. At other times, the same substance may have no effect at

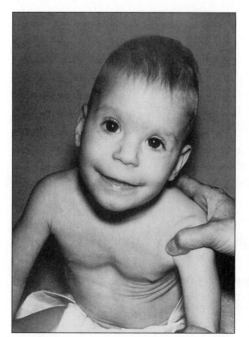

Children born with fetal alcohol syndrome often exhibit facial deformities, heart defects, stunted growth, and cognitive impairments that can last throughout life. The syndrome is entirely preventable, but not curable.

all. For example, if a woman contracts rubella (German measles) during the first three months of pregnancy, the effects can range from death of the fetus to a child who is born deaf. If she gets rubella during the final three months of pregnancy, however, severe damage to the fetus is unlikely, because the critical period for the formation of major body parts has passed.

Pregnancy is most likely to have a favorable outcome when the mother gets good nutrition and good medical care, and when she avoids exposure to substances that could be harmful to her baby, including alcohol and nicotine. Alcohol is the drug most often abused by pregnant women, and with potentially devastating consequences (Lee, Mattson, & Riley, 2004; Riley et al., 2003). Pregnant women who consume large amounts of alcohol risk giving birth to a child with **fetal alcohol syndrome (FAS)**, a condition characterized by facial deformities, heart defects, stunted growth, and cognitive impairments (Mattson, Riley, Gramling, Delis, & Jones, 1998; Shaffer, 1999). Even smaller amounts of alcohol can cause neurological problems (Hunt, Streissguth, Kerr, & Olson, 1995; Shriver & Piersel, 1994). For that reason, doctors recommend that pregnant women and those who are trying to become pregnant abstain from drinking alcohol altogether.

Pregnant women are also wise not to smoke. Smoking restricts the oxygen supply to the fetus, slows its breathing, and speeds up its heartbeat. These changes are associated with a significantly increased risk of miscarriage (Ness et al., 1999). In this country alone, smoking may cause over 100,000 miscarriages a year. Babies of mothers who smoke are also more likely to suffer low birth weight, which puts the child at risk for other developmental problems (DiFranza & Lew, 1995; Visscher, Feder, Burns, Brady, & Bray, 2003).

Many other maternal factors can affect the health of the newborn, including prenatal care and nutrition. Differences in access to good nutrition and health care help explain why the infant death rate in this country is over twice as high for African Americans as it is for whites. (see **Figure 7–2**; Singh & Yu, 1995.) A much higher percentage of African Americans live in poverty, and it is often harder for poor women to eat a healthy diet and see a doctor regularly during pregnancy (Aved, Irwin, Cummings, & Findeisen, 1993; Roussy, 2000).

The mother's level of psychological stress during pregnancy and the way she copes with it also appear to be related to the health of a newborn (Huizink, Mulder, & Buitelaar, 2004). For example, one study (Rini, Dunkel–Schetter, Wadhwa, & Sandman, 1999) found that the risks of prematurity and low birth weight were higher in mothers with low self-esteem who felt pessimistic, stressed, and anxious during pregnancy.

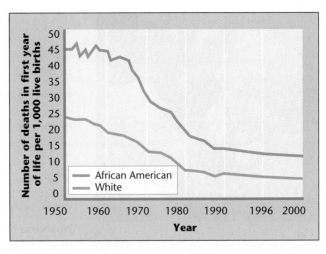

Figure 7–2

Mortality rates for white and African-American infants.

Source: National Center for Health Statistics, 1995 (through 1990); www.BlackHealthCare.com, 2000 (for 1991–1996); Centers for Disease Control (for 2000).

► CHECK YOUR UNDERSTANDING

Match each of the following terms with the appropriate definition:

1. ___ fetus
2. ___ prenatal development
3. ___ teratogens
4. ___ embryo
5. ___ critical periods
6. ___ placenta

a. substances that cross the placenta, causing birth defects.
b. times at which harmful agents can do major damage to the fetus.
c. the fertilized egg, two weeks after conception.
d. the developing organism, after three months.
e. the period from conception to birth.
f. the organ that nourishes the fetus.

Answers: 1. d, 2. e, 3. a, 4. c, 5. b, 6. f.

► APPLY YOUR UNDERSTANDING

1. Sue has just discovered that she is pregnant. She asks you whether you think it would be all right if she drinks a beer or two with her friends at the end of the week. Based on what you have read in this chapter, which of the following would be the most appropriate reply?
   a. "Not during the first three months of pregnancy, and no more than one drink a week thereafter."
   b. "Not during the last six months of pregnancy, but it would be okay prior to that."
   c. "Avoid alcohol at all times during pregnancy."
   d. "Only one drink a week, and then only if she gets good nutrition and good medical care."

2. Mary Jane is pregnant and a heavy smoker. If her baby has a health problem due to Mary Jane's smoking, it is most likely to _____.
   a. have mild mental retardation.
   b. have a low birth weight.
   c. be blind.
   d. have a weak immune system.

Answers: 1. c, 2. b.

If they are raised in a compatible environment, easy, uninhibited babies will most likely grow to be outgoing children and adults.

The Newborn

7.2 Describe the role heredity plays in shaping the newborn's reflexes, temperament, and perceptual abilities.

Research has disproved the old idea that **neonates**, or newborn babies, do nothing but eat, sleep, and cry, while remaining oblivious to the world. True, newborns can sleep up to 20 hours a day, but when awake they are much more aware and competent than they may seem at first glance.

REFLEXES

What early reflexes enable newborns to respond to their environment?

Newborns come equipped with a number of useful reflexes. Many of these reflexes, such as those that control breathing, are essential to life outside the uterus. Some enable babies to nurse. The baby's tendency to turn his or her head toward anything that touches the cheek is called the *rooting reflex*. The rooting reflex is very useful in helping the baby find the mother's nipple. The *sucking reflex* is the tendency to suck on anything that enters the mouth, and the *swallowing reflex* enables the baby to swallow milk and other liquids without choking.

Other reflexes have purposes that are less obvious. The *grasping reflex* is the tendency to cling vigorously to an adult's finger or to any other object placed in the baby's hands. The *stepping reflex* refers to the fact that very young babies take what looks like walking steps if they are held upright with their feet just touching a flat surface. These two reflexes normally disappear after two or three months, reemerging later as voluntary grasping (at around five months of age) and real walking (at the end of the first year).

Very young babies are also capable of a surprisingly complex kind of behavior: Imitating the facial expressions of adults (Bower, 2003). If an adult opens his or her mouth or sticks out his or her tongue, newborn babies often respond by opening their mouths or sticking out their tongues (Meltzoff & Moore, 1989). When this ability to imitate was first noted in newborns, psychologists could hardly believe it. How could babies carry out such complex responses at an age when they can have no idea how their own face looks, much less how to make specific facial expressions? It now appears that this early imitation is only a primitive reflex, like the grasping and stepping reflexes. The behavior disappears after a few weeks and then reemerges in a more complex form many months later (Bjorklund, 1989; Wyrwicka, 1988).

Almost all newborns respond to the human face, the human voice, and the human touch. This behavior improves their chances of survival. After all, babies are totally dependent on the people who take care of them, so it is essential that their social relationships get off to a good start. From the very beginning, they have a means of communicating their needs: They can cry. And very soon—in only about six weeks—they have an even better method of communication, one that serves as a thank you to the people who are working so hard to keep them happy: They can smile.

TEMPERAMENT

Is your temperament the same as when you were a newborn?

We may be tempted to talk about babies as if they are all the same, but babies display individual differences in **temperament** (Gartstein & Rothbart, 2003; Goldsmith & Harman, 1994). Some cry much more than others; some are much more active. Some babies love to be cuddled; others seem to wriggle uncomfortably when held. Some are highly reactive to stimuli around them, whereas others are quite placid no matter what they see or hear.

In a classic study of infant temperament, Alexander Thomas and Stella Chess (1977) identified three types of babies: "easy," "difficult," and "slow to warm up."

- "Easy" babies are good natured and adaptable, easy to care for and to please.
- "Difficult" babies are moody and intense, with strong, negative reactions to new people and situations.

neonates Newborn babies.

temperament Characteristic patterns of emotional reactions and emotional self-regulation.

- "Slow to warm up" babies are relatively inactive and slow to respond to new things; when they do react, their reactions are mild.

To these three types, Jerome Kagan and his associates (Kagan, Reznick, Snidman, Gibbons, & Johnson, 1988; Kagan & Snidman, 1991) have added a fourth: The "shy child." Shy children are timid and inhibited, fearful of anything new or strange. Considerable research evidence supports the view that basic temperament is the result of hereditary factors (Kagan, 1994) (Kagan, Arcus, & Snidman, 1993). Additional evidence to support the notion that temperament is largely biologically based and stable comes from neuroimaging studies showing that the amygdala (see **Figure 2–7**) of shy infants overreacts (compared with infants who are less shy and inhibited) when the shy infants are presented with a novel stimulus or situation, a response that continues into adolescence (Schwartz et al., 2003; Schwartz, Christopher, Shin, Kagan, & Rauch, 2003).

Some evidence suggests, however, that differences in temperament also may be due to prenatal influences. In particular, maternal stress produces reliable changes in heartbeat and movement in the fetus, and these, in turn, are correlated with temperament in the child. Some psychologists believe that the mix of hormones in the womb may be as important in determining temperament as the genes the child inherits (Azar, 1997b; DiPietro, Hodgson, Costigan, & Johnson, 1996; Huizink et al., 2002).

Regardless of what initially causes a baby's temperament, it often remains quite stable over time (Rothbart, Derryberry, & Hershey, 2000). In one study that asked mothers to describe their children's temperaments, characteristics such as degree of irritability, flexibility, and persistence were all relatively stable from infancy through age eight (Pedlow, Sanson, Prior, & Oberklaid, 1993). Other studies have found that fussy or difficult infants are likely to become "problem children" who are aggressive and have difficulties in school (Guérin, 1994; Patterson & Bank, 1989; Persson-Blennow & McNeil, 1988). As we've noted, longitudinal studies have shown that most shy infants continue to be relatively shy and inhibited, just as most uninhibited infants remained relatively outgoing and bold (Kagan & Snidman, 1991).

A combination of biological and environmental factors generally contributes to this stability in behavior. For example if a newborn has an innate predisposition to cry often and react negatively to things, the parents may find themselves tired, frustrated, and often angry. These reactions in the parents may serve to reinforce the baby's difficult behaviors, and so they tend to endure. Even if children are born with a particular temperament, they need not have that temperament for life. Each child's predispositions interact with his or her experiences, and how the child turns out is the result of that interaction (Kagan, 1989, 1994; Kagan, Snidman, & Arcus, 1992; Karrass & Braungart–Rieker, 2003; Maccoby, 2000).

A child's temperament—which usually can be categorized as easy, difficult, slow to warm-up, or shy is often a relatively stable characteristic across the lifespan.

PERCEPTUAL ABILITIES

Which senses are the most developed at birth, and which are the least developed?

Newborns can see, hear, and understand far more than previous generations gave them credit for. Their senses work fairly well at birth and rapidly improve to near-adult levels. Neonates begin to absorb and process information from the outside world as soon as they enter it—in some cases, even before.

VISION Unlike puppies and kittens, human babies are born with their eyes open and functioning, even though the world looks a bit fuzzy to them at first. They see most clearly when faces or objects are only 8 to 10 inches away from them. Visual acuity (the clarity of vision) improves rapidly, however, and so does the ability to focus on objects at different distances. By six or eight months of age, babies can see almost as well as the average college student, though their visual system takes another three or four years to develop fully (Maurer & Maurer, 1988).

Even very young babies already have visual preferences. They would rather look at a new picture or pattern than one they have seen many times before. If given a choice between two pictures or patterns, both of which are new to them, they generally prefer the one with the clearer contrasts and simpler patterns. As babies get older and their vision improves, they prefer more and more complex patterns, perhaps reflecting their need for an increasingly complex environment (Acredolo & Hake, 1982; Fantz, Fagan, & Miranda, 1975; Slater, 2000).

In general, infants find human faces and voices particularly interesting (Flavell, 1999; Turati, 2004). They not only like to look at another person's face, but they also will follow the other person's gaze. Hood, Willen, and Driver (1998) presented a photograph of a human face on a video monitor. Sometimes the adult depicted looked straight ahead, sometimes to the left or right. The researchers found that infants as young as three months noticed the direction of the adult's gaze and shifted their gaze accordingly. Newborns also prefer to look at their own mother rather than at a stranger (Walton, Bower, & Bower, 1992).

DEPTH PERCEPTION Depth perception is the ability to see the world in three dimensions, with some objects nearer, others farther away. Although researchers have been unable to find evidence of depth perception in babies younger than 4 months (Aslin & Smith, 1988), the ability to see the world in three dimensions is well developed by the time a baby learns to crawl, between 6 and 12 months of age.

This finding was demonstrated in a classic experiment using a device called a *visual cliff* (Walk & Gibson, 1961). Researchers divided a table into three parts. The center was a solid runway, raised above the rest of the table by about an inch. On one side of this runway was a solid surface decorated in a checkerboard pattern and covered with a sheet of clear glass. The other side was also covered with a thick sheet of clear glass, but on this side—the visual cliff—the checkerboard surface was not directly under the glass, but 40 inches below it. An infant of crawling age was placed on the center runway, and the mother stood on one side or the other, encouraging the baby to crawl toward her across the glass. In the original study, all of the 6- to 14-month-old infants tested refused to crawl across the visual cliff, even though they were perfectly willing to cross the "shallow" side of the table. When the "deep" side separated the baby from the mother, some of the infants cried; others peered down at the surface below the glass or patted the glass with their hands. Although not all babies refuse to cross the visual cliff in subsequent experiments such as this, their behaviors clearly show that even at quite young ages, babies can perceive depth.

OTHER SENSES Even before babies are born, their ears are in working order (Fernald, 2001). Fetuses in the uterus can hear sounds and will startle at a sudden, loud noise in the mother's environment. After birth, babies show signs that they remember sounds they heard in the womb. Babies also are born with the ability to tell the direction of a sound. They show this by turning their heads toward the source of a sound (Muir, 1985).

Infants are particularly tuned in to the sounds of human speech. One-month-olds can distinguish among similar speech sounds such as "pa-pa-pa" and "ba-ba-ba" (Eimas & Tartter, 1979). In some ways, young infants are even better at distinguishing speech sounds than are older children and adults. As children grow older, they often lose their ability to hear the difference between two very similar speech sounds that are not distinguished in their native language (Werker & Desjardins, 1995). For example, young Japanese infants have no trouble hearing the difference between "ra" and "la," sounds that are not heard as being different in the Japanese language. By the time they are one year old, however, Japanese infants can no longer tell these two sounds apart (Werker, 1989).

With regard to taste and smell, newborns have clear-cut likes and dislikes. They like sweet flavors, a preference that persists through childhood. Babies only a few hours old will show pleasure at the taste of sweetened water but will screw up their faces in disgust at the taste of lemon juice (Steiner, 1979).

As infants grow older, their perceptions of the world become keener and more meaningful. Two factors are important in this development. One is physical maturation of the sense organs and the nervous system; the other is gaining experience in the world.

When placed on a visual cliff, babies of crawling age (about 6 to 14 months) will not cross the deep side, even to reach their mothers. This classic experiment tells us that by the time they can crawl, babies can also perceive depth.

Infancy and Childhood

7.3 Identify the major physical, cognitive, and social transitions that characterize infancy and childhood and describe how Piaget's theory of cognitive development and Erikson's theory of social development can be used as organizing frameworks for understanding this developmental period.

During the first dozen or so years of life, a helpless baby becomes a competent member of society. Many important kinds of developments occur during these early years. Here we discuss physical and motor changes as well as cognitive and social ones.

PHYSICAL DEVELOPMENT

Do children grow at a steady pace?

In the first year of life, the average baby grows 10 inches and gains 15 pounds. By four months, birth weight has doubled, and by the first birthday, birth weight has tripled. During the second year, physical growth slows considerably. Rapid increases in height and weight will not occur again until early adolescence.

An infant's growth does not occur in the smooth, continuous fashion depicted in growth charts. Rather, growth takes place in fits and starts (Lampl, Veidhuis, & Johnson, 1992). When babies are measured daily over their first 21 months, most show no growth 90 percent of the time, but when they do grow, they do so rapidly—sometimes startlingly so. Incredible though it may sound, some older children gain as much as one inch in height overnight!

Marked changes in body proportions accompany changes in a baby's size. During the first two years after birth, as the brain undergoes rapid growth, children have heads that are large relative to their bodies. A child's brain reaches three-quarters of its adult size by about the age of two, at which point head growth slows down, and the body does most of the growing. Head growth is virtually complete by age 10, but the body continues to grow for several more years. (see **Figure 7–3**.)

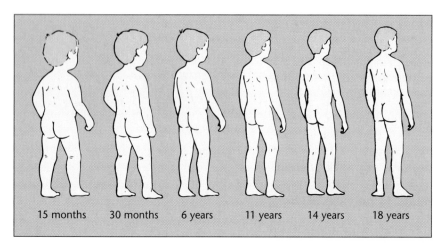

Figure 7–3

Body proportions at various ages. Young children are top heavy: They have large heads and small bodies. As they get older, the body and legs become longer, and the head is proportionately smaller.

Source: From Bayley, *Individual Patterns of Development.* Copyright © 1956 by the Society for Research in Child Development. Adapted with permission.

---

developmental norms The average ages at which specific skills, such as walking, are archieved.

MOTOR DEVELOPMENT

Is walking at an early age a sign of future athletic ability?

Motor development refers to the acquisition of skills involving movement, such as grasping, crawling, and walking. Much early motor development consists of substituting voluntary actions for reflexes (Clark, 1994). The newborn grasping and stepping reflexes, for example give way to voluntary grasping and walking in the older baby.

The average ages at which such skills are achieved are called **developmental norms**. By about nine months, for example, the average infant can stand up while holding onto something. Crawling occurs, on average, at 10 months, and walking at about one year. However, some normal infants develop much faster than average, whereas others develop more slowly. A baby who is three or four months behind schedule may be perfectly normal, and one who is three or four months ahead is not necessarily destined to become a star athlete. To some extent, parents can accelerate the acquisition of motor skills in children by providing them with ample training, encouragement, and practice. Differences in these factors seem to account for most of the cross-cultural differences in the average age at which children reach certain milestones in motor development (Hopkins & Westra, 1989, 1990).

Motor development proceeds in a *proximodistal* fashion—that is, from nearest the center of the body (proximal) to farthest from the center (distal). For example, the infant initially has much greater control over gross arm movements than over movements of the fingers. Babies start batting at nearby objects as early as one month, but they cannot reach accurately until they

The normal sequence of motor development. At birth, babies have grasping and stepping reflexes. At about 2 months, they can lift their head and shoulders. They can sit up by themselves at about 6 ½ months and can stand (while holding on to something) at about 9 months. Crawling begins, on average, at 10 months, and walking at 1 year.

are about four months old. It takes them another month or two before they are consistently successful in grasping objects (von Hofsten & Fazel–Zandy, 1984). At first, they grasp with the whole hand, but by the end of the first year, they can pick up a tiny object with the thumb and forefinger.

Maturation refers to biological processes that unfold as a person grows older and that contribute to orderly sequences of developmental changes, such as the progression from crawling to toddling to walking. Psychologists used to believe that maturation of the central nervous system largely accounted for many of the changes in early motor skills—that environment and experience played only a minor part in their emergence. But this view has been changing (Thelen, 1994, 1995). Many researchers now see early motor development as arising from a combination of factors both within and outside the child. The child plays an active part in the process by exploring, discovering, and selecting solutions to the demands of new tasks. A baby who is learning to crawl, for example, must figure out how to position the body with belly off the ground and to coordinate arm and leg movements to maintain balance while managing to proceed forward (Bertenthal et al., 1994). What doesn't work must be discarded or adapted; what does work must be remembered and called on for future use. This process is a far cry from seeing the baby as one day starting to crawl simply because he or she has reached the point of maturational "readiness."

As coordination improves, children learn to run, skip, and climb. At three and four, they begin to use their hands for increasingly complex tasks, learning how to put on mittens and shoes, then grappling with buttons, zippers, shoelaces, and pencils. Gradually, through a combination of practice and the physical maturation of the body and the brain, they acquire increasingly complex motor abilities, such as bike riding, roller blading, and swimming. By the age of about 11, some children begin to be highly skilled at such tasks (Clark, 1994).

COGNITIVE DEVELOPMENT

How does a child's ability to reason change over time?

The most influential theorist in the area of cognitive development was the Swiss psychologist Jean Piaget (1896–1980). Piaget observed and studied children, including his own three. He watched them play games, solve problems, and perform everyday tasks, and he asked them questions and devised tests to learn how they thought. As a result of his observations, Piaget believed that cognitive development is a way of adapting to the environment. In Piaget's view, children are intrinsically motivated to explore and understand things. As they do so, according to Piaget, they progress through four basic stages of cognitive development. These are outlined in the "**Summary Table.**"

SENSORY-MOTOR STAGE (BIRTH TO TWO YEARS) According to Piaget, babies spend the first two years of life in the **sensory-motor stage** of development. They start out by simply applying the skills with which they were born—primarily sucking and grasping—to a broad range of activities. Young babies delight in taking things into their mouths—their mother's breast, their own thumb, or anything else within reach. Similarly, young babies will grasp a rattle reflexively. When they eventually realize that the noise comes from the rattle, they begin to shake everything they can get hold of in an effort to reproduce the sound. Eventually, they distinguish between things that make noise and things that do not. In this way,

maturation The automatic biologically programmed unfolding of development in an organism that occurs with the passage of time.

sensory-motor stage In Piaget's theory, the stage of cognitive development between birth and 2 years of age in which the individual develops object permanence and acquires the ability to form mental representations.

Jean Piaget (center, in the dark suit) based his theory of cognitive development on case studies of children.

SUMMARY TABLE

PIAGET'S STAGES OF COGNITIVE DEVELOPMENT

STAGE	APPROXIMATE AGE	KEY FEATURES
Sensory-motor	0–2 years	Object permanence Mental representations
Preoperational	2–7 years	Representational thought Fantasy play Symbolic gestures Egocentrism
Concrete-operational	7–11 years	Conservation Complex classification
Formal-operational	Adolescence–adulthood	Abstract and hypothetical thought

infants begin to organize their experiences, fitting them into rudimentary categories called *schema*, such as "suckable" and "not suckable," or "noisemaking" and "not noisemaking" (see Chapter 5: "Cognitive and Mental Abilities").

Another important outcome of the sensory-motor stage, according to Piaget, is the development of **object permanence**, an awareness that objects continue to exist even when out of sight. For a newborn child, objects that disappear simply cease to exist—"out of sight, out of mind." But as children gain experience with the world, they develop a sense of object permanence. By the time they are 18 to 24 months old, they can even imagine the movement of an object that they do not actually see move. This last skill depends on the ability to form **mental representations** of objects and to manipulate those representations in their heads. This is a major achievement of the late sensory-motor stage.

By the end of the sensory-motor stage, toddlers have also developed a capacity for self-recognition—that is, they are able to recognize the child in the mirror as "myself." In one famous study, mothers put a dab of red paint on their child's nose while pretending to wipe the child's face. Then each child was placed in front of a mirror. Babies under one year of age stared in fascination at the red-nosed baby in the mirror; some of them even reached out to touch the nose's reflection. But babies between 21 and 24 months reached up and touched their own reddened noses, thereby showing that they knew the red-nosed baby in the mirror was "me" (Brooks–Gunn & Lewis, 1984).

PREOPERATIONAL STAGE (2 TO 7 YEARS) When children enter the **preoperational stage** of cognitive development, their thought is still tightly bound to their physical and perceptual experiences. But their increasing ability to use mental representations lays the groundwork for the development of language—using words as symbols to represent events and to describe, remember, and reason about experiences. (We will say much more about language development shortly.) Representational thought also lays the groundwork for two other hallmarks of this stage—engaging in *fantasy play* (a cardboard box becomes a castle) and using *symbolic gestures* (slashing the air with an imaginary sword to slay an imaginary dragon).

Although children of this age have made advances over sensory-motor thought, in many ways they don't yet think as do older children and adults. For example, preschool children are **egocentric**. They have difficulty seeing things from another person's point of view or putting themselves in someone else's place.

Children of this age are also easily misled by appearances (Flavell, 1986). They tend to concentrate on the most outstanding aspect of a display or an event, ignoring everything else. In a famous experiment, Piaget showed preoperational children two identical glasses, filled to the same level with juice. The children were asked which glass held more juice, and they replied (correctly) that both had the same amount. Then Piaget poured the juice from

---

object permanence The concept that things continue to exist even when they are out of sight.

mental representations Mental images or symbols (such as words) used to think about or remember an object, a person, or an event.

preoperational stage In Piaget's theory, the stage of cognitive development between 2 and 7 years of age in which the individual becomes able to use mental representations and language to describe, remember, and reason about the world, though only in an egocentric fashion.

egocentric Unable to see things from another's point of view.

one glass into a taller, narrower glass. (See the accompanying photo.) Again the children were asked which glass held more juice. They looked at the two glasses, saw that the level of the juice in the tall, narrow one was much higher, and then replied that the narrow glass had more. According to Piaget, children at this stage cannot consider the past (Piaget simply poured all the juice from one container into another) or the future (if he poured it back again, the levels of juice would be identical). Nor can they consider a container's height and width at the same time. Thus, they can't understand how an increase in one dimension (height) might be offset by a decrease in another dimension (width).

CONCRETE-OPERATIONAL STAGE (7 TO 11 YEARS) During the **concrete-operational stage**, children become more flexible in their thinking. They learn to consider more than one dimension of a problem at a time and to look at a situation from someone else's viewpoint. This is the age at which they become able to grasp **principles of conservation**, such as the idea that the volume of a liquid stays the same regardless of the size and shape of the container into which it is poured. Other related conservation concepts have to do with number, length, area, and mass. All involve an understanding that basic amounts remain constant despite superficial changes in appearance, which can always be reversed.

Another accomplishment of this stage is the ability to grasp complex classification schemes such as those involving superordinate and subordinate classes. For instance, if you show a preschooler four toy dogs and two toy cats and ask whether there are more dogs or more animals, the child will almost always answer "more dogs." It is not until age seven or eight that children are able to think about objects as being simultaneously members of two classes, one more inclusive than the other. Yet even well into the elementary school years, children's thinking is still very much stuck in the "here and now." Often, they are unable to solve problems without concrete reference points that they can handle or imagine handling.

FORMAL-OPERATIONAL STAGE (ADOLESCENCE—ADULTHOOD) This limitation is overcome in the **formal-operational stage** of cognitive development, often reached during adolescence. Youngsters at this stage can think in abstract terms. They can formulate hypotheses, test them mentally, and accept or reject them according to the outcome of these mental experiments. Therefore, they are capable of going beyond the here and now to understand things in terms of cause and effect, to consider possibilities as well as realities, and to develop and use general rules, principles, and theories.

MORAL DEVELOPMENT

How do gender and ethnic background affect moral development?

Piaget's theory provides a useful way of explaining how changes in cognition happen as children develop. Although some researchers suggest that children may be more competent than Piaget believed (Gopnick, Meltzoff, & Kuhl, 1999; Baillargeon, 1994) and that social learning may be more important than he described (Vygotsky, 1978; Daehler, 1994), most psychologists find Piaget's view to be a good foundation for understanding the child's development of thought.

Several pscyhologists have expanded on Piaget's theory of cognitive development, including Lawrence Kohlberg, whose work focused on understanding how people make moral decisions about right and wrong. Kohlberg (1979, 1981) studied moral reasoning by telling his participants stories that illustrate complex moral issues. The "Heinz dilemma" is the best known of these stories:

> In Europe, a woman was near death from cancer. One drug might save her, a form of radium that a druggist in the same town had recently discovered. The druggist was charging $2,000, ten times what the drug cost him to make. The sick woman's husband, Heinz, went to everyone he knew to borrow the money, but he could only get together about half of what it cost.

In Piaget's famous experiment, the child has to judge which glass holds more liquid: the tall, thin one or the short, wide one. Although both glasses hold the same amount, children in the preoperational stage say that the taller glass holds more, since they focus their attention on only one thing—the height of the column of liquid.

concrete-operational stage In Piaget's theory, the stage of cognitive development between 7 and 11 years of age in which the individual can attend to more than one thing at a time and understand someone else's point of view, though thinking is limited to concrete matters.

principles of conservation The concept that the quantity of a substance is not altered by reversible changes in its appearance.

formal-operational stage In Piaget's theory, the stage of cognitive development between adolescence and adulthood in which the individual becomes capable of abstract thought.

He told the druggist that his wife was dying and asked him to sell it cheaper or let him pay later. But the druggist said, "No." The husband got desperate and broke into the man's store to steal the drug for his wife (Kohlberg, 1969, p. 379).

The children and adolescents who heard this story were asked, "Should the husband have done that? Why?"

On the basis of his participants' replies to these questions (particularly the second one, "Why?"), Kohlberg theorized that moral reasoning develops in stages, much like Piaget's account of cognitive development:

- *Preconventional level* Preadolescent children are at what Kohlberg called the preconventional level of moral reasoning: They tend to interpret behavior in terms of its concrete consequences. Younger children at this level base their judgments of "right" and "wrong" behavior on whether it is rewarded or punished. Somewhat older children, still at this level, guide their moral choices on the basis of what satisfies needs, particularly their own.

- *Conventional level* With the arrival of adolescence and the shift to formal-operational thought, the stage is set for progression to the second level of moral reasoning, the conventional level. At this level, the adolescent at first defines right behavior as that which pleases or helps others and is approved by them. Around mid-adolescence, there is a further shift toward considering various abstract social virtues, such as being a "good citizen" and respecting authority. Both forms of conventional moral reasoning require an ability to think about such abstract values as "duty" and "social order," to consider the intentions that lie behind behavior, and to put oneself in the "other person's shoes."

- *Postconventional level* The third level of moral reasoning, the postconventional level, requires a still more abstract form of thought. This level is marked by an emphasis on abstract principles such as justice, liberty, and equality. Personal and strongly felt moral standards become the guideposts for deciding what is right and wrong. Whether these decisions correspond to the rules and laws of a particular society at a particular time is irrelevant. For the first time, people may become aware of discrepancies between what they judge to be moral and what society has determined to be legal.

Kohlberg's views have been criticized on several counts. First, research indicates that many people in our society, adults as well as adolescents, never progress beyond the conventional level of moral reasoning (Conger & Petersen, 1991). Does this finding mean that these people are morally "underdeveloped," as Kohlberg's theory implies?

Second, Kohlberg's theory does not take account of cultural differences in moral values (Nucci, 2002). Kohlberg put considerations of "justice" at the highest level of moral reasoning. In Nepal, however, researchers discovered that a group of adolescent Buddhist monks placed the highest moral value on alleviating suffering and showing compassion, concepts that have no place in Kohlberg's scheme of moral development (Huebner, Garrod, & Snarey, 1990).

Third, Kohlberg's theory has been criticized as sexist. Kohlberg found that boys usually scored higher than girls on his test of moral development. According to Carol Gilligan (1982, 1992), this was the case because boys are more inclined to base their moral judgments on the abstract concept of justice, whereas girls tend to base theirs more on the

Only when people have reached Kohlberg's postconventional level of moral reasoning can they understand that there may be a difference between what is moral and what is legal.

criteria of caring about other people and the importance of maintaining personal relationships. In Gilligan's view, there is no valid reason to assume that one of these perspectives is morally superior to the other. Although subsequent research has found that gender differences in moral thinking tend to diminish in adulthood (L. D. Cohn, 1991), concerns about gender bias in Kohlberg's theory still remain.

More recent research on moral development has moved in the direction of broadening Kohlberg's focus on changes in moral reasoning. These researchers are interested in the factors that influence moral choices in everyday life, and the extent to which those choices are actually put into action. In other words, they want to understand moral behavior as much as moral thinking (Power, 1994).

LANGUAGE DEVELOPMENT

How does a child develop language skills?

The development of language follows a predictable pattern. At about two months of age, an infant begins to *coo* (a nondescript word for nondescript sounds). In another month or two, the infant enters the **babbling** stage and starts to repeat sounds such as *da* or even meaningless sounds that developmental psychologists refer to as "grunts"; these sounds are the building blocks for later language development (Dill, 1994). A few months later, the infant may string together the same sound, as in *dadadada*. Finally, the baby will form combinations of different sounds, as in *dabamaga* (Ferguson & Macken, 1983).

Even deaf babies with deaf parents who communicate with sign language engage in a form of babbling (Pettito & Marentette, 1991). Similar to hearing infants, these babies begin to babble before they are 10 months old—but they babble with their hands! Just as hearing infants utter sounds over and over, deaf babies make repetitive movements of their hands, like those of sign language. Such behaviors suggest that human language has been shaped by evolutionary forces and is biologically based (Pinker, 1994; 1999; 2002) (see Chapter 5: "Cognition and Mental Abilities").

Gradually, an infant's babbling takes on certain features of adult language. At about age four to six months, the infant's vocalizations begin to show signs of *intonation*, the rising and lowering of pitch that allows adults to distinguish, for example, between questions ("You're tired?") and statements ("You're tired."). Also around this time, babies learn the basic sounds of their native language and can distinguish them from the sounds of other languages (Cheour et al., 1998). By six months, they may recognize commonly used words, such as their own names (Kuhl, Williams, & Lacerda, 1992; Mandel, Jusczyk, & Pisoni, 1995) and the words *mommy* and *daddy* (Tincoff & Jusczyk, 1999).

By around their first birthday, babies begin to use intonation to indicate commands and questions (Greenfield & Smith, 1976). At about the same age, they show signs of understanding what is said to them, and they begin not only to imitate what others say but also to use sounds to get attention. Vocalization also becomes more and more communicative and socially directed. Caregivers facilitate this process by speaking to their babies in what is called *infant directed speech*. The parents speak slowly and use simple sentences, a higher-pitched voice, repetition, and exaggerated intonations—all of which engage babies' attention and help them to distinguish the sounds of their language (Hampson & Nelson, 1993).

All this preparation leads up to the first word at about age one. During the next six to eight months, children build a vocabulary of one-word sentences called **holophrases**: "Up!"; "Out!"; "More!" Children may also use compound words such as *awgone* [all gone]. To these holophrases, they add words used to address people—*Bye-bye* is a favorite—and a few exclamations, such as *Ouch!*

In the second year of life, children begin to distinguish between themselves and others. Possessive words become a big part of the vocabulary: [The shoes are] "Daddy's." But the overwhelming passion of children from 12 to 24 months old is naming. With little or no prompting, they will name virtually everything they see, though not always correctly! Children at this age are

babbling A baby's vocalizations, consisting of repetition of consonant–vowel combinations.

holophrases One-word sentences commonly used by children under 2 years of age.

From 12 to 24 months, babies typically point at and name, although not always correctly, whatever object interests them.

fascinated by objects. If they don't know the name of an object, they will simply invent one or use another word that is almost right. Feedback from parents ("No, that's not a dog, it's a cow.") enhances vocabulary and helps children understand what names can and cannot be assigned to classes of things ("dog" is not used for big four-legged animals that live on farms and moo rather than bark).

During the third year of life, children begin to form two- and three-word sentences such as "See daddy," "Baby cry," "My ball," and "Dog go woof woof." Recordings of mother–child conversations show that children from 24 to 36 months old noticeably omit auxiliary verbs and verb endings ([Can] "I have that?"; "I [am] eat[ing] it up."), as well as prepositions and articles ("It [is] time [for] Sarah [to] take [a] nap.") (Bloom, 1970). Apparently, children this age seize on the most important parts of speech, those that contain the most meaning.

After three years of age, children begin to fill in their sentences ("Nick school." becomes "Nick goes to school."), and language production increases dramatically. Children start to use the past tense as well as the present. Sometimes they *overregularize* the past tense, by applying the regular form when an irregular one is called for (saying "goed" instead of "went," for example). Such mistakes are signs that the child has implicitly grasped the basic rules of language (Marcus, 1996). Preschoolers also ask more questions and learn to employ "Why?" effectively (sometimes monotonously so). By the age of five or six, most children have a vocabulary of over 2,500 words and can construct sentences of 6 to 8 words.

The importance of the social environment to language development was documented in a study by Betty Hart and Todd Risley (1995); (for a summary, see Chance, 1997). Over a three-year period, these researchers studied the linguistic environment provided in the homes of preschool youngsters. They found that both the quality and quantity of language experiences varied with the educational level of the parents. For example, the most-educated parents directed over three times as many words to their children as did the least-educated parents. The well-educated parents also did more explaining, asked more questions, and provided more feedback. The best educated parents were also far more likely to give positive feedback, such as, "That's right." or "Good." The least educated parents were more likely to comment negatively about a child's behavior (saying, "No" or "Stop that") than to comment positively. These differences in environment predicted differences in academic achievement years later, especially in language skills.

SOCIAL DEVELOPMENT

According to Erickson's theory, what are the major developmental milestones in childhood?

Along with developing more sophisticated ways of thinking about the world, infants and children also become increasingly more capable in their social relationships. One theorist who emphasized and described how social relationships affect development was Erik Erikson (1902–1994).

ERIKSON'S STAGE THEORY Erik Erikson viewed human social development as being comprised of a sequence of eight stages, beginning at birth and ending in old age. In each stage, the individual faces a central conflict or "crisis," which must be resolved. If the conflict is resolved favorably, this sets the stage for successful development in the following periods of development.

In early development especially, parent-child interactions are critically important, because the family constitutes the child's first brush with society. As the child grows older, peer relationships become more important. In adulthood, the central conflicts begin to center less on relationships with others, and more on how the person interprets the patterns of his or her life. **Table 7–1** summarizes Erikson's eight stages of development, which are described in more detail as follows:

1. **Trust versus mistrust.** During the first year of life, babies are torn between trusting and not trusting their parents. If their needs are generally met, infants come to trust the environment and themselves. This process leads to faith in the predictability of the

>TABLE 7-1 ERIKSON'S EIGHT STAGES OF DEVELOPMENT

Stage	Development Period
Trust versus Mistrust	Infancy (age 0–1)
Autonomy versus Shame and Doubt	Toddlerhood (age 1–3)
Initiative versus Guilt	Early Childhood (age 3–6)
Industry versus Inferiority	Later Childhood (age 6–13)
Identity versus Role Confusion	Adolescence (age 13–18)
Intimacy versus Isolation	Young Adulthood (age 18–25)
Generativity versus Stagnation	Adulthood (age 25–60)
Integrity versus Despair	Maturity (age 60–end of life)

environment and optimism about the future. Frustrated infants become suspicious, fearful, and overly concerned with security.

2. **Autonomy versus shame and doubt.** During their first three years, as physical development proceeds, children gain increasing autonomy and begin to explore their surroundings. They learn to walk, hold onto things, and control their excretory functions. If the child repeatedly fails to master these skills, self-doubt may take root. One response to self-doubt is the practice of abiding compulsively by fixed routines. At the other extreme is the hostile rejection of all controls, both internal and external. If parents and other adults belittle a child's efforts, the child may also begin to feel shame and may acquire a lasting sense of inferiority.

3. **Initiative versus guilt.** Between the ages of three and six, children become increasingly active, undertaking new projects, manipulating things in the environment, making plans, and conquering new challenges. Parental support and encouragement for these initiatives lead to a sense of joy in exercising initiative and taking on new challenges. However, if the child is scolded for these initiatives, strong feelings of guilt, unworthiness, and resentment may take hold and persist.

4. **Industry versus inferiority.** During the next six or seven years, children encounter a new set of expectations at home and at school. They must learn the skills needed to become well-rounded adults, including personal care, productive work, and independent social living. If children are stifled in their efforts to become part of the adult world, they may conclude that they are inadequate, mediocre, or inferior, and may lose faith in their power to become self-sufficient.

5. **Identity versus role confusion.** At puberty, childhood ends and the responsibilities of adulthood loom just ahead. The critical problem at this stage is to find one's identity. In Erikson's view, identity is achieved by integrating a number of roles—student, sister or brother, friend, and so on—into a coherent pattern that gives the young person a sense of inner continuity or identity. Failure to forge an identity leads to role confusion and despair.

According to Erik Erikson, the central developmental task in early adulthood is to form one or more meaningful intimate relationships.

6. **Intimacy versus isolation.** During young adulthood, men and women must resolve a critical new issue: the question of intimacy. To love someone else, Erikson argued, we must have resolved our earlier crises successfully and feel secure in our own identities. To form an intimate relationship, lovers must be trusting, autonomous, and capable of initiative, and must exhibit other hallmarks of maturity. Failure at intimacy brings a painful sense of loneliness and the feeling of being incomplete.

7. **Generativity versus stagnation.** During middle adulthood, roughly between the ages of 25 and 60, the challenge is to remain productive and creative in all aspects of one's life. People who have successfully negotiated the six earlier stages are likely to find meaning and joy in all the major activities of life—career, family, and community. For others, life becomes a drab routine, and they feel dull and resentful.

8. **Integrity versus despair.** With the onset of old age, people must try to come to terms with their approaching death. For some, this is a period of despair at the loss of former roles, such as employee and parent. Yet, according to Erikson, this stage also represents an opportunity to attain full selfhood. By this, he meant an acceptance of one's life, a sense that it is complete and satisfactory. People who have gained full maturity by resolving the conflicts in all the earlier stages possess the integrity to face death with a minimum of fear.

Because Erikson's theory provides a useful context for the study of human development across the entire lifespan, we will refer to it throughout the remainder of this chapter.

PARENT–CHILD RELATIONSHIPS IN INFANCY: DEVELOPMENT OF ATTACHMENT

Young animals of many species follow their mothers around because of **imprinting**. Shortly after they are born or hatched, they form a strong bond to the first moving object they see. In nature, this object is normally the mother, the first source of nurturance and protection. But in laboratory experiments, certain species of animals, such as geese, have been hatched in incubators and have imprinted on decoys, mechanical toys, and even human beings (Hoffman & DePaulo, 1977; Lorenz, 1935). These goslings faithfully follow their human "mother," showing no interest whatever in adult females of their own species.

Human newborns do not imprint on first-seen moving objects, but they do gradually form an **attachment**, or emotional bond, to the people who take care of them (regardless of the caregiver's gender). As we saw in Chapter 6, "Motivation and Emotion," classic studies of baby monkeys suggest that the sense of security engendered by physical contact and closeness is one important root of attachment (Harlow, 1958; Harlow & Zimmerman, 1959).

In humans, of course, this attachment is built on many hours of interaction during which baby and parent come to form a close relationship. Signs of attachment are evident by the age of six months or even earlier. The baby will react with smiles and coos at the caregiver's appearance and with whimpers and doleful looks when the caregiver goes away. At around seven months, attachment behavior becomes more intense. The infant will reach out to be picked up by the caregiver, and will cling to the caregiver, especially when tired, frightened, or hurt. The baby will also begin to be wary of strangers, sometimes reacting with loud wails at even the friendliest approach by an unfamiliar person. If separated from the caregiver even for a few minutes in an unfamiliar place, the baby will usually become quite upset.

Parents are often puzzled by this new behavior in their previously nonchalant infants, but it is perfectly normal. In fact, anxiety over separation from the mother indicates that the infant has developed a sense of "person permanence" along with a sense of object permanence. For five-month-olds, it's still "out of sight, out of mind" when mom or dad leaves the room, but for nine-month-olds, the memory of their parent lingers, and they announce at the top of their lungs that they want mommy or daddy to come back!

Ideally, infants learn in their first year of life that their primary caregivers can be counted on to be there when needed. As described in the previous section of this chapter, Erik Erikson called this result the development of *basic trust*. If babies' needs are generally met, they develop faith in other people and also in themselves. They see the world as a secure, dependable place and have optimism about the future. In contrast, babies whose needs are not usually met, perhaps because of an unresponsive or often absent caregiver, develop what Erikson referred to as *mistrust*. They grow to be fearful and overly anxious about their own security. This view is supported by research showing that children who grow up in well-adjusted families generally form stronger attachments to their parents than do children who grow up in strife-filled families (Frosch, Mangelsdorf, & McHale, 2000).

As infants develop basic trust, they are freed from preoccupation with the availability of the caregiver. They come to discover that there are other things of interest in the world. Cautiously at first, then more boldly, they venture away from the caregiver to investigate objects and other people around them. This exploration is a first indication of children's developing

Konrad Lorenz discovered that goslings will follow the first moving object they see, regardless of whether it is their mother, a mechanical toy, or a human. Here, Lorenz is trailed by ducklings who have imprinted on him.

imprinting The tendency in certain species to follow the first moving thing (usually its mother) it sees after it is born or hatched.

attachment Emotional bond that develops in the first year of life that makes human babies cling to their caregivers for safety and comfort.

autonomy, or a sense of independence. Autonomy and attachment may seem to be opposites, but they are actually closely related. The child who has formed a secure attachment to a caregiver can explore the environment without fear. Such a child knows that the caregiver will be there when really needed, and so the caregiver serves as a "secure base" from which to venture forth (Ainsworth, 1977).

Children who are insecurely attached to their mothers are less likely to explore an unfamiliar environment, even when their mother is present. Moreover, if left in a strange place, most young children will cry and refuse to be comforted, but the insecurely attached child is more likely to continue crying even after the mother returns, either pushing her away angrily or ignoring her altogether. In contrast, a securely attached 12-month-old is more likely to rush to the returning mother for a hug and words of reassurance and then happily begin to play again (Ainsworth, Blehar, Waters, & Wall, 1978).

The importance of secure attachment early in life is evident for many years afterward (Weinfield, Whaley, & Egeland, 2004). For example, studies of children from one through six years of age have shown that those who formed a secure attachment to their mothers by the age of 12 months later tended to be more at ease with other children, more interested in exploring new toys, and more enthusiastic and persistent when presented with new tasks (Harris & Liebert, 1991).

At about age 7 months, infants develop "stranger anxiety," a fearful reaction to unfamiliar people caused by the baby's developing cognitive abilities and attachment to primary caregivers.

At about two years of age, children begin to assert their growing independence, becoming very negative when interfered with by parents. They refuse everything: getting dressed ("No!"), going to sleep ("No!"), using the potty ("No!"). The usual outcome of these first declarations of independence is that the parents begin to discipline the child. Children are told they have to eat and go to bed at a particular time, they must not pull the cat's tail or kick their sister, and they must respect other people's rights. The conflict between the parents' need for peace and order and the child's desire for autonomy often creates difficulties. But it is an essential first step in **socialization**, the process by which children learn the behaviors and attitudes appropriate to their family and their culture.

Erikson saw two possible outcomes of this early conflict: *autonomy versus shame and doubt*. If a toddler fails to acquire a sense of independence and separateness from others, self-doubt may take root. The child may begin to question his or her own ability to act effectively in the world. If parents and other adults belittle a toddler's efforts, the child may also begin to feel ashamed. The need for both autonomy and socialization can be met if parents allow the child a reasonable amount of independence, while insisting that the child follow certain rules.

PARENT-CHILD RELATIONSHIPS IN CHILDHOOD As children grow older, their social worlds expand. They play with siblings and friends, they go off to nursery school or day care, and they eventually enter kindergarten. Erikson saw the stage between ages three and six as one of growing initiative, surrounded by a potential for guilt (*initiative versus guilt*). Children of this age become increasingly involved in independent efforts to accomplish goals—making plans, undertaking projects, mastering new skills—from bike riding to table setting to drawing, painting, and writing simple words. Parental encouragement of these initiatives leads to a sense of joy in taking on new tasks. But if children are repeatedly criticized and scolded for things they do wrong, they may develop strong feelings of unworthiness, resentment, and guilt. In Erikson's view, avoiding these negative feelings is the major challenge of this stage.

The effect of parenting style on a child's outlook and behavior has been the subject of extensive research. For example, Diana Baumrind (1972, 1991, 1996) identified four basic parenting styles:

- *Authoritative* parents, according to Baumrind, represent the most successful parenting style. Authoritative parents provide firm structure and guidance without being overly controlling. They listen to their children's opinions and give explanations for their decisions, but it is clear that they are the ones who make and enforce the rules. Parents who use this approach are most likely to have children who are self-reliant and socially responsible.
- *Authoritarian* parents control their children's behavior rigidly and insist on unquestioning obedience. They are high on control, but low on warmth dimensions of parenting. Authoritarian parents are likely to produce children who generally have poor

autonomy Sense of independence; a desire not to be controlled by others.

socialization Process by which children learn the behaviors and attitudes appropriate to their family and culture.

communication skills and are moody, withdrawn, and distrustful. They also may act out when their parents are not around to police their behavior.

- *Permissive* parents are high in warmth, but low on control. They are very supportive of their children, but fail to set appropriate limits on their behavior. The children of permissive-indulgent parents tend to be immature, disrespectful, impulsive, and out of control.
- *Indifferent* parents exert too little control, failing to set limits on their children's behavior. They are also neglectful and inattentive, providing little emotional support to their children. The children of permissive-indifferent parents tend to be overly dependent and lacking in social skills and self-control.

Although there are many studies such as Baumrind's that show a relationship between parent behavior and child development, it is important to be cautious when drawing conclusions about cause and effect from these data. First, parents do not determine the parent–child relationship on their own: Children also affect it (Collins, Maccoby, Steinberg, Hetherington, & Bornstein, 2000). Parents do not act the same way toward every child in the family (even though they may try to), because each child is a different individual. A thoughtful, responsible child is more likely to elicit authoritative parenting, whereas an impulsive child who is difficult to reason with is more likely to elicit an authoritarian style. Thus, children influence the behavior of their caregivers at the same time that the caregivers are influencing them.

Second, there is a great deal of research that indicates that the importance of parents may be overestimated. An extreme version of this position is described in a controversial book titled *The Nurture Assumption*, by Judith Rich Harris (1998). Harris contends that parents have little influence on their child's personality (except for their genetic contribution). Instead, she argues that peers are the key factor in shaping adult personality. In the next section of the chapter, we will examine peer influences on development and then return to an evaluation of Harris's position.

RELATIONSHIPS WITH OTHER CHILDREN At a very early age, infants begin to show an interest in other children, but the social skills required to play with them develop only gradually (Pellegrini & Galda, 1994). Children first play alone; this activity is called *solitary play*. Then, between 18 month and two years, they begin to engage in *parallel play*—that is, they play side by side, doing the same or similar things, but not interacting much with each other. Around the age of two, imitation becomes a game: One child throws a toy into the air, the other does the same, and then they both giggle. At around age two and a half, children begin to use language to communicate with their playmates, and their play becomes increasingly imaginative. By age three or three and a half, they are engaging in *cooperative play*, including games that involve group imagination such as "playing house" (Eckerman, Davis, & Didow, 1989).

Peer influences outside the family increase greatly when children start school. Now they are under a great deal of pressure to be part of a **peer group** of friends. In peer groups, children learn many valuable things, such as how to engage in cooperative activities aimed at collective goals and how to negotiate the social roles of leader and follower (Rubin, Coplan, Chen, & McKinnon, 1994).

As children get older, they develop a deeper understanding of the meaning of friendship (Rubin et al., 1994). For preschoolers, a friend is simply "someone I play with," but around age seven, children begin to realize that friends "do things" for one another. At this still egocentric age, however, friends are defined largely as people who "do things for *me*." Later, at about age nine, children come to understand that friendship is a two-way street and that, although friends do things for us, we are also expected to do things for them. During these early years, friendships often come and go at dizzying speed; they endure only as long as needs are being met. It is not until late childhood or early adolescence that friendship is viewed as a stable and continuing social relationship requiring mutual support, trust, and confidence (Selman, 1981).

Successfully making friends is one of the tasks that Erikson saw as centrally important to children between the ages of 7 and 11, the stage of *industry versus inferiority*. At this age, children must master many increasingly difficult skills, social interaction with peers being

When young children engage in parallel play, each plays alone, but near the other.

peer group A network of same-aged friends and acquaintances who give one another emotional and social support.

only one of them. Others have to do with mastering academic skills at school, meeting growing responsibilities placed on them at home, and learning to do various tasks that they will need as independent-living adults. In Erikson's view, if children become stifled in their efforts to prepare themselves for the adult world, they may conclude that they are inadequate or inferior and lose faith in their power to become self-sufficient. Those whose industry is rewarded develop a sense of competence and self-assurance.

We have seen that peers can have a significant effect on development. Does it follow, as Harris argued in *The Nurture Assumption*, that parents matter very little? Harris holds that children logically are more likely to imitate the behaviors of their peers, because peers are their future collaborators and are responsible for creating the culture in which they ultimately will live. To support her position, she cites studies such as one showing that the best predictor of adolescents becoming smokers is whether or not their peers smoke, not the smoking habits of their parents. Most psychologists reject extreme positions such as Harris's (Collins, Maccoby, Steinberg, Hetherington, & Bornstein, 2000; Maccoby, 2000; Parke & O'Neil, 1999; Williams, 1999). They point to studies showing that even in the face of strong peer influence, parents can significantly affect a child's personality by monitoring and by buffering the negative effects of peers (Ary, Duncan, Duncan, & Hops, 1999; Voydanoff & Donnelly, 1999).

Moreover, most developmental psychologists believe that peer influence is just one example of a much broader class of environmental factors called the **nonshared environment** (Plomin, 1999; Rose et al., 2003; Turkheimer & Waldron, 2000). Even children who grow up in the same home, with the same parents, are likely to have very different day-to-day human relationships, and this nonshared environment can have a significant effect on their development. For example, as we describe in the next section, children of many working parents regularly spend part of their time in childcare settings away from home, which may not necessarily be the same for all siblings. "The message is not that family experiences are unimportant," concludes one review of the research. Instead, the crucial environmental influences that shape personality development are "specific to each child, rather than general to an entire family" (Plomin & Rende, 1991, p. 180).

CHILDREN IN DUAL-CAREER FAMILIES Most dual-career families must entrust their young children to the care of someone else for a sizable percentage of the children's waking hours. In America, over half of the children between birth and the third grade spend some time being regularly cared for by persons other than their parents (America's Children: Key National Indicators of Well-Being, 2000). Is it a good idea to leave infants and very young children with substitute caregivers?

Some researchers have expressed concern that being entrusted to caregivers outside the immediate family may interfere with the development of secure attachments and put children at greater risk for emotional maladjustment (Barglow, Vaughn, & Molitor, 1987; Belsky & Rovine, 1988). But according to the findings of one large-scale longitudinal study (NICHD, 1996), placing a baby in full-time day care even in the first few months of life doesn't in itself undermine attachment. Working parents and their babies still have ample opportunity to engage in the daily give-and-take of positive feelings on which secure attachments are built. Day care, however, can be a negative factor, if working parents generally provide insensitive and unresponsive care. Such behavior is, in itself, associated with insecure attachment, but these babies are even *more* likely to form an insecure attachment if they also experience extensive day care, especially poor-quality care or frequently changing day-care arrangements.

One conclusion, then, is that *quality of care counts* (Brobert, Wessels, Lamb, & Hwang, 1997; Scarr, 1999; Votruba, Coley, & Chase–Lansdale, 2004). A secure, affectionate, stimulating environment is likely to produce children who are healthy, outgoing, and ready to learn, just as an environment that encourages fears and doubts is likely to stunt development. Research shows, for example, that children of working mothers who are placed in a quality day care, even at very early ages, are no more likely to develop behavior problems or have problems with their self-esteem than children reared at home (Harvey, 1999). Furthermore, some research shows clear benefits for the children of mothers who work, even if the children are still very young (Greenstein, 1993). For example, the children of employed mothers tend to be more independent and self-confident and to have less stereotyped views of males and females (Harris & Liebert, 1991).

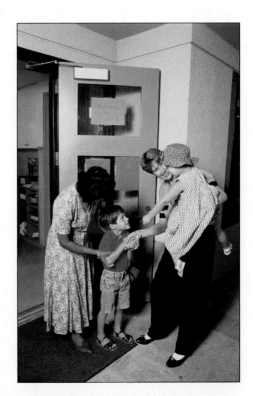

Studies have shown that working parents can instill feelings of trust and attachment in their children even when the children are in full-time day care.

nonshared environment The unique aspects of the environment that are experienced differently by siblings, even though they are reared in the same family.

GENDER-ROLE DEVELOPMENT

When do children learn about their gender?

Children's understanding of the differences between males and females follows the patterns established by their developing cognitive abilities and social interactions. By about age three, both boys and girls have developed a **gender identity**—that is, a little girl knows that she is a girl, and a little boy knows that he is a boy. At this point, however, children have little understanding of what that means. A three-year-old boy might think that he could grow up to be a mommy or that if you put a dress on him and a bow in his hair, he will turn into a girl. By the age of four or five, most children know that gender depends on what kind of genitals a person has (Bem, 1989). They have also acquired **gender constancy**, the realization that gender cannot be changed.

At quite a young age, children also start to acquire **gender-role awareness**, a knowledge of what behaviors are expected of males and of females in their society (Lewin, 1996). As a result, they develop **gender stereotypes**, or oversimplified beliefs about what the "typical" male and female are like (Sinnott, 1994; Steele, 2003). Girls are supposed to be clean, neat, and careful, whereas boys are supposed to like rough, noisy, physical play; women are kind, caring, and emotional, whereas men are strong, dominant, and aggressive. There is much consistency across cultures regarding the gender stereotypes that children develop (Williams & Best, 1990). This is the case partly because gender roles tend to be similar in many different cultures and because gender stereotypes tend to "match" the tasks thought appropriate for the sexes.

At the same time that children acquire gender-role awareness and gender stereotypes, they also develop their own **gender-typed behavior**: Girls play with dolls, and boys play with trucks; girls put on pretty clothes and fuss with their hair, and boys run around and wrestle with each other. Although the behavioral differences between boys and girls are minimal in infancy, quite major differences tend to develop as children grow older (Prior, Smart, Sanson, & Oberklaid, 1993). Boys become more active and physically aggressive, and tend to play in larger groups. Girls talk more, shove less, and tend to interact in pairs. If aggression is displayed among girls, it is more likely to take the form of spiteful words and threats of social isolation (Zuger, 1998). Of course, there are some active, physically aggressive girls and some quiet, polite boys, but they are not in the majority. The source of such gender-typed behavior is a matter of considerable debate.

Because gender-related differences in styles of interaction appear very early in development (even before the age of three), Eleanor Maccoby, a specialist in this area, believes that they are at least partly biological in origin. In addition to the influence of genes, some evidence suggests that prenatal exposure to hormones plays a part (Collaer & Hines, 1995). But Maccoby thinks that biologically based differences are small at first and later become exaggerated because of the different kinds of socialization experienced by boys and girls. She suggests that a lot of gender-typical behavior is the product of children playing with others of their sex (Maccoby, 1998). Undoubtedly, popular culture—especially as portrayed on television—also influences the norms of gender-appropriate behavior that develop in children's peer groups. And parents, too, can sometimes add input, especially during critical transitions in the child's life when parents feel it is important for children to behave in more gender-stereotyped ways (Fagot, 1994). The end result is substantial gender-typed behavior by middle childhood. Research on this topic continues, but the growing consensus is that both biology and experience contribute to gender differences in behavior (Collaer & Hines, 1995; Collins, Maccoby, Steinberg, Hetherington, & Bornstein, 2000).

TELEVISION AND CHILDREN

Is watching TV a good or bad influence on the development of children?

American children spend more time watching television than they do engaging in any other activity besides sleeping (Huston, Watkins, & Kunkel, 1989). Not surprisingly, psychologists, educators, and parents are very concerned about the influence TV may have on children (Funk, Baldacci, Pasold, & Baumgardner, 2004). Indeed, the American Academy of Pediatrics (1999) goes so far as to say that children under the age of 2

---

gender identity A little girl's knowledge that she is a girl, and a little boy's knowledge that he is a boy.

gender constancy The realization that gender does not change with age.

gender-role awareness Knowledge of what behavior is appropriate for each gender.

gender stereotypes General beliefs about characteristics that men and women are presumed to have.

gender-typed behavior Socially prescribed ways of behaving that differ for boys and girls.

should not watch television at all and that older children should not have television sets in their bedrooms.

One concern is the violence that pervades much TV entertainment. Children who watch two hours of TV daily (well below our national average) will see about 8,000 murders and 100,000 other acts of violence by the time they leave elementary school (Kunkel et al., 1996). Even Saturday-morning cartoons average more than 20 acts of violence per hour (Seppa, 1997). Does witnessing this violence make children more aggressive, and if so, does TV violence account, at least in part, for the rapid rise in violent crime among adolescents? The answer appears to be "Yes." In a comprehensive review of research in this area, Anderson et al. (2003) concluded, "First, media violence has a modest direct effect . . . on serious forms of violent behavior. Second, a more extensive body of research documents a larger impact of media violence on aggression (including violence. . .)" (p. 104). The authors point out that the effects of media violence can extend well into adulthood even for people who are not highly aggressive. Finally, although some people are more affected than others by viewing media violence, the authors conclude ". . . no one is exempt from the deleterious effects of media violence; neither gender, nor nonaggressive personality, nor superior upbringing, nor higher social class, nor greater intelligence provides complete protection" (p. 104).

Another area of concern about children who watch too much television is that excessive TV viewing can lead to a variety of sleep disturbances, including night wakings, daytime sleepiness, increased anxiety at bedtime, shortened sleep duration, and difficulty falling asleep (Van den Bulck, 2004). Children who watch television before bedtime or who have a television in their bedroom appear to have the highest risk for developing sleep problems (Owens et al., 1999).

In addition, every moment spent watching TV is a moment not engaging in other activities, such as chatting with friends or playing board games and sports, that may be more beneficial. For instance, obesity in children has been correlated with the amount of time spent watching TV (Vandewater, Shim, & Caplovitz, 2004).

But there is evidence that children can learn worthwhile things from watching television (Anderson, 1998; Wright et al., 1999). In one long-term study, the TV viewing habits of five-year-olds were monitored and recorded by parents and electronic devices. Years later, an examination of the high school records of these same children found that the more time they had spent viewing such educational programs as *Sesame Street* and *Mr. Rogers*, the higher their high school grades were. In contrast, children who watched a lot of noneducational and violent programming at the age of five had comparatively lower high school grades than their peers (Anderson, Huston, Wright, & Collins, 1998). However, these data are correlational and leave open the question of cause and effect.

To summarize, television can be a significant influence on children's development. It presents both "good" and "bad" models for them to copy, and it provides vast amounts of information. In the end, whether television's influence is largely positive or largely negative may depend as much on what children watch as on how much they watch.

▶ CHECK YOUR UNDERSTANDING

1. The average ages at which developmental skills, such as walking, are mastered are called

_____ _____.

2. List, in order, Piaget's four stages of cognitive development.

Match each phase of childhood with its major challenge, according to Erik Erikson's theory.

3. ___ infancy
4. ___ toddlerhood
5. ___ preschool years
6. ___ elementary school years

a. industry versus inferiority
b. trust versus mistrust
c. autonomy versus shame and doubt
d. initiative versus guilt

Answers: 1. developmental norms, **2.** sensory-motor, preoperational, concrete-operations, formal-operations, **3.** b, **4.** c, **5.** d, **6.** a.

1. At age 10 months, a child watches a red ball roll under a chair, but fails to search for it. At two years, the same child watches the same event, but now searches systematically for the ball. What change most likely accounts for the different reactions?
   a. The 10-month-old lacks depth perception.
   b. The 10-month-old does not yet understand the principle of conservation.
   c. The two-year-old has acquired a sense of object permanence.
   d. All of the above are equally likely explanations.

2. At work, Frank takes longer breaks than he should. When asked why, he responds that "everyone else does, so it's o.k." Frank's reasoning reflets moral development characteristic of which of Kohlberg's stages?
   a. preconventional
   b. conventional
   c. postconventional
   d. meta-conventional

3. Three preschoolers of different ages are sitting in a room watching a playful puppy. Child 1 exclaims, "I play puppy tail." Child 2 reaches for the dog and cries out, "Gimme!" Child 3 asks, "Who left the puppy here?" On the basis of your knowledge of language development, which child is most likely to be the youngest and which is most likely to be the oldest?
   a. Child 3 is youngest, child 1 is oldest.
   b. Child 3 is youngest, child 2 is oldest.
   c. Child 2 is youngest, child 3 is oldest.
   d. Child 1 is youngest, child 3 is oldest.

4. Roberta is concerned about leaving her baby in day care because she is afraid the child will fail to "connect" with her, a developmental task psychologists call _____.
   a. attachment
   b. object permanence
   c. conservation
   d. concrete thinking

Answers: 1. c., 2. b., 3. c., 4. a.

Adolescence

7.4   Describe the major changes that occur in adolescence and suggest why identity formation is critical to both cognitive and social development in this developmental period.

Today, the demarcation points for moving into and out of adolescence are becoming increasingly fuzzy for many young people living in the United States. Although the period called adolescence is often thought of as corresponding to the "teenage" years, children often begin to expect the freedom and autonomy associated with adolescence at younger ages than did their parents and grandparents. In some families, children as young as 10 have considerable personal freedoms and no curfew. A small but significant number are sexually active. And many 10- to 12-year-olds are involved in other activities that formerly required adult, or at least adolescent, status. Adolescence likewise has expanded at the other end of this period into the years formerly associated with adulthood. In generations past, the typical expectation was for young people to graduate from high school, get a job, get married, and establish a family and professional life, all by the time they were in their early 20s. As was described in the opening of this chapter, increasing numbers of young adults in their 20s are moving back in with their parents, assuming at least some of the lifestyle habits that correspond more closely to adolescent, rather than adult, status. Adolescence, thus, is a period of the lifespan that is defined as much by social expectations and personal circumstances as by biological and cognitive changes. In general, we consider adolescence to be the period of the lifespan from about age 10 to age 20, although when an individual enters and leaves adolescence is highly specific to the circumstances of that person's life. For however long it lasts, it is the period in which the individual is transformed from a child into an adult.

PHYSICAL CHANGES

What are the consequences of going through puberty early or late?

A series of dramatic physical milestones ushers in adolescence. The most obvious is the **growth spurt**, a rapid increase in height and weight that begins, on average, at about age 10 in girls and age 12 in boys, and reaches its peak at age 12 in girls and 14 in boys. The typical adolescent attains his or her adult height about 6 years after the start of the growth spurt (Tanner, 1978).

growth spurt A rapid increase in height and weight that occurs during adolescence.

Teenagers are acutely aware of the changes taking place in their bodies. Many become anxious about whether they are the "right" shape or size and obsessively compare themselves with the models and actors they see on television and in magazines. Because few adolescents can match these ideals, it is not surprising that when young adolescents are asked what they most dislike about themselves, physical appearance is mentioned more often than anything else (Conger & Petersen, 1991). These concerns can lead to serious eating disorders, as we saw in Chapter 6, "Motivation and Emotion."

In both sexes, changes also occur in the face. The chin and nose become more prominent, and the lips get fuller. Increases in the size of oil glands in the skin can contribute to acne; sweat glands produce a more odorous secretion. The heart, lungs, and digestive system all expand.

SEXUAL DEVELOPMENT The visible signs of **puberty**—the onset of sexual maturation—occur in a different sequence for boys and girls. In boys, the initial sign is growth of the testes, which starts, on average, at around age 11, about a year before the beginning of the growth spurt in height. Along with the growth spurt comes enlargement of the penis. Development of pubic hair takes a little longer, and development of facial hair longer still. Deepening of the voice is one of the last noticeable changes of male maturation.

In females, the beginning of the growth spurt is typically the first sign of approaching puberty. Shortly thereafter, the breasts begin to develop; some pubic hair appears at around the same time. **Menarche**, the first menstrual period, occurs about a year or so later—between age 12 and 13 for the average American girl (Powers, Hauser, & Kilner, 1989). The timing of menarche is affected by health and nutrition, with heavier girls maturing earlier than thinner ones. Smoking and drinking alcohol also are associated with early menarche (Danielle, Rose, Viken, & Kaprio, 2000; Graber, 2003).

Individuals differ greatly in the age at which they go through the changes of puberty. Some 12-year-old girls and 14-year-old boys still look like children, whereas others their age already look like young women and men (Weichold, Silbereisen, & Schmitt–Rodermund, 2003). Among boys, early maturing typically has psychological advantages. Boys who mature earlier usually do better in sports and in social activities and receive greater respect from their peers (Conger & Petersen, 1991). For girls, early maturation appears to be a mixed blessing. A girl who matures early may be admired by other girls but is likely to be subjected to embarrassing treatment as a sex object by boys (Clausen, 1975).

The onset of menstruation does not necessarily mean that a girl is biologically capable of becoming a mother. It is uncommon (though not unheard of) for a girl to become pregnant during her first few menstrual cycles. Female fertility increases gradually during the first year after menarche. The same is true of male fertility. Boys achieve their first ejaculation at an average age of 13, often during sleep. But first ejaculations contain relatively few sperm (Tanner, 1978). Nevertheless, pregnancy can occur, even when parents are very young.

By school age, boys and girls tend to play by the rules of sex-typed behavior. Typically, girls play nonaggressive games, in pairs or small groups, whereas boys prefer more active group games.

Psychologists used to believe that the beginnings of sexual attraction and desire in young people coincided with the physical changes of puberty, but recent research may be changing this view. Hundreds of case histories that researchers have collected tend to put the first stirrings of sexual interest in the fourth and fifth grade. The cause may be increases in an adrenal sex hormone that begin at age 6 and reach a critical level around age 10 (McClintock & Herdt, 1996). Other pubertal hormones may also begin their rise much earlier than was formerly known (Marano, 1997). If so, the onset of the obvious physical changes that we now call puberty may actually be more of a mid-way point than a start along the path toward sexual maturity.

ADOLESCENT SEXUAL ACTIVITY The achievement of the capacity to reproduce is probably the single most important development in adolescence. But sexuality is a confusing issue for adolescents in our society. Fifty years ago, young people were expected to postpone expressing their sexual needs until they were responsible, married adults. Since then, major changes have occurred in sexual customs. Three-fourths of all males and more than half of all females between the ages of 15 and 19 have had intercourse; the average age for first intercourse is 16 for boys and 17 for girls (Stodghill, 1998).

puberty The onset of sexual maturation, with accompanying physical development.

menarche First menstrual period.

Boys and girls tend to view their early sexual behavior in significantly different ways (Lewin, 1994a). Fewer high school girls than boys report feeling good about their sexual experiences (46 percent versus 65 percent). Similarly, more girls than boys said that they should have waited until they were older before having sex (65 percent compared with 48 percent).

One of the possible consequences of sexual activity is that it will lead to pregnancy. The United States has the highest teen birth rate in the industrialized world: nearly 7 times the rate in France and 13 times the rate in Japan. One reason for our higher teen birth rate may be ignorance among our young people of the most basic facts concerning reproduction (Guthrie & Bates, 2003). In countries such as Norway, Sweden, and the Netherlands, which have extensive programs of sex education, teenage pregnancy rates are much lower (Hechtman, 1989). Another explanation for some unwanted teenage pregnancies may be the adolescent tendency to believe that "nothing bad will happen to me." This sense of invulnerability, especially in the absence of sex education, may blind some teenagers to the possibility of pregnancy (Quadrel, Prouadrel, Fischoff, & Davis, 1993).

COGNITIVE CHANGES

What are two common fallacies that characterize adolescent thinking?

Just as bodies mature during adolescence, so do patterns of thought. Piaget (1969) saw the cognitive advances of adolescence as an increased ability to reason abstractly, called formal-operational thought. Adolescents can understand and manipulate abstract concepts, speculate about alternative possibilities, and reason in hypothetical terms. This process allows them to debate such problematical issues as abortion, sexual behavior, and AIDS. Of course, not all adolescents reach the stage of formal operations, and many of those who do fail to apply formal-operational thinking to the everyday problems they face (Flavell, Miller, & Miller, 2002). Younger adolescents especially are unlikely to be objective about matters concerning themselves and have not yet achieved a deep understanding of the difficulties involved in moral judgments.

Moreover, in those who do achieve formal-operational thinking, this advance has its hazards, among them overconfidence in new mental abilities and a tendency to place too much importance on one's own thoughts. Some adolescents also fail to realize that not everyone thinks the way they do and that other people may hold different views (Harris & Liebert, 1991). Piaget called these tendencies the "egocentrism of formal operations" (Piaget, 1967).

David Elkind (1968, 1969) used Piaget's notion of adolescent egocentrism to account for two fallacies of thought that he noticed in this age group. The first is the **imaginary audience**—the tendency of teenagers to feel that they are constantly being observed by others, that people are always judging them on their appearance and behavior. This feeling of being perpetually "onstage" may be the source of much self-consciousness, concern about personal appearance, and showing off in adolescence (Bell & Bromnick, 2003).

The other fallacy of adolescent thinking is the **personal fable**—adolescents' unrealistic sense of their own uniqueness. For example, a teenager might feel that others couldn't possibly understand the love that the teenager feels toward a boyfriend or girlfriend because that love is so unique and special. This view is related to the feeling of invulnerability we mentioned earlier. Many teenagers believe that they are so different from other people that they won't be touched by the negative things that happen to others. This feeling of invulnerability is consistent with the reckless risk taking in which many people in this age group engage. (Arnett, 1991; Korinek, 2003).

PERSONALITY AND SOCIAL DEVELOPMENT

What important tasks do adolescents face in their personal and social lives?

Adolescents are eager to establish independence from their parents, but at the same time, they fear the responsibilities of adulthood. They have many important tasks ahead of them and many important decisions to make. Particularly in a technologically advanced society like ours, this period of development is bound to involve some stress.

imaginary audience Elkind's term for adolescents' delusion that they are constantly being observed by others.

personal fable Elkind's term for adolescents' delusion that they are unique, very important, and invulnerable.

HOW "STORMY AND STRESSFUL" IS ADOLESCENCE? Early in the 20th century, many people saw adolescence as a time of great instability and strong emotions. For example, G. Stanley Hall (1904), one of the first developmental psychologists, portrayed adolescence as a period of "storm and stress," fraught with suffering, passion, and rebellion against adult authority. Recent research, however, suggests that the "storm and stress" view greatly exaggerates the experiences of most teenagers (Arnett, 1999). The great majority of adolescents do not describe their lives as filled with turmoil and chaos (Eccles et al., 1993). Most adolescents manage to keep stress in check, experience little disruption in their everyday lives, and generally develop more positively than is commonly believed (Bronfenbrenner, 1986; Galambos & Leadbeater, 2002). For example, a cross-cultural study that sampled adolescents from 10 countries, including the United States, found that over 75 percent of them had healthy self-images, were generally happy, and valued the time they spent at school and at work (Offer, Ostrov, Howard, & Atkinson, 1988).

Still, adolescence is inevitably accompanied by some stress related to school, family, and peers, and this stress can at times be difficult to manage (Crystal et al., 1994). Individuals differ in their ability to cope. Some young people are particularly *resilient* and able to overcome even the worst conditions, partly because of a strong belief in their own ability to make things better (Werner, 1995). In contrast, those whose prior development has already been stressful are likely to experience even greater stress during adolescence. Thus, the degree of struggle growing up that any given adolescent faces is due to an interaction of developmental challenges on the one hand and factors that promote resilience on the other (Compas, Hinden, & Gerhardt, 1995).

FORMING AN IDENTITY To make the transition from dependence on parents to dependence on oneself, the adolescent must develop a stable sense of self. This process is called **identity formation**, a term derived from Erik Erikson's theory, which sees the major challenge of this stage of life as *identity versus role confusion* (Erikson, 1968). The overwhelming question for the young person becomes "Who am I?" In Erikson's view, the answer comes by integrating a number of different roles—say, talented math student, athlete, and artist; or, political liberal and aspiring architect—into a coherent whole that "fits" comfortably. Failure to form this coherent sense of identity leads to confusion about roles.

As the students in this middle-school group show, the age at which adolescents reach sexual maturity varies widely. Differences can lead to problems for teenagers of both sexes.

James Marcia (1980) believes that finding an identity requires a period of intense self-exploration called an **identity crisis**. He recognizes four possible outcomes of this process. One is *identity achievement*. Adolescents who have reached this status have passed through the identity crisis and succeeded in making personal choices about their beliefs and goals. They are comfortable with those choices because the choices are their own. In contrast are adolescents who have taken the path of *identity foreclosure*. They have prematurely settled on an identity that others provided for them. They have become what those others want them to be without ever going through an identity crisis. Other adolescents are in *moratorium* regarding the choice of an identity. They are in the process of actively exploring various role options, but they have not yet committed to any of them. Finally, there are teens who are experiencing *identity diffusion*. They avoid considering role options in any conscious way. Many are dissatisfied with this condition but are unable to start a search to "find themselves." Some of them resort to escapist activities such as drug or alcohol abuse (Adams & Gullota, 1983). Of course, any given adolescent's identity status can change over time as the person matures or even regresses. Some evidence suggests that identity development varies by social class or ethnic background. For example, teens from poor families are often less likely to experience a period of identity moratorium, probably because financial constraints make it harder for them to explore many different role options (Holmbeck, 1994).

RELATIONSHIPS WITH PEERS For most adolescents, the peer group provides a network of social and emotional support that helps enable both the movement toward greater independence from adults and the search for personal identity. But peer relationships change during the adolescent years. Friendship groups in early adolescence

identity formation Erickson's term for the development of a stable sense of self necessary to make the transition from dependence on others to dependence on oneself.

identity crisis A period of intense self-examination and decision making; part of the process of identity formation.

cliques Groups of adolescents with similar interests and strong mutual attachment.

tend to be small unisex groups, called **cliques**, of three to nine members. Especially among girls, these unisex friendships increasingly deepen and become more mutually self-disclosing as the teens develop the cognitive abilities to better understand themselves and one another (Holmbeck, 1994). Then, in mid-adolescence, unisex cliques generally break down and give way to mixed-sex groups. These, in turn, are usually replaced by groups consisting of couples. At first, adolescents tend to have short-term heterosexual relationships within the group that fulfill short-term needs without exacting the commitment of "going steady" (Sorensen, 1973). Such relationships do not demand love and can dissolve overnight. But between the ages of 16 and 19, most adolescents settle into more stable dating patterns.

RELATIONSHIPS WITH PARENTS While they are still searching for their own identity, striving toward independence, and learning to think through the long-term consequences of their actions, adolescents require guidance and structure from adults, especially from their parents. In their struggle for independence, adolescents question everything and test every rule. Unlike young children who believe that their parents know everything and are all-powerful and good, adolescents are all too aware of their parents' shortcomings. It takes many years for adolescents to see their mothers and fathers as real people with their own needs and strengths as well as weaknesses (Smollar & Youniss, 1989). In fact, many young adults are surprised that their parents have gotten so much smarter in the last seven or eight years!

The low point of parent–child relationships generally occurs in early adolescence, when the physical changes of puberty are occurring; then the warmth of the parent–child relationship ebbs, and conflict rises. Warm and caring relationships with adults outside the home, such as those at school or at a supervised community center, are valuable to adolescents during this period (Eccles et al., 1993); however, conflicts with parents tend to be over minor issues and are usually not intense (Holmbeck, 1994). In only a small minority of families does the relationship between parents and children markedly deteriorate in adolescence (Paikoff & Brooks–Gunn, 1991).

► CHECK YOUR UNDERSTANDING

1. The most obvious indication that adolescence is starting is a rapid increase in height and weight, known as the _____ _____. This is combined with a series of physical changes leading to sexual maturation, the onset of which is called _____.

2. Erikson's view of the major challenge in adolescence is one of _____ versus _____.

3. List the four identity statuses described by James Marcia.

4. True (T) or false (F): The most difficult time in the relationship between a teenager and parents is usually in late adolescence, when the young person is anxious to leave the family "nest."

Answers: 1. growth spurt; puberty, 2. identity; role confusion, 3. identity achievement, identity foreclosure, identity moratorium, identity diffusion, 4. (F).

► APPLY YOUR UNDERSTANDING

1. Beth is 14 years old. In the last year or two, she has begun to enjoy debating complex issues such as human rights, poverty, and justice. Which of the following is most likely to be true?
   a. Beth has become capable of formal-operational thought.
   b. Beth is experiencing identity foreclosure.
   c. Beth is experiencing identity diffusion.
   d. Beth's thinking demonstrates adolescent egocentrism.

2. Your adolescent brother is very self-conscious. He feels that he is constantly being observed by others who are judging him on his appearance and his behavior. As a result, he is overly concerned about his behavior and often shows off. You recognize this as a common characteristic of teenagers that is known as ____.
   a. ___ the personal fable.
   b. ___ egocentric distortion.
   c. ___ role confusion.
   d. ___ the imaginary audience.

Answers: 1. a., 2. d.

Early and Middle Adulthood

7.5   List the major changes that typically occur during the periods of early and middle adulthood and evaluate Erikson's contention that intimacy and generativity are the major developmental tasks of these periods of development.

Compared with adolescent development, development during adulthood is much less predictable, much more a function of the individual's decisions, circumstances, and even luck. In adulthood, as distinct from childhood and somewhat from adolescence, most developmental milestones do not occur at particular ages. Consider the "boomerang" children described in the opening paragraph of this chapter, who leave home as young adults, only to return and live with their parents as they continue to prepare for the responsibilities of full adulthood. Still, certain experiences and changes take place sooner or later in nearly everyone's life, and nearly every adult tries to fulfill certain needs, including those for nurturing partnerships and satisfying work.

LOVE, PARTNERSHIPS, AND PARENTING

What factors are important in forming satisfying relationships in adulthood?

Nearly all adults form a long-term, loving partnership with another adult at some point in their lives. Such a partnership can happen at any stage in the life course, but it is especially common in young adulthood. According to Erik Erikson, the major challenge of young adulthood is *intimacy versus isolation*. Failure to form an intimate partnership with someone else can cause a young adult to feel painfully lonely and incomplete. However, Erikson also believed that a person is not ready to commit to an intimate relationship until he or she has developed a firm sense of personal identity, the task of the preceding stage of life.

FORMING PARTNERSHIPS Almost 90 percent of Americans eventually get married (U.S. Bureau of the Census, 2002a), but those who marry are waiting longer to do so. For example, in 1970, the median age of an American woman marrying for the first time was 20.8 years; this increased to 25.3 years by 2002. Similarly, for American men, the median age for first marriages was 23.2 years in 1970, increasing to 26.9 years by 2002 (U.S. Bureau of the Census, 2002b). This postponement of marriage is even greater among African Americans than among whites (Balaguer & Markman, 1994).

Although heterosexual marriage is still the statistical norm in our society, other types of partnerships are increasingly meeting the needs of a diverse population. Cohabiting relationships are one example, though most such relationships last no longer than two years (Doyle, 2004). Contrary to popular belief, the greatest recent increase in cohabiting couples is not among the very young, but rather among people over age 35 (Steinhauer, 1997). Among elderly widows and widowers, cohabitation is increasingly seen as a way of enjoying a life together without financial complications and tax penalties.

Homosexual couples are another example of intimate partnerships outside the tradition of heterosexual marriage. Studies show that most gays and lesbians seek the same loving, committed, and meaningful partnerships as most heterosexuals seek (Peplau & Cochran, 1990). Moreover, successful relationships among gay or lesbian couples have the same characteristics as successful relationships in the heterosexual world: High levels of mutual trust, respect, and appreciation; shared decision making; good communication; and good skills at resolving conflicts (Birchler & Fals–Stewart, 1994; Kurdek, 1991, 1992; Laird, 2003; see "**Understanding Ourselves**: Resolving Conflicts in Intimate Relationships").

PARENTHOOD For most parents, loving and being loved by their children is an unparalleled source of fulfillment; however, the birth of the first child is also a major turning point

Peer groups help adolescents develop identities apart from family influences. Cliques are small groups of friends that offer closeness, but can also exert significant control over adolescents' lives.

[UNDERSTANDING OURSELVES]

RESOLVING CONFLICTS IN INTIMATE RELATIONSHIPS

Even the closest, most loving couples have disagreements. People, after all, are different. They have different desires, approaches, and priorities—and different points of view. For those reasons, conflict is inevitable in every intimate relationship. But conflict does not necessarily mean destructive forms of fighting. Conflict can be resolved in constructive ways that don't tear a couple apart. Constructive fighting can actually bring people closer together in search of mutually satisfactory solutions.

Psychologists who have studied intimate relationships often suggest a number of steps that lead to constructive conflict resolution:

1. *Carefully choose the time and place for an argument.* People who start airing a grievance at some inappropriate time shouldn't be surprised when the outcome is unsatisfactory. Try not to begin a major disagreement while your partner is in the middle of completing some important task or is ready to fall asleep after a long, tiring day.

2. *Be a good listener.* Don't go on the defensive as soon as your partner brings up a concern or complaint. Listen carefully without interrupting. Try to understand what your partner is saying from his or her point of view. Listening calmly, without anger, will help to get the discussion off to a good start. Don't let your body give nonverbal cues that contradict good listening. For example, don't continue to do chores or watch television while your partner is speaking. Don't shrug your shoulders or roll your eyes as if discounting your partner's view.

3. *Give feedback regarding your understanding of the other person's grievance.* Restate what your partner has told you in your own words. To help clarify and avoid misunderstandings, ask questions if you are unsure of anything. For example, if a wife says she is fed up with the amount of time her husband spends watching television sports, he might respond by saying, "I know you don't like me watching sports a lot, but do you expect me to stop entirely?" Such feedback helps to clarify and avoid misunderstandings.

4. *Be candid. Level with your partner about your feelings.* Say what you really think. If you are angry, don't make your partner guess your feelings by giving the silent treatment or showing anger in indirect ways. Of course, being candid does not mean being tactless or hurtful. Don't engage in name calling, sarcasm, mockery, or insults. Such tactics are counterproductive.

5. *Use "I" rather than "you" statements.* For example, if you're angry with your partner for being late, say, "I've been really worried and upset for the last hour," rather than "You're a whole hour late!" "You" statements sound like accusations and tend to put people on the defensive. "I" statements sound more like efforts to communicate feelings in nonjudgmental ways.

6. *Focus on behavior, not on the person.* For example, focus on your partner's lateness as a problem. Don't accuse your partner of being thoughtless and self-centered.

7. *Don't overstate the frequency of a problem or overgeneralize about it.* Don't tell your partner that he's always late or that she's exactly like her mother.

8. *Focus on a limited number of specific issues.* Don't overwhelm your partner with a barrage of grievances. Stick to current concerns of high priority. Don't dredge up a long list of complaints from the past.

9. *Don't find scapegoats for every grievance against you.* We all tend to explain away our shortcomings by blaming them on circumstances or sometimes on other people. Take responsibility for your actions and encourage your partner to do the same.

10. *Suggest specific, relevant changes to solve a problem.* Both participants in the conflict should propose at least one possible solution. A proposed solution should be reasonable and consider the other person's viewpoint as well as your own.

11. *Be open to compromise.* Settling disputes successfully often involves negotiation. Both people must be willing to give in a little. Don't back your partner into a corner by making an ultimatum. Partners need to be willing to change themselves to some extent in response to each other's feelings. This willingness is the essence of being in an intimate relationship.

12. *Don't think in terms of winner and loser.* A competitive approach to conflict resolution doesn't work in intimate relationships. Strive for solutions that are satisfactory to both parties. Think of each other as allies attacking a mutual problem. In this way, your relationship will become stronger.

in a couple's relationship, one that requires many adjustments. Romance and fun often give way to duty and obligations. Because young children demand a lot of time and energy, parents may be left with little time or energy for each other.

Parenthood may also heighten conflicts between pursuit of careers and responsibilities at home. This outcome is especially likely among women who have had an active career outside the home. They may be torn between feelings of loss and resentment at the prospect of leaving their job, and anxiety or guilt over the idea of continuing to work. This conflict is added to the usual worries about being an adequate wife and mother (Warr & Perry, 1982). It is no wonder that women feel the need for their partner's cooperation more strongly during this period of life than men do (Belsky, Lang, & Rovine, 1985). Today's fathers spend more time with their children than their fathers did, but in most families mothers still bear the greater responsibility for both child rearing and housework.

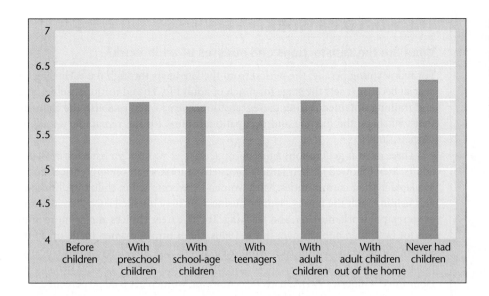

Figure 7–4
Marital satisfaction. This graph shows when married people are most and least content with their marriage, on a scale of 1 (very unhappy) to 7 (very happy).

Source: American Sociological Association; adapted from *USA Today*, August 12, 1997, p. D1.

Given the demands of child rearing, it isn't surprising that marital satisfaction tends to decline after the arrival of the first child (Ruble, Fleming, Hackel, & Stangor, 1988; see **Figure 7–4**). But after children leave home, many parents experience renewed satisfaction in their relationship as a couple. Rather than lamenting over their "empty nests," many women breathe a sigh of relief (Rovner, 1990) and experience an increase in positive mood and well-being (Dennerstein, Dudley, & Guthrie, 2002). For the first time in years, the husband and wife can be alone together and enjoy one another's company (Orbuch, Houser, Mero, & Webster, 1996). In cases where adult children return home to live, parents must again adjust to their presence and their demands. As noted in the opening paragraphs of this chapter, "boomerang" children require adaptations by all members of the family.

ENDING A RELATIONSHIP Intimate relationships frequently break up. Although this is the case for all types of couples—married and unmarried, heterosexual and homosexual—most of the research on ending relationships has focused on married, heterosexual couples. The U.S. divorce rate has risen substantially since the 1960s, as it has in many other developed nations (Lewin, 1995). Although the divorce rate appears to have stabilized, it has stabilized at quite a high level. Almost half of American marriages eventually end in divorce (U.S. Bureau of the Census, 2002a).

Rarely is the decision to separate a mutual one. Most often, one partner takes the initiative in ending the relationship after a long period of slowly increasing unhappiness. Making the decision does not necessarily bring relief. In the short term, it often brings turmoil, animosity, and apprehension. In the longer term, however, most divorced adults report that the divorce was a positive step that eventually resulted in greater personal contentment and healthier psychological functioning, although a substantial minority seem to suffer long-term negative effects (Kelly, 1982; Stack, 1994).

Divorce can have serious and far-reaching effects on children—especially on their school performance, self-esteem, gender-role development, emotional adjustment, relationships with others, and attitudes toward marriage (Barber & Eccles, 1992; Collins, Maccoby, Steinberg, Hetherington, & Bornstein, 2000; Forgatch & DeGarmo, 1999; Vaughn, 1993). And children who have been involved in multiple divorces are placed at an even greater risk (Kurdek, Fine, & Sinclair, 1995). Children adapt more successfully to divorce when they have good support systems, when the divorcing parents maintain a good relationship, and when sufficient financial resources are made available to them. The effects of divorce also vary with the children themselves: Those who have easygoing temperaments and who were generally well behaved before the divorce usually have an easier time adjusting (Davies & Cummings, 1994; Edwards, 1995; Hetherington, Bridges, & Insabella, 1998; Miller, Kliewer, & Burkeman, 1993).

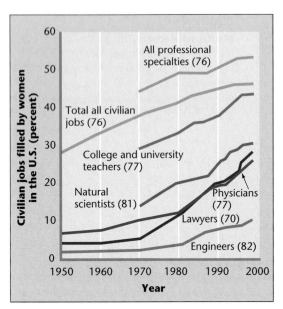

Figure 7–5

Percentage of selected jobs filled by women in the United States, 1950–2000. This graph shows the percentage of each job filled by women. The figures in parentheses indicate women's earnings as a percentage of men's in the given field.

Source: Copyright © 2000 Rodger Doyle. Reprinted with permission.

THE WORLD OF WORK

What are the satisfactions and stresses of adult work?

For many young people, the period from the late teens through the early twenties is crucial because it sets the stage for much of adult life. The educational achievements and training obtained during these transitional years often establish the foundation that will shape the income and occupational status for the remainder of adult life (Arnett, 2000).

Three or four generations ago, choosing a career was not an issue for most young adults. Men followed in their fathers' footsteps or took whatever apprenticeships were available in their communities. Most women were occupied in child care, housework, and helping with the family farm or business, or they pursued such "female" careers as secretarial work, nursing, and teaching. Today, career choices are far more numerous for both men and women. In the 1990s, for example, women made up approximately 20 percent of full-time employed physicians and lawyers, and nearly 40 percent of college professors. All told, women accounted for about 39 percent of the labor force (Gilbert, 1994). On average, however, women get paid 30 percent less than men, partly because they hold more junior-level positions and partly because they work in lower-paying careers. Women are less likely than men to advance to high-level managerial and executive positions (Valian, 1998; see **Figure 7–5**).

Although women hold 53 percent of the professional jobs in the United States, most are in the less-well-paid fields, such as education. Only 28 percent of the professional jobs that paid over $40,000 in 1998 were held by women (Doyle, 2000). Moreover, some women experience discrimination and sexual harassment at work (Valian, 1998) and therefore have fewer opportunities to change jobs or receive promotions (Aranya, Kushnir, & Valency, 1986), despite the fact that discrimination based on sex is illegal (see Chapter 11: "Psychology Applied to Work"). Career opportunities in the underrepresented fields of engineering and computer technology are especially promising for women.

DUAL-CAREER FAMILIES Over the last 50 years, the number of married women in the paid labor force has increased dramatically: 71 percent of married women with school-aged children and 60 percent of women with children under six now have jobs outside the home (Gilbert, 1994; Harris & Liebert, 1991). The two-paycheck family is not always a matter of choice. This increasing role of women as economic providers is a worldwide trend (Elloy & Mackie, 2002).

As we noted earlier, balancing the demands of career and family is a problem in many families, especially for women (Caplan, 2003). Even when the wife has a full-time job outside the home, she is likely to end up doing far more than half of the housework and child care. The "double shift"—one at paid work outside the home and another at unpaid household labor—is the common experience of millions of women throughout the world (Mednick, 1993). True equality—the hopeful goal of the dual-career movement—has yet to be achieved (Viers & Prouty, 2001).

Despite the pressures associated with the double shift, most women report increases in self-esteem when they have a paid job (Baruch & Barnett, 1986). They also tend to experience less anxiety and depression than childless working women do (Barnett, Brennan, & Marshall, 1994). The vast majority of working mothers say that they would continue to work even if they didn't need the money (Schwartz, 1994). Those women most apt to feel stressed by a double shift are those who do not find satisfaction in their various roles (Barnett, 1994).

PHYSICAL CHANGES

What is menopause, and what changes accompany it?

As people move through adulthood and approach midlife, changes do occur. Some of these changes reflect physical aspects of development, the most obvious of which involves a decline in the function of the reproductive organs and the hormones that regulate sexual response. In women, the amount of estrogen (the principal female hormone) produced by the ovaries drops sharply at around age 45, although the exact age varies considerably from woman to woman. Breasts, genital tissues, and the uterus begin to shrink, and menstrual periods become irregular and then cease altogether at around age 50. The cessation of menstruation is called **menopause**.

The hormonal changes that accompany menopause often cause certain physical symptoms; the most noticeable are "hot flashes." In some women, menopause also leads to a serious thinning of the bones called *osteoporosis*, making them more vulnerable to fractures. While both of these symptoms can be prevented by hormone replacement therapy (a pill or a skin patch that must be prescribed by a physician), recent studies have shown that taking hormones to reduce the symptoms of menopause may also place woman at a higher risk for heart disease and breast cancer (Rymer, Wilson, & Ballard, 2003). Because the severity of menopausal symptoms varies from woman to woman, as do the risk factors associated with breast cancer and heart disease, it is important for women to approach hormone therapy carefully under the supervision of a physician.

Experts disagree about whether a "male menopause" exists. Men never experience as severe a drop in testosterone (the principal male hormone) as women do in estrogen. Instead, studies have found a more gradual decline—perhaps 30 to 40 percent—in testosterone in men between age 48 and age 70 (Brody, 2004; Crooks & Bauer, 2002). Recent evidence also confirms the common belief that with increasing age, male fertility slowly decreases as well (Ford et al., 2000).

COGNITIVE CHANGES

In what ways do adults think differently than adolescents?

Only recently have researchers begun to explore the ways in which an adult's thinking differs from that of an adolescent. Nonetheless, a few conclusions have begun to emerge from the research literature. Although adolescents are able to test alternatives and to arrive at what they see as the "correct" solution to a problem, adults gradually come to realize that there isn't a single correct solution to every problem—there may, in fact, be no correct solution, or there may be several. Adolescents rely on authorities to tell them what is "true," but adults realize that "truth" often varies according to the situation and one's viewpoint. Adults are also more practical: They know that a solution to a problem must be realistic as well as reasonable (Cavanaugh, 1990). No doubt these changes in adult thinking derive from greater experience of the world. Dealing with the kinds of complex problems that arise in adult life requires moving away from the literal, formal, and somewhat rigid thinking of adolescence and young adulthood (Labouvie–Vief, 1986).

Most of the measurable cognitive changes that do take place during adulthood do not simply involve a rise or fall in general ability. Instead, for most people, some cognitive skills, such as vocabulary and verbal memory, increase steadily through the sixth decade of life. Other cognitive skills, such as reasoning and spatial orientation, generally peak during the 40s, falling off only slightly with increasing age. Perceptual speed and the ability to perform mathematical computations show the largest declines with age. Perceptual speed (which involves the ability to make quick and accurate visual discriminations) begins to decline as early as 25, while the ability to perform mathematical computations does not begin to decline until approximately 40 years of age (Schaie, 1983, 1996; Schaie & Willis, 2001; Willis & Shaie, 1999).

It is important to note that the cognitive declines that do occur in adulthood can usually be offset by the use of better, more efficient strategies and by the greater base of knowledge that older adults possess. And just as physical exercise is necessary for optimal physical development, so mental exercise is necessary for optimal cognitive development. Although some decline in cognitive skills is inevitable as people age, the decline can be minimized if people stay mentally active (Schaie, 1994).

PERSONALITY CHANGES

What changes in personality occur as adults move into midlife?

Psychological health generally is better in adulthood than in adolescence. (Jones & Meredith, 2000; Shiner, Masten, & Roberts, 2003). Both men and women tend to become less

menopause The time in a woman's life when menstruation ceases.

Many mothers who also work outside the home experience increased self esteem.

midlife crisis A time when adults discover they no longer feel fulfilled in their jobs or personal lives and attempt to make a decisive shift in career or lifestyle.

midlife transition According to Levinson, a process whereby adults assess the past and formulate new goals for the future.

self-centered and develop better coping skills with age (Neugarten, 1977). One longitudinal study found that people are more sympathetic, giving, productive, and dependable at age 45 than they were at age 20 (Block, 1971). Another found that people in their middle years feel an increasing commitment to and responsibility for others, develop new ways of adapting, and are more comfortable in interpersonal relationships (Vaillant, 1977). Such findings suggest that the majority of people are successfully meeting what Erik Erikson saw as the major challenge of middle adulthood: *generativity versus stagnation*. Generativity refers to the ability to continue being productive and creative, especially in ways that guide and encourage future generations. For those who fail to achieve this state, life becomes a drab and meaningless routine, and the person feels stagnant and bored.

Feelings of boredom and stagnation in middle adulthood may be part of what is called a **midlife crisis**. The person in midlife crisis feels painfully unfulfilled and ready for a radical, abrupt shift in career, personal relationships, or lifestyle. Research shows, however, that the midlife crisis is not typical; most people do not make sudden dramatic changes in their lives in middle adulthood (Martino, 1995; Lachman, 2004). In fact, only about 10 percent reported experiencing a midlife crisis (Brim, 1999). Furthermore, one large-scale study found that the majority of middle-aged adults reported lower levels of anxiety and worry than young adults, and generally felt positively about their lives. Daniel Levinson, who studied personality development in men and women throughout adulthood (Levinson, 1978, 1986, 1987), preferred the term **midlife transition** for the period when people tend to take stock of their lives. Many of the men and women in his studies, confronted with the first signs of aging, began to think about the finite nature of life. They realized that they may never accomplish all that they had hoped to do, and they questioned the value of some of the things they had accomplished so far, wondering how meaningful they were. As a result, some gradually reset their life priorities, establishing new goals based on their new insights.

▶ CHECK YOUR UNDERSTANDING

1. According to Erik Erikson, the major challenge of young adulthood is _____ versus _____, whereas the major challenge of middle adulthood is _____ versus _____.

2. The cessation of menstruation in middle-age women is called _____.

Answers: 1. intimacy, isolation; generativity, stagnation. **2.** menopause.

▶ APPLY YOUR UNDERSTANDING

1. If you were to poll a group of couples in middle adulthood, you would expect to find that most of them say that their marital satisfaction _____
   a. has steadily decreased over the years.
   b. has not changed over the years.
   c. declined during the child-rearing years, but has increased since then.
   d. has steadily increased over the years.

2. Imagine that you survey a large group of women who have both full-time jobs outside the home and families (the so-called "double shift"). Compared with women who do not have paying jobs outside the home, what would you expect to find about this group of dual-career women?
   a. They are more likely to be anxious and depressed.
   b. They are more likely to have higher self-esteem.

   c. They are more likely to say they wouldn't work if they didn't need the money.
   d. Both (a) and (c) are correct.

3. In comparison to younger workers, middle-aged workers have more difficulty with?
   a. physical tasks that must be performed quickly
   b. tasks involving vocabulary and verbal skills
   c. tasks involving reasoning and problem-solving
   d. tasks that require judgement

4. Jackson is arguing that "almost everyone experiences a midlife crisis" and it is only natural for people to want to experience radical changes in their lives at this age. After reading your text, you should conclude that Jackson's statement is
   a. correct.
   b. incorrect.

Answers: 1. c, **2.** b, **3.** a, **4.** b.

Later Adulthood

7.6 Describe the typical pattern of aging in older adulthood and identify the primary developmental challenges of this period.

Older adults constitute the fastest-growing segments of the U.S. population. Indeed, during the 20th century, the percentage of Americans over age 65 more than tripled, and those over age 85 now represent the fastest-growing segment of the population (APA's Task Force on Diversity, 1998). In the 2000 census, 35 million Americans were over age 65; by the year 2030, it is expected that there may be more than 70 million in this age group.

THE DEMOGRAPHICS OF AGING

What factors are related to life expectancy?

This dramatic rise in the number of older adults in the U.S. stems from the aging of the large baby-boom generation, coupled with increases in life expectancy due primarily to better health care and nutrition (Downs, 1994; see **Figure 7–6**). However, a sizable gender gap exists in life expectancy. The average woman today enjoys a life span that is seven years longer than that of the average man. The reasons for this gender gap are still unclear, but likely factors include differences in hormones, exposure to stress, health-related behaviors (Moeller-Leimkuehler, 2003), and genetic makeup. There is also a gap in life expectancy between whites and African Americans in this country. The average white American child is likely to live to age 76, whereas the average African-American child is likely to live only to age 71. This difference seems to stem largely from disparities in socioeconomic well-being.

Because older adults are becoming an increasingly visible part of American society, it is important to understand their development. Unfortunately, our views of older adults are often heavily colored by myths. For example, many people believe that most older adults are lonely, poor, and troubled by ill health. Even health-care professionals sometimes assume that it is natural for elderly people to feel ill. As a result, symptoms that would indicate a treatable medical problem in younger people are taken as inevitable signs of decay in the elderly and thus frequently go untreated. The false belief that "senility" is inevitable in old age is another damaging myth, as is the belief that most older adults are helpless and dependent on their families for care and financial support. All the research on late adulthood contradicts these stereotypes. Increasingly, people age 65 and over are healthy, productive, and able (Cutler, 2001; Kolata, 1996b; Manton & Gu, 2001).

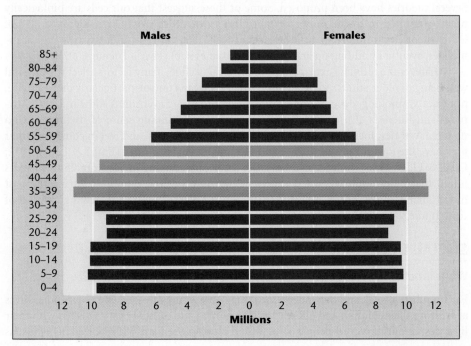

Figure 7–6

Population age structure, 1999. The U.S. population will continue to age over the next several decades, as the huge baby-boom generation moves through the population.

Source: U.S. Census Bureau. Available online at http://www.census.gov/population/www.dbna/db-aging-toc.html.

Studies suggest that older adults experience more positive emotions than do younger adults, a finding that is contrary to the stereotype that many people associate with aging.

PHYSICAL CHANGES

Why does the body deteriorate with age?

Despite describing themselves as being in poor physical condition, most people in midlife have few serious illnesses. Beginning in middle adulthood and continuing through late adulthood, however, physical appearance and the functioning of every organ change. The hair thins and turns white or gray. The skin wrinkles. Bones become more fragile. Muscles lose power, and joints stiffen or wear out. Circulation slows, blood pressure rises, and because the lungs hold less oxygen, the older adult has less energy. Body shape and posture change, and the reproductive organs atrophy. Difficulties in falling asleep and staying asleep become more common, and reaction times are slower. Vision, hearing, and the sense of smell all become less acute (Cavanaugh, 1990; Whitbourne, 1998). Most people are at first unaware of these changes because they occur gradually. But the decline eventually becomes undeniable.

It is curious that we do not yet know why physical aging happens (DiGiovanna, 1994). Several theories have been proposed. Some of these suggest that our cells are biologically preprogrammed to divide only a certain number of times (Saretzki & Zglinicki, 2002). Other theories emphasize that the "wear-and-tear" that our cells undergo as we age accumulates, eventually adding up and making death inevitable (De la Fuente, 2002).

Whatever the ultimate explanation for physical decline, many factors affect the physical well-being of older adults. Some are things that they can control, particularly diet, exercise, health care, smoking, drug use, and overexposure to sun (Levenson & Aldwin, 1994). Attitudes and interests also matter. People who have a continuing sense of usefulness, who maintain old ties, investigate new ideas, take up new activities, and feel in control of their lives have the lowest rates of disease and the highest survival rates (Butler & Lewis, 1982; Caspi & Elder, 1986). Indeed, a survey of 2,724 people ranging in age from 25 to 74 years found that older adults reported experiencing more positive emotions during the past month than younger adults reported (Mroczek & Kolarz, 1998). So there's a good deal of truth in the saying, "You're only as old as you feel."

SOCIAL DEVELOPMENT

What kind of lifestyle and sex life can be expected after age 65?

Far from being weak and dependent, most men and women over 65 live independent lives apart from their children and outside nursing homes, and most are very satisfied with their lifestyles. In one survey of people 65 years and older, more than half reported being just as happy as they were when they were younger. Three-quarters said they were involved in activities that were as interesting to them as any they had experienced during their younger years (Birren, 1983). Moreover, those who remain physically and mentally active, travel, exercise, and attend meetings are more likely to report being happier and more satisfied with their lives than those who stay at home (George, 2001).

Still, gradual social changes do take place in late adulthood. In general, older people interact with fewer people and perform fewer social roles. Behavior becomes less influenced by social rules and expectations than it was earlier in life. Most older people step back and assess life, realize there is a limit to their capacity for social involvement, and learn to live comfortably with those restrictions. This process does not necessarily entail a psychological "disengagement" from the social world, as some researchers have contended. Instead, older people may simply make sensible choices that suit their more limited time frames and physical capabilities (Carstensen, 1995).

RETIREMENT Another major change that most people experience in late adulthood is retiring from paid employment. People's reactions to retirement differ greatly, partly because society has no clear expectations of what retirees are supposed to do (Schlossberg, 2004). Should they sit in rocking chairs and watch life go by, or should they play golf, become foster grandparents, and study Greek? The advantage to this lack of clear social expectations is that older adults have the flexibility to structure their retirement as they please. Men and women often go about this process differently. Men generally see retirement as a time to slow down and do less, whereas women often view it as a time to learn new things and explore new possibilities (Helgesen, 1998). This difference can cause obvious problems for retired couples (Moen, Kim, & Hofmeister, 2001).

Of course, the nature and quality of retired life depend in part on financial status. If retirement means a major decline in a person's standard of living, that person will be less eager to retire and will lead a more limited life after retirement. Another factor in people's attitudes toward retirement is their feelings about work. People who are fulfilled by their jobs are usually less interested in retiring than people whose jobs are unrewarding (Atchley, 1982). Similarly, people who have very ambitious, hard-driving personalities tend to want to remain in the work force longer than those who are more relaxed.

SEXUAL BEHAVIOR A common misconception about older adults is that they have outlived their sexuality. This myth reflects our stereotypes. To the extent that we see the elderly as physically unattractive and frail, we find it difficult to believe that they are sexually active. However, while older people respond more slowly and are less sexually active than younger people, the majority of older adults can enjoy sex and have orgasms. One survey revealed that 37 percent of married people over age 60 have sex at least once a week, 20 percent have sex outdoors, and 17 percent swim in the nude (Woodward & Springen, 1992). Another study of people age 65 to 97 found that about half the men still viewed sex as important, and slightly over half of those in committed relationships were satisfied with the quality of their sex lives (Clements, 1996).

COGNITIVE CHANGES

Is memory loss inevitable in old age?

Healthy people who remain intellectually active maintain a high level of mental functioning in old age (Schaie, 1984; Shimamura, Berry, Mangels, Rusting, & Jurica, 1995). Far from the common myth that the brain cells of elderly people are rapidly dying, the brain of the average person shrinks only about 10 percent in size between the ages of 20 and 70 (Goleman, 1996). This finding means that, for a sizable number of older adults, cognitive abilities remain largely intact. Although the aging mind works a little more slowly (Birren & Fisher, 1995; Salthouse, 1991), and certain types of memories are a little more difficult to

Older adults who exercise regularly are better able to avoid the physical problems that sometimes occur with aging.

"Then it's moved and seconded that the compulsory retirement age be advanced to ninety-five."

Source: © The New Yorker Collection, 1963. Peter Arnold from www.cartoonbank.com. All Rights Reserved.

Because people with Alzheimer's disease suffer memory loss, signs can remind them to perform ordinary activities.

store and retrieve (Craik, 1994), any associated decline in functioning is usually offset by the experience that accumulates with age. If there are gradual declines in the ability to process and attend to information, these changes usually are not serious enough to interfere significantly with the ability to enjoy an active, independent life (Li, 2002). Moreover, older adults who stay both mentally and physically active generally experience significantly less cognitive decline than those who do not (Bosma, vanBoxtel, Ponds, Houx, & Jolles, 2003; Colcombe & Kramer, 2003; Vaillant, 2003). Training and practice on cognitive tasks can also help greatly reduce the decline in cognitive performance in later adulthood (Guenther, Schaefer, Holzner, & Kemmler, 2003; Saczynski, Willis, & Schaie, 2002; Willis & Schaie, 1986), though the benefits of training are often limited only to those skills that are practiced (Kramer & Willis, 2002).

ALZHEIMER'S DISEASE For people suffering from **Alzheimer's disease**, the picture is quite different. They forget the names of their children or are unable to find their way home from the store. Some even fail to recognize their lifelong partners. Named for the German neurologist Alois Alzheimer, the disease causes brain changes that result in the progressive loss of the ability to communicate and reason (Glenner, 1994).

For many years, Alzheimer's disease was considered rare, and it was diagnosed only in people under 60 who developed symptoms of memory loss and confusion. But now Alzheimer's is recognized as a common disorder in older people, many of whom used to be called "senile." According to current estimates, about 10 percent of adults over 65 and nearly half of adults over 85 suffer from Alzheimer's disease (Bennett & Knopman, 1994). Factors that put people at risk for developing the disorder include having a genetic predisposition (Lleo, Berezovska, Growdon, & Hyman, 2004), having a family history of dementia (a general decline in physical and cognitive abilities), having Down syndrome or Parkinson's disease, being born to a woman over the age of 40, and suffering a head trauma (especially one that caused unconsciousness) (Kokmen, 1991; Myers, 1996). In addition, people who are not active (both physically and intellectually) during their middle years increase their risk for developing Alzheimer's disease (Friedland et al., 2001; Vaillant, 2003; Wilson & Bennett, 2003).

Alzheimer's usually begins with minor memory losses, such as difficulty in recalling words and names or in remembering where something was placed. As the disease progresses—and this process may take anywhere from 2 to 20 years—personality changes are also likely. First, people may become emotionally withdrawn. Later, they may suffer from delusions, such as thinking that relatives are stealing from them; they often become confused and may not know where they are or what time of day it is. Eventually, Alzheimer's disease robs people of the ability to speak, to care for themselves, and to recognize family members. If they do not die of other causes, Alzheimer's will eventually be fatal (Wolfson et al., 2001).

Early diagnosis of Alzheimer's disease is usually based on questions that healthy people can typically answer with ease, but these questions usually give those in the early stages of Alzheimer's trouble (Petersen et al., 2001; Solomon et al., 1998). At present, there is no known cure for Alzheimer's, but breakthroughs in research are occurring so fast that a drug to slow the progress of the disorder or even a vaccine to prevent it may be developed in the near future (Henry, 1996; Kolata, 2004; Novak, 1999; Pennisi, 1999).

FACING THE END OF LIFE

How well do most elderly people cope with the end of life?

The end of life—whenever it comes—is the final deveopmental event. Coping with the end of life is often difficult, especially if the dying person is young. A classic study of how people adjust to their impending death was conducted by psychiatrist Elisabeth Kübler–Ross (1969), who interviewed more than 200 dying people of all ages to try to understand the psychological aspects of dying. From these interviews, she described a sequence of five stages that she believed people pass through as they react to their own impending death:

1. **Denial**—The person denies the diagnosis, refuses to believe that death is approaching, insists that an error has been made, and seeks other, more acceptable opinions or alternatives.

Alzheimer's disease A neurological disorder, most commonly found in late adulthood, characterized by progressive losses in memory and cognition and by changes in personality.

2. **Anger**—The person now accepts the reality of the situation but expresses envy and resentment toward those who will live to fulfill a plan or dream. The question becomes "Why me?" Anger may be directed at the doctor or directed randomly. The patience and understanding of other people are particularly important at this stage.

3. **Bargaining**—The person desperately tries to buy time, negotiating with doctors, family members, clergy, and God in a healthy attempt to cope with the realization of death.

4. **Depression**—As bargaining fails and time is running out, the person may succumb to depression, lamenting failures and mistakes that can no longer be corrected.

5. **Acceptance**—Tired and weak, the person at last enters a state of "quiet expectation," submitting to fate.

According to Kübler–Ross, Americans have a greater problem coping with death than people in some other cultures. She observes that whereas some cultures are *death affirming*, American culture is *death denying:* "We are reluctant to reveal our age; we spend fortunes to hide our wrinkles; we prefer to send our old people to nursing homes" (1975, p. 28). We also shelter children from knowledge of death and dying. By trying to protect them from these unpleasant realities, however, we may actually make them more fearful of death.

Fear of death seems to be a particular problem for young adults or those in middle age, when the first awareness of mortality coincides with a greater interest in living (Tomer, 2000). But the elderly do have some major fears associated with dying. They fear the pain, indignity, and depersonalization that they might experience during a terminal illness, as well as the possibility of dying alone. They also worry about burdening their relatives with the expenses of their hospitalization or nursing care. Sometimes, too, relatives are not able to provide much support for the elderly as they decline, either because they live too far away or because they may be unable to cope either with the pain of watching a loved one die or with their own fears of mortality (Kübler–Ross, 1975).

Of particular concern to people in later adulthood is the loss of one's mate. The death of one's spouse may be the most severe challenge that people face during late adulthood. Especially if the death was unexpected, people respond to such a loss with initial disbelief, followed by numbness. Only later is the full impact of the loss felt, and that can be severe. The incidence of depression rises significantly following the death of a spouse (Norris & Murrell, 1990). Moreover, a long-term study of several thousand widowers 55 years of age and older revealed that nearly 5 percent of them died in the six-month period following their wife's death, a figure that is well above the expected death rate for men that age. Thereafter, the mortality rate of these men fell gradually to a more normal level (Butler & Lewis, 1982).

The burden of widowhood is heavy for both men and women (Feinson, 1986; Wilcox et al., 2003). Perhaps because they are not as used to taking care of themselves, men seem to suffer more than women from the loss of a mate. But because women have a longer life expectancy, there are many more widows than widowers. Thus, men have a better chance of remarrying. More than half the women over age 65 are widowed, and half of them will live another 15 years without remarrying.

Those who cope best with the grief and adjustment associated with the loss of a spouse or mate are often the same people who have developed successful coping mechanisms throughout their lives. The development of a healthy, stable personality is linked to positive adjustment at the end of life, as it has been throughout earlier developmental transitions.

> ▶ CHECK YOUR UNDERSTANDING

Indicate whether the following statements are true (T) or false (F):

1. ____ The average man lives as long as the average woman.

2. ____ The physical changes of aging become incapacitating for most older adults.

3. ____ Most elderly people are dependent on their adult children.

4. ____ Healthy people who remain intellectually involved generally maintain a high level of mental functioning in old age.

5. List in order the five stages of dying described by Elisabeth Kübler-Ross.

Answers: 1. (F), 2. (F), 3. (F), 4. (T), 5. Denial, anger, bargaining, depression, acceptance.

► APPLY YOUR UNDERSTANDING

1. You are having a discussion about cognitive changes in late adulthood, during which people make the claims that follow. Based on what you have learned in this chapter, you agree with all of them EXCEPT _____.
   a. "If you are healthy and remain intellectually active, you are likely to maintain a high level of mental functioning in old age."
   b. "As you get older, it usually becomes more difficult to process and attend to information."
   c. "If you practice mental tasks, you can help to minimize the decline in those skills."
   d. "Alzheimer's disease involves the decline of cognitive functions, while personality dimensions remain intact."

2. Elisabeth Kübler–Ross notes that Americans "are reluctant to reveal our age; we spend fortunes to hide our wrinkles; we prefer to send our old people to nursing homes." She suggests that this is because American culture is _____.
   a. death affirming.
   b. death denying.
   c. moratorial.
   d. foreclosed.

Answers: 1. d., 2. b.

>KEY TERMS<

developmental psychology, *p. 233*
cross-sectional approach, *p. 233*
cohort, *p. 233*
longitudinal approach, *p. 233*

Prenatal development

prenatal development, *p. 233*
embryo, *p. 234*
fetus, *p. 234*
critical period, *p. 234*
fetal alcohol syndrome (FAS), *p. 234*

The newborn

neonates, *p. 236*

temperament, *p. 236*

Infancy and childhood

developmental norms, *p. 240*
maturation, *p. 241*
sensory-motor stage, *p. 241*
object permanence, *p. 242*
mental representations, *p. 242*
preoperational stage, *p. 242*
egocentric, *p. 242*
concrete-operational stage, *p. 243*
principles of conservation, *p. 243*
formal-operational stage, *p. 243*
babbling, *p. 245*

holophrases, *p. 245*
imprinting, *p. 248*
attachment, *p. 248*
autonomy, *p. 249*
socialization, *p. 249*
peer group, *p. 250*
nonshared environment *p. 251*
gender identity, *p. 252*
gender constancy, *p. 252*
gender-role awareness, *p. 252*
gender stereotypes, *p. 252*
gender-typed behavior, *p. 252*

Adolescence

growth spurt, *p. 254*

puberty, *p. 255*
menarche, *p. 255*
imaginary audience, *p. 256*
personal fable, *p. 256*
identity formation, *p. 257*
identity crisis, *p. 257*
cliques, *p. 258*

Adulthood

menopause, *p. 263*
midlife crisis, *p. 264*
midlife transition, *p. 264*

Late adulthood

Alzheimer's disease, *p. 268*

>CHAPTER REVIEW<

Prenatal Development

What major events take place during the fetal and embryonic stages of prenatal development? Human development is studied using a variety of methods. **Cross-sectional studies** involve studying different age groups of people, whereas **longitudinal studies** involve studying the same group of individuals at different times in their lives. Longitudinal studies are more time consuming, but do account for **cohort** differences in the typical experiences of members of different generations.

The period of development from conception to birth is called **prenatal development**. It is often broken into stages: the latter part of the first three months is referred to as the embryonic stage and the last six months is the fetal stage. Most major organ systems and physical structures, such as arms and legs, are formed by the end of the embryonic stage, although at the beginning of the fetal period, the baby is only about one inch long.

Why can a toxic agent cause devastating effects at one point in prenatal development but not at others? During prenatal development, teratogens—disease-producing organisms or potentially harmful substances, such as drugs—can pass through the placenta and cause irreparable harm to the **embryo** or **fetus**. This harm is greatest if the drug or other substance is introduced at the same time that some major developmental process is occurring. If the same substance is introduced outside this critical period, little or even no harm may result.

What early reflexes enable newborns to respond to their environment? Although newborn babies, called **neonates**, appear helpless, they are much more competent and aware than they seem. Newborns see and hear, are capable of reflexive behavior, and are distinctly unique in their underlying temperaments. Newborns come equipped with a number of reflexes that help them to respond to their environments. Those that help them to breathe and nurse are critical to survival. For example, the *rooting reflex* causes newborns, when touched on the cheek, to turn their head in that direction and grope around with their mouth. This helps them to locate a nipple. Nursing is further facilitated by the *sucking reflex*, which causes newborns to suck on anything placed in their mouth, and the *swallowing reflex*, which enables them to swallow liquids without choking.

Is your temperament the same as it was when you were a newborn? Babies are born with individual differences in personality called **temperament** differences. Often a baby's temperament remains quite stable over time due to a combination of genetic and environmental influences. But stability in temperament is not inevitable; changes in temperament can also take place. Your own temperament, therefore, may be both similar to and different from the temperament you displayed as a newborn.

Which senses are the most developed at birth, and which are the least developed? All of a baby's senses are functioning at birth: sight, hearing, taste, smell, and touch. Although it is hard to tell exactly what a baby's sensory world is like, newborns seem particularly adept at discriminating speech sounds, which suggests that their hearing is quite keen. Their least developed sense is probably vision, which takes 6 to 8 months to become as good as the average college student's.

Infancy and Childhood

Do children grow at a steady pace? During the first dozen years of life, a helpless infant becomes a competent older child. This transformation encompasses many important kinds of changes, including physical, motor, cognitive, and social developments. Growth of the body is most rapid during the first year, with the average baby growing approximately 10 inches and gaining about 15 pounds. It then slows down considerably until early adolescence. When growth does occur, it often happens suddenly—almost overnight—rather than through small, steady changes.

Is walking at an early age a sign of future athletic ability? This is a question about motor development, the acquisition of skills involving movement. Babies tend to reach the major milestones in early motor development at broadly similar ages, give or take a few months. These average ages are called **developmental norms**. Those who are somewhat ahead of their peers are not necessarily destined for athletic greatness. Motor development that is slower or faster

than the norm tells us little or nothing about a child's future characteristics. **Maturation**, the biological process that leads to developmental changes, also is shaped by experiences with the environment.

How does a child's ability to reason change over time? According to the Swiss psychologist Jean Piaget, children undergo qualitative changes in thinking as they grow older. Piaget depicted these changes as a series of stages. During the **sensory-motor stage** (from birth to age two), children acquire **object permanence**, the understanding that things continue to exist even when they are out of sight. In the **preoperational stage** (ages two to seven), they become increasingly adept at using mental representations, and language assumes an important role in describing, remembering, and reasoning about the world. Children in the **concrete-operational stage** (ages 7 to 11) are able to pay attention to more than one factor at a time and can understand someone else's point of view, as **conservation** skills improve and **egocentrism** declines. Finally, in the **formal-operational stage** (adolescence to adulthood), teenagers acquire the ability to think abstractly and test ideas mentally using logic.

How do gender and ethnic background affect moral development? Like Piaget, Lawrence Kohlberg developed a stage theory about the development of thinking, but he focused exclusively on moral thinking. He proposed that children at different levels of moral reasoning base their moral choices on different factors: first a concern about physical consequences, later a concern about what other people think, and finally a concern about abstract principles. One problem with Kohlberg's view, however, is that it doesn't consider how gender and ethnic background affect moral development. The cultural values associated with being female, African American, Japanese, and so on may affect the ways in which people determine what is right and wrong, good and bad.

How does a child develop language skills? Chidlren learn language in a predicatable series of stages, beginning with cooing, and then **babbling**, first words, **holophrases**, and increasingly more complex sentences. Because all humans learn language in much the same way, language is thought to be biologically based, although social and environmental factors also have an impact on which language is learned.

According to Erikson's theory, what are the major developmental milestones in childhood? According to Erik Erikson, development proceeds through eight stages, each involving a central conflict to be resolved. Infants need to establish a sense of *basic trust*. Toddlers focus on developing *autonomy*, which involves independence from parents. Young children develop a sense of *initiative* when they find they are competent in the world; older children experience a sense of *industry* when they work on important developmental skills.

Infants form emotional bonds, called **attachments**, with their caregivers. If attachments are secure, they can go on to develop a healthy sense of independence, called **autonomy**. As children develop, they learn the behavior and attitudes of their culture, a process called **socialization**. Play, which develops from *solitary play* (ages one to two), to *parallel play* (ages two to three), to *cooperative play* (around age three), has an important role in socialization. Parents also influence socialization, and children often benefit most when they have *authoritative* parents, who provide firm structure but are not overly controlling.

When do children learn about their gender? Children develop **gender-typed behavior**, or behavior appropriate to their gender, through a process of **gender-role awareness** and the formation of **gender stereotypes** reflected in their culture.

Is watching TV a good or bad influence on the development of children? Watching television can be worthwhile when programs have educational context and provide positive role models; however, TV also reduces the time children could spend on other positive activities and perhaps contributes to a decline in academic skills, especially reading. When it contains aggressive content and negative role models, TV can encourage aggressive behavior.

Adolescence

What are the consequences of going through puberty early or late? The physical changes of adolescence—rapid growth and sexual maturation—are just part of the transformation that occurs during this period. The child turns into an adult, not only physically, but also cognitively, socially, and personally. Although **puberty**, the onset of sexual maturation, starts earlier in girls than in boys, there are substantial individual differences in exactly when it begins. Very early maturing girls face both advantages and disadvantages. They may like the admiration they get from other girls but dislike the embarrassing sexual attention given to them by boys. Boys who mature early usually do better in sports and in social activities and receive greater respect from their peers, so early maturation may be advantageous for boys.

What are two common fallacies that characterize adolescent thinking? In terms of cognitive development, teenagers often reach the level of formal-operational thought, in which they can reason abstractly and speculate about alternatives. These newfound abilities may make them overconfident that their own ideas are right, turning adolescence into a time of cognitive egocentrism. Frequent focus on the self may also make teens prone to feeling constantly watched and judged by others, a phenomenon called the **imaginary audience**. In addition, adolescents may think of themselves as so unique as to be untouched by the negative things that happen to other people. This **personal fable** may encourage them to take needless risks.

What important tasks do adolescents face in their personal and social lives? Many adolescents undertake a search for personal identity in which they ideally acquire a solid sense of who they are. In Erik Erikson's theory, *identity versus role confusion* is the major challenge of this period. Teenagers also work toward developing romantic interests that can build a foundation for strong, intimate relationships in adulthood. Parent–child relationships may become temporarily rocky during adolescence as teenagers become aware of their parents' faults and question parental rules. These conflicts are most common during early adolescence and tend to resolve themselves by the later adolescent years.

Early and Middle Adulthood

What factors are important in forming satisfying relationships in adulthood? Reaching developmental milestones in adulthood is much less predictable than in earlier years; it is much more a function of the individual's decisions, circumstances, and even luck. Still, there are certain experiences and changes that take place sooner or later in nearly everyone's life and certain needs that nearly every adult tries to fulfill. Almost every adult forms a long-term loving partnership with at least one other adult at some point in life. According to Erik Erikson, the task of finding *intimacy* versus being isolated and lonely is especially important during young adulthood. Erikson believed that people are not ready for love until they have formed a firm sense of identity.

What are the satisfactions and stresses of adult work? The vast majority of adults are moderately or highly satisfied with their jobs and would continue to work even if they didn't need to work for financial reasons. Balancing the demands of job and family is often difficult, however, especially for women, because they tend to have most of the responsibility for housework and child care. Yet despite this stress of a "double shift," a job outside the home is a positive, self-esteem–boosting factor in most women's lives.

What is menopause, and what changes accompany it? Middle adulthood brings a decline in the functioning of the reproductive organs. In women, this is marked by **menopause**, the cessation of menstruation, accompanied by a sharp drop in estrogen levels. Although estrogen-replacement therapy can alleviate some negative symptoms (such as thinning bones and "hot flashes"), it is associated with cancer and heart risks; thus, women should seek medical advice and supervision. Men experience a slower, less dramatic decline in testosterone levels.

In what ways do adults think differently than adolescents? An adult's thinking is more flexible and practical than an adolescent's. Whereas adolescents search for the one "correct" solution to a problem, adults realize that there may be several "right" solutions or none at all. Adults also place less faith in authorities than adolescents place in them.

What changes in personality occur as adults move into midlife? Certain broad patterns of personality change occur in adulthood. As people grow older, they tend to become less self-centered and more comfortable in interpersonal relationships. They also develop better coping skills and new ways of adapting. By middle age, many adults feel an increasing commitment to, and responsibility for, others. This suggests that many adults are successfully meeting what Erik Erikson saw as the major challenge of middle adulthood: *generativity* (the ability to continue being productive and creative, especially in ways that guide and encourage future generations) *versus stagnation* (a sense of boredom or lack of fulfillment, sometimes called a **midlife crisis**). Most adults, however, do not experience dramatic upheaval in their middle years, and this period may be better thought of as one of **midlife transition**.

Later Adulthood

What factors are related to life expectancy? Over the past century, life expectancy in America has increased mainly because of improved health care and nutrition. There is, however, a sizable gender gap, with women living an average of seven years longer than men. There is also a sizable racial gap, with white Americans living an average of five years longer than African Americans.

Why does the body deteriorate with age? The physical changes of late adulthood affect outward appearance and the functioning of every organ. We don't yet know why these changes happen. Perhaps our cells are programmed to eventually deteriorate and die, or perhaps our body parts wear out after repeated use. Whatever the reason, physical aging is inevitable, although it can be slowed by a healthy lifestyle.

What kind of lifestyle and sex life can be expected after age 65? Most older adults have an independent lifestyle and engage in activities that interest them. Although their sexual responses may be slowed, most continue to enjoy sex in their 60s and 70s. Still, gradual social changes occur in late adulthood. Older adults start to interact with fewer people and perform fewer social roles. They may also become less influenced by social rules and expectations. Realizing that there is a limit to the capacity for social involvement, they learn to live with some restrictions.

Is memory loss inevitable in old age? The aging mind works a little more slowly, and certain kinds of memories are more difficult to store and retrieve, but these changes are generally not extensive enough to interfere with most everyday tasks. Healthy older adults who engage in intellectually stimulating activities usually maintain a high level of mental functioning, unless they develop a degenerative condition, such as **Alzheimer's disease**, that affects memory.

How well do most elderly people cope with the end of life? Most elderly people fear death less than younger people fear it. However, they do fear the pain, indignity, depersonalization, and loneliness associated with a terminal illness. They also worry about becoming a financial burden to their families. The death of a spouse may be the most severe challenge that the elderly face.

Concept Map

7.1 PRENATAL DEVELOPMENT

STAGES
- Embryonic stage: Conception—3 months
- Fetal stage: 3 months—birth

CRITICAL PERIODS
- When major development events occur
- When harmful substances have most disruptive effects

7.2 THE NEWBORN

- **Reflexes:** Inborn and adaptive for survival—rooting, sucking, grasping, imitation
- **Temperament:** Largely inborn—easy, difficult, slow to warm up, shy
- **Perceptual Abilities:** Vision becomes clearer over first few months; depth perception by age 6 months; other senses develop during first few months

7.3 INFANCY AND CHILDHOOD

PHYSICAL GROWTH AND MOTOR DEVELOPMENT
- Growth is rapid in first year, slow during childhood, spurts in adolescence
- **Developmental norms:** Average ages for development milestones
- Proximodistal development: From body center outward
- **Maturation:** Biological processes that unfold as development proceeds

SOCIAL DEVELOPMENT
- **Erikson's Eight Stages**

Trust vs Mistrust (infancy)	Identity vs Role confusion (adolescence)
Autonomy vs Shame and Doubt (toddlerhood)	Intimacy vs Isolation (early adulthood)
Initiative vs Guilt (early childhood)	Generativity vs Stagnation (adulthood)
Industry vs Inferiority (later childhood)	Integrity vs Despair (later adulthood)

- **Types of Parenting**

Authoritarian (high control, low warmth)	Permissive-indulgent (low control, high warmth)
Permissive-indifferent (low control, low warmth)	Authoritative (moderate control, high warmth)

- **Development of Play**
  Solitary: Until age 1 1/2 or 2
  Parallel: From age 2 to 3
  Cooperative: At about age 3

COGNITIVE, MORAL, AND LANGUAGE DEVELOPMENT
- **Cognitive development (Piaget)**

Sensory-motor Stage (Birth-2 years)	Concrete Operational Stage (7-11 years)
Preoperational Stage (2-7 years)	Formal Operational Stage (adolescence-adult)

- **Moral Development (Kohlberg)**

  Preconventional: Morality determined by consequences

  Conventional: Morality determined by approval of others

  Postconventional: Morality determined by abstract principles

- **Language Development:** Cooing, **babbling**, words (usually names), **holophrases:** single words with complex meanings, first sentences

GENDER-ROLE DEVELOPMENT
- **Gender identity:** Knowledge of one's gender
- **Gender constancy:** Awareness that gender will not change
- **Gender-role awareness:** What behaviors are expected of girls versus boys
- **Gender stereotypes:** Oversimplified beliefs about "masculine" and "feminine"
- **Gender-typed behavior:** Development of behavior that fits gender stereotypes

7.4 ADOLESCENCE

PHYSICAL CHANGES

- **Growth spurt:** Rapid increase in height and weight signals onset of puberty
- **Puberty:** Onset of sexual maturation
- Sexual behavior follows sexual maturation

COGNITIVE CHANGES

- **Imaginary audience:** Teenagers feel they are constantly being observed
- **Personal fable:** Adolescents' sense of their own uniqueness and invulnerability

PERSONALITY DEVELOPMENT

- Identity formation
- Small unisex cliques, then mixed-sex groups, and eventually couples
- Most adolescents have good relationships with their parents

7.5 EARLY AND MIDDLE ADULTHOOD

PARTNERSHIPS

- 90% of Americans marry, and many others cohabitate
- Homosexual couples seek the same loving commitments as most heterosexuals
- About half of marriages end in divorce

WORK

- Women still earn 30% less than men and do more "double shift" work at home
- 71% of women with school-aged children work outside the home

PHYSICAL, COGNITIVE, AND PERSONALITY CHANGES

- **Menopause:** In women, the ceasing of menstruation
- Adult thinking is more complex, more practical, and more likely to correctly assess the situation
- Cognitive abilities are best maintained by staying physically and mentally active
- The **midlife crisis** is overstated; people more likely make a midlife transition

7.6 LATER ADULTHOOD

DEMOGRAPHIC TRENDS

- Elderly are the fastest growing group in the U.S. population
- Women live 7 years longer than men, on average
- White Americans live 5 years longer than African-Americans

PHYSICAL CHANGES: AGING

- Cells are preprogrammed to divide a fixed number of times
- Wear and tear on our bodies accumulates over time

SOCIAL DEVELOPMENT

- Most older adults are as happy as they were at younger ages
- Retirement is harder for those whose incomes decline and who enjoyed their jobs
- Older adults often enjoy sexual activity

COGNITIVE CHANGES

- Healthy people usually maintain high cognitive functioning in older adulthood
- Small declines can often be offset by training, practice, and greater experience
- **Alzheimer's disease** involves brain deterioration leading to progressive cognitive and personality decline

END OF LIFE

- Kubler-Ross's five stages of coping with impending death: denial, anger, bargaining, depression, acceptance
- Older adults often fear the loss of function and mate more than death
- Older adults who cope best with impending death are those with healthy personalities throughout life

Concept Map

[CHAPTER 8]

Personality, Stress, and Health

Overview

Try sitting for 12 hours at a stretch while navigating a traffic-choked, potholed city populated by jaywalking pedestrians, traffic police and kamikaze drivers—many of them fellow [New York City] cabbies. Add a steady dose of stinging insults and haughty demands from backseat drivers. Top off the day with a profusion of fried food and sugared coffee, and it makes sense that cabbies suffer from soaring rates of high blood pressure, diabetes, lower back pain and shredded nerves.

"I know so many drivers with big bellies," said Shahzad Butt, a 13-year veteran of the road. "They all carry medicine around in their pocket." But when fares grow scarcer after midnight, he and about 100 other cabbies head to a 24-hour health club in Queens, where a brightly illuminated awning beckons drivers along the Brooklyn-Queens Expressway. The gym, BQE Fitness Complex overlooking Exit 40 in Woodside, has become something of a service station for broken and bedraggled cabbies whose white-knuckle jobs leave them tightly wound, their bodies and souls aching." (Andrew Jacobs, "From the Wheel to the Treadmill," *New York Times*, December 28, 2005, p. B.1.)

The decision to sacrifice one's health for one's livelihood takes its toll on overworked and stressed-out employees around the globe. Stress is a state of psychological tension or strain, and as you'll see in this chapter, too much stress over too long a period may contribute to both physical and psychological problems. That's why 45-year-old Bangladeshi driver Mohammed Raju Ahmad is switching back and forth from one treadmill to another. His shirt sopping, the once roly-poly driver power-walked a BQE Fitness Complex treadmill and said, "When health is good, mind is good. When mind is good, passenger feels good because I don't lose my temper so much." Ahmad's sentiment is one that more and more companies are adopting as a powerful rationale for creating workplace wellness programs: Healthy employees = happy employees = happy customers = healthy profits.

About 20 percent of employers have some kind of dedicated stress-reduction program in place, and a recent UK survey found that workplace wellness programs can generate a return on investment of nearly 400 percent for employers in terms of increased productivity and lower insurance premiums. That's why the UK's leading satellite broadcaster, Sky, thinks the £90,000 (about $160,000) it's spending on its Feel Karma wellness program is well spent. Unlike NY cabbies who must wait until their shift ends to pump some iron (and on their own dime, as well), Sky's 11,500 employees can jump on trampolines, do Tai Chi, or participate in Pilates, all during working hours. And to encourage them to exercise for half an hour three times a week, Sky issues pedometers to every employee—from hairdressers to journalists—as well as opportunities to check blood pressure, body mass, and cholesterol. Yet, while making employees more fit is the goal, the last thing the Human Resources team wanted to be was the "health police." Employees choose activities based on their own health shortcomings and goals.

Employee control is key in a larger sense. When it comes to job stress, control over one's work may be the most important factor, said Dr. Peter L. Schall of the Center for Occupational and Environmental Health at the University of California at Irvine. His research has shown that workers most likely to develop high blood pressure are those who work under deadlines with little control over their workday. Contrast these workers to employees at Genentech, the biotech giant voted the "Best Company to Work for in 2006" by Fortune magazine. Aside from enjoying perks like in-house daycare, a concierge service that arranges birthday parties and Friday afternoon keggers, Genentech's researchers have an incredible amount of autonomy. To keep creativity alive and employees happy, Genentech encourage its scientists and engineers to spend fully 20 percent of each workweek pursuing pet projects. The company also awards sabbaticals to reduce stress and stave off burnout.[1]

This chapter includes a discussion of three interrelated topics—personality, stress, and health. Many psychologists define **personality** as an individual's unique pattern of thoughts, feelings, and behaviors that persists over time and across situations. Notice that there are two important parts to this definition. One the one hand, personality refers to *unique differences*—those aspects that distinguish a person from everyone else. In addition, the definition asserts that personality is relatively *stable* and *enduring*—that these unique differences persist through time and across situations. If you could view yourself at various ages in home movies or videos, you might notice that some of the same characteristics are always evident. Maybe you are a natural "actor," always showing off for the camera; or perhaps you are a director type who, at age 4, as well as at age 14, was telling the camera operator what to do. Because we expect people's personalities to be relatively consistent, we generally suspect that something is wrong with a person when that is not the case.

One of the factors that can bring into focus the stability or the inconsistencies with an individual's personality is the accumulation of **stress**, defined here to mean the psychological tension or strain—the uncomfortable emotional and bodily responses—to difficult

personality An individual's unique pattern of thoughts, feelings, and behaviors that persists over time and across situations.

stress A state of psychological tension or strain.

situations. Stress is part of life. We all feel stressed when the car breaks down, when we lose our wallet, when our computer crashes, or when we're under pressure to meet a deadline and there just aren't enough hours in the day to get everything done. Sometimes, we must cope with acute stress, such as the death of a parent or spouse. As we cope, we undergo a process called **adjustment**, which refers to any attempt—successful or not—to cope with stress.

Stress, of course, isn't always "bad"; it can have positive as well as negative consequences. Indeed, most people would be bored with an existence that held no challenges or surprises. Moreover, stress may stimulate effort and spark creativity. Even when a situation is hopeless and a happy ending is impossible, people often report that they have grown, acquired new coping skills and resources, and perhaps experienced a spiritual or religious transformation as a result of stressful experiences (Folkman & Moskowitz, 2000).

Too much stress, over too long a period, however, may contribute to both physical and psychological problems. **Health psychology** focuses on how the mind and body interact. Specifically, health psychologists seek to understand how psychological factors influence wellness and illness. Numerous studies have found that people suffering from acute or chronic stress may be more vulnerable to everything from the common cold to cancer (S. Cohen et al., 1998; Spiegel & Kato, 1996). As you will learn, new research is uncovering the biological mechanisms that link stress to lowered immunity and poor health. The challenge for health psychologists is to find ways both to prevent stress from becoming physically and emotionally debilitating and to *promote* healthy behavior and well-being (Baum, Revenson, & Singer, 2001).

This chapter begins by looking at the major theoretical perspectives that attempt to explain the development and basic structure of personality. It then explores the common, everyday sources of stress in our lives and why some individuals seem particularly vulnerable to stress and others are stress-hardy and resilient. Next, we look at how people cope with stress, and we explore the relationship between stress and our body's response to it. Last, we consider what psychologists mean when they say that a person is well-adjusted.

Theories of Personality

8.1 Compare and contrast the ways in which the four major theories on personality (Psychodynamic, Humanistic, Trait, and Cognitive-Social) explain the structure and development of personality.

Psychologists approach the study of personality in a number of ways. Some set out to identify the most important characteristics of personality. Others seek to understand why there are differences in personality. Among the latter group, some psychologists identify the family as the most important factor in the development of the individual's personality. Others emphasize environmental influences outside the family, and still others see personality as the result of how we learn to think about ourselves and our experiences.

THE PSYCHODYNAMIC THEORY OF SIGMUND FREUD

What are the major ideas in Freud's psychodynamic theory?

Psychodynamic theories see behavior as the product of psychological forces that interact within the individual, often outside conscious awareness. Many personality theorists have developed views that are consistent with the psychodynamic viewpoint, but the best known and most influential among them is Sigmund Freud (Solms, 2004). As we saw in Chapter 1, Freud created an entirely new perspective on the study of human behavior. Up to his time, psychology had focused on consciousness—that is, on those thoughts and feelings of which we are aware. In a radical departure, Freud stressed the **unconscious**—all the ideas, thoughts, and feelings of which we are *not* normally aware. Freud's ideas form the basis of **psychoanalysis**, a term that refers both to his theory of personality and to the form of therapy that he invented.

adjustment Any effort to cope with stress.

health psychology A subfield of psychology concerned with the relationship between psychological factors and physical health and illness.

psychodynamic theories Personality theories contending that behavior results from psychological forces that interact within the individual, often outside conscious awareness.

unconscious In Freud's theory, all the ideas, thoughts, and feelings of which we are not and normally cannot become aware.

psychoanalysis The theory of personality Freud developed, as well as the form of therapy he invented.

According to Freud, human behavior is based on unconscious instincts, or drives. Some instincts are aggressive and destructive; others, such as hunger, thirst, self-preservation, and sex, are necessary to the survival of the individual and the species. Freud used the term *sexual instincts* to refer not just to erotic sexuality, but also to the desire for virtually any form of pleasure. In this broad sense, Freud regarded the sexual instinct as the most critical factor in the development of personality.

HOW PERSONALITY IS STRUCTURED

Freud theorized that personality is formed around three structures: the *id*, the *ego*, and the *superego*. The **id** is the only structure present at birth and is completely unconscious (see **Figure 8–1**.) In Freud's view, the id consists of all the unconscious urges and desires that continually seek expression. It operates according to the **pleasure principle**—that is, it tries to obtain immediate pleasure and to avoid pain. As soon as an instinct arises, the id seeks to gratify it. Because the id is not in contact with the real world,

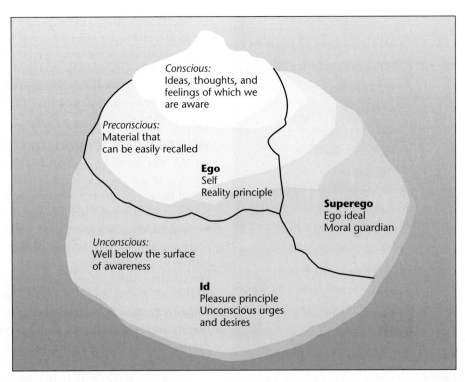

however, it has only two ways of obtaining gratification. One way is by reflex actions, such as coughing, which relieve unpleasant sensations at once. The other is through fantasy, or what Freud referred to as *wish fulfillment*: A person forms a mental image of an object or a situation that partially satisfies the instinct and relieves the uncomfortable feeling. This kind of thought occurs most often in dreams and daydreams, but it may take other forms. For example, if someone insults you and you spend the next half hour imagining clever retorts, you are engaging in wish fulfillment.

Mental images of this kind provide fleeting relief, but they cannot fully satisfy most needs. For example, just thinking about being with someone you love is a poor substitute for actually being with that person. Therefore, the id by itself is not very effective at gratifying instincts. It must link to reality if it is to relieve its discomfort. The id's link to reality is the ego.

Freud conceived of the **ego** as the psychic mechanism that controls all thinking and reasoning activities. The ego operates partly consciously, partly *preconsciously*, and partly unconsciously. ("Preconscious" refers to material that is not currently in awareness but can easily be recalled.) The ego learns about the external world through the senses and sees to the satisfaction of the id's drives in the external world. But instead of acting according to the pleasure principle, the ego operates by the **reality principle**: By means of intelligent reasoning, the ego tries to delay satisfying the id's desires until it can do so safely and successfully. For example, if you are thirsty, your ego will attempt to determine how best to obtain something to quench your thirst effectively and safely. Today, ego functions are often referred to as the "Self."

A personality that consists only of ego and id would be completely selfish. It would behave effectively, although unsociably. Fully adult behavior is governed not only by reality, but also by morality—that is, by the individual's conscience or by the moral standards that the individual develops through interaction with parents and society. Freud called this moral watchdog the **superego**.

The superego is not present at birth. In fact, young children are amoral and do whatever is pleasurable. As we mature, however, we *assimilate*, or adopt as our own, the judgments of our parents about what is "good" and "bad." In time, the external restraint applied by our parents gives way to our own internal self-restraint. The superego, eventually acting as our conscience, takes over the task of observing and guiding the ego, just as our parents once observed and guided us in childhood. Like the ego, the superego works at the conscious, preconscious, and unconscious levels.

Figure 8–1

The structural relationship formed by the id, ego, and superego. Freud's conception of personality is often depicted as an iceberg to illustrate how the vast workings of the mind occur beneath the level of conscious awareness. Notice that the ego is partly conscious, partly unconscious, and partly preconscious; it derives knowledge of the external world through the senses. The superego also works at all three levels. But the id is an entirely unconscious structure.

Source: Adapted from *New Introductory Lectures on Psychoanalysis*, by Sigmund Freud, 1933, New York: Carlton House.

id In Freud's theory of personality, the collection of unconscious urges and desires that continually seek expression.

pleasure principle According to Freud, the way in which the id seeks immediate gratification of an instinct.

ego Freud's term for the part of the personality that mediates between environmental demands (reality), conscience (superego), and instinctual needs (id); now often used as a synonym for "self."

reality principle According to Freud, the way in which the ego seeks to satisfy instinctual demands safely and effectively in the real world.

superego According to Freud, the social and parental standards the individual has internalized.

Freud believed that during the oral stage, babies are dependent on others to fulfill their needs, and they derive pleasure from the mouth, lips, and tongue.

libido According to Freud, the energy generated by the sexual instinct.

fixation According to Freud, a partial or complete halt at some point in the individual's psychosexual development.

oral stage First stage in Freud's theory of personality development, in which the infant's erotic feelings center on the mouth, lips, and tongue.

anal stage Second stage in Freud's theory of personality development, in which a child's erotic feelings center on the anus and on elimination.

phallic stage Third stage in Freud's theory of personality development, in which erotic feelings center on the genitals.

Oedipus complex and Electra complex According to Freud, a child's sexual attachment to the parent of the opposite sex and jealousy toward the parent of the same sex; generally occurs in the phallic stage.

latency period In Freud's theory of personality, a period in which the child appears to have no interest in the other sex; occurs after the phallic stage.

genital stage In Freud's theory of personality development, the final stage of normal adult sexual development, which is usually marked by mature sexuality.

Ideally, our id, ego, and superego work in harmony, the ego satisfying the demands of the id in a reasonable, moral manner that is approved by the superego. We are then free to love and hate and to express our emotions sensibly and without guilt. When our id is dominant, our instincts are unbridled, and we are likely to endanger both ourselves and society. When our superego dominates, our behavior is checked too tightly, and we are inclined to judge ourselves too harshly or too quickly, impairing our ability to act on our own behalf and enjoy ourselves.

HOW PERSONALITY DEVELOPS Freud's theory of personality development focuses on the way in which we satisfy the sexual instinct during the course of life. Freud thought of the sexual instinct broadly, as a craving for sensual pleasure of all kinds. He called the energy generated by the sexual instinct **libido**. As infants mature, their libido becomes focused on different sensitive parts of the body during sequential stages of development. According to Freud, children's experiences at each of these stages stamp their personality with tendencies that endure into adulthood. If a child is deprived of pleasure (or allowed too much gratification) from the part of the body that dominates a certain stage, some sexual energy may remain permanently tied to that part of the body, instead of moving on in normal sequence to give the individual a fully integrated personality. This is called **fixation**, and as we shall see, Freud believed that it leads to immature forms of sexuality and to certain characteristic personality traits. Let's look more closely at the psychosexual stages that Freud identified and their presumed relationship to personality development.

In the **oral stage** (birth to 18 months), infants, who depend completely on other people to satisfy their needs, relieve sexual tension by sucking and swallowing; when their baby teeth come in, they obtain oral pleasure from chewing and biting. According to Freud, infants who receive too much oral gratification at this stage grow into overly optimistic and dependent adults; those who receive too little may turn into pessimistic and hostile people later in life. Fixation at this stage is linked to such personality characteristics as lack of confidence, gullibility, sarcasm, and argumentativeness.

During the **anal stage** (roughly 18 months to 3 years), the primary source of sexual pleasure shifts from the mouth to the anus. Just about the time children begin to derive pleasure from holding in and excreting feces, toilet training takes place, and they must learn to regulate this new pleasure. In Freud's view, if parents are too strict in toilet training, some children throw temper tantrums and may live in self-destructive ways as adults. Others become obstinate, stingy, and excessively orderly. If parents are too lenient, their children may become messy, unorganized, and sloppy.

When children reach the **phallic stage** (roughly age 3 to age 5), they discover their genitals and develop a marked attachment to the parent of the opposite sex while becoming jealous of the same-sex parent. In boys, Freud called this the **Oedipus complex**, after the character in Greek mythology who killed his father and married his mother. Girls go through a corresponding **Electra complex**, involving possessive love for their father and jealousy toward their mother. Most children eventually resolve these conflicts by identifying with the parent of the same sex. Freud contended, however, that fixation at this stage leads to vanity and egotism in adult life, with men boasting of their sexual prowess and treating women with contempt, and with women becoming flirtatious and promiscuous. Phallic fixation may also prompt feelings of low self-esteem, shyness, and worthlessness.

At the end of the phallic period, Freud believed, children lose interest in sexual behavior and enter a **latency period**. During this period, which begins around the age of 5 or 6 and lasts until age 12 or 13, boys play with boys, girls play with girls, and neither sex takes much interest in the other.

At puberty, the individual enters the last psychosexual stage, which Freud called the **genital stage**. At this time, sexual impulses reawaken. Through lovemaking, the person is able to satisfy unfulfilled desires from infancy and childhood. Ideally, the immediate gratification of desires demanded in earlier stages yields to mature sexuality, in which postponed gratification, a sense of responsibility, and caring for others all play a part.

>TABLE 8-1 MAJOR PSYCHODYNAMIC PERSPECTIVES

Theorist	Basic Views
Sigmund Freud (1856–1939)	• Personality consists of the *id* (unconscious urges and drives), the *ego* (which is reality-based), and the *superego* (which reflects moral standards) • Much of human nature is motivated by unconscious (out of our awareness) forces, especially those involving the libido (sexual instinct) • Personality is developed for the most part in childhood, and incomplete development can result in *fixation* (incomplete development) that can affect adult behavior
Carl Jung (1875–1961)	• The role of the unconscious was expanded to include the *personal unconscious* (our own repressed thoughts, feelings and memories) and the *collective unconscious* (species-wide, shared memories, inherited through our evolutionary past.) • *Archetypes* (which are mental images shared by all humans, such as "mother" or "hero") shape personality and are reflected in myths that often are common across many cultures • People can be divided into *introverts* (who are caught up in their private world, and *extroverts* (who turn their attention to the external world). • Psychic development comes to fruition in middle age (not childhood).
Alfred Adler (1870–1937)	• People possess innate positive motives and they strive for personal and social perfection • People can become fixated on their feelings of inferiority and develop an *inferiority complex*, or they may engage in *compensation*, which involves overcoming their weaknesses by developing other abilities
Karen Horney (1885–1952)	• Environmental and social factors are the most influential in shaping personality, especially those involving human relationships during childhood • Needs for security and to feel love are emphasized and are especially important in childhood • Individuals respond to anxiety caused by fear of abandonment by *moving toward people* (submission), *moving against people* (aggression), or *moving away from people* (detachment) • Culture and social conditions play a major role in shaping personality, and this largely accounts for the existence of gender differences
Erik Erikson (1902–1994)	• Emphasized ego development, and the importance of parent-child relationships • Viewed human development as a sequence of eight age-related stages, each of which centers on resolving a specific conflict, or crisis (see Chapter 7: "Human Development Across the Lifespan")

Freud is certainly not without his critics. Feminists have assailed Freud's male-centered, phallic view of personality development, especially because he also hypothesized that all little girls feel inferior because they do not have a penis. Many people now see *penis envy* as much less central to female personality development than Freud thought (Dahl, 1996; Gelman, 1990). In fact, the whole notion that male and female personality development proceeds along similar lines is being challenged. If gender differences in development exist, then the unique developmental tasks encountered by girls may leave them with important skills and abilities that were overlooked or minimized in Freud's theory.

Moreover, Freud's beliefs, particularly his emphasis on sexuality, were not completely endorsed even by members of his own psychoanalytic school. Carl Jung and Alfred Adler, two early associates of Freud, eventually broke with him and formulated their own psychodynamic theories of personality. Jung expanded the scope of the unconscious well beyond the selfish satisfactions of the id. Adler believed that human beings have positive—and conscious—goals that guide their behavior. Other psychodynamic theorists put greater emphasis on the ego and its attempts to gain mastery over the world. These neo-Freudians, principally Karen Horney and Erik Erikson, also focused more on the influence of social interaction on personality. The basic premises of these psychodynamic theorists are briefly outlined in **Table 8–1**: Major Psychodynamic Perspectives.

COMMON FEATURES OF PSYCHODYNAMIC THEORIES

What ideas do all psychodynamic theories have in common?

Despite their differences, theorists who subscribe to the psychodynamic view do share certain beliefs about the nature of personality. All, for example, agree that personality results from the interplay of forces that direct our psychic (or mental) energy. For Freud, the source of energy is primarily sexual (the libido) and it is directed by the id, ego, and superego. Other theories focus on somewhat different forces (perhaps striving for perfection (Alfred Alder) or for security (Karen Horney), but all psychodynamic views emphasize the *dynamic* or continually changing, quality of personality. All psychodynamic theories also emphasize the role of unconscious processes in determining personality and, hence, behavior.

A useful way to conceptualize the basic tenets of the psychodynamic approach is to consider the common threads that these theories share. The following five propositions are central to all psychodynamic theories and have stood the test of time (Westen, 1998):

1. Much of mental life is unconscious, and as a result, people may behave in ways that they themselves do not understand.

2. Mental processes (such as emotions, motivations, and thoughts) operate in parallel and thus may lead to conflicting feelings.

3. Stable personality patterns begin to form in childhood, and early experiences strongly affect personality development.

4. Our mental representations of ourselves, of others, and of our relationships tend to guide our interactions with other people.

5. The development of personality involves learning to regulate sexual and aggressive feelings as well as becoming socially interdependent rather than dependent.

HUMANISTIC PERSONALITY THEORIES

What are the major ways that humanistic personality theories differs from psychodynamic theories?

Freud believed that personality grows out of the resolution of unconscious conflicts and developmental crises. Many of his followers—including some who modified his theory and others who broke away from his circle—also embraced this basic viewpoint. But others, including Alfred Adler, came to emphasize a very different view of human nature. Adler focused on forces that contribute to positive growth and move the person toward personal perfection. For these reasons, Adler is sometimes called the first *humanistic* personality theorist.

Humanistic personality theories emphasize that we are positively motivated and progress toward higher levels of functioning—in other words, that there is more to human existence than dealing with hidden conflicts. Humanistic psychologists believe that life is a process of opening ourselves to the world around us and experiencing joy in living. Humanists stress people's potential for growth and change as well as the ways that they subjectively experience their lives right now, rather than dwelling on how they felt or acted in the past. This approach holds all of us personally responsible for our lives. Finally, humanists also believe that given reasonable life conditions, people will develop in desirable directions (Cloninger, 1993). Adler's concept of striving for perfection laid the groundwork for later humanistic personality theorists such as Abraham Maslow and Carl Rogers. We discussed Maslow's theory of the hierarchy of needs leading to self-actualization in Chapter 6, "Motivation and Emotion." We now turn to Rogers's theory of self-actualization.

CARL ROGERS'S HUMANISTIC VIEW

According to Rogers, how can thinking of yourself as self-assured help you to become so?

One of the most prominent humanistic theorists, Carl Rogers (1902–1987), contended that men and women develop their personalities in the service of positive goals. According to

humanistic personality theories Personality theories that assert the fundamental goodness of people and their striving toward higher levels of functioning.

Rogers, every organism is born with certain innate capacities, capabilities, or potentialities—"a sort of genetic blueprint, to which substance is added as life progresses" (Maddi, 1989, p. 102). The goal of life, Rogers believed, is to fulfill this genetic blueprint, to become the best of whatever each of us is inherently capable of becoming. Rogers called this biological push toward fulfillment the **actualizing tendency**. Although Rogers maintained that the actualizing tendency characterizes all organisms—plants, animals, and humans—he noted that human beings also form images of themselves, or *self-concepts*. Just as we try to fulfill our inborn biological potential, so, too, we attempt to fulfill our self-concept, our conscious sense of who we are and what we want to do with our lives. Rogers called this striving the **self-actualizing tendency**. If you think of yourself as "intelligent" and "athletic," for example, you will strive to live up to those images of yourself.

When our self-concept is closely matched with our inborn capacities, we are likely to become what Rogers called a **fully functioning person**. Such people are self-directed: They decide for themselves what it is they want to do and to become, even though their choices may not always be sound ones. They are not unduly swayed by other people's expectations for them. Fully functioning people are also open to experience—to their own feelings as well as to the world and other people around them—and thus find themselves "increasingly willing to be, with greater accuracy and depth, that self which [they] most truly [are]" (Rogers, 1961, pp. 175–176).

According to Rogers, people tend to become more fully functioning if they are brought up with **unconditional positive regard**, or the experience of being treated with warmth, respect, acceptance, and love regardless of their own feelings, attitudes, and behaviors.

But often parents and other adults offer children what Rogers called **conditional positive regard**: They value and accept only certain aspects of the child. The acceptance, warmth, and love that the child receives from others then depend on the child's behaving in certain ways and fulfilling certain conditions. In the process, self-concept comes to resemble the inborn capacity less and less, and the child's life deviates from the genetic blueprint.

When people lose sight of their inborn potential, they become constricted, rigid, and defensive. They feel threatened and anxious, and experience considerable discomfort and uneasiness. Because their lives are directed toward what other people want and value, they are unlikely to experience much real satisfaction in life. At some point, they may realize that they don't really know who they are or what they want.

TRAIT THEORIES OF PERSONALITY

What is the key focus of trait theories?

The psychodynamic and humanistic personality theories that we have examined so far all emphasize early childhood experiences, and all attempt to explain the varieties of human personality. Other personality theorists focus on the present, describing the ways in which already developed adult personalities differ from one another. These *trait theorists* assert that people differ according to the degree to which they possess certain **personality traits**, such as dependency, anxiety, aggressiveness, and sociability. Although traits cannot be observed directly, we can infer a trait from how a person behaves. If, for example, someone consistently throws parties and regularly participates in groups, we might conclude that the person possesses a high degree of sociability.

Psychologist Gordon Allport believed that traits—or "dispositions," as he called them—are literally encoded in the nervous system as structures that guide consistent behavior across a wide variety of situations. Allport also believed that whereas traits describe behaviors that are common to many people, each individual personality consists of a unique group of traits (Allport & Odbert, 1936). Raymond Cattell (1965), using a statistical technique called **factor analysis**, has demonstrated that various traits tend to cluster in groups. For example, a person who is described as persevering or determined is also likely to be thought of as responsible, ordered, attentive, and stable, and probably would not be described as frivolous, neglectful, and changeable (Cattell & Kline, 1977). According to Cattell, each individual personality consists of a relatively unique constellation of 16 or so basic traits.

This parent is showing warmth and love to her child. Carl Rogers believed that people become more fully functioning if parents provide *unconditional positive regard* by showing warmth, respect, love, and acceptance of all of their children's feelings, attitudes, and behaviors.

actualizing tendency According to Rogers, the drive of every organism to fulfill its biological potential and become what it is inherently capable of becoming.

self-actualizing tendency According to Rogers, the drive of human beings to fulfill their self-concepts, or the images they have of themselves.

fully functioning person According to Rogers, an individual whose self-concept closely resembles his or her inborn capacities or potentials.

unconditional positive regard In Rogers's theory, the full acceptance and love of another person regardless of his or her behavior.

conditional positive regard In Rogers's theory, acceptance and love that are dependent on another's behaving in certain ways and on fulfilling certain conditions.

personality traits Dimensions or characteristics on which people differ in distinctive ways.

factor analysis A statistical technique that identifies groups of related objects; it was used by Cattell to identify clusters of traits.

Big Five Five basic personality traits currently considered to be of central importance in describing personality.

Other theorists thought that Cattell used too many traits to describe personality. Eysenck (1976) argued that personality could be reduced to three basic dimensions: *Emotional stability, introversion–extroversion,* and *psychoticism.* According to Eysenck, *emotional stability* refers to how well a person controls emotions. On a continuum, individuals at one end of this trait would be seen as poised, calm, and composed, whereas people at the other end might be described as anxious, nervous, and excitable. *Introversion–extroversion* refers to the degree to which a person is inwardly or outwardly oriented. At one end of this dimension would be the socially outgoing, talkative, and affectionate people, known as *extroverts. Introverts*—generally described as reserved, silent, shy, and socially withdrawn—would be at the other extreme. Eysenck used the term *psychoticism* to describe people characterized by insensitivity and uncooperativeness at one end and warmth, tenderness, and helpfulness at the other end.

THE FIVE FACTOR MODEL OF PERSONALITY

What five basic traits describe most differences in personality?

Many personality theorists today believe that important dimensions of job performance are linked to basic personality traits, such as conscientiousness.

Contemporary trait theorists have boiled personality traits down to five basic dimensions: *extroversion, agreeableness, conscientiousness, emotional stability,* and *openness to experience* (see **Table 8–2**; Botwin & Buss, 1989; Goldberg, 1993; Wiggins, 1996). Research has shown that these five traits can be used to describe people all over the world. This and other research has led to a growing consensus today that these **Big Five** personality dimensions, also known as the *five-factor model,* capture the most salient dimensions of human personality (Funder, 1991; McCrae & Costa, 1996; Wiggins, 1996), although there is some disagreement about whether the fifth dimension should be called "culture" or "openness to experience" (McCrae & Costa, 1985, 1987, 1989) or "intellect" (Digman & Takemoto–Chock, 1981; Peabody & Goldberg, 1989). Recently, each of the Big Five traits has been shown to have at least six *facets,* or components, as shown in **Table 8–2** (Jang, Livesey, McCrae, Angleitner, & Riemann, 1998). The 30 identified facets are not an exhaustive listing of all aspects of personality; rather, they represent a broad sample of important traits (Costa & McCrae, 1992, 1995).

>TABLE 8–2 THE "BIG FIVE" DIMENSIONS OF PERSONALITY

Traits	Facets of Each Big Five Trait
Extroversion	Warmth, gregariousness, assertiveness, activity, excitement seeking, positive emotions
Agreeableness	Trust, straightforwardness, altruism, compliance, modesty, tender mindedness
Conscientiousness/Dependability	Competence, order, dutifulness, achievement-striving, self-discipline, deliberation
Emotional Stability	Anxiety, hostility, depression, self-consciousness, impulsiveness, vulnerability
Openness to Experience/Culture/Intellect	Fantasy, aesthetics, feelings, actions, ideas, values

Source: Adapted from Jang, K. L., Livesley, W. J., McCrae, R. R., Angleitner, A., & Riemann, R. (1998). Heritability of facet-level traits in a cross-cultural twin sample: Support for a hierarchical model of personality. *Journal of Personality and Social Psychology, 74,* 1556–1565. Table 3, p. 1560. Copyright © 1998 by the American Psychological Association. Adapted with permission.

One survey of the literature found that the Big Five dimensions of personality may have some important real-world applications—particularly as they relate to employment decisions (Hogan, Hogan, & Roberts, 1996). For example, one study (Ones, Viswesvaran, & Schmidt, 1993) found that the dimensions of conscientiousness and emotional stability were reliable predictors of job performance in a wide variety of occupational settings. In another study, the measures of agreeableness and emotional stability predicted performance for employees in customer service positions (McDaniel & Frei, 1994). The Big Five personality traits have also been shown to be useful in predicting the job performance of police officers (Schneider, 2002). In addition, research has shown that absenteeism in the workplace is related to the conscientiousness, extraversion, and emotional stability scales (Conte & Jacobs, 2003). Thus, the Big Five dimensions of personality show promise as reliable predictors of job performance, especially when other criteria (such as technical skills and experience) are also considered (Hogan et al., 1996).

The Big Five personality traits have proven useful in describing and predicting behavior across a wide range of age groups and social settings. For example, one nine-year longitudinal study of grade-school children demonstrated the validity and consistency of the Big Five personality traits throughout childhood (Asendorpf & Van–Aken, 2003). In another study, the Big Five reliably predicted alcohol consumption and grade point average among college students (Paunonen, 2003).

Recent evidence shows that the Big Five, and many of their individual facets, are strongly influenced by heredity (Azar, 2002; Livesley, Jang, & Vernon, 2003; Loehlin, McCrae, Costa, & John, 1998). One study divided the relative contribution of genetic and environmental influences in almost 1,000 sets of identical twins; this study found that genetics accounted for a substantial portion of the differences between scores on 26 of the 30 facets tested (Jang, Livesley, Angleitner, Riemann, & Vernon, 2002). Researchers have also confirmed that genetic factors play a significant role in shaping abnormal and dysfunctional personality traits (Markon, Krueger, Bouchard, & Gottesman, 2002), such as those that predispose individuals toward alcohol abuse (Mustanski, Viken, Kaprio, & Rose, 2003), eating disorders (Klump, McGue, & Iacono, 2002), depression, marijuana dependence, and antisocial personality disorder (Fu et al., 2002).

One of the questions raised by the Five Factor theory, as well as by other trait theories of personality, is whether traits can really describe and predict behavior. Are "agreeable" people always agreeable? Are they agreeable in all situations? Of course not. So then, how useful is the trait designation of "agreeable"? The issue of consistency in human behavior has long intrigued personality theorists who are interested in the interaction of personality traits with the person's social environment. For this group, behavior is a product of the person *and* the situation (Mischel, Shoda, & Mendoza–Denton, 2002). That interaction, the blending of the self and the social, is the focus of cognitive–social learning theorists.

COGNITIVE–SOCIAL LEARNING THEORIES

How do personal and situational factors combine to shape behavior?

In contrast to personality trait theories, **cognitive–social learning theories** hold that people's actions are influenced by their situations, including the people around them. Thus, although individuals may have basic predispositions to respond in characteristic ways, their actual behavior is heavily influenced by their particular environment. Furthermore, experiences help shape not only how people interact with others, but also how they come to think about these interactions and about themselves.

Cognitive-social learning theories emphasize that people internally organize their expectancies and values to guide their own behavior. This set of personal standards is unique to each one of us, growing out of our own life history. Our behavior is the product of the interaction of *cognitions* (how we think about a situation and how we view our behavior in that situation), *learning and past experiences* (including reinforcement, punishment, and modeling), and the *immediate environment*. Thus, cognitive-social learning theories emphasize the role that our expectations and our self-concept play in establishing our unique personalities.

PETER WAS A BORN WORRIER ...

I HOPE THIS GUY KNOWS WHAT HE'S DOING.

Source: Tee and Charles Addams Foundation.

cognitive–social learning theories Personality theories that view behavior as the product of the interaction of cognitions, learning and past experiences, and the immediate environment.

According to cognitive–social learning theorists, people who meet their own internal standards of performance develop a sense of self-efficacy, a confidence that they can meet their goals.

expectancies In Bandura's view, what a person anticipates in a situation or as a result of behaving in certain ways.

performance standards In Bandura's theory, standards that people develop to rate the adequacy of their own behavior in a variety of situations.

self-efficacy According to Bandura, the expectancy that one's efforts will be successful.

locus of control According to Rotter, an expectancy about whether reinforcement is under internal or external control.

EXPECTANCIES, SELF-EFFICACY, AND LOCUS OF CONTROL Albert Bandura (1977, 1986, 1997) asserts that people evaluate a situation according to certain internal **expectancies**, such as personal preferences, and this evaluation affects their behavior. Environmental feedback that follows the actual behavior, in turn, influences future expectancies. These experience-based expectancies lead people to conduct themselves according to unique **performance standards**, individually determined measures of excellence by which they judge their own behavior. Those who succeed in meeting their own internal performance standards develop an attitude that Bandura calls **self-efficacy** (Bandura & Locke, 2003). For example, two young women trying a video game for the first time may experience the situation quite differently, even if their scores are similarly low. One with a high sense of self-efficacy may find the experience fun and be eager to gain the skills necessary to go on to the next level, whereas the one with a lower sense of self-efficacy may be disheartened by getting a low score, assume she will never be any good at video games, and never play again. Similarly, a person with high self-efficacy who interprets math problems as opportunities to succeed will approach the math SAT with a different expectancy than someone who sees math problems as opportunities to fail.

In our example, the two young women approach the experience with different expectancies. To Rotter (1954), **locus of control** is a prevalent expectancy, or cognitive strategy, by which people evaluate situations. People with an *internal locus* of control are convinced they can control their own fate. They believe that through hard work, skill, and training, they can find reinforcements and avoid punishments. People with an *external locus* of control do not believe they control their fate. Instead, they are convinced that chance, luck, and the behavior of others determine their destiny and that they are helpless to change the course of their lives.

Both Bandura and Rotter have tried to combine personal variables (such as expectancies) with situational variables in an effort to understand the complexities of human behavior. Both theorists believe that expectancies become part of a person's *explanatory style*, which, in turn, greatly influences behavior. Explanatory style, for example, separates optimists from pessimists. It is what causes two beginners who get the same score on a video game to respond so differently.

General expectancies or explanatory styles, such as optimism or pessimism, can have a significant effect on behavior. Some research shows that children as young as eight years old have already developed a habitual explanatory style. In one study, third-graders were asked to read descriptions of 12 good and 12 bad events and then come up with reasons the events happened. Their scores reflected their degree of pessimism or optimism. Pessimists tended to believe that negative events were due to personal characteristics they could not change; optimists viewed negative events as unfortunate incidents they could remedy. Children with a more pessimistic style were found to be more prone to depression and to do worse on achievement tests (Nolen–Hoeksema, Girgus, & Seligman, 1986).

In a now-famous study, researchers tracked 99 students from the Harvard graduation classes of 1939 to 1944. The men were interviewed about their experiences and underwent physical checkups every five years. When researchers analyzed the men's interviews for signs of pessimism or optimism, they found that the explanatory style demonstrated in those interviews predicted the state of an individual's health decades later. Those men who were optimists at age 25 tended to be healthier at age 65, whereas the health of the pessimists had begun to deteriorate at about age 45 (Peterson, Vaillant, & Seligman, 1988). Although the reasons for these findings are not yet clear, a separate investigation that used a checklist about health habits found that the pessimists in this study were less careful about their health than were optimists. They tended to smoke and drink more and reported twice as many colds and visits to doctors. Another study looked at insurance agents in their first two years on the job (Seligman & Schulman, 1986). Explanatory style predicted which agents would become excellent agents and which would quit the company (three-fourths of all agents quit within three years). Optimists sold 37 percent more insurance than pessimists in the first two years and persisted through the difficulties of the job.

HOW CONSISTENT ARE WE? We have seen that trait theorists tend to believe that behavior is relatively consistent across situations. For example, "agreeable" people tend to be agreeable in most situations nearly all the time. In contrast, cognitive–social learning theorists view personality as the relatively stable cognitive processes that underlie behavior that are the product of the person and the situation: At any time, our actions are influenced by the people around us, and by the way we think we are supposed to behave in a given situation. According to this latter view, although underlying personality is relatively stable, behavior is likely to be more inconsistent than consistent from one situation to another.

If behavior is relatively inconsistent across situations, why does it *appear* to be more consistent than it actually is? Why is the trait view of personality so compelling? One explanation is that, because we see a person only in those situations that tend to elicit the same behavior, we tend to assume that they are consistent across a wide range of situations. Moreover, there is considerable evidence that people need to find consistency and stability even in the face of inconsistency and unpredictability. We therefore see consistency in the behavior of others even when there is none (Hayden & Mischel, 1976; Mischel, 2003; Mischel & Shoda, 1998).

COMPARING AND EVALUATING PERSONALITY THEORIES

What are the major contributions and limitations of each of the four major theoretical perspectives on personality?

The previous sections of this chapter make clear that there are a wide variety of approaches to the understanding of what constitutes personality. It is important to recognize that each theoretical perspective makes important contributions to our understanding of human nature. All have had a major impact on how psychologists, as well as people working in other fields, conceptualize personality. Each approach also has certain limitations, and each is subject to criticism. Some of the more important contributions and limitations of the four major theoretical views of personality are outlined in **Table 8–3**.

Each theoretical tradition has spawned an array of research programs and each has also given rise to important and effective psychotherapy techniques and approaches. We will explore the basis of several of these approaches to psychotherapy in Chapter 9: "Psychological Disorders and Their Treatments." Additionally, the theoretical perspectives that describe personality have generated a host of personality tests and assessment techniques. We describe some of the more widely used methods of personality assessment in the next section.

>TABLE 8-3 CONTRIBUTIONS AND CRITICISMS ASSOCIATED WITH MAJOR PERSONALITY THEORIES

Perspective	Major Contributions	Criticisms
Psychodynamic Theories	• Notions of unconscious urges, sexual instincts, and the importance of childhood experience have fundamentally changed the way human nature is viewed, in psychology, literature, and the arts and humanities • Psychotherapy techniques based on this theory can be effective	• May give too little attention to social and environmental events as determinants of personality. (For example, the role that culture plays in gender-expectations) • Difficult to test ideas scientifically
Humanistic Theories	• Provides a very optimistic view of human potential and growth • Emphasize the important role of a nurturing, supportive family and environment	• May fail to adequately consider the "darker" more destructive aspects of personality, and may foster self-centered approaches • Difficult to test ideas scientifically
Trait Theories	• Have considerable "common sense" appeal since personality traits are commonly used to describe individuals • Provide a useful way to describe personality differences among individuals and are useful for research on personality	• Tell us little about how traits develop • Simplicity of trait theories may not adequately represent the real complexity of the construct of personality
Cognitive-Social Learning Theories	• Emphasize the mental processes that are involved in personality and focus on conscious behavior and experience • Provide useful explanations for the *inconsistencies* of behavior	• May give inadequate attention to unconscious processes and personality development • May be too narrow in scope

► CHECK YOUR UNDERSTANDING

1. According to Freud, the primary source of psychic energy is generated by the sexual instinct and is called the _____.

Indicate whether the following are true (T) or false (F).

2. ___ Humanistic personality theory emphasizes that we are motivated by conflicts, whereas psychodynamic personality theory emphasizes positive strivings.

3. ___ The ultimate goal of life, Carl Rogers believed, is to become the best person that we can inherently become.

4. ___ Personality traits are almost entirely determined by the environment.

5. According to cognitive–social learning theorists, _____ _____ is what separates optimists from pessimists.

► APPLY YOUR UNDERSTANDING

1. An angry parent imagines hitting a child for misbehaving, but decides instead to discuss the misbehavior with the child and to point out why the behavior was wrong. After hearing the child's explanation for the behavior, the parent feels guilty for having been so angry. According to Freud's psychodynamic theory, the parent's anger and fantasy are the result of the _____; the decision to discuss the problem is the result of the _____, and the guilt derives from the _____.

   a. ego; superego; id
   b. id; ego; superego
   c. ego; id; superego
   d. id; superego; ego

2. Your friend has always known that she wants to be a doctor. When you ask her how she knows that, she says, "That's just who I am. It's what I want to do with my life." Rogers calls the push toward fulfilling this sense of who she is _____.
   a. being fully functioning
   b. engaging in a compensatory process
   c. expressing a high need for achievement
   d. the self-actualizing tendency

3. According to research, if you wanted to hire highly productive people, you would want to hire people who score high on all of the following factors EXCEPT
   a. introversion
   b. conscientiousness
   c. emotional stability
   d. agreeableness

4. Rey Ramos grew up in the South Bronx, an urban ghetto where young males are more likely to go to jail than they are to graduate from high school. He said, "My father always said you can't change anything; destiny has everything written for you. But, I rebelled against that, and I told him I was going to make my own destiny." According to cognitive–social learning theories of personality, which of the following is most descriptive of Rey?
   a. He has an internal locus of control
   b. He has a low sense of self-efficacy
   c. He is compensating for feelings of inferiority
   d. He has an external locus of control

Personality Assessment

8.2 Describe how personality is assessed and measured and note the theoretical perspectives aligned with these various assessment methods.

In some ways, testing personality is much like testing intelligence. In both cases, we are trying to measure something intangible and invisible. And in both cases, a "good test" is one that is both *reliable* and *valid*: It gives dependable and consistent results, and it measures what it claims to measure. (See Chapter 5, "Cognition and Mental Abilities.") But there are special difficulties in measuring personality.

Because personality reflects *characteristic* behavior, we are not interested in someone's *best* behavior. We are interested in *typical* behavior—how a person usually behaves in ordinary situations. Further complicating the measurement process, such factors as fatigue, the desire to impress the examiner, and the fear of being tested can profoundly affect a person's behavior in a personality-assessment situation. For the intricate task of measuring personality, psychologists use four basic tools: the personal interview, direct observation of behavior, objective tests, and projective tests. The tools most closely associated with each of the major theories of personality are shown in the "**Summary Table.**"

SUMMARY TABLE

THEORIES AND ASSESSMENTS OF PERSONALITY

THEORY	ROOTS OF PERSONALITY	METHODS OF ASSESSING
Psychodynamic	Unconscious thoughts, feelings, motives, and conflicts; repressed problems from early childhood	Projective tests, personal interviews
Humanistic	A drive toward personal growth and higher levels of functioning	Objective tests, personal interviews
Trait	Relatively permanent dispositions within the individual that cause the person to think, feel, and act in characteristic ways	Objective tests
Social Learning	Determined by past reinforcement and punishment as well as by observing what happens to other people	Interviews, objective tests, observations

THE PERSONAL INTERVIEW

What are the purposes of structured and unstructured interviews?

An interview is a conversation with a purpose: to obtain information from the person being interviewed. Interviews are often used in clinical settings to learn, for example, why someone is seeking treatment and to help diagnose the person's problem. Such interviews are generally *unstructured*—that is, the interviewer asks the client questions about any issues that arise and asks follow-up questions whenever appropriate. The interviewer may also pay attention to the person's behavior—manner of speaking, poise, or tenseness when certain topics are raised. The most effective interviewers are warm, interested in what the respondent has to say, calm, relaxed, and confident (Feshbach & Weiner, 1982).

When conducting systematic research on personality, investigators more often rely on the *structured* interview (van-Iddekinge, Raymark, Eidson, & Attenweiler, 2004). Structured interviews also are commonly used techniques in personnel selection (see Chapter 11: "Psychology Applied to Work"). In structured interviews, the order and content of the questions are fixed, and the interviewer adheres to the set format. Although less personal, this kind of interview allows the interviewer to obtain comparable information from everyone interviewed. Generally speaking, structured interviews are usually more reliable than unstructured interviews and allow examiners to draw out information about sensitive topics that might not come up in an unstructured interview.

DIRECT OBSERVATION

What are the advantages and limits of the observational method?

Another way to find out how a person usually behaves is to observe that person's actions in everyday situations over a long period. Behaviorists and social learning theorists prefer this method of assessing personality because it allows them to see how situation and environment influence behavior and to note the range of behaviors that the person is capable of exhibiting.

In *direct observation*, observers watch people's behavior firsthand. Systematic observation allows psychologists to look at aspects of personality (e.g., traits, moods, or motives) as they are expressed in real life (Ozer & Reise, 1994). Ideally, the observers' unbiased accounts of the subjects' behavior paint an accurate picture of that behavior, but an observer runs the risk of misinterpreting the true meaning of an act. For example, the observer may think that children are being hostile when they are merely protecting themselves from the class bully. An expensive and time-consuming method of research, direct observation may also yield faulty results if, as noted earlier, the presence of the observer affects people's behavior.

objective tests Personality tests that are administered and scored in a standard way.

OBJECTIVE TESTS

Why are objective tests preferred by trait theorists?

To avoid depending on the skills of an interviewer or the interpretive abilities of an observer in assessing personality, psychologists devised **objective tests**, or personality inventories. Generally, these are written tests that are administered and scored according to a standard procedure. The tests are usually constructed so that the person merely chooses a "yes" or "no" response, or selects one answer among many choices. Objective tests are the most widely used tools for assessing personality, but they have two serious drawbacks. First, they rely entirely on self-report. If people do not know themselves well, or cannot be entirely objective about themselves, or want to paint a particular picture of themselves, self-report questionnaire results have limited usefulness (Funder, 1991). In fact, some research indicates that peers who know you well often do a better job characterizing you than you do yourself (Funder, 1995). Second, if people have taken other personality questionnaires, their familiarity with the test format may affect their responses to the present questionnaire. This is a particular problem on college campuses, where students are likely to participate in many research studies that rely on personality inventories (Council, 1993) (see "Understanding Ourselves: Evaluating Your Personality.")

[UNDERSTANDING OURSELVES]

EVALUATING YOUR PERSONALITY

The following scales provide a way for you to assess your own personality on the Big Five. They also will allow you to examine the extent to which others agree with your assessment, the extent to which your behavior is consistent across a range of situations, and the extent to which your personality has been stable over time. (see **Table 8–2**.)

For each of the adjectives, indicate the extent to which you think it applies to you. If you write your answers on a separate sheet of paper, you can then ask others to rate you on the same dimensions and compare their answers to your own. Friends, close relatives, and others who know you well are likely to provide the most useful information. You also might try to get ratings from people who see you in different situations—perhaps some people who see you only in class, some who see you only in informal social situations, and others who have known you for a very long time in a wide variety of situations. That will give you an opportunity to see the extent to which different situations cause you to behave in different ways; in turn, this could lead others, who see you only in narrowly defined situations, to conclude that your *personality* is different than perhaps it really is.

You might also fill out the form, or have others fill it out, as you were in the past, and compare that with how you are today. It would be interesting to speculate on the reasons for any significant changes over time.

Use the following scales to rate yourself on each adjective:

1: Very true of me
2: Often true of me
3: Sometimes true of me
4: Seldom true of me
5: Almost never true of me

EXTROVERSION

Outgoing	1	2	3	4	5
Sociable	1	2	3	4	5
Forceful	1	2	3	4	5
Energetic	1	2	3	4	5
Adventurous	1	2	3	4	5
Enthusiastic	1	2	3	4	5

AGREEABLENESS

Forgiving	1	2	3	4	5
Not demanding	1	2	3	4	5
Warm	1	2	3	4	5
Not stubborn	1	2	3	4	5
Modest	1	2	3	4	5
Sympathetic	1	2	3	4	5

CONSCIENTIOUSNESS

Efficient	1	2	3	4	5
Organized	1	2	3	4	5
Responsible	1	2	3	4	5
Thorough	1	2	3	4	5
Self-disciplined	1	2	3	4	5
Deliberate	1	2	3	4	5

EMOTIONAL STABILITY

Tense	1	2	3	4	5
Irritable	1	2	3	4	5
Depressed	1	2	3	4	5
Self-conscious	1	2	3	4	5
Moody	1	2	3	4	5
Not self-confident	1	2	3	4	5

OPENNESS TO EXPERIENCE

Curious	1	2	3	4	5
Imaginative	1	2	3	4	5
Artistic	1	2	3	4	5
Wide interests	1	2	3	4	5
Excitable	1	2	3	4	5
Unconventional	1	2	3	4	5

Because of their interest in accurately measuring personality traits, trait theorists favor objective tests. For example, objective tests such as the **NEO-PI-R** have been developed to assess the Big Five major personality traits (Costa & McCrae, 1992, 1995). The NEO-PI-R divides each of the Big Five traits into six facets and yields scores for each facet and each trait. For each of over 200 questions, the person indicates to what degree he or she disagrees with the statement made. The primary use of the test is to assess the personality of a normal adult, although recent studies suggest it may also prove useful in some clinical and organizational settings (Sanderson & Clarkin, 2002) (see Chapter 11: "Psychology Applied to Work.")

The most widely used and thoroughly researched objective personality test, however, is the **Minnesota Multiphasic Personality Inventory (MMPI-2)** (Dorfman & Leonard, 2001). The MMPI was originally developed as an aid in diagnosing psychiatric disorders (Hathaway & McKinley, 1942), and remains in use today as a means of effectively distinguishing between different types of mental disorders (Egger, Delsing, & DeMey, 2003) and detecting malingering (faking a mental disorder) (Kucharski, Johnsen, & Procell, 2004). The person taking the test is asked to answer "true," "false," or "cannot say" to such questions as: "Once in a while I put off until tomorrow what I ought to do today," "At times I feel like swearing," and "There are people who are trying to steal my thoughts and ideas." Some of the items repeat very similar thoughts in different words: For example, "I tire easily" and "I feel weak all over much of the time." This redundancy provides a check on the possibility of false or inconsistent answers.

Researchers have derived several personality scales from this test, including ratings for schizophrenia, depression, and hypochondriasis. These elements of the MMPI-2 are highly regarded as useful tools for differentiating among psychiatric populations (Anastasi & Urbina, 1997). The MMPI-2 is also used to differentiate among more normal personality dimensions, such as extroversion–introversion, masculinity-femininity, and assertiveness, but with less success.

PROJECTIVE TESTS

What do projective tests try to measure?

Psychodynamic theorists, who believe that people are often unaware of the determinants of their behavior, tend to discount objective personality tests that rely on self-reports. Instead, they prefer **projective tests** of personality. Most projective tests consist of simple ambiguous stimuli that can elicit an unlimited number of responses. The test taker looks at some essentially meaningless material or at a vague picture and then explains what the material means to him or her. Or the person may be asked to complete a sentence fragment, such as "When I see myself in the mirror, I . . ." The tests offer no clues regarding the "best way" to interpret the material or to complete the sentence.

Projective tests have several advantages: Because these tests are flexible and can even be treated as games or puzzles, people can take them in a relaxed atmosphere, without the tension and self-consciousness that sometimes accompany objective tests. Often, the person being examined doesn't even know the true purpose of the test, so responses are less likely to be faked. Some psychologists believe that a projective test can uncover unconscious thoughts and fantasies, such as latent sexual or family problems. In any event, the accuracy and usefulness of projective tests depend largely on the skill of the examiner in eliciting and interpreting responses.

The **Rorschach test** is the best known and one of the most frequently used projective personality tests (Ball, Archer, & Imhof, 1994; C. E. Watkins, Campbell, Nieberding, & Hallmark, 1995). It is named for Hermann Rorschach, a Swiss psychiatrist who in 1921 published the results of his research on interpreting inkblots as a key to personality (see **Figure 8–2.**) Each inkblot design is printed on a separate card and is unique in form, color, shading, and white space. People are asked to specify what they see in each blot. Test instructions are minimal, so people's responses will be completely their own. After interpreting all the blots, the person goes over the cards again with the examiner and

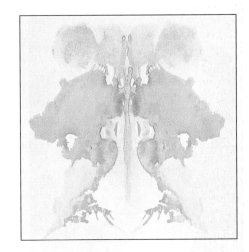

Figure 8–2

Two of the inkblots used in the Rorschach projective test.

NEO-PI-R An objective personality test designed to assess the Big Five personality traits.

Minnesota Multiphasic Personality Inventory (MMPI-2) The most widely used objective personality test, originally intended for psychiatric diagnosis.

projective tests Personality tests, such as the Rorschach inkblot test, consisting of ambiguous or unstructured material.

Rorschach test A projective test composed of ambiguous inkblots; the way people interpret the blots is thought to reveal aspects of their personality.

Figure 8–3

A sample item from the Thematic Appercep-tion Test (TAT). In the lower photo, the person is making up a story to explain the scene in the picture she is describing (presented above). The examiner then interprets and evaluates the person's story for what it reveals about her personality.

Source: Reprinted by permission of the publishers from Henry A. Murray, *Thematic Apperception Test,* Plate 12F, Cambridge, Mass.: Harvard University Press, Copyright © 1943 by the President and Fellows of Harvard College, © 1971 by Henry A. Murray.

explains which part of each blot prompted each response. There are different methods of interpreting a person's responses to the blots on the Rorschach test, and some produce more valid results than others (Exner, 1996; Masling, 2002; Viglione & Taylor, 2003; Weiner, 1996, 1997).

Somewhat more demanding is the **Thematic Apperception Test (TAT)**. It consists of 20 cards picturing one or more human figures in deliberately ambiguous situations (see **Figure 8–3**; Morgan, 2002.) A person is shown the cards one by one and asked to write a complete story about each picture, including what led up to the scene depicted, what the characters are doing at that moment, what their thoughts and feelings are, and what the outcome will be.

Although various scoring systems have been devised for the TAT (Aranow, Weiss, & Rezikoff, 2001; Hibbard, Farmer, Wells, Difillipo, & Barry, 1994), examiners usually interpret the stories in the light of their personal knowledge of the storyteller. One key in evaluating the TAT is whether the person identifies with the hero or heroine of the story or with one of the minor characters. The examiner then determines what the attitudes and feelings of the character reveal about the storyteller. The examiner also assesses each story for content, language, originality, organization, and consistency. Certain themes, such as the need for affection, repeated failure, or parental domination, may recur in several plots.

Both the Rorschach and the TAT may open up a conversation between a clinician and a person who is reluctant or unable to talk about personal problems. Both tests may also provide useful information about motives, events, or feelings of which the person is unaware. However, because projective tests are often not administered in a standard fashion, their validity and reliability, especially in cross-cultural settings, have been called into question (Dawes, 1994; Hofer & Chasiotis, 2004; Wierzbicki, 1993). As a result, their use has declined since the 1970s. Still, when interpreted by a skilled examiner, these tests can offer valuable insights into a person's attitudes and feelings. Oftentimes, such tests can lead clinicians to a clearer understanding of the problems faced by a patient or client. Sometimes these problems are linked to the stress the client is experiencing. In some cases, stressful events in the person's life may be producing much of the discomfort being experienced. In other cases, stress may be a consequence of other psychological issues. Indeed, stress is a common feature of life, as we will see in the next sections of this chapter.

> ► **CHECK YOUR UNDERSTANDING**

1. ___ tests require people to fill out questionnaires, which are then scored according to a standardized procedure.

2. In _____ tests of personality, people are shown ambiguous stimuli and asked to describe them or to make up a story about them.

Answers: 1. objective. **2.** projective.

> ► **APPLY YOUR UNDERSTANDING**

1. You are consulting a psychologist who asks you to take a personality test. She shows you pictures of people and asks you to write a complete story about each picture. The test is most likely the
   a. Minnesota Multiphasic Personality Inventory
   b. Rorschach Test
   c. Thematic Apperception Test
   d. NEO-PI-R

2. "They are often not administered in a standard fashion, they are seldom scored objectively, but when interpreted by a skilled examiner, they can provide insight into a person." To what does this quotation most likely refer?
   a. Structured interviews
   b. Objective personality tests
   c. Projective personality tests
   d. The NEO-PI-R and the MMPI-2

Answers: 1. c. **2.** c.

Thematic Apperception Test (TAT) A projective test composed of ambiguous pictures about which a person is asked to tell a complete story.

Stress can be generated by positive, as well as negative, events. Here, the happy addition of a new baby to the family will likely cause some stress for the mother, father, and the baby's older brother.

Sources of Stress

8.3 Identify the major sources of chronic stress that most people experience.

The term **stressor** refers to any environmental demand that creates a state of tension or threat and requires change or adaptation. Many situations prompt us to change our behavior in some way, but only some cause stress. Consider, for example, stopping at a traffic signal that turns red. Normally, this involves no stress. But now imagine that you are rushing to an important appointment and the red light will surely make you late. Here, stress is triggered because the situation not only requires adaptation, but it also produces tension and distress as well.

We will see later in this chapter that some events, such as wars and natural disasters, are inherently stressful. Danger is real, lives are threatened, and often there is little or nothing people can do to save themselves. Stress is not limited, however, to dangerous situations or even to unpleasant situations. Things that happen to many of us every day can cause stress. Good things can also cause stress, because they "require change or adaptation if an individual is to meet his or her needs" (Morris, 1990, p. 72). For example, a wedding is often a stressful as well as an exciting event. A promotion at work is gratifying, but it demands that we relate to new people in new ways, learn to carry more responsibility, and perhaps work longer hours.

CHANGE

Why is change so stressful for most people?

All of these stressful events involve change. Most people have a strong preference for order, continuity, and predictability in their lives. Therefore, anything—good or bad—that requires change can be experienced as stressful. The more change required, the more stressful the situation.

Questionnaires, such as the College Life Stress Inventory (CLSI), have been constructed to measure the amount of change and, hence the amount of stress, that is present in an individual's life (Renner & Macklin, 1998, 2002). As you can see in **Table 8–4**, both positive and negative life events can cause stress, and the more of these life events that are experienced, the higher the overall "stress rating."

stressor Any environmental demand that creates a state of tension or threat and requires change or adaptation.

>TABLE 8-4   COLLEGE LIFE STRESS INVENTORY

Copy the "stress rating" number into the column titled "Your Items" for any item that has happened to you in the last year, and then add these numbers for your total.

Event	Stress Ratings	Your Items
Being raped	100	
Finding out that you are HIV positive	100	
Being accused of rape	98	
Death of a close friend	97	
Death of a close family member	96	
Contracting a sexually transmitted disease (other than AIDS)	94	
Concerns about being pregnant	91	
Finals week	90	
Concerns about your partner being pregnant	90	
Oversleeping for an exam	89	
Flunking a class	89	
Having a boyfriend or girlfriend cheat on you	85	
Ending a steady dating relationship	85	
Serious illness in a close friend or family member	85	
Financial difficulties	84	
Writing a major term paper	83	
Being caught cheating on a test	83	
Drunk driving	82	
Sense of overload in school or work	82	
Two exams in one day	80	
Cheating on your boyfriend or girlfriend	77	
Getting married	76	
Negative consequences of drinking or drug use	75	
Depression or crisis in your best friend	73	
Difficulties with parents	73	
Talking in front of a class	72	
Lack of sleep	69	
Change in housing situation (hassles, moves)	69	
Competing or performing in public	69	
Getting into a physical fight	66	
Difficulties with a roommate	66	
Job changes (applying, new job, work hassles)	65	
Declaring a major or having concerns about future plans	65	
A class you hate	62	
Drinking or use of drugs	61	
Confrontations with professors	60	
Starting a new semester	58	
Going on a first date	57	
Registration	55	
Maintaining a steady dating relationship	55	
Commuting to campus or work, or both	54	
Peer pressures	53	
Being away from home for the first time	53	
Getting sick	52	
Concerns about your appearance	52	
Getting straight A's	51	
A difficult class that you love	48	
Making new friends; getting along with friends	47	
Attending a fraternity or sorority "rush"	47	
Falling asleep in class	40	
Attending an athletic event (e.g., football game)	20	
Total	——	

Source: Renner, M. J., & Macklin, R. S. (1998). A life stress instrument for classroom use. *Teaching of Psychology, 25* (1), p. 47. Copyright © 1998 by Lawrence Erlbaum Associates, Inc. Reprinted with permission.

In Renner and Macklin's work, college students' scores on the CLSI ranged from a low of 182 to a high of 2,571, but two-thirds had scores between 800 and 1,700. You may find it interesting to compute your score and see how you compare. Although there is considerable individual variation in how well people adapt to life changes such as those represented in the CLSI, in general, very high scores correspond to an enhanced risk of developing a stress-induced illness.

EVERYDAY HASSLES

How can everyday hassles contribute to stress?

Many of the items on the College Life Stress Inventory concern stress that arises from fairly dramatic, relatively infrequent events; however, many psychologists have pointed out that much stress is generated by "hassles," life's petty annoyances, irritations, and frustrations (Chang & Sanna, 2003; Ruffin, 1993; Safdar & Lay, 2003; Whisman & Kwon, 1993). Such seemingly minor matters as having a zipper break, waiting in long lines, or having a petty argument with a friend take their toll. Richard Lazarus believed that big events matter so much because they trigger numerous little hassles that eventually overwhelm us with stress. People who have recently suffered a major traumatic event are more likely than other people to be plagued by minor stressors or hassles (Pillow, Zautra, & Sandler, 1996). Both major and minor events are stressful because they lead to feelings of pressure, frustration, and conflict.

Much of the stress in everyday life is generated by daily "hassles", such as getting stuck in traffic, because they contribute to feelings of pressure, frustration, and conflict.

PRESSURE Pressure occurs when we feel forced to speed up, intensify, or shift direction in our behavior, or when we feel compelled to meet a higher standard of performance. Pressure on the job or in school is a familiar example. Psychologists who study the effects of corporate "downsizing," which requires that production levels are maintained, but with fewer workers, often find that these workers report increased stress and depression, increased injuries on the job, and lower job satisfaction (Crawford, 2002). This pressure also contributes to poor job performance (Clay, 1999; Kaminski, 1999). In our private lives, trying to live up to social and cultural norms about what we *should* be doing, as well as our family's and friends' expectations, also adds pressure to meeting our personal needs.

FRUSTRATION Frustration occurs when a person is prevented from reaching a goal because something or someone stands in the way. Morris (1990) identified five sources of frustration that are especially common in American life. *Delays* are annoying because our culture puts great stock in the value of time. *Lack of resources* is frustrating to those Americans who cannot afford the things they need or desire. *Losses*, such as the end of a love affair or a cherished friendship, cause frustration because they often make us feel helpless, unimportant, or worthless. *Failure* generates intense frustration—and accompanying guilt—in our competitive society. We imagine that if we had done things differently, we might have succeeded; thus, we usually feel personally responsible for our setbacks and tend to assume that others blame us for not trying harder or being smarter. *Discrimination* also frustrates us: Being denied opportunities or recognition simply because of one's sex, age, religion, ethnicity or racial background is extremely frustrating.

CONFLICT Of all life's troubles, conflict is probably the most common. A manager does not want to go to her boss to ask for overtime, but neither does she want to listen to her subordinates complain about overwork with no extra pay. A student finds that both of the required courses she wanted to take this semester are scheduled at the same hours on the same days. **Conflict** arises when we face two or more incompatible demands, opportunities, needs, or goals. We can never completely resolve conflict. We must either give up some of our goals, modify some of them, delay our pursuit of some of them, or resign ourselves to not attaining all of our goals. Whatever we do, we are bound to experience some frustration, thereby adding to the stressfulness of conflicts.

pressure A feeling that one must speed up, intensify, or change the direction of one's behavior or live up to a higher standard of performance.

frustration The feeling that occurs when a person is prevented from reaching a goal.

conflict Simultaneous existence of incompatible demands, opportunities, needs, or goals.

SELF-IMPOSED STRESS

How do we create stress?

So far, we have considered sources of stress outside the individual. Sometimes, however, people create problems for themselves quite apart from stressful events in their environment. Some psychologists argue that many people carry around a set of irrational, self-defeating beliefs that add unnecessarily to the normal stresses of living (Ellis & Harper, 1975). For example, some people believe that "it is essential to be loved or approved of by almost everyone for everything I do." For such people, any sign of disapproval will be a source of considerable stress. Others believe that "I must be competent, adequate, and successful at everything I do." For them, the slightest sign of failure or inadequacy means that they are worthless human beings. Still other people believe that "it is disastrous if everything doesn't go the way I would like." These people feel upset, miserable, and unhappy when things don't go perfectly. As we describe in Chapter 9, "Psychological Disorders and their Treatments," self-defeating thoughts like these can contribute to depression, as well as do feelings of stress (Beck, 1984, 2002).

STRESS AND INDIVIDUAL DIFFERENCES

Do people who are resistant to stress share certain traits?

Why do some children living in adverse conditions remain troubled throughout their lives, while more resilient children in the same circumstances become well-adjusted adults? Here, the children of migrant workers in Beijing, China, play in front of their ramshackle housing.

Just as some people create more stress for themselves than others do, some people cope well with major life stresses, whereas others are thrown by even minor problems. What accounts for these individual differences? How much stress we experience depends partly on the way we interpret our situation. Self-confident people who feel capable of coping with life will feel less stress in a given situation than will those who lack self-assurance (Kessler, Price, & Wortman, 1985). Also, seeing a challenging situation as an opportunity for success rather than for failure is typically associated with positive emotions such as eagerness, excitement, and confidence (Folkman & Moskovitz, 2000). For example, students who know they can study when they have to and who have done well on exams in the past tend to be calmer the night before an important test than students who have done poorly on previous exams.

People's overall view of the world is also related to how well they can cope with stress. As noted earlier in this chapter, *optimists* tend to appraise events as challenges rather than threats and are, in general, better able to cope with stressful events than are *pessimists*, who are more likely to dwell on failure (Peterson, 2000). Similarly, people with an *internal locus of control* see themselves as being able to affect their situations. As a consequence, they are more likely to see difficult circumstances as challenges rather than as threats. Those with an *external locus of control* are more likely to appraise events negatively because they perceive themselves as helpless victims of circumstances and believe that they cannot affect their situations (Ryan & Deci, 2000).

HARDINESS AND RESILIENCE People with a trait we call *hardiness* tolerate stress exceptionally well or seem to thrive on it (Kobasa, 1979). They also feel that they control their own destinies and are confident about being able to cope with change (Kessler, Price, & Wortman, 1985; Taylor, 2003). Conversely, individuals who have little confidence that they can master new situations and can exercise control over events feel powerless and apathetic (Peterson, Maier, & Seligman, 1993b). (Recall our discussion of learned helplessness in Chapter 4, "Learning and Memory.") Even when change offers new opportunities for taking charge of their situation, they remain passive.

Psychologists are also interested in *resilience*: the ability to "bounce back," recovering one's self-confidence, good spirits, and hopeful attitude after extreme or prolonged stress (Beasley, Thompson, & Davidson, 2003). Resilience may partially explain why some children who grow up in adverse circumstances (such as extreme poverty, dangerous neighborhoods, with abusive parents, or exposure to drugs and alcohol) become well-adjusted adults, whereas others remain troubled—and frequently get into trouble—throughout their lives (Bonanno, 2004; Feinauer, Hilton, & Callahan, 2003; Leifer, Kilbane, & Kalick, 2004). On the basis of research that followed high-risk children into adulthood, it appears that two ways to foster resilience are mentor programs (such as Big Brother/Big Sister, which pairs an adult volunteer with an "at-risk" child) and after-school programs that offer a range of activities (Brown, cited in Huang, 1998; Clauss & Caroline, 2003; Werner, 1996).

▶ CHECK YOUR UNDERSTANDING

Indicate whether the following statements are true (T) or false (F):

1. ___ Change that results from "good" events, such as marriage or job promotion, does not produce stress.

2. ___ Stressful events almost always involve changes in our lives.

3. ___ Big events in life are always much more stressful than everyday hassles.

4. ___ Coping refers to successful efforts to deal with stress.

Answers: 1. (F), 2. (T), 3. (F), 4. (F).

▶ APPLY YOUR UNDERSTANDING

1. Four people are confronted with the same stressful situation. Other things being equal, which one would be expected to cope most successfully?
   a. Al, who is an optimist with an internal locus of control.
   b. Bill, who is an optimist with an external locus of control.
   c. Dan, who is a pessimist with an internal locus of control.
   d. Mike, who is a pessimist with an external locus of control.

2. LaShondra is a caterer. She has just finished the prep work for a 15-person dinner that is scheduled for 7:30 P.M. that night. At 4:00 P.M., the client calls to tell her that there will actually be 30 people, and they need to start dinner at 7:00 P.M. instead of 7:30 P.M. LaShondra feels stressed because this call creates _____.
   a. frustration
   b. pressure
   c. self-imposed stress
   d. conflict

Answers: 1. a., 2. b.

Extreme Stress

8.4 Identify the most common major sources of extreme stress and describe the symptoms of posttraumatic stress disorder.

Extreme stress marks a radical departure from everyday life, such that a person cannot continue life as before and, in some cases, can never fully recover. What are some major causes of stress? What effect do they have on people? How do people cope?

SOURCES OF EXTREME STRESS

What are some sources of extreme stress, and what impact do they have?

Extreme stress has a variety of sources, ranging from unemployment to wartime combat, from violent natural disaster to rape. More common events, too, can be sources of extreme stress, including bereavement, separation, and divorce.

UNEMPLOYMENT Joblessness is a major source of stress. In fact, when the jobless rate rises, there is also an increase in first admissions to psychiatric hospitals, infant mortality, deaths from heart disease, alcohol-related diseases, and suicide (Almgren, Guest, Immerwahr, & Spittel, 2002; Brenner, 1973, 1979; Rayman & Bluestone, 1982; White & Waghorn,

2004). In a study involving aircraft workers who lost their jobs, many workers reported high blood pressure, alcoholism, heavy smoking, and anxiety. Other studies found that family strain increases. "Things just fell apart," one worker said after both he and his wife suddenly found themselves unemployed.

Finally, two studies have shown that death rates increase and psychiatric symptoms worsen not just during periods of unemployment, but also during short, rapid upturns in the economy (Brenner, 1979; Eyer, 1977; Hart, 1985; Hutschemaekers & van de Vijver, 1989). These findings lend support to the point we discussed earlier: Change, whether good or bad, causes stress.

DIVORCE AND SEPARATION "The deterioration or ending of an intimate relationship is one of the more potent of stressors and one of the more frequent reasons why people seek psychotherapy" (Coleman et al., 1987, p. 155). After a breakup typically both partners feel they have failed at one of life's most important endeavors, but strong emotional ties often continue to bind the pair. If only one spouse wants to end the marriage, the initiator may feel sadness and guilt at hurting the other partner; the rejected spouse may feel anger, humiliation, and guilt over his or her role in the failure. Even if the separation was a mutual decision, ambivalent feelings of love and hate can make life turbulent. Of course, adults are not the only ones who are stressed by divorce. A national survey of the impact of divorce on children (Cherlin, 1992) found that a majority suffer intense emotional stress at the time of divorce. Although most recover within a year or two (especially, if the custodial parent establishes a stable home and the parents do not fight about child rearing), a minority experience long-term problems (Wallerstein, Blakeslee, & Lewis, 2000).

The death of a loved one is a source of extreme stress for many people. Recently, psychologists have questioned traditional notions about the grieving process.

BEREAVEMENT For decades, it was widely held that following the death of a loved one, people go through a necessary period of intense grief during which they work through their loss and, about a year later, pick up and go on with their lives. Psychologists (Janis, Mahl, & Holt, 1969) and physicians, as well as the public at large, have endorsed this cultural wisdom. But some researchers have challenged this view of loss (C. G. Davis, Wortman, Lehman, & Silver, 2000; Wortman & Silver, 1989).

According to Wortman and her colleagues, the first myth about bereavement is that people should be intensely distressed when a loved one dies; this suggests that people who are not devastated are behaving abnormally, perhaps pathologically. Often, however, people have prepared for the loss, said their goodbyes, and feel little remorse or regret. Indeed, they may be relieved that their loved one is no longer suffering. The second myth—that people need to work through their grief—may lead family, friends, and even physicians to (consciously or unconsciously) encourage the bereaved to feel or act distraught. Moreover, physicians may deny those mourners who are deeply disturbed necessary antianxiety or antidepressant medication "for their own good." The third myth holds that people who find meaning in the death, who come to a spiritual or existential understanding of why it happened, cope better than those who do not. In reality, people who do not seek greater understanding are the best adjusted and least depressed. The fourth myth—that people should recover from a loss within a year or so—is perhaps the most damaging. Parents trying to cope with the death of an infant and adults whose spouse or child died suddenly in a vehicle accident often continue to experience painful memories and wrestle with depression years later. But because they have not recovered "on schedule," members of their social network may become unsympathetic. Unfortunately, the people who need support most may hide their feelings because they do not want to make other people uncomfortable. Often they fail to seek treatment because they, too, believe they should recover on their own.

Not all psychologists agree with this "new" view of bereavement. But most agree that research on loss must consider individual (and group or cultural) differences, as well as variations in the circumstances surrounding a loss (Bonanno & Kaltman, 1999; Harvey & Miller, 1998).

CATASTROPHES Catastrophes, natural and otherwise—including floods, earthquakes, violent storms, fires, plane crashes, and terrorist attacks—produce certain psychological reactions common to all stressful events. At first, in the *shock stage*, "the victim is stunned, dazed, and apathetic" and sometimes even "stuporous, disoriented, and amnesic for the traumatic event." Then, in the *suggestible stage*, victims are passive and quite ready to do whatever rescuers tell them to do. In the third phase, the *recovery stage*, emotional balance is regained, but anxiety often persists, and victims may need to recount their experiences over and over again (Morris, 1990). In later stages, survivors may feel irrationally guilty because they lived while others died.

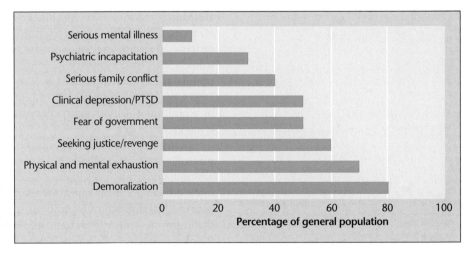

Figure 8–4

Mental trauma in societies at war. In societies that have undergone the stress of war, nearly everyone suffers some psychological reaction, ranging from serious mental illness to feelings of demoralization. Rates of clinical depression are as high as 50 percent.

Source: Mollica, R. F. (2000, June). Invisible wounds. *Scientific American*, p. 54. Figure by Laurie Grace.

COMBAT AND OTHER THREATENING PERSONAL ATTACKS Wartime experiences often cause soldiers intense and disabling combat stress that persists long after they have left the battlefield. Similar reactions—including bursting into rage over harmless remarks, sleep disturbances, cringing at sudden loud noises, psychological confusion, uncontrollable crying, and silently staring into space for long periods—are also frequently seen in survivors of serious accidents, especially children, and of violent crimes such as rapes and muggings. **Figure 8–4** shows the traumatic effects of war on the civilian population, based on composite statistics obtained after recent civil wars (Mollica, 2000).

REACTIONS TO EXTREME STRESS

What experiences can lead to posttraumatic stress disorder?

In many extremely stressful situations, the time of greatest stress is not when danger is actually present. *Anticipating* the danger is actually the time of greatest stress. Parachutists, for example, are most afraid as the time for the jump approaches. Once in line, unable to turn back, they calm down. During the most dangerous part of the jump—in free fall, waiting for their chutes to open—they are much less frightened (Epstein, 1962).

We also need to be concerned about reactions after danger has passed. Severely stressful events can cause a psychological disorder known as **posttraumatic stress disorder (PTSD)**.

The experiences of soldiers have heightened interest in PTSD. For example, more than one-third of the soldiers who served in Vietnam experienced PTSD at some point afterward (Ozer, Best, Lipsey, & Weiss, 2003). Many veterans of World War II, who are now older adults, still have nightmares from which they awaken sweating and shaking. The memories of combat continue to torment them after more than half a century (Gelman, 1994). Recently, therapists have begun to observe a new phenomenon: Veterans who seemed to be healthy and well adjusted throughout their postwar lives suddenly develop symptoms of PTSD when they retire and enter their "golden years" (Sleek, 1998).

Soldiers are not the only victims of war. Indeed, during the 20th century, civilian deaths outnumbered military deaths in most wars. Yet only in the last decade, especially following the tragedy of the September 11th attacks, have medical researchers begun to investigate the psychological and physiological effects of war and terrorism on civilian survivors. They are finding that civilians also experience long lasting and severe problems, such as exhaustion, hatred, mistrust, and the symptoms of PTSD (Gurwitch, Sitterle, Young, & Pfefferbaum, 2002; Mollica, 2000).

Yet not everyone who is exposed to severely stressful events (such as heavy combat or childhood sexual abuse) develops PTSD. Although more than half of the American population is exposed to a severely traumatic event at some time, less than 10 percent will develop symptoms of PTSD (Ozer et al., 2003). Individual characteristics—including gender (Curle & Williams, 1996; Rabasca, 1999b), personality, a family history of mental disorders

Soldiers who have been in combat, such as the ones who served in Iraq, are at risk for developing posttraumatic stress disorder.

posttraumatic stress disorder (PTSD)
Psychological disorder characterized by episodes of anxiety, sleeplessness, and nightmares resulting from some disturbing past event.

(Friedman, Schnurr, & McDonagh–Coyle, 1994), substance abuse among relatives (Gurvits, Gilbertson, Lasko, Orr, & Pittman, 1997), and even preexisting neurological disorders—appear to predispose some people to PTSD more than others. Both men and women who have a history of emotional problems are more likely to experience severe trauma and to develop PTSD as a consequence of trauma (Breslau, Davis, & Andreski, 1995). Not surprisingly, people who may already be under extreme stress (perhaps caused by a health problem or interpersonal difficulties) prior to experiencing a traumatic event are at greatest risk.

Interestingly, some psychologists have found that following a significant trauma, a few particularly stable individuals experience a *positive* form of personal growth called *posttraumatic growth* (Calhoun & Tedeschi, 2001). In the rare instances where posttraumatic growth occurs, it appears to emerge largely from an individual's struggle to reconcile personal loss through religious or existential understanding. When it does occur, posttraumatic growth is more likely to be seen in young adults than in older people (Powell, Rosner, Butollo, Tedeschi, & Calhoun, 2003).

▶ CHECK YOUR UNDERSTANDING

Is each of the following statements true (T) or false (F)?

1. ___ If people who are bereaved following the death of a spouse or child have not recovered by the end of one year, this outcome indicates that they are coping abnormally.

2. ___ Catastrophes—including floods, earthquakes, violent storms, fires, and plane crashes—produce different psychological reactions than do other kinds of stressful events.

3. ___ Most children whose parents divorce experience serious and long-term problems.

4. ___ Posttraumatic stress disorder can appear months or even years after a traumatic event.

Answers: 1. (F), 2. (F), 3. (F), 4. (T).

▶ APPLY YOUR UNDERSTANDING

1. According to research on myths about bereavement, which of the following person's arguments is accurate?
   a. Ruth, who argues that there are large cultural and individual differences in how people cope with the death of a loved one.
   b. Lara, who argues that people should be distressed at the death of a loved one, and if they are not something is wrong.
   c. Cassie, who argues that people who have not recovered by the end of a year following death have serious psychological problems.
   d. Maddie, who states that people who find "meaning" in a loved one's death cope better than those who don't.

2. Brent was in a serious car accident, and appeared to be fully recovered. Six months later, however, he began to have trouble sleeping and concentrating, and he began having vivid, terrifying nightmares about the crash. The most likely name of Brent's problem would be _____.
   a. panic disorder
   b. paranoid coping disorder
   c. posttraumatic growth disorder
   d. posttraumatic stress disorder

Answers: 1. a., 2. d.

Coping with Stress

8.5 Differentiate between direct and defensive methods of coping and suggest several factors that are related to the successful ability to cope.

Whatever its source, stress requires that we cope—that is, it requires us to make cognitive and behavioral efforts to manage psychological stress (Lazarus, 1993). There are many different ways of coping with stress (Skinner, Edge, Altman, & Sherwood, 2003), but two general types of adjustment stand out: direct coping and defensive coping.

DIRECT COPING

What are three strategies that deal directly with stress?

Direct coping refers to intentional efforts to change an uncomfortable situation. Direct coping tends to be problem oriented and to focus on the immediate issue. When we are threatened, frustrated, or in conflict, we have three basic choices for coping directly: *confrontation, compromise,* or *withdrawal.*

Consider the case of a woman who has worked hard at her job for years, but has not been promoted. She learns that she has not been promoted due to her stated unwillingness to temporarily move to a branch office in another part of the country to acquire more experience. Her unwillingness to move stands between her and her goal of advancing in her career. She has several choices, which we will explore.

CONFRONTATION Acknowledging that there is a problem for which a solution must be found, attacking the problem head-on, and pushing resolutely toward the goal is called **confrontation**. The hallmark of the "confrontational style" is making intense efforts to cope with stress and to accomplish one's aims (Morris, 1990). Doing so may involve learning skills, enlisting other people's help, or just trying harder. Or it may require steps to change either oneself or the situation. The woman who wants to advance her career might decide that if she wants to move up in the company, she will have to relocate. Or she might challenge the assumption that working at the branch office would give her the kind of experience that her supervisor thinks she needs. She might try to persuade her boss that even though she has never worked in a branch office, she nevertheless has acquired enough experience to handle a better job in the main office. Or she might remind her supervisor of the company's stated goal of promoting more women to top-level positions.

Confrontation may also include expressions of anger. Anger may be effective, especially if we really have been treated unfairly and if we express our anger with restraint instead of exploding in rage.

COMPROMISE **Compromise** is one of the most common and effective ways of coping directly with conflict or frustration. We often recognize that we cannot have everything we want and that we cannot expect others to do just what we would like them to do. In such cases, we may decide to settle for less than we originally sought. In our example, the woman might agree to take a less desirable position that doesn't require branch office experience, or she might strike a bargain to go to the branch office for a shorter time.

WITHDRAWAL In some circumstances, the most effective way of coping with stress is to withdraw from the situation. The woman whose promotion depends on temporarily relocating, for example, might quit her job and join another company. When we realize that our adversary is more powerful than we are, that there is no way we can effectively modify ourselves or the situation, that there is no possible compromise, and that any form of aggression would be self-destructive, **withdrawal** is a positive and realistic response. In seemingly hopeless situations, such as submarine and mining disasters, few people panic (Mintz, 1951). Believing that there is nothing they can do to save themselves, they give up. If a situation is hopeless, resignation may be the most effective way of coping with it.

Perhaps the greatest danger of coping by withdrawal is that the person may begin to avoid all similar situations. The woman who did not want to take a job at her company's branch office may not only quit her present job, but may leave without even looking for a new one. In such cases, coping by withdrawal can become maladaptive avoidance. Moreover, people who have given up on a situation are in a poor position to take advantage of an effective solution if one should come along.

Withdrawal, in whatever form, is a mixed blessing. Although it can be an effective method of coping, it has built-in dangers. The same characteristic tends to be true of defensive coping, to which we now turn.

Sometimes confronting a problem head on provides the best outcome in a situation in which conflict is inevitable.

confrontation Coping by acknowledging a stressful situation directly and attempting to find a solution to the problem or to attain the difficult goal.

compromise Coping by deciding on a more realistic solution or goal when an ideal solution or goal is not practical.

withdrawal Coping by avoiding a conflict-oriented situation.

defense mechanisms Self-deceptive techniques for reducing stress, including denial, repression, projection, identification, regression, intellectualization, reaction formation, displacement, and sublimation.

DEFENSIVE COPING

What are the major ways of coping defensively?

Thus far, we have discussed coping with stress that arises from recognizable sources. But there are times when we either cannot identify or cannot deal directly with the source of our stress. For example, you return to a parking lot to discover that your car has been damaged. In other cases, a problem is so emotionally threatening that it cannot be faced directly: Perhaps someone close to you is terminally ill, or after four years of hard work, you have failed to gain admission to medical school and may have to abandon your plan to become a doctor.

In such situations, people may turn to **defense mechanisms** as a way of coping. Defense mechanisms are techniques for *deceiving* oneself about the causes of a stressful situation to reduce pressure, frustration, conflict, and anxiety. Self-deception can take many forms (see "**Summary Table: Defense Mechanisms**.") The self-deceptive nature of such adjustments led Freud to conclude that they are entirely unconscious, but not all psychologists agree that they always spring from unconscious conflicts over which we have little or no control. Often we realize that we are pushing something out of our memory or are otherwise deceiving ourselves. For example, all of us have blown up at someone when we *knew* we were really angry at someone else. Whether defense mechanisms operate consciously or unconsciously, they provide a means of coping with stress that might otherwise be unbearable.

Does defensive coping mean that a person is immature, unstable, or on the edge of a "breakdown"? Is direct coping adaptive, and is defensive coping maladaptive? Not necessarily (Cramer, 2000). In some cases of prolonged and severe stress, lower level defenses may not only contribute to our overall ability to adjust but also may even become essential to survival. Defenses are "essential for softening failure, alleviating tension and anxiety, repairing emotional hurt, and maintaining our feelings of adequacy and worth" (Coleman,

SUMMARY TABLE

DEFENSE MECHANISMS

Denial	Refusing to acknowledge a painful or threatening reality: Ray, whose best friend has just been killed in a car accident, insists that it is a case of mistaken identity and that his friend is still alive.
Repression	Excluding uncomfortable thoughts from consciousness: Lisa, whose grandmother died of breast cancer, is at higher-than-average risk for developing breast cancer herself; still, she routinely forgets to get a mammogram.
Projection	Attributing one's repressed motives, feelings, or wishes to others: Marilyn is unfairly passed over for a promotion; she denies that she is angry about this situation but is certain that her supervisor is angry with her.
Identification	Taking on the characteristics of someone else to avoid feeling inadequate: Anthony, uncertain of his own attractiveness, takes on the dress and mannerisms of a popular co-worker.
Regression	Reverting to childlike behavior and defenses: Furious because his plan to reorganize his division has been rejected, Bob throws a tantrum, slams his office door, and throws his papers on the floor.
Intellectualization	Thinking abstractly about stressful problems as a way of detaching oneself from them: After learning that she has not been asked to a co-worker's costume party, Tina coolly discusses the ways in which social cliques form and the ways that they serve to regulate and control office life.
Reaction formation	Expression of exaggerated ideas and emotions that are the opposite of one's repressed beliefs or feelings: At work, Michael loudly professes that he would never take advantage of a rival employee, though his harassing behavior indicates quite the opposite.
Displacement	Shifting repressed motives from an original object to a substitute object: Nelson is infuriated at his boss's unreasonable request that he rewrite his marketing plan, but he is afraid to say anything for fear that he will make his boss angry, so he comes home and yells at his housemates for telling him what to do.
Sublimation	Redirecting repressed motives and feelings into more socially acceptable channels: The child of parents who never paid attention to him, Bill is running for public office.

Glaros, & Morris, 1987, p. 190). Defenses can also be adaptive for coping with more serious problems. In the short run, especially if there are few other options, defenses may reduce anxiety and thus allow for the highest possible level of adaptation. Over the long run, however, defenses can hinder successful adjustment. Defense mechanisms are maladaptive when they interfere with a person's ability to deal directly with a problem or when they create more problems than they solve.

SOCIOECONOMIC AND GENDER DIFFERENCES IN COPING WITH STRESS

Who experiences the most stress?

Individuals use various coping strategies in different combinations and in different ways to deal with stressful events. It is tempting to conclude that styles of coping, such as personality, reside within the individual. Yet, a good deal of research indicates that how much stress people encounter and how they cope depend to a significant degree on the environment in which they live (S. E. Taylor & Repetti, 1997).

The defense mechanism of sublimation occurs when people redirect their repressed motives into socially acceptable channels. For instance, a person interested in starting fires may become a firefighter as a way to redirect such urges.

Consider the impact of socioeconomic status on stress and coping. In poor neighborhoods, addressing even the basic tasks of living is stressful. Housing is often substandard and crowded; there are fewer stores, and they offer lower quality goods; crime and unemployment rates are likely to be high; and schools have high student-teacher ratios, high staff turnover, and more part-time teachers. In short, poor people have to deal with more stress than people who are financially secure (N. Adler et al., 1994; S. Cohen & Williamson, 1988; Evans & English, 2002). Moreover, some data indicate that people in low-income groups cope less effectively with stress and that, as a result, stressful events have a stronger impact on their emotional lives (Kessler, 1979). People in lower income groups are significantly more depressed, anxious, hopeless, and hostile. As we will see, those negative emotions are associated with worse physical and mental health (Gallo & Matthews, 2003). Psychologists have offered possible explanations for these data. People in lower socioeconomic classes often have fewer means for coping with hardship and stress (Pearlin & Schooler, 1978; Gallo & Matthews, 2003). Low-income people also have fewer people to turn to and fewer community resources to draw on for support during stressful times (Liem & Liem, 1978). These factors help explain why stress often takes a greater toll on people in lower socioeconomic classes.

Are there gender differences in coping with stress? At present, the answer seems to be unclear. Some research indicates that when faced with equally stressful situations, men and women generally use quite similar coping strategies (Porter & Stone, 1995). However other research suggests the opposite—that in at least some circumstances, men and women use rather different coping strategies (Bellman, Forster, Still, & Cooper, 2003; Ptacek, Smith, & Dodge, 1994; Anshel, Porter, & Quek, 1998; Narayanan, Shanker, & Spector, 1999). For example, one recent study (Nolen-Hoeksema, 1999) found that when men are down or depressed, they are more likely than women to turn to alcohol; when women are blue, sad, or mad, they are more likely to ruminate about the problem, revisiting negative emotions and the events that led up to them in their minds. Given that gender-related expectations and stereotypes still exist within our culture, it is not surprising that sometimes different coping styles are adopted by men and women.

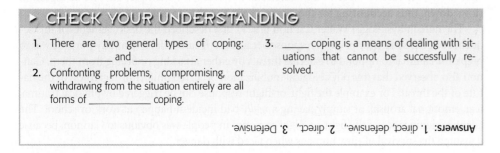

► CHECK YOUR UNDERSTANDING

1. There are two general types of coping: _____ and _____.

2. Confronting problems, compromising, or withdrawing from the situation entirely are all forms of _____ coping.

3. _____ coping is a means of dealing with situations that cannot be successfully resolved.

Answers: 1. direct, defensive, 2. direct, 3. Defensive.

► APPLY YOUR UNDERSTANDING

1. You're approaching a deadline by which a project must be finished. Your stress level rises when you realize that it will be nearly impossible to meet the deadline. Which of the following is NOT one of your choices for coping *directly* with the stressful situation?

   a. Trying harder and enlisting the help of others.

   b. Denying that you will be unable to finish the project on time and continuing to work away frantically.

   c. Admitting defeat and withdrawing from the situation.

   d. Working out an arrangement through which you submit part of the project on time and get additional time for submitting the rest of it.

2. Bill is very frustrated because he did quite poorly on several midterm exams. After returning from an especially difficult exam, he yells at his roommate for leaving clothes strewn around the floor. Bill's reaction is most likely the result of which defense mechanism?

   a. Projection

   b. Reaction formation

   c. Sublimation

   d. Displacement

Answer: 1. b., 2. d.

How Stress Affects Health

8.6 Describe the biological mechanisms involved in the link between stress and illness.

"We know that 50% of deaths are directly related to human behaviors, and yet we spend too little time doing research and implementing programs related to them," said David Satcher, the U.S. Surgeon General (Satcher, 1999, p. 16). Physicians and psychologists agree that stress management is an essential part of programs to prevent disease and promote health.

THE BODY'S RESPONSE TO STRESS

What long-lasting effects of stress do we need to be concerned with?

To understand how our body responds to stress, we must first examine how we react to danger. Suppose you are walking alone down an unfamiliar street late at night when you notice that a suspicious stranger is following you. Suddenly your heart begins to pound, your respiration increases, and you develop a queasy feeling in your stomach. What is happening to you? The hypothalamus, a center deep in your brain, is reacting to your perception of danger by organizing a generalized response that affects several organs throughout your body (see **Figure 8–5**.) Almost immediately the hypothalamus stimulates the sympathetic branch of the autonomic nervous system and the adrenal glands to release stress hormones such as *adrenaline* and *norepinephrine* into the blood. This process in turn leads to increases in heart rate, blood pressure, respiration, and perspiration. Other organs also respond; for example, the liver increases the available sugar in the blood for extra energy, and the bone marrow increases the white blood cell count to combat infection. Conversely, the rate of some bodily functions decreases; for example, the rate of digestion slows down, thus accounting for the queasy feeling in the stomach.

The noted physiologist Walter Cannon (1929) first described the basic elements of this sequence of events as a *fight-or-flight* response because it appeared that its primary purpose was to prepare an animal to respond to external threats by either attacking or fleeing from them. Cannon also observed that this physiological mobilization occurred uniformly regardless of the nature of the threat. For example the fight-or-flight response can be triggered by physical trauma, fear, emotional arousal, or simply having a *really* bad incident happen at work or school. The adaptive significance of the fight-or-flight response in people was obvious to Cannon, because it assured the survival of early humans when faced with danger.

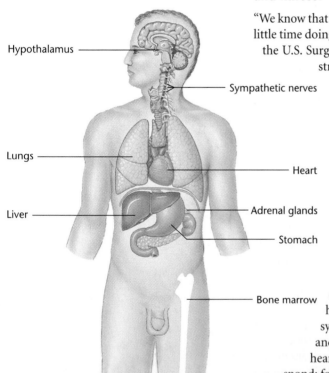

Hypothalamus

Sympathetic nerves

Lungs

Heart

Liver

Adrenal glands

Stomach

Bone marrow

Figure 8–5

The physiological response to stress. When the body is confronted with a stressful situation, the hypothalamus stimulates the sympathetic nervous system and the adrenal glands to release stress hormones. Other organs, including the stomach and liver, also respond.

Source: Mollica, R. F. (June 2000). Invisible wounds. *Scientific American*, p. 54. Figure by Laurie Grace.

Extending Cannon's theory of the fight-or-flight response, the Canadian physiologist Hans Selye (pronounced SAY-lee) (1907–1982) contended that we react to physical and psychological stress in three stages that he collectively called the **general adaptation syndrome (GAS)** (Selye, 1956, 1976). These three stages are alarm reaction, resistance, and exhaustion.

Stage 1, *alarm reaction*, is the first response to stress. It begins when the body recognizes that it must fend off some physical or psychological danger. Emotions run high. Activity of the sympathetic nervous system is increased, resulting in the release of hormones from the adrenal gland. We become more sensitive and alert, our respiration and heartbeat quicken, our muscles tense, and we experience other physiological changes as well. All of these changes help us to mobilize our coping resources in order to regain self-control. At the alarm stage, we might use either direct or defensive coping strategies. If neither of these approaches reduces the stress, we eventually enter the second stage of adaptation.

During Stage 2, *resistance*, physical symptoms and other signs of strain appear as we struggle against increasing psychological disorganization. We intensify our use of both direct and defensive coping techniques. If we succeed in reducing the stress, we return to a more normal state. But if the stress is extreme or prolonged, we may turn in desperation to inappropriate coping techniques and cling to them rigidly, despite the evidence that they are not working. When that happens, physical and emotional resources are further depleted, and signs of psychological and physical wear and tear become even more apparent.

In the third stage, *exhaustion*, we draw on increasingly ineffective defense mechanisms in a desperate attempt to bring the stress under control. Some people lose touch with reality and show signs of emotional disorder or mental illness at this stage. Others show signs of "burnout," including the inability to concentrate, irritability, procrastination, and a cynical belief that nothing is worthwhile (Freudenberger, 1983; Maslach & Leiter, 1982, 1997). Physical symptoms such as skin or stomach problems may erupt, and some victims of burnout turn to alcohol or drugs to cope with the stress-induced exhaustion. If the stress continues, the person may suffer irreparable physical or psychological damage or even death.

Selye's contention that stress can be linked to physical illness has been well supported by research. But how can psychological stress lead to or influence physical illness? First, when we experience stress, our heart, lungs, nervous system, and other physiological systems are forced to work harder. The human body is not designed to be exposed for long periods to the powerful biological changes that accompany alarm and mobilization; so when stress is prolonged, we are more likely to experience some kind of physical disorder. Second, stress has a powerful negative effect on the body's immune system, and prolonged stress can destroy the body's ability to defend itself from disease. Stress, too, may lead to unhealthy behavior, such as smoking, drinking, overeating, or skipping meals, not getting enough sleep and exercise, and avoiding regular medical checkups. These behaviors can, in turn, lead to illness and poor overall health.

If stress persists for a long enough time, the person eventually will enter a stage of exhaustion, according to Selye's general adaptation syndrome theory.

STRESS AND HEART DISEASE

How is Type A behavior related to heart disease?

Stress is a major contributing factor in the development of coronary heart disease (CHD), the leading cause of death and disability in the United States (McGinnis, 1994). Heredity also affects the likelihood of developing CHD, but even among identical twins, the incidence of CHD is closely linked to attitudes toward work, problems in the home, and the amount of leisure time available (Kringlen, 1981; O'Callahan, Andrews, & Krantz, 2003). Frequent or chronic stress can damage the heart and blood vessels (Heinz et al., 2003). For example, the stress hormone cortisol increases blood pressure (which weakens the walls of blood vessels), can trigger arrhythmias (erratic heartbeats that may lead to sudden death), and increases cholesterol levels (which causes a plaque buildup and, over time, arteriosclerosis or "hardening" of the arteries). Generally, life stress and social isolation are significant predictors of mortality among

general adaptation syndrome (GAS) According to Selye, the three stages the body passes through as it adapts to stress: alarm reaction, resistance, and exhaustion.

Evidence appears to show that the chronic anger and hostility associated with Type A behavior can predict heart disease.

those who have suffered heart attacks for whatever reason (Ruberman, Weinblatt, Goldberg, & Chaudhary, 1984).

Mental stress on the job is linked to CHD, as is individual personality. Negative emotions are also associated with higher levels of cardiovascular disease (Gallo & Matthews, 2003a). A great deal of research has been done, for example, on people who exhibit the **Type A behavior pattern**—that is, who respond to life events with impatience, hostility, competitiveness, urgency, and constant striving (M. Friedman & Rosenman, 1959). Type A people are distinguished from people with the more easygoing **Type B behavior pattern**. The two cardiologists who first identified the characteristics of Type A personalities were convinced that this behavior pattern was most likely to surface in stressful situations.

A number of studies have shown that Type A behavior predicts CHD (Booth–Kewley & Friedman, 1987; Carmona, Sanz, & Marin, 2002; T. Q. Miller, Tuner, Tindale, Posavac, & Dugoni, 1991). For example, when Type A personalities were subjected to harassment or criticism their heart rate and blood pressure were much higher than those of Type B personalities under the same circumstances (Lyness, 1993). Both high heart rate and high blood pressure are known to contribute to CHD.

Other studies maintain that the link between Type A behavior and CHD is less direct—that the tendency toward Type A behavior may influence people to engage in behaviors, such as smoking or overeating, that directly contribute to heart disease (K. A. Matthews, 1988). On the basis of the preponderance of evidence, however, it seems clear that *chronic anger* and *hostility* (both components of Type A behavior) do indeed predict heart disease (T. Q. Miller, Smith, Turner, Guijavo, & Hallet, 1996; Williams, 2001). For example, people who scored high on an anger scale were 2.5 times more likely to have heart attacks or sudden cardiac deaths than their calmer peers (J. C. Williams et al., 2000). Counseling designed to diminish the intensity of time urgency and hostility in patients with Type A behavior has been moderately successful in reducing the incidence of CHD (Friedman et al., 1996).

Depression, too, appears to increase the risk of heart disease and premature death (McCabe, Schneiderman, Field, & Wellens, 2000; Rugulies, 2002; Schwartzman & Glaus, 2000). Here, the link to heart disease is through the long-term exposure to stress-produced hormones that, over time, damage the heart and blood vessels.

Because long-term stress increases the likelihood of developing CHD, reducing stress has become part of the treatment used to slow the progress of atherosclerosis, or blockage of the arteries, which can lead to a heart attack. A very low-fat diet and stress-management techniques, such as yoga and deep relaxation, also have been effective in treating this disease (Ornish, 1990).

STRESS AND THE IMMUNE SYSTEM

Why do so many students get sick during finals?

Scientists have long suspected that stress also affects the functioning of the immune system. Recall that the immune system is strongly affected by hormones and signals from the brain. The field of **psychoneuroimmunology (PNI)** studies the interaction between stress on the one hand and immune, endocrine, and nervous system activity on the other (Azar, 1999a; Dougall & Baum, 2004; Stowell, McGuire, Robles, & Kiecolt–Glaser, 2003). To the extent that stress disrupts the functioning of the immune system, it can impair health (S. Cohen & Herbert, 1996). Chronic stress, such as caring for an elderly parent, living in poverty, depression (Kiecolt–Glaser & Glaser, R. 2002; Oltmanns & Emery, 1998), or even the stress associated with college exams (O'Leary, 1990), has been linked to suppressed functioning of the immune system (Irwin, 2002).

Increased stress may make us more susceptible to upper respiratory infections, such as the common cold (Cohen, 1996). For example, volunteers who reported being under severe stress and who had experienced two or more major stressful events during the previous year were more likely to develop a cold when they were exposed to a cold virus (Cohen, Tyrrell, & Smith, 1991). A control group of volunteers who reported lower levels of stress were less likely to develop cold symptoms even though they were equally exposed to the

Type A behavior pattern *A general pattern of behavior characterized by impatience, hostility, competitiveness, urgency, and constant striving.*

Type B behavior pattern *A general pattern of behavior characterized by patience, flexibility, and lower intensity of attitudes and competitiveness.*

psychoneuroimmunology (PNI) *A new field that studies the interaction between stress on the one hand, and immune, endocrine, and nervous system activity on the other.*

virus. People who report experiencing many positive emotions (for example, happiness, pleasure, or relaxation) are also less likely to develop colds when exposed to the virus than those who report many negative emotions (for example, anxiety, hostility, or depression) (Cohen, Doyle, Turner, Alper, & Skoner, 2003a).

Psychoneuroimmunologists have also established a possible relationship between stress and cancer (Herberman, 2002). Stress does not cause cancer, but it apparently impairs the immune system so that cancerous cells are better able to establish themselves and spread throughout the body. Current animal research is focused on finding the exact cellular mechanisms that link stress to cancer (Herberman, 2002; Quan et al., 1999).

Establishing a direct link between stress and cancer in humans is more difficult. For obvious reasons, researchers cannot conduct similar experiments with human participants. Some early research showed a correlation between stress and incidence of cancer (McKenna, Zevon, Corn, & Rounds, 1999; O'Leary, 1990), but more recent research has not confirmed these findings (Maunsell, Brisson, Mondor, Verreault, & Deschenes, 2001). However, several new cancer drugs work by boosting the immune system, although even this does not necessarily mean that damage to the immune system makes people more vulnerable to cancer (Azar, 1999b). Thus, the jury is still out on whether stress contributes to cancer in humans.

Many medical practitioners agree that psychologists can play a vital role in improving the quality of life for cancer patients (McGuire, 1999; Rabasca, 1999a). For example, women faced with the diagnosis of late-stage breast cancer understandably experience high levels of depression and mental stress. Many physicians now routinely recommend that their breast-cancer patients attend group therapy sessions, which are effective in reducing depression, mental stress, hostility, insomnia, and the perception of pain (Giese–Davis, et al., 2002; Goodwin, et al., 2001; Kissane et al., 1997; Quesnel, 2003; Spiegel, 1995). Some initial reports also showed that breast-cancer patients who attended group therapy sessions actually had an increased survival rate (Spiegel & Moore, 1997), although more recent investigations have not supported this claim (DeAngelis, 2002; Edelman, Lemon, Bell, & Kidman, 1999; Goodwin et al., 2001).

▶ CHECK YOUR UNDERSTANDING

1. _____ is the term given to the set of characteristics, such as hostility and a sense of urgency, that many people believe make a person more susceptible to coronary heart disease.

Indicate whether the following statements are true (T) or false (F):

2. ___ Research has been unable to find a relationship between stress and the strength of the body's immune system.

3. ___ Increased stress may make us more susceptible to the common cold.

4. ___ Prolonged stress has been shown to increase vulnerability to cancer.

5. ___ If a person typically reacts to stress with a calm, problem-solving response, she would probably be labeled as having a type B behavior pattern.

Answers: 1. Type A behavior patterns. 2. (F), 3. (T), 4. (T), 5. (T).

▶ APPLY YOUR UNDERSTANDING

1. You are going through a particularly stressful event. According to Selye's *general adaptation syndrome*, your first response to the stress is likely to be _____.
   a. increased activity in the sympathetic nervous system and heightened sensitivity and alertness
   b. reliance on defense mechanisms in an effort to bring the stress quickly under control
   c. inability to concentrate, irritability, and procrastination
   d. increased activity in the immune system to ward off potential diseases

2. Beth plans on entering a career field that involves the study of how stress interacts with physiological processes such as immune, endocrine, and nervous systems activities. Her interests fall closest to those of _____.
   a. psychoneuroimmunology
   b. psychobiosocial medicine
   c. psychopathology
   d. forensic psychology

Answers: 1. a, 2. a.

Staying Healthy

8.7 Suggest several ways in which individuals can minimize stress and pursue a healthy, well-adjusted lifestyle.

Stress may be part of life, but there are proven ways to reduce the negative impact of stress on your body and your health. The best method, not surprisingly, is to reduce stress. A healthy lifestyle can also prepare you to cope with the unavoidable stress in your life.

REDUCING STRESS

What steps can people take to reduce stress?

The field of health psychology is focused on understanding the relationships between our life-style behaviors and our health. Health psychologists often provide advice on how to reduce stress and stay healthy.

CALM DOWN *Exercise* is a good beginning. Running, walking, biking, swimming, or other aerobic exercise lowers your resting heart rate and blood pressure, so that your body does not react as strongly to stress and recovers more quickly. As we discuss later, exercise is also part of a healthy lifestyle. Moreover, numerous studies show that people who exercise regularly and are physically fit have higher self-esteem than those who do not; are less likely to feel anxious, depressed, or irritable; and have fewer aches and pains, as well as fewer colds (Biddle, 2000; Sonstroem, 1997).

Relaxation training is another stress buster. A number of studies indicate that relaxation techniques lower stress (Pothier, 2002) and improve immune functioning (Andersen, Kiecolt–Glaser, & Glaser, 1994). Relaxation is more than flopping on the couch with the TV zapper, however. Healthful physical relaxation requires lying quietly and alternately tensing and relaxing every voluntary muscle in your body—from your head to your toes—to learn how to recognize muscle tension, as well as to learn how to relax your body. Breathing exercises can have the same effect: If you are tense, deep, rhythmic breathing is difficult, but learning to do so relieves bodily tension (see also Chapter 3, "Sensation, Perception, and Consciousness," for a discussion of meditation.)

REACH OUT A strong network of friends and family who provide *social support* can help to maintain good health (Uchino, Cacioppo, & Kiecolt–Glaser, 1996; Cohen, Doyle, Turner, Alper, & Skoner, 2003b). One review of the literature concluded that the positive relationship between health and social support is on par with the negative relationship between health and such well-established risk factors as physical inactivity, smoking, and high blood pressure (House, Landis, & Umberson, 1988). Exactly why the presence of a strong social support system is related to health is not fully understood. Some researchers contend that social support may directly affect our response to stress and health by producing physiological changes in endocrine, cardiac, and immune functioning (Uchino, et al., 1996). Whatever the underlying mechanism, most people can remember times when other people made a difference in their lives by giving them good advice (informational support), helping them to feel better about themselves (emotional support), providing assistance with chores and responsibilities or financial help (tangible support), or simply by "hanging out" with them (belonging support) (Uchino, Uno, & Holt–Lunstad, 1999; R. B. Williams et al., 1992).

A strong network of supportive family and friends can provide many kinds of social support that help reduce stress.

Not all relationships are alike, however. Knowing a lot of people or having a partner may or may not be a stress buffer; what matters are the characteristics of friends and partners and the quality of the relationships (Hartup & Stevens, 1999). For example, studies have found that married couples who argue in a hostile way—criticizing, belittling, and insulting one another—have suppressed immune function compared with couples who interact in more constructive ways—listening to one another's points of view, seeking common ground and compromise, as well as using humor to break up tension (Hobfoll, Cameron, Chapman, & Gallagher, 1996; Kiecolt–Glaser, Malarkey, Chee, Newton, & Cacioppo, 1993; Kiecolt–Glaser, Bane, Glaser, & Malarkey, 2003).

BE PART OF A COMMUNITY Health psychologists are also investigating the role religion may play in reducing stress and bolstering health (Freedland, 2004; Rabin & Koenig, 2002; Siegel, Anderman, & Schrimshaw, 2001; Smith, 2000). For example, research has found that elderly people who pray or attend religious services regularly enjoy better health and markedly lower rates of depression than those who do not (Koenig, McCullough, & Larson, 2000). Other studies have shown that having a religious commitment may also help to moderate high blood pressure and hypertension (Levin & Vanderpool, 1989).

It is unclear why there is an association between health and religion (Contrada et al., 2004). One explanation holds that religion provides a system of social support that includes caring friends and opportunities for close personal interactions. As previously described, a strong network of social support can reduce stress in a variety of ways, and in turn, reduced stress is associated with better health (Urchino et al., 1996, 1999). Other possible explanations are that regular attendance at religious services encourages people to help others, which in turn increases feelings of personal control and reduces feelings of depression; that frequent attendance at religious services increases positive emotions; and that most religions encourage healthy lifestyles (Powell, Shababi, & Thoresen, 2003).

Altruism—reaching out and giving to others because this brings *you* pleasure—is one of the more effective ways to reduce stress (Vaillant, 2000). Caring for others tends to take our minds off our own problems, to make us realize that there are others who are worse off than we are, and to foster the feeling that we're involved in something larger than our own small slice of life (Folkman, Chesney, & Christopher–Richards, 1994). Interestingly, altruism is a component of most religions, suggesting that altruism and religious commitment may have something in common that helps to reduce stress. Altruism may also channel loss, grief, or anger into constructive action. An example is *Mothers Against Drunk Driving* (MADD), an organization founded by a mother whose son was killed by a drunken driver.

Managers who are able to create a work environment where co-workers feel supported and small errors are taken in stride can help their subordinates deal more effectively with stressful situations that arise at work.

LEARN TO COPE EFFECTIVELY How you appraise events in your environment—and how you appraise your ability to cope with potentially unsettling, unpredictable events—can minimize or maximize stress and its impact on health.

Proactive coping is the psychological term for anticipating stressful events and taking advance steps to avoid them or to minimize their impact (Aspinwall & Taylor, 1997). Proactive coping does not mean "expect the worst"; constant vigilance actually increases stress and may damage health. Rather, proactive coping means (as in the Boy Scout motto), "Be prepared." This may include accumulating resources (time, money, social support, and information), recognizing potential stress in advance, and making realistic plans. For example, a recent widower anticipates that his first Christmas without his late wife will be lonely and makes plans to spend the holidays with friends. A woman who is moving to a new city knows the transition may be stressful. She finds out as much as she can about her new location before she moves—whether her friends have friends there, where she can participate in activities she enjoys (such as taking classes in drawing or karate), where there are places and groups or organizations where she might meet people who share her interests (a house of worship, the best jazz clubs, the local animal shelter), and so on.

In many cases, you cannot change or escape stressful circumstances, but you can change the way you think about things. *Positive reappraisal* helps people to make the best of a tense or painful situation. A low grade can be seen as a warning sign, not a catastrophe; a job you hate provides information on what you really want in your career; instead of brooding about a nasty remark from your sister, ask what does this tell you about *her*? Positive reappraisal does not require you to become a "Pollyanna" (the heroine of a novel who was optimistic to the point of being naive). Rather, it requires finding new meaning in a situation, or finding a perspective or insight that you had overlooked. After his partner died, one HIV caregiver told researchers, "What his death did was snap a certain value into my behavior, which is, 'Listen, you don't know how long you've got. You've just lost another one. Spend more time with the people who mean something to you'" (S. E. Taylor, Kemeny, Reed, Bower, & Gruenwald, 2000, p. 105).

One of the most effective, stress-relieving forms of reappraisal is *humor*. As Shakespeare so aptly put it in *The Winter's Tale*: "A merry heart goes all the day/ Your sad tires in a mile" (*Act IV, Scene 3*). Journalist Norman Cousins (1981) attributed his recovery from a life-threatening disease to regular "doses" of laughter. Watching classic comic films, he believed, reduced both his pain and the inflammation in his tissues. He wrote:

> What was significant about the laughter . . . was not just the fact that it provides internal exercise for a person flat on his or her back—a form of jogging for the innards—but that it creates a mood in which the other positive emotions can be put to work, too. In short, it helps make it possible for good things to happen (pp. 145–146).

Some health psychologists agree that a healthy body and a sense of humor go hand in hand (Salovey, Rothman, Detweiler, & Steward, 2000; Vaillant, 2000), while others believe that more research is needed before any firm conclusions can be drawn (Martin, 2002). Most are in agreement, however, that doing what we can to maintain a healthy body helps us both reduce and cope with stress.

ADOPTING A HEALTHY LIFESTYLE

What are the elements of a healthy lifestyle?

While learning how to avoid and cope with stress is important, the positive psychology movement (see Chapter 1: "The Science of Psychology"), has prompted many health psychologists to explore other ways to promote good health by adopting a healthier lifestyle. Developing healthy habits like eating a well-balanced diet, getting regular exercise, not smoking, and avoiding high-risk behaviors are all important to maintaining health (Friedman, 2002).

EAT A NUTRITIOUS DIET A good diet of nutritious foods is important because it provides the energy necessary to sustain a vigorous lifestyle while promoting healthy growth and development. Although there is some disagreement about what *exactly* constitutes a well-balanced diet, most experts advise eating a wide variety of fruits, vegetables, nuts, whole grain breads, and cereals, accompanied by small portions of fish and lean meats. Several studies have documented that eating a healthy diet can improve the quality of life, increase longevity, and reduce the risk of heart disease, cancer, and stroke (Trichopoulou, Costacou, Bamia, & Trichopoulos, 2003). Conversely, eating excessive amounts of fatty meats, deep-fried foods, dairy products that are high in cholesterol (such as whole milk and butter), and foods high in sugars (such as soda and candy, which often lack vitamins and minerals) are generally considered unhealthy (Friedman, 2002).

EXERCISE REGULARLY The importance of regular aerobic exercise (such as jogging, brisk walking, or swimming) for maintaining a healthy body has been well established. In addition, health psychologists have shown that regular aerobic exercise can also help peo-

Doing yoga exercises regularly is a direct way of coping with stress that can enhance feelings of well-being while improving balance and flexibility.

ple cope better with stress, as well as help them feel less depressed, more vigorous, and more energetic. One study, for example, randomly divided mildly depressed college women into three groups. One group participated in regular aerobic exercise, one group received relaxation therapy, and the last group (a control group) received no treatment at all. After 10 weeks, the mildly depressed women in the aerobic activity group reported a marked decrease in their depression when compared to the no treatment group. The relaxation group also showed benefits from relaxation therapy, but they were not as significant as the group that had engaged in the regular aerobic exercise program (McCann & Holmes, 1984). Numerous other studies have also demonstrated a link between regular exercise, reduced stress, increased self-confidence, and improved sleep quality (Gandhi, Depauw, Dolny, & Freson, 2002; Rice, 1997; Weinberg & Gould, 1999).

QUIT SMOKING Fewer Americans smoke today than in the past, and over half of those who did smoke have quit; however, cigarette smoking still poses a serious health threat to the millions of people who continue to smoke (Millis, 1998). Smoking is linked to chronic lung disease, heart disease, and cancer. In addition, smoking can reduce the quality of life by decreasing lung efficiency.

Interestingly, the tendency to start smoking occurs almost exclusively during the adolescent years. Almost no one over the age of 21 takes up the habit for first time, but teenagers who seriously experiment with cigarettes or have friends who smoke are more likely to start smoking than those who do not (Choi, Pierce, Gilpin, Farkas, & Berry, 1997). For these reasons, health psychologists realize that initiatives aimed at preventing smoking should primarily focus their efforts on young people.

Most adults who smoke want to quit, but their addiction to nicotine (discussed in Chapter 4) makes quitting very difficult. Fortunately, several alternative methods to help people quit smoking have been developed in recent years. For example, prescription antidepressant medications such as *Zyban*, *Wellbutrin*, and *Effexor*, which work at the neurotransmitter level, have proven useful in helping people stop smoking. Nicotine substitutes, usually in the form of chewing gum, patches, or inhalers, have also produced encouraging results. Many people who are attempting to quit also find that modifying the environment that they have come to associate with smoking is important. For example, because people often smoke in bars or during coffee breaks, changing routines that signal lighting up can also help. Finally, some people succeed in quitting "cold turkey." They simply decide to stop smoking without any external support or change in their lifestyle. Regardless of how people quit smoking, studies have shown that quitting will generally add years to a smoker's life.

AVOID HIGH RISK BEHAVIORS Every day, we make dozens of small, seemingly insignificant choices that can potentially affect our health and well-being. For example, choosing to wear a seat belt every time you ride in a car is one of the more significant measures to reduce the risk of injury and early death. Similarly, refusing to have unprotected sex reduces your chances of contracting a sexually transmitted disease.

Health psychologists, working with public agencies, are designing intervention programs to help people make safer choices in their everyday lives. For example, John Jemmott and his colleagues (Jemmott, Jemmott, Fong, & McCaffree, 2002) studied the impact of a *safer sex* program that stressed the importance of condom use and other safer sex practices on a sample of 496 high-risk inner city African-American adolescents. Six months after the program began, a follow-up evaluation of the participants revealed that they reported a lower incidence of high-risk sexual behavior, including unprotected intercourse, than did adolescents who did not participate in the program. Research like this underscores the important role that health psychologists can play in helping people learn to avoid risky behavior and improve their quality of life.

THE WELL-ADJUSTED PERSON

What qualities describe a well-adjusted person?

We noted at the beginning of the chapter that adjustment is any effort to cope with stress. Psychologists disagree, however, about what constitutes *good* adjustment. Some think it is the ability to live according to social norms. Thus, a woman who grows up in a small

self-actualization Highest level of need in Maslow's hierarchy, which involves the desire for personal growth and fulfillment.

town, attends college, teaches for a year or two, and then settles down to a peaceful family life might be considered well adjusted because she is living by the predominant values of her community.

Other psychologists disagree strongly with this view. They argue that society is not always right. Thus, if we accept its standards blindly, we renounce the right to make individual judgments. Barron (1963) argues that well-adjusted people enjoy the difficulties and ambiguities of life, treating them as challenges to be overcome. Such people are aware of their strengths and weaknesses; this awareness enables them to live in harmony with their inner selves.

We may also evaluate adjustment by using specific criteria, such as the following (Morris, 1990), to judge an action:

1. Does the action realistically meet the demands of the situation, or does it simply postpone resolving the problem?
2. Does the action meet the individual's needs?
3. Is the action compatible with the well-being of others?

Abraham Maslow, whose hierarchy of needs was discussed in Chapter 6: "Motivation and Emotion," believed that well-adjusted people strive to achieve **self-actualization**. That is, they live in a way that enhances their own growth and fulfillment, regardless of what others might think. According to Maslow, well-adjusted people are unconventional and creative thinkers, perceive people and events realistically, and set goals for themselves. They also tend to form deep, close relationships with a few chosen individuals.

As we have seen, there are many standards for judging whether an individual is well adjusted. A person deemed well adjusted by one standard might not be considered well adjusted by other standards. The same principle holds true when we try to specify what behaviors are "abnormal"—the topic of the next chapter.

► CHECK YOUR UNDERSTANDING

Mark the following statements as being True (T) or False (F).

1. ___ People who are religious and attend religious services regularly are more resistant to stress-related illnesses.

2. ___ When people engage in positive reappraisal, they first identify all of the major problems in their life and then figure out what the "worst case scenario" is for each of them

3. ___ Engaging in regular aerobic exercise has been shown to be an effective way of coping with stress.

4. ___ Antidepressant medications such as Zyban and Wellbutrin have been used successfully to help people quit smoking.

5. According to the text, the well-adjusted person has learned to balance
   a. conformity and nonconformity
   b. self-control and spontaneity
   c. flexibility and structure
   d. all of the above

Answers: 1. (T), 2. (F), 3. (T), 4. (T); 2. d.

► APPLY YOUR UNDERSTANDING

1. Jeff is experiencing prolonged and intense stress at work. To counteract this stress, he has taught himself some exercises that involve first tensing, then relaxing, his muscles. He has also learned to breathe deeply and regularly as a way to reduce stress. The term that describes Jeff's approach is _____.
   a. psychoneuroimmunology
   b. positive reappraisal
   c. self-actualization
   d. relaxation training

2. Mary lives in a way that enhances her own growth and fulfillment regardless of what others think. In many ways, she is unconventional, is a creative thinker, and has close relationships with only a few chosen individuals. According to Maslow, Mary is most likely _____.
   a. a well-adjusted, self-actualizing person
   b. engaging in positive reappraisal
   c. a Type A personality
   d. making excessive use of intellectualization

Answers: 1. d., 2. a.

>KEY TERMS<

personality, *p. 277*
stress, *p. 277*
adjustment, *p. 278*
health psychology, *p. 278*

Theories of personality

psychodynamic theories, *p. 278*
unconscious, *p. 278*
psychoanalysis, *p. 278*
id, *p. 279*
pleasure principle, *p. 279*
ego, *p. 279*
reality principle, *p. 279*
superego, *p. 279*
libido, *p. 280*
fixation, *p. 280*
oral stage, *p. 280*
anal stage, *p. 280*
phallic stage, *p. 280*

Oedipus complex and Electra complex, *p. 280*
latency period, *p. 280*
genital stage, *p. 280*
humanistic personality theories, *p. 282*
actualizing tendency, *p. 283*
self-actualizing tendency, *p. 283*
fully functioning person, *p. 283*
unconditional positive regard, *p. 283*
conditional positive regard, *p. 283*
personality traits, *p. 283*
factor analysis, *p. 283*
Big Five, *p. 284*
cognitive–social learning theories, *p. 285*
expectancies, *p. 286*

performance standards, *p. 286*
self-efficacy, *p. 286*
locus of control, *p. 286*

Personality assessment

objective tests, *p. 290*
NEO-PI-R, *p. 291*
Minnesota Multiphasic Personality Inventory (MMPI-2), *p. 291*
projective tests, *p. 291*
Rorschach test, *p. 291*
Thematic Apperception Test (TAT), *p. 292*

Sources of stress

stressor, *p. 293*
pressure, *p. 295*
frustration, *p. 295*
conflict, *p. 295*

Extreme stress

posttraumatic stress disorder (PTSD), *p. 299*

Coping with stress

confrontation, *p. 301*
compromise, *p. 301*
withdrawal, *p. 301*
defense mechanisms, *p. 302*

How stress affects health

general adaptation syndrome (GAS), *p. 305*
type A behavior pattern, *p. 306*
type B behavior pattern, *p. 306*
psychoneuroimmunology (PNI), *p. 306*

Staying healthy

self-actualization, *p. 312*

>CHAPTER REVIEW<

Personality refers to an individual's unique pattern of thoughts, feelings, and behaviors that persists over time and across situations. The key elements in this definition are unique differences—those aspects that distinguish a person from everyone else—and the idea that personality is relatively stable and enduring.

We experience **stress** when we are faced with a tense or threatening situation that requires us to change or adapt our behavior (a **stressor**). Some life-and-death situations, like war and natural disasters, are inherently stressful. Even events that are usually viewed as positive, like a wedding or a job promotion, can be stressful, because they require change or adaptation. How we adjust to the stresses in our lives affects our health, since prolonged or severe stress can contribute to physical and psychological disorders. **Health psychologists** try to find ways to prevent stress from becoming debilitating and to promote healthy behaviors.

Theories of Personality

What are the major ideas in Freud's psychodynamic theory? Freud believed that our personality includes the **id**, which operates according to the **pleasure principle** and seeks immediate gratification, the **ego**, which operates according to the **reality principle** and controls reasoning, and the **superego**, which is the moral watchdog.

Freud called energy generated by the sexual instinct **libido**. As infants mature, their libido becomes focused on different sensitive parts of the body. A **fixation** occurs if a child is deprived of or receives too much pleasure from the part of the body that dominates one of the

five developmental stages—**oral**, **anal**, **phallic**, **latency**, and **genital**—and some sexual energy may lodge in that part of the body. Strong attachment to the parent of the opposite sex and jealousy of the parent of the same sex—which develops during the phallic stage—is termed the **Oedipus complex** in boys and the **Electra complex** in girls. At the end of the phallic stage, the child enters the latency period, characterized by a loss of interest in sexual behavior. Finally, at puberty, the individual enters the genital stage of mature sexuality.

What ideas do all psychodynamic theories have in common? **Psychodynamic theories** of personality consider behavior to be the result of psychological dynamics within the individual. Often these dynamics are **unconscious** processes. Early life experiences are particularly important in personality development.

What are the major ways that humanistic personality theories differs from psychodynamic theories? Freud and many of his followers believed that personality grows out of the resolution of unconscious conflicts and developmental crises from the past. **Humanistic personality theories** emphasize that we are positively motivated and progress toward higher levels of functioning, and they stress people's potential for growth and change in the present.

According to Rogers, how can thinking of yourself as self-assured help you to become so? Rogers contended that every person is born with an **actualizing tendency**, which propels us toward realizing our biological potential. A **fully functioning person** is one whose self-concept closely matches his or her inborn capabilities, and it is encouraged when a child is raised in an atmosphere characterized by **unconditional positive regard**.

What is the key focus of trait theories? Trait theorists reject the notion that there are just a few distinct personality types. Instead, they insist that each person possesses a unique constellation of fundamental **personality traits**, which can be inferred from how the person behaves.

What five basic traits describe most differences in personality? Recent research suggests that there may be five overarching and universal personality traits: extroversion, agreeableness, conscientiousness, emotional stability, and openness to experience (also called culture or intellect). Research shows that these traits have some real world applications and are strongly influenced by heredity.

How do personal and situational factors combine to shape behavior? **Cognitive–social learning theories** of personality view behavior as the product of the interaction of cognitions, learning and past experiences, and the immediate environment. Albert Bandura maintains that certain internal **expectancies** determine how a person evaluates a situation and that this evaluation has an effect on the person's behavior. **Expectancies** prompt people to conduct themselves according to unique **performance standards**, which are individually determined measures of excellence by which people judge their behavior. Those who succeed in meeting their own internal performance standards develop an attitude that Bandura calls **self-efficacy**. According to Rotter, people with an internal **locus of control**—one type of expectancy—believe that they can control their own fate through their actions.

What are the major contributions and limitations of each of the four theoretical perspectives on personality? The **psychoanalytic perspective** revolutionized the way that psychologists and others view unconscious urges, sexual instincts, and childhood experiences, but gives little attention to cultural and social forces as determinants of personality. **Humanistic theories** emphasize the positive aspects of human nature, but may foster self-centeredness and not give sufficient attention to more negative human qualities and urges. **Trait theories** provide convenient and useful descriptions of personality, but may be oversimplified and tell us little about how traits develop. **Cognitive-social learning theories** provide useful explanations for inconsistencies in our behavior, but may be too narrow in scope and give too little attention to unconscious processes and personality development. All theoretical perspectives have led to useful psychotherapeutic and personality assessment techniques.

Personality Assessment

What are the purposes of structured and unstructured interviews? During an unstructured interview, the interviewer asks questions about any material that arises during the conversation as well as follow-up questions where appropriate, but the behavior of the interviewer may affect the results. In a structured interview, the order and the content of the questions are fixed, and the interviewer does not deviate from the format, so it may not address some of the issues that come up in an unstructured interview. Structured interviews are more likely to be used for systematic research on personality because they solicit comparable information from all interviewees.

What are the advantages and limits of the observational method? Direct observation of a person over a period of time to determine the environmental influence on that person's behavior has the advantage of not relying on people's self-reports of their behavior. However, the subject's behavior may be affected by the observer's presence in ways that can be misinterpreted.

Why are objective tests preferred by trait theorists? **Objective personality tests** ask respondents to answer "yes–no" questions about their own behavior and thoughts. The **NEO-PI-R** reports scores for each of the Big Five traits and their associated facets. The **Minnesota Multiphasic Personality Inventory** (**MMPI-2**) is typically used as an aid to diagnose mental disorders, and it includes questions that measure the truthfulness of a person's response.

What do projective tests try to measure? Psychodynamic theorists, who believe that much behavior is determined by unconscious processes, tend to discount tests that rely on self-reports. They are more likely to use **projective tests**, which consist of ambiguous stimuli that can draw out an unlimited number of interpretations based on these unconscious processes. Two such tests are the **Rorschach test** and the **Thematic Apperception Test** (**TAT**).

Sources of Stress

Why is change so stressful for most people? Environmental demands that create a state of tension or threat and require adaptations are called **stressors**. Because most people have a strong desire to maintain order in their lives, any event, either good or bad, that involves change will be experienced as stressful.

How can everyday hassles contribute to stress? Many psychologists believe day-to-day petty annoyances and irritations—such as being stuck in traffic, misplacing car keys, and getting into trivial arguments—to be as stressful as major life events, because, although seemingly minor, these incidents give rise to feelings of pressure, frustration, conflict, and anxiety.

When we experience **pressure** from either internal or external forces, we feel forced to intensify our efforts or to perform at higher levels. Internal forces include meeting our personal standards; external forces include competition or imposed standards in jobs, grades, and parental demands. We feel frustrated when someone or something stands between us and our goal. Five basic sources of **frustration** are delays, lack of resources, losses, failure, and discrimination. **Conflict** arises when we are faced with two or more incompatible demands, opportunities, needs, or goals.

How do we create stress? Sometimes we subject ourselves to stress by internalizing a set of irrational, self-defeating beliefs that add unnecessarily to the normal stresses of living and that are independent of outside forces.

Do people who are resistant to stress share certain traits? People who cope well with stress tend to be self-confident and optimistic. They also see themselves as being able to affect their situations, a trait referred to as having an internal locus of control.

Stress-resistant people share a trait called *hardiness*—a tendency to experience difficult demands as challenging rather than threatening. People who feel that they have some control over an event are far less susceptible to stress than are those who feel powerless in the same situation. *Resilience*, the ability to bounce back after a stressful event, is also related to positive adjustment.

Extreme Stress

What are some sources of extreme stress, and what impact do they have? People experiencing extreme stress cannot continue their everyday life as they did before the stress and, in some cases, never fully recover. Extreme stress derives from a number of sources, including unemployment, divorce and separation, bereavement, combat, and catastrophes. One of the impediments to effective coping occurs when the stressed or grieving person feels compelled to adjust in socially prescribed ways that do not provide effective relief.

What experiences can lead to posttraumatic stress disorder? Extreme traumas may result in **posttraumatic stress disorder (PTSD)**, a disabling emotional disorder which includes symptoms of anxiety, sleeplessness, and nightmares. Combat veterans and people with a history of emotional problems are especially vulnerable to PTSD.

Coping with Stress

What are three strategies that deal directly with stress? People generally adjust to stress in one of two ways: *Direct coping* describes any action people take to change an uncomfortable situation, whereas *defensive coping* denotes the various ways people convince themselves—through a form of self-deception—that they are not really threatened or do not really want something they cannot get.

When we cope directly with a particular threat or conflict, we do it in one of three ways: **Confrontation**, **compromise**, or **withdrawal**. When we confront a stressful situation and admit to ourselves that there is a problem that needs to be solved, we may learn new skills, enlist other people's aid, or try harder to reach our goal. Confrontation may also include expressions of anger. Compromise usually requires adjusting expectations or desires; the conflict is resolved by settling for less than what was originally sought. Sometimes the most effective way of coping with a stressful situation is to distance oneself from it. The danger of withdrawal, however, is that it may become a maladaptive habit.

What are the major ways of coping defensively? When a stressful situation arises and there is little that can be done to deal with it directly, people often turn to **defense mechanisms** as a way of coping. Defense mechanisms are ways of deceiving ourselves about the causes of stressful events, thus reducing immediate sources of conflict, frustration, pressure, and anxiety. Although defensive coping can contribute to our overall ability to adjust to difficult circumstances, it can also lead to maladaptive behavior if it interferes with the person's ability to deal constructively with a difficult situation.

Who experiences the most stress? How people handle stress is determined to a significant degree by the environment in which they live. People in low-income groups often experience more stress and also have fewer means of coping, lower self-concepts, and an external locus of control. Men and women may cope differently with stress.

How Stress Affects Health

What long-lasting effects of stress do we need to be concerned with? Physiologist Hans Selye contends that people react to physical and psychological stress in three stages that he called the **general adaptation syndrome (GAS)**. In Stage 1, *alarm reaction*, the body recognizes that it must fight off some physical or psychological danger. This recognition results in quickened respiration and heart rate, increased sensitivity and alertness, and a highly charged emotional state—a physical adaptation that augments our coping resources and helps us to regain self-control. If neither direct nor defensive coping mechanisms succeed in reducing the stress, we move on to Selye's second stage of adaptation. During this *resistance stage*, physical symptoms of strain appear as we intensify our efforts to cope both directly and defensively. If these attempts to regain psychological equilibrium fail, psychological disorganization rages out of control until we reach *exhaustion*, Selye's third stage. In this phase, we use increasingly ineffective defense mechanisms to bring the stress under control. At this point, some people lose touch with reality, whereas others show signs of "burnout," such as shorter attention spans, irritability, procrastination, and general apathy.

How is Type A behavior related to heart disease? Stress is known to be an important factor in the development of coronary heart disease. The **Type A behavior pattern**—a set of high-stress characteristics that includes hostility, urgency, competitiveness, and striving—has been linked to a greater likelihood of coronary heart disease. People with the more relaxed **Type B behavior pattern** are less likely to experience stress-related disorders.

Why do so many students get sick during finals? Stress—such as that experienced by students during examination periods—can suppress the functioning of the immune system. Stress can also increase one's susceptibility to the common cold, and it appears to be linked to the development of some forms of cancer. The relatively new field of **psychoneuroimmunology (PNI)** investigates the relationships between psychological factors and our immune response.

Staying Healthy

What steps can people take to reduce stress? We can reduce the negative impact of stress on our health by trying to reduce stress and by maintaining a healthy lifestyle, which equips the body to cope with stress that is unavoidable. Exercising regularly and learning to relax reduce the body's responses to stress. Having a strong network of friends and family that provide social support is also related to healthier adjustment. People who are religious and who are altruistic also typically experience less stress, although the mechanism involved is not clear. Finally, people can improve their ability to cope by taking steps to minimize the impact of stressful events (proactive coping), by making the best of difficult situations (positive reappraisal), and by maintaining a sense of humor.

What are the elements of a healthy lifestyle? The positive psychology movement has prompted many psychologists to explore ways to promote good health by adopting a healthier lifestyle. Developing healthy habits like eating a well-balanced diet, getting regular exercise, not smoking, and avoiding high-risk behaviors are all important to maintaining health.

What qualities describe a well-adjusted person? Psychologists disagree on what constitutes good adjustment. Some believe that well-adjusted people live according to social norms, having learned to control socially forbidden impulses and to limit their goals to those that society allows. Others disagree, arguing that well-adjusted people enjoy overcoming challenging situations and that this ability leads to growth and self-fulfillment, a need referred to by Maslow and other humanistic psychologists as **self-actualization**. Finally, some psychologists use specific criteria to evaluate a person's ability to adjust, such as how well the adjustment solves the problem and satisfies both personal needs and the needs of others.

> CHAPTER 8 < Personality, Stress, and Health

8.1 THEORIES OF PERSONALITY

PSYCHODYNAMIC PERSPECTIVES

- Much of mental life is unconscious
- Early childhood experiences have a strong impact on personality formation
- Psychoanalysis: Sigmund Freud's theory and approach to therapy
- In Freud's theory, three processes shape personality: id, ego, superego

HUMANISTIC PERSPECTIVES

- Humans are motivated toward positive growth and higher levels of functioning
- Carl Rogers: Humans have a biological push toward fulfilling the self-actualizing tendency
- Unconditional positive regard: Full acceptance and love of another person

COGNITIVE–SOCIAL LEARNING PERSPECTIVES

- People organize expectancies and values to guide behavior
- Cognitions, learning, and past experiences shape personality
- Important concepts: Expectancies, self-efficacy, locus of control

TRAIT PERSPECTIVES

- Personality traits: Dimensions or characteristics on which people differ in distinctive ways
- Factor analysis: Statistical technique that allows researchers to identify basic personality traits
- The Five Factor Model: Extroversion, agreeableness, conscientiousness, emotional stability, openness to experience

8.2 PERSONALITY ASSESSMENT

ASSESSMENT METHODS

- Personal Interview: unstructured, structured
- Direct Observation
- Objective Tests: Self-report paper and pencil questions; MMPI
- Projective Tests: Ambiguous figures against which people "project" unconcious urges and drives; Rorschach Inkblot Test, Thematic Apperception Test (TAT)

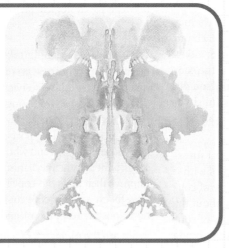

8.3 SOURCES OF STRESS

STRESSOR

Environmental demand that
- creates a state of tension or threat
- requires change or adaptation

SOURCES

- Change
- Accumulated daily hassles
- Major traumas
- Chronic sources: Pressure, frustration, conflict

8.4 EXTREME STRESS

COMMON SOURCES

- Unemployment
- Divorce and separation
- Bereavement
- Catastrophes and natural disasters
- War and combat

POSTTRAUMATIC STRESS DISORDER (PTSD):

Psychological disorder characterized by episodes of anxiety, sleeplessness, and nightmares resulting from some disturbing past event

8.5 COPING WITH STRESS

DIRECT METHODS

- **Confrontation:** Acknowledging there is a problem, attacking the problem head-on, and pushing resolutely toward the goal
- **Compromise:** Deciding on a more realistic solution when an ideal solution is not practical
- **Withdrawal:** Avoiding a conflict-oriented situation

DEFENSIVE METHODS

- Self-deceptive techniques including denial, repression, projection, identification, regression, intellectualization, reaction formation, displacement, and sublimation
- Can be adaptive or maladaptive, depending on circumstances

DIFFERENCES IN COPING WITH STRESS

- **Socioeconomic:** People in lower socioeconomic classes have fewer resources for coping with hardship and stress, often cope less effectively, and have poorer physical and mental health
- **Gender:** Given the gender-related stereotypes that still exist in our culture, men and women sometimes use different coping styles

8.6 HOW STRESS AFFECTS HEALTH

SEQUENCE

Perception of stress leads to physical responses such as

- increase in heart rate
- rise in blood pressure
- faster respiration
- perspiration

GENERAL ADAPTATION SYNDROME (GAS)

- **Alarm:** Initial reaction, including the activation of the sympathetic nervous system
- **Resistance:** Physical symptoms and signs of strain result from prolonged stress
- **Exhaustion:** Mental or physical breakdown begins

TYPE A BEHAVIOR PATTERN

- Response pattern characterized by impatience, hostility, competitiveness, urgency, and constant striving
- Linked to higher risk of stress-related illness

8.7 STAYING HEALTHY

REDUCE STRESS

- Regular exercise and relaxation training
- Social support systems
- Altruism—helping others
- Using effective coping techniques

ADOPT A HEALTHY LIFESTYLE

- Eat a diet high in fruits, vegetables, nuts, whole grains
- Get regular aerobic exercise
- Quit (or don't start) smoking
- Avoid high-risk behaviors
- Pursue self-actualization

Concept Map

[CHAPTER 9]

Psychological Disorders and Their Treatments

Overview

Perspectives on Psychological Disorders

- Defining Abnormality
- Models of Abnormality
- The Prevalence of Psychological Disorders
- Classifying Abnormal Behavior

Mood Disorders

- Depression
- Suicide
- Mania and Bipolar Disorder
- Causes of Mood Disorders

Anxiety Disorders

- Phobias
- Panic Disorder
- Other Anxiety Disorders

Psychosomatic, Somatoform, and Dissociative Disorders

- Mind-Body Disorders

Schizophrenic Disorders

- Symptoms of Schizophrenia
- Subtypes of Schizophrenia
- Causes of Schizophrenia

Other Common Disorders

- Sexual and Gender-Identity Disorders
- Personality Disorders
- Childhood Disorders

Psychotherapies

- Insight Therapies
- Behavior Therapies
- Cognitive-Based Therapies
- Group Therapies
- Effectiveness of Psychotherapy

Biological Treatments

- Drug Therapies
- Electroconvulsive Therapy
- Psychosurgery

Challenges in Therapy

- Client Diversity and Treatment
- Matching Treatments to Individuals

"I am now the most miserable man living. If what I feel were equally distributed to the whole human family, there would not be one cheerful face on the earth. Whether I shall ever be better I can not tell; I awfully forebode I shall not. To remain as I am is impossible; I must die or be better, it appears to me."

On January 23, 1841, Abraham Lincoln, then an Illinois state legislator, wrote these words to his law partner, John T. Stuart, in Washington. A number of forces had conspired to bring Lincoln to the point of utter despair that winter. Lincoln's political career was foundering. He was bound to a woman, Mary Todd, whom he didn't love. And a stretch of unseasonably cold weather proved to be, as Lincoln wrote "very severe on defective nerves." Yet Lincoln had also suffered a mental breakdown in the summer of 1835, and what was then called Lincoln's "melancholy" was to recur throughout his life.

Modern clinical psychologists would probably agree that Abraham Lincoln suffered from what we now call "clinical depression." Not just a case of the blues, Lincoln's depression probably met today's criteria for diagnosis: depressed mood, a marked decrease in pleasure, or both, for at least two weeks, and symptoms including agitation, fatigue, feelings of worthlessness, and thoughts of death or suicide. Indeed in that winter of 1841, Lincoln's closest friend, Joshua Speed, recalled: "Lincoln went Crazy—had to remove razors from his room—take away all Knives and other such dangerous things-&-it was terrible." Although suicide was a recurrent theme in Lincoln's thoughts and the verses he liked to both read and compose, he never actually attempted to take his life, and he went on to become one of the country's most effective, revered, and beloved presidents.

How did Abraham Lincoln handle or even treat his "melancholy?" The author of *Lincoln's Melancholy*, Joshua Wolf Shenk, says that although Lincoln had a charge account at the local Springfield pharmacy for medications including camphor, sarsaparilla, and even opiates, Lincoln mainly toughed it out, to our country's great good fortune. Shenk says, "the suffering he had endured lent him clarity and conviction, creative skills in the face of adversity, and a faithful humility, that helped him guide the nation through its greatest peril," the civil war that threatened to destroy it. Ironically, in our day, one of the greatest presidents of all time would have been subjected to a battery of medical and psychiatric tests and immediately declared a "political liability," and "unfit for office."[1] How would history have changed had Lincoln been on Prozac, one of today's most widely prescribed medications for treating clinical depression?

Today depressive disorders affect approximately 18.8 million American adults or about 9.5 percent of the U.S. population age 18 or older in a given year. Although Abraham Lincoln may have been able to function quite impressively while depressed, most Americans cannot. Depression costs employers more than $51 billion per year in absenteeism and lost productivity, not including high medical and pharmacy bills. Fortunately, however, the depressed have a myriad of treatment options that were not available in Lincoln's day—options ranging from various kinds of psychotherapy to pharmaceuticals, such as Prozac, that are part of a group of psychoactive drugs known as selective serotonin reuptake inhibitors (SSRIs). In this chapter, we will identify and describe the major forms that psychological disorders take and the types of treatments that are available to those affected. We begin with a brief discussion about what characteristics define a psychological disorder. ◼

Perspectives on Psychological Disorders

9.1   Compare and contrast the central assumptions and features of the major models that explain psychological disorders: biological, psychoanalytic, cognitive-behavioral, diathesis-stress, and systems.

When is a person's behavior abnormal? It is not always easy to determine. There is no doubt about the abnormality of a man who dresses in flowing robes and accosts pedestrians on the street, claiming to be Jesus Christ, or a woman who dons an aluminum-foil helmet to prevent space aliens from "stealing" her thoughts. But other instances of abnormal behavior aren't always clear. Some people exhibit unusual behavior. But does their behavior deserve to be labeled "abnormal"? Do any of them have a genuine psychological disorder? Consider the following individuals (Nevis, Tathus, & Green, 2005):

- Lindsay was a very successful chemical engineer known for the meticulous accuracy of her work. But Lindsay also had a "little quirk." She constantly felt compelled to double-, triple-, and even quadruple-check things to assure herself that they were done properly. For example, when leaving her apartment in the morning, she occasionally got as far as the garage—but invariably she would go back to make certain that the door was securely locked and the stove, lights, and other appliances were all turned off. Going on a vacation was particularly difficult for her because her checking routine was so exhaustive and time consuming. Yet Lindsay insisted that she would never want to give up this chronic checking. Doing so, she said, would make her "much too nervous."

- Jonathan was a 22-year-old auto mechanic whom everyone described as a loner. He seldom engaged in conversation and seemed lost in his own private world. At work, the other mechanics took to whistling sharply whenever they wanted to get his attention. Jonathan also had a "strange look" on his face that could make customers feel uncomfortable. But his oddest behavior was his assertion that he sometimes had the distinct feeling his dead mother was standing next to him, watching what he did. Although Jonathan realized that his mother was not really there, he nevertheless felt reassured by the illusion of her presence. He took great care not to look or reach toward the spot where he felt his mother was because doing so inevitably made the feeling go away.

DEFINING ABNORMALITY

How does a mental health professional define a psychological disorder?

Although individuals often define abnormality in terms of personal unhappiness or lack of well-being, mental health professionals generally take another perspective. They assess abnormality chiefly by looking for *maladaptive personality traits, psychological discomfort* regarding a particular behavior, and evidence that the behavior is preventing the person from *functioning well in life.* From the perspective of a mental health professional, both Lindsay and Jonathan show evidence of a psychological disorder. Note that people with disorders may not always be distressed by their own behavior, but that behavior does impair their ability to function well in everyday settings or in social relationships. Consequently, both Lindsay and Jonathan most likely would be judged as meeting the criteria for diagnosis with some sort of psychological disorder. However, it is important to note that there is no hard and fast rule as to what constitutes abnormal behavior.

Identifying behavior as abnormal is also a matter of degree. To understand why, imagine that each of our two cases is slightly less extreme. Lindsay is still prone to double-checking, but she doesn't check over and over again. As for Jonathan, he only occasionally withdraws from social contact, and he has had the sense of his dead mother's presence just twice over the last three years. In these less severe situations, a mental health professional would not be so ready to diagnose a mental disorder. Clearly, great care must be taken when separating mental health and mental illness into two *qualitatively* different categories. It is often more accurate to think of mental illness as simply being *quantitatively* different from normal behavior—that is, different in degree. The line between one and the other is often somewhat arbitrary. Cases are always much easier to judge when they fall at the extreme end of a dimension than when they fall near the "dividing line."

The place and times also contribute to how we define mental disorders. Throughout history, various explanations—ranging from possession by evil spirits to physical illness—have been used to explain why some people behave abnormally. In fact, the basic reason for the failed—and sometimes abusive—treatment of mentally disturbed people throughout history has been the lack of understanding of the nature and causes of psychological disorders. Although our knowledge is still inadequate, important advances in understanding abnormal behavior can be traced to the late 19th and early 20th centuries, when three influential but conflicting models of abnormal behavior emerged: The biological model, the psychoanalytic model, and the cognitive–behavioral model.

MODELS OF ABNORMALITY

How have the biological, psychoanalytic, cognitive-behavioral, diathesis-stress, and systems models each attempted to explain psychological disorders?

THE BIOLOGICAL MODEL The **biological model** holds that psychological disorders are caused by physiological malfunctions—for example, of the nervous system or the endocrine glands—often stemming from hereditary factors. As we saw in Chapter 2,

---

biological model View that psychological disorders have a biochemical or physiological basis.

"The Biological Basis of Behavior," neuroscientists have provided important insights into the biological factors that underlie normal behavior. Not surprisingly, research in this area has also contributed to our understanding of abnormal behavior. New techniques in neuroimaging, for example, have enabled researchers to pinpoint specific regions of the brain that are involved in disorders such as schizophrenia (Callicott, 2003; Chance, Esiri, & Timothy, 2003; Yotsutsuji et al., 2003) and antisocial personality disorder (Anderson, Bechara, Damasio, Tranel, & Damasio, 1999). Advances in the field of behavior genetics have begun to identify specific genes that are involved in the development of complex disorders such as schizophrenia (Gerber et al., 2003; Hashimoto et al., 2003; Williams et al., 1999) and autism (Lamb, Moore, Bailey, & Monaco, 2000; Nurmi et al., 2003).

THE PSYCHOANALYTIC MODEL Freud and his followers developed the **psychoanalytic model** at the end of the 19th and during the first half of the 20th centuries (see Chapter 8.) According to this model, behavior disorders are symbolic expressions of unconscious conflicts, which can usually be traced to childhood. For example, a man who behaves violently toward women may be unconsciously expressing rage at his mother for not being affectionate toward him during his childhood. The psychoanalytic model argues that in order to resolve their problems effectively, people must become aware that the source of their problems usually lies in their childhood and infancy.

Although Freud and his followers profoundly influenced both the mental health disciplines and Western culture, only weak and scattered scientific evidence supports their theories about the causes and effective treatment of mental disorders.

THE COGNITIVE-BEHAVIORAL MODEL A third model of abnormal behavior grew out of 20th-century research on learning and cognition. The **cognitive–behavioral model** suggests that psychological disorders, like all behavior, result from learning. From this perspective, fear, anxiety, sexual deviations, and other maladaptive behaviors are learned—and they can be unlearned.

The cognitive–behavioral model stresses both internal and external learning processes in the development and treatment of psychological disorders. For example, a bright student who believes that he is academically inferior to his classmates and can't perform well on a test may not put much effort into studying. Naturally, he performs poorly, and his poor test score both punishes his minimal effort and confirms his belief that he is academically inferior. This student is caught up in a vicious cycle (Turk & Salovey, 1985). A cognitive–behavior therapist might try to modify both the young man's dysfunctional studying behavior and his inaccurate and maladaptive cognitive processes.

The cognitive–behavioral model has led to innovations in the treatment of psychological disorders, but the model has been criticized for its limited perspective, especially its emphasis on environmental causes and treatments.

NEWER THEORETICAL APPROACHES Each of the three major competing theories is useful in explaining the causes of certain types of disorders. The most exciting recent developments, however, emphasize integration of the various theoretical models to discover specific causes and specific treatments for different mental disorders.

The **diathesis–stress model** is one promising approach to integration (Fowles, 1992; Rende & Plomin, 1992; Walker & Diforio, 1997). This model suggests that a biological predisposition called a **diathesis** must combine with some kind of stressful circumstance before the predisposition to a mental disorder shows up as behavior (D. Rosenthal, 1970). According to this model, some people are biologically prone to developing a particular disorder under stress, whereas others are not.

The **systems approach** examines how biological, psychological, and social risk factors combine to produce psychological disorders. It is also known as the *biopsychosocial model*. According to this model, emotional problems are "lifestyle diseases" that, much like heart disease and many other physical illnesses, result from a combination of biological risks, psychological stresses, and social pressures and expectations. As we saw in Chapter 8: "Personality, Health, and Stress," heart disease can result from a combination

The cognitive–behavioral view of mental disorders suggests that people can learn—and unlearn—thinking patterns that affect their lives unfavorably. For example, an athlete who is convinced she will not win may not practice as hard as she should and end up "defeating herself."

psychoanalytic model View that psychological disorders result from unconscious internal conflicts.

cognitive–behavioral model View that psychological disorders result from learning maladaptive ways of thinking and behaving.

diathesis–stress model View that people biologically predisposed to a mental disorder (those with a certain diathesis) will tend to exhibit that disorder when particularly affected by stress.

diathesis Biological predisposition.

systems approach View that biological, psychological, and social risk factors combine to produce psychological disorders. Also known as the biopsychosocial model of psychological disorders.

of genetic predisposition, personality styles, poor health habits (such as smoking), and stress. In the systems approach, too, psychological problems result from several risk factors that influence one another. In this chapter, we follow the systems approach in examining the causes and treatments of abnormal behavior.

THE PREVALENCE OF PSYCHOLOGICAL DISORDERS

How common are mental disorders?

How common are psychological disorders in the United States? Are they increasing or decreasing over time? Are some population groups more prone to these disorders than others? These questions interest psychologists and public-health experts, who are concerned with both the prevalence and the incidence of mental health problems. *Prevalence* refers to the frequency with which a given disorder occurs at a given time. If there were 100 cases of depression in a population of 1,000, the prevalence of depression would be 10 percent. The *incidence* of a disorder refers to the number of new cases that arise in a given period. If there were 10 *new* cases of depression in a population of 1,000 in a single year, the incidence rate would be 1.0 percent per year.

The American Psychiatric Association funded an ambitious and wide-ranging study of the prevalence of psychological disorders, which involved interviewing more than 20,000 people around the country. The results were surprising: 15 percent of the population was found to be experiencing a clinically significant mental disorder, and 6 percent was experiencing a significant substance abuse disorder (Narrow, Rae, Robins, & Regier, 2001). The most common mental disorders were anxiety disorders, followed by phobias and mood disorders. (All of these are described in detail later in this chapter.) Schizophrenia, a severe mental disorder that often involves hospitalization, was found to afflict 1 percent of the population, or over 2 million people. Substance abuse problems were found in 6 percent of the population, with abuse of alcohol being three times more prevalent than abuse of all other drugs combined.

CLASSIFYING ABNORMAL BEHAVIOR

Why is it useful to have a manual of psychological disorders?

Given the finding that perhaps as much as 20 percent of U.S. population will experience a mental disorder severe enough to be considered abnormal, the question becomes, how can such disorders be treated? The first step in formulating a treatment plan is to identify the most likely cause of the disorder, a process referred to as *diagnosis*. Diagnosis of mental disorders follows a process parallel to that used to diagnose physical illness such as strep throat or lung cancer. The first step is to identify the pattern of symptoms present and to classify these, identifying a specific disorder thought to be present.

For nearly 40 years, the American Psychiatric Association (APA) has issued a manual describing and classifying the various kinds of psychological disorders. This publication, the **Diagnostic and Statistical Manual of Mental Disorders (DSM)**, has been revised four times. The fourth edition, text revision *DSM-IV-RT* (American Psychiatric Association, 2000), was coordinated with the 10th edition of the World Health Organization's *International Classification of Diseases*, which also provides a model for diagnosing mental disorders.

The DSM-IV-RT includes a complete list of mental disorders, with each diagnostic category painstakingly defined in terms of significant behavior patterns so that diagnoses based on it will be reliable (Nathan & Langenbucher, 1999). Although the manual provides careful descriptions of symptoms of different disorders to improve consistent diagnosis, it is generally silent on cause and treatment. The DSM has gained increasing acceptance because its detailed criteria for diagnosing mental disorders have made diagnosis much more reliable. Today, it is the most widely used classification of psychological disorders. The next several sections of this chapter will briefly outline some of the more common disorders identified in the DSM, organized according to the major categories used in this classification system.

Diagnostic and Statistical Manual of Mental Disorders (DSM) Manual that lists and describes the various kinds of psychological disorders.

Mood Disorders

9.2 Cite the major symptoms associated with depression, dysthymia, mania, and bipolar disorder and suggest what factors most likely cause these various mood disorders.

Mood disorders are relatively common and characterized by disturbances in mood or in a prolonged emotional state, sometimes referred to as *affect*. Most people have a wide emotional range; they can be happy or sad, animated or quiet, cheerful or discouraged, or overjoyed or miserable, depending on the circumstances. In some people with mood disorders, this range is greatly restricted. They seem stuck at one or the other end of the emotional spectrum—either consistently excited and euphoric or consistently sad—regardless of the circumstances of their lives. Other people with a mood disorder alternate between the extremes of euphoria and sadness.

Feelings of sadness, apathy, worthlessness, confusion, and failure are symptoms associated with depression, a relatively common mood disorder that affects people of all ages.

DEPRESSION

How does clinical depression differ from ordinary sadness?

The most common mood disorder is **depression**, a state in which a person feels overwhelmed with sadness. Depressed people lose interest in the things they normally enjoy. Intense feelings of worthlessness and guilt leave them unable to feel pleasure. They are tired and apathetic, sometimes to the point of being unable to make the simplest decisions. Many depressed people feel as if they have failed utterly in life, and they tend to blame themselves for their problems. Consider the words that Abraham Lincoln used to describe his depression, which are quoted in the opening sentences of this chapter: "I am now the most miserable man living." Seriously depressed people often have insomnia and lose

mood disorders Disturbances in mood or prolonged emotional state.

depression A mood disorder characterized by overwhelming feelings of sadness, lack of interest in activities, and perhaps excessive guilt or feelings of worthlessness.

[UNDERSTANDING OURSELVES]

RECOGNIZING DEPRESSION

From time to time, almost everyone feels depressed. Failing a major exam, breaking up with a boyfriend or girlfriend, even leaving home and friends to attend college can all produce a temporary state of "the blues." More significant life events can have an even greater impact: The loss of one's job or the loss of a loved one can produce a sense of hopelessness about the future that feels very much like a slide into depression.

The preceding instances would typically be considered "normal" reactions to negative life events. But at what point do these normal responses cross the line into clinical depression? How do clinicians determine whether the hopelessness and despair being expressed by a person constitute a major depressive episode or just a period of sadness that will eventually get better on its own?

The DSM-IV-RT provides the framework for making this distinction. Clinical depression is characterized by depressed mood, by the loss of interest and pleasure in usual activities, or both. Clinicians also look for some significant impairment or distress in social, occupational, or other important areas of functioning. People suffering from depression not only feel sad or empty, but also have significant problems carrying on a normal lifestyle.

Clinicians look, too, for other explanations of the symptoms: Could they be due to substance abuse or the side effects of medication that the person is taking? Could they be the re-sult of a medical condition, such as hypothy-roidism (the inability of the thyroid gland to produce an adequate amount of its hor-mones)? Could the symptoms be better inter-preted as an intense grief reaction?

If the symptoms do not seem to be ex-plained by the preceding causes, how do clini-cians make a diagnosis of depression? The DSM-IV-RT notes that at least five of the follow-ing symptoms, including at least one of the first two, must be present:

1. Depressed mood: Does the person feel sad or empty for most of the day, most every day, or do others observe these symptoms?

2. Loss of interest in pleasure: Has the per-son lost interest in performing normal ac-tivities, such as working or going to social events? Does the person seem to be "just going through the motions" of daily life without deriving any pleasure from them?

3. Significant weight loss or gain: Has the person gained or lost more than 5% of body weight in a month? Has the person lost interest in eating or complain that food has lost its taste?

4. Sleep disturbances: Is the person having trouble sleeping? Or, conversely, is the person sleeping too much?

5. Disturbances in motor activities: Do oth-ers notice a change in the person's activi-ty level? Does the person just "sit around," or does the person's behavior reflect agi-tation or unusual restlessness?

6. Fatigue: Does the person complain of being constantly tired and having no energy?

7. Feelings of worthlessness or excessive guilt: Does the person express feelings such as "You'd be better off without me" or "I'm evil and I ruin everything for every-body I love"?

8. Inability to concentrate: Does the person complain of memory problems ("I just can't remember anything anymore") or the inability to focus attention on simple tasks, such as reading a newspaper?

9. Recurrent thoughts of death: Does the person talk about committing suicide or express the wish that he or she were dead?

If you or someone you know well seems to have these symptoms, that person should consult a doctor or mental health profession-al. When these symptoms are present and are not due to other medical conditions, a di-agnosis of major depression is typically the result, and appropriate treatment can be pre-scribed.

Source: Diagnostic and Statistical Manual of Mental Disorders, 4th Edition, Text Revision. Washington, DC, American Psychiatric Association, 2000.

interest in food and sex. They may have trouble thinking or concentrating—even to the extent of finding it difficult to read a newspaper. In fact, difficulty in concentrating and subtle changes in short-term memory are sometimes the first signs of the onset of depression (Williams et al., 2000). In very serious cases, depressed people may be plagued by suicidal thoughts or may even attempt suicide (Cicchetti & Toth, 1998).

We want to point out that *clinical depression* is different from the "normal" kind of depression that all people experience from time to time. It is entirely normal to become sad when a loved one has died, when romantic relationships end, when you have problems on the job or at school—even when the weather is bad or you don't have a date for Saturday night. Most psychologically healthy people also get "the blues" occasionally for no apparent reason. But in all of these instances, either the mood disturbance is a normal reaction to a "real world" problem (for example, grief), or it passes quickly. Only when depression is long lasting and goes well beyond the typical reaction to a stressful life event is it classified as a mood disorder (APA, 2000). (See Box "Understanding Ourselves.")

DSM-IV-RT distinguishes between two forms of depression: *Major depressive disorder* is an episode of intense sadness that may last for several months; in contrast, *dysthymia* involves less intense sadness (and related symptoms), but persists with little relief for a period of two years or more. Depression is two to three times more prevalent in women than in men (Kessler et al., 2003; Simpson, Nee, & Endicott, 1997; Weissman & Olfson, 1995). One of the most severe hazards of depression, as well as some of the other disorders described in this chapter, is that people may become so miserable that they no longer want to live.

SUICIDE

What factors are related to a person's likelihood of committing suicide?

Nearly 30,000 people in the United States commit suicide each year; this makes it the 11th leading cause of death. Indeed, suicides outnumber homicides by five to three in the United States, and more than twice as many people die of suicide than of HIV/AIDS (NIMH, 2000). More women than men attempt suicide, but more men succeed, partly because men tend to choose violent and lethal means, such as guns.

Although the largest number of suicides occurs among older white males, since the 1960s, the rates of suicide attempts have been rising among adolescents and young adults (see **Figure 9–1**). In fact, adolescents account for 12 percent of all suicide attempts in the United States, and suicide is the third leading cause of death in that age group (Centers for Disease Control and Prevention, 1999; Hoyert et al., 1999). We cannot as yet explain the increase, though the stresses of leaving home, meeting the demands of college or a career, and surviving loneliness or broken romantic attachments seem to be particularly great at this stage of life. Although external problems such as unemployment and financial strain may also contribute to personal problems, suicidal behavior is most common among adolescents with psychological problems.

Several myths concerning suicide can be quite dangerous:

Myth: Someone who talks about committing suicide will never do it.

Fact: Most people who kill themselves have talked about it. Such comments should always be taken seriously.

Myth: Someone who has tried suicide and failed is not serious about it.

Fact: Any suicide attempt means that the person is deeply troubled and needs help immediately. A suicidal person may well try again, picking a more deadly method the second or third time around.

Myth: Only people who are life's losers—those who have failed in their careers and in their personal lives—commit suicide.

Fact: Many people who kill themselves have prestigious jobs, conventional families, and a good income. Physicians, for example, have a suicide rate several times higher than that for the general population; in some cases, the tendency to commit suicide may be related to work stresses.

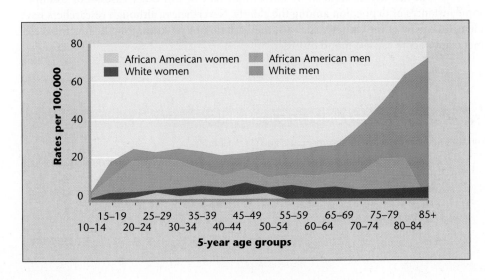

Figure 9–1

Gender and race differences in the suicide rate across the life span. The suicide rate for white males, who commit the largest number of suicides at all ages, shows a sharp rise beyond the age of 65. In contrast, the suicide rate for African-American females, which is the lowest for any group, remains relatively stable throughout the life span.

Source: Suicide and Life-Threatening Behavior by Moscicki, E. K. Copyright 1995 by Guilford Publications Inc. Reproduced with permission of Guilford Publications, Inc. in the format Textbook via Copyright Clearance Center.

mania A mood disorder characterized by euphoric states, extreme physical activity, excessive talkativeness, distractedness, and sometimes grandiosity.

bipolar disorder A mood disorder in which periods of mania and depression alternate, sometimes with periods of normal mood intervening.

People considering suicide are overwhelmed with hopelessness. They feel that things cannot get better and see no way out of their difficulties. This perception is depression in the extreme, and it is not easy to talk someone out of this state of mind. Telling a suicidal person that things aren't really so bad does no good; in fact, the person may only view this as further evidence that no one understands his or her suffering. But most suicidal people do want help, however much they may despair of obtaining it. If a friend or family member seems at all suicidal, getting professional help is urgent. A community mental health center is a good starting place, as are the national suicide hotlines.

MANIA AND BIPOLAR DISORDER

What is mania, and how is it involved in bipolar disorder?

Another mood disorder, which is less common than depression, is **mania**, a state in which the person becomes euphoric or "high," extremely active, excessively talkative, and easily distracted. People suffering from mania may become grandiose—that is, their self-esteem is greatly inflated. They typically have unlimited hopes and schemes, but little interest in realistically carrying them out. People in a manic state sometimes become aggressive and hostile toward others as their self-confidence grows more and more exaggerated. At the extreme, people going through a manic episode may become wild, incomprehensible, or violent until they collapse from exhaustion.

The mood disorder in which both mania and depression are present is known as bipolar disorder. In people with **bipolar disorder**, periods of mania and depression alternate (each lasting from a few days to a few months), sometimes with periods of normal mood in between. Occasionally, bipolar disorder occurs in a mild form, with moods of unrealistically high spirits followed by moderate depression. Research suggests that bipolar disorder is much less common than depression and, unlike depression, occurs equally in men and women. Bipolar disorder also seems to have a stronger biological component than depression: It is more strongly linked to heredity and is most often treated with drugs (Gershon, 1990; Maj, 2003; Konradi et al., 2004).

CAUSES OF MOOD DISORDERS

What causes some people to experience extreme mood changes?

Most psychologists believe that mood disorders, like most other disorders, result from a combination of risk factors (see **Table 9–1**: Major Psychological Disorders and Their Associated Causes.) Biological factors seem to be most important in some cases—for example, bipolar disorder—whereas psychological factors appear to be chiefly responsible in other cases—for example, depression following the experience of a loss (Katz & McGuffin, 1993). Social factors seem to be most important in still other cases—for example, some instances of depression among the elderly. Nevertheless, although researchers have identified many of the causative factors, they still do not yet know exactly how these elements interact to cause a mood disorder.

> ► CHECK YOUR UNDERSTANDING

Indicate whether the following statements are true (T) or false (F):

1. ___ People with a mood disorder always alternate between the extremes of euphoria and sadness.

2. ___ More men attempt suicide, but more women actually kill themselves.

3. ___ Mania is the most common mood disorder.

4. ___ Most psychologists now believe that mood disorders result from a combination of risk factors.

Answers: 1. (F), 2. (F), 3. (F), 4. (T).

> APPLY YOUR UNDERSTANDING

1. Bob has been "down in the dumps" for the last three months. He is having a difficult time dealing with any criticism he receives at work or at home. Most days he feels that he is a failure, despite the fact that he is successful in his job and his family is happy. Although he participates in various activities outside the home, he finds no joy in anything. He says he is constantly tired, but he has trouble sleeping. It is most likely that Bob is suffering from _____.

   a. major depressive disorder
   b. mania
   c. dysthymia
   d. bipolar disorder

2. Mary almost seems to be two different people. At times, she is hyperactive and talks nonstop (sometimes so fast that nobody can understand her). At those times, her friends say she is "bouncing off the walls." But then she changes: She becomes terribly sad, loses interest in eating, spends much of her time in bed, and rarely says a word. It is most likely that Mary is suffering from_____.

   a. major depressive disorder
   b. mania
   c. dysthymia
   d. bipolar disorder

Answers: 1. a, 2. d.

> TABLE 9–1 CATEGORIES OF MAJOR PSYCHOLOGICAL DISORDERS AND THEIR ASSOCIATED CAUSES

Disorder	Biological Factors	Psychological Factors	Social Factors
Mood disorders • Major clinical depression • Mania • Dysthymia • Bipolar disorder	• Genes are implicated, especially in bipolar disorder, and also some forms of depression • Levels of neurotransmitters (primarily serotonin and norepinephrine) are disrupted	• Cognitive distortions can lead to inaccurate feelings of incompetence and unworthiness • Negative self-perceptions and cognitions become learned and perpetuated	• Difficulties in personal relationships or life situations cause stress which in vulnerable individuals can lead to depression
Anxiety Disorders • Phobia • Panic Disorder • Generalized anxiety disorder • Obsessive-compulsive disorder • Acute stress disorder • Posttraumatic stress disorder	• Anxiety disorders run in families suggesting a genetic vulnerability in this disorder • Evolutionary forces may have "prepared" humans to easily learn some anxiety responses (e.g., fear of snakes and the dark)	• Strong fears can become conditioned and generalized, giving rise to phobias and other anxiety responses • Overuse of defense mechanism (defensive coping–see Chapter 8) creates anxiety, which can take the form of an anxiety disorder	• People living in highly stressful environments generally experience more anxiety in their lives
Psychosomatic, Somatoform, and Dissociative Disorders • Conversion disorder • Hypochondriasis • Body dysmorphic disorder • Dissociative identity disorder	• Some conversion disorders may be cases of misdiagnosed physical illness, such as epilepsy or multiple sclerosis • Amnesia and dissociative experiences may result from brain injury or disease	• Unconscious processes and overuse of defense mechanisms may give rise to symptoms • Symptoms may be learned responses to extreme or traumatic events, which are maintained via reinforcement	• Trauma, especially during childhood, may be involved, and cause defensive coping
Schizophrenia • Several subtypes are diagnosed	• Genes are probably involved in creating a vulnerability to this disease • May involve the faulty regulation of dopamine and glutamate neurotransmitters • Brain structural abnormalities may be involved	• Prenatal disturbances may produce brain changes • Early learning experiences may contribute in vulnerable individuals	• Disturbed family relations can contribute to the severity of symptoms

Anxiety Disorders

9.3 Describe the common features shared by the anxiety disorders and identify how the major types of disorders in this category differ from each other.

All of us are afraid from time to time, but we usually know why we are fearful. Our fear is caused by something appropriate and identifiable, and it passes with time. In the case of **anxiety disorders**, however, either the person does not know why he or she is afraid, or the anxiety is inappropriate to the circumstances. In either case, the person's fear and anxiety just don't seem to make sense.

As we noted earlier in this chapter, surveys have found that anxiety disorders are more common than any other form of mental disorder (Kessler et al., 1994; Narrow, Rae, Robins, & Regier, 2001). Anxiety disorders can be subdivided into several diagnostic categories, including specific phobias, panic disorder, and other anxiety disorders, such as generalized anxiety disorder, obsessive-compulsive disorder, and disorders caused by specific traumatic events. The major explanations for what causes anxiety disorders to develop are outlined in **Table 9–1**.

PHOBIAS

Into what three categories are phobias usually grouped?

A **specific phobia** is an intense, paralyzing fear of something that perhaps should be feared, but the fear is excessive and unreasonable. In fact, the fear in a specific phobia is so great that it leads the person to avoid routine or adaptive activities and thus interferes with life functioning. For example, it may appropriate to be a bit fearful as an airplane takes off or lands, but people with a phobia about flying refuse to get on or even go near an airplane. Other common phobias focus on animals, heights, closed places, blood, needles, and injury. About 10 percent of people in the United States suffer from at least one specific phobia.

Most people feel some mild fear or uncertainty in many social situations, but when these fears interfere significantly with life functioning, they are considered to be **social phobias**. Intense fear of public speaking is a common form of social phobia. In other cases, simply talking with people or eating in public causes such severe anxiety that the phobic person will go to great lengths to avoid these situations.

Agoraphobia is much more debilitating than most other social phobias. This term comes from Greek and Latin words that literally mean "fear of the marketplace," but the disorder typically involves multiple, intense fears, such as the fear of being alone, of being in public places from which escape might be difficult, of being in crowds, of traveling in an automobile, or of going through tunnels or over bridges. The common element in all of these situations seems to be a great dread of being separated from sources of security, such as the home or a loved one with whom the person feels safe.

Agoraphobia can greatly interfere with life functioning: Some sufferers are so fearful that they will venture only a few miles from home; others will not leave their homes at all. Although agoraphobia is less common than social phobia (it affects about 3 percent of the population), because of the severity of its effects, it is more likely to cause the sufferer to seek treatment (Robins & Regier, 1991).

PANIC DISORDER

How does a panic attack differ from fear?

Another type of anxiety disorder is **panic disorder**, characterized by recurring episodes of a sudden, unpredictable, and overwhelming fear or terror called *panic attacks* occur without any reasonable cause and are accompanied by feelings of impending doom, chest pain, dizziness or fainting, sweating, difficulty breathing, and fear of losing control or dying. Panic attacks usually last only a few minutes, but they may recur for no apparent reason. For example, consider the following description:

> A 31-year-old stewardess . . . had suddenly begun to feel panicky, dizzy, had trouble breathing, started to sweat, and trembled uncontrollably. She excused herself and sat in the back of the plane and within 10 minutes the symptoms had subsided. Two similar episodes had occurred in the past:

anxiety disorders Disorders in which anxiety is a characteristic feature or the avoidance of anxiety seems to motivate abnormal behavior.

specific phobia Anxiety disorder characterized by an intense, paralyzing fear of something.

social phobia An anxiety disorder characterized by excessive, inappropriate fears connected with social situations or performances in front of other people.

agoraphobia An anxiety disorder that involves multiple, intense fears of crowds, public places, and other situations that require separation from a source of security such as the home.

panic disorder An anxiety disorder characterized by recurrent panic attacks in which the person suddenly experiences intense fear or terror without any reasonable cause.

The first, four years previously, when the plane had encountered mild turbulence; the second, two years earlier, during an otherwise uneventful flight, as in this episode (Spitzer et al., 1981, p. 219).

Panic attacks not only cause tremendous fear while they are happening, but also leave a dread of having another panic attack, which can persist for days or even weeks after the original episode. In some cases, this dread is so overwhelming that it can lead to the development of agoraphobia: To prevent a recurrence, people may avoid any circumstance that might cause anxiety, clinging to people or situations that help keep them calm.

OTHER ANXIETY DISORDERS

How do generalized anxiety disorder and obsessive-compulsive disorder differ from specific phobias?

In the various phobias and in panic attacks, there is a specific source of anxiety, such as fear of heights, fear of social situations, or fear of being in crowds. In contrast, **generalized anxiety disorder** is defined by prolonged vague but intense fears that are not attached to any particular object or circumstance. Generalized anxiety disorder perhaps comes closest to the everyday meaning attached to the term *neurotic*. Its symptoms include the inability to relax, muscle tension, rapid heartbeat or pounding heart, apprehensiveness about the future, constant alertness to potential threats, and sleeping difficulties.

A very different form of anxiety disorder is **obsessive-compulsive disorder**, or **OCD**. *Obsessions* are involuntary thoughts or ideas that keep recurring despite the person's attempts to stop them, whereas *compulsions* are repetitive, ritualistic behaviors that a person feels compelled to perform (Patrick, 1994). Obsessive thoughts are often horrible and frightening. One patient, for example, reported that "when she thought of her boyfriend, she wished he were dead"; when her mother went down the stairs, she "wished she'd fall and break her neck"; when her sister spoke of going to the beach with her infant daughter, she "hoped that they would both drown" (Carson & Butcher, 1992, p. 190).

Truly compulsive behaviors may be equally dismaying to the person who feels driven to perform them. They often take the form of washing or cleaning, as if the compulsive behavior were the person's attempt to "wash away" the contaminating thoughts. One patient reported that her efforts to keep her clothes and body clean eventually took up six hours of her day, and even then, "washing my hands wasn't enough, and I started to use rubbing alcohol" (Spitzer et al., 1981, p. 137). Another common type of compulsion is checking: repeatedly performing some kind of behavior to make sure that something was or was not done. For example, Lindsay, the engineer who was described at the beginning of the chapter, felt compelled to double- and triple-check whether her doors were locked or her lights were off.

People who experience obsessions and compulsions often do not seem particularly anxious, so why is this disorder considered an anxiety disorder? The answer is that if such people try to stop their irrational behavior—or if someone else tries to stop them—they experience severe anxiety. In other words, the obsessive–compulsive behavior seems to have developed to keep anxiety under control. **Table 9–2** lists several major types of anxiety disorders and their associated major symptoms.

generalized anxiety disorder An anxiety disorder characterized by prolonged vague but intense fears that are not attached to any particular object or circumstance.

obsessive-compulsive disorder (OCD) An anxiety disorder in which a person feels driven to think disturbing thoughts or to perform senseless rituals.

>TABLE 9–2 COMMON ANXIETY DISORDERS

Disorder	Major Symptoms
Phobia	Intense, irrational fear of an object (specific phobia) or a social setting (social phobia)
Panic Disorder	Recurrent episodes of sudden, unpredictable, overwhelming fear or terror
Generalized Anxiety Disorder	Prolonged, vague fears not associated with particular objects or circumstances
Obsessive-compulsive disorder (OCD)	Disorder in which the person feels driven to think disturbing thoughts (obsessions) or perform senseless rituals, usually involving cleaning or checking (compulsions)
Acute Stress Disorder	Extreme anxiety reaction following soon after a traumatic event
Post-traumatic Stress Disorder	Anxiety reaction that is long-lasting or delayed following a traumatic event (See Chapter 8: "Personality, Stress, and Health.")

Psychosomatic, Somatoform, and Dissociative Disorders

9.4 Distinguish between psychosomatic disorders, somatoform disorders, and dissociative disorders and describe two examples of each.

Several psychological disorders involve symptoms that mimic those commonly associated with neurological disorders such as multiple sclerosis, stroke, and epilepsy. When neurological problems do not have a physical cause, but rather occur as the result of psychological forces, they are typically diagnosed as being psychosomatic, dissociative, or somatoform disorders.

MIND-BODY DISORDERS

What are the differences among psychosomatic disorders, somatoform, and dissociative disorders?

PSYCHOSOMATIC DISORDERS The term *psychosomatic* perfectly captures the interplay of *psyche* (mind) and *soma* (body), which characterizes these disorders. A **psychosomatic disorder** is a real, physical disorder, but one that has, at least in part, a psychological cause. Tension headaches are an example of a psychosomatic disorder. They are caused by muscle contractions brought on by stress. The headache is real, but it is called "psychosomatic" because psychological factors (such as stress and anxiety) appear to play an important role in causing the symptoms. People suffering from tension headaches are often taught relaxation techniques that relieve stress and reduce muscle tension.

Scientists used to believe that psychological factors contributed to the development of some physical illnesses, principally headaches, allergies, asthma, and high blood pressure, but not others, such as infectious diseases. Today modern medicine leans toward the idea that all physical ailments are to some extent "psychosomatic"—in the sense that stress, anxiety, and various states of emotional arousal alter body chemistry, the functioning of bodily organs, and the body's immune system (which is vital in fighting

Tension headaches, resulting from muscles clenched in response to stress, are a classic psychosomatic disorder. Many physicians now believe that nearly all diseases have a psychosomatic component and that the mind contributes in many ways to the health of the body.

psychosomatic disorders Disorders in which there is real physical illness that is largely caused by psychological factors such as stress and anxiety.

infections) (see Chapter 8: "Personality, Stress, and Health"). Because virtually every physical disease can be linked to psychological stress, DSM-IV does not contain a separate list of psychosomatic disorders.

SOMATOFORM DISORDERS Psychosomatic disorders involve genuine physical illnesses, but in **somatoform disorders**, physical symptoms occur without any identifiable physical cause. Common complaints are back pain, dizziness, abdominal pain, and sometimes anxiety and depression. People suffering from somatoform disorders believe that they are physically ill and describe symptoms that sound like physical illnesses, but medical examinations reveal no organic problems. Nevertheless, people who suffer from these disorders are not consciously seeking to mislead others about their physical condition. The symptoms are real to them and are not under voluntary control (APA, 2000).

One of the more dramatic forms of somatoform disorder involves complaints of paralysis, blindness, deafness, seizures, loss of feeling, or pregnancy. In these **conversion disorders**, no physical causes appear, yet the symptoms are very real. Yet another somatoform disorder is **hypochondriasis**. Here, the person interprets some small symptom—perhaps a cough, a bruise, or perspiration—as a sign of a serious disease. Although the symptom may actually exist, there is no evidence that the serious illness does. Repeated assurances have little effect, and the person is likely to visit one doctor after another, searching for a medical authority who will share his or her conviction.

Body dysmorphic disorder, or imagined ugliness, is a recently diagnosed and poorly understood type of somatoform disorder. Cases of body dysmorphic disorder can be very striking. One man, for example, felt that people stared at his "pointed ears" and "large nostrils" so much that he eventually could not face going to work, so he quit his job. Clearly, people who become that preoccupied with their appearance cannot lead a normal life. Ironically, most people who suffer body dysmorphic disorder are not ugly. They may be average looking or even attractive, but they are unable to evaluate their looks realistically. Many people with this disorder seek physical treatment (such as plastic surgery) rather than psychotherapy.

DISSOCIATIVE DISORDERS **Dissociative disorders** are among the most puzzling forms of mental disorders, both to the observer and to the sufferer. *Dissociation* means that part of an individual's personality appears to be separated from the rest. The disorder usually involves memory loss, called *amnesia*, and a complete, though generally temporary, change in identity. Rarely, several distinct personalities appear in one person.

Loss of memory without an organic cause can occur as a reaction to an extremely stressful event or period. During World War II, for example, some hospitalized soldiers could not recall what their names were, where they lived, where they were born, or how they came to be in battle. But war and its horrors are not the only causes of *dissociative amnesia*. The person who betrays a friend in a business deal or the victim of rape may also forget, selectively, what has happened. Sometimes an amnesia victim leaves home and assumes an entirely new identity, although this phenomenon, known as *dissociative fugue*, is very unusual.

In **dissociative identity disorder**, commonly known as *multiple personality disorder*, several distinct personalities emerge at different times. Although this dramatic disorder has been the subject of popular fiction and films, most psychologists believe it to be extremely rare, although in recent years, the number of cases appears to be increasing (Eich, Macaulay, Loewenstein, & Dihle, 1997). In the true multiple personality, the various personalities are distinct people with their own names, identities, memories, mannerisms, speaking voices, and even IQs. Sometimes the personalities are so separate that they don't know they inhabit a body with other "people." At other times, the personalities do know of the existence of other "people" and even make disparaging remarks about them. Typically, the personalities contrast sharply with one another, as if each one represents different aspects of the same person—one being the more socially acceptable, "nice" side of the person and the other being the darker, more uninhibited or "evil" side.

somatoform disorders Disorders in which there is an apparent physical illness for which there is no organic basis.

conversion disorders Somatoform disorders in which a dramatic specific disability has no physical cause but instead seems related to psychological problems.

hypochondriasis A somatoform disorder in which a person interprets insignificant symptoms as signs of serious illness in the absence of any organic evidence of such illness.

body dysmorphic disorder A somatoform disorder in which a person becomes so preoccupied with his or her imagined ugliness that normal life is impossible.

dissociative disorders Disorders in which some aspect of the personality seems separated from the rest.

dissociative identity disorder (Formerly called multiple personality disorder.) Disorder characterized by the separation of the personality into two or more distinct personalities.

When she was found by a Florida park ranger, Jane Doe was suffering from amnesia. She could not recall her name, her past, or how to read and write. She never regained her memory of the past.

► CHECK YOUR UNDERSTANDING

Indicate whether the following statements are true (T) or false (F):

1. ___ Modern medicine leans toward the idea that all physical ailments are to some extent "psychosomatic."

2. ___ People who suffer from somatoform disorders do not consciously seek to mislead others about their physical condition.

3. ___ Research has shown that at least some diagnosed somatoform disorders actually were real physical illnesses that were overlooked or misdiagnosed.

4. _____ _____ usually involve memory loss and a complete—though generally temporary—change in identity.

5. Dissociative disorders, like conversion disorders, seem to involve _____ processes.

Answers: 1. (T), 2. (T), 3. (T), 4. dissociative disorders, 5. unconscious.

► APPLY YOUR UNDERSTANDING

1. Bob is concerned about a few warts that have appeared on his arms. His doctor says that they are just warts and are not a concern, but Bob believes they are cancerous and that he will die from them. He consults another doctor and then another, both of whom tell him they are just normal warts, but he remains convinced they are cancerous and he is going to die. It appears that Bob is suffering from _____.
   a. hypochondriasis
   b. a psychosomatic disorder
   c. a somatoform disorder
   d. a phobia

2. John is a writer, but work on his latest novel has come to a halt because he has lost all feeling in his arm and his hand. His doctor can find no physical cause for his problem; however, there is no question that he no longer has feeling in his arm and that he can no longer hold a pencil or type on a keyboard. It seems likely that John is suffering from _____.
   a. body dysmorphic disorder
   b. hypochondriasis
   c. conversion disorder
   d. dissociative disorder

3. A person who was being interrogated by the police confessed on tape to having committed several murders. When the alleged killer was brought to trial, his lawyers agreed that the voice on the tape belonged to their client. But they asserted that the person who confessed was another personality that lived inside the body of their client. In other words, they claimed that their client was suffering from _____.
   a. depersonalization disorder
   b. dissociative identity disorder
   c. conversion disorder
   d. body dysmorphic disorder

4. You are reading the newspaper and come across a story of a young man who was found wandering the streets with no recollection of who he was, where he came from, or how he got there. You suspect that he is most likely suffering from _____.
   a. depersonalization disorder
   b. dissociative amnesia
   c. conversion disorder
   d. body dysmorphic disorder

Answers: 1. a., 2. c., 3. b., 4. b.

Schizophrenic Disorders

9.5   List the symptoms commonly seen in cases of schizophrenia and explain why this disorder is usually considered to involve psychosis.

Schizophrenic disorders are severe conditions marked by disordered thoughts and communications, inappropriate emotions, and bizarre behavior that lasts for months or even years. People with schizophrenia are out of touch with reality, which is to say that they are **psychotic**. *Psychosis* is sometimes confused with insanity, but the terms are not synonymous. **Insanity** is the legal term for people who are found not to be responsible for their criminal actions.

SYMPTOMS OF SCHIZOPHRENIA

How is schizophrenia different from dissociative identity disorder?

A common misconception is that *schizophrenia* means "split personality." But, as we have seen, split personality (or multiple personality) is actually a dissociative identity disorder.

schizophrenic disorders Severe disorders in which there are disturbances of thoughts, communications, and emotions, including delusions and hallucinations.

psychotic (psychosis) Behavior characterized by a loss of touch with reality.

insanity Legal term for mentally disturbed people who are not considered responsible for their criminal actions.

The misunderstanding comes from the fact that the root *schizo* derives from the Greek verb meaning "to split." What is split in schizophrenia is not so much personality as the connections among thoughts.

People with schizophrenia often suffer from **hallucinations**, false sensory perceptions that usually take the form of hearing voices that are not really there. (Visual, tactile, or olfactory hallucinations are more likely to indicate substance abuse or organic brain damage.) They also frequently have **delusions**—false beliefs about reality with no factual basis—that distort their relationships with their surroundings and with other people. Typically, these delusions are *paranoid*: People with schizophrenia often believe that someone is out to harm them. They may think that a doctor wants to kill them or that they are receiving radio messages from aliens invading from outer space. They often regard their own bodies—as well as the outside world—as hostile and alien. Because their world is utterly different from reality, people with schizophrenia usually cannot live a normal life unless they are successfully treated with medication. Often, they are unable to communicate with others, because their words are incoherent when they speak. The following case illustrates some of the major characteristics of schizophrenia:

> For many years [a 35-year-old widow] has heard voices, which insult her and cast suspicion on her chastity. . . . The voices are very distinct, and in her opinion, they must be carried by telescope or a machine from her home. Her thoughts are dictated to her; she is obliged to think them, and hears them repeated after her. She ... has all kinds of uncomfortable sensations in her body, to which something is "done." In particular, her "mother parts" are turned inside out, and people send a pain through her back, lay ice water on her heart, squeeze her neck, injure her spine, and violate her. There are also hallucinations of sight—black figures and the altered appearance of people—but these are far less frequent. (Spitzer et al., 1981, pp. 308–309)

SUBTYPES OF SCHIZOPHRENIA

How do the subtypes of schizophrenia differ from each other?

There are actually several kinds of schizophrenic disorders, which have different characteristic symptoms.

Disorganized schizophrenia includes some of the more bizarre symptoms of schizophrenia, such as giggling, grimacing, and frantic gesturing. People suffering from disorganized schizophrenia show a childish disregard for social conventions and may urinate or defecate at inappropriate times. They are active, but aimless, and they are often given to incoherent conversations.

In **catatonic schizophrenia**, motor activity is severely disturbed. People in this state may remain immobile, mute, and impassive. They may behave in a robotlike fashion when ordered to move, and they may even let doctors put their arms and legs into uncomfortable positions that they maintain for hours. At the opposite extreme, they may become excessively excited, talking and shouting continuously.

Paranoid schizophrenia is marked by extreme suspiciousness and complex delusions. People with paranoid schizophrenia may believe themselves to be Napoleon or the Virgin Mary, or they may insist that Russian spies with laser guns are constantly on their trail because they have learned some great secret. As they are less likely to be incoherent or to look or act "crazy," these people can appear more "normal" than people with other schizophrenic disorders when their delusions are compatible with everyday life. They may, however, become hostile or aggressive toward anyone who questions their thinking or delusions. Note that this disorder is far more severe than paranoid personality disorder, which does not involve bizarre delusions or loss of touch with reality.

Finally, **undifferentiated schizophrenia** is the classification developed for people who have several of the characteristic symptoms of schizophrenia—such as delusions, hallucinations, or incoherence—yet do not show the typical symptoms of any other subtype of the disorder.

hallucinations Sensory experiences in the absence of external stimulation.

delusions False beliefs about reality that have no basis in fact.

disorganized schizophrenia Schizophrenic disorder in which bizarre and childlike behaviors are common.

catatonic schizophrenia Schizophrenic disorder in which disturbed motor behavior is prominent.

paranoid schizophrenia Schizophrenic disorder marked by extreme suspiciousness and complex, bizarre delusions.

undifferentiated schizophrenia Schizophrenic disorder in which there are clear schizophrenic symptoms that do not meet the criteria for another subtype of the disorder.

CAUSES OF SCHIZOPHRENIA

Is schizophrenia inherited?

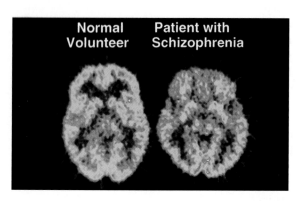

Normal Volunteer **Patient with Schizophrenia**

Figure 9–2

Neuroimages of a normal person's and a Schizophrenic's brain. Neuroimaging technique, such as this PET scan, often reveal important differences between the brains of people with schizophrenia and normal volunteers. Still, neuroimaging does not provide a decisive diagnostic test for schizophrenia.

Because schizophrenia is a very serious disorder, considerable research has been directed at trying to discover its causes (Heinrichs, 2001). Many studies indicate that schizophrenia has a genetic component (Gerber et al., 2003; Gottesman, 1991; Hashimoto et al., 2003). People with schizophrenia are more likely than other people to have children with schizophrenia, even when those children have lived with adoptive parents since early in life. If one identical twin suffers from schizophrenia, the chances are almost 50 percent that the other twin will also develop this disorder. In fraternal twins, if one twin has schizophrenia, the chances are only about 17 percent that the other twin will develop it.

Recent research suggests that the biological predisposition to schizophrenia may involve the faulty regulation of the neurotransmitters dopamine and glutamate in the central nervous system (Goff & Coyle, 2001; Javitt & Coyle, 2004; Koh et al., 2003). Some research also indicates that pathology in various structures of the brain may influence the onset of schizophrenia (Chance, Esiri, & Timothy, 2003; Flashman & Green, 2004; van Elst & Trimble, 2003; Weiss et al., 2004; Yotsutsuji et al., 2003)(see **Figure 9–2**). Other studies link schizophrenia to some form of early prenatal disturbance (Wolf & Weinberger, 1996). Nevertheless, scientists typically find only nonsignificant differences in brain structure and chemistry between schizophrenic and healthy people (Noga, Bartley, Jones, Torrey, & Weinberger, 1996). As yet, no laboratory tests can diagnose schizophrenia on the basis of brain abnormalities alone. In fact, studies of identical twins in which only one suffers from schizophrenia have sometimes found more evidence of brain abnormalities in the well twin than in the sick twin.

Studies of identical twins have also been used to identify the importance of environment in causing schizophrenia. Because identical twins are genetically identical and because half of the identical twins of people with schizophrenia do not develop schizophrenia themselves, this severe and puzzling disorder cannot be caused by genetic factors alone. Environmental factors—ranging from disturbed family relations to taking drugs to biological damage that may occur at any age, even before birth—must also figure in determining whether a person will develop schizophrenia.

Schizophrenia appears to be a complex disorder with multiple causes. Consequently, models that propose that both biological and environmental explanations are involved seem most appropriate. Recall that the diathesis-stress model would predict that environment and experience can increase or decrease the effects of any inherited tendency. According to the systems model, it is a combination of biological, psychological, and social factors that produce the symptoms of schizophrenia in vulnerable individuals.

> **CHECK YOUR UNDERSTANDING**

Indicate whether the following statements are true (T) or false (F):

1. ___ Schizophrenia is almost the same thing as multiple personality disorder.

2. ___ Psychotic symptoms, or loss of contact with reality, are indicators that a person suffers from disorders other than schizophrenia.

3. ___ Studies indicate that a biological predisposition to schizophrenia may be inherited.

4. ___ *Insanity* is the legal term for mentally disturbed people who are found not to be responsible for their criminal actions.

5. ___ Laboratory tests can be used to diagnose schizophrenia on the basis of brain abnormalities.

Answers: 1. (F), 2. (F), 3. (T), 4. (T), 5. (F).

Other Common Disorders

9.6   Describe the major features of the sexual and gender-identity disorders, the personality disorders, and the most common disorders of childhood and identify two examples of specific disorders in each category.

The DSM identifies several categories of disorders. Along with those already discussed are disorders involving unusual sexual behavior or gender-identity issues, those that center on a personality disorder, and those that typically occur during childhood.

SEXUAL AND GENDER-IDENTITY DISORDERS

What are the three main types of sexual disorders?

Ideas about what is normal and abnormal in sex vary with the times—and the individual. Alfred Kinsey and his associates showed years ago that many Americans enjoy a variety of sexual activities, some of which were, and still are, forbidden by law (1948, 1953). As psychologists became more aware of the diversity of "normal" sexual behaviors, they increasingly narrowed their definition of what constitutes abnormal sexual behavior. Today the DSM-IV-RT recognizes only three main types of sexual disorders: sexual dysfunction, paraphilias, and gender-identity disorders.

Sexual dysfunction is the loss or impairment of the ordinary physical responses of sexual function. In men, this usually takes the form of *erectile disorder* (ED), the inability to achieve or maintain an erection. In women, it often takes the form of *female sexual arousal disorder*, the inability to become sexually excited or to reach orgasm. (These conditions were once called "impotence" and "frigidity," respectively, but professionals in the field have rejected these terms as too negative and judgmental.) Occasional problems with achieving or maintaining an erection in men or with lubrication or reaching orgasm in women are common. Only when the condition is frequent or constant and when enjoyment of sexual relationships becomes impaired should it be considered serious. The incidences of ED are quite high, even among otherwise healthy men. In one survey, 25 percent of 40- to 70-year-old men had moderate ED. Less than half the men in this age group reported having no ED (Lamberg, 1998). Fortunately, new medications, such as Viagra, Levitra, and Cialis, are extremely effective in treating ED (Dinsmore et al., 1999; Goldstein et al., 1998; Marks, Duda, Dorey, Macairan, & Santos, 1999; Meston & Frohlich, 2000). But although these medications can help a man keep an erection, they will not produce an erection unless a man is also sexually aroused.

Repeated use of nonhuman objects, such as shoes, underwear, or leather goods, as the preferred or exclusive method of achieving sexual excitement is known as fetishism.

sexual dysfunction Loss or impairment of the ordinary physical responses of sexual function.

A second group of sexual disorders, known as **paraphilias**, involves the use of unconventional sex objects or situations to obtain sexual arousal. Most people have unusual sexual fantasies at some time, and this kind of fantasizing can be a healthy stimulant of normal sexual enjoyment. **Fetishism**—the repeated use of a nonhuman object such as a shoe or underwear as the preferred or exclusive method of achieving sexual excitement—is considered a sexual disorder, however. Fetishes are typically articles of women's clothing or items made out of rubber or leather (Junginger, 1997; Mason, 1997). Most people who practice fetishism are male, and the fetish frequently begins during adolescence. At least one theorist has suggested that fetishes derive from unusual learning experiences: As their sexual drive develops during adolescence, some boys learn to associate arousal with inanimate objects, perhaps as a result of early sexual exploration while masturbating or because of difficulties in social relationships (Bertolini, 2001; Wilson, 1987).

One of the most serious paraphilias is **pedophilia**, which is technically defined as "recurrent, intense sexually arousing fantasies, sexual urges, or behaviors involving sexual activity with a prepubescent child" (APA, 1994, p. 528). Child sexual abuse is shockingly common in the United States, and the abuser usually is someone close to the child. Pedophiles are almost invariably men under age 40 (Barbaree & Seto, 1997). Although there is no single cause of pedophilia, some of the most common explanations are that pedophiles cannot adjust to the adult sexual role and have been interested exclusively in children as sex objects since adolescence; they turn to children as sexual objects in response to stress in adult relationships in which they feel inadequate; or they have records of unstable social adjustment and generally commit sexual offenses against children in response to a temporary aggressive mood. Studies also indicate that the majority of pedophiles have histories of sexual frustration and failure, tend to perceive themselves as immature, and are rather dependent, unassertive, lonely, and insecure (Cohen & Galynker, 2002).

Gender-identity disorders involve the desire to become—or the insistence that one really is—a member of the other sex. Some little boys, for example, want to be girls instead. They may reject boys' clothing, desire to wear their sister's clothes, and play only with girls and with toys that are considered "girls' toys." Similarly, some girls wear boys' clothing and play only with boys and "boys' toys." When such children are uncomfortable being a male or a female and are unwilling to accept themselves as such, the diagnosis is *gender-identity disorder in children*.

The causes of gender-identity disorders are not known. Both animal research and the fact that these disorders are often apparent from early childhood suggest that biological factors, such as prenatal hormonal imbalances, are major contributors. Family dynamics and learning experiences, however, may also be contributing factors.

PERSONALITY DISORDERS

Which personality disorder creates the most significant problems for society?

In Chapter 8, we saw that personality is the individual's unique and enduring pattern of thoughts, feelings, and behavior. We also saw that despite having certain characteristic views of the world and ways of doing things, people normally can adjust their behavior to fit different situations. But some people, starting at some point early in life, develop inflexible and maladaptive ways of thinking and behaving that are so exaggerated and rigid that they cause serious distress to themselves or problems to others. People with such **personality disorders** range from harmless eccentrics to cold-blooded killers. A personality disorder may also coexist with one of the other problems already discussed in this chapter: Someone with a personality disorder may also become depressed, develop sexual problems, and so on. Several major personality disorders and their descriptions are presented in **Table 9–3**.

ANTISOCIAL PERSONALITY DISORDER One of the most widely studied personality disorders is **antisocial personality disorder**. People who exhibit this disorder lie, steal, cheat, and show little or no sense of responsibility, although they often seem intelligent and charming at first. The "con man" exemplifies many of the features of the antisocial person-

paraphilias Sexual disorders in which unconventional objects or situations cause sexual arousal.

fetishism A paraphilia in which a nonhuman object is the preferred or exclusive method of achieving sexual excitement.

pedophilia Desire to have sexual relations with children as the preferred or exclusive method of achieving sexual excitement.

gender-identity disorders Disorders that involve the desire to become, or the insistence that one really is, a member of the other biological sex.

personality disorders Disorders in which inflexible and maladaptive ways of thinking and behaving learned early in life cause distress to the person or conflicts with others.

antisocial personality disorder Personality disorder that involves a pattern of violent, criminal, or unethical and exploitative behavior and an inability to feel affection for others.

> TABLE 9-3 MAJOR PERSONALITY DISORDERS

Personality Disorder	Primary Symptoms
schizoid personality disorder	Person affected is withdrawn and lacks feelings for others
paranoid personality disorder	Person affected is inappropriately suspicious and mistrustful of others
dependent personality disorder	Person affected is unable to make choices and decisions independently and cannot tolerate being alone
avoidant personality disorder	Fear of rejection experienced by the person affected leads to social isolation
narcissistic personality disorder	Person affected has an exaggerated sense of self-importance and needs constant admiration
borderline personality disorder	Person affected experiences marked instability in self-image, mood, and interpersonal relationships
antisocial personality disorder	Person affected exhibits a pattern of violent, criminal, or unethical and exploitative behavior and an inability to feel affection for others

ality, as does the person who compulsively cheats business partners, because she or he knows their weak points. Antisocial personalities rarely show any anxiety or guilt about their behavior. Indeed, they are likely to blame society or their victims for the antisocial actions that they themselves commit.

People with antisocial personality disorder, such as the man in the following description, are responsible for a good deal of crime and violence:

> Although intelligent, [G.] was a poor student and was frequently accused of stealing from his schoolmates. At the age of 14, he stole a car, and at the age of 20, he was imprisoned for burglary. After he was released, he spent another two years in prison for drunk driving and then eleven years for a series of armed robberies. Released from prison yet one more time in 1976, he tried to hold down several jobs, but succeeded at none of them. He moved in with a woman whom he had met one day earlier, but he drank heavily (a habit that he had picked up at age 10) and struck her children until she ordered him out of the house at gunpoint. "It seems like things have always gone bad for me," he later said. "It seems like I've always done dumb things that just caused trouble for me." (Spitzer, Skodal, Gibbon, & Williams, 1983, p. 68)

On psychiatric evaluation, this man was found to have a superior IQ of 129 and considerable general knowledge. He slept and ate well and showed no significant changes of mood. He admitted to having "made a mess of life," but added that "I never stew about the things I have done." This person, Gary Gilmore, was executed for murder in 1977.

Approximately 3 percent of American men and less than 1 percent of American women suffer from antisocial personality disorder. It is not surprising that prison inmates show high rates of antisocial personality disorder: One study identified it in 50 percent of the populations of two prisons (Hare, 1983). Not all people with antisocial personality disorder are convicted criminals, however. Many manipulate others for their own gain while avoiding the criminal justice system.

Similar to many other serious psychological disorders, antisocial personality disorder seems to result from a combination of biological predisposition, difficult life experiences, and an unhealthy social environment (Moffitt, 1993). Some findings suggest that heredity is a risk factor for the later development of antisocial behavior (Fu et al., 2002; Lyons et al., 1995). Impulsive violence and aggression have also been linked with abnormal levels of certain neurotransmitters (Virkkunen, 1983). Although none of this research is definitive, the weight of evidence suggests that some people with antisocial personalities are less responsive to stress and thus are more likely to engage in thrill-seeking behaviors that may be harmful to themselves or others (Patrick, 1994). Because they respond less emotionally to

Gary Gilmore, who was attracted to a life of crime including the murder of at least two people, exhibited the central characteristics of antisocial personality disorder. He was found guilty of murder and executed in 1977, after a highly publicized trial.

stress, punishment does not affect them as it does other people (Hare, 1993). Another intriguing explanation for the cause of antisocial personality disorder is that it arises as a consequence of damage to the prefrontal region of the brain during infancy (Anderson, Bechara, Damasio, Tranel, & Damasio, 1999).

Some psychologists feel that emotional deprivation in early childhood predisposes people to antisocial personality disorder. The child for whom no one cares, say psychologists, cares for no one. Respect for others is the basis of our social code, but when you cannot see things from another person's perspective, behavior "rules" seem like nothing more than an assertion of adult power to be defied.

Family influences may also prevent the normal learning of rules of conduct in the preschool and school years. A child who has been rejected by one or both parents is not likely to develop adequate social skills or appropriate social behavior. Further, the high incidence of antisocial behavior in people with an antisocial parent suggests that antisocial behavior may be partly learned and partly inherited. After serious misbehavior begins in childhood, there is an almost predictable progression: The child's conduct leads to rejection by peers and failure in school, followed by affiliation with other children who have behavior problems. By late childhood or adolescence, the deviant patterns that will later show up as a full-blown antisocial personality disorder are well established (Hill, 2003; Patterson, DeBaryshe, & Ramsey, 1989).

Cognitive theorists emphasize that in addition to the failure to learn rules and develop self-control, moral development may be arrested among children who are emotionally rejected and inadequately disciplined (Soyguet & Tuerkcapar, 2001). For example, between the ages of about 7 and 11, all children are likely to respond to unjust treatment by behaving unjustly toward someone else who is vulnerable. At about age 13, when they are better able to reason in abstract terms, most children begin to think more in terms of fairness than vindictiveness, especially if new cognitive skills and moral concepts are reinforced by parents and peers (M. W. Berkowitz & Gibbs, 1983). Some theorists suggest that people with antisocial personality disorder may not have successfully completed this moral transition.

CHILDHOOD DISORDERS

Why do stimulants appear to slow down hyperactive children and adults?

Children, like adults, may suffer from many of the conditions already discussed in this chapter—for example, depression and anxiety disorders. But other disorders are either characteristic of children or are first evident in childhood. The DSM-IV-RT contains a long list of "disorders usually first diagnosed in infancy, childhood, or adolescence." Two of these disorders are attention-deficit/hyperactivity disorder and autistic disorder.

Attention-deficit/hyperactivity disorder (ADHD) was once known simply as *hyperactivity*. The new name reflects the fact that children with the disorder typically have trouble focusing their attention in the sustained way that other children do. Instead, they are easily distracted, often fidgety and impulsive, and almost constantly in motion. Many theorists believe that this disorder—which affects nearly 5 percent of all school-age children and is much more common in boys than girls—is present at birth, but becomes a serious problem only after the child starts school. The class setting demands that children sit quietly, pay attention as instructed, follow directions, and inhibit urges to yell and run around. The child with ADHD simply cannot conform to these demands.

We do not yet know what causes ADHD, but most theorists assume that biological factors are influential (Filipek et al., 1997; Vaidya et. al., 1998). Family interaction and other social experiences may be more important in preventing the disorder than in causing it. That is, some exceptionally competent parents and patient, tolerant teachers may be able to teach "difficult" children to conform to the demands of schooling. Although some psychologists train the parents of children with ADHD in these management skills, the most frequent treatment for these children is a type of drug known as a *psychostimulant*. Psychostimulants do not work by "slowing down" hyperactive children; rather, they appear to increase the children's ability to focus their attention so that they can attend to the task at hand, which decreases their hyperactivity (Barkley, 1990). Unfortunately, psychostimulants often produce only short-term benefits, and their use is controversial (Panksepp, 1998).

attention-deficit/hyperactivity disorder (ADHD) A childhood disorder characterized by inattention, impulsiveness, and hyperactivity.

A different and profoundly serious disorder that usually becomes evident in the first few years of life is **autistic disorder**. Autistic children fail to form normal attachments to parents, remaining distant and withdrawn into their own separate worlds. As infants, they may even show distress at being picked up or held. As they grow older, they typically do not speak, or they develop a peculiar speech pattern called *echolalia*, in which they repeat the words said to them. Autistic children typically show strange motor behavior, such as repeating body movements endlessly or walking constantly on tiptoe. They don't play as normal children do; they are not at all social and may use toys in odd ways, constantly spinning the wheels on a toy truck or tearing paper into strips. Autistic children often display the symptoms of retardation (LaMalfa, Lassi, Bertelli, Salvini, & Placidi, 2004), but it is hard to test their mental ability, because they generally don't talk. The disorder lasts into adulthood in the great majority of cases.

We don't know what causes autism, although most theorists believe that it results almost entirely from biological conditions (Goode, 2004). Some causes of mental retardation, such as fragile X syndrome (see Chapter 7), also seem to increase the risk of autistic disorder. Recent evidence suggests that genetics also play a strong role in causing the disorder (Bailey et al., 1995; Cook et al., 1998; Lamb, Moore, Bailey, & Monaco, 2000; Nurmi et al., 2003; Rodier, 2000).

autistic disorder A childhood disorder characterized by lack of social instincts and strange motor behavior.

▶ CHECK YOUR UNDERSTANDING

Match each of the following terms with the appropriate description:

1. ___ pedophilia
2. ___ gender-identity disorder
3. ___ female sexual arousal disorder
4. ___ paraphilias
   a. The inability for a woman to become sexually excited or to reach orgasm.
   b. Involve the use of unconventional sex objects or situations to obtain sexual arousal.
   c. Recurrent, intense sexually arousing fantasies, sexual urges, or behaviors involving sexual activity with a prepubescent child.

d. The desire to become—or the insistence that one really is—a member of the other biological sex.

Indicate whether the following statements are true (T) or false (F):

5. ___ ADHD is much more common in boys than in girls.
6. ___ Psychostimulants work by slowing down the activity of the nervous systems of hyperactive children.
7. ___ Most theorists believe that autistic disorder results almost entirely from biological conditions.

Answers: 1. c., 2. d., 3. a., 4. b., 5. (T), 6. (F), 7. (T).

▶ APPLY YOUR UNDERSTANDING

1. A man is arrested for stealing women's underwear from clotheslines and adding them to the large collection he has hidden in his home. He says that he finds the clothing sexually exciting. It would appear that he is suffering from _____.
   a. erectile disorder
   b. gender-identity disorder
   c. pedophilia
   d. fetishism

2. John represents himself as a stockbroker who specializes in investing the life savings of elderly people, but he never invests the money. Instead, he puts it into his own bank account and then flees the country. When he is caught and asked how he feels about financially destroying elderly people, he explains, "Hey, if they were stupid enough to give me their money, they deserved what they got." John is most likely suffering from
   _____.
   a. multiple personality disorder
   b. autism
   c. antisocial personality disorder
   d. paraphilia

3. Harry is a child who is usually distant and withdrawn. He doesn't seem to form attachments with anyone, even his parents. He plays by himself. He rarely talks; when he does, it is usually to repeat what someone else just said to him. It is most likely that Harry is suffering from _____.
   a. attention-deficit/hyperactivity disorder
   b. autistic disorder
   c. bipolar disorder
   d. disorganized personality disorder

Answers: 1. d., 2. c., 3. b.

psychotherapy The use of psychological techniques to treat personality and behavior disorders.

insight therapies A variety of individual psychotherapies designed to give people a better awareness and understanding of their feelings, motivations, and actions in the hope that this will help them to adjust.

psychoanalysis The theory of personality Freud developed, as well as the form of therapy he invented.

free association A psychoanalytic technique that encourages the person to talk without inhibition about whatever thoughts or fantasies come to mind.

transference The client's carrying over to the analyst feelings held toward childhood authority figures.

The consulting room where Freud met his clients. Note the position of Freud's chair at the head of the couch. In order to encourage free association, the psychoanalyst has to function as a blank screen onto which the client can project his or her feelings. To accomplish this, Freud believed, the psychoanalyst has to stay out of sight of the client.

Psychotherapies

9.7 Compare and contrast the philosophies and techniques of insight therapies, behavior therapies, cognitive therapies, and group therapies, and suggest how each works to help clients deal with psychological disorders.

The previous sections of this chapter identify and briefly describe several of the major types of psychological disorders that individuals experience. As you have seen, such disorders can result from multiple causes—inherited and biological abnormalities in the structure or functioning of the brain, psychological difficulties including poor self-concept and inadequate coping skills, and social factors such as trauma and abuse, especially if these occur in childhood. In the remaining sections of this chapter, we describe some of the more commonly used treatments for these disorders. As you will see, biologically-based treatments, including drug therapies, are sometimes helpful in alleviating symptoms. Before we discuss biological forms of therapy, however, we first present an overview of some of the various types of **psychotherapy** that have been developed to help people cope with the disorders they experience. Many of these therapies are linked to the theoretical traditions discussed in earlier chapters, especially Chapter 8: "Personality, Stress, and Health."

INSIGHT THERAPIES

What do insight therapies have in common?

Several of the individual psychotherapies used in both private practice and institutions fall under the heading of **insight therapies**. Although the various insight therapies differ in their details, their common goal is to give people a better awareness and understanding of their feelings, motivations, and actions in the hope that this will lead to better adjustment (Pine, 1998). In this section, we consider three major insight therapies: psychoanalysis, client-centered therapy, and Gestalt therapy.

PSYCHOANALYSIS **Psychoanalysis** is designed to bring hidden feelings and motives to conscious awareness so that the person can deal with them more effectively.

In Freudian psychoanalysis, the client is instructed to talk about whatever comes to mind, with as little editing as possible and without inhibiting or controlling thoughts and fantasies. This process is called **free association**. Freud believed that the resulting "stream of consciousness" would provide insight into the person's unconscious mind. During the early stages of psychoanalysis, the analyst remains impassive, mostly silent, and out of the person's sight. In classical psychoanalysis, the client lies on a couch while the analyst sits quietly behind the client. The analyst's silence is a kind of "blank screen" onto which the person projects unconscious thoughts and feelings.

Eventually, clients may test their analyst by talking about desires and fantasies that they have never revealed to anyone else. But the analyst maintains neutrality throughout, showing little of his or her own feelings and personality. When clients discover that their analyst is not shocked or disgusted by their revelations, they are reassured and transfer to their analyst feelings they have toward authority figures from their childhood. This process is known as **transference**. It is said to be *positive transference* when the person feels good about the analyst.

As people continue to expose their innermost feelings, they begin to feel increasingly vulnerable. They want reassurance and affection, but their analyst remains silent. Their anxiety builds. Threatened by their analyst's silence and by their own thoughts, clients may feel cheated and perhaps accuse their analyst of being a money grabber. Or they may suspect that their analyst is really disgusted by their disclosures or is laughing about them behind their backs. This *negative transference* is thought to be a crucial step in psychoanalysis, for it presumably reveals negative feelings toward authority figures and resistance to uncovering repressed emotions.

As therapy progresses, the analyst takes a more active role and begins to *interpret* or suggest alternative meanings for clients' feelings, memories, and actions. The goal of interpretation is to help people to gain **insight**—to become aware of what was formerly outside their awareness. As what was unconscious becomes conscious, clients may come to see how their childhood experiences have determined how they currently feel and act. Analysts encourage their clients to confront childhood events and to recall them fully. As these clients relive their childhood traumas, they become able to resolve conflicts they could not resolve in the past. *Working through* old conflicts is thought to provide people with the chance to review and revise the feelings and beliefs that underlie their problems.

Only a handful of people who seek therapy go into traditional psychoanalysis. As Freud himself recognized, analysis requires great motivation to change and an ability to deal rationally with whatever the analysis uncovers. Moreover, traditional analysis may take five years or longer, with three, sometimes five, sessions a week. Few people can afford this kind of treatment. Fewer still possess the verbal and analytical skills necessary to discuss thoughts and feelings in this detailed way. And many want more immediate help for their problems. Moreover, for those with severe disorders, psychoanalysis generally is not effective.

LASSIE! GET HELP!!

CLIENT-CENTERED THERAPY Carl Rogers, the founder of **client-centered** (or **person-centered**) **therapy**, took bits and pieces of the psychoanalytic view and revised and rearranged them into a radically different approach. According to Rogers, the goal of therapy is to help people to become fully functioning, to open them up to all of their experiences and to all of themselves. Such inner awareness is a form of insight, but for Rogers, insight into current feelings was more important than insight into unconscious wishes with roots in the distant past. Rogers called his approach to therapy *client centered* because he placed the responsibility for change on the person with the problem. Rogers's ideas about therapy are quite specific. He believed that people's defensiveness, rigidity, anxiety, and other signs of discomfort stem from their experiences of what he called conditional positive regard. They have learned that love and acceptance are contingent on conforming to what other people want them to be. The cardinal rule in person-centered therapy is for the therapist to express *unconditional positive regard*—that is, to show true acceptance of clients no matter what they may say or do. Rogers felt that this was a crucial first step toward getting clients to accept themselves.

Carl Rogers (far right) leading a group therapy session. Rogers was the founder of client-centered therapy.

Rather than taking an objective approach, Rogerian therapists try to understand things from the clients' point of view. They are also emphatically *nondirective*. They do not suggest reasons why clients feel as they do or how they might better handle a difficult situation. Instead, they try to reflect clients' statements, sometimes asking questions and sometimes hinting at feelings that clients have not put into words. Rogers felt that when therapists provide an atmosphere of openness and genuine respect, clients can find themselves. Consistent with Rogers' viewpoint, research has shown that a therapist's warmth and understanding increase success, no matter what therapeutic approach is used (Frank & Frank, 1991).

insight Awareness of previously unconscious feelings and memories and how they influence present feelings and behavior.

client-centered (or person-centered) therapy Nondirectional form of therapy developed by Carl Rogers that calls for unconditional positive regard of the client by the therapist with the goal of helping the client become fully functioning.

SHORT-TERM PSYCHODYNAMIC THERAPY Although Freud and Rogers originated the two major forms of insight therapy, others have developed hundreds of variations on this theme. Most involve a therapist who is far more active and emotionally engaged with clients than traditional psychoanalysts thought fit. These therapists give clients direct guidance and feedback, commenting on what they are told rather than just listening to their clients in a neutral manner. Most of these newer therapies are also much shorter-term than traditional psychoanalysis.

Insight remains the goal of so-called **short-term psychodynamic therapy**, but there is usually a time limit on treatment—for example, a limit of 25 sessions (Coren, 2001; Olfson, Marcus, Druss, & Pincus, 2002; Winston & Winston, 2002). This trend is based on research showing that most people (75 percent) experience improvement in this time frame (Howard, Kopta, Krause, & Orlinsky, 1986), even though longer therapy may be even more beneficial (Seligman, 1995). Health insurance plans typically offer coverage for psychotherapy for only a limited number of visits, so short-term therapies are often elected for this reason as well.

Corresponding to the trend toward a time-limited framework, insight therapies have become more symptom oriented, trying to help clients correct the *immediate* problems in their lives. Today's insight therapists see people as less at the mercy of early childhood events than Freud did. Although they do not discount childhood experiences, they typically focus on the client's current life situation and relationships.

BEHAVIOR THERAPIES

What do behaviorists believe should be the focus of psychotherapy?

Behavior therapies sharply contrast with insight-oriented approaches. They concentrate on changing people's *behavior*, rather than on discovering insights into their thoughts and feelings. Behavior therapies are based on the belief (described in Chapter 4: "Learning and Memory") that all behavior, both normal and abnormal, is learned (Tryon, 2000). People suffering from hypochondriasis *learn* that they get attention when they are sick; people with paranoid personalities *learn* to be suspicious of others. Behavior therapists also assume that maladaptive behaviors *are* the problem, not symptoms of deeper underlying causes. If behavior therapists can teach people to behave in more appropriate ways, they believe that they have cured the problem. The therapist does not need to know exactly how or why a client learned to behave abnormally in the first place. The job of the therapist is simply to teach the person new, more satisfying ways of behaving on the basis of scientifically studied principles of learning, such as classical conditioning, operant conditioning, and modeling.

THERAPIES BASED ON CLASSICAL CONDITIONING As you saw in Chapter 4, "Learning and Memory," classical conditioning involves the repeated pairing of a neutral stimulus with one that evokes a certain reflex response. Eventually, the formerly neutral stimulus alone comes to elicit the same response. The approach is one of learned stimulus-response associations. Several variations on classical conditioning have been used to treat psychological problems.

Systematic desensitization, a method for gradually reducing fear and anxiety, is one of the oldest behavior therapy techniques (Wolpe, 1990). The method works by gradually associating a new response (relaxation) with stimuli that have been causing anxiety. For example, an aspiring politician might seek therapy because he is anxious about speaking to crowds. The therapist explores the kinds of crowds that are most threatening: Is an audience of 500 worse than one of 50? Is it harder to speak to men than it is to women? Is there more anxiety facing strangers than a roomful of friends? From this information the therapist develops a *hierarchy of fears*—a list of situations from the least to the most anxiety provoking. The therapist then teaches the client how to relax, including both mental and physical techniques of relaxation. Once the person has mastered deep relaxation, she or he begins work at the bottom of the hierarchy of fears. The person is told to relax while imagining the least threatening situation on the list, then the next most threatening, and so on, until the most fear-arousing one is reached and the client can still remain calm.

short-term psychodynamic therapy Insight therapy that is time limited and focused on trying to help clients correct the immediate problems in their lives.

behavior therapies Therapeutic approaches that are based on the belief that all behavior, normal and abnormal, is learned, and that the objective of therapy is to teach people new, more satisfying ways of behaving.

systematic desensitization A behavioral technique for reducing a person's fear and anxiety by gradually associating a new response (relaxation) with stimuli that have been causing the fear and anxiety.

This commonsense approach of working step-by-step through a hierarchy of fears in real life is probably familiar to you. For example, folk wisdom says that if you fall off a horse, the best way to get over your fear of riding is to get right back on the horse and continue to ride until the fear is gone. That is an example of desensitization in the real world.

The technique of **flooding** is a less familiar and more frightening method of desensitization. It involves full-intensity exposure to a feared stimulus for a prolonged period of time (O'Leary & Wilson, 1987; Wolpe, 1990). For example, someone with a powerful fear of snakes might be forced to handle dozens of snakes, or someone with an overwhelming fear of spiders might be forced to stroke a tarantula and allow it to crawl up an arm. If you think that flooding is an unnecessarily harsh method, remember how debilitating many untreated anxiety disorders can be to a person.

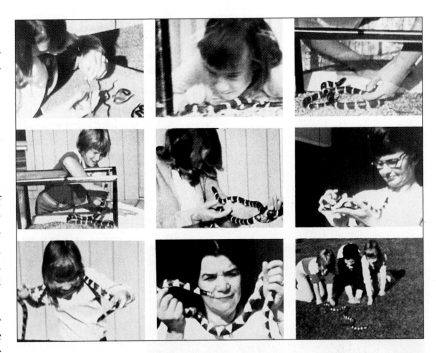

The clients in these photographs are overcoming a simple phobia: fear of snakes. After practicing a technique of deep relaxation, clients in desensitization therapy work from the bottom of their hierarchy of fears up to the situation that provokes the greatest fear or anxiety. Here, clients progress from handling rubber snakes (top left) to viewing live snakes through a window (top center) and finally to handling live snakes. This procedure can also be conducted vicariously in the therapist's office, where clients combine relaxation techniques with imagining anxiety-provoking scenes.

THERAPIES BASED ON OPERANT CONDITIONING In *operant conditioning*, a person learns to behave in a certain way because that behavior is reinforced, or rewarded. One therapy based on the principle of reinforcement is called **behavior contracting**. The therapist and the client agree on behavioral goals and on the reinforcement that the client will receive when he or she reaches those goals. These goals and reinforcements are often written in a contract that binds both the client and the therapist, as if by legal agreement. For example, a contract to help a person stop smoking might read as follows: "For each day that I smoke fewer than 20 cigarettes, I will earn 30 minutes of time to go bowling. For each day that I exceed the goal, I will lose 30 minutes from the time that I have accumulated." Behavior contracting has also been used effectively in schools to assist students with emotional and behavior difficulties. Contracts specify which negative behaviors (such as aggressiveness or disruptiveness) will be followed by penalties, and which positive behaviors (such as completing class work on time or classroom participation) will be followed by rewards (Ruth, 1996).

Another therapy based on operant conditioning is called the token economy. **Token economies** are usually used in schools and hospitals where controlled conditions are most feasible (Boniecki & Moore, 2003; Comaty, Stasio, & Advokat, 2001; O'Leary & Wilson, 1987). People are rewarded with tokens or points for behaviors that are considered appropriate and adaptive. The tokens or points can be exchanged for desired items and privileges. On the ward of a mental hospital, for example, improved grooming habits might earn points that can be used to purchase special foods or weekend passes. Token economies have proven effective in modifying the behavior of people who are resistant to other forms of treatment, such as people with chronic schizophrenia (Kopelowicz, Liberman, & Zarate, 2002; Paul, 1982). The positive changes in behavior, however, do not always generalize to everyday life outside the hospital or clinic.

THERAPIES BASED ON SOCIAL LEARNING Modeling—the process of learning a behavior by watching someone else perform it—can also be used to treat problem behaviors. For example, one group of researchers helped people to overcome a snake phobia by showing films in which models confronted snakes and gradually moved closer and closer to them (Bandura, Blanchard, & Ritter, 1969). Similar techniques have succeeded in reducing such common phobias as fear of dental work (Melamed, Hawes, Heiby, & Glick, 1975). Moreover, a combination of modeling and positive reinforcement was successful in helping people with schizophrenia to learn and use appropriate behavior both inside and outside the hospital (Bellack, Hersen, & Turner, 1976). Modeling has also been used extensively to teach people with mental retardation job skills and independent living skills (LaGreca, Stone, & Bell, 1983; Matson, Smalls, Hampff, Smiroldo, & Anderson, 1998; Sundel, 1991).

flooding A behavioral technique involving full-intensity exposure to a feared stimulus for a prolonged time.

behavior contracting Form of operant conditioning therapy in which the client and therapist set behavioral goals and agree on reinforcements that the client will receive on reaching those goals.

token economy An operant conditioning therapy in which people earn tokens (reinforcers) for desired behaviors and exchange them for desired items or privileges.

modeling A behavior therapy in which the person learns desired behaviors by watching others perform those behaviors.

COGNITIVE-BASED THERAPIES

How can people overcome irrational and self-defeating beliefs about themselves?

Cognitive-based therapies are focused on the belief that if people can change their distorted ideas about themselves and the world, they can also change their problem behaviors and make their lives more enjoyable (Bleijenberg, Prins, & Bazelmans, 2003). The task facing cognitive therapists is to identify erroneous ways of thinking and to correct them. This focus on learning new ways of thinking shares many similarities with behavior therapies, which also focus on learning. In fact, many professionals consider themselves to be *cognitive behavior therapists*—therapists who combine both cognitive and behavior therapies (Brewin, 1996). Three popular forms of cognitive-based therapy are stress-inoculation therapy, rational-emotive therapy, and Aaron Beck's cognitive approach.

According to cognitive therapists, the confidence this person is showing stems from the positive thoughts she has about herself. Stress-inoculation therapy helps replace negative, anxiety-evoking thoughts with confident self-talk.

STRESS-INOCULATION THERAPY As we go about our lives, we talk to ourselves constantly—proposing courses of action, commenting on our performance, expressing wishes, and so on. **Stress-inoculation therapy** makes use of this self-talk to help people cope with stressful situations (Meichenbaum & Cameron, 1982). The client is taught to suppress any negative, anxiety-evoking thoughts and to replace them with positive, "coping" thoughts. Take a student with exam anxiety who faces every test telling herself, "Oh no, another test. I'm so nervous. I'm sure I won't think calmly enough to remember the answers. If only I'd studied more. If I don't get through this course, I'll never graduate!" This pattern of thought is highly dysfunctional because it only makes anxiety worse. With the help of a cognitive therapist, the student learns a new pattern of self-talk: "I studied hard for this exam, and I know the material well. I looked at the textbook last night and reviewed my notes. I should be able to do well. If some questions are hard, they won't all be, and even if it's tough, my whole grade doesn't depend on just one test." Then the person tries out the new strategy in a real situation, ideally one of only moderate stress (such as a short quiz). Finally, the person is ready to use the strategy in a more stressful situation (such as a final exam). Stress-inoculation therapy works by turning the client's thought patterns into a kind of vaccine against stress-induced anxiety.

RATIONAL–EMOTIVE THERAPY Another type of cognitive-based therapy, **rational-emotive therapy (RET)**, developed by Albert Ellis (1973, 2001), is based on the view that most people in need of therapy hold a set of irrational and self-defeating beliefs (Overholser, 2003). They believe that they should be competent at *everything*, liked by *everyone*, *always* treated fairly, quick to find solutions to *every* problem, and so forth. Such beliefs involve absolutes—"musts" and "shoulds"—that allow for no exceptions, making no room for mistakes. When people with such irrational beliefs come up against real-life struggles, they often experience excessive psychological distress. For example, when a telemarketer who believes that he must be the most successful employee in his unit has a week of low sales volume, he may view his non-stellar performance as a catastrophe and become deeply depressed rather than just feeling disappointed.

Rational-emotive therapists confront such dysfunctional beliefs vigorously, using a variety of techniques, including persuasion, challenge, commands, and theoretical arguments (Ellis & MacLaren, 1998). Studies have shown that RET often does enable people to reinterpret their negative beliefs and experiences in a more positive light, decreasing the likelihood of becoming depressed (Blatt, Zuroff, Quinlan, & Pilkonis, 1996; Bruder et al., 1997).

BECK'S COGNITIVE THERAPY One of the most important and promising forms of cognitive-based therapy for treating depression is known simply as **cognitive therapy** (Cahill et al., 2003). Sometimes it is referred to as "Beck's cognitive therapy," after Aaron Beck, who developed it (1967), to avoid confusion with the broader category of cognitive-based therapies.

Beck believes that depression results from inappropriately self-critical patterns of thought about the self. Such people have unrealistic expectations, magnify their failures, make sweeping negative generalizations about themselves from little evidence, notice only negative feedback from the outside world, and interpret anything less than total success as

cognitive-based therapies Psychotherapies that emphasize changing clients' perceptions of their life situation as a way of modifying their behavior.

stress-inoculation therapy A type of cognitive therapy that trains clients to cope with stressful situations by learning a more useful pattern of self-talk.

rational-emotive therapy (RET) A directive cognitive therapy based on the idea that clients' psychological distress is caused by irrational and self-defeating beliefs and that the therapist's job is to challenge such dysfunctional beliefs.

cognitive therapy Therapy that depends on identifying and changing inappropriately negative and self-critical patterns of thought. Also known as Beck's cognitive therapy, after Aaron Beck, its founder.

failure. This negative chain of thinking may often spiral downward from small setbacks, until the person concludes that he or she is worthless. According to Beck, the downward spiral of negative, distorted thoughts is at the heart of depression.

Beck's assumptions about the cause of depression are very similar to those underlying RET, but the style of treatment differs considerably. Cognitive therapists are much less challenging and confrontational than rational-emotive therapists. Instead, they try to help clients examine each dysfunctional thought in a supportive, but objectively scientific manner ("Are you *sure* your whole life will be totally ruined if you break up with Frank? What is your evidence for that? Didn't you once tell me how happy you were *before* you met him?"). Like RET, Beck's cognitive therapy tries to lead the person to more realistic and flexible ways of thinking.

GROUP THERAPIES

What are some advantages of group therapies?

Some therapists believe that treating several people simultaneously is preferable to treating each alone. Such **group therapy** allows both client and therapist to see how the person acts around others. If a person is painfully anxious and tongue-tied, chronically self-critical, or hostile and aggressive, these tendencies will show up quickly in a group.

Group therapies have other advantages, too. A good group offers social support, a feeling that one is not the only person in the world with problems. Group members can also help one another learn useful new behaviors (how to express feelings, how to disagree without antagonizing others). Interactions in a group can lead people toward insights into their own behavior, such as why they are so defensive or feel compelled to complain constantly. Finally, because group therapy consists of several clients "sharing" a therapist, it is less expensive than individual therapy (Fejr, 2003; Yalom, 1995).

Group therapy can help to identify problems that a person has interacting with other people. The group also offers social support, helping people to feel less alone with their problems.

There are many kinds of group therapy. Some groups follow the general outlines of the therapies we have already mentioned. Others are oriented toward a very specific goal, such as stopping smoking, drinking, or overeating. Alcoholics Anonymous (AA) is perhaps the best known *self-help group*, but self-help groups are available for virtually every life problem. Local chapters of many groups can be identified in your telephone directory or by searching the Internet.

Do these self-help groups work? In many cases, they apparently do. Alcoholics Anonymous has developed a reputation for helping people cope with alcoholism. Most group members express strong support for their groups (Riordan & Beggs, 1987), and studies have demonstrated that they can indeed be effective (Galanter, 1984; McKellar, Stewart, & Humphreys, 2003; Ouimette et al., 2001; Pisani, Fawcett, Clark, & McGuire, 1993).

FAMILY THERAPY Family therapy is another form of group therapy (Lebow & Gurman, 1995; Molineux, 1985). Family therapists believe that if one person in the family is having problems, it is often a signal that the entire family needs assistance. Therefore, it would be a mistake to treat a client without making an attempt to meet the person's parents, spouse, and children. Family therapists do not try to reshape the personalities of family members (Gurman & Kniskern, 1991). Instead, the primary goals of family therapy are improving family communication, encouraging family members to become more empathetic, getting them to share responsibilities, and reducing conflict within the family. To achieve these goals, all family members must believe that they will benefit from changes in their behavior.

Although family therapy is especially appropriate when there are problems between husband and wife or parents and children, it is increasingly used when only one family member has a clear psychological disorder, such as schizophrenia, agoraphobia, or in some cases, depression (Keitner, Archambault, Ryan, & Miller, 2003; Lebow & Gurman, 1995). The goal of treatment in these circumstances is to help the mentally healthy members of the family cope more effectively with the impact of the disorder on the family unit. The improved coping of the well-adjusted family members may in turn help the troubled person. Family therapy is

group therapy Type of psychotherapy in which clients meet regularly to interact and help one another achieve insight into their feelings and behavior.

family therapy A form of group therapy that sees the family as at least partly responsible for the individual's problems and that seeks to change all family members' behaviors to the benefit of the family unit as well as the troubled individual.

also called for when a person's progress in individual therapy is slowed by the family (often because other family members have trouble adjusting to that person's improvement).

Unfortunately, not all families benefit from family therapy. Sometimes the problems are too entrenched. In the other cases, important family members may be absent or unwilling to cooperate. In still others, one family member monopolizes sessions, making it hard for anyone else's views to be heard. In all these cases, a different therapeutic approach is needed.

COUPLE THERAPY Another type of group therapy is **couple therapy**, which is designed to assist partners who are having difficulties with their relationship. In the past, this therapy was generally called *marital therapy*, but the term "couple therapy" is considered more appropriate today because it captures the broad range of partners who may seek help (Oltmanns & Emery, 2001).

Most couple therapists concentrate on improving patterns of communication and mutual expectations. In *empathy training*, for example, each member of the couple is taught to share inner feelings and to listen to and understand his or her partner's feelings before responding to them. This technique requires that people spend more time listening, trying to grasp what is really being said, and less time in self-defensive rebuttal. Other couple therapists use behavioral techniques. For example, a couple might be helped to develop a schedule for exchanging specific caring actions, such as helping with chores around the house, making time to share a special meal together, or remembering special occasions with a gift or card. This approach may not sound very romantic, but proponents say it can break a cycle of dissatisfaction and hostility in a relationship, and hence, it is an important step in the right direction (Margolin, 1987). Couple therapy for both partners is generally more effective than therapy for only one of them (Dunn & Schwebel, 1995; Johnson, 2003).

EFFECTIVENESS OF PSYCHOTHERAPY

How much better off is a person who receives psychotherapy than one who gets no treatment at all?

We have noted that some psychotherapies are generally effective, but how much better are they than no treatment at all? Researchers have found that about one-third of people who receive no treatment for their mental disorders improve on their own; about two-thirds of those who are treated improve (Borkovec & Costello, 1993; Lambert, Shapiro, & Bergin, 1986). Furthermore, many people who do not receive formal therapy get therapeutic help from friends, clergy, physicians, and teachers. Thus, the recovery rate for people who receive *no* therapeutic help at all is quite possibly even less than one-third. Perhaps if Abraham Lincoln, whose recurring bouts of depression are described in the opening paragraphs of this chapter, had received some form of the psychotherapies available today, he might have suffered less.

Other attempts to study the effectiveness of psychotherapy have generally agreed that psychotherapy is effective (Hartmann & Siegfried, 2003; Leichsenring & Leibing, 2003; Lipsey & Wilson, 1993; Shapiro & Shapiro, 1982; Wampold et al., 1997), although its value appears to be related to a number of other factors. For instance, psychotherapy works best for relatively mild psychological problems (Kopta, Howard, Lowry, & Beutler, 1994) and seems to provide the greatest benefits to people who really *want* to change (Orlinsky & Howard, 1994). There also seems to be greater improvement among people who have undergone long-term therapy than among those who have received short-term treatments (Seligman, 1995). This last finding is illustrated in **Figure 9–3**.

Another important question is whether some forms of psychotherapy are more effective than others. Is behavior therapy, for example, more effective than insight therapy? In general, the answer seems to be "not much" (Garfield, 1983; Hanna, 2002; Michelson, 1985; Smith, Glass, & Miller, 1980; Wampold et al., 1997). Most of the benefits of treatment seem to come from being in *some* kind of therapy, regardless of the particular type.

As we have seen, the various forms of psychotherapy are based on very different views about what causes mental disorders and, at least on the surface, approach the treatment of mental disorders in different ways. Why, then, is there no substantial difference in their effectiveness? To answer this question, some psychologists have focused their attention on what the various forms of psychotherapy have in common, rather than emphasizing their differences (Barker, Funk, & Houston, 1988; Roberts, Kewman, Mercer, & Hovell, 1993):

couple therapy A form of group therapy intended to help troubled partners improve their problems of communication and interaction.

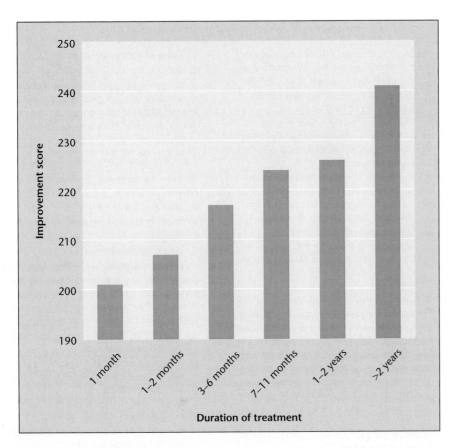

Figure 9–3
Duration of therapy and improvement. One of the most dramatic results of the *Consumer Reports* (1995) study on the effectiveness of psychotherapy was the strong relationship between reported improvement and the duration of therapy.

Source: Adapted from Seligman, M. E. P. (1995). The effectiveness of psychotherapy: The *Consumer Reports* study. *American Psychologist, 50,* 965–974. Copyright © 1995 by the American Psychological Association. Adapted with permission.

1. All forms of psychotherapy provide people with an *explanation for their problems.* Along with this explanation often comes a new perspective, providing people with specific actions to help them cope more effectively.

2. Most forms of psychotherapy offer people *hope.* Because most people who seek therapy have low self-esteem and feel demoralized and depressed, hope and the expectation for improvement increase their feelings of self-worth.

3. All major types of psychotherapy engage the client in a *therapeutic alliance* with a therapist. Although their therapeutic approaches may differ, effective therapists are warm, empathetic, and caring people who understand the importance of establishing a strong emotional bond with their clients that is built on mutual respect and understanding (Blatt, Zuroff, Quinlan, & Pilkonis, 1996; Wampold, 2001).

Together, these nonspecific factors common to all forms of psychotherapy appear, at least in part, to explain why most people who receive any form of therapy show some benefits as compared with those who receive no therapeutic help at all (Klein et al., 2003).

▶ CHECK YOUR UNDERSTANDING

1. The process called _____ involves having clients project their feelings toward authority figures onto their therapist.

2. Rogerian therapists show that they value and accept their clients by providing them with _____ _____ regard.

3. The technique of _____ involves intense and prolonged exposure to something feared.

4. Some therapy involves learning desired behaviors by watching others perform those actions, which is also known as _____.

5. Developing new ways of thinking that lead to more adaptive behavior lies at the heart of all _____ therapies.

6. Most researchers agree that psychotherapy helps about _____-_____ of the people treated.

Answers: 1. transference, **2.** unconditional positive, **3.** flooding, **4.** modeling, **5.** cognitive or cognitive-based, **6.** two-thirds

> **APPLY YOUR UNDERSTANDING**

1. Which of the following choices best illustrates client-centered therapy with a depressed person?

   a. The client is encouraged to give up her depression by interacting with a group of people in a self-help group.

   b. The therapist tells the client that her depression is self-defeating and gives the client "assignments" to develop self-esteem and enjoy life.

   c. The therapist encourages the client to say anything that comes into his head, to express her innermost fantasies, and to talk about critical childhood events.

   d. The therapist offers the client his unconditional positive regard and, once this open atmosphere is established, tries to help her discover why she feels depressed.

2. Robert is about to start a new job, but it is in a tall building and he is deathly afraid of riding in elevators. He sees a therapist who first teaches him how to relax. After he has mastered that skill, the therapist asks him to relax while imagining that he is entering the office building. When he can do that without feeling anxious, the therapist asks him to relax while imagining standing in front of the elevator doors, and so on until Robert can completely relax while imagining riding in elevators. This therapeutic technique is known as _____.

   a. transference

   b. desensitization

   c. behavior contracting

   d. flooding

3. Sarah applies for a job promotion, but she is passed over. She has great difficulty accepting this fact and as a consequence she becomes deeply depressed. She sees a therapist who vigorously challenges and confronts her in an effort to show her that her depression comes from an irrational, self-defeating belief that she will never be successful. This therapist is most likely engaging in _____.

   a. rational-emotive therapy

   b. stress-inoculation therapy

   c. flooding

   d. desensitization therapy

4. Your friend is experiencing anxiety attacks, but doesn't want to see a therapist because "they don't do any good." Which of the following replies most accurately reflects what you have learned about the effectiveness of therapy?

   a. "You're right. Psychotherapy is no better than no treatment at all."

   b. "Actually, even a brief course of therapy usually has a beneficial effect compared with doing nothing."

   c. "Only insight therapy is likely to help."

   d. "Therapy could help you, but you'd probably have to stick with it for at least a year before it has any effect."

Answers: 1. d, 2. b, 3. a, 4. b.

Biological Treatments

9.8   Describe how drug therapy, electroconvulsive therapy, and psychosurgery can be used to treat psychological disorders.

Biological treatments—a group of approaches including medication, electroconvulsive therapy, and psychosurgery—may be used to treat psychological disorders in addition to, or instead of, psychotherapy. Clients and therapists select biological treatments for several reasons. First, some people are too agitated, disoriented, or unresponsive to be helped by psychotherapies. Second, biological treatment is virtually always used for disorders that have a strong biological component. Third, biological treatment is often used for people who are dangerous to themselves and to others.

The only mental health professionals licensed to offer biological treatments are psychiatrists, who are physicians, but therapists who are not medical doctors often work with physicians who prescribe medication for their clients. In many cases where biological treatments are used, psychotherapy is also recommended. For example, medication and psychotherapy used together work better for treating major depression and for preventing a recurrence than either treatment used alone (Keller et al., 2000; Reynolds et al., 1999).

DRUG THERAPIES

What has been the impact of psychoactive theories on the treatment of psychological disorders?

Medication is frequently and effectively used to treat a number of different psychological problems. The medications used to treat psychological disorders are prescribed not only by psychi-

---

biological treatments A group of approaches, including medication, electroconvulsive therapy, and psychosurgery, that are sometimes used to treat psychological disorders in conjunction with, or instead of, psychotherapy.

>TABLE 9–4 CATEGORIES OF DRUG THERAPIES

Category	Common Therapeutic Uses	Examples
Antianxiety Drugs	• Some anxiety disorders such as generalized anxiety disorder • Situation-induced stress (short-term)	• Minor tranquilizers, such as *Valium* (diazepam) and *Atavan* (lorazepan)
Antidepressant Drugs	• Depression and dysthymia • Some anxiety disorders, such as obsessive-compulsive disorder and panic disorder	• Monoamine oxidase inhibitors • Tricyclics • Selective serotonin reuptake inhibitors (SSRIs), such as *Prozac, Paxil,* and *Zoloft*
Antipsychotic Drugs	• Disorders with psychotic features, such as schizophrenia and mania	• Major tranquilizers, such as *Thorazine*
Lithium	• Bipolar disorder	• lithium carbonate

atrists, but even more commonly by primary-care physicians such as family practitioners, pediatricians, and gynecologists. Drug therapies are widely used, in part, because newer generations of drugs are quite effective for many people and also because drug therapies can cost less than psychotherapy. Critics suggest, however, that another reason is our society's "pill mentality," or belief that we can take a medicine to fix any problem.

TYPES OF PSYCHOACTIVE DRUGS Generally speaking, the drugs used to treat mental disorders work by regulating the action of specific neurotransmitter mechanisms in the brain (see Chapter 2: "The Biological Basis of Behavior"). Although there are dozens of drugs commonly prescribed by physicians for the treatment of mental health disorders, most can be organized into general categories based on the types of disorders for which they are effective (see **Table 9–4**).

The most commonly prescribed drugs for the treatment of mental disorders are the antidepressants. As the opening paragraphs of this chapter note, drugs have long been used as a treatment for depression. Early drugs, however, like those used by Abraham Lincoln, only masked the symptoms of this disorder, without addressing its biological source. In the 1950s and 1960s, researchers developed the first antidepressant drugs that worked by altering the neurotransmitter mechanisms in the brain that are disrupted in cases of depression. Until the end of the 1980s, however, there were only two main types of antidepressant drugs (both named for their chemical properties): *monoamine oxidase inhibitors (MAO inhibitors)* and *tricyclics*. Both work by increasing the concentration of the neurotransmitters serotonin and norepinephrine in the brain (McKim, 1997). Both are effective for most people with serious depression, but both produce a number of serious and troublesome side effects.

In 1988, Prozac (fluoxetine) came onto the market. This drug works by reducing the uptake of serotonin in the nervous system, thus increasing the amount of serotonin active in the brain at any given moment (see **Figure 9–4**.) For this reason, Prozac is part of a group of psychoactive drugs known as *selective serotonin reuptake inhibitors (SSRIs)*. Today, a number of second-generation SSRIs are available to treat depression, including *Paxil* (paroxetine), *Zoloft* (sertraline), and *Effexor* (venlafaxine HCl). In addition to increasing serotonin, *Effexor* also raises the levels of norepinephrine in the brain, so it is technically known as an *SNRI* (serotonin and norepinephrine reuptake inhibitor). For many patients, correcting the imbalance in these chemicals in the brain reduces their symptoms of depression and also relieves the

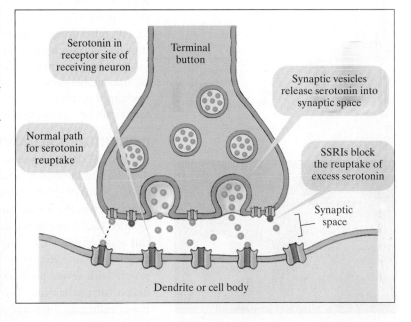

Figure 9–4

How do the SSRIs work? Antidepressants such as Prozac, Paxil, Zoloft, and Effexor belong to a class of drugs called SSRIs (selective serotonin reuptake inhibitors). These drugs reduce the symptoms of depression by blocking the reabsorption (or reuptake) of serotonin in the synaptic space between neurons. The increased availability of serotonin to bind to receptor sites on the receiving neuron is thought to be responsible for the ability of these drugs to relieve symptoms of depression.

associated symptoms of anxiety. Moreover, because these drugs have fewer side effects than MAO inhibitors or tricyclics (Nemeroff & Schatzberg, 2002), they have been heralded in the popular media as "wonder drugs" for the treatment of depression.

IMPACT OF PSYCHOACTIVE DRUGS Today, antidepressant drugs are not only used to treat depression, but also have shown promise in treating generalized anxiety disorder, panic disorder, obsessive–compulsive disorder, social phobia, and posttraumatic stress disorder (Bourin, 2003; Donnelly, 2003; Shelton & Hollon, 2000). Antidepressant drugs like the SSRIs do not work for everyone, however. At least a quarter of the patients with major depressive disorder do not respond to antidepressant drugs (Shelton & Hollon, 2000). Moreover, for some patients, these drugs produce unpleasant side effects, including nausea, insomnia, headaches, anxiety, and impaired sexual functioning. They can also cause severe withdrawal symptoms in patients who stop taking them abruptly (Balon, 2002; Clayton, McGarvey, Abouesh, & Pinkerton, 2001).

Oftentimes, psychoactive drugs can have dramatic effects. For example, some of the people who suffer from schizophrenia and take an appropriate antipsychotic drug can go from being perpetually frightened, angry, confused, and plagued by auditory and visual hallucinations to being totally free of such symptoms (Grinspoon, Ewalt, & Schader, 1972). Antipsychotic drugs do not, however, cure schizophrenia; they only alleviate the symptoms while the person is taking the drug. Therefore, most people with schizophrenia must take antipsychotics for years—perhaps for the rest of their lives (Mueser & Glynn, 1995; Oltmanns & Emery, 1998). This can lead to discomfort, because antipsychotic drugs can also have a number of undesirable side effects (Kane & Lieberman, 1992; McKim, 1997). Blurred vision and constipation are among the common complaints, as are temporary neurological impairments such as muscular rigidity or tremors. A very serious potential side effect is *tardive dyskinesia*, a permanent disturbance of motor control, particularly of the face (uncontrollable smacking of the lips, for instance), which can be only partially alleviated with other drugs (Diaz, 1997). The risk of tardive dyskinesia increases with the length of time that antipsychotics are taken.

Another problem is that antipsychotics are of little value in treating the problems of social adjustment that people with schizophrenia face outside an institutional setting. Because many discharged people fail to take their medications, relapse is common. The relapse rate, however, can usually be reduced if drug therapy is effectively combined with psychotherapy.

DEINSTITUTIONALIZATION Prior to the introduction of the antipsychotic drugs in the mid-1950s, most people with severe forms of mental disorders lived in institutions dedicated to their care, many of which were funded and run by state governments. The development of effective drug therapies starting in the 1950s, however, led to a number of changes in these state-run mental hospitals (Shorter, 1997). First, people who were agitated could now be sedated with drugs. Although the drugs often produced lethargy, this was considered an improvement over the use of physical restraints. The second major, and more lasting, result of the new drug therapies was the widespread release of people with severe psychological disorders back into the community—a policy called **deinstitutionalization**. The practice of placing people in smaller, more humane facilities or returning them under medication to care within the community intensified during the 1960s and 1970s.

In recent years, however, deinstitutionalization has created serious problems (Lamb & Weinberger, 2001). Discharged people often are assigned to poorly funded community mental health centers—or to none at all. Many of these former patients are not prepared to live in the community with support, and they receive little guidance in coping with the mechanics of daily life. Those who return home can become a burden to their families, especially when they don't get adequate follow-up care. Residential centers, such as halfway houses, vary in quality, but many provide poor care and minimal contact with the outside world. Insufficient sheltered housing forces many former patients into nonpsychiatric facilities—often rooming houses located in dirty, unsafe, isolated neighborhoods. The suicide rate among deinstitutionalized

Recent surveys indicate that about 40 percent of the homeless people in the United States are mentally ill.

---

deinstitutionalization Policy of treating people with severe psychological disorders in the larger community or in small residential centers such as halfway houses, rather than in large public hospitals.

patients is increasing (Goldney, 2003), and some surveys indicate that about 40 percent of the homeless people in the U.S. are mentally ill (Burt et al., 1999). People diagnosed with mental illness are further burdened by the social stigma of their illness, which may be the largest single obstacle to rehabilitation. Moreover, although outpatient care is presumed to be a well-established national policy objective in mental health, health insurance typically discourages outpatient care by requiring substantial copayments and by limiting the number of treatment visits. Despite these difficulties, however, the development of new generations of more effective psychoactive medicines offers promise to those who suffer from mental disorders.

ELECTROCONVULSIVE THERAPY

How is the electroconvulsive therapy of today different from that of the past?

Another mode of biological treatment is **electroconvulsive therapy** (**ECT**), which is most often used for cases of prolonged and severe depression that do not respond to other forms of treatment (Birkenhaeger, Pluijms, & Lucius, 2003; Olfson, Marcus, Sackeim, Thompson, & Pincus, 1998). The ECT technique involves briefly passing an electric current through the brain or, perhaps, through only one hemisphere of the brain (unilateral ECT) (Thomas & Kellner, 2003). The electric current triges convulsions and a brief and temporary loss of consciousness. Treatment normally consists of 10 or fewer sessions of ECT.

No one knows exactly why ECT works, but evidence clearly shows that it does. Still, ECT has many critics, and its use remains controversial (Krystal, Holsinger, Weiner, & Coffey, 2000). The side effects of ECT include some brief confusion, as well as disorientation and memory impairment, though research suggests that unilateral ECT produces fewer side effects and is only slightly less effective than the traditional method (Diaz, 1997; Khan, 1993). In view of the side effects, ECT is usually considered a "last-resort" treatment when all other methods have failed.

PSYCHOSURGERY

What is psychosurgery, and how is it used today?

Psychosurgery refers to brain surgery performed to change a person's behavior and emotional state. This is a drastic step, especially because the effects of psychosurgery are difficult to predict. In a *prefrontal lobotomy*, the frontal lobes of the brain are severed from the deeper centers beneath them. The assumption is that in extremely disturbed people, the frontal lobes intensify emotional impulses from the lower brain centers (chiefly, the thalamus and hypothalamus). Unfortunately, lobotomies can work with one person and fail completely with another—possibly producing permanent, undesirable side effects, such as the inability to inhibit impulses or a near-total absence of emotion.

Prefrontal lobotomies are rarely performed today. In fact, very few psychosurgical procedures are done nowadays, except as desperate measures, to control such conditions as intractable psychoses, Parkinson's disease, epilepsy that does not respond to other treatments (see Chapter 2, "Biological Bases of Behavior"), severe obsessive–compulsive disorders, and pain in a terminal illness (Baer, Rauch, & Ballantine, 1995; Weingarten & Cummings, 2001).

electroconvulsive therapy (ECT) Biological therapy in which a mild electrical current is passed through the brain for a short period, producing convulsions and temporary loss of consciousness; used to treat severe, prolonged depression.

psychosurgery Brain surgery performed to change a person's behavior and emotional state; a biological therapy rarely used today.

▶ CHECK YOUR UNDERSTANDING

1. The only mental health professionals licensed to provide drug therapy are _____.
2. Schizophrenia is often treated with drugs belonging to the category of _____ drugs.
3. Although it is considered effective in treating depression, electroconvulsive therapy (ECT) is considered a treatment of last resort because of its potential negative side effects. Is this statement true (T) or false (F)?
4. The more general term used for surgeries such as the prefrontal lobotomy is_____.

Answers: 1. psychiatrists, 2. antipsychotic, 3. (T), 4. psychosurgery.

Challenges in Therapy

9.9 Identify the most important ways in which a therapist should attempt to match a specific therapeutic approach to an individual client.

Although we all share certain basic human characteristics as individuals and as groups, we also have our own distinctive traits, our own distinctive ways of responding to the world. Does individual uniqueness influence the treatment of psychological problems? In many cases, the answer is, "yes."

CLIENT DIVERSITY AND TREATMENT

Are there particular groups of people who may require special approaches in the treatment of psychological problems?

Imagine the following scenario: As a Native American client is interviewed by a psychologist, the client stares at the floor. He answers questions politely, but during the entire consultation, he looks away continually, never meeting the doctor's eye. This body language might lead the psychologist to suppose that the man is depressed or has low self-esteem, unless, that is, the psychologist knows that in this person's culture, avoiding eye contact is a sign of respect.

Our ideas of what constitutes normal behavior are culture bound. When psychotherapist and client come from different cultures, misunderstandings of speech, body language, and customs are almost inevitable (Cardemil & Battle, 2003; Helms & Cook, 1999). Even when client and therapist are of the same nationality and speak the same language, there can be striking differences if they belong to different racial and ethnic groups (Casas, 1995). Some African-American people, for example, are wary of confiding in a white therapist—so much so that their wariness is sometimes mistaken for paranoia. For this reason, many black people seek out a black therapist, a tendency that is becoming more common (Williams, 1989).

In recent years a particular challenge for U.S. therapists has been to treat refugees from foreign countries, many of whom have fled such horrifying circumstances at home that they arrive in the United States exhibiting posttraumatic stress disorder (Paunovic & Oest, 2001). These refugees must overcome not only the effects of past trauma, but also the new stresses of settling in a strange country, which often include separation from their families, ignorance of the English language and culture, and inability to practice their traditional occupations. Therapists in such circumstances must learn something of their clients' culture. Often they have to conduct interviews through an interpreter—hardly an ideal circumstance for therapy. To be effective, treatment and prevention approaches must reflect the beliefs and cultural practices of the person's ethnic group.

MATCHING TREATMENTS TO INDIVIDUALS

How should individuals evaluate which therapy is best for them?

Even when cultural differences are not involved in determining a specific treatment approach for an individual, therapy should reflect both that person's preferences and the type of prob-

Research suggests that many African-American clients are more comfortable dealing with a therapist of the same racial background.

SUMMARY TABLE

MAJOR PERSPECTIVES ON THERAPY

TYPE OF THERAPY	CAUSE OF DISORDER	GOAL	TECHNIQUES
Insight therapies			
Psychoanalysis	Unconscious conflicts and motives; repressed problems from childhood.	To bring unconscious thoughts and feelings to consciousness; to gain insight.	Free association, dream analysis, interpretation, transference.
Client-centered therapy	Experiences of conditional positive regard.	To help people become fully functioning by opening them up to all of their experiences.	Regarding clients with unconditional positive regard.
Short-term psychodynamic	Varies among individuals.	To help people correct the more immediate problems in their lives.	Providing direct guidance and feedback to correct problems.
Behavior therapies	Reinforcement for maladaptive behavior.	To learn new and more adaptive behavior patterns.	Classical conditioning (systematic desensitization, extinction, flooding); aversive conditioning; operant conditioning (behavior contracting, token economies); modeling.
Cognitive-based therapies	Misconceptions; negative, self-defeating thinking.	To identify erroneous ways of thinking and to correct them.	Stress-inoculation therapy; rational-emotive therapy; Beck's cognitive therapy.
Group therapies	Interpersonal problems; addictions.	To use group's input and support to develop insight into one's personality and behavior.	Group interaction and mutual therapy; couple therapy; support; family interacting with others in self-help groups.
Biological treatments	Physiological imbalance or malfunction.	To eliminate symptoms; prevent recurrence.	Drugs, electroconvulsive therapy, psychosurgery.

lem being treated. As noted previously, many of the most severe mental disorders probably involve a biological dimension. People with these disorders often respond favorably to biological treatments, and oftentimes drugs are the therapy of first choice in these cases. Because there usually are several medications that might be effective, the choice of the particular drug prescribed is usually based on the physician's judgment about the specific characteristics of the individual's disorder as well as the preferences of the person being treated.

Even if medications are effective, their success can often be improved by providing psychotherapy. And, in some cases, medicines are not appropriate so psychotherapy is used alone. As you saw earlier in this chapter, many methods of psychotherapy are available, including those emphasizing insight, behavioral approaches, and cognitive restructuring. The choice of therapeutic styles can sometimes depend on the specific characteristics of a disorder. For example, behavioral therapies are often used when the problems involve specific anxieties or other well-defined problems. Cognitive therapies are particularly useful when depression is involved (Merrill, Tolbert, & Wade, 2003), and can also be effective in the treatment of anxiety disorders (Dugas, 2003). Insight therapies are often chosen when the person is seeking self-understanding or is having relationship issues, and group therapies can be effective in these situations as well.

The choice of therapies should be based on the therapists' appraisal of the individual's specific problems. It should also reflect the person's preferences for treatment. For example, some patients prefer to be treated with medications; others are opposed to the use of these medicines or react badly to their side effects and prefer a psychotherapeutic approach instead. A skilled clinician will evaluate both the disorder and the patient's preferences and lifestyle to craft the treatment program that is likely to be most effective. A summary of the major treatment options available is presented in the **Summary Table**.

▶ CHECK YOUR UNDERSTANDING

Indicate whether the following statements are true (T) or false (F):

1. ___ Our ideas about what constitutes normal behavior are culture bound.

2. ___ Trained mental health professionals rarely misinterpret the body language of a client from another culture.

3. ___ There is usually one best approach to treatment.

Answers: 1. (T)., 2. (F)., 3. (F).

▶ APPLY YOUR UNDERSTANDING

1. Preventing and treating psychological disorders is especially challenging in a society such as ours which has a culturally diverse population. Which of the following is **NOT** a constructive way of dealing with this challenge?

    a. Therapists need to recognize that some disorders that afflict people from other cultures may not exist in Western culture at all.

    b. Therapists from many different backgrounds need to receive training so that people who wish to do so can be treated by a therapist who shares their cultural background.

    c. Clients should be treated by therapists who represent the dominant, majority culture so that they can best adapt to their new environment.

    d. Intervention programs need to take into account the cultural norms and values of the group being served.

2. Suppose that Frank is experiencing symptoms associated with anxiety and depression. He should _____.

    a. work out these problems himself because therapies are no more effective than personal effort at resolving them

    b. see a psychiatrist and begin taking medication

    c. see a cognitive psychologist and pursue insight therapy

    d. see a trained clinician who will prescribe a treatment consistent with his symptoms and preferences

Answers: 1. c., 2. d.

>KEY TERMS<

Perspectives on psychological disorders

biological model, *p. 320*
psychoanalytic model, *p. 321*
cognitive–behavioral model, *p. 321*
diathesis–stress model, *p. 321*
diathesis, *p. 321*
systems approach, *p. 321*
Diagnostic and Statistical Manual of Mental Disorders (DSM), *p. 322*

Mood disorders

mood disorders, *p. 323*
depression, *p. 323*
mania, *p. 326*
bipolar disorder, *p. 326*

Anxiety disorders

anxiety disorders, *p. 328*
specific phobia, *p. 328*
social phobia, *p. 328*
agoraphobia, *p. 328*
panic disorder, *p. 328*

generalized anxiety disorder, *p. 329*
obsessive–compulsive disorder (OCD), *p. 329*

Psychosomatic, somatoform, and dissociative disorders

psychosomatic disorders, *p. 330*
somatoform disorders, *p. 331*
conversion disorders, *p. 331*
hypochondriasis, *p. 331*
body dysmorphic disorder, *p. 331*
dissociative disorders, *p. 331*
dissociative identity disorder, *p. 331*

Schizophrenic disorders

schizophrenic disorders, *p. 332*
psychotic (psychosis), *p. 332*
insanity, *p. 332*
hallucinations, *p. 333*
delusions, *p. 333*
disorganized schizophrenia, *p. 333*
catatonic schizophrenia, *p. 333*
paranoid schizophrenia, *p. 333*

undifferentiated schizophrenia, *p. 333*

Other common disorders

sexual dysfunction, *p. 335*
paraphilias, *p. 336*
fetishism, *p. 336*
pedophilia, *p. 336*
gender-identity disorders, *p. 336*
personality disorders, *p. 336*
antisocial personality disorder, *p. 336*
attention-deficit/hyperactivity disorder (ADHD), *p. 338*
autistic disorder, *p. 339*

Psychotherapies

psychotherapy, *p. 340*
insight therapies, *p. 340*
psychoanalysis, *p. 340*
free association, *p. 340*
transference, *p. 340*
insight, *p. 341*
client-centered (or person-centered) therapy, *p. 341*

short-term psychodynamic therapy, *p. 342*
behavior therapies, *p. 342*
systematic desensitization, *p. 342*
flooding, *p. 343*
behavior contracting, *p. 343*
token economy, *p. 343*
modeling, *p. 343*
cognitive-based therapies, *p. 344*
stress-inoculation therapy, *p. 344*
rational-emotive therapy (RET), *p. 344*
cognitive therapy, *p. 344*
group therapy, *p. 345*
family therapy, *p. 345*
couple therapy, *p. 346*

Biological treatments

biological treatments, *p. 348*
deinstitutionalization, *p. 350*
electroconvulsive therapy (ECT), *p. 351*
psychosurgery, *p. 351*

>CHAPTER REVIEW<

Perspectives on Psychological Disorders

How does a mental health professional define a psychological disorder? Mental health professionals define a psychological disorder as a condition that either seriously impairs a person's ability to function in life or creates a high level of inner distress (or sometimes both). This view does not mean that the category "disordered" is always easy to distinguish from the category "normal." In fact, it may be more accurate to view abnormal behavior as merely quantitatively different from normal behavior.

How have the biological, psychoanalytic, cognitive-behavioral, diathesis-stress, and systems models each attempted to explain psychological disorders? The **biological model** holds that abnormal behavior is caused by some physiological malfunction, especially of the brain. It is assumed that these malfunctions are often hereditary in origin. The **psychoanalytic model**, which Freud originated, holds that abnormal behavior is a symbolic expression of unconscious conflicts that generally can be traced to childhood. The **cognitive–behavior model** states that psychological disorders arise when people learn maladaptive ways of thinking and acting. What has been learned can be unlearned, however. Cognitive–behavior therapists therefore strive to modify their patients' dysfunctional behaviors and distorted, self-defeating processes of thought.

The **diathesis–stress model** holds that psychological disorders develop when a **diathesis** (or biological predisposition) is set off by stressful circumstances. The **systems approach** contends that psychological disorders are "lifestyle diseases" that arise from a combination of biological risk factors, psychological stresses, and societal pressures on people. This approach, too, can help to explain why a family background of a disorder doesn't always mean that the disorder will develop.

How common are mental disorders? According to research, at least 20 percent of Americans will suffer from one or more mental disorders in their lifetime. At any given point in time, about 15 percent of the population is experiencing a clinically significant mental disorder, and another 6 percent is experiencing substance abuse problems.

Why is it useful to have a manual of psychological disorders? For nearly 40 years, the American Psychiatric Association has published the **Diagnostic and Statistical Manual of Mental Disorders (DSM)**. The current fourth edition, known as DSM-IV-RT, provides careful descriptions of the symptoms of different disorders so that diagnoses based on them will be reliable from one mental health professional to another. The DSM-IV-RT includes little information on causes and treatments.

Mood Disorders

How does clinical depression differ from ordinary sadness? **Mood disorders**, also called affect disorders, involve disturbances in emotional states. The most common mood disorder is **depression**, a state in which a person feels overwhelmed with sadness, loses interest in activities, and displays other symptoms, such as excessive guilt or feelings of worthlessness. The DSM-IV-RT distinguishes between two forms of clinical depression. *Major depressive disorder* is an episode of intense sadness that may last for several months; in contrast, *dysthymia* involves less intense sadness but persists with little relief for a period of two years or more.

What factors are related to a person's likelihood of committing suicide? More women than men attempt suicide, but more men succeed. Suicide rates among American adolescents and young adults have been rising, and suicide is the third leading cause of death among adolescents. A common feeling associated with suicide is hopelessness, which is also typical of depression.

What is mania, and how is it involved in bipolar disorder? People suffering from **mania** become euphoric ("high"), extremely active, excessively talkative, and easily distracted. They typically have unlimited hopes and schemes, but little interest in realistically carrying them out. At the extreme, they may collapse from exhaustion. Manic episodes rarely appear by themselves; rather, they usually alternate with depression. Such a mood disorder, in which both mania and depression are alternately present and are sometimes interrupted by periods of normal mood, is known as **bipolar disorder**.

What causes some people to experience extreme mood changes? Mood disorders can result from a combination of biological, psychological, and social factors.

Anxiety Disorders

Into what three categories are phobias usually grouped? A **specific phobia** is an intense, paralyzing fear of something that it is unreasonable to fear so excessively. A **social phobia** is excessive, inappropriate fear connected with social situations or performances in front of other people. **Agoraphobia** is an especially debilitating social phobia that involves multiple, intense fears such as the fear of being alone or of being in public places or other situations that require separation from a source of security.

How does a panic attack differ from fear? **Panic disorder** is characterized by recurrent panic attacks, which are sudden, unpredictable, and overwhelming experiences of intense fear or terror without any reasonable cause.

How do generalized anxiety disorder and obsessive–compulsive disorder differ from specific phobias? **Generalized anxiety disorder** is defined by prolonged vague but intense fears that, unlike phobias, are not attached to any particular object or circumstance. In contrast, **obsessive–compulsive disorder** involves either involuntary thoughts that recur despite the person's attempt to stop them or compulsive rituals that a person feels compelled to perform.

Psychosomatic, Somatoform, and Dissociative Disorders

What are the differences among psychosomatic, somatoform, and dissociative disorders? **Psychosomatic disorders** are illnesses that have a valid physical basis, but are largely caused by psychological factors such as excessive stress and anxiety. In contrast, **somatoform disorders** are characterized by physical symptoms without any identifiable physical cause. Examples are **conversion disorder** (a dramatic specific disability without organic cause), **hypochondriasis** (insistence that minor symptoms mean serious illness), and **body dysmorphic disorder** (imagined ugliness in some part of the body).

In **dissociative disorders**, some part of a person's personality or memory is separated from the rest. Dissociative amnesia involves the loss of at least some significant aspects of memory. When an amnesia victim leaves home and assumes an entirely new identity, the disorder is known as *dissociative fugue*. In **dissociative identity disorder**, commonly known as *multiple personality disorder*, a person has several distinct personalities that emerge at different times.

Schizophrenic Disorders

How is schizophrenia different from dissociative identity disorder? In dissociative identity disorder, consciousness is split into two or more distinctive personalities, each of which is coherent and intact. This condition is different from **schizophrenic disorders**, which involve dramatic disruptions in thought and communication, inappropriate emotions, and bizarre behavior that lasts for years. People with schizophrenia are out of touch with reality and usually cannot live a normal life unless successfully treated with medication. They often suffer from **hallucinations** (false sensory perceptions) and **delusions** (false beliefs about reality).

How do the subtypes of schizophrenia differ from each other? Subtypes of schizophrenic disorders include **disorganized schizophrenia** (childish disregard for social conventions), **catatonic schizophrenia** (mute immobility or excessive excitement), **paranoid schizophrenia** (extreme suspiciousness related to complex delusions), and **undifferentiated schizophrenia** (characterized by a diversity of symptoms).

Is schizophrenia inherited? Based on findings obtained in twin and family studies, most researchers believe that there is a genetic basis for schizophrenia. However, the diathesis-stress model and systems model point out that psychological and social factors are also involved.

Other Common Disorders

What are the three main types of sexual disorders? DSM-IV recognizes three main types of sexual disorders. One is **sexual dysfunction**—loss or impairment of the ability to function effectively during sex. In men, this may take the form of erectile disorder (inability to achieve or keep an erection); in women, it often occurs as female sexual arousal disorder (inability to become sexually excited or to reach orgasm). Another main class of sexual disorders consists of the **paraphilias**, in which the person has sexual interest in unconventional objects or situations. One example is **fetishism**, or repeated use of a nonhuman object to achieve sexual excitement. Another is **pedophilia**, or sexual arousal that involves a prepubescent child. **Gender-identity disorders** make up the third main type of sexual disorder. These involve the desire to become, or the insistence that one really is, a member of the other sex.

Which personality disorder creates the most significant problems for society? **Personality disorders** are enduring, inflexible, and maladaptive ways of thinking and behaving that are so exaggerated and rigid that they cause serious inner distress or conflicts with others. Several types of personality disorders exist, each involving specific symptoms. People with **antisocial personality disorder** chronically lie, steal, and cheat with little or no remorse. Because this disorder is responsible for a good deal of crime and violence, it creates the greatest problems for society.

Why do stimulants appear to slow down hyperactive children and adults? DSM-IV-RT contains a long list of disorders usually first diagnosed in infancy, childhood, or adolescence. Two disorders discussed in this chapter are **attention-deficit/hyperactivity disorder (ADHD)** and **autistic disorder**. Children with ADHD are highly distractible, often fidgety and impulsive, and almost constantly in motion. The psychostimulants frequently prescribed for ADHD appear to increase the child's ability to focus attention on routine tasks. Autistic disorder is a profound problem identified in the first few years of life. It is characterized by a failure to form normal social attachments, by severe speech impairment, and by strange motor behaviors.

Psychotherapies

What do insight therapies have in common? **Psychotherapies** involve the use of psychological techniques to treat personality and behavior disorders, and several forms have been developed. **Insight therapy** is a major category of treatment for psychological problems. Insight therapies have the common goal of providing people with better awareness and understanding of their feelings, motivations, and actions in the hope that this will lead to better adjustment. Three examples of insight therapies are psychoanalysis, client-centered therapy, and short-term psychodynamic therapy.

Psychoanalysis is based on the belief that psychological problems stem from feelings and conflicts repressed during childhood. One way of uncovering what has been repressed is through the process of **free association**, in which the client discloses whatever thoughts or fantasies come to mind without editing or otherwise inhibiting them. As therapy progresses, the analyst takes a more active role and begins to interpret or suggest meanings for the clients' feelings, memories, and actions.

The insight therapy founded by Carl Rogers is built on the idea that treatment for psychological problems should be based on the client's view of the world rather than on the therapist's. For that reason, it is called **client-centered** or **person-centered therapy**. The therapist's most important task is to provide unconditional positive regard for clients so that they will learn to accept themselves.

Contemporary insight therapists are more active than traditional psychoanalysts, giving clients direct guidance and feedback. They are also more focused on clients' immediate problems than on their childhood traumas. An especially significant development is the trend toward **short-term psychodynamic therapy**, which recognizes that most people can be successfully treated within a limited time frame.

What do behaviorists believe should be the focus of psychotherapy? **Behavior therapies** are based on the belief that all behavior, normal and abnormal, is learned and that the goal of therapy is to teach people more satisfying ways of behaving. To behaviorists, the focus of psychotherapy should be the problem behaviors themselves, not some deeper, underlying conflicts that are presumably causing those behaviors.

When therapies attempt to evoke new conditioned responses to old stimuli, they are using classical conditioning as a basis for treatment. One example is a technique called **systematic desensitization**, in which people learn to remain in a deeply relaxed state while confronting situations that they fear. **Flooding**, which exposes phobic people to feared situations at full intensity for a prolonged period, is a harsh, but effective, method of desensitization.

Therapies based on operant conditioning encourage or discourage behaviors by reinforcing or punishing them, respectively. In the technique called **behavior contracting**, client and therapist agree on certain behavioral goals and on the reinforcement that the client will receive on reaching them. In another technique, which is called the **token economy**, tokens that can be exchanged for rewards are used for positive reinforcement.

In **modeling**, which is based on social learning principles, a person learns new behaviors by watching others perform them.

How can people overcome irrational and self-defeating beliefs about themselves? **Cognitive therapies** focus not so much on maladaptive behaviors as on maladaptive ways of thinking. By changing people's distorted, self-defeating ideas about themselves and the world, cognitive therapies help to encourage better coping skills and adjustment.

The things we say to ourselves as we go about our daily lives can encourage either success or failure, a self-confident outlook or acute anxiety. **Stress-inoculation therapy** takes advantage of this fact by teaching clients how to use self-talk to "coach" themselves through stressful situations.

Rational-emotive therapy (RET) is based on the idea that people's emotional problems derive from a set of irrational and self-defeating beliefs that they hold about themselves and the world. They think in terms of absolutes—they must be liked by *everyone*, be competent at *everything, always* be treated fairly, *never* be stymied by a problem. The therapist vigorously challenges these beliefs until the client comes to see just how irrational and dysfunctional these beliefs are.

Aaron Beck believes that depression results from negative patterns of thought—patterns that are strongly and inappropriately self-critical. Beck's **cognitive therapy** tries to help such people think more objectively and positively about themselves and their life situations.

What are some advantages of group therapies? **Group therapies** are based on the idea that psychological problems are at least partly interpersonal and are therefore best approached in a group. Group therapies offer a circle of support for clients, shared insights into problems, and the opportunity to obtain psychotherapy at a lower cost. Among the many different kinds of group therapy are self-help groups, family therapy, and couple therapy. As the cost of private psychotherapy has risen, self-help groups have become increasingly popular because of their low cost. In such groups, people share their concerns and feelings with others who are experiencing similar problems. For example, Alcoholics Anonymous is a very effective self-help group.

Family therapy is based on the idea that a person's psychological problems are to some extent also family problems. Therefore, the therapist treats the entire family, rather than just the individual reportedly having difficulties. The major goals are to improve communication and empathy and to reduce conflict within the family. **Couple therapy** concentrates on improving patterns of communication and interaction between couples. Similar to family therapy, it attempts to change relationships, not just individuals. Empathy training and scheduled exchanges of rewards are two of the techniques used to turn a hostile, unsatisfying relationship around.

How much better off is a person who receives psychotherapy than one who gets no treatment at all? Most researchers agree that psychotherapy helps about two-thirds of the people treated. Although there is some debate over how many untreated people also recover, the consensus is that those who get therapy are generally better off than those who don't. Each kind of therapy, however, works better for some problems than for others.

Biological Treatments

What has been the impact of psychoactive drugs on the treatment of psychological disorders? **Biological treatments**—including medication, electroconvulsive therapy, and psychosurgery—are sometimes used when psychotherapy does not work or when a client has a disorder for which biological treatment is known to be safe and effective. Medication, especially, is very often used in conjunction with psychotherapy. Psychiatrists (who are also physicians) are the only mental health professionals licensed to offer biological treatments.

Drugs are the most common form of biological therapy and psychoactive drugs are often categorized according to the disorders for which they are generally used. For example, antidepressant drugs alleviate depression, though some also have serious side effects. Antipsychotic drugs are valuable in treating schizophrenia. They do not cure the disorder, but they reduce its symptoms, although side effects can be severe. Many types of medications are used to treat psychological disorders, and in general they work by modifying various neurotransmitter mechanisms in the brain.

Before the development of effective medications in the 1950's, institutionalization in large mental hospitals was the most common approach to caring for people with serious mental disorders. Then, with the advent of antipsychotic drugs, a trend began toward **deinstitutionalization** (integrating people with serious mental disorders back into the community). The idea behind deinstitutionalization was that people would be cared for in a community setting, but community mental health centers and other support services proved inadequate to the task. As a result, many former patients stopped taking their medication, became homeless, and ended up suffering from psychosis and living on the streets. Thus, although deinstitutionalization may have been a good idea in principle, in practice it has not worked out well for many patients or for society.

How is the electroconvulsive therapy of today different from that of the past? **Electroconvulsive therapy (ECT)** is used for cases of severe depression that do not respond to other treatments. An electric current briefly passed through the brain of the patient produces convulsions and temporary loss of consciousness, but depression often lifts afterward.

What is psychosurgery, and how is it used? **Psychosurgery** is brain surgery performed to change a person's behavior and emotional state. It is rarely used today, and then only as a last, desperate measure on people who have severe and intractable problems and don't respond to any other form of treatment.

Challenges in Therapy

Are there particular groups of people who may require special approaches in the treatment of psychological problems? Given that human beings differ as much as they do, it isn't surprising that a one-size-fits-all concept isn't always appropriate in the treatment of psychological problems. In recent years, the special needs of people from other cultures have gained the attention of mental health professionals.

How should individuals evaluate which therapy is best for them? The choice of which particular therapy to use should be based not only on a person's symptoms, but also on the preferences of the individual receiving treatment.

Psychological Disorders and Their Treatments

>CHAPTER 9<

9.1 PERSPECTIVES ON PSYCHOLOGICAL DISORDERS

MODELS OF ABNORMALITY

- **Biological model:** Biochemical or physiological causes that often involve faulty neurotransmitter systems
- **Psychoanalytic model:** Unconscious internal conflicts and issues
- **Cognitive-Behavioral model:** Learned maladaptive ways of thinking and behaving
- **Diathesis-stress model:** Biological predispositions (diatheses) make some people more vulnerable to stress
- **Systems models:** Combine biological, psychological, and social risk factors

9.2 MOOD DISORDERS

DISRUPTIONS OF NORMAL MOOD

- **Depression:** Overwhelming feeling of sadness, lack of interest in activities, guilt, feelings of worthlessness
- **Dysthymia:** Milder but longer lasting feelings of depression
- **Mania:** Euphoric (high) mood, extreme physical activity and distractedness, grandiosity
- **Bipolar Disorder:** Alternating periods of depression and mania

CAUSES

- Biological: Genes (bipolar disorder and depression); neurotransmitter imbalances
- Cognitive distortions and negative self-perceptions
- For vulnerable individuals, stressful situations

9.3 ANXIETY DISORDERS

MAJOR ANXIETY DISORDERS

- **Specific phobia:** Intense, paralyzing fear of something
- **Panic disorder:** Recurrent and unpredictable panic attacks
- **Generalized anxiety disorder:** Prolonged vague but intense fears
- **Obsessive-compulsive disorder (OCD):** Disturbing thoughts (obsessions) or senseless rituals (compulsions)
- **Post-traumatic stress disorder (PTSD):** Long-lasting anxiety reaction following a traumatic event
- **Acute stress disorder:** Extreme anxiety reaction soon after a traumatic event

9.4 PSYCHOSOMATIC, SOMATOFORM, DISSOCIATIVE DISORDERS

PSYCHOSOMATIC DISORDERS

- Real physical illness largely caused by psychological forces
- Examples: Tension headaches and immune system disorders
- Not included in the DSM listing

SOMATOFORM DISORDERS

- Physical symptoms, no identifiable biological cause
- Conversion disorder: Specific disability such as paralysis or blindness
- Hypochondriasis: Insignificant symptoms perceived as a sign of serious illness
- Body dysmorphic disorder: Extreme preoccupation with imagined ugliness or deformity

DISSOCIATIVE DISORDERS

- Separation of some aspects of the personality from others
- Dissociative identity disorder ("multiple personality disorder")

9.5 SCHIZOPHRENIC DISORDERS

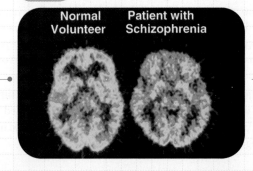

Normal Volunteer   Patient with Schizophrenia

MAJOR SYMPTOMS AND SUBTYPES

- Disturbances of thoughts, communications, and emotions, including delusions and hallucinations
- Psychosis: Behavior characterized by loss of touch with reality
- Subtypes: Disorganized, catatonic, paranoid, undifferentiated

CAUSES

- Faulty genes
- Problems regulating neurotransmitters
- Structural problems in the brain
- Stress and other psychological factors

9.6 OTHER COMMON DISORDERS

SEXUAL AND GENDER-IDENTITY DISORDERS

- **Sexual dysfunction:** Loss or impairment of ordinary sexual function
- **Paraphilias:** Using unconventional objects or situations to achieve sexual arousal
- **Gender-identity disorder:** The desire to become, or the insistence that one is, a member of the opposite sex

PERSONALITY DISORDERS

- Inflexible and maladaptive ways of thinking and behaving
- **Antisocial personality disorder:** Lack of guilt or remorse for criminal acts

CHILDHOOD DISORDERS

- **Attention-deficit/hyperactivity disorder (ADHD):** Inattention, impulsiveness, and hyperactivity
- **Autistic disorder:** Lack of social instincts and strange motor behavior

9.7 PSYCHOTHERAPIES

INSIGHT THERAPIES: Psychoanalysis (Freud); Client-centered (person-centered) therapy (Rogers); Gestalt therapy (Perls); short-term psychodynamic therapy (common modern approach)

BEHAVIOR THERAPIES: Systematic desensitization, flooding, behavioral contracting, token economies, modeling

COGNITIVE-BASED THERAPIES: Stress-inoculation therapy, rational-emotive therapy (RET), cognitive therapy (Beck)

GROUP THERAPIES: Self-help groups, family therapy, couple therapy

DESENSITIZATION THERAPY These photos show people overcoming a simple phobia: fear of snakes

9.8 BIOLOGICAL TREATMENTS

DRUG THERAPIES

- Antianxiety drugs
- Antidepressant drugs
- Antipsychotic drugs
- Lithium

ELECTROCONVULSIVE THERAPY

- Passing a mild electric current through the brain, producing a seizure
- Used to treat severe, prolonged depression

PSYCHOSURGERY

- Brain surgery performed to change behavior or emotional state
- Used rarely and as a last resort

9.9 CHALLENGES IN THERAPY

- Therapists must be sensitive to their clients' cultural differences
- Therapists must match therapies to the symptoms and preferences of clients

Concept Map

Overview

Social Psychology

You and your boss are interviewing two people for a spot on your project management team. One is a well-dressed young white man. The other is a middle-aged white woman, overweight and wearing colorful clothes. It turns out they are equally qualified and both very smart and personable, although the older woman has several more years of actual experience in your field. Still, your boss tells you, "I don't think that she'll be a good fit with the team." You find yourself agreeing, though you just can't put your finger on why.

This little scenario illustrates one of the most hard-to-fight causes of discriminatory behavior: hidden biases. Even when people are outwardly committed to egalitarian behavior or work hard to behave without prejudice with regard to age, race, appearance or sexual orientation, they often harbor unconscious negative prejudices or stereotypes. Not only do hidden biases derail careers and lead to damaging consequences everywhere from schoolrooms to banks, they can also affect split-second, life-or-death decisions. Shootings of black men incorrectly thought to be holding guns—an immigrant in New York, a cop in Rhode Island—have brought this issue into public debate.

There's certainly no denying that hidden bias has a corrosive effect in the workplace. A bright young woman with an MBA from Columbia University, Peggy Knoll has a reputation as a top performer. Like many of her B-school peers, she wants to reach the top echelons of corporate life; however, unlike most men and women in her graduating class, Knoll has characteristics that block her path to the top. She wears cornrows and laughs loudly. According to her boss, Knoll has an appearance and persona that undermines her leadership potential. In other words, Knoll looks and acts black, which she is, instead of white, and this spurs those around her—like her boss—to act on hidden biases they would never, ever, admit to having.

A now classic experiment showed that white interviewers sat farther away from black applicants than from other white applicants, made more speech errors, and ended the interviews 25 percent sooner. This kind of behavior on the part of an interviewer would certainly diminish the performance of anyone treated that way. Knoll, who was a focus-group participant in a recent survey on bias, is one of many black professionals who say her career has been derailed by hidden-bias discrimination tied to characteristics such as hairstyles, speech patterns, mannerisms, or wardrobe. In fact, in a survey of more than 1,600 minority professionals, over 40 percent of professional women in large corporations say they feel excluded and constrained by "style compliance"— the need to blend into a corporate culture dominated by white men. "Asian women executives were convinced that they weren't commanding enough in their tone of voice, and were not assertive," says economist Sylvia Ann Hewlett, co-investigator of the study. "African-American managers were quite sure they spoke too loudly, were too threatening." And as for professionals from India, one survey participant said: "There's a stereotype that they're very good technically...but they're not really the leaders of tomorrow."

Not only do victims of hidden biases suffer, but workplaces do, too. Hidden biases can reduce a company's productivity by affecting employees' ability to work in teams. They affect employee turnover and quality of life and can also leave employers out of step with the country's shifting demographics. In a nation where the Hispanic population is growing by leaps and bounds, white men still account for 98 percent of CEOs and 95 percent of top earners in Fortune 500 companies. With increasing spending power, minorities are starting to look at companies and say, "Why should we spend our money here if your senior staff is a totally different color?"

So if biases are hidden, how can we possibly get rid of them? The first step is rooting them out. A team of researchers from Harvard University, the University of Virginia, and the University of Washington have developed the Implicit Association Test (IAT) as part of a project designed to detect bias based on several factors, including race, gender, age, sexual orientation, weight, and national origin. One of the test's developers, Tony Greenwald, was one of the first to take the test. He was surprised and dismayed to discover that even he held hidden biases. Want to test your own? It's easy to take the test yourself by going to http://www.tolerance.org/hidden_bias/index.html.[1]

Greenwald and his fellow researchers specialize in the field of social psychology, which is the topic of this chapter. **Social psychology** is the scientific study of how people's thoughts, feelings, and behaviors are influenced by the behaviors and characteristics of other people, whether real, imagined, or inferred. Every day, we all make judgments concerning other people that are often based on very little "real" evidence. The process by which we form such impressions, whether accurate or not, is part of a fascinating area of social psychology known as social cognition. ◻

Social Cognition

10.1 Identify and describe the common errors humans commit and the biases they hold when they make attributions about the causes of their own and others' actions.

Part of the process of being influenced by other people involves organizing and interpreting information about them. We use this information to form first impressions, to try to understand their behavior, and to determine to what extent we are attracted to them. This collecting and assessing of information about other people is called **social cognition**. Social cognition is a major area of interest to social psychologists.

social psychology The scientific study of the ways in which the thoughts, feelings, and behaviors of one individual are influenced by the real, imagined, or inferred behavior or characteristics of other people.

social cognition Knowledge and understanding concerning the social world and the people in it (including oneself).

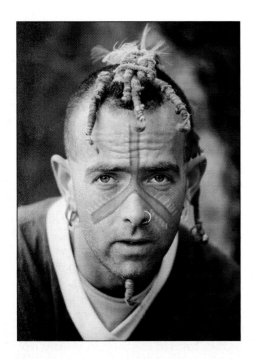

First impressions are important, since we construct schemata that are heavily influenced by the primacy effect. What first impressions do you think are triggered by the hair and adornments of this young man?

FORMING IMPRESSIONS

How do we form first impressions of people?

Forming first impressions of people is more complex than you may think. You must direct your attention to various aspects of the person's appearance and behavior and then make a rapid assessment of what those characteristics mean. How do you complete this process? What cues do you interpret? How accurate are your impressions? The concept of *schemata* helps to answer these questions.

SCHEMATA When we meet someone for the first time, we notice a number of things about that person—clothes, gestures, manner of speaking, body build, and facial features. We then draw on these cues to fit the person into a category. No matter how little information we have or how contradictory it is, no matter how many times our initial impressions have been wrong, we still categorize people after meeting them only briefly. Associated with each category is a **schema**—a set of beliefs and expectations based on past experience that is presumed to apply to all members of that category (Fiske & Taylor, 1991). Schemata (the plural of schema) flesh out our impressions after we have pegged people into categories. For example, if a woman is wearing a white coat and has a stethoscope around her neck, you could reasonably categorize her as a doctor. Associated with this category is a schema of various beliefs and expectations: highly trained professional, knowledgeable about diseases and their cures, qualified to prescribe medication, and so on. By applying this schema, you expect that this particular woman has these traits. As the opening paragraphs of this chapter make clear, our schemata at times reflect subtle—or perhaps not to subtle—biases that have been incorporated into our schemata.

Our reliance on schemata reflects a desire to lessen our mental effort. Humans have been called "cognitive misers" (Fiske & Taylor, 1991). Instead of exerting ourselves to interpret every detail that we learn about a person, we are stingy with our mental efforts. Generally speaking, once we have formed an impression about someone, we do not exert the mental effort to change it, even if that impression was formed by jumping to conclusions or through prejudice (Fiske, 1995). Over time, however, as we continue to interact with people, we do add new information about them to our mental files. Our later experiences, though, generally do not influence us nearly so much as our earliest impressions. This phenomenon is called the **primacy effect**. For example, if you already like a new acquaintance, you may excuse something that annoys you later. Conversely, if someone makes an early *bad* impression, subsequent evidence of that person's good qualities will do little to change your feelings, again reflecting the power of the primacy effect.

Schemata also help us create the behavior we expect from other people. In one study, pairs of participants played a competitive game (Snyder & Swann, 1978). The researchers told one member of each pair that his or her partner was either hostile or friendly. The players who were led to believe that their partner was hostile behaved differently toward the partner than did the players led to believe that their partner was friendly. In turn, those treated as hostile actually began to display hostility. In fact, these people continued to show hostility later, when they were paired with new players who had no expectations about them at all. The expectation of hostility seemed to produce actual aggressiveness, and this behavior persisted. When we bring about expected behavior in another person in this way, our impression becomes a **self-fulfilling prophecy** (Rosenthal, 2002).

STEREOTYPES Just as schemata shape our impressions of others, so do stereotypes. A **stereotype** is a set of characteristics presumed to be shared by all members of a social category. A stereotype is actually a special kind of schema, one that is simplistic, but very strongly held, and not necessarily based on firsthand experience. A stereotype can involve almost any distinguishing feature of a person—age, sex, race, occupation, place of residence, or membership in a certain group (Hilton & Von Hipple, 1996).

When our first impression of a person is governed by a stereotype, we tend to infer things about that person solely on the basis of some key distinguishing feature and to ignore facts that are inconsistent with the stereotype, no matter how apparent they are. As a result, we may perceive things about the person selectively or inaccurately, thereby perpet-

schema (plural: schemata) A set of beliefs or expectations about something that is based on past experience.

primacy effect The fact that early information about someone weighs more heavily than later information in influencing one's impression of that person.

self-fulfilling prophecy The process in which a person's expectation about another elicits behavior from the second person that confirms the expectation.

stereotype A set of characteristics presumed to be shared by all members of a social category.

uating our initial stereotype. For example, after you have categorized someone as male or female, you may rely more on your stereotype of that gender than on your own observations of how the person acts. Because women are traditionally stereotyped as more emotional and submissive and men as more rational and assertive (Deaux & Kite, 1993; Williams & Best, 1990), you may come to see these traits in men and women more than they really exist. Clearly, stereotypes can reflect hidden biases, like those described in the opening paragraphs of this chapter.

Recent studies (Macrae & Bodenhausen, 2000) indicate that sorting people into categories is not automatic or inevitable. People are more likely to apply stereotyped schemata in a chance encounter than in a structured, task-oriented situation (such as a classroom or the office); more likely to pay attention to individual signals than to stereotypes when they are pursuing a goal; and consciously, or unconsciously, to suppress stereotypes that violate social norms. For example, a man who has operated according to stereotyped schemata may expect women in gender-typed roles, such as a nurse or secretary or his wife, to be warm and gentle, but may not hold these expectations toward women he meets in his work life or in their professional roles (as lawyer, executive, or telephone repair person).

ATTRIBUTION

How do we decide why people act as they do?

Suppose that you run into a friend at the supermarket. You greet him warmly, but he barely acknowledges you, mumbles "Hi," and walks away. You feel snubbed and try to figure out why he acted like that. Did he behave that way because of something in the situation? Did you say something to offend him? Was he somehow embarrassed by meeting you at the particular time and place? Or is his behavior more correctly attributed to something within him—to some personal trait such as moodiness or arrogance?

Stereotypes can be complex. Would most people see this construction worker as possessing more stereotypically female, or male, personal qualities?

EXPLAINING BEHAVIOR Social interaction is filled with these types of occasions—occasions that invite us to make judgments about the causes of behavior. When something unexpected or unpleasant occurs, we wonder about it and try to understand it. Social psychologists' observations about how we go about attributing causes to behavior form the basis of **attribution theory**.

One way of thinking about the causes of behavior is to view them as arising from *internal* versus *external* causes. Thus, we might conclude that a classmate's lateness was caused by his laziness (a personal factor, which is an internal attribution) or by traffic congestion (a situational factor, which is an external attribution). To explain behavior further, we rely on three kinds of information about the behavior: distinctiveness, consistency, and consensus. For example, if your instructor asks you to stay briefly after class so that she can talk with you, you will probably try to figure out what lies behind her request by asking yourself three questions.

First, how *distinctive* is the instructor's request? Does she often ask students to stay and talk (low distinctiveness) or is such a request unusual (high distinctiveness)? If she often asks students to speak with her, you will probably conclude that she has personal reasons for talking with you. But if her request is highly distinctive, you will probably conclude that something about you, not her, underlies her request.

Second, how *consistent* is the instructor's behavior? Does she regularly ask you to stay and talk (high consistency), or is this a first for you (low consistency)? If she has consistently made this request of you before, you will probably guess that this occasion is like those others. But if her request is inconsistent with past behavior, you will probably wonder whether some particular event—perhaps something you said in class—motivated her to request a private conference.

Finally, what degree of *consensus* among teachers exists regarding this behavior? Do your other instructors ask you to stay and talk with them (high consensus), or is this instructor unique in making such a request (low consensus)? If it is common for instructors in your school to ask to speak with you, this instructor's request is probably due to some external factor. But if she is the only instructor ever to ask to speak privately with you, it must

attribution theory The theory that addresses question of how people make judgments about the causes of behavior.

Did this accident happen because of poor driving or because the driver swerved to avoid a child in the street? The fundamental attribution error says that we are more likely to attribute the bad behavior of others to internal causes, such as poor driving, rather than situational factors, such as a child in the street.

be something about this particular person—an internal motive or a concern—that accounts for her behavior (Iacobucci & McGill, 1990).

If you conclude that the instructor has her own reasons for wanting to speak with you, you may feel mildly curious for the remainder of class until you can find out what she wants. But if you think external factors—like your own actions—have prompted her request, you may worry about whether you are in trouble and nervously wait for the end of class.

BIASES Unfortunately, the causal attributions we make are often vulnerable to *biases*. For example, imagine that you are at a party and you see an acquaintance, Ted, walk across the room carrying several plates of food and a drink. As he approaches his chair, Ted spills food on himself. You may attribute the spill to Ted's personal characteristics—he is clumsy. Ted, however, is likely to make a very different attribution. He will likely attribute the spill to an external factor—he was carrying too many other things. Your explanation for this behavior reflects the **fundamental attribution error**—the tendency to attribute the behavior of others to causes within themselves (Aronson, Wilson, & Akert, 1999; Gilbert & Malone, 1995; Ross & Nisbett, 1991). The fundamental attribution error is part of the *actor–observer bias*—the tendency to explain the behavior of others as caused by internal factors, while attributing *one's own* behavior to *external* forces (Fiske & Taylor, 1991).

A related type of biases is called **defensive attribution**. Defensive attributions occur when we are motivated to present ourselves well, either to impress others or to feel good about ourselves (Agostinelli, Sherman, Presson, & Chassin, 1992). One example of a defensive attribution is the *self-serving bias*, which is a tendency to attribute our successes to our personal attributes while chalking up our failures to external forces beyond our control (Schlenker & Weigold, 1992; Sedikides, Campbell, Reeder, & Elliot, 1998). Students do this all the time. They tend to regard exams on which they do well as good indicators of their abilities and exams on which they do poorly as bad indicators (Davis & Stephan, 1980). Similarly, teachers are more likely to assume responsibility for students' successes than for their failures (Arkin, Cooper, & Kolditz, 1980). In one survey of more than 800,000 high school seniors, less than 1 percent said they were below average in "ability to get along with others," while more than half said they were in the top 10 percent. In another survey, less than 80 percent of the respondents said that Mother Teresa was likely to go to heaven, though 87 percent said that they themselves were likely to do so (Shermer, 2004).

A second type of defensive attribution comes from thinking that people get what they deserve: Bad things happen to bad people, and good things happen to good people. This is called the **just-world hypothesis** (Lerner, 1980). When misfortune strikes someone, we often jump to the conclusion that the person deserved it, rather than giving full weight to situational factors that may have been responsible. Why do we behave this way? One reason is that doing so gives us the comforting illusion that such a thing could never happen to us. By reassigning the blame for a terrible misfortune from a chance event (something that could happen to us) to the victim's own negligence (a trait that *we*, of course, do not share), we delude ourselves into believing that we could never suffer such a fate (Dalbert, 2001).

fundamental attribution error The tendency of people to overemphasize personal causes for other people's behavior and to underemphasize personal causes for their own behavior.

defensive attribution The tendency to attribute our successes to our own efforts or qualities and our failures to external factors.

just-world hypothesis Attribution error that is based on the assumption that bad things happen to bad people and good things happen to good people.

INTERPERSONAL ATTRACTION

Do "birds of a feather flock together," or do "opposites attract"?

A third aspect of social cognition involves interpersonal attraction. When people meet, what determines whether they will like each other or not? This is the subject of much speculation and even mystification, with popular explanations running the gamut from fate to compatible astrological signs. Romantics believe that irresistible forces propel individuals toward an inevitable meeting with their beloved, but social psychologists take a more hardheaded view. They have found that attraction and the tendency to like someone else are closely linked to such factors as *proximity*, *physical attractiveness*, *similarity*, *exchange*, and *intimacy*.

PROXIMITY **Proximity** is usually the most important factor in determining attraction (Berscheid & Reis, 1998; Brehm, 2002). The closer two people live to each other, the more likely they are to interact; the more frequent their interaction, the more they will tend to like each other. Conversely, two people separated by considerable geographic distance are not likely to run into each other and thus have little chance to develop a mutual attraction. The proximity effect has less to do with simple convenience than with the security and comfort we feel with people and things that have become familiar. Familiar people are predictable and safe—thus more likable (Bornstein, 1989).

PHYSICAL ATTRACTIVENESS Physical attractiveness can powerfully influence the conclusions that we reach about a person's character. We actually give attractive people credit for more than their beauty. We presume them to be more intelligent, interesting, happy, kind, sensitive, moral, and successful than people who are not perceived as attractive. They are also thought to make better spouses and to be more sexually responsive (Dion, 1972; Feingold, 1992; Katz, 2003; Zuckerman, Miyake, & Elkin, 1995). As we saw in the opening paragraphs of this chapter, physical attractiveness is often part of the hidden biases people hold.

Not only do we tend to credit physically attractive people with a wealth of positive qualities, but we also tend to like them more than we do less attractive people. One reason is that physical attractiveness itself is generally considered a positive attribute (Baron & Byrne, 1991). Research has found that mothers of more attractive infants tend to show their children more affection and to play with them more often than mothers of unattractive infants (Langlois, Ritter, Casey, & Sawin, 1995). Even in hospitals, premature infants rated as more attractive by attending nurses thrived better and gained weight faster than those judged as less attractive, presumably because they received more nurturing (Badr & Abdallah, 2001). Attractive children are more likely to be treated leniently by teachers (McCall, 1997), and attractive adults are generally judged to be more productive by their employers (Hosoda, Stone, & Coats, 2003).

In general, we tend to give good-looking people the benefit of the doubt: If they don't live up to our expectations during the first encounter, we give them a second chance, ask for or accept a second date, or seek further opportunities for interaction. These reactions can give attractive people substantial advantages in life and can lead to self-fulfilling prophecies: physically attractive people may come to think of themselves as good or lovable because they are continually treated as if they are. Conversely, unattractive people may begin to see themselves as bad or unlovable because they have always been regarded that way—even as children.

SIMILARITY Attractiveness, however, isn't everything. In the abstract, people might prefer extremely attractive individuals, but in reality they usually chose friends and partners who are close to their own level of attractiveness (Harvey & Pauwells, 1999). Similarity—of attitudes, interests, values, backgrounds, and beliefs, as well as looks—underlies much interpersonal attraction (AhYun, 2002; P. M. Buss, 1985; Sano, 2002; Tan & Singh, 1995). When we know that someone shares our attitudes and interests, we tend to have more positive feelings toward that person.

We value similarity because it is important to us to have others agree with our choices and beliefs. By comparing our opinions with those of other people, we clarify our understanding of and reduce our uncertainty about social situations. Finding that others agree with us strengthens our convictions and boosts our self-esteem (Suls & Fletcher, 1983).

If similarity is such a critical determinant of attraction, what about the notion that opposites attract? Aren't people sometimes attracted to others who are completely different from them? Extensive research has failed to confirm this notion. In long-term

What factors are most important in the formation of romantic relationships: proximity? physical attractiveness? similarity in attitudes or circumstances? Social psychologists have found that interpersonal attractiveness depends on each of these factors, and others as well.

proximity How close two people live to each other.

exchange The concept that relationships are based on trading rewards among partners.

equity Fairness of exchange achieved when each partner in the relationship receives the same proportion of outcomes to investments.

Self-disclosure—revealing personal experiences and opinions—is essential to all close relationships.

relationships, where attraction plays an especially important role, people overwhelmingly prefer to associate with people who are similar to themselves (D. M. Buss, 1985).

EXCHANGE According to the *reward theory of attraction*, we tend to like people who make us feel rewarded and appreciated. The reward theory of attraction is based on the concept of **exchange**. In social interactions, people make exchanges. For example, you may agree to help a friend paint his apartment if he prepares dinner for you. Every exchange involves both rewards (you get a free dinner; he gets his apartment painted) and costs (you have to paint first; he then has to cook you dinner).

Exchanges work only insofar as they are fair or equitable. A relationship is based on **equity** when what one person "gets out of it" is equal to what the other gets (Walster, Walster, & Berscheid, 1978; van Yperen & Buunk, 1990) (see also Chapter 11: "Psychology Applied to Work"). As long as both parties find their interactions more rewarding than costly, and continue to feel the relationship is equitable, their exchanges are likely to continue (Cook & Rice, 2003; Takeuchi, 2000; Van Yperen & Buunk, 1990). When exchanges are consistently unfair, the one who reaps fewer rewards feels cheated, and the one who gains is apt to feel guilty. This result may undermine the attraction that once drew the two people together.

INTIMACY When does liking someone become something more? *Intimacy* is the quality of genuine closeness and trust in another person. People become closer and stay closer through a continuing reciprocal pattern where each person tries to know the other and allows the other to know him or her (Harvey & Pauwells, 1999). When people communicate, they do more than just interact—they share deep-rooted feelings and ideas. When you are first getting to know someone, you communicate about "safe," superficial topics like the weather, sports, or shared activities. As you get to know each other better over time, your conversation progresses to more personal subjects: your personal experiences, memories, hopes and fears, goals and failures (Altman & Taylor, 1973).

Intimate communication is based on the process of *self-disclosure* (Prager, 1995). As you talk with friends, you disclose, or reveal, personal experiences and opinions that you might conceal from strangers. Because self-disclosure is possible only when you trust the listener, you will seek—and usually receive—a reciprocal disclosure to keep the conversation balanced. For example, after telling your roommate about something that embarrassed you, you may expect him or her to reveal a similar episode; you might even ask directly, "Has anything like that ever happened to you?" Such reciprocal intimacy keeps you "even" and makes your relationship more emotionally satisfying (Collins & Miller, 1994). The pacing of disclosure is important. If you "jump levels" by revealing too much too soon—or to someone who is not ready to make a reciprocal personal response—the other person will probably retreat, and communication will go no further.

▶ CHECK YOUR UNDERSTANDING

1. Associated with the many categories into which we "peg" people are sets of beliefs and expectations called _____ that are assumed to apply to all members of a category. When these are quite simplistic, but deeply held, they are often referred to as _____.

2. When the first information we receive about a person weighs more heavily in forming an impression than later information does, we are experiencing the _____ effect.

3. The tendency to attribute the behavior of others to internal causes and one's own behavior to external causes is called the _____ _____.

4. The belief that people must deserve the bad things that happen to them reflects the _____-_____ _____.

5. The tendency to attribute the behavior of others to personal characteristics is the _____-_____ bias.

6. Jonas dates Lucy because she is funny, outgoing, and intelligent; she dates him because he is attractive and supportive. Their relationship is best explained by which view?
   a. primacy theory
   b. the self-fulfilling prophecy
   c. attractiveness bias
   d. equity theory

Answers: 1. schemata, stereotypes, 2. primacy, 3. fundamental attribution error, 4. just-world hypothesis, 5. actor-observer, 6. d.

1. You meet someone at a party who is outgoing, entertaining, and has a great sense of humor. A week later, your paths cross again, but this time the person seems very shy, withdrawn, and humorless. Most likely, your impression of this person after the second meeting is that he or she _____.
   a. is actually shy, withdrawn, and humorless, despite your initial impression
   b. is actually outgoing and entertaining but was just having a bad day
   c. is low in social cognition
   d. has just engaged in a self-fulfilling prophecy

2. Your classmate tells you she did really well on her mathematics midterm exam because she studied hard and "knew the material cold." But she says she did poorly on her psychology midterm because the exam was unfair and full of ambiguous questions. On the basis of what you have learned in this portion of the chapter, this may be an example of _____.
   a. the fundamental attribution bias
   b. the primacy effect
   c. the self-fulfilling prophecy
   d. stereotyping

Answers: 1. b., 2. a.

Attitudes

10.2 Distinguish between prejudice and discrimination and describe the factors that cause and reduce these attitudes and behaviors.

The phrase "I don't like his attitude" is a telling one. People are often told to "change your attitude" or make an "attitude adjustment." An **attitude** is a relatively stable organization of beliefs, feelings, and tendencies toward something or someone—called an attitude object. Attitudes are important mainly because they often influence our behavior. Discrimination, for example, is often caused by prejudiced attitudes. Psychologists wonder how attitudes are formed and how they can be changed.

THE NATURE OF ATTITUDES

What are attitudes and why are they important?

An attitude has three major components: *evaluative beliefs* about the object, *feelings* about the object, and *behavior tendencies* toward the object. Beliefs include facts, opinions, and our general knowledge. Feelings encompass love, hate, like, dislike, and similar sentiments. Behavior tendencies refer to our inclinations to act in certain ways toward the object—to approach it, avoid it, and so on. For example, our attitude toward a political candidate includes our beliefs about the candidate's qualifications and positions on crucial issues and our expectations about how the candidate will vote on those issues. We also have feelings about the candidate—like or dislike, trust or mistrust. And because of these beliefs and feelings, we are inclined to behave in certain ways toward the candidate—to vote for or against the candidate, to contribute time or money to the candidate's campaign, to make a point of attending or staying away from rallies for the candidate, and so forth.

As we will see shortly, these three aspects of an attitude are often consistent with one another. For example, if we have positive feelings toward something, we tend to have positive beliefs about it and to behave positively toward it. This tendency does not mean, however, that our every action will accurately reflect our attitudes.

ATTITUDES AND BEHAVIOR The relationship between attitudes and behavior is not always straightforward (Andrich & Styles, 1998). Variables such as the strength of the attitude, how easily it comes to mind, how salient (or noticeable) a particular attitude is in a given situation, and how relevant the attitude is to the particular behavior in question help to determine whether a person will act in accordance with an attitude (Eagly, 1992; Eagly & Chaiken, 1998; Kraus, 1995).

Personality traits are also important. Some people consistently match their actions to their attitudes (R. Norman, 1975). Others have a tendency to override their own attitudes to behave properly in a given situation. As a result, attitudes predict behavior better for

attitude Relatively stable organization of beliefs, feelings, and behavior tendencies directed toward something or someone—the attitude object.

Workers who are high on the trait of self-monitoring are more likely to behave in ways that their managers expect, rather than to openly, but honestly, disagree.

some people than for others (M. Snyder & Tanke, 1976). People who rate highly on **self-monitoring** are especially likely to override their attitudes to behave in accordance with others' expectations. Before speaking or acting, high self-monitors observe the situation for clues about how they should react. Then they try to meet those "demands," rather than behave according to their own beliefs or sentiments. In contrast, low self-monitors express and act on their attitudes with great consistency, showing little regard for situational clues or constraints. Thus, a high self-monitor who disagrees with the politics of a fellow dinner guest may keep her thoughts to herself in an effort to be polite and agreeable, whereas a low self-monitor who disagrees might dispute the speaker openly, even though doing so might disrupt the social occasion (Snyder, 1987).

ATTITUDE DEVELOPMENT How do we acquire our attitudes? Where do they come from? Many of our basic attitudes derive from early, direct personal experience. Children are rewarded with smiles and encouragement when they please their parents, and they are punished through disapproval when they displease them. These early experiences give children enduring attitudes (Oskamp, 1991). Attitudes are also formed by imitation. Children mimic the behavior of their parents and peers, acquiring attitudes even when no one is deliberately trying to shape them.

But parents are not the only source of attitudes. Teachers, friends, and even famous people are also important in shaping our attitudes. A student who idolizes a teacher may adopt many of the teacher's attitudes toward controversial subjects, even if they run counter to attitudes of parents or friends. The mass media, particularly television, also have a great impact on attitude formation. Television bombards us with messages—not merely through its news and entertainment, but also through commercials. Without experience of their own against which to measure the merit of these messages, children are particularly susceptible to the influence of television on their attitudes (see Chapter 7: "Human Development Across the Lifespan").

PREJUDICE AND DISCRIMINATION

How does a person develop a prejudice toward someone else?

Although the terms *prejudice* and *discrimination* are often used interchangeably, they actually refer to different concepts. **Prejudice**—an attitude—is an unfair, intolerant, or unfavorable view of a group of people. **Discrimination**—a behavior—is an unfair act or a series

self-monitoring The tendency for an individual to observe the situation for cues about how to react.

prejudice An unfair, intolerant, or unfavorable attitude toward a group of people.

discrimination An unfair act or series of acts taken toward an entire group of people or individual members of that group.

When interviewing job applicants, it is important to be aware of the influence of prejudice, so that decisions are based on each candidate's skills, experiences, and abilities, not on attributes unrelated to job performance.

of acts directed against an entire group of people or individual members of that group. To discriminate is to treat an entire class of people in an unfair way.

Prejudice and discrimination do not always occur together. It is possible to be prejudiced against a particular group without openly behaving in a hostile or discriminatory manner toward its members. Discrimination, the expression of prejudice, is determined by a variety of factors. Some factors encourage suppressing prejudice and others encourage or justify its expression (Crandall & Eshleman, 2003): A prejudiced store owner may smile at an African-American customer, for example, to disguise opinions that could hurt his business. Likewise, many institutional practices can be discriminatory even though they are not based on prejudice. For example, regulations establishing a minimum height requirement for police officers may discriminate against women and certain ethnic groups whose average height falls below the arbitrary standard, even though the regulations do not stem from sexist or racist attitudes.

PREJUDICE Like attitudes in general, prejudice has three components: beliefs, feelings, and behavioral tendencies. Prejudicial beliefs are virtually always negative stereotypes, and as mentioned earlier, reliance on stereotypes can lead to erroneous thinking about other people. When a prejudiced white employer interviews an African-American job applicant, for example, the employer may attribute to the candidate all the traits associated with the employer's African-American stereotype. Qualities of the candidate that do not match the stereotype are likely to be ignored or quickly forgotten (Allport, 1954). For example, the employer whose stereotype includes the belief that African-Americans are lazy may belittle the candidate's hard-earned college degree by thinking, "I never heard of that college. It must be an easy school."

This thinking, which is similar to the fundamental attribution error, is known as the **ultimate attribution error**. The error refers to the tendency for a person with stereotyped beliefs about a particular group of people to make internal attributions for group members' shortcomings and external attributions for their successes. In the preceding example, the employer is making an external attribution (an easy school) for the college success of the African-American job seeker. The other side of the ultimate attribution error is to make internal attributions for the failures of people who belong to groups we dislike. For instance, many white Americans believe that lower average incomes among black Americans as compared with white Americans are due to lack of ability or low motivation, rather than to unequal opportunities (Kluegel, 1990). The ultimate attribution error oftentimes reflects the kinds of subtle, hidden biases described in the opening paragraphs of this chapter.

ultimate attribution error The tendency for a person with stereotyped beliefs to make internal attributions for group members' shortcomings and external attributions for their successes.

frustration–aggression theory The theory that, under certain circumstances, people who are frustrated in their goals turn their anger away from the proper, powerful target and toward another, less powerful target that is safer to attack.

in-group bias The tendency to see the members of one's own group as superior to members of the out-group, who are not members of one's group.

racism Prejudice and discrimination directed at a particular racial group.

Along with stereotyped beliefs, prejudiced attitudes are usually marked by strong emotions, such as dislike, fear, hatred, or loathing. For example, on learning that a person whom they like is a homosexual, heterosexuals may suddenly view the person as undesirable, sick, a sinner, or a pervert. (See Herek, 2000.)

SOURCES OF PREJUDICE Many theories attempt to sort out the causes and sources of prejudice. According to the **frustration–aggression theory**, prejudice is the result of people's frustrations (Allport, 1954). As you saw in Chapter 8, "Motivation and Emotion," under some circumstances frustration can spill over into anger and hostility. People who feel exploited and oppressed often cannot vent their anger against an identifiable or proper target, so they displace their hostility onto those even "lower" on the social scale than themselves. The result is prejudice and discrimination. The people who are the victims of this displaced aggression become *scapegoats* and are blamed for the problems of the times.

For example, after the 2001 terrorist attacks in the United States, many Arabs, Muslims, or even people who looked Middle Eastern, became scapegoats for some Americans' frustration about the violence. African-Americans have long been scapegoats for the economic frustrations of some lower income white Americans who feel powerless to improve their own condition. Latin-Americans, Asian-Americans, Jewish-Americans, and women are also scapegoated—at times by African-Americans. Like kindness, greed, and all other human qualities, prejudice is not restricted to a particular race or ethnic group.

There are also cognitive sources of prejudice. As we saw earlier, people are "cognitive misers" who try to simplify and organize their social thinking as much as possible. Too much simplification—*oversimplification*—leads to erroneous thinking, stereotypes, prejudice, and discrimination. For example, a stereotyped view of women as indecisive or weak will prejudice an employer against hiring a qualified woman as a manager. Belief in a just world—where people get what they deserve and deserve what they get—also oversimplifies one's view of the victims of prejudice as somehow "deserving" their plight (Fiske & Neubers, 1990).

Prejudice is often tied to either–or thinking: Either you are one of "us," or you are one of "them." An *in-group* is any group of people who feels a sense of solidarity and exclusivity in relation to nonmembers. An *out-group*, in contrast, is a group of people who are outside this boundary and are viewed as competitors, enemies, or different and unworthy of respect. These terms can be applied to opposing sports teams, rival gangs, and political parties, or to entire nations, regions, religions, and ethnic or racial groups. According to the **in-group bias**, members see themselves not just as different, but also as superior to members of out-groups. In extreme cases, members of an in-group may see members of an out-group as less than human and feel hatred that may lead to violence, civil war, and even genocide.

RACISM **Racism** is a form of prejudice based in the belief that members of certain racial or ethnic groups are *innately* inferior. Racists believe that intelligence, industry, morality, and other valued traits are biologically determined and therefore cannot be changed. The most blatant forms of racism in the United States have declined in the last several decades. For example, today 9 out of 10 white Americans say that they would vote for a black president. But racism still exists in subtle forms. For example, many whites say that they approve of interracial marriage, but would be "uncomfortable" if someone in their own family married an African American. Many whites also support racial integration of schools, but become "uneasy" if the percentage of black students in their own child's class or school increases significantly (Jaynes & Williams, 1989). Hidden biases such as these, which were also noted in the opening paragraphs of this chapter, can have a dramatic impact on our attitudes.

When people of varying racial, ethnic, or religious backgrounds work cooperatively together, prejudice and discrimination typically are reduced.

Thus, it is not surprising that black and white Americans have different views of how minority group members are treated in our society. In one survey, two out of three whites agreed with the statement, "Blacks have as good a chance as white people . . . to get any job for which they are qualified"; about the same proportion of blacks disagreed. (See **Figure 10–1** for other differences from the same survey.)

STRATEGIES FOR REDUCING PREJUDICE AND DISCRIMINATION How can we use our knowledge of prejudice, stereotypes, and discrimination to reduce prejudice and its expression? Three strategies appear promising: recategorization, controlled processing, and improving contact between groups.

- When we *recategorize*, we try to expand our schema of a particular group—such as viewing people from different races or genders as sharing similar qualities. These more inclusive schemata become *superordinate categories*. For example, both Catholics and Protestants in the United States tend to view themselves as Christians, rather than as separate competing groups (as in Northern Ireland). If people can create such superordinate, overarching categories, they can often reduce stereotypes and prejudice (Dovidio & Gaertner, 1999; Hewstone, Islam, & Judd, 1993).
- Some researchers believe that we all learn the stereotypes in our culture, so the primary difference between someone who is prejudiced and someone who is not is the ability to suppress prejudiced beliefs through *controlled processing* (Devine, 1989; Devine, Monteith, Zuwerink, & Elliot, 1991). We can train ourselves to be more "mindful" of people who differ from us. For example, a group of sixth-graders was taught to be more understanding of the handicapped by having them view slides of handicapped people and to think about their situations, answering such questions as "How might a handicapped person drive a car?" The group showed far less prejudice toward the handicapped after this procedure (Langer, Bashner, & Chanowitz, 1985).
- Finally, we can reduce prejudice and tensions between groups by bringing them together (Pettigrew, 1998). This was one of the intentions of the famous 1954 U.S. Supreme Court's decision in *Brown v. Board of Education of Topeka, Kansas*, which mandated that public schools become racially integrated.
  Intergroup contact alone is not enough, however (Taylor & Moghaddam, 1994). To reduce prejudice when different groups are combined, certain conditions usually must be met. First, groups must have equal status. When members of the majority group retain special privileges, prejudice often accelerates rather than dissolves. Second, people need to have direct contact with members of the other group. Third, this contact should take place in a cooperative, rather than a competitive, environment: Working together to achieve a common goal is an excellent strategy for breaking down the walls of prejudice. Finally, prejudice is most successfully reduced when social and organizational norms encourage cooperative, intergroup contact among members. Organizations that promote such programs are best able to structure an environment of shared respect and productivity.

In all of these suggestions, the primary focus is on changing behavior, not on changing attitudes directly. But changing behavior is often a first step toward changing attitudes. This is not to say that attitude change follows automatically. Attitudes can be difficult to budge because they are often so deeply rooted. Eliminating deeply held attitudes, then, can be very difficult. That is why social psychologists have concentrated so much effort to understand the factors that encourage attitude change. The section that follows examines some of the major findings in the psychological research on attitude change.

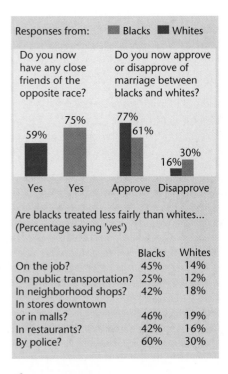

Figure 10–1

Racial attitudes in the United States.

As the figure illustrates, black and white Americans have different views of how minority group members are treated in this country.

Source: Gelles, R. J., & Levine, A. (1999). *Sociology: An Introduction*, 6/e, Fig. 9–7, p. 338; data from *USA Today*, June 11, 1997, p. 9a.

> CHECK YOUR UNDERSTANDING

1. A(n) _____ is a fairly stable organization of beliefs, feelings, and behavioral tendencies directed toward some object, such as a person or group.

Are the following statements true (T) or false (F)?

2. ___ The three components of an attitude are: evaluative belief, evaluative opinions, and evaluative facts.

3. ___ People who are high in self-monitoring are better able to override their attitudes and adapt their behavior to the situation.

4. ___ If we can measure attitudes, we can predict behavior.

5. ___ Prejudice is the act of treating someone unfairly.

Answers: 1. attitude, 2. (F), 3. (T), 4. (F), 5. (F)

> APPLY YOUR UNDERSTANDING

1. John has been passed over for promotion four times, and each time a female coworker has been chosen over him. John becomes prejudiced against women in his profession. This situation is best explained as an example of _____.
   a. in-group bias
   b. out-group bias
   c. the ultimate attribution error
   d. the frustration-aggression theory

2. You are asked to advise an elementary school on ways to reduce prejudice in an integrated third grade classroom. On the basis of what you have read, which of the following is most likely to be effective?
   a. Seating black and white children alternately around the drawing table.
   b. Talking to the group regularly about the unfairness of prejudice and discrimination.
   c. Holding frequent competitions to see whether the black students or the white students perform classroom work better.
   d. Assigning pairs consisting of one black student and one white student to do interdependent parts of homework assignments.

Answers: 1. d, 2. d.

Changing Attitudes

10.3 Describe how attitudes can be changed through persuasion and through self-persuasion that involves cognitive dissonance reduction.

A man watching television on Sunday afternoon ignores scores of beer commercials, but listens to a friend who recommends a particular brand. A political speech convinces one woman to change her vote in favor of the candidate, but leaves her next-door neighbor determined to vote against him. Why would a personal recommendation have greater persuasive power than an expensively produced television commercial? How can two people with similar initial views derive completely different messages from the same speech? What makes one attempt to change attitudes fail and another succeed? Are some people more resistant to attitude change than others? We begin answering these questions by looking at the process of persuasion.

THE PROCESS OF PERSUASION

What factors encourage someone to change an attitude?

Persuasion involves the conscious attempt for one person or group to change another's attitudes. The first step in persuasion is to seize and retain the audience's attention (Albarracin, 2002). To be persuaded, an individual must first pay attention to the message (Perloff, 2003).

In the world of persuasive advertising, attempts to influence the attitudes and buying habits of the public have become more creative (Clay, 2002). Advertisers use many techniques to capture the audience's attention. For example, ads that arouse emotions, especially feelings that make audience members want to act, can be memorable and thus persuasive (DeSteno & Braverman, 2002; Engel, Black, & Miniard, 1986). Humor, too, is an effective way to keep audience members watching or reading an ad that they would otherwise ignore (Conway & Dube, 2002; Scott, Klein, & Bryant, 1990). Other ads "hook" the audience by involving them in a narrative. A commercial might open with a dramatic scene or situation—for example, two people seemingly "meant" for each other but not yet making eye contact—and the viewer stays tuned to find out what happens. Even ads that are annoying can still be effective in capturing attention, because people tend to notice them when they appear (Aaker & Bruzzone, 1985).

With so many clever strategies focused on seizing and holding our attention, how can we shield ourselves from unwanted influences and resist persuasive appeals? We can start by reminding ourselves that these are deliberate attempts to influence us and to change our behavior. Research shows that to a great extent, "forewarned is forearmed" (Wood & Quinn, 2003). Another strategy for resisting persuasion is to analyze ads to identify which attention-getting strategies are at work. We can make a game of deciphering the advertisers' "code" instead of falling for the ad's appeal. In addition, we can raise our standards for the kinds of messages that are worthy of our attention and commitment.

THE COMMUNICATION MODEL

In communicating a message, why are the source, the message, the medium, and the audience important to consider?

The second and third steps in persuasion—comprehending and then accepting the message—are influenced by both the message itself and the way in which it is presented (Perloff, 2003). The *communication model* of persuasion spotlights four key elements to achieve these goals: the source, the message itself, the medium of communication, and characteristics of the audience. Persuaders manipulate each of these factors in the hopes of changing of their audience's members attitudes.

The effectiveness of a persuasive message first depends on its *source*, the author or communicator who appeals to the audience to accept the message. Credibility makes a big difference, at least initially (Ito, 2002; Jain & Posavac, 2001). For example, we are less likely to change our attitude about the oil industry's antipollution efforts if the president of a major refining company tells us about them than if we hear the same information from an impartial commission appointed to study the situation. However, over a period of time, the message may nonetheless be influential. In many instances, we are inclined to forget the source, while remembering the content. This is known as the *sleeper effect* (Kumkale & Albarracín, 2004).

The credibility of the source is most important when we are not inclined to pay attention to the message (Cooper & Croyle, 1984; Petty & Cacioppo, 1981, 1986). But in cases in which we have some interest in the message, the message itself plays the greater role in determining whether we change our attitudes (Petty & Cacioppo, 1986). Researchers have discovered that we frequently tune out messages that simply contradict our own point of view (Jacks & Cameron, 2003). Thus, messages are generally more successful when they present both sides of an argument and when they present novel arguments, rather than when they rehash old standbys, heard many times before. A two-sided presentation generally makes the speaker seem less biased and thus enhances credibility. We have greater respect and trust for a communicator who acknowledges that there is another side to a controversial issue. Messages that create fear sometimes work well, too, although if a message generates too much fear, it may turn off the audience and be ignored (Worchel, Cooper, & Goethals, 1991).

When it comes to choosing an effective *medium* of persuasion, written documentation is best suited to helping people understand complex arguments, whereas videotapes or live presentations are more effective with an audience that already grasps the gist of an argument. Most effective, however, are face-to-face appeals or the lessons of our own experience. Salespeople who sell products door to door rely on the power of personal contact.

The most critical factors in changing attitudes—and the most difficult to control—have to do with the *audience*. Attitudes are most resistant to change if (1) the audience has a strong commitment to its present attitudes, (2) those attitudes are shared by others, and (3) the attitudes were instilled during early childhood by such pivotal groups as the family.

LAST CALL.

When closing time comes around, don't get behind the wheel.
Get in front of a phone. Call a friend, or call a cab.

MADD
Mothers Against Drunk Driving

For an ad to affect our behavior, it must first attract our attention. This one also generates fear, which can sometimes be effective.
Source: © MADD. Used by permission.

The discrepancy between the content of the message and the present attitudes of the audience also affects how well the message will be received. Up to a point, the greater the difference between the two, the greater the likelihood of attitude change, as long as the person delivering the message is considered an expert on the topic. If the discrepancy is too great, however, the audience may reject the new information altogether, even though it comes from an expert.

Finally, certain personal characteristics make some people more susceptible to attitude change than others. People with low self-esteem are more easily influenced, especially when the message is complex and hard to understand. Highly intelligent people tend to resist persuasion because they can think of counterarguments.

COGNITIVE DISSONANCE THEORY

How do people deal with contradictory and competing beliefs?

One of the more fascinating approaches to understanding the process of attitude change is the theory of **cognitive dissonance**, developed by Leon Festinger (1957). Cognitive dissonance exists whenever a person holds two contradictory cognitions, or beliefs, at the same time. "I am a considerate and loyal friend" is one cognition; "Yesterday I repeated some juicy gossip I heard about my friend Chris" is another cognition. These two cognitions are *dissonant*—each one implies the opposite of the other. According to Festinger, cognitive dissonance creates unpleasant psychological tension, which motivates us to try to resolve the dissonance in some way.

Sometimes changing one's attitude is the easiest way to reduce the discomfort of dissonance. I cannot easily change the fact that I have repeated gossip about a friend; therefore, it is easier to change my attitude toward my friend. If I conclude that Chris is not really a friend but simply an acquaintance, then my new attitude now fits my behavior—spreading gossip about someone who is *not* a friend does not contradict the fact that I am loyal and considerate to those who *are* my friends. Similarly, one way to reduce the discomfort or guilt associated with cheating in school is to show support for other students who engage in academic dishonesty (Storch & Storch, 2003).

Discrepant behavior that contradicts an attitude does not necessarily bring about attitude change, however, because there are other ways a person can reduce cognitive dissonance. One alternative is to *increase the number of consonant elements*—that is, the thoughts that are consistent with one another. For example, I might recall the many times I defended Chris when others were critical of him. Now my repeating a little bit of gossip seems less at odds with my attitude toward Chris as a friend. Another option is to reduce the importance of one or both dissonant cognitions. For instance, I could tell myself, "The person I repeated the gossip to was Terry, who doesn't really know Chris very well. Terry doesn't care and won't repeat it. It was no big deal, and Chris shouldn't be upset about it." By reducing the significance of my disloyal action, I reduce the dissonance that I experience and so make it less necessary to change my attitude toward Chris.

Face-to-face attempts to persuade are often the most effective, especially if the persuasive message is offered by a credible source.

But why would someone engage in behavior that goes against an attitude in the first place? One answer is that cognitive dissonance is a natural part of everyday life. Simply choosing between two or more desirable alternatives leads inevitably to dissonance. Suppose you are in the market for a computer, but can't decide between a PC and a Mac. If you choose one, you must accept all of its bad features and forego the good features of the brand not chosen. This causes dissonance. You can reduce this dissonance by changing your attitude: You might decide that the other keyboard wasn't "quite right" and that some of the "bad" features of the computer you bought aren't so bad after all.

In the final analysis, the most effective means of changing attitudes—especially important attitudes, behaviors, or lifestyle choices—may be self-persuasion (Aronson, 1999). In

cognitive dissonance Perceived inconsistency between two cognitions.

contrast to traditional, direct techniques of persuasion, people are put in situations in which they are motivated to persuade themselves to change their attitudes or behavior. For example, many educators hoped that school integration would reduce racial prejudices. But often the reverse proved true: Although they attended the same schools and classes, black and white children tended to "self-segregate." However, when children were assigned to small, culturally diverse study groups in which they were *forced to cooperate*, attitudes changed—albeit slowly. Insults and put-downs, often ethnically based, decreased. Having learned both to teach and to listen to "others," students emerged from the experience with fewer group stereotypes and greater appreciation of individual differences. This outcome, in turn, made them less likely to stereotype others. In a nutshell, working with diverse individuals who did not fit preconceived notions made it difficult to maintain prejudice, because of cognitive dissonance.

▶ CHECK YOUR UNDERSTANDING

Are the following statements true (T) or false (F)?

1. ___ The sleeper effect occurs when over time we remember the content of a message, even though we may forget the actual communication.

2. ___ A speaker usually gains credibility when she presents both sides of an argument.

3. ___ Messages are always persuasive when they are delivered by highly credible sources.

4. ___ A person who has two contradictory beliefs at the same time is experiencing cognitive dissonance.

5. The message that most likely will result in a change in attitude is one with _____.
   a. high fear from a highly credible source
   b. high fear from a moderately credible source
   c. moderate fear from a highly credible source
   d. moderate fear from a moderately credible source

Answers: 1. (T), 2. (T), 3. (F), 4. (T), 5. c

▶ APPLY YOUR UNDERSTANDING

1. If you wanted to communicate most effectively you would choose to use _____.
   a. a speaker with moderate rather than high credibility
   b. a written advertisement rather than a live presentation
   c. a message that was consistent with the biases of the audience
   d. a message that conveys many highly discrepant ideas and points of view

2. Your supervisor has assigned you to work closely on a project with a person you do not like. Over time, you convince yourself that the person actually has many good qualities. This situation is best explained as an example of _____.
   a. the fundamental attribution error
   b. the ultimate attributions bias
   c. increasing cognitive dissonance
   d. decreasing cognitive dissonance

Answers: 1. c, 2. d.

Social Influence

10.4 Distinguish among conformity, compliance, and obedience and suggest how group norms are involved in all of these types of social influence.

In social psychology, **social influence** refers to the process by which others—individually or collectively—affect our perceptions, attitudes, and actions (Nowak, Vallacher, & Miller, 2003; Petty, Wegener, & Fabrigar, 1997). In the previous section, we examined one form of social influence: attitude change. In this section, we focus on how the presence or actions of others can control behavior without regard to underlying attitudes.

CULTURAL INFLUENCES

How does your culture influence how you dress or what you eat?

Culture exerts an enormous influence on our attitudes and behavior. As such, culture is a major form of social influence. Consider for a moment the many aspects of day-to-day living that are derived from culture:

social influence The process by which others individually or collectively affect one's perceptions, attitudes, and actions.

norm A shared idea or expectation about how to behave.

conformity Voluntarily yielding to social norms, even at the expense of one's preferences.

- **Our culture dictates how we dress.** A Saudi woman covers her face before venturing outside her home; a North-American woman freely displays her face, arms, and legs; and women in some other societies roam completely naked (Myers, 1992).
- **Our culture specifies what we eat—and what we do not eat.** Americans do not eat dog meat, Chinese eat no cheese, and Hindus refuse to eat beef. Culture further guides *how* we eat: with a fork, chopsticks, or our bare hands.
- **People from different cultures seek different amounts of personal space.** Latin Americans, French people, and Arabs get closer to one another in most face-to-face interactions than do Americans, the British, or Swedes.

In the course of comparing and adapting our own behavior to that of others, we learn the norms of our culture. A **norm** is a culturally shared idea or expectation about how to behave (Cialdini & Trost, 1998). As in the preceding examples, norms are often steeped in tradition and strengthened by habit. Cultures seem strange to us if their norms are very different from our own. It is tempting to conclude that *different* means "wrong," simply because unfamiliar patterns of behavior can make us feel uncomfortable. To transcend our differences and get along better with people from other cultures, we must find ways to overcome such discomfort.

One technique for understanding other cultures is the *cultural assimilator*, a strategy for perceiving the norms and values of another group (Baron, Graziano & Stangor, 1991; Brislin, Cushner, Cherries, & Yong, 1986). This technique teaches by example, asking students to explain why a member of another culture has behaved in a particular way. For example, why do the members of a Japanese grade school class silently follow their teacher single file through a park on a lovely spring day? Are they afraid of being punished for disorderly conduct if they do otherwise? Are they naturally placid and compliant? Once you understand that Japanese children are raised to value the needs and feelings of others over their own selfish concerns, their orderly, obedient behavior seems much less perplexing. Cultural assimilators encourage us to remain open-minded about others' norms and values by challenging such cultural truisms as "Our way is the right way."

Why do Japanese schoolchildren behave in such an orderly way? How does your answer compare with the discussion of cultural influences?

CONFORMITY

What increases the likelihood that someone will conform?

Accepting the norms of one's culture should not be confused with conformity. For instance, millions of Americans drink coffee in the morning, but they do not do so because they are conforming. They drink coffee because through cultural experience, they have learned to like and desire it. **Conformity**, in contrast, implies a conflict between an individual and a group—a conflict that is resolved when the individual yields her or his own preferences or beliefs to the norms or expectations of the larger group.

Since the early 1950s, when Solomon Asch conducted the first systematic study of the subject, conformity has been a major topic of research in social psychology. Asch demonstrated in a series of experiments that under some circumstances, people will conform to group pressures even if this action forces them to deny obvious physical evidence. His studies ostensibly tested visual judgment by asking people to view cards with several lines of differing lengths; then, people were asked to choose the card with the line most similar to the line on a comparison card (see **Figure 10–2**). The lines were deliberately drawn so that the comparison was obvious and the correct choice was clear. In each group of people, all but one of the participants were actually confederates of the experimenter. On certain trials, these confederates were secretly instructed to deliberately give the same wrong answer. This procedure put the lone dissenter on the spot: Should he conform to what he knew to be a wrong decision and agree with the group, thereby denying the evidence of his own eyes, or should he disagree with the group, thereby risking the social consequences of nonconformity?

Overall, participants conformed by giving obviously incorrect answers on about 35 percent of the trials. Some people never conformed, however, and in subsequent research, experimenters discovered that two sets of factors influenced the likelihood that a person would conform: characteristics of the situation and characteristics of the person.

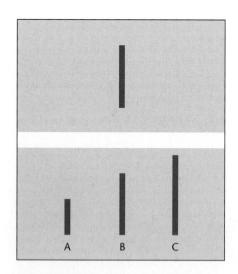

Figure 10–2

Asch's experiment on conformity. In Asch's experiment on conformity, participants were shown a comparison card like the top one and asked to indicate which of the three lines on the bottom card was the most similar. Participants frequently chose the wrong line in order to conform to the group choice.

The *size* of the group is one situational factor that has been studied extensively. Asch (1951) found that the likelihood of conformity increased with group size until four confederates were present. After that point, the number of others made no difference to the frequency of conformity. Another important situational factor is the degree of *unanimity* in the group. If just one confederate broke the perfect agreement of the majority by giving the correct answer, conformity among participants in the Asch experiments fell from an average of 35 percent to about 25 percent (Asch, 1956). Apparently, having just one "ally" eases the pressure to conform. The ally does not even have to share the person's viewpoint—just breaking the unanimity of the majority is enough to reduce conformity (Allen & Levine, 1971).

The *nature of the task* is still another situational variable that affects conformity. For example, conformity has been shown to vary with the difficulty and ambiguity of a task. When the task is difficult or poorly defined, conformity tends to be higher (Blake, Helson, & Mouton, 1956). In an ambiguous situation, people are less sure of their own opinion and more willing to conform to the majority view. *Cultural norms and expectations* can also influence conforming behavior. Individuals who live in collectivist cultures, such as those in China, Fiji, Lebanon, and Brazil, generally conform more to group expectations (B.P. Smith & Bond, 1994) than do people fully assimilated into U.S. culture.

Sometimes we can be misled by what we think are group norms and conform to what is not, in fact, a norm. Perception, more than reality, for example, may influence the dangerous practice of "binge drinking," discussed in the "Understanding Ourselves" box. Personal characteristics also influence conforming behavior. The more a person is attracted to the group, expects to interact with its members in the future, holds a position of relatively low status, and does not feel completely accepted by the group, the more that person tends to conform. The fear of rejection apparently motivates conformity when a person scores high on one or more of these factors.

[UNDERSTANDING OURSELVES]

BELIEFS AND BINGE DRINKING

Her friends believe that Leslie Baltz, a senior honors student at the University of Virginia, was following a school tradition of the "fourth-year fifth"—drinking a fifth of liquor to celebrate the last home football game. When friends found her unconscious that evening, they rushed her to the hospital. But it was too late. She died the next day, another victim of alcohol poisoning through binge drinking (Winerip, 1998).

Binge drinking, defined as taking five or more alcoholic drinks in a row, has been identified as the number one health hazard for college students (Wechsler, Fulop, Padilla, Lee, & Patrick, 1997). Not only do binge drinkers risk their lives, but their drinking has also been linked to higher rates of drunk driving, unplanned and unsafe sexual activity, physical and sexual assault, unintentional injuries, interpersonal problems, physical or cognitive impairment, and poor academic performance (Harford, Wechsler, & Muthen, 2003; Oesterle, Hill, Hawkins, Guo, Catalano, & Abbott, 2004; Wechsler, Davenport, Dowdall, Moeykens,

& Castillo, 1994). The consequences of alcohol abuse are so alarming that today virtually all American four-year colleges have established alcohol task forces and alcohol education programs targeted at high-risk students (Wechsler, Seibring, Liu, & Ahl, 2004). Yet, attempts to reduce binge drinking by teaching social skills, increasing awareness of support systems, improving coping skills,

Source: AP Photo/Victor R. Caivano.

and raising self-esteem have met with relatively little success. What more can be done?

It may be as simple as relying on students' tendency to conform to social norms and making them aware that most of their peers do *not* indulge in binge drinking (Johnston & White, 2003). Serious the problem may be, binge drinking is not as prevalent as many students believe it to be. In some surveys, students estimate that as many as 70 percent of their classmates binge drink (Gose, 1997). Yet, national surveys indicate that the actual figure may be closer to 40 percent (Wechsler, Lee, Kuo, Seibring, Nelson, & Lee, 2002; Winerip, 1998). Even more encouraging is the fact that binge-drinking rates among high school students have declined over 30 percent in recent years (Johnson, O'Malley, & Bachman, 2003). When students realize that binge drinking is less common than they think, they are considerably less likely to try it themselves (Donaldson et al., 1994; Gose, 1997; Haines & Spear, 1996; Hansen, 1993; Hansen & Graham, 1991).

compliance Change of behavior in response to an explicit request from another person or group.

obedience Change of behavior in response to a command from another person, typically an authority figure.

COMPLIANCE

How could a salesperson increase a customer's compliance in buying a product?

Conformity is a response to pressure exerted by norms that are generally left unstated. In contrast, **compliance** is a change of behavior in response to an explicitly stated request. One technique for inducing compliance is the so-called *foot-in-the-door effect*. Every salesperson knows that the moment a prospect allows the sales pitch to begin, the chances of making a sale improve greatly. The same effect operates in other areas of life: After people have agreed to a small request, they are more likely to comply with a larger one.

In the most famous study of this phenomenon, Freedman and Fraser (1966) approached certain residents of Palo Alto, California, posing as members of a committee for safe driving. They asked residents to place a large, ugly sign reading "Drive Carefully" in their front yards. Only 17 percent agreed to do so. Then other residents were asked to sign a petition calling for more safe-driving laws, which nearly everyone agreed to do. When these same people were later asked to place the ugly "Drive Carefully" sign in their yards, an amazing 55 percent agreed. Compliance with the first small request more than tripled the rate of compliance with the larger request.

Why does the foot-in-the-door technique work so well? One possible explanation is that agreeing to the token act (signing the petition) realigns the person's self-perception to that of someone who more strongly favors the cause. When presented with the larger request, the person then feels obligated to comply (Cialdini & Trost, 1998).

Another strategy commonly used by salespeople is the *lowball* procedure (Cialdini & Trost, 1998). The first step is to induce a person to agree to do something. The second step is to then raise the cost of compliance. Among new-car dealers, lowballing works like this: The dealer persuades the customer to buy a new car by reducing the price well below that offered by competitors. Once the customer has agreed to buy the car, however, the terms of the sale shift abruptly (for example, the trade-in value promised by the used-car manager is cut); in the end, the car is more costly than it would be at other dealerships. Despite the added costs, many customers follow through on their commitment to buy. Although the original inducement was the low price (the "lowball" that the salesperson originally pitched), once committed, the buyer remains committed to the now pricier car.

Under certain circumstances, a person who has refused to comply with one request may be more likely to comply with a second. For example, if saying no to the first request made you feel guilty, you may say yes to something else. This phenomenon has been dubbed the *door-in-the-face effect* (Cialdini, 1995). In one study, researchers approached students and asked them to make an unreasonably large commitment: Would they counsel delinquent youths at a detention center for two years? Nearly everyone declined, thus effectively "slamming the door" in the researcher's face. But when later asked to make a much smaller commitment—supervising children during a trip to the zoo—many of the same students quickly agreed. The door-in-the-face effect may work because people interpret the smaller request as a concession and feel pressured to comply.

OBEDIENCE

How does the "power of the situation" affect obedience?

Compliance is agreement to change behavior in response to a request. **Obedience** is compliance with a command. Like compliance, it is a response to an explicit message; in this case, however, the message is a direct order, generally from a

Nazi concentration camps are a shocking example of the extremes to which people will go to obey orders. How do you explain the behaviors of the people who ran these camps?

person in authority, such as a police officer, principal, or parent, who can back up the command with some sort of force if necessary. Obedience embodies social influence in its most direct and powerful form.

Several studies by Stanley Milgram, mentioned in Chapter 1, "The Science of Psychology," showed how far many people will go to obey someone in authority (Milgram, 1963; Blass, 2002; Meyer, 2003). People who agreed to participate in what they believed was a learning experiment administered what they thought were severe electrical shocks to the "learners." Milgram's research has been replicated in different cultures and with both male and female participants (Smith & Bond, 1999). What factors influence the degree to which people will do what they are told? Studies in which people were asked to put a dime in a parking meter by people wearing uniforms show that one important factor is the amount of power vested in the person giving the orders. People obeyed a guard whose uniform looked like that of a police officer more often than they obeyed a man dressed either as a milkman or as a civilian. Another factor is surveillance. If we are ordered to do something and then left alone, we are less likely to obey than if we are being watched, especially if the act seems unethical to us. Milgram, for example, found that his "teachers" were less willing to give severe shocks when the experimenter was out of the room.

Milgram's experiments revealed other factors that influence a person's willingness to follow orders. When the victim was in the same room as the "teacher," obedience dropped sharply. When another "teacher" who refused to give shocks was present, obedience also dropped. But when responsibility for an act was shared, so that the person was only one of many doing it, the degree of obedience was much greater.

Why do people willingly obey an authority figure, even if doing so means violating their own principles? Milgram (1974) suggested that people come to see themselves as the agents of *another* person's wishes and therefore as not responsible for the obedient actions or their consequences. Once this shift in self-perception has occurred, obedience follows, because in their own minds, people who obey have relinquished control of their actions.

► CHECK YOUR UNDERSTANDING

1. A(n) _____ is a shared idea or expectation about how to behave.
2. Many people are more likely to comply with a smaller request after they have refused a larger one. This is called the _____ effect.

Are the following statements true (T) or false (F)?

3. ___ Research shows that compliance is often higher in collectivist cultures than in noncollectivist ones.
4. ___ Milgram's research shows that many people are willing to obey an authority figure, even if doing so means violating their own principles.
5. ___ A person is more likely to conform to the group when the group's task is ambiguous or difficult than when it is easy and clear.

Answers: 1. norm, 2. door-in-the-face, 3. (T), 4. (T), 5. (T)

► APPLY YOUR UNDERSTANDING

1. You answer the telephone and hear the caller say, "Good morning. My name is _____ and I'm calling on behalf of XYZ. How are you today?" Right away you know this caller is using which of the following social influence techniques?
   a. The lowball technique
   b. The assimilator technique
   c. The foot-in-the-door technique
   d. The door-in-the-face technique
2. You would like to say something in class. You raise your hand and wait to be recognized, even though the teacher has not mentioned that hand-raising is the appropriate way to indicate your desire to speak. This is best considered to be an example of _____.
   a. compliance
   b. conformity
   c. obedience
   d. the self-fulfilling prophecy

Answers: 1. c, 2. b.

deindividuation A loss of personal sense of responsibility sometimes experienced by individuals when they are in a group.

Social Action

10.5 Identify and describe the psychological processes involved in deindividuation and the bystander effect, and suggest the major factors that are involved in determining whether individuals in groups will help others in need.

The various kinds of social influence that we have just discussed may take place even when no one else is physically present. We refrain from playing our stereo at full volume when our neighbors are sleeping, comply with jury notices that we received in the mail, and obey traffic signals even when no one is on the road to enforce them. We now turn to processes that *do* depend on the presence of others. Specifically, we examine processes that occur when people interact one-on-one and in groups. One of these social actions is called *deindividuation.*

DEINDIVIDUATION

Do we behave differently when other people are present?

We all have seen cases of social influence in which people act differently in the presence of others from the way they would if they were alone. The most striking and frightening instance of this phenomenon is *mob behavior.* Some well-known violent examples of mob behavior are the beatings and lynchings of African Americans, the looting that sometimes accompanies urban rioting, and the wanton destruction of property that mars otherwise peaceful protests and demonstrations. One reason for mob behavior is that people can lose their personal sense of responsibility in a group, especially in a group subjected to intense pressures and anxiety. This process is called **deindividuation** because people respond not as individuals, but as anonymous parts of a larger group. In general, the more anonymous that people feel in a group, the less responsible they feel as individuals (Aronson, Wilson, & Akert, 2002).

But deindividuation only partly explains mob behavior. Another contributing factor is that, in a group, one dominant and persuasive person can convince people to act through a *snowball effect*: If the persuader convinces just a few people, those few will convince others, who will convince still others, and the group becomes an unthinking mob. Moreover, large groups provide *protection.* Anonymity makes it difficult to press charges. If 2, or even 10, people start smashing windows, they will probably be arrested. If a thousand people do so, very few of them will be caught or punished.

After natural disasters, such as the hurricanes in Florida and New Orleans, strangers often reach out to help each other with physical and financial support.

HELPING BEHAVIOR

What factors make us more inclined to help a person in need?

Research on deindividuation seems to support the unfortunate—and inaccurate—notion that when people get together, they become more destructive and irresponsible than they would be individually. But human society depends on people's willingness to work together and help one another. In fact, instances of cooperation and mutual assistance are just as abundant as examples of human conflict and hostility. We need only to recall the behavior of people all over the country in the aftermath of the September 11, 2001, terrorist attacks on the World Trade Center and the Pentagon to find hundreds of examples of people working together and helping each other (Ballie, 2001). If, as we saw in Chapter 6, "Motivation and Emotion," our willingness to harm others is influenced by social forces, so is our willingness to help others.

What are some of the social forces that can promote helping behavior? One is perceived self-interest. We offer our boss a ride home from the office because we know that our next promotion depends on how much she likes us. We volunteer to feed a neighbor's cat while he is away because we want him to do the same for us. But when helpful actions are not linked to such personal gain, they are considered **altruistic behavior** (Batson & Powell, 2003). A person who acts in an altruistic way does not expect any recognition or reward in return, except perhaps the good feeling that comes from helping someone in need. Many people direct altruistic acts, including many charitable contributions, at strangers and make them anonymously (M. L. Hoffman, 1977).

Under what conditions is helping behavior most likely to occur? Like other things that social psychologists study, altruism is influenced by two sets of factors: those in the situation and those in the individual.

The most important situational variable is the *presence of other people*. In a phenomenon called the **bystander effect**, the likelihood that a person will help someone else in trouble *decreases* as the number of bystanders present increases (Clarkson, 1996; Chekroun & Brauer, 2002). In one experiment, people filling out a questionnaire heard a taped "emergency" in the next room, complete with a crash and screams. Of those who were alone, 70 percent offered help to the unseen female victim, but of those who waited with a companion—a stranger who did nothing to help—only 7 percent offered help (Latané & Rodin, 1969). Another key aspect of the situation is its *ambiguity*. Any factors that make it harder for others to recognize a genuine emergency reduce the probability of altruistic actions (Clark & Word, 1974).

The *personal characteristics* of bystanders also affect helping behavior. Not all bystanders are equally likely to help a stranger. Increasing the amount of personal responsibility that one person feels for another boosts the likelihood that help will be extended (Moriarty, 1975). The amount of *empathy* that we feel toward another person affects our willingness to help, too (Krebs, 1975). *Mood* also makes a difference: A person in a good mood is more likely to help another in need than is someone who is in a neutral or bad mood (Salovey, Mayer, & Rosenhan, 1991; Isen & Levin, 1972). In addition, helping behavior is increased when people don't *fear embarrassment* by offering assistance that isn't really needed (McGovern, 1976).

HELPING BEHAVIOR ACROSS CULTURES People often assume that there is a "helping personality" or a set of traits that determines who is helpful and who is not. This is unlikely. Several conditions, both individual and situational, combine to determine when help will be offered. Similarly, it is doubtful that there is such a thing as a "helpful culture"—that is, a society, nation, or group whose members are invariably "more helpful" than those of other groups. Psychologists have instead focused on the cultural factors that make helping more or less likely to take place.

Individualism/collectivism is an important dimension in this area: It seems plausible that members of individualist cultures feel less obligated to help other people than do members of collectivist cultures. A study using Indian and American participants investigated this possibility (Miller, Bersoff, & Harwood, 1990). Participants were presented with helping scenarios involving either a stranger, a friend, or a close relative whose need was either minor, moderate, or extreme. There were no cultural differences in cases of extreme need; members of both cultures reported being equally willing to help. But the two groups differed in cases of minor needs. Almost three times as many Indians (from a collectivist culture) as Americans (from an individualist culture) felt obligated to help in a scenario involving a close friend or a stranger asking for minor assistance. Even within collectivist cultures, however, the prediction of when help will be offered can be difficult (Triandis, 1994). Some members of collectivist societies are reluctant to offer help to anyone outside their in-group. They are therefore less likely to help strangers. Other cultures treat a stranger as a member of their group until that person's exact status can be determined.

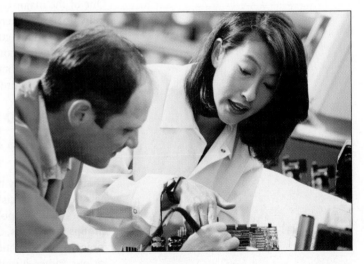

Factors linked to culture—including corporate culture and management style—can make it more, or less, likely that workers will be given help by others.

altruistic behavior Helping behavior that is not linked to personal gain.

bystander effect The tendency for an individual's helpfulness in an emergency to decrease as the number of passive bystanders increases.

1. _____ is a process by which people feel anonymous in a large group.

2. In a mob, one dominant person can often convince other people to engage in an action they wouldn't otherwise do as a result of the _____ effect.

3. _____ behavior is helping other people with no expectation of personal gain.

4. According to the bystander effect, the likelihood that someone will help another person in trouble _____ as the number of passive bystanders present increases.

Answers: 1. Deindividuation, 2. snowball, 3. Altruistic, 4. decreases.

1. Jennifer believes that workplace violence is unacceptable, yet she finds herself participating in a labor strike that involves smashing windows at the corporate office. Her participation is best explained according to the basic principle of _____.
   a. deindividuation
   b. the bystander effect
   c. cognitive dissonance
   d. the ultimate attribution error

2. Jeremy contributes money anonymously to the United Way in a completely unselfish act. His behavior is best described by the psychological term _____.
   a. the snowball effect
   b. deindividuation
   c. polarization
   d. altruism

Answers: 1. a., 2. d.

Social Forces in Organizations

10.6 Describe how group processes and social forces influence decisions, leadership, productivity, and communication in work-based organizations.

One of the major contributions of social psychology is to help us better understand how individuals act when they work together. To be effective members of their organizations, people must make good decisions, form functional work teams, provide leadership, and become productive contributors toward the organization's goals. Social psychologists study all of these behaviors, and results of their studies can lead toward improved organizational effectiveness and productivity.

GROUPS AND DECISION MAKING

How is making a decision in a group different from making a decision on your own?

There is a tendency in our society to turn important decisions over to groups. In the business world, key decisions are often made around a conference table rather than behind one person's desk. In politics, major policy decisions are seldom vested in just one person. Groups of advisers, cabinet officers, committee members, or aides meet to deliberate and forge a course of action. In the courts, a defendant may request a trial by jury, and for some serious crimes, jury trial is required by law. The nine-member U.S. Supreme Court renders group decisions on legal issues affecting the entire nation.

Many people trust these group decisions more than decisions made by individuals. Yet, the dynamics of social interaction within groups sometimes conspire to make group decisions *less* sound than those made by someone acting alone. Social psychologists are intrigued by how this outcome happens.

POLARIZATION IN GROUP DECISION MAKING People often assume that an individual acting alone is more likely to take risks than a group considering the same issue. This assumption remained unchallenged until the early 1960s. At that time, James Stoner (1961) designed an experiment to test the idea. He asked participants individually to counsel imaginary people who had to choose between a risky, but potentially rewarding course of action and a conservative, but less rewarding alternative. Next, the participants met in small groups to discuss each decision until they reached unanimous agreement. Surprisingly, the groups consistently recommended a riskier course of action than the people working alone did. This phenomenon is known as the **risky shift**.

The risky shift is simply one aspect of a more general group phenomenon called **polarization**—the tendency for people to become more extreme in their attitudes as a result of group discussion. Polarization begins when group members discover during discussion that they share views to a greater degree than they realized. Then, in an effort to be seen in a positive light by the others, at least some group members become strong advocates for what is potentially the dominant sentiment in the group. Arguments leaning toward one extreme or the other not only reassure people that their initial attitudes are correct, but they also intensify those attitudes so that the group as a whole becomes more extreme in its position (Liu & Latane, 1998). So, if you want a group decision to be made in a cautious, conservative direction, you should make sure that the members of the group hold cautious and conservative views in the first place. Otherwise, the group decision may polarize in the opposite direction.

THE EFFECTIVENESS OF GROUPS "Two heads are better than one" reflects the common assumption that members of a group will pool their abilities and arrive at a better decision than will individuals working alone. In fact, groups are more effective than individuals only under certain circumstances (Turner, 2001). For one thing, their success depends on the task they face. If the requirements of the task match the skills of the group members, the group is likely to be more effective than any single individual.

Even if task and personnel are perfectly matched, however, the ways in which group members *interact* may reduce the group's efficiency. For example, high-status individuals tend to exert more influence in groups, so if they do not possess the best problem-solving skills, group decisions may suffer (Torrance, 1954). Another factor affecting group interaction and effectiveness is group size. The larger the group, the more likely it is to include someone who has the skills needed to solve a difficult problem. On the other hand, it is much harder to coordinate the activities of a large group. In addition, large groups may be more likely to encourage **social loafing**, the tendency of group members to exert less individual effort on the assumption that others in the group will do the work (Miller, 2002). Finally, the quality of group decision making also depends on the *cohesiveness* of a group. When the people in a group like one another and feel committed to the goals of the group, cohesiveness is high. Under these conditions, members may work hard for the group, spurred by high morale. But cohesiveness can undermine the quality of group decision making. If the group succumbs to **groupthink**, according to Irving Janis (1982, 1989), strong pressure to conform prevents its members from criticizing the emerging group consensus. In such a group, amiability and morale supersede judgment. Members with doubts may hesitate to express them. The result may be disastrous decisions—such as the Bay of Pigs invasion, the Watergate burglary and cover-up, or the ill-fated *Columbia* and *Challenger* space flights (Kruglanski, 1986; Raven, 1998; Vaughn, 1996).

LEADERSHIP

What makes a great leader?

Most groups have leaders, but how do group leaders come to the fore? For many years, the predominant answer was the **great person theory**, which states that leaders are extraordinary people who assume positions of influence and then shape events around them. In this view, people like George Washington, Winston Churchill, and Nelson Mandela were "born leaders" who would have led any nation at any time in history.

Most historians and psychologists now regard this theory as naive, because it ignores social and economic factors. An alternative theory holds that leadership emerges when the right person is in the right place at the right time. For instance, in the late 1950s and early 1960s, Dr. Martin Luther King, Jr., rose to lead the black civil rights movement. Dr. King was clearly a "great person"—intelligent, dynamic, eloquent, and highly motivated. Yet, had the times not been right (for instance, had he lived 30 years earlier), it is doubtful that he would have been as successful as he was.

Groups can make decisions and perform tasks very effectively under the right conditions.

risky shift Greater willingness of a group than an individual to take substantial risks.

polarization Shift in attitudes by members of a group toward more extreme positions than the ones held before group discussion.

social loafing The tendency of indivuals to exert less effort when they are working as part of a group.

groupthink The tendency for people to withhold contradictory opinions due to pressure to conform to group opinions, thereby leading to poorer decisions.

great person theory The theory that leadership is a result of personal qualities and traits that qualify one to lead others.

One theory of leadership holds that the particularly effective leader is the right person in the right place at the right time. For the American civil rights movement, Martin Luther King, Jr., was such a leader.

Recently, social scientists have argued that there is more to leadership than either the great person theory or the right-place-at-the-right-time theory implies. Rather, the leader's traits, certain aspects of the situation in which the group finds itself, and the response of the group and the leader to each other are all important considerations (Bennis, Spreitzer, & Cummings, 2001). **Contingency theories of leadership** are based on such transactional views of leadership.

According to Fred Fiedler's *contingency* theory (Fiedler, 1993, 2002), personal characteristics are important to the success of a leader. One kind of leader is *task oriented*, concerned with doing the task well—even at the expense of worsening relationships among group members. Other leaders are *relationship oriented*, concerned with maintaining group cohesiveness and harmony. Which style is most effective depends on three sets of situational factors. One is the nature of the task (whether it is clearly structured or ambiguous). The second consideration is the relationship between leader and group (whether the leader has good or bad personal relations with the group members). The third consideration is the leader's ability to exercise great or little power over the group.

Fiedler has shown that if conditions are either very favorable (good leader–member relations, structured tasks, high leader power) or very unfavorable (poor leader–member relations, unstructured task, low leader power) for the leader, the most effective leader is the one who is task oriented. However, when conditions within the group are only moderately favorable for the leader, the most effective leader is one who is concerned about maintaining good interpersonal relations.

Fiedler's contingency view of leadership, which has received a great deal of support from research conducted in the laboratory as well as in real-life settings, clearly indicates that there is no such thing as an ideal leader for all situations (Ayman et al., 1998; Graen & Hui, 2001; Hughes, Ginnett, & Curphy, 1998). "Except perhaps for the unusual case," Fiedler states, "it is simply not meaningful to speak of an effective or of an ineffective leader; we can only speak of a leader who tends to be effective in one situation and ineffective in another" (Fiedler, 1967, p. 261). Contingency theories of leadership are discussed further in Chapter 11: "Psychology Applied to Work."

LEADERSHIP ACROSS CULTURES The distinction between task-oriented and relationship-oriented leaders seems to be a main operating principle in most work groups in the United States. Someone who is explicitly appointed as a manager or crew chief is charged with making sure that the job gets done, whereas someone else usually emerges informally to act as the relationship-oriented specialist who tells jokes, remembers everyone's birthday, smoothes disputes, and generally maintains morale (Bales, 1951). In the Western world, this division of leadership often operates in informal social groups as well. Yet, it is not the only approach to leadership. Consider a collectivist culture that values cooperation and interdependence among group members. In such an environment, it is unlikely that individuals would emerge to serve specific functions within a group. Although one member may be named "the manager," there is less need for individuals to have clearly defined roles as "this type of leader" or "that type of leader." All members see themselves as working together to accomplish the group's goals.

Leadership in U.S. businesses has undergone a transformation during the past three decades through the introduction of a management style that has proven successful in Japan and other Eastern collectivist cultures (J. W. Dean & Evans, 1994; McFarland, Senn, & Childress, 1993). This approach emphasizes decision-making input from all group members, small work teams that promote close cooperation, and a style of leadership in which managers receive much the same treatment as any other employee. In the West, it is not uncommon for executives to have their own parking spaces, dining facilities, and fitness and social clubs, as well as separate offices and independent schedules. Most Japanese executives consider this privileged style of management very strange. In many Eastern cultures, managers and executives share the same facilities as their workers, hunt for parking spaces like everyone else, and eat and work side by side with their employees. It is interesting that the Japanese model has effectively combined the two leadership approaches—task oriented and relationship oriented—into a single overall style. By being a part of the group, the leader can simultaneously work toward

contingency theory of leadership The theory that effective leadership depends on the match between the personal characteristics of the leader and important aspects of the situation.

and direct the group's goals, while also contributing to the group's morale and social climate. Combining these roles is an effective strategy for Japanese leaders in such diverse workplaces as banks, bus companies, shipyards, coal mines, and government offices (Misumi, 1985).

WOMEN IN LEADERSHIP POSITIONS Just as leadership styles differ across cultures, research has shown that the leadership styles of men and women can also vary considerably. For example, one five-year study of 2,482 managers in more than 400 organizations found that both female and male co-workers often say that women make better managers than men (Kass, 1999). The reason seems to be that female managers have added such traditionally "masculine" task-oriented traits as decisiveness, planning, and setting standards to such "feminine" relationship-oriented assets as communication, feedback, and empowering other employees, whereas male managers still rely on an autocratic style that emphasizes individual competition and achievement (Eagly, 2003). Indeed, one review concluded that, in contrast to the directive and task-oriented leadership style common among men, women tend to have a more democratic, collaborative, and interpersonally oriented style of managing employees (O'Leary & Flanagan, 2001).

Another large-scale review of 45 studies on gender and leadership found that the styles of leadership adopted by women are generally more effective than traditional male leadership styles (Eagly, Johannesen–Schmidt, & van-Engen, 2003). This study found that female leaders are generally more effective than male leaders at winning acceptance for their ideas and instilling self-confidence in their employees (Lips, 2002). Results like these have prompted some experts to call for specialized women-only leadership training programs, to assist women in developing their full feminine leadership potential independent of the male influence (Vinnicombe & Singh, 2003).

ORGANIZATIONAL BEHAVIOR

Can psychology help to increase worker output and satisfaction?

The places where we work and the various organizations to which we belong shape much of our behavior. **Industrial organizational (I/O) psychology** spotlights the influence on human interaction of large, complex organizational settings, with special emphasis on behavior in the workplace. Although the final chapter of this book outlines the major topics addressed by I/O psychologists in more detail, we provide an introduction to this field in brief sections that follow.

PRODUCTIVITY I/O psychologists focus on practical problems, such as how to reduce employee turnover, improve worker morale, and increase productivity. One of the first studies of the relationship between productivity and working conditions was conducted in the late 1920s by Elton Mayo and his colleagues, who gradually increased the lighting in the Western Electric Hawthorne plant in Cicero, Illinois. The researchers were testing the hypothesis that better lighting would boost worker output. But their results showed something else entirely: Productivity increased not only with better lighting, but also with too much lighting, and with too little lighting. In what has become known as the **Hawthorne effect**, the workers' efficiency rose no matter what was done to their conditions, simply because of the attention that the researchers were giving to them.

The methods of Mayo's team have since come under criticism, but their study was one of the first to highlight the importance of psychological and social factors on behavior in the workplace. Since the 1930s, I/O psychologists have attempted to analyze person-job relationships in more specific terms. For example, workers whose jobs call for a greater variety of skills are more likely to think of their work as meaningful and to exhibit increased motivation and satisfaction, and workers whose jobs entail more autonomy generally produce work of a higher quality (Melamed, Ben–Avi, Luz, & Green, 1995). Thus, motivation, satisfaction, and productivity in the workplace can all be improved by making the right changes in job components.

Research by I/O psychologists has also found that small, cohesive work groups are usually more productive than large, impersonal ones (Craig, 2002). Putting this idea into

Some research suggests that women can be particularly effective in management roles, since they can bring together the masculine style of decisiveness with the feminine style that emphasizes winning group acceptance and increasing group members' self-confidence. Do you think that Dr. Condoleezza Rice, the U.S. Secretary of State under the Bush administration, possesses both types of leadership skills?

industrial/organizational (I/O) psychology The area of psychology concerned with the application of psychological principles to the problems of human organizations, especially work organizations.

Hawthorne effect The principle that people will alter their behavior because of researchers' attention and not necessarily because of any specific treatment condition.

Research in I/O psychology suggests that productivity is usually higher when employees work in smaller, more cohesive groups, which are often called work teams.

practice, managers of assembly-line workers have developed the autonomous work group, replacing, in some factories, the massive assembly line with small groups of workers who produce an entire unit (a whole car, for example) and periodically alternate their tasks. Additional benefits derived from this approach include greater worker satisfaction, higher quality output, and decreased absenteeism and turnover (Pearson, 1992), all of which are described in more detail in Chapter 11: "Psychology Applied to Work."

COMMUNICATION AND RESPONSIBILITY The way in which communications are handled within an organization also has an impact on organizational efficiency and the attitudes of its members (Parker, Axtell, & Turner, 2001). A system in which members communicate with just one person in authority—a centralized system—typically works well in solving simple problems. Complex problems, in contrast, are better handled in a decentralized way, with group members freely communicating with one another (Porter & Roberts, 1976).

Decision making in groups is another process that I/O psychologists study. Although some groups make better decisions than others, group decision making generally enhances member satisfaction (Cotton, 1993). If people believe that they had an input into a decision, they are more satisfied with the outcome and their membership in the group, although their productivity may not increase. Increasingly, as we discuss in Chapter 11, corporations are turning to I/O psychologists for advice on issues ranging from helping employees balance work and family to teaching employees at all levels more effective ways to communicate and work productively (Murray, 1999).

▶ **CHECK YOUR UNDERSTANDING**

1. The tendency for people to become more extreme in their attitudes as a result of group discussion is called _____.

2. When individuals work less hard in group projects then on individual tasks, this is called _____ _____.

3. The poor decisions made in the Watergate cover-up, the *Challenger* space flight, and the Bay of Pigs invasion were due primarily to a process called _____.

4. The view that there are people who are "born" to be leaders is referred to as the _____ _____ theory.

Answers: 1. polarization, 2. social loafing, 3. groupthink, 4. great person.

▶ **APPLY YOUR UNDERSTANDING**

1. Your boss says that she needs to convene a group to discuss a controversial proposal and she wants to be sure that their decision is made in a cautious, conservative direction. You recommend that she make sure that the members of the group are already cautious and conservative if she wishes to avoid which of the following problems:
   a. the Hawthorne effect
   b. risky shift
   c. deindividuation
   d. the primacy effect

2. In a work setting, the situation is very favorable for the leader. The task is clear, the leader has good relations with the members of the work group, and the leader has considerable power. According to Fiedler's contingency model, what style of leadership is likely to be most effective in this situation?
   a. task oriented
   b. relationship oriented
   c. both styles would be equally effective.

Answers: 1. b., 2. a.

>KEY TERMS<

>CHAPTER REVIEW<

Social Cognition

How do we form first impressions of people? Forming impressions, explaining others' behavior, and experiencing interpersonal attraction are all examples of **social cognition**, the process of taking in and assessing information about other people. It is one way in which we are influenced by the thoughts, feelings, and behaviors of others.

When forming impressions of others, we rely on **schemata**, or sets of expectations and beliefs about categories of people. Impressions are also affected by the order in which information is acquired. First impressions are the strongest (the **primacy effect**), probably because we prefer not to expend a great deal of cognitive effort analyzing large amounts of subsequent data. This same preference also encourages us to form impressions by using simplistic, but strongly held, schemata called **stereotypes**.

How do we decide why people act as they do? **Attribution theory** holds that people seek to understand human behavior by attributing it either to causes within the person or causes in the situation. Biases in perception can lead to the **fundamental attribution error**, in which we overemphasize personal traits in attributing causes to others' behavior. **Defensive attribution** motivates us to explain our own actions in ways that protect our self-esteem. We tend to attribute our successes to internal factors and our failures to external ones. The **just-world hypothesis** may lead us to blame the victim when bad things happen to other people.

Do "birds of a feather flock together" or do "opposites attract"? When it comes to interpersonal attraction, the adage "Birds of a feather flock together" has more validity than "Opposites attract."

People who are similar in attitudes, interests, backgrounds, and values tend to like one another. **Proximity** is another factor that promotes liking. The more we are in contact with certain people, the more we tend to like them. We also tend to like people who make us feel appreciated and rewarded, an idea based on the concept of **exchange**. Most people also tend to like physically attractive people, as well as attributing to them, correctly or not, many positive personal characteristics.

Attitudes

What are attitudes and why are they important? An **attitude** is a relatively stable organization of beliefs, feelings, and tendencies toward something or someone—called an attitude object. Attitudes are important because they often influence behavior. We cannot always tell people's attitudes from their actions, however. Furthermore, people who rate highly on **self-monitoring** are better able to override their attitudes to behave properly in a situation. The three major components of attitudes are (1) evaluative beliefs about the attitude object, (2) feelings about that object, and (3) behavioral tendencies toward it. These three components are very often (but not always) consistent with one another.

How does a person develop a prejudice toward someone else? **Prejudice** is an unfair negative attitude directed toward a group and its members, whereas **discrimination** is behavior based on prejudice. One explanation of prejudice is the **frustration–aggression theory**, which states that people who feel exploited and oppressed displace their hostility toward the powerful onto people who are "lower" on the social scale than they are. Another theory proposes a cognitive source of prejudice—oversimplified or stereotyped thinking about categories of people. Such thinking can lead to the **ultimate attribution error,** when people make internal attributions for others' shortcomings and external attributions for their successes. Finally, conformity to the prejudices of one's social group can help to explain prejudice.

Prejudice can be reduced by recategorizing and expanding our out schema of a particular group, by using controlled processing to intentionally try to be less prejudiced, and by interacting cooperatively with members of a minority group in a situation in which all group members have equal status.

Changing Attitudes

What factors encourage someone to change an attitude? Attitudes may be changed in response to efforts at persuasion. The first step in persuasion is to get the audience's attention. Then the task is to get the audience to comprehend and accept the message.

In communicating a message, why are the source, the message, the medium, and the audience important to consider? According to the communication model, persuasion is a function of the source of the message, the content of the message itself, the medium of communication, and the characteristics of the audience. Persuasion is usually maximized when the source is credible, the message presents both sides of an issue, the medium is appropriate to the message, and the audence is open-minded.

How do people deal with contradictory and competing beliefs? When people hold competing, contradictory cognitions, this causes a state of psychological tension called **cognitive dissonance.** According to Leon Festinger, cognitive dissonance can be reduced by changing attitudes or behaviors or by focusing attention on consonant, rather than dissonant, elements in the situation. This form of self-persuasion may be the most effective means of changing attitudes, especially when they are formed early in life and deeply held.

Social Influence

How does your culture influence how you dress or what you eat? **Social influence** is the process by which people's thoughts, feelings, and actions are affected by the behavior and characteristics of other people. The culture in which you are immersed has an enormous influence on your thoughts and actions. Culture dictates differences in diet, dress, and personal space. The fact that you eat pizza and shun rattlesnake meat, dress in jeans and a T-shirt instead of a loincloth or sari, and feel uncomfortable when others stand very close to you when they speak are all results of culture. In the course of adapting our behavior to that of others, we learn the **norms** of our culture, as well as its beliefs and values.

What increases the likelihood that someone will conform? Voluntarily yielding one's preferences, beliefs, or judgments to those of a larger group is called **conformity.** Research by Solomon Asch and others has shown that characteristics of both the situation and the person influence the likelihood of conforming. There are also cultural influences on the tendency to conform, with people in collectivist cultures often being more prone to conformity than those in noncollectivist ones, like the U.S.

How could a salesperson increase a customer's compliance in buying a product? **Compliance** is a change in behavior in response to an explicit request from someone else. One technique to encourage compliance is the foot-in-the-door approach, or getting people to go along with a small request in order to make them more likely to comply later with a larger one. For example, a salesperson might get you to agree to try a product "free" for 30 days to make you more likely to buy the product later. Another technique is the lowball procedure: initially offering a low price to win commitment, and then gradually escalating the cost. Also effective is the door-in-the-face tactic, or initially making an unreasonable request, which is bound to be turned down, but will perhaps generate enough guilt to make compliance with smaller second request more likely.

How does the "power of the situation" affect obedience? Classic research by Stanley Milgram showed that many people were willing to obey orders to administer harmful shocks to other people. This **obedience** to an authority figure was more likely when certain situational factors were present. For example, people found it harder to disobey when the authority figure issuing the order was nearby. They were also more likely to obey the command when the person being given the shock was some distance from them. According to Milgram, obedience is dependent on the constraints of the situation.

Social Action

Do we behave differently when other people are present? Conformity, compliance, and obedience may take place even when no one else is physically present, but other processes of social influence depend on the presence of others. Immersion in a large, anonymous group may lead to **deindividuation,** the loss of a sense of personal responsibility for one's actions. Deindividuation can sometimes lead to violence or other forms of irresponsible behavior. The greater the sense of anonymity, the more this effect occurs.

What factors make us more inclined to help a person in need? Helping someone in need without expectation of a reward is called **altruistic behavior.** Altruism is influenced by situational factors such as the presence of other people. According to the **bystander effect,** a person is less apt to offer assistance when other potential helpers are present; conversely, being the only person to spot someone in trouble tends to encourage helping. Helping behavior is encouraged when emergencies are unambiguous, and when the helper is an empathetic person and is in a good mood.

Social Forces in Organizations

How is making a decision in a group different from making a decision on your own? Group decisions are often more extreme than decisions made by individuals, a phenomenon called **polarization.** Groups also tend to take riskier positions than individuals, a finding referred to as the **risky shift.** People deliberating in groups may also display **social loafing,** a tendency to exert less effort on the assumption that others will do most of the work. In very cohesive groups, there is a tendency toward **groupthink**, an unwillingness to criticize the emerging group consensus even when it seems misguided.

What makes a great leader? According to the **great person theory**, leadership is a function of personal traits that qualify one to lead others. According to **contingency theories of leadership**, traits of the leader and traits of the group interact with certain aspects of the situation to determine what kind of leader will come to the fore. Fred Fiedler focused on two contrasting leadership styles: task oriented and relationship oriented. The effectiveness of each style depends on the nature of the task, the relationship of the leader with group members, and the leader's power over the group.

The task-oriented leadership style typical of American businesses is being transformed through the introduction of a management style that emphasizes small work teams and input from all members of the group. Recent research indicates that women in leadership positions tend to have a more democratic, collaborative and interpersonally oriented style of managing employees than do men in similar positions.

Can psychology help to increase worker output and satisfaction? **Industrial/organizational (I/O) psychology** studies behavior in organizational settings such as the workplace. Research in this field shows that worker output and satisfaction can be raised by a variety of situational changes. For example, worker output often increases simply because of attention from others, a phenomenon called the **Hawthorne effect**. Research findings have led organizations to establish autonomous work groups to replace less efficient assembly-line arrangements. Productivity and morale may also be improved by increasing worker responsibility and facilitating communication in the workplace.

>CHAPTER 10< Social Psychology

10.1 SOCIAL COGNITION

SOCIAL COGNITION

- Knowledge and understanding of the social world and the people in it
- **Schema:** Categories that help organize information about the world
- **Stereotypes:** Common characteristics we associate with groups of people
- **Self-fulfilling prophecy:** Situation created by one's expectations, which in turn influences behavior

ATTRIBUTION THEORY

- **Attribution:** Making judgments about the causes of behavior
- **Fundamental attribution error:** Making personal (internal) attributions for other people's behavior but not for our own behavior
- **Defensive attribution:** Attributions that involve enhanced self-presentation
- **Just-world hypothesis:** Bad things happen to bad people and good things happen to good people

INTERPERSONAL ATTRACTION

- We like those who are similar in values, attractiveness, and background
- We like those who provide rewards, especially if exchanges are equitable

10.2 ATTITUDES

ATTITUDE

- Relatively stable organization of beliefs, feelings, and behavioral tendencies
- People high in self-monitoring are more likely to behave according to others' expectations

RACIAL ATTITUDES IN THE UNITED STATES

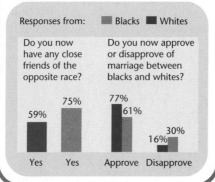

Responses from: Blacks Whites

Do you now have any close friends of the opposite race?

Do you now approve or disapprove of marriage between blacks and whites?

59% Yes | 75% Yes | 77% Approve | 61% Approve | 16% Disapprove | 30% Disapprove

PREJUDICE AND DISCRIMINATION

- **Prejudice:** An unfair, intolerant, or unfavorable attitude toward a group of people
- **Discrimination:** Unfair actions against a person or group of people because of their group membership
- **Ultimate attribution error:** Tendency to make internal attributions for group members' shortcomings but external attributions for their successes

10.3 CHANGING ATTITUDES

PERSUASIVE COMMUNICATIONS

- Source: Who presents the message?
- Message: What does the message say?
- Medium: What form does the message take?
- Audience: What are the attitudes and characteristics of those who hear the message?

COGNITIVE DISSONANCE THEORY

- Contradictory beliefs and actions cause a state of psychological tension
- Cognitive dissonance can be reduced by changing beliefs or actions, or by focusing on other aspects of the situation

Concept Map

10.4 SOCIAL INFLUENCE

SOCIAL INFLUENCE

- Process by which others affect our perceptions, attitudes, and actions
- **Norms:** Common ideas about how to behave

CONFORMITY

- Voluntarily acting in accordance with social norms
- Likelihood of conformity increases with group size
- Conformity varies with the difficulty and ambiguity of a task
- Fear of rejection can motivate conformity

COMPLIANCE

- Changing behavior in response to a specific request by another
- Foot-in-the-door effect: Getting agreement to a small request makes it more likely to get agreement to a large request
- Lowball technique: Getting agreement to a small request and then changing the request to a larger one
- Door-in-the-face effect: Beginning with a large request, which makes it more likely to get agreement to a later small request

OBEDIENCE

- Changing behavior in response to a command from another person
- Most direct and powerful form of social influence

10.5 SOCIAL ACTION

DEINDIVIDUATION

- Loss of a sense of personal responsibility as a member of a group
- Example: Mob behavior

ALTRUISTIC BEHAVIOR

- Behavior intended to help others with no extrinsic reward or recognition
- **Bystander effect:** The more bystanders present in an emergency, the less likely one individual will offer to help
- **Culture effect:** Members of collectivist cultures are more likely to offer help in response to minor needs than are members of individualist cultures

10.6 SOCIAL FORCES IN ORGANIZATIONS

GROUP INFLUENCES

- **Risky shift:** Groups recommend riskier decisions
- **Polarization:** People in groups shift to more extreme positions
- **Social loafing:** Individuals exert less effort when they are part of a group
- **Groupthink:** Social pressure to conform limits effective decision making

LEADERSHIP THEORIES

- **Great person theory:** Leaders are extraordinary people with special traits
- **Contingency theory:** Effective leadership depends on the leader's traits, features of the situation, and interaction of leadership style and group characteristics
- **Culture effect:** Leadership in collectivist cultures is more cooperative and less hierarchical than in individualist cultures
- Women have both "masculine" task-oriented traits and "feminine" relationship-oriented skills

Concept Map

Psychology Applied to Work

Snaking past impulse items like dark chocolate mini-pretzels and smoked salmon jerky, customers approaching the cashier at a Trader Joe's grocery store might notice an interesting help wanted plea. "Join our crew" the hand-lettered sign implores, "and you'll get: custom nametags, 3 fashionable t-shirts, 200 new friends, health insurance, a retirement plan, a cool box cutter, and 10% discount on all grocery items."

These are not typical benefits or perks for part-time grocery store clerks—and nor is the generous compensation—but then Trader Joe's is not your typical grocery store. The quirky specialty grocery chain from Southern California has created a loyal (even passionate) following among customers who crave its bargain gourmet items. From its beginnings in 1958 as a convenience store, Trader Joe's has grown into a $3 billion a year national chain with 217 stores across the United States from Encinitas, CA to Swampscott, Massachusetts.

Yet, however innovative, cheap, and tasty its food items, Trader Joe's runaway success relies just as much on its knowledgeable, upbeat and friendly employees in their trademark Hawaiian T-shirts. Consider the following example, which is par for the course at Trader Joe's. Tugging a cart full of flowers and wine in his Ann Arbor, Michigan, Trader Joe's, Mike Losey is stopped by an employee who wants to know if he is throwing a dinner party. When Losey said yes, the "crew member" spent several minutes discussing Losey's menu and then recommended a three-minute crème brulee. "Why is everyone so happy and positive here?" is one of the Frequently Asked Questions on the employment portion of the Trader Joe's Web-site "Hmmm…. We get this one a lot," begins the company's cheeky reply. "Understand, we can neither confirm nor deny any reports of 'something in the water'. But one taste of all the terrific food and beverages in our stores and we think

you'll be smiling, too!" This offhand answer belies the company's carefully planned efforts to create a culture in which employees have fun and know they are highly valued. In the retail industry, Trader Joe's culture is nothing short of revolutionary. "Trader Joe's is one of a handful of companies responsible for what is seen as a paradigm shift in the retail industry," according to human resources expert Mel Kleiman. "They've taken the approach that the employee is number one. They feel that if they treat employees the way they want employees to treat customers, odds are stores will have a better shot at providing a unique shopping experience for people as soon as they walk through the door."

Generous compensation and benefits may lure Trader Joe employees in, but it won't keep them smiling and going the extra mile for every customer. One huge reason employees stay is that the grocery chain has created a truly collaborative environment in which everyone does the same job at one time or another, and where employees' opinions are respected. It's not unusual for store managers to sweep the floors, stock shelves, and work the cash registers, if needed. This collaborative culture may sound haphazard or like the old hippie communes, but it's one of the things employees learn at the company's training program. At Trader Joe's University everyone—from "captains" and "first mates" (store managers and assistant managers) to "crew" (all part-timers)—learns management, leadership, and communication skills all geared toward placing the employee/customer relationship first. The store also gives employees a high degree of autonomy, and cultivates a club-like atmosphere—think "200 new friends"—that is the opposite of what a store clerk at somewhere such as Shop Rite would experience.[1]

How are psychologists involved in creating organizations like Trader Joe's? The field of study within psychology that emphasizes the application of psychological principles and theories to real-world settings is **industrial/organizational (I/O) psychology**, which studies how individuals and organizations work and how psychological principles can be applied to such settings to improve their effectiveness.

As the name of the field implies, the focus of I/O psychology is twofold. Professionals working in the subfield of **industrial psychology** usually are involved with managing *human resources* in organizations. Organizations rely on people to do work, and the quality and quantity of work that can be done depends heavily on having a well-trained, knowledgeable, productive workforce. Industrial psychologists study the various jobs in organizations to identify the knowledge, skills, abilities, and other traits required to perform them. In general, **organizational psychology** is focused more broadly on factors that affect the organization, rather than on the individuals who work in organizations, although the distinction between industrial psychology and organizational psychology is fuzzy at best. Organizational psychologists, for example, study the ways in which different organizational systems and structures affect productivity.

Industrial/organizational psychologists also play an important role in forming national social policies pertaining to work. For example, there is a strong link between personnel selection issues in psychology and legal and social policy issues involved in employment (Tenopyr, 1996; Zedeck & Goldstein, 2000). The areas of greatest concern to industrial psychologists typically deal with performing accurate job analysis, hiring a productive and representative work force, and assessing performance using unbiased methods. I/O psychologists also can help develop appropriate organizational policies and procedures to address these concerns and help organizations meet both productivity and fair employment goals. ◼

Matching People to Jobs

11.1   Define the procedures by which a job analysis is conducted, suggest how a job analysis serves as a basis for personnel selection, identify which selection factors predict high levels of job performance, and discuss the basic protections guaranteed by fair employment laws.

industrial/organizational (I/O) psychology
The field of psychology that includes the scientific study of how individuals and organizations work, and of how psychological principles can be applied to such settings to improve their effectiveness.

industrial psychology Subfield of industrial/organizational psychology involved with effectively managing the human resources in organizations.

organizational psychology Subfield of industrial/organizational psychology that focuses on factors that pertain to the organization, rather than to the individuals who work within it.

job analysis A procedure or set of procedures that identifies the various tasks required by a job and the human qualifications that are required to perform that job.

job Positions in an organization that involve the performance of the same set of tasks.

functional job analysis (FJA) A method of conducting a job analysis that involves identifying the procedures and processes that workers use in the performance of the job.

JOB ANALYSIS

What is a job and how is a job defined?

Common wisdom, as well as psychological research, suggests that organizational productivity is enhanced when workers are assigned to the jobs that best fit their abilities and interests. To determine which people should be assigned to specific jobs in an organization, managers need to understand the requirements of each job. This is usually accomplished with a **job analysis**.

To understand how a job analysis is conducted, it is first necessary to understand how jobs are structured and defined. In any organization, workers perform *tasks*, the basic units of work (see **Figure 11–1**). Usually, workers perform many tasks in their jobs (Clifford, 1994). As a store manager, for example, you might select and order merchandise, supervise a staff of salespeople, keep track of sales and how merchandise moves out of the store, deal with customer problems, and see that the store is clean and the displays attractive. A **job** is defined as including all positions in the organization that involve the performance of the same set of tasks: Typing memos, letters, and other correspondence; scheduling meetings; and receiving and screening visitors and phone calls are tasks that fit into the job of "secretary" in most organizations.

Job analysis usually involves collecting data about two aspects of a job: the behaviors that are performed by workers while doing the job, and the characteristics of the work environment in which the job is performed (the physical, mechanical, social, and informational elements of the job) (Harvey, 1991). A good job analysis documents the tasks workers must perform, and it notes the job-related aspects of the environment in which the work is done. It also identifies the human attributes that are necessary to perform the job at a satisfactory level (Harvey & Wilson, 2000).

CONDUCTING A JOB ANALYSIS One common method for conducting a job analysis is **functional job analysis (FJA)**, which identifies how workers perform the tasks that make up their jobs. In FJA, job tasks are rated according to three basic dimensions: the ways in which workers in the job must manipulate *things*, the ways in which workers need to respond to and analyze *data*, and the ways in which workers must relate to other *people* (Gatewood & Field, 1998) (see **Figure 11–2**).

Job Family	Clerical	
Job	**Secretary**	**Receptionist**
Job Tasks	Type correspondence	Answer corporate phone line and direct calls appropriately
	Arrange meetings and schedule appointments as requested by supervisor	Greet guests and direct them to the appropriate offices
	Keep records of expenses and disbursements from office budgets	Arrange for transportation (cabs and car services) for officers and visitors
	Open and sort mail	Mail and accept packages

Figure 11–1

Sample of Representative Job Tasks Assigned to Two Jobs in the Same Job Family Jobs include a defined set of tasks, which vary from job to job. Jobs that include similar tasks can be grouped into job families.

A second method of job analysis, the **KSAO system**, focuses on understanding the human characteristics required to perform the job successfully. These characteristics are most often classified into four categories: knowledge (K), skills (S), abilities (A), and other characteristics (O) (Harvey, 1991). Job *knowledge* refers to the specific information a person needs to perform the job. For example, to work as a massage therapist, a person needs to have a thorough knowledge of human anatomy and physiology as well as the various techniques used in massage. *Skills* refers to the specific techniques and behaviors required to perform the tasks the job entails. Skills often involve psychomotor activities, such as the ability to type, or to operate a machine. *Abilities* are considered to be relative stable characteristics a person possesses, such as artistic talent or intelligence. *Other characteristics* include all other personal traits, such as emotional stability or conscientiousness, that may be required to perform a particular job.

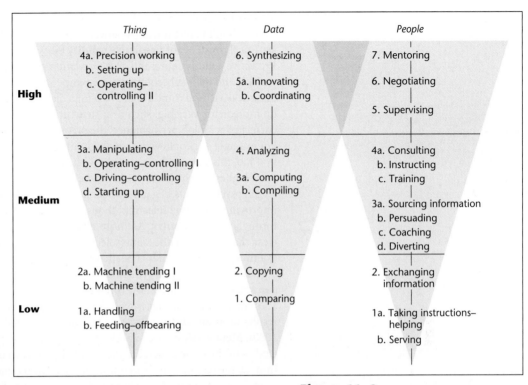

Figure 11–2

People–Data–Things Dimensions of a Functional Job Analysis

This figure notes the types of skills workers use in jobs of low, medium, and high complexity, as they interact with things, data, and people.

Source: Functional Job Analysis Scales: A Desk Aid (rev. ed.) by S. Fine, 1989. Dryden. Reprinted with permission from Dryden, a division of Thomson Learning, Inc.

USES OF A JOB ANALYSIS A job analysis has a number of uses (Van Iddekinge, Putka, Raymark, & Eidson, 2005). For example, a **job description** can be prepared based on the specific tasks a job requires. Job descriptions identify the core tasks required by the job and list the knowledge, skills, abilities, and other characteristics people must have to perform the job. The U. S. Department of Labor maintains a listing of job descriptions for every job in the economy in a database called O*NET, available online free of charge. It includes career exploration tools to assist individuals in evaluating their career interests, as well as information about the job-related skills and training needed for different jobs (U.S. Department of Labor, 2006a). O*NET also provides a "skills search" function that individuals can use to match their own skills to jobs in which they might be interested. If you would like to explore your own career interests, you can log onto the O*NET Website at *http://online.onetcenter.org*.

Job analysis is also used when organizations develop training programs. It serves a particularly important function in developing performance evaluation systems, which are used to measure how successfully each employee is performing the job. In addition, job analysis can play a role in establishing the level of compensation or pay associated with a new or existing job.

Job analysis thus lays the foundation for many functions of a business: recruiting, hiring and training employees, and evaluating their performance. Accurate job analysis is a critical human resources function. It has been estimated, for example, that large organizations spend between $150,000 and $4,000,000 annually on job analysis (Levine, Sistrunk, McNutt, & Gael, 1988). Because qualifications the employee needs and the job analysis provides both the company and the worker with an understanding of the duties or responsibilities expected, it serves as the starting point for matching employees to jobs—the organizational function referred to as personnel selection.

PREDICTING JOB PERFORMANCE

Which human characteristics best predict performance on the job?

Personnel selection is the process of selecting from a pool of job applicants those who will be offered a job (Muchinsky, 2006). The purpose of personnel selection is to hire applicants who will be the most productive employees. Thus, personnel selection specialists need to

---

KSAO system of job analysis A method of conducting a job analysis that relies on identifying the human characteristics of knowledge, skills, abilities, and other characteristics that are required for the job.

job description Identifies the core tasks required by the job and lists the knowledge, skills, abilities, and other characteristics that are necessary for people to perform the job.

personnel selection The process of selecting from a pool of job applicants those who will be hired to perform a job.

identify the characteristics that will *predict* future performance. The central concept for understanding the relationships between applicant characteristics and job performance is the statistical construct of **predictive validity** (see Chapter 5: "Cognition and Mental Abilities"). Predictive validity represents the correlation between job applicants' scores on a predictor variable and their subsequent performance on the job. (See Appendix A: "Measurement and Statistical Methods" and **Figure A–9** for a discussion of correlational statistics.) When scores on a predictor variable, such as a structured interview or personnel test, are substantially correlated with job performance, the predictor variable can be used in the selection process. For example, if people who score high on a test of conscientiousness also are better workers in a job, this test can be a useful tool in a personnel selection system. Job applicants who score highest on the predictor are those who shoud be hired (Schmidt & Hunter, 1998).

As psychologists began to understand the significance of predictive validity studies for improving personnel selection, thousands of these studies were conducted in organizations throughout the country. As more and more validity studies were performed, it became clear that studies of the same selection procedures produced widely different results. For example, in some studies, a particular test of cognitive ability might be found to be highly correlated with job performance; in other studies of the same test in nearly identical circumstances, no such relationship was found.

Industrial psychologists were unable to explain this seemingly unpredictable pattern of results until an advanced statistical technique called meta-analysis was developed in the 1980s. **Meta-analysis** is a sophisticated way of analyzing the combined results of multiple studies of the same general topic. Simply put, meta-analysis involves examining the results from all the research studies conducted on a given topic, then statistically "correcting" these results for various sorts of errors and biases, and finally "averaging" the corrected results to arrive at a single, best estimate of the underlying, or "true," relationship.

In the case of predictive validity studies of various personnel selection methods, meta-analysis has enabled psychologists to arrive at good estimates of the real predictive relationship between each of these selection techniques and employees' performance (see **Table 11–1**). Several of the major methods used in personnel selection today are discussed in the paragraphs that follow.

EMPLOYMENT INTERVIEWS One of the most frequently used selection predictors is the **employment interview**. Interviews typically involve having job applicants answer questions asked by one or more interviewers. Selection interviews vary widely in both the content of the specific questions asked and the framework in which the interview is conducted. For research purposes, interview techniques often are divided into those using structured formats versus those that rely on unstructured, open-ended procedures.

A *structured job interview* is one in which all job applicants who are interviewed are asked a uniform, consistent set of questions, usually in a fixed order, by the same individual or team of interviewers (Campion, Purcell, & Brown, 1988). The questions are usually derived from the job analysis, and pertain directly to the applicant's abilities to perform the tasks of the job. In a structured interview, the applicant's responses usually are scored, often numerically, using a consistent scoring scheme. An *unstructured job interview* is in most respects the opposite approach. Unstructured interviews have no fixed format, and the questions may vary widely from person to person. Furthermore, in unstructured interviews there usually is no specified method of scoring responses. More often a general rating or ranking is assigned to each applicant based on the interviewer's subjective impression and judgment.

In terms of predictive validity, structured interviews are more highly correlated with measures of subsequent job performance than are unstructured interviews (see again **Table 11–1**). In fact, when interviews are conducted in a highly structured setting and are scored using a consistent method, they are among the most valid of all selection techniques. Although unstructured interviews are somewhat less strongly related to subsequent job performance, they, too, can be used to predict which applicants are likely to be the highest performing workers on the job.

Employment interviews can be used for several other purposes. For example, interviews can provide an effective means of communicating the content of the job and allow applicants to see what will be expected of them should they be hired (Schultz & Shultz,

---

predictive validity Correlation between individuals' scores on a predictor variable and their subsequent performance on some criterion, such as job performance.

---

meta-analysis A sophisticated statistical technique for analyzing the combined results of multiple studies of the same general topic which yields an estimate of the true relationship these studies are attempting to measure.

---

employment interview Selection method that consists of asking questions to which the job applicant responds, either in a structured or an unstructured setting.

> TABLE 11-1 SUMMARY OF PREDICTIVE VALIDITY COEFFICIENTS ASSOCIATED WITH COMMONLY USED SELECTION METHODS

Selection Method	Predictive Validity Coefficient (Correlation between Selection Method Scores and Job Performance)[2]
Structured Interview	.51
Unstructured Interview	.38
Cognitive (General Mental) Ability	.51
Conscientiousness	.31
Reference Checks	.26
Years of Education	.10
Interests	.10
Job Knowledge tests	.48
Work Sample tests	.54
Assessment Centers	.37
Graphology (Hand writing analysis)	.02
Age	−.01

Adapted from: Frank L. Schmidt and John E. Hunter (1998). "The validity and utility of selection methods in personnel psychology: Practical and theoretical implications of 85 years of research findings." **Psychological Bulletin, 124** (2), 262–274.

[2] *Note:* The numbers in this column represent the mean true predictive validity (expressed as a correlation coefficient) of each of the predictors listed for measures of job performance. The higher the number in this column, the stronger is the relationship between the Selection Method and subsequent Job Performance by those hired.

1998; Gatewood & Field, 1998). By giving applicants a realistic picture of the job, employers provide an opportunity for applicants to evaluate whether or not a job will be a good match for their interests and skills. Skilled interviewers can also use the interview setting as an opportunity to recruit an applicant to accept the job.

EMPLOYMENT TESTS Interviews are a fairly expensive method of selecting employees. When there are many more applicants than can be hired, organizations often rely on objective, paper-and-pencil tests as a first step in screening applicants. A further advantage of employment tests is that most of them are *objective*. Therefore, the possibility for bias in

In structured interviews, every job applicant is asked the same set of questions. Responses usually are recorded and often are scored according to a numerical scoring scheme. Structured interviews are highly valid predictors of future job performance.

favor of applicants who managers personally like or who are similar to them is greatly reduced (Stanley, 2004).

The most important argument in favor of the use of objective employment tests in personnel selection, however, is that they have proven to be valid and important predictors of performance (Schmidt & Hunter, 1998). I/O psychologists routinely use a wide variety of employment tests. In general, these tests can be categorized into those that measure cognitive abilities and those that measure personality characteristics. Meta-analytic studies have shown both types of tests to be highly valid predictors of job performance (Ree, Earles, & Teachout, 1994; Barrick & Mount, 1991; Schmidt & Hunter, 1998).

Tests of cognitive ability. Of all the methods used in personnel selection, tests of cognitive abilities have the highest overall validity for predicting job performance and the lowest financial cost associated with their use (Schmidt & Hunter, 2004). Furthermore, they are a quick, easy-to-use means of selecting applicants who are most likely to be high performers. Tests of cognitive ability, for the most part, measure general intelligence (see Chapter 5: "Cognition and Mental Abilities"), which is usually referred to by industrial/organizational psychologists as *general mental ability (GMA)*. Tests that measure GMA are widely used in the United States and include the General Aptitude Test Battery (GATB), used to select employees in the U. S. government, and the Armed Services Vocational Aptitude Battery (ASVAB), taken by all enlisted military personnel. A similar, but much shorter, test widely used in private industry is the Wonderlic Personnel Test. This test takes 12 minutes to administer and includes 50 questions that cover a wide variety of problem types, including vocabulary tasks, number comparisons, analysis of geometric figures, and story problems requiring math or logic (Wonderlic Personnel Test, Inc., 1992). Questions similar to those asked in the Wonderlic Personnel Test are presented in **Table 11–2**.

The ability of cognitive ability tests to predict job performance in a wide variety of jobs is impressive (see again **Table 11–1**), (Hunter, 1980; Hunter and Hunter, 1984; Reeve & Hakel, 2002). Although tests of general mental ability are better at predicting performance in complex jobs, even in the simplest jobs in the U. S. economy, general mental ability is substantially correlated with job performance.

> **TABLE 11–2 EXAMPLES OF QUESTIONS SIMILAR TO THOSE USED IN THE WONDERLIC PERSONNEL TEST**

1. INITIATE is the opposite of:
   a. Lose   c. Quit
   b. Continue   d. Irrelevant

2. If one cup of coffee costs $1.29, how much will 3 cups of coffee cost?

3. How many of the items listed below are exact duplicates of each other?

3850	3850
49657	49657
540863	540663
5840211	5840211
91588257	91583257

4. INCORPORATE   INCLUDE – Do these words:
   a. have similar meanings
   b. have contradictory meanings
   c. mean neither the same nor opposite

5. Which number would be the next to occur in the following series:
   2, 8, 14, 20, 26, _____

Answers: 1. c., 2. $3.87, 3. (3), 4. a., 5. 32

Tests of cognitive ability, however, are not without their problems. Foremost among these is the charge that they may be unfair to members of certain disadvantaged racial and ethnic groups.

Tests of personality Tests of personality generally include self-descriptive statements about job applicants' preferences ("I would rather go to a baseball game than read a book.") and typical behaviors ("I am able to set clear goals and work effectively to achieve them."). In recent years, most researchers working in the field of industrial/organizational psychology have used the Five Factor Theory (see Chapter 8: "Personality, Stress, and Health") to explore the relationship between the major dimensions of personality and job performance. One commonly used test that measures these five factors—*Conscientiousness, Emotional Stability, Agreeableness, Openness to Experience*, and *Extraversion*—is the NEO-PI. (See Table 11–3 for examples of questions similar to those asked on the NEO-PI.)

Which of the five factors do you believe would be correlated with performance on the job? It is easy to imagine that all five could be valid predictors of performance. For example, we generally like to work with people who finish the projects they start (conscientiousness), who are neither too anxious or unstable nor overly compulsive and paranoid (emotional stability), who are easy to like and who like us (agreeableness), who like to learn new things and aren't afraid to try new approaches to solving problems (openness to experience), and who enjoy interacting with other people (extraversion).

Yet research has shown that among these traits, the one that is most closely tied to performance on the job is **conscientiousness**, the ability to finish projects, to attend to detail without becoming absorbed by it, and to care about the quality of the work. Although the other personality traits may be related to performance in some types of settings (Hogan & Holland, 2003), conscientiousness is a valid predictor of job performance in all jobs (Barrick & Mount, 1991; Barrick, Mount, & Judge, 2001). Furthermore, conscientiousness is not significantly correlated with general mental ability. Therefore, when both a test of general mental ability and a test of conscientiousness are used to predict the future performance of job applicants, an even better, more accurate prediction can be made (Schmidt & Hunter, 2004).

Integrity tests Tests of personality and general mental ability attempt to predict which applicants will become high-performing employees. Employment tests also have been designed to predict which employees are most likely to engage in negative, *counterproductive,* behavior. These tests are generally called **integrity tests**.

Paper-and-pencil integrity tests became much more popular after 1988, the year in which a bill was passed by Congress that prohibited the widespread use of polygraphs (lie detectors) for selecting people for jobs. A *polygraph* measures several physiological responses, such as breathing rate, blood pressure, and perspiration, that are usually accelerated when people tell a lie.

conscientiousness The personality trait that refers to a person's ability to finish projects that are started, to attend to detail without becoming absorbed by it, and to care enough about the quality of work that it is not compromised by inattention or lack of effort.

integrity tests Paper-and-pencil tests that predict the likelihood that a job applicant will engage in counterproductive behavior in the workplace.

> **TABLE 11–3 EXAMPLES OF QUESTIONS SIMILAR TO THOSE USED IN THE NEO-PI TEST OF THE FIVE FACTORS OF PERSONALITY**

Respond to the following statements by choosing the answer that best corresponds to your agreement or disagreement: Strongly Agree, Agree, Neutral, Disagree, Strongly Disagree.

1. I am a person who likes to be in charge of others.
2. I find that I sometimes lose my temper more easily than others do.
3. I have a hard time leaving a partially-completed task undone.
4. I seem to worry a good deal more than other people do.
5. I find there are relatively few people I meet that I would like to get to know better.
6. I enjoy learning new things.

Adapted from: NEO-PI-R, published by Paul T. Costa, Jr. and Robert R. McCrae (1992). Odessa, FL: Psychological Assessment Resources, Inc.

Job knowledge and work sample tests are good methods for evaluating the level of skill that job applicants bring with them from their previous jobs.

Prior to 1988, polygraphs were widely used in private industry to screen job applicants, usually for jobs that involved security or handling large sums of money. Although polygraph tests can still be used in some job interview settings, especially for jobs in government and in the military that involve national security, they are no longer allowed in most non-governmental organizations. Employers are increasingly turning to integrity tests to predict which potential employees are most likely to engage in counterproductive behavior in the workplace.

Counterproductive behaviors can be defined narrowly and broadly (Dunn, Mount, Barrick, & Ones, 1995). Narrow definitions usually identify specific behaviors that are clearly harmful to the organization, such as stealing, lying, or hurting another employee. More broadly defined counterproductivity includes such behaviors as the abuse of sick leave, drug and alcohol abuse, chronic tardiness, and general uncooperativeness.

Integrity tests can predict both kinds of counterproductive behaviors, although they are better at predicting the broad behaviors that disrupt work place productivity (Ones, Viswesvaran, & Schmidt, 1993). How do they do this? Integrity tests include questions that measure three of the five factors of personality that are linked to counterproductive behavior: *conscientiousness*, *agreeableness*, and *emotional stability* (Schmidt & Hunter, 2004). By identifying which applicants score low on these three dimensions, integrity tests can help employers screen out potentially difficult employees before they are hired.

MEASURES OF PREVIOUS PERFORMANCE One of the long-standing dictums in psychology is this: *The best predictor of future performance is past performance.* In an organizational context, this basic principle means that, in general, people who have performed at a high level in previous positions will most likely perform at a high level in future positions. Thus, personnel selection specialists often pay particular attention to previous work histories of job applicants and look for evidence of prior performance.

One method of doing this involves having each job applicant complete an *application blank* that includes questions about prior job history. Application blanks also request general information about each employee (name, phone number, and so forth), and they are the most frequently used method of selection (Schultz & Schultz, 1998).

Another means of identifying previous level of job performance is reference checking. Job applicants can be required to identify previous employers and to provide the names of former work supervisors. However, many employers are reluctant to provide information about the quality of a previous employee's work because any negative information that prevents the employee from securing a new job may result in a lawsuit that is expensive to defend (Fishman, 2005). Consequently, companies sometimes adopt the policy that they will verify a previous worker's employment, but make no comment about the quality of his or her work. Nevertheless, sometimes important information can be gathered by checking references, either in writing or by phone, and most organizations do check references before extending a job offer (Kerrison, 2006; Weiss, 2006).

A third means of identifying the quality of previous work experience can sometimes be obtained via *job knowledge* or *work sample tests*. These tests involve asking applicants to demonstrate their knowledge of the job for which they are applying, or to actually perform the skills required by the job in question. For example, a job knowledge test for a press operator might involve asking questions about how the press operates and how it can be repaired when it breaks down. A work sample test might involve having the job applicant go onto the factory floor and actually operate the press. The validity of job knowledge and work sample tests is, understandably, very high (see again **Table 11–1**). However, relatively few jobs allow for the use of these procedures in personnel selection.

ASSESSMENT CENTERS Many of selection methods previously outlined are appropriate for positions at all levels in an organization. However for jobs that involve substantial leadership and management responsibility, some organizations prefer to include an *assessment center* evaluation as part of their personnel selection strategy.

Assessment centers typically place applicants for high-level management positions into a simulated and highly structured group setting. Here, applicants participate in group exercises where their interactions and decisions are observed and evaluated by professional evaluators who look for how they approach and solve organizational problems. The typical assessment center lasts two days, involves several group exercises and the administration of a variety of ability and personality tests, and includes a lengthy and detailed structured interview (Gaugler, Rosenthal, Thornton, & Benson, 1987). Companies use assessment centers because advancement in management is related to skills that are difficult to evaluate using traditional selection methods (Jansen & Stoop, 2001).

The validity of assessment centers for predicting the long-term performance of individuals in upper management is reasonably good (see again **Table 11–1**); however, much of the ability of an assessment center to predict which employees will make the best top-level managers is also predicted by the tests of general mental ability and personality typically administered as part of the assessment center exercise. Despite this finding, many large organizations continue to use assessment centers to select individuals for high-level managerial positions because they believe the exercises can provide a wide range of insights about these candidates and can suggest the level their career may reach (Schmidt & Hunter, 2004).

OVERVIEW OF PERSONNEL SELECTION Industrial psychologists often recommend that organizations use a combination of predictors in their personnel selection process. In general, the most effective combinations include a test of general mental ability along with either a structured interview or a test of conscientiousness (Schmidt & Hunter, 2004). Regardless of the specific methods an organization adopts, the way in which the selection system is implemented will also have an impact on hiring success.

Research shows, for example, that applicants who develop a favorable attitude about the way they are treated in the hiring process are more likely to hold positive attitudes about the company (Hausknecht, Day, & Thomas, 2004). They also are more likely to accept a job if it is offered, and are more likely to recommend the employer to others as a good place to work. In general, interviews and work samples are perceived most favorably by job applicants as valid means by which to select employees, followed by cognitive ability tests. Personality tests and integrity tests are viewed by applicants less fair.

One of the most significant challenges faced by industrial psychologists in the 21st century will be to devise systems that are fair to all applicants, that are easily integrated into organizational processes, and that maximize the productivity of the labor force. The issue of fairness includes abiding by federal legislation designed to eradicate discriminatory practices.

LAWS DEFINING FAIR EMPLOYMENT

What does it mean to be a member of a "protected class" and what protections are guaranteed to members of these groups?

In the United States as well as abroad, companies have, at times, refused to hire employees based on gender, age, race, and religious beliefs (Brinkley, 1999). Today, most industrialized nations have developed legislation to guard against employment practices that otherwise would be considered discriminatory. In the United States, one of the most important sets of such laws, the Civil Rights Act of 1964, was established by an act of Congress.

The **Civil Rights Act of 1964** is a sweeping set of laws and regulations aimed at protecting the rights of individuals and groups of people who had historically experienced discrimination because they were women or belonged to certain racial, ethnic, or religious groups (see

assessment center Method used to select high-level managers that places applicants in a simulated and highly structured group setting where they are given personnel tests and extensive interviews and they engage in various role playing activities.

Civil Rights Act of 1964 A sweeping set of laws and regulations aimed at protecting the rights of people who had, because they were members of certain racial, ethnic, or religious groups, experienced discrimination.

President Lyndon B. Johnson, seated, signed into law the Civil Rights Act of 1964, which dramatically broadened individuals' protection from unfair discrimination. In this photo, Dr. Martin Luther King, Jr., and others involved in the civil rights movement look on as President Johnson signs this historic bill.

Chapter 10: "Social Psychology"). The Civil Rights Act (CRA) includes an array of provisions that define and prohibit discriminatory practices in all walks of life. The particular set of regulations that pertain most directly to employees and businesses are contained in Title VII. Title VII expressly prohibits discrimination against employees because of their membership in certain named **protected classes (or groups)**, which are defined to include individuals whose group membership is based on race, color, religion, sex, or national origin. The major theme of Title VII is captured by these specific provisions (U. S. Equal Employment Opportunity Commission, 2006):

It shall be an unlawful employment practice for an employer:

(1) to fail or refuse to hire or to discharge any individual, or otherwise to discriminate against any individual with respect to his compensation, terms, conditions, or privileges of employment, because of such individual's race, color, religion, sex, or national origin; or (2) to limit, segregate, or classify his employees or applicants for employment in any way which would deprive or tend to deprive any individual of employment opportunities or otherwise adversely affect his status as an employee, because of such individual's race, color, religion, sex, or national origin.

The CRA of 1964 was a major step forward in protecting the rights of individuals against illegal discrimination. In the years since it was passed, both its scope and the number and types of groups it identifies as "protected" have been extended through a series of federal laws (see **Table 11–4**).

> ► CHECK YOUR UNDERSTANDING

1. The primary distinction between industrial and organizational psychology is their relative focus on:
   a. the individual versus the organization
   b. personnel selection versus job analysis
   c. job analysis versus job design
   d. hierarchical leadership versus team leadership

2. A _____ _____ is the process businesses go through to develop a thorough and accurate job description

Indicate whether the following statements are True (T) or False (F):

3. A job is defined as the set of tasks that an individual worker performs.

4. The job analysis system that focuses on people-data-things is called the KSAO system.

5. The technique of meta-analysis is used to summarize the results of many research studies on the same topic.

6. The most valid means of selecting people for jobs is the unstructured interview.

7. Job applicants express the most favorable attitudes about the personality test as a method of personnel selection.

8. Under the Civil Rights Act of 1964, which of the following groups is NOT identified as a protected class?
   a. people with a gay or lesbian sexual preference
   b. people of different color
   c. people who are members of different religious groups
   d. people who belong to different racial groups

Answers: 1. a., 2. job analysis, 3. F, 4. F, 5. T, 6. F, 7. F, 8. a.

> ► APPLY YOUR UNDERSTANDING

1. Ms. Washington wants to create a personnel selection system that has the highest possible validity. She would be advised to use which of the following selection methods:
   a. assessment center and structured job interview
   b. test of general mental ability and structured job interview
   c. test of conscientiousness and assessment center
   d. work sample and job application blank

2. Integrity tests are generally used to predict:
   a. job performance
   b. turnover
   c. counterproductivity
   d. general mental ability

3. Which of the following terms best describes the focus of the CRA of 1964?
   a. predictive validity
   b. consistent leadership
   c. adequate training for the job
   d. protection from discrimination

Answers: 1. b., 2. c., 3. d.

protected classes (or groups) Groups of people who are guaranteed legal protection against discrimination under the provisions of the Civil Rights Act of 1964 and subsequent acts and laws.

>TABLE 11-4 MAJOR LEGISLATIVE ACTS THAT ADDRESS DISCRIMINATION IN THE WORKPLACE

Legislation	Year	Decision
Civil Rights Act, Title VII	1964	Prohibits discrimination based on race, color, religion, sex and national origin
Age Discrimination Act	1967	Protects workers against discrimination based on age.
Rehabilitation Act	1973	Expands coverage of the Civil Rights Act and Age Discrimination Act to further include issues of age and disability.
Pregnancy Discrimination Act	1978	An amendment to the 1964 Civil Rights Act that makes discrimination against pregnant women a form of sex discrimination.
Americans with Disabilities Act	1990	Protects disabled workers from discrimination based on disability. Workers can and should be considered for a job as long as their disability does not interfere with the duties of that job.
Federal Medical Leave Act	1993	Allows employees up to 12 weeks of unpaid leave without reprisal should they or a member of their family become sick or in distress.

Note: This table was prepared by John Gambon, Ph.D. Professor of Psychology, Ozarks Technical College, 1000 East Chestnut Expressway, Springfield, MO 65802

Measuring Performance on the Job

11.2   Identify several methods by which job performance can be measured, and suggest the limitations associated with each method.

Individual job performance is important to evaluate for a wide variety of reasons. From an organizational point of view, effective methods for evaluating performance improve the quality of organizational decisions, including pay raises, promotions, and terminations; they enhance employees' understanding of how much success they are having in their job; they serve to either encourage or erode the loyalty workers feel toward their organization (Murphy & Cleveland, 1995). Formal performance appraisals also can provide a legally defensible rationale for making personnel decisions.

STRATEGIES FOR EVALUATING PERFORMANCE

What circumstances determine whether it is better to use an objective or a subjective performance appraisal system?

Performance appraisal systems, the formal methods for evaluating performance, have as their goal an unbiased assessment of the *quantity* and *quality* of work contributed by each individual within an organization. Depending somewhat on the type of work being performed, several methods of performance appraisal can be effectively used.

When productivity can be measured directly, an **objective performance appraisal** system is usually employed. Objective methods are based on *quantitative* measurement, such as by counting the number of goods produced, the number of pieces assembled, or the dollars of product sold. Although it might seem that objective measures of performance are accurate and valid, objective performance data may not tell the entire story of an individual's effectiveness and contribution to the organization. For example, one machine operator might be able to produce more units because her machine is newer and faster than the machine assigned to a co-worker; one pharmaceutical sales agent may have a better territory to cover than another agent selling the same drugs. Another problem with objective performance appraisal strategies is that they seldom cover all the work an individual does for the company. A press operator may not produce the highest number of units in his division, but he may be the person most often called on to fix machines when they fail to operate correctly. His value to the organization should not be measured solely in how many units he produces. Similarly, a data entry worker may enter the most data of any person in the division, but may also make the most errors.

performance appraisal system Formal methods used to assess the quantity and quality of work contributed by each individual within an organization.

objective performance appraisal Method of performance appraisal based on quantitative measurement of the amount of work done.

Organizations use a variety of techniques to ensure that performance evaluations are based on productivity, rather than on factors that are not directly related to job performance.

When objective measures fail to capture important dimensions of job performance, *subjective* methods are usually used. **Subjective performance appraisal** methods rely on *judgments* about the *quality* of work an employee contributes. These systems are used extensively in all types of organizations, often because jobs do not involve work that can be measured objectively. Teachers, managers, nurses, and many other employees do important work that cannot be "counted."

TYPES OF ERRORS IN PERFORMANCE ASSESSMENT

What kinds of rating errors commonly occur in performance appraisal systems?

When individuals make subjective judgments about their own work, or about the work of peers, supervisors, or subordinates, their judgments are always open to error. Industrial psychologists are concerned with three major types of errors in subjective judgments of productivity.

One type of error is known as **halo error**, or the *halo effect*. A halo error occurs when evaluators base their ratings of many dimensions of an employee's performance on how they assess a single characteristic. For example, if an employee is judged to be cooperative and pleasant toward co-workers, raters may evaluate her as also being more proficient at her assigned tasks than she actually is, as having more regular work attendance than she actually does, and as possessing higher levels of skill than she actually has. Her warm personal style acts as a "halo" that biases the evaluations of her other work-related behaviors. The "horns" effect is similar: If a supervisor finds a worker resists taking directions, she may also rate the worker unfairly low on a number of dimensions of job performance instead of only one. Recent research suggests, however, that even when halo error is present in performance evaluations, those evaluations may still be accurate (Viswesvaran, Schmidt, & Ones, 2005; Jackson & Furnham, 2001).

Another error that sometimes occurs in subjective performance evaluations is **recency error**, which occurs when evaluations of performance rely too extensively on the most recent behavior of the employee. Usually formal performance appraisals are done only once or, at most, a few times during the year. When evaluators fail to consider the general level of work done by employees throughout the entire period of time since the last review, their evaluations may well be biased by the recency error. Employees who work harder in the days just before a performance appraisal may be trying to take advantage of the recency error.

A third type of error involves the tendency of evaluators to judge all employees as being more similar to each other than they actually are. The **central tendency error** occurs when raters evaluate all, or nearly all, employees as being "average" despite the presence of real differences in levels of performance. *Leniency errors* are committed when employees are all rated high; *severity errors* are committed when all employees receive low ratings. Research suggests that personality variables are linked to leniency and severity rating errors. Perhaps not surprisingly, raters who score high on the personality trait of conscientiousness are more likely to rate others severely; those who score high in agreeableness are more likely to make leniency errors (Bernardin, Cooke, & Villanova, 2000).

Central tendency, leniency, and severity errors are a special problem when workers from different appraisal groups are compared in terms of performance. Assuming that all workers are actually equally productive, those who were rated leniently, and therefore received higher ratings, will likely be treated more favorably than those rated severely: Perhaps they will receive bigger raises or more recognition for their work. Errors of central tendency, leniency, or severity can thus lead employers to distribute rewards unfairly.

LIMITING THE IMPACT OF RATING ERRORS

How can errors made in evaluating employee performance be reduced or eliminated?

Several techniques can be helpful in reducing rating errors. Recency errors, for example, can be reduced by requiring raters to maintain ongoing records of evaluation, perhaps noting overall performance at the end of each pay period or at the end of each month. At

subjective performance appraisal Methods of performance appraisal that rely on judgments about the quality of work an employee contributes.

halo error (halo effect) A rating error that occurs when evaluators generalize their ratings on multiple dimensions of an employee's performance from how they assess a single characteristic.

recency error A rating error that occurs when evaluations of performance rely too extensively on the most recent behavior of the employee.

central tendency error A rating error that occurs when raters evaluate all, or nearly all, employees as being average when in fact their levels of performance differ.

whatever point in the annual cycle that performance appraisal occurs, raters can consult their ongoing record and make an evaluation that reflects ratings across several points in time. Central tendency errors can be reduced by requiring evaluators to rank order employees, from highest-performing to lowest-performing. Although rank ordering imposes an artificial distinction between higher- and lower-performing employees, and therefore does not allow for the possibility that all workers might be equally productive, it does require that raters pay attention to subtle distinctions in the quality and quantity of work each employee contributes.

Other types of errors can be addressed by creating performance appraisal systems that require evaluators to focus on employee *behaviors*, rather than rating less directly observable attitudes and intentions. Multiple evaluators can also be used in the process.

BEHAVIOR-BASED PERFORMANCE APPRAISAL One of the greatest challenges in creating an appraisal system that is fair and unbiased is to identify exactly what is expected of individuals who hold a given job. For example, for most U.S. jobs, employers likely would agree that it would be unfair to require that employees belong to a particular political party. But it would be fair to expect employees to work cooperatively with coworkers, regardless of their political affiliations. Generally speaking, evaluations based on observable *behaviors*, rather than on attitudes or intentions, are less prone to error.

One commonly used performance appraisal method that is based on the raters' observations of behaviors is called the **behaviorally anchored ratings scale (BARS)**. A BARS system identifies specific behaviors that would be associated with high performance, average performance, and substandard performance for the job being evaluated. These behaviors are then arranged into a rating scale so that each is associated with a particular rating on that scale (see **Figure 11–3**). When evaluators use a BARS scale to rate a particular employee, that employee's typical behavior is assessed in the context of the positive and negative incidents identified on the scale. In this way, evaluators' ratings reflect the job-related behaviors employees characteristically display in their work.

A similar method of performance appraisal that also is based on rating behaviors is called the **behavioral observation scale (BOS)**. A behavioral observation scale is similar to the BARS method in that both involve assessment of job-related behaviors. Although a BARS requires the rater to choose which behavior listed is most representative of the work of the employee, a BOS focuses on the *frequency* of various behaviors that are expected on the job (see **Figure 11–4**). The use of the BOS method is based on establishing an agreed upon list of relevant and important work behaviors, which are then evaluated by managers.

Both BARS and BOS systems do not eliminate the possibility that evaluators may be biased or make errors in their ratings. By focusing the performance appraisal on clearly identified behaviors in the workplace, however, rating errors generally are reduced. Furthermore, when there are disagreements

behaviorally anchored ratings scale (BARS)
A performance appraisal method that specifies specific behaviors that would be associated with high performance, average performance, and substandard performance for the job being evaluated, arranges these behaviors into a rating scale, and matches employee behavior to the appropriate scaled behaviors that best correspond.

behavioral observation scale (BOS)
A performance appraisal method that identifies important work-related behaviors and requires raters to specify the *frequency* at which the employee performs those behaviors.

Figure 11–3

Example of a BARS Performance Evaluation
This BARS profile assesses the job performance of police officers, their knowledge of proper procedures related to the legal requirements.

Source: Psychology of Work Behavior, red.ed. by F.J. Landy and D.A. Trumbo, 1980. Brooks/Cole.

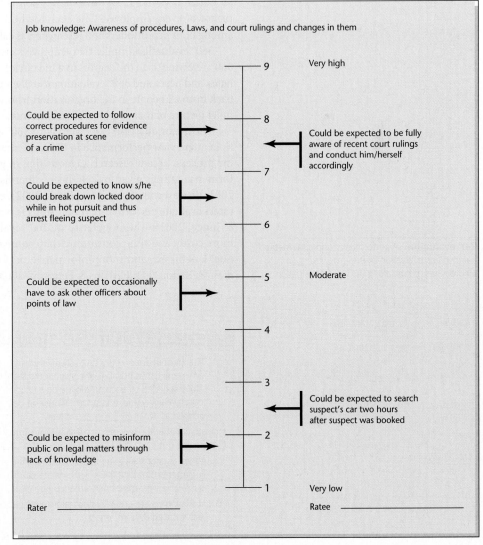

Figure 11–4

Example of a BOS scale The following is an example of a BOS scale for a *grocery store employee* in two categories of behavior: *customer assistance*, and *operating a check-out machine*.

Mark the number that best corresponds to this employee's behavior:

1. Uses good eye contact and smiles when customers ask where a product is located.

Never	Seldom	Sometimes	Frequently	Always
1	2	3	4	5

2. Operates the scanning machine and the cash register at check-out accurately and efficiently.

Never	Seldom	Sometimes	Frequently	Always
1	2	3	4	5

between a rater's and an employee's evaluation of the employee's work, behavior-based systems also have the advantage of encouraging clear communication about what is expected of the employee and about how managers can help the employee achieve the expected standards. An additional benefit of systems such as BARS and BOS is that they require both workers and managers to be involved in developing the rating scales used for each job. This collaboration can improve communication and clarify for all parties what the most important dimensions of job performance are.

360° EVALUATION SYSTEMS In any performance evaluation system in which employees are evaluated by only one rater, there is always the possibility that the rater's biases will result in an unfair assessment. An obvious solution is to have more than one rater assess the performance of every employee. One such method that is attracting considerable attention today among both practitioners and researchers is called the 360° evaluation.

360° evaluation implies that employees are rated from every perspective (hence the term, 360°, referring to all the degrees in a full circle). Assessments are made by supervisors, subordinates, and peers, and 360° evaluation usually includes self-evaluation as well. By soliciting feedback from all people in the organization who work with an employee, management can get a fuller picture of that employee's performance.

The major question associated with 360° evaluation concerns the degree to which multiple raters view performance in the same way. If raters agree, this supports the accuracy of the process. Recent research suggests that in general there is a high correspondence of performance ratings given by self, peer, supervisor, and subordinate raters (Facteau & Craig, 2001; Viswesvaran, Schmidt, & Ones, 2002), even though the way in which these groups of raters evaluate performance dimensions is not presently well understood (Scullen, Mount, & Judge, 2003). The popularity of 360° evaluation is growing. Although this method is more costly and time consuming than some others, it also generally results in more accurate, less biased, and more informative performance evaluations (Kuzmits, Adams, Sussman, & Raho, 2004; Luthans & Peterson, 2003).

360° evaluation A performance appraisal method that involves evaluation by supervisors, subordinates, peers, along with a self-evaluation.

> ► CHECK YOUR UNDERSTANDING

1. If a performance appraisal system is based on counting the number of components that are assembled by each employee on average during a work cycle, that system would be described as a(n) _____ system.

Indicate whether the following statements are True (T) or False (F):

2. When performance appraisals rely on the judgments of raters, these systems are called *subjective* systems of performance appraisal.

3. If all workers are unfairly rated below average, this is called a "horn" effect.

4. BARS methods require that raters respond to the frequency with which employees perform certain behaviors.

5. Performance appraisal systems that involve evaluations by self, supervisors, subordinates, and peers are called:
   a. BOS systems
   b. BARS systems
   c. 360° evaluation
   d. halo systems

Answers: 1. objective, 2. T, 3. F, 4. F, 5. c.

training The organized approach that organizations undertake to instruct employees in relevant job-related attitudes and behaviors.

▶ APPLY YOUR UNDERSTANDING

1. If supervisors are commiting a *recency error*, which of the following approaches is the best solution for minimizing this problem?
   a. Supervisors can rely on a ranking system of employees to ensure not everyone will be evaluated the same.
   b. Supervisors can ask other supervisors to review their evaluation to determine if they are accurate.
   c. Supervisors can keep records of both good and bad behavior observed at specific and regular points in time.

   d. Supervisors can rate employees on their behavior rather than on their attitudes and intentions.

2. Despite the fact that the employees in Lucy's work group vary widely in their job performance, Lucy gives them all average performance ratings so that none of the workers will feel unfairly treated. The rating error Lucy is making is referred to as:
   a. halo
   b. recency
   c. leniency
   d. central tendency

Answers: 1. c, 2. d.

Behavior within Organizations

11.3   Describe the various methods used by I/O psychologists to train workers and suggest how the structure of an organization influences its operation.

Industrial/organizational psychologists are not only concerned with selecting employees and ensuring that they are treated fairly. They also are involved in preparing those workers to perform the work required to the best of their ability. Oftentimes, this means that employees must be *trained* to perform specific parts of the job for which they are hired.

TRAINING EMPLOYEES

What methods are commonly used to train workers to be more effective in their jobs?

The work that employees are hired to do often requires specialized skills that must be learned on the job. In other cases, organizations want all employees to develop particular attitudes or patterns of behavior. **Training** is the organized approach to instructing employees in relevant job-related attitudes and behaviors.

DETERMINING TRAINING NEEDS Sometimes the need for training is obvious. In many organizations, employees are hired for jobs even though they do not have some of the necessary job skills at the time they are hired. New employees may also need to learn about various aspects of the organizational culture. For example, when speaking with clients, does the new receptionist refer to corporate officers by their first names, or by Mr. or Ms.? Consider the opening paragraphs of this chapter—even experienced food store workers must learn a new corporate culture and new ways of interacting with customers when they go to work at Trader Joe's. In many organizations, training is an ongoing function, because experienced workers also can benefit from learning about new ways of working and from different ways of thinking about organizational processes.

Assessing an organization's training needs can be thought of as a three-step process (Landy & Conte, 2004; Ostroff & Ford, 1989). First, an *organizational analysis* is done in which the company's goals are examined and problems are identified. Next, for those problems that lend themselves to training-based solutions, a *task analysis* is performed. Task analysis identifies which job tasks can be addressed through training and examines the KSAOs required to perform those tasks successfully. As you might expect, the

Performance evaluations that are based on behavioral ratings scales, such as BARS and BOS assessments, can provide valuable feedback to employees about how to improve in their work.

on-the-job training (OJT) The training method in which the employee being trained learns the new job tasks while actually performing the job.

job rotation The training method that teaches employees to perform each job in their work.

vestibule training The training method that allows employees to learn techniques and behaviors in a simulated work place.

techniques used in task analysis often overlap substantially with those used in job analysis. Finally, a *person analysis* is conducted to examine the knowledge, skills, and current performance of workers to determine who needs additional training.

Training programs can be designed to teach workers the necessary skills, behaviors, or attitudes that will allow them to perform job tasks at an acceptable level. After training is complete, an assessment of training outcomes should be performed, so managers can evaluate which training needs have been successfully addressed, and which remain (Goldstein & Ford, 2002; Alliger & Janak, 1989).

ON-THE-JOB TRAINING (OJT) One of the most common methods of teaching new workers the skills they need to perform their job is **on-the-job training**. The key element of on-the-job training, or OJT, is that the employee being trained learns the new job tasks while actually performing the job (Berings, Poell, & Simon, 2005). For example, a new assistant chef may be unfamiliar with how the head chef in a particular restaurant wants foods to be plated and sauced. The new worker can be given specific, step-by-step instructions, and can be shown by an experienced employee exactly how these tasks are to be performed.

One of the oldest programs of on-the-job training is *apprenticeship*, which is still used extensively in the crafts and trades. Today, there are about 37,000 apprentice programs in the United States that involve nearly a half-million trainees, called *apprentices* (U. S. Department of Labor, 2006b). Apprentices go through a formal and extensive program of on-the-job training, which includes both instruction and supervision by a skilled worker in the field. Sometimes apprenticeship programs are offered through trade schools, career colleges, or community colleges that offer both classroom instruction and on-the-job experience.

Another type of on-the-job training is **job rotation**. In job rotation programs, workers are trained to perform each of the different jobs in a particular supervisory unit. For example, in an assembly unit in which five different workers each perform a specific part of the assembly of a machine, each worker would learn each of the five jobs involved. Job rotation programs provide an effective way of staffing jobs that have high turnover, because workers are already trained to take over the job of a person who quits (Riggio, 2003). When jobs are rotated among work team members on a regular basis, this also can provide some relief from the boredom associated with performing the same task over and over. Job rotation is often part of supervisors' training. Research suggests that supervisors who are rotated through several jobs are more apt to remain with a company than those who receive no such training (Grensing-Pophal, 2005; Pooley, 2005).

VESTIBULE AND SIMULATION TRAINING Sometimes new job skills cannot be learned while performing the actual job itself. An alternative approach in such instances is vestibule training. **Vestibule training** allows employees to learn to perform job tasks at work stations similar to those used in production, but that are located in a training facility rather than on the actual production floor.

In other cases, *training simulators* are used. For example, flight simulators are used to teach U. S. military pilots how to fly. Flight simulators operate like real airplanes, with fully-equipped cockpits and pitch-and-roll machines that move the simulator to replicate the actual movements of an aircraft. The only major difference between flying a simulator versus a real airplane is that the simulator doesn't have wings or leave the ground.

Computer-based simulations can provide yet another vehicle for some types of training needs. One such example of computer-simulated training is discussed in the opening paragraphs of Chapter 4: "Learning and Memory," which describe how U. S. soldiers are being trained to assess the risks associated with various combat situations by playing computer games. Today, computer-based simulations are being used to train firefighters, medical personnel, and heavy equipment operators, as well as workers in many

Pilot training is greatly enhanced when flight simulators are used. Here, high risk, dangerous situations can be simulated, and pilots can learn and practice corrective actions without endangering themselves or others.

other jobs. (Bliss, Scerbo, Schmidt, & Thompson, 2006; Smith 2006; Foundry Management and Technology, 2006; Construction Equipment, 2006).

MANAGEMENT DEVELOPMENT Over 90 percent of companies offer management development programs to their managerial employees (Baldwin & Padgett, 1993). In fact, providing managers with opportunities to develop their skills is one factor that distinguishes excellent companies (Kotter, 1988).

Both *personal* and *interpersonal skills* are involved in managing the work of other people (Whetton & Cameron, 1991). Personal skills that appear to be especially important for managers include the ability to solve problems, to manage stress effectively, and to understand how their own actions and decisions affect their subordinates. Interpersonal skills often involve the ability to communicate effectively, to motivate subordinates, to manage conflict, and to gain the power and influence necessary to be effective in directing the work of others.

The most commonly used method for management training is the technique called **case study analysis**, where managers read case studies that describe conflict situations in an organization, develop strategies for effectively managing these cases, and then discuss their approaches to the problem in a group setting (Berger, 1983). Case study analysis teaches managers how to analyze problems logically, to consider their various dimensions, and solve problems in a manner consistent with management's goals.

Other methods used in management training and development programs involve similar approaches. *Role playing* or *management games*, for example, give managers practice in solving the kinds of problems they must deal with on the job. The same kinds of tasks and simulations often are used in assessment centers.

CHANGING ATTITUDES IN THE WORKPLACE

How can organizations use training to promote a more tolerant, non-discriminatory work environment?

Sometimes organizations need to develop their workforce not in terms of skills, but rather in terms of attitudes and interpersonal behaviors. Cultural diversity training and sexual harassment training are used to accomplish these goals.

Cultural diversity training is used to help workers adapt their actions and their attitudes so that they can work effectively in a multicultural work environment. The U.S. workplace broadly reflects the demographic trends within the population overall, and both are becoming much more diverse. For example, of all new additions to the work force in the decade of the 1990s, nearly half (45 percent) were non-white, and nearly two-thirds were women. Consequently, most industrial/organizational psychologists predict that cultural diversity training will become even more important in future years (Bhawuk & Brislin, 2000).

Why is it important for organizations to offer programs in cultural diversity training? First, organizations must maintain an atmosphere that is fair and non-discriminatory for all employees; not doing so puts companies at risk for lawsuits filed under anti-discrimination laws such as The Civil Rights Act of 1964. Cultural diversity training alerts workers to how their actions may be offensive to others and helps them learn to work cooperatively with co-workers of different cultures or genders. Second, and equally important, cultural diversity in the work force "captures the benefits in creativity and problem-solving capabilities that a diverse workforce provides" (Chrobot-Mason & Quinones, 2002). When workers are able to appreciate and embrace various points of view, productivity is enhanced. Finally, the ever-increasing globalization of the workplace means that more employees are taking assignments abroad, which also leads to a need for cultural diversity training (Speitzer, McCall, & Mahoney, 1997).

Apprenticeship programs are widely used in the trade professions to teach new employees complex skills.

case study analysis The management training method where managers read about conflict situations in an organization, develop strategies for effectively managing these cases, and then discuss their approaches to the problem in a group setting.

cultural diversity training Training that helps workers understand how people from other cultures think and act, and how to adjust their own attitudes and actions so all employees can work effectively in a multi-cultural work environment.

Most employers offer cultural diversity training and sexual harassment training to encourage employees to be more tolerant and accepting of others with whom they work.

Cultural diversity training relies on many of the same techniques used in management development programs. Often programs begin by having co-workers representing various cultural, ethnic, racial, or gender groups discuss their perceptions about how they are similar to and different from each other; then discussion, which may involve the reading of case studies, role playing, or games, is focused on identifying and correcting behaviors that are discriminatory or unfair and on developing attitudes that do not involve unfair stereotypes and prejudices.

A similar type of training is aimed at reducing sexual harassment in the work place. According to the law, **sexual harassment** can be defined in either of two ways. *Quid pro quo* harassment is defined as behavior in which sexual favors are solicited in return for favorable treatment. An example of quid pro quo harassment might involve a manager offering a salary increase or a promotion to a subordinate in exchange for sexual attention. Sexual harassment is also involved when managers or co-workers create a *hostile work environment*, perhaps by telling sexist jokes, by posting nude "pin-up" photos in lockers, or by teasing of a sexual nature. The goals of sexual harassment training parallel those of cultural diversity training: to protect the organization from lawsuits and to create an environment where every worker is able to perform to his or her maximum level of creativity, effort, and productivity.

> ### ▶ CHECK YOUR UNDERSTANDING

1. When workers learn to perform all jobs in their work unit, this type of training is called _____.
2. The biggest disadvantage to vestibule or simulator training typically is the _____.
3. Which of the following techniques would be least likely to be used to train newly hired managers:

a. vestibule training
b. case study analysis
c. cultural diversity and sexual harassment training
d. job rotation

Answers: 1. job rotation, 2. cost, 3. a.

> ### ▶ APPLY YOUR UNDERSTANDING

1. Which of the following training approaches would most likely be used to encourage production workers to treat their coworkers with more respect?
   a. vestibule training
   b. case study analysis
   c. cultural diversity and sexual harassment training
   d. job rotation
2. Which of the following situations is the best example of *quid pro quo* sexual harassment?

a. Bob continually makes "lesbian" jokes that offend his assistant.
b. Bob is afraid to tell his boss that her comments about his physical attractiveness make him uncomfortable.
c. Bob tells his co-worker that he will help her get a promotion if she will have dinner and drinks with him.
d. Bob makes it clear that he is not "gay" and won't tolerate any "homosexual" jokes.

Answers: 1. c, 2. c.

Organizational Culture

11.4   Describe how an organization's approach to the use of teams, its philosophy of leadership, and the attitudes of its employees about their work each contribute to its organizational culture.

The topics discussed so far in this chapter—job analysis, personnel selection, fair employment practices, and training—occur in the context of a particular organization. Organizations have their own **corporate, or organizational, culture**, which refers to the formal and informal rules, procedures, and expectations that define the values, attitudes, beliefs, and customs of an organization (Ostroff, Kinicki, & Tamkins, 2003). Organizations differ, sometimes in rather dramatic ways, as the description of Trader Joe's in the opening paragraphs of this chapter makes clear.

Most organizations today also are quite different than they were a generation ago, when most jobs were relatively simple and most workers performed the same narrowly defined set of tasks over and over, sometimes for entire careers. For example, in a classically structured assembly plant in the 1960s, a five-step assembly process would most likely be broken down into

---

sexual harassment Behaviors that involve either soliciting sexual favors in exchange for favorable treatment or creating a hostile work environment.

corporate (organizational) culture The formal and informal rules, procedures, and expectations that define the values, attitudes, beliefs, and customs of an organization.

five separate jobs, with one person assigned to perform each. The efficiency in such a "line" oriented approach to production came from having each worker perform a specific job, over and over, as quickly as possible. Yet many factors prevent line-based assembly organizations from operating at maximum efficiency. For example, if a worker is absent and a substitute worker is assigned, the substitute may not be able to perform the job as fast as the experienced person, thereby slowing down the entire line. Also, when individuals do not understand the entire manufacturing process, they often have difficulty solving work-related problems. So companies have developed new techniques to resolve these problems.

TEAMS AND TEAMWORK

Why do organizations sometimes organize workers into teams?

As jobs have become more complex, line-based organizations have adapted to meet changing work conditions. To address many of the issues raised by technological advances in the workplace and by the shifting expectations of workers, many organizations have adopted a "team-based" approach to work.

The basic idea behind work teams is that productivity is enhanced when several people work together cooperatively to solve problems (Kozlowski & Bell, 2003). Teams are particularly effective when problems must be solved by the workers themselves. A good team generally outperforms individuals in tasks that require experience, judgment, and multiple skills (Salas, Stagl, & Burke, 2004).

Organizing workers into teams can also address some of the motivational problems experienced in work that is routine. Oftentimes, workers on a team are trained to perform all jobs in their unit (a technique discussed earlier in this chapter as job rotation) and they regularly exchange jobs, which keeps their skills sharp and also helps relieve boredom. Research suggests that those who work in teams are more satisfied with their work and are more productive (Glassop, 2002). Depending somewhat on the goals team-based organizations are working toward, there are many different ways that work teams can be organized and several different functions they can perform (Sunstrom, DeMeuse, & Futrell, 1990).

TYPES OF WORK TEAMS Among the first team-based approaches to emerge in the work place were *problem-solving teams*. These teams usually consist of approximately 5 to 15 employees who gather regularly to discuss concerns about safety, productivity, and efficiency. At their meetings, team members can share concerns and come up with remedies to fix problems. Most problem-solving teams are advisory in nature and do not have the ability to pressure management into accepting their ideas. Nonetheless, team discussions and recommendations can help management see where change is needed and improvement can occur. (Verespej, 1992).

As the success of problem-solving teams became apparent, many organizations expanded the autonomy and responsibility given to work teams, allowing them to perform many of the functions formerly assigned to managers. *Self-managed teams* work as individual units within the organization. Self-managed teams not only identify problems and develop solutions, they also have the power to implement their ideas. In some self-managed teams, team members hire new co-workers or discipline team members who are not performing up to standard (Nichols, Lane, & Brechu, 1993). Self-managed teams may also order materials, research new ideas, develop products, and solve internal problems with little or no help from management. Self-managed teams ultimately are responsible for the success or failure of the group's work (Cohen, Ledford & Spreitzer, 1996).

Cross-functional teams are often employed when complex work requires the cooperative effort of workers with different types of expertise. Such teams usually are made up of employees from many disciplines or corporate divisions. For example, if a college is having difficulty retaining students from the first to the second semester, the president may organize a team that includes members from the admissions staff, the residential life staff, the academic affairs office, and the business office to discuss such things as admission standards, housing problems, preparation for college-level work, and financial aid needs. Cross-functional teams frequently share information, develop new ideas, coordinate projects, and solve complex, multi-dimensional problems by relying on the diverse nature of the group and the information each member brings.

Virtual teams are the newest form of team development. When members of a work team are unable to gather in person because they do not work in the same geographical area, team members may be able to interact via various types of information technology. Communication via electronic media is a hallmark of a virtual team (Avolio, Kahai, Dumdum, & Sivasubramanian, 2001; Cascio, 1999). Interaction may occur through video conferencing, e-mail, chat rooms, phone conferencing, or wide-area networks. Considering the rapid advances in information technologies, such as the use of instant messaging and streaming video, most I/O psychologists predict the use of virtual teams is likely to increase (Axtell, Fleck, & Turner, 2004; Heneman & Greenberger, 2002).

Virtual teams face many of the same challenges other types of teams encounter. For example, some team members may engage in *social loafing* (see Chapter 10: "Social Psychology"), minimizing their own efforts and allowing their co-workers to cover for their low level of contribution. Virtual teams also involve unique challenges. For example, the lack of face-to-face contact may make forming a sense of group identity and group trust more difficult. Also, because team members do not interact outside of their formal role, they have little opportunity to develop the personal relationships that can sometimes help members of groups get through particularly difficult periods. Because virtual team members do not meet in person, they cannot rely as extensively on social and nonverbal cues in problem solving situations, and the development of group cohesion may be slower (Weisband & Atwater, 1999). Managing virtual teams also poses some challenges, because managers may find it difficult to monitor and supervise the work of people they can't see or with whom they do not directly interact (Cascio, 1999).

CHARACTERISTICS OF TEAM-BASED APPROACHES Regardless of their specific structure and purpose, effective work teams typically are guided by five general principles (McIntyre & Salas, 1995):

- Team members communicate with each other, providing and receiving feedback about the job.
- Team members are willing to offer assistance to other team members when it is needed and to take direction from team members without feeling that their performance is in some way deficient.
- Team members view their work success as coming from the effort of the team, not from the independent contributions of the team members. Thus, they identify their own success with that of the work team.
- Team members view interdependence—the need for team members to depend on each other to be successful—as a core employment value.
- Team leadership is an important dimension of the team's success. When the team leader participates in team-oriented behavior, such as by providing and accepting feedback, the effectiveness of the team is enhanced.

The use of team-based approaches in organizations has been gaining popularity (Borman, Ilgen, & Klimoski, 2003). Businesses today exist within a complex, information-rich culture in which no employee can know or master all of the areas of knowledge needed to run a successful enterprise. In addition, today's workforce is better educated and is better able to perform complex decision-making functions. Furthermore, workers today at every level of the organization expect to find challenge in their work, and most are unwilling to work at repetitive tasks that do not provide intellectual stimulation. Finally, the work performed in modern organizations has itself changed. Most jobs no longer consist of performing the same set of simple repetitive tasks; rather, they involve flexible approaches to rapidly changing technologies and business climates (Muchinsky, 2006). All these factors encourage the use of work teams (Kinlaw, 1990).

A discussion of team approaches to organizational structure and operation raises the question of leadership. Although the work team concept implies that workers within a group are interdependent and share responsibilities, the success of work teams also depends on effective leadership (Salas, Bowers, & Edens, 2002). Regardless of the degree to which workers perform independent, autonomous tasks within an organization or work as members of fully-integrated work teams, leadership is of central importance in understanding how organizations operate.

LEADERSHIP

What is the central feature of any "contingency" theory of leadership?

The study of leadership has long been a focus of organizational psychology. As we saw in Chapter 10: "Social Psychology," several theories of leadership have emerged to explain why some individuals become leaders and others do not. In recent years, contingency theories of leadership have become more popular. Contingency theories are based on the assumption that leadership is the product of both the characteristics of the leader and those of the worker and the work place. Fred Fiedler's contingency theory (see Chapter 10: "Social Psychology") is one example of a leadership theory that emphasizes multiple factors in leadership effectiveness.

LEADER-MEMBER EXCHANGE THEORY Another contingency theory that emphasizes the traits and behaviors of both leaders and followers is **leader-member exchange theory (LMX)** (Dansereau, Graen & Haga, 1975). According to the basic assumptions of the LMX model, leaders evaluate each of their subordinates according to three dimensions: their competence and skill, the degree to which they are trustworthy, and their interest in assuming greater responsibility within the work group. Subordinates who are skilled, can be trusted to perform even when they are not directly supervised, and are motivated to assume responsibility are considered by the leader to be members of the *in-group*. Those who lack these skills are relegated to the *out-group*.

According to the LMX model, after leaders have categorized subordinates into these two groups, they use different strategies to motivate and manage them. For members of the in-group, leaders are more likely to use a style that provides workers with considerable autonomy and decision-making authority. In exchange, in-group members are expected to take on additional duties and to contribute more than out-group members (Graen & Uhl-Bien, 1998; Yukl, 2002). Leaders also are more likely to spend time with in-group members, to mentor them, to be more flexible in setting expectations for them, and to provide them with greater rewards. Leaders are more likely to use formal, authoritarian methods of supervising the work of out-group members.

The LMX model suggests that leadership involves a complex set of *exchanges* between leader and subordinates; subordinates evaluate the leader in much that same way as the

leader-member exchange theory (LMX) Theory of leadership in which leaders evaluate their subordinates on their competence and skill, the degree to which they are trustworthy, and their interest in assuming greater responsibility within the work group and divide workers into in-groups and out-groups, which they lead differently.

According to the LMX model, leaders are more likely to mentor and encourage subordinates who are members of their "in-group."

leader evaluates them. Both parties evaluate the other's contributions and their loyalty, and judge them according to how much they are liked and respected (Dienesch & Liden, 1986; Liden & Maslyn, 1998). Various dimensions of organizational culture and the specific tasks required on the job also influence leader-members exchanges. LMX theory provides a framework for understanding a variety of work relationships, including not only leaders and subordinates, but co-workers and team members as well (Sherony & Green, 2002; Liden, Wayne, & Sparrowe, 2000).

SUCCESS IN LEADERSHIP An obvious, but nevertheless important, point to make about leadership is that no specific set of traits, skills, abilities, or attitudes will guarantee a person success in a leadership position. The major premise of contingency theories such as Fiedler's theory and the LMX model is that, to be effective, the characteristics of the leader must match those demanded by the situation. Consequently, a person who is very effective as a leader in one group may not be effective in another. This situation is often observed in sales-based organizations that promote managers from within. There is no certainty that the highest-producing sales agent possesses the talents that will translate into excellent management skills. Likewise, a person who can effectively lead one team of workers may not be as successful if promoted to a different division or a different level within the organization.

There are, however, some characteristics that seem to generalize across different types of organizational settings. For example, leaders who are *charismatic*—who exude confidence and have a vision that followers can relate to—are oftentimes effective in a wide array of settings (Yukl, 2002). They are especially effective in motivating the productivity of work teams (Keller, 2006). Charismatic leaders, who in some organizations are called "transformational leaders," seem to inspire higher levels of job satisfaction in employees as well (Judge & Bono, 2000). Leaders who establish clear expectations for how work is to be performed are also generally effective (Keller, 2006). And leaders can learn to improve their effectiveness by participating in management training programs such as those described earlier in this chapter.

ORGANIZATIONAL ATTITUDES

What factors contribute to high levels of job satisfaction and the sense that an organization is fair and just?

Effective leadership contributes to organizational productivity in many ways. For example, a leader can have an important impact on the attitudes that workers develop about their jobs and the organizations for which they work. Among the attitudes that organizational psychologists are most interested in are the degree to which workers derive satisfaction from their jobs, and the extent to which they develop an appreciation that their organization's processes and procedures are fair.

JOB SATISFACTION. **Job satisfaction** refers to the amount of pleasure an employee derives from a job (Muchinsky, 2006). Job satisfaction is determined by the degree to which employees feel their expectations about their jobs are met (Hulin & Judge, 2003). Job satisfaction is not defined by the specific tasks and working conditions associated with a particular job or by the expectations any particular individual brings to the work place. Rather, job satisfaction is the result of how the worker's expectations match the realities of the job. When expectations are met or exceeded, levels of job satisfaction are generally high. Job satisfaction, of course, can vary over time and in response to particular circumstances (Dawis, 2004).

Organizational psychologists are interested in job satisfaction because it is linked to many important organizational variables. Perhaps the most closely studied relationship between job satisfaction and work behavior is the link between satisfaction and job performance. It makes sense to think that workers who are satisfied with their jobs perform at higher levels than those who are unhappy in their work. Hundreds of research studies have been conducted to explore the relationship between these two variables. A recent meta-analysis suggests that the true correlation between job satisfaction and job performance is .30 (Judge, Thoresen, Bono, & Patton, 2001), a statistic perhaps not as high as would seem intuitively reasonable. A correlation of this magnitude suggests that job satisfaction accounts for about 9 percent of differences in productivity, with the remaining 91 percent being attributable to other factors. Other studies have

job satisfaction The degree of pleasure an employee derives from his or her job.

suggested even lower correlations. So job satisfaction is, at best, only slightly predictive of productivity. Nevertheless, most employees want satisfying jobs and most employers seek to create a workplace that contributes to high job satisfaction.

For decades, organizational psychologists have focused on understanding the link between job satisfaction and various aspects of the work environment. Working conditions do play an important role, although many other variables come into play. For example, when psychologists measure the degree to which workers are "involved" in their work—that is, they view their work as important to their self-image—they generally find that workers who are highly involved are somewhat more satisfied with their jobs (Brown, 1996). Workers who are highly committed to their organizations also are more likely to experience greater satisfaction with their jobs (Brown, 1996). Job satisfaction may be improved when "daily hassles" are removed from the work place (Muchinsky, 2000), thereby reducing overall levels of stress.

More recently, research has focused on the notion that job satisfaction may result as much from personality variables as from the characteristics of a particular environment. Research using the Five Factor Theory as a means of understanding personality (see Chapter 8: "Personality, Stress, and Health") has demonstrated a significant link between job satisfaction and four of the "big five" personality traits: *conscientiousness, emotional stability, extraversion,* and *agreeableness*. It seems that at least some important dimensions of job satisfaction may have an inherited basis (Ilies & Judge, 2003). Individuals who are optimistic about life in general report higher levels of job satisfaction than do those with a more pessimistic world view (Thoresen, Kaplan, Barsky, Warren, & deCharmont, 2003).

Job satisfaction also is somewhat dependent on life circumstances outside the job. Research demonstrates that factors such as employee age, the number of years worked, overall health, personal motivation, and marital status are all positively correlated with job satisfaction; even an employee's leisure activities can influence satisfaction on the job (Schultz & Schultz, 1998). Job satisfaction is a complex variable, influenced by personal characteristics and personality traits, outside-the-job life circumstances, and conditions that the worker encounters on the job.

Even though job satisfaction is only modestly linked to job performance, employers often want to understand how their employees feel about their jobs. This is particularly the case during times of corporate transition, when employers want to know how changes in the organization are being received by employees. When employers want to measure the degree to which employees are satisfied with their jobs, they often rely on professionally developed surveys.

One of the most commonly used measures of job satisfaction is the **Job Description Index**, or **JDI** (Kinicki, McKee-Ryan, Schrieshein, & Carson, 2002). The JDI measures workers' views of five different facets of the job: pay, promotion opportunities, supervision, co-workers, and the work itself (see **Figure 11–5**). It also provides a measure of overall, or *global*, job satisfaction. Another survey that assesses job satisfaction is the *Minnesota Satisfaction Questionnaire* (see **Figure 11–6**). Both surveys are widely used by employers. Questionnaires such as these are also used to explore other topics of interest to organizational psychologists, including the attitudes employees hold about the fairness that exists within their workplace.

ORGANIZATIONAL JUSTICE In recent years, organizational psychologists have become interested in how employees think about issues of fairness and justice in the work place. Such topics often are referred to as issues of **organizational justice**.

To better understand the complex dimensions involved in organizational justice, it is useful to consider its various components. One aspect of organizational justice involves the employee's perception of *distributive justice*, which refers to the fairness of the outcomes that employees receive in recognition for what they

Job Description Index (JDI) Standardized questionnaire that measures global job satisfaction and also workers' levels of satisfaction with five facets of the job: pay, promotion opportunities, supervision, co-workers, and the work itself.

organizational justice Organizational constructs concerned with the fair treatment of people in organizations.

In today's business climate, more workers are expressing concerns about organizational justice.

Sample items from the Job Descriptive Index (JDI)

Think of the work you do at present. How well does each of the following words or phrases describe your work? In the blank beside each word below, write

___Y___ for "Yes" if it describes your work

___N___ for "No" if it does NOT describe it

___?___ if you cannot decide

WORK ON PRESENT JOB

_____ Routine

_____ Satisfying

_____ Good

Think of the pay you get now. How well does each of the following words or phrases describe your present pay? In the blank beside each word below, write

___Y___ for "Yes" if it describes your pay

___N___ for "No" if it does NOT describe it

___?___ if you cannot decide

PRESENT PAY

_____ Income adequate for normal expenses

_____ Insecure

_____ Less than I deserve

Think of the opportunities for promotion that you have now. How well does each of the following words or phrases describe these? In the blank beside each word below, write

___Y___ for "Yes" if it describes your opportunities for promotion

___N___ for "No" if it does NOT describe them

___?___ if you cannot decide

OPPORTUNITIES FOR PROMOTION

_____ Dead-end job

_____ Unfair promotion policy

_____ Regular promotions

Think of the kind of supervision that you get on your job. How well does each of the following words or phrases describe this? In the blank each word below, write

___Y___ for "Yes" if it describes the supervision you get on your job

___N___ for "No" if it does NOT describe it

___?___ If you cannot decide

SUPERVISION

_____ Impolite

_____ Praises good work

_____ Doesn't supervise enough

Think of the majority of the people that you work with now or the people you meet in connection with your work. How well does each of the following words or phrases describe these people? In the blank beside each word below, write

___Y___ for "Yes" if it describes the people you work with

___N___ for "No" if it does NOT describe them

___?___ if you cannot decide

CO-WORKERS (PEOPLE)

_____ Boring

_____ Responsible

_____ Intelligent

Figure 11–5

Sample items from the Job Description Index

The JDI measures global job satisfaction, and also satisfaction with pay, promotion opportunities, supervision, co-workers, and the work itself.

Source: Copyright © Bowling Green StateUniversity

contribute to the organization (see Box "Understanding Ourselves: How do we determine what is fair?") Most employees expect that when they work hard and contribute positively to the productivity of the organization, they should receive rewards for their hard work (Shore, 2004).

Another dimension of organizational justice involves *procedural justice*, the fairness of the policies and procedures used within the organization. Procedural justice requires that organizational rules are clearly stated and applied equally to all workers. A key component involves leadership: In general, employees expect to "follow their leader," assuming that corporate leaders will act in the organization's, and hence the employees', best interests (Hosmer, 1995; Mayer, Davis, & Schoorman, 1995).

A third type of justice is often called *interactional justice*, because it pertains to how organizations address the concerns of employees. Interactional justice takes two forms.

Sample Items from the Minnesota Satisfaction Questionnaire

Ask yourself: How satisfied am I with this aspect of my job?

0 means I am very satisfied with this aspect of my job.

Sat. means I am satisfied with this aspect of my job.

N means I can't decide whether I am satisfied or not with this aspect of my job.

Dissat. means I am dissatisfied with this aspect of my job.

Very Dissat means I am very dissatisfied with this aspect of my job.

On my present job, this is how I feel about...	Very Dissat.	Dissat.	N	Sat	Very Sat.
1. Being able to keep busy all the time					
2. The chance to work alone on the job					
3. The chance to do different things from time to time					
4. The chance to be "somebody" in the community					
5. The way my boss handles subordinates					
6. The competence of my supervisor in making decisions					
7. Being able to do things that don't go against my conscience					
8. The way my job provides for steady employment					
9. The chance to do things for other people					
10. The chance to tell people what to do					
11. The chance to do something that makes use of my abilities					
12. The way company policies are put into practice					
13. My pay and the amount of work I do					
14. The chances for advancement on this job					
15. The freedom to use my own judgment					
16. The chance to try my own methods of doing the job					
17. The working conditions					
18. The way my coworkers get along with each other					
19. The praise I get for doing a good job					
20. The feeling of accomplishment I get from the job					

Figure 11–6

Sample Items from the Minnesota Satisfaction Questionnaire

Source: From Manual for the Minnesota Satisfaction Questionnaire by Vocational Psychology Research, University of Minnesota.

Interpersonal justice is high when organizations show concern for workers as individuals—for example, when a manager sends a get-well card to a subordinate following a surgery or attends the wedding of a worker in his or her unit. *Informational justice* involves establishing procedures and policies that recognize and are responsive to the feelings of employees. For example, if an organization needs to eliminate a position within a unit, informational justice is served by providing advance notification about the reasons why the position must be terminated, outlining the criteria for deciding which position will be affected and the timeline for making this change, and providing an appeal process for workers to use to voice any concerns they might have.

Research clearly demonstrates that all three forms of organizational justice contribute to employees' perceptions of fairness (Colquitt, Conlon, Wesson, Porter, & Ng, 2001). When workers are treated fairly, other positive dimensions of organizational

[UNDERSTANDING OURSELVES]

HOW DO WE DETERMINE WHAT IS FAIR?

Why do we work? For many people, at least part of the answer to this question involves the response: To get paid. Although most people agree that pay should correspond to the work a person does in some abstract way, there often is substantial disagreement about how pay should be awarded. What, after all, is *fair* payment for the work that one performs?

Consider the following hypothetical situation. Suppose you are a manager who supervises a work unit of 10 people. Your supervisor has given you a pool of money equal to 5 percent of the total salaries in your unit (a total of $10,000) to use for annual raises. You can distribute this money to these 10 people in any way you see fit. How would you determine who gets how much of the pool?

Organizational psychologists often consider three different rules that guide decisions about

What rule of reward distribution do you think would be favored by Donald Trump: equality, equity, or need?

how to distribute rewards in a fair manner (Muchinsky, 2006). Some organizations embrace the *rule of equality*: This rule specifies that all workers should receive equal rewards, regardless of the work each performs. According to the rule of equality, all workers performing a particular job should be compensated at the same level, regardless of the quality of work they produce or their other work place behaviors. Thus, two workers who both hold the job of "carpenter" would be paid the same hourly rate, regardless of individual differences in the effort they expend on the job or the quality or quantity of work they produce. Many union contracts specify that compensation should be assigned primarily according to equality: If a worker performs at a satisfactory level, he or she should be paid an equivalent wage to other workers performing the same job. Equality rules often are invoked when performance distinctions among workers are difficult to make.

The *rule of equity* is another way of dispersing rewards within an organization. Equity-based rules specify that workers should receive compensation according to their contributions to the organization: Thus, those who perform at a higher level should receive more rewards. Piece-rate systems rely on equity rules to distribute rewards, because workers are paid directly in accordance with their productivity; workers who produce more are paid more. Many other equity-based compensation systems have been developed that match rewards to the effort and performance of individual employees. In organizations that rely on the rule of equity for distribution of compensation, performance appraisal is a critically important organizational function.

Finally, the *rule of need* specifies that individuals with greater needs should receive more compensation; however, fair employment laws such as the Civil Rights Acts prohibit the use of many need-based compensation systems because they involve disparate treatment of individuals based on their group membership. For example, it is con-

trary to the intent of Title VII (and other laws such as the Equal Pay Act) to pay male workers more than female workers for the same job because men are the "head" of their households and therefore "need" more money. Need-based systems, however, are sometimes used in organizations when needs are job-related. For example, workers with higher needs for training may be selected and referred to training programs.

So how would you distribute the $10,000 of salary increases to your employees? Would you give each of the 10 workers in your unit a 5 percent increase in their salaries, a strategy prescribed by the equality rule? Would you apply the equality rule in a different way, and award each employee a raise of $1,000? Or would you use the equity rule, and base the raises you give on your estimation of the quality and quantity of work each employee contributes to the organization? In this case, some workers in your unit might get a 0 percent raise, and others receive an increase well in excess of the 5 percent average. Or would you consider need? For example, would you award higher raises to employees at the bottom end of the pay scale since they might have a harder time covering their basic expenses with their salaries?

As this example demonstrates, achieving a fair distribution of rewards is not a simple task; however the perception of fairness in the distribution of rewards is an important motivator for performance, not only among humans, but in other primate species as well: Even monkeys make less effort when they see other monkeys get more reward for equal work (Brosnan, 2003). And research suggests that, in general, people prefer being over-rewarded to being equitably rewarded, and they become distressed when they believe they are under-rewarded for their work (Shore, 2004). There is no single "correct" method of distributing rewards that is considered by all parties to be fair: What one employee considers to be "fair" often varies substantially from how other employees define fairness.

behavior—such as job satisfaction, job commitment, and productivity—are increased, and negative behaviors—such as absenteeism and sabotage—are diminished (Simons & Roberson, 2003). Research on the topic of organizational justice is likely to continue as organizational psychologists work to better understand how to enhance workplace productivity while maintaining a positive environment.

► CHECK YOUR UNDERSTANDING

1. When work teams are composed of members from several different divisions within an organization, each with a specialized skill needed by the team, these teams are called _____ teams.

2. On what three dimensions do leaders using the LMX model evaluate their employees?

3. The pleasure an employee derives from the job is called _____ _____.

Respond to the following statements as being either True (T) or False (F):

4. Charismatic leaders are also sometimes called transformational leaders.

5. Job satisfaction can be measured with the NEO-PI.

6. When employees believe that an organization's rules and procedures are fair, this defines the concept of interactional justice.

Answers: 1. cross-functional; 2. competence and skill, trustworthiness, and willingness to assume responsibility; 3. job satisfaction; 4. (T), 5. (F), 6. (F).

► APPLY YOUR UNDERSTANDING

1. A manager needs to solve a problem with production so he calls together a lead engineer, two production managers, a leader of the worker's union, an efficiency expert, and two employees who work on the production line to work with him to solve the problem. This "team" the manager has assembled is best considered to be a:
   a. virtual team
   b. self-managed team
   c. cross-functional team
   d. leaderless team

2. According to the LMX model, leaders are most likely to use a strict, directive approach with employees who are:
   a. highly skilled
   b. not very trustworthy

   c. willing to take on extra responsibility
   d. all of the above

3. People who experience high levels of job satisfaction are likely to be high in all of the following traits except:
   a. emotional stability
   b. conscientiousness
   b. agreeableness
   d. openness to experience

4. Sam is a manager who decides that if he pays all workers the same wage they will think that he is fair. Sam is focusing on which of the following dimensions of organizational justice?
   a. distributive justice
   b. procedural justice
   c. interpersonal justice
   d. informational justice

Answers: 1. c., 2. b., 3. d., 4. a.

Creating a Healthy Work Environment

11.5 Identify several ways that industrial/organizational psychologists apply psychological principles to improve working conditions for employees.

Industrial/organizational psychologists are involved in applying psychological principles to every aspect of the work environment. One way they improve the work environment is by designing procedures and equipment so that workers' safety and efficiency is maximized. Psychologists in the field of **human factors psychology**, sometimes called *engineering psychology* or *ergonomics*, emphasize how human skills and abilities can best be utilized in work applications.

HUMAN FACTORS PSYCHOLOGY

What is the primary goal of human factors psychology?

Human factors psychologists focus on several aspects of the work environment as they try to design more efficient and safer ways of performing jobs. Among the types of problems they work on are those that involve operator-machine systems and those that pertain to work space design (Hancock, 1999).

OPERATOR-MACHINE SYSTEMS If you have flown in an airplane and had the opportunity to look into the cockpit, chances are that you have been impressed with the large number of

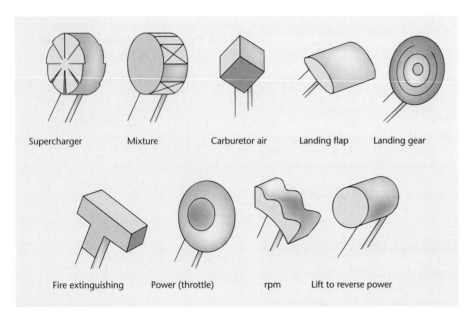

Figure 11–7

Various Aircraft Control Knobs

Source: United States Air Force, *Air Force System Command Design Handbook 1-3: Human Factors Engineering,* 1980.

dials and levers pilots must learn to operate. Flying a plane is a complex task: To land a plane, for example, the pilot must control the aircraft's speed, establish the correct glide path and rate of descent, and be in near-constant communication with the control tower to monitor the location of other planes in the area. A minor error, such as pulling back on the throttle rather than pushing in or failing to lower the landing gear, could easily end in disaster. How do pilots learn the function of each gauge, switch, and knob in the cockpit without getting them confused?

One way that psychologists have contributed to complex *operator-machine systems* such as aircraft cockpits is to design control panels that are matched to the way humans think and solve problems (Wickens & Hollands, 2003). Consider the design of knobs and levers. If every knob in the cockpit were the same size and shape, it would be difficult for pilots to discriminate which levers controlled which functions; this would be particularly true in an emergency or if no lighting were available. Consequently, on control panels, different shaped knobs are used for different operations: For example, engine power is delivered with a lever attached to a round knob, landing flaps have a wing-shaped knob, engine speed (rpm) is controlled with a knob shaped with ripples along the top (see **Figure 11–7**).

Levers also are located according to the importance of the function they control. Power levers, for example, are located low and between the pilot and co-pilot seats, so that in an emergency either the pilot or the co-pilot can access the power control quickly, easily, and with a minimum of effort; because there is just one control lever, the pilot and co-pilot cannot be working against each other in adding or backing off the power of the aircraft. Levers also operate according to consistent patterns of movement; pushing away or up always increases the function being controlled, pulling back slows things down.

Operator-machine systems often are designed to reduce accidents (Wickens & Hollands, 2003). For example, most industrial machines have large, clearly labeled, easily accessible "on-off" switches so that machines can be quickly switched off if a malfunction occurs. Human factors psychologists also design guards to protect workers from the hazardous parts of equipment. Modern lawnmowers, for example, now require that a bar be depressed on the handle for the blade to operate; if an accident occurs, the operator will most likely let up on the bar and the blade will stop, thereby limiting the potential for serious injury.

INFORMATION PROCESSING AND PHYSICAL MOBILITY As we saw in Chapter 4: "Learning and Memory," the human information processing system is limited. At any given time, our attention is usually focused on only one message and our working memory is able to consider only a few pieces of information. Furthermore, our body movements are limited both by our physical structure as well as the way in which our brain communicates to various parts of the body. Human factors psychologists consider these limitations as they design machines and equipment (Hancock, 1999).

Consider, for example, the computer keyboard. Perhaps it has occurred to you that the standard keyboard, often referred to as the "QWERTY" keyboard after the first six letters on the upper-left alphabetic row of keys, is not well designed to accommodate the hand movement limitations our bodies impose. In fact, the QWERTY keyboard was designed specifically to slow the typing speed of accomplished typists at a time when mechanical typewriter technology could not match the speed with which keys could be struck. A more efficient design would place the letters we use the most in our language, such as the vowels and the most frequently used consonants like "s," "t," and "r," in locations where our fingers could reach them most quickly. Several such keyboards have been designed (see **Figure**

Oftentimes, human factors psychologists can suggest minor changes to work space configurations that enhance productivity. Here, a desk at the proper height and with roll-in access helps accommodate the needs of an employee in a wheel chair.

11–8), but none have caught on, probably because workers are reluctant to re-learn a new arrangement of keys (Riggio, 2003).

Many other examples of how machines are engineered to accommodate the limitations of human movement and thinking are available. For example, auditory signals often are used for emergency warnings, because in most settings, visual signals do not command the same degree of attention. When we need specific information about a machine's output, quantitative displays are used to report precise temperatures, speeds, and so forth. When we need to know only whether output is increasing or decreasing, or is approaching some critical level, dials usually display a signal, such as "danger," or "low battery." Human factors psychologists direct their efforts at understanding how the human body receives, processes, and transmits information, and at how the body is limited in its movements to design machines that are as efficient as possible yet are safe to operate (Wickens & Hollands, 2003). The development of computer technology and the need to enter, store, and retrieve large quantities of information has provided human factors psychologists with many new work design challenges (Hancock, 1999).

WORKPLACE DESIGN Much of the work done by human factors psychologists involves the design of display panels, operating controls, and work tasks associated with operating specific pieces of equipment. However, human factors psychologists also are involved in designing the larger work environment. For example, a psychologist may be consulted to design the arrangement of offices or office cubicles in a space, where consideration must be given to privacy, work flow, communication networks, and so forth. Psychologists also make recommendations for how work stations are designed: Should workers perform their jobs while seated or standing; which materials should workers be able to reach without getting out of their chairs, and which can be located at more distant sites?

In general, human factors psychologists consider several general principles in determining how to structure the work space (Riggio, 2003). First, the work space should be designed so the most important job functions involve the least effort and movement for the worker and the most important controls and displays are located directly in front of the worker. Second, machines, tools, or materials that are used more frequently should be located most conveniently. Third, job components that involve the same functions should be grouped together. For example, if workers need to attend to several dials measuring the speed with which a machine is producing a product and several others that monitor the machine's internal operation, the speed dials should be located together, and the operational dials should be grouped in a separate location. Finally, if there is a sequence in which tools or machines are used, work stations should be arranged in space according to this sequence. For example, if a carpenter first saws a board, then planes it, then sands it, and then glues it, these four work stations should be arranged so that the carpenter can move directly from one to the next without backtracking.

MANAGING WORK-RELATED STRESS

What factors contribute to work place stress and what can organizations do to address the stressful components of workers' jobs?

Creating and maintaining a safe work environment involves more than thoughtful design of the workplace (Griffen & Neal, 2000). It also involves consideration of the stress that employees experience in their jobs and in their lives.

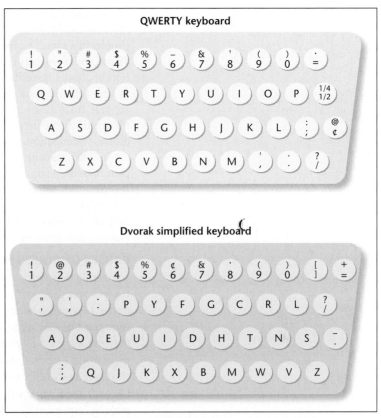

Figure 11–8

The QWERTY and Dvorak keyboards As you can see, the most commonly used letters in the English alphabet are scattered across the keyboard in the QWERTY system, but are located on the more easily accessed center keys on the Dvorak keyboard. After users learn the Dvorak system, skilled typists can type anywhere from 5 to 20 percent faster using the Dvorak keyboard (Sanders & McCormick, 1993).

Sanders, M. S., & McCormick, E. J. (1993). *Human factors in engineering and design* (7th ed.). New York: McGraw-Hill.

The general topic of stress and health was discussed more fully in Chapter 8: "Personality, Stress, and Health." However, work is a source of significant amounts of stress for many people. In a survey published by the National Institute on Occupational Safety and Health, 40 percent of workers reported their job to be either "very stressful" or "extremely stressful" (Occupational Hazards, 2006). Seventy-five percent of Americans now describe their jobs as stressful, and work-related stress is directly linked to high health care costs: In a recent six-year study of over 46,000 workers from 22 major organizations, depression and unmanaged stress emerged as the top two most costly risk factors in terms of medical expenditures (Occupational Hazards, 2006).

In 2005, the annual premium that a health insurer charged an employer for a health plan covering a family of four averaged $10,800 (National Coalition on Health Care, 2006). It is clear that work-related stress is expensive, not only in terms of money spent for health care and work time lost on the job, but also because it causes distress which can carry over into other parts of workers' lives. I/O psychologists are working hard to understand what factors cause stress in the workplace and to develop ways to deal with it.

CAUSES OF STRESS IN THE WORKPLACE Many aspects of the work environment can contribute to feelings of stress (Quick & Tetrick, 2003). For example, when workers have no control over their working conditions, the result is often stress. **Job autonomy** refers to the degree to which workers in a job have control over their work and their work environment. Autonomous jobs are those in which workers have some say in how they structure the tasks they are assigned to perform and some flexibility about how they go about performing their work. As noted earlier in this chapter, one advantage that members of most work teams, and especially self-managing teams, enjoy is some sense of autonomy in determining how their work will be done. When workers are given some degree of discretion in making important decisions in their work, research has demonstrated that accident rates decline and job stress is reduced (Parker, Axtell, & Turner, 2001).

Work-related stress is also reduced when role conflict and role overload are minimized. **Role conflict** results when workers are expected to perform mutually exclusive activities or when the assigned work conflicts with other personal or professional responsibilities (Muchinsky, 2006). When workers are directed to finish a project on an unrealistic time frame or within an inadequate budget, but yet are held responsible for producing work of an uncompromised level of quality, these two demands conflict: Both objectives cannot be met at the same time. Another example of role conflict might involve work assignments that conflict with family responsibilities: When mandatory overtime work is assigned on short notice, this may cause considerable difficulty for workers who have inflexible child care arrangements, and they may have to choose between missing work or leaving children with unhappy relatives or perhaps at home alone with no adult supervision.

Role overload occurs when there is more work assigned than can be accomplished (Hoffmann & Stetzer, 1996; Frone, 1998). Most students are familiar with the feelings of stress that are triggered when more work is assigned in a class than can reasonably be accomplished. Employees who have too many assigned tasks likewise are victims of role overload.

Several other characteristics of the workplace also have been shown to contribute to stress (Neal & Griffen, 2004). One important contributor is job uncertainty. When workers are unsure about their job security, or about how their work is being evaluated, they experience more stress. Also, when supervision is unsupportive, employees experience more stress in their jobs (Quick & Tetrick, 2003). Leaders can have an important impact on reducing job stress for their subordinates (Griffen & Neal, 2000). One way in which successful leaders reduce stress and enhance workplace safety is through clear communication. Work stress also is reduced when workers have sufficient training for their jobs.

DEALING WITH WORKPLACE STRESS There are several reasons why organizations undertake programs to minimize workplace stress. First, as noted earlier, it is clear that work stress is costly for an organization. Also, the same solutions that allow employees to manage work stress also enhance organizational productivity (Kelloway

---

job autonomy The degree to which workers have control over their work and their work environment.

---

role conflict Conflict that results when workers are expected to perform mutually exclusive activities or when the work assigned conflicts with other personal or professional responsibilities.

---

role overload Situation that occurs when there is more work assigned than can be accomplished.

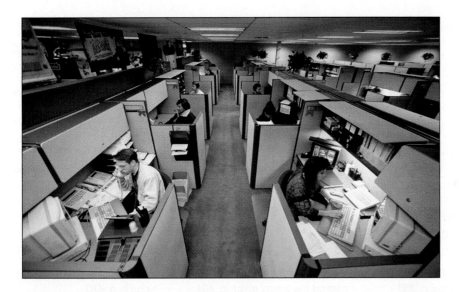

I/O psychologists strive to design work environments that both optimize productivity and minimize employees' stress.

& Day, 2005). For example, organizational effectiveness is enhanced when jobs are designed so that ambiguity, role conflict and overload, and uncertainty are reduced and organizational leadership and management practices are of high quality (Parker & Wall, 1998; Fried & Ferris, 1987).

Today, many organizational psychologists are working to develop programs that *prevent* workplace stress before it becomes a problem. The new field of *occupational health psychology* focuses on the prevention of occupational stress, illness, and injury (National Institute for Occupational Safety and Health, 2006). Occupational health psychologists often recommend that organizations consider how work-related stress can be prevented. For example, jobs can sometimes be redesigned so they include increased levels of autonomy and less role conflict and role overload. In job redesign, tasks are clarified and work is reorganized so that duties can be performed more efficiently. Job redesign has been shown to have clear benefits in terms of increased employee motivation and productivity, as well as decreased levels of stress (Parker & Wall, 1998).

Leadership training can also address workplace stress. When employees have a clear sense of organizational direction, believe they are being treated fairly, and feel they play an important role in the organization's success, their sense of well-being is enhanced (Barling, Weber, & Kelloway, 1996). As the science of psychology advances, industrial/organizational psychologists will learn new and more effective ways to apply principles, findings, and techniques from all areas of psychology. Their goal will be to create work environments conducive not only to health and high levels of job satisfaction for workers, but to high levels of organizational productivity as well.

▶ CHECK YOUR UNDERSTANDING

1. The division of psychology that addresses the interface between people and the environment in which they work is called _____ _____ psychology.

2. When workers are assigned tasks that require incompatible actions, these involve role _____; when they are given more tasks to do than they can accomplish, this is called role _____.

Identify which of the following statements are True (T) and False (F).

3. The primary goal of human factors psychologists is to reduce work place stress.

4. Work space should be designed so that the most important job functions involve the least amount of effort and are located in the most convenient places for workers to perform.

5. Job autonomy is higher when jobs can be simplified.

Answers: 1. human factors, **2.** conflict; overload, **3.** (F), **4.** (T), **5.** (F),

>KEY TERMS<

industrial/organizational (I/O) psychology, *p. 393*
industrial psychology, *p. 393*
organizational psychology, *p. 394*
job analysis, *p. 394*
job, *p. 394*
functional job analysis (FJA), *p. 394*
KSAO system, *p. 395*
job description, *p. 395*
personnel selection *p. 395*
predictive validity, *p. 396*
meta-analysis, *p. 396*

employment interview, *p. 396*
conscientiousness, *p. 399*
integrity tests, *p. 399*
assessment center, *p. 401*
Civil Rights Act of 1964, *p. 401*
protected classes (or groups), *p. 402*
performance appraisal system, *p. 403*
objective appraisal system, *p. 403*
subjective performance appraisal, *p. 404*
halo error, *p. 404*

recency error, *p. 404*
central tendency error, *p. 404*
behaviorally anchored ratings scale (BARS), *p. 405*
behavioral observation scale (BOS), *p. 405*
360° evaluation, *p. 406*
training, *p. 407*
on-the-job training, *p. 408*
job rotation, *p. 408*
vestibule training, *p. 408*
case study analysis, *p. 409*
cultural diversity training, *p. 409*
sexual harassment, *p. 410*

corporate, or organizational, culture, *p. 410*
leader-member exchange theory (LMX), *p. 413*
job satisfaction, *p. 414*
Job Description Index JDI, *p. 415*
organizational justice, *p. 415*
human factors psychology, *p. 419*
job autonomy, *p. 422*
role conflict, *p. 422*
role overload, *p. 422*

>CHAPTER REVIEW<

Matching People to Jobs

What is a job and how is a job defined? A **job** is defined as including all positions in the organization that involve the same set of tasks. **Job analysis** identifies the tasks and skills needed to perform a job. **Functional job analysis** identifies jobs according to the skills people need to manage things, data, and people. The **KSAO method** of job analysis identifies the knowledge, skills, abilities, and other characteristics that people need to successfully perform the job. Job analysis lays the foundation for many other organizational functions, such as preparing job descriptions, identifying training needs, and determining performance appraisal systems.

Which human characteristics best predict performance on the job? The **predictive validity** of a **personnel selection** method is the correlation between how people score on a predictor, such as an interview or personnel test, and how they perform on the job. The statistical technique of **meta-analysis**, which identifies the average true predictive validity of personnel selection methods, is used to understand which methods are most closely tied to subsequent job performance.

In general, personnel interviews have high predictive validity, although structured interviews are more closely linked to job performance than are unstructured interviews. Tests of general mental ability

and conscientiousness also are predictive of job performance. **Integrity tests**, which measure conscientiousness, agreeableness, and emotional stability, can predict which workers are more likely to engage in counterproductive behaviors. Previous job performance also predicts future job performance, as do tests of job knowledge and work sample tests. **Assessment centers** are sometimes used to select applicants for high-level management positions.

What does it mean to be a member of a "protected class" and what protections are guaranteed to members of these groups? The **Civil Rights Act (CRA) of 1964** protects members of groups who historically experienced discrimination. The groups identified in the CRA of 1964 are called **protected classes**, and are identified as including individuals whose group membership is based on race, color, religion, sex, and national origin. Title VII of the CRA protects such individuals from discrimination in all aspects of employment. Subsequent laws have expanded the definition of what constitutes a protected class.

Measuring Performance on the Job

What circumstances determine whether it is better to use an objective or a subjective performance appraisal system? **Objective methods** of performance appraisal, such as piece-rate systems and commission-based systems, are sometimes used when productivity can be measured quantitatively. Objective measures can be biased, however, such as when one worker has newer equipment, or when some workers have work assignments beyond those directly associated with production. In such cases, or when work is not directly tied to quantitative performance, **subjective methods** based on supervisor judgments are used to evaluate performance.

What kinds of rating errors commonly occur in performance appraisal systems? **Halo error** occurs when a positive evaluation of one trait carries over to the evaluation of other traits. **Recency errors** occur when raters rely too extensively on recent performance, rather than on typical performance. **Central tendency errors** occur when raters evaluate all, or nearly all, employees as being "average."

How can errors made in evaluating employee performance be reduced or eliminated? When raters evaluate behavior, rather than attitudes or intentions, rating errors are usually reduced. **Behaviorally-anchored rating scales (BARS)** and **behavior observation scales (BOS)** are used to focus evaluators' attention on specific work place behaviors (BARS) or on the frequency that workers engage in such behaviors (BOS). **360° evaluation** involves self-evaluation and ratings from peers, supervisors, and subordinates, thereby providing multiple ratings of performance, which can also reduce the impact of bias.

Behavior within Organizations

What methods are commonly used to train workers to be more effective in their jobs? **Training** is used to instruct employees in relevant job-related attitudes and behaviors. The need for training is established by performing an organizational analysis (to identify corporate problems), a task analysis (to determine the KSAOs needed to perform jobs identified as having training needs), and a person analysis (to determine which employees would benefit from training).

On-the-job training consists of having employees learn new skills while performing their job. **Job rotation** involves having employees learn several jobs, so that they can rotate among them. **Vestibule training** consists of having employees learn job skills on machines in a training facility before they actually perform them on the production floor. New skills also can be learned through simulations, either with machines or on computers.

Managerial training often is based on the **case study method**, where managers read about a hypothetical problem and discuss in groups how it can be solved most effectively.

How can organizations use training to promote a more tolerant, non-discriminatory work environment? **Cultural diversity training** and **sexual harassment training** are used to change attitudes of workers so that they can work more productively with co-workers who represent an increasingly diverse work force.

Organizational Culture

Why do organizations sometimes organize workers into teams? **Corporate,** or **organizational, culture** refers to the formal and informal rules, procedures, and expectations that define the values, attitudes, beliefs, and customs of an organization. Because jobs are becoming more complex and most workers are well-educated and expect challenge in their work, many organizations have employees work in teams, rather than on assembly lines. Members of work teams communicate with each other, offer assistance, identify their own success with the work of the team, are interdependent, and look to the team leader for guidance.

What is the central feature of any "contingency" theory of leadership? Contingency theories of leadership emphasize that leadership depends on characteristics of the leader and also on characteristics of the followers and the situation in which work occurs. The **leader-member exchange (LMX) theory** states that leaders evaluate their subordinates and engage in a series of exchanges with them that vary depending on whether the leader identifies them as members of the in-group or the out-group. Subordinates also evaluate their leader and enter into different exchanges based on the leader's style and effectiveness. In general, leaders who are charismatic are effective in a wide range of situations.

What factors contribute to high levels of job satisfaction and the sense that an organization is fair and just? **Job satisfaction**, which refers to the amount of pleasure an employee derives from work, is only modestly related to job performance. Yet, many organizations want employees to be satisfied with their jobs. Job satisfaction is associated with four of the "Big Five" personality traits: conscientiousness, emotional stability, extraversion, and agreeableness. Workers who are optimists also report higher levels of job satisfaction. Job satisfaction is often measured by questionnaires, such as the **Job Description Index (JDI)**, which examines satisfaction with pay, promotion opportunities, supervision, co-workers, and the work itself, and also reports an overall level of job satisfaction.

Organizational justice is established according to how workers think about the fairness and justice of their work place. Organizational justice depends on distributive justice (rewards are dispensed fairly), procedural justice (policies and procedures are fair to all workers), and interpersonal justice (the organization shows concern for workers and is responsive to their feelings). All three forms of justice are important to workers, and are linked to positive work behaviors.

Creating a Healthy Work Environment

What is the primary goal of human factors psychology? **Human factors psychologists** study how machines and the overall work environment can best be matched to human skills and abilities. For example, in designing operator-machine systems, human factors psychologists attempt to have machines provide feedback to operators in highly visible form. They often design controls to have single functions so that operators are not confused. Because humans have limited attention and information processing abilities, human factors psychologists try to design machines that accommodate these human limitations. They also arrange work operations so that efficiency is maximized.

What factors contribute to work place stress and what can organizations do to address the stressful components of workers' jobs? Seventy-five percent of U.S. workers report that their jobs are stressful, and this work-related stress is expensive in terms of the health care costs it generates, the productivity decline it leads to, and the degree of worker unhappiness it produces. Work stress is heightened when jobs lack **autonomy** (workers have little control over their work), involve **role conflict** (tasks assigned conflict with each other or with personal obligations), or when they produce **role overload** (too many tasks are assigned). Occupational health psychologists focus on preventing work place stress from occurring, often by redesigning jobs so they have more autonomy and less role conflict and role overload. Effective leadership can also prevent work place stress from becoming overwhelming.

Concept Map

11.1 MATCHING PEOPLE TO JOBS

JOB ANALYSIS
- Identifying the tasks and skills required in a job
- **Functional job analysis:** Tasks involving people, data, and things
- **KSAO system** (Knowledge, Skills, Abilities, Other Characteristics): Characteristics of workers

PREDICTORS OF JOB PERFORMANCE
- Employment Interviews
- Employment Tests
- Measures of Previous Performance
- Assessment Centers

LAWS DEFINING FAIR EMPLOYMENT
- **Civil Rights Act (CRA) of 1964:** Made it unlawful to discriminate against members of **protected classes**
- Title VII: Section of the CRA of 1964 that pertains most directly to employment

11.2 MEASURING PERFORMANCE ON THE JOB

OBJECTIVE AND SUBJECTIVE MEASURES
- Objective: Used when productivity can be measured quantitatively
- Subjective: Used when judgments are used to assess productivity

ERRORS IN SUBJECTIVE RATINGS
- **Halo error:** Positive evaluation of one trait causes other traits to be evaluated more positively
- **Recency error:** Ratings are based on most recent performance
- **Central tendency error:** Workers are evaluated as more similar than they actually are
- **Techniques for reducing errors:** BARS, BOS, 360° evaluation

11.3 BEHAVIOR WITHIN ORGANIZATIONS

TRAINING
- Organizational analysis: Identifies corporate goals and training needs
- Task analysis: Identifies which job tasks and skills can be addressed through training
- Person analysis: Identifies which workers will benefit from training

TRAINING METHODS
- **On-the-job training:** Learning new skills on the job
- **Vestibule training:** Learning jobs in training work stations
- **Simulation training:** Learning in simulators or using computer simulation programs
- **Management development:** Helping managers improve personal and interpersonal skills
- **Cultural diversity training:** Learning to work with people from different cultural backgrounds
- **Sexual harassment training:** Training to prevent sexual harassment

11.4 ORGANIZATIONAL CULTURE

TYPES OF WORK TEAMS

- **Problem-solving teams:** Work unit members meet regularly to discuss problems and find solutions
- **Self-managed teams:** Team members are responsible for most management tasks
- **Cross-functional teams:** Team members have different skills they use to solve group problems
- **Virtual teams:** Team members from different locations communicate electronically

LEADERSHIP

- Leader-member exchange (LMX) theory: Emphasizes exchanges between workers and leader
- Charismatic (transformational) leaders are effective in a wide array of settings

JOB SATISFACTION

- Tied to conscientiousness, emotional stability, extraversion, agreeableness
- Measured with the Job Descriptive Index or the Minnesota Satisfaction Questionnaire

ORGANIZATIONAL JUSTICE

- Distributive justice: Fairness of outcomes
- Procedural justice: Fairness of work policies and procedures
- Interpersonal justice: Concern for employees and responsiveness to their feelings

11.5 CREATING A HEALTHY WORK ENVIRONMENT

HUMAN FACTORS PSYCHOLOGY

- Study of how to maximize worker safety and productivity in the workplace
- Operator-machine systems: Designing machines to match human abilities and limitations

WORK-RELATED STRESS

- **Lack of job autonomy:** Workers have little control over work or working conditions
- **Role conflict:** Workers are asked to perform mutually exclusive tasks, or work conflicts with other responsibilities
- **Role overload:** More work is assigned than can be performed
- **Job uncertainty:** Workers are uncertain about job security or how they are evaluated

MANAGING WORK-RELATED STRESS

- Psychologists emphasize prevention
- **Occupational health psychology:** New field that focuses on preventing work-related stress

Concept Map

MEASUREMENT AND STATISTICAL METHODS

Scales of Measurement	The Normal Curve	Measures of Correlation
Measurements of Central Tendency	• Skewed Distributions	Using Statistics to Make Predictions
• Differences Between the Mean, Median, and Mode	Measures of Variation	• Probability
	• Range	
	• The Standard Deviation	

Most of the experiments described in this book involve measuring one or more variables and then analyzing the data statistically. The design and scoring of all the tests we have discussed are also based on statistical methods. **Statistics** is a branch of mathematics. It provides techniques for sorting out quantitative facts and ways of drawing conclusions from them. Statistics let us organize and describe data quickly; they guide the conclusions we draw and help us to make inferences.

Statistical analysis is essential to conducting an experiment or designing a test, but statistics can only handle numbers—groups of them. To use statistics, the psychologist first must measure things—that is, count and express them in quantities.

Scales of Measurement

No matter what we are measuring—height, noise, intelligence, or attitudes—we have to use a scale. The data we want to collect determine the scale we use, and, in turn, the scale we use helps to determine the conclusions we can draw from our data.

NOMINAL SCALES A nominal scale is a set of arbitrarily named or numbered categories. If we decide to classify a group of people by the color of their eyes, we are using a **nominal scale**. We can count how many people have blue eyes, how many have green eyes, how many have brown eyes, and so on, but we cannot say that one group has more or less eye color than the other. The colors are simply different. Because a nominal scale is more of a way of classifying than of measuring, it is the least informative kind of scale. If we want to compare our data more precisely, we will have to use a scale that tells us more.

ORDINAL SCALES If we list horses in the order in which they finish a race, we are using an **ordinal scale**. On an ordinal scale, data are ranked from first to last, according to some criterion. An ordinal scale tells the order, but nothing about the distances between what is ranked first and second or ninth and tenth. It does not tell us how much faster the winning horse ran than the horse that placed or showed. If a person ranks her preferences for various kinds of soup—pea soup first, then tomato, then onion, and so on—we know what soup she likes most and what soup she likes least, but we have no idea how much better she likes tomato than onion, or whether pea soup is far more favored than either one of them. Because we do not know the distances between the items ranked on an ordinal scale, we cannot add or subtract ordinal data. If mathematical operations are necessary, we need a still more informative scale.

INTERVAL SCALES An **interval scale** is often compared to a ruler that has been broken off at the bottom—it only goes from, say, $5\frac{1}{2}$ to 12. The intervals between 6 and 7, 7 and 8, 8 and 9, and so forth are equal, but there is no zero. A thermometer is an interval scale—even though a certain degree registered on a Fahrenheit or Centigrade thermometer specifies a certain state of cold or heat, there is no such thing as no temperature at all. One day is never twice as hot as another; it is only so many equal degrees hotter.

statistics A branch of mathematics that psychologists use to organize and analyze data.

nominal scale A set of categories for classifying objects.

ordinal scale Scale indicating order or relative position of items according to some criterion.

interval scale Scale with equal distances between the points or values, but without a true zero.

An interval scale tells us how many equal-size units that one thing lies above or below another thing of the same kind, but it does not tell us how many times bigger, smaller, taller, or fatter one thing is than another. An intelligence test cannot tell us that one person is three times as intelligent as another, only that he or she scored so many points above or below someone else.

RATIO SCALES We can only say that a measurement is two times as long as another or three times as high when we use a **ratio scale** that has a true zero. For instance, if we measure the snowfall in a certain area over several winters, we can say that six times as much snow fell during the winter in which we measured a total of 12 feet as during a winter in which only 2 feet fell. This scale has a zero—there may be no snow.

Measurements of Central Tendency

Usually, when we measure a number of instances of anything—from the popularity of television shows to the weights of 8-year-old boys to the number of times a person's optic nerve fires in response to electrical stimulation—we get a distribution of measurements that ranges from smallest to largest or lowest to highest. The measurements will usually cluster around some value near the middle. This value is the **central tendency** of the distribution of the measurements.

Suppose, for example, that you want to keep 10 children busy tossing rings around a bottle. You give them three rings to toss each turn, the game has six rounds, and each player scores one point every time he or she gets the ring around the neck of the bottle. The highest possible score is 18. The distribution of scores might end up like this: 11, 8, 13, 6, 12, 10, 16, 9, 12, 3.

What could you quickly say about the ring-tossing talent of the group? First, you could arrange the scores from lowest to highest: 3, 6, 8, 9, 10, 11, 12, 12, 13, 16. In this order, the central tendency of the distribution of scores becomes clear. Many of the scores cluster around the values between 8 and 12. There are three ways to describe the central tendency of a distribution. We usually refer to all three as the *average*.

The arithmetical average is called the **mean**—the sum of all of the scores in the group divided by the number of scores. If you add up all the scores and divide by 10 (the total number of scores in this group of ring tossers), you find that the mean for the group is 10.

The **median** is the point that divides a distribution in half—50 percent of the scores fall above the median, and 50 percent fall below. In the ring-tossing scores, five scores fall at 10 or below, five at 11 or above. The median is thus halfway between 10 and 11—which is 10.5.

The point at which the largest number of scores occurs is called the **mode**. In our example, the mode is 12. More people scored 12 than any other number.

DIFFERENCES BETWEEN THE MEAN, MEDIAN, AND MODE

If we take many measurements of anything, we are likely to get a distribution of scores in which the mean, median, and mode are all about the same—the score that occurs most often (the mode) will also be the point that half the scores are below and half above (the median). The same point will be the arithmetical average (the mean). This is not always true, of course, and small samples rarely come out so symmetrically. In these cases, we often have to decide which of the three measures of central tendency—the mean, the median, or the mode—will tell us what we want to know.

For example, a shopkeeper wants to know the general incomes of passersby so that he can stock the right merchandise. He might conduct a rough survey by standing outside his store for a few days from 12:00 P.M. to 2:00 P.M. and asking every 10th person who walks by to check a card showing the general range of his or her income. Suppose that most of the people checked the ranges between $15,000 and $25,000 a year. A couple of the people, however, made a lot of money—one checked the $100,000–$150,000 box and the other checked the $200,000-or-above box. The mean for the set of income figures would be pushed higher by those two large figures and would not really tell the shopkeeper what he wants to know about his potential customers. In this case, he would be wiser to use the median or the mode.

ratio scale Scale with equal distances between the points or values and with a true zero.

central tendency Tendency of scores to congregate around some middle value.

mean Arithmetical average calculated by dividing a sum of values by the total number of cases.

median Point that divides a set of scores in half.

mode Point at which the largest number of scores occurs.

Suppose that instead of meeting two people whose incomes were so great, he noticed that people from two distinct income groups walked by his store—several people checked the box for $15,000–$17,000 and several others checked $23,000–$25,000. The shopkeeper would find that his distribution was bimodal. It has two modes—$16,000 and $24,000. This might be more useful to him than the mean, which could lead him to think his customers were a unit with an average income of about $20,000.

Another way of approaching a set of scores is to arrange them into a **frequency distribution**—that is, to select a set of intervals and count how many scores fall into each interval. A frequency distribution is useful for large groups of numbers; it puts the number of individual scores into more manageable groups.

Suppose that a psychologist tests memory. She asks 50 college students to learn 18 non-sense syllables and then records how many syllables each student can recall two hours later. She arranges her raw scores from lowest to highest in a rank distribution:

2	6	8	10	11	14
3	7	9	10	12	14
4	7	9	10	12	15
4	7	9	10	12	16
5	7	9	10	13	17
5	7	9	11	13	
6	8	9	11	13	
6	8	9	11	13	
6	8	10	11	13	

The scores range from 2 to 17, but 50 individual scores are too cumbersome to use. So the psychologist chooses a set of two-point intervals and tallies the number of scores in each interval:

Interval	Tally	Frequency
1–2	|	1
3–4	|||	3
5–6	|||| |	6
7–8	|||| ||||	9
9–10	|||| |||| |||	13
11–12	|||| |||	8
13–14	|||| ||	7
15–16	||	2
17–18	|	1

Now the psychologist can tell at a glance the results of her experiment. Most of the students had scores near the middle of the range, and very few had scores in the high or low intervals. She can see these results even better if she uses the frequency distribution to construct a bar graph—a **frequency histogram**. Marking the intervals along the horizontal axis and the frequencies along the vertical axis would give her the graph shown in **Figure A–1**. Another way is to construct a **frequency polygon**, a line graph. A frequency polygon drawn from the same set of data is shown in **Figure A–2**. Note that the figure is not a smooth curve, as the points are

frequency distribution A count of the number of scores that fall within each of a series of intervals.

frequency histogram Type of bar graph that shows frequency distributions.

frequency polygon Type of line graph that shows frequency distributions.

Figure A–1

A frequency histogram for a memory experiment. The bars indicate the frequency of scores within each interval.

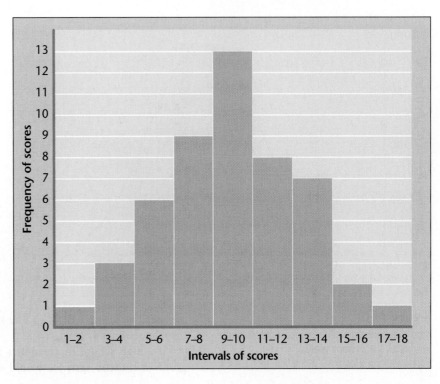

Figure A–2

A frequency polygon drawn from data used in Figure A–1. The dots, representing the frequency of scores in each interval, are connected by straight lines.

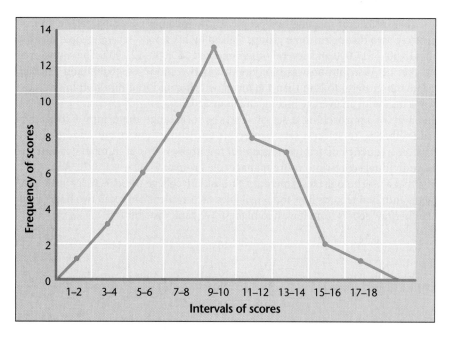

connected by straight lines. With many scores, however, and with small intervals, the angles would smooth out, and the figure would resemble a rounded curve.

The Normal Curve

normal curve Hypothetical bell-shaped distribution curve that occurs when a normal distribution is plotted as a frequency polygon.

Ordinarily, if we take enough measurements of almost anything, we get a *normal distribution*. Tossing coins is a favorite example of statisticians. If you tossed 10 coins into the air 1,000 times and recorded the heads and tails on each toss, your tabulations would reveal a normal distribution. Five heads and five tails would occur most often, six heads/four tails and four heads/six tails would be the next most frequent, and so on down to the rare all heads or all tails.

Plotting a normal distribution on a graph yields a particular kind of frequency polygon, called a **normal curve**. **Figure A–3** shows data on the heights of 1,000 men. Superimposed over the yellow bars that reflect the actual data is an "ideal" normal curve for the same data. Note that the curve is absolutely symmetrical—the left slope parallels the right slope exactly. Moreover, the mean, median, and mode all fall on the highest point on the curve.

The normal curve is a hypothetical entity. No set of real measurements shows such a smooth gradation from one interval to the next, or so purely symmetrical a shape. But because so many things do approximate the normal curve so closely, the curve is a useful model for much that we measure.

SKEWED DISTRIBUTIONS

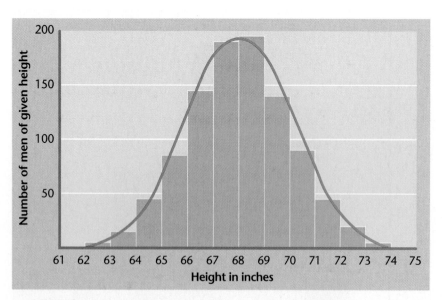

Figure A–3

A normal curve based on measurements of the heights of 1,000 adult males.

Source: From Hill, 1966.

If a frequency distribution is asymmetrical—if most of the scores are gathered at either the high end or the low end—the frequency polygon will be *skewed*. The hump will sit to one side or the other, and one of the curve's tails will be disproportionately long.

If a high school mathematics instructor, for example, gives her students a sixth-grade arithmetic test, we would expect nearly all the scores to be quite high. The frequency polygon would probably look like the one in **Figure A–4**. But if a sixth-grade class is asked to do advanced algebra, the scores would probably be quite low. The frequency polygon would be very similar to the one shown in **Figure A–5**.

Note, too, that the mean, median, and mode fall at different points in a skewed distribution, unlike in the normal curve, where they coincide. Usually, if you know that the mean is greater than the median of a distribution, you can predict that the frequency polygon will be skewed to the right. If the median is greater than the mean, the curve will be skewed to the left.

Measures of Variation

Sometimes it is not enough to know the distribution of a set of data and their mean, median, and mode. Suppose that an automotive safety expert feels that too much damage occurs in tail-end accidents because automobile bumpers are not all the same height. It is not enough to know the average height of an automobile bumper. The safety expert also wants to know about the variation in bumper heights: How much higher is the highest bumper than the mean? How do bumpers of all cars vary from the mean?

RANGE

The simplest measure of variation is the **range**—the difference between the largest and smallest measurements. Perhaps the safety expert measured the bumpers of 1,000 cars two years ago and found that the highest bumper was 18 inches from the ground, and the lowest was only 12 inches from the ground. The range was thus 6 inches—18 minus 12. This year, the highest bumper is still 18 inches high, and the lowest is still 12 inches from the ground. The range is still 6 inches. Moreover, our safety expert finds that the means of the two distributions are the same—15 inches off the ground. But look at the two frequency polygons in **Figure A–6**—there is still something the expert needs to know, as the measurements cluster around the mean in drastically different ways. To find out how the measurements are distributed around the mean, our safety expert has to turn to a slightly more complicated measure of variation—the standard deviation.

THE STANDARD DEVIATION

The **standard deviation**, in a single number, tells us much about how the scores in any frequency distribution are dispersed around the mean. Calculating the standard deviation is one of the most useful and widely employed statistical tools.

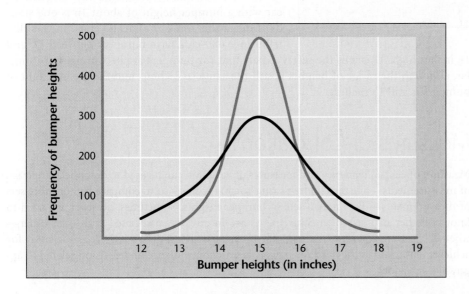

range Difference between the largest and smallest measurements in a distribution.

standard deviation Statistical measure of variability in a group of scores or other values.

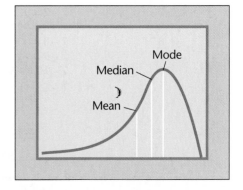

Figure A–4

A skewed distribution. Most of the scores are gathered at the high end of the distribution, causing the hump to shift to the right. Because the tail on the left is longer, we say that the curve is skewed to the left. Note that the mean, median, and mode are different.

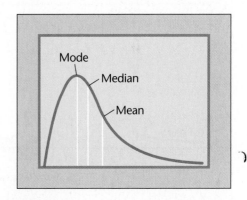

Figure A–5

In this distribution, most of the scores are gathered at the low end, so the curve is skewed to the right. The *mean*, *median*, and *mode* do not coincide.

Figure A–6

Frequency polygons for two sets of measurements of automobile bumper heights. Both are normal curves; in each distribution, the *mean*, *median*, and *mode* are 15. But the variation from the mean is different, causing one curve to be flattened and the other to be much more sharply peaked.

Number of scores = 10		Mean = 7
Scores	Difference from mean	Difference squared
4	7 − 4 = 3	$3^2 = 9$
5	7 − 5 = 2	$2^2 = 4$
6	7 − 6 = 1	$1^2 = 1$
6	7 − 6 = 1	$1^2 = 1$
7	7 − 7 = 0	$0^2 = 0$
7	7 − 7 = 0	$0^2 = 0$
8	7 − 8 = −1	$-1^2 = 1$
8	7 − 8 = −1	$-1^2 = 1$
9	7 − 9 = −2	$-2^2 = 4$
10	7 − 10 = −3	$-3^2 = 9$

Sum of squares = 30
÷
Number of scores = 10
Variance = 3
Standard deviation = $\sqrt{3}$ = 1.73

Figure A–7

Step-by-step calculation of the *standard deviation* for a group of 10 scores with a mean of 7.

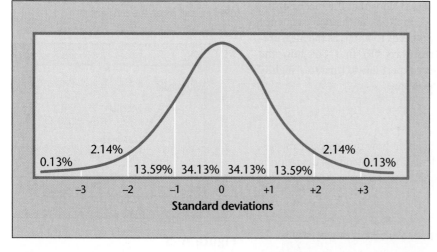

Figure A–8

A normal curve divided to show the percentage of scores that fall within each *standard deviation* from the *mean*.

To find the standard deviation of a set of scores, we first find the mean. Then we take the first score in the distribution, subtract it from the mean, square the difference, and jot it down in a column to be added up later. We do the same for all the scores in the distribution. Then we add up the column of squared differences, divide the total by the number of scores in the distribution (which gives us the variance among scores), and find the square root of that number. **Figure A–7** shows the calculation of the standard deviation for a small distribution of scores.

In a normal distribution, however peaked or flattened the curve, about 68 percent of the scores fall between one standard deviation above the mean and one standard deviation below the mean. (See **Figure A–8**.) Another 27 percent fall between one standard deviation and two standard deviations on either side of the mean, and 4 percent more between the second and third standard deviations on either side. Overall, then, more than 99 percent of the scores fall between three standard deviations above and three standard deviations below the mean. This makes the standard deviation useful for comparing two different normal distributions.

Now let us see what the standard deviation can tell our automotive safety expert about the variations from the mean in the two sets of data. The standard deviation for the cars measured two years ago is about 1.4. A car with a bumper height of 16.4 is one standard deviation above the mean of 15; one with a bumper height of 13.6 is one standard deviation below the mean. Because the engineer knows that the data fall into a normal distribution, he or she can figure that about 68 percent of the 1,000 cars he or she measured will fall somewhere between these two heights: 680 cars will have bumpers between 13.6 and 16.4 inches high. For the more recent set of data, the standard deviation is just slightly less than one. A car with a bumper height of about 14 inches is one standard deviation below the mean; a car with a bumper height of about 16 is one standard deviation above the mean. Thus, in this distribution, 680 cars have bumpers between 14 and 16 inches high. This tells the safety expert that car bumpers are becoming more similar, although the range of heights is still the same (6 inches), and the mean height of bumpers is still 15 inches.

Measures of Correlation

Measures of central tendency and measures of variation can be used to describe a single set of measurements—like the children's ring-tossing scores—or to compare two or more sets of measurements—like the two sets of bumper heights. Sometimes, however, we need to know whether two sets of measurements are in any way associated with each other—whether they are *correlated*. Is parental IQ related to children's IQ? Does the need for achievement relate to the need for power? Is watching violence on television related to aggressive behavior?

One fast way to determine whether two variables are correlated is to draw a **scatter plot**. We assign one variable (X) to the horizontal axis of a graph, the other variable (Y) to the vertical axis. Then we plot a person's score on one characteristic along the horizontal axis, and his or her score on the second characteristic along the vertical axis. Where the two scores intersect, we draw a dot. When several scores have been plotted in this way, the pattern of dots tells whether the two characteristics are in any way correlated with each other.

If the dots on a scatter plot form a straight line running between the lower-left corner and the upper-right corner, as they do in **Figure A–9a**, we have a perfect positive correlation—a high score on one of the characteristics is always associated with a high score on the other. A straight line running between the upper-left corner and the lower-right corner, as in **Figure A–9b**, is the sign of a perfect negative correlation—a high score on one of the characteristics is always associated with a low score on the other. If the

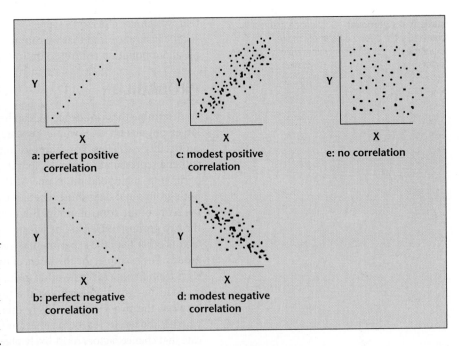

pattern formed by the dots generally clusters around a line, as in **Figure A–9c** and **d**, we have a modest correlation—the two characteristics are related, but not highly correlated. If the dots spread out over the whole graph, forming a circle or a random pattern, as they do in **Figure A–9e**, there is no correlation between the two characteristics.

A scatter plot can give us a general idea whether a correlation exists and how strong it is. To describe the relation between two variables more precisely, we need a **correlation coefficient**—a statistical measure of the degree to which two variables are associated. The correlation coefficient tells us the degree of association between two sets of matched scores—that is, to what extent high or low scores on one variable tend to be associated with high or low scores on another. It also provides an estimate of how well we can predict from a person's score on one characteristic how high he or she will score on another. If we know, for example, that a test of mechanical ability is highly correlated with success in engineering courses, we could predict that success on the test would also mean success as an engineering major.

Correlation coefficients can run from +1.0 to −1.0. The highest possible value (+1.0) indicates a perfect positive correlation—high scores on one variable are always and systematically related to high scores on a second variable. The lowest possible value (−1.0) represents a perfect negative correlation—high scores on one variable are always and regularly related to low scores on the second variable. In life, most things are far from perfect, so most correlation coefficients fall somewhere between +1.0 and −1.0. A correlation smaller than ±0.20 is considered very low, from ±0.20 to ±0.40 is low, from ±0.40 to ±0.60 is moderate, from ±0.60 to ±0.80 is high, and from ±0.80 to ±1.0 is very high. A correlation of zero indicates that there is no correlation between two sets of scores—no regular relation between them at all.

Correlation tells us nothing about causality. If we found a high positive correlation between participation in elections and income levels, for example, we still could not say that being wealthy made people vote or that voting made people wealthy. We would still not know which came first or whether some third variable explained both income levels and voting behavior. Correlation tells us only that we have found some association between scores on two specified characteristics.

Using Statistics to Make Predictions

Behind the use of statistics is the hope that we can generalize from our results and use them to predict behavior. We hope, for example, that we can use the record of how well a group of rats run through a maze today to predict how another group of rats will do tomorrow,

Figure A–9
Scatter plots provide a picture of the strength and direction of a correlation.

---

scatter plot Diagram showing the association between scores on two variables.

correlation coefficient Statistical measure of the strength of association between two variables.

statistical significant Confidence that results obtained were due to differences in the experimental manipulation, rather than to chance factors.

that we can use a person's scores on a sales aptitude test to predict how well she or he will sell life insurance, and that we can measure the attitudes of a relatively small group of people about pollution control to indicate the attitudes of the whole country.

PROBABILITY

To determine the confidence we can have that the results of a single study will apply to the larger population as a whole, psychologists depend on statistical analyses that relay on probability estimates. For example, in the simplest kind of experiment, a psychologist will gather a representative sample, split it randomly into two groups, and then apply some experimental manipulation to one of the groups. Afterward, the psychologist will measure both groups and determine whether the experimental group's score is now different from the score of the control group. But even if there is a large difference between the scores of the two groups, it may still be wrong to attribute the difference to the manipulation. Many factors other than the experimental treatment could produce score differences between the groups. For example, the members of one group may be different in one or more important ways from members of the other group.

Statistics give the psychologist a means to determine whether the observed difference between the two groups is likely due to chance factors, such as sample differences, or whether the results reflect the effect of the experimental manipulation. If the statistics indicate that chance factors most likely play a small role in explaining the results obtained, psychologists conclude that these results are **statistically significant**. Although chance factors can never be ruled out entirely in explainig the results of a study—just as it is always possible to flip 100 coins and get 100 heads in a row—statistics allow psychologists to estimate the confidence they should have in drawing conclusions about their research.

COMMONLY USED PSYCHOACTIVE DRUGS AND THEIR EFFECTS

Depressants: Alcohol, Barbiturates, and the Opiates • Alcohol • Barbiturates • Opiates	**Stimulants: Caffeine, Nicotine, Amphetamines, and Cocaine** • Caffeine • Nicotine • Amphetamines	• Cocaine **Hallucinogens and Marijuana** • Hallucinogens • Marijuana

Because they involve the alteration of how we normally experience sensation, perception, and other mental processes, several types of drugs are called "psychoactive." These drugs typically are categorized according to their primary effects on the nervous system into three general groups: the **depressants**, which slow down behavior or cognitive processes, the **stimulants**, which speed up mental processes, especially those governed by the sympathetic nervous system; and the **hallucinogens**, which trigger significant distortions of various mental processes, especially perception. This appendix outlines the most important features of the most commonly used drugs in each of these categories.

Depressants: Alcohol, Barbiturates, and the Opiates

Depressants are chemicals that retard behavior and thinking by slowing down the activity of the central nervous system. Generally speaking, alcohol, barbiturates, and the opiates have depressant effects. People take depressants to reduce tension, to forget their troubles, or to relieve feelings of inadequacy, loneliness, or boredom.

ALCOHOL The most frequently used psychoactive drug in Western societies is **alcohol**. The effects of alcohol depend on the individual, the social setting, and cultural attitudes, as well as on how much a person consumes and how fast.

In spite of, or perhaps because of, the fact that it is legal and socially approved, alcohol is the number-one drug problem in the United States. More than 30 percent of high school seniors say that they get drunk, and alcohol is also a significant problem among middle-school students. (See **Figure B–1**.) Alcohol is a highly addictive drug with potentially devastating long-term effects. At least 14 million Americans (more than 7 percent of the population ages 18 and older) have problems with drinking, including more than 8 million alcoholics, who are addicted to alcohol. Three times as many men as women are problem drinkers. For both sexes, alcohol abuse and addiction is highest in the 18- to 29-year-old age group (National Institute on Alcohol Abuse and Alcoholism, 2000b).

Heavy, chronic drinking can harm virtually every organ in the body, beginning with the brain. Chronic and excessive alcohol use is associated with impairments in perceptual-motor skills, visual-spatial processing, problem solving, and abstract reasoning (Nixon, 1999). Alcohol is the leading cause of liver disease and kidney damage, is a major factor in cardiovascular disease, increases the risk of certain cancers, and can lead to sexual dysfunction and infertility. Alcohol is particularly damaging to the nervous system during the teenage years. Areas of the brain that are not fully developed until age 21 are especially susceptible to damage from high levels of alcohol intoxication (Ballie, 2001). Approximately 100,000 Americans die each year as a result of using alcohol with other drugs or from alcohol-related problems, making it the third leading cause of preventable death after tobacco and diet-activity patterns (Van Natta, Malin, Bertolucci, & Kaelbert, 1985).

The social costs of abusing alcohol are high. Alcohol is involved in a substantial proportion of violent and accidental deaths, including suicides, which makes it the leading contributor (after AIDS) to death among young people. Alcohol is implicated in more than

depressants Chemicals that slow down behavior or cognitive processes.

stimulants: Chemicals that speed up mental processes.

hallucinogens: Chemicals that trigger significant distortions of various mental processes, especially perception.

alcohol Depressant that is the intoxicating ingredient in whiskey, beer, wine, and other fermented or distilled liquors.

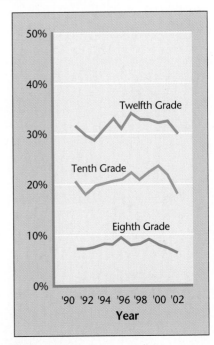

Figure B–1

Teenage use of alcohol (% drunk in past 30 days). A national survey found that use of alcohol by American teenagers began to diminish slightly after 1999. Thirty percent of 12th graders reported getting drunk during the past 30 days in 2002, down from approximately 32 percent in 2001.

Source: Johnston, L.D., O'Malley, P.M., & Bachman, J.G. (2003). Monitoring the future national survey results on adolescent drug use. *www.monitoringthefuture.com.*

> TABLE B-1 THE BEHAVIORAL EFFECTS OF BLOOD-ALCOHOL LEVELS

Levels of Alcohol in the Blood	Behavioral Effects
0.05%	Feels good; less alert
0.10%	Is slower to react; less cautious
0.15%	Reaction time is much slower
0.20%	Sensory-motor abilities are suppressed
0.25%	Is staggering (motor abilities severely impaired); perception is limited as well
0.30%	Is in semistupor
0.35%	Is at level for anesthesia; death is possible
0.40%	Death is likely (usually as a result of respiratory failure)

Source: Data from *Drugs, Society, and Human Behavior,* 3d ed., by Oakey Ray, 1983, St. Louis, MO: The C. V. Mosby Co.

two-thirds of all fatal automobile accidents, two-thirds of all murders, two-thirds of all spouse beatings, and more than half of all cases of violent child abuse. Moreover, the use of alcohol during pregnancy has been linked to a variety of birth defects, the most notable being fetal alcohol syndrome. (See Chapter 7, "Human Development across the lifespan.") More than 40 percent of all heavy drinkers die before the age of 65 (compared with less than 20 percent of nondrinkers). In addition, there is the untold cost in psychological trauma suffered by the nearly 30 million children of alcohol abusers.

What makes alcohol so powerful? Alcohol first affects the frontal lobes of the brain (Adams & Johnson-Greene, 1995), which figure prominently in inhibitions, impulse control, reasoning, and judgment. As consumption continues, alcohol impairs functions of the cerebellum, the center of motor control and balance (Johnson-Greene et al., 1997). Eventually, alcohol consumption affects the spinal cord and medulla, which regulate such involuntary functions as breathing, body temperature, and heart rate. A blood-alcohol level of 0.25 percent or more may cause this part of the nervous system to shut down and may severely impair functioning; slightly higher levels can cause death from alcohol poisoning. (See **Table B–1**.)

Even in moderate quantities, alcohol affects perception, motor processes, memory, and judgment. It diminishes the ability to see clearly, to perceive depth, and to distinguish the differences between bright lights and colors, and it generally affects spatial-cognitive functioning—all clearly necessary for driving a car safely (Matthews, Best, White, Vandergriff, & Simson, 1996). Alcohol interferes with memory storage: Heavy drinkers may also experience *blackouts*, which make them unable to remember anything that occurred while they were drinking; but even long-term alcoholics show improvements in memory, attention, balance, and neurological functioning after three months of sobriety (Sullivan, Rosenbloom, Lim, & Pfefferbaum, 2000).

Heavy drinkers have difficulty focusing on relevant information and ignoring inaccurate, irrelevant information, thus leading to poor judgments (Nixon, 1999). For example, dozens of studies demonstrate that alcohol is correlated with increases in aggression, hostility, violence, and abusive behavior (Bushman, 1993; Bushman & Cooper, 1990; Ito, Miller, & Pollock, 1996). Thus, intoxication makes people less aware of and less concerned about the negative consequences of their actions. The same principle applies to potential victims. One study demonstrated that when women are intoxicated, their ability to accurately evaluate a dangerous situation with a potential male aggressor is diminished, so that their risk of being sexually assaulted increases (Testa, Livingston, & Collins, 2000). Similarly, people who are intoxicated are more likely to engage in unprotected sex than if they were sober (MacDonald, Fong, Zanna, & Martineau, 2000; MacDonald, MacDonald, Zanna, & Fong, 2000).

Women are especially vulnerable to the effects of alcohol (National Institute on Alcohol Abuse and Alcoholism, 2000). Because women generally weigh less than men, the same dose of alcohol has a stronger effect on the average woman than on the average man (York & Welte, 1994). In addition, most women have lower levels of the stomach enzyme that regulates alcohol metabolism. The less of this enzyme in the stomach, the greater the amount of alcohol that passes into the bloodstream and spreads through the body. (This is the reason why drinking on an empty stomach has more pronounced effects than drinking with meals Frezza et al., 1990.) As a rough measure, one drink is likely to have the same effects on a woman as two drinks have on a man.

The dangers of alcohol notwithstanding, alcohol continues to be popular because of its short-term effects. As a depressant, it calms the users system, much like a general anesthetic (McKim, 1997). Alcohol also inhibits centers in the brain that govern critical judgment and impulsive behavior. Alcohol makes people feel more courageous, less inhibited, more spontaneous, and more entertaining (Steele & Josephs, 1990). Thus, although the action of alcohol is to slow the nervous system, users often *feel* as if it stimulates, rather than inhibits, cognitive processes, making it an attractive drug. To drinkers, the long-term negative consequences of alcoholism pale beside these short-term positive consequences.

The good news is that since 1977, overall consumption of alcohol has dropped by 17 percent and consumption of hard liquor by almost 40 percent (Knapp, 1999). Alcohol-related traffic deaths, while still too common, are declining, too (Yi, Willimas, & Dufour, 2002.) (See **Figure B–2**). The alarming news is that drinking in high school (and earlier) is still common: More than 30 percent of high school seniors say they get drunk, and binge drinking has become a dangerous "tradition" on college campuses.

BARBITURATES Barbiturates, commonly known as "downers," include such medications as Amytal, Nembutal, Seconal, and phenobarbital. Discovered about a century ago, this class of depressants was first prescribed for its sedative and anticonvulsant qualities. But after researchers recognized in the 1950s that barbiturates had potentially deadly effects—particularly in combination with alcohol—their use declined, though they are still sometimes prescribed to treat such diverse conditions as insomnia, anxiety, epilepsy, arthritis, and bed-wetting (Reinisch & Sanders, 1982). Although barbiturates are often prescribed to help people sleep, they actually disrupt the body's natural sleep patterns and cause dependence when used for long periods. Frequently prescribed for elderly people, who tend to take them chronically along with their other medications, barbiturates may produce significant side effects such as confusion and anxiety (Celis, 1994).

The general effects of barbiturates are strikingly similar to those of alcohol: Taken on an empty stomach, a small dose causes light-headedness, silliness, and poor motor coordination (McKim, 1997), whereas larger doses may bring on slurred speech, loss of inhibition, and increases in aggression (Aston, 1972). When taken during pregnancy, barbiturates, like alcohol, can produce such birth defects as a cleft palate and malformations of the heart, skeleton, and central nervous system (Wilder & Bruni, 1981).

OPIATES Psychoactive substances derived from, or resembling, sap taken from the seedpod of the opium poppy, **opiates** have a long history of use—though not always abuse. A Sumerian tablet from 4000 B.C. refers to the "joy plant." Originating in Turkey, opium spread west around the Mediterranean and east through India into China, where it was used in pill or liquid form in folk medicines for thousands of years. But changes in the way opium and its derivative, morphine, were used opened the door to abuse. In China during the mid seventeenth century, users began to smoke opium, and addiction often followed the use of this more potent form of the drug. During the U. S. Civil War, physicians used a new invention, the hypodermic needle, to administer morphine, a much-needed

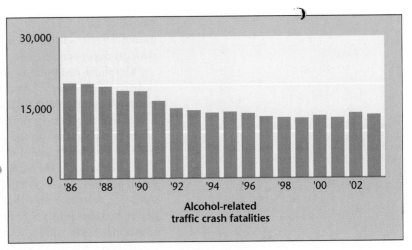

Figure B–2

Alcohol-related motor vehicle traffic crash fatalities. Alcohol-related motor vehicle traffic crash deaths have generally declined since the 1980s, although the total number for the most recent year is still tragically high.

Source: http://www.niaaa.nih.gov/databases/crash01.htm; (2002–2003): *http://www-nrd.nhtsa.dot.gov/pdf/ nrd-30/NCSA/PPT/2003AARelease.pdf*

barbiturates Potentially deadly depressants, first used for their sedative and anticonvulsant properties, now used only to treat such conditions as epilepsy and arthritis.

opiates Drugs, such as opium and heroin, derived from the opium poppy, that dull the senses and induce feelings of euphoria, well-being, and relaxation. Synthetic drugs resembling opium derivatives are also classified as opiates.

painkiller for soldiers. In this form, morphine was far more addictive than smoking opium. Heroin—introduced in 1898 as a cure for morphine addiction—created an even stronger dependency.

Morphine compounds are still used in painkillers and other medications, such as codeine cough syrups. The nonmedicinal distribution of opiates was banned early in the twentieth century. After that, a black market for heroin developed. In the public mind, the heroin addict became synonymous with the "dope fiend," the embodiment of social evil.

Heroin and other opiates resemble endorphins, the natural painkillers produced by the body, and occupy many of the same nerve-receptor sites. (See Chapter 2, "The Biological Basis of Behavior.") Heroin users report a surge of euphoria soon after taking the drug, followed by a period of "nodding off" and clouded mental functioning. Regular use leads to tolerance; tolerance may lead to physical dependence. In advanced stages of addiction, heroin becomes primarily a painkiller to stave off withdrawal symptoms. These symptoms, which may begin within hours of the last dose, include profuse sweating; alternating hot flashes and chills with goose bumps resembling the texture of a plucked turkey (hence the term *cold turkey*); severe cramps, vomiting, and diarrhea; and convulsive shaking and kicking (as in "kicking the habit").

Heroin abuse is associated with serious health conditions, including fatal overdose, spontaneous abortion, collapsed veins, pulmonary problems, and infectious diseases, especially HIV/AIDS and hepatitis, as a result of sharing needles (Bourgois, 1999). The mortality rate of heroin users is almost 15 times higher than that of nonusers (Inciardi & Harrison, 1998). No longer an inner-city problem, its use is growing in suburbs and among young people and women, who often inhale or smoke heroin in the mistaken belief that it is not dangerous in this form (Kantrowitz, Rosenberg, Rogers, Beachy, & Holmes, 1993; National Institute on Drug Abuse, 2000c).

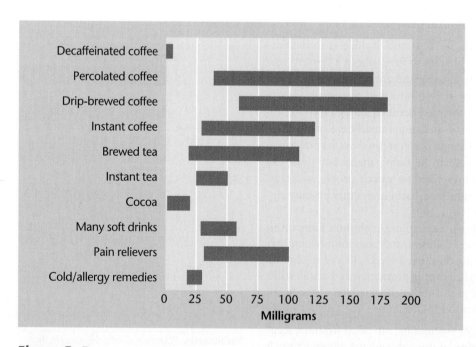

Figure B–3

The amount of caffeine in some common preparations. Caffeine occurs in varying amounts in coffee, tea, soft drinks, and many nonprescription medications. On average, Americans consume about 200 mg of caffeine each day.

Source: August 7, 1991 by the *New York Times*.

Stimulants: Caffeine, Nicotine, Amphetamines, and Cocaine

The drugs classified as *stimulants*—caffeine, nicotine, amphetamines, and cocaine—have legitimate uses, but because they produce feelings of optimism and boundless energy, the potential for abuse is high.

CAFFEINE Caffeine, which occurs naturally in coffee, tea, and cocoa, belongs to a class of drugs known as *xanthine stimulants*. The primary ingredient in over-the-counter stimulants, caffeine is popularly believed to enhance performance, but many of its stimulant effects are illusory. In one study, research participants performing motor and perceptual tasks thought that they were doing better when they were on caffeine, but their actual performance was no better than without it. In terms of wakefulness, caffeine reduces the total number of sleep minutes and increases the time it takes to fall asleep. It is interesting that it is the only stimulant that does not appear to alter sleep stages or cause REM rebound, making it somewhat safer than amphetamines.

Caffeine is found in many beverages and nonprescription medications, including pain relievers and cold and allergy remedies. (See **Figure B–3**.) It is generally considered a benign drug, although large doses—more than five or six cups of strong coffee, for example—may cause caffeinism, or "coffee nerves": anxiety, headaches, heart palpitations, insomnia, and diarrhea. Caffeine interferes with many prescribed medications, such as tranquilizers and sedatives, and appears to aggravate the symptoms of many psychiatric disorders. It is not clear what percentage of coffee drinkers are dependent on caffeine. Those who are dependent experience tolerance, difficulty in giving it up, and physical and psychological distress, such as headaches, lethargy, and depression, whether the caffeine is in soda, coffee, or tea (Blakeslee, 1994).

NICOTINE Nicotine, the psychoactive ingredient in tobacco, is probably the most dangerous and addictive stimulant in use today. Recent studies have found that the neurochemical properties of nicotine are similar to those of cocaine, amphetamines, and morphine (Glassman & Koob, 1996; Pontieri, Tanda, Orzi, & DiChiara, 1996). When smoked, nicotine tends to arrive at the brain all at once following each puff—a rush similar to the "high" experienced by heroin users. The smoker's heart rate increases and blood vessels constrict, causing dull skin and cold hands and accelerating the process of wrinkling and aging (Daniell, 1971). Nicotine affects levels of several neurotransmitters, including norepinephrine, dopamine, and serotonin, and depending on the time, the amount smoked, and other factors, may have sedating or stimulating effects. Symptoms of withdrawal from nicotine include nervousness, difficulty concentrating, both insomnia and drowsiness, headaches, irritability, and intense craving, which continue for weeks and may recur months or even years after a smoker has quit (Brandon, 1994). Despite well-known health risks and strong social pressures (Edwards, 2004), millions of Americans continue to smoke, either for the pleasure of the combined stimulant-sedative effects or to prevent cravings and withdrawal symptoms. Particularly worrisome is that the number of teenagers who start smoking each year has hardly changed. Youth aged 12 to 17 who smoke are about 12 times more likely to use illicit drugs, and 16 times more likely to drink heavily, than their nonsmoking peers and have an increased risk of depression (National Household Survey on Drug Abuse, 1998; D. Smith, 2001).

AMPHETAMINES Amphetamines are powerful synthetic stimulants, first marketed in the 1930s as a nasal spray to relieve symptoms of asthma. At the chemical level, **amphetamines** resemble epinephrine, a hormone that stimulates the sympathetic nervous system. (See Chapter 2, "The Biological Basis of Behavior.") During World War II, the military routinely gave soldiers amphetamines in pill form to relieve fatigue. After the war, the demand for "pep pills" grew among night workers, truck drivers, students, and athletes. Because amphetamines tend to suppress the appetite, they also were widely prescribed as "diet pills." Today, the only legitimate medical uses for amphetamines are to treat narcolepsy and attention deficit disorder. (Paradoxically, amphetamines have a calming effect on hyperactive children.) They are, however, widely used for nonmedical, "recreational" reasons.

Amphetamines not only increase alertness, but also produce feelings of competence and well-being. People who inject them intravenously report a "rush" of euphoria. After the drug's effects wear off, however, users may "crash" into a state of exhaustion and depression (Gunne & Anggard, 1972). Amphetamines are habit forming: Users may come to believe that they cannot function without them. High doses can cause sweating, tremors, heart palpitations, anxiety, and insomnia—which may lead people to take barbiturates or other drugs to counteract these effects. Excessive use of amphetamines may cause personality changes, including paranoia, homicidal and suicidal thoughts, and aggressive, violent behavior (Leccese, 1991). Chronic users may develop amphetamine psychosis, which resembles paranoid schizophrenia and is characterized by delusions, hallucinations, and paranoia. The label "dope fiend" more accurately describes the behavior of amphetamine addicts than that of heroin addicts!

Methamphetamine—known on the street as "speed" and "fire," or in a crystal, smokable form as "ice," "crystal," and "crank"—is easily produced in home laboratories from ingredients available over the counter. An increasingly popular variation, Ecstasy (methylenedioxymethamphetamine, or MDMA), acts as both a stimulant and an hallucinogen. The name "Ecstasy" reflects the users' belief that the drug makes people love and trust one another, puts them in touch with their own emotions, and heightens sexual pleasure.

Short-term physical effects associated with the use of "X" include involuntary teeth clenching (which is why users sometimes wear baby pacifiers around their neck or suck lollipops),

amphetamines Stimulant drugs that initially produce "rushes" of euphoria often followed by sudden "crashes" and, sometimes, severe depression.

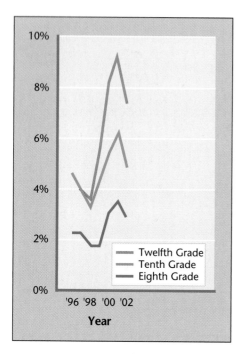

Figure B–4

Teenage use of Ecstasy in past year. Teenage use of Ecstasy has dropped sharply in recent years, after rising steadily after 1998.

Source: Johnston, L.D., O'Malley, P.M., & Bachman, J.G. (2003). Monitoring the Future national survey results on adolescent drug use. *www.monitoringthefuture.com.*

faintness, and chills or sweating. Although early research on Ecstasy with primates suggested that even short-term recreational use could have long-term harmful consequences, more recent studies have not verified evidence of permanent damage from short-term use (Navarro & Maldonado, 2004; also see Ricaurte, Yuan, Hatzidimitriou, Cord, & McCann, 2003; Sumnall, Jerome, Doblin, & Mithoefer, 2004). There is still some reason to be concerned, however, especially with heavy use. Animal research going back more than 20 years shows that high doses of methamphetamine damage the axon terminals of dopamine- and serotonin-containing neurons (National Institute on Drug Abuse, 2000b). One study also found that the recreational use of Ecstasy may lead to a decrease in intelligence test scores (Gouzoulis-Mayfrank et al., 2000), and heavy use has been associated with a decline in visual memory (Back-Madruga et al., 2003). Moreover, the use of Ecstasy during pregnancy has been associated with birth defects (McElhatton, Bateman, Evans, Pughe, & Thomas, 1999). Increased public awareness of the potential dangers associated with Ecstasy explains in part the very recent and sharp decline in its usage (Johnston, O'Malley, & Bachman, 2003). (See **Figure B–4**.)

COCAINE First isolated from coca leaves in 1885, **cocaine** came to be used widely as a topical anesthetic for minor surgery (and still is, for example, in the dental anesthetic Novocain). Around the turn of the century, many physicians believed that cocaine was beneficial as a general stimulant, as well as a cure for excessive use of alcohol and morphine addiction. Among the more famous cocaine users was Sigmund Freud. When he discovered how addictive cocaine was, Freud campaigned against it, as did many of his contemporaries, and ingesting the drug fell into disrepute.

Cocaine made a comeback in the 1970s in such unlikely places as Wall Street, where investment bankers and others found that the drug not only made them high, but also allowed them to wheel and deal around the clock with little sleep (Califano, 1999). In the white-powdered form that is snorted (street names include "coke" and "snow"), it became a status drug, the amphetamine of the wealthy. In the 1980s, a cheaper, smokable, crystallized form known as "crack" (made from the by-products of cocaine extraction) appeared in inner-city neighborhoods. Crack reaches the brain in less than 10 seconds, producing a high that lasts from 5 to 20 minutes, followed by a swift and equally intense depression. Users report that crack leads to almost instantaneous addiction. Addiction to powdered cocaine, which has longer-lasting effects, is not inevitable, but is likely. Babies born to women addicted to crack or cocaine often are premature or have low birthweight, may have withdrawal symptoms, and are at risk for subtle deficits in intelligence and language skills (Inciardi, Surratt, & Saum, 1997; Nelson, Lerner, Needlman, Salvator & Singer, 2004).

On the biochemical level, cocaine blocks the reabsorption of the neurotransmitter dopamine, which is associated with awareness, motivation, and, most significantly, pleasure (Swan, 1998), thereby keeping it available in the synaptic cleft. From an evolutionary perspective, dopamine rewards such survival-related activities as eating, drinking, and engaging in sex. Excess dopamine intensifies and prolongs feelings of pleasure—hence the cocaine user's feelings of euphoria. Normally, dopamine is reabsorbed, leading to feelings of satiety or satisfaction; dopamine reabsorption tells the body, "That's enough." But cocaine short-circuits this feeling of satisfaction, in effect telling the body, "More!" The addictive potential of cocaine may be related to the fact that it damages the brain cells that produce dopamine, thus increasing the amount of cocaine needed to get the same high in the future (Little, Krowlewski, Zhang, & Cassin, 2003).

Hallucinogens and Marijuana

Certain drugs can cause striking perceptual experiences that resemble hallucinations; for this reason they are known as *hallucinogens*. The hallucinogens include lysergic acid diethylamide (LSD, also known as "acid"), mescaline, peyote, and psilocybin. Marijuana is sometimes included in this group, although its effects are normally less powerful. In large enough doses, many other drugs bring on hallucinatory or delusional experiences, mimic-

cocaine Drug derived from the coca plant that, although producing a sense of euphoria by stimulating the sympathetic nervous system, also leads to anxiety, depression, and addictive cravings.

king those that occur in severe mental illnesses; hallucinogens do so in small doses, usually without toxic effects.

HALLUCINOGENS *Hallucinogens* are natural or synthetic drugs that cause shifts in perception of the outside world or, in some cases, experience of imaginary landscapes, settings, and beings that may seem more real than the outside world. How many cultural groups have used hallucinogens is not known. Historians believe that Native Americans have used mescaline, a psychedelic substance found in the mushroom-shaped tops or "buttons" of peyote cactus, for at least 8,000 years.

By contrast, the story of **lysergic acid diethylamide (LSD)**, the drug that triggered the current interest in the hallucinogens, begins in the 20th century. In 1943, an American pharmacologist synthesized LSD, and after ingesting it, he reported experiencing "an uninterrupted stream of fantastic pictures and extraordinary shapes with an intense, kaleidoscopic play of colors." His report led others to experiment with LSD as an artificial form of psychosis, a painkiller for terminal cancer patients, and a cure for alcoholism in the 1950s (Ashley, 1975). LSD came to public attention in the 1960s, when Harvard psychologist Timothy Leary, after trying the related hallucinogen psilocybin, began spreading the "Turn On, Tune In, Drop Out" gospel of the hippie movement. Use of LSD and marijuana declined steadily in the 1970s, but became popular once again in the 1990s, especially with high school and college students (Janofsky, 1994).

About an hour after ingesting LSD, people begin to experience an intensification of sensory perception, loss of control over their thoughts and emotions, and feelings of depersonalization and detachment, as if they were watching themselves from a distance. Some LSD users say that things never looked or sounded or smelled so beautiful; others have terrifying, nightmarish visions. Some users experience a sense of extraordinary mental lucidity; others become so confused that they fear they are losing their minds. The effects of LSD are highly variable, even for the same person on different occasions.

"Bad trips," or unpleasant experiences, may be set off by a change in dosage or an alteration in setting or mood. During a bad trip, the user may not realize that the experiences are being caused by the drug and thus may panic. Flashbacks, or recurrences of hallucinations, may occur weeks after ingesting LSD. Other consequences of frequent use may include memory loss, paranoia, panic attacks, nightmares, and aggression (Gold, 1994; Seligmann et al., 1992).

Unlike depressants and stimulants, LSD and the other hallucinogens do not appear to produce withdrawal effects. If LSD is taken repeatedly, tolerance builds up rapidly: After a few days, no amount of the drug will produce its usual effects, until its use is suspended for about a week (McKim, 1997). This effect acts as a built-in deterrent to continuous use, which helps explain why LSD is generally taken episodically, rather than habitually. After a time, users seem to get tired of the experience and so decrease or discontinue their use of the drug, at least for a period of time.

MARIJUANA Marijuana is a mixture of dried, shredded flowers and leaves of the hemp plant *Cannabis sativa* (which is also a source of fiber for rope and fabrics). Unlike LSD, marijuana usage has a long history. In China, cannabis has been cultivated for at least 5,000 years. The ancient Greeks knew about its psychoactive effects, and it has been used as an intoxicant in India for centuries. But only in the twentieth century did marijuana become popular in the United States. Today, marijuana is the most frequently used illegal drug in the United States and the fourth most popular drug among students, after alcohol, caffeine, and nicotine (Treaster, 1994). **Figure B–5** shows the increase in marijuana use by adolescents in recent years.

Although the active ingredient in marijuana, *tetrahydrocannabinol* (THC), shares some chemical properties with hallucinogens like LSD, it is far less potent. Marijuana smokers report feelings of relaxation; heightened enjoyment of food, music, and sex; a loss of awareness of time; and on occasion, dreamlike experiences. As with LSD, experiences are varied. Many users experience a sense of well-being, and some feel euphoric, but others become suspicious, anxious, and depressed.

lysergic acid diethylamide (LSD) Hallucinogenic or "psychedelic" drug that produces hallucinations and delusions similar to those occurring in a psychotic state.

marijuana A mild hallucinogen that produces a "high" often characterized by feelings of euphoria, a sense of well-being, and swings in mood from gaiety to relaxation; may also cause feelings of anxiety and paranoia.

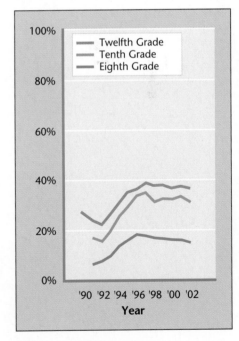

Figure B–5

Teenage use of marijuana in past years.
A national survey found that use of marijuana by American teenagers has leveled off in recent years after rising steadily in the 1990s.

Source: Johnston, L.D., O'Malley, P.M., & Bachman, J.G. (2003). Monitoring the Future national survey results on adolescent drug use. *www.monitoringthefuture.com.*

Marijuana has direct physiological effects, including dilation of the blood vessels in the eyes, making the eyes appear bloodshot; a dry mouth and coughing (because it is generally smoked); increased thirst and hunger; and mild muscular weakness, often in the form of drooping eyelids (Donatelle & Davis, 1993). The major physiological dangers of marijuana are potential respiratory and cardiovascular damage, including triggering heart attacks (Mittleman, 2000; Sridhar, Ruab, & Weatherby, 1994). Among the drug's psychological effects is a distortion of time (Chait & Pierri, 1992), which appears to be related to the impact marijuana has on specific regions of the brain (O'Leary et al., 2003): Feelings that minutes occur in slow motion or that hours flash by in seconds are common. In addition, marijuana may produce alterations in short-term memory and attention.

While under the influence of marijuana, people often lose the ability to remember and coordinate information, a phenomenon known as *temporal disintegration.* For instance, someone who is "high" on marijuana may forget what he or she was talking about in midsentence. Such memory lapses may trigger anxiety and panic (Hollister, 1986; Leccese, 1991). While high, marijuana users have shortened attention spans and delayed reactions, which contribute to concerns about their ability to drive a car or to study or work effectively (Chait & Pierri, 1992; National Institute on Drug Abuse, 1998).

Is marijuana a "dangerous" drug? This question is the subject of much debate in scientific circles as well as public forums. On the one hand are those who hold that marijuana can be psychologically if not physiologically addictive (Haney et al., 2004; Levin et al., 2004); that frequent, long-term use has a negative impact on learning and motivation; and that legal prohibitions against marijuana should be continued. The evidence for cognitive or psychological damage is mixed. One study of college students showed that critical skills related to attention, memory, and learning are impaired among people who use marijuana heavily, even after discontinuing its use for at least 24 hours (National Institute on Drug Abuse, 2000a). On the other hand are those who maintain that marijuana is less harmful than the legal drugs, alcohol and nicotine. They argue that the criminalization of marijuana forces people to buy unregulated cannabis from illegal sources, which means that they might smoke "pot" contaminated with more harmful substances. Moreover, some evidence indicates that marijuana can relieve some of the unpleasant side effects of chemotherapy and can reduce suffering among terminal cancer patients. Scientists have recently begun to develop new medicines modeled on the psychoactive ingredient in marijuana (THC) to allow patients to achieve similar positive medical effects without using marijuana (Kathuria et al., 2003; Piomelli, 2001). In short, the jury is still out, and the debate over marijuana is likely to continue (Stein, 2002).

>GLOSSARY<

360° evaluation   A performance appraisal method that involves evaluation by supervisors, subordinates, peers, along with a self-evaluation.

absolute threshold   The least amount of energy that can be detected as a stimulation 50 percent of the time.

achievement motive   The need to excel, to overcome obstacles.

actualizing tendency   According to Rogers, the drive of every organism to fulfill its biological potential and become what it is inherently capable of becoming.

adaptation   An adjustment of the senses to the level of stimulation they are receiving.

additive color mixing   The process of mixing lights of different wavelengths to create new hues.

adjustment   Any effort to cope with stress.

adoption studies   Research carried out on children, adopted at birth by parents not genetically related to them, to determine the relative influence of heredity and environment on human behavior.

afferent neurons   Neurons that carry messages from sense organs to the spinal cord or brain.

affiliation motive   The need to be with others.

afterimage   Sensory experience that occurs after a visual stimulus has been removed.

aggression   Behavior intented to do harm to others; also, the motive to behave aggressively.

agoraphobia   An anxiety disorder that involves multiple, intense fears of crowds, public places, and other situations that require separation from a source of security such as the home.

algorithm   A step-by-step method of problem solving that guarantees a correct solution.

all-or-none law   Principle that the action potential in a neuron does not vary in strength; either the neuron fires at full strength, or it does not fire at all.

altered states of consciousness   Mental states that differ noticeably from normal waking consciousness.

altruistic behavior   Helping behavior that is not linked to personal gain.

Alzheimer's disease   A neurological disorder, most commonly found in late adulthood, characterized by progressive losses in memory and cognition and by changes in personality.

amplitude   The magnitude of a wave; in sound, the primary determinant of loudness.

anal stage   Second stage in Freud's theory of personality development, in which a child's erotic feelings center on the anus and on elimination.

anorexia nervosa   A serious eating disorder that is associated with an intense fear of weight gain and a distorted body image.

antisocial personality disorder   Personality disorder that involves a pattern of violent, criminal, or unethical and exploitative behavior and an inability to feel affection for others.

anxiety disorders   Disorders in which anxiety is a characteristic feature or the avoidance of anxiety seems to motivate abnormal behavior.

apnea   Sleep disorder characterized by breathing difficulty during the night and feelings of exhaustion during the day.

arousal theory   Theory of motivation that proposes that organisms seek an optimal level of arousal.

assessment center   Method used to select high-level managers that places applicants in a simulated and highly structured group setting where they are given personnel tests and extensive interviews and they engage in various role playing activities.

association areas   Areas of the cerebral cortex where incoming messages from the separate senses are combined into meaningful impressions and outgoing messages from the motor areas are integrated.

attachment   Emotional bond that develops in the first year of life that makes human babies cling to their caregivers for safety and comfort.

attention   The selection of some incoming information for further processing in memory.

attention-deficit/hyperactivity disorder (ADHD)   A childhood disorder characterized by inattention, impulsiveness, and hyperactivity.

attitude   Relatively stable organization of beliefs, feelings, and behavior tendencies directed toward something or someone—the attitude object.

attribution theory   The theory that addresses question of how people make judgments about the causes of behavior.

auditory nerve   The bundle of axons that carries signals from each ear to the brain.

autistic disorder   A childhood disorder characterized by lack of social instincts and strange motor behavior.

autonomic nervous system   The part of the peripheral nervous system that carries messages between the central nervous system and the internal organs.

autonomy Sense of independence; a desire not to be controlled by others.

availability A heuristic by which a judgment or decision is based on information that is most easily retrieved from memory.

axon Single long fiber extending from the cell body; it carries outgoing messages.

babbling A baby's vocalizations, consisting of repetition of consonant–vowel combinations.

basilar membrane Membrane in the cochlea of the inner ear that responds to vibrations; it contains sense receptors for sound.

behavior contracting Form of operant conditioning therapy in which the client and therapist set behavioral goals and agree on reinforcements that the client will receive on reaching those goals.

behavior genetics Study of the relationship between heredity and behavior.

behavior therapies Therapeutic approaches that are based on the belief that all behavior, normal and abnormal, is learned, and that the objective of therapy is to teach people new, more satisfying ways of behaving.

behavioral observation scale (BOS) A performance appraisal method that identifies important work-related behaviors and requires raters to specify the *frequency* at which the employee performs those behaviors.

behaviorally anchored ratings scale (BARS) A performance appraisal method that specifies specific behaviors that would be associated with high performance, average performance, and substandard performance for the job being evaluated, arranges these behaviors into a rating scale, and matches employee behavior to the appropriate scaled behaviors that best correspond.

behaviorism School of psychology that studies only observable and measurable behavior.

Big Five Five basic personality traits currently considered to be of central importance in describing personality.

binaural cue Cue to sound location that involves both ears working together.

binocular cues Visual cues requiring the use of both eyes.

biological model View that psychological disorders have a biochemical or physiological basis.

biological treatments A group of approaches, including medication, electroconvulsive therapy, and psychosurgery, that are sometimes used to treat psychological disorders in conjunction with, or instead of, psychotherapy.

biopsychosocial theory The theory that the interaction of biological, psychological, and cultural factors influences the intensity and duration of pain.

bipolar cells Neurons that have only one axon and one dendrite; in the eye, these neurons connect the receptors on the retina to the ganglion cells.

bipolar disorder A mood disorder in which periods of mania and depression alternate, sometimes with periods of normal mood intervening.

blind spot The place on the retina where the axons of all the ganglion cells leave the eye and where there are no receptors.

body dysmorphic disorder A somatoform disorder in which a person becomes so preoccupied with his or her imagined ugliness that normal life is impossible.

brainstorming A problem-solving strategy in which an individual or a group produces numerous ideas and evaluates them only after all ideas have been collected.

bulimia nervosa An eating disorder characterized by binges of eating followed by self-induced vomiting or the excessive use of laxatives.

bystander effect The tendency for an individual's helpfulness in an emergency to decrease as the number of passive bystanders increases.

case study Intensive description and analysis of a single individual or just a few individuals.

case study analysis The management training method where managers read about conflict situations in an organization, develop strategies for effectively managing these cases, and then discuss their approaches to the problem in a group setting.

catatonic schizophrenia Schizophrenic disorder in which disturbed motor behavior is prominent.

central nervous system (CNS) Division of the nervous system that consists of the brain and spinal cord.

central tendency Tendency of scores to congregate around some middle value.

central tendency error A rating error that occurs when raters evaluate all, or nearly all, employees as being average when in fact their levels of performance differ.

cerebellum Structure in the hindbrain that controls certain reflexes and coordinates the body's movements.

cerebral cortex The outer surface of the two cerebral hemispheres that regulates most complex behavior.

childhood amnesia The difficulty adults have remembering experiences from their first two years of life.

chromosomes Pairs of threadlike bodies within the cell nucleus that contain the genes.

chunking The grouping of information into meaningful units for easier handling by short-term memory.

circadian rhythm A regular biological rhythm with a period of approximately 24 hours.

Civil Rights Act of 1964 A sweeping set of laws and regulations aimed at protecting the rights of people who had, because they were members of certain racial, ethnic, or religious groups, experienced discrimination.

classical (or Pavlovian) conditioning The type of learning in which a response naturally elicited by one stimulus comes to be elicited by a different, formerly neutral stimulus.

client-centered (or person-centered) therapy Nondirectional form of therapy developed by Carl Rogers that calls for unconditional positive regard of the client by the therapist with the goal of helping the client become fully functioning.

cliques Groups of adolescents with similar interests and strong mutual attachment.

cochlea Part of the inner ear containing fluid that can vibrate, which in turn causes the basilar membrane to vibrate.

cognition The processes whereby we acquire and use knowledge.

cognitive dissonance Perceived inconsistency between two cognitions.

cognitive learning Learning that depends on mental processes that are not directly observable.

cognitive map A learned mental image of a spatial environment that may be called on to solve problems when stimuli in the environment change.

cognitive psychology School of psychology devoted to the study of mental processes in the broadest sense.

cognitive therapy Therapy that depends on identifying and changing inappropriately negative and self-critical patterns of thought. Also known as Beck's cognitive therapy, after Aaron Beck, its founder.

cognitive-based therapies Psychotherapies that emphasize changing clients' perceptions of their life situation as a way of modifying their behavior.

cognitive–behavioral model View that psychological disorders result from learning maladaptive ways of thinking and behaving.

cognitive–social learning theories Personality theories that view behavior as the product of the interaction of cognitions, learning and past experiences, and the immediate environment.

cohort A group of people born during the same period in historical time.

color blindness Partial or total inability to perceive hues.

compensatory model A rational decision-making model in which choices are systematically evaluated on various criteria.

compliance Change of behavior in response to an explicit request from another person or group.

compromise Coping by deciding on a more realistic solution or goal when an ideal solution or goal is not practical.

concept A mental category for classifying objects, people, or experiences.

concrete-operational stage In Piaget's theory, the stage of cognitive development between 7 and 11 years of age in which the individual can attend to more than one thing at a time and understand someone else's point of view, though thinking is limited to concrete matters.

conditional positive regard In Rogers's theory, acceptance and love that are dependent on another's behaving in certain ways and on fulfilling certain conditions.

conditioned response (CR) After conditioning, the response an organism produces when a conditioned stimulus is presented.

conditioned stimulus (CS) An originally neutral stimulus that is paired with an unconditioned stimulus and eventually produces the desired response in an organism when presented alone.

conditioned taste aversion Learned revulsion of certain foods because they have been associated with subseguent nausea, based on classical conditioning, conditioned teste a versions are acquired very quickly, sometimes in only one trial.

cones Receptor cells in the retina responsible for color vision.

confirmation bias The tendency to look for evidence in support of a belief and to ignore evidence that would disprove a belief.

conflict Simultaneous existence of incompatible demands, opportunities, needs, or goals.

conformity Voluntarily yielding to social norms, even at the expense of one's preferences.

confrontation Coping by acknowledging a stressful situation directly and attempting to find a solution to the problem or to attain the difficult goal.

conscientiousness The personality trait that refers to a person's ability to finish projects that are started, to attend to detail without becoming absorbed by it, and to care enough about the quality of work that it is not compromised by inattention or lack of effort.

consciousness Our awareness of how we think, feel, perceive, and experience the world.

content validity Refers to a test's having an adequate sample of questions measuring the skills or knowledge it is supposed to measure.

contingency A reliable "if–then" relationship between two events, such as a CS and a US.

contingency theory of leadership The theory that effective leaderhsip depends on the match between the personal characteristics of the leader and important aspects of the situation.

control group In a controlled experiment, the group not subjected to a change in the independent variable; used for comparison with the experimental group.

convergence A visual depth cue that comes from muscles controlling eye movement as the eyes turn inward to view a nearby stimulus.

convergent thinking Thinking that is directed toward one correct solution to a problem.

conversion disorders Somatoform disorders in which a dramatic specific disability has no physical cause but instead seems related to psychological problems.

cornea The transparent protective coating over the front part of the eye.

corporate (organizational) culture The formal and informal rules, procedures, and expectations that define the values, attitudes, beliefs, and customs of an organization.

corpus callosum A thick band of nerve fibers connecting the left and right cerebral cortex.

correlation coefficient Statistical measure of the strength of association between two variables.

correlational research Research technique based on the naturally occurring relationship between two or more variables.

counterfactual thinking Thinking about alternative realities and things that never happened.

couple therapy A form of group therapy intended to help troubled partners improve their problems of communication and interaction.

creativity The ability to produce novel and socially valued ideas or objects.

criterion-related validity Validity of a test as measured by a comparison of the test score and independent measures of what the test is designed to measure.

critical period A time when certain internal and external influences have a major effect on development; at other periods, the same influences will have little or no effect.

cross-sectional approach A method of studying developmental changes by comparing people of different ages at about the same time.

cultural diversity training Training that helps workers understand how people from other cultures think and act, and how to adjust their own attitudes and actions so all employees can work effectively in a multi-cultural work environment.

culture The tangible goods and the values, attitudes, behaviors, and beliefs that are passed from one generation to another.

culture-fair tests Intelligence tests designed to eliminate cultural bias by minimizing skills and values that vary from one culture to another.

dark adaptation Increased sensitivity of rods and cones in darkness.

daydreams Apparently effortless shifts in attention away from the here and now into a private world of make-believe.

decay theory A theory that argues that the passage of time causes forgetting.

defense mechanisms Self-deceptive techniques for reducing stress, including denial, repression, projection, identification, regression, intellectualization, reaction formation, displacement, and sublimation.

defensive attribution The tendency to attribute our successes to our own efforts or qualities and our failures to external factors.

deindividuation A loss of personal sense of responsibility sometimes experienced by individuals when they are in a group.

deinstitutionalization Policy of treating people with severe psychological disorders in the larger community or in small residential centers such as halfway houses, rather than in large public hospitals.

delusions False beliefs about reality that have no basis in fact.

dendrites Short fibers that branch out from the cell body and pick up incoming messages.

deoxyribonucleic acid (DNA) Complex molecule in a double-helix configuration that is the main ingredient of chromosomes and genes and that forms the code for all genetic information.

dependent variable In an experiment, the variable that is measured to see how it is changed by manipulations in the independent variable.

depressants Chemicals that slow down the action of the nervous system and its associated behaviors and cognitive processes.

depressants Chemicals that slow down behavior or cognitive processes.

depression A mood disorder characterized by overwhelming feelings of sadness, lack of interest in activities, and perhaps excessive guilt or feelings of worthlessness.

desensitization therapy A conditioning technique designed to gradually reduce anxiety about a particular object or situation.

developmental norms The average ages at which specific skills, such as walking, are archieved.

developmental psychology The study of the changes that occur in people from conception to death.

Diagnostic and Statistical Manual of Mental Disorders (DSM) Manual that lists and describes the various kinds of psychological disorders.

diathesis Biological predisposition.

diathesis–stress model View that people biologically predisposed to a mental disorder (those with a certain diathesis) will tend to exhibit that disorder when particularly affected by stress.

difference threshold or just-noticeable difference (jnd) The smallest change in stimulation that can be detected 50 percent of the time.

discrimination An unfair act or series of acts taken toward an entire group of people or individual members of that group.

disorganized schizophrenia Schizophrenic disorder in which bizarre and childlike behaviors are common.

display rules   Culture-specific rules that govern how, when, and why expressions of emotion are appropriate.

dissociative disorders   Disorders in which some aspect of the personality seems separated from the rest.

dissociative identity disorder   (Formerly called multiple personality disorder.) Disorder characterized by the separation of the personality into two or more distinct personalities.

divergent thinking   Thinking that meets the criteria of originality, inventiveness, and flexibility and is directed at generating many possible solutions.

dreams   Vivid visual and auditory experiences that occur primarily during REM periods of sleep.

drive   State of tension or arousal that motivates behavior.

drive-reduction theory   States that motivated behavior is aimed at reducing a state of bodily tension or arousal and at returning the organism to homeostasis.

efferent neurons   Neurons that carry messages from the spinal cord or brain to the muscles and glands.

ego   Freud's term for the part of the personality that mediates between environmental demands (reality), conscience (superego), and instinctual needs (id); now often used as a synonym for "self."

egocentric   Unable to see things from another's point of view.

elaborative rehearsal   The linking of new information in short-term memory to familiar material stored in long-term memory.

electroconvulsive therapy (ECT)   Biological therapy in which a mild electrical current is passed through the brain for a short period, producing convulsions and temporary loss of consciousness; used to treat severe, prolonged depression.

embryo   A developing human between 2 weeks and 3 months after conception.

emotion   Feeling, such as fear, joy, or surprise, that underlies behavior.

emotional intelligence   According to Goleman, a form of intelligence that refers to how effectively people perceive and understand their own emotions and the emotions of others, and how well they can regulate and manage their emotional behavior.

emotional memory   Learned emotional responses to various stimuli.

employment interview   Selection method that consists of asking questions to which the job applicant responds, either in a structured or an unstructured setting.

endocrine glands   Glands of the endocrine system that release hormones into the bloodstream.

episodic memory   The portion of long-term memory that stores personally experienced events.

equity   Fairness of exchange achieved when each partner in the relationship receives the same proportion of outcomes to investments.

equity theory   Theory of motivation that emphasizes the belief that effort expended should match rewards received for work.

ethical standards   Ethical requirements that psychologists who offer therapy or other professional services must adhere to.

ethnicity   A common cultural heritage—including religion, language, or ancestry—that is shared by a group of individuals.

evolutionary psychology   An approach to, and subfield of, psychology that is concerned with the evolutionary origins of behaviors and mental processes, their adaptive value, and the purposes they continue to serve.

exchange   The concept that relationships are based on trading rewards among partners.

expectancies   In Bandura's view, what a person anticipates in a situation or as a result of behaving in certain ways.

expectancy theory   Theory of motivation that emphasizes workers' awareness of the value of work-related rewards and of how their behaviors are linked to receiving those rewards.

experimental group   In a controlled experiment, the group subjected to a change in the independent variable.

experimental method   Research technique in which an investigator deliberately manipulates selected events or circumstances and then measures the effects of those manipulations on subsequent behavior.

experimenter bias   Expectations by the experimenter that might influence the results of an experiment or its interpretation.

explicit memory   Memory for information that we can readily express in words and are aware of having; these memories can be intentionally retrieved from memory.

extinction   A decrease in the strength or frequency, or stopping, of a learned response because of failure to continue pairing the US and CS (classical conditioning) or withholding of reinforcement (operant conditioning).

extrinsic motivation   A desire to perform a behavior to obtain an external reward or avoid punishment.

factor analysis   A statistical technique that identifies groups of related objects; it was used by Cattell to identify clusters of traits.

family studies   Studies of heritability in humans based on the assumption that if genes influence a certain trait, close relatives should be more similar on that trait than distant relatives.

family therapy   A form of group therapy that sees the family as at least partly responsible for the individual's problems and that seeks to change all family members' behaviors to the benefit of the family unit as well as the troubled individual.

feature detectors Specialized brain cells that only respond to particular elements in the visual field such as movement or lines of specific orientation.

feminist theory Feminist theories offer a wide variety of views on the social roles of women and men, the problems and rewards of those roles, and prescriptions for changing those roles.

fetal alcohol syndrome (FAS) A disorder that occurs in children of women who drink alcohol during pregnancy; this disorder is characterized by facial deformities, heart defects, stunted growth, and cognitive impairments.

fetishism A paraphilia in which a nonhuman object is the preferred or exclusive method of achieving sexual excitement.

fetus A developing human between 3 months after conception and birth.

fixation According to Freud, a partial or complete halt at some point in the individual's psychosexual development.

fixed-interval schedule A reinforcement schedule in which the correct response is reinforced after a fixed length of time since the last reinforcement.

fixed-ratio schedule A reinforcement schedule in which the correct response is reinforced after a fixed number of correct responses.

flooding A behavioral technique involving full-intensity exposure to a feared stimulus for a prolonged time.

flow According to Csikszentmihalyi, a state of mind characterized by complete and consuming focus on an activity that provides a sense of internalized motivation and happiness.

formal-operational stage In Piaget's theory, the stage of cognitive development between adolescence and adulthood in which the individual becomes capable of abstract thought.

fovea The area of the retina that is the center of the visual field.

framing The perspective from which we interpret information before making a decision.

fraternal twins Twins developed from two separate fertilized ova and therefore different in genetic makeup.

free association A psychoanalytic technique that encourages the person to talk without inhibition about whatever thoughts or fantasies come to mind.

frequency The number of cycles per second in a wave; in sound, the primary determinant of pitch.

frequency distribution A count of the number of scores that fall whithin each of a series of intervals.

frontal lobe Part of the cerebral cortex that is responsible for voluntary movement; it is also important for attention, goal-directed behavior, and appropriate emotional experiences.

frustration The feeling that occurs when a person is prevented from reaching a goal.

frustration–aggression theory The theory that, under certain circumstances, people who are frustrated in their goals turn their anger away from the proper, powerful target and toward another, less powerful target that is safer to attack.

fully functioning person According to Rogers, an individual whose self-concept closely resembles his or her inborn capacities or potentials.

functional fixedness The tendency to perceive only a limited number of uses for an object, thus interfering with the process of problem solving.

functional job analysis (FJA) A method of conducting a job analysis that involves identifying the procedures and processes that workers use in the performance of the job.

functionalist theory Theory of mental life and behavior that is concerned with how an organism uses its perceptual abilities to function in its environment.

fundamental attribution error The tendency of people to overemphasize personal causes for other people's behavior and to underemphasize personal causes for their own behavior.

ganglion cells Neurons that connect the bipolar cells in the eyes to the brain.

gate-control theory The theory that a "neurological gate" in the spinal cord controls the transmission of pain messages to the brain.

gender The psychological and social meanings attached to being biologically male or female.

gender constancy The realization that gender does not change with age.

gender identity A little girl's knowledge that she is a girl, and a little boy's knowledge that he is a boy.

gender stereotypes General beliefs about characteristics that men and women are presumed to have.

gender-identity disorders Disorders that involve the desire to become, or the insistence that one really is, a member of the other biological sex.

gender-role awareness Knowledge of what behavior is appropriate for each gender.

gender-typed behavior Socially prescribed ways of behaving that differ for boys and girls.

general adaptation syndrome (GAS) According to Selye, the three stages the body passes through as it adapts to stress: alarm reaction, resistance, and exhaustion.

generalized anxiety disorder An anxiety disorder characterized by prolonged vague but intense fears that are not attached to any particular object or circumstance.

genes Segments of DNA that control the transmission of traits; they are found on the chromosomes.

genetics Study of how traits are transmitted from one generation to the next.

genital stage In Freud's theory of personality development, the final stage of normal adult sexual development, which is usually marked by mature sexuality.

Gestalt psychology School of psychology that studies how people perceive and experience objects as whole patterns.

giftedness Refers to superior IQ combined with demonstrated or potential ability in such areas as academic aptitude, creativity, and leadership.

glial cells (or glia) Cells that insulate and support neurons by holding them together, provide nourishment and remove waste products, prevent harmful substances from passing into the brain, and form the myelin sheath.

Goal-setting theory Theory of motivation that emphasizes that when goals are clearly stated, and when workers believe that their efforts on the job will lead to the attainment of these goals, their behavior will be highly motivated toward meeting the goals.

Golgi tendon organs Receptors that sense movement of the tendons, which connect muscle to bone.

graded potential A shift in the electrical charge in a tiny area of a neuron.

grammar The language rules that determine how sounds and words can be combined and used to communicate meaning within a language.

great person theory The theory that leadership is a result of personal qualities and traits that qualify one to lead others.

group tests Written intelligence tests administered by one examiner to many people at one time.

group therapy Type of psychotherapy in which clients meet regularly to interact and help one another achieve insight into their feelings and behavior.

groupthink The tendency for people to withhold contradictory opinions due to pressure to conform to group opinions, thereby leading to poorer decisions.

growth spurt A rapid increase in height and weight that occurs during adolescence.

hallucinations Sensory experiences in the absence of external stimulation.

hallucinogens Chemicals that produce a significant disruption in waking consciousness.

halo error (halo effect) A rating error that occurs when evaluators generalize their ratings on multiple dimensions of an employee's performance from how they assess a single characteristic.

Hawthorne effect The principle that people will alter their behavior because of researchers' attention and not necessarily because of any specific treatment condition.

health psychology A subfield of psychology concerned with the relationship between psychological factors and physical health and illness.

heritability Degree to which a given trait results from hereditary, genetic instructions.

heuristics Rules of thumb that help in simplifying and solving problems, although they do not guarantee a correct solution.

hindbrain Area containing the medulla, pons, and cerebellum.

hindsight bias The tendency to see outcomes as inevitable and predictable after we know the outcome.

holophrases One-word sentences commonly used by children under 2 years of age.

homeostasis State of balance and stability in which the organism functions effectively.

hormones Chemical substances released by the endocrine glands; they help regulate bodily activities.

human factors psychology The scientific study of how peoples' skills and abilities can best be utilized in work applications.

human genome The full complement of genes within a human cell.

humanistic personality theories Personality theories that assert the fundamental goodness of people and their striving toward higher levels of functioning.

humanistic psychology School of psychology that emphasizes mental health and well-being, self-understanding, and realizing one's full human potential.

hypnosis Trancelike state in which a person responds readily to suggestions.

hypochondriasis A somatoform disorder in which a person interprets insignificant symptoms as signs of serious illness in the absence of any organic evidence of such illness.

hypothesis A specific, testable prediction derived from a theory.

id In Freud's theory of personality, the collection of unconscious urges and desires that continually seek expression.

identical twins Twins developed from a single fertilized ovum and therefore identical in genetic makeup at the time of conception.

identity crisis A period of intense self-examination and decision making; part of the process of identity formation.

identity formation Erickson's term for the development of a stable sense of self necessary to make the transition from dependence on others to dependence on oneself.

image A mental representation of a sensory experience.

imaginary audience Elkind's term for adolescents' delusion that they are constantly being observed by others.

implicit memory Memory for information that we cannot readily express in words and may not be aware of having; these memories cannot be intentionally retrieved from memory.

imprinting The tendency in certain species to follow the first moving thing (usually its mother) it sees after it is born or hatched.

incentive External stimulus that prompts goal-directed behavior.

independent variable In an experiment, the variable that is manipulated to test its effects on the other, dependent variable.

industrial psychology Subfield of industrial/organizational psychology involved with effectively managing the human resources in organizations.

industrial/organizational (I/O) psychology The area of psychology concerned with the application of psychological principles to the problems of human organizations, especially work organizations.

industrial/organizational (I/O) psychology The field of psychology that includes the scientific study of how individuals and organizations work, and of how psychological principles can be applied to such settings to improve their effectiveness.

information-processing model A computerlike model used to describe the way humans encode, store, and retrieve information.

in-group bias The tendency to see the members of one's own group as superior to members of the out-group, who are not members of one's group.

insanity Legal term for mentally disturbed people who are not considered responsible for their criminal actions.

insight Learning that occurs rapidly as a result of understanding all the elements of a problem.

insight therapies A variety of individual psychotherapies designed to give people a better awareness and understanding of their feelings, motivations, and actions in the hope that this will help them to adjust.

insomnia Sleep disorder characterized by difficulty in falling asleep or remaining asleep throughout the night.

instinct Inborn, inflexible, goal-directed behavior that is characteristic of an entire species.

integrity tests Paper-and-pencil tests that predict the likelihood that a job applicant will engage in counterproductive behavior in the workplace.

intelligence A general term referring to the ability or abilities involved in learning and adaptive behavior.

intelligence quotient (IQ) A numerical value given to intelligence that is determined from the scores on an intelligence test on the basis of a score of 100 for average intelligence.

interneurons (or association neurons) Neurons that carry messages from one neuron to another.

interposition Monocular distance cue in which one object, by partly blocking a second object, is perceived as being closer.

intrinsic motivation A desire to perform a behavior that stems from the enjoyment derived from the behavior itself.

ions Electrically charged particles found both inside and outside the neuron.

iris The colored part of the eye that regulates the size of the pupil.

job Positions in an organization that involve the performance of the same set of tasks.

job analysis A procedure or set of procedures that identifies the various tasks required by a job and the human qualifications that are required to perform that job.

job autonomy The degree to which workers have control over their work and their work environment.

job description Identifies the core tasks required by the job and lists the knowledge, skills, abilities, and other characteristics that are necessary for people to perform the job.

Job Description Index (JDI) Standardized questionnaire that measures global job satisfaction and also workers' levels of satisfaction with five facets of the job: pay, promotion opportunities, supervision, co-workers, and the work itself.

job rotation The training method that teaches employees to perform each job in their work.

job satisfaction The degree of pleasure an employee derives from his or her job.

just-world hypothesis Attribution error that is based on the assumption that bad things happen to bad people and good things happen to good people.

kinesthetic senses Senses of muscle movement, posture, and strain on muscles and joints.

KSAO system of job analysis A method of conducting a job analysis that relies on identifying the human characteristics of knowledge, skills, abilities, and other characteristics that are required for the job.

language A flexible system of communication that uses sounds, rules, gestures, or symbols to convey information.

latency period In Freud's theory of personality, a period in which the child appears to have no interest in the other sex; occurs after the phallic stage.

latent learning Learning that is not immediately reflected in a behavior change.

law of effect Thorndike's theory that behavior consistently rewarded will be "stamped in" as learned behavior, and behavior that brings about discomfort will be "stamped out."

leader-member exchange theory (LMX) Theory of leadership in which leaders evaluate their subordinates on their competence and skill, the degree to which they are trustworthy, and their interest in assuming greater responsibility within the work group and divide workers into in-groups and out-groups, which they lead differently.

learned helplessness Failure to take steps to avoid or escape from an unpleasant or aversive stimulus that occurs as a result of previous exposure to unavoidable painful stimuli.

learning The process by which experience or practice results in a relatively permanent change in behavior or potential behavior.

learning set The ability to become increasingly more effective in solving problems as more problems are solved.

lens The transparent part of the eye behind the pupil that focuses light onto the retina.

libido According to Freud, the energy generated by the sexual instinct.

light adaptation Decreased sensitivity of rods and cones in bright light.

limbic system Ring of structures that play a role in learning and emotional behavior.

linguistic relativity hypothesis Whorf's idea that patterns of thinking are determined by the specific language one speaks.

locus of control According to Rotter, an expectancy about whether reinforcement is under internal or external control.

longitudinal approach A method of studying developmental changes by evaluating the same people at different points in their lives.

long-term memory (LTM) The portion of memory that is more or less permanent, corresponding to everything we "know."

long-term potentiation (LTP) A long-lasting change in the structure or function of a synapse that increases the efficiency of neural transmission and is thought to be related to how information is stored by neurons.

mania A mood disorder characterized by euphoric states, extreme physical activity, excessive talkativeness, distractedness, and sometimes grandiosity.

maturation The automatic biologically programmed unfolding of development in an organism that occurs with the passage of time.

meditation Any of the various methods of concentration, reflection, or focusing of thoughts undertaken to suppress the activity of the sympathetic nervous system.

memory The ability to remember the things that we have experienced, imagined, and learned

menarche First menstrual period.

menopause The time in a woman's life when menstruation ceases.

mental representations Mental images or symbols (such as words) used to think about or remember an object, a person, or an event.

mental retardation Condition of significantly subaverage intelligence accompanied by deficiencies in adaptive behavior.

mental set The tendency to perceive and to approach problems in certain ways.

meta-analysis A sophisticated statistical technique for analyzing the combined results of multiple studies of the same general topic which yields an estimate of the true relationship these studies are attempting to measure.

midbrain Region between the hindbrain and the forebrain; it is important for hearing and sight, and it is one of several places in the brain where pain is registered.

midlife crisis A time when adults discover they no longer feel fulfilled in their jobs or personal lives and attempt to make a decisive shift in career or lifestyle.

midlife transition According to Levinson, a process whereby adults assess the past and formulate new goals for the future.

Minnesota Multiphasic Personality Inventory (MMPI-2) The most widely used objective personality test, originally intended for psychiatric diagnosis.

mnemonics Techniques that make material easier to remember.

modeling A behavior therapy in which the person learns desired behaviors by watching others perform those behaviors.

monaural cue Cue to sound location that requires just one ear.

monocular cues Visual cues requiring the use of one eye.

mood disorders Disturbances in mood or prolonged emotional state.

morphemes The smallest meaningful units of speech, such as simple words, prefixes, and suffixes.

motion parallax Monocular distance cue in which objects closer than the point of visual focus seem to move in the direction opposite to the viewer's moving head, and objects beyond the focus point appear to move in the same direction as the viewer's head.

motive Specific need or desire, such as hunger, thirst, or achievement, that prompts goal-directed behavior.

motor (or efferent) neurons Neurons that carry messages from the spinal cord or brain to the muscles and glands.

myelin sheath White fatty covering found on some axons.

narcolepsy Hereditary sleep disorder characterized by sudden nodding off during the day and sudden loss of muscle tone, often following moments of emotional excitement.

naturalistic observation Research method involving the systematic study of animal or human behavior in natural settings rather than in the laboratory.

negative reinforcer Any event whose reduction or termination increases the likelihood that ongoing behavior will recur.

neonates Newborn babies.

NEO-PI-R An objective personality test designed to assess the Big Five personality traits.

nerve (or tract) Group of axons bundled together.

neural impulse (or action potential) The firing of a nerve cell.

neural plasticity The ability of the brain to change in response to experience.

neurogenesis The growth of new neurons.

neurons Individual cells that are the smallest unit of the nervous system.

neuropsychologists Psychobiologists who study the brain's influence on behavior.

neuroscience The study of the brain and the nervous system.

neurotransmitters Chemicals released by the synaptic vesicles that travel across the synaptic space and affect adjacent neurons.

night terrors Frightening, often terrifying dreams that occur during NREM sleep from which a person is difficult to awaken and doesn't remember the content.

nightmares Frightening dreams that occur during REM sleep and are remembered.

nominal scale A set of categories for classifying objects.

non-REM (NREM) sleep Non-rapid-eye-movement stages of sleep that alternate with REM stages during the sleep cycle.

nonshared environment The unique aspects of the environment that are experienced differently by siblings, even though they are reared in the same family.

norm A shared idea or expectation about how to behave.

obedience Change of behavior in response to a command from another person, typically an authority figure.

object permanence The concept that things continue to exist even when they are out of sight.

objective performance appraisal Method of performance appraisal based on quantitative measurement of the amount of work done.

objective tests Personality tests that are administered and scored in a standard way.

observational (or vicarious) learning Learning by observing other people's behavior.

observer bias Expectations or biases of the observer that might distort or influence his or her interpretation of what was actually observed.

obsessive-compulsive disorder (OCD) An anxiety disorder in which a person feels driven to think disturbing thoughts or to perform senseless rituals.

occipital lobe Part of the cerebral hemisphere that receives and interprets visual information.

Oedipus complex and Electra complex According to Freud, a child's sexual attachment to the parent of the opposite sex and jealousy toward the parent of the same sex; generally occurs in the phallic stage.

olfactory bulb The smell center in the brain.

on-the-job training (OJT) The training method in which the employee being trained learns the new job tasks while actually performing the job.

operant (or instrumental) conditioning The type of learning in which behaviors are emitted (in the presence of specific stimuli) to earn rewards or avoid punishments.

operant behavior Behavior designed to operate on the environment in a way that will gain something desired or avoid something unpleasant.

opponent-process theory Theory of color vision that holds that three sets of color receptors (yellow–blue, red–green, black–white) respond to determine the color you experience.

optic chiasm The point near the base of the brain where some fibers in the optic nerve from each eye cross to the other side of the brain.

optic nerve The bundle of axons of ganglion cells that carries neural messages from each eye to the brain.

oral stage First stage in Freud's theory of personality development, in which the infant's erotic feelings center on the mouth, lips, and tongue.

organ of Corti Structure on the surface of the basilar membrane that contains the receptor cells for hearing.

organizational justice Organizational constructs concerned with the fair treatment of people in organizations.

organizational psychology Subfield of industrial/organizational psychology that focuses on factors that pertain to the organization, rather than to the individuals who work within it.

oval window Membrane across the opening between the middle ear and inner ear that conducts vibrations to the cochlea.

panic disorder An anxiety disorder characterized by recurrent panic attacks in which the person suddenly experiences intense fear or terror without any reasonable cause.

paranoid schizophrenia Schizophrenic disorder marked by extreme suspiciousness and complex, bizarre delusions.

paraphilias Sexual disorders in which unconventional objects or situations cause sexual arousal.

parasympathetic division Branch of the autonomic nervous system; it calms and relaxes the body.

parietal lobe Part of the cerebral cortex that receives sensory information from throughout the body.

participants Individuals whose reactions or responses are observed in an experiment.

pedophilia Desire to have sexual relations with children as the preferred or exclusive method of achieving sexual excitement.

peer group A network of same-aged friends and acquaintances who give one another emotional and social support.

perception The brain's interpretation of sensory information so as to give it meaning.

perceptual constancy A tendency to perceive objects as stable and unchanging despite changes in sensory stimulation.

performance appraisal system Formal methods used to assess the quantity and quality of work contributed by each individual within an organization.

performance standards In Bandura's theory, standards that people develop to rate the adequacy of their own behavior in a variety of situations.

performance tests Intelligence tests that minimize the use of language.

peripheral nervous system (PNS) Division of the nervous system that connects the central nervous system to the rest of the body.

personal fable Elkind's term for adolescents' delusion that they are unique, very important, and invulnerable.

personality An individual's unique pattern of thoughts, feelings, and behaviors that persists over time and across situations.

personality disorders Disorders in which inflexible and maladaptive ways of thinking and behaving learned early in life cause distress to the person or conflicts with others.

personality traits Dimensions or characteristics on which people differ in distinctive ways.

personnel selection The process of selecting from a pool of job applicants those who will be hired to perform a job.

perspective Monocular distance and depth cues that involve the convergence of lines, the haziness of images, and the relative elevation of objects.

phallic stage Third stage in Freud's theory of personality development, in which erotic feelings center on the genitals.

pheromones Chemicals that communicate information to other organisms through smell.

phonemes The basic sounds that make up any language.

pitch Auditory experience corresponding primarily to frequency of sound vibrations, resulting in a higher or lower tone.

pleasure principle According to Freud, the way in which the id seeks immediate gratification of an instinct.

polarization The condition of a neuron when the inside is negatively charged relative to the outside; for example, when the neuron is at rest.

polarization Shift in attitudes by members of a group toward more extreme positions than the ones held before group discussion.

polygenic inheritance Process that occurs when traits are determined through the combined action of several genes.

positive psychology An emerging field of psychology that focuses on positive experiences, including subjective well-being, self-determination, the relationship between positive emotions and physical health, and the factors that allow individuals, communities, and societies to flourish.

positive reinforcer Any event whose presence increases the likelihood that ongoing behavior will recur.

posttraumatic stress disorder (PTSD) Psychological disorder characterized by episodes of anxiety, sleeplessness, and nightmares resulting from some disturbing past event.

predictive validity Correlation between individuals' scores on a predictor variable and their subsequent performance on some criterion, such as job performance.

prejudice An unfair, intolerant, or unfavorable attitude toward a group of people.

prenatal development Development from conception to birth.

preoperational stage In Piaget's theory, the stage of cognitive development between 2 and 7 years of age in which the individual becomes able to use mental representations and language to describe, remember, and reason about the world, though only in an egocentric fashion.

preparedness A biological readiness to learn certain associations because of their survival advantages.

pressure A feeling that one must speed up, intensify, or change the direction of one's behavior or live up to a higher standard of performance.

primacy effect The fact that early information about someone weighs more heavily than later information in influencing one's impression of that person.

primary drive An unlearned drive, such as hunger, that is based on a physiological state.

primary emotions Emotions, such as fear, anger, and pleasure, that are found in all cultures.

primary motor cortex The section of each frontal lobe responsible for voluntary movement.

primary reinforcer A reinforcer that is rewarding in itself, such as food, water, and sex.

primary somatosensory cortex Area of the parietal lobe where messages from the sense receptors are registered.

principle of reinforcement Same as law of effect

principles of conservation The concept that the quantity of a substance is not altered by reversible changes in its appearance.

proactive interference   The process by which information already in memory interferes with new information.

problem representation   The first step in solving a problem; it involves interpreting or defining the problem.

procedural memory   The portion of long-term memory that stores information relating to skills, habits, and other perceptual-motor tasks.

projective tests   Personality tests, such as the Rorschach inkblot test, consisting of ambiguous or unstructured material.

protected classes (or groups)   Groups of people who are guaranteed legal protection against discrimination under the provisions of the Civil Rights Act of 1964 and subsequent acts and laws.

prototype   According to Rosch, a mental model containing the most typical features of a concept.

proximity   How close two people live to each other.

psychoactive drugs   Chemical substances that change moods and perceptions.

psychoanalysis   The theory of personality Freud developed, as well as the form of therapy he invented.

psychoanalytic model   View that psychological disorders result from unconscious internal conflicts.

psychobiology   The area of psychology that focuses on the biological foundations of behavior and mental processes.

psychodynamic theories   Personality theories contending that behavior results from psychological forces that interact within the individual, often outside conscious awareness.

psychology   The scientific study of behavior and mental processes.

psychoneuroimmunology (PNI)   A new field that studies the interaction between stress on the one hand and immune, endocrine, and nervous system activity on the other.

psychosomatic disorders   Disorders in which there is real physical illness that is largely caused by psychological factors such as stress and anxiety.

psychosurgery   Brain surgery performed to change a person's behavior and emotional state; a biological therapy rarely used today.

psychotherapy   The use of psychological techniques to treat personality and behavior disorders.

psychotic (psychosis)   Behavior characterized vby a loss of touch with reality.

puberty   The onset of sexual maturation, with accompanying physical development.

punisher   A stimulus that follows a behavior and decreases the likelihood that the behavior will be repeated.

punishment   Any event whose presence decreases the likelihood that ongoing behavior will recur.

pupil   A small opening in the iris through which light enters the eye.

race   A subpopulation of a species, defined according to an identifiable characteristic (that is, geographic location, skin color, hair texture, genes, facial features, and so forth).

racism   Prejudice and discrimination directed at a particular racial group.

random sample   Sample in which each potential participant has an equal chance of being selected.

rational-emotive therapy (RET)   A directive cognitive therapy based on the idea that clients' psychological distress is caused by irrational and self-defeating beliefs and that the therapist's job is to challenge such dysfunctional beliefs.

reality principle   According to Freud, the way in which the ego seeks to satisfy instinctual demands safely and effectively in the real world.

recency error   A rating error that occurs when evaluations of performance rely too extensively on the most recent behavior of the employee.

receptor cell   A specialized cell that responds to a particular type of energy.

receptor sites   Locations on a receptor neuron into which a specific neurotransmitter fits like a key into a lock.

reinforcement theory   Theory based on the principles of operant conditioning which specifies that workers will modify their behavior based on the outcomes that are associated with it.

reinforcer   A stimulus that follows a behavior and increases the likelihood that the behavior will be repeated.

reliability   Ability of a test to produce consistent and stable scores.

REM (paradoxical) sleep   Sleep stage characterized by rapid-eye movements and increased dreaming.

representative sample   Sample carefully chosen so that the characteristics of the participants correspond closely to the characteristics of the larger population.

representativeness   A heuristic by which a new situation is judged on the basis of its resemblance to a stereotypical model.

response generalization   Giving a response that is somewhat different from the response originally learned to that stimulus.

resting potential   Electrical charge across a neuron membrane resulting from more positive ions concentrated on the outside and more negative ions on the inside.

retina   The lining of the eye containing receptor cells that are sensitive to light.

retinal disparity   Binocular distance cue based on the difference between the images cast on the two retinas when both eyes are focused on the same object.

retroactive interference   The process by which new information interferes with information already in memory.

retrograde amnesia   The inability to recall events preceding an accident or injury, but without loss of earlier memory.

risky shift   Greater willingness of a group than an individual to take substantial risks.

rods   Receptor cells in the retina responsible for night vision and perception of brightness.

role conflict   Conflict that results when workers are expected to perform mutually exclusive activities or when the work assigned conflicts with other personal or professional responsibilities.

role overload   Situation that occurs when there is more work assigned than can be accomplished.

Rorschach test   A projective test composed of ambiguous inkblots; the way people interpret the blots is thought to reveal aspects of their personality.

rote rehearsal   Retaining information in memory simply by repeating it over and over.

schedule of reinforcement   In operant conditioning, the rule for determining when and how often reinforcers will be delivered.

schema   (plural: schemata) A set of beliefs or expectations about something that is based on past experience.

schizophrenic disorders   Severe disorders in which there are disturbances of thoughts, communications, and emotions, including delusions and hallucinations.

scientific method   An approach to knowledge that relies on collecting data, generating a theory to explain the data, producing testable hypotheses based on the theory, and testing those hypotheses empirically.

secondary drive   A learned drive, such as ambition, that is not based on a physiological state.

secondary emotions   Emotions found in some but not all cultures.

secondary reinforcer   A reinforcer whose value is acquired through association with other primary or secondary reinforcers.

self-actualization   Highest level of need in Maslow's hierarchy, which involves the desire for personal growth and fulfillment.

self-actualizing tendency   According to Rogers, the drive of human beings to fulfill their self-concepts, or the images they have of themselves.

self-efficacy   According to Bandura, the expectancy that one's efforts will be successful.

self-fulfilling prophecy   The process in which a person's expectation about another elicits behavior from the second person that confirms the expectation.

self-monitoring   The tendency for an individual to observe the situation for cues about how to react.

semantic memory   The portion of long-term memory that stores general facts and information.

sensation   The process of receiving sensory data from the environment and translating it to the brain.

sensory (or afferent) neurons   Neurons that carry messages from sense organs to the spinal cord or brain.

sensory registers   Entry points in memory for raw information from the senses.

sensory-motor stage   In Piaget's theory, the stage of cognitive development between birth and 2 years of age in which the individual develops object permanence and acquires the ability to form mental representations.

serial position effect   The finding that, when asked to recall a list of unrelated items, performance is better for the items at the beginning and end of the list than for items in the middle.

sexual dysfunction   Loss or impairment of the ordinary physical responses of sexual function.

sexual harassment   Behaviors that involve either soliciting sexual favors in exchange for favorable treatment or creating a hostile work environment.

sexual orientation   Refers to the direction of one's sexual interest toward members of the same sex, the other sex, or both sexes.

shadowing   Monocular cue to distance and depth based on the fact that shadows often appear on the parts of objects that are more distant.

shape constancy   A tendency to see an object as the same shape no matter what angle it is viewed from.

shaping   Reinforcing successive approximations to a desired behavior.

short-term memory (STM)   Working memory; briefly stores and processes selected information from the sensory registers.

short-term psychodynamic therapy   Insight therapy that is time limited and focused on trying to help clients correct the immediate problems in their lives.

size constancy   The perception of an object as the same size regardless of the distance from which it is viewed.

Skinner box   A box often used in operant conditioning of animals; it limits the available responses and thus increases the likelihood that the desired response will occur.

social cognition   Knowledge and understanding concerning the social world and the people in it (including oneself).

social influence   The process by which others individually or collectively affect one's perceptions, attitudes, and actions.

social learning theorists Psychologists whose view of learning emphasizes the ability to learn by observing a model or receiving instructions, without firsthand experience by the learner.

social loafing The tendency of indivuals to exert less effort when they are working as part of a group.

social phobia An anxiety disorder characterized by excessive, inappropriate fears connected with social situations or performances in front of other people.

social psychology The scientific study of the ways in which the thoughts, feelings, and behaviors of one individual are influenced by the real, imagined, or inferred behavior or characteristics of other people.

socialization Process by which children learn the behaviors and attitudes appropriate to their family and culture.

somatic nervous system The part of the peripheral nervous system that carries messages from the senses to the central nervous system and between the central nervous system and the skeletal muscles.

somatoform disorders Disorders in which there is an apparent physical illness for which there is no organic basis.

sound A psychological experience created by the brain in response to changes in air pressure that are received by the auditory system.

sound waves Changes in pressure caused when molecules of air or fluid collide with one another and then move apart again.

specific phobia Anxiety disorder characterized by an intense, paralyzing fear of something.

spinal cord Complex cable of neurons that runs down the spine, connecting the brain to most of the rest of the body.

split-half reliability A method of determining test reliability by dividing the test into two parts and checking the agreement of scores on both parts.

spontaneous recovery The reappearance of an extinguished response after the passage of time, without training.

Stanford-Binet Intelligence Scale Test of intelligence, developed from Binet and Simon's original scale, which set the average intelligence quotient (IQ) at 100.

state-dependent memory The finding that people who learn material in a particular physiological state tend to recall that material better if they return to the same state they were in during learning.

stereoscopic vision Combination of two retinal images to give a three-dimensional perceptual experience.

stereotype A set of characteristics presumed to be shared by all members of a social category.

stimulants Chemicals that speed up the action of the nervous system and its associated behaviors and cognitive processes.

stimulus control Control of conditioned responses by cues or stimuli in the environment.

stimulus discrimination Learning to respond to only one stimulus and to inhibit the response to all other stimuli.

stimulus generalization The transfer of a learned response to different but similar stimuli.

stimulus motive Unlearned motive, such as curiosity or contact, that prompts us to explore or change the world around us.

stress A state of psychological tension or strain.

stress-inoculation therapy A type of cognitive therapy that trains clients to cope with stressful situations by learning a more useful pattern of self-talk.

stressor Any environmental demand that creates a state of tension or threat and requires change or adaptation.

stretch receptors Receptors that sense muscle stretch and contraction.

structuralism School of psychology that stresses the basic units of experience and the combinations in which they occur.

subjective performance appraisal Methods of performance appraisal that rely on judgments about the qualify of work an employee contributes.

substance abuse A pattern of drug use that diminishes the ability to fulfill responsibilities at home, work, or school; that results in repeated use of a drug in dangerous situations; or that leads to legal difficulties related to drug use.

substance dependence A pattern of compulsive drug-taking that results in tolerance, withdrawal symptoms, or other specific symptoms for at least a year.

superego According to Freud, the social and parental standards the individual has internalized.

survey research Research technique in which questionnaires or interviews are administered to a selected group of people.

sympathetic division Branch of the autonomic nervous system; it prepares the body for quick action in an emergency.

synapse Area composed of the axon terminal of one neuron, the synaptic space, and the dendrite or cell body of the next neuron.

synaptic space (or synaptic cleft) Tiny gap between the axon terminal of one neuron and the dendrites or cell body of the next neuron.

synaptic vesicles Tiny sacs in a terminal button that release chemicals into the synapse.

systematic desensitization A behavioral technique for reducing a person's fear and anxiety by gradually associating a new response (relaxation) with stimuli that have been causing the fear and anxiety.

systems approach View that biological, psychological, and social risk factors combine to produce psychological disorders. Also known as the biopsychosocial model of psychological disorders.

taste buds Structures on the tongue that contain the receptor cells for taste.

temperament Characteristic patterns of emotional reactions and emotional self-regulation.

temporal lobe Part of the cerebral hemisphere that helps regulate hearing, balance and equilibrium, and certain emotions and motivations.

terminal button (or synaptic knob) Structure at the end of an axon terminal branch.

texture gradient Monocular cue to distance and depth based on the fact that objects seen at greater distances appear to be smoother and less textured.

Thematic Apperception Test (TAT) A projective test composed of ambiguous pictures about which a person is asked to tell a complete story.

theory General, systematic explanation of a phenomenon that organizes known facts and allows us to predict relationships.

theory of multiple intelligences Howard Gardner's theory that there is not one intelligence, but rather many intelligences, each of which is relatively independent of the others.

threshold of excitation The level an impulse must exceed to cause a neuron to fire.

timbre The quality or texture of sound; caused by overtones.

token economy An operant conditioning therapy in which people earn tokens (reinforcers) for desired behaviors and exchange them for desired items or privileges.

training The organized approach that organizations undertake to instruct employees in relevant job-related attitudes and behaviors.

transference The client's carrying over to the analyst feelings held toward childhood authority figures.

triarchic theory of intelligence Sternberg's theory that intelligence involves mental skills (analytical intelligence), insight and creative adaptability (creative intelligence), and environmental responsiveness (practical intelligence).

trichromatic theory The theory of color vision that holds that all color perception derives from three different color receptors in the retina (usually red, green, and blue receptors).

twin studies Studies of identical and fraternal twins to determine the relative influence of heredity and environment on human behavior.

Type A behavior pattern A general pattern of behavior characterized by impatience, hostility, competitiveness, urgency, and constant striving.

Type B behavior pattern A general pattern of behavior characterized by patience, flexibility, and lower intensity of attitudes and competitiveness.

ultimate attribution error The tendency for a person with stereotyped beliefs to make internal attributions for group members' shortcomings and external attributions for their successes.

unconditional positive regard In Rogers's theory, the full acceptance and love of another person regardless of his or her behavior.

unconditioned response (UR) A response that takes place in an organism whenever an unconditioned stimulus occurs.

unconditioned stimulus (US) A stimulus that invariably causes an organism to respond in a specific way.

unconscious In Freud's theory, all the ideas, thoughts, and feelings of which we are not and normally cannot become aware.

undifferentiated schizophrenia Schizophrenic disorder in which there are clear schizophrenic symptoms that do not meet the criteria for another subtype of the disorder.

validity Ability of a test to measure what it has been designed to measure.

variable-ratio schedule A reinforcement schedule in which a varying number of correct responses must occur before reinforcement is presented.

vestibular senses The senses of equilibrium and body position in space.

vestibule training The training method that allows employees to learn techniques and behaviors in a simulated work place.

visual acuity The ability to distinguish fine details visually.

waking consciousness Mental state that encompasses the thoughts, feelings, and perceptions that occur when we are awake and reasonably alert.

Weber's law The principle that the jnd for any given sense is a constant fraction or proportion of the stimulation being judged.

Wechsler Adult Intelligence Scale—Third Edition (WAIS-III) An individual intelligence test developed especially for adults; measures both verbal and performance abilities.

Wechsler Intelligence Scale for Children—Third Edition (WISC-III) An individual intelligence test developed especially for school-aged children; measures verbal and performance abilities and also yields an overall IQ score.

withdrawal Coping by avoiding a conflict-oriented situation.

Yerkes–Dodson law States that there is an optimal level of arousal for the best performance of any task; the more complex the task, the lower the level of arousal that can be tolerated before performance deteriorates.

Aaker, D. A., & Bruzzone, D. E. (1985). Causes of irritation in advertising. *Journal of Marketing, 49,* 47–57.

Abbar, M., Courltet, P., Bellivier, F., Leboyer, M., Boulenger, J. P., Castelhau, et al. (2001). Suicide attempts and the tryptophan hydroxylase gene. *Molecular Psychiatry, 6,* 268–273.

Acebo, C., & Carskadon, M. A. (2002). Influence of irregular sleep patterns on waking behavior. In M. A. Carskadon (Ed.), *Adolescent sleep patterns: Biological, social and psychological influences* (pp. 220–235). New York: Cambridge University Press.

Achter, J. A., Lubinski, D., & Benbow, C. P. (1996). Multipotentiality among intellectually gifted: "It was never there and already it's vanishing." *Journal of Counseling Psychology, 43,* 65–76.

Ackerman, J. (2004, January-February). Untangling the brain: The search for the causes and cures of dyslexia. *Yale Alumni Magazine,* 47–55.

Acredolo, L. P., & Hake, J. L. (1982). Infant perception. In B. B. Wolman (Ed.), *Handbook of developmental psychology* (pp. 244–283). Englewood Cliffs, NJ: Prentice Hall.

Adams, A. J., Kuzmits, F. E., Sussman, L., & Raho, L. E. (2004). 360-Feedback in health care management. *Healthcare manager, 23* (4), 321–328.

Adams, J. L. (1980). *Conceptual blockbusting: A guide to better ideas* (2nd ed.). New York: Norton.

Adams, G. R., & Gullota, T. (1983). *Adolescent life experiences.* Monterey, CA: Brooks/Cole.

Adelson, R. (2002). Figure this: Deciding what's figure, what's ground. *Monitor on Psychology, 33,* 44–45.

Adler, N., Boyce, T., Chesney, M. A., Cohen, S., Folkman, S., Kahn, R. I., et al. (1994). Socioeconomic status and health. The challenge of the gradient. *American Psychologist, 49,* 15–24.

Aeschleman, S. R., Rosen, C. C., & Williams, M. R. (2003). The effect of non-contingent negative and positive reinforcement operations on the acquisition of superstitious behaviors. *Behavioural Processes, 61,* 37–45.

Age Discrimination in Employment Act of 1967 (29 U.S.C. 633A)

Agostinelli, G., Sherman, S. J., Presson, C. C., & Chassin, L. (1992). Self-protection and self-enhancement biases in estimates of population prevalence. *Personality and Social Psychology Bulletin, 18*(5), 631–642.

AhYun, K. (2002). Similarity and attraction. In M. Allen & R. W. Raymond (Eds.), *Interpersonal communication research: Advances through meta-analysis. LEA's communication series* (pp. 145–167). Mahwah, NJ: Lawrence Earlbaum Associates, Publishers.

Ainsworth, M. D., Blehar, M. C., Waters, E., & Wall, S. (1978). *Patterns of attachment.* New York: Halstead Press.

Aiken, L. R. (1988). *Psychological testing and assessment* (6th ed.). Boston: Allyn & Bacon.

Albarracin, D. (2002). Cognition in persuasion: An analysis of information processing in response to persuasive communications. In M. P. Zanna (Ed.), *Advances in experimental social psychology* (Vol. 34, pp. 61–130). San Diego, CA: Academic Press, Inc.

Albus, M. (1989). Cholecystokinin. *Progress in Neuro-Psychopharmacology and Biological Psychiatry, 12*(Suppl.), 5–21.

Alexander, C. N., Robinson, P., & Rainforth, N. (1994). Treating and preventing alcohol, nicotine, and drug abuse through Transcendental Meditation: A review and statistical meta-analysis. *Alcoholism Treatment Quarterly* [Special Issue], *11*(1–2), 13–87.

Allen, L. S., & Gorski, R. A. (1992). Sexual orientation and size of the anterior commissure in the human brain. *Proceedings of the National Academy of Sciences, 89,* 7199–7202.

Allen, V. L., & Levine, J. M. (1971). Social support and conformity: The role of independent assessment of reality. *Journal of Experimental Social Psychology, 7,* 48–58.

Alliger, G. M. & Janak, E. A. (1989). Kirkpatrick's levels of training criteria: Thirty years later. *Personnel Psychology, 42* (2), 331–342.

Allport, G. W. (1954). *The nature of prejudice.* New York: Anchor.

Allport, G. W., & Odbert, H. S. (1936). Trait-names: A psycholexical study. *Psychological Monographs, 47*(1, Whole No. 211).

Almgren, G., Guest, A., Immerwahr, G., & Spittel, M. (2002). Joblessness, family disruption, and violent death in Chicago, 1970–90. *Social Forces, 76,* 1465–1493.

Altman, I., & Taylor, D. A. (1973). *Social penetration: The development of interpersonal relationships.* New York: Holt, Rinehart & Winston.

Amabile, T. M. (1983). The social psychology of creativity: A comparative conceptualization. *Journal of Personality and Social Psychology, 45,* 357–376.

American Academy of Pediatrics. (1999, August 2). *AAP discourages television for very young children.* Press release.

American Psychiatric Association (2000). *Diagnostic and statistical manual of mental disorders* (4th ed. TR). Washington, DC: American Psychiatric Press.

American Psychiatric Association (APA). (1994). *Diagnostic and statistical manual of mental disorders* (4th ed.). Washington, DC: American Psychiatric Press.

American Psychological Association (APA). (1992). *Ethical principles of psychologists and code of conduct.* Washington. DC: Author.

American Psychological Association (APA). (2000, November). Facts & figures. *Monitor on Psychology, 31,* 10.

Americans with Disabilities Act of 1990, Titles I and V (42 U.S.C. 12101)

America's Children: Key National Indicators of Well-Being. (2000). A report from the National Maternal and Child Health Clearinghouse. Retrieved November 10, 2000, from the World Wide Web: http://childstats.gov

Anastasi, A., & Urbina, S. (1997). *Psychological testing* (7th ed.). Upper Saddle River, NJ: Prentice Hall.

Anch, A. M., Browman, C. P., Mitler, M. M., & Walsh, J. K. (1988). *Sleep: A scientific perspective.* Englewood Cliffs, NJ: Prentice Hall.

Andersen, B. L., Kiecolt-Glaser, J. K., & Glaser, R. (1994). A biobehavioral model of cancer stress and disease course. *American Psychologist, 49,* 389–404.

Anderson, D. R., Huston, A. C., Wright, J. C., & Collins, P. A. (1998). Initial findings on the long term impact of Sesame Street and educational television for children: The Recontact Study. In R. Noll & M. Price (Eds.), *A communications cornucopia: Markle Foundation essays on information policy* (pp. 279–296). Washington, DC: Brookings Institution.

Anderson, S. W., Bechara, A., Damasio, H., Tranel, D., & Damasio, A. R. (1999). Impairment of social and moral behavior related to early damage in human prefrontal cortex. *Nature Neuroscience, 2,* 1032–1037.

Andrich, D., & Styles, I. M. (1998). The structural relationship between attitude and behavior statements from the unfolding perspective. *Psychological Methods, 3,* 454–469.

Anshel, M. H., Porter, A., & Quek, J-J. (1998). Coping with acute stress in sports as a function of gender: An exploratory study. *Journal of Sport Behavior, 21,* 363–376.

Aranow, E., Weiss, K. A., & Rezikoff, M. (2001). *A practical guide to the Thematic Apperception Test: The TAT in clinical practice.* Philadelphia: Brunner–Routledge.

Aranya, N., Kushnir, T., & Valency, A. (1986). Organizational commitment in a male dominated profession. *Human Relations, 39,* 433–438.

Archer, J. (1996). Sex differences in social behavior: Are the social role and evolutionary explanations compatible? *American Psychologist, 51*(9), 909–917.

Arkin, R. M., Cooper, H., & Kolditz, T. (1980). A statistical review of literature concerning the self-serving attribution bias in interpersonal influence situations. *Journal of Personality, 48,* 435–448.

Arndt, J., Greenberg, J., Pyszczynski, T., & Solomon, S. (1997). Subliminal exposure to death-related stimuli increases defense of the cultural worldview. *Psychological Science, 8,* 379–385.

Aronson, E. (1999). The power of self-persuasion. *American Psychologist, 54,* 875–884.

Aronson, E., Wilson, T. D., & Akert, R. (1999). *Social psychology* (3d ed.). New York: Addison-Wesley Longman.

Aronson, E., Wilson, T. D., & Akert, R. M. (2002). *Social psychology* (4th ed.). Upper Saddle River, NJ: Prentice Hall.

Arrigo, J. M., & Pezdek, K. (1997). Lessons from the study of psychogenic amnesia. *Current Directions in Psychological Science, 6,* 148–152.

Ary, D. V., Duncan, T. E., Duncan, S. C., & Hops, H. (1999). Adolescent problem behavior: The influence of parents and peers. *Behaviour Research and Therapy, 37,* 217–230.

Asch, S. E. (1951). Effects of group pressure upon the modification and distortion of judgments. In H. Guetzkow (ed.), *Groups, leadership, and men.* Pittsburgh: Carnegie Press.

Asch, S. E. (1956). Studies of independence and conformity: I. A minority of one against a unanimous majority. *Psychological Monographs, 70*(9, Whole No. 416).

Asendorpf, J. B., & Van-Aken, M. A. G. (2003). Validity of Big Five personality judgements in childhood: A 9 year longitudinal study. *European Journal of Personality, 17,* 1–17.

Aspinwall, L. G., & Taylor, S. E. (1997). A stitch in time: Self-regulation and proactive coping. *Psychological Bulletin, 121,* 417–436.

Aslin, R. N., & Smith, L. B. (1988). Perceptual development. *Annual Review of Psychology, 39,* 435–473.

Astur, R. S., Taylor, L. B., Marnelak, A. N., Philpott, L., & Sutherland, R. J. (2002). Humans with hippocampus damage display severe spatial memory impairments in a virtual Morris water task. *Behavioural Brain Research, 132,* 77–84.

Atchley, R. C. (1982). Retirement as a social institution. *Annual Review of Sociology, 8,* 263–287.

Auvergne, R., Lere, C., El-Bahh, B., Arthaud, S., Lespinet, V., Rougier, A., & Le-Gal-La-Salle, G. (2002). Delayed kindling epileptogenesis and increased neurogenesis in adult rats housed in an enriched environment. *Brain Research, 954,* 277–285.

Aved, B. M., Irwin, M. M., Cummings, L. S., & Findeisen, N. (1993). Barriers to prenatal care for low-income women. *Western Journal of Medicine, 158,* 493–498.

Avolio, B. J. Kahai, S., Dumbum, R. & Sivasubramanaim, N. (2001). Virtual teams: Implications for e-leadership and team development. In M. London (E.), How people evaluate others in organizations (pp. 337–358). Mahwah, NJ: Erlbaum.

Axtell, C. M., Fleck, S. J., & Turner, N. (2004). Virtual teams: Collaborating across distance. In C. L. Cooper & I. T. Robertson (Eds.), *International review of industrial and organizational psychology 2004* (Vol. 19, pp. 205–249). West Sussex: Wiley.

Ayas, N. T., White, D. P., Manson, J. E., Stampfer, M. J., Speizer, F. E., Malhotra, A., & Hu, F. B. (2003). A prospective study of sleep duration and coronary heart disease in women. *Archives of Internal Medicine, 163,* 205–209.

Ayman, R., Chemers, M. M., Fiedler, F., Romano, R., Vecchio, R. P., & Zaccaro, S. J. (1998). Contingency model. In F. Dansereau & F. J. Yammarino (Eds.), *Leadership: The multiple-level approaches: Classical and new wave monographs in organizational behavior and industrial relations* (Vol. 24, pp. 73–143). Stamford, CT: JAI Press, Inc.

Azar, B. (1999a, March). "Decade of Behavior" moves forward. *APA Monitor,* p. 16.

Azar, B. (1999b, May). Decision researchers split, but prolific. *APA Monitor,* p. 14.

Azar, B. (2002, September). Searching for genes that explain our personalities. *Monitor on Psychology,* pp. 44–46.

Baars, B. J., & McGovern, K. (1994). Consciousness. In V. S. Ramachandran (Ed.), *Encyclopedia of human behavior* (Vol. 1, pp. 687–699). San Diego, CA: Academic Press.

Babkoff, H., Caspy, T., Mikulincer, M., & Sing, H. C. (1991). Monotonic and rhythmic influences: A challenge for sleep deprivation research. *Psychological Bulletin, 109,* 411–428.

Baddeley, A. D. (1986). *Working memory.* Oxford: Clarendon Press.

Baddeley, A. D. (1987). Amnesia. In R. L. Gregory (ed.), *The Oxford companion to the mind* (pp. 20–22). Oxford: Oxford University Press.

Baddeley, A. D. (1994). The magical number seven: Still magic after all these years? *Psychological Review, 101,* 353–356.

Baddeley, A. D. (2002). Is working memory still working? *European Psychologist, 7,* 85–97.

Baddeley, A. D., & Hitch, G. J. (1994). Developments in the concept of working memory. *Neuropsychology, 6*, 485–493.

Badr, L. K., & Abdallah, B. (2001). Physical attractiveness of premature infants affects outcome at discharge from NICU. *Infant Behavior and Development, 24*, 129–133.

Baer, L., Rauch, S. L., & Ballantine, T. (1995). Cingulotomy for intractable obsessive-compulsive disorder: Prospective long-term follow-up of 18 patients. *Archives of General Psychiatry, 52*, 384–392.

Bagemihl, B. (2000). *Biological exuberance: Animal homosexuality and natural diversity.* New York: St. Martin's Press.

Bahrick, H. P. (1984). Semantic memory in permastore: Fifty years of memory for Spanish learned in school. *Journal of Experimental Psychology: General, 113*, 1–31.

Bahrick, H. P., Bahrick, P. O., & Wittlinger, R. P. (1974, December). Those unforgettable high school days. *Psychology Today*, pp. 50–56.

Bailey, A., LeCouteur, A., Gottesman, I., Bolton, P., Simonoff, E., Yuzda, E., et al. (1995). Autism as a strongly genetic disorder: Evidence from a British twin study. *Psychological Medicine, 25*(1), 63–77.

Balaguer, A., & Markman, H. (1994). Mate selection. In V. S. Ramachandran (Ed.), *Encyclopedia of human behavior* (Vol. 3, pp. 127–135). San Diego, CA: Academic Press.

Baldwin, T. T., & Padgett, M. Y. (1993). Management development: A review and commentary. In C. L. Cooper & I. T. Robertson (Eds.), *International review of industrial and organizational psychology* (Vol. 8, pp. 35–85). London: Wiley.

Bales, R. F. (1951). *Interaction Process Analysis: A method for the study of small groups.* Reading, MA: Addison-Wesley.

Ball, J. D., Archer, R. P., & Imhof, E. A. (1994). Time requirements of psychological testing: A survey of practitioners. *Journal of Personality Assessment, 63*, 239–249.

Ballie, R. (2001). Teen drinking more dangerous than previously thought. *Monitor on Psychology, 32*, 12.

Balon, R. (2002). Emotional blunting, sexual dysfunction, and SSRIs. *International Journal of Neuropsychopharmacology, 5*, 415–416.

Bandura, A. (1977). *Social learning theory.* Englewood Cliffs, NJ: Prentice Hall.

Bandura, A. (1986). *Social foundations of thought and action: A social cognitive theory.* Englewood Cliffs, NJ: Prentice Hall.

Bandura, A. (1997). *Self-efficacy: The exercise of control.* New York: Freeman.

Bandura, A., Blanchard, E. B., & Ritter, B. (1969). Relative efficacy of desensitization and modeling approaches for inducing behavioral, affective, and attitudinal changes. *Journal of Personality and Social Psychology, 13*, 173–199.

Bandura, A., & Locke, E. A. (2003). Negative self-efficacy and goal effects revisited. *Journal of Applied Psychology, 8*, 87–99.

Banich, M. T. (1998). Integration of information between the cerebral hemispheres. *Current Directions in Psychological Science, 7*, 32–37.

Bar, M., & Biederman, I. (1998). Subliminal visual priming. *Psychological Science, 9*, 464–469.

Bar–On, R., & Parker, J. D. A. (Eds.) (2000). *The handbook of emotional intelligence: Theory, development, assessment, and application at home, school, and in the workplace.* San Francisco: Jossey–Bass.

Barbaree, H. E., & Seto, M. C. (1997). Pedophilia: Assessment and treatment. In D. R. Laws & W. T. O'Donohue (eds.), *Handbook of sexual deviance: Theory and application.* New York: Guilford.

Barber, B. L., & Eccles, J. E. (1992). Long-term influence of divorce and single parenting on adolescent family- and work-related values, behaviors and aspirations. *Psychological Bulletin, 111*, 108–126.

Barglow, P., Vaughn, B. E., & Molitor, N. (1987). Effects of maternal absence due to employment on the quality of infant-mother attachment in a low-risk sample. *Child Development, 58*, 945–954.

Barinaga, M. (2000a, March 3). Asilomar revisited: Lessons for today. *Science, 287*, 1584–1585.

Barker, S. L., Funk, S. C., & Houston, B. K. (1988). Psychological treatment versus nonspecific factors: A meta-analysis of conditions that engender comparable expectations for improvement. *Clinical Psychology Review, 8*, 579–594.

Barkley, R. A. (1990). *Hyperactive children: A handbook for diagnosis and treatment* (2nd ed.). New York: Guilford.

Barling, J., Weber, T., & Kelloway, E. K. (1996). Effects of transformational leadership training on attitudinal and financial outcomes: A field experiment. *Journal of Applied Psychology, 81* (6), 827–832.

Barnett, R. C., Brennan, R. T., & Marshall, N. L. (1994). Gender and the relationship between parent role quality and psychological distress: A study of men and women in dual-earner couples. *Journal of Family Issues, 15*, 229–252.

Barnett, R. C., & Rivers, C. (1998). *She works/he works: How two-income families are happy, healthy, and thriving.* Cambridge, MA: Harvard University Press.

Barnett, W. S. (1998). Long-term effects on cognitive development and school success. In W. S. Barnett & S. S. Boocock (Eds.), *Early care and education for children in poverty (pp. 11–44).* Albany, NY: State University of New York Press.

Baron, R. A., & Byrne, D. (1991). *Social psychology: Understanding human interaction* (6th ed.). Boston: Allyn & Bacon.

Baron, R. M., Graziano, W. G., & Stangor, C. (1991). Social psychology. Fort Worth: Holt, Rinehart & Winston.

Barrick, M. R., & Mount, M. K. (1991). The Big Five personality dimensions and job performance: A meta-analysis. *Personnel Psychology, 44*, 1–26.

Barrick M. R., Mount, M. K., & Judge, T. A. (2001). Personality and performance at the beginning of the next millennium: What do we know and where do we go? *International Juornal of Selection and Assessment, 9* (1–2), 9–30.

Barron, F. (1963). *Creativity and psychological health.* Princeton, NJ: Van Nostrand.

Bartlett, F. C. (1932). *Remembering: A study in experimental and social psychology.* New York: Macmillan.

Bartoshuk, L. M., & Beauchamp, G. K. (1994). Chemical senses. *Annual Review of Psychology, 45*, 419–449.

Baruch, F., & Barnett, R. (1986). Role quality, multiple role involvement, and psychological well-being in mid-life women. *Journal of Personality and Social Psychology, 51*, 578–585.

Bassetti, C., & Aldrich, M. S. (1996). Narcolepsy. *Neurological Clinics, 14*, 545–571.

Batson, C. D., & Powell, A. A. (2003). Altruism and prosocial behahavior. In T. Millon & M. J. Lerner (Eds.), *Handbook of psychology:*

Personality and social psychology (Vol. 5, pp. 463–484). New York: John Wiley & Sons, Inc.

Baum, A., Revenson, T. A., & Singer, J. E. (2001). *Handbook of health psychology.* Mahwah, NJ: Erlbaum.

Baumrind, D. (1985). Research using intentional deception. *American Psychologist, 40,* 165–174.

Beasley, M., Thompson, T., & Davidson, J. (2003). Resilience in response to life stress: The effects of coping style and cognitive hardiness. *Personality and Individual Differences, 34,* 77–95.

Beatty, S. E., & Hawkins, D. I. (1989). Subliminal stimulation: Some new data and interpretation. *Journal of Advertising, 18,* 4–8.

Bechara, A., Damasio, H., Tranel, D., & Damasio, A. R. (1997, February 28). Deciding advantageously before knowing the advantageous strategy. *Science, 275,* 1293–1295.

Beck, A. T. (1984). Cognition and therapy. *Archives of General Psychiatry, 41,* 1112–1114.

Beck, A. T. (2002). Cognitive models of depression. In R. L Leahy & T. E. Dowd (Eds.), *Clinical advances in cognitive psychotherapy: Theory and Application* (pp. 29–61). New York: Springer Publishing Co.

Beirne-Smith, M., Patton, J., & Ittenbach, R. (1994). *Mental retardation* (4th ed.). New York: Macmillan.

Bellack, A. S., Hersen, M., & Turner, S. M. (1976). Generalization effects of social skills training in chronic schizophrenics: An experimental analysis. *Behavior Research and Therapy, 14,* 391–398.

Bellman, S., Forster, N., Still, L., & Cooper, C. L. (2003). Gender differences in the use of social support as a moderator of occupational stress. *Stress and Health: Journal of the International Society for the Investigation of Stress, 19,* 45–58.

Belsky, J., Lang, M. E., & Rovine, M. (1985). Stability and change in marriage across the transition to parenthood: A second study. *Journal of Marriage and the Family, 97,* 855–865.

Belsky, J., & Rovine, M. (1988). Nonmaternal care in the first year of life and infant parent attachment security. *Child Development, 59,* 157–167.

Beniczky, S., Keri, S., Voeroes, E., Ungurean, A., Benedek, G., Janka, Z., & Vecsei, L. (2002). Complex hallucinations following occipital lobe damage. *European Journal of Neurology, 9,* 175–176.

Benjamin, L. T., Jr. (2000). The psychology laboratory at the turn of the 20th century. *American Psychologist, 55,* 318–321.

Bennett, D. A., & Knopman, D. S. (1994). Alzheimer's disease: A comprehensive approach to patient management. *Geriatrics, 49*(8), 20–26.

Bennis, W., Spreitzer, G. M., & Cummings, T. G. (Eds.) (2001). *The future of leadership: Today's top leadership thinkers speak to tomorrow's leaders.* San Francisco: Jossey–Bass.

Benson, E. (February, 2003). Intelligent intelligence testing. *Monitor on Psychology, 34,* 48–58.

Benson, H. (1975). *The relaxation response.* New York: William Morrow.

Berger, M. A. (1983). Studying enrollment decline (and other timely issues) via the case study. *Educational evaluation and policy analysis, 5* (3), 307–316.

Berger, R. J. (1969). The sleep and dream cycle. In A. Kales (ed.), *Sleep: Physiology and pathology.* Philadelphia: Lippincott.

Berings, M. G. M. C., Poell, R. F., & Simons, P. R-J. (2005). Conceptualizing on-the-job learning styles. *Human resource development review, 4* (4), 373–400.

Berkowitz, M. W., & Gibbs, J. C. (1983). Measuring the developmental features of moral discussion. *Merrill-Palmer Quarterly, 29,* 399–410.

Berlin, B., & Kay, P. (1969). *Basic color terms: Their universality and evolution.* Berkeley: University of California Press.

Bernardin, H. J., Cooke, D. K., & Villanova, P. (2000). Conscientiousness and Agreeableness as Predictors of Rating Leniency. *Journal of Applied Psychology, 85* (2), 232–234.

Bernhard, F., & Penton-Voak, I. (2002). The evolutionary psychology of facial attractiveness. *Current Directions in Psychological Science, 11,* 154–158.

Berscheid, E., & Reis, H. T. (1998). Attraction and close relationships. In D. Gilbert, S. T. Fiske, & G. Lindzey (Eds.) *Handbook of social psychology* (4th ed., Vol. 2, pp. 193–381). New York: Mc-Graw-Hill.

Bertenthal, B. I., Campos, J. J., & Kermoian, R. (1994). An epigenetic perspective on the development of self-produced locomotion and its consequences. *Current Directions in Psychological Science, 3,* 140–145.

Bertolini, M. (2001). Central masturbatory fantasy, fetish and transitional phenomenon. In M. Bertolini & A. Giannakoulas (Eds.), *Squiggles and spaces: Revisiting the work of D. W. Winnicott,* Vol. 1 (pp. 210–217). London: Whurr Publishers, Ltd.

Betancourt, H., & López, S. R. (1993). The study of culture, ethnicity, and race in American psychology. *American Psychologist, 48,* 629–637.

Bhawuk, D. P., & Brislin, R. W. (2000). Cross-cultural training: A review. *Applied Psychology: An International Review, 49,* (1), 162–191.

Biddle, S. (2000). Exercise, emotions, and mental health. In Y. Hanin (Ed.), *Emotions in sport* (pp. 267–291). Champaign, IL: Human Kinetics.

Birchler, G. R., & Fals-Stewart, W. S. (1994). Marital dysfunction. In V. S. Ramachandran (Ed.), *Encyclopedia of human behavior* (Vol. 3, pp. 103–113). San Diego: Academic Press.

Birkenhaeger, T. K., Pluijms, E. M., & Lucius, S. A. P. (2003). ECT response in delusional versus non-delusional depressed inpatients. *Journal of Affective Disorders, 74,* 191–195.

Birren, J. E. (1983). Aging in America: Role for psychology. *American Psychologist, 38,* 298– 299.

Birren, J. E., & Fisher, L. M. (1995). Aging and speed of behavior: Possible consequences for psychological functioning. *Annual Review of Psychology, 46,* 329–353.

Bjorklund, D. F. (2003). Evolutionary psychology from a developmental systems perspective: Comment on Lickliter and Honeycutt (2003). *Psychological Bulletin, 129,* 836–841.

Bjornson, C. R. R., Rietze, R. L., Reynolds, B. A., Magli, M. C., & Vescovi, A. L. (1999, January 22). Turning brain into blood: A hematopoietic fate adopted by adult neural stem cells in vivo. *Science, 283,* 534–537.

Blackmore, S. (1999). *The meme machine.* Oxford, UK: Oxford University Press.

Blagrove, M., & Akehurst, L. (2000). Effects of sleep loss on confidence-accuracy relationships for reasoning and eyewitness memory. *Journal of Experimental Psychology: Applied, 6,* 59–73.

Blagrove, M., & Akelhurst, L. (2001). Personality and the modulation of effects of sleep loss on mood and cognition. *Personality and Individual Differences, 30,* 819–828.

Blake, R. R., Helson, H., & Mouton, J. (1956). The generality of conformity behavior as a function of factual anchorage, difficulty of task and amount of social pressure. *Journal of Personality, 25,* 294–305.

Blanchard, E. B., Appelbaum, K. A., Radnitz, C. L., Morrill, B., Michultka, D., Kirsch, C., et al. (1990). A controlled evaluation of thermal biofeedback and thermal biofeedback combined with cognitive therapy in the treatment of vascular headache. *Journal of Consulting & Clinical Psychology, 58,* 216–224.

Blanck, D. C., Bellack, A. S., Rosnow, R. L., Rotheram-Borus, M. J., & Schooler, N. R. (1992). Scientific rewards and conflicts of ethical choices in human subjects research. *American Psychologist, 47,* 959–965.

Blass, T. (2002). Perpetrator behavior as destructive obedience: An evaluation of Stanley Milgram's perspective, the most influential social–psychological approach to the Holocaust. In L. S. Newman & R. Erber (Eds.), *Understanding genocide: The social psychology of the Holocaust* (pp. 91–109). London: Oxford University Press.

Blatt, S. J., Zuroff, D. C., Quinlan, D. M., & Pilkonis, P. (1996). Interpersonal factors in brief treatment of depression: Further analysis of the NIMH Treatment of Depression Collaborative Research Program. *Journal of Consulting and Clinical Psychology, 64,* 162–171.

Bleijenberg, G., Prins, J., & Bazelmans, E. (2003). Cognitive–behavioral therapies. In L. A. Jason & P. A. Fennell (Eds.), *Handbook of chronic fatigue syndrome* (pp. 493–526). New York: John Wiley & Sons, Inc.

Bliss, J. P., Scerbo, M. W., Schmidt, E. A., & Thompson, S. N. (2006). The efficacy of a medical virtual reality simulator for training phlebotomy. *Human factors, 48* (1), 72–84.

Bloom, L. (1970). *Language development: Form and function in emerging grammar.* Cambridge, MA: MIT Press.

Blouin, J. L., Dombroski, B. A., Nath, S. K., Lasseter, V. K., Wolyniec, P. S., Nestadt, G., Thornquist, M., Ullrich, G., McGrath, J., Kasch, L., Lamacz, M., Thomas, M. G., Gehrig, C., Radhakrishnan, U., Snyder, S. E., Balk, K. G., Neufeld, K., Swartz, K. L., DeMarchi, N., Papadimitriou, G. N., Dikeos, D. G., Stefanis, C. N., Chakravarti, A., Childs, B., & Pulver, A. E. (1998). Schizophrenia susceptibility loci on chromosomes 13q32 and 8p21. *Nature Genetics, 20,* 70–73.

Blum, J. M. (1979). *Pseudoscience and mental ability: The origins and fallacies of the IQ controversy.* New York: Monthly Review Press.

Blundell, J. E., & Halford, J. C. G. (1998). Serotonin and appetite regulation: Implications for the pharmacological treatment of obesity. *CNS Drugs, 9,* 473–495.

Bohart, A. C., & Greening, T. (2001). Humanistic psychology and positive psychology. *American Psychologist, 56,* 81–82.

Bonanno, G. A. (2004). Loss, trauma, and human resilience: Have we underestimated the human capacity to thrive after extremely aversive events? *American Psychologist, 59,* 20–28.

Bonanno, G. A., & Kaltman, S. (1999). Toward an integrative perspective on bereavement. *Psychological Bulletin, 125,* 760–776.

Boniecki, K., & Moore, S. (2003). Breaking the silence: Using a token economy to reinforce classroom participation. *Teaching of Psychology, 30,* 224–227.

Boomsma, D. I., Koopmans, J. R., Van Doornen, L. J. P., & Orlebeke, J. M. (1994). Genetic and social influences on starting to smoke: A study of Dutch adolescent twins and their parents. *Addiction, 89,* 219–226.

Booth-Kewley, S., & Friedman, H. S. (1987). Psychological predictors of heart disease: A quantitative review. *Psychological Bulletin, 101,* 343–362.

Borkovec, T. D., & Costello, E. (1993). Efficacy of applied relaxation and cognitive-behavioral therapy in the treatment of generalized anxiety disorder. *Journal of Consulting and Clinical Psychology, 61,* 611–619.

Borman, W. C., Ilgen, D. R., & Klimoski, R. J. (2003). *Industrial and organizational psychology.* New York: Wiley.

Bornstein, R. F., & Masling, J. M. (Eds.). (1998). Empirical studies of the therapeutic hour. Empirical studies of psychoanalytic theories (Vol. 8). Washington, DC: American Psychological Association.

Bosworth, R. G., & Dobkins, K. R. (1999). Left-hemisphere dominance for motion processing in deaf signers. *Psychological Science, 10,* 256–262.

Bornstein, R. F. (1989). Exposure and affect: Overview and meta-analysis of research, 1968–1987. *Psychological Reports, 106,* 265–289.

Botwin, M. D., & Buss, D. M. (1989). The structure of act report data: Is the five factor model of personality recaptured? *Journal of Personality and Social Psychology, 56,* 988–1001.

Bouchard, C., Tremblay, A., Despres, J. P., Nadeau, A., Lupien, P. J., Theriault, G., et al. (1990). The response to long-term overfeeding in identical twins. *New England Journal of Medicine, 322,* 1477–1482.

Bouchard, T. J., Jr. (1984). Twins reared together and apart: What they tell us about human diversity. In S. W. Fox (Ed.), *Individuality and determinism* (pp. 147–178). New York: Plenum.

Bourin, M. (2003). Use of paroxetine for the treatment of depression and anxiety disorders in the elderly: A review. *Human Psychopharmacology, 18,* 185–190.

Bourne, L. E., Dominowski, R. L., Loftus, E. F., & Healy, A. F. (1986). *Cognitive process* (2nd ed.). Englewood Cliffs, NJ: Prentice Hall.

Bowden, E. M., & Beeman, M. J. (1998). Getting the right idea: Semantic activation in the right hemisphere may help solve insight problems. *Psychological Science, 9,* 435–440.

Bowden, E. M., & Jung-Beeman, M. (2003). Aha! Insight experience correlates with solution activation in the right hemisphere. *Psychonomic Bulletin and Review, 10,* 730–737.

Bower, B. (2003, April 19). Words get in the way: Talk is cheap, but it can tax your memory. *Science News, 163,* 250–251.

Bower, G. H., & Mann, T. (1992). Improving recall by recoding interfering material at the time of recall. *Journal of Experimental Psychology: Learning, Memory, and Cognition, 18,* 1310–1320.

Brainerd, C. J., & Reyna, V. F. (1998). When things that were never experienced are easier to "remember" than things that were. *Psychological Science, 9,* 484–489.

Braun, A. R., Balkin, T. J., Wesensten, N. J., Gwadry, F., Varga, M., Baldwin, P., et al. (1998, January 2). Dissociated pattern of activity in visual cortices and their projections during human rapid eye movement sleep. *Science, 279,* 91–95.

Bredemeier, B., & Shields, D. (1985, October). Values and violence in sports today. *Psychology Today*, pp. 23–32.

Brehm, S. S. (2002). *Intimate relationships* (3d ed.). New York: McGraw-Hill.

Bremner, J. D., & Marmar, C. R. (Eds.). (1998). *Trauma, memory and dissociation*. Washington, DC: American Psychiatric Press.

Brenner, M. H. (1973). *Mental illness and the economy*. Cambridge, MA: Harvard University Press.

Brenner, M. H. (1979). Influence of the social environment on psychopathology: The historic perspective. In J. E. Barrett (ed.), *Stress and mental disorder*. New York: Raven Press.

Breslau, N., Davis, G. C., & Andreski, P. (1995). Risk factors for PTSD-related traumatic events: A prospective analysis. *American Journal of Psychiatry, 152*, 529–535.

Brewer, J. B., Zhao, Z., Desmond, J. E., Glover, G. H., & Gabriel, J. D. E. (1998, August 21). Making memories: Brain activity that predicts how well visual experience will be remembered. *Science, 281*, 1185–1187.

Brewin, C. R. (1996). Theoretical foundations of cognitive-behavior therapy for anxiety and depression. *Annual Review of Psychology, 47*, 33–57.

Brinkley, A. (1999). *American history: A survey* (10th ed.). New York: McGraw Hill.

Brislin, R. W., Cushner, K., Cherries, C., & Yong, M. (1986). Intercultural interactions: A practical guide. Beverly Hills, CA: Sage.

Brobert, A. G., Wessels, H., Lamb, M. E., & Hwang, C. P. (1997). Effects of day care on the development of cognitive abilities in 8-year-olds: A longitudinal study. *Developmental Psychology, 33*, 62–69.

Bronfenbrenner, U. (1986). Ecology of the family as a context for human development: Research perspectives. *Developmental Psychology, 22*, 723–742.

Brooks, D. C., Bowker, J. L., Anderson, J. E., & Palmatier, M. I. (2003). Impact of brief or extended extinction of a taste aversion on inhibitory associations: Evidence from summation, retardation and preference tests. *Learning and Behavior, 31*, 69–84.

Brooks-Gunn, J. (1993). *Adolescence*. Paper presented at the meeting of the Society for Research in Child Development, Kansas City, MO.

Brooks-Gunn, J., & Lewis, M. (1984). The development of early visual self-recognition. *Developmental Review, 4*, 215–239.

Brosnan, S. F. (2003). Monkeys reject unequal pay. *Nature, 425* (6955), 297–299.

Brown, B., & Grotberg, J. J. (1981). Head Start: A successful experiment. *Courrier*. Paris: International Children's Centre.

Brown, N. R., & Schopflocher, D. (1998). Event clusters: An organization of personal events in autobiographical memory. *Psychological Science, 9*, 470–475.

Brown, S. P. (1996). A meta-analysis and review of organizational research in job involvement. *Psychological Bulletin, 120*, (2), 235–255.

Bruder, G. E., Stewart, M. W., Mercier, M. A., Agosti, V., Leite, P., Donovan, S., et al. (1997). Outcome of cognitive-behavioral therapy for depression: Relation to hemispheric dominance for verbal processing. *Journal of Abnormal Psychology, 106*, 138–144.

Brunner, H. G., Nelen, M., Breakefield, X. O., Ropers, H. H., & Van Oost, B. A. (1993a, October 22). Abnormal behavior associated with a point mutation in the structural gene for monoamine oxidase A. *Science, 262*, 578–580.

Bushman, B. J., Baumeister, R. F., & Stack, A. D. (1999). Catharsis, aggression, and persuasive influence: Self-fulfilling or self-defeating prophecies? *Journal of Personality & Social Psychology, 76*, 367–376.

Buist, C. M. (2002). Reducing essential hypertension in the elderly using biofeedback assisted self-regulatory training. *Dissertation Abstracts International: Section B: The Sciences and Engineering, 63*, 516.

Buss, D. M., & Shackelford, T. K. (1997). Human aggression in evolutionary perspective. *Clinical Psychology Review, 17*, 605–619.

Bulik, C. M., Sullivan, P. F., & Kendler, K. S. (2003). Genetic and environmental contributions to obesity and binge eating. *International Journal of Eating Disorders, 33*, 293–298.

Bursik, K. (1998). Moving beyond gender differences: Gender role comparisons of manifest dream content. *Sex Roles, 38*, 203–214.

Burt, M. R., Aron, L. Y., Douglas, T., Valente, J., Lee, E., & Iwen, B. (1999). Homelessness: Programs and the people they serve. Retrieved September 18, 2003, from *http://www.urban.org/UploadedPDF/homelessness.pdf*.

Buss, D. M. (1985). Human mate selection. *American Scientist, 73*, 47–51.

Buss, D. M. (2000a). The evolution of happiness. *American Psychologist, 55*, 15–23.

Buss, D. M. (2000b). *The dangerous passion: Why jealousy is as necessary as love and sex*. New York: Free Press.

Buss, D. M., & Malamuth, N. M. (Eds.). (1996). *Sex, power, conflict: Evolutionary and feminist perspectives*. New York: Oxford University Press.

Buss, D. M., & Reeve, H. K. (2003). Evolutionary psychology and developmental dynamics: Comment on Lickliter and Honeycutt (2003). *Psychological Bulletin, 129*, 848–853.

Butler, R. N., & Lewis, M. I. (1982). *Aging and mental health: Positive psychological and biomedical approaches*. St. Louis, MO: Mosby.

Byne, W. (1994). The biological evidence challenged. *Scientific American, 270*(5), 50–55.

Byrne, R. W. (2002). *Evolutionary psychology and primate cognition*. Cambridge, Mass: MIT Press.

Cabeza, R., & Nyberg, L. (2000). Imaging cognition II: An empirical review of 275 PET and fMRI studies. *Journal of Cognitive Neuroscience, 12*, 1–47.

Cacioppo, J. T., Hawkley, L. C., Berntson, G. G., Ernst, J. M., Gibbs, A. C., Strickgold, R., & Hobson, A. (2002). Do lonely days invade the nights? Potential social modulation of sleep efficiency. *Psychological Science, 13*, 384–387.

Cahill, J., Barkham, M., Hardy, G., Rees, A., Shapiro, D. A., Stiles, W. B., & Macaskill, N. (2003). Outcomes of patients completing and not completing cognitive therapy for depression. *British Journal of Clinical Psychology, 42*, 133–143.

Cahill, L., & McGaugh, J. L. (1998). Mechanisms of emotional arousal and lasting declarative memory. *Trends in Neurosciences, 21*, 294–299.

Calhoun, L. G., & Tedeschi, R. G. (2001). Posttraumatic growth: The positive lessons of loss. In R. A. Neimeyer (Ed.), *Meaning recon-*

struction & the experience of loss (pp. 157–172). Washington, DC: American Psychological Association.

Callicott, J. H. (2003). An expanded role for functional neuroimaging in schizophrenia in schizophrenia. *Current Opinions in Neurobiology, 13,* 256–260.

Campion, M. A., Purcell, E., & Brown, B. K. (1988). Structured interviewing: Raising the psychometric properties of the employment interview. *Personnel psychology, 41* (1), 25–42.

Cannon, W. B. (1929). *Bodily changes in pain, hunger, fear, and rage,* rev.ed. New York: Appleton-Century.

Caporael, L. R. (2001). Evolutionary psychology: Toward a unifying theory and a hybrid science. *Annual Review of Psychology, 52,* 607–628.

Capron, C., & Duyme, M. (1989). Assessment of effects of socioeconomic status on IQ in a full cross-fostering study. *Nature (London), 340,* 552–554.

Cardemil, E. V., & Battle, C. L. (2003). Guess who's coming to therapy? Getting comfortable with conversations about race and ethnicity in psychotherapy. *Professional Psychology: Research and Practice, 34,* 278–286.

Carello, C., & Turvey, M. T. (2003). Physics and psychology of the muscle sense. *Current Directions in Psychological Science, 13(1),* 25–28.

Carlson, N. R. (2000). *Physiology of behavior* (7th ed.). Boston: Allyn & Bacon.

Carmona, F. J., Sanz, L. J., & Marin, D. (2002). Type-A behaviour pattern and coronary heart disease. *Psiquis: Revista de Psiquiatria, Psicologia Medica y Psicosomatica, 23,* 22–30.

Carpenter, S. (2001). Research confirms the virtue of 'sleeping on it'. *Monitor on Psychology, 32,* 49–51.

Carr, M., Borkowski, J. G., & Maxwell, S. E. (1991). Motivational components of underachievement. *Developmental Psychology, 27,* 108–118.

Carskadon, M. A. (2002). Risks of driving while sleepy in adolescents and young adults. In M. A. Carskadon (Ed.), *Adolescent sleep patterns: Biological, social, and psychological influences* (pp. 148–158). New York: Cambridge University Press.

Carskadon, M. A., & Dement, W. C. (1982). Nocturnal determinants of daytime sleepiness. *Sleep, 5* (Suppl. 2), 73–81.

Carson, R. C., & Butcher, J. N. (1992). *Abnormal psychology and modern life.* New York: HarperCollins.

Carstensen, L. (1995). Evidence for a life-span theory of socioemotional selectivity. *Current Directions in Psychological Science, 4,* 151–156.

Carter, T., Hardy, C. A., & Hardy, J. C. (2001). Latin vocabulary acquisition: An experiment using information processing techniques of chunking and imagery. *Journal of Instructional Psychology, 28,* 225–228.

Cartwright, J. (2000). *Teaching evolutionary psychology.* Cambridge, MA: MIT Press.

Cartwright, R. D. (1996). Dreams and adaptation to divorce. In D. Barrett (Ed.), *Trauma and dreams* (pp. 179–185). Cambridge, MA: Harvard University Press.

Casas, J. M. (1995). Counseling and psychotherapy with racial/ethnic minority groups in theory and practice. In B. Bongar & L. E. Beutler

(eds.), *Comprehensive handbook of psychotherapy* (pp. 311–335). New York: Oxford University Press.

Cascio, W. F. (1999). Virtual workplaces: Implications for organizational behavior. In C. L. Cooper & D.M. Rousseau (Eds.), *Trends in organizational behavior: The virtual organization* (Vol. 6, pp. 1–14). New York: Wiley.

Caspi, A., & Elder, G. H., Jr. (1986). Life satisfaction in old age: Linking social psychology and history. *Journal of Psychology and Aging, 1,* 18–26.

Cattell, R. B. (1965). *The scientific analysis of personality.* Baltimore: Penguin.

Cattell, R. B., & Kline, P. (1977). *The specific analysis of personality and motivation.* New York: Academic Press.

Cavanaugh, J. C. (1990). *Adult development and aging.* Belmont, CA: Wadsworth.

Ceci, S. J., & Williams, W. M. (1997). Schooling, intelligence, and income. *American Psychologist, 52,* 1051–1058.

Centers for Disease Control and Prevention. (1999). Suicide deaths and rates per 100,000 [On-line]. Available: *http://www.cdc.gov/ncipc/data/us9794/suic.htm.*

Chance, S. A., Esiri, M. M., & Timothy, J. C. (2003). Ventricular enlargement in schizophrenia: A primary change in the temporal lobe? *Schizophrenia Research, 62,* 123–131.

Chang, E. C., & Sanna, L. J. (2003). Experience of life hassles and psychological adjustment among adolescents: Does it make a difference if one is optimistic or pessimistic? *Personality and Individual Differences, 34,* 867–879.

Chassin, L., Pitts, S. C., DeLucia, C., & Todd, M. (1999). A longitudinal study of children of alcoholics: Predicting young adult substance use disorders, anxiety, and depression. *Journal of Abnormal Psychology, 108,* 106–119.

Chekroun, P., & Brauer, M. (2002). The bystander effect and social control behavior: the effect of the presence of others on people's reactions to norm violations. *European Journal of Social Psychology, 32,* 853–866.

Chen, P., Goldberg, D. E., Kolb, B., Lanser, M., & Benowitz, L. I. (2002). Inosine induces axonal rewiring and improves behavioral outcome after stroke. *Proceedings of the National Academy of Sciences USA, 99,* 9031–9036.

Cheour, M., Ceponiene, R., Lehtokoski, A., Luuk, A., Allik, J., Alho, K., & Näätänen, R. (1998). Development of language-specific phoneme representations in the infant brain. *Nature Neuroscience, 1,* 351–353.

Cherlin, A. (1992). *Marriage, divorce, remarriage.* Boston, MA: Harvard University Press.

Cherniss, C., & Goleman, D. (2001). *The emotionally intelligent workplace.* San Francisco: Jossey–Bass.

Cherry, C. (1966). *On human communication: A review, a survey, and a criticism* (2nd ed.). Cambridge, MA: MIT Press.

Chervin, R. D., Killion, J. E., Archbold, K. H., & Ruzicka, D. L. (2003). Conduct problems and symptoms of sleep disorders in children. *Journal of the American Academy of Child and Adolescent Psychiatry, 42,* 201–208.

Chester, J. A., Lumeng, L., Li, T. K., & Grahame, N. J. (2003). High and low alcohol preferring mice show differences in conditioned taste aversion to alcohol. *Alcoholism: Clinical and Experimental Research, 27*, 12–18.

Choi, W. S., Pierce, J. P., Gilpin, E. A., Farkas, A. J., & Berry, C. C. (1997). Which adolescent experimenters progress to established smoking in the United States. *American Journal of Preventive Medicine, 13*, 385–391.

Chomsky, N. (1957). *Syntactic structures*. The Hague: Mouton.

Chomsky, N., Place, U., & Schoneberger, T. (2000). The Chomsky–Place correspondence 1993–1994. *Analysis of Verbal Behavior, 17*, 7–38.

Chrobot-Mason, D., & Quinones, M. A. (2002). Training for a diverse workplace. In K. Kraiger (Ed.), *Creating, implementing, and managing effective training and development* (pp. 117–159). San Francisco: Jossey-Bass.

Chua, S. C., Chung, W. K., Wu-Peng, X. S., Zhang, Y., Liu, S. M., Tartaglia, L., & Leibel, R. L. (1996, February 16). Phenotypes of mouse diabetes and rat fatty due to mutations in OB (leptin) receptor. *Science, 271*, 994–996.

Cialdini, R. B. (1995). Principles and techniques of social influence. In A. Tesser (Ed.), *Advanced social psychology* (pp. 257–282). New York: McGraw-Hill.

Cialdini, R. B., & Trost, M. (1998). Social influence: Social norms, conformity, and compliance. In D. Gilbert, S. T. Fiske, & G. Lindzey (Eds.), *Handbook of social psychology* (4th ed., Vol. 2, pp. 151–192). Boston: McGraw-Hill.

Cicchetti, D., & Toth, S. L. (1998). The development of depression in children and adolescents. *American Psychologist, 53*, 221–241.

Civil Rights Act of 1964 (42 U.S.C. 88–352)

Civil Rights Act of 1991 (42 U.S.C. 102–166)

Clark, G. M. (1998). Research advances for cochlear implants. *Auris Nasus Larynx, 25*, 73–87.

Clark, R. D., & Word, L. E. (1974). Where is the apathetic bystander? Situational characteristics of the emergency. *Journal of Personality and Social Psychology, 29*, 279–287.

Clarkson, P. (1996). *To act or not to act: That is the question*. London: Whurr.

Clausen, J. A. (1975). The social meaning of differential physical and sexual maturation. In S. E. Dragastin & G. H. Elder, Jr. (Eds.), *Adolescence in the life cycle: Psychological change and social context* (pp. 25–47). New York: Wiley.

Clauss, E., & Caroline, C. C. (2003). Promoting ecologic health resilience for minority youth: Enhancing health care access through the school health center. *Psychology in the Schools, 40*, 265–278.

Clay, R. A. (1999, January). "Lean production" may also be a lean toward injuries. *APA Monitor*, p.26.

Clay, R. A. (2002, October). Advertising as science. *Monitor on Psychology, 33*, 38–41.

Clayton, A. H., McGarvey, E. L., Abouesch, A. L., & Pinkerton, R. C. (2001). Substitution of an SSRI with bupropion sustained release following SSRI-induced sexual dysfunction. *Journal of Clinical Psychiatry, 62*, 185–190.

Clifford, J. P. (1994). Job analysis: Why do it, and how should it be done? *Public Personnel Management, 23* (2), 321–338.

Cloninger, S. C. (1993). *Theories of personality. Understanding persons.* Englewood Cliffs, NJ: Prentice Hall.

Cocchini, G., Logie, R. H., Sala, S. D., MacPherson, S. E., & Baddeley, A. D. (2002). Concurrent performance of two memory tasks: Evidence for domain-specific working memory systems. *Memory and Cognition, 30*, 1086–1095.

Cohen, A., & Raffal, R. D. (1991). Attention and feature integration: Illusory conjunctions in a patient with a parietal lobe lesion. *Psychological Science, 2*, 106–110.

Cohen, L. J., & Galynker, I. I. (2002). Clinical features of pedophilia and implications for treatment. *Journal of Psychiatric Practice, 8*, 276–289.

Cohen, S. (1996). Psychological stress, immunity, and upper respiratory infections. *Current Directions in Psychological Science, 5*(3), 86–88.

Cohen, S. G., Ledford, G. E., & Spreitzer, G. M. (1996). A predictive model of self-managing work team effectiveness. *Human relations, 49* (5), 643–676.

Cohen, S., Doyle, W. J., Turner, R. B., Alper, C. M., & Skoner, D. P. (2003a). Emotional styles and susceptibility to the common cold. *Psychosomatic Medicine, 65*, 652–657.

Cohen, S., Doyle, W. J., Turner, R., Alper, C. M., & Skoner, D. P. (2003b). Sociability and susceptibility to the common cold. *Psychological Science, 14*, 389–396.

Cohen, S., Frank, E., Doyle, W. J., Skoner, D. P., Rabin, B. S., & Gwaltney, J. M., Jr. (1998). Types of stressors that increase susceptibility to the common cold in healthy adults. *Health Psychology, 17*, 214–223.

Cohen, S., & Herbert, T. B. (1996). Health psychology: Psychological factors and physical disease from the perspective of human psychoneuroimmunology. *Annual Review of Psychology, 47*, 113–142.

Cohen, S., Tyrrell, D. A., & Smith, A. P. (1991). Psychological stress and susceptibility to the common cold. *New England Journal of Medicine, 325* (9), 606–612.

Cohen, S., & Williamson, G. M. (1988). Stress and infectious disease in humans. *Psychological Bulletin, 109*, 5–24.

Coleman, J., Glaros, A., & Morris, C. G. (1987). *Contemporary psychology and effective behavior* (6th ed.). Glenview, IL: Scott, Foresman.

Collaer, M. L., & Hines, M. (1995). Human behavioral sex differences: A role for gonadal hormones during early development? *Psychological Bulletin, 118*, 55–107.

Collins, N. L., & Miller, L. C. (1994). Self-disclosure and liking: A meta-analytic review. *Psychological Bulletin, 116*, 457–475.

Collins, R. C. (1993). Head Start: Steps toward a two-generation program strategy. *Young Children, 48*(2), 25–73.

Collins, W. A., Maccoby, E. E., Steinberg, L., Hetherington, E. M., & Bornstein, M. H. (2000). Contemporary research on parenting: The case for nature and nurture. *American Psychologist, 55*, 218–232.

Collins, W. A., Maccoby, E. E., Steinberg, L., Hetherington, E. M., & Bornstein, M. H. (2001). Toward nature WITH nurture. *American Psychologist, 56*, 171–172.

Colquitt, J. A., Conlon, D. E., Wesson, M. J., Porter, C. O., & Ng, K. Y. (2001). Justice at the millennium: A meta-analytic review of 25 years of organizational justice research. *Journal of Applied Psychology, 86* (3), 425–445.

Comaty, J. E., Stasio, M., & Advokat, C. (2001). Analysis of outcome variables of a token economy system in a state psychiatric hospital:

A program evaluation. *Research in Developmental Disabilities, 22,* 233–253.

Compas, B. E., Hinden, B. R., & Gerhardt, C. A. (1995). Adolescent development: Pathways and processes of risk and resilience. *Annual Review of Psychology, 46,* 265–293.

Conger, J. J., & Petersen, A. C. (1991). *Adolescence and youth* (4th ed.). New York: HarperCollins.

Conroy, J. W. (1996). The small ICF/MR program: Dimensions of quality and cost. *Mental Retardation, 34,* 13–26.

Construction equipment. (2006). Train operators with a PC-based simulator. *Construction equipment, 10* (3), 23.

Conte, J. J., & Jacobs, R. R. (2003). Validity evidence linking polychronicity and Big Five personality dimensions to absence, lateness, and supervisory performance ratings. *Human Performance, 16,* 107–129.

Contrada, F. (2004, August 4). Parents recount tale of Marine's suicide. *The Republican.* Available online at *www.masslive.com/chico peeholyoke/republican/index.ssf?/base/news-5/1091621886289650.xml*

Conway, A. R. A., Cowan, N., & Bunting, M. F. (2001). The cocktail party phenomenon revisited: The importance of working memory capacity. *Psychonomic Bulletin and Review, 8,* 331–335.

Conway, M., & Dube, L. (2002). Humor in persuasion on threatening topics: Effectiveness is a function of audience sex role orientation. *Personality and Social Psychology Bulletin, 28,* 863–873.

Cook, E. H., Courchesne, R. Y., Cox, N. J., Lord, C., Gonen, D., Guter, S. J., et al. (1998). Linkage-disequilibrium mapping of autistic disorder, with 15q1113 markers. *American Journal of Human Genetics, 62,* 1077–1083.

Cook, K. S., & Rice, E. (2003). Social exchange theory. In J. Delamater (Ed.), *Handbook of social psychology. Handbooks of sociology and social research,* (pp. 53–76). New York: Kluwer Academic/Plenum Publishers.

Cooper, J., & Croyle, R. T. (1984). Attitudes and attitude change. *Annual Review of Psychology, 35,* 395–426.

Cooper, M. L., Frone, M. R., Russell, M., & Mudar, P. (1995). Drinking to regulate positive and negative emotions: A motivational model of alcohol use. *Journal of Personality & Social Psychology, 69,* 990–1005.

Corder, B., Saunders, A. M., Strittmatter, W. J., Schmechel, D. E., Gaskell, P. C., & Small, D. E. (1993, August 13). Gene dose of apolipoprotein E type 4 allele and the risk of Alzheimer's disease in late onset families. *Science, 261,* 921–923.

Coren, A. (2001). *Short-term psychotherapy: A psychodynamic approach.* New York: Palgrave.

Cornelius, R. R. (1996). *The science of emotion: Research and tradition in the psychology of emotions.* Upper Saddle River, NJ: Prentice Hall.

Cosmides, L., Tooby, J., & Barkow, J. (1992). *The adapted mind: Evolutionary psychology and the generation of culture.* New York: Oxford.

Costa, A., Peppe, A., Dell'Agnello, G., Carlesimo, G., Murri, L., Bonuccelli, U., & Caltagirone, C. (2003). Dopaminergic modulation of visual-spatial working memory in Parkinson's disease. *Dementia and Geriatric Cognitive Disorders, 15,* 55–66.

Costa, P. T., & McCrae, R. R. (1995). Domains and facets: Hierarchical personality assessment using the Revised NEO Personality Inventory. *Journal of Personality Assessment, 64,* 21–50.

Costa, P. T., Jr., & McCrae, R. R. (1992). *Revised NEO Personality Inventory (NEO-PI-R) and NEO Five-Factor Inventory (NEO-FFI) professional manual.* Odessa, FL: Psychological Assessment Resources, Inc.

Cotton, J. L. (1993). *Employee involvement: Methods for improving performance and work attitudes.* Newbury Park, CA: Sage.

Council, J. R. (1993). Context effects in personality research. *Current Directions, 2,* 31–34.

Cousins, N. (1981). *Anatomy of an illness as perceived by the patient.* New York: Bantam.

Cowan, N. (1988). Evolving conceptions of memory storage, selective attention, and their mutual constraints within the human information-processing system. *Psychological Bulletin, 104,* 163–191.

Craig, A. D., & Bushnell, M. C. (1994, July 8). The thermal grill illusion: Unmasking the burn of cold pain. *Science, 265,* 252–255.

Craig, C. D. (2002). Ripples: Group work in different settings. *Social Work with Groups, 25,* 94–97.

Craighead, L. (1990). Supervised exercise in behavioral treatment for moderate obesity. *Behavior Therapy, 20,* 49–59.

Craik, F. I. M. (2002). Levels of processing: Past, present . . . and future? *Memory, 10,* 305–318.

Craik, F. I. M., & Lockhart, R. S. (1972). Levels of processing: A framework for memory research. *Journal of Verbal Learning and Verbal Behavior, 11,* 671–684.

Craik, F. I. M., Moroz, T. M., Moscovitch, M., Stuss, D. T., Winocur, G., Tulving, E., et al. (1999). In search of the self: A positron emission tomography study. *Psychological Science, 10,* 26–34.

Cramer, P. (2000). Defense mechanisms in psychology today: Further processes for adaptation. *American Psychologist, 55,* 637–646.

Crandall, C. S., & Eshleman, A. (2003). A justification-suppression model of the expression and experience of prejudice. *Psychological Bulletin, 129,* 414–446.

Crawford, C. B. (2003). A prolegomenon for a viable evolutionary psychology—the myth and the reality: Comment on Lickliter and Honeycutt (2003). *Psychological Bulletin, 129,* 854–857.

Crawford, N. (2002, June). Employees' longer working hours linked to family conflict, stress-related health problems. *Monitor on Psychology,* p. 17.

Crick, F., & Mitchison, G. (1995). REM sleep and neural nets. *Behavioural Brain Research [Special Issue: The function of sleep], 69,* 147–155.

Cronan, T. A., Walen, H. R., & Cruz, S. G. (1994). The effects of community-based literacy training on Head Start parents. *Journal of Community Psychology, 22,* 248–258.

Cronbach, L. J. (1990). *Essentials of psychological testing* (5th ed.). New York: HarperCollins.

Crosby, F. J., & VanDeVeer, C. (Eds.) (2000). *Sex, race, & merit.* Ann Arbor: University of Michigan Press.

Crutchfield, R. A. (1955). Conformity and character. *American Psychologist, 10,* 191–198.

Crystal, D. S., Chen, C., Fuligini, A. J., Stevenson, H., Hus, C., Ko, H., Kitamura, S., & Kimura, S. (1994). Psychological maladjustments and academic achievement: A cross-cultural study of Japanese, Chinese, and American high school students. *Child Development, 65,* 738–753.

Csikszentmihalyi, M. (1990). *Flow: The Psychology of Optimal Experience.* New York: Harper Collins.

Csikszentmihalyi, M. (1996). *Creativity.* New York: Harper Collins.

Csikszentmihalyi, M. (1999). Implications of a systems perspective for the study of creativity. In R. J. Sternaberg (Ed.), *Handbook of Creativity.* New York: Cambridge University Press.

Csikszentmihalyi, M., Rathunde, K., & Whalen, S. (1993). *Talented teenagers: The roots of success and failure.* New York: Cambridge University Press.

Cunningham, J. E. C. (2003). Neuropsychology, genetic liability, and psychotic symptoms in those at high risk of schizophrenia. *Journal of Abnormal Psychology, 112,* 38–48.

Curle, C. E., & Williams, C. (1996). Post-traumatic stress reactions in children: Gender differences in the incidence of trauma reactions at two years and examination of factors influencing adjustment. *British Journal of Clinical Psychology, 35,* 297–309.

Cutler, W. B., Friedmann, E., & McCoy, N. L. (1998). Pheromonal influences on sociosexual behavior in men. *Archives of Sexual Behavior, 27,* 1–13.

Czeisler, C. A., Duffy, J. F., & Shanahan, T. L. (1999, June 25). Stability, precision, and near-24-hour period of human circadian pacemaker. *Science, 284,* 2177–2181.

Dahl, E. K. (1996). The concept of penis envy revisited: A child analyst listens to adult women. *Psychoanalytic Study of the Child, 51,* 303–325.

Dahlström, W. G. (1993). Tests: Small samples, large consequences. *American Psychologist, 48,* 393–399.

Dalbert, C. (2001). *Just world beliefs as a personal resource: Dealing with challenges and critical life events.* New York: Kluwer Academic/Plenum.

Daley, T. C., Whaley, S. E., Sigman, M. D., Espinosa, M. P., & Neumann, C. (2003). IQ on the rise: The Flynn Effect in rural Kenyan children. *Psychological Science, 14,* 215–219.

Damas, A. (2002). A factorial invariance analysis of intellectual abilities in children across different age and cultural groups using the Wechsler Intelligence Scale for Children. *Dissertation Abstracts International: Section B: The Sciences and Engineering, 62,* 4832.

Damasio, H., Grabowski, T. J., Tranel, D., Hichawa, R. D., & Damasio, A. R. (1996). A neural basis for lexical retrieval. *Nature, 380,* 499–505.

Danielle, D. M., Rose, R. J., Viken, R. J., & Kaprio, J. (2000). Pubertal timing and substance use: Associations between and within families across late adolescence. *Developmental Psychology, 36,* 180–189.

Dansereau, F., Graen, G., & Haga, W. J. (1975). A vertical dyad linkage approach to leadership within formal organzations: A longitudinal investigation of the role making process. *Organizational Behavior & Human Performance, 13* (1), 46–78.

Davidson, P. S. R., & Glisky, E. L. (2002). Is flashbulb memory a special instance of source memory? Evidence from older adults. *Memory, 10,* 99–111.

Davies, P. T., & Cummings, E. M. (1994). Marital conflict and child adjustment: An emotional security hypothesis. *Psychological Bulletin, 166,* 387–411.

Davies, M., Stankov, L., & Roberts, R. D. (1998). Emotional intelligence: In search of an elusive construct. *Journal of Personality and Social Psychology, 75,* 989–1015.

Davis, C. G., Wortman, C. B., Lehman, D. R., & Silver, R. C. (2000). Searching for meaning in loss: Are clinical assumptions correct? *Death Studies, 24,* 497–540.

Davis, M. H., & Stephan, W. G. (1980). Attributions for exam performance. *Journal of Applied Social Psychology, 10,* 235–248.

Dawes, R. M. (1994). *House of cards: The collapse of modern psychotherapy.* New York: Free Press.

Dawis, R. V. (2004). Job satisfaction. In J. C. Thomas (Ed), *Comprehensive handbood of psychological assessment* (Vol. 4, pp. 470–481). Hoboken, NJ: Wiley.

Dean, J. W., Jr., & Evans, J. R. (1994). *Total quality: Management, organization, and strategy.* St. Paul, MN: West.

DeAngelis, T. (2002, June). How do mind–body interventions affect breast cancer? *Monitor on Psychology,* 51–53.

Deaux, K., & Kite, M. (1993). Gender stereotypes. In F. L. Denmark & M. A. Paludi (eds.), *Psychology of women: A handbook of issues and theories* (pp. 107–139). Westport, CT: Greenwood.

Deci, E. L., Koestner, R., & Ryan, R. M. (1999). A meta-analytic review of experiments examining the effects of extrinsic rewards on intrinsic motivation. *Psychological Bulletin, 125,* 627–668.

Dehaene, S., Spelke, E., Stanescu, R., Pinel, P., & Tsivkin, S. (1999, May 7). Sources of mathematical thinking: Behavioral and brain-imaging evidence. *Science, 284,* 970–974.

Deikman, A. J. (1973). Deautomatization and the mystic experience. In R. W. Ornstein (ed.), *The nature of human consciousness.* San Francisco: Freeman.

DeKay, W. T., & Buss, D. M. (1992). Human nature, individual differences and the importance of context: Perspectives from evolutionary psychology. *Current Directions in Psychological Science, 1,* 184–189.

de-l'Etoile, S. K. (2002). The effect of musical mood induction procedure on mood state-dependent word retrieval. *Journal of Music Therapy, 39,* 145–160.

DePaulo, B. M., & Pfeifer, R. L. (1986). On-the-job experience and skill detecting deception. *Journal of Applied Social Psychology, 16,* 249–267.

D'Esposito, M., Zarahn, E., & Aguirre, G. K. (1999). Event-related functional MRI: Implications for cognitive psychology. *Psychological Bulletin, 125,* 155–164.

DeSteno, D., & Braverman, J. (2002). Emotion and persuasion: Thoughts on the role of emotional intelligence. In L. F. Barrett & P. Salovey, *The wisdom in feeling: Psychological processes in emotional intelligence* (pp. 191–210). New York: Guilford Press.

Devine, P. G. (1989). Stereotypes and prejudice: Their automatic and controlled components. *Journal of Personality & Social Psychology, 56,* 5–18.

Devine, P. G., Monteith, M. J., Zuwerink, J. R., & Elliot, A. J. (1991). Prejudice with and without compunction. *Journal of Personality & Social Psychology, 60,* 817–830.

Dhami, M. K. (2003). Psychological models of professional decision making. *Psychological Science, 14,* 175–180.

Diamond, J. (1994). Race without color. *Discover, 15,* 82–92.

Diaz, J. (1997). *How drugs influence behavior: Neuro-behavioral approach.* Upper Saddle River, NJ: Prentice Hall.

Dick, D. M., & Rose, R. J. (2002). Behavior genetics: What's new? What's next? *Current Directions in Psychological Science, 11,* 70–74.

Dienesch, R. M., & Liden, R. C. (1986). Leader-member exchange model of leadership: A critique and further development. *Academy of Management Review, 11* (3), 618–634.

Dieter, J., Field, T., Hernandez, R. M., Emory, E. K., & Redzepi, M. (2003). Stable preterm infants gain more weight and sleep less after five days of massage therapy. *Journal of Pediatric Psychology, 28,* 403–411.

DiFranza, J. R., & Lew, R. A. (1995). Effect of maternal cigarette smoking on pregnancy complications and sudden infant death syndrome. *Journal of Family Practice, 40,* 385–394.

DiGiovanna, A. G. (1994). *Human aging: Biological perspectives.* New York: McGraw-Hill.

Digman, J. M., & Takemoto-Chock, N. K. (1981). Factors in the natural language of personality: Re-analysis and comparison of six major studies. *Multivariate Behavioral Research, 16,* 149–170.

Dill, S. (1994, July). Baby's grunts may mean more than parents think. *American Weekend,* p.10C.

DiMatteo, M. R., & Friedman, H. S. (1982). *Social psychology and medicine.* Cambridge, MA: Oelgeschlager, Gunn, & Hain.

Dinsmore, W. W., Hodges, M., Hargreaves, C., Osterloh, I. H., Smith, M. D., & Rosen, R. C. (1999). Sildenafil citrate (Viagra) in erectile dysfunction: Near normalization in men with broad-spectrum erectile dysfunction compared with age-matched healthy control subjects. *Urology, 53,* 800–805.

Dion, K. K. (1972). Physical attractiveness and evaluations of children's transgressions. *Journal of Personality and Social Psychology, 24,* 285–290.

DiPietro, J. A., Hodgson, D. M., Costigan, K. A., & Johnson, T. R. (1996). Fetal antecedents of infant temperament. *Child Development, 67,* 2568–2583.

Domhoff, G. W. (1996). *Finding meaning in dreams: A quantitative approach.* New York: Plenum Press.

Domjan, M., & Purdy, J. E. (1995). Animal research in psychology: More than meets the eye of the general psychology student. *American Psychologist, 50,* 496–503.

Donnelly, C. L. (2003). Pharmacologic treatment approaches for children and adolescents with posttraumatic stress disorder. *Child and Adolescent Psychiatric Clinics of North America, 12,* 251–269.

Donovan, J. J. (2001). Work motivation. In N. Anderson, D. S. Ones, H. K. Sinangil, & C. Visvesvaran (Eds.), *Handbook of industrial, work, and organizational psychology* (Vol. 2, pp. 53–76). London: Sage.

Dorfman, W. I., & Leonard, S. (2001). The Minnesota Multiphasic Personality Inventory-2 (MMPI-2). In W. I. Dorfman & M. Hersen (Eds.), *Understanding psychological assessment: Perspectives on individual differences* (pp. 145–171). Dordrecht, Netherlands: Kluwer Academic Publishers.

Dougall, A. L., & Baum, A. (2004). Psychoneuroimmunology and trauma. In P. P. Schnurr & B. L. Green (Eds.), *Trauma and health: Physical health consequences of exposure to extreme stress.* (pp. 129–155). Washington, DC: American Psychological Association.

Dovidio, J. F., & Gaertner, S. I. (1999). Reducing prejudice: Combating intergroup biases. *Current Directions in Psychological Science, 8,* 101–105.

Doyle, R. (2000). By the numbers: Women and the professions. *Scientific American, 282*(4), 30–32

Du, L., Faludi, G., Palkovits, M., Demeter, E., Bakish, D., Lapierre, Y. D., et al. (1999). Frequency of long allele in serotonin transporter gene is increased in depressed suicide victims. *Biological Psychiatry, 46,* 196–201.

Dugas, M. J., Ladouceur, R., Leger, E., Freeston, M. H., Langolis, F., Provencher, M. D., & Boisvert, J. M. (2003). Group cognitive behavioral therapy for generalized anxiety disorder: Treatment outcome and long-term follow-up. *Journal of Consulting and Clinical Psychology, 71,* 821–825.

Duncan, J., Seitz, R. J., Kolodny, J., Bor, D., Herzog, H., Ahmed, A., et al. (2000, July 21). A neural basis for general intelligence. *Science, 285,* 457–460.

Dunkle, T. (1982, April). The sound of silence. *Science, 82,* pp. 30–33.

Dunn, R. L., & Schwebel, A. I. (1995). Meta-analytic review of marital therapy outcome research. *Journal of Family Psychology, 9,* 58–68.

Dunn, W. S., Mount, M. K., Barrick, M. R., & Ones, D. S. (1995). Relative importance of personality and general mental ability in managers' judgments of applicant qualifications. *Journal of Applied Psychology, 80* (4), 500–509.

Eagly, A. H. (1992). Uneven progress: Social psychology and the study of attitudes. *Journal of Personality and Social Psychology, 63*(5), 693–710.

Eagly, A. H. (2003). The rise of female leaders. *Zeitschrift-fur-Sozialpsychologie, 34,* 123–132.

Eagly, A. H., & Carli, L. L. (1981). Sex of researchers and sex-typed communications as determinants of sex differences in influenceability: A meta-analysis of social influence studies. *Psychological Bulletin, 90,* 1–20.

Eagly, A. H., & Chaiken, S. (1998). Attitude structure and function. In D. Gilbert, S. T. Fiske, & G. Lindzey (Eds.), *Handbook of Social Psychology* (4th ed., Vol. 2, pp. 269–322). New York: McGraw-Hill.

Eagly, A. H., Johannesen–Schmidt, & van-Engen, M. L. (2003). Transformational, transactional, and laissez-faire leadership styles: A meta analysis comparing women and men. *Psychological Bulletin, 129,* 569–591.

Eaves, L. J., Heath, A. C., Neale, M. C., Hewitt, J. K., & Martin, N. G. (1993). *Sex differences and non-additivity in the effects of genes on personality.* Unpublished manuscript, cited in F. S. Mayer & K. Sutton. (1996). *Personality: An integrative approach.* Upper Saddle River, NJ: Prentice Hall.

Eccles, J., Midgley, C., Wigfield, A., Buchanan, C. M., Reuman, D., Flanagan, C., & MacIver, D. (1993). Development during adolescence: The impact of stage-environment fit on young adolescents' experiences in school and families. *American Psychologist: Special Issue: Adolescence, 48,* 90–101.

Ecker, K. (2005). Employees take RAC to court over psychological testing. *Corporate legal times, 15* (168), 68.

Eckerman, C. O., Davis, C. C., & Didow, S. M. (1989). Toddlers' emerging ways of achieving social coordinations with a peer. *Child Development, 60,* 440–453.

Edelman, S., Lemon, J., Bell, D. R., & Kidman, A. D. (1999). Effects of group CBT on the survival time of patients with metastatic breast cancer. *Psycho-Oncology, 8,* 474–481.

Edery, H. G., & Nachson, I. (2004). Distinctiveness in flashbulb memory: Comparative analysis of five terrorist attacks. *Memory, 12,* 147–157.

Edwards, A. J., (1995). A theory of adolescent sexual behavior. Edmonton: Department of Educational Psychology, University of Alberta. *Memory, 12,* 147–157.

Egeth, H., & Lamy, D. (2003). Attention. In A. F. Healy & R. W. Proctor (Eds.), *Handbook of Psychology: Experimental Psychology,* Vol. 4 (pp. 269–292). New York: John Wiley & Sons.

Egger, J. I. M., Delsing, P. A. M., & DeMey, H. R. A. (2003). Differential diagnosis using the MMPI-2: Goldberg's index revisited. *European Psychiatry, 18,* 409–411.

Eich, E., Macaulay, D., Loewenstein, R. J., & Dihle, P. H. (1997). Memory, amnesia, and dissociative identity disorder. *Psychological Science, 8,* 417–422.

Eichenbaum, H., & Cohen, N. J. (2001). *From conditioning to conscious recollection: Memory systems of the brain.* New York: Oxford University Press.

Eimas, P. D., & Tartter, V. C. (1979). On the development of speech perception: Mechanisms and analogies. In H. W. Reese & L. P. Lipsitt (Eds.), *Advances in child development and behavior* (Vol. 13, pp. 155–193). New York: Academic Press.

Eisenberg, N., & Lennon, R. (1983). Sex differences in empathy and related capacities. *Psychological Bulletin, 94,* 100–131.

Eisenberger, R., & Cameron, J. (1996). Detrimental effects of reward. *American Psychologist, 51,* 1153–1166.

Eisenberger, R., & Rhoades, L. (2001). Incremental effects of reward on creativity. *Journal of Personality and Social Psychology 81,* 728–741.

Eisenberger, R., Rhoades, L., & Cameron, J. (1999). Does pay for performance increase or decrease perceived self-determination and intrinsic motivation, *Journal of Personality and Social Psychology. 77* (5), 1026–1040.

Elbert, T., Pantev, C., Wienbruch, C., Rockstroh, B., & Taub, E. (1995, October 13). Increased cortical representation of the fingers of the left hand in string players. *Science, 270,* 305–307.

Eley, T. C., Lichenstein, P., & Stevenson, J. (1999). Sex differences in the etiology of aggressive and nonaggressive antisocial behavior: Results from two twin studies. *Child Development, 70,* 155–168.

Eley, T. C., Bishop, D. V. M., Dale, P. S., Oliver, B., Petrill, S. A., Price, T. S., Saudino, K. J., Simonoff, E., Stevenson, J., Plomin, R., & Purcell, S. (1999). Genetic and environmental origins of verbal and performance components of cognitive delay in 2-year olds. *Developmental Psychology, 35,* 1122–1131.

Eley, T. C., & Stevenson, J. (1999). Exploring the covariation between anxiety and depression symptoms: A genetic analysis of the effects of age and sex. *Journal of Child Psychology & Psychiatry & Allied Disciplines, 40,* 1273–1282.

Eley, T. C., Bishop, D. V. M., Dale, P. S., Oliver, B., Petrill, S. A., Price, T. S., Saudino, K. J., Simonoff, E., Stevenson, J., Plomin, R., & Purcell, S. (1999). Genetic and environmental origins of verbal and performance components of cognitive delay in 2-year olds. *Developmental Psychology, 35,* 1122–1131.

Elkins, G. R., & Rajab, M. H. (2004). Clinical hypnosis for smoking cessation: Preliminary results of a three-session intervention. *International Journal of Clinical and Experimental Hypnosis, 52,* 73–81.

Ellis, A., & Harper, R. A. (1975). *A new guide to rational living.* North Hollywood, CA: Wilshire Book Co.

Ellis, A., & MacLaren, C. (1998). *Rational emotive behavior therapy: A therapist's guide.* San Luis Obispo, CA: Impact.

Ellsworth, P. C. (2002). Appraisal processes in emotion. In R. R. Davidson, K. R. Scherer, & H. H. Goldsmith (Eds.), *Handbook of affective science* (pp. 233–248). New York: Oxford University Press.

Engel, J. F., Black, R. D., & Miniard, P. C. (1986). *Consumer behavior.* Chicago: Dryden Press.

Engle, R. W. (2002). Working memory capacity as executive attention. *Current Directions in Psychological Science, 11,* 19–23.

Epstein, R., Kirshnit, C. E., Lanza, R. P., & Rubin, L. C. (1984). "Insight" in the pigeon: Antecedents and determinants of an intelligent performance. *Nature (London), 308,* 61–62.

Epstein, S. (1962). The measurement of drive and conflict in humans: Theory and experiment. In M. R. Jones (Ed.), *Nebraska Symposium on Motivation*: Vol. 10 (pp. 127–209). Lincoln: University of Nebraska Press.

Esposito, M. D., Zarahn, E., & Aguirre, G. K. (1999). Event-related functional MRI: Implications for Cognitive Psychology. *Psychological Bulletin, 125,* 155–164.

Esterson, A. (2002). The myth of Freud's ostracism by the medical community in 1896–1905: Jeffrey Masson's assault on truth. *History of Psychology, 5,* 115–134.

Evans, G. W., & English, K. (2002). The environment of poverty: Multiple stressor exposure, psychophysiological stress, and socioemotional adjustment. *Child Development, 73,* 1238–1248.

Evans, R. B. (1999, December). A century of psychology. *APA Monitor,* pp. 14–30.

Everly, G. S., & Lating, J. M. (2004). Neurologic desensitization in the treatment of posttraumatic stress. In G. S. Everly & J. M. Lating (Eds.) *Personality guided therapy for posttraumatic stress disorder* (pp. 161–176). Washington, DC: American Psychological Association.

Exner, J. E. (1996). A comment on "the comprehensive system for the Rorschach: A critical examination." *Psychological Science, 7,* 11–13.

Eyer, J. (1977). Prosperity as a cause of death. *International Journal of Health Services, 7,* 125–150.

Eysenck, H. J. (1976). *The measurement of personality.* Baltimore, MD: University Park Press.

Facteau, J. D. & Craig, S. B. (2001). Are performance appraisal ratings from different rating sources comparable? *Journal of Applied Psychology, 86* (2), 215–227.

Fagot, B. I. (1994). Parenting. In V. S. Ramachandran (Ed.), *Encyclopedia of human behavior* (Vol. 3, pp. 411–419). San Diego, CA: Academic Press.

Fairburn, C. G., & Wilson, G. T. (Eds.). (1993). *Binge eating: Nature, assessment and treatment.* New York: Guilford Press.

Fallon, A., & Rozin, P. (1985). Sex differences in perceptions of desirable body states. *Journal of Abnormal Psychology, 84,* 102–105.

Fantz, R. L., Fagan, J. F., & Miranda, S. B. (1975). Early visual selectivity. In L. B. Cohen & P. Salapatek (Eds.), *Infant perception: From sensation to cognition* (Vol. 1, pp. 249–346). New York: Academic Press.

Farber, S. (1981, January). Telltale behavior of twins. *Psychology Today*, pp. 58–62, 79–80.

Farthing, C. W. (1992). *The psychology of consciousness*. Englewood Cliffs, NJ: Prentice Hall.

Featherstone, R. E., Fleming, A. S., & Ivy, G. O. (2000). Plasticity in the maternal circuit: Effects of experience and partum condition on brain astrocyte number in female rats. *Behavioral Neuroscience, 114*, 158–172.

Fehr, B. (1994). Prototype-based assessment of laypeople's views of love. *Personal Relationships, 1*, 309–331.

Feinauer, L., Hilton, H. G., & Callahan, E. H. (2003). Hardiness as a moderator of shame associated with childhood sexual abuse. *American Journal of Family Therapy, 31*, 65–78.

Feingold, A. (1992). Good-looking oeioke are not what we think. *Psychological Bulletin, 111*, 304–341.

Feinson, M. C. (1986). Aging widows and widowers: Are there mental health differences? *International Journal of Aging and Human Development, 23*, 244–255.

Feldman, R. S., Salzinger, S., Rosario, M., Alvarado, L., Caraballo, L., & Hammer, M. (1995). Parent, teacher, and peer ratings of physically abused and nonmaltreated children's behavior. *Journal of Abnormal Child Psychology, 23*, 317–334.

Ferguson, C. A., & Macken, M. A. (1983). The role of play in phonological development. In K. E. Nelson (Ed.), *Children's language* (Vol. 4). Hillsdale, NJ: Erlbaum.

Feshbach, S., & Weiner, B. (1982). *Personality*. Lexington, MA: D. C. Heath.

Festinger, L. (1957). *A theory of cognitive dissonance*. Evanston, IL: Row, Peterson.

Fiedler, F. E. (1967). *A theory of leadership effectiveness*. New York: McGraw-Hill.

Fiedler, F. E. (1993). The leadership situation and the black box contingency theories. In M. Chemers & R. Ayman (eds.), *Leadership theory and research: Perspective and directions* (pp. 1–28). San Diego, CA: Academic Press.

Fiedler, F. E. (2002). The curious role of cognitive resources in leadership. In R. E. Riggio & S. E. Murphy (Eds.), *Multiple intelligences and leadership. LEA's organization and management series* (pp. 91–104). Mahwah, NJ: Lawrence Erlbaum Associates, Publishers.

Field, T. (2001). *Touch*. Cambridge, MA: MIT Press.

Field, T. M. (1986). Interventions for premature infants. *Journal of Pediatrics, 109*, 183–191.

Filipek, P. A., Semrund-Clikeman, M., Steingard, R. J., Renshaw, P. R., Kennedy, D. N., & Biederman, J. (1997). Volumetric MRI analysis comparing subjects having attention-deficit hyperactivity disorder with normal controls. *Neurology, 48*, 589–601.

Finn, P. R., Sharkansky, E. J., Brandt, K. M., & Turcotte, N. (2000). The effects of familial risk, personality, and expectancies on alcohol use and abuse. *Journal of Abnormal Psychology, 109*, 122–133.

Fire extinguisher training simulator. (2006). *Foundry management and technology, 1334* (2), 22.

Fischetti, M. (2003, June). To hear again. *Scientific American*, 82–83.

Fischhoff, B. (1975). Hindsight & foresight: The effect of outcome knowledge on the judgment under uncertainty. *Journal of Experimental Psychology: Human Perception and Performance, 1*, 288–299.

Fischhoff, B., & Downs, J. (1997). Accentuate the relevant. *Psychological Science, 8*, 154–158.

Fischman, J. (1985, September). Mapping the mind. *Psychology Today*, pp. 18–19.

Fishman, N. (2005, June 13). Risky business: Making hiring decisions without background checks can lead to costly mistakes. *Nation's Restaurant News, 13*, 12. Retrieved February 27, 2006, from ProQuest (85731143).

Fiske, S. T., & Neuberg, S. L. (1990). A continuum of impression formation, from category-based to individuating processes: Influence of information and motivation on attention and interpretation. In M. P. Zanna (Ed.), Advances in experimental social psychology (Vol. 23, pp. 399–427). New York: Academic Press.

Fiske, S. T., & Taylor, S. E. (1991). *Social cognition* (2nd ed.). New York: McGraw-Hill.

Fiske, S. (1995). Social cognition. In A. Tesser (Ed.), Advanced social psychology (pp. 149–194). New York: McGraw-Hill.

Flashman, L. A., & Green, M. F. (2004). Review of cognition and brain structure in schizophrenia: Profiles, longitudinal course, and effects of treatment. *Psychiatric Clinics of North America, 27*, 1–18.

Flieller, A. (1999). Comparison of the development of formal thought in adolescent cohorts aged 10-15 years. *Developmental Psychology, 35*, 1048–1058.

Flier, J. S., & Maratos-Flier, E. (1998). Obesity and the hypothalamus: Novel peptides for new pathways. *Cell, 92*, 437–440.

Flor, H., Elbert, T., Knecht, S., Wienbruch, C., & Pantev, C. (1995). Phantom-limb pain as a perceptual correlate of cortical reorganization following arm amputation. *Nature, 375*, 482–484.

Flynn, G. (1999). Pre-employment testing can be unlawful. *Workforce, 78* (7), 82–87.

Folkman, S., Chesney, M. A., & Christopher-Richards, A. (1994). Stress and coping in partners of men with AIDS. *Psychiatric Clinics of North America, 17*, 33–55.

Folkman, S., & Moskowitz, S. T. (2000). Positive affect and the other side of coping. *American Psychologist, 55*, 647–654.

Ford, B. D. (1993). Emergenesis: An alternative and a confound. *American Psychologist, 48*, 1294.

Ford-Mitchell, D. (1997, November 12). Daydream your way to better health. *Ann Arbor News*, p.C3.

Forgatch, M. S., & DeGarmo, D. S. (1999). Parenting through change: An effective prevention program for single mothers. *Journal of Consulting and Clinical psychology, 67*, 711–724.

Fowles, D. C. (1992). Schizophrenia: Diathesis-stress revisited. *Annual Review of Psychology, 43*, 303–336.

Frank, J. D., & Frank, J. B. (1991). *Persuasion and healing* (3rd ed.). Baltimore: Johns Hopkins University Press.

Freedland, K. E. (2004). Religious beliefs shorten hospital stays? Psychology works in mysterious ways: Comment on Contrada et al. (2004). *Health Psychology, 23*, 239–242.

Freedman, J. L., & Fraser, S. C. (1966). Compliance without pressure: The foot-in-the-door technique. *Journal of Personality and Social Psychology, 4*, 195–202.

Freeman, W., Brebner, K., Lynch, W., Patel, K., Robertson, D., Roberts, D. C., & Vrana, K. E. (2002). *Molecular Brain Research, 104*, 11–20.

Freudenberger, H. J. (1983). Hazards of psychotherapeutic practice. Psychotherapy in Private Practice, 1, 83–89.

Fried, Y., & Ferris, G. R. (1987). The validity of the job characteristics model: A review and meta-analysis. *Personnel Psychology, 40* (2), 287–322.

Friedman, H. S. (2002). *Health Psychology* (2nd ed.) Upper Saddle River, NJ: Prentice Hall.

Friedman, M., & Rosenman, R. H. (1959). Association of specific overt behavior patterns with blood and cardiovascular findings: Blood cholesterol level, blood clotting time, incidence of arcus senilis and clinical coronary artery disease. *JAMA, Journal of the American Medical Association, 169*, 1286–1296.

Friedman, M., Breall, W. S., Goodwin, M. L., Sparagon, B. J., Ghandour, G., & Fleischmann, N. (1996). Effect of Type A behavioral counseling on frequency of episodes of silent myocardial ischemia in coronary patients. *American Heart Journal, 132*(5), 933–937.

Friedman, M. J., Schnurr, P. P., & McDonagh-Coyle, A. (1994). Posttraumatic stress disorder in the military veteran. *Psychiatric Clinics of North America, 17*, 265–277.

Friman, P. C., Allen, K. D., Kerwin, M. L. E., & Larzelere, R. (1993). Changes in modern psychology. *American Psychology, 48*, 658–664.

Froelich, L., & Hoyer, S. (2002). The etiological and pathogenetic heterogeneity of Alzheimer's disease. *Nervenarzi, 73*, 422–427.

Frosch, C. A., Mangelsdorf, S. C., McHale, J. L. (2000). Marital behavior and the security of preschooler-parent attachment relationships. *Journal of Family Psychology, 14*, 144–161.

Frone, M. R. (1998). Predictors of work injuries among employed adolescents. *Journal of Applied Psychology, 83* (4), 565–576.

Frosch, C. A., Mangelsdorf, S. C., McHale, J. L. (2000). Marital behavior and the security of preschooler-parent attachment relationships. *Journal of Family Psychology, 14*, 144–161.

Fu, Q., Heath, A. C., Bucholz, K. K., Nelson, E., Goldberg, J., Lyons, M. J., True, W. R., Jacob, T., Tsuang, M. T., & Eisen, S. A. (2002). Shared genetic risk of major depression, alcohol dependence, and marijuana dependence: Contribution of antisocial personality disorder in men. *Archives of General Psychiatry, 59*, 1125–1132.

Funder, D. C. (1991). Global traits: A neo-Allportian approach to personality. *Psychological Science, 2*, 31–39.

Funder, D. C. (1995). On the accuracy of personality judgment: A realistic approach. *Psychological Review, 102*(4), 652–670.

Gabrieli, J. D., Desmond, J. E., Bemb, J. B.,Wagner, A. D., Stone, M.V.,Vaidya, C. J. & Glover, G. H. (1996). Functional magnetic resonance imaging of semantic memory processes in the frontal lobes. *Psychological Science, 7*, 278–283.

Gabrieli, J. D. E. (1998). Cognitive neuroscience of human memory. *Annual Review of Psychology, 49*, 87–115.

Gage, F. H. (2000, February 25). Mammalian neural stem cells. *Science, 287*, 1433–1438.

Gage, F. H. (2003, September). Brain, repair yourself. *Scientific American*, 46–53.

Galanter, M. (1984). Self-help large-group therapy for alcoholism: A controlled study. *Alcoholism, Clinical and Experimental Research, 8*(1), 16–23.

Gallistel, C. R. (1981). Bell, Magendie, and the proposals to restrict the use of animals in neurobehavioral research. *American Psychologist, 36*, 357–360.

Gallo, L. C., & Matthews, K. A. (2003). Understanding the association between socioeconomic status and physical health: Do negative emotions play a role? *Psychological Bulletin, 129*, 10–51.

Gandhi, N., Depauw, K. P., Dolny, D. G., & Freson, T. (2002). Effect of an exercise program on quality of life of women with fibromyalgia. *Women and Therapy, 25*, 91–103.

Gardner, H. (1983a). *Frames of mind: The theory of multiple intelligences.* New York: Basic Books.

Gardner, H. (1993). *Multiple intelligences: The theory in practice.* New York: Basic Books.

Gardner, H. (1999). *Intelligence reframed: Multiple intelligences for the 21st century.* New York: Basic Books, Inc.

Garfield, S. L. (ed.). (1983). Special section: Meta-analysis and psychotherapy. *Journal of Consulting and Clinical Psychology, 51*, 3–75.

Garlick, D. (2003). Integrating brain science with intelligence research. *Current Directions in Psychological Science, 12*, 185–189.

Garry, M., & Polaschek, D. L. L. (2000). Imagination and memory. *Current Directions in Psychological Science, 9*, 6–10.

Gatewood, R. D. & Field, H. S. (1998). *Human Resource Selection.* Fort Worth, TX: Harcourt College Publishers.

Gathchel, R. J., & Oordt, M. S. (2003). Insomnia. In R. J. Gathchel & M. S. Oordt (Eds.), *Clinical health psychology and primary care: Practical advice and clinical guidance for successful collaboration* (pp. 135–148). Washington, D.C.: American Psychological Association.

Gaugler, B. B., Rosenthal, D. B., Thronton, G. C., & Bentson, C. (1987). Meta-analysis of assessment center validity. *Journal of Applied Psychology, 72* (3), 493–511.

Gécz, J., & Mulley, J. (2000). Genes for cognitive function: Developments on the X. *Genome Research, 10*, 157–163.

Gelman, D. (1990, October 29). A fresh take on Freud. *Newsweek*, pp. 84–86.

Gelman, D. (1994, June 13). Reliving the painful past. *Newsweek*, pp. 20–22.

Gerber, D. J., Hall, D., Miyakawa, T., Demars, S., Gogos, J. A., Karayiorgou, M., & Tonegawa, S. (2003). Evidence for association of schizophrenia with genetic variation in 8p21.3 gene, PPP3ccc, encoding the calcineurin gamma subunit. *Proceedings of the National Academy of Sciences, 100*, 8993–8998.

Gergen, K. J. (1973). The codification of research ethics—views of a Doubting Thomas. *American Psychologist, 28*, 907–912.

Gernsbacher, M. A., & Kaschak, M. P. (2003). Neuroimaging studies of language production and comprehension. *Annual Review of Psychology, 54*, 91–114.

Gershoff, E. T. (2002). Corporal punishment by parents and associated child behaviors and experiences.: A meta-analytic and theoretical review. *Psychological Bulletin, 128*, 539–579.

Gershon, E. S. (1990). Genetics. In F. K. Goodwin & K. R. Jamison (eds.), *Manic depressive illness* (pp. 373–401). New York: Oxford University Press.

Getzels, J. W. (1975). Problem finding and the inventiveness of solutions. *Journal of Creative Behavior, 9*, 12–18.

Giese–Davis, J., Koopman, C., Butler, L. D., Classen, C., Cordova, M., Fobair, P., Benson, J., Draemer, H. C., & Spiegel, D. (2002). Change in emotion-regulation strategy for women with metastic breast cancer following supportive-expressive group therapy. *Journal of Consulting and Clinical Psychology, 70*, 916–925.

Gilbert, D. T., & Malone, P. S. (1995). The correspondence bias. *Psychological Bulletin, 117*, 21–38.

Gilovich, T. (1991). *How we know what isn't so: The fallibility of human reason in everyday life.* New York: Free Press.

Ginsberg, H. (1972). *The myth of the deprived child.* Englewood Cliffs, NJ: Prentice Hall.

Giovanni, B. (2003). Language, mind, and culture: From linguistic relativity to representational modularity. In M. Mack & M. T. Banich (Eds.), *Mind, brain, and language: Multidisciplinary perspectives* (pp. 23–59). Mahwah, NJ: Lawrence Erlbaum Associates.

Glassop, L. I. (2002). The organizational benefits of teams. *Human relations, 55* (2), 225–250.

Gleaves, D. H., Smith, S. M., Butler, L. D., & Spiegel, D. (2004). False and recovered memories in the laboratory and clinic: A review of experimental and clinical evidence. *Clinical Psychology: Science and Practice, 11*, 3–28.

Glenner, G. G. (1994). Alzheimer's disease. In V. S. Ramachandran (Ed.), *Encyclopedia of human behavior* (Vol. 1, pp. 103–111). San Diego, CA: Academic Press.

Gobet, F. L., Peter, C. R., Croker, S., Cheng, P., Jones, G., Oliver, I., & Pine, J. M. (2001). Chunking mechanisms in human learning. *Trends in Cognitive Sciences, 5*, 236–243.

Goff, D. C., & Coyle, J. T. (2001). The emerging role of glutamate in the pathophysiology and treatment of schizophrenia. *American Journal of Psychiatry, 158*, 1367–1377.

Gold, P. E., & Greenough, W. T. (2001). *Memory consolidation: Essays in honor of James L. McGaugh.* Washington, DC: American Psychological Association.

Goldberg, L. R. (1993). The structure of phenotypic personality traits. *American Psychologist, 48*, 26–34.

Goldney, R. D. (2003). Deinstitutionalization and suicide. *Crisis, 24*, 39–40.

Goldstein, E. B. (1999). *Sensation and perception* (5th ed.). Pacific Grove, CA: Brooks-Cole.

Goldstein, I. L., & Ford, J. K. (2002). *Training in organizations* (4th ed.). Belmont, CA: Wadsworth.

Goldstein, I., Lue, T. F., Padma-Nathan, H., Rosen, R. C., Steers, W. D., & Wicker, P. A. (1998). Oral sildenafil in the treatment of erectile dysfunction. Sildenafil study group. *New England Journal of Medicine, 338*, 1397–1404.

Goleman, D. (1997). *Emotional intelligence.* New York: Bantam Books.

Goleman, D., Boyatzis, R., & McKee, A. (2002). *Primal leadership: Realizing the power of emotional intelligence.* Boston: Harvard Business School Press.

Golomb, J., Kluger, A., de Leon, M. J., Ferris, S. H., Convit, A., Mittelman, M. S., et al. (1994). Hippocampal formation size in normal human aging: A correlate of delayed secondary memory performance. *Learning & Memory, 1*, 45–54.

Gonsalkorale, W. M., Miller, V., Afzal, A., & Whorwell, P. J. (2003). Long term benefits of hypnotherapy for irritable bowel syndrome. *Gut, 52*, 1623–9.

Goode, E. (2000b, March 14). Human nature: born or made? *New York Times*, pp. F1, F9.

Goode, E. (2004, February 24). Lifting the veils of autism, one by one. The *New York Times*, pp. D1, D4.

Goodwin, P. J., Leszcz, M., Ennis, M., Koopmans, J., Vincent, L., Guther, H., Drysdale, E., Hundleby, M., Chochinov, H. M., Navarro, M., Speca, M., & Hunter, J. (2001). The effect of group psychosocial support on survival in metastatic breast cancer. *New England Journal of Medicine, 345*, 1719–1726.

Gopnik, A., Neltzoff, A. N., & Kuhl, P. (1999). *The scientist in the crib: Minds, brains and how children learn.* New York: William Morrow.

Gordis, E. (1996). Alcohol research: At the cutting edge. *Archives of General Psychiatry, 53*, 199–201.

Gose, B. (1997, October 24). Colleges try to curb excessive drinking by saying moderation is okay. *Chronicle of Higher Education*, pp. A61–A62.

Gottesman, I. I. (1991). *Schizophrenia genesis: The origins of madness.* New York: Freeman.

Graen, G. B., & Hui, C. (2001). Approaches to leadership: Toward a complete contingency model of face-to-face leadership. In M. Erez & U. Kleinbeck (Eds.), *Work motivation in the context of a globalizing economy* (pp. 211–225). Mahwah, NJ: Lawrence Erlbaum Associates, Publishers.

Graen, G. B. & Uhl-Bien, M. (1998). Relationship-based approach to leadership: Development of Leader-Member Exchange (LMX) theory of leadership over 25 years: Applying a multi-levle multi-domain perspective. In F. Dansereau & F. J. Yammarino (Eds.), Leaderhips: *The multiple-level appraoches: Contemporary and alternative* (pp. 103–155). Stamford, CT: JAI Press.

Grafton, S. T., Mazziotta, J. C., Presty, S., Friston, K. J., Frackowiak, R. S., J., & Phelps, M. E. (1992). Functional anatomy of human procedural learning determined with regional cerebral blood flow and PET. *Journal of Neuroscience, 12*, 2542–2548.

Graham, S. (1992). Most of the subjects were white and middle class. *American Psychologist, 47*, 629–639.

Grandey, A. A. (2000). Emotional regulation in the workplace: A new way to conceptualize emotional labor. *Journal of Occupational Health Psychology, 5*, 95–110.

Green, J. P., & Lynn, S. J. (2000). Hypnosis and suggestion-based approaches to smoking cessation: An examination of the evidence. *International Journal of Clinical & Experimental Hypnosis [Special Issue: The Status of Hypnosis as an Empirically Validated Clinical Intervention], 48*, 195–224.

Greene, J., & Haidt, J. (2002). How (and where) does moral judgment work? *Trends in Cognitive Sciences, 6*, 517–523.

Greene, R. L. (1987). Effects of maintenance rehearsal on human memory. *Psychological Bulletin, 102*, 403–413.

Greenfield, P. M., & Smith, J. H. (1976). *The structure of communication in early language development.* New York: Academic Press.

Greenstein, T. H. (1993). Maternal employment and child behavioral outcomes. *Journal of Family Issues, 14*, 323–354.

Greenwald, A. G., & Banaji, M. R. (1995). Implicit social cognition: Attitudes, self-esteem, and stereotypes. *Psychological Review, 102,* 4–27.

Greenwald, A. G., Spangenberg, E. R., Pratkanis, A. R., & Eskenazi, J. (1991). Double-blind tests of subliminal self-help audiotapes. *Psychological Science, 2,* 119–122.

Grensing-Pophal, L. (2005). Job rotation. *Credit union management, 28* (7), 50–53.

Griffen, M. A. & Neal, A. (2000). Perceptions of safety at work: A framework for linking safety climate to safety performance, knowledge, and motivation. *Journal of Occupational Health Psychology, 5* (3), 347–358.

Griffiths, R. A., & Channon-Little, L. D. (1995). Dissociation, dieting disorders and hypnosis: A review. *European Eating Disorders Review [Special Issue: Dissociation and the Eating Disorders], 3,* 148–159.

Grinspoon, L., Ewalt, J. R., & Shader, R. I. (1972). *Schizophrenia: Pharmacotherapy and psychotherapy.* Baltimore: Williams & Wilkins.

Guérin, D. (1994, August). *Fussy infants at risk.* Paper presented at the meeting of the American Psychological Association, Los Angeles.

Guilford, J. P. (1967). *The nature of human intelligence.* New York: McGraw-Hill.

Gurman, A. S., & Kniskern, D. P. (Eds.). (1991). *Handbook of Family Therapy, Vol 2.* Philadelphia, PA: Brunner/Mazel.

Gurvits, T. V., Gilbertson, M. W., Lasko, N. B., Orr, S. P., & Pitman, R. K. (1997). Neurological status of combat veterans and adult survivors of sexual abuse PTSD. *Annals of the New York Academy of Sciences, 821,* 468–471.

Gurwitch, R. H., Sitterle, K. A., Young, B. H., & Pfefferbaum, B. (2002). The aftermath of terrorism. In A. M. La Greca & W. K. Silverman (Eds.), *Helping children cope with disasters and terrorism* (pp. 327–357). Washington, DC: American Psychological Association.

Guthrie, R. (1976). *Even the rat was white.* New York: Harper & Row.

Gutman, A. (2004). Ground rules for adverse impact. *The Industrial-Organizational Psychologist, 41* (3), 109–119.

Haberlandt, K. (1997). *Cognitive psychology.* Boston: Allyn & Bacon.

Haier, R. J. (1993). Cerebral glucose metabolism and intelligence. In P. A. Vernon (Ed.), *Biological approaches to the study of human intelligence* (pp. 317–332). Norwood, NJ: Ablex.

Haines, M., & Spear, S. F. (1996). Changing the perception of the norm: A strategy to decrease binge drinking among college students. *Journal of American College Health, 45,* 134–140.

Hall, E. T., & Hall, M. R. (2003). Subtle conformance to internalized culture: The sounds of silence. In J. M. Henslin (Ed.). *Down to earth sociology: Introductory readings* (12th Ed.) (pp. 100–108). New York: Free Press.

Hamann, S. B., Ely, T. D., Hoffman, J. M., & Kilts, C. D. (2002). Ecstasy and agony: Activation of the human amygdala in positive and negative emotion. *Psychological Science, 13,* 135–141.

Hameroff, S. R., Kaszniak, A. W., & Scott, A. C. (Eds.). (1996). *Toward a science of consciousness: The first Tucson discussions and debates.* Cambridge, MA: MIT Press.

Hammen, C., Gitlin, M., & Altshuler, L. (2000). Predictors of work adjustment in bipolar I patients. A naturalistic longitudinal follow-up. *Journal of Consulting & Clinical Psychology, 68,* 220–225.

Hampson, J., & Nelson, K. (1993). The relation of maternal language to variation in rate and style of language acquisition. *Journal of Child Language, 20,* 313–342.

Hancock, P. A. (1999). *Human performance and ergonomics.* San Diego: Academic Press.

Hanna, F. J. (2002). *Therapy with difficult clients: Using the precursors model to awaken change.* Washington, DC: American Psychological Association.

Hansen, W. B. (1993). School-based alcohol prevention programs. *Alcohol, Health and Research World, 17,* 54–60.

Hansen, W. B., & Graham, J. W. (1991). Preventing alcohol, marijuana, and cigarette use among adolescents: Peer pressure resistance training versus establishing conservative norms. *Preventive Medicine, 20,* 414–430.

Harburg, E., Gleiberman, L., DiFranceisco, W., Schork, A. & Weissfeld, L. A. (1990b). Familial transmission of alcohol use: III. Impact of imitation/non-imitation of parent alcohol use (1960) on the sensible/problem drinking of their offspring (1977). *British Journal of Addiction, 85,* 1141–1155.

Hare, R. D. (1983). Diagnosis of antisocial personality disorder in two prison populations. *American Journal of Psychiatry, 140,* 887–890.

Hare, R. D. (1993). *Without conscience: The disturbing world of the psychopaths among us.* New York: Pocket Books.

Harford, T. C., Wechsler, H., & Muthen, B. O. (2003). Alcohol related aggression and drinking at off-campus parties and bars: A national study of current drinkers in college. *Journal of Studies on Alcohol, 64,* 704–711.

Harlow, H. F., & Zimmerman, R. R. (1959, August). Affectional responses in the infant monkey. *Science, 130,* 421–432.

Harris, J. R. (1998). *The nurture assumption: Why children turn out the way they do.* New York: Free Press.

Harris, J. R., & Liebert, R. M. (1991). *The child: A contemporary view of development* (3rd ed.). Englewood Cliffs, NJ: Prentice Hall.

Hart, N. (1985). *The sociology of health and illness.* London: Causeway Books.

Hart, B., & Risley, T. R. (1995). *Meaningful differences in the everyday experience of young American children.* Baltimore: Brookes.

Hartmann, S., & Zepf, S. (2003). Effectiveness of psychotherapy in Germany: A replication of the *Consumer Reports* study. *Psychotherapy Research, 13,* 235–242.

Hartup, W. W., & Stevens, N. (1999). Friendships and adaptation across the lifespan. Current Directions in Psychological Science, 8, 76–79.

Harvey, J. H., & Miller, E. D. (1998). Toward a psychology of loss. *Psychological Science, 9,* 429–434.

Harvey, J. H., & Pauwells, B. G. (1999). Recent developments in close-relationships theory. *Current Directions in Psychological Science, 8,* 93–95.

Harvey, R. J. (1991). Job analysis. In M. D. Dunnette & L. M. Hough (Eds.), *Handbook of industrial and organizational psychology,* (2nd ed., Vol. 2, pp. 71–163). Palo Alto, CA: Consulting Psychologists Press.

Harvey, R. J., & Wilson, M. A. (2000). Point/Counterpoint Introduction – Yes Virginia, there is an objective reality in job analysis. *Journal of Organizational Behavior, 21* (7), 829–855.

Hashimoto, T., Volk, D. W., Eggan, S. M., Mirnics, K., Pierri, J. N., Sun, Z., Sampson, A. R., & Lewis, D. A. (2003). Gene expression deficits in a subclass of GABA neurons in the prefrontal cortex of subjects with schizophrenia. *Journal of Neuroscience, 16*, 6315–6326.

Hasson, D., Arnetz, B., Jelveus, L., & Edelstam, B. (2004). A randomized clinical trial of the treatment effects of massage compared to relaxation tape recordings on diffuse long-term pain. *Psychotherapy and Psychosomatics, 73*, 17–24.

Hathaway, S. R., & McKinley, J. C. (1942). A multiphasic personality schedule (Minnesota): III. The measurement of symptomatic depression. *Journal of Psychology, 14*, 73–84.

Hauri, P. (1982). *Sleep disorders.* Kalamazoo, MI: Upjohn.

Hausknecht, J. P., Day, D. V., & Thomas, S. C. (2004). Applicant reactions to selection procedures: An updated model and meta-analysis. *Personnel Psychology, 57* (3), 639–683.

Hayden, T., & Mischel, W. (1976). Maintaining trait consistency in the resolution of behavioral inconsistency: The wolf in sheep's clothing? *Journal of Personality, 44*, 109–132.

Heath, A. C., & Martin, N. G. (1993). Genetic models for the natural history of smoking: Evidence for a genetic influence on smoking persistence. *Addictive Behavior, 18*, 19–34.

Heath, R. C. (1972). Pleasure and brain activity in man. *Journal of Nervous and Mental Disease, 154*, 3–18.

Hébert, R. (2003, July). NINR sleep research means wake-up call for policy. *APS Observer,* pp. 1, 9–12.

Hechtman, L. (1989). Teenage mothers and their children: Risks and problems: A review. *Canadian Journal of Psychology, 34*, 569–575.

Heider, E. R. (1972). Universals in color naming and memory. *Journal of Experimental Psychology, 93*, 10–20.

Heider, E. R., & Oliver, D. C. (1972). The structure of the color space in naming and memory in two languages. *Cognitive Psychology, 3*, 337–354.

Heinrichs, R. W. (2001). *In search of madness: Schizophrenia and neuroscience.* New York: Oxford University Press.

Heinz, A., Hermann, D., Smolka, M. N., Rieks, M., Graef, K. J., Poehlau, D., Kuhn, W., & Bauer, M. (2003). Effects of acute psychological stress on adhesion molecules interleukins and sex hormones: Implications for coronary heart disease. *Psychopharmacology, 165*, 111–117.

Helgesen, S. (1998). *Everyday revolutionaries: Working women and the transformation of American life.* New York: Doubleday.

Hellige, J. B. (1990). Hemispheric asymmetry. *Annual Review of Psychology, 41*, 55–80.

Hellige, J. B. (1993). *Hemispheric asymmetry: What's right and what's left.* Cambridge, MA: Harvard University Press.

Helms, J. E. (1992). Why is there no study of cultural equivalence in standardized cognitive ability testing? *American Psychologist, 47*, 1083–1101.

Helms, J. E., & Cook, D. A. (1999). *Using race and culture in counseling and psychotherapy: Theory and process.* Needham Heights, MA: Allyn & Bacon.

Helmreich, R., & Spence, J. (1978). The Work and Family Orientation Questionnaire: An objective instrument to assess components of achievement motivation and scientific attainment. *Personality and Social Psychology Bulletin, 4*, 222–226.

Hendrick, S., & Hendrick, C. (1992). *Liking, loving and relating* (2nd ed.). Pacific Grove, CA: Brooks/Cole.

Heneman, R. L., & Greenberger, D. B. (Eds.). (2002). *Human resource management in virtual organizations.* Greenwich, CT: Information Age.

Henkel, L. A., Franklin, N., & Johnson, M. K. (2000). Cross-modal source monitoring confusions between perceived and imagined events. *Journal of Experimental Psychology: Learning, Memory, & Cognition, 26*, 321–335.

Henriques, J. B., & Davidson, R. J. (1990). Regional brain electrical asymmetries discriminate between previously depressed and healthy control subjects. *Journal of Abnormal Psychology, 99*, 22–31.

Herberman, R. B. (2002). Stress, natural killer cells, and cancer. In H. G. Koenig & H. J. Cohen (Eds.), *The link between religion and health: Psychoneuroimmunology and faith factor* (pp. 69–83). London: Oxford University Press.

Herek, G. M. (2000). The psychology of sexual prejudice. *Current Directions in Psychological Science, 9*, 19–22.

Hermann, C., & Blanchard, E. B. (2002). Biofeedback in the treatment of headache and other childhood pain. *Applied Psychophysiology and Biofeedback, 27*, 143–162.

Herrnstein, R. J., & Murray, C. (1994). *The bell curve.* New York: Free Press.

Hetherington, E. M., Bridges, M., & Insabella, G. M. (1998). What matters? What does not? Five perspectives on the association between marital transitions and children's adjustment. *American Psychologist, 53*, 167–184.

Herzog, H. A. (1995). Has public interest in animal rights peaked? *American Psychologist, 50*, 945–947.

Hewstone, M., Islam, M. R., & Judd, C. M. (1993). Models of cross categorization and intergroup relations. *Journal of Personality and Social Psychology, 64*, 779–793.

Hibbard, S. R., Farmer, L., Wells, C., Difillipo, E., & Barry, W. (1994). Validation of Cramer's defense mechanism manual for the TAT. *Journal of Personality Assessment, 63*, 197–210.

Hildebrandt, H., Brokate, B., Eling, P., & Lanz, M. (2004). Response shifting and inhibition, but not working memory, are impaired after long-term heavy alcohol consumption. *Neuropsychology, 18*, 203–211.

Hilgard, E. R., Hilgard, J. R., & Kaufmann, W. (1983). *Hypnosis in the relief of pain* (2nd ed.). Los Altos, CA: Kaufmann.

Hill, C. E., Zack, J. S., Wonnell, T. L., Hoffman, M. A., Rochlen, A. B., Goldberg, J. L., et al. (2000). Structured brief therapy with a focus on dreams or loss for clients with troubling dreams and recent loss. *Journal of Counseling Psychology, 47*, 90–101.

Hill, J. (2003). Early identification of individuals at risk for antisocial personality disorder. *British Journal of Psychiatry, 182* (Suppl. 44).

Hilton, J., & von Hipple, W. (1996). Stereotypes. *Annual Review of Psychology, 47*, 237–271.

Hobfoll, S. E., Cameron, R. P., Chapman, H. A., & Gallagher, R. W. (1996). Social support and social coping in couples. In G. R. Pierce, B. R. Sarason, & I. G. Sarason (Eds.), The handbook of social support and the family (pp. 413–433). New York: Plenum.

Hobson, J. A. (1994). *The chemistry of conscious states: How the brain changes its mind.* Boston: Little, Brown.

Hochschild, A. R. (1983). *The managed heart.* Berkeley: University of California Press.

Hofer, J., & Chasiotis, A. (2004). Methodological considerations of applying a TAT-type picture-story test in cross-cultural research. *Journal of Cross Cultural Psychology, 35*, 224–241.

Hoffman, D. A., & Stetzer, A. (1996). A cross-level investigation of factors influencing unsafe behaviors and accidents. *Personnel Psychology, 49* (2), 307–339.

Hoffman, H. S., & DePaulo, P. (1977). Behavioral control by an imprinting stimulus. *American Scientist, 65*, 58–66.

Hoffman, M. L. (1977). Personality and social development. *Annual Review of Psychology, 28*, 295–321.

Hoffman, R. E., Hawkins, K. A., Gueorguieva, R., Boutros, N. N., Rachid, F., Carroll, K., & Krystal, J. H. (2003). Transcranial magnetic stimulation of left temporoparietal cortex and medication-resistant auditory hallucinations. *Archives of General Psychiatry, 60*, 49–56.

Hoffrage, U., Hertwig, R., & Gigerenzer, G. (2000). Hindsight bias: A by-product of knowledge updating? *Journal of Experimental Psychology: Learning, Memory & Cognition, 26*, 566–581.

Hogan, J., & Holland, B. (2003). Using theory to evaluate personality and job-performance relations: A socioanalytic perspective. *Journal of Applied Psychology, 88* (1), 100–112.

Hogan, R., Hogan, J., & Roberts, B. W. (1996). Personality measurement and employment decisions: Questions and answers. *American Psychologist, 51*(5), 469–477.

Holmbeck, G. N. (1994). Adolescence. In V. S. Ramachandran (Ed.), *Encyclopedia of human behavior* (Vol. 1, pp. 17–28). San Diego, CA: Academic Press.

Hood, B. M., Willen, J. D., & Driver, J. (1998). Adult's eyes trigger shifts of visual attention inhuman infants. *Psychological Science, 9*, 131–134.

Hoptman, M. J., & Davidson, R. J. (1994). How and why do the two cerebral hemispheres interact? *Psychological Bulletin, 116*, 195–219.

Horn, J. (1983). The Texas Adoption Project: Adopted children and their intellectual resemblance to biological and adoptive parents. *Child Development, 54*, 268–275.

Horne, J. A., Reyner, L. A., & Barrett, P. R. (2003). Driving impairment due to sleepiness is exacerbated by low alcohol intake. *Occupational and Environmental Medicine, 60*, 689–692.

Hosmer, L. (1995). Trust: The connecting link between organizational theory and philosophical ethics. *Academy of management review, 20* (2), 379–403.

Hosoda, M., Stone, R. E., & Coats, G. (2003). The effects of physical attractiveness on job-related outcomes: A meta-analysis of experimental studies. *Personnel Psychology, 56*, 431–462.

House, J. S., Landis, K. R., & Umberson, D. (1988). Social relationships and health. *Science, 241* (4865), 540–545.

Howard, K. I., Kopta, S. M., Krause, M. S., & Orlinsky, D. E. (1986). The dose-effect relationship in psychotherapy. American Psychologist, 41, 159–164.

Howell, W. C. (2003). Human factors and ergonomics. In W. C. Borman, D. R. Ilgen, & R. J. Klimoski (Eds.), *Handbook of psychology: Industrial and organizational psychology* (Vol. 12, pp. 541–564). Hoboken, NJ: Wiley.

Hoyert, D. L., Kochanek, K. D., & Murphy, S. L. (1999). Deaths: Final data for 1997. *National Vital Statistics Reports, 47*(9). Hyattsville, MD: National Center for Health Statistics.

HR Focus, (2003). Eight steps to better on-the-job training. *HR Focus, 80* (7), 11–14.

Huang, T. (1998, February 3). Weathering the storms. *Charlotte Observer,* pp. 1–2E.

Hubel, D. H., & Wiesel, T. N. (1979). Brain mechanisms of vision. *Scientific American, 241*(3), 150–162.

Hubel, D. H., & Livingstone, M. S. (1990). Color and contrast sensitivity in the lateral geniculate body and primary visual cortex of the macaque monkey. *Journal of Neuroscience, 10*, 2223–2237.

Huffman, C. J., Matthews, T. D., & Gagne, P. E. (2001). The role of part-set cuing in the recall of chess positions: Influence of chunking in memory. *North American Journal of Psychology, 3*, 535–542.

Huebner, A. M., Garrod, A., & Snarey, J. (1990). *Moral development in Tibetan Buddhist monks: A cross-cultural study of adolescents and young adults in Nepal.* Paper presented at the meeting of the Society for Research in Adolescence, Atlanta, GA.

Hughes, R. L., Ginnett, R. C., & Curphy, G. J. (1998). Contingency theories of leadership. In G. R. Hickman (Ed.), *Leading organizations: Perspectives for a new era* (pp. 141–157). Thousand Oaks, CA: Sage Publications, Inc.

Hulin, C. L., & Judge, T. A. (2003). Job attitudes. In W. C. Borman, D. R. Ilgen, & R. J. Klimoski (Eds.), *Handbook of psychology* (Vol. 12): *Industrial and organizational psychology* (pp. 255–276). Hoboken, NJ: Wiley.

Humphreys, L. G. (1992). Commentary: What both critics and users of ability tests need to know. *Psychological Science, 3*, 271–274.

Hunt, M. (1994). *The story of psychology.* New York: Anchor/Random House.

Hunt, E., Streissguth, A. P., Kerr, B., & Olson, H. C. (1995). Mothers' alcohol consumption during pregnancy: Effects on spatial-visual reasoning in 14-year-old children. *Psychological Science, 6*, 339–342.

Hunter, J. E. (1980). *Test validation for 12,000 jobs: An application of synthetic validity and validity generalization to the General Aptitude Test Battery (GATB).* Washington, DC: U.S. Employment Service, U. S. Department of Labor.

Hunter, J. E., & Hunter, R. F. (1984). Validity and utility of alternative predictors of job performance. *Psychological Bulletin, 96* (1), 72–98.

Huston, A. C., Watkins, B. A., & Kunkel, D. (1989). Public policy and children's television. *American Psychologist, 44*, 424–433.

Hutchison, K. E., Stallings, M., McGeary, J., & Bryan, A. (2004). Population stratification in the candidate gene study: Fatal threat or red herring? *Psychological Bulletin, 130*, 66–79.

Hutschemaekers, G. J. M., & van de Vijver, F. J. R. (1989). Economic recessions and neurotic problems: The Netherlands 1930–1985. In R. Veenhoven & A. Hagenaars (Eds.), *Did the crisis really hurt? Effects of the 1980–1982 economic recession on satisfaction, mental health and mortality.* Rotterdam: Universitaire Pers Rotterdam, 1989.

Hyde, J. S. (1982). *Understanding human sexuality* (2nd ed.). New York: McGraw-Hill.

Hyde, J. S. (1984a). Children's understanding of sexist language. *Developmental Psychology, 20*, 697–706.

Hyman, I. E., Husband, T. H., & Billings, F. J. (1995). False memories of childhood experiences. *Applied Cognitive Psychology, 9*, 181–197.

Iacobucci, D., & McGill, A. L. (1990). Analysis of attribution data: Theory testing and effects estimation. *Journal of Personality and Social Psychology, 59*(3), 426–441.

Ilies, R., & Judge, T. A. (2003). On the heritability of job satisfaction: The mediating role of personality. *Journal of Applied Psychology, 88* (4), 750–759.

Imrie, R. (1999, September 3). $850,000 awarded in repressed-memory case. *Charlotte Observer*, p.8A.

Irwin, M. (2002). Psychoneuroimmunology of depression: Clinical implications. *Brain, Behavior and Immunity, 16*, 1–16.

Isen, A. M., & Levin, P. F. (1972). The effect of feeling good on helping: Cookies and kindness. *Journal of Personality and Social Psychology, 21*, 384–388.

Ito, K. (2002). Additivity of heuristic and systematic processing persuasion: Effects of source credibility, argument quality, and issue involvement. *Japanese Journal of Experimental Social Psychology, 41*, 137–146.

Iwamasa, G. Y., & Smith, S. K. (1996). Ethnic diversity in behavioral psychology: A review of the literature. *Behavioral Modification, 20*, 45–59.

Jacks, J. Z., & Cameron, K. A. (2003). Strategies for resisting persuasion. *Basic and Applied Social Psychology, 25*, 145–161.

Jackson, C. J., & Furnham, A. (2001). Appraisal Ratings, halo, and selection: A study using sales staff. *European Journal of Psychological Assessment, 17* (1), 17–24.

Jackson, D. C., Mueller, C. J., Dolski, I., Dalton, K. M., Nitschke, J. B., Urry, H. L., Rosenkranz, M. A., Ryff, C. D., Singer, B. H., & Davidson, R. J. (2003). Now you feel it, now you don't: Frontal brain electrical asymmetry and individual differences in emotion regulation. *Psychological Science, 14*, 612–617.

Jacobs, W. J., & Nadel, L. (1998). Neurobiology of reconstructed memory. *Psychology, Public Policy, & Law, 4*, 1110–1134.

Jacobsen, P. B., Bovbjerg, D. H., Schwartz, M. D., & Andrykowski, M. A. (1994). Formation of food aversions in patients receiving repeated infusions of chemotherapy. *Behaviour Research & Therapy, 38*, 739–748.

Jain, S., & Posavac, S. S. (2001). Prepurchase attribute verifiability, source credibility, and persuasion. *Journal of Consumer Psychology, 11*, 169–180.

Jang, K. L., Livesley, W. J., Angleitner, A., Riemann, R., & Vernon, P. A. (2002). Genetic and environmental influences on the convariance of facets defining the domains of the five-factor model of personality. *Personality and Individual Differences, 33*, 83–101.

Jang, K. L., Livesley, W. J., McCrae, R. R., Angleitner, A., & Riemann, R. (1998). Heritability of facet-level traits in a cross-cultural twin sample: Support for a hierarchical model of personality. *Journal of Personality and Social Psychology, 74*, 1556–1565.

Janis, I. (1982). *Groupthink: Psychological studies of policy decisions and fiascoes* (2nd ed.). Boston: Houghton Mifflin.

Janis, I. L. (1989). *Crucial decisions: Leadership in policymaking and crisis management*. New York: Free Press.

Janis, I. L., Mahl, G. G., & Holt, R. R. (1969). *Personality: Dynamics, development and assessment*. New York: Harcourt Brace Jovanovich.

Janos, P. M., & Robinson, N. M. (1985). Psychosocial development in intellectually gifted children. In F. D. Horowitz & M. O'Brien (Eds.), *Gifted and talented: Developmental perspectives* (pp. 149–195). Washington, DC: American Psychological Association.

Jansen, P. G. W., & Stoop, B. A. M. (2001). The dynamics of assessment center validity: Results of a 7-year study. *Journal of Applied Psychology, 86* (4), 741–753.

Javitt, D. C., & Coyle, J. T. (January 2004). Decoding schizophrenia. *Scientific American*, pp. 48–55.

Jaynes, G. D., & Williams, R. M. (Eds.). (1989). *Common destiny: Blacks and American society*. Washington, DC: National Academy Press.

Jemmott, J. B., III, Jemmott, L. S., Fong, G. T., & McCaffree, K. (2002). Reducing HIV risk-associated sexual behavior among African-American adolescents: Testing the generality of intervention effects. *American Journal of Community Psychology, 27*, 161–187.

Jensen, A. R. (1992). Commentary: Vehicles of g. *Psychological Science, 3*, 275–278.

Johansson, M., & Arlinger, S. D. (2003). Prevalence of hearing impairment in a population in Sweden. *International Journal of Audiology, 42*, 18–28.

Johnsen, B. H., Laberg, J. C., Eid, J., & Hugdahl, K. (2002). Dichotic listening and sleep deprivation: Vigilance effects. *Scandinavian Journal of Psychology, 43*, 413–417.

Johnson, A. (2003). Procedural memory and skill acquisition. In A. F. Healy & R. W. Proctor (Eds.), *Handbook of Psychology: Experimental Psychology*, Vol. 4 (pp. 499–523). New York: John Wiley & Sons.

Johnson, D. (1990). Can psychology ever be the same again after the human genome is mapped? *Psychological Science, 1*, 331–332.

Johnson, D. M., & Erneling, C. A. (Eds.). (1997). *The future of the cognitive revolution*. New York: Oxford University Press.

Johnson, L. D., O'Malley, P. M., & Bachman, J. G. (2003, December 19). *Data from in-school surveys of 8th, 10th, and 12th grade students. Drug and Alcohol press release and associated tables*. Ann Arbor, MI: University of Michigan News and Information Services.

Johnson, S., & Leach, J. (2001). Using expert employees to train on the job. *Advances in developing human resources, 3* (4), 425–435.

Johnston, K. L., & White, K. M. (2003). Binge-drinking: A test of the role of group norms in the theory of planned behaviour. *Psychology and Health, 18*, 63–77.

Jones, C. J., & Meredith, W. (2000). Developmental paths of psychological health from early adolescence to later adulthood. *Psychology & Aging, 15*, 351–360.

Jones, L. W., Sinclair, R. C., & Courneya, K. S. (2003). The effects of source credibility and message framing on exercise intentions, behaviors and attitudes: An integration of the elaboration likelihood model and prospect theory. *Journal of Applied Social Psychology, 33*, 179–196.

Jones, M. C. (1924). Elimination of children's fears. *Journal of Experimental Psychology, 7*, 381–390.

Judge, T. A. & Bono, J. E. (2000). Five-factor model of personality and transformational leadership. *Journal of Applied Psychology, 85* (5), 751–765.

Judge, T. A., Thoresen, C. J., Bono, J. E., & Patton, G. K. (2001). The job satisfaction-job performance relationship: A qualitative and quantitative review. *Psychological Bulletin, 127* (3), 376–407.

Junginger, J. (1997). Fetishism. In D. R. Laws & W. T. O'Donohue (eds.), *Handbook of sexual deviance: Theory and application.* New York: Guilford.

Kadotani, H., Kadotani, T., Young, T., Peppard, P. E., Finn, L., Colrain, I. M., et al. (2001). Association between apolipoprotein E C 4 and sleep-disordered breathing in adults. *Journal of the American Medical Association, 285,* 2888–2890.

Kahneman, D., & Tversky, A. (1996). On the reality of cognitive illusions. *Psychological Review, 103*(3), 582–591.

Kalat, J. W. (1988). *Biological psychology* (3rd ed.). Belmont, CA: Wadsworth.

Kaminski, M. (1999). *The team concept: A worker-centered alternative to lean production.* APA Public Interest Directorate. Available online at: *www.apa.org/pi/wpo/niosh/abstract22.html.*

Kane, J., & Lieberman, J. (1992). *Adverse effects of psychotropic drugs.* New York: Guilford Press.

Kanfer, R., & Ackerman, P. L. (2000). Individual differences in work motivation: Further explorations of a trait framework. *Applied Psychology: An International Review, 49 (3),* 470–482.

Kaplan, C. A., & Simon, H. A. (1990). In search of insight. *Cognitive Psychology, 22,* 374–419.

Kass, S. (1999, September). Employees perceive women as better managers than men, finds five-year study. *APA Monitor,* p.6.

Kassebaum, N. L. (1994). Head Start: Only the best for America's children. *American Psychologist, 49,* 123–126.

Katz, R., & McGuffin, P. (1993). The genetics of affective disorders. In D. Fowles (ed.), *Progress in experimental personality and psychopathology research.* New York: Springer.

Katz, S. (2003). Physical appearance: The importance of being beautiful. In J. M. Henslin (Ed.), *Down to earth sociology: Introductory readings* (12th ed.; pp. 313–320). New York: Free Press.

Keitner, G. I., Archambault, R., Ryan, C. E., & Miller, I. W., (2003). Family therapy and chronic depression. *Journal of Clinical Psychology, 59,* 873–884.

Kelemen, W. L., & Creeley, C. E. (2003). State-dependent memory effects using caffeine and placebo do not extend to metamemory. *Journal of General Psychology, 130,* 70–86.

Kelley, H. H. (1967). Attribution theory in social psychology. In D. Levine (Ed.), *Nebraska Symposium on Motivation: Vol. 15* (pp. 192–238). Lincoln: University of Nebraska Press.

Keller, A., & Vosshall, L. B. (2004). A psychophysical test of the vibration theory of olfaction. *Nature Neuroscience, 7,* 337–338.

Keller, M. B., McCullough, J. P., Klein, D. N., Arnow, B., Dunner, D. L., Gelenberg, A. J., et al. (2000). A comparison of Nefazodone, the cognitive behavioral-analysis system of psychotherapy, and their combination for the treatment of chronic depression. *New England Journal of Medicine, 342,* 1462–1470.

Keller, R. T. (2006). Transformational leadership, initiating structure, and substitutes for leadership: A longitudinal study of research and development project team performance. *Journal of Applied Psychology, 91 (1),* 202–210.

Kelloway, E. K., & Day, A. (2005). Building healthy workplaces: Where we need to be. *Canadian Journal of behavioural Science, 37 (4),* 309–312.

Kendler, K. S., Neale, M. C., Kessler, R. C., Heath, A. C., & Eaves, L. J. (1992). Generalized anxiety disorder in women: A population-based twin study. *Archives of General Psychiatry, 49,* 267–272.

Keppel, B. (2002). Kenneth B. Clark in patterns of American culture. *American Psychologist, 57,* 29–37.

Kerrison, D. (2006). Do you really know who you are hiring. *InFinsia, 120* (1), 42–53.

Kessler, R. C. (1979). Stress, social status, and psychological distress. *Journal of Health and Social Behavior, 20,* 259–272.

Kessler, R. C., Berglund, P., Demler, O., Jin, R., Koretz, D., Merikangas, K. R., Rush, A. J., Walters, E. E., & Wang, P. S. (2003). The epidemiology of major depressive disorder: Results from the National Comorbidity Survey Replication (NCS-R). *Journal of the American Medical Association, 289,* 3095–3105.

Kessler, R. C., McGonagle, K. A., Zhao, S., Nelson, C. R., Highes, M., Eshleman, S., et al. (1994). Lifetime and 12-month prevalence of DSM-III-R psychiatric disorders in the United States: Results from the National Comorbidity Survey. *Archives of General Psychiatry, 51,* 8–19.

Kessler, R. C., Price, R. H., & Wortman, C. B. (1985). Social factors in psychopathology: Stress, social support, and coping processes. *Annual Review of Psychology, 36,* 531–572.

Khan, A. (1993). Electroconvulsive therapy: Second edition. *Journal of Nervous and Mental Disease, 181*(9), n.p.

Kiecolt–Glaser, J. K., Bane, C., Glaser, R., & Malarkey, W. B. (2003). Love, marriage, and divorce: Newlyweds' stress hormones foreshadow relationship changes. *Journal of Consulting and Clinical Psychology, 71,* 176–188.

Kiecolt–Glaser, J. K., & Glaser, R. (2002). Depression and immune function: Central pathways to morbidity and mortality. *Journal of Psychosomatic Research, 53,* 873–876.

Kiecolt-Glaser, J. K., Malarkey, W. B., Chee, M., Newton, T., & Cacioppo, J. T. (1993). Negative behavior during marital conflict is associated with immunological down-regulation. Psychosomatic Medicine, 55, 395–409.

Kihlström, J. F. (1998). Dissociations and dissociation theory in hypnosis: Comment on Kirsch and Lynn (1998). *Psychological Bulletin, 123,* 186–191.

Kileny, P. R., Zwolan, T. A., & Ashbaugh, C. (2001). The influence of age at implantation on performance with a cochlear implant in children. *Otology and Neurotology, 22,* 42–46.

Kilpatrick, D. G., Acierno, R., Saunders, B., Resnick, H. S., Best, C. L., & Schnurr, P. P. (2000). Risk factors for adolescent substance abuse and dependence: Data from a national sample. *Journal of Consulting & Clinical Psychology, 68,* 19–30.

Kimberg, D. Y., D'Esposito, M. D., & Farah, M. J. (1997). Cognitive functions in the prefrontal cortex–working memory and executive control. *Current Directions in Psychological Science, 6,* 185–192.

Kingstone, A., Enns, J. T., Mangun, G. R., & Gazzaniga, M. S. (1995). Right-hemisphere memory superiority: Studies of a split-brain patient. *Psychological Science, 6,* 118–121.

Kinicki, A. J., McKee-Ryan, F. M., Schriesheim, C. A., & Carson, K. P. (2002). Assessing the construct validity of the job descriptive index: A review and meta-analysis. *Journal of Applied Psychology, 87 (1),* 14–32.

Kinlaw, D. C. (1990). *Developing superior work teams*. New York: Simon and Schuster.

Kirsch, I., & Braffman, W. (2001). Imaginative suggestibility and hypnotizability. *Current Directions in Psychological Science, 10*, 57–60.

Kirsch, I., Montgomery, G., & Saperstein, G. (1995). Hypnosis as an adjunct to cognitive behavioral psychotherapy: A meta analysis. *Journal of Consulting and Clinical Psychology, 63*, 214–220.

Kissane, D. W., Bloch, S., Miach, P., Smith, G. C., Seddon, A., & Keks, N. (1997). Cognitive-existential group therapy for patients with primary breast cancer–techniques and themes. *Psychooncology, 6*(1), 25–33.

Kite, M. E., Russo, N. F., Brehm, S. S., Fouad, N. A., Hall, C. C., Hyde, J. S., & Keita, G. P. (2001). Women psychologists in academe. *American Psychologist, 56*, 1080–1098.

Kleim, J. A., Vij, K., Ballard, D. H., & Greenough, W. T. (1997). Learning-dependent synaptic modifications in the cerebellar cortex of the adult rat persist for at least four weeks. *Journal of Neuroscience, 17*, 717–721.

Klein, D. N., Schwartz, J. E., Santiago, N. J., Vivian, D., Vocisano, C., Castonguay, L. G., Arnow, B., Blalock, J. A., Manber, R., Markowitz, J. C., Riso, L. P., Rothbaum, B., McCullough, J. P., Thase, M. T., Borian, F. E., Miller, I. W., & Keller, M. B. (2003). Therapeutic alliance in depression treatment: Controlling for prior change and patient characteristics. *Journal of Consulting and Clinical Psychology, 71*, 997–1006.

Kleinmuntz, D. N. (1991). Decision making for professional decision makers. *Psychological Science, 2*, 135, 138–141.

Klingenspor, B. (1994). Gender identity and bulimic eating behavior. *Sex Roles, 31*, 407–432.

Klinger, E. (1990). *Daydreaming: Using waking fantasy and imagery for self-knowledge and creativity*. New York: J.P. Tarcher.

Kluckhohn, C. (1949). *Mirror for man: The relation of anthropology to modern life*. New York: Whittlesey House.

Kluckholm, C., Murray, H. A., & Schneider, D. M., (Eds.) (1961). *Personality in nature, society, and culture*. New York: Knopf.

Kluegel, J. R. (1990). Trends in white's explanations of the black–white gap in socioeconomic status, 1977–89. *American Sociological Review, 55*, 512–525.

Klump, K. L., McGue, M., & Iacono, W. G. (2002). Genetic relationships between personality and eating attitudes and behaviors. *Journal of Abnormal Psychology, 111*, 380–389.

Kobasa, S. C. (1979). Stressful life events, personality, and health: An inquiry into hardiness. *Journal of Personality and Social Psychology, 37*, 1–11.

Koenig, H. G., McCullough, M. E., & Larson, D. B. (2000). *Handbook of religion and health*. New York: Oxford University Press.

Koh, P. O., Bergson, C., Undie, A., S., Goldman, R., Patricia, S., & Lidow, M. S. (2003). Up regulation of D1 dopamine receptor interacting protein, calcyon, in patients with schizophrenia. *Archives of General Psychiatry, 60*, 311–319.

Kohn, A. (1993). *Punished by rewards*. Boston: Houghton Mifflin.

Kokmen, E. (1991). The EURODEM collaborative re-analysis of case-control studies of Alzheimer's disease: Implications for clinical research and practice. *International Journal of Epidemiology, 20*(Suppl. 2), S65–S67.

Kolata, G. (1996a, April 3). Can it be? Weather has no effect on arthritis. *New York Times*, p. B9.

Kolb, B., Gibb, R., & Robinson, T. E. (2003). Brain plasticity and behavior. *Current Directions in Psychological Science, 12*, 1–5.

Kolchakian, M. R., & Hill, C. E. (2002). Dream interpretation with heterosexual dating couples. *Dreaming: Journal of the Association For the Study of Dreams, 12*, 1–16.

Komaki, J. L. (1986). Toward effective supervision: An operant analysis and comparison of managers at work. Journal of Applied Psychology, 71 (2), 270–279.

Komaki, J. L. (2003). Reinforcement theory at work: Enhanceing and explaining what employees do. In L. W. Porter, Ga. A. Bigley, & R. M Steers (Eds.), *Motivation and work behavior* (7ᵗʰ ed., pp. 95–112). Boston: McGraw-Hill Irwin.

Komatsu, L. K. (1992). Recent views of conceptual structure. *Psychological Bulletin, 112*, 500–526.

Komiya, N., Good, G. E., & Sherrod, N. B. (2000). Emotional openness as a predictor of college students' attitudes toward seeking psychological help. *Journal of Counseling Psychology, 47*, 138–143.

Konradi, C., Eaton, M., MacDonald, M. L., Walsh, J., Benes, F. M., & Heckers, S. (2004). Molecular evidence for mitochondrial dysfunction in bipolar disorder. *Archives of General Psychiatry, 61*, 300–308.

Kopelowicz, A., Liberman, R. P., & Zarate, R. (2002). Psychosocial treatments for schizophrenia. In P. E. Nathan & J. M. Gorman (Eds.), *A guide to treatments that work* (2d ed., pp. 201–228). London: Oxford University Press.

Kopta, S. M., Howard, K. I., Lowry, J. L., & Beutler, L. E. (1994). Patterns of symptomatic recovery in psychotherapy. *Journal of Consulting and Clinical Psychology, 62*, 1009–1016.

Kozlowski, S. J., & Bell, B. S. (2003). Work groups and teams in organizations. In W. C. Borman, D. R. Ilgen, & R. J. Klimoski (Eds.), *Handbook of psychology: Industrial and organizational psychology* (Vol. 12, pp. 333–375). Hoboken, NJ: Wiley.

Krasne, F. B., & Glanzman, D. L. (1995). What we can learn from invertebrate learning. *Annual Review of Psychology, 46*, 585–624.

Kraus, S. J. (1995). Attitudes and the prediction of behavior: A meta-analysis of the empirical literature. *Personality and Social Psychology Bulletin, 21*, 58–75.

Krebs, D. (1975). Empathy and altruism. *Journal of Personality and Social Psychology, 32*, 1134–1140.

Krebs, D. L. (2003). Fictions and fact about evolutionary approaches to human behavior: Comment on Lickliter and Honeycutt (2003). *Psychological Bulletin, 129*, 842–847.

Kreiman, G., Koch, C., & Fried, I. (2000). Imagery neurons in the human brain. *Nature, 408*, 357–361.

Kringlen, E. (1981). *Stress and coronary heart disease. Twin research 3: Epidemiological and clinical studies*. New York: Alan R. Liss.

Krosnick, J. A. (1999). Survey research. *Annual Review of Psychology, 50*, 537–567.

Kruglanski, A. W. (1986, August). Freeze-think and the Challenger. *Psychology Today*, pp. 48–49.

Krystal, A. D., Holsinger, T., Weiner, R. D., & Coffey, C. E. (2000). Prediction of the utility of a switch from unilateral to bilateral ECT in the elderly using treatment 2 ictal EEG indices. Journal of ECT, 16, 327–337.

Kucharski, L. T., Johnsen, D., & Procell, S. (2004). The utility of the MMPI-2 infrequency psychopathology F(p) and the revised infrequency psychopathology scales in the detection of malingering. *American Journal of Forensic Psychology, 22*, 33–40.

Kuhl, P. K., Williams, K. A., & Lacerda, F. (1992, January 31). Linguistic experience alters phonetic perception in infants by 6 months of age. *Science, 255*, 606–608.

Kulik, J., & Brown, R. (1979). Frustration, attribution of blame, and aggression. *Journal of Experimental Social Psychology, 15*, 183–194.

Kumkale, G. T., & Albarracín, D. (2004). The sleeper effect: A meta-analytic review. *Psychological Bulletin, 130*, 143–172.

Kuncel, N. R., Hezlett, S. A., & Ones, D. S. (2004). Academic performance, career potential, creativity, and job performance: Can one construct predict them all? *Journal of Personality and Social Psychology, 86*, 148–161.

Kunkel, D., Wilson, B. J., Linz, D., Potter, J., Donnerstein, E., Smith, S. L., Blumenthal, E., & Gray, T. (1996). *The national television violence study*. Studio City, CA: Mediascope.

Kunst-Wilson, W. R., & Zajonc, R. B. (1980). Affective discrimination of stimuli that cannot be recognized. *Science, 207*, 557–558.

Kupfermann, I. (1991). Hypothalamus and limbic system motivation. In E. R. Kandel, J. H. Schwartz, & T. M. Jessel (eds.), *Principles of neural science* (3rd ed., pp. 750–760). New York: Elsevier.

Kurdek, L. A., Fine, M. A., & Sinclair, R. J. (1995). School adjustment in sixth graders: Parenting transitions, family climate, and peer norm effects. *Child Development, 66*, 430–445.

Laan, E., Everaerd, W., van Berlo, R., & Rijs, L. (1995). Mood and sexual arousal in women. *Behavior Research Therapy, 33*, 441–443.

Labouvie-Vief, G. (1986). Modes of knowledge and the organization of development. In M. L. Commons, L. Kohlberg, F. A. Richards, & J. Sinnott (Eds.), *Beyond formal operations: 2. Models and methods in the study of adult and adolescent thoughts*. New York: Praeger.

LaGreca, A. M., Stone, W. L., & Bell, C. R., III. (1983). Facilitating the vocational-interpersonal skills of mentally retarded individuals. *American Journal of Mental Deficiency, 88*, 270–278.

Lal, S. (2002). Giving children security. *American Psychologist, 57*, 20–28.

LaMalfa, G., Lassi, S., Bertelli, M., Salvini, R., & Placidi, G. F. (2004). Autism and intellectual disability: A study of prevalence on a sample of the Italian population. *Journal of Intellectual Disability Research, 48*, 262–267.

Lamb, H. R., & Weinberger, L. E. (2001). *Deinstitutionalization: Promise and problems*. San Francisco: Jossey–Bass.

Lamb, J. A., Moore, J., Bailey, A., & Monaco, A. P. (2000). Autism: Recent molecular genetic advances. *Human Molecular Genetics, 9*, 861–868.

Lamberg, L. (1998). New drug for erectile dysfunction boon for many, "viagravation" for some. *JAMA: Medical News & Perspectives, 280*, 867–871.

Lambert, M. J., Shapiro, D. A., & Bergin, A. E. (1986). The effectiveness of psychotherapy. In S. L. Garfield & A. E. Bergin (eds.), *Handbook of psychotherapy and behavior change* (3rd ed., pp. 157–212). New York: Wiley.

Lampl, M., Veldhuis, J. D., & Johnson, M. L. (1992, October 30). Saltation and stasis: A model of human growth. *Science, 258*, 801–803.

Landesman, S., & Butterfield, E. C. (1987). Normalization and deinstitution of mentally retarded individuals: Controversy and facts. *American Psychologist, 42*, 809–816.

Landy, F. J. & Conte, J. M. (2004). *Work in the 21st Century*. New York: McGraw-Hill.

Lange, K., Williams, L. M., Young, A. W., Bullmore, E. T., Brammer, M. J., Williams, S. C. R., Gray, J. A., & Philips, M. L. (2003). Task instructions modulate neural responses to fearful facial expressions. *Biological Psychiatry, 53*, 226–232.

Lange, T., Perras, B., Fehm, H. L., & Born, J. (2003). Sleep enhances the human antibody response to hepatitis A vaccination. *Psychosomatic Medicine, 65*, 831–835.

Langer, E. J., Bashner, R. S., & Chanowitz, B. (1985). Decreasing prejudice by increasing discrimination. *Journal of Personality and Social Psychology, 49*, 113–120.

Langlois, J. H., Ritter, J. M., Casey, R. J., & Sawin, D. B. (1995). Infant attractiveness predicts maternal behaviors and attitudes. *Developmental Psychology, 31*, 464–472.

Lantz, M. S., Buchalter, E. N., & McBee, L. (1997). The wellness group: A novel intervention for coping with disruptive behavior in elderly nursing home residents. *Gerontologist, 37*, 551–556.

Latané, B., & Rodin, J. (1969). A lady in distress: Inhibiting effects of friends and strangers on bystander intervention. *Journal of Experimental Social Psychology, 5*, 189–202.

Laumann, E. O., Gagnon, J. H., Michael, R. T., & Michaels, S. (1994). *The social organization of sexuality: Sexual practices in the United States*. Chicago: University of Chicago Press.

Lazarus, R. S. (1993). From psychological stress to the emotions: A history of changing outlooks. *Annual Review of Psychology, 44*, 1–21.

Leary, W. E. (1990, January 25). Risk of hearing loss is growing, panel says. *New York Times*, Sec.B.

LeBoeuf, R. A., & Shafir, E. (2003). Deep thoughts and shallow frames on the susceptibility to framing effects. *Journal of Behavioral Decision Making, 16*, 77–92.

Lebow, J. L., & Gurman, A. S. (1995). Research assessing couple and family therapy. *Annual Review of Psychology, 46*, 27–57.

Leibowitz, H. W., & Owens, D. A. (1977). Nighttime driving accidents and selective visual degradation. *Science, 197*, 422–423.

Leichsenring, F., & Leibing, E. (2003). The effectiveness of psychodynamic therapy and cognitive behavior therapy in the treatment of personality disorders: A meta-analysis. *American Journal of Psychiatry, 160*, 1223–1232.

Leifer, M., Kilbane, T., & Kalick, S. (2004). Vulnerability or resilience to inter-generational sexual abuse: The role of maternal factors. *Child Maltreatment: Journal of the American Professional Society on the Abuse of Children, 9*, 78–91.

Leigh, R. J. (1994). Human vestibular cortex. *Annals of Neurology, 35*, 383–384.

Leitenberg, H., & Henning, K. (1995). Sexual fantasy. *Psychological Bulletin, 117*, 469–496.

Lerman, C., Caporaso, N. D., Audrain, J., Main, D., Bowman, E. D., Lockshin, B., et al. Evidence suggesting the role of specific genetic factors in cigarette smoking. *Health Psychology, 18*, 14–20.

Lerner, M. J. (1980). *The belief in a just world: A fundamental delusion*. New York: Plenum.

Leroy, P., Dessolin, S., Villageois, P., Moon, B. C., Friedman, J. M., Ailhaud, G., & Dani, C. (1996). Expression of ob gene in adipose cells. Regulation by insulin. *Journal of Biological Chemistry, 271,* 2365–2368.

LeVay, S., & Hamer, D. H. (1994). Evidence for a biological influence in male homosexuality. *Scientific American, 270*(5), 44–49.

Levenson, M. R., & Aldwin, C. M. (1994). Aging, personality, and adaptation. In V. S. Ramachandran (Ed.), *Encyclopedia of human behavior* (Vol. 1, pp. 47–55). San Diego, CA: Academic Press.

Levin, J. S., & Vanderpool, H. Y. (1989). Is religion therapeutically significant for hypertension? *Social Science and Medicine, 29* (1), 69–78.

Levine, E. L., Sistrunk, F., McNutt, K. J., & Gael, S. (1988). Exploring job analysis systems in selected organizations: A description of process and outcomes. *Journal of Business and Psychology, 3* (1), 3–21.

Lewy, A. J., Ahmed, S., Latham, J. J., & Sack R. (1992). Melatonin shifts human circadian rhythms according to a phase-response curve. *Chronobiology International 9,* 380–392.

Li, Y. J., & Low, W. C. (1997). Intraretrosplenial cortical grafts of fetal cholinergic neurons and the restoration of spatial memory function. *Cell Transplant, 6,* 85–93.

Lichstein, K. L., Wilson, N. M., & Johnson, C. T. (2000). Psychological treatment of secondary insomnia. *Psychology & Aging, 15,* 232–240.

Lichtenstein, E. (1999). Nicotine Anonymous: Community resource and research implications. *Psychology of Addictive Behaviors, 13,* 60–68.

Lickliter, R., & Honeycutt, H. (2003a). Developmental dynamics: Toward a biologically plausible evolutionary psychology. *Psychological Bulletin, 129,* 819–835.

Lickliter, R., & Honeycutt, H. (2003b). Developmental dynamics and contemporary evolutionary psychology: Status quo or irreconcilable views? Reply to Bjorklund (2003), Krebs (2003), Buss and Reeve (2003), Crawford (2003), and Tooby et al. (2003). *Psychological Bulletin, 129,* 866–872.

Liden, R. C., & Maslyn, J. M. (1998). Multidimensionality of leader-member exchange: An empirical assessment through scale development. *Journal of Management, 24* (1), 43–72.

Liden, R. C., Wayne, S. J., & Sparrowe, R. T. (2000). An examination of the mediating role of psychological empowerment on the relations between the job, interpersonal relationships, and work outcomes. *Journal of Applied Psychology, 85* (3), 407–416.

Liem, R., & Liem, J. V. (1978). Social class and mental illness reconsidered: The role of economic stress and social support. *Journal of Health and Social Behavior, 19,* 139–156.

Liggett, D. R. (2000). *Sport hypnosis.* Champaign, IL: Human Kinetics.

Li, Y. J., & Low, W. C. (1997). Intraretrosplenial cortical grafts of fetal cholinergic neurons and the restoration of spatial memory function. *Cell Transplant, 6,* 85–93.

Lindsay, D. S., & Johnson, M. K. (1989). The eyewitness suggestibility effect and memory for source. *Memory & Cognition, 17,* 349–358.

Lin, L., Umahara, M., York, D. A., & Bray, G. A. (1998). Beta-casomophins stimulate and enterostatin inhibits the intake of dietary fat in rats. *Peptides, 19,* 325–331.

Linn, R. L. (1982). Admissions testing on trial. *American Psychologist, 37,* 279–291.

Lips, H. M. (2002). *A new psychology of women: Gender, culture, and ethnicity* (2nd ed.). New York: McGraw-Hill.

Lipsey, M., & Wilson, D. (1993). The efficacy of psychological, educational, and behavioral treatment: Confirmation from meta-analysis. *American Psychologist, 48,* 1181–1209.

Lipsky, D. K., & Gartner, A. (1996). Inclusive education and school restructuring. In W. Stainback & S. Stainback (Eds.), *Controversial issues confronting special education: Divergent perspectives* (pp. 3–15). Baltimore: Brookes.

Liu, C., Weaver, D. R., Jin, X., Shearman, I. P., Pieschl, R. I., Gribkoff, V. K., et al. (1997). Molecular dissection of two distinct actions of melatonin on the suprachiasmatic circadian clock. *Neuron, 19,* 99–102.

Liu, J. H., & Latane, B. (1998). Extremitization of attitudes: Does thought- and discussion-induced polarization cumulate? *Basic and Applied Social Psychology, 20,* 103–110.

Livesley, W. J., Jang, K. L., & Vernon P. A. (2003). Genetic basis of personality structure. In T. Millon & M. J. Lerner, (Eds.), *Handbook of psychology: Personality and social psychology,* Vol. 5 (pp. 59–83). New York: John Wiley & Sons, Inc.

Locke, E. A., & Latham, G. P. (1990). *A theory of goal setting task performance.* Englewood Cliffs, NJ: Prentice Hall.

Locke, E. A., & Latham, G. P. (2002). Building a practically useful theory of goal setting and task motivation: A 35-year odyssey. *American Psychologist, 57* (9), 705–717.

Loehlin, J. C., Horn, J. M., & Willerman, L. (1997). Heredity, environment, and IQ in the Texas adoption study. In R. J. Sternberg & E. Grigorenko (eds.), *Intelligence: Heredity and environment.* New York: Cambridge University Press.

Loehlin, J. C., McCrae, R. R., Costa, P. T., & John, O. P. (1998). Heritability of common and measure-specific components of the Big Five personality traits. *Journal of Research in Personality, 32,* 431–453.

Loftus, E. F. (1997). Repressed memory accusations: Devastated families and devastated patients. *Applied Cognitive Psychology, 11*(1), 25–30.

Loftus, E. F., Coan, J. A., & Pickrell, J. E. (1996). Manufacturing false memories using bits of reality. In L. Reder (Ed.), *Implicit memory and metacognition* (pp. 195–220). Mahwah, NJ: Erlbaum.

Loftus, E. F., & Pickrell, J. E. (1995). The formation of false memories. *Psychiatric Annals, 25,* 720–725.

Lorenz, K. (1968). *On aggression.* New York: Harcourt.

Louie, T. A., Curren, M. T., & Harich, K. R. (2000). "I knew we could win": Hindsight bias for favorable and unfavorable decision outcomes. *Journal of Applied Psychology, 85,* 264–272.

Lubinski, D. (2000). Scientific and social significance of assessing individual differences: "Sinking shafts at a few critical points." *Annual Review of Psychology, 51,* 405–444.

Luthans, F., & Peterson, S. (2003). 360-Degree feedback with systematic coaching: Empirical analysis suggests a winning combination. *Human resource management, 42* (3), 243–256.

Lyness, S. A. (1993). Predictors of differences between Type A and B individuals in heart rate and blood pressure reactivity. *Psychological Bulletin, 114,* 266–295.

Lyons, M. J., True, W. R., Eisen, S. A., Goldberg, J., Meyer, J. M., Faraone, S. V., et al. (1995). Differential heritability of adult and juvenile antisocial traits. *Archives of General Psychiatry, 52,* 906–915.

Lyubomirsky, S., & Ross, L. (1999). Changes in attractiveness of elected, rejected and precluded alternatives: A comparison of happy and unhappy individuals. *Journal of Personality and Social Psychology, 76,* 988–1007.

Maas, J. (1998). *Power sleep: The revolutionary program that prepares your mind for peak performance.* New York: Villard.

Macionis, J. J. (1993). *Sociology* (4th ed.). Englewood Cliffs, NJ: Prentice Hall.

MacLean, P. D. (1970). The limbic brain in relation to the psychoses. In P. Black (ed.), *Physiological correlates of emotion* (pp. 129–146). New York: Academic Press.

MacLeod, D. I. A. (1978). Visual sensitivity. Annual Review of *Psychology, 29,* 613–645.

Macmillan, M. (2000). *An odd kind of fame: Stories of Phineas Gage.* Cambridge, MA: MIT Press.

Macrae, C. N., & Bodenhausen, G. V. (2000). Social cognition: Thinking categorically about others. *Annual Review of Psychology, 51,* 93–120.

Mackworth, N. (1965). Originality. *American Psychologist, 20,* 51–66.

Maddi, S. R. (1989). *Personality theories: A comparative approach* (5th ed.). Homewood, IL: Dorsey.

Madsen, P. L. (1993). Blood flow and oxygen uptake in the human brain during various states of sleep and wakefulness. *Acta Paediatrica Scandinavica, 148* (Suppl.), 3–27.

Maier, S. F., & Seligman, M. E. (1976). Learned helplessness: Theory and evidence. *Journal of Experimental Psychology: General, 105,* 3–46.

Maisto, A. A., & Hughes, E. (1995). Adaptation to group home living for adults with mental retardation as a function of previous residential placement. *Journal of Intellectual Disability Research, 39,* 15–18.

Maloney, M. P., & Ward, M. P. (1976). *Psychological assessment: A conceptual approach.* New York: Academic Press.

Maj, M. (2003). The effect of lithium in bipolar disorder: A review of recent research evidence. *Bipolar Disorders, 5,* 180–188.

Mandel, D. R., Jusczyk, P. W., & Pisoni, D. B. (1995). Infants' recognition of the sound patterns of their own names. *Psychological Science, 6,* 314–317.

Mann, T., Sherman, D., & Updegraff, J. (2004). Dispositional motivations and message framing: A test of the congruency hypothesis in college students. *Health Psychology, 23,* 330–334.

Manns, J. R., Hopkins, R. O., & Squire, L. R. (2003). Semantic memory and the human hippocampus. *Neuron, 38,* 127–133.

Maquet, P., Laureys, S., Peigneus, P., Fuchs, S., Petiau, C., Phips, C., Aerts, J., Fiore, G. D., Degueldre, C., Meulemans, T., Luxen, A., Franck, G., VanDerLinden, M., Smith, C., & Axel, C. (2000). Experience-dependent changes in cerebral activation during human REM sleep. *Nature: Neuroscience, 3,* 831–836.

Marano, H. E. (1997, July 1). Puberty may start at 6 as hormones surge. *New York Times,* pp. C1, C6.

Marcus, G. F. (1996). Why do children say "breaked"? *American Psychological Society, 5,* 81–85.

Margolin, G. (1987). Marital therapy: A cognitive-behavioral-affective approach. In N. S. Jacobson (ed.), *Psychotherapists in clinical practice* (pp. 232–285). New York: Guilford.

Mark, A. (2003). Inattentional blindness: Looking without seeing. *Current Directions in Psychological Science, 12,* 180–184.

Markel, H. (2003, September 2). Lack of sleep takes its toll on student psyches. *New York Times,* p. D6.

Markon, K. E., Krueger, R. F., Bouchard, T. J., Jr., & Gottesman, I. I. (2002). Normal and abnormal personality traits: Evidence for genetic and environmental relationships in the Minnesota Study of Twins Reared Apart. *Journal of Personality, 70,* 661–693.

Marks, L. S., Duda, C., Dorey, F. J., Macairan, M. L., & Santos, P. B. (1999). Treatment of erectile dysfunction with sildenafil. *Urology, 53,* 19–24.

Martin, R. A. (2002). Is laughter the best medicine? Humor, laughter, and physical health. *Current Directions in Psychological Science, 11,* 216–220.

Martino, A. (1995, February 5). Mid-life usually brings positive change, not crisis. *Ann Arbor News.*

Maslach, C., & Leiter, M. P. (1997). *The truth about burnout.* San Francisco: Jossey-Bass.

Masling, J. (2002). How do I score thee? Let me count the ways. Or some different methods of categorizing Rorschach responses. *Journal of Personality Assessment, 79,* 399–421.

Mason, F. L. (1997). Fetishism: Psychopathology and theory. In D. R. Laws & W. T, (1977). *Sexual deviance: Theory, assessment, and treatment.* New York: Guilford Press.

Massaro, D. W., & Cowan, N. (1993). Information processing models: Microscopes of the mind. *Annual Review of Psychology, 44,* 383–425.

Mateo, J. M. (2002). Kin-recognition abilities and nepotism as a function of sociality. *Proceedings: Biological Sciences, 269,* 721–727.

Mateo, J. M., & Johnston, R. E. (2000). Kin recognition and the "armpit effect": Evidence of self-referent phenotype matching. *Proceedings of the Royal Society: Biological Sciences, 267,* 695–700.

Mather, M., Shafir, E., & Johnson, M. (2000). Misremembrance of options past: Source monitoring and choice. *Psychological Science, 11,* 132–138.

Matlin, M. W. (1989). *Cognition* (2nd ed.). Fort Worth, TX: Holt, Rinehart & Winston.

Matson, J. L., Smalls, Y., Hampff, A., Smiroldo, B. B., & Anderson, S. J. (1998). A comparison of behavioral techniques to teach functional independent-living skills to individuals with severe and profound mental retardation. *Behavior Modification, 22,* 298–306.

Matsumoto, D. (1996). *Culture and psychology.* Pacific Grove, CA: Brooks/Cole.

Matthews, K. A. (1988). Coronary heart disease and Type A behaviors: Update on and alternative to the Booth-Kewley and Friedman (1987) quantitative review. *Psychological Bulletin, 104,* 373–380.

Mattson, S. N., Riley, E. P., Gramling, L., Delis, D. C., & Jones, K. L. (1998). Neuropsychological comparison of alcohol-exposed children with or without physical features of fetal alcohol syndrome. *Neuropsychology, 12,* 146–153.

Maunsell, E., Brisson, J., Mondor, M., Verreault, R., & Deschenes, L. (2001). Stressful life events and survival after breast cancer. *Psychosomatic Medicine, 63,* 306–315.

Maurer, D., & Maurer, C. (1988). *The world of the newborn.* New York: Basic Books.

Mayer, R. C., Davis, C. & Schoorman, J. H. (1995). An integrative model of organizational trust. *Academy of management review, 20* (3), 709–734.

Mazzoni, G., & Memon, A. (2003). Imagination can create false autobiographical memories. *Psychological Science, 14,* 186–188.

Mazzoni, G. A. L., Lombardo, P., Malvagia, S., & Loftus, E. F. (1999). Dream interpretation and false beliefs. *Professional Psychology: Research & Practice, 30,* 45–50.

McBurney, D. H., & Collings, V. B. (1984). *Introduction to sensation/perception* (2nd ed.). Englewood Cliffs, NJ: Prentice Hall.

McCabe, P. M., Schneiderman, N., Field, T., & Wellens, A. R. (2000). *Stress, coping, and cardiovascular disease.* Mahwah, NJ: Erlbaum.

McCall, M. (1997). Physical attractiveness and access to alcohol: What is beautiful does not get carded. *Journal of Applied Social Psychology, 27*(5), 453–462.

McCann, I. L., & Holmes, D. S. (1984). Influence of aerobic exercise on depression. *Journal of Personality and Social Psychology, 46,* 1142–1147.

McClearn, G. E., Plomin, R., Gora-Maslak, G., & Crabbe, J. C. (1991). The gene chase in behavioral science. *Psychological Science, 2,* 222–229.

McClintock, M. K. (1999). Reproductive biology. Pheromones and regulation of ovulation. *Nature, 401,* 232–233.

McClintock, M. K., & Herdt, G. (1996). Rethinking puberty: The development of sexual attraction. *Current Directions in Psychological Science, 5,* 178–183.

McClure, E. B. (2000). A meta-analytic review of sex differences in facial expression processing and their development in infants, children, and adolescents. *Psychological Bulletin, 126,* 424–453

McCrae, R. R., & Costa, P. T., Jr. (1985). Updating Norman's "adequate taxonomy": Intelligence and personality dimensions in natural language and in questionnaires. *Journal of Personality and Social Psychology, 49,* 710–721.

McCrae, R. R., & Costa, P. T., Jr. (1987). Validation of the five-factor model of personality across instruments and observers. *Journal of Personality and Social Psychology, 52,* 81–90.

McCrae, R. R., & Costa, P. T., Jr. (1989). More reasons to adopt the five-factor model. *American Psychologist, 44,* 451–452.

McCrae, R. R., & Costa, P. T., Jr. (1996). Toward a new generation of personality theories: Theoretical contexts for the five-factor model. In J. S. Wiggins (ed.), *The five-factor model of personality: Theoretical perspectives* (pp. 51–87). New York: Guilford Press.

McDaniel, M. A., & Frei, R. L. (1994). Validity of customer service measures in personnel selection: A review of criterion and construct evidence. (Cited in Hogan, R., Hogan, J., & Roberts, B. W. [1996]. Personality measurement and employment decisions: Questions and answers. *American Psychologist, 51*[5], 469–477.)

McDonald, J. W. (1999, September). Repairing the damaged spinal cord. *Scientific American, 281,* 65–73.

McFarland, L. J., Senn, L. E., & Childress, J. R. (1993). *21st century leadership: Dialogues with 100 top leaders.* Los Angeles: The Leadership Press.

McGinnis, M. (1994). The role of behavioral research in national health policy. In S. Blumenthal, K. Matthews, & Weiss (eds.), *New research frontiers in behavioral medicine: Proceeding of the National Conference.* Washington, DC: NIH Publications.

McGlynn, R. P., McGurk, D., Effland, V. S., Johll, N. L., & Harding, D. J. (2004). Brainstorming and task performance in groups constrained by evidence. *Organizational Behavior and Human Decision Processes, 93,* 75–87.

McGovern, L. P. (1976). Dispositional social anxiety and helping behavior under three conditions of threat. *Journal of Personality, 44,* 84–97.

McGue, M. (1993). From proteins to cognitions: The behavioral genetics of alcoholism. In R. Plomin & G. E. McClearn (Eds.), *Nature, nurture & psychology* (pp. 245–268). Washington, DC: American Psychological Association.

McGuire, M. T., Wing, R. R., Klem, M. L., Lang, W., & Hill, J. O. (1999). What predicts weight regain in a group of successful weight losers? *Journal of Consulting & Clinical Psychology, 67,* 177–185.

McGuire, S. (2001). Are behavioral genetic and socialization research compatible? *American Psychologist, 56,* 171.

McIntyre, C. K., Marriott, L. K., & Gold, P. E. (2003). Cooperation between memory systems: Acetylcholine release in the amygdala correlates positively with performance on a hippocampus-dependent task. *Behavioral Neuroscience, 117,* 320–326.

McIntyre, R. M., & Salas, E. (1995). Measuring and managing for team performance: Lessons from complex environments. In R. A. Guzzo & E. Salas (Eds.), *Team effectiveness and decision making in organizations* (pp. 9–45). San Francisco: Jossey-Bass.

McKay, R. (1997, April 4). Stem cells in the nervous system. *Science, 276,* 66–71.

McKellar, J., Stewart, E., & Humphreys, K. (2003). Alcoholics Anonymous involvement and positive alcohol-related outcomes: Cause, consequence, or just a correlate? A prospective 2-year study of 2,319 alcohol-dependent men. *Journal of Consulting and Clinical Psychology 71,* 302–308.

McKenna, M. C., Zevon, M. A., Corn, B., & Rounds, J. (1999). Psychosocial factors and the development of breast cancer: A meta-analysis. *Health Psychology, 18,* 520–531.

McKim, W. A. (1997). *Drugs and behavior* (3rd ed.). Upper Saddle River, NJ: Prentice Hall.

McMillan, T. M., Robertson, I. H., & Wilson, B. A. (1999). Neurogenesis after brain injury: Implications for neurorehabilitation. *Neuropsychological Rehabilitation, 9,* 129–133.

McNally, R. J. (2003a). Experimental approaches to the recovered memory controversy. In M. F. Lenzenweger & J. M. Hooley (Eds.), *Principles of experimental psychopathology: Essays in honor of Brendan A. Maher* (pp. 269–277). Washington, DC: American Psychological Association.

McNally, R. J. (2003b). Recovering memories of trauma: A view from the laboratory. *Current Directions in Psychological Science, 12,* 32–35.

McNeil, B. J., Pauker, S. G., Sox, H. C., Jr., & Tversky, A. (1982). On the elicitation of preferences for alternative therapies. *New England Journal of Medicine, 306,* 1259–1262.

Mednick, S. C., Nakayama, K., Cantero, J. L., Atienza, M., Levin, A. A., Pathak, N., & Stickgold, R. (2002). The restorative effect of naps on perceptual deterioration. *Nature Neuroscience, 5,* 677–681.

Meichenbaum, D., & Cameron, R. (1982). Cognitive-behavior therapy. In G. T. Wilson & C. M. Franks (eds.), *Contemporary behavior therapy: Conceptual and empirical foundations.* New York: Guilford.

Melamed, B. G., Hawes, R. R., Heiby, E., & Glick, J. (1975). Use of filmed modeling to reduce uncooperative behavior of children during dental treatment. *Journal of Dental Research, 54,* 797–801.

Melamed, S., Ben-Avi, I., Luz, J., & Green, M. (1995). Objective and subjective work monotony: Effects on job satisfaction, psychological distress, and absenteeism in blue-collar workers. *Journal of Applied Psychology, 80,* 29–42.

Mellers, B. A., Schwartz, A., & Cooke, A. D. J. (1998). Judgment and decision making. *Annual Review of Psychology, 49,* 447–477.

Meltzoff, A. N., & Moore, M. K. (1985). Cognitive foundations and social functions of imitation and intermodal representation in infancy. In J. Mehler & R. Fox (Eds.), *Neonate cognition: Beyond the blooming, buzzing confusion.* Hillsdale, NJ: Erlbaum.

Melzack, R. (1980). Psychological aspects of pain. In J. J. Bonica (ed.), *Pain.* New York: Raven Press.

Mendez, B., & Martha, M. (2001). Changes in parental sense of competence and attitudes in low-income Head Start parents as a result of participation in a Parent Education Workshop. *Dissertation Abstracts International: Section B: The Sciences and Engineering, 62,* 2976.

Merrill, K. A., Tolbert, V. E., & Wade, W. A. (2003). Effectiveness of cognitive therapy for depression in a community mental health center: A benchmarking study. *Journal of Consulting and Clinical Psychology, 71,* 404–409.

Meston, C. M., & Frohlich, M. A. (2000). The neurobiology of sexual function. *Archives of General Psychiatry, 57,* 1012–1030.

Metcalfe, J., Funnell, M., & Gazzaniga, M. S. (1995). Guided visual search is a left-hemisphere process in split-brain patient. *Psychological Science, 6,* 157–173.

Meyer, G. J., Finn, S. E., Eyde, L. D., Kay, G. G., Moreland, K. L., Dies, R. R., et al. (2001). Psychological testing and psychological assessment: A review of evidence and issues. *American Psychologist, 56,* 128–165.

Meyer, P. (2003). Conformity and group pressure: If Hitler asked you to electrocute a stranger would you? Probably. In J. M. Henslin (Ed), *Down to earth sociology: Introductory readings* (12th ed.; pp. 253–260). New York: Free Press.

Michael, R. T., Gagnon, J. H., Laumann, E. O., & Kolata, G. (1994). *Sex in America: A definitive survey.* Boston: Little, Brown.

Meyers, D. G. (1996). *Social Psychology,* (5th ed.) New York: McGraw-Hill.

Michael, R. T., Laumann, E. O., & Kolata, G. B. (1995). *Sex in America: A definitive survey.* New York: Warner Books.

Michelson, L. (ed.). (1985). Meta-analysis and clinical psychology [special issue.] *Clinical Psychology Review, 5*(1).

Migliaccio, E., Giorgio, M., Mele, S., Pelicci, G., Reboldi, P., Pandolfi, P. P., et al. (1999). The p66shu adaptor protein controls oxidative stress response and life span in mammals. *Nature, 402,* 309–313.

Milgram, S. (1963). Behavioral study of obedience. *Journal of Abnormal and Social Psychology, 67,* 371–378.

Milgram, S. (1974). *Obedience to authority: An experimental view.* New York: Harper & Row.

Miller, A. I. (1992). Scientific creativity: A comparative study of Henri Poincare and Albert Einstein. *Creativity Research Journal, 5,* 385–418.

Miller, G. (2000). *The mating mind: Why our ancestors scribbled on cave walls.* New York: Doubleday.

Miller, J. A. (2002). Individual motivation loss in group settings: An exploratory study of the social-loafing phenomenon. *Dissertation Abstracts International Section A: Humanities and Social Sciences, 62,* 2972.

Miller, J. G., Bersoff, D. M., & Harwood, R. L. (1990). Perceptions of social responsibilities in India and the United States: Moral imperatives or personal decisions? *Journal of Personality and Social Psychology, 58,* 33–47.

Miller, T. Q., Smith, T. W., Turner, C. W., Guijarro, M. L., & Hallet, A. J. (1996). A meta-analytic review of research on hostility andphysical health. *Psychological Bulletin, 119*(2), 322–348.

Miller, T. Q., Turner, C. W., Tindale, R. S., Posavac, E. J., & Dugoni, B. L. (1991). Reasons for the trend toward null findings in research on Type A behavior. *Psychological Bulletin, 110,* 469–485.

Millis, R. M. (1998). Smoking. In H. S. Friedman (Ed.), *Encyclopedia of mental health,* Vol. 3. San Diego: Academic Press.

Milner, B. (1959). The memory defect in bilateral hippocampal lesions. *Psychiatric Research Reports, 11,* 43–52.

Milner, B., Corkin, S., & Teuber, H. H. (1968). Further analysis of the hippocampal amnesic syndrome: 14-year follow-up study of H. M. *Neuropsychologia, 6,* 215–234.

Milton, J., & Wiseman, R. (1999). Does psi exist? Lack of replication of an anomalous process of information transfer. *Psychological Bulletin, 125,* 387–391.

Mineka, S., & Oehman, A. (2002). Phobias and preparedness: The selective, autonomic, and encapsulated nature of fear. *Biological Psychiatry, 51,* 927–937.

Minton, H. L. (2002). Psychology and gender at the turn of the century. *American Psychologist, 55,* 613–615.

Minton, H. L., & Schneider, F. W. (1980). *Differential psychology.* Monterey, CA: Brooks/Cole.

Mintun, M. A., Sheline, Y. I., Moerlein, S. M., Vlassenko, A. G., Huang, Y., & Snyder, A. Z. (2004). Decreased hippocampal 5-HT2A receptor binding in major depressive disorder: In vivo measurement with [18F]altanserin positron emission tomography. *Biological Psychiatry, 55,* 217–224.

Mischel, W. (2003). Challenging the traditional personality psychology paradigm. In R. J. Sternberg (Ed.), *Psychologists defying the crowd: Stories of those who battled the establishment and won* (pp. 139–156). Washington, DC: American Psychological Association.

Mischel, W., Shoda, Y., & Mendoza-Denton, R. Situation-behavior profiles as a locus of consistency in personality. *Current Directions in Psychological Science, 11*, 50–54.

Misumi, J. (1985). *The behavioral science of leadership: An interdisciplinary Japanese leadership program.* Ann Arbor: University of Michigan Press.

Mitchell, T. R., & Daniels, D. (2003). Motivation. In W. C. Borman, D. R. Ilgen, & R. J. Klimoski (Eds.), *Handbook of psychology* (Vol. 12): *Industrial and organizational psychology* (pp. 225–254). Hoboken, NJ: Wiley.

Moffitt, T. W. (1993). Adolescence-limited and life-course-persistent antisocial behavior: A developmental taxonomy. *Psychological Review, 100*, 674–701.

Molineux, J. B. (1985). *Family therapy: A practical manual.* Springfield, IL: Charles C. Thomas.

Mollica, R. F. (2000, June). Invisible wounds. *Scientific American, 282*, 54–57.

Monahan, J. L., Murphy, S. T., & Zajonc, R. B. (2000). Subliminal mere exposure: Specific, general and diffuse effects. *Psychological Science, 11*, 462–466.

Monastra, V. J., Monastra, D. M., & George, S. (2002). The effects of stimulant therapy, EEG biofeedback, and parenting style on the primary symptoms of attention-deficit hyperactivity disorder. *Applied Psychophysiology and Biofeedback, 27*, 231–249.

Montgomery, G. H., DuHamel, K. N., & Redd, W. H. (2000). A meta-analysis of hypnotically induced analgesia: How effective is hypnosis? *International Journal of Clinical & Experimental Hypnosis [Special Issue: The Status of Hypnosis as an Empirically Validated Clinical Intervention], 48*, 138–153.

Moore, R. Y. (1999, June 25). A clock for the ages. *Science, 284*, 2102–2103.

Moore-Ede, M. C., Czeisler, C. A., & Richardson, G. S. (1983). Circadian time keeping in health and disease: I. Basic properties of circadian pacemakers. *New England Journal of Medicine, 309*, 469–476.

Morgan, W. G. (2002). Origin and history of the earliest thematic apperception test pictures. *Journal of Personality Assessment, 79*, 422–445.

Moriarty, T. (1975). Crime, commitment and the responsive bystander: Two field experiments. *Journal of Personality and Social Psychology, 31*, 370–376.

Morin, C. M., Bastien, C. H., Brink, D., & Brown, T. R. (2003). Adverse effects of temazepam in older adults with chronic insomnia. *Human Psychopharmacology Clinical and Experimental, 18*, 75–82.

Morris, C. (1990). *Contemporary psychology and effective behavior* (7th ed.). Glenview, IL: Scott, Foresman.

Moyer, C. A., Rounds, J., & Hannum, J. W. (2004). A meta-analysis of massage therapy research. *Psychological Bulletin, 130*, 3–18.

Mroczek, D. K., & Kolarz, C. M. (1998). The effect of age on positive and negative affect: A developmental perspective on happiness. *Journal of Personality & Social Psychology, 75*, 1333–1349.

Muchinsky, P. M. (2000). Emotions in the workplace: The neglect of organizational behavior. *Journal of Organizational Behavior, 21* (7), 801–805.

Muchinsky, P. M. (2006*). Psychology Applied to Work* (8th Ed.). Belmont, CA: Thompson Wadsworth.

Mueser, K. T., & Glynn, S. M. (1995). *Behavioral family therapy for psychiatric disorders.* Boston: Allyn & Bacon.

Mumford, M. D., & Gustafson, S. B. (1988). Creativity syndrome: Integration, application, and innovation. *Psychological Bulletin, 103*, 27–43.

Muir, D. W. (1985). The development of infants' auditory spatial sensitivity. In S. Trehub & B. Schneider (Eds.), *Auditory development in infancy.* New York: Plenum.

Muris, P., Merchelbach, H., Gadet, B., & Moulaert, V. (2000). Fears, worries, and scary dreams in 4- to 12-year-old children: Their content, developmental pattern, and origins. *Journal of Clinical Child Psychology, 29*, 43–52.

Murphy, K. R. & Cleveland, J. N. (1995). *Understanding performance appraisal: Social, organizational, and goal-based perspectives.* Thousand Oaks, CA: Sage.

Murray, B. (1999, October). Psychologists can boost the corporate bottom line. *APA Monitor*, p. 17.

Murray, H. G., & Denny, J. P. (1969). Interaction of ability level and interpolated activity in human problem solving. *Psychological Reports, 24*, 271–276.

Mustanski, B. S., Viken, R. J., Kaprio, J., & Rose, R. J. (2003). Genetic influences on the association between personality risk factors and alcohol use and abuse. *Journal of Abnormal Psychology, 112*, 282–289.

Muth, E. R., Stern, R. M., Uijtdehaage, S. H. J., & Koch, K. L. (1994). Effects of Asian ancestry on susceptibility to vection-induced motion sickness. In J. Z. Chen & R. W. McCallum (eds.), *Electrogastrography: Principles and applications* (pp. 227–233). New York: Raven Press.

Myers, D. G. (1996). *Social psychology* (5th ed.). New York: Mc-Graw-Hill.

Nairne, J. S. (2003). Sensory and working memory. In A. F. Healy & R. W. Proctor (Eds.), *Handbook of Psychology: Experimental Psychology*, Vol. 4 (pp. 423–444). New York: John Wiley & Sons.

Narayanan, L., Shanker, M., & Spector, P. E. (1999). Stress in the workplace: A comparison of gender and occupations. *Journal of Organizational Behavior, 20*, 63–73.

Narrow, W. E., Rae, D. S., Robins, L. N., & Regier D. A. (2001). Revised prevalence estimates of mental disorders in the United States: Using a clinical significance criterion to reconcile 2 survey estimates. *Archives of General Psychiatry, 59*, 115–123.

Nash, M. (2004). Salient findings: Pivotal reviews and research on hypnosis, soma, and cognition. *International Journal of Clinical and Experimental Hypnosis, 52*, 82–88.

Nash, M. R. (2001, July). The truth and the hype of hypnosis. *Scientific American*, pp. 47–54.

Nathan, P. E., & Langenbucher, J. W. (1999). Psychopathology: Description and classification. *Annual Review of Psychology, 50*, 79–107.

National Coalition on Health Care. (2006). *Health insurance cost.* Accessed June 13, 2006 from http://www.nchc.org/facts/cost.shtml

National Institute for Occupational Safety and Health (NIOSH). (2006). *Stress at work.* Accessed June 27, 2006, from: http://www.cdc.gov/niosh/ohp.html

National Institute of Neurological Disorders and Stroke. (2003). *Brain basics: Understanding sleep.* Retrieved from http://

www.ninds.nih.gov/health_and_medical/pubs/understand-ing_ sleep_brain_basic_.htm.

National Institute on Drug Abuse. (2000a). *Marijuana*. Retrieved September 9, 2000, from the World Wide Web: *http://165. 112.78.61/Infofax/ marijuana.html.*

Neal, A & Griffin, M. A. (2004). Safety climate and safety at work. In J. Barling, & M. R. Frone (Eds.), *The psychology of workplace safety*, (pp. 15–34). Washington, DC: American Psychological Association.

Nehlig, A., Daval, J. L., & Debry, G. (1992). Caffeine and the central nervous system: Mechanisms of action, biochemical, metabolic and psychostimulant effects. *Brain Research Reviews, 17,* 139–170.

Neisser, U. (1998). Introduction: Rising test scores and what they mean. In U. Neisser (Ed.), *The rising curve: Long-term gains in IQ and related measures* (pp. 3–22). Washington, DC: American Psychological Association.

Neisser, U., Boodoo, G., Bouchard, T. J., Jr., Boykin, A. W., Brody, N., Ceci, S. J., Halpern, D. F., Loehlin, J. C., Perloff, R., Sternberg, R. J., & Urbina, S. (1996). Intelligence: Knowns and unknowns. *American Psychologist, 51,* 77–101.

Nelson, C. A., Monk, C. S., Lin, J., Carver, L. C., Thomas, K. M., & Truwit, C. L. (2000). Functional neuroanatomy of spatial working memory in children. *Developmental Psychology, 36,* 109–116.

Nelson, D. L. (1999). Implicit memory. In D. E. Morris & M. Gruneberg (eds.), *Theoretical aspects of memory*. London: Routledge.

Nemeroff, C. B., & Schatzberg, A. F. (2002). Pharmacological treatments for unipolar depression. In P. Nathan & J. M. Gorman (Eds.), *A guide to treatments that work* (2d ed., pp. 212–225). New York: Oxford University Press.

Ness, R. B., Grisso, J. A., Hirschinger, N., Markovic, N., Shaw, L. M., Kay, N. L., (1999) Cocaine and tobacco use and the risk of spontaneous abortion. *New England Journal of Medicine, 340,* 333–339.

Nestler, E. J., & Malenka, R. C. (2004, March). The addicted brain. *Scientific American,* 78–85.

Neugarten, B. L. (1977). Personality and aging. In I. Birren & K. W. Schaie (Eds.), *Handbook of the psychology of aging* (pp. 626–649). New York: Van Nostrand.

NICHD Early Child Care Research Network. (1997). The effects of infant child care on infant-mother attachment security: Results of the NICHD study of early child care. *Child Development, 68,* 860–879.

Nicholls, C. E., Lane, H. W., & Brechu, M. B. (1993). Taking self-managed teams to Mexico. *Academy of management executive, 13* (3), 15–25.

Nickerson, R. S., & Adams, M. J. (1979). Long-term memory for a common object. *Cognitive Psychology, 11,* 287–307.

Nissani, M. (1990). A cognitive reinterpretation of Stanley Milgram's observations on obedience to authority. *American Psychologist, 45,* 1384–1385.

Noga, J. T., Bartley, A. J., Jones, D. W., Torrey, E. F., & Weinberger, D. R. (1996). Cortical gyral anatomy and gross brain dimensions in monozygotic twins discordant for schizophrenia. *Schizophrenia Research, 22*(1), 27–40.

Nolen-Hoeksema, S. (1999, October). Men and women handle negative situations differently, study suggests. *APA Monitor.*

Nolen-Hoeksema, S., Girgus, J. S., & Seligman, M. E. P. (1986). Learned helplessness in children: A longitudinal study of depression, achievement, and explanatory style. *Journal of Personality and Social Psychology, 51,* 435–442.

Norman, R. (1975). Affective-cognitive consistency, attitudes, conformity, and behavior. *Journal of Personality and Social Psychology, 32,* 83–91.

Norris, F. H., & Murrell, S. A. (1990). Social support, life events, and stress as modifiers of adjustment to bereavement by older adults. *Psychology and Aging, 45,* 267–275.

Novak, M. A. (1991, July). "Psychologists care deeply" about animals. *APA Monitor,* p.4.

Novick, L. R., & Sherman, S. J. (2003). On the nature of insight solutions: Evidence from skill differences in anagram solution. *Quarterly Journal of Experimental Psychology: Human Experimental Psychology, 56A,* 351–382.

Nowak, A., Vallacher, R. R., & Miller, M. E. (2003). Social influence and group dynamics. In T. Millon & M. J. Lerner (Eds.), *Handbook of psychology: Personality and social psychology* (Vol. 5, pp. 383–417). New York: John Wiley & Sons, Inc.

Nurmi, E. L., Amin, T., Olson, L. M., Jacobs, M. M., McCauley, J. L., Lam, A. Y., Organ, E. L., Folstein, S. E., Haines, J. L., & Sutcliffe, J. S. (2003). Dense linkage disequilibrium mapping in the 15q11-q13 maternal expression domain yields evidence for association in autism. *Molecular Psychiatry, 8,* 624–634.

Nyberg, L., Marklund, P., Persson, J., Cabeza, R., Forkstarn, C., Petersson, K. M., & Ingvar, M. (2003). Common prefrontal activations during working memory, episodic memory, and semantic memory. *Neuropsychologia, 41,* 371–377.

O'Callahan, M., Andrews, A. M., & Krantz, D. S. (2003). Coronary heart disease and hypertension. In A. M. Nezu & C. M. Nezu (Eds.), *Handbook of psychology: Health psychology,* Vol. 9 (pp. 339–364). New York: John Wiley & Sons, Inc.

Ocampo, C., Prieto, L. R., Whittlesey, V., Connor, J., Janco-Gidley, J., Mannix, S., & Sare, K. (2003). Diversity research in *Teaching of Psychology*: Summary and recommendations. *Teaching of Psychology, 30,* 5–18.

Occupational Hazards. (2002). High stress linked to spiraling health care costs. *Occupational Hazards.* Accessed June 13, 2006, from http://www.occupationalhazards.com/articles/index.php?id=4411

O'Connor, T. G., McGuire, S., Reiss, D., Hetherington, E. M., & Plomin, R. (1998). Co-occurrence of depressive symptoms and antisocial behavior in adolescence: A common genetic liability. *Journal of Abnormal Psychology, 107,* 27–37.

Oesterle, S., Hill, K. G., Hawkins, J. D., Guo, J., Catalano, R. F., & Abbott, R. D. (2004). Adolescent heavy episodic drinking trajectories and health in young adulthood. *Journal of Studies on Alcohol, 65,* 204–212.

Ojemann, G., Ojemann, J., Lettich, E., & Berger, M. (1989). Cortical language localization in left, dominant hemisphere: An electrical stimulation mapping investigation in 117 patients. *Journal of Neurosurgery, 71,* 316–326.

Olds, M. E., & Forbes, J. L. (1981). The central basis of motivation: Intracranial self-stimulation studies. *Annual Review of Psychology, 32,* 523–574.

O'Leary, A. (1990). Stress, emotion, and human immune function. *Psychological Bulletin, 108,* 363–382.

O'Leary, K. D., & Wilson, G. T. (1987). *Behavior therapy: Application and outcome.* Englewood Cliffs, NJ: Prentice Hall.

O'Leary, V. E., & Flanagan, E. H. (2001). Leadership. In J. Worell (Ed.), *Encyclopedia of gender. Volume Two* (pp. 245–257). San Diego, CA: Academic Press.

Olfson, M., Marcus, S. C., Druss, B., & Pincus, H. A. (2002). National trends in the use of outpatient psychotherapy. *American Journal of Psychiatry, 19,* 1914–1920.

Olfson, M., Marcus, S., Sackeim, H. A., Thompson, J., & Pincus, H. A. (1998). Use of ECT for the inpatient treatment of recurrent major depression. *American Journal of Psychiatry, 155,* 22–29.

Oltmanns, T. F., & Emery, R. E. (1998). *Abnormal psychology* (2nd ed.). Upper Saddle River, NJ: Prentice Hall.

Oltmanns, T. F., & Emery, R. E. (2001). *Abnormal psychology* (3rd ed.) Upper Saddle River, NJ: Prentice Hall.

Omi, M., & Winant, H. (1994). *Racial formation in the United States: From the 1960s to the 1990s* (2nd ed). New York: Routledge.

Ones, D. S., Viswesvaran, C., & Schmidt, F. L. (1993). Comprehensive meta-analysis of integrity test validities: Findings and implications for personnel selection and theories of job performance. *Journal of Applied Psychology, 78* (4), 679–703.

Orbuch, T. L., House, J. S., Mero, R. P., & Webster, P. S. (1996). Marital quality over the life course. *Social Psychology Quarterly, 59,* 162–171.

Orlinsky, D. E., & Howard, K. I. (1994). Unity and diversity among psychotherapies: A comparative perspective. In B. Bonger & L. E. Beutler (eds.), *Foundations of psychotherapy: Theory, research, and practice.* New York: Basic Books.

Ortar, G. (1963). Is a verbal test cross-cultural? *Scripta Hierosolymitana, 13,* 219–235.

Oskamp, S. (1991). *Attitudes and opinions* (2nd ed.). Englewood Cliffs, NJ: Prentice Hall.

Ostroff, C., & Ford, J. K. (1989). Assessing training needs: Critical levels of analysis. In I.L. Goldstein & Associates (Eds.) *Training and Development in Organizations* (pp. 25–62), San Francisco: Jossey-Bass.

Ostroff, C., Kinicki, A. J., & Tamkins, M. M. (2003). Organizational culture and climate. In W. C. Borman, D. R. Ilgen, & R. J. Klimoski (Eds.), *Handbook of psychology: Industrial and organizational psychology* (Vol. 12, pp. 565–593). Hoboken, NJ: Wiley.

Ouimette, P., Humphreys, K., Moos, R. H., Finney, J. W., Cronkite, R., & Federman, B. (2001). Self-help group participation among substance use disorder patients with posttraumatic stress disorder. *Journal of Substance Abuse Treatment, 20,* 25–32.

Overholser, J. C. (2003). Rational–emotive behavior therapy: An interview with Albert Ellis. *Journal of Contemporary Psychotherapy, 33,* 187–204.

Owens, J., Maxim R., McGuinn, M., Nobile, C., Msall, M., & Alario, A. (1999). Television-viewing habits and sleep disturbance in school children. *Pediatrics, 104,* 27.

Oyer, P., & Schaefer, S. (2002). Sorting quotas and the civil rights act of 1991: Who hires when its hard to fire? *Journal of law and economics, 45*(1), 41–68.

Ozer, D. J., & Reise, S. P. (1994). Personality assessment. *Annual Review of Psychology, 45,* 357–388.

Ozer, E. J., Best, S. R., Lipsey, T. L., & Weiss, D. S. (2003). Predictors of posttraumatic stress disorder and symptoms in adults: A meta-analysis. *Psychological Bulletin, 2003,* 52–73.

Pace, R. (1994, July 28). Christy Henrich, 22, gymnast plagued by eating disorders. *New York Times,* p. A12.

Paivio, A. (1986). *Mental representations: A dual coding approach.* New York: Oxford University Press.

Panksepp, J. (1998). Attention deficit hyperactivity disorders, psychostimulants, and intolerance of childhood playfulness: A tragedy in the making? *Current Directions in Psychological Science, 7,* 91–98.

Panskepp, J. (1986). The neurochemistry of behavior. *Annual Review of Pscychology, 37,* 77–107.

Papassotiropoulos, A., Luetjohann, D., Bagli, M., Locatelli, S., Jessen, F., Buschfort, R., Ptok, U., Bjoerkhem, I., von Bergmann, K., & Heun, R. (2002). 24S-hydroxycholesterol in cerebrospinal fluid is elevated in early stages of dementia. *Journal of Psychiatric Research, 36,* 27–32.

Pare, D., Collins, D. R., & Guillaume, P. J. (2002). Amygdala oscillations and the consolidation of emotional memories. *Trends in Cognitive Sciences, 6,* 306–314.

Park–Gates, S. L. (2002). Effects of group interactive brainstorming on creativity. *Dissertation Abstracts International: Section A: Humanities and Social Science, 62,* 2363.

Parke, R. D., & O'Neil, R. (1999). Social relationships across contexts: Family-peer linkages. In A. W. Collins & B. Laursen (Eds.), *Relationships as developmental contexts. The Minnesota symposia on child psychology* (Vol. 30, pp. 211–239). Mahwah, NJ: Lawrence Erlbaum.

Parker, S. K., Axtell, C. M., & Turner, N. (2001). Designing a safer workplace: importance of job autonomy, communication quality, and supportive supervisors. *Journal of Occupational Health Psychology, 6* (3), 211–228.

Parker, S. K., & Wall, T. D. (1998). *Job and work design: Organizing work to promote well-being and effectiveness.* Thousand Oaks, CA: SAGE Publications.

Parnetti, L., Senin, U., & Mecocci, P. (1997). Cognitive enhancement therapy for Alzheimer's disease: The way forward. *Drugs, 53,* 752–768.

Patenaude, A. F., Guttmacher, A. E., & Collins, F. S. (2002). Genetic testing and psychology: New roles, new responsibilities. *American Psychologist, 5,* 271–282.

Patrick, C. J. (1994). Emotion and psychopathy: Startling new insights. *Psychophysiology, 31,* 319–330.

Patterson, D. R., & Jensen, M. P. (2003). Hypnosis and clinical pain. *Psychological Bulletin, 129,* 495–521.

Patterson, D. R., & Ptacek, J. T. (1997). Baseline pain as a moderator of hypnotic analgesia for burn injury treatment. *Journal of Consulting & Clinical Psychology, 65,* 60–67.

Patterson, G. R., & Bank, L. (1989). Some amplifying mechanisms for pathologic processes in families. In M. R. Gunnar & E. The-len (eds.), *Systems and development: The Minnesota Symposia on Child Psychology* (Vol. 22). Hillsdale, NJ: Erlbaum.

Paul, G. L. (1982). The development of a "transportable" system of behavioral assessment for chronic patients. Invited address, University of Minnesota, Minneapolis.

Paunonen, S. V. (2003). Big Five factors of personality and replicated predictions of behavior. *Journal of Personality and Social Psychology, 84*, 411–422.

Paunovic, N., & Oest, L. G. (2001). Cognitive behavior therapy versus exposure therapy in the treatment of PTSD in refugees. *Behaviour Research and Therapy, 39*, 1183–1197.

Pavlov, I. P. (1927). *Conditional reflexes* (G. V. Anrep, trans.). London: Oxford University Press.

Peabody, D., & Goldberg, L. R. (1989). Some determinants of factor structures from personality-trait descriptors. *Journal of Personality and Social Psychology, 57*, 552–567.

Pearlin, L. I., & Schooler, C. (1978). The structure of coping. *Journal of Health and Social Behavior, 19*, 2–21.

Pearson, C. A. L. (1992). Autonomous workgroups: An evaluation at an industrial site. *Human Relations, 9*, 905–936.

Pedlow, R., Sanson, A., Prior, M., & Oberklaid, F. (1993). Stability of maternally reported temperament from infancy to 8 years. *Developmental Psychology, 29*, 998–1007.

Pennisi, E. (1999, October 22). Enzymes point way to potential Alzheimer's therapies. *Science, 286*, 650–651.

Peplau, L. A., & Cochran, S. D. (1990). A relationship perspective on homosexuality. In D. P. McWhirter, S. A. Sanders, & J. M. Reinisch (Eds.), *Homosexuality/heterosexuality: The Kinsey scale and current research* (pp. 321–349). New York: Oxford University Press.

Perloff, R. M. (2003). *The dynamics of persuasion: Communication and attitudes in the 21st century* (2d ed.). Mahwah, NJ: Lawrence Erlbaum Associates, Publishers.

Persky, H. (1983). Psychosexual effects of hormones. *Medical Aspects of Human Sexuality, 17*, 74–101.

Persson-Blennow, I., & McNeil, T. F. (1988). Frequencies and stability of temperament types in childhood. *Journal of the American Academy of Child and Adolescent Psychiatry, 27*, 619–622.

Peterson, C. (2000). The future of optimism. *American Psychologist, 55*, 44–55.

Peterson, C., Maier, S. F., & Seligman, M. E. P. (1993). Explanatory style and helplessness. *Social Behavior and Personality, 20*, 1–14.

Peterson, C., Maier, S. F., & Seligman, M. E. P. (1993b). *Learned helplessness: A theory for the age of personal control.* New York: Oxford University Press.

Peterson, C., Vaillant, G. E., & Seligman, M. E. P. (1988). Explanatory style as a risk factor for illness. *Cognitive Therapy and Research, 12*, 119–132.

Peterson, L. R., & Peterson, M. J. (1959). Short-term retention of individual verbal items. *Journal of Experimental Psychology, 58*, 193–198.

Pettigrew, T. F. (1998). Intergroup contact theory. *Annual Review of Psychology, 49*, 65–85.

Petitto, L. A., & Marentette, P. F. (1991, March 22). Babbling in the manual mode: Evidence for the ontogeny of language. *Science, 251*, 1493–1496.

Petty, R. E., & Cacioppo, J. T. (1981). *Attitudes and persuasion: Classic and contemporary approaches.* Dubuque, IA: Wm. C. Brown.

Petty, R. E., & Cacioppo, J. T. (1986b). Communication and persuasion: Central and peripheral routes to attitude change. New York: Springer-Verlag.

Petty, R. E., Wegener, D. T., & Fabrigar, L. R. (1997). Attitudes and attitude change. *Annual Review of Psychology, 48*, 609–647.

Phelps, J. A., Davis, J. O., & Schartz, K. M. (1997). Nature, nurture, and twin research strategies. *Current Directions in Psychological Science, 6*, 117–121.

Phelps, L., & Bajorek, E. (1991). Eating disorders of the adolescent: Current issues in etiology, assessment, and treatment. *School Psychology Review, 20*, 9–22.

Phinney, J. S. (1996). When we talk about American ethnic groups, what do we mean? *American Psychologist, 51*, 918–927.

Pickren, W. E. (2004). Between the cup of principle and the lip of practice: Ethnic minorities and American psychology, 1966–1980. *History of Psychology, 7*, 45–64.

Pillow, D. R., Zautra, A. J., & Sandler, I. (1996). Major life events and minor stressors: Identifying mediational links in the stress process. *Journal of Personality and Social Psychology, 70*, 381–394.

Pine, F. (1998). *Diversity and direction in psychoanalytic techniques.* New Haven, CT: Yale University Press.

Pisani, V. D., Fawcett, J., Clark, D. C., & McGuire, M. (1993). The relative contributions of medication adherence and AA meeting attendance to abstinent outcome for chronic alcoholics. *Journal of Studies on Alcohol, 54*, 115–119.

Plomin, R. (1994). *Genetics and experience: The interplay between nature and nurture.* Thousand Oaks, CA: Sage.

Plomin, R. (1997). Identifying genes for cognitive abilities and disabilities. In R. J. Sternberg & E. Grigorenko (eds.), *Intelligence: Heredity and environment.* New York: Cambridge University Press.

Plomin, R. (1999). Parents and personality. *Contemporary Psychology, 44*, 269–271.

Plomin, R., Corley, R., DeFries, J. C., & Fulker, D. W. (1990). Individual differences in television watching in early childhood: Nature as well as nurture. *Psychological Science 1*(6), 371–377.

Plomin, R., & Crabbe, J. (2000). DNA. *Psychological Bulletin, 126*, 806–828.

Plomin, R., DeFries, J. C., Craig, I. W., & McGuffin, P. (2003). Behavioral genomics. In R. Plomin & J. C. DeFries (Eds.). *Behavioral genetics in the postgenomic era* (pp. 531–540). Washington, DC: American Psychological Association.

Plomin, R., DeFries, J. C., & McClearn, G. E. (1990). *Behavioral genetics: A primer* (2nd ed.). New York: Freeman.

Plomin, R., & Rende, R. (1991). Human behavioral genetics. *Annual Review of Psychology, 42*, 161–190.

Plous, S. (1996). Attitudes toward the use of animals in psychology research and education: Results from a national survey of psychologists. *American Psychologist, 51*(11), 1167–1180.

Plutchik, R. (1994). The psychology and biology of emotion. New York: HarperCollins.

Pogarsky, G., & Piquero, A. R. (2003). Can punishment encourage offending? Investigating the "resetting" effect. *Journal of Research in Crime and Delinquency, 40*, 95–120.

Pohl, R. F., Schwarz, S., Sczesny, S., & Stahlberg, D. (2003). Hindsight bias in gustatory judgements. *Experimental Psychology, 50*, 107–115.

Pollatasek, A., Rayner, K., & Lee, H. W. (2000). Phonological coding in word perception and reading. In A. Kennedy & R. Radach (Eds.), *Reading as a perceptual process* (pp. 399–425). Amsterdam: North-Holland/Elsevier Science Publishers.

Pooley, E. (2005). Job rotation. *Canadian business, 78* (21), 109.

Pope, H. (2000). *The Adonis complex: The secret crisis of male obsession.* New York: Free Press.

Porter, L. S., & Stone, A. A. (1995). Are there really gender differences in coping? A reconsideration of previous results from a daily study. *Journal of Social and Clinical Psychology, 14*, 184–202.

Porter, L. W., & Roberts, K. H. (1976). Communication in organizations. In M. D. Dunnette (ed.), *Handbook of industrial and organizational psychology.* Chicago: Rand McNally.

Postman, L. (1975). Verbal learning and memory. *Annual Review of Psychology, 26*, 291–335.

Pothier, P. K. T. (2002). Effect of relaxation on neuro-immune responses of persons undergoing chemotherapy. *Dissertation Abstracts International: Section B: The Sciences and Engineering, 62*, 4471.

Powell, L. H., Shababi, L., & Thoresen, C. E. (2003). Religion and spirituality: Linkages to physical health. *American Psychologist, 58*, 36–52.

Powell, N. B., Schechtman, K. B., Riley, R. W., Li, K., Troell, R., Guilleminault, C., (2001). The road to danger: The comparative risks of driving while sleepy. *Laryngoscope, 111*, 887–893.

Powell, S., Rosner, R., Butollo, W., Tedeschi, R. G., & Calhoun, L. G. (2003). Postraumatic growth after a war: A study with former refugees and displaced people in Sarajevo. *Journal of Clinical Psychology, 59*, 71–83.

Powell, D. H., & Driscoll, P. F. (1973). Middle class professionals face unemployment. *Society, 10(2)*, 18–26.

Power, F. C. (1994). Moral development. In V. S. Ramachandran (Ed.), *Encyclopedia of human behavior* (Vol. 3, pp. 203–212). San Diego, CA: Academic Press.

Powers, S. I, Hauser, S. T., & Kilner, L. A. (1989). Adolescent mental health. *American Psychologist, 44*, 200–208.

Prager, K. J. (1995). *The psychology of intimacy.* New York: Guilford Press.

Prickaerts, J., Koopmans, G., Blokland, A., & Scheepens, A. (2004). Learning and adult neurogenesis: Survival with or without proliferation? *Neurobiology of Learning and Memory, 81*, 1–11.

Prior, M., Smart, D., Sanson, A., & Obeklaid, F. (1993). Sex differences in psychological adjustment from infancy to 8 years. *Journal of the American Academy of Child and Adolescent Psychiatry, 32*, 291–304.

Ptacek, J. T., Smith R. E., & Dodge, K. L. (1994). Gender differences in coping with stress: When stressor and appraisals do not differ. *Personality and Social Psychology Bulletin, 20*, 421–430.

Quadrel, M. J., Prouadrel, Fischoff, B., & Davis, W. (1993). Adolescent (In)vulnerability. *American Psychologist, 2*, 102–116.

Quan, N., Zhang, Z. B., Demetrikopoulos, M. K., Kitson, R. P., Chambers, W. H., Goldfarb, R. H., et al. (1999). Evidence for involvement of B lymphocytes in the surveillance of lung metastases in the rat. *Cancer Research, 59*, 1080–1089.

Quesnel, C., Savard, J., Simard, S., Ivers, H., & Morin, C. M. (2003). Efficacy of cognitive-behavioral therapy for insomnia in women treated for non-metastatic breast cancer. *Journal of Consulting and Clinical Psychology, 71*, 189–200.

Quick, J. C. & Tetrick, L. E. (2003). *Handbook of occupational health psychology.* Washington, DC: American Psychological Association.

Rabasca, L. (1999a, June). Improving life for the survivors of cancer. *APA Monitor*, pp. 28–29.

Rabasca, L. (1999b, November). Is it depression? Or could it be a mild traumatic brain injury? *APA Monitor*, pp. 27–28.

Rabasca, L. (2000a, March). Lessons in diversity [and] helping American Indians earn psychology degrees. *Monitor on Psychology, 31*, 50–53.

Rabin, B. S., & Koenig, H. G. (2002). Immune, neuroendocrine, and religious measures. In *The link between religion and health: Psychoneuroimmunology and the faith factor* (pp. 197–249). London: Oxford University Press.

Rainer, G., & Miller, E. K. (2002). Timecourse of object-related neural activity in the primate prefrontal cortex during a short-term memory task. *European Journal of Neuroscience, 15*, 1244–1254.

Ramey, S. L. (1999). Head Start and preschool education: Toward continued improvement. *American Psychologist, 54*, 344–346.

Rasika, S., Alvarez-Buylla, A., & Nottebohm, F. (1999). BDNF mediates the effects of testosterone on the survival of new neurons in an adult brain. *Neuron, 22*, 53–62.

Raven, B. H. (1998). Groupthink: Bay of Pigs and Watergate reconsidered. *Organizational Behavior and Human Decision Processes, 73*, 352–361.

Ravussin, E., Pratley, R. E., Maffei, M., Wang, H., Friedman, J. M., Bennett, P. H., & Bogardus, C. (1997). Relatively low plasma leptin concentrations precede weight gain in Pima Indians. *Nature Medicine 3*, 238–240.

Rayman, P., & Bluestone, B. (1982). *The private and social response to job loss: A metropolitan study.* Final report of research sponsored by the Center for Work and Mental Health, National Institute of Mental Health.

Ree, M. J., & Earles, J. A. (1992). Intelligence is the best predictor of job performance. *Current Directions in Psychological Science, 1*, 86–89.

Ree, M. J., Earles, J. A., & Teachout, M. S. (1994). Predicting job performance: Not much more than g. *Journal of Applied Psychology, 79* (4), 518–524.

Reed, S. K. (1996). *Cognition: Theory and applications* (4th ed.). Pacific Grove, CA: Brooks/Cole.

Reeve, C. L., & Hakel, M. D. (2002). Asking the right questions about g. *Human Performance, 15* (1–2), 47–74.

Refinetti, R. (2000). *The clocks within us.* Boca Raton, FL: CRC Press.

Rende, R., & Plomin, R. (1992). Diathesis-stress models of psychopathology: A quantitative genetic perspective. *Applied & Preventive Psychology, 1*, 177–182.

Renner, M. J., & Mackin, R. S. (1998). A life stress instrument for classroom use. *Teaching of Psychology, 25*, 46–48.

Renner, M. J., & Mackin, R. S. (2002). A life stress instrument for classroom use. In R. A. Griggs (Ed.), *Handbook for teaching introductory psychology*, Vol. 3 (pp. 236–238). Mahwah, NJ: Erlbaum.

Rensink, R. A. (2004). Visual sensing without seeing. *Psychological Science, 13*, 27–32.

Renzulli, J. S. (1978). What makes giftedness? Reexamining a definition. *Phi Delta Kappan, 60,* 180–184, 216.

Rescorla, R. A. (1966). Predictability and number of pairings in Pavlovian fear conditioning. *Psychonomic Science, 4,* 383–384.

Rescorla, R. A. (1967). Pavlovian conditioning and its proper control procedures. *Psychological Review, 74,* 71–80.

Rescorla, R. A. (1988). Pavlovian conditioning: It's not what you think. *American Psychologist, 43,* 151–160.

Resing, W. C., & Nijland, M. I. (2002). Are children becoming more intelligent? Twenty-five years' research using the Leiden Diagnostic Test. *Kind-en-Adolescent, 23,* 42–49.

Reuter-Lorenz, P. A., & Miller, A. C. (November 1998). The cognitive neuroscience of human laterality: Lessons from the bisected brain. *Current Directions in Psychological Science, 7,* 15–20.

Reyna, V. F., & Titcomb, A. L. (1997). Constraints on the suggestibility of eyewitness testimony: A fuzzy-trace theory analysis. In D. G. Payne & F. G. Conrad (eds.), *Intersections in basic and applied memory research.* Mahwah, NJ: Erlbaum.

Reynolds, C. F., Frank, E., Perel, J. M., Imber, S. D., Cornes, C., Miller, M. D., et al. (1999). Nortriptyline and interpersonal psychotherapy as maintenance therapies for recurrent major depression. *Journal of the American Medical Association, 281,* 39–45.

Rhue, J. W., Lynn, S. J., & Kirsch, I. (1993). *Handbook of clinical hypnosis.* Washington, DC: American Psychological Association.

Riccio, D. C., Millin, P. M., & Gisquet-Verrier, P. (2003). Retrograde amnesia: Forgetting back. *Current Directions in Psychological Science, 12,* 41–44.

Rice, B. J. (1997). Effects of aerobic exercise on stress and depression. *Dissertation Abstracts International: Section B: The Sciences and Engineering, 58,* 2697.

Richardson, G. S., Miner, J. D., & Czeisler, C. A. (1989–90). Impaired driving performance in shiftworkers: The role of the circadian system in a multifactional model. *Alcohol, Drugs & Driving, 5*(4), 6(1), 265–273.

Richey, W. (2001, May 20). Disabled golfer wins right to ride. *Christian Science Monitor.* n.p.

Riggio, R. E. (2003). *Introduction to Industrial/Organizational Psychology (4th ed.).* Upper Saddle River, NJ: Prentice Hall.

Riley, V. (1981). Psychoneuroendocrine influences on immunocompetence and neoplasia. *Science, 212,* 1100–1109.

Rilling, M. (2000). John Watson's paradoxical struggle to explain Freud. *American Psychologist, 55,* 301–312.

Rini, C. K., Dunkel-Schetter, C., Wadhwa, P. D., & Sandman, C. A. (1999). Psychological adaptation and birth outcomes: The role of personal resources, stress, and sociocultural context in pregnancy. *Health Psychology, 18,* 333–345.

Riordan, R. J., & Beggs, M. S. (1987). Counselors and self-help groups. *Journal of Counseling and Development, 65,* 427–429.

Ripple, C. H., Gilliam, W. S., Chanana, N., & Zigler, E. (1999). Will fifty cooks spoil the broth? The debate over entrusting Head Start to the states. *American Psychologist, 54,* 327–343.

Roberson, D., Davies, I., & Jules, D. (2000). Color categories are not universal: Replications and new evidence from a stone-age culture. *Journal of Experimental Psychology: General, 129,* 369–398.

Roberts, A. H., Kewman, D. G., Mercer, L., & Hovell, M. (1993). The power of nonspecific effects in healing: Implications for psychosocial and biological treatments. *Clinical Psychology Review, 13,* 375–391.

Robertson, R. G., Rolls, E. T., & Georges-Francois, P. (1998). Spatial view cells in the primate hippocampus: Effects of removal of view details. *Journal of Neurophysiology, 79,* 1145–1156.

Robins, L. N., & Regier, D. A. (1991). *Psychiatric disorders in America: The Epidemiologic Catchment Area Study.* New York: Free Press.

Robins, R. W., Gosling, S. D., & Craik, K. H. (1999). An empirical analysis of trends in psychology. *American Psychologist, 54,* 117–128.

Robinson, A., & Clinkenbeard, P. R. (1998). Giftedness: An exceptionality examined. *Annual Review of Psychology, 49,* 117–139.

Rodier, P. M. (2000, February). The early origins of autism. *Scientific American, 282,* 56–63.

Rodin, J. (1985). Insulin levels, hunger, and food intake: An example of feedback loops in body weight regulation. *Health Psychology, 4,* 1–24.

Roese, N. J. (1997). Counterfactual thinking. *Psychological Bulletin, 121,* 133–148.

Rofe, Y. (1984). Stress and affiliation: A utility theory. *Psychological Review, 91,* 251–268.

Rofe, Y., Hoffman, M., & Lewin, I. (1985). Patient affiliation in major illness. *Psychological Medicine, 15,* 895–896.

Rogers, C. R. (1961). *On becoming a person: A therapist's view of psychotherapy.* Boston: Houghton Mifflin.

Roitbak, A. I. (1993). *Glia and its role in nervous activity.* Saint Petersburg, Russia: Nauka.

Rolls, E. T. (2000). Memory systems in the brain. *Annual Review of Psychology, 51,* 599–630.

Roncadin, C., Guger, S., Archibald, J., Barnes, M., & Dennis, M. (2004). Working memory after mild, moderate, or severe childhood closed head injury. *Developmental Neuropsychology, 25,* 21–36.

Rosch, E. (1998). Principles of categorization. In A. M. Collens & E. E. Smith (Eds.), *Readings in cognitive science: A perspective from psychology and artificial intelligence* (pp. 312–322). San Mateo, CA: Morgan Kaufman, Inc.

Rosch, E. (2002). Principles of categorization. In D. J. Levitin (Ed.), *Foundations of Cognitive Psychology: Core Readings* (pp. 251–270). Cambridge, MA: MIT Press.

Rosch, E. H. (1973). Natural categories. *Cognitive Psychology, 4,* 328–350.

Rosch, E. H. (1978). Principles of categorization. In E. H. Rosch & B. B. Lloyd (eds.), *Cognition and categorization.* Hillsdale, NJ: Erlbaum.

Rosenthal, D. (1970). *Genetic theory and abnormal behavior.* New York: McGraw-Hill.

Rosenthal, R. (2002). Covert communications in classrooms, clinics, courtrooms, and cubicles. *American Psychologist, 57,* 839–849.

Rosenzweig, M. R., & Leiman, A. L. (1982). *Physiological psychology.* Lexington, MA: D. C. Heath.

Ross, L., & Nisbett, R. E. (1991). *The person and the situation.* New York: McGraw-Hill.

Ross, P. (2003, September). Mind readers. *Scientific American,* 74–77.

Ross, P. E. (April, 2004). Draining the language out of color. *Scientific American*, 46–47.

Rotenberg, V. S. (2004). The peculiarity of the right-hemisphere function in depression: Solving paradoxes. *Progress in Neuro Psychopharmacology and Biological Psychiatry, 28*, 1–13.

Rottenstreich, Y., & Tversky, A. (1997). Unpacking, repacking, and anchoring: Advances in support theory. *Psychological Review, 104*(2), 406–415.

Rotter, J. B. (1954). *Social learning and clinical psychology*. Englewood Cliffs, NJ: Prentice Hall.

Rovner, S. (1990, December 25). The empty nest myth. *Ann Arbor News*, p. D3.

Rowan, A., & Shapiro, K. J. (1996). Animal rights, a bitten apple. *American Psychologist, 51*(11), 1183–1184.

Ruberman, J. W., Weinblatt, E., Goldberg, J. D., & Chaudhary, B. S. (1984). Psychological influences on mortality after myocardial infarction. *New England Journal of Medicine, 311*, 552–559.

Rubin, K. H., Coplan, R. J., Chen, X., & McKinnon, J. E. (1994). Peer relationships and influences in childhood. In V. S. Ramachandran (Ed.), *Encyclopedia of human behavior* (Vol. 3, pp. 431–439). San Diego, CA: Academic Press.

Ruffin, C. L. (1993). Stress and health-little hassles vs. major life events. *Australian Psychologist, 28*, 201–208.

Rugulies, R. (2002). Depression as a predictor for coronary heart disease: A review and meta-analysis. *American Journal of Preventive Medicine, 23*, 51–61.

Russell, T. G., Rowe, W., & Smouse, A. D. (1991). Subliminal self-help tapes and academic achievement: An evaluation. *Journal of Counseling and Development, 69*, 359–362.

Ruth, W. (1996). Goal setting and behavior contracting for students with emotional and behavioral difficulties: Analysis of daily, weekly, and total goal attainment. *Psychology in the Schools, 33*, 153–158.

Ryan, R. M., & Deci, E. L. (2000). Self-determination theory and the facilitation of intrinsic motivation, social development, and well-being. *American Psychologist, 55*, 68–78.

Sack, R. L., Brandes, R. W., Kendall, A. R., & Lewy, A. J. (2001). Entrainment of free-running circadian rhythms by melatonin in blind people. *The New England Journal of Medicine, 343*, 1070–1077.

Sadeh, A., Raviv, A., & Gruber, R. (2000). Sleep patterns and sleep disruptions in school-age children. *Developmental Psychology, 36*, 291–301.

Sadoski, M., & Paivio, A. (2001). *Imagery and text: A dual coding theory of reading and writing*. Mahwah, NJ: Lawrence Erlbaum.

Sagario, D. (2003, December 1). Here's what to do if you find yourself fired. *Des Moines Register*, p. D1. Retrieved February 27, 2006, from News Bank Inc.

Saint-Amour, D., Lepore, F., Lassonde, M., & Guillemot, J. P. (2004). Effective binocular integration at the midline requires the corpus callosum. *Neuropsychologia, 43*, 164–174.

Salas, E., Bowers, C. A., & Edens, E. (2002). *Improving teamwork in organizations: Applications of resource management training*. Mahwah, NJ: Lawrence Erlbaum.

Salas, E., Stagl, K. C., & Burke, C. S. (2004). 25 years of team effectiveness in organizations: Research, themes, and emerging needs. In C. L. Cooper & I. T. Robertson (Eds.), *International review of industrial and organizational psychology 2004* (Vol. 19, pp. 47–91). West Sussex: Wiley.

Salovey, P., Mayer, J. D., & Rosenhan, D. L. (1991). Mood behavior. In M. S. Clark (Ed.), *Review of personality and social psychology: Prosocial behavior* (Vol. 12, pp. 215–237). Newbury Park, CA: Sage.

Salovey, P., Rothman, A. J., Detweiler, J. B., & Steward, W. T. (2000). Emotional states and physical health. *American Psychologist, 55*, 110–121.

Salthouse, T. A. (1991). Mediation of adult age differences in cognition by reductions in working memory and speed of processing. *Psychological Science, 2*, 179–183.

Sanders, M. S. & McCormick, E. J. (1993). Human factors in engineering design (7th ed.). New York: McGraw-Hill.

Sanderson, C., & Clarkin, J. F. (2002). Further use of the NEO-PI-R personality dimensions in differential treatment planning. In P. T. Costa, Jr. & T. A. Widiger (Eds.), *Personality disorders and the five-factor model of personality* (2d ed.) (pp. 351–375). Washington, DC: American Psychological Association.

Sano, D. L. (2002). Attitude similarity and marital satisfaction in long-term African American and Caucasian marriages. *Dissertation Abstracts International Section A: Humanities and Social Sciences, 62*, 289.

Satcher, D. (1999, October). A report of the surgeon general–executive summary. APA Monitor, p. 16.

Sattler, J. M. (1992). *Assessment of children* (3rd ed.). San Diego: Jerome M. Sattler.

Sattler, J. M. (2002). *Assessment of children: Behavioral and clinical applications* (4th ed.). La Mesa, CA: Jerome M. Sattler, Publisher, Inc.

Savage-Rumbaugh, S., & Brakke, K. E. (1996). Animal language: Methodological and interpretive issues. In D. Jamieson & M. Bekoff (Eds.), *Readings in animal cognition* (pp. 269–288). Cambridge, MA: MIT Press.

Scarr, S., & Weinberg, R. (1983). The Minnesota Adoption Study: Genetic differences and malleability. *Child Development, 54*, 260–267.

Schacter, D. L. (1999). The seven sins of memory: Insights from psychology and cognitive neuroscience. *American Psychologist, 54*, 182–203.

Schacter, D. L., Norman, K. A., & Koutstaal, W. (1998). The cognitive neuroscience of constructive memory. *Annual Review of Psychology, 49*, 289–318.

Schlenker, B. R., & Weigold, M. F. (1992). Interpersonal processes involving impression regulation and management. *Annual Review of Psychology, 43*, 133–168.

Schmidt, F. L., & Hunter, J. (2004). General mental ability in the world of work: Occupational attainment and job performance. *Journal of Personality and Social Psychology, 86* (1), 162–173.

Schmidt, F. L., & Hunter, J. E. (1998). The validity and utility of selection methods in personnel psychology: Practical and theoretical implications of 85 years of research findings, *Psychological Bulletin, 124* (2), 262–274.

Schmuck, P., & Sheldon, K. M. (2001). *Life goals and well-being: Towards a positive psychology of human striving*. Seattle, WA: Hogrefe & Huber.

Schneider, B. M. (2002). Using the Big-Five Personality Factors in the Minnesota Multiphasic Personality Inventory, California Psychological

Inventory, and Inwald Personality Inventory to predict police performance. *Dissertation Abstracts International: Section B: The Sciences and Engineering, 63*, 2098.

Scholey, A. B., Bosworth, J. A. J., & Dimitrakaki, V. (1999). The effects of exposure to human pheromones on mood and attraction. *Proceedings of the British Psychological Society, 7(1)*, 77.

Schroeder, S. R., Schroeder, C. S., & Landesman, S. (1987). Psychological services in educational setting to persons with mental retardation. *American Psychologist, 42*, 805–808.

Schultz, D. P., & Schultz, S. E. (1998). *Psychology and work today: An introduction to industrial and organizational psychology.* 7th ed. Prentice Hall: Upper Saddle River.

Schwartz, B. (1989). *Psychology of learning and behavior* (3rd ed.). New York: Norton.

Schwartz, G. E. (1974, April). TM relaxes some people and makes them feel better. *Psychology Today*, pp. 39–44.

Schwartzman, J. B., & Glaus, K. D. (2000). Depression and coronary heart disease in women: Implications for clinical practice and research. Professional Psychology: Research & Practice, 31, 48–57.

Schwarz, N., & Vaughn, L. A. (2002). The availability heuristic revisited: Ease of recall and content of recall as distinct sources of information. In T. Gilovich & D. Griffin (Eds.), *Heuristics and biases: The psychology of intuitive judgment* (pp. 103–119). New York: Cambridge University Press.

Schweinhart, L. J., Barnes, H. V., & Weikart, D. P. (1993). *Significant benefits: The High/Scope Perry Study through age 27* (Monographs of the High/Scope Educational Research Foundation, No. 10). Ypsilanti, MI: High/Scope Press.

Scott, C., Klein, D. M., & Bryant, J. (1990). Consumer response to humor in advertising: A series of field studies using behavioral observation. *Journal of Consumer Research, 16*, 498–501.

Scott, J. (2002, April 21). Once bitten, twice shy: A world of eroding trust. *New York Times*, p. WK5.

Scullen, S. E., Mount, M. K., & Judge, T. A. (2003). Evidence of the construct validity of developmental ratings of managerial performance. *Journal of Applied Psychology, 88* (1), 50–66.

Scupin, R. (1995). *Cultural anthropology* (2nd ed.). Englewood Cliffs, NJ: Prentice Hall.

Seamon, J. G., & Kenrick, D. T. (1992). *Psychology.* Englewood Cliffs, NJ: Prentice Hall.

Sears, D. O. (1994). On separating church and lab. *Psychological Science, 5*, 237–339.

Sedikides, C., Campbell, W. K., Reeder, G. D., & Elliot, A. J. (1998). The self-serving bias in relational context. *Journal of Personality and Social Psychology, 74* (2), 378–386.

Seeley, R. J., & Schwartz, J. C. (1997). The regulation of energy balance: Peripheral hormonal signals and hypothalamic neuropeptides. *Current Directions in Psychological Science, 6*, 39–44.

Segura, S., & McCloy, R. (2003). Counterfactual thinking in everyday life situations: Temporal order effects and social norms. *Psicologica, 24*, 1–15. p. 65.

Seligman, J., Rogers, P., & Annin, P. (1994, May 2). The pressure to lose. *Newsweek*, pp. 60, 62.

Seligman, M. E. P. (1995). The effectiveness of psychotherapy: The *Consumer Reports* study. *American Psychologist, 50*(12), 965–974.

Seligman, M. E. P., & Csikzentmihalyi, M. (2000). Positive psychology. *American Psychologist, 55*, 5–14.

Seligman, M. E., & Maier, S. F. (1967). Failure to escape traumatic shock. *Journal of Experimental Psychology, 74*, 1–9.

Seligman, M. E., & Schulman, P. (1986). Explanatory styles as a predictor of productivity and quitting among life insurance sales agents. *Journal of Personality and Social Psychology, 50*, 832–838.

Sell, R. L., Wells, J. A., & Wypij, D. (1995). The prevalence of homosexual behavior and attraction in the United States, the United Kingdom and France: Results of national population-based samples. *Archives of Sexual Behavior, 24*, 235–238.

Selman, R. (1981). The child as friendship philosopher. In S. R. Asher & J. M. Gottman (Eds.), *The development of children's friendships* (pp. 242–272). New York: Cambridge University Press.

Selye, H. (1956). *The stress of life.* New York: McGraw-Hill.

Selye, H. (1976). *The stress of life* (rev. ed.). New York: McGraw-Hill.

Semrud-Clikeman, M., & Hynd, G. W. (1990). Right hemispheric dysfunction.

Seppa, N. (1997, June). Children's TV remains steeped in violence. *APA Monitor*, p. 36.

Sewards, T. V., & Sewards, M. A. (2003). Representations of motivational drives in mesial cortex, medial thalamus, hypothalamus and midbrain. *Brain Research Bulletin, 61*, 25–49.

Shapiro, D., & Shapiro, D. (1982). Meta-analysis of comparative therapy outcome studies: A replication and refinement. *Psychological Bulletin, 92*, 581–604.

Shapiro, K. (1991, July). Use morality as basis for animal treatment. *APA Monitor*, p. 5.

Shaywitz, S. E., Shaywitz, B. A., Pugh, K. R., Fulbright, R. K., Constable, R. T., Mencl, W. E., et al. (1998). Functional disruption in the organization of the brain for reading in dyslexia. *Neurobiology, 95*, 2636–2641.

Sheldon, K. M., & King, L. (2001). Why positive psychology is necessary. *American Psychologist, 56*, 216–217.

Shelton R. C., & Hollon, S. D. (2000). Antidepressants. In A. Kazdin (Ed.), *Encyclopedia of psychology.* Washington, DC: American Psychological Association.

Shepard, R. N. (1978). Externalization of mental images and the act of creation. In B. S. Randhawa & W. E. Coffman (Eds.), *Visual learning, thinking, and communication* (pp. 138–189). New York: Academic Press.

Sherman, R. A. (1996). *Unraveling the mysteries of phantom limb sensations.* New York: Plenum Press.

Shermer, M. (2004, May). The enchanted glass. *Scientific American, 290*, 46.

Sherony, K. M., & Green, S. G. (2002). Coworker exchange: Relationships between coworkers, leader-member exchange, and work attitudes. *Journal of Applied Psychology, 87* (3), 542–548.

Shimamura, A. P., Berry, J. M., Mangels, J. A., Rusting, C. L., & Jurica, P. J. (1995). Memory and cognitive abilities in university professors: Evidence for successful aging. *Psychological Science, 6*, 271–277.

Shore, L. M., Cleveland, J. N., & Goldberg, C. B. (2003). Work attitudes and decisions as a function of manager age and employee age. *Journal of Applied Psychology, 88* (3), 529–537.

Shore, T. H. (2004). Equity sensitivity theory: Do we all want more than we deserve? *Journal of Managerial Psychology, 19* (7), 722–728.

Shorter, E. (1997). *A history of psychiatry: From the era of the asylum to the age of Prozac.* New York: Wiley.

Shriver, M. D., & Piersel, W. (1994). The long-term effects of intrauterine drug exposure: Review of recent research and implications for early childhood special education. *Topics in Early Childhood Special Education, 14,* 161–183.

Siegel, K., Anderman, S. J., & Schrimshaw, E. W. (2001). Religion and coping with health stress. *Psychology and Health, 16,* 631–653.

Siegert, R. J., & Ward, T. (2002). Evolutionary psychology: Origins and criticisms. *Australian Psychologist, 37,* 20–29.

Simon, H. A. (1974). How big is a chunk? *Science, 165,* 482–488.

Simons, T., & Roberson, Q. (2003). Why managers should care about fairness: The effects of aggregate justice perceptions on organizational outcomes. *Journal of Applied Psychology, 88* (3), 432–443.

Simpson, H. B., Nee, J. C., & Endicott, J. (1997). First-episode major depression. Few sex differences in course. *Archives of General Psychiatry, 54*(7), 633–639.

Singh, G. K., & Yu, S. M. (1995). Infant mortality in the United States: Trends, differentials, and projections, 1950 through 2010. *American Journal of Public Health, 85,* 957–964.

Sinnott, J. D. (1994). Sex roles. In V. S. Ramachandran (Ed.), *Encyclopedia of human behavior* (Vol. 4, pp. 151–158). San Diego, CA: Academic Press.

Skeels, H. M. (1938). Mental development of children in foster homes. *Journal of Consulting Psychology, 2,* 33–43.

Skeels, H. M. (1942). The study of the effects of differential stimulation on mentally retarded children: A follow-up report. *American Journal of Mental Deficiencies, 46,* 340–350.

Skeels, H. M. (1966). Adult status of children with contrasting early life experiences. *Monographs of the Society for Research in Child Development, 31*(3), 1–65.

Skinner, B. F. (1938). *The behavior of organisms.* New York: Appleton-Century-Crofts.

Skinner, B. F. (1953). Some contributions of an experimental analysis of behavior to psychology as a whole. *American Psychologist, 8*(2), 69–78.

Skinner, B. F. (1987). Whatever happened to psychology as the science of behavior? *American Psychologist, 42,* 780–786.

Skinner, B. F. (1989). The origins of cognitive thought. *American Psychologist, 44,* 13–18.

Skinner, B. F. (1990). Can psychology be a science of mind? *American Psychologist, 45,* 1206–1210.

Skinner, E. A., Edge, K., Altman, J., & Sherwood, H. (2003). Searching for the structure of coping: A review and critique of category systems for classifying ways of coping. *Psychological Bulletin, 129,* 216–269.

Sleek, S. (1998, May). Older vets just now feeling pain of war. *APA Monitor,* pp.1, 28.

Sleek, S. (1999, February). Programs aim to attract minorities to psychology. *APA Monitor,* p. 47.

Smith, B. W. (2000). Noah revisited: Religious coping by church members and the impact of the 1993 Midwest flood. *Journal of Community Psychology, 28,* 169–186.

Smith, C. T. (1985). Sleep states and learning: A review of the animal literature. *Neuroscience & Biobehavioral Reviews, 9,* 157–168.

Smith, C. T., & Kelly, G. (1988). Paradoxical sleep deprivation applied two days after end of training retards learning. *Physiology & Behavior, 43,* 213–216.

Smith, C. T., & Lapp, L. (1986). Prolonged increase in both PS and number of REMS following a shuttle avoidance task. *Physiology & Behavior, 36,* 1053–1057.

Smith, D. (2001). Impairment on the job. *Monitor on Psychology, 32,* 52–53.

Smith, D. E., Roberts, J., Gage, F. H., & Tuszynski, M. H. (1999). Age-associated neuronal atrophy occurs in the primate brain and is reversible by growth factor gene therapy. *Proceedings of the National Academy of Sciences, 96,* 10893–10898.

Smith, J. M. (2006). Mobile training unit: A cost-effective live fire option. *Fire engineering, 159* (4), 133–134.

Smith, M. L., Glass, G. V., & Miller, T. I. (1980). *The benefits of psychotherapy.* Baltimore: Johns Hopkins University Press.

Smith, M. T., Perlis, M. L., Park, A., Smith, M. S., Pennington, J., Giles, D. E., & Buysee, D. (2002). Comparative meta-analysis of pharmacotherapy and behavior therapy for persistent insomnia. *American Journal of Psychiatry, 159,* 5–11.

Smith, P. B., & Bond, M. H. (1994). *Social psychology across cultures: Analysis and perspectives.* Boston: Allyn & Bacon.

Smith, P. B., & Bond, M. H. (1999). *Social psychology across cultures: Analysis and perspectives* (2nd ed.). Boston: Allyn & Bacon.

Smith, S. M., Gleaves, D. H., Pierce, B. H., Williams, T. L., Gilliland, T. R., & Gerkens, D. R. (2003). Eliciting and comparing false and recovered memories: An experimental approach. *Applied Cognitive Psychology, 17,* 251–279.

Smollar, J., & Youniss, J. (1989). Transformations in adolescents' perceptions of parents. *International Journal of Behavioral Development, 12,* 71–84.

Snodgrass, S. E. (1992). Further effects of role versus gender on interpersonal sensitivity. *Journal of Personality and Social Psychology, 62,* 154–158.

Snyder, M. (1987). *Public appearances/private realities: The psychology of self-monitoring.* New York: Freeman.

Snyder, M., & Swann, W. B., Jr. (1978). Behavioral confirmation in social interaction: From social perception to social reality. *Journal of Experimental Social Psychology, 14,* 148–162.

Snyder, M., & Tanke, E. D. (1976). Behavior and attitude: Some people are more consistent than others. *Journal of Personality, 44,* 501–517.

Snyder, S. H. (1977, March). Opiate receptors and internal opiates. *Scientific American, 236,* 44–56.

Solms, M. (2004, May). Freud returns. *Scientific American,* pp. 82–88.

Somer, E. (2002). Maladaptive daydreaming: A qualitative inquiry. *Journal of Contemporary Psychotherapy, 32,* 197–212.

Sonstroem, R. J. (1997). Physical activity and self-esteem. In W. P. Morgan (Ed.), *Physical activity and mental health* (pp. 127–143). Philadelphia, PA: Taylor & Francis.

Sorensen, R. C. (1973). *Adolescent sexuality in contemporary America.* New York: World.

Sowell, E. R., Thompson, P. M., Welcome, S. E., Henkenius, A. L., Toga, A. W., & Peterson, B. S. (2003). Cortical abnormalities in children and adolescents with attention-deficit hyperactivity disorder. *Lancet, 362,* 1699–1707.

Soyguet, G., & Tuerkcapar, H. (2001). Assessment of interpersonal schema patterns in antisocial personality disorder: A cognitive interpersonal perspective. *Turk Psikoloji Dergisi, 16,* 55–69.

Spanos, N. P. (1996). *Multiple identities and false memories.* Washington, DC: American Psychological Association.

Spanos, N. P., Burgess, C. A., Burgess, M. F., Samuels, C., & Blois, W. O. (1997). *Creating false memories of infancy with hypnotic and nonhypnotic procedures.* Unpublished manuscript, Carlton University, Ottawa, Canada.

Spehar, B., & Gillam, B. (2002). Modal completion in the Poggendorff illusion: Support for the depth-processing theory. *Psychological Science, 13,* 306–312.

Sperling, G. (1960). The information available in brief visual presentations. *Psychological Monographs, 74,* 1–29.

Sperry, R. W. (1964, January). The great cerebral commissure. *Scientific American, 210,* 42–52.

Sperry, R. W. (1968). Hemisphere disconnection and unity in conscious awareness. *American Psychologist, 23,* 723–733.

Sperry, R. W. (1970). *Perception in the absence of neocortical commissures. In Perception and its disorders* (Res. Publ. A.R.N.M.D., Vol. 48). New York: The Association for Research in Nervous and Mental Disease.

Sperry, R. W. (1988). Psychology's mentalists paradigm and the religion/science tension. *American Psychologist, 43,* 607–613.

Sperry, R. W. (1995). The future of psychology. *American Psychologist, 5*(7), 505–506.

Spiegel, D. (1995). Essentials of psychotherapeutic intervention for cancer patients. *Support Care Cancer, 3*(4), 252–256.

Spiegel, D., & Kato, P. M. (1996). Psychological influences on cancer incidence and progression. *Harvard Review of Psychiatry, 4,* 10–26.

Spiegel, D., & Moore, R. (1997). Imagery and hypnosis in the treatment of cancer patients. Oncology, 11, 1179–1189.

Spinath, F. M., Harlaar, N., Ronald, A., & Plomin, R. (2004). Substantial genetic influence on mild mental impairment in early childhood. *American Journal of Mental Retardation, 109,* 34–43.

Spitzer, R. L., Skodal, A. E., Gibbon, M., & Williams, J. B. W. (1981). *DSM-III case book.* Washington, DC: American Psychiatric Association.

Spitzer, R. L., Skodal, A. E., Gibbon, M., & Williams, J. B. W. (1983). *Psychopathology: A casebook.* New York: McGraw-Hill.

Spoendlin, H. H., & Schrott, A. (1989). Analysis of the human auditory nerve. *Hearing Research, 43,* 25–38.

Spreitzer, G. M., McCall, M. M., & Mahoney, J. D. (1997). Early identification of international executive potential. *Journal of Applied Psychology, 82* (1), 6–29.

Squire, L. R., & Kandel, E. R. (1999). *Memory: From mind to molecules.* New York: Scientific American Library.

Stack, S. (1994). Divorce. In V. S. Ramachandran (Ed.), *Encyclopedia of human behavior* (Vol. 2, pp. 153–163). San Diego, CA: Academic Press.

Stajkovic, A. D. & Luthans, F. (1997). Business ethics across cultures: A social cognitive model. *Journal of World Business, 32* (1), 17–34.

Stancliffe, R. J. (1997). Community residence size, staff presence and choice. *Mental Retardation, 35,* 1–9.

Stanley, T. L. (2004). The wisdom of employment testing. *Supervision, 65* (2), 11–13.

Stauffer, J. M., & Buckley, M. R. (2005). The existence and nature of racial bias in supervisory ratings. *Journal of Applied Psychology, 90* (3), 586–591.

Steele, C. M., & Josephs, R. A. (1990). Alcohol myopia: Its prized and dangerous effects. *American Psychologist, 45,* 921–933.

Stern, K., & McClintock, M. K. (1998, March 12). Regulation of ovulation by human pheromones. *Nature, 392,* 177.

Steiger, H., Gauvin, L., Jabalpurwala, S., Seguin, J. R., & Stotland, S. (1999). Hypersensitivity to social interactions in bulimic syndromes: Relationships to binge eating. *Journal of Consulting & Clinical Psychology, 67,* 765–775.

Steinhauer, J. (1997, July 6). Living together without marriage or apologies. *New York Times,* p. A9.

Stern, L. (1985). *The structures and strategies of human memory.* Homewood, IL: Dorsey Press.

Stern, R. M., & Koch, K. L. (1996). Motion sickness and differential susceptibility. *Current Directions in Psychological Science, 5,* 115–120.

Sternberg, R. J. (1986). *Intelligence applied.* Orlando, FL: Harcourt Brace Jovanovich.

Sternberg, R. J. (2001). What is the common thread of creativity? Its dialectical relation to intelligence and wisdom. *American Psychologist, 56,* 360–362.

Stickgold, R., Rittenhouse, C. D., & Hobson, J. A. (1994). Dream splicing: A new technique for assessing thematic coherence in subjective reports of mental activity. *Consciousness and Cognition, 3,* 114–128.

Stodghill, R. (1998, June 15). Where'd you learn that? *Time,* 52–59.

Stoner, J. A. F. (1961). *A comparison of individual and group decisions involving risk.* Unpublished master's thesis, School of Industrial Management, MIT.

Storch, E. A., & Storch, J. B. (2003). Academic dishonesty and attitudes towards academic dishonest acts: Support for cognitive dissonance theory. *Psychological Reports, 92,* 174–176.

Storm, L., & Ertel, S. (2001). Does Psi exist? Comments on Milton and Wise-man's (1999) meta-analysis of Ganzfeld research. *Psychological Bulletin, 12,* 424–433.

Stowell, J. R., McGuire, L., Robles, T., Glaser, R., & Kiecolt-Glaser, J. K. (2003). Psychoneuroimmunology. In A. M. Nezu & C. M. Nezu (Eds.), *Handbook of psychology: Health psychology,* Vol. 9 (pp. 75–95). New York: John Wiley & Sons, Inc.

Strickland, B. R. (2000). Misassumptions, misadventures, and the misuse of psychology. *American Psychologist, 55,* pp. 331–338.

Stylianou, D. A. (2002). On the interaction of visualization and analysis: The negotiation of a visual representation in expert problem solving. *Journal of Mathematical Behavior, 21,* 303–317.

Subotnik, R. F., & Arnold, K. D. (1994). *Beyond Terman: Contemporary longitudinal studies of giftedness and talent.* Norwood, NJ: Ablex.

Suls, J., & Fletcher, B. (1983). Social comparison in the social and physical sciences: An archival study. *Journal of Personality and Social Psychology, 44,* 575–580.

Sumova, A., Saladek, M., Jac, M., & Illnervoa, H. (2002). The circadian rhythm of Per1 gene product in rat's suprachiasmatic nucleus and its modulation by seasonal changes in daylight. *Brain Research, 947,* 260–270.

Sunstrom, E., DeMeuse, K., & Futrell, D. (1990). Work teams: Applications and effectiveness. *American psychologist, 31* (3), 120–133.

Sundel, S. S. (1991). The effects of videotaped modeling on the acquisition, performance, and generalization of job-related social skills in adults with mental retardation living in group homes. *Dissertation Abstracts International, 51,* 2522.

Surguladze, S. A., Young, A. W., Senior, C., Brebion, G., Travis, M. J., & Phillips, M. L. (2004). Recognition accuracy and response bias to happy and sad facial expressions in patients with major depression. *Neuropsychology, 18,* 212–218.

Swaab, D. F., & Hoffman, M. A. (1995). Sexual differentiation of the human hypothalamus in relation to gender and sexual orientation. *Trends in Neuroscience, 18,* 264–270.

Symons, C. S., & Johnson, B. T. (1997). The self-reference effect in memory: A meta-analysis. *Psychological Bulletin, 121,* 371–394.

T. O'Donohue (eds.), *Handbook of sexual deviance: Theory and application.* New York: Guilford.

Tagano, D. W., Moran, D. J., III, & Sawyers, J. K. (1991). *Creativity in early childhood classrooms.* Washington, DC: National Education Association.

Takaki, A., Nagai, K., Takaki, S., & Yanaihara, N. (1990). Satiety function of neurons containing CCKK-like substance in the dorsal parabrachial nucleus. *Physiology & Behavior, 48,* 865–871.

Takeuchi, S. A. (2000). If I don't look good, you don't look good? Toward a new matching theory of interpersonal attraction based on the behavioral and the social exchange principles. *Dissertation Abstracts International Section A: Humanities and Social Sciences, 60,* 4198.

Tanner, J. M. (1978). *Foetus into man: Physical growth from conception to maturity.* Cambridge, MA: Harvard University Press.

Tan, D. T. Y., & Singh, R. (1995). Attitudes and attraction: A developmental study of the similarity-attraction and dissimilarity-repulsion hypotheses. *Personality and Social Psychology Bulletin, 21*(9), 975–986.

Tanofsky, M. B., Wilfley, D. E., Spurrell, E. B., Welch, R., & Brownell, K. D. (1997). Comparison of men and women with binge eating disorder. International Journal of Eating Disorders, 21, 49–54.

Taylor, D. M., & Moghaddam, F. M. (1994). *Theories of intergroup relations: International social psychological perspectives.* Westport, CT: Praeger.

Taylor, S. E. (2003). *Health Psychology* (5th ed.) New York: McGraw-Hill.

Taylor, S. E., Klein, L. C., Lewis, B. P., Gruenewald, T. L., Gurung, R. A. R., & Updegraff, J. A. (2000). Biobehavioral responses to stress in females: Tend-and-befriend, not fight-or-flight. *Psychological Review, 107,* 411–429.

Taylor, S. E., Pham, L. B., Rivkin, I. D., & Armor, D. A. (1998). Harnessing the imagination: Mental simulation, self-regulation, and coping. *American Psychologist, 53,* 429–439.

Taylor, S. E., & Repetti, R. L. (1997). Health psychology: What is an unhealthy environment and how does it get under the skin? *Annual Review of Psychology, 48,* 411–447.

Tenopyr, M. L. (1996). The complex interactions between measurement and national employment policy. *Psychology, Public Policy, and Law, 2,* 348–362.

Thierry, N., Willeit, M., Praschak-Rieder, N., Zill, P., Hornik, K., Neumeister, A., Lenzinger, E., Stastny, J., Hilger, E., Konstantinidis, A., Aschauer, H., Ackenheil, M., Bondy, B., & Dasper, S. (2004). Serotonin transporter promoter gene polymorphic region (5-HT-TLPR) and personality in female patients with seasonal affective disorder and in healthy controls. *European Neuropsychopharmacology, 14,* 53–58.

Thomas, S. G., & Kellner, C. H. (2003). Remission of major depression and obsessive-compulsive disorder after a single unilateral ECT. *Journal of ECT, 19,* 50–51.

Thompson, J. K., & Thompson, C. M. (1986). Body size distortion and self-esteem in asymptomatic, normal weight males and females. *International Journal of Eating Disorders, 5,* 1061–1068.

Thoresen, C. J., Kaplan, S. A., Barsky, A. P., Warren, C. R., & deCharmont, K. (2003). The affective underpinnings of job perceptions and attitudes: A meta-analytic review and interpretation. *Psychological Bulletin, 129* (2), 914–945.

Thorndike, E. L. (1898). Animal intelligence. *Psychological Review Monograph, 2*(4, Whole No. 8).

Tincoff, R., & Jusczyk, P. W. (1999). Some beginnings of word comprehension in 6-month-olds. *Psychological Science, 10,* 172–176.

Tobler, I. (1997). *What do we know about the evolution of sleep—when it arose and why?* Retrieved from *www.sciam.com/askexpert/biology/biology24.html.*

Tolman, E. C., & Honzik, C. H. (1930). Introduction and removal of reward, and maze performance in rats. University of California Publications in *Psychology, 4,* 257–275.

Tooby, J., & Cosmides, L. (2003). The second law of thermodynamics is the first law of psychology: Evolutionary developmental psychology and the theory of tandem, coordinated inheritances: Comment on Lickliter and Honeycutt (2003). *Psychological Bulletin, 129,* 858–865.

Torrance, E. P. (1954). Leadership training to improve air-crew group performance. *USAF ATC Instructor's Journal, 5,* 25–35.

Tourangeau, R., Rips, J. L., & Rasinski, K. (2000). *Stalking the cognitive measurement error.* New York: Cambridge University Press.

Triandis, H. C. (1994). *Culture and social behavior.* New York: McGraw-Hill.

Trice, A. D. (1986). Ethical variables? *American Psychologist, 41,* 482–483.

Trichopoulou, A, Costacou, T., Bamia, C., & Trichopoulos, D. (2003). Adherence to a Mediterranean diet and survival in a Greek population. *The New England Journal of Medicine, 348,* 2599–2608.

Tryon, W. W. (2000). Behavior therapy as applied learning theory. *Behavior Therapist, 23,* 131–133.

Tucker, C. M., & Herman, K. C. (2002). Using culturally sensitive theories and research to meet the academic needs of low-income African American children. *American Psychologist, 57,* 762–773.

Tulving, E. (1985). How many memory systems are there? *American Psychologist, 40,* 385–398.

Tulving, E., Kapur, S., Markowitsch, H. J., Craik, F. I. M., Habib, R., & Houle, S. (1994). Neuroanatomical correlates of retrieval in episodic memory: Auditory sentence recognition. *Proceedings of the National Academy of Sciences of the U.S.A., 91,* 2012–2015.

Turk, D. C., & Salovey, P. (1985). Cognitive structures, cognitive processes, and cognitive behavior modification: II. Judgments and inferences of the clinician. *Cognitive Therapy and Research, 9,* 19–34.

Turkeltaub, P. E., Gareau, L., Flowers, D. L., Zeffiro, T. A., & Eden, G. F. (2003). Development of neural mechanisms for reading. *Nature Neuroscience, 6,* 767–773.

Turkheimer, E. (1991). Individual and group differences in adoption studies of IQ. *Psychological Bulletin, 110,* 392–405.

Turner, M. E. (2001). *Groups at work: Theory and research.* Mahwah, NJ: Erlbaum.

U.S. Department of Justice (2006). *The Americans with Disabilities Act.* Accessed June 26, 2006 from: http://www.ada.gov/adahom1.htm

U.S. Department of Labor (2006a). *O*NET Online.* Accessed June 28, 2006, from: http://www.online.onetcenter.org

U.S. Department of Labor (2006b). *Training: Apprenticeship.* Accessed June 29, 2006 from: http://www.dol.gov/dol/topic/training/apprenticeship.htm#doltopics

U.S. Equal Employment Opportunity Commission (2006). *Title VII of the Civil Rights Act of 1964.* Accessed June 26, 2006 from: http://www.eeoc.gov/policy/vii.html

Uchino, B. N., Cacioppo, J. T., & Kiecolt-Glaser, J. K. (1996). The relationship between social support and physiological processes: A review with emphasis on underlying mechanisms and implications for health. *Psychological Bulletin, 119*(3), 488–531.

Uchino, B. N., Uno, D., & Holt-Lunstad, J. (1999). Social support, psychological processes, and health. *Current Directions in Psychological Science, 8,* 145–148.

Uhl, G., Blum, K., Nobel, E. P., & Smith, S. (1993). Substance abuse vulnerability and D2 dopamine receptor gene and severe alcoholism. *Trends in Neuroscience, 16,* 83–88.

Ulrich, R., & Azrin, N. (1962). Reflexive fighting in response to aversive stimulation. *Journal of Experimental Analysis of Behavior, 5,* 511–520.

Underwood, G. (1994). Subliminal perception on TV. *Nature, 370,* 103.

Underwood, G. (1996). *Implicit cognition.* New York: Oxford University.

Urbaniak, A. (2004). Training employees. *Supervision, 65* (2), 6–17.

Vaidya, C. J., Austin, G., Kirkorian, G., Ridlehuber, H. W., Desmond, J. E., Glover, G. H., et al. (1998). Selective effects of methylphenidate in attention deficit hyperactivity disorder: A functional magnetic resonance study. *Proceedings of the National Academy of Sciences, U.S.A., 96,* 8301–8306.

Vaillant, G. E. (2000). Adaptive mental mechanisms: Their role in positive psychology. *American Psychologist, 55,* 89–98.

Vaisse, C., Halaas, J. L., Horvath, C. M., Darnell, J. E., Stoffel, M., & Friedman, J. M. (1996). Leptin activation of Stat3 in the hypothalamus of wild-type and ob/ob mice but not db/db mice. *Nature Genetics, 14,* 95–97.

Valian, V. (1998). *Why so slow?: The advancement of women.* Cambridge, MA: MIT Press.

Van Dongen, H. P. A., Maislin, G., Mullington, J. M., & Dinges, D. F. (2003). The cumulative cost of additional wakefulness: Dose-response effects on neurobehavioral functions and sleep physiology from chronic sleep restriction and total sleep deprivation. *Sleep, 26,* 117–126.

Van Eerde, W., & Thierry, H. (1996). Vroom's expectancy models and work-related criteria: A meta-analysis. *Journal of Applied Psychology, 81* (5), 575–586.

van Elst, L. T., & Trimble, M. R. (2003). Amygdala pathology in schizophrenia and psychosis of epilepsy. *Current Opinion in Psychiatry, 16,* 321–326.

Van Iddekinge C. H., Putka, D. J., Raymark, P. H., & Eidson Jr., C. E. (2005). Modeling error variance in job specification ratings: The influence of rater, job, and organization-level factors. *Journal of Applied Psychology, 90* (2), 323–334.

Van Praag, H., & Gage, F. H. (2002). Stem cell research, part 1: New neurons in the adult brain. *Journal of the American Academy of Child and Adolescent Psychiatry, 41,* 354–356.

Van Yperen, N. W., & Buunk, B. P. (1990). A longitudinal study of equity and satisfaction in intimate relationships. *European Journal of Social Psychology, 54,* 287–309.

van-Iddekinge, C. H., Raymark, P. H., Eidson, C. E. Jr., & Attenweiler, W. J. (2004). What do structured selection interviews really measure? The construct validity of behavior description interviews. *Human Performance, 17,* 71–93.

Vastag, B. (2003). Addiction poorly understood by clinicians: Experts say attitudes, lack of knowledge hinder treatment. *Journal of the American Medical Association, 290,* 1299–1303.

Vaughn, D. (1996). *The Challenger launch decision: Risky technology, culture, and deviance at NASA.* Chicago, IL: University of Chicago Press.

Vecera, S. P., Vogel, E. K., & Woodman, G. F. (2002). Lower region: A new cue for figure-ground assignment. *Journal of Experimental Psychology: General, 131,* 194–205.

Verespej, M. A. (1992). When workers get new roles. *Industry week,* 11.

Vermetten, E., & Bremner, J. D. (2002). Circuits and systems in stress: II. Applications to neurobiology and treatment in posttraumatic stress disorder. *Depression and Anxiety, 16,* 14–38.

Vgontzas, A. N., & Kales, A. (1999). Sleep and its disorders. *Annual Review of Medicine, 50,* 387–400.

Viding, E., Spinath, F. M., Price, T. S., Bishop, D. V. M., Dale, P. S., & Plomin, R. (2004). Genetic and environmental influence on language impairment in 4-year-old same-sex and opposite-sex twins. *Journal of Child Psychology and Psychiatry and Allied Disciplines, 45,* 315–325.

Viglione, D. J., & Taylor, N. (2003). Empirical support for interrater reliability of Rorschach comprehensive system coding. *Journal of Clinical Psychology, 59,* 111–121.

Vingerhoets, G., Berckmoes, C., & Stroobant, N. (2003). Cerebral hemodynamics during discrimination of prosodic and semantic emotion in speech studied by transcranial Doppler ultrasonography. *Neuropsychology, 17,* 93–99.

Vinnicombe, S., & Singh, V. (2003). Women-only management training: An essential part of women's leadership development. *Journal of Change Management, 3,* 294–306.

Virkkunen, M. (1983). Insulin secretion during the glucose tolerance test in antisocial personality. *British Journal of Psychiatry, 142,* 598–604.

Viswesvaran, C., Schmidt, F. L., & Ones, D. S. (2005). Is there a general factor in ratings of job performance? A meta-analytic framework for distangling substantive and error influences. *Journal of Applied Psychology, 90* (1), 108–131.

Viswesvaran, C., Schmidt, F. L., & Ones, D. S. (2002). The moderating influence of job performance dimensions on convergence of supervisory and peer ratings of job performance: Unconfounding construct-level convergence and rating difficulty. *Journal of Applied Psychology, 87* (2), 345–354.

von Hofsten, C., & Fazel-Zandy, S. (1984). Development of visually guided hand orientation in reaching. *Journal of Experimental Child Psychology, 38,* 208–219.

Vygotsky, L. S. (1979). *Mind in society: The development of higher mental processes.* Cambridge, MA: Harvard University Press. (Original works published in 1930, 1933, and 1935.)

Vroom, V. H. (1964). *Work and motivation.* New York: Wiley.

Wadden, T. S., Vogt, R. A., Anderson, R. E., Bartlett, S. F., Foster, G. D., Kuehnel, R. H., Wilk, F., Weinstock, R., Buckenmeyer, P., Berkowitz, R. I., & Steen, S. N. (1997). Exercise in the treatment of obesity: Effects of four interventions on body composition, resting energy expenditure, appetite and mood. *Journal of Consulting and Clinical Psychology, 65,* 269–277.

Wagar, B. M., & Thagard, P. (2004). Spiking Phineas Gage: A neurocomputational theory of cognitive–affective integration in decision making. *Psychological Review, 111,* 67–79.

Wagner, U., Gais, S., Haider, H., Verleger, R., & Born, J. (2004). Sleep inspires insight. *Nature, 427,* 352–355.

Wahlsten, D. (1999). Single-gene influences on brain and behavior. *Annual Review of Psychology, 50,* 599–624.

Walchle, S. B., & Landman, J. (2003). Effects of counterfactual thought on post-purchase consumer affect. *Psychology and Marketing, 20,* 23–46.

Wald, M. L. (1997, September 11). "Truckers are driving with too little sleep, research shows." *New York Times,* p. A22.

Walker, E. F., & Diforio, D. (1997). Schizophrenia: A neural diathesis-stress model. *Psychological Review, 104,* 667–685.

Walters, E. E., & Kendler, K. S. (1995). Anorexia nervosa and anorexic-like syndromes in a population-based female twin sample. *American Journal of Psychiatry, 152,* 64–67.

Wall, P. D., & Melzack, R. (1996). *The challenge of pain* (2nd ed.). Harmondworth, UK: Penguin.

Wall, R. P., & Melzack, R. (eds.). (1989). *Textbook of pain* (2nd ed.). Edinburgh: Churchill Livingston.

Wallerstein, J. S., Blakeslee, S., & Lewis, J. (2000). *The unexpected legacy of divorce: Twenty-five year landmark study.* New York: Hyperion.

Walster, E., Walster, G. W., & Berscheid, E. (1978). *Equity: Theory and research.* Boston: Allyn & Bacon.

Walton, G. E., Bower, N. J. A., & Bower, T. G. R. (1992). Recognition of familiar faces by newborns. *Infant Behavior and Development, 15,* 265–269.

Waltz, J. A., Knowlton, B. J., Holyoak, K. J., Boone, K. B., Mishkin, F. S., Santos, M. M., et al. (1999). A system for relational reasoning in human prefrontal cortex. *Psychological Science, 10,* 119–125.

Wampold, B. E. (2001). *The great psychotherapy debate: Models, methods, and findings.* Mahwah, NJ: Erlbaum.

Wampold, B. E., Mondin, G. W., Moody, M., Stich, F., Benson, K., & Ahn, H. (1997). A meta-analysis of outcome studies comparing bona fide psychotherapies: Empirically, "all must have prizes." *Psychological Bulletin, 122,* 203–215.

Warr, P., & Perry, G. (1982). Paid employment and women's psychological well-being. *Psychological Bulletin, 91,* 498–516.

Waters, A. J., Gobet, F., & Leyden, G. (2002). Visuospatial abilities of chess players. *British Journal of Psychology, 93,* 557–565.

Watkins, C. E., Campbell, V. L., Nieberding, R., & Hallmark, R. (1995). Contemporary practice of psychological assessment by clinical psychologists. *Professional Psychological Research & Practice, 26,* 54–60.

Watson, J. B. (1924). *Behaviorism.* Chicago: University of Chicago Press.

Watson, J. B., & Rayner, R. (1920). Conditioned emotional reactions. *Journal of Experimental Psychology, 3,* 1–14.

Webb, W. B., & Levy, C. M. (1984). Effects of spaced and repeated total sleep deprivation. *Ergonomics, 27,* 45–58.

Wechsler, H., Davenport, A., Dowdall, G., Moeykens, B., & Castillo, S. (1994). Health and behavioral consequences of binge drinking in college. *Journal of the American Medical Association, 272,* 1672–1677.

Wechsler, H., Fulop, M., Padilla, A., Lee, H., & Patrick, K. (1997). Binge drinking among college students: A comparison of California with other states. *Journal of American College Health, 45,* 273–277.

Wechsler, H., Lee, J. E., Kuo, M., Seibring, M., Nelson, T. F., Lee, H. (2002). Trends in college binge drinking during a period of increased prevention efforts: Erratum. *Journal of American College Health, 51* (1), 37.

Wechsler, H., Seibring, M., Liu, I. C., & Ahl, M. (2004). Colleges respond to student binge drinking: Reducing student demand or limiting access. *Journal of American College Health, 52,* 159–168.

Weinberg, M. K., Tronick, E. Z., Cohn, J. F., & Olson, K. L. (1999). Gender differences in emotional expressivity and self-regulation during early infancy. *Developmental Psychology, 35,* 175–188.

Weiner, I. B. (1996). Some observations on the validity of the Rorshach Inkblot Method. *Psychological Assessment, 8,* 206–213.

Weiner, I. B. (1997). Current status of the Rorshach Inkblot Method. *Journal of Personality Assessment, 68,* 5–19.

Weingarten, S. M., & Cummings, J. L. (2001). Psychosurgery of frontal–subcortical circuits. In D. G. Lichter & J. L. Cummings (Eds.), *Frontal-subcortical circuits in psychiatric and neurological disorders* (pp. 421–435). New York: Guilford Press.

Weinstein, S. (1968). Intensive and extensive aspects of tactile sensitivity as a function of body part, sex, and laterality. In D. R. Kenshalo (ed.), *The skin senses.* Springfield, IL: Charles C. Thomas.

Weisband, S., & Atwater, L. (1999). Evaluating self and others in electronic and face-to-face groups. *Journal of Applied Psychology, 84* (4), 632–639.

Weiss, A. P., Zalesak, M., DeWitt, L., Goff, D., Kunkel, L., & Heckers, S. (2004). Impaired hippocampal function during the detection of novel words in schizophrenia. *Biological Psychiatry, 55,* 668–675.

Werker, F. J., & Desjardins, R. N. (1995). Listening to speech in the 1st year of life: Experiential influences on phoneme perception. *Current Directions in Psychological Science, 4,* 76–81.

Weiss, G. (2006). Doing a reference check. *Medical economics, 83* (5), 50.

Werner, E. E. (1996). Vulnerable but invincible: High risk children from birth to adulthood. *European Child & Adolescent Psychiatry, 5* (Suppl. 1), 47–51.

Westen, D. (1998b). Unconscious thought, feeling and motivation: The end of a century-long debate. In R. F. Bornstein & J. M. Masling (Eds.), *Empirical perspectives on the psychoanalytic unconscious* (pp. 1–43). Washington, DC: American Psychological Association.

Wheeler, M. A., Stuss, D. T., & Tulving. E. (1997). Toward a theory of episodic memory: The frontal lobes and autonoetic consciousness. *Psychological Bulletin, 121,* 331–354.

Whetten, D. A., & Cameron, K. S. (1991). *Developing management skills* (2nd ed.). New York: HarperCollins.

Whisman, M. A., & Kwon, P. (1993). Life stress and dysphoria: The role of self-esteem and hopelessness. *Journal of Personality and Social Psychology, 65,* 1054–1060.

White, P., & Waghorn, G. (2004). Mental illness and employment status. *Australian and New Zealand Journal of Psychiatry, 38,* 174–175.

Wickens, C. D. & Hollands, J. G. (2003). *Engineering psychology and human performance (3rd edition).* Upper Saddle River, NJ: Prentice Hall.

Wierzbicki, M. (1993). *Issues in clinical psychology: Subjective versus objective approaches.* Boston: Allyn & Bacon.

Wiggins, J. S. (ed.). (1996). *The five-factor model of personality: Theoretical perspectives.* New York: Guilford Press.

Williams, J. C., Paton, C. C., Siegler, I. C., Eigenbrodt, M. L., Nieto, F. J., & Tyroles, H. A. (2000). Anger proneness predicts coronary heart disease risk: Prospective analysis from the atherosclerosis risk in communities (ARIC) study. *Circulation, 101,* 2034–2039.

Williams, J. E., & Best, D. L. (1990). *Measuring sex stereotypes: A multinational study.* Newbury Park, CA: Sage.

Williams, L. (1989, November 22). Psychotherapy gaining favor among blacks. *New York Times.*

Williams, R. A., Hagerty, B. M., Cimprich, B., Therrien, B., Bay, E., & Oe, H. (2000). Changes in directed attention and short-term memory in attention. Journal of Psychiatric Research, 34, 227–238.

Williams, R. B. (2001). Hostility and other psychological risk factors: Effects on health and the potential for successful behavioral approaches to prevention and treatment. In A. Baum, T. A. Revenson, & J. E. Singer (Eds.), *Handbook of health psychology.* Mahwah, NJ: Erlbaum.

Williams, R. B., Barefoot, J. C., Califf, R. M., Haney, T. L., Saunders, W. B., Pryor, D. B., et al. (1992). Prognostic importance of social and economic resources among medically treated patients with angiographically documented coronary artery disease. *Journal of the American Medical Association, 267,* 520–524.

Willis, S. L., & Schaie, K. W. (1986). Training the elderly on the ability factors of spatial orientation and inductive reasoning. *Psychology and Aging, 1,* 239–247.

Wilson, G. D. (1987). An ethological approach to sexual deviation. In G. D. Wilson (ed.), *Variant sexuality: Research and theory* (pp. 84–115). London: Croom Helm.

Winerip, M. (1998, January 4). Binge nights: The emergency on campus. *Education Life (New York Times* supplement), Section 4A, pp. 28–31, 42.

Winn, P. (1995). The lateral hypothalamus and motivated behavior: An old syndrome reassessed and a new perspective gained. *Current Directions in Psychological Science, 4,* 182–187.

Winson, J. (1990, November). The meaning of dreams. *Scientific American, 263,* 94–96.

Winston, A., & Winston, B. (2002). *Handbook of integrated short-term psychotherapy.* Washington, DC: American Psychiatric Association.

Wolf, S. S., & Weinberger, D. R. (1996). Schizophrenia: A new frontier in developmental neurobiology. *Israel Journal of Medical Science, 32*(1), 51–55.

Wolpe, J. (1973). *The practice of behavior therapy* (2nd ed.). New York: Pergamon.

Wolpe, J. (1982). *The practice of behavior therapy* (3rd ed.). New York: Pergamon.

Wolpe, P. R. (1990). The holistic heresy: Strategies of ideological challenge in the medical profession. *Social Science & Medicine, 31*(8), 913–923.

Wonderlic Personnel Test. (1992). *Wonderlic Personnel Test & Scholastic Level Exam: User's manual.* Libertyville, MO: Wonderlic Personnel Test, Inc.

Wood, N. L., & Cowan, N. (1995). The cocktail party phenomenon revisited: Attention and memory in the classic selective listening procedure of Cherry (1953). *Journal of Experimental Psychology: General, 124,* 243–262.

Wood, W., & Quinn, J. M. (2003). Forewarned and forearmed? Two meta-analytic syntheses of forewarnings of influence appeals. *Psychological Bulletin, 129,* 119–138.

Worchel, S., Cooper, J., & Goethals, G. R. (1991). *Understanding social psychology* (5th ed.). Pacific Grove, CA: Brooks/Cole.

Wortman, C. B., & Silver, R. C. (1989). The myths of coping with loss. *Journal of Consulting & Clinical Psychology, 57,* 349–357.

Wright, R. (1994). *The moral animal: The new science of evolutionary psychology.* New York: Pantheon.

Wyatt, W. J. (1993, December). Identical twins, emergenesis, and environments. *American Psychologist,* pp. 1294–1295.

Wyrwicka, W. (1988). Imitative behavior: A theoretical view. Pavlovian *Journal of Biological Science, 23,* 125–131.

Yalom, I. D. (1995). *The theory and practice of group psychotherapy* (4th ed.). New York: Basic Books.

Yang, C. C., Chen, H., & Hong, K. (2003). Visualization of large category map for Internet browsing. *Decision Support Systems, 35,* 89–102.

Yanovski, S. Z. (1993). Binge eating disorder. Current knowledge and future directions. *Obesity Research, 1,* 306–324.

Yotsutsuji, T., Saitoh, O., Suzuki, M., Hagino, H., Mori, K., Takahashi, T., Kurokawa, K., Matsui, M., Seto, H., & Kurachi, M. (2003). Quantification of lateral ventricular subdivisions in schizophrenia by high-resolution three-dimensional magnetic resonance imaging. *Psychiatry Research: Neuroimaging, 122,* 1–12.

Young, Q. W., Hellawell, D. J., Wan de Wal, C., & Johnson, M. (1996). Facial expression processing after amygdalotomy. *Neuropsychologia, 34*, 31–39.

Yukl, G. A. (2002). *Leadership in Organizations*. Upper Saddle River: Prentice-Hall.

Yukl, G. A. & Latham, G. P. (1975). Consequences of reinforcement schedules and incentive magnitudes for employee performance: Problems encountered in an industrial setting. *Journal of Applied Psychology, 60* (3), 294–298.

Zadra, A., & Donderi, D. C. (2000). Nightmares and bad dreams: Their prevalence and relationship to well-being. *Journal of Abnormal Psychology, 109*, 273–281.

Zedeck, S., & Goldstein, I. L. (2000). The relationship between I/O psychology and public policy: A commentary. In J. F. Kehoe (Ed.), *Managing selection in changing organizations* (pp. 371–396). San Francisco: Jossey-Bass.

Zehr, D. (2001). Portrayals of Wundt and Titchener in introductory psychology texts: A content analysis. *Teaching of Psychology, 27*, 122–123.

Zigler, E. (1998). By what goals should Head Start be assessed? *Children's Services: Social Policy, Research, and Practice, 1*, 5–18.

Zigler, E. (2003). What would draw a basic scientist into Head Start (and why would he never leave)? In R. J. Sternberg (Ed.), *Psychologists defying the crowd: Stories of those who battled the establishment and won* (pp. 273–282). Washington, DC: American Psychological Association.

Zigler, E. F., Finn–Stevenson, M., & Hall, N. W. (2002). *The first three years & beyond: Brain development and social policy*. New Haven, CT: Yale University Press.

Zigler, E., & Muenchow, S. (1992). *Head Start: The inside story of America's most successful educational experiment*. New York: Basic Books.

Zigler, E., & Styfco, S. J. (1994). Head Start: Criticisms in a constructive context. *American Psychologist, 49*, 127–132.

Zigler, E., & Styfco, S. J. (2001). Extended childhood intervention prepares children for school and beyond. *Journal of the American Medical Association, 285*, 2378–2380.

Zigler, E., & Styfco, S. J. (eds.). (1993). *Head Start and beyond*. New Haven, CT: Yale University Press.

Zubieta, J., Heitzeg, M. M., Smith, Y. R., Bueller, J. A., Yanjun Xu, K. X., Koeppe, R. A., Stohler, C. S., & Goldman, D. (2003, February 21). COMT val[158]met genotype affects -Opioid neurotransmitter responses to a pain stressor. *Science, 299*, 1240–1243.

Zucker, R. A., & Gomberg, E.S.L. (1990). Etiology of alcoholism reconsidered: The case for a biopsychosocial process. *American Psychologist, 41*, 783–793.

Zuckerman, M., Miyake, K., & Elkin, C. S. (1995). Effects of attractiveness and maturity of face and voice on interpersonal impression. *Journal of Research in Personality, 29*, 253–272.

Zuger, A. (1998, July 28). A fistful of aggression is found among women. *New York Times*, p. B8

Case Study References
Chapter 1: Toyota
Sources:

Anonymous, "Problem Solving at Toyota," *Fabricating and Metalworking*, October 2005, Vol.4, Iss.9, pp. 42–43.

Anonymous, "Can Benchmarking Produce Evidence?" *Harvard Business Review*, January 2006, Vol. 84, Iss.1, p. 69.

Fujio Cho, Mariko Mikami, "5. Act.Improve.Repeat," *Business 2.0*, January/February 2005. Vol.6, Iss.1, p. 72.

Alex Taylor III, "How Toyota Does It: The Birth of the Prius," *Fortune*, March 6, 2006, Vol. 153. No.4, pp.107–124.

Chapter 2: Brain Scans
Sources:

Sandra Blakeslee, "If You Have a ëBuy Button' in Your Brain, What Pushes It?" *The New York Times*, October 19, 2004, p. F5.

Robert Lee Hotz, "MAPPING THE MIND; Searching for the Why of buy; Researchers scan for insight into how marketing may brand the brain's preference for products and politicians. Series: ABOUT THIS SERIES/ First in a series of occasional articles about scientists' efforts to explore the creation of beliefs and behavior in the synapses of the brain.'" *Los Angeles Times*, February 27, 2005, p. A1.

Alisdair Reid, "MRI scanners can improve advertising effectiveness," *Knight Ridder Tribune Business News*, January 18, 2006, p. 1.

Julie Tamaki, "Researchers Get a Super Handle on Ads That Work; A study at UCLA employs brain scans to gauge responses to the $2.5 million, 30-second television commercials during the big game," *Los Angeles Times*, February 6, p. C1.

Chapter 3:
Sources:

Lockwood Tooher, N. (2006, April 10). Ambien users are filing lawsuits. *Lawyer's Weekly USA*, 1.

Song, S. (2006, January 16). Sleeping your way to the top. *Time, 167*(3), 83.

Graham, J. (2006, April 5). Sleepless in Seattle and rest of U.S. too: The inability to get a good night's rest has become an epidemic in America, according to a new U.S. report. *Knight Ridder Tribune Business News*, p. 1.

Brody, J. E. (2006, April 11). What's holding up the sandman? *New York Times*, p. F6.

Stein, S. (2005, October 9). Scientists find out what losing sleep does to a body. *Washington Post*, p. A1.

Saul, S. (2006, February, 7). Record sales of sleep pills cause worry. *New York Times*, p. A1.

Saul R. (with Nixon, R.). (2006, March 8). Some sleeping pill users range far beyond bed. *New York Times*, p. C1.

Chapter 4:
Sources:

Edwards, A. J. (1995). *A theory of adolescent sexual behavior*. Edmonton: Department of Educational Psychology, University of Alberta.

Edwards, C. (2006, February 20). Class, take out your games. *Business Week*, 70.

Peck, M. (2005, July) Army game strives to turn soldiers into sensors. *National Defense, 90*(620), 22.

McLester, S. (2005, October 25). *Technology & Learning, 26*(3), 18–20, 22, 24, 26.

Frauenheim, E. (2006, April 10). Can video games win points as teaching tools? *Workforce Management, 85*(7), 12.

Johnson, S. (2005). Everything bad is good for you (pp. 36–37). New York: Riverhead Books.

Chapter 5: Cognition and Mental Abilities

Sources:

Anonymous. (2006, April 23). The leadership thing; what they don't teach in college can hurt us. *Boston Globe*, p. A3.

Anonymous. (2005).Yale psychologist designs test, a challenger to the SAT. *USA Today*.

Benderly, B. L. Looking beyond the SAT. *Association for Psychological Science Observer, 17*(5).

Yates, L. (2005, September 14). Faculty focus: Sternberg's success, a message to students. *Tuftsdaily.com*, Retrivied from http://www.tuftsdaily.com/media/storage/paper856/news/2005/09/14/Features/Faculty.Focus.Sternbergs.Success.A.Message.To.Students-1491288.shtml?norewrite200605041323&sourcedomain=www.tuftsdaily.com

Boone, C. (2004, November 27). Looking for common sense Ben Franklin was noted for his brains and practicality, but in a high-tech world is that mix harder to find? [Home Edition]. *Atlanta Journal-Constitution*, p. D1.

Hall, L. & Skocay, M. (2005, September 23). An interview with Dean Sternberg," *The Tufts Observer Online.*

Chapter 6: Motivation and Emotion

Sources:

O'Neal, S. & Gebauer, J. (2006, First Quarter). Talent management in the 21st century: Attracting, retaining and engaging employees of choice. *World at Work Journal, 15*(1), 6–17.

Shaw, M. E. (2006, May 2). For college grads, job satisfaction is as vital as salary. *Knight Ridder Tribune Business News*, p. 1.

Green, G. T. (2005, November). Recognition and the generational divide. *Workspan, 48*(11), 10.

Sullivan, J. (2006, March 27). Personalizing motivation. *Workforce Management, 85*(6), 50.

Anonymous. (2005, November 4). Motivation: Pay in the balance [Special Report]. *Employee Benefits*, 69–70.

Chapter 7: Human Development Across the Life Span

Sources:

Roberts, A. (2006, March 18). Grown but not gone: They're back—or they never left. Many young adults like living with folks—and movies, TV are taking notice. *Knight Ridder Tribune Business News*, p. 1.

Trunk, P. (2005, May 15). Believe it or not, moving back home is now in. *Boston Globe*, p. G1.

Brown, E. (2005, July) Mom and Dad, we're baaack. *Money, 34*(7), 39.

El Nasser, H. (2005, January 11) Why grown kids come home; high rents, college loans drive "boomerang kids" back to nest. *USA Today*, p. A1.

Chapter 8: Personality and Stress

Sources:

Millar, M. (25 October). Survey proves fitter employees lead to healthier balance sheets. *Personnel Today*, 3.

Carey, B. (2004, September 7).Working long hours? Take a massage break, courtesy of your boss [Sick of work—second of three articles: The yoga cure]. *New York Times*, p. F.1.

Moore, A. (2006, February 28). The sky is the limit. *Personnel Today*, 22–23.

Chapter 9: Psychological Disorders and Their Treatments

Sources:

Shenk, J. W. (2005, October). Lincoln's great depression. *Atlantic Monthly*, pp. 52–57.

Rand Corporation. (2004) Statistics on depression in U.S.: NIHM. The numbers count: Mental illness in America. Science on Our Minds Fact Sheet Series.

Chapter 10: Social Psychology

Sources:

Babcock, P. (2006, February). Detecting hidden bias, *HR Magazine, 51*(2), 50–55. Available online at: http://www.tolerance.org/hidden_bias

Gardner, M. (2005, October 31) Is "white" the only color of success?; Minorities can have their careers derailed by their tone of voice or hairstyle, a new study shows [Entire issue]. *Christian Science Monitor*, 13.

Harris, W. (2006, March) Hidden bias. *Black Enterprise, 36*(8), 62.

Wallace, L. S. (2005, November 18). Social bias still in the workplace. *Houston Chronicle*, p.5.

Chapter 11: Psychology Applied to Work

Sources:

Lewis, L. (2005). *Trader Joe's adventure: Turning a unique approach to business into a retail and cultural phenomenon.* Chicago: Dearborn.

McGregor, J. (2004, October). Leading listener Trader Joe's. *Fast Company, 87*, 82. Trader Joe's: Your neighorhood grocery store. Accessed online on November 22, 2006 at www.traderjoes.com

Speizer, I. (2004, September). Shopper's special. *Workforce Management, 83*(9), 51. Information also from my visit to Trader Joe's newest store in New York City's Union Square and from their Web site www.traderjoes.com

Chapter 8

Opener: Robert Brenner; Robert Brenner/HOTOEDIT; p. 280 Jim Craigmyle/Masterfile Corporation; p. 283 Jose Louis Pelaez/CORBIS – NY; p. 284 Tony Freeman/PhotoEdit Inc.; p. 285 © Tee and Charles Addams Foundation; p. 286 (T) Corbis – Comstock Images Royalty Free; p. 286 (B) Warren Morgan/CORBIS – NY; p. 291 Bob Daemmrich/Stock Boston; p. 292 (T) Reprinted by permission of the publishers from Henry A. Murray, THEMATIC APPERCEPTION TEST, Plate 12F, Cambridge, Mass.: Harvard University Press, Copyright © 1943 by the President and Fellows of Harvard College, © 1971 by Henry A. Murray; p. 292 (B) Ken Karp/Pearson Education/PH College; p. 293 Tim Brown/Getty Images Inc. – Stone Allstock; p. 295 Andrew Bret Wallis/Taxi; Andrew Bret Wallis/Taxi/Getty Images; p. 296 Peter Rogers/Getty Images, Inc – Liaison; p. 298 Lawrence Migdale/Getty Images Inc. – Stone Allstock; p. 299 Joe Raedle; Getty Images, Inc.; p. 301 Michael Newman/PhotoEdit Inc.; p. 303 Vince Streano/CORBIS – NY; p. 305 Peter Dazeley; Peter Dazeley/Image Bank/Getty Images; p. 306 Christopher Bissell/Getty Images Inc. – Stone Allstock; p. 308 Barbara Stitzer/PhotoEdit Inc.; p. 309 David Young – Wolff/PhotoEdit Inc.; p. 310 Philip North–Coombes/Getty Images Inc. – Stone Allstock

Chapter 9

Opener: © Bettmann/CORBIS All Rights Reserved; p. 321 Jim Cummins; Getty Images, Inc.; p. 323 Suzie Packard/Alamy Images; p. 330 Jon Feingersh/Masterfile Corporation; p. 331 Susan Greenwood/Getty Images, Inc – Liaison; p. 334 Monte S. Buchsbaum, M.D., Mt. Sinai School of Medicine, New York, NY; p. 335 B. Sporre/zefa/Masterfile Corporation; p. 340 The Freud Museum/Corbis/Sygma; p. 337 Getty Images Inc. – Hulton Archive Photos; p. 341 © The New Yorker Collection 1989 Danny Shanahan from cartoonbank.com. All Rights Reserved; p. 341 Michael Rougier/Getty Images/Time Life Pictures; p. 343 Albert Bandura; p. 344 Corbis – Comstock Images Royalty Free; p. 345 Bob Daemmrich/Stock Boston; p. 350 Laima E. Druskis/Pearson Education/PH College; p. 352 Spencer Grant/PhotoEdit Inc.

Chapter 10

Opener: Dan Lamont; © Dan Lamont / CORBIS All Rights Reserved; p. 362 The Cover Story; © The Cover Story / CORBIS All Rights Reserved; p. 363 John Burke/Index Stock Imagery, Inc.; p. 364 Robert J. Bennett/Robert J. Bennett; p. 365 Image Source; Photodisc/Getty Images; p. 366 Sidney/The Image Works; p. 368 Serge Krouglikoff/zefa; © Serge Krouglikoff / zefa / CORBIS All Rights Reserved; p. 369 Rachel Epstein/PhotoEdit Inc.; p. 370 Art Montes De Oca; [Photographer]/Photographer's Choice/Getty Images; p. 374 Kayte M. Deioma/PhotoEdit Inc.; p. 374 © MADD. Used by permission; p. 376 Alain Oddie/PhotoEdit Inc.; p. 377 AP Photo/Victor R. Caivano; p. 378 Getty Images Inc. – Hulton Archive Photos; p. 380 AP Wide World Photos; p. 381 Walter Hodges/Getty Images Inc. – Stone Allstock; p. 383 Walter Hodges/Getty Images Inc. – Stone Allstock; p. 384 William Langley/Getty Images, Inc. – Taxi; p. 385 Win McNamee; Getty Images, Inc.; p. 386 ADEK BERRY/AFP; ADEK BERRY/AFP/Getty Images.

Chapter 11

Opener: Michael Nagle; Getty Images, Inc.; p. 397 Michael Newman/PhotoEdit Inc.; p. 400 Photos.com; p. 401 Cecil Stoughton; LBJ Library. Photo by Cecil Stoughton; p. 404 IImageDJ/www.indexopen.com; p. 407 David Mager/Pearson Learning Photo Studio; p. 408 Upitis, Alvis/Getty Images Inc. – Image Bank; p. 409 (T) Michael Newman/PhotoEdit Inc.; p. 409 (B) Masterfile Corporation; p. 413 Churchill & Klehr Photography; p. 415 Richard Carson / Reuters NewMedia Inc./Corbis/Bettmann; p. 418 AP Wide World Photos; p. 420 BSIP/Phototake NYC; p. 423 Ed Kashi/Corbis/Bettmann.